Your Companion Site — Even More Help for Studying!

bedfordstmartins.com/roarkunderstanding

FREE Online Study Guide— Improve Your Understanding!

Get immediate feedback on your progress with

- Quizzing
- Key terms review
- Map and visual activities
- Timeline activities
- Note-taking outlines
- Chapter study guide steps

FREE History Research and Writing Help

Refine your research skills, evaluate sources, and organize your findings with

- A database of useful images, maps, documents and more at *Make History*
- A guide to online sources for history
- Help with writing history papers
- A tool for building a bibliography
- Tips on avoiding plagiarism

Understanding
the
American Promise

A BRIEF HISTORY

Understanding
the
American Promise

A BRIEF HISTORY

James L. Roark
Emory University

Michael P. Johnson
Johns Hopkins University

Patricia Cline Cohen
University of California, Santa Barbara

Sarah Stage
Arizona State University

Alan Lawson
Boston College

Susan M. Hartmann
The Ohio State University

Bedford / St. Martin's
Boston • New York

For Bedford/St. Martin's

Publisher for History: Mary Dougherty
Executive Editor for History: William J. Lombardo
Director of Development for History: Jane Knetzger
Developmental Editor: Kathryn Abbott
Senior Production Editor: Bridget Leahy
Assistant Production Manager: Joe Ford
Executive Marketing Manager: Jenna Bookin Barry
Editorial Assistant: Robin Soule
Copy Editor: Linda McLatchie
Indexer: Leoni Z. McVey
Photo Researcher: Picture Research Consultants, Inc.
Permissions Manager: Kalina Ingham Hintz
Senior Art Director: Anna Palchik
Text Designer: Jerilyn Bockorick
Cover Designer: Donna Lee Dennison
Cover Photo: Immigrant worker. © CORBIS.
Cartography: Mapping Specialists Limited
Composition: Nesbitt Graphics, Inc.
Printing and Binding: RR Donnelley and Sons

President: Joan E. Feinberg
Editorial Director: Denise B. Wydra
Director of Marketing: Karen R. Soeltz
Director of Production: Susan W. Brown
Associate Director, Editorial Production: Elise S. Kaiser
Managing Editor: Elizabeth M. Schaaf

Library of Congress Control Number: 2010936410

Manufactured in the United States of America.

6   5   4   3   2   1
f   e   d   c   b   a

For information, write: Bedford/St. Martin's, 75 Arlington Street, Boston, MA 02116
(617-399-4000)

ISBN: 978–0–312–64518–2   (Combined edition)
ISBN: 978–0–312–64519–9   (Vol. I)
ISBN: 978–0–312–64520–5   (Vol. II)

PREFACE

In *Understanding the American Promise,* we set out solve a couple of problems that had come to us over the years. First, we knew that, although many students dutifully read their survey texts, they came away confused. They couldn't tell what was most important and they felt overwhelmed. At the same time, their instructors felt that some texts didn't show students what was so exciting and even fun about history. These teachers wanted a way to give their students a grounding in the basics and to show how historians think and work, a text that would show that history is a discipline based upon inquiry, interpretation, and debate. With these issues in mind, we took a hard look at the survey course from all directions. We reflected on our own classes and students and how they've changed. We reviewed state-of-the-art scholarship on effective teaching. We consulted learning experts and instructional designers. We talked to students. And, most importantly, we talked to you—instructors teaching the course—and asked about your needs. *Understanding the American Promise* is the product of these efforts.

With *Understanding the American Promise,* we offer something new—an abridged narrative of U.S. history that concentrates on major developments, combined with an innovative design and pedagogy orchestrated to work together to foster students' comprehension and historical thinking. This brief narrative and distinctive format will help your students grasp important developments and begin to think like historians.

This means that, in *Understanding,* design, pedagogy and narrative work together to help students learn, and then reinforce and retain their knowledge. We started with *The American Promise,* our full-length survey textbook acclaimed for its effective braiding together of political and social history, and reduced the length by over thirty percent. This abridged narrative will better help students discern overarching trends and connect them with the individuals—from Presidents to pipefitters and sharecroppers to suffragettes—that animate the past.

Then, we joined our prose with an innovative pedagogy and a well-crafted design to make a compelling new teaching and learning tool. *Understanding's* chapter architecture supports students' comprehension and helps them to grasp key themes and ideas. To this end, all chapters open with a succinct, single paragraph–length statement about the main themes and events of the chapter, designed to establish clear learning outcomes. At the beginning of each chapter, we also ask students a "Did You Know?" question to invite them to connect what they already know (or think they know) to each chapter's big theme. Chapters are then organized into three to six main sections, with all section titles crafted as big questions to facilitate active reading and to emphasize that history is an inquiry-based discipline. These main sections end with quick review questions that prompt students to check their comprehension and reflect on what they've read. Throughout, chronology boxes show the sequence of events, and marginal definitions highlight key terms, providing on-the-page reinforcement and a handy tool for review. We hope that this structure will help students to grasp meaning as they read and also model how historians think, how they pose questions, and how they answer those questions with evidence and interpretation.

We've also reconsidered the traditional review that comes at the end of the chapter. We've provided a three-step chapter review that will help students with the basic material but also help them go beyond a basic understanding of what happened. In step one, students identify key terms and explain why each matters. In step two, they apply their understanding of basic terms to questions about cause and effect, change over time, and comparison. And in step three, students pull it all together with analytical and synthetic questions that treat the whole chapter. Finally, an active recitation question asks students to consider what is truly important to understand about what they have just read.

As teachers, our guiding principle is to promote intelligent engagement as a catalyst toward historical understanding. This means giving our students an effective textbook that is enjoyable to read and that provides the tools to help them develop their skills of historical analysis and interpretation, and it is our hope that this new approach provides just such a tool. It is our article of faith that when we empower students to engage meaningfully with the past, we encourage habits of thinking essential for a well-rounded general education at any college or university—and beyond. Historical knowledge and the ability to think critically provide a rock-solid foundation for informed and active citizenship, whether that citizen was born in the United States or is a first generation immigrant, as many of our students are.

As always, our use of *American Promise* in our title reflects our emphasis on human agency and our conviction that American history is an unfinished story. For millions, the nation has held out the promise of a better life, unfettered worship, representative government, democratic politics, and other freedoms seldom found elsewhere. But none of these promises has come with guarantees. As we see it, much of American history is a continuing struggle over the definition and realization of the nation's promise. Abraham Lincoln, in the midst of what he termed the "fiery trial" of the Civil War, pronounced the nation "the last best hope of Earth." Kept alive by countless sacrifices, that hope has been marred by compromises, disappointments, and denials, but it lives still. We hope that *Understanding the American Promise* will help students become aware of the legacy of hope bequeathed to them by previous generations of Americans stretching back nearly four centuries, a legacy that is theirs to preserve and build on.

We trust you'll agree that *Understanding the American Promise* achieves its goal of giving students a smart alternative for *understanding* American history. If we help you stir in your students a lifelong passion for history and the habits of critical thinking, the pleasure is ours.

Acknowledgments

We gratefully acknowledge all the helpful suggestions from those who have read and taught from previous editions of *The American Promise: A History of the United States* and *The American Promise: A Compact History*. We would like specifically to acknowledge those scholars and teachers who gave their time and expertise to the draft for this first edition of *Understanding the American Promise:* Cary W. Blankenship, *University of Kentucky;* Roland Frankum Jr., *Millersville*

University; Cecilia Gowdy-Wygant, *Front Range Community College;* Pauline S. Johnson, *Mars Hill College;* Carol A. Keller, *San Antonio College;* Tracy A. Lai, *Seattle Central Community College;* Peggy Lambert, *Lone Star College-Kingwood;* John Mack, *Labette Community College;* Anne Paulet, *Humboldt State University,* Jeffrey Smith, *Lindenwood University;* and Julie Winch, *University of Massachusetts-Boston.*

A project as complex as this requires the talents of many individuals. First, we would like to acknowledge our families for their support, forbearance, and toleration of our textbook responsibilities. Pembroke Herbert and Sandi Rygiel of Picture Research Consultants, Inc., contributed their unparalleled knowledge, soaring imagination, and diligent research to make possible the extraordinary illustration program. Pauline Johnson of Mars Hill College reviewed each chapter's pedagogy with the astute eye of a lifelong teacher.

We would also like to thank the many people at Bedford/St. Martin's who have been crucial to this project. Developmental editor Kathryn Abbott oversaw the development of each chapter and added value at every step. Thanks also go to editorial assistant Robin Soule, who provided unflagging assistance and who coordinated the review program and the turnover of manuscript. We are also grateful to Jane Knetzger, director of development for history, William Lombardo, executive editor, and Mary Dougherty, publisher, for their support and guidance. For their imaginative and tireless efforts to promote the book, we want to thank Jenna Bookin Barry, executive marketing manager, Sally Constable, market development manager, John Hunger, senior history specialist, Sean Blest, eastern history specialist, and Stephen Watson, marketing assistant. With great skill and professionalism, Bridget Leahy, senior production editor, pulled together the many pieces related to copyediting, design, and typesetting, with the able assistance of Lidia MacDonald-Carr and Laura Winstead and the guidance of managing editor Elizabeth Schaaf and assistant managing editor John Amburg. Assistant production manager Joe Ford oversaw the manufacturing of the book. Designer and page makeup artist Jerilyn Bockorick, copyeditor Linda McLatchie, and proofreaders Jan Cocker and Melissa Clark attended to the myriad details that help make the book shine. Leoni McVey provided an outstanding index. The book's covers were designed by Donna Dennison. New media editor Marissa Zanetti, associate editor Jack Cashman, and media producer Nancy Hiney, made sure that *Understanding the American Promise: A Brief History* remains at the forefront of technological support for students and instructors. Editorial director Denise Wydra provided helpful advice throughout the course of the project. Finally, Charles H. Christensen, former president, took a personal interest in *The American Promise* from the start, and Joan E. Feinberg, president, has guided all editions through every stage of development.

James Roark
Michael Johnson
Patricia Cohen
Sarah Stage
Alan Lawson
Susan Hartmann

BRIEF CONTENTS

CONTENTS

1

UNDERSTANDING ANCIENT AMERICA

BEFORE 1492 *3*

2

ENCOUNTERING THE NEW WORLD

1492–1600 *31*

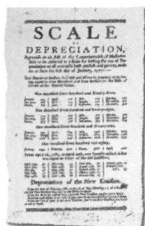

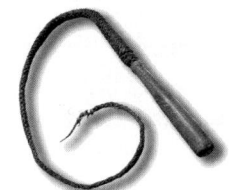

15
THE CRUCIBLE OF WAR

1861–1865 *395*

16
RECONSTRUCTING A NATION

1863–1877 *427*

17
CONTESTING THE WEST

1870–1900 *455*

MAPS, FIGURES, AND TABLES

VERSIONS AND SUPPLEMENTS

Understanding the American Promise: A Brief History is supported by loads of resources—study tools for students, instructor materials, and many options for packaging the book with documents readers, trade books, atlases, and other guides—for free or at a substantial discount. Descriptions follow, but for more information, visit the book's catalog site at bedfordstmartins.com/roarkunderstanding/catalog or contact your local Bedford/St. Martin's sales representative.

Available Versions of This Book

To accommodate different course lengths and course budgets, this title is available in several different formats. The e-books are available at a substantial discount.

Combined Volume (Chapters 1–31)—available in paperback and e-book formats
Volume I: To 1877 (Chapters 1–16)—available in paperback and e-book formats
Volume II: From 1865 (Chapters 16–31)—available in paperback and e-book formats

With our innovative e-books your students get the content you want in a convenient format—for about half the cost of a print book. **Bedford/St. Martin's e-Books** have been optimized for reading and studying online. **CourseSmart e-Books** can be downloaded or used online, whichever is more convenient for your students.

Companion site at bedfordstmartins.com/ roarkunderstanding

Our new companion sites gather free and premium resources, giving students a way to extend their Bedford book, online. These book-specific sites provide one destination to practice, read, write, and study—and to find and access quizzes and activities, study aids, and history research and writing help.

▶ **FREE Online Study Guide.** Available at the companion site, this popular resource provides students with self-review quizzes and activities for each chapter, including a multiple-choice self-test that focuses on important concepts; an identification quiz that helps students remember key people, places, and events; a flashcard activity that tests students' knowledge of key terms; and map activities intended to strengthen students' geography skills. It also includes downloadable versions of the textbook chapter study guides. Instructors can monitor students' progress through an online Quiz Gradebook or receive email updates.

▶ **FREE History Research and Writing Help.** Also available on the companion site, this resource includes the textbook authors' **Suggested References** organized by chapter; **History Research and Reference Sources,** with links to history-related databases, indexes, and journals; **More Sources and How to Format a History**

Paper, with clear advice on how to integrate primary and secondary sources into research papers and how to cite and format sources correctly; ***Build a Bibliography,*** a simple Web-based tool that generates bibliographies in four commonly used documentation styles; and ***Tips on Avoiding Plagiarism,*** an online tutorial that reviews the consequences of plagiarism and features exercises to help students practice integrating sources and recognize acceptable summaries.

Instructor Resources

Bedford/St. Martin's has developed a wide range of teaching resources for this book and for this course. They range from lecture and presentation materials to assessment tools and course management options. Most can be downloaded or ordered at bedfordstmartins.com/roarkunderstanding/catalog.

▶ ***HistoryClass for Understanding the American Promise.*** *HistoryClass,* a Bedford/St. Martin's Online Course Space, puts the online resources available with this textbook in one convenient place—an interactive e-book and primary sources reader; maps, images, documents and links; chapter review quizzes; interactive multimedia exercises; and research and writing help. Get into HistoryClass and get all our premium content and tools in one completely customizable course space; then assign, rearrange, and mix our resources with yours. For more information visit yourhistoryclass.com.

▶ **Bedford/St. Martin's Course Cartridges.** Whether you use Blackboard, WebCT, Desire2Learn, Angel, Sakai, or Moodle, we have free content and support available for you to plug our content into your course management system. Registered instructors can download cartridges with no hassle, no strings attached. Content includes our most popular free resources and book-specific content for this title. Visit bedfordstmartins.com/cms to get a demo, find your versions, or download your cartridge.

▶ **NEW PowerPoint Maps, Images, Lecture Outlines, and i>clicker Content.** Look good and save time with *The Bedford Lecture Kit.* These presentation materials are downloadable individually from the Media and Supplements tab at bedfordstmartins.com/roarkunderstanding/catalog, and they are available on *The Bedford Lecture Kit Instructor's Resource CD-ROM.* They include ready-made and fully customizable PowerPoint multimedia presentations built around lecture outlines that are embedded with maps, figures, and selected images from the textbook and are supplemented by more detailed instructor notes on key points. Also available are maps and selected images in JPEG and PowerPoint format; content for i>clicker, a classroom response system, in Microsoft Word and PowerPoint formats; the Instructor's Resource Manual in Microsoft Word format; and outline maps in PDF format for quizzing or handouts. All files are suitable for copying onto transparency acetates.

▶ **Instructor's Resource Manual.** The instructor's manual offers both experienced and first-time instructors tools for presenting textbook material in engaging ways. It includes chapter review material, teaching strategies, and a guide to chapter-specific supplements available for the text.

- **Computerized Test Bank.** The test bank includes a mix of fresh, carefully crafted multiple-choice, fill-in-the-blank, short-answer, and essay questions for each chapter. The questions appear in Microsoft Word format and in easy-to-use test bank software that allows instructors to easily add, edit, re-sequence, and print questions and answers. Instructors can also export questions into a variety of formats, including WebCT and Blackboard.

- *Make History*—**Free Documents, Maps, Images, and Web Sites.** *Make History* combines the best Web resources with hundreds of maps and images, to make finding the source material you need simple. Browse the collection of thousands of resources by course or by topic, date, and type. Each item has been carefully chosen and helpfully annotated to make it easy to find exactly what you need. Available at bedfordstmartins.com/makehistory.

- *Reel Teaching* **Video clips.** This DVD provides a large collection of short video clips for classroom presentation. Designed as engaging "lecture launchers" varying in length from 1 to 15 or more minutes, the 59 documentary clips were carefully chosen for use in both semesters of the U.S. survey course. The clips feature compelling images, archival footage, personal narratives, and commentary by noted historians.

- **NEW** *America in Motion: Video clips for U.S. History.* Set history in motion with *America in Motion*, an instructor DVD containing dozens of short digital movie files of twentieth-century American historical events. From the wreckage of the battleship *Maine,* to FDR's Fireside Chats, to Oliver North testifying before Congress, *America in Motion* engages your students with dynamic scenes from key events and challenges them to think critically. All files are classroom-ready, edited for brevity, and easily integrated with PowerPoint or other presentation software for electronic lectures or assignments. An accompanying guide provides each clip's historical context, ideas for use, and suggested questions.

- **Videos and Multimedia.** A wide assortment of videos and multimedia CD-ROMs on various topics in U.S. history is available to qualified adopters through your Bedford/St. Martin's sales representative.

Packaging Opportunities

Save your students money and package your favorite text with more! For information on free packages and discounts up to 50%, contact your local Bedford/St. Martin's sales representative.

- **e-Book.** The e-book for this title can be packaged with the print text at no additional cost. For a complete list of titles, visit bedfordstmartins.com/ebooks/catalog.

- *Reading the American Past: Selected Historical Documents*, **Fourth Edition.** Edited by Michael P. Johnson (Johns Hopkins University), one of the authors of *The American Promise,* and designed to complement the textbook, *Reading the American Past* provides a broad selection of over 150 primary source documents, as well as editorial apparatus to help students analyze the sources. Emphasizing the important social, political, and economic themes of U.S. history courses, these documents provide a wide range of perspectives on environmental, western, ethnic, and gender history. Available free when packaged with the text. For more information, visit bedfordstmartins.com/roarksources/catalog.

▶ *Reading the American Past e-Book.* The reader is available as an e-book. When packaged with the print or electronic version of the textbook, it is available for free. For more information, visit bedfordstmartins.com/ebooks/catalog.

▶ *Rand McNally Atlas of American History.* This collection of more than eighty full-color maps illustrates key events and eras from early exploration, settlement, expansion, and immigration to U.S. involvement in wars abroad an on U.S. soil. Introductory pages for each section include brief overview, timelines, graphs, and photos to quickly establish a historical context. Available for $3.00 when packaged with the text. For a complete list of titles, visit bedfordstmartins.com/americanatlas/catalog.

▶ *Maps in Context: A Workbook for American History.* Written by historical cartography expert Gerald A. Danzer (University of Illinois at Chicago), this skill-building workbook helps students comprehend essential connections between geographic literacy and historical understanding. Organized to correspond to the typical U.S. history survey course, Maps in Context presents a wealth of map-centered projects and convenient pop quizzes that give students hands-on experience working with maps. Available free when packaged with the text. For a complete list of titles, visit bedfordstmartins.com/mapsincontext/catalog.

▶ *The Bedford Glossary for U.S. History.* This handy supplement for the survey course gives students historically contextualized definitions for hundreds of terms—from *abolitionism* to *zoot suit*—that students will encounter in lectures, reading, and exams. Available free when packaged with the text. For a complete list of titles, visit bedfordstmartins.com/usgloss/catalog.

▶ *U.S. History Matters: A Student Guide to World History Online.* This resource, written by Alan Gevinson, Kelly Schrum, and the late Roy Rosenzweig (all of George Mason University), provides an illustrated and annotated guide to 250 of the most useful Web sites for student research in U.S. history as well as advice on evaluating and using Internet sources. This essential guide is based on the acclaimed "History Matters" Web site developed by the American Social History Project and the Center for History and New Media. Available free when packaged with the text. For a complete list of titles, visit bedfordstmartins.com/ushistory matters/catalog.

▶ **The Bedford Series in History and Culture.** More than one hundred titles in this highly praised series combine first-rate scholarship, historical narrative, and important primary documents for undergraduate courses. Each book is brief, inexpensive, and focused on a specific topic or period. For a complete list of titles, visit bedfordstmartins.com/history/series. Package discounts are available.

▶ **Trade Books.** Titles published by sister companies Hill and Wang; Farrar, Strauss and Giroux; Henry Holt and Company; St. Martin's Press; Picador; and Palgrave Macmillan are available at a 50 percent discount when packaged with Bedford/St. Martin's textbooks. For more information, visit bedfordstmartins.com/tradeup.

▶ *Going to the Source: The Bedford Reader in American History.* Developed by Victoria Bissell Brown and Timothy J. Shannon, this reader's strong pedagogical framework helps students learn how to ask fruitful questions in order to evaluate documents effectively and develop critical reading skills. The reader's wide variety of chapter topics that complement the survey course and its rich diversity of sources—from personal letters to political cartoons—provoke students' interest as it teaches them the skills they need to successfully interrogate historical sources. Package discounts are available. For more information, visit bedfordstmartins.com/brownshannon/catalog.

▶ *America Firsthand.* With its distinctive focus on ordinary people, this primary documents reader, by Robert D. Marcus, David Burner, and Anthony Marcus, offers a remarkable range of perspectives on America's history from those who lived it. Popular Points of View sections expose students to different perspectives on a specific event or topic, and Visual Portfolios invite analysis of the visual record. Package discounts are available. For more information, visit bedfordstmartins.com/marcusburner/catalog.

▶ *A Pocket Guide to Writing in History.* This portable and affordable reference tool by Mary Lynn Rampolla provides reading, writing, and research advice useful to students in all history courses. Concise yet comprehensive advice on approaching typical history assignments, developing critical reading skills, writing effective history papers, conducting research, using and documenting sources, and avoiding plagiarism—enhanced with practical tips and examples throughout—have made this slim reference a best-seller. Package discounts are available. For more information, visit bedfordstmartins.com/rampolla/catalog.

▶ *A Student's Guide to History.* This complete guide to success in any history course provides the practical help students need to be effective. In addition to introducing students to the nature of the discipline, author Jules Benjamin teaches a wide range of skills from preparing for exams to approaching common writing assignments, and he explains the research and documentation process with plentiful examples. Package discounts are available. For more information, visit bedfordstmartins.com/benjamin/catalog.

How to use this book to figure out what's **really** important

Memorizing facts and dates for a history class won't get you very far. That's because history isn't just about "facts." It's also about understanding cause-and-effect and the significance of people, places, and events from the past that still have relevance to your world today. This textbook is designed to help you focus on what's truly significant in U.S. history and to give you practice in thinking like a historian.

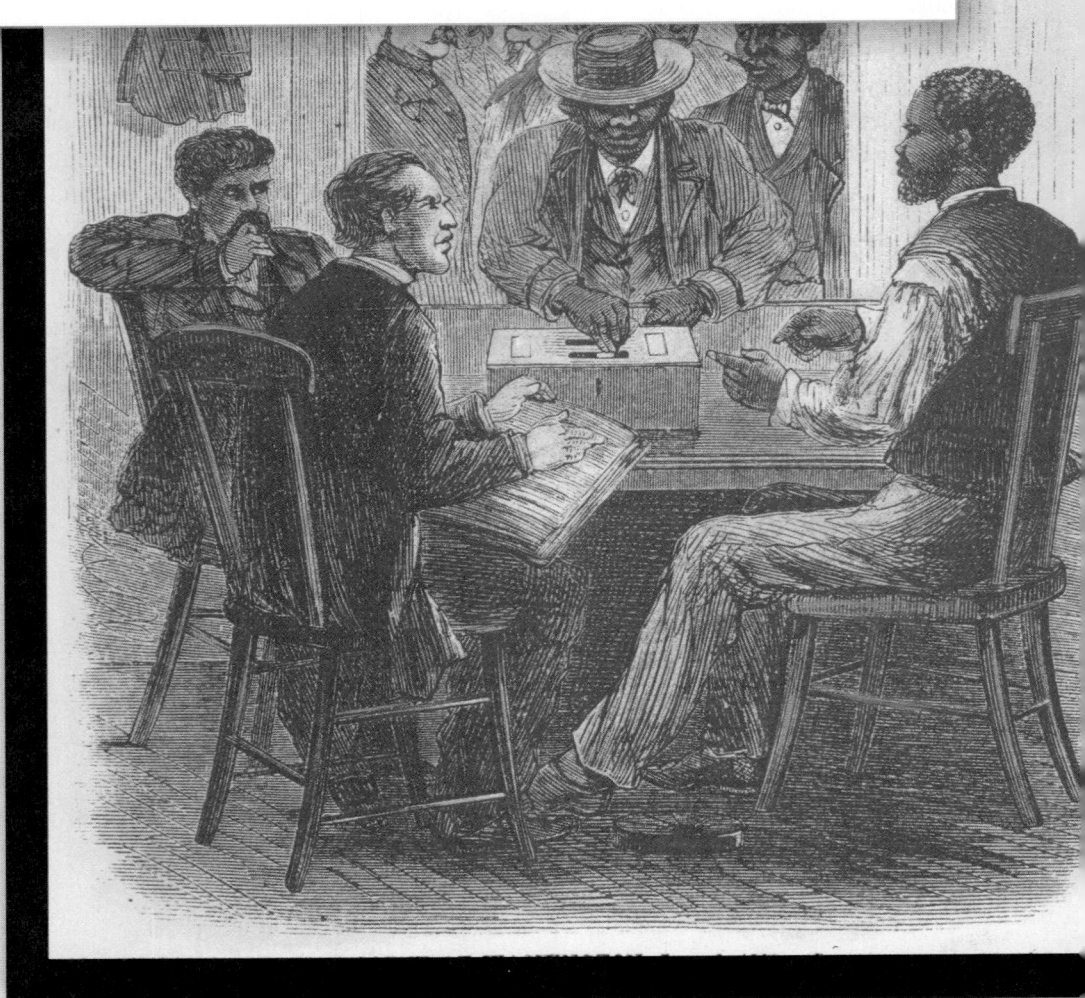

The opening page gives you a preview of the entire chapter.

The title tells you the subject of the chapter and identifies the time span that will be covered.

16 RECONSTRUCTING A NATION

1863–1877

> This chapter explores the period known as Reconstruction, in which the nation struggled to define the defeated South's status within the Union and the meaning of freedom for ex-slaves. Despite the end of the Civil War, the nation entered one of its most violent eras, as victorious Northerners, defeated white Southerners, and newly freed African

The opening paragraph identifies the themes that will be explored, such as the continuing struggle between North and South, the meaning of freedom for ex-slaves, and erupting violence.

> What were Lincoln's plans for wartime reconstruction?

> What vision did Andrew Johnson have for presidential reconstruction?

> How radical was congressional reconstruction?

Each question opens a new section of the chapter and will be addressed in turn on the following pages.

> How was the battle over reconstruction fought in the South?

> Why did reconstruction collapse?

> Conclusion: What were the achievements and failures of reconstruction?

SAML. DOVE wishes to know of the whereabouts of his mother, Areno, his sisters Maria, Neziah, and Peggy, and his brother Edmond, who were owned by Geo. Dove, of Rockingham county, Shenandoah Valley, Va. Sold in Richmond, after which Saml. and Edmond were taken to Nashville, Tenn., by Joe Mick; Areno was left at the Eagle Tavern, Richmond
Respectfully yours,
SAML. DOVE.
Utica, New York, Aug. 5, 1865—3m
U. S. Christian Commission,
Nashville, Tenn., July 19, 1865.

DID YOU KNOW?

The priorities for newly freed African Americans were to locate family members, acquire land, and worship in their own churches.

Voting day, June 5, 1867. Black freedmen line up to vote in Washington, D.C.

427

Each section has tools that help you focus on what's important.

The question in red is the specific topic discussed in this section.

> ## What vision did Andrew Johnson have for presidential reconstruction?

The Black Codes

Titled "Selling a Freeman to Pay His Fine at Monticello, Florida," this 1867 drawing from a northern magazine equates black codes with the reinstitution of slavery. The ascension of Andrew Johnson to the presidency emboldened many southern states to pass laws severely restricting blacks' freedom. Granger Collection.

Marginal key terms give you background on important people, ideas, and events. Use them for reference while you read but also pay attention to which terms are emphasized.

Andrew Johnson
► President of the United States from 1865 to 1869, Vice President Johnson became president after the assassination of Abraham Lincoln. Like Lincoln, Johnson sought the quick restoration of civil government in the South and pardoned most ex-Confederates. Johnson battled with Congress over the course of Reconstruction and was the first president in U.S. history to be impeached by the House of Representatives. He barely escaped removal from office by the Senate.

WITH ABRAHAM LINCOLN'S death on April 15, 1865, Vice President Andrew Johnson of Tennessee became the new president. Congress had adjourned in March and would not reconvene until December. Thus, throughout the summer and fall, Johnson drew up and executed a plan of reconstruction without congressional advice.

Congress reconvened in December to find that, as far as the president and former Confederates were concerned, reconstruction was completed. Most Republicans, however, thought Johnson's puny demands of ex-rebels encouraged the rebirth of the Old South at the expense of black liberty. They proceeded to dismantle Johnson's program and substitute a program of their own.

Johnson's Program of Reconciliation

Born in 1808 in Raleigh, North Carolina, **Andrew Johnson** was the son of illiterate parents. Self-educated and ambitious, Johnson moved to Tennessee, where he built a career in politics championing the South's common white people and assailing its "illegitimate, swaggering, bastard, scrub aristocracy." The only senator from a Confederate state to remain loyal to the Union, Johnson held the planter class responsible for secession.

A Democrat all his life, Johnson occupied the White House only because the Republican Party in 1864 had needed a vice presidential candidate who would appeal to loyal, Union-supporting Democrats. Johnson vigorously defended states' rights (but not secession) and opposed Republican efforts to expand the power of the federal government. A steadfast supporter of slavery, Johnson grudgingly accepted emancipation more because he hated planters than because he sympathized with slaves. "Damn the negroes," he said. "I am fighting those traitorous aristocrats, their masters." The new president harbored unshakable racist convictions. Africans, Johnson said, were "inferior to the white man in point of intellect—better calculated in physical structure to undergo drudgery and hardship."

CHAPTER LOCATOR | What were Lincoln's plans for wartime reconstruction?

Like Lincoln, Johnson stressed the rapid restoration of civil government in the South. Like Lincoln, he promised to pardon most, but not all, ex-rebels. Johnson recognized the state governments created by Lincoln but set out his own requirements for restoring the other rebel states to the Union. All that the citizens of a state had to do was to renounce the right of secession, deny that the debts of the Confederacy were legal and binding, and ratify the Thirteenth Amendment, abolishing slavery, which became part of the Constitution in December 1865.

Johnson also returned to pardoned ex-Confederates all confiscated and abandoned land, even if it was in the hands of freedmen. Reformers were shocked. Instead of punishing planters as Republicans expected, his instructions canceled the promising beginnings made by General Sherman and the Freedmen's Bureau to settle blacks on land of their own. As one freedman observed, "Things was hurt by Mr. Lincoln getting killed."

White Southern Resistance and Black Codes

In the summer of 1865, delegates across the South gathered to draw up the new state constitutions required by Johnson's plan of reconstruction. Rather than accept Johnson's plan, delegates balked at even the president's mild requirements to renounce secession, disown their war debts, and ratify the Thirteenth Amendment. Despite this defiance, Johnson did nothing. White Southerners began to think that by standing up for themselves they could define the terms of reconstruction.

State governments across the South adopted a series of laws known as **black codes**, which made a travesty of black freedom. The codes sought to keep ex-slaves subordinate to whites by subjecting them to every sort of discrimination.

Black Codes

Several states made it illegal for blacks to own a gun.

Mississippi made insulting gestures and language by blacks a criminal offense.

The codes barred blacks from jury duty.

Not a single southern state granted any black the right to vote.

At the core of the black codes, however, lay the matter of labor and the desire to force freedmen back to the plantations. South Carolina attempted to limit blacks to either farmwork or domestic service by requiring them to pay annual taxes of $10 to $100 to work in any other occupation. Mississippi declared that blacks who did not possess written evidence of employment could be declared vagrants and be subject to involuntary plantation labor. Under so-called apprenticeship laws, courts bound thousands of black children—orphans and others whose parents they deemed unable to support them—to work for planter "guardians."

CHRONOLOGY

1865
- President Abraham Lincoln is shot; dies on April 15; is succeeded by Andrew Johnson.
- Johnson carries out rapid restoration of civil government in the South.
- Johnson returns confiscated and abandoned land to pardoned ex-Confederates.
- Southern states enact black codes.
- The Thirteenth Amendment, abolishing slavery, becomes part of Constitution.

1866
- Civil Rights Act nullifies black codes and extends civil rights to blacks.

Chronologies for each major section show the sequence of events in this section.

black codes
▶ Laws passed by state governments in the South in 1865 that sought to keep ex-slaves subordinate to whites. At the core of the black codes lay the desire to force freedmen back to the plantations.

The quick review helps you check your recall of the section.

QUICK REVIEW

Why and how did the aims of Congress and the president diverge? What specifically were the issues over which they clashed?

| What vision did Andrew Johnson have for presidential reconstruction? | How radical was congressional reconstruction? | How was the battle over reconstruction fought in the South? | Why did reconstruction collapse? | Conclusion: What were the achievements and failures of reconstruction? |

The chapter locator at the bottom of the page puts this section in the context of the chapter as a whole, so you can see how this section relates to what's coming next.

The Chapter Study Guide provides a 3-step process that will build your understanding and your historical skills.

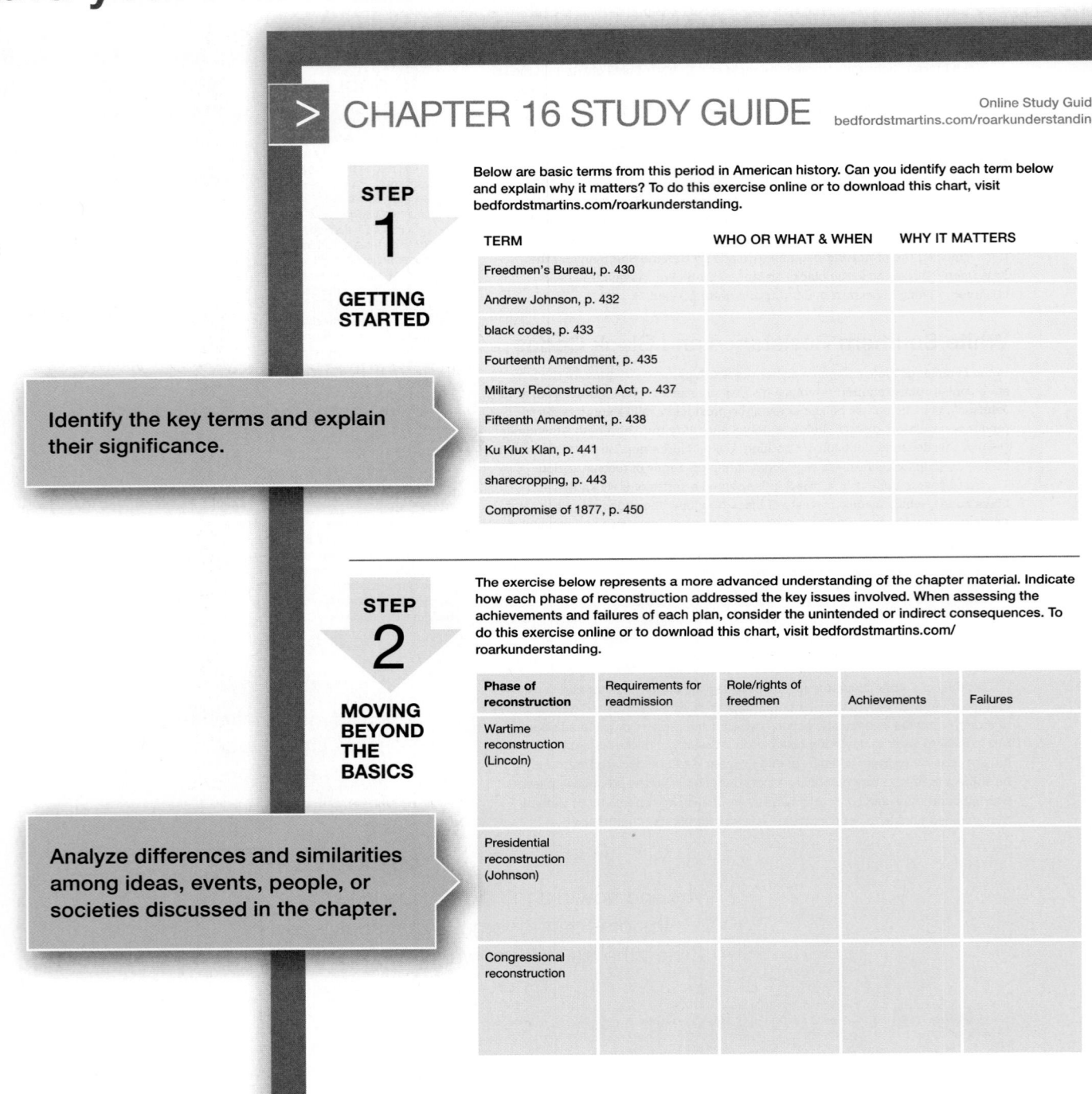

Online Study Guide
bedfordstmartins.com/roarkunderstanding

CHAPTER 16 STUDY GUIDE

STEP 1

GETTING STARTED

Below are basic terms from this period in American history. Can you identify each term below and explain why it matters? To do this exercise online or to download this chart, visit bedfordstmartins.com/roarkunderstanding.

TERM	WHO OR WHAT & WHEN	WHY IT MATTERS
Freedmen's Bureau, p. 430		
Andrew Johnson, p. 432		
black codes, p. 433		
Fourteenth Amendment, p. 435		
Military Reconstruction Act, p. 437		
Fifteenth Amendment, p. 438		
Ku Klux Klan, p. 441		
sharecropping, p. 443		
Compromise of 1877, p. 450		

> Identify the key terms and explain their significance.

STEP 2

MOVING BEYOND THE BASICS

The exercise below represents a more advanced understanding of the chapter material. Indicate how each phase of reconstruction addressed the key issues involved. When assessing the achievements and failures of each plan, consider the unintended or indirect consequences. To do this exercise online or to download this chart, visit bedfordstmartins.com/roarkunderstanding.

Phase of reconstruction	Requirements for readmission	Role/rights of freedmen	Achievements	Failures
Wartime reconstruction (Lincoln)				
Presidential reconstruction (Johnson)				
Congressional reconstruction				

> Analyze differences and similarities among ideas, events, people, or societies discussed in the chapter.

452

STEP

3

PUTTING IT ALL TOGETHER

Now that you've reviewed various parts of the chapter, take a step back and try to see the big picture by answering these questions. Remember to use specific examples from the chapter in your answers. To do this exercise online, visit bedfordsmartins.com/roarkunderstanding.

Answer the big-picture questions using specific examples or evidence from the chapter.

SOUTHERN RECONSTRUCTION IN ACTION

► How did white Southerners respond during Reconstruction? Consider both Democrats and Republicans in your response.

► How did southern African Americans attempt to shape their own lives during Reconstruction?

PRESIDENTIAL AND CONGRESSIONAL RECONSTRUCTION

► What role did the black codes play in shaping the course of reconstruction?

► What steps did Congress take between 1865 and 1869 to assist ex-slaves in their lives as freedmen? How effective were these actions?

LOOKING BACKWARD, LOOKING AHEAD

► How did long-held racial views among whites, in both the South and the North, shape Reconstruction?

► What were the lasting accomplishments of Reconstruction? What were its most important failures?

THE END OF RECONSTRUCTION

► How and why did the decline of northern support for Reconstruction help southern Democrats "redeem" the South?

► Why did white supremacy become the foundation of southern politics in the 1870s?

IN YOUR OWN WORDS

Imagine that you must explain chapter 16 to someone who hasn't read it. What would be the most important points to include and why?

Explain the important points in your own words to make sure you have a firm grasp of the chapter material.

Visit the **FREE Online Study Guide** at bedfordstmartins.com/roarkunderstanding to do these steps on-line and to check how much you've learned.

xxxvii

Understanding the American Promise

A BRIEF HISTORY

1
UNDERSTANDING ANCIENT AMERICA

BEFORE 1492

> This chapter charts the history of ancient Native American peoples from their migration out of Asia to the eve of European contact in 1492. It explores the development of distinct Native American cultures, as well as the common characteristics they shared.

> What is the connection between archaeology and history?

> Who were the first Americans?

> How did Archaic Americans adapt to changing conditions?

> How did agriculture change Native American societies?

> How were native societies organized in the 1490s?

> What were the characteristics of Mexican culture?

> Conclusion: How do we understand the worlds of ancient Americans?

DID YOU KNOW?

In 1492, central Mexico had three times as many people as Spain and Portugal combined.

The Great Tenochtitlan. Detail of the 1945 fresco by Mexican artist Diego Rivera.

What is the connection between archaeology and history?

Mississippian Wooden Mask

Sometime between AD 1200 and 1350, a Native American in what is now central Illinois fashioned this mask from red cedar. Originally, a thin sheet of copper covered the mask, leaving a greenish residue that is still visible today. The mask was used in rituals by Mississippian people connected to Cahokia, a vast ceremonial site located in southern Illinois, just across the Mississippi River from present-day St. Louis. Photograph © 2002 John Bigelow Taylor www.johnbigelowtaylor.com. Illinois State Museum, Springfield, Cat. no. 273.

ARCHAEOLOGISTS AND HISTORIANS share the desire to learn about people who lived in the past, but they usually employ different methods to obtain information. Both archaeologists and historians study artifacts as clues to the activities and ideas of the humans who created them. They concentrate, however, on different kinds of artifacts. Archaeologists tend to focus on physical objects such as bones, spear points, pots, baskets, jewelry, clothing, and buildings. Historians

CHAPTER LOCATOR | What is the connection between archaeology and history? | Who were the first Americans?

4 CHAPTER 1 UNDERSTANDING ANCIENT AMERICA

direct their attention mostly to writings, including personal and private jottings such as letters and diary entries, and an enormous variety of public documents, such as laws, speeches, newspapers, and court cases. Although historians are interested in other artifacts and archaeologists do not neglect written sources if they exist, the concentration of historians on writings and of archaeologists on other physical objects denotes a rough cultural and chronological boundary between the human beings studied by the two groups of scholars, a boundary marked by the use of writing.

Writing is defined as a system of symbols that record spoken language. Writing originated among ancient peoples in China, Egypt, and Central America about eight thousand years ago, within the most recent 2 percent of the four hundred millennia that modern human beings (*Homo sapiens*) have existed. Writing came into use even later in most other places in the world. The ancient Americans who inhabited North America in 1492, for example, possessed many forms of symbolic representation, but not writing.

The people who lived during the millennia before writing were biologically nearly identical to us. Their DNA was the template for ours. But unlike us, they did not use writing to communicate across space and time. They invented hundreds of spoken languages; they moved across the face of the globe, learning to survive in almost every natural environment; they chose and honored leaders; they traded, warred, and worshipped; and, above all, they learned from and taught one another. Much of what we would like to know about their experiences remains unknown because it took place before writing existed.

Archaeologists specialize in learning about people who did not document their history in writing. They study the millions of artifacts these people created. They also scrutinize soil, geological strata, pollen, climate, and other environmental features to reconstruct as much as possible about the world ancient peoples inhabited. Although no documents chronicle the day-to-day lives of ancient Americans, archaeologists have learned to make artifacts, along with their natural and human environment, tell a great deal about the people who used them.

This chapter relies on studies by archaeologists to sketch a brief overview of ancient America, the long first phase of the history of the United States. Ancient Americans and their descendants resided in North America for thousands of years before Europeans arrived. For their own reasons and in their own ways, they created societies and cultures of remarkable diversity and complexity.

KEY FACTORS

Archaeologists
– Focus on physical objects such as bones, spear points, and pottery.

Historians
– Tend to focus more on written records.

QUICK REVIEW <

Why must historians rely on the work of archaeologists to write the history of ancient America?

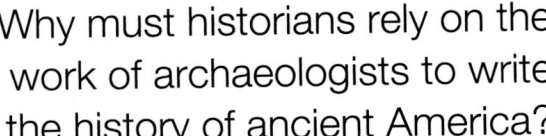

How did Archaic Americans adapt to changing conditions?

How did agriculture change Native American societies?

How were native societies organized in the 1490s?

What were the characteristics of Mexican culture?

Conclusion: How do we understand the worlds of ancient Americans?

> Who were the first Americans?

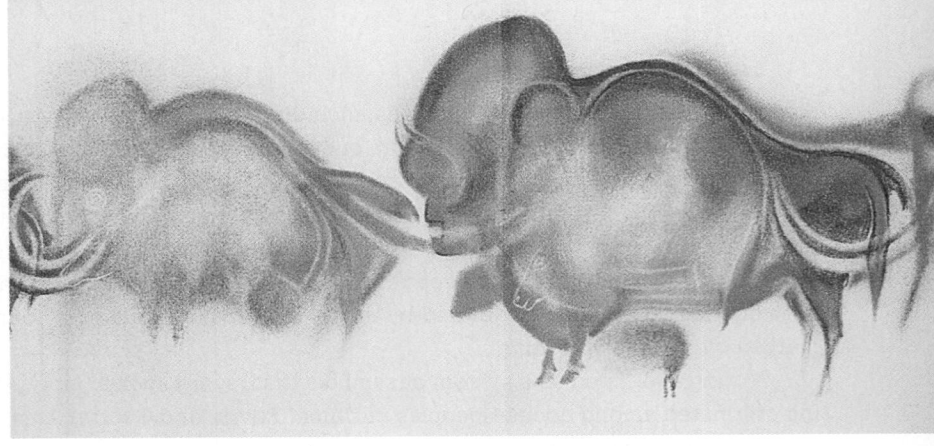

Mammoth Cave Painting Like Clovis peoples in ancient America, human beings elsewhere in the world hunted mammoths. An ancient artist painted this portrait of mammoths on the wall of a cave in southern France about 16,000 BP. North American mammoths stood about fourteen feet tall at the shoulder and weighed eight to ten tons. Hunters armed with stone-tipped wooden spears needed to study such formidable prey to identify their vulnerabilities. Musée de l'Homme.

THE FIRST HUMAN BEINGS to arrive in the Western Hemisphere emigrated from Asia. They brought with them hunting skills, weapon- and tool-making techniques, and a full range of other forms of human knowledge developed millennia earlier in Africa, Europe, and Asia. These first Americans hunted large mammals, such as the mammoths they had learned in Europe and Asia to kill, butcher, and process for food, clothing, building materials, and many other purposes. Most likely, these first Americans wandered into the Western Hemisphere more or less accidentally, hungry and in pursuit of their prey.

African and Asian Origins

Human beings lived elsewhere in the world for hundreds of thousands of years before they reached the Western Hemisphere. They lacked a way to travel to the Western Hemisphere because millions of years before humans existed anywhere on the globe, North and South America became detached from the gigantic common landmass scientists now call Pangaea. About 240 million years ago, powerful forces deep within the earth fractured Pangaea and slowly pushed the continents apart to approximately their present positions (**Map 1.1**). This process of continental drift encircled the land of the Western Hemisphere with large oceans that isolated it from the other continents long before early human beings (*Homo erectus*) first appeared in Africa about two million years ago. (Hereafter in this chapter, the abbreviation *BP*—archaeologists' notation for "years before the present"—is used to indicate dates earlier than two thousand years ago. Dates more recent than two thousand years ago are indicated with the common and familiar notation *AD*—for example, AD 1492.)

More than a million and a half years after *Homo erectus* appeared, or about 400,000 BP, modern humans (*Homo sapiens*) evolved in Africa. All human beings throughout the world today are descendants of these ancient Africans. Slowly, over many millennia, *Homo sapiens* migrated out of Africa and into Europe and

CHAPTER LOCATOR | What is the connection between archaeology and history? | Who were the first Americans?

6 CHAPTER 1 UNDERSTANDING ANCIENT AMERICA

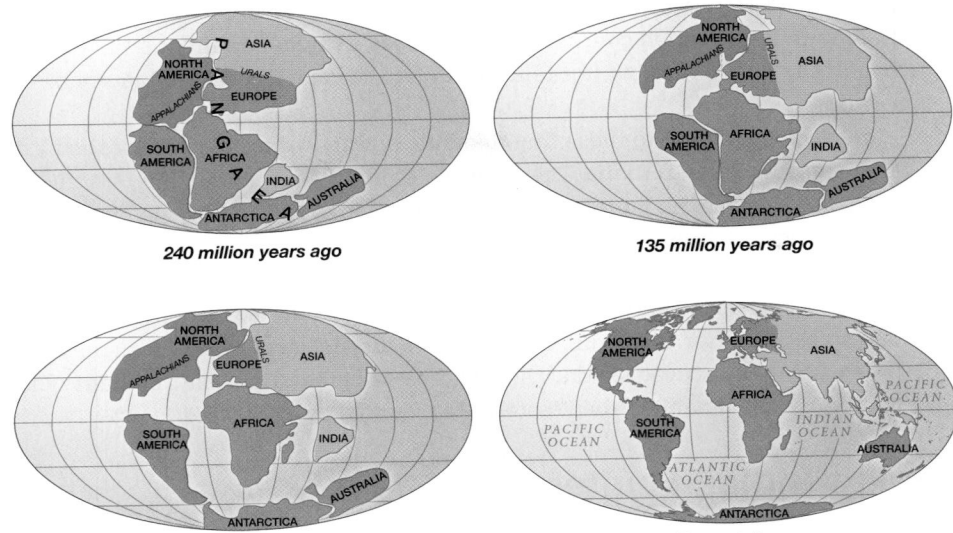

240 million years ago

135 million years ago

65 million years ago

Present day

MAP 1.1 ■ Continental Drift
Massive geological forces separated North and South America from other continents eons before human beings evolved in Africa in the past 1.5 million years.

Asia. Unlike North and South America, Europe and Asia retained land connections to Africa, making this migration possible.

Two major developments made it possible for human beings to migrate to the Western Hemisphere. First, humans successfully adapted to the frigid environment near the Arctic Circle. Second, changes in the earth's climate reconnected North America to Asia.

By about 25,000 BP, *Homo sapiens* had spread from Africa throughout Europe and Asia. People, probably women, had learned to use bone needles to sew animal skins into warm clothing that permitted them to become permanent residents of extremely cold regions such as northeastern Siberia. A few of these ancient Siberians walked to North America on land that now lies submerged beneath the sixty miles of water that currently separates easternmost Siberia from westernmost Alaska. During the last global cold spell—the Wisconsin glaciation, which endured from about 25,000 to 14,000 BP—snow piled up in glaciers, causing the sea level to drop as much as 350 feet below its current level. The falling sea level exposed a land bridge between Asian Siberia and American Alaska as well as a long coastline (now underwater). This land bridge and exposed coastline, which scientists call **Beringia**, opened a pathway hundreds of miles wide between the Eastern and Western Hemispheres.

Siberian hunters presumably roamed Beringia for centuries in search of game animals. As the hunters ventured farther and farther east, and probably also along the Alaskan coastline, they eventually became pioneers of human life

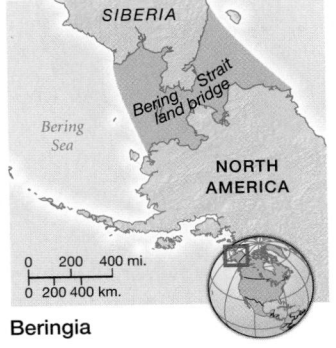

Beringia

CHRONOLOGY

c. 240 million BP
– Pangaea fractures, and continents begin their drift toward present positions.

c. 400,000 BP
– Modern humans (*Homo sapiens*) evolve in Africa.

c. 25,000 BP
– *Homo sapiens* have spread from Africa to Europe and Asia.

c. 25,000–14,000 BP
– Wisconsin glaciation exposes Beringia land bridge between Siberia and Alaska.

c. 15,000 BP
– First humans arrive in North America.

c. 13,500–13,000 BP
– Paleo-Indians in North and Central America use Clovis points to hunt big game.

c. 11,000 BP
– Mammoths and many other big-game prey of Paleo-Indians become extinct.

NOTE: BP is an abbreviation used by archaeologists for "years before the present."

Beringia
▶ Land bridge that was exposed between Asian Siberia and American Alaska when sea levels fell during the Wisconsin glaciation (25,000–14,000 BP), opening a pathway for the migration of Siberian peoples to the Americas.

How did Archaic Americans adapt to changing conditions? | How did agriculture change Native American societies? | How were native societies organized in the 1490s? | What were the characteristics of Mexican culture? | Conclusion: How do we understand the worlds of ancient Americans?

7

in the Western Hemisphere. Their migrations probably had very little influence on their own lives, which continued more or less as they had in Siberia. Although they did not know it, their migrations revolutionized the history of the world.

Archaeologists refer to these first migrants and their descendants for the next few millennia as **Paleo-Indians**. They speculate that these Siberian hunters traveled in small bands of no more than twenty-five people. How many such bands arrived in North America before Beringia disappeared beneath the sea will never be known.

When they came is hotly debated by experts. The first migrants probably arrived sometime after 15,000 BP. Scattered and inconclusive evidence suggests that they may have arrived several thousand years earlier. Certainly, humans who originated in Asia inhabited the Western Hemisphere by 13,500 BP.

Paleo-Indians

▶ The first ancient Americans. Paleo-Indians concentrated their hunting activities on big game, such as mammoths and bison.

Paleo-Indian Hunters

When humans first arrived in the Western Hemisphere, massive glaciers covered most of present-day Canada. A narrow corridor not entirely obstructed by ice ran along the eastern side of Canada's Rocky Mountains, and most archaeologists believe that Paleo-Indians probably migrated through the ice-free passageway in pursuit of game. They may also have traveled along the Pacific coast in small boats, hunting marine life and hopscotching from one desirable landing spot to another. At the southern edge of the glaciers, Paleo-Indians entered a hunters' paradise. North, Central, and South America teemed with wildlife. Ample food permitted the Paleo-Indian population to grow. Within a thousand years or so, Paleo-Indians had migrated to the tip of South America and virtually everywhere else in the Western Hemisphere, as proved by discoveries of their spear points.

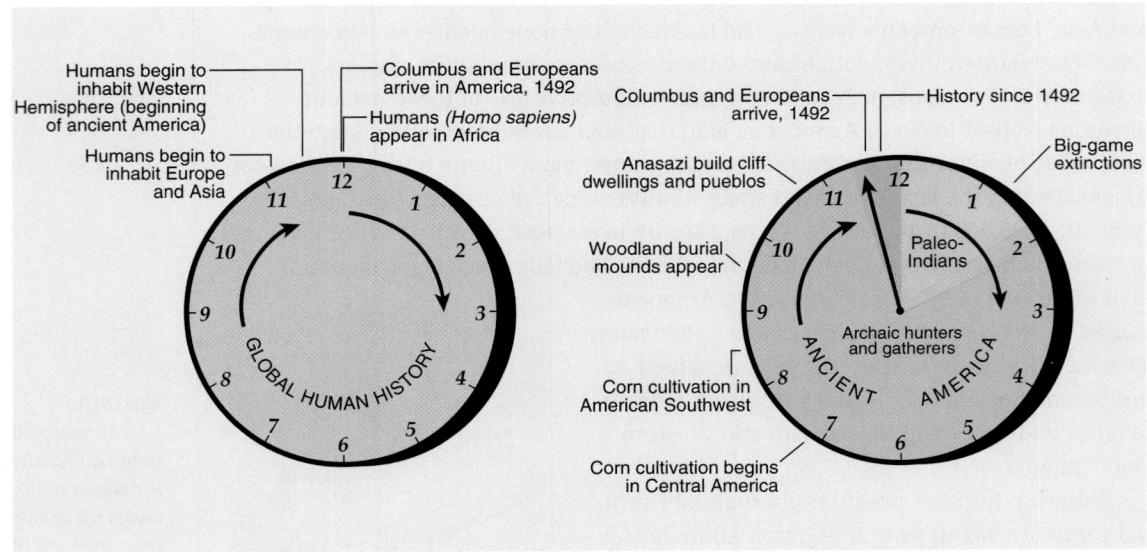

FIGURE 1.1 ■ **Human Habitation of the World and the Western Hemisphere**
These clock faces illustrate the long global history of modern humans (left) and of human history in the Western Hemisphere since the arrival of the first ancient Americans (right).

CHAPTER LOCATOR | What is the connection between archaeology and history? | Who were the first Americans?

8 CHAPTER 1 UNDERSTANDING ANCIENT AMERICA

Early Paleo-Indians used distinctively shaped spearheads known as **Clovis points**, named for the place in New Mexico where they were first excavated. Archaeologists' discovery of Clovis points throughout North and Central America in sites occupied between 13,500 BP and 13,000 BP provides evidence that these nomadic hunters shared a common ancestry and way of life. Paleo-Indians hunted mammoths and bison—judging from the artifacts and bones that have survived from this era—but they probably also hunted smaller animals. Concentration on large animals, when possible, made sense because just one mammoth kill supplied hunters with meat for weeks or, if dried, for months. In addition to food, mammoth kills provided hides and bones for clothing, shelter, tools, and much more.

About 11,000 BP, Paleo-Indians confronted a major crisis. The mammoths and other large mammals they hunted became extinct. The extinction was gradual, stretching over several hundred years. Scientists are not completely certain why it occurred, although environmental change probably contributed to it. About this time, the earth's climate warmed, glaciers melted, and sea levels rose. Mammoths and other large mammals probably had difficulty adapting to the warmer climate. Many archaeologists also believe, however, that Paleo-Indians probably contributed to the extinctions in the Western Hemisphere by killing large animals more rapidly than they could reproduce. Whatever the causes, within just a few thousand years of their arrival in the Western Hemisphere, Paleo-Indian hunters faced a radical change in the natural environment—namely, the extinction of large mammals.

Paleo-Indians adapted to the drastic environmental change of the big-game extinction by making at least two important changes in their way of life. First, hunters began to prey more intensively on smaller animals. Second, Paleo-Indians devoted more energy to foraging—that is, to collecting wild plant foods such as roots, seeds, nuts, berries, and fruits. When Paleo-Indians made these changes, they replaced the apparent uniformity of the big-game-oriented Clovis culture with great cultural diversity adapted to the many natural environments throughout the hemisphere, ranging from icy tundra to steamy jungles.

These post-Clovis adaptations to local environments resulted in the astounding variety of Native American cultures that existed when Europeans arrived in AD 1492. By then, more than three hundred major tribes and hundreds of lesser groups inhabited North America alone. Hundreds more lived in Central and South America. Hundreds of other ancient American cultures had disappeared or transformed themselves as their people constantly adapted to environmental change and other challenges.

Clovis points

▶ Distinctly shaped spearheads used by Paleo-Indians. The discovery of Clovis points throughout North and Central America is evidence that Paleo-Indian hunters shared a common ancestry and way of life.

Clovis Spear Straightener

Clovis hunters used this bone spear straightener about 11,000 BP at a campsite in Arizona. Presumably Clovis hunters stuck their spear shafts through the opening and then grasped the handle of the straightener and moved it back and forth along the length of the shaft to remove imperfections and make the spear a more effective weapon. Arizona State Museum, University of Arizona.

QUICK REVIEW

Why and how did humans migrate to North America?

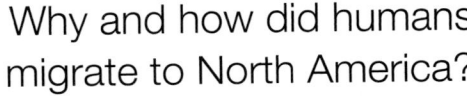

| How did Archaic Americans adapt to changing conditions? | How did agriculture change Native American societies? | How were native societies organized in the 1490s? | What were the characteristics of Mexican culture? | Conclusion: How do we understand the worlds of ancient Americans? |

How did Archaic Americans adapt to changing conditions?

Folsom Point at Wild Horse Arroyo

In 1927, paleontologist J. D. Figgins found this spear point embedded between the fossilized ribs of a bison that had been extinct for 10,000 years. Subsequently named the Folsom point, this discovery stimulated archaeologists to rethink the history of ancient Americans and to uncover fresh evidence of their many cultures.

ARCHAEOLOGISTS use the term *Archaic* to describe the many different hunting and gathering cultures that descended from Paleo-Indians and the long period of time when those cultures dominated the history of ancient America, roughly from 10,000 BP to somewhere between 4000 BP and 3000 BP. The term usefully describes the era in the history of ancient America that followed the Paleo-Indian big-game hunters and preceded the development of agriculture. It denotes a **hunter-gatherer** way of life that persisted in North America long after European colonization.

Like their Paleo-Indian ancestors, **Archaic Indians** hunted with spears, but they also took smaller game with traps, nets, and hooks. Unlike their Paleo-Indian predecessors, most Archaic peoples used a variety of stone tools to prepare food from wild plants. A characteristic Archaic artifact is a grinding stone used to pulverize seeds into edible form. Most Archaic Indians migrated from place to place to harvest plants and hunt animals. They usually did not establish permanent villages, although they often returned to the same river valley or fertile meadow from year to year. In certain regions with especially rich resources—such as present-day California and the Pacific Northwest—they developed permanent settlements. Archaic peoples followed these practices in distinctive ways in the different environmental regions of North America (**Map 1.2**).

hunter-gatherer

▶ A nomadic way of life centered on hunting animals and gathering plants for food. For much of their history, ancient Americans were hunter-gatherers.

Archaic Indians

▶ Members of the many different hunting and gathering cultures that descended from Paleo-Indians. The Archaic period lasted roughly from 10,000 BP to somewhere between 4000 BP and 3000 BP.

CHAPTER LOCATOR | What is the connection between archaeology and history? | Who were the first Americans?

10 CHAPTER 1 UNDERSTANDING ANCIENT AMERICA

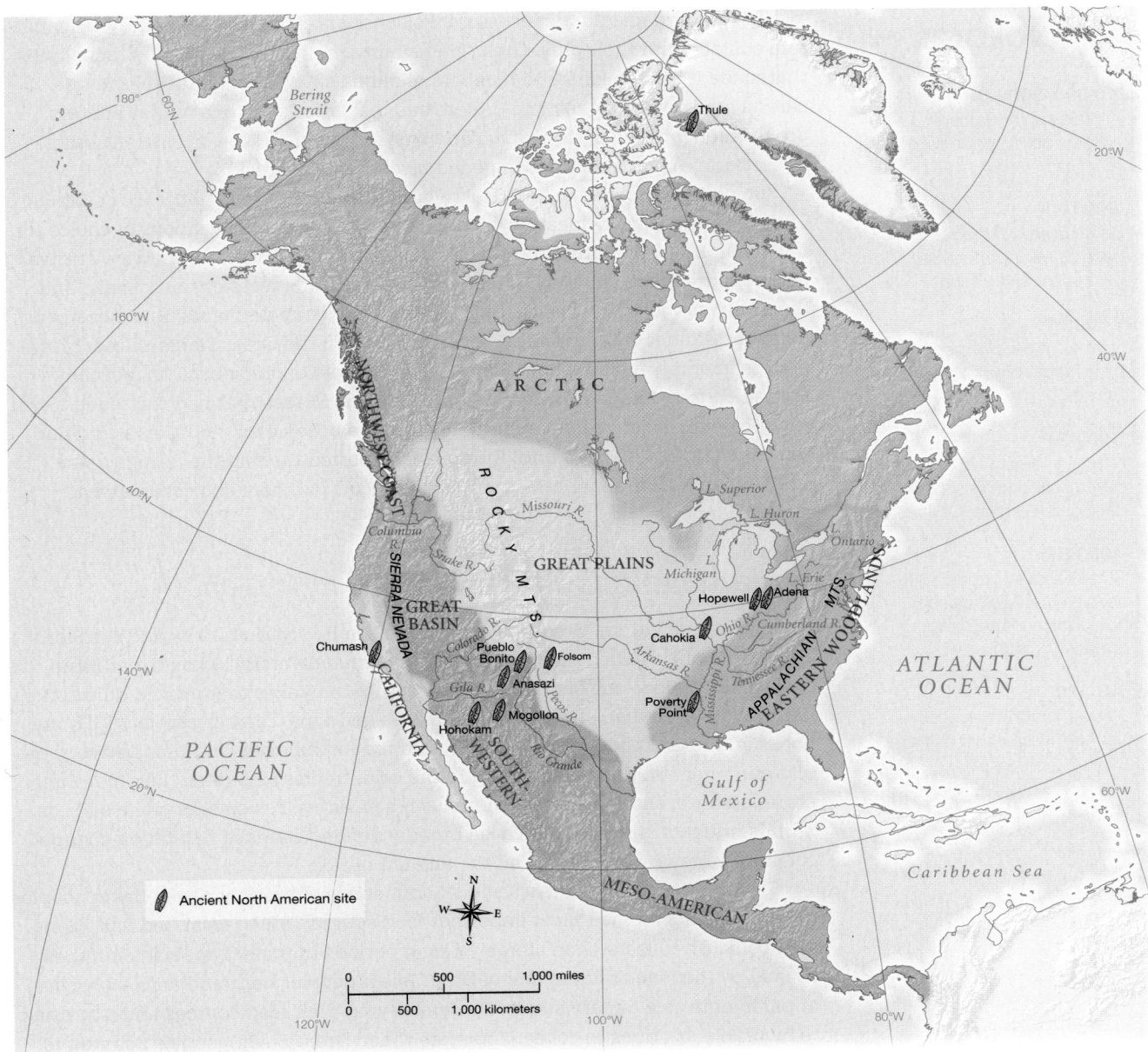

MAP 1.2 ■ Native North American Cultures
Environmental conditions defined the boundaries of the broad zones of cultural similarity among ancient North Americans.

▶ FOR MORE HELP ANALYZING THIS MAP, see the map activity for this chapter in the Online Study Guide at bedfordstmartins.com/roarkunderstanding.

Great Plains Bison Hunters

After the extinction of large game animals, some hunters began to concentrate on bison in the huge herds that grazed the grassy, arid plains stretching for hundreds of miles east of the Rocky Mountains. For almost a thousand years after the big-game extinctions, Archaic Indians hunted bison with spears tipped with flint spear points known as **Folsom points** (named after the site near Folsom, New Mexico, where they were first discovered).

Folsom points
▶ Flint spear points used by some Archaic Indians. Folsom points are named for the site in Folsom, New Mexico, where they were first discovered.

| How did Archaic Americans adapt to changing conditions? | How did agriculture change Native American societies? | How were native societies organized in the 1490s? | What were the characteristics of Mexican culture? | Conclusion: How do we understand the worlds of ancient Americans? |

c. 10,000–3000 BP
- Archaic hunter-gatherer cultures dominate ancient America.

c. 6000 BP
- Some Eastern Woodland peoples begin to establish permanent settlements.

c. 5500 BP
- Northwest peoples begin to concentrate on whaling and fishing.

c. 5000 BP
- Chumash emerge in the region surrounding present-day Santa Barbara, California.

c. 4000 BP
- Some Eastern Woodland peoples grow gourds and pumpkins and begin making pottery.

c. AD 500
- Bows and arrows appear in North America south of the Arctic.

Like their nomadic predecessors, Folsom hunters moved constantly to maintain contact with their prey. Great Plains hunters developed trapping techniques that made it easy to kill large numbers of animals. At the original Folsom site, careful study of the bones found there suggests that early one winter hunters drove bison into the narrow gulch and speared twenty-three of them. At other sites, Great Plains hunters stampeded bison herds over cliffs.

Bows and arrows reached Great Plains hunters from the north about AD 500. They largely replaced spears, which had been the hunters' weapons of choice for millennia. Bows permitted hunters to wound animals from farther away, arrows made it possible to shoot repeatedly, and arrowheads were easier to make and therefore less costly to lose than the larger, heavier spear points. But these new weapons did not otherwise alter bison hunting on the Great Plains. Although we tend to imagine ancient Great Plains bison hunters on horseback, in fact they hunted on foot, like their Paleo-Indian ancestors. Horses that had existed in North America millions of years earlier had long since become extinct. Horses did not return to the Great Plains until Europeans imported them in the decades after 1492, when Native American bison hunters acquired them and soon became expert riders.

Great Basin Cultures

Archaic peoples in the Great Basin between the Rocky Mountains and the Sierra Nevada inhabited a region of great environmental diversity. Some Great Basin Indians lived along the shores of large marshes and lakes that formed during rainy periods. They ate fish of every available size and type, catching them with bone hooks and nets. Other cultures survived in the foothills of mountains between the blistering heat on the desert floor and the cold, treeless mountain heights. Hunters killed deer, antelope, and sometimes bison, as well as smaller game such as rabbits, rodents, and snakes. These broadly defined zones of habitation changed constantly, depending largely on the amount of rain.

Despite the variety and occasional abundance of animals, Great Basin peoples relied on plants as their most important food source. Unlike meat and fish, plant food could be collected and stored for long periods to protect against shortages caused by the fickle rainfall. Many Great Basin peoples gathered ample supplies of piñon nuts as a dietary staple. By diversifying their food sources and migrating to favorable locations to collect and store them, Great Basin peoples adapted to the severe environmental challenges of the region and maintained their Archaic hunter-gatherer way of life for centuries after Europeans arrived in AD 1492.

Pacific Coast Cultures

The richness of the natural environment made present-day California the most densely settled area in all of ancient North America. The land and ocean offered such ample food that California peoples remained hunters and gatherers for hundreds of years after AD 1492. California's diverse environment also encouraged corresponding diversity among native peoples. Archaic settlements in California included about five hundred separate tribes speaking some ninety languages, each with local dialects. No other region of comparable size in North America exhibited such cultural variety.

CHAPTER LOCATOR | What is the connection between archaeology and history? | Who were the first Americans?

12 CHAPTER 1 UNDERSTANDING ANCIENT AMERICA

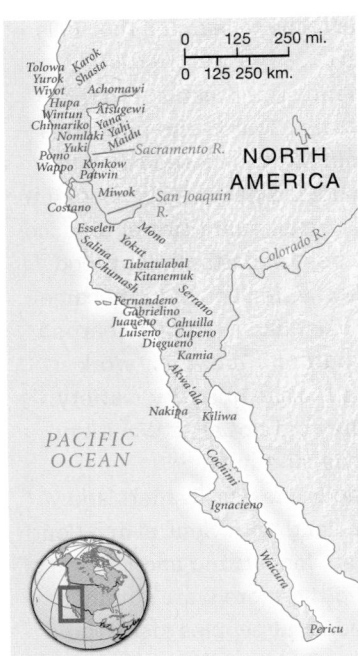

Ancient California Peoples

The Chumash, one of the many California cultures, emerged in the region surrounding what is now Santa Barbara about 5000 BP. Comparatively plentiful food resources—especially acorns—permitted Chumash people to establish relatively permanent villages. Conflict, evidently caused by competition for valuable acorn-gathering territory, frequently broke out among the villages, as documented by Chumash skeletons that display signs of violent deaths. Although few other California cultures achieved the population density and village settlements of the Chumash, all shared the hunter-gatherer way of life and reliance on acorns as a major food source.

Another rich natural environment lay along the Pacific Northwest coast. Like the Chumash, Northwest peoples built more or less permanent villages. After about 5500 BP, they concentrated on catching whales and large quantities of salmon, halibut, and other fish, which they dried to last throughout the year. They also traded with people who lived hundreds of miles from the coast. Fishing freed Northwest peoples to develop sophisticated woodworking skills. They fashioned elaborate wood carvings that denoted wealth and status, as well as huge canoes for fishing, hunting, and conducting warfare against neighboring tribes. Much of the warfare among Archaic northwesterners grew out of attempts to defend or gain access to prime fishing sites.

Eastern Woodland Cultures

East of the Mississippi River, Archaic peoples adapted to a forest environment that included many local variants, such as the major river valleys of the Mississippi, Ohio, Tennessee, and Cumberland; the Great Lakes region; and the Atlantic coast (see Map 1.2, page 11). Throughout these diverse locales, Archaic peoples followed similar survival strategies.

Woodland hunters stalked deer as their most important prey. Deer supplied Woodland peoples with food as well as hides and bones that they crafted into clothing, weapons, needles, and many other tools. Like Archaic peoples elsewhere, Woodland Indians gathered edible plants, seeds, and nuts. About 6000 BP, some Woodland groups established more or less permanent settlements of 25 to 150 people, usually near a river or lake that offered a wide variety of plant and animal resources. The existence of such settlements has permitted archaeologists to locate numerous Archaic burial sites that suggest Woodland people had a life

Chumash Necklace

Long before the arrival of Europeans, ancient Chumash people in southern California made this elegant necklace of abalone shell. Its iridescent splendor demonstrates that Chumash people wore beautiful as well as useful adornments. Natural History Museum of Los Angeles County.

How did Archaic Americans adapt to changing conditions?	How did agriculture change Native American societies?	How were native societies organized in the 1490s?	What were the characteristics of Mexican culture?	Conclusion: How do we understand the worlds of ancient Americans?

expectancy of about eighteen years, a relatively short time to learn all the skills necessary to survive, reproduce, and adapt to change.

Around 4000 BP, Woodland cultures added two important features to their basic hunter-gatherer lifestyles: agriculture and pottery. Gourds and pumpkins that were first cultivated thousands of years earlier in Mexico spread north to Woodland peoples through trade and migration. Woodland peoples also began to cultivate local species such as sunflowers, as well as small quantities of tobacco, another import from South America. Corn was the most important plant food carried to North America by traders and migrants from Mexico, and it became a significant Woodland food crop around 2500 BP. Most likely, women learned how to plant, grow, and harvest these crops as an outgrowth of their work gathering edible wild plants. Cultivated crops added to the quantity, variety, and predictability of Woodland food sources, but they did not alter Woodland peoples' dependence on gathering wild plants, seeds, and nuts.

Like agriculture, pottery also probably originated in Mexico. Traders and migrants probably brought pots into North America along with Central and South American seeds. Pots were more durable than baskets for cooking and storage of food and water, but they were also much heavier and therefore were shunned by nomadic peoples. The permanent settlements of Woodland peoples made the heavy weight of pots much less important than their advantages compared to leaky and fragile baskets. While pottery and agriculture introduced changes in Woodland cultures, ancient Woodland Americans retained the other basic features of their Archaic hunter-gatherer lifestyle, which persisted in most areas to 1492 and beyond.

> QUICK REVIEW

Why did Archaic Indians shift from big-game hunting to foraging and smaller-game hunting?

CHAPTER LOCATOR | What is the connection between archaeology and history? | Who were the first Americans?

14 CHAPTER 1 UNDERSTANDING ANCIENT AMERICA

How did agriculture change Native American societies?

Ancient Agriculture

Dropping seeds into holes punched in cleared ground by a pointed stick, known as a "dibble," this ancient American farmer sows a new crop. Created by a sixteenth-century European artist, the drawing misrepresents who did the agricultural work in many ancient American cultures—namely, women rather than men. However, the three-foot dibble would have been used as shown here.

The Pierpont Morgan Library/Art Resource, NY; Jerry Jacka Photography.

> ► FOR MORE HELP ANALYZING THIS IMAGE, see the visual activity for this chapter in the Online Study Guide at bedfordstmartins.com/roarkunderstanding.

AMONG EASTERN WOODLAND PEOPLES and most other Archaic cultures, agriculture supplemented, but did not replace, hunter-gatherer subsistence strategies. Reliance on wild animals and plants required most Archaic groups to remain small and mobile. But beginning about 4000 BP, distinctive southwestern cultures slowly began to depend on agriculture and to build permanent settlements. Later, around 2500 BP, Woodland peoples in the vast Mississippi valley began to construct **burial mounds** and other earthworks that suggest the existence of social and political hierarchies that archaeologists term **chiefdoms**. Although the hunter-gatherer lifestyle never entirely disappeared, the development of agricultural settlements and chiefdoms represented important innovations to the Archaic way of life.

burial mounds
► Large earthworks constructed by the Woodland peoples of the Mississippi valley, beginning around 2500 BP. Burial mounds provide evidence of social and political hierarchy among Woodland peoples.

chiefdoms
► The term archaeologists use for the social and political hierarchies that emerged among some ancient Americans toward the end of the Archaic period.

| How did Archaic Americans adapt to changing conditions? | How did agriculture change Native American societies? | How were native societies organized in the 1490s? | What were the characteristics of Mexican culture? | Conclusion: How do we understand the worlds of ancient Americans? |

c. 7000 BP
- Corn cultivation begins in Central and South America.

c. 4000 BP
- Distinctive southwestern cultures slowly begin to depend on agriculture and to build permanent settlements.

c. 3500 BP
- Southwestern cultures begin corn cultivation.

c. 2500 BP
- Eastern Woodland cultures start to build burial mounds.
- Some Eastern Woodland peoples begin to cultivate corn.

c. 2500–2100 BP
- Adena culture develops in Ohio.

c. 2100 BP–AD 400
- Hopewell culture emerges in Ohio and Mississippi valleys.

c. AD 200–900
- Mogollon culture develops in New Mexico.

c. AD 500–1400
- Hohokam culture develops in Arizona.

c. AD 800–1500
- Mississippian culture flourishes in Southeast.

c. AD 1000–1200
- Anasazi peoples build cliff dwellings at Mesa Verde and pueblos at Chaco Canyon.

pueblos
▶ Multiunit dwellings that are characteristic of ancient Americans in the Southwest. The ruins of Anasazi pueblos at Mesa Verde, Colorado, and Chaco Canyon, New Mexico, still exist today.

Southwestern Cultures

Ancient Americans in present-day Arizona, New Mexico, and southern portions of Utah and Colorado developed cultures characterized by agriculture and multiunit dwellings called **pueblos**. All southwestern peoples confronted the challenge of a dry climate and unpredictable fluctuations in rainfall that made the supply of wild plant food very unreliable. These ancient Americans probably adopted agriculture in response to this basic environmental condition.

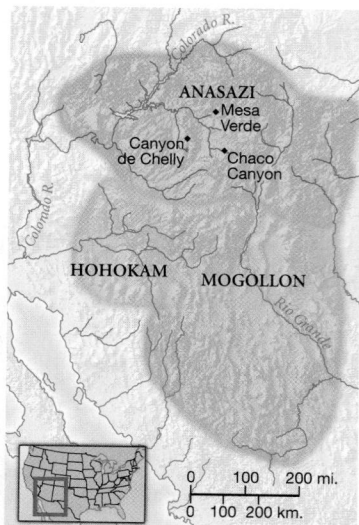

Southwestern Cultures

About 3500 BP, southwestern hunters and gatherers began to cultivate corn. Corn had been grown in Central and South America since about 7000 BP, and it slowly traveled up to North America with migrants and traders. In the centuries after 3500 BP, corn eventually became the most important cultivated crop for ancient Americans throughout North America. In the Southwest, the demands of corn cultivation encouraged hunter-gatherers to restrict their migratory habits in order to tend the crop. A vital consideration was access to water. Southwestern Indians became irrigation experts, conserving water from streams, springs, and rainfall and distributing it to thirsty crops.

About AD 200, small farming settlements began to appear throughout southern New Mexico, marking the emergence of the Mogollon culture. Typically, a Mogollon settlement included a dozen pit houses, each made by digging out a rounded pit about fifteen feet in diameter and a foot or two deep and then erecting poles to support a roof of branches or dirt. Larger villages usually had one or two bigger pit houses that may have been the predecessors of the circular kivas, the ceremonial rooms that became a characteristic of nearly all southwestern settlements. About AD 900, Mogollon culture began to decline, for reasons that remain obscure. Its descendants included the Mimbres people in southwestern New Mexico, who crafted spectacular pottery adorned with human and animal designs. By about AD 1250, the Mimbres culture disappeared, for reasons unknown.

Around AD 500, while the Mogollon culture prevailed in New Mexico, other ancient people migrated from Mexico to southern Arizona and established the distinctive Hohokam culture. Hohokam settlements used sophisticated grids of irrigation canals to plant and harvest crops twice a year. Hohokam settlements reflected the continuing influence of Mexican cultural practices that migrants brought with them as they traveled north. Hohokam people built sizable platform mounds and ball courts characteristic of many Mexican cultures. About AD 1400, Hohokam culture declined for reasons that remain a mystery, although the rising salinity of the soil caused by centuries of irrigation probably caused declining crop yields and growing food shortages.

North of the Hohokam and Mogollon cultures, in a region that encompassed southern Utah and Colorado and northern Arizona and New Mexico, the Anasazi

CHAPTER LOCATOR | What is the connection between archaeology and history? | Who were the first Americans?

16 CHAPTER 1 UNDERSTANDING ANCIENT AMERICA

Pueblo Bonito, Chaco Canyon, New Mexico About AD 1000, Pueblo Bonito stood at the center of Chacoan culture, which extended over more than 20,000 square miles in the region at the intersection of present-day Utah, Colorado, Arizona, and New Mexico. The numerous circular kivas show the significance of ceremonies and rituals to the people of Chaco Canyon. Richard Alexander Cooke III.

▶ FOR MORE HELP ANALYZING THIS IMAGE, see the visual activity for this chapter in the Online Study Guide at bedfordstmartins.com/roarkunderstanding.

culture began to flourish about AD 100. The early Anasazi built pit houses on mesa tops and used irrigation much like their neighbors to the south. Beginning around AD 1000 (again, it is not known why), some Anasazi began to move to large, multistory cliff dwellings whose ruins still exist at Mesa Verde, Colorado, and elsewhere. Other Anasazi communities erected huge stone-walled pueblos with enough rooms to house everyone in the settlement. Pueblo Bonito at Chaco Canyon, New Mexico, for example, contained more than eight hundred rooms. Anasazi pueblos and cliff dwellings typically included one or more kivas used for secret ceremonies, restricted to men, that sought to communicate with the supernatural world.

Drought began to plague the region about AD 1130, and it lasted for more than half a century, triggering the disappearance of Anasazi culture. By AD 1200, the large Anasazi pueblos had been abandoned. The prolonged drought probably intensified conflict among pueblos and made it impossible to depend on the techniques of irrigated agriculture that had worked for centuries. Some Anasazi migrated toward regions with more reliable rainfall and settled in Hopi, Zuñi, and Acoma pueblos that their descendants in Arizona and New Mexico have occupied ever since.

Woodland Burial Mounds and Chiefdoms

No other ancient Americans created dwellings similar to pueblos, but around 2500 BP, Woodland cultures throughout the vast area drained by the Mississippi River began to build burial mounds. The size of the mounds, the labor and organization required to erect them, and differences in the artifacts buried with certain individuals suggest the existence of a social and political hierarchy that

How did Archaic Americans adapt to changing conditions? | How did agriculture change Native American societies? | How were native societies organized in the 1490s? | What were the characteristics of Mexican culture? | Conclusion: How do we understand the worlds of ancient Americans?

17

archaeologists term a chiefdom. Experts do not know the name of a single chief, nor do they know the organizational structure a chief headed. But the only way archaeologists can account for the complex and labor-intensive burial mounds and artifacts found in them is to assume that one person—whom scholars term a chief—commanded the labor and obedience of very large numbers of other people, who made up the chief's chiefdom.

Between 2500 BP and 2100 BP, Adena people built hundreds of burial mounds radiating from central Ohio. In the mounds, the Adena usually buried the dead with grave goods that included spear points and stone pipes as well as thin sheets of mica (a glasslike mineral) crafted into the shapes of birds, beasts, and human hands. Over the body and grave goods, Adena people piled dirt into a mound. Sometimes burial mounds were constructed all at once, but often they were built up slowly over many years. About 2100 BP, Adena culture evolved into the more elaborate Hopewell culture, which lasted about five hundred years. Centered in Ohio, Hopewell culture extended throughout the enormous drainage of the Ohio and Mississippi rivers. Hopewell people built larger mounds than their Adena predecessors had and filled them with more magnificent grave goods.

Burial was probably reserved for the most important members of Hopewell groups. Burial rituals appear to have brought many people together to honor the dead person and to help build the mound. Hopewell mounds were often one hundred feet in diameter and thirty feet high. Grave goods at Hopewell sites testify to the high quality of Hopewell crafts and to a thriving trade network that ranged from Wyoming to Florida. Archaeologists believe that Hopewell chiefs probably played an important role in this interregional trade.

Hopewell culture declined about AD 400 for reasons that are obscure. Archaeologists speculate that bows and arrows, along with an increasing reliance on agriculture, made small settlements more self-sufficient and, therefore, less

Ceramic Jar

This handsome jar, crafted about 2000 BP by a Woodland potter (probably a woman), illustrates the usefulness of ceramic pots for storage and cooking and exhibits the human delight in decorative artistry. Gilcrease Museum, Tulsa, Oklahoma.

CHAPTER LOCATOR | What is the connection between archaeology and history? | Who were the first Americans?

18 CHAPTER 1 UNDERSTANDING ANCIENT AMERICA

dependent on the central authority of the Hopewell chiefs who were responsible for the burial mounds.

Four hundred years later, another mound-building culture flourished. The Mississippian culture emerged in the floodplains of the major southeastern river systems about AD 800 and lasted until about AD 1500. Major Mississippian sites included huge mounds with platforms on top for ceremonies and for the residences of great chiefs. Most likely, the ceremonial mounds and ritual practices derived from Mexican cultural expressions that were carried north by traders and migrants. The largest Mississippian site was **Cahokia**, whose remnants can be seen in Illinois near the confluence of the Mississippi and Missouri rivers.

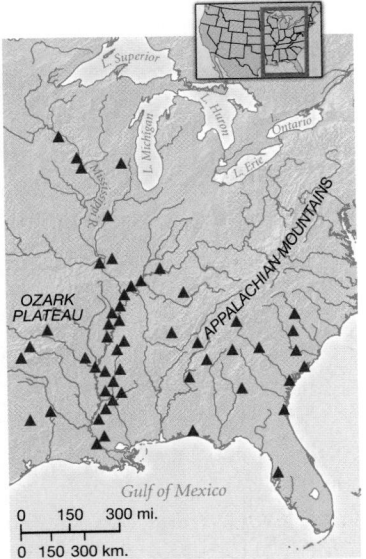

Major Mississippian Mounds, AD 800–1500

Cahokia

Featured one hundred mounds grouped around large open plazas
May have had as many as thirty thousand inhabitants
Residents of Cahokia worshipped a sun god
Evidence of mass human sacrifices demonstrates the coercive power of Cahokia's elites

Cahokia

▶ A flourishing urban area that lasted from about AD 800 until about AD 1500. The largest of the Mississippian sites, Cahokia included huge mounds for ceremonies and for the residences of the chiefs. It may have had as many as thirty thousand residents.

Cahokia and other Mississippian cultures had dwindled by AD 1500. When Europeans arrived, most of the descendants of Mississippian cultures lived in small, dispersed villages supported by hunting and gathering supplemented by agriculture. Clearly, the conditions that caused large chiefdoms to emerge—whatever they were—had changed, and chiefs no longer commanded the powers they had once enjoyed.

QUICK REVIEW

How and why did the societies of the Southwest differ from eastern societies?

How did Archaic Americans adapt to changing conditions?

How did agriculture change Native American societies?

How were native societies organized in the 1490s?

What were the characteristics of Mexican culture?

Conclusion: How do we understand the worlds of ancient Americans?

How were native societies organized in the 1490s?

ABOUT THIRTEEN MILLENNIA after Paleo-Indians first migrated to the Western Hemisphere, a new migration—this time from Europe—began in 1492 with the journey of Christopher Columbus. In the decades before 1492, Native Americans continued to employ their ancestors' time-tested survival strategies of hunting, gathering, and agriculture. Those strategies succeeded in both populating and shaping the new world Europeans encountered.

By the 1490s, Native Americans lived throughout North America, but their total population is a subject of spirited debate among scholars. Some experts claim Native Americans numbered 18 million to 20 million, while others place the population at no more than a million. A prudent estimate is about 4 million. On the eve of European colonization, the small island nation of England had about the same number of people as all of North America. The vastness of North America meant that the population density was low, just 60 people per hundred square miles, compared to more than 8,000 in England. Compared to England and elsewhere in Europe, Native Americans were spread thin across the land because of their survival strategies of hunting, gathering, and agriculture.

CHAPTER LOCATOR | What is the connection between archaeology and history? | Who were the first Americans?

20 CHAPTER 1 UNDERSTANDING ANCIENT AMERICA

Regions in North America with abundant resources had relatively high populations. About one-fifth of Native Americans lived along the West Coast in food-rich California and the Pacific Northwest, where the population density was, respectively, six times greater and four times greater than the average for the whole continent (**Figure 1.2**). The food-scarce Great Plains, Great Basin, and Arctic regions held about one-quarter of Native Americans, but the population density was extremely low, roughly one-tenth the continental average. About a quarter of Native Americans resided in the arid Southwest, where irrigation and intensive agriculture permitted a population density about twice the continental average. But even in California, the most densely inhabited region of North America, population density was just one-twentieth of England's.

The enormous Woodland region east of the Mississippi River was home to about one-third of Native Americans, whose population density approximated the continental average. Eastern Woodland peoples clustered into three broad linguistic and cultural groups: Algonquian, Iroquoian, and Muskogean.

Algonquian tribes inhabited the Atlantic seaboard, the Great Lakes region, and much of the upper Midwest (**Map 1.3**). The relatively mild climate along the Atlantic permitted the coastal Algonquians to grow corn and other crops as well as to hunt and fish. Around the Great Lakes and in northern New England, however, cool summers and severe winters made agriculture impractical.

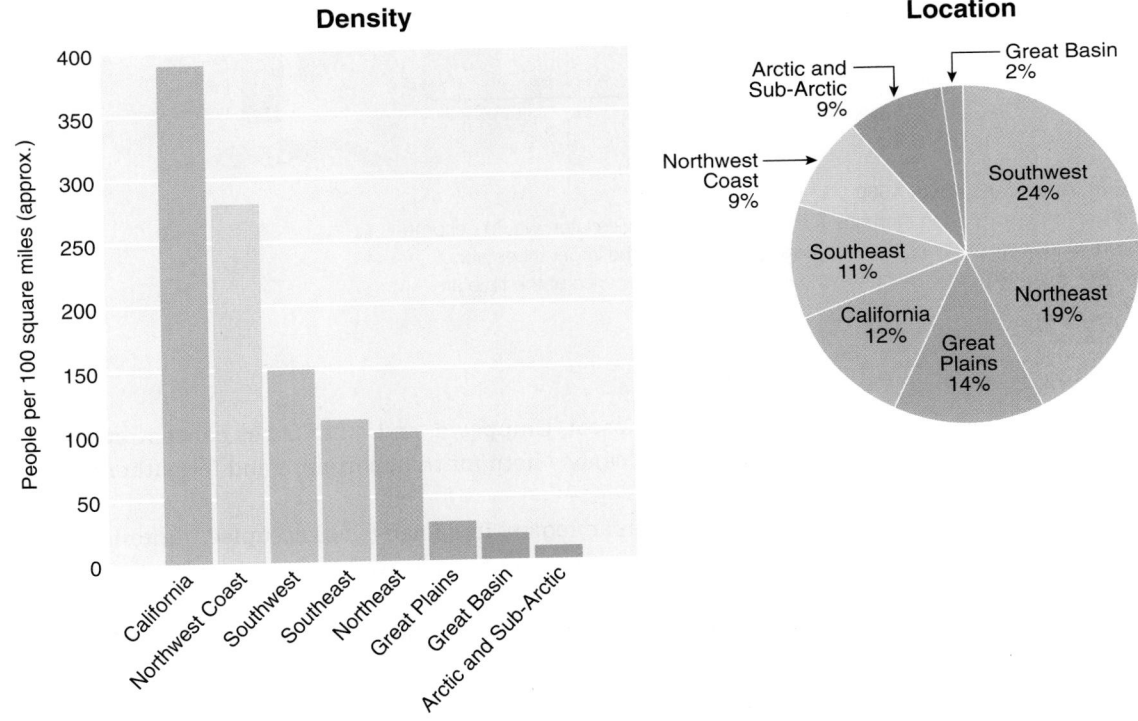

FIGURE 1.2 ■ Native American Population in North America about 1492 (Estimated)
The population density on the enormous expanses of the Great Plains, Great Basin, and Arctic regions was very low, although in total about a quarter of all native North Americans resided in these areas. Overall, the population density in North America was less than 1 percent of the population density of England, a fact that helps explain why European colonists tended to view North America as a comparatively empty wilderness.

| How did Archaic Americans adapt to changing conditions? | How did agriculture change Native American societies? | **How were native societies organized in the 1490s?** | What were the characteristics of Mexican culture? | Conclusion: How do we understand the worlds of ancient Americans? |

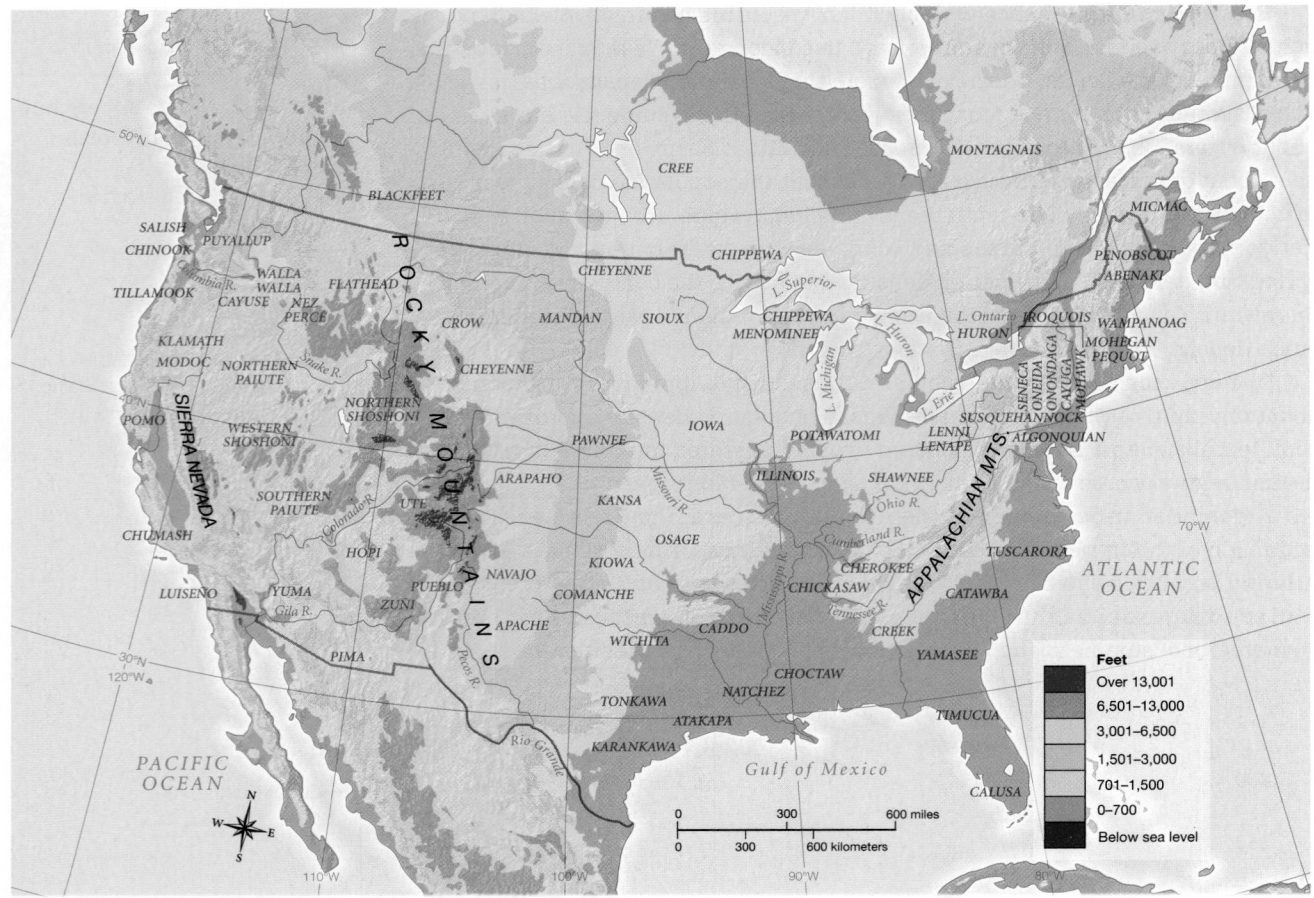

MAP 1.3 ■ Native North Americans about 1500
Distinctive Native American peoples resided throughout the area that, centuries later, would become the United States. This map indicates the approximate location of some of the larger tribes about 1500. In the interest of legibility, many other peoples who inhabited North America at the time are omitted from the map.

Instead, the Abenaki, Penobscot, Chippewa, and other tribes concentrated on hunting and fishing, using canoes both for transportation and for gathering wild rice.

Inland from the Algonquian region, Iroquoian tribes occupied territories centered in Pennsylvania and upstate New York, as well as the hilly upland regions of the Carolinas and Georgia. Three features distinguished Iroquoian tribes from their neighbors. First, their success in cultivating corn and other crops allowed them to build permanent settlements, usually consisting of several bark-covered longhouses up to one hundred feet long and housing five to ten families. Second, Iroquoian societies adhered to matrilineal rules of descent. Property of all sorts belonged to women. Women headed family clans and even selected the chiefs (normally men) who governed the tribes. Third, for purposes of war and diplomacy, an Iroquoian confederation—including the Seneca, Onondaga, Mohawk, Oneida, and Cayuga tribes—formed the League of Five Nations, which remained powerful well into the eighteenth century.

CHAPTER LOCATOR · What is the connection between archaeology and history? · Who were the first Americans?

22 CHAPTER 1 UNDERSTANDING ANCIENT AMERICA

Muskogean peoples spread throughout the woodlands of the Southeast, south of the Ohio River and east of the Mississippi. Including the Creek, Choctaw, Chickasaw, and Natchez tribes, Muskogeans inhabited a region that provided abundant food from hunting, gathering, and agriculture. Remnants of the earlier Mississippian culture still existed in Muskogean religion.

Great Plains peoples accounted for about one out of seven Native Americans. Inhabiting the huge region west of the Eastern Woodlands and east of the Rocky Mountains, many tribes had migrated to the Great Plains within the past two hundred years, forced westward by Iroquoian and Algonquian tribes. Some Great Plains tribes—especially the Mandan and Pawnee—farmed successfully, growing both corn and sunflowers. But the Teton Sioux, Blackfeet, Comanche, Cheyenne, and Crow on the northern plains and the Apache and other nomadic tribes on the southern plains depended on buffalo (American bison) for their subsistence.

Southwestern cultures included about a quarter of all native North Americans. These descendants of the Mogollon, Hohokam, and Anasazi cultures lived in settled agricultural communities, many of them pueblos. They continued to grow corn, beans, and squash using methods they had refined for centuries. However, their communities came under attack by a large number of warlike Athabascan tribes who invaded the Southwest beginning around AD 1300. The Athabascans—principally Apache and Navajo—were skillful warriors who preyed on the sedentary pueblo Indians.

About a fifth of all native North Americans resided along the Pacific coast. In California, abundant acorns and nutritious marine life continued to support high population densities, but they retarded the development of agriculture. Similar dependence on hunting and gathering persisted along the Northwest coast. Salmon was so abundant that at The Dalles, a prime fishing site on the Columbia River on the border of present-day Oregon and Washington, Northwest peoples caught millions of pounds of salmon every summer and traded it as far away as California and the Great Plains. Although important trading centers existed throughout North America, particularly in the Southwest, it is likely that The Dalles was the largest Native American trading center in North America.

While trading was common, all native North Americans in the 1490s still depended on hunting and gathering for a major portion of their food. Most of them also practiced agriculture. Some used agriculture to supplement hunting and gathering; for others, the balance was reversed. People throughout North America used bows, arrows, and other weapons for hunting and warfare. None of them employed writing, expressing themselves instead in many other ways: drawings sketched on stones, wood, and animal skins; patterns woven in baskets and textiles; designs painted on pottery, crafted into beadwork, or carved into effigies; and songs, dances, religious ceremonies, and burial rites.

These rich and varied cultural resources of Native Americans did not include features of life common in Europe during the 1490s. Native Americans did not use wheels; sailing ships were unknown to them; they had no large domesticated animals such as horses, cows, or oxen; their use of metals was restricted to copper. However, the absence of these European conveniences mattered less to native North Americans than their own cultural adaptations to the natural environment local to each tribe and their adaptations to the social environment among neighboring peoples. That great similarity—adaptation to natural and social environments—underlay all the cultural diversity among native North Americans.

How did Archaic Americans adapt to changing conditions?

How did agriculture change Native American societies?

How were native societies organized in the 1490s?

What were the characteristics of Mexican culture?

Conclusion: How do we understand the worlds of ancient Americans?

23

It would be a mistake, however, to conclude that native North Americans lived in blissful harmony with nature and one another. Archaeological sites provide ample evidence of violent conflict among Native Americans. Skeletons bear the marks of wounds as well as of ritualistic human sacrifice and even cannibalism. Religious, ethnic, economic, and familial conflicts must have occurred, but they remain in obscurity because they left few archaeological traces.

Native Americans not only adapted to the natural environment; they also changed it in many ways. They built thousands of structures, from small dwellings to massive pueblos and enormous mounds, permanently altering the landscape. Their gathering techniques selected productive and nutritious varieties of plants, thereby shifting the balance of local plants toward useful varieties. The first stages of North American agriculture, for example, probably resulted from Native Americans gathering wild seeds and then sowing them in a meadow for later harvest. It is almost certain that fertile and hardy varieties of corn were developed this way, first in Mexico and later in North America. To clear land for planting corn, Native Americans set fires that burned off thousands of acres of forest.

Native Americans also used fires for hunting. Great Plains hunters often started fires to force buffalo together and make them easy to slaughter. Eastern Woodland, Southwest, and Pacific coast Indians also set fires to hunt deer and other valuable prey. Throughout North America, Indians started fires along the edges of woods to burn off shrubby undergrowth and encroaching tree seedlings. These burns encouraged the growth of tender young plants that attracted deer and other game animals, bringing them within convenient range of hunters' weapons. The burns also encouraged the growth of food plants that Indians relished, such as blackberries, strawberries, and raspberries.

Because fires set by Native Americans usually burned until they ran out of fuel or were extinguished by rain or wind, enormous regions of North America were burned over. In the long run, fires created and maintained meadows for hunting and agriculture, cleared underbrush from forests, and promoted a diverse and productive natural environment. Fires, like other activities of Native Americans, shaped the landscape of North America long before Europeans arrived in 1492.

> QUICK REVIEW

What common characteristics underlay Native American diversity in the 1490s?

CHAPTER LOCATOR | What is the connection between archaeology and history? | Who were the first Americans?

24 CHAPTER 1 UNDERSTANDING ANCIENT AMERICA

What were the characteristics of Mexican culture?

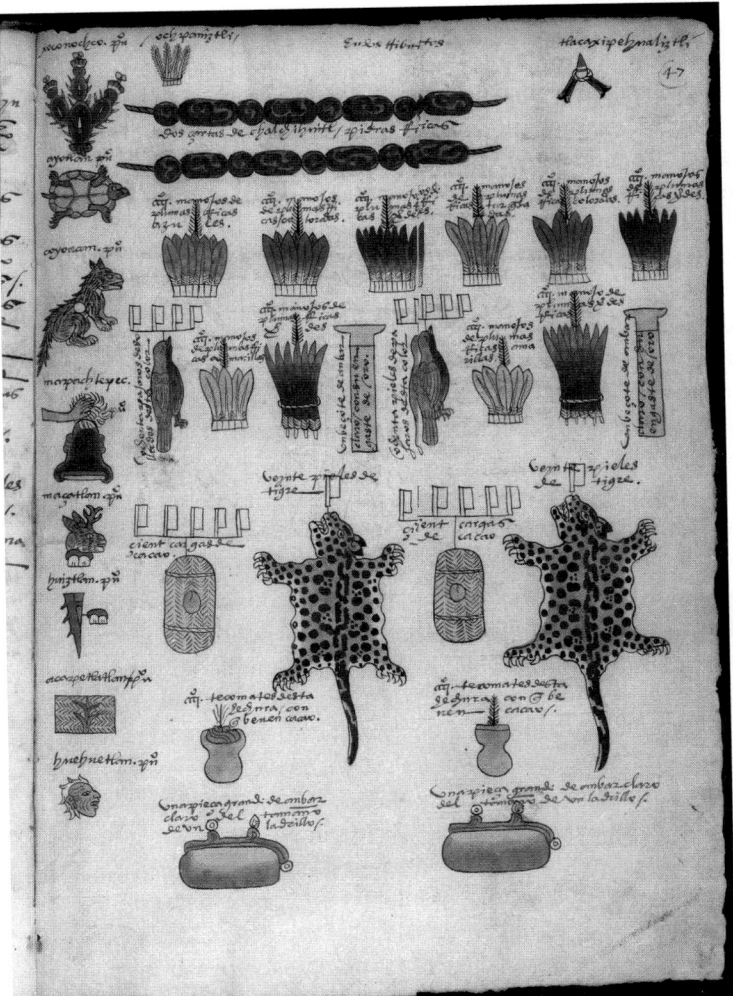

Mexican Tribute Account

This page from the *Codex Mendoza* records the tribute paid to the Mexican capital by the Xoconochco province, a tropical region near present-day Chiapas near the Guatemalan border. In this case, the tribute includes, among many other things, two large strings of green stones, fourteen hundred bundles of rich feathers, and eighty complete bird skins. The tribute exacted by the Mexicans from their empire made them wealthy and created resentment among conquered peoples. Bodleian Library, Oxford, U.K., MS Arch.Self.A1.Fol.47r.

THE INDIGENOUS POPULATION of the New World (the Western Hemisphere) numbered roughly 80 million in the 1490s, about the same as the population of Europe. Almost all these people lived in Mexico and Central and South America. Like their much less numerous North American counterparts, they too lived in a natural environment of tremendous diversity. They too developed hundreds of cultures. But among all these cultures, the **Mexica** stood out. (Europeans often called these people Aztecs, a name the Mexica did not use.) Their empire stretched from coast to coast across central Mexico, encompassing between 8 million and 25 million people (experts disagree about the total population). We know more about the Mexica than about any other Native American society of the time, principally because of their massive monuments and their Spanish conquerors' well-documented interest in subduing them.

The Mexica began their rise to prominence about 1325, when small bands settled on a marshy island in Lake Texcoco, the site of the future city of Tenochtitlán, the capital of the Mexican empire. Resourceful, courageous, and cold-blooded warriors, the Mexica often hired out as mercenaries for richer, more settled tribes.

Mexica

▶ Native peoples who, by 1490, had built an empire in central Mexico. Also known as Aztecs, the Mexica were a warrior people whose society was built around conquest and the extraction of tribute from conquered peoples.

How did Archaic Americans adapt to changing conditions?

How did agriculture change Native American societies?

How were native societies organized in the 1490s?

What were the characteristics of Mexican culture?

Conclusion: How do we understand the worlds of ancient Americans?

25

c. AD 1325
- Small bands of Mexica settle on a marshy island in Lake Texcoco.

c. AD 1430
- Mexica succeed in asserting their dominance over their former allies and leading their own military campaigns.

c. 1490
- Mexican empire stretches from coast to coast in central Mexico and encompasses between 8 and 25 million people.

AD 1492
- Christopher Columbus arrives in New World, beginning European colonization.

By 1430, the Mexica succeeded in asserting their dominance over their former allies and leading their own military campaigns in an ever-widening arc of empire building. By the 1490s, the Mexica ruled an empire that covered more land than Spain and Portugal combined and contained almost three times as many people.

The empire exemplified the central values of Mexican society. The Mexica worshipped the war god Huitzilopochtli. Warriors held the most exalted positions in the social hierarchy, even above the priests who performed the sacred ceremonies that won Huitzilopochtli's favor. In the almost constant battles necessary to defend and to extend the empire, young Mexican men exhibited the courage and daring that would allow them to rise in the carefully graduated ranks of warriors. The Mexica considered capturing prisoners the ultimate act of bravery. Warriors usually turned over the captives to Mexican priests, who sacrificed them to Huitzilopochtli by cutting out their hearts. The Mexica believed that human sacrifice fed the sun's craving for blood, preventing a fatal descent into everlasting darkness and chaos.

The empire contributed far more to Mexican society than victims for sacrifice. At the most basic level, the empire functioned as a military and political system that collected tribute from subject peoples. The Mexica forced conquered tribes to pay tribute in goods, not money. Tribute redistributed to the Mexica as much as one-third of the goods produced by conquered tribes and included everything from textiles to basic food products such as corn and beans, as well as exotic luxury items such as gold, turquoise, and rare bird feathers.

Tribute reflected the fundamental relations of power and wealth that pervaded the Mexican empire. The relatively small nobility of Mexican warriors, supported by a still smaller priesthood, possessed the military and religious power to command the obedience of thousands of non-noble Mexicans and of millions of other non-Mexicans in subjugated provinces. The Mexican elite exercised their power to obtain tribute and thereby to redistribute wealth from the conquered to the conquerors, from the commoners to the nobility, from the poor to the rich. This redistribution of wealth made possible the achievements of Mexican society that eventually amazed the Spaniards: the huge cities, fabulous temples, teeming markets, and luxuriant gardens, not to mention the storehouses stuffed with gold and other treasures.

On the whole, the Mexica did not interfere much with the internal government of conquered regions. Instead, they usually permitted the traditional ruling elite to stay in power—so long as they paid tribute. The conquered provinces received very little in return from the Mexica, except immunity from punitive raids. Subjugated communities felt exploited by the constant payment of tribute to the Mexica. By depending on military conquest and the constant collection of tribute, the Mexica failed to create among their subjects a belief that Mexican domination was, at some level, legitimate and equitable. After 1492, Spanish intruders would exploit this high level of discontent to conquer the Mexica.

> ## QUICK REVIEW

How did the conquest and creation of an empire exemplify the central values of Mexican society?

CHAPTER LOCATOR | What is the connection between archaeology and history? | Who were the first Americans?

26 CHAPTER 1 UNDERSTANDING ANCIENT AMERICA

Conclusion: How do we understand the worlds of ancient Americans?

© Charles and Josette Lenars/Corbis.

ANCIENT AMERICANS SHAPED the history of human beings in the New World for more than twelve thousand years. They established continuous human habitation in the Western Hemisphere from the time the first big-game hunters crossed Beringia until 1492 and beyond. Ancient Americans achieved their success through resourceful adaptation to the hemisphere's ever-changing natural environments. Their creativity and artistry are unmistakably documented in the artifacts they left at kill sites, camps, and burial mounds.

In the five centuries after 1492—just 4 percent of the time human beings have inhabited the Western Hemisphere—Europeans and their descendants began to shape and eventually to dominate American history. Native American peoples continued to influence major developments of American history for centuries after 1492. But the new wave of strangers that at first trickled and then flooded into the New World from Europe and Africa forever transformed the peoples and places of ancient America.

SO NOW YOU KNOW

At the beginning of the chapter, you were asked if you knew that central Mexico had three times as many people in 1492 as did Spain and Portugal combined. Now you know that the Americas were rich, diverse, and fully populated, some areas very densely, others much less so. Ancient Americans had their own cultures, values, religious beliefs, and ways of understanding the world that were sometimes as varied from one another as they would be from those of the Europeans and Africans whom they would soon encounter.

| How did Archaic Americans adapt to changing conditions? | How did agriculture change Native American societies? | How were native societies organized in the 1490s? | What were the characteristics of Mexican culture? | Conclusion: How do we understand the worlds of ancient Americans? |

27

CHAPTER 1 STUDY GUIDE

Online Study Guide
bedfordstmartins.com/roarkunderstanding

STEP 1

GETTING STARTED

Below are basic terms from this period in American history. Can you identify each term below and explain why it matters? To do this exercise online or to download this chart, visit bedfordstmartins.com/roarkunderstanding.

TERM	WHO OR WHAT & WHEN	WHY IT MATTERS
Beringia, p. 7		
Paleo-Indians, p. 8		
Clovis points, p. 9		
hunter-gatherer, p. 10		
Archaic Indians, p. 10		
Folsom points, p. 11		
burial mounds, p. 15		
chiefdoms, p. 15		
pueblos, p. 16		
Cahokia, p. 19		
Mexica, p. 25		

STEP 2

MOVING BEYOND THE BASICS

The exercise below represents a more advanced understanding of the chapter material. Consider the differences between the major Indian cultural groups in 1490. As you fill in the chart, consider the relationship between the information you include under the three column headings for each cultural group. How, for instance, did geography and climate shape the group's economy and lifestyle? How did economy and lifestyle shape the group's social and political organization? To do this exercise online or to download this chart, visit bedfordstmartins.com/roarkunderstanding.

Indian peoples in 1490	Geography and climate	Economy and lifestyle (sources of food and material goods, economic organization, trade)	Social/political organization (religion, family structures, social hierarchy)
Southwestern cultures			
Eastern Woodland cultures			
Pacific coast cultures			
Great Basin cultures			
Great Plains cultures			

Now that you have reviewed key elements of the chapter, take a step back and try to explain the big picture. Remember to use specific examples from the chapter in your answers. To do this exercise online, visit bedfordstmartins.com/roarkunderstanding.

THE FIRST AMERICANS

▶ When and how did humans first arrive in the Americas?

▶ Describe the lifestyle of the Paleo-Indians. How did they adapt to the extinction of mammoths and other large mammals around 11,000 BP?

AGRICULTURE AND ADAPTATION

▶ How did Archaic Indians differ from their Paleo-Indian ancestors?

▶ How did the advent of agriculture change the settlement patterns and social organization of some Indian groups?

NATIVE AMERICAN CULTURES IN 1490

▶ What factors shaped population density across North America?

▶ What set the Mexica apart from the other Indian cultures of North America?

LOOKING BACKWARD, LOOKING AHEAD

▶ What accounts for the diversity of Indian peoples on the eve of European contact?

IN YOUR OWN WORDS

Imagine that you must explain chapter 1 to someone who hasn't read it. What would be the most important points to include and why?

2

ENCOUNTERING THE NEW WORLD

1492–1600

> This chapter examines the causes, course, and impact of Europeans' exploration of parts of the world previously unknown to them, from early Portuguese efforts to chart the coast of Africa to the establishment of a Spanish colonial empire in the New World. It explores the many changes in both the New World and the Old World caused by Europeans' encounters with Native Americans during the sixteenth century.

> What factors led to European exploration in the fifteenth century?

> What did Spanish explorers discover in the western Atlantic?

> How did Spaniards explore, conquer, and colonize New Spain?

> How did New Spain influence sixteenth-century Europe?

> Conclusion: What promise did the New World offer Europeans?

DID YOU KNOW?

The conquest of the Americas made Spain the most powerful European country in the sixteenth century.

"Europeans Encountering Indians," unknown artist, ca. 1700.

What factors led to European exploration in the fifteenth century?

HISTORICALLY, the East—not the West—attracted Europeans. Around the year 1000, Norsemen crossed the North Atlantic and founded a small fishing village at L'Anse aux Meadows on the tip of Newfoundland that lasted only a decade or so. Viking sagas memorialized the Norse "discovery," but it had virtually no other impact in the New World or in Europe. Instead, wealthy Europeans developed a taste for luxury goods from Asia and Africa, and merchants competed to satisfy that taste. As Europeans traded with the East and with one another, they acquired new information about the world they inhabited. A few people—sailors, merchants, and aristocrats—took the risks of exploring beyond the limits of the world known to Europeans.

Mediterranean Trade and European Expansion

From the twelfth through the fifteenth centuries, spices, silk, carpets, ivory, gold, and other exotic goods traveled overland from Persia, Asia Minor, India, and Africa and then funneled into continental Europe through Mediterranean trade routes (**Map 2.1**). Dominated primarily by the Italian cities of Venice, Genoa, and Pisa, this trade enriched Italian merchants and bankers, who fiercely defended their near monopoly of access to Eastern goods. The vitality of the Mediterranean trade offered participants few incentives to look for alternatives.

In the mid-fourteenth century, Europeans suffered a catastrophic epidemic of bubonic plague. The Black Death, as it was called, killed about a third of the European population. The plague had major long-term consequences. By drastically reducing the population, it made Europe's limited supply of food more plentiful for survivors. Many survivors inherited property from plague victims, giving them new chances for advancement.

Understandably, most Europeans perceived the world as a place of alarming risks where the delicate balance of health, harvests, and peace could quickly be tipped toward disaster by epidemics, famine, and violence. Most people protected themselves from the constant threat of calamity by worshipping the supernatural, by living amid kinfolk and friends, and by maintaining good relations with the rich and powerful. But the insecurity and uncertainty of fifteenth-century European life also encouraged a few people to take greater risks, such as embarking on dangerous sea voyages through uncharted waters to points unknown.

In European societies, exploration promised fame and fortune to those who succeeded. Monarchs such as Isabella of Spain who hoped to enlarge their realms

CHAPTER LOCATOR | What factors led to European exploration in the fifteenth century?

32 CHAPTER 2 ENCOUNTERING THE NEW WORLD

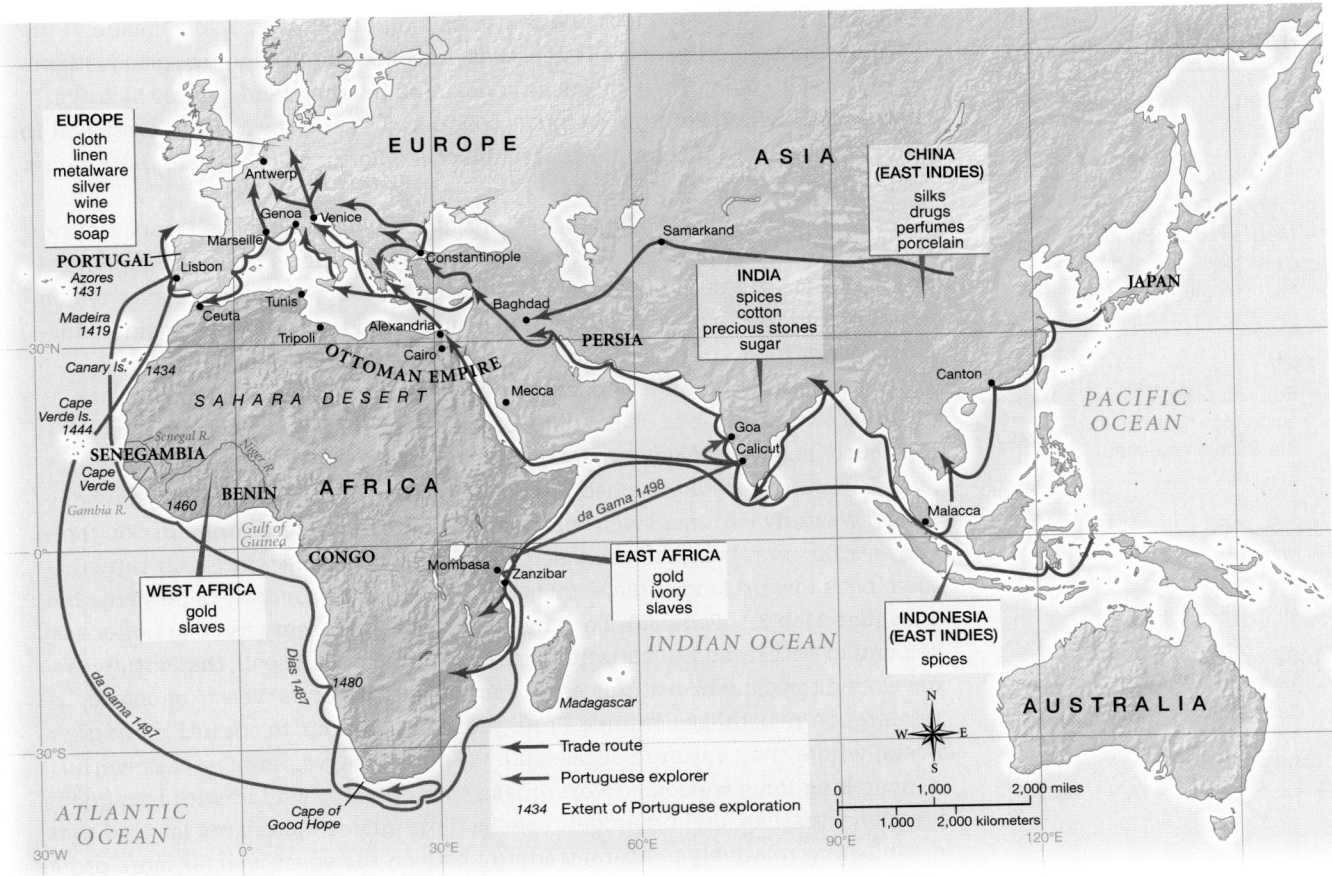

MAP 2.1 ■ European Trade Routes and Portuguese Exploration in the Fifteenth Century
The strategic geographic position of Italian cities as a conduit for overland trade from Asia was slowly undermined during the fifteenth century by Portuguese explorers who hopscotched along the coast of Africa and eventually found a sea route that opened the rich trade of the East to Portuguese merchants.

and enrich their dynasties also had reasons to sponsor journeys of exploration. More territory meant more subjects who could pay more taxes, provide more soldiers, and participate in more commerce, magnifying a monarch's power and prestige. Voyages of exploration also could stabilize a monarch's regime by diverting unruly noblemen toward distant lands. Some explorers, such as Columbus, were commoners who hoped to be elevated to the aristocracy as a reward for their daring achievements.

Scientific and technological advances also helped set the stage for exploration. The invention of movable type by Johannes Gutenberg around 1450 in Germany made printing easier and cheaper, stimulating the diffusion of information, including news of discoveries, among literate Europeans. By 1400, crucial navigational aids employed by maritime explorers were already available: compasses; hourglasses, useful in estimating speed; and the astrolabe and quadrant, devices for determining latitude. While many people knew about these and other advances, the Portuguese were the first to use them in a campaign to sail beyond the limits of the world known to Europeans.

A Century of Portuguese Exploration

Portugal devoted far more energy and wealth to the geographic exploration of the world between 1415 and 1460 than all the other countries of Europe combined. Facing the Atlantic on the Iberian Peninsula, the Portuguese lived on the fringes of the thriving Mediterranean trade. As a Christian kingdom, Portugal cooperated

What did Spanish explorers discover in the western Atlantic?	How did Spaniards explore, conquer, and colonize New Spain?	How did New Spain influence sixteenth-century Europe?	Conclusion: What promise did the New World offer Europeans?

33

c. 1000
- Norsemen found small village on the tip of Newfoundland.

c. 1100–1500
- Mediterranean trade routes dominate European trade with Asia, India, Africa, and the Middle East.

1347
- Bubonic plague epidemic known as the Black Death reaches Europe.

1415–1460
- Prince Henry the Navigator works to advance Portuguese trade and exploration.

1488
- Bartolomeu Dias rounds Cape of Good Hope.

1498
- Vasco da Gama sails to India.

Prince Henry the Navigator

▶ Portuguese prince who, between 1415 and 1460, collected information about sailing techniques and geography, sought new sources of trade for Portugal, and financed voyages of exploration. His efforts contributed to Portugal's creation of a commercial empire in Africa, India, Indonesia, and China in the early sixteenth century.

with Spain in the Reconquest, the centuries-long drive to expel Muslims from the Iberian Peninsula. The religious zeal that propelled the Reconquest also justified expansion into what the Portuguese considered heathen lands. A key victory came in 1415 when Portuguese forces conquered Ceuta, the Muslim bastion at the mouth of the Strait of Gibraltar that had blocked Portugal's access to the Atlantic coast of Africa.

The most influential advocate of Portuguese exploration was **Prince Henry the Navigator**, son of the Portuguese king (and great-uncle of Queen Isabella of Spain). From 1415 until his death in 1460, Henry collected the latest information about sailing techniques and geography, supported new crusades against Muslims, sought fresh sources of trade, and pushed explorers to go farther still.

Neither the Portuguese nor anybody else in Europe knew the immensity of Africa or the length or shape of its coastline. At first, Portuguese mariners cautiously hugged the west coast of Africa, seldom venturing beyond sight of land. By 1434, they had reached the northern edge of the Sahara Desert, where strong westerly currents swept them out to sea. They soon learned to ride those currents far away from the coast before catching favorable winds that turned them back toward land, a technique that allowed them to reach Cape Verde by 1444 (See Map 2.1, Page 33). To stow the supplies necessary for long periods at sea and to withstand the battering of waves in the open ocean, the Portuguese developed the caravel, a sturdy ship that became explorers' vessel of choice.

African resistance confined Portuguese expeditions to coastal trading posts, where they bartered successfully for gold, slaves, and ivory. Powerful African kingdoms welcomed Portuguese trading ships loaded with iron goods, weapons, textiles, and ornamental shells. Portuguese merchants learned that establishing relatively peaceful trading posts on the coast was far more profitable than attempting the violent conquest and colonization of inland regions. In the 1460s, the Portuguese used African slaves to develop sugar plantations on the Cape Verde Islands, inaugurating an association between enslaved Africans and plantation labor that would be transplanted to the New World.

About 1480, Portuguese explorers began a conscious search for a sea route to Asia. In 1488, Bartolomeu Dias sailed around the Cape of Good Hope at the southern tip of Africa and hurried back to Lisbon with the exciting news that it appeared to be possible to sail on to India and China. In 1498, after ten years of careful preparation, Vasco da Gama commanded the first Portuguese fleet to sail to India. Portugal quickly capitalized on the commercial potential of da Gama's new sea route. By the early sixteenth century, the Portuguese controlled a far-flung commercial empire in India, Indonesia, and China (collectively referred to as the East Indies). Their new sea route to the East eliminated overland travel and allowed Portuguese merchants to charge much lower prices for the Eastern goods they imported and still make handsome profits.

> ## QUICK REVIEW

Why did European exploration expand dramatically in the fifteenth century?

CHAPTER LOCATOR | What factors led to European exploration in the fifteenth century?

34   CHAPTER 2
ENCOUNTERING THE NEW WORLD

What did Spanish explorers discover in the western Atlantic?

IN RETROSPECT, the explorations of the African coast and the East Indies during the fifteenth century seemed to make the Portuguese ideally qualified to venture across the Atlantic. However, Portuguese and most other experts believed that sailing west across the Atlantic to Asia was literally impossible. The European discovery of America required someone bold enough to believe that the experts were wrong and that the risks could be overcome. That person was **Christopher Columbus**. His explorations inaugurated a geographic revolution that forever altered Europeans' understanding of the world and its peoples, including themselves. Columbus's landfall in the Caribbean originated a thriving exchange between the people, ideas, cultures, and institutions of the Old and New Worlds that continues to this day.

Christopher Columbus
▶ Genoese sailor who, under Spanish auspices beginning in 1492, made a series of voyages across the Atlantic Ocean in search of a western route to Asia. His discovery of the Americas began the process of European expansion in the New World.

The Explorations of Columbus

Columbus went to sea when he was about fourteen, and he eventually made his way to Lisbon, where he married Felipa Moniz, whose father had been raised in the household of Prince Henry the Navigator. Through Felipa, Columbus gained access to explorers' maps and information about the tricky currents and winds encountered in sailing the Atlantic. Columbus himself ventured into the Atlantic frequently and sailed at least twice to the central coast of Africa.

CHRONOLOGY

1492
– Christopher Columbus lands on Caribbean island that he names San Salvador.

1493
– Columbus makes second voyage to New World.

1494
– Portugal and Spain negotiate Treaty of Tordesillas.

1497
– John Cabot searches for Northwest Passage.

1513
– Vasco Núñez de Balboa crosses Isthmus of Panama.

1519
– Ferdinand Magellan sets out to sail around the world.

Like other educated Europeans, Columbus believed that the earth was a sphere and that theoretically it was possible to reach the East Indies by sailing west. With flawed calculations, he estimated that Asia was only about 2,500 miles away, a shorter distance than Portuguese ships routinely sailed between Lisbon and the Congo. In fact, the shortest distance to Japan from Europe's jumping-off point was nearly 11,000 miles. Convinced by his erroneous calculations, Columbus set out to prove he was right.

In 1492, after years of unsuccessful lobbying in Portugal and Spain, plus overtures to England and France, Columbus finally won financing for his journey from the Spanish monarchs, Isabella and Ferdinand. They saw Columbus's venture as an inexpensive gamble: The potential loss was small, but the potential gain was huge.

After scarcely three months of preparation, Columbus and his small fleet—the *Niña*, the *Pinta*, and the *Santa María*—headed west. Six weeks after leaving the Canary Islands, where he stopped for supplies, Columbus landed on a tiny Caribbean island about three hundred miles north of the eastern tip of Cuba.

Columbus claimed possession of the island for Isabella and Ferdinand and named it San Salvador, in honor of the Savior, Jesus Christ. He called the islanders "Indians," assuming that they inhabited the East Indies somewhere near Japan or China. The islanders called themselves Tainos, which in their language meant "good" or "noble." The Tainos inhabited most of the Caribbean islands Columbus visited on his first voyage. An agricultural people, the Tainos grew cassava, corn, cotton, tobacco, and other crops. Instead of dressing in the finery Columbus had expected to find in the East Indies, the Tainos "all . . . go around as naked as their mothers bore them," Columbus wrote. Although Columbus concluded that the Tainos "had no religion," in reality they worshipped gods they called *zemis*, ancestral spirits who inhabited natural objects such as trees and stones. The Tainos mined a little gold, but they had no riches. "It seemed to me that they were a people very poor in everything," Columbus wrote.

At first, Columbus got the impression that the Tainos believed the Spaniards came from heaven. But after six weeks of encounters, Columbus decided that "the people of these lands do not understand me nor do I, nor anyone else that I have with me, [understand] them. And many times I understand one thing said by these Indians . . . for another, its contrary." The confused communication between the Spaniards and the Tainos suggests how strange each group seemed to the other. Columbus's perceptions of the Tainos were shaped by European attitudes, ideas, and expectations, just as the Tainos' perceptions of the Europeans were no doubt colored by their own culture.

Columbus's First Voyage to the New World, 1492–1493

Taino Zemi Basket

Crafted sometime between 1492 and about 1520, this basket is an example of the effigies Tainos made to represent *zemis*, or deities. The basket maker used African ivory and European mirrors as well as Native American fibers, dyes, and designs. Archivio Fotografico del Museo Preistorico Etnografico L. Pigorini, Roma.

CHAPTER LOCATOR | What factors led to European exploration in the fifteenth century?

Columbus and his men understood that they had made a momentous discovery, but they found it frustrating. Although the Tainos proved friendly, they did not have the riches Columbus expected to find in the East. In mid-January 1493, he started back to Spain, where Queen Isabella and King Ferdinand were overjoyed by his news. With one voyage, Columbus appeared to have made Spain a serious challenger to Portugal in the race for a sea route to Asia. The Spanish monarchs elevated Columbus to the nobility and awarded him the title "Admiral of the Ocean Sea."

Soon after Columbus returned to Spain, the Spanish monarchs rushed to obtain the pope's support for their claim to the new lands in the West. When the pope, a Spaniard, complied, the Portuguese feared their own claims to recently discovered territories were in jeopardy. To protect their claims, the Portuguese and Spanish monarchs negotiated the Treaty of Tordesillas in 1494. The treaty drew an imaginary line eleven hundred miles west of the Canary Islands (**Map 2.2**). Land discovered

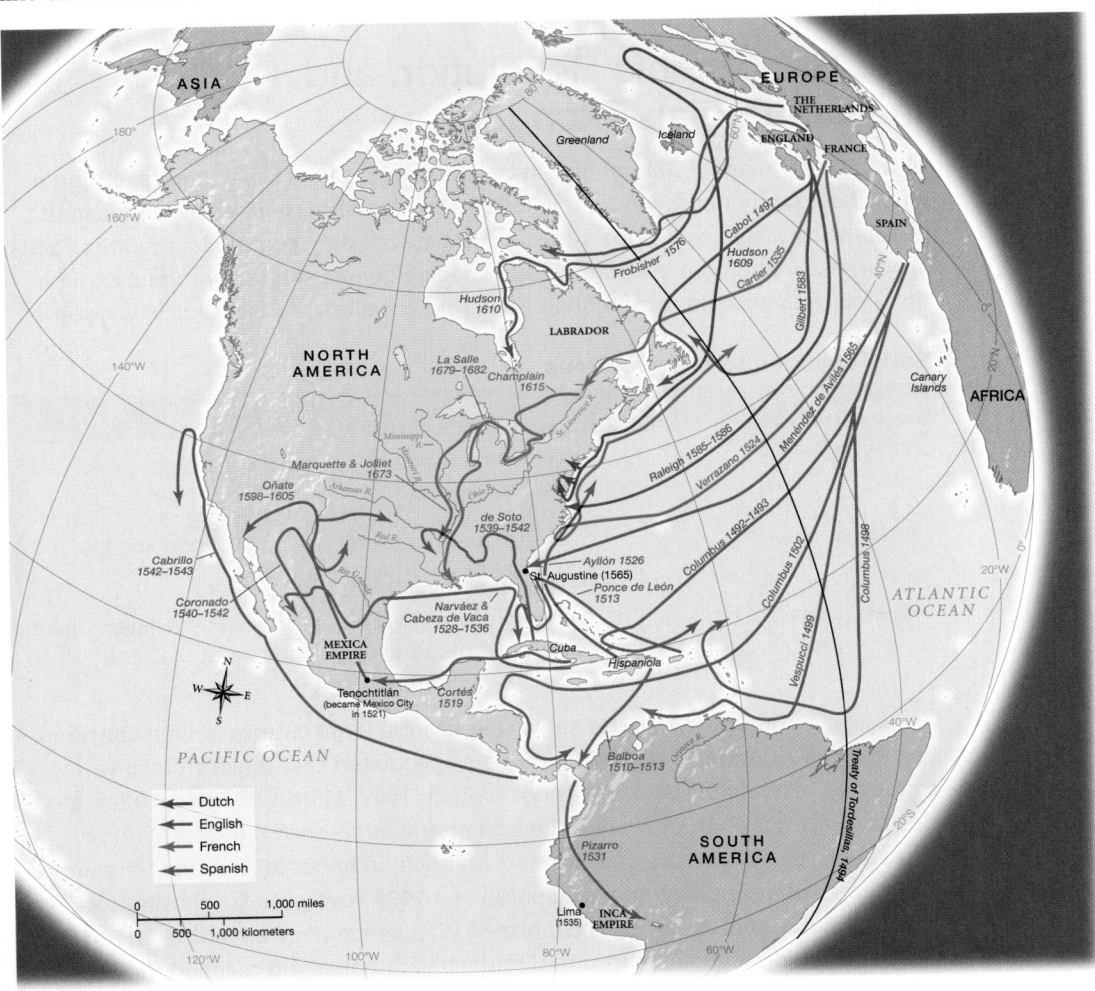

MAP 2.2 ■ European Exploration in Sixteenth-Century America
This map illustrates the approximate routes of early European explorations of the New World.

▶ FOR MORE HELP ANALYZING THIS MAP, see the map activity for this chapter in the Online Study Guide at bedfordstmartins.com/roarkunderstanding.

What did Spanish explorers discover in the western Atlantic?	How did Spaniards explore, conquer, and colonize New Spain?	How did New Spain influence sixteenth-century Europe?	Conclusion: What promise did the New World offer Europeans?

west of the line (namely, the islands that Columbus discovered and any additional land that might be located) belonged to Spain; Portugal claimed land to the east (namely, its African and East Indian trading empire).

Isabella and Ferdinand moved quickly to realize the promise of their new claims. In the fall of 1493, they dispatched Columbus once again, this time with a fleet of seventeen ships and more than a thousand men who planned to locate the Asian mainland, find gold, and get rich. Before Columbus died in 1506, he returned to the New World two more times (in 1498 and 1502) without relinquishing his belief that the East Indies were there, someplace. Other explorers continued to search for a passage to the East or some other source of profit without success. Nonetheless, Columbus's discoveries forced sixteenth-century Europeans to think about the world in new ways: It really was possible to sail from Europe to the western rim of the Atlantic and return to Europe. And, most important, across the Atlantic lay lands and peoples entirely unknown to Europeans.

The Geographic Revolution and the Columbian Exchange

Within thirty years of Columbus's initial discovery, Europeans' understanding of world geography underwent a revolution. An elite of perhaps twenty thousand people with access to Europe's royal courts and trading centers learned the exciting news about global geography. But it took a generation of additional exploration before they could comprehend the larger contours of Columbus's discoveries.

Early Voyages to the Americas

Explorer	Voyage
John Cabot	Reached Newfoundland in 1497 while searching for a Northwest Passage to Asia.
Amerigo Vespucci	Participated in a Spanish expedition that landed on the northern coast of South America in 1499.
Pedro Álvars Cabral	Commanded a Portuguese fleet bound for the Indian Ocean that accidentally made landfall on the coast of Brazil.

By 1500, European experts knew that several large chunks of land cluttered the western Atlantic. A few cartographers speculated that these chunks were connected in a landmass that was not Asia. In 1507, Martin Waldseemüller, a German cartographer, published the first map that showed the New World separate from Asia. He named the land America, in honor of Amerigo Vespucci, an Italian businessman who participated in a 1499 voyage to South America.

Two additional discoveries confirmed Waldseemüller's speculation. In 1513, Vasco Núñez de Balboa crossed the Isthmus of Panama and reached the Pacific Ocean. Clearly, more water lay between the New World and Asia. Ferdinand Magellan discovered how much water there was when he led an expedition to circumnavigate the globe in 1519. Sponsored by King Charles I of Spain, Magellan's voyage took him first to the New World, around the southern tip of South America, and into the Pacific late in November 1520. Crossing the Pacific took almost four months, decimating his crew with hunger and thirst. Magellan himself was killed by Philippine tribesmen. A remnant of his expedition continued on to the Indian Ocean and managed to transport a cargo of spices back to Spain in 1522.

In most ways, Magellan's voyage was a disaster. One ship and 18 men crawled back from an expedition that had begun with five ships and more than 250 men. But the geographic information it provided left no doubt that America was a continent separated from Asia by the enormous Pacific Ocean. Magellan's voyage made clear that it was possible to sail west to reach the East Indies, but that route was a terrible way to go. After Magellan, most Europeans who sailed west set their sights on the New World, not on Asia.

Columbus's arrival in the Caribbean anchored the western end of what might be imagined as a sea bridge that spanned the Atlantic, connecting the Western Hemisphere to Europe. This new sea bridge launched the **Columbian exchange**, a transatlantic trade of goods, people, and ideas that has continued ever since.

Spaniards brought novelties to the New World that were commonplace in Europe, including Christianity, iron technology, sailing ships, firearms, wheeled vehicles, horses and other domesticated animals, and much else. Unknowingly, they also brought many Old World diseases that caused devastating epidemics of smallpox, measles, and other maladies that killed the vast majority of Indians during the sixteenth century and continued to decimate survivors in later centuries. European diseases made the Columbian exchange catastrophic for Native Americans. In the long term, these diseases were decisive in transforming the dominant peoples of the New World from descendants of Asians, who had inhabited the hemisphere for millennia, to descendants of Europeans and Africans, the recent arrivals from the Old World by way of the newly formed sea bridge.

Ancient American goods, people, and ideas made the return trip across the Atlantic. Europeans were introduced to New World foods such as corn and potatoes that became important staples in European diets, especially for poor people. Columbus's sailors became infected with syphilis in sexual encounters with New World women and unwittingly carried the deadly disease back to Europe. New World tobacco created a European fashion for smoking. But for almost a generation after 1492, this Columbian exchange did not reward the Spaniards with the riches they yearned to find.

Columbian exchange
▶ The transatlantic trade of goods, people, ideas, and diseases initiated by Columbus's arrival in the Caribbean. The Columbian exchange transformed both the Americas and Europe.

QUICK REVIEW

How did Columbus's landfall in the Caribbean help revolutionize Europeans' understanding of world geography?

What did Spanish explorers discover in the western Atlantic?

How did Spaniards explore, conquer, and colonize New Spain?

How did New Spain influence sixteenth-century Europe?

Conclusion: What promise did the New World offer Europeans?

How did Spaniards explore, conquer, and colonize New Spain?

Cortés Arrives in Tenochtitlán This portrayal of the arrival of Cortés and his army in the Mexican capital illustrates the Spaniards' military advantages of horses, armor, and Indian supporters. Bibliothèque Nationale de France.

DURING THE SIXTEENTH CENTURY, the New World helped Spain become the most powerful monarchy in both Europe and the Americas. Initially, Spanish expeditions reconnoitered the Caribbean, scouted stretches of the Atlantic coast, and established settlements on the large islands of Hispaniola, Puerto Rico, Jamaica, and Cuba. Spaniards enslaved Caribbean tribes and put them to work growing crops and mining gold. But the profits from these early ventures barely covered the costs of maintaining the settlers. After almost thirty years of exploration, the promise of Columbus's discovery seemed illusory.

In 1519, however, that promise was fulfilled, spectacularly, by Hernán Cortés's march into Mexico. By about 1545, Spanish conquests extended from northern Mexico to southern Chile, and New World riches filled Spanish treasure chests. Cortés's expedition served as the model for Spaniards' and other Europeans' expectations that the New World could yield bonanza profits for its conquerors.

The Conquest of Mexico

Hernán Cortés, an obscure nineteen-year-old Spaniard, arrived in the New World in 1504. He fought in the conquest of Cuba and elsewhere in the Caribbean. In 1519, the governor of Cuba authorized Cortés to organize an expedition of about six hundred men and eleven ships to investigate rumors of a wealthy kingdom somewhere in the interior of the mainland.

Landing first on the Yucatán peninsula, Cortés had the good fortune to receive from a local chief the gift of a fourteen-year-old girl named **Malinali**, who spoke several native languages, including Mayan and Nahuatl, the language of the

Hernán Cortés
▶ Spanish conquistador who, along with his followers, conquered the Mexica in 1521. The conquest of the Mexican empire brought enormous wealth to Spain and prompted other would-be conquerors to explore the Americas.

Malinali
▶ Fourteen-year-old girl from the Yucatán peninsula who served as Cortés's interpreter during his 1519 march through Mexico. Malinali, whom the Spaniards called Marina, was given to Cortés by a local chief. Her fluency in a number of the region's languages proved indispensable to Cortés and his men.

CHAPTER LOCATOR | What factors led to European exploration in the fifteenth century?

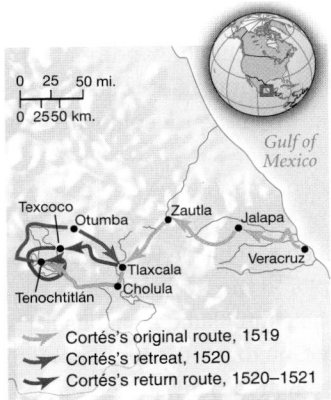

Cortés's Invasion of Tenochtitlán, 1519–1521

Map legend:
- 0 25 50 mi.
- 0 2550 km.
- Gulf of Mexico
- Texcoco, Otumba, Zautla, Jalapa, Veracruz, Tlaxcala, Cholula, Tenochtitlán
- Cortés's original route, 1519
- Cortés's retreat, 1520
- Cortés's return route, 1520–1521

Mexica, the most powerful people in what is now Mexico and Central America (see chapter 1). Malinali, whom the Spaniards called Marina, soon learned Spanish and became Cortés's interpreter. "Without her help," wrote one of the Spaniards who accompanied Cortés, "we would not have understood the language of New Spain and Mexico." With her help, Cortés talked and fought with Indians along the Gulf coast of Mexico, trying to discover the location of the fabled kingdom.

In Tenochtitlán, the capital of the **Mexican empire**, the emperor **Montezuma** heard about some strange creatures sighted along the coast. (Montezuma and his people are often called Aztecs, but they called themselves Mexica.) Montezuma sent representatives to bring the strangers large quantities of food and perhaps postpone their dreaded arrival in the capital. Before the Mexican messengers served food to the Spaniards, they sacrificed several hostages and soaked the food in their blood. This fare disgusted the Spaniards and might have been enough to turn them back to Cuba. But along with the food, the Mexica also brought the Spaniards another gift, a "disk in the shape of a sun, as big as a cartwheel and made of very fine gold," as one of the Mexica recalled.

In August 1519, Cortés marched inland to find Montezuma. Leading about 350 men armed with swords, lances, and muskets and supported by ten cannons, four smaller guns, and sixteen horses, Cortés had to live off the land, establishing peaceful relations with indigenous tribes when he could and killing them when he thought necessary. On November 8, 1519, Cortés reached Tenochtitlán. Montezuma came out to welcome the Spaniards. After presenting Cortés with gifts, Montezuma ushered the Spaniards to the royal palace. Quickly, Cortés took Montezuma hostage and held him under house arrest, hoping to make him a puppet through whom the Spaniards could rule the Mexican empire. This uneasy peace existed for several months until one of Cortés's men led a massacre of many Mexican nobles, causing the people of Tenochtitlán to revolt. They murdered Montezuma, who seemed to them a Spanish puppet, and they mounted a ferocious assault on the Spaniards. On June 30, 1520, Cortés and about a hundred other Spaniards fought their way out of Tenochtitlán and retreated about one hundred miles to Tlaxcala, a stronghold of bitter enemies of the Mexica. The Tlaxcalans allowed Cortés to regroup, obtain reinforcements, and plan a strategy to conquer Tenochtitlán.

In the spring of 1521, Cortés and tens of thousands of Indian allies laid siege to the Mexican capital. With a relentless, scorched-earth strategy, Cortés finally defeated the last Mexican defenders on August 13, 1521. The great capital of the Mexican empire "looked as if it had been ploughed up," one of Cortés's soldiers remembered.

The Search for Other Mexicos

Conquistadors quickly fanned out from Tenochtitlán in search of other sources of treasure. The most spectacular prize fell to Francisco Pizarro, who conquered the **Incan empire** in Peru. The Incas controlled a vast, complex region that contained more than nine million people and stretched along the western coast of South America for more than two thousand miles. In 1532, Pizarro and his army of

Mexican empire

▶ An empire, ruled by the Mexica, stretching from coast to coast in what is now Mexico and Central America. Often called Aztecs, the Mexica were the most powerful people in that area. With the help of Tlaxcala Indian allies, the Spanish, led by conquistador Hernán Cortés, conquered the Mexican empire in 1521.

Montezuma

▶ Emperor of the Mexican empire at the time of Cortés's 1519 expedition. Montezuma saw the Europeans as a potential threat, but in November 1519, he allowed Cortés and his men to enter Tenochtitlán and invited them into his palace. Presented with this opportunity, Cortés took Montezuma hostage, beginning a chain of events that ended with Spanish conquest of the Mexican empire.

conquistadors

▶ Soldiers who led Spain's initial efforts to conquer and control the wealth of the Americas. In addition to defeating native peoples in battle, conquistadors played a key role in extracting labor from indigenous populations.

Incan empire

▶ Vast empire of more than nine million people that stretched along the western coast of South America. Along with the Mexican empire, the Inca empire provided the gold and silver that contributed to Spain's preeminence in the sixteenth century.

1519
– Hernán Cortés leads expedition to find wealth in Mexico.

1520
– Mexica in Tenochtitlán revolt against Spaniards.

1521
– Cortés conquers Mexica at Tenochtitlán.

1532
– Francisco Pizarro begins conquest of Peru.

1539
– Hernando de Soto begins exploring southeastern North America.

1540
– Francisco Vásquez de Coronado starts to explore Southwest and Great Plains.

1542
– Juan Rodríguez Cabrillo explores California coast.

1549
– Repartimiento reforms begin to replace encomienda.

c. 1560
– Major centers of Indian civilization are conquered and colonized by the Spaniards.

1565
– St. Augustine, Florida, is settled.

1598
– Juan de Oñate explores New Mexico.

1599
– Pueblos revolt against Oñate.

fewer than two hundred men captured the Incan emperor Atahualpa and held him hostage. As ransom, the Incas gave Pizarro gold and silver equivalent to half a century's worth of precious-metal production in Europe. With the ransom safely in their hands, the Spaniards executed Atahualpa.

Other would-be conquistadors came up empty-handed. Juan Ponce de León had sailed along the Florida coast in 1513. Encouraged by Cortés's success, he went back to Florida in 1521 to find riches, only to be killed in a battle with Calusa Indians. A few years later, Lucas Vázquez de Ayllón explored the Atlantic coast north of Florida to present-day South Carolina. In 1526, he established a small settlement on the Georgia coast that he named San Miguel de Gualdape, the first Spanish attempt to establish a foothold in what is now the United States. This settlement was soon swept away by sickness and hostile Indians. Pánfilo de Narváez surveyed the Gulf coast from Florida to Texas in 1528. The Narváez expedition ended disastrously with a shipwreck on the Texas coast near present-day Galveston.

In 1539, Hernando de Soto, who had taken part in the conquest of Peru, set out with nine ships and more than six hundred men to find another Peru in North America. Landing in Florida, de Soto spent three years searching for the rich civilizations he believed were there. After the brutal slaughter of many Native Americans and much hardship, de Soto died in 1542, and his men turned back to Mexico, disappointed.

Tales of the fabulous wealth of the mythical Seven Cities of Cíbola lured Francisco Vásquez de Coronado to search the Southwest and Great Plains of North America. In 1540, Coronado left northern Mexico with more than three hundred Spaniards, a thousand Indians, and a priest who claimed to know the way to what he called "the greatest and best of the discoveries." Cíbola turned out to be a small Zuñi pueblo of about a hundred families. When the Zuñi shot arrows at the Spaniards, Coronado attacked the pueblo and routed the defenders after a hard battle. Convinced that the rich cities must lie somewhere over the horizon, Coronado kept moving all the way to central Kansas before deciding in 1542 to abandon his search.

Juan Rodríguez Cabrillo led a maritime expedition in 1542 that sailed along the coast of California. Cabrillo died on Santa Catalina Island, offshore from present-day Los Angeles, but his men sailed on to Oregon, where a ferocious storm forced them to turn back toward Mexico.

These probes into North America by de Soto, Coronado, and Cabrillo persuaded other Spaniards that although enormous territories stretched northward, their inhabitants had little to loot or exploit. After a generation of vigorous exploration, the Spaniards concluded that there was only one Mexico and one Peru.

New Spain in the Sixteenth Century

For all practical purposes, Spain was the dominant European power in the Western Hemisphere during the sixteenth century (**Map 2.3**). Portugal claimed the giant territory of Brazil under the Tordesillas treaty but was far more concerned with exploiting its hard-won trade with the East Indies than in colonizing the New World. England and France were absorbed by domestic and diplomatic concerns in Europe and largely lost interest in America until late in the century. In the decades after 1519, the Spaniards created the distinctive colonial society of New Spain, which showed other Europeans how the New World could be made to serve the purposes of the Old.

CHAPTER LOCATOR | What factors led to European exploration in the fifteenth century?

42 CHAPTER 2 ENCOUNTERING THE NEW WORLD

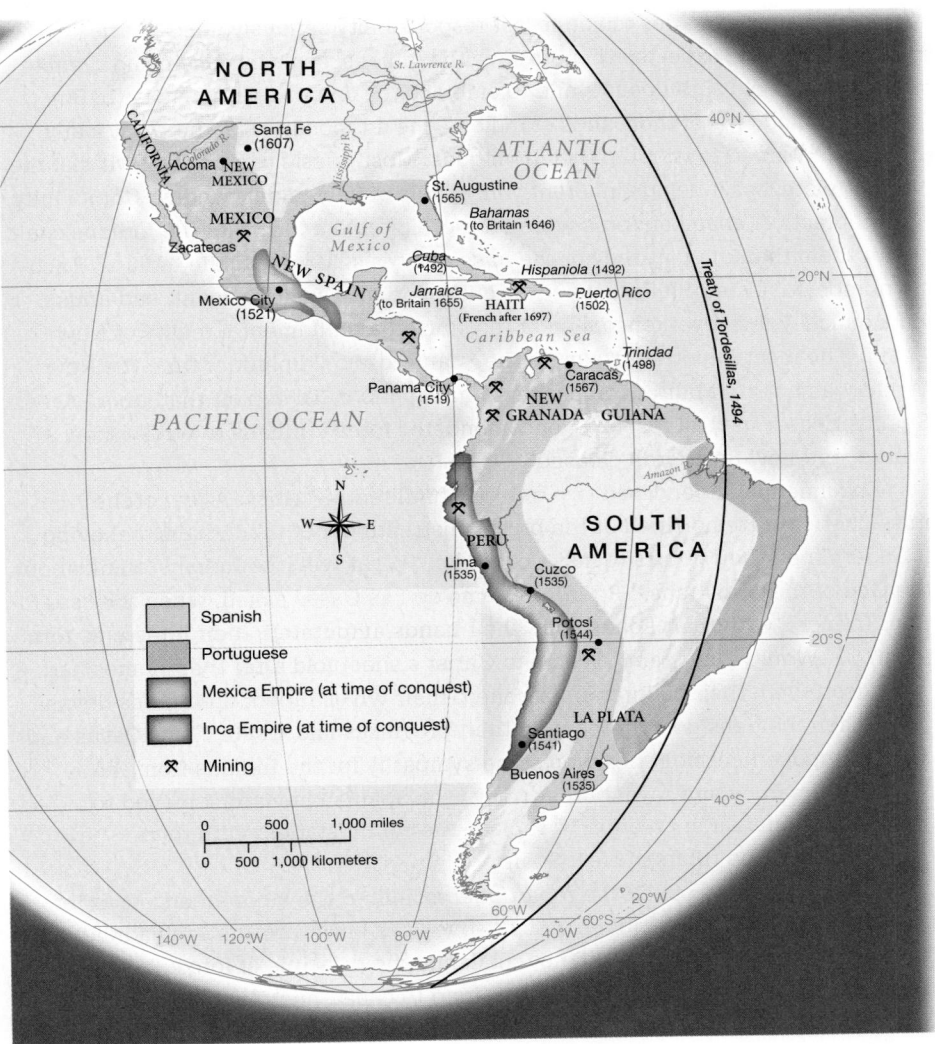

MAP 2.3 ■ Sixteenth-Century European Colonies in the New World
Spanish control spread throughout Central and South America during the sixteenth century, with the important exception of Portuguese Brazil. North America, though claimed by Spain under the Treaty of Tordesillas, remained peripheral to Spain's New World empire.

The Spanish monarchy claimed ownership of most of the land in the Western Hemisphere and gave the conquistadors permission to explore and plunder. The crown took one-fifth of any loot confiscated and allowed the conquistadors to divide the rest. In the end, most conquistadors received very little after the plunder was divided among leaders such as Cortés and his favorite officers. To compensate his disappointed soldiers, Cortés gave them towns the Spaniards had subdued.

The distribution of conquered towns institutionalized the system of *encomienda*, which empowered the conquistadors to rule the Indians and the lands in and around their towns. Encomienda transferred to the Spanish *encomendero* (the man who "owned" the town) the tribute that the town had previously paid to the Mexican empire. In theory, encomienda involved a reciprocal relationship between the encomendero and "his" Indians. In return for the tribute and labor of the Indians, the encomendero was supposed to be responsible for their material well-being, to guarantee order and justice in the town, and to encourage the Indians to convert to Christianity.

encomienda
▶ The system in which conquered towns were distributed to conquistadors who were empowered to rule the Indians and surrounding lands. *Encomenderos*, conquistadors who had been granted towns, subjected the Indians under their control to chronic overwork, mistreatment, and abuse.

Catholic missionaries took this last responsibility seriously. Missionaries believed that God expected them to save the Indians' souls by convincing them to abandon their old sinful beliefs and to embrace the one true Christian faith. But after baptizing tens of thousands of Indians, the missionaries learned that many Indians continued to worship their own gods. Most priests came to believe that the Indians were lesser beings inherently incapable of fully understanding Christianity.

In practice, encomenderos were far more interested in what the Indians could do for them than in what they or the missionaries could do for the Indians. Encomenderos subjected the Indians to chronic overwork, mistreatment, and abuse. Economically, however, encomienda recognized a fundamental reality of New Spain: The most important treasure the Spaniards could plunder from the New World was not gold but uncompensated Indian labor. To exploit that labor, New Spain's richest natural resource, encomenderos forced Indians to work when, where, and how Spaniards pleased.

Encomienda engendered two groups of influential critics. A few of the missionaries were horrified at the brutal mistreatment of the Indians, believing it undermined their efforts to make converts. "What will [the Indians] think about the God of the Christians," Friar Bartolomé de Las Casas asked, when they see their friends "with their heads split, their hands amputated, their intestines torn open? . . . Would they want to come to Christ's sheepfold after their homes had been destroyed, their children imprisoned, their wives raped, their cities devastated, their maidens deflowered, and their provinces laid waste?" Las Casas and other outspoken missionaries won some sympathy for the Indians from the Spanish monarchy and royal bureaucracy. The Spanish monarchy moved to abolish encomienda in an effort to replace the conquistadors with royal bureaucrats as the rulers of New Spain.

In 1549, a reform called the *repartimiento* limited the labor an encomendero could command from his Indians to forty-five days per year from each adult male. The repartimiento, however, did not challenge the principle of forced labor, nor did it prevent encomenderos from continuing to cheat, mistreat, and overwork their Indians. Slowly, repartimiento replaced encomienda as the basic system of exploiting Indian labor.

The practice of coerced labor in New Spain grew directly out of the Spaniards' assumption that they were superior to the Indians. As one missionary put it, the Indians "are incapable of learning. . . . [They] are more stupid than asses and refuse to improve in anything." Therefore, most Spaniards assumed, Indians' labor should be organized by and for their conquerors. Spaniards seldom hesitated to use violence to punish and intimidate recalcitrant Indians.

From the viewpoint of Spain, the single most important economic activity in New Spain after 1540 was silver mining. Spain imported more New World gold than silver in the early decades of the century, but that changed with the discovery of major silver deposits at Potosí, Bolivia, in 1545 and at Zacatecas, Mexico, in 1546 (**Figure 2.1**). The mines required large capital investments and many miners. Typically, a few Spaniards supervised large groups of Indian miners, who were supplemented by African slaves later in the sixteenth century.

For Spaniards, life in New Spain after the conquests was relatively easy. Encomienda gave them a comfortable, leisurely life that was the envy of many Spaniards back in Europe. As one colonist wrote to his brother in Spain, "Don't hesitate [to come]. . . . This land [New Spain] is as good as ours [in Spain], for God has given us more here than there, and we shall be better off."

CHAPTER LOCATOR | What factors led to European exploration in the fifteenth century?

44 CHAPTER 2 ENCOUNTERING THE NEW WORLD

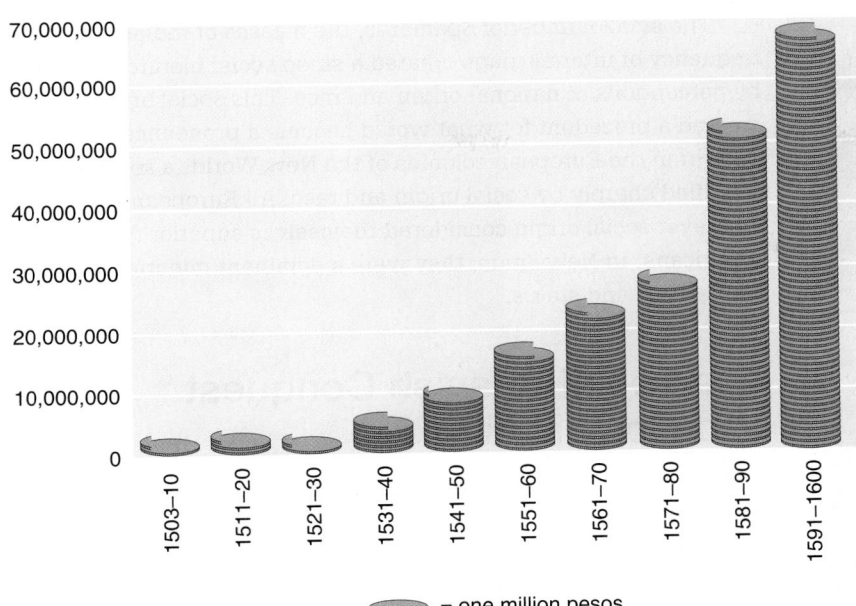

FIGURE 2.1 ■ New World Gold and Silver Imported into Spain during the Sixteenth Century, in Pesos
Spain imported more gold than silver during the first three decades of the sixteenth century, but the total value of this treasure was quickly eclipsed during the 1530s and 1540s, when rich silver mines were developed. Silver accounted for most of Spain's precious-metal imports from the New World.

= one million pesos

During the century after 1492, about 225,000 Spaniards settled in the colonies. Virtually all of them were poor young men who came directly from Spain. Laborers and artisans made up the largest proportion, but soldiers and sailors were also numerous. Throughout the sixteenth century, men vastly outnumbered women, although the proportion of women grew from about one in twenty before 1519 to nearly one in three by the 1580s.

The gender and number of Spanish settlers shaped two fundamental features of the society of New Spain. First, Europeans never made up more than 1 or 2 percent of the total population. Although Spaniards ruled New Spain, the population was almost wholly Indian. Second, the shortage of Spanish women meant that Spanish men frequently married Indian women or used them as concubines. For the most part, the relatively few women from Spain married Spanish men, contributing to a tiny elite defined by European origins.

Social and Racial Hierarchy in New Spain

Peninsulares	People born on the Iberian Peninsula. Peninsulares enjoyed the highest social status in New Spain.
Creoles	The children born in the New World to Spanish men and women. Creoles were below peninsulares but still considered part of the white elite. Together, peninsulares and creoles made up between 1 and 2 percent of the population of New Spain.
Mestizos	The offspring of Spanish men and Indian women, who accounted for 4 or 5 percent of the population. A few mestizos rose into the ranks of the elite, especially if their Indian ancestry was not obvious from their skin color.
Indians	The largest group in New Spain, who made up the bottom of the social pyramid. Indians comprised more than 90 percent of the population of New Spain.

What did Spanish explorers discover in the western Atlantic? | **How did Spaniards explore, conquer, and colonize New Spain?** | How did New Spain influence sixteenth-century Europe? | Conclusion: What promise did the New World offer Europeans?

45

Español con India,
Mestizo.

Mestizo con Española,
Castizo.

Castizo con Española,
Español.

Español con Mora,
Mulato.

5

Mulato con Española,
Morisco.

6

Morisco con Española,
Chino.

7

Chino con India,
Salta atras.

Salta atras con Mulata,
Lobo.

Mixed Races

These eighteenth-century paintings illustrate forms of racial mixture common in sixteenth-century New Spain. In the first painting, a Spanish man and an Indian woman have a mestizo son; in the fourth, a Spanish man and a woman of African descent have a mulatto son; in the fifth, a Spanish woman and a mulatto man have a *morisco* daughter. Bob Schalkwijk/INAH.

▶ FOR MORE HELP ANALYZING THIS IMAGE, see the visual activity for this chapter in the Online Study Guide at bedfordstmartins.com/roarkunderstanding.

The small number of Spaniards, the masses of Indians, and the frequency of intermarriage created a steep social hierarchy defined by perceptions of national origin and race. This social arrangement created a precedent for what would become a pronounced pattern in the European colonies of the New World: a society stratified sharply by social origin and race. All Europeans of whatever social origin considered themselves superior to Native Americans; in New Spain, they were a dominant minority in both power and status.

The Toll of Spanish Conquest and Colonization

By 1560, the major centers of Indian civilization had been conquered, their leaders overthrown, their religion held in contempt, and their people forced to work for the Spaniards. Profound demoralization pervaded Indian society. As a Mexican poet wrote:

> Nothing but flowers and songs of sorrow are left in Mexico . . .
> where once we saw warriors and wise men. . . .
> We are crushed to the ground; we lie in ruins.
> There is nothing but grief and suffering in Mexico.

Adding to the culture shock of conquest and colonization was the deadly toll of European diseases. As conquest spread, Indians succumbed to epidemics of measles, smallpox, and respiratory illnesses. They had no immunity to these diseases because they had not been exposed to them before the arrival of Europeans. The isolation of the Western Hemisphere before 1492 had protected ancient Americans from the contagious diseases that had raged throughout Eurasia for millennia. The new post-1492 sea bridge eliminated that isolation, and by 1570, the Indian population of New Spain had fallen about 90 percent from what it was when Columbus arrived. The destruction of the Indians was a catastrophe unequaled in human history. A Mayan Indian recalled that when sickness struck his village, "great was the stench of the dead. . . . The dogs and vultures devoured the bodies. The mortality was terrible." For most Indians, New Spain was a graveyard.

For Spaniards, Indian deaths meant that the most valuable resource of New Spain—Indian labor—dwindled rapidly. By the last quarter of the sixteenth century, Spanish colonists felt the pinch of a labor shortage. To help supply laborers, the colonists

CHAPTER LOCATOR | What factors led to European exploration in the fifteenth century?

46 CHAPTER 2 ENCOUNTERING THE NEW WORLD

began to import African slaves. In the years before 1550, while Indian labor was still adequate, only 15,000 slaves were imported from Africa. Even after Indian labor began to decline, the relatively high cost of African slaves kept imports low, totaling approximately 36,000 from 1550 to the end of the century. During the sixteenth century, New Spain continued to rely primarily on a shrinking number of Indians.

Spanish Outposts in Florida and New Mexico

After the explorations of de Soto, Coronado, and Cabrillo, officials in New Spain lost interest in North America. The monarchy claimed that Spain owned North America and insisted that a few North American settlements be established to give some tangible reality to its claims. Settlements in Florida also served to protect Spanish ships from pirates and privateers who hoped to prey on the Spanish treasure fleet sailing toward Spain.

In 1565, the Spanish king sent Pedro Menéndez de Avilés to create settlements along the Atlantic coast of North America. In early September, Menéndez founded St. Augustine in Florida, the first permanent European settlement within what became the United States. By 1600, St. Augustine had a population of about five hundred, the only remaining Spanish beachhead on the vast Atlantic shoreline of North America.

More than sixteen hundred miles west of St. Augustine, the Spaniards founded another outpost in 1598. Juan de Oñate led an expedition of about five hundred people to settle northern Mexico, now called New Mexico, and to claim the booty rumored to exist there. After a two-month journey from Mexico, Oñate and his companions reached pueblos near present-day Albuquerque and Santa Fe. From there, Oñate sent out scouting parties to find the legendary treasures of the region and to locate the ocean, which he believed must be nearby. Meanwhile, many of his soldiers planned to mutiny, and relations with the Indians deteriorated. When Indians in the Acoma pueblo revolted against the Spaniards, Oñate ruthlessly suppressed the uprising, killing eight hundred men, women, and children. Although Oñate's response to the Acoma pueblo revolt reconfirmed the Spaniards' military superiority, he did not bring peace or stability to the region. After another pueblo revolt occurred in 1599, many of Oñate's settlers returned to Mexico, leaving New Mexico as a small, dusty assertion of Spanish claims to the North American Southwest.

QUICK REVIEW

Why did New Spain develop a society highly stratified by race and national origin?

What did Spanish explorers discover in the western Atlantic?

How did Spaniards explore, conquer, and colonize New Spain?

How did New Spain influence sixteenth-century Europe?

Conclusion: What promise did the New World offer Europeans?

How did New Spain influence sixteenth-century Europe?

▶ FOR MORE HELP ANALYZING THIS IMAGE, see the visual activity for this chapter in the Online Study Guide at bedfordstmartins.com/roarkunderstanding.

Algonquian Ceremonial Dance
When the English artist John White visited the coast of present-day North Carolina in 1585 as part of Raleigh's expedition, he painted this watercolor portrait of an Algonquian ceremonial dance. This and White's other portraits are the only surviving likenesses of sixteenth-century North American Indians that were drawn from direct observation in the New World. The British Museum, London, UK/The Bridgeman Art Library.

THE RICHES OF NEW SPAIN helped make the sixteenth century the Golden Age of Spain. After the deaths of Queen Isabella and King Ferdinand, their sixteen-year-old grandson became King Charles I of Spain in 1516. Three years later, just as Cortés ventured into Mexico, Charles I was selected as Holy Roman Emperor Charles V. His empire encompassed more territory than that of any other European monarch. He used the wealth of New Spain to protect this empire and to promote his interests in the fierce dynastic battles of sixteenth-century Europe. He also sought to defend orthodox Christianity from the insurgent heresy of the Protestant Reformation. In short, the Spanish monarchy used New World wealth to bankroll Old World ambitions.

The Protestant Reformation and the European Order

In 1517, Martin Luther, an obscure Catholic priest in central Germany, initiated the **Protestant Reformation** by publicizing his criticisms of the Catholic Church. Luther's ideas won the sympathy of many Catholics, but they were considered

Protestant Reformation
▶ Multifaceted religious movement launched by the Catholic priest Martin Luther that divided Europe in the sixteenth century. The end of the Catholic Church's monopoly on European religious authority had long-lasting religious, cultural, and political consequences.

CHAPTER LOCATOR | What factors led to European exploration in the fifteenth century?

extremely dangerous by church officials and monarchs such as Charles V who believed that, just as the church spoke for God, they ruled for God.

Luther preached a doctrine known as "justification by faith": Individual Christians could obtain salvation and life everlasting only by having faith that God would save them. Giving offerings to the church, following the orders of priests, or participating in church rituals would not put believers one step closer to heaven. Also, the only true source of information about God's will was the Bible, not the church. By reading the Bible, any Christian could learn as much about God's commandments as any priest. Indeed, Luther called for a "priesthood of all believers."

In effect, Luther charged that the Catholic Church was in many respects fraudulent. He insisted that priests were unnecessary for salvation and that they encouraged Christians to violate God's will by promoting religious practices not specifically commanded by the Bible. The church, Luther declared, had neglected its true purpose of helping individual Christians understand the spiritual realm revealed in the Bible and had wasted its resources in worldly conflicts of politics and wars. Luther hoped his ideas would reform the Catholic Church, but instead they ruptured forever the unity of Christianity in western Europe.

Charles V pledged to exterminate Luther's Protestant heresies. The wealth pouring into Spain from the New World fueled his efforts to defend orthodox Catholic faith against Protestants, as well as against Muslims in eastern Europe and against any nation that contested Spain's supremacy. As the wealthiest and most powerful monarch in Europe, Charles V, followed by his son and successor Philip II, assumed responsibility for upholding the existing order of sixteenth-century Europe.

New World Treasure and Spanish Ambitions

Both Charles V and Philip II fought wars throughout the world during the sixteenth century. Mexican silver funneled through the royal treasury and was dissipated in military adventures that served the goals of the monarchy but did little to benefit most Spaniards. Moreover, Charles V's and Philip II's expenses for constant warfare far outstripped the revenues arriving from New Spain. To help meet military expenditures, both kings raised taxes in Spain more than fivefold during the sixteenth century. When taxes failed to produce enough revenue to fight its wars, the monarchy borrowed heavily from European bankers. By the end of the sixteenth century, interest payments on royal debts swallowed two-thirds of the crown's annual revenues. In retrospect, the riches from New Spain proved a short-term blessing but a long-term curse.

Sixteenth-century Spaniards did not see it that way. As they looked at their accomplishments in the New World, they saw unmistakable signs of progress. They had added enormously to their knowledge and wealth. They had built mines, cities, Catholic churches, and even universities on the other side of the Atlantic. Their military, religious, and economic achievements gave them great pride and confidence.

Europe and the Spanish Example

The lessons of sixteenth-century Spain were not lost on Spain's European rivals. Spain proudly displayed the fruits of its New World conquests. In 1520, for example, the German artist Albrecht Dürer wrote in his diary that he "marveled over the

CHRONOLOGY

1517
- Protestant Reformation begins in Germany.

1519
- King Charles of Spain is selected as Holy Roman Emperor.

1524
- Giovanni da Verrazano scouts the Atlantic coast of North America for France.

1535
- Jacques Cartier explores St. Lawrence River.

1576
- Martin Frobisher explores northern Canadian waters.

1587
- English settle Roanoke Island.

What did Spanish explorers discover in the western Atlantic?	How did Spaniards explore, conquer, and colonize New Spain?	**How did New Spain influence sixteenth-century Europe?**	Conclusion: What promise did the New World offer Europeans?

subtle ingenuity of the men in these distant lands" who created such "things . . . [as] a sun entirely of gold, a whole fathom [six feet] broad." But the most exciting news about "the men in these distant lands" was that they could serve the interests of Europeans, as Spain had shown. With a few notable exceptions, Europeans saw the New World as a place for the expansion of European influence, a place where, as one Spaniard wrote, Europeans could "give to those strange lands the form of our own."

France and England tried to follow Spain's example. Both nations warred with Spain in Europe, preyed on Spanish treasure fleets, and ventured to the New World, where they too hoped to find an undiscovered passageway to the East Indies or another Mexico or Peru.

In 1524, France sent Giovanni da Verrazano to scout the Atlantic coast of North America from North Carolina to Canada, looking for a Northwest Passage (see Map 2.2, page 37). Eleven years later, France probed farther north with Jacques Cartier's voyage up the St. Lawrence River. Encouraged, Cartier returned to the region with a group of settlers in 1541, but the colony they established—like the search for a Northwest Passage—came to nothing.

English attempts to follow Spain's lead were slower but equally ill-fated. Not until 1576, almost eighty years after John Cabot's voyages, did the English try again to find a Northwest Passage. This time Martin Frobisher sailed into the waters of northern Canada (see Map 2.2, page 37). His sponsor was the Cathay Company, which hoped to open trade with China. Like many other explorers, Frobisher was mesmerized by the Spanish example and was sure he had found gold. But the tons of "ore" he hauled back to England proved worthless, the Cathay Company collapsed, and English interests shifted southward to the giant region on the northern margins of New Spain.

English explorers' attempts to establish North American settlements were no more fruitful than was their search for a northern route to China. Sir Humphrey Gilbert led expeditions in 1578 and 1583 that made feeble efforts to found colonies in Newfoundland until Gilbert vanished at sea. Sir Walter Raleigh organized an expedition in 1585 to settle Roanoke Island off the coast of present-day North Carolina. The first group of explorers left no colonists on the island, but two years later, Raleigh sent a contingent of more than one hundred settlers to Roanoke under John White's leadership. White went back to England for supplies, and when he returned to Roanoke in 1590, the colonists had disappeared, leaving only the word *Croatoan* (whose meaning is unknown) carved in a tree. The Roanoke colonists most likely died from a combination of natural causes and unfriendly Indians. By the end of the century, England had failed to secure a New World beachhead.

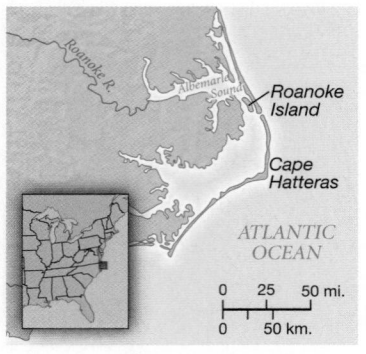

Roanoke Settlement, 1585–1590

> **QUICK REVIEW**

How did Spain's conquests in the New World shape Spain's position in Europe?

CHAPTER LOCATOR | What factors led to European exploration in the fifteenth century?

50 CHAPTER 2
ENCOUNTERING THE NEW WORLD

Private Collection/Picture Research Consultants & Archives.

Conclusion: What promise did the New World offer Europeans?

THE SIXTEENTH CENTURY in the New World belonged to the Spaniards who employed Columbus and to the Indians who greeted him as he stepped ashore. Isabella of Spain helped initiate the Columbian exchange between the New World and the Old that massively benefited first Spain and later other Europeans and that continues to this day. The exchange also subjected Native Americans to the ravages of European diseases and Spanish conquest. The exchange illustrated one of the most important lessons of the sixteenth century: After millions of years, the Atlantic no longer was an impassable barrier separating the Eastern and Western Hemispheres.

Spain remained a New World power for almost four centuries, and its language, religion, culture, and institutions left a permanent imprint. By the end of the sixteenth century, however, other European monarchies began to contest Spain's dominion in Europe and to make forays into the northern fringes of Spain's New World preserve. To reap the benefits the Spaniards enjoyed from their New World domain, the others had to learn a difficult lesson: how to deviate from Spain's example. That discovery lay ahead.

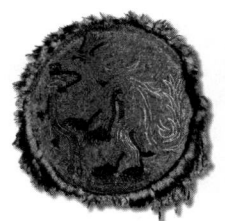

SO NOW YOU KNOW

The conquest and colonization of the New World made Spain the most powerful nation in sixteenth-century Europe. Columbus's voyages and Spanish efforts of exploration and aggressive colonization funneled the vast wealth of the Mexican and Incan empires to Spain, making it *the* nation that other Europeans competed with and sought somehow to emulate.

CHAPTER 2 STUDY GUIDE

Online Study Guide
bedfordstmartins.com/roarkunderstanding

STEP 1

GETTING STARTED

Below are basic terms from this period in American history. Can you identify each term below and explain why it matters? To do this exercise online or to download this chart, visit bedfordstmartins.com/roarkunderstanding.

TERM	WHO OR WHAT & WHEN	WHY IT MATTERS
Prince Henry the Navigator, p. 34		
Christopher Columbus, p. 35		
Columbian exchange, p. 39		
Hernán Cortés, p. 40		
Malinali, p. 40		
Mexican empire, p. 41		
Montezuma, p. 41		
conquistadors, p. 41		
Incan empire, p. 41		
encomienda, p. 43		
Protestant Reformation, p. 48		

STEP 2

MOVING BEYOND THE BASICS

The exercise below represents a more advanced understanding of the chapter material. In this exercise, you will reflect on the nature and impact of exploration and conquest in the Age of Exploration. What were the motives behind expansion across the Atlantic? Why did monarchs support overseas expeditions? Why did men like Columbus undertake such dangerous journeys? Identify key conquests and discoveries for each nation. Finally, describe the impact of exploration and colonization in the Americas both in the New World and in Europe. To do this exercise online or to download this chart, visit bedfordstmartins.com/roarkunderstanding.

EXPLORATION, 1492–1600	Motives for exploration and settlement	Conquests and discoveries	Impact in New World	Impact in Europe
Portugal				
Spain				
France				
England				

Now that you have reviewed key elements of the chapter, take a step back and try to explain the big picture. Remember to use specific examples from the chapter in your answers. To do this exercise online, visit bedfordstmartins.com/roarkunderstanding.

EXPANSION AND EXPLORATION

▶ Why was Portuguese maritime exploration focused on the west coast of Africa? What did Portugal hope to gain from such journeys?

▶ What was the Columbian exchange, and what were its consequences for both the peoples of the Americas and those from the Old World?

CONQUEST AND COLONIZATION

▶ Describe the government and society of New Spain. How did New Spain reflect the values, beliefs, and goals of the Spanish conquerors?

▶ How did Spanish conquest and colonization affect the peoples of the Americas?

THE IMPACT OF DISCOVERY IN EUROPE

▶ What role did New World wealth play in the clash between Protestants and Catholics in sixteenth-century Europe?

▶ What lessons did other European powers draw from Spain's experience in the New World?

LOOKING BACKWARD, LOOKING AHEAD

▶ How did the isolation of the peoples of the Americas before 1492 affect the course and consequences of European expansion in the New World?

▶ How did Spanish success in the New World influence European competition for control of the Americas?

IN YOUR OWN WORDS

Imagine that you must explain chapter 2 to someone who hasn't read it. What would be the most important points to include and why?

King Powhatan co̅mands C. Smith to be slayne
his daughter Pokahontas beggs his life his thank
.d by James River   and how he subiected 30 of their kings. read P

3
FOUNDING THE SOUTHERN COLONIES

1601–1700

> This chapter examines the growth of England's southern mainland colonies in the seventeenth century, as well as the small Spanish borderland outposts in Florida and New Mexico. It explores the early years of the Virginia colony, the rise of tobacco culture in the Chesapeake, its impact on the region's social and political environment, tensions in the Spanish borderland, and the transition to African slaves as a major labor force.

> What challenges faced early Chesapeake colonists?

> How did a tobacco society take shape?

> How and why did Chesapeake society change in the late seventeenth century?

> What caused tensions in the Spanish borderland?

> When and why did the southern colonies move toward a slave labor system?

> Conclusion: Why were export crops and slave labor important in the growth of the southern colonies?

DID YOU KNOW?

Tobacco made Virginia a successful colony.

Scene from Captain John Smith, *A General Historie of Virginia,* in which Pocohontas "saves" Smith's life, 1624.

What challenges faced early Chesapeake colonists?

In 1612, John Smith published a detailed map that showed not only geographic features of early Virginia but also the limits of exploration (indicated by small crosses), the locations of the houses of the Indian "kings" (indicated by red boxes), and "ordinary houses" of indigenous people (indicated by dots). The map shows the early settlers' intense interest in knowing where the Indians were—and were not. Notice the location of Jamestown (upriver from Point Comfort) and of Powhatan's residence at the falls (just to the right of the large P outside the hut on the upper left side). Princeton University Libraries, Department of Rare Books and Special Collections.

WHEN JAMES I became king of England in 1603, he eyed North America as a possible location for English colonies that could be as profitable as the Spanish colonies. Although Spain claimed all of North America under the 1494 Treaty of Tordesillas (see chapter 2), King James believed that England could encroach on the outskirts of Spain's New World empire.

In 1606, London investors organized the Virginia Company, a joint-stock company. English merchants had pooled their capital and shared risks for many years by using joint-stock companies for trading voyages to Europe, Asia, and Africa. The Virginia Company, however, had larger ambitions: to establish a colony in North America that might somehow benefit England as Spain's New World empire had

CHAPTER LOCATOR | What challenges faced early Chesapeake colonists?

rewarded Spain. King James granted the company more than six million acres in North America. In effect, the king's land grant was a royal license to poach on both Spanish claims and Native Americans' possessions.

The Virginia Company investors hoped to found an empire that would strengthen England both overseas and at home. Richard Hakluyt, a strong proponent of colonization, claimed that a colony would provide work for poor "valiant youths rusting and hurtfull by lack of employment" in England. Colonists could buy English goods and supply products that England now had to import from other nations. Of course, the primary reason the Virginia Company investors risked their capital was that they hoped to reap quick profits from the new colony.

Enthusiastic reports from the Roanoke voyages twenty years earlier (see chapter 2) claimed that in Virginia, "the earth bringeth foorth all things in abundance . . . without toile or labour." Even if these reports were exaggerated, investors hoped that some ready source of large profits would be found in North America. Such hopes failed to address the difficulties of adapting European desires and expectations to the New World already inhabited by Native Americans. The Jamestown settlement struggled to survive for nearly two decades, until the royal government replaced the private Virginia Company, which never earned a penny for its investors.

The Fragile Jamestown Settlement

On April 26, 1607, 144 Englishmen aboard the ships *Susan Constant, Discovery,* and *Godspeed* arrived at the mouth of the Chesapeake Bay. That night, while the colonists rested on shore, a band of Indians attacked and dangerously wounded two men. The attackers were followers of **Powhatan**, the Algonquian chief who dominated the region. The attack gave the colonists an early warning that the North American wilderness was not quite the paradise described by the Virginia Company's publications in England. A few weeks later, they went ashore on a small peninsula in the midst of Powhatan's chiefdom. There, they quickly built a fort, the first building in the settlement they named **Jamestown**.

The Jamestown fort showed the settlers' awareness that they needed to protect themselves from Indians and Spaniards. Spain planned to wipe out Jamestown when the time was ripe, but that time never came. Powhatan's people defended Virginia as their own. For weeks, the settlers and Powhatan's warriors skirmished repeatedly. English muskets and cannons repelled Indian attacks on Jamestown, but the Indians' superior numbers and knowledge of the Virginia wilderness made it risky for the settlers to venture far beyond the peninsula. Late in June 1607, Powhatan sensed a stalemate and made peace overtures.

The settlers soon confronted dangerous, invisible threats: disease and starvation. During the summer, many of the Englishmen lay "night and day groaning in every corner of the Fort most pittiful to heare," wrote George Percy, one of the settlers. By September, fifty colonists had died. The colonists increased their misery by bickering among themselves, leaving crops unplanted and food supplies shrinking. "For the most part [the settlers] died of meere famine," Percy wrote.

Powhatan's people came to the rescue of the weakened and demoralized Englishmen. Early in September 1607, they began to bring corn to the colony for barter. Accustomed to eating food derived from wheat, English people considered

CHRONOLOGY

1606
– Virginia Company receives royal charter.

1607
– English colonists found Jamestown settlement.

1607–1610
– Starvation plagues Jamestown.

1618
– Powhatan dies; Opechancanough becomes chief of the Algonquians.

1619
– House of Burgesses begins to meet in Virginia.

1622
– Opechancanough leads first Indian uprising against Virginia colonists.

1624
– Virginia becomes royal colony.
– Population of Virginia reaches 1,200.

Powhatan
▶ The supreme chief of about fourteen thousand Algonquian Indians who inhabited the coastal plain of present-day Virginia, near the Chesapeake Bay. Without the help of Powhatan, the Jamestown colony would not have survived.

Jamestown
▶ The colony established by the joint-stock company called the Virginia Company in 1607. Mortality rates in the early years of the colony were high, as disease, famine, and Indian attacks took their toll.

| How did a tobacco society take shape? | How and why did Chesapeake society change in the late seventeenth century? | What caused tensions in the Spanish borderland? | When and why did the southern colonies move toward a slave labor system? | Conclusion: Why were export crops and slave labor important in the growth of the southern colonies? |

corn the food "of the barbarous Indians which know no better . . . a more convenient food for swine than for man." The famished Jamestown colonists soon overcame their prejudice against corn. Indians' corn acquired by both trade and plunder managed to keep 38 of the original settlers alive until a fresh supply of food and 120 more colonists arrived from England in January 1608.

It is difficult to exaggerate the fragility of the early Jamestown settlement. Although the Virginia Company sent hundreds of new settlers to Jamestown each year, few survived. When a new group of colonists arrived in 1610, they found only 60 of the 500 previous settlers still alive. The Virginia Company continued to pour people into the colony, promising in a 1609 pamphlet that "the place will make them rich." But most settlers went instead to early graves.

Cooperation and Conflict between Natives and Newcomers

Powhatan's people stayed in contact with the English settlers but maintained their distance. Few Indians converted to Christianity, and the English devoted scant effort to proselytizing. Marriage between Indian women and English men also was rare, despite the acute shortage of English women in Virginia in the early years. Few settlers other than John Smith bothered to learn the Indians' language.

The miscommunication and misunderstandings between the settlers and Powhatan's people are illustrated by the story of the capture and release of **Captain John Smith**. In December 1607, Smith was captured by warriors of Powhatan. According to Smith, Powhatan "feasted him after their best barbarous manner." Then, Smith recalled, "two great stones were brought before Powhatan: then as many [Indians] as could layd hands on [Smith], dragged him to [the stones], and thereon laid his head, and being ready with their clubs, to beate out his braines." At that moment, **Pocahontas**, Powhatan's eleven-year-old daughter, rushed forward and "got [Smith's] head in her armes, and laid her owne upon his to save him from death." Pocahontas, Smith wrote, "hazarded the beating out of her owne braines to save mine, and . . . so prevailed with her father, that I was safely conducted [back] to James towne."

Historians believe that this episode happened more or less as Smith described it. But Smith did not understand why Pocahontas acted as she did. Most likely, when Pocahontas intervened to save Smith, she was a knowing participant in an Algonquian ceremony that expressed Powhatan's supremacy and his ritualistic adoption of Smith as a subordinate chief, or *werowance*. What Smith interpreted as Pocahontas's saving him from certain death was instead a ceremonial enactment of Powhatan's willingness to incorporate Smith and the white strangers at Jamestown into Powhatan's empire.

In 1613, after relations between Powhatan and the English colonists had deteriorated into bloody raids by both parties, the colonists captured Pocahontas and held her hostage at Jamestown. Within a year, she converted to Christianity and married one of the colonists, a widower named John Rolfe. After giving birth to a son named Thomas, Pocahontas, her husband, and the new baby sailed for England in the spring of 1616. Pocahontas died in England in 1617. Her son, Thomas, however, ultimately returned to Virginia.

Captain John Smith
▶ Leader of the Jamestown colony. Smith learned the Algonquian language of his Indian neighbors; however, this did not prevent him from misunderstanding the meaning behind his capture and redemption by Powhatan and his daughter Pocahontas in 1607.

Pocahontas
▶ The daughter of Powhatan. Pocahontas played a key role in a ceremonial enactment of incorporating Captain John Smith into Powhatan's society. Later captured and held hostage at Jamestown, Pocahontas converted to Christianity and married John Rolfe, the man who helped develop the tobacco crop that resulted in Virginia's success.

CHAPTER LOCATOR | What challenges faced early Chesapeake colonists?

Events like the capture of Pocahontas gave Powhatan's people good reason to regard the English with suspicion. Although the settlers often made friendly overtures to the Indians, they did not hesitate to use their guns and swords to enforce English notions of proper Indian behavior. More than once, the Indians refused to trade their corn to the settlers, evidently hoping to starve them out. Each time, the English broke the boycott by attacking the uncooperative Indians, pillaging their villages, and confiscating their corn.

The Indians retaliated against English violence, but for fifteen years they did not organize an all-out assault on the European intruders, probably for several reasons. Although Christianity held few attractions for the Indians, the power of the settlers' God impressed them. One chief told John Smith that "he did believe that our [English] God as much exceeded theirs as our guns did their bows and arrows." Powhatan probably concluded that these powerful strangers would make better allies than enemies. As allies, the English strengthened Powhatan's dominance over the tribes in the region. They also traded with his people, usually exchanging European goods for corn. Native Virginians had some copper weapons and tools before the English arrived, but they quickly recognized the superiority of the intruders' iron and steel knives, axes, and pots. The trade that supplied the Indians with European conveniences provided the English settlers with a necessity: food.

But why were the settlers unable to feed themselves for more than a decade? First, as the staggering death rate suggests, many settlers were too sick to be productive members of the colony. Second, very few farmers came to Virginia in the early years. Instead, most of the newcomers were gentlemen and their servants. The proportion of gentlemen in Virginia in the early years was six times greater than in England, a reflection of the Virginia Company's urgent need for investors and settlers. John Smith declared repeatedly that in Virginia "there is no country to pillage [as in New Spain]. . . . All you can expect from [Virginia] must be by labor." For years, however, colonists clung to English notions that gentlemen should not work with their hands and that tradesmen should work only in trades for which they had been trained. These ideas made more sense in labor-rich England than in labor-poor Virginia. In the meantime, the colonists depended on the Indians' corn for food.

The persistence of the Virginia colony created difficulties for Powhatan's chiefdom. Steady contact between natives and newcomers spread European diseases among the Indians, who suffered deadly epidemics in 1608 and between 1617 and 1619. The settlers' need for corn introduced other tensions within Powhatan's villages. To produce enough corn for their own survival and for trade

Ætatis suæ 21. Aᵒ. 1616.

Matoaks als Rebecka daughter to the mighty Prince Powhatan Emperour of Attanoughkomouck als Virginia converted and baptized in the Christian faith, and Wife to the wor.¹¹ Mr Tho: Rolff.

Pocahontas in England

Shortly after Pocahontas and her husband, John Rolfe, arrived in England in 1616, she posed for this portrait dressed in English clothing suitable for a princess. The portrait captures the dual novelty of England for Pocahontas and of Pocahontas for the English. The mutability of Pocahontas's identity is displayed in the identification of her as "Matoaks" or "Rebecka." National Portrait Gallery, Smithsonian Institution/Art Resource, NY.

| How did a tobacco society take shape? | How and why did Chesapeake society change in the late seventeenth century? | What caused tensions in the Spanish borderland? | When and why did the southern colonies move toward a slave labor system? | Conclusion: Why were export crops and slave labor important in the growth of the southern colonies? |

with the English required the Indians to spend more time and effort growing crops. Since Native American women did most of the agricultural work, their burden increased along with the cultural significance of their chief crop. The corn surplus grown by Indian women was bartered for desirable English goods such as iron pots, which replaced the baskets and ceramic jugs that Native Americans had used for millennia. But from the Indians' viewpoint, the most important fact about the English colonists was that they were not going away.

Powhatan died in 1618, and his brother Opechanca-nough replaced him as supreme chief. In 1622, Opechan-canough organized an all-out assault on the English settlers. As an English colonist observed, "When the day appointed for the massacre arrived [March 22], a number of savages visited many of our people in their dwellings, and while partaking with them of their meal[,] the savages, at a given signal, drew their weapons and fell upon us murdering and killing everybody they could reach[,] sparing neither women nor children, as well inside as outside the dwellings." In all, the Indians killed 347 colonists, nearly a third of the English population. But the attack failed to dislodge the colonists. In the aftermath, the settlers unleashed a murderous campaign of Indian extermination that in a few years pushed the Indians beyond the small circumference of white settle-ment. Before 1622, the settlers knew that the Indians, though dangerous, were necessary to keep the colony alive. After 1622, most colonists considered the Indians their perpetual enemies.

From Private Company to Royal Government

The 1622 uprising prompted a royal investigation of affairs in Virginia. The investigators discovered that the appalling mortality among the colonists was caused more by disease and mismanagement than by Indian

Advertisement for Jamestown Settlers

Virginia imported thousands of indentured servants to labor in the tobacco fields, but the colony also advertised in 1631 for settlers like those pictured here. The notice features men and women equally, although men heavily outnumbered women in the Chesapeake region. Harvard Map Collection, Pusey Library, Harvard University.

raids. In 1624, King James revoked the charter of the Virginia Company and made Virginia a royal colony, subject to the direction of the royal government rather than to the company's private investors, an arrangement that lasted until 1776.

The king now appointed the governor of Virginia and his council, but most other features of local government established under the Virginia Company remained intact. In 1619, for example, the company had inaugurated the **House of Burgesses**, an assembly of representatives (called burgesses) elected by the colony's inhabitants. (Historians do not know exactly which settlers were considered inhabitants and were thus qualified to vote.) Under the new royal government, laws passed by the burgesses had to be approved by the king's bureaucrats in England rather than by the company. Otherwise, the House of Burgesses continued as before, acquiring distinction as the oldest representative legislative assembly in the English colonies. Under the new royal government, all free adult men in Virginia could vote for the House of Burgesses, giving it a far broader and more representative constituency than the English House of Commons.

The demise of the Virginia Company marked the end of the first phase of colonization of the Chesapeake region. From the first 105 adventurers in 1607, the population had grown to about 1,200 by 1624. Despite mortality rates higher than during the worst epidemics in London, new settlers still came. Their arrival and King James's willingness to take over the struggling colony reflected a fundamental change in Virginia. After years of fruitless experimentation, it was becoming clear that English settlers could make a fortune in Virginia by growing tobacco.

House of Burgesses

▶ An assembly of representatives (called burgesses) established by the Virginia Company in 1619. After 1624 and until 1670, all free adult men in Virginia could vote for the House of Burgesses, regardless of landownership.

QUICK REVIEW

Why was the Jamestown settlement so dependent on Powhatan's people for survival during its first decade?

How did a tobacco society take shape?

In Europe, tobacco smokers congregated in clubs to enjoy the intoxicating weed. In this seventeenth-century satirical print, a dog cleans up after those who cannot hold their smoke. Koninklijke Bibliotheek, The Hague.

TOBACCO GREW WILD in the New World, and Native Americans used it for thousands of years before Europeans arrived. During the sixteenth century, Spanish colonists in the New World sent tobacco to Europe, where it was an expensive luxury used sparingly by a few. During the next century, English colonists in North America sent so much tobacco to European markets that it became an affordable indulgence used often by many people.

Initially, the Virginia Company had no plans to grow and sell tobacco. John Rolfe—the husband-to-be of Pocahontas—planted West Indian tobacco seeds in 1612 and learned that they flourished in Virginia. By 1617, the colonists had grown enough tobacco to send the first commercial shipment to England, where it sold for a high price. After that, Virginia changed from a colony of rather aimless adventurers who had difficulty growing enough corn to feed themselves into a society of dedicated planters who grew as much tobacco as possible.

By 1700, nearly 100,000 colonists lived in the Chesapeake region, encompassing Virginia, Maryland, and northern North Carolina (**Map 3.1**). They exported more than 35 million pounds of tobacco, a fivefold increase in per capita production since 1620. Clearly, Chesapeake colonists mastered the demands of tobacco agriculture, and the "Stinkinge Weede" (a seventeenth-century Marylander's term for tobacco) also mastered the colonists. Settlers lived by the rhythms of tobacco agriculture, and their endless need for labor attracted droves of English indentured servants to work in the tobacco fields.

Tobacco Agriculture

A demanding crop, tobacco required close attention and a great deal of hand labor year-round. Like the Indians, the colonists "cleared" fields by cutting a ring of bark from each tree (a procedure known as "girdling"), thereby killing the tree.

CHAPTER LOCATOR | What challenges faced early Chesapeake colonists?

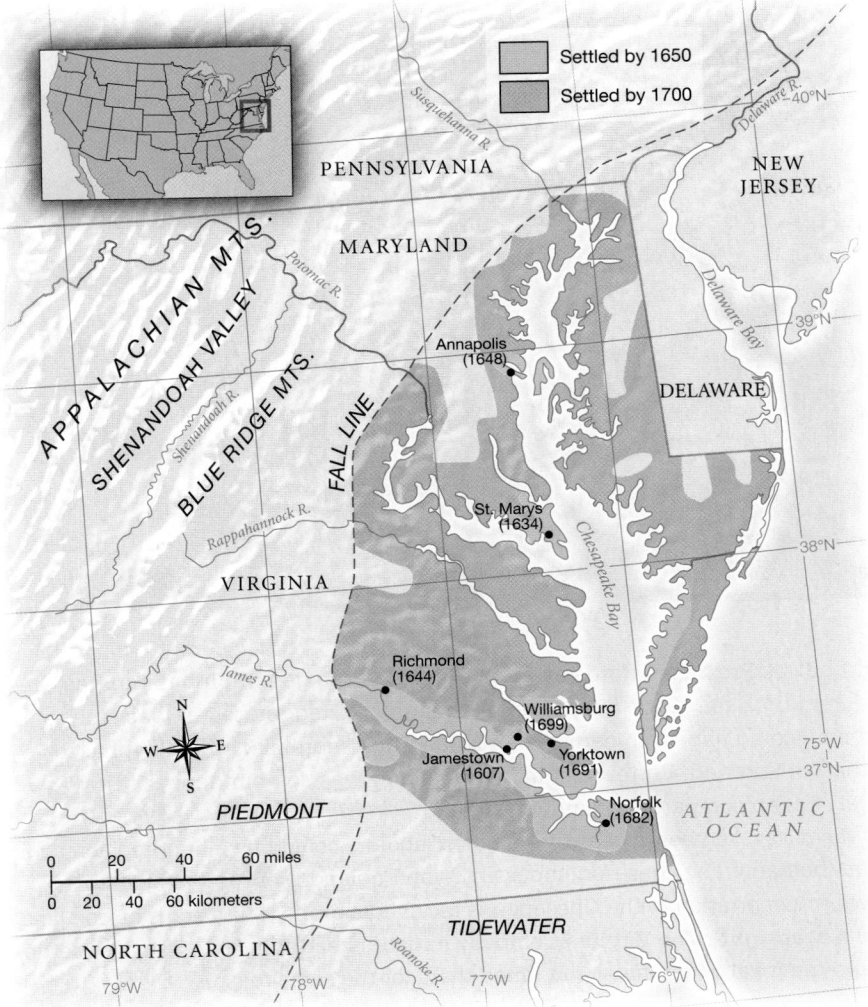

Settled by 1650
Settled by 1700

CHRONOLOGY

1612
– John Rolfe begins to plant tobacco in Virginia.

1617
– First commercial tobacco shipment leaves Virginia for England.

1619
– First Africans arrive in Virginia.

1632
– King Charles I grants Lord Baltimore land for colony of Maryland.

1634
– Colonists begin to arrive in Maryland.

1700
– Population of the Chesapeake region reaches 100,000.
– Chesapeake region exports 35 million pounds of tobacco to England.

MAP 3.1 ■ Chesapeake Colonies in the Seventeenth Century
The intimate association between land and water in the settlement of the Chesapeake in the seventeenth century is illustrated by this map. Although Delaware had excellent access to navigable water, it was claimed and defended by the Dutch colony at New Amsterdam (see chapter 4) rather than by the English settlements in Virginia and Maryland shown on this map.

▶ FOR MORE HELP ANALYZING THIS MAP, see the map activity for this chapter in the Online Study Guide at bedfordstmartins.com/roarkunderstanding.

Girdling brought sunlight to clearings but left fields studded with tree stumps, making the use of plows impractical. Instead, colonists used heavy hoes to till their tobacco fields. To plant, a visitor observed, they "just make holes [with a stick] into which they drop the seeds," much as the Indians did. Growing tobacco with such methods left little time for idleness, but the colonists enjoyed the fruits of their labor. "Everyone smokes while working or idling," one traveler reported, including "men, women, girls, and boys, from the age of seven years."

The English settlers worked hard because their labor promised greater rewards in the Chesapeake region than in England. One colonist proclaimed that

How did a tobacco society take shape?	How and why did Chesapeake society change in the late seventeenth century?	What caused tensions in the Spanish borderland?	When and why did the southern colonies move toward a slave labor system?	Conclusion: Why were export crops and slave labor important in the growth of the southern colonies?

This print illustrates the processing of tobacco on a seventeenth-century plantation. Workers cut the mature plants and put the leaves in piles to wilt (left foreground and center background). After the leaves dried somewhat, they were suspended from poles in a drying barn (right foreground), where they were seasoned before being packed in casks for shipping. Sometimes, tobacco leaves were left to dry in the fields (center background). From "About Tobacco," Lehman Brothers.

headright

▶ A grant of fifty acres of free land to new English settlers who could pay their own passage to Virginia. Most new Virginians, however, could not afford passage and arrived as indentured servants.

indentured servants

▶ English immigrants who agreed to work for four to seven years as servants in exchange for passage to America. Indentured servitude was the primary source of labor in seventeenth-century Virginia.

"the dirt of this Province affords as great a profit to the general Inhabitant, as the Gold of Peru doth to . . . the Spaniard." Although he exaggerated, it was true that a hired man could expect to earn two or three times more in Virginia's tobacco fields than in England. Better still, in Virginia land was so abundant that it was extremely cheap compared to land in England.

By the mid-seventeenth century, common laborers could buy a hundred acres for less than their annual wages—an impossibility in England. New settlers who paid their own transportation to the Chesapeake received a grant of fifty acres of free land (termed a **headright**). The Virginia Company initiated headrights to encourage settlement, and the royal government continued them for the same reason.

A Servant Labor System

Headrights, cheap land, and high wages gave poor English folk powerful incentives to immigrate to the New World. Yet many potential immigrants could not afford to pay for a trip across the Atlantic. Their poverty and the colonists' crying need for labor formed the basic context for the creation of a servant labor system.

About 80 percent of the immigrants to the Chesapeake during the seventeenth century were **indentured servants**. Twenty Africans arrived in Virginia in 1619, but scanty records make it impossible to know their fate. Until the 1670s, however, only a small number of slaves labored in Chesapeake tobacco fields. (Large numbers of slaves came in the eighteenth century, as chapter 5 explains.) A few indentured servants of African descent served out their terms of servitude and became free. A few slaves purchased their way out of bondage and lived as free people, even owning land and using the local courts to resolve disputes, much as freed white servants did. A small number of Native Americans also became servants. But the overwhelming majority of indentured servants were white immigrants from England. Instead of a slave society, the seventeenth-century Chesapeake region was fundamentally a society of white servants and ex-servants.

CHAPTER LOCATOR | What challenges faced early Chesapeake colonists?

To buy passage aboard a ship bound for the Chesapeake, an English immigrant had to come up with about £5, roughly a year's wages for an English servant or laborer. Unable to pay for their trip across the Atlantic, poor immigrants agreed to a contract called an indenture, which functioned as a form of credit. By signing an indenture, an immigrant borrowed the cost of transportation to the Chesapeake from a merchant or ship captain in England. To repay this loan, the indentured person agreed to work as a servant for four to seven years in North America.

Once the indentured person arrived in the colonies, the merchant or ship captain sold his right to the immigrant's labor to a local tobacco planter. To obtain the servant's labor, the planter paid about twice the cost of transportation and agreed to provide the servant with food and shelter during the term of the indenture. When the indenture expired, the planter owed the former servant "freedom dues," usually a few barrels of corn and a suit of clothes.

Ideally, indentures allowed poor immigrants to trade their most valuable assets—their freedom and their ability to work—for a trip to the New World and a period of servitude followed by freedom in a land of opportunity. Planters reaped more immediate benefits. A planter expected a servant to grow enough tobacco in one year to cover the price the planter paid for the indenture. Servants' labor during the remaining three to six years of the indenture promised a handsome profit for the planter. No wonder one Virginian declared, "Our principall wealth . . . consisteth in servants." But roughly half of all servants became sick and died before serving out their indentures, reducing planters' gains and destroying the servants' hopes. Planters still profited, however, since they received a headright of fifty acres of land from the colonial government for every newly purchased servant.

About three out of four servants were men between the ages of fifteen and twenty-five when they arrived in the Chesapeake. Typically unemployed and often homeless, most servants had no special training or skills, although the majority had some experience with agricultural work. "Hunger and fear of prisons bring to us onely such servants as have been brought up to no Art or Trade," one Virginia planter complained. A skilled craftsman could obtain a shorter indenture, but few risked coming to the colonies since their prospects were better in England.

Women were almost as rare as skilled craftsmen in the Chesapeake and more ardently desired. In the early days of the tobacco boom, the Virginia Company shipped young single women servants to the colony as prospective wives for male settlers willing to pay "120 weight [pounds] of the best leaf tobacco for each of them," in effect getting both a wife and a servant. The company reasoned that, as one official wrote in 1622, "the plantation can never flourish till families be planted, and the respect of wives and children fix the people on the soil." The company's efforts as a marriage broker proved no more successful than its other ventures. Women remained a small minority of the Chesapeake population until late in the seventeenth century.

The servant labor system perpetuated the gender imbalance. Although female servants cost about the same as males and generally served for the same length of time, only about one servant in four was a woman. Planters preferred male servants for field work, although many servant women hoed and harvested tobacco fields. Most women servants also did household chores such as cooking, washing, cleaning, gardening, and milking.

How did a tobacco society take shape?	How and why did Chesapeake society change in the late seventeenth century?	What caused tensions in the Spanish borderland?	When and why did the southern colonies move toward a slave labor system?	Conclusion: Why were export crops and slave labor important in the growth of the southern colonies?

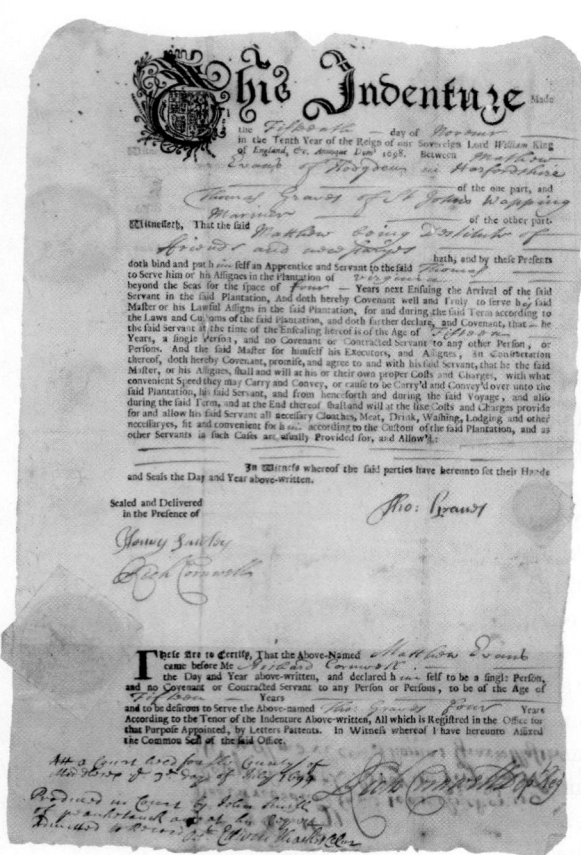

Indenture Contract

Indenture contracts were so common that forms were printed with blank spaces for details to be written in. In this 1698 contract, fifteen-year-old Matthew Evans agreed to serve mariner Thomas Graves, or anybody to whom Graves sold his rights, for four years in Virginia. The Library of Virginia.

Servants—whether men or women, whites or blacks, English or African—tended to work together and socialize together. During the first half century of settlement, racial intermingling occurred, although the small number of blacks made it infrequent. Courts punished sexual relations between blacks and whites, but the number of court cases shows that sexual desire readily crossed the color line. In general, the commonalities of servitude caused servants—regardless of their race and gender—to consider themselves apart from free people, whose ranks they longed to join eventually.

Servant life was harsh by the standards of seventeenth-century England and even by the frontier standards of the Chesapeake. Unlike servants in England, Chesapeake servants had no control over who purchased their labor for the period of their indenture. Many servants were bought and sold several times before their indenture expired. A Virginia servant protested in 1623 that his master "hath sold me for £150 sterling like a damnd slave."

For servants, the dreams of a new life that prompted them to leave England withered when they confronted the rigors of labor in the tobacco fields. James Revel, an eighteen-year-old thief punished by being indentured to a Virginia tobacco planter, declared he was a "slave" sent to hoe "tobacco plants all day" from dawn to dark. Severe laws aimed to keep servants in their place. Punishments for petty crimes stretched servitude far beyond the original terms of indenture. After midcentury, the Virginia legislature added three or more years to the indentures of most servants by requiring them to serve until they were twenty-four years old.

Women servants were subject to special restrictions and risks. They were prohibited from marrying until their servitude had expired. A servant woman, the law assumed, could not serve two masters at the same time: one who owned her indentured labor and another who was her husband. However, the predominance of men in the Chesapeake population inevitably pressured women to engage in sexual relations. About a third of immigrant women were pregnant when they married. As a rule, if a woman servant gave birth to a child, she had to serve two extra years and pay a fine. However, for some servant women, premarital pregnancy was a path out of servitude: The father of an unborn child sometimes purchased the indenture of the servant mother-to-be, then freed and married her.

Harsh punishments reflected four fundamental realities of the servant labor system. First, planters' hunger for labor caused them to demand as much labor as they could get from their servants, including devising legal ways to extend the period of servitude. Second, servants hoped to survive their servitude and use their freedom to obtain land and start a family. Third, servants' hopes frequently conflicted with planters' demands. Since servants saw themselves as free people in a temporary status of servitude, they often made grudging, halfhearted workers. Finally, planters put up with this contentious arrangement because the alternatives were less desirable.

Planters could not easily hire free men and women because land was readily available and free people preferred to work for themselves on their own land. Nor could planters depend on much labor from family members. The preponderance of men in the population meant that families were few, were started late, and thus had few children. And, until the 1680s and 1690s, slaves were expensive and hard to come by. Before then, masters who wanted to expand their labor force and grow more tobacco had few alternatives to buying indentured servants.

Cultivating Land and Faith

Villages and small towns dotted the rural landscape of seventeenth-century England, but in the Chesapeake, acres of wilderness were interrupted here and there by tobacco farms. Tobacco was such a labor-intensive crop that one field worker could tend only about two acres of the plants in a year (an acre is slightly smaller than a football field), plus a few more acres for food crops. A successful farmer needed a great deal more land, however, because tobacco quickly exhausted the fertility of the soil. Since each farmer cultivated only 5 or 10 percent of his land at any one time, a "settled" area comprised swatches of cultivated land surrounded by forest. Arrangements for marketing tobacco also contributed to the dispersion of settlements. Tobacco planters sought land that fronted a navigable river in order to minimize the work of transporting the heavy barrels of tobacco onto ships. A settled region thus resembled a lacework of farms stitched around waterways.

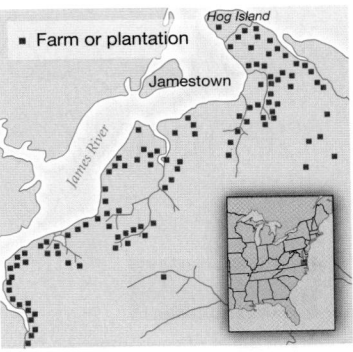

Settlement Patterns along the James River

Most Chesapeake colonists were nominally Protestants. Attendance at Sunday services and conformity to the doctrines of the Church of England were required of all English men and women. Few clergymen migrated to the Chesapeake, however, and too few of those who did were models of righteousness and piety. Certainly, some colonists took their religion seriously. Church courts punished fornicators, censured blasphemers, and served notice on parishioners who spent Sundays "goeing a fishing." But on the whole, religion did not awaken the zeal of Chesapeake settlers, certainly not as it did the zeal of New England settlers in these same years (see chapter 4).

The situation was similar in the Catholic colony of Maryland. In 1632, England's King Charles I granted his Catholic friend Lord Baltimore about six and a half million acres in the northern Chesapeake region. Lord Baltimore intended to create a refuge for Catholics, who suffered severe discrimination in England. He fitted out two ships; gathered about 150 settlers; and sent them to the new colony, where they arrived on March 25, 1634. However, Maryland failed to live up to Baltimore's hopes. The colony's population grew very slowly for twenty years, and most settlers were Protestants rather than Catholics. The religious turmoil of the Puritan Revolution in England (discussed in chapter 4) spilled across the Atlantic, creating conflict between Maryland's few Catholics—most of them wealthy and prominent—and the Protestant majority, most of them neither wealthy nor prominent. During the 1660s, Maryland began to attract settlers, mostly Protestants, as readily as Virginia. Although Catholics and the Catholic faith continued to exert influence in Maryland, the colony's society, economy, politics, and culture became nearly indistinguishable from Virginia's. Both colonies shared a devotion to tobacco, the true faith of the Chesapeake.

QUICK REVIEW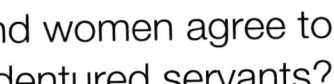

Why did so many English men and women agree to come to the Chesapeake as indentured servants?

How did a tobacco society take shape?	How and why did Chesapeake society change in the late seventeenth century?	What caused tensions in the Spanish borderland?	When and why did the southern colonies move toward a slave labor system?	Conclusion: Why were export crops and slave labor important in the growth of the southern colonies?

How and why did Chesapeake society change in the late seventeenth century?

Inside a Poor Planter's House

The houses of seventeenth-century Chesapeake settlers were typically "earth-fast": The structural timbers that framed the house were simply placed in holes in the ground, and the floor was packed dirt. No seventeenth-century house was substantial enough to survive until today. This photo shows a carefully documented reconstruction of the interior of a poor planter's house at Historic St. Mary's City, Maryland. Image courtesy of Historic St. Mary's City.

THE SYSTEM OF INDENTURED SERVITUDE sharpened inequality in Chesapeake society by the mid-seventeenth century, propelling social and political polarization that culminated in 1676 with Bacon's Rebellion. The rebellion prompted reforms that stabilized relations between elite planters and their lesser neighbors and paved the way for a social hierarchy that muted differences of landholding and wealth and amplified racial differences. Amid this social and political evolution, one thing did not change: Chesapeake colonists' dedication to growing tobacco.

Social and Economic Polarization

The first half of the seventeenth century in the Chesapeake was the era of the **yeoman**—a farmer who owned a small plot of land sufficient to support a family and tilled largely by servants and a few family members. A small number of elite planters had larger estates and commanded ten or more servants. But for the first several decades, few men lived long enough to accumulate fortunes sufficient to set them much apart from their neighbors.

Until midcentury, the principal division in Chesapeake society was less between rich and poor planters than between free farmers and unfree servants. Although these two groups contrasted sharply in their legal and economic status, their daily lives had many similarities. Servants looked forward to the time when their indentures would expire and they would become free and eventually own land.

yeoman

▶ A farmer who owned a small plot of land sufficient to support a family and tilled largely by servants and a few family members. During the first half of the seventeenth century in the Chesapeake, nearly all farmers were yeomen.

CHAPTER LOCATOR | What challenges faced early Chesapeake colonists?

During the third quarter of the century, three major developments splintered the equality. First, as planters grew more and more tobacco, the ample supply depressed tobacco prices in European markets. Cheap tobacco reduced planters' profits and made saving enough to become landowners more difficult for freed servants. Second, because the mortality rate in the Chesapeake colonies declined, more and more servants survived their indentures, and landless freemen became more numerous and grew more discontented. Third, declining mortality also encouraged the formation of a planter elite. By living longer, the most successful planters compounded their success. The wealthiest planters also began to serve as merchants, marketing crops for their less successful neighbors, importing English goods for sale, and extending credit to hard-pressed customers.

By the 1670s, the society of the Chesapeake had become polarized. Landowners—the planter elite and the more numerous yeoman planters—clustered around one pole. Landless colonists, mainly freed servants, gathered at the other. Each group eyed the other with suspicion and mistrust. For the most part, planters saw landless freemen as a dangerous rabble rather than as fellow colonists with legitimate grievances. Governor William Berkeley feared the political threat to the governing elite posed by "six parts in seven [of Virginia colonists who] . . . are poor, indebted, discontented, and armed."

Government Policies and Political Conflict

In general, government and politics strengthened the distinctions in Chesapeake society. The most vital distinction separated servants and landowners, and the colonial government enforced it with an iron fist. As discontent mounted among the poor during the 1660s and 1670s, colonial officials tried to keep political power in safe hands. Beginning in 1661, for example, Governor William Berkeley did not call an election for the House of Burgesses for fifteen years. In 1670, the House of Burgesses outlawed voting by poor men, permitting only men who headed households and owned land to vote.

The king also began to tighten the royal government's control of trade and to collect substantial revenue from the Chesapeake. A series of navigation acts funneled the colonial trade exclusively into the hands of English merchants and shippers. The **Navigation Acts of 1650 and 1651** specified that colonial goods had to be transported in English ships with predominantly English crews. A 1660 act required colonial products to be sent only to English ports, and a 1663 law stipulated further that all goods sent to the colonies must pass through English ports and be carried in English ships manned by English sailors. Taken together, these navigation acts reflected the English government's mercantilist assumptions about the colonies: What was good for England should determine colonial policy.

CHRONOLOGY

c. 1600–1650
– Yeoman farmers predominate in the Chesapeake region.

1644
– Opechancanough leads second Indian uprising against Virginia colonists.

1660
– Navigation Act imposes an import tax on colonial tobacco brought into England.

1661–1676
– No elections called in the House of Burgesses.

1670
– House of Burgesses outlaws voting by poor men.

1676
– Bacon's Rebellion.

Navigation Acts of 1650 and 1651

▶ Acts of Parliament that specified that colonial goods had to be transported in English ships with predominantly English crews. The acts reflected the English government's belief that the interests of England should determine colonial policy.

How did a tobacco society take shape?	**How and why did Chesapeake society change in the late seventeenth century?**	What caused tensions in the Spanish borderland?	When and why did the southern colonies move toward a slave labor system?	Conclusion: Why were export crops and slave labor important in the growth of the southern colonies?

mercantilism

▶ Economic policies that regulated colonial commerce for the enrichment of the mother country. Seventeenth-century English colonial policy was based on mercantilist assumptions.

Assumptions about **mercantilism** also underlay the import duty on tobacco inaugurated by the Navigation Act of 1660. The law assessed an import tax of two pence on every pound of colonial tobacco brought into England, about the price a Chesapeake tobacco farmer received. The tax gave the king a major financial interest in the size of the tobacco crop. During the 1660s, these tobacco import taxes yielded about a quarter of all English customs revenues, an impressive sign of the growing importance of the Chesapeake colonies in England's Atlantic empire.

Bacon's Rebellion

Bacon's Rebellion

▶ A colonial uprising in 1676 sparked by Virginia's Indian policy. Although Indian attacks triggered the rebellion, it was also the result of underlying social and political tensions in the colony.

Colonists, like residents of European monarchies, accepted social hierarchy and inequality as long as they believed that government officials ruled for the general good. When rulers violated that precept, ordinary people felt justified in rebelling. In 1676, **Bacon's Rebellion** erupted as a dispute over Virginia's Indian policy. Before it was over, the rebellion convulsed Chesapeake politics and society, leaving in its wake death, destruction, and a legacy of hostility between the great planters and their poorer neighbors.

Opechancanough, the Algonquian chief who had led the Indian uprising of 1622 in Virginia, mounted another surprise attack in 1644 and killed about five hundred Virginia colonists in two days. During the next two years of bitter fighting, the colonists eventually gained the upper hand, capturing and murdering the old chief. The treaty that concluded the war established policies toward the Indians that the government tried to maintain for the next thirty years. The Indians relinquished all claims to land already settled by the English. Wilderness land beyond the fringe of English settlement was supposed to be reserved exclusively for Indian use. The colonial government hoped to minimize contact between settlers and Indians and thereby maintain the peace.

If the Chesapeake population had not grown, the policy might have worked. But the number of land-hungry colonists, especially poor, recently freed servants, continued to multiply. In their quest for land, they pushed beyond the treaty limits of English settlement and steadily encroached on Indian land. During the 1660s and 1670s, violence between colonists and Indians repeatedly flared along the advancing frontier. The government, headquartered in the tidewater region near the coast, far from the danger of Indian raids, took steps to calm the disputes and reestablish the peace. Frontier settlers thirsted for revenge against what their leader, Nathaniel Bacon, termed "the protected and Darling Indians." Bacon proclaimed his "Design not only to ruine and extirpate all Indians in Generall but all Manner of Trade and Commerce with them." Indians were not the only enemies Bacon and his men singled out. Bacon also urged the colonists to "see what spounges have suckt up the Publique Treasure." He charged that grandees, or elite planters, operated the government for their private gain, a charge that made sense to many colonists. Bacon crystallized the grievances of the small planters and poor farmers against both the Indians and the colonial rulers in Jamestown.

Hoping to maintain the fragile peace on the frontier in 1676, Governor Berkeley pronounced Bacon a rebel, threatened to punish him for treason, and called for new elections of burgesses who, Berkeley believed, would endorse his get-tough policy. To Berkeley's surprise, the elections backfired. Almost all the old burgesses were voted out of office, and they were replaced by local leaders, including Bacon. The legislature was now in the hands of minor grandees who, like Bacon, chafed at the rule of the elite planters.

CHAPTER LOCATOR | What challenges faced early Chesapeake colonists?

In June 1676, the new legislature passed a series of reform measures known as Bacon's Laws. Among other changes, the laws gave local settlers a voice in setting tax levies, forbade officeholders from demanding bribes or other extra fees for carrying out their duties, placed limits on holding multiple offices, and restored the vote to all freemen. Under pressure, Berkeley pardoned Bacon and authorized his campaign of Indian warfare. But elite planters soon convinced Berkeley that Bacon and his men were a greater threat than the Indians.

When Bacon learned that Berkeley had once again branded him a traitor, he declared war against Berkeley and the other grandees. For three months, Bacon's forces fought the Indians, sacked the grandees' plantations, and attacked Jamestown. Berkeley's loyalists retaliated by plundering the homes of Bacon's supporters. The fighting continued until late October, when Bacon unexpectedly died, most likely from dysentery, and several English ships arrived to bolster Berkeley's strength. With the rebellion crushed, Berkeley hanged several of Bacon's allies and destroyed farms that belonged to Bacon's supporters.

The rebellion did nothing to dislodge the grandees from their positions of power. If anything, it strengthened them. When the king learned of the turmoil in the Chesapeake and its devastating effect on tobacco exports and customs duties, he ordered an investigation. Royal officials replaced Berkeley with a governor more attentive to the king's interests, nullified Bacon's Laws, and instituted an export tax on every hogshead of tobacco as a way of paying the expenses of government without having to obtain the consent of the House of Burgesses.

In the aftermath of Bacon's Rebellion, tensions between great planters and small farmers gradually lessened. Bacon's Rebellion showed, a governor of Virginia said, that it was necessary "to steer between . . . either an Indian or a civil war." The ruling elite concluded that it was safer for the colonists to fight the Indians than to fight each other, and the government made little effort to restrict settlers' encroachment on Indian land. Tax cuts also were welcomed by all freemen. The export duty on tobacco imposed by the king allowed the colonial government to reduce taxes by 75 percent between 1660 and 1700. In the long run, however, the most important contribution to political stability was the declining importance of the servant labor system. During the 1680s and 1690s, fewer servants arrived in the Chesapeake, partly because of improving economic conditions in England. Accordingly, the number of poor, newly freed servants also declined, reducing the size of the lowest stratum of free society. In 1700, as many as one-third of the free colonists still worked as tenants on land owned by others, but the social and political distance between them and the great planters did not seem as important as it had been in 1660. The main reason was that by 1700, the Chesapeake was in the midst of transition to a slave labor system that minimized the differences between poor farmers and rich planters and magnified the differences between whites and blacks.

QUICK REVIEW

Why did Chesapeake colonial society become increasingly polarized between 1650 and 1670?

How did a tobacco society take shape?

How and why did Chesapeake society change in the late seventeenth century?

What caused tensions in the Spanish borderland?

When and why did the southern colonies move toward a slave labor system?

Conclusion: Why were export crops and slave labor important in the growth of the southern colonies?

What caused tensions in the Spanish borderland?

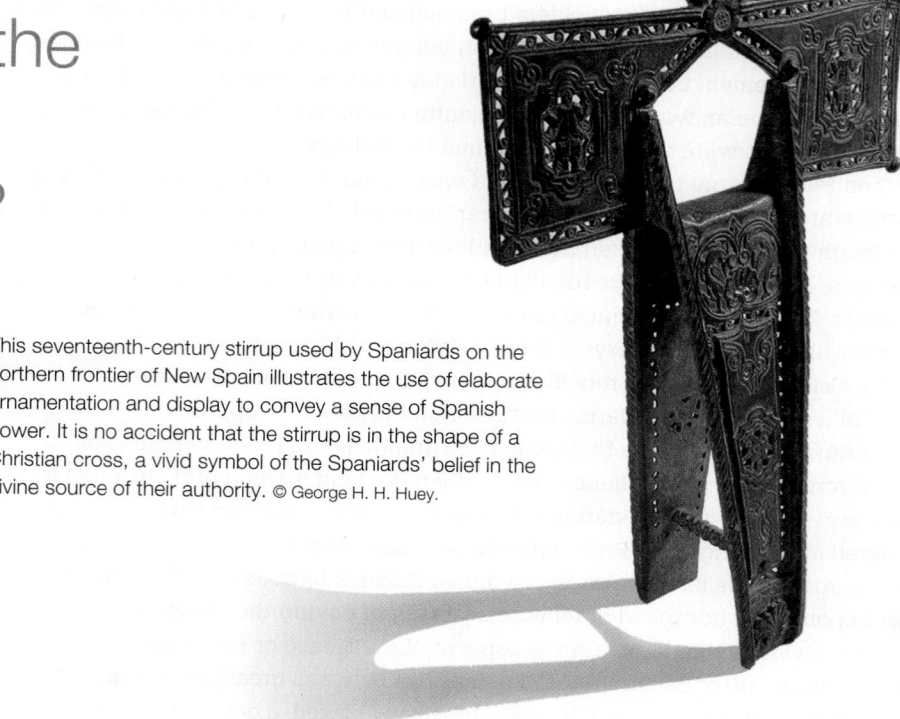

Spanish Stirrup This seventeenth-century stirrup used by Spaniards on the northern frontier of New Spain illustrates the use of elaborate ornamentation and display to convey a sense of Spanish power. It is no accident that the stirrup is in the shape of a Christian cross, a vivid symbol of the Spaniards' belief in the divine source of their authority. © George H. H. Huey.

WHILE ENGLISH COLONIES in the Chesapeake grew and prospered with the tobacco trade, the northern outposts of the Spanish empire in New Mexico and Florida stagnated. Instead of attracting settlers and growing crops for export, New Mexico and Florida appealed to Spanish missionaries seeking to harvest Indian souls. The missionaries baptized thousands of Indians in Spanish North America during the seventeenth century, but they also planted the seeds of Indian uprisings against Spanish rule.

The Spanish Borderlands

Only about 4,500 Spanish colonists lived in the borderlands: 1,500 in Florida and 3,000 in New Mexico.

Indians outnumbered Spanish colonists ten or twenty to one.

Royal officials considered eliminating both colonies because their costs greatly exceeded their benefits.

Missionaries persuaded the Spanish government to continue to support the colonies.

Royal officials hoped that the missionaries' efforts would pacify the Indians and preserve Spanish footholds in North America.

CHAPTER LOCATOR | What challenges faced early Chesapeake colonists?

Dozens of missionaries came to Florida and New Mexico, as one announced, to free the Indians "from the miserable slavery of the demon and from the obscure darkness of their idolatry." The missionaries believed that the Indians' religious beliefs and rituals were idolatrous devil worship and that their way of life was barbaric. The missionaries followed royal instructions that Indians should be taught "to live in a civilized manner, clothed and wearing shoes . . . [and] given the use of . . . bread, linen, horses, cattle, tools, and weapons, and all the rest that Spain has had." In effect, the missionaries sought to convert the Indians not just into Christians but also into imitation Spaniards.

The missionaries supervised the building of scores of Catholic churches across Florida and New Mexico. Typically, they conscripted Indian women and men to do the construction. Adopting practices common elsewhere in New Spain, they forced the Indians both to work and to pay tribute in the form of food, blankets, and other goods. Although the missionaries congratulated themselves on the many Indians they converted, their coercive methods subverted their goals. A missionary reported that an Indian in New Mexico asked him, "If we [missionaries] who are Christians caused so much harm and violence [to Indians], why should they become Christians?"

The Indians retaliated repeatedly against Spanish exploitation, but the Spaniards suppressed the violent uprisings by taking advantage of the disunity among the Indians, much as Cortés did in the conquest of Mexico (see chapter 2). In 1680, however, Pueblo Indians organized a unified revolt under the leadership of Popé, who ordered his followers, as one recounted, to "break up and burn the images of the holy Christ, the Virgin Mary, and the other saints, the crosses, and everything pertaining to Christianity." During the **Pueblo Revolt**, the Indians desecrated churches, killed two-thirds of the Spanish missionaries, and drove the Spaniards out of New Mexico to present-day El Paso, Texas. The Spaniards managed to return to New Mexico by the end of the seventeenth century, but only by restraining the missionaries and reducing labor exploitation. Florida Indians never mounted a unified attack on Spanish rule, but they too organized sporadic uprisings and resisted conversion, causing a Spanish official to report by the end of the seventeenth century that "the law of God and the preaching of the Holy Gospel have now ceased."

KEY EVENT

1680
– Pueblo Revolt

Pueblo Revolt

▶ A 1680 Indian uprising in colonial New Mexico led by Popé. The rebels killed two-thirds of the Spanish missionaries and drove Spaniards out of New Mexico for several years until they returned at the end of the seventeenth century.

QUICK REVIEW

Why did the Pueblo Indians revolt against Spanish missionaries in 1680?

| How did a tobacco society take shape? | How and why did Chesapeake society change in the late seventeenth century? | What caused tensions in the Spanish borderland? | When and why did the southern colonies move toward a slave labor system? | Conclusion: Why were export crops and slave labor important in the growth of the southern colonies? |

When and why did the southern colonies move toward a slave labor system?

This portrait of a Brazilian sugar plantation shows the house of the Brazilian owners, attended by numerous slaves. Courtesy of the John Carter Brown Library at Brown University.

DURING THE SIXTEENTH CENTURY, Spaniards and Portuguese in the New World supplemented Indian laborers with enslaved Africans. On this foundation, European colonizers built African slavery into the most important form of coerced labor in the New World. During the seventeenth century, English colonies in the West Indies followed the Spanish and Portuguese examples and developed sugar plantations with slave labor. In the English North American colonies, however, a slave labor system did not emerge until the last quarter of the seventeenth century. During the 1670s, settlers from Barbados brought slavery to the new English mainland colony of Carolina, where the imprint of the West Indies remained strong for decades. In Chesapeake tobacco fields at about the same time, slave labor began to replace servant labor, marking the transition toward a society of freedom for whites and slavery for Africans.

The West Indies: Sugar and Slavery

The most profitable part of the English New World empire in the seventeenth century lay in the Caribbean (**Map 3.2**). Barbados, colonized in the 1630s, was the

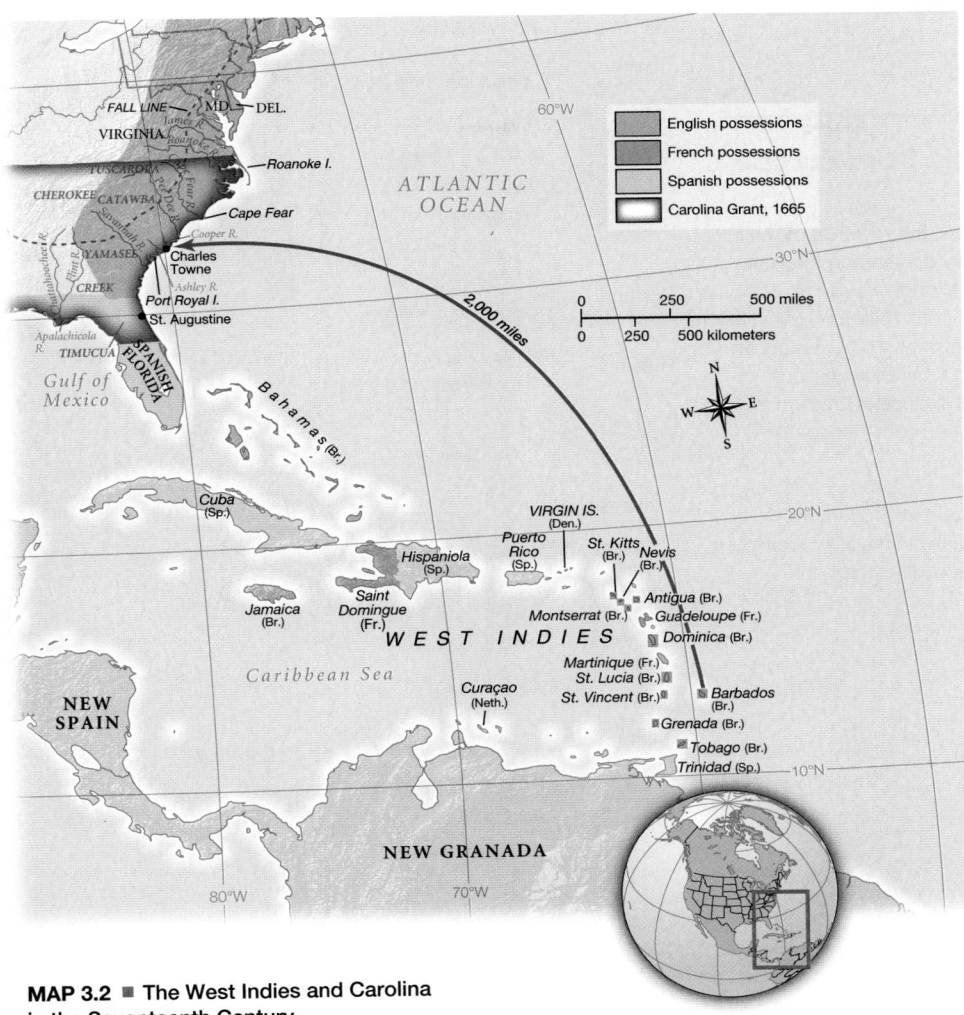

CHRONOLOGY

1640s
- Barbados colonists begin to grow sugarcane with labor of African slaves.

1663
- Royal charter is granted for Carolina colony.

1670
- Charles Towne, South Carolina, is founded.

1670s
- Settlers from Barbados bring slavery to Carolina.

1670–1700
- Slave labor system emerges in Carolina and Chesapeake colonies.

1690s
- Carolinians begin to grow rice with labor of African slaves.

1700
- Slaves make up about half of the population of Carolina.

MAP 3.2 ■ The West Indies and Carolina in the Seventeenth Century

Although Carolina was geographically near the Chesapeake colonies, it was culturally closer to the West Indies in the seventeenth century because its early settlers—both blacks and whites—came from Barbados. South Carolina maintained strong ties to the West Indies for more than a century, long after the arrival of many later settlers from England, Ireland, France, and elsewhere.

jewel of the English West Indies. During the 1640s, Barbadian planters began to grow sugarcane with such success that a colonial official proclaimed Barbados "the most flourishing Island in all those American parts, and I verily believe in all the world for the production of sugar."

Sugar commanded high prices in England, and planters rushed to grow as much as they could. By midcentury, annual sugar exports from the English Caribbean totaled about 150,000 pounds; by 1700, exports reached nearly 50 million pounds.

Sugar transformed Barbados and other West Indian islands. Poor farmers could not afford the expensive machinery that extracted and refined sugarcane juice. Planters with the necessary capital to grow and process sugarcane got rich. By 1680, the wealthiest Barbadian sugar planters were, on average, four times richer than tobacco grandees in the Chesapeake. The sugar grandees differed

How did a tobacco society take shape?	How and why did Chesapeake society change in the late seventeenth century?	What caused tensions in the Spanish borderland?	When and why did the southern colonies move toward a slave labor system?	Conclusion: Why were export crops and slave labor important in the growth of the southern colonies?

Migration to the New World from Europe and Africa, 1492–1700

Before 1640, Spain and Portugal reaped the rewards of their sixteenth-century voyages of discovery by sending four out of five European migrants to the New World, virtually all of them bound for New Spain or Brazil. But from 1640 to 1700, more migrants came from England than from any other European nation and nearly as many as from all other European nations combined, a measure of the growing significance of England's colonies in both the Caribbean and North America during the seventeenth century.

While few enslaved Africans were carried across the Atlantic before 1580, from the voyages of Columbus to 1700, more Africans than Europeans crossed the Atlantic to the New World, and virtually all of them were slaves. What might explain the shifting destinations of enslaved Africans?

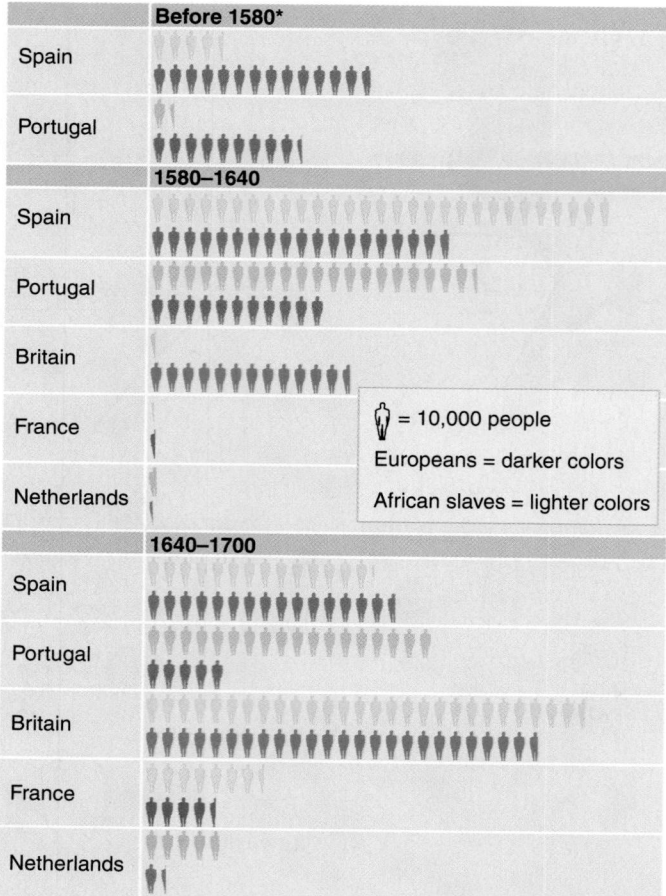

= 10,000 people

Europeans = darker colors

African slaves = lighter colors

*Note: Before 1580, migration from Britain, France, and the Netherlands was negligible.

from their Chesapeake counterparts in another crucial way: The average sugar baron in Barbados owned 115 slaves in 1680.

African slaves planted, cultivated, and harvested the sugarcane that made West Indian planters wealthy. Beginning in the 1640s, Barbadian planters purchased thousands of slaves to work their plantations, and the African population on the island mushroomed. For slaves, work on a sugar plantation was a life sentence to brutal, unremitting labor. Slaves suffered high death rates. Since slave men outnumbered slave women two to one, few slaves could form families and have children. These grim realities meant that in Barbados and elsewhere in the West Indies, the slave population did not grow by natural reproduction. Instead, planters continually purchased enslaved Africans. Although sugar plantations did not gain a foothold in North America in the seventeenth century, the West Indies nonetheless exerted a powerful influence on the development of slavery in the mainland colonies.

Carolina: A West Indian Frontier

The early settlers of what became South Carolina were immigrants from Barbados. In 1663, a Barbadian planter named John Colleton and a group of seven

CHAPTER LOCATOR | What challenges faced early Chesapeake colonists?

other men obtained a charter from England's King Charles II to establish a colony south of the Chesapeake and north of the Spanish territories in Florida. The men, known as "proprietors," hoped to siphon settlers from Barbados and other colonies and encourage them to develop a profitable export crop comparable to West Indian sugar and Chesapeake tobacco. Following the Chesapeake example, the proprietors offered headrights of up to 150 acres of land for each settler. In 1670, they established the colony's first permanent English settlement, Charles Towne (later spelled Charleston) (see Map 3.2, page 75).

As the proprietors had planned, most of the early settlers were from Barbados. In fact, Carolina was the only seventeenth-century English colony to be settled principally by colonists from other colonies rather than directly from England. The Barbadian immigrants brought their slaves with them. More than a fourth of the early settlers were slaves, and as the colony continued to attract settlers from Barbados, the black population multiplied. By 1700, slaves made up about half the population of Carolina.

The Carolinians experimented unsuccessfully to match their semitropical climate with profitable export crops of tobacco, cotton, indigo, and olives. In the mid-1690s, colonists identified a hardy strain of rice and took advantage of the knowledge of rice cultivation among their many African slaves to build rice plantations. Settlers also sold livestock and timber to the West Indies, as well as another "natural resource": They captured and enslaved several thousand local Indians and sold them to Caribbean planters. Both economically and socially, seventeenth-century Carolina was a frontier outpost of the West Indian sugar economy.

Slave Labor Emerges in the Chesapeake

By 1700, more than eight out of ten people in the southern colonies of English North America lived in the Chesapeake. Until the 1670s, almost all Chesapeake colonists were white people from England. By 1700, however, one out of eight people in the region was a black person from Africa. A few black people had lived in the Chesapeake since the 1620s, but the black population grew fivefold between 1670 and 1700 as hundreds of tobacco planters made the transition from servant to slave labor.

For planters, slaves had several obvious advantages over servants. Although slaves cost three to five times more than servants, slaves never became free. Since the mortality rate had declined by the 1680s, planters could reasonably expect a slave to live longer than a servant's period of indenture. Slaves also promised to be a perpetual labor force, since children of slave mothers inherited the status of slavery.

Slaves had another important advantage over servants: They could be controlled politically. Bacon's Rebellion had demonstrated how disruptive former servants could be when their expectations were not met. A slave labor system promised to avoid the political problems caused by the servant labor system.

The slave labor system polarized Chesapeake society along lines of race and status: All slaves were black, and nearly all blacks were slaves; almost all free people were white, and all whites were free or only temporarily bound in indentured servitude. Unlike Barbados, where slaves constituted more than three-fourths of the population by the end of the seventeenth century, the Chesapeake

| How did a tobacco society take shape? | How and why did Chesapeake society change in the late seventeenth century? | What caused tensions in the Spanish borderland? | **When and why did the southern colonies move toward a slave labor system?** | Conclusion: Why were export crops and slave labor important in the growth of the southern colonies? |

77

retained a vast white majority. Among whites, huge differences of wealth and status still existed. By 1700, more than three-quarters of white families had neither servants nor slaves. Nonetheless, poor white farmers enjoyed the privileges of free status. They could own property, get married, have families, and bequeath their property and their freedom to their descendants; they could move when and where they wanted; they could associate freely with other people; they could serve on juries, vote, and hold political office; and they could work, loaf, and sleep as they chose. These privileges of freedom—none of them possessed by slaves—made lesser white folk feel they had a genuine stake in the existence of slavery, even if they did not own a single slave. By emphasizing the privileges of freedom shared by all white people, the slave labor system reduced the tensions between poor folk and grandees that had plagued the Chesapeake region in the 1670s.

In contrast to slaves in Barbados, most slaves in the seventeenth-century Chesapeake colonies had frequent and close contact with white people. Slaves and white servants performed the same tasks on tobacco plantations, often working side by side in the fields. Slaves took advantage of every opportunity to slip away from white supervision and seek out the company of other slaves. Planters often feared that slaves would turn such seemingly innocent social pleasures to political ends, either to run away or to conspire to strike against their masters. Slaves often did run away, but they were usually captured or returned after a brief absence. Despite planters' nightmares, slave insurrections did not occur.

Although slavery resolved the political unrest caused by the servant labor system, it created new political problems. By 1700, the bedrock political issue in the southern colonies was keeping slaves in their place, at the end of a hoe. The slave labor system in the southern colonies stood roughly midway between the sugar plantations and black majority of Barbados to the south and the small farms and homogeneous villages that developed in seventeenth-century New England to the north (see chapter 4).

> **QUICK REVIEW**

Why had slave labor largely displaced indentured servant labor by 1700 in Chesapeake tobacco production?

Conclusion: Why were export crops and slave labor important in the growth of the southern colonies?

HIP/Art Resource, NY.

BY 1700, the colonies of Virginia, Maryland, and Carolina were firmly established. Their societies differed markedly from English society in most respects, yet the colonists considered themselves English people who happened to live in North America. They claimed the same rights and privileges as English men and women, while they denied those rights and privileges to Native Americans and African slaves.

The English colonies also differed from the example of New Spain. Settlers and servants flocked to English colonies, in contrast to the small number of Spaniards who trickled into New Spain. Few English missionaries sought to convert Indians to Protestant Christianity, unlike the numerous Catholic missionaries in the Spanish settlements in New Mexico and Florida. Large quantities of gold and silver never materialized in English North America. English colonists never adopted the Spanish system of forced labor known as encomienda (see chapter 2). Yet some forms of coerced labor and racial distinction that developed in New Spain had North American counterparts, as English colonists employed servants and slaves and defined themselves as superior to Indians and Africans.

By 1700, the remnants of Powhatan's people still survived. As English settlement pushed north, west, and south of the Chesapeake Bay, the Indians faced the new colonial world that Powhatan and Pocahontas had encountered when John Smith and the first colonists had arrived at Jamestown. By 1700, the many descendants of Pocahontas's son, Thomas, as well as other colonists and Native Americans, understood that the English had come to stay.

The Virginia Planters Beft TOBACCO.

SO NOW YOU KNOW

Tobacco made the Virginia colony a success. It transformed life in Virginia and the rest of the Chesapeake region. Large plantations producing rice developed in Carolina while even larger plantations grew sugarcane in Barbados. By the end of the seventeenth century, all these plantation societies relied heavily on African slaves for their success.

| How did a tobacco society take shape? | How and why did Chesapeake society change in the late seventeenth century? | What caused tensions in the Spanish borderland? | When and why did the southern colonies move toward a slave labor system? | Conclusion: Why were export crops and slave labor important in the growth of the southern colonies? |

STEP 1

GETTING STARTED

Below are basic terms from this period in American history. Can you identify each term below and explain why it matters? To do this exercise online or to download this chart, visit bedfordstmartins.com/roarkunderstanding.

TERM	WHO OR WHAT & WHEN	WHY IT MATTERS
Powhatan, p. 57		
Jamestown, p. 57		
Captain John Smith, p. 58		
Pocahontas, p. 58		
House of Burgesses, p. 61		
headright, p. 64		
indentured servants, p. 64		
yeoman, p. 68		
Navigation Acts of 1650 and 1651, p. 69		
mercantilism, p. 70		
Bacon's Rebellion, p. 70		
Pueblo Revolt, p. 73		

STEP 2

MOVING BEYOND THE BASICS

The exercise below represents a more advanced understanding of the chapter material. In this exercise, you will reflect on the social and economic development of the English colonies and the Spanish borderland. Begin by identifying the important economic activities of each region. What was involved in making each colony a financial success? What resources (both material and human) were necessary? How did each settlement develop socially? What were the challenges and successes, both political and social, that occurred as each colony developed? To do this exercise online or to download this chart, visit bedfordstmartins.com/roarkunderstanding.

Colony	Economy (including labor, land use and distribution, resources, crops)	Population and social hierarchy	Challenges	Successes
Chesapeake				
New Mexico				
Barbados				
Carolina				

To do this exercise online, visit bedfordsmartins.com/roarkunderstanding.

STEP 3

PUTTING
IT ALL
TOGETHER

Now that you've reviewed various parts of the chapter, take a step back and try to see the big picture by answering these questions. Remember to use specific examples from the chapter in your answers. To do this exercise online, visit bedfordsmartins.com/roarkunderstanding.

JAMESTOWN AND THE CHESAPEAKE

▶ How did interactions with the Algonquians shape the Jamestown colony's early history?

▶ How did the development of tobacco cultivation transform the Chesapeake?

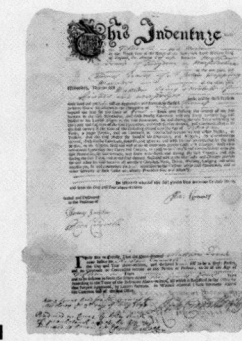

INDENTURED SERVITUDE AND BACON'S REBELLION

▶ What role did indentured servants play in the transformation of the Chesapeake in the early seventeenth century?

▶ What events led to Bacon's Rebellion, and why did Virginia erupt into violence in 1676?

SLAVERY

▶ What role did sugar play in the development of African slavery in the New World?

▶ How did the introduction of African slaves affect the development of Chesapeake society?

LOOKING BACKWARD, LOOKING AHEAD

▶ How did the seventeenth-century English colonies differ from their sixteenth-century Spanish counterparts?

▶ How did the introduction of African slaves contribute to the emergence of a distinct southern colonial society?

IN YOUR OWN WORDS

Imagine that you must explain chapter 3 to someone who hasn't read it. What would be the most important points to include and why?

Why why should the minding
within a World of Evils Finding thy Times
Then Fam'd World: Fam'd thy Warrs
Us Joies thy Foies thy soe,
This Sceane Retreat: I am yet sorye,
the Eternall Dramae to him thy hard
Faith (which end thy Force Subvert)
(after more) with Glory.

4
CREATING THE NORTHERN COLONIES

1601–1700

> This chapter explores the development of the northern colonies in the seventeenth century, examining the factors that gave each colony its unique character. It gives particular emphasis to the importance of religion in the evolution of New England and to England's attempts to control colonial trade.

> How did the English Reformation influence Puritans?

> What was distinctive about the settlement of New England?

> How did New England society change during the seventeenth century?

> What was distinctive about the middle colonies?

> What was the role of the North American colonies in the English empire?

> Conclusion: What made the English colonization of North America distinctive?

DID YOU KNOW?

New England Puritans did not celebrate Christmas or Easter.

Thomas Smith, a New England mariner, created colonial America's oldest known self-portrait around 1680.

How did the English Reformation influence Puritans?

Queen Elizabeth's Funeral Procession

The death of Elizabeth I in 1603 created uncertainty about the balance of Protestantism and Catholicism in England. Since Elizabeth had no children, James, Elizabeth's nephew and the son of the staunch Catholic Queen Mary (Elizabeth's sister), assumed the throne and soon cracked down on Protestants, especially Puritans. Courtesy of the Trustees of the British Library.

Puritans
▶ Dissenting members of the Church of England who sought to purify the Church of England of remnants of Catholicism. Puritanism was less an organized movement than a set of ideas and religious principles.

English Reformation
▶ The break between the English church and the Catholic Church. The English Reformation began in 1534 when Henry VIII outlawed the Catholic Church and made himself head of the Church of England.

THE RELIGIOUS ROOTS of the **Puritans** who founded New England reached back to the Protestant Reformation, which arose in Germany in 1517 (see chapter 2). The Reformation spread quickly to other countries, but the English church initially remained within the Catholic fold and continued its allegiance to the pope in Rome. King Henry VIII, who reigned from 1509 to 1547, understood that the Reformation offered him an opportunity to break with Rome and take control of the church in England. In 1534, Henry formally initiated the **English Reformation**. At his insistence, Parliament passed the Act of Supremacy, which outlawed the Catholic Church and proclaimed the king "the only supreme head on earth of the Church of England." Henry seized the vast properties of the Catholic Church in England as well as the privilege of appointing bishops and others in the church hierarchy.

In the short run, the English Reformation allowed Henry VIII to achieve his political goal of controlling the church. In the long run, however, the Reformation brought to England the political and religious turmoil that Henry had hoped to avoid. Henry himself sought no more than a halfway Reformation, one that preserved Catholic religious beliefs and practices while giving control of the church to the English crown. Many English Catholics wanted to revoke the English Reformation. But many other English people insisted on a genuine, thoroughgoing Reformation; these people came to be called Puritans.

During the sixteenth century, Puritanism was less an organized movement than a set of ideas and religious principles that appealed strongly to many dissenting members of the Church of England. They sought to purify the Church of England by eliminating what they considered the offensive features of Catholicism. For example, they demanded that the church hierarchy be abolished and that ordinary Christians be given greater control over religious life. They wanted to do away with the rituals of Catholic worship and instead emphasize an individual's relationship with God developed through Bible study, prayer, and introspection. Although there were many varieties and degrees of Puritanism, all Puritans shared a desire to make the English church thoroughly Protestant.

The fate of Protestantism waxed and waned under the monarchs who succeeded Henry VIII. When he died in 1547, the advisers of the new king, Edward VI—the nine-year-old son of Henry and his third wife, Jane Seymour—initiated religious reforms that moved in a Protestant direction. The tide of reform reversed in 1553 when Edward died and was succeeded by Mary I, the daughter of Henry and Catherine of Aragon, his first wife. Mary was a steadfast Catholic, and shortly after becoming queen, she married Philip II of Spain, Europe's most powerful guardian of Catholicism. Mary attempted to restore the pre-Reformation Catholic Church. She outlawed Protestantism in England and persecuted those who refused to conform, sentencing almost three hundred to burn at the stake.

The tide turned again in 1558 when Mary died and was succeeded by Elizabeth I, the daughter of Henry and his second wife, Anne Boleyn. During her long reign, Elizabeth reaffirmed the English Reformation and tried to position the English church between the extremes of Catholicism and Puritanism. Above all, she desired a church that would strengthen the monarchy and the nation. By the time Elizabeth died in 1603, many people in England looked on Protestantism as a defining feature of national identity.

When Elizabeth's successor, James I, became king, English Puritans petitioned for further reform of the Church of England. James authorized a new translation of the Bible, known ever since as the King James version. However, neither James I nor his son Charles I, who became king in 1625, was receptive to the ideas of Puritan reformers. In 1629, Charles I dissolved Parliament—where Puritans were well represented—and initiated aggressive anti-Puritan policies. Many Puritans despaired about continuing to defend their faith in England and began to make plans to emigrate. Some left for Europe, others for the West Indies. The largest number set out for America.

CHRONOLOGY

1534
- King Henry VIII breaks with Roman Catholic Church; English Reformation begins.

1547
- Edward VI becomes king of England; Church of England moves in the direction of Protestantism.

1553
- Mary I becomes queen of England and attempts to restore Catholicism.

1558
- Elizabeth I becomes queen of England and establishes moderate Protestantism as the state religion.

QUICK REVIEW

How did Henry VIII seek to benefit from the English Reformation?

| What was distinctive about the settlement of New England? | How did New England society change during the seventeenth century? | What was distinctive about the middle colonies? | What was the role of the North American colonies in the English empire? | Conclusion: What made the English colonization of North America distinctive? |

What was distinctive about the settlement of New England?

In 1629, the Massachusetts Bay Company designed this seal depicting an Indian man inviting English settlers to "come over and help us." The seal was an attempt to lend an aura of altruism to the Massachusetts Bay Company's colonization efforts. In reality, colonists in Massachusetts and elsewhere were far less interested in helping Indians than in helping themselves. For the most part, that suited the Indians, who wanted no "help" from the colonists. Courtesy of Massachusetts Archives.

> ► FOR MORE HELP ANALYZING THIS IMAGE, see the visual activity for this chapter in the Online Study Guide at bedfordstmartins.com/roarkunderstanding.

PURITANS WHO IMMIGRATED to New England aspired to escape the turmoil and persecution of England and to build a new, orderly, Puritan version of English society. Puritans established the first small settlement in New England in 1620, followed a few years later by additional settlements by the Massachusetts Bay Company. Allowed self-government through royal charter, these Puritans were in a unique position to direct the new colonies according to their faith. Their faith shaped the colonies they established in almost every way.

CHAPTER LOCATOR | How did the English Reformation influence Puritans?

The Pilgrims and Plymouth Colony

One of the first Protestant groups to emigrate, later known as **Pilgrims**, espoused an unorthodox view known as separatism. These Separatists sought to withdraw—or separate—from the Church of England, which they considered hopelessly corrupt. In 1608, they moved to Holland; by 1620, they realized that they could not live and worship there as they had hoped. William Bradford, a leader of the Separatists, believed that America promised to better protect their children's piety and preserve their community. Separatists obtained permission to settle in the extensive territory granted to the Virginia Company (see chapter 3). To finance their journey, they formed a joint-stock company with English investors. In August 1620, 102 Pilgrim immigrants boarded the *Mayflower*, arriving eleven weeks later at the outermost tip of Cape Cod, in present-day Massachusetts.

The Pilgrims realized immediately that they had landed far north of the Virginia grants and had no legal authority to settle in the area. To provide order and security as well as a claim to legitimacy, they drew up the Mayflower Compact on the day they arrived. They pledged to "covenant and combine ourselves together into a civil Body Politick, for our better Ordering and Preservation." The signers (all men) agreed to enact and obey necessary and just laws.

The Pilgrims settled at Plymouth in 1620 and elected William Bradford their governor. That first winter "was most sad and lamentable," Bradford wrote later. "In two or three months' time half of [our] company died . . . being the depth of winter, and wanting houses and other comforts [and] being infected with scurvy and other diseases." In the spring, Wampanoag Indians rescued the floundering Plymouth settlement. First Samoset and then Squanto befriended the settlers. Samoset arranged for the Pilgrims to meet and establish good relations with Massasoit, the Wampanoag chief whose territory included Plymouth. Squanto, Bradford recalled, "was a special instrument sent of God for their [the Pilgrims'] good. . . . He directed them how to set their corn, where to take fish, and to procure other commodities, and was also their pilot to bring them to unknown places." With the Indians' guidance, the Pilgrims managed to harvest enough food to guarantee their survival through the coming winter, an occasion they celebrated in the fall of 1621 with a feast of thanksgiving attended by Massasoit and other Wampanoags.

Still, the Plymouth colony remained precarious. The colonists quarreled with their London investors, who became frustrated when Plymouth failed to produce the expected profits. These struggles to survive constantly frustrated the London investors, but the Pilgrims persisted, living simply and coexisting in relative peace with the Indians. They paid the Wampanoags when settlers gradually encroached on Indian land. By 1630, Plymouth had become a small permanent settlement, but it failed to attract many other English Puritans.

The Founding of Massachusetts Bay Colony

In 1629, shortly before Charles I dissolved Parliament, a group of Puritan merchants and country gentlemen obtained a royal charter for the **Massachusetts Bay Company**. In addition to the usual privileges granted to joint-stock companies, the charter included a unique provision that permitted the government of the Massachusetts Bay Company to be located in the colony rather than in England.

CHRONOLOGY

1620
– Plymouth colony is founded.

1621
– Thanksgiving feast is attended by Pilgrims and Wampanoags.

1629
– Massachusetts Bay Company receives royal charter.

1630
– John Winthrop leads Puritan settlers to Massachusetts Bay.

Pilgrims
▶ Puritan Separatists who founded the Plymouth colony in Massachusetts in 1620. The Pilgrims believed that the Church of England could not be reformed and hoped to create their own religious community outside of England.

Massachusetts Bay Company
▶ Joint-stock company that established settlements around present-day Boston in 1630. The company's charter included a unique provision that permitted its government to be located in the colony rather than in England.

| What was distinctive about the settlement of New England? | How did New England society change during the seventeenth century? | What was distinctive about the middle colonies? | What was the role of the North American colonies in the English empire? | Conclusion: What made the English colonization of North America distinctive? |

To lead the emigrants, the stockholders of the Massachusetts Bay Company elected **John Winthrop**, a prosperous lawyer and landowner, to serve as governor. In March 1630, eleven ships crammed with seven hundred passengers sailed for Massachusetts; six more ships and another five hundred emigrants followed a few months later. Winthrop's fleet arrived in Massachusetts Bay in early June. Unlike the Separatists, Winthrop's Puritans aspired to reform the corrupt Church of England (rather than separate from it) by setting an example of godliness in the New World. Winthrop and a small group chose to settle on the peninsula that became Boston, and other settlers clustered at promising locations nearby (**Map 4.1**).

In a sermon to his companions aboard the *Arbella* while they were still at sea, Winthrop proclaimed the cosmic significance of their journey. The Puritans had "entered into a covenant" with God to "work out our salvation under the power and purity of his holy ordinances," Winthrop declared. This sanctified agreement with God meant that the Puritans had to make "extraordinary" efforts to "bring into familiar and constant practice" religious principles that most people in England merely preached. To achieve their pious goals, the Puritans had to subordinate their individual interests to the common good. "We must be knit together in this work as one man," Winthrop preached. "We must delight in each other, make others' conditions our own, rejoice together, mourn together, labor and suffer together." The stakes could not be higher, Winthrop told his listeners: "We must consider that we shall be as a city upon a hill. The eyes of all people are upon us."

That belief shaped seventeenth-century New England as profoundly as tobacco shaped the Chesapeake. Winthrop's vision of a city on a hill fired the Puritans' fierce determination to keep their covenant and live according to God's laws.

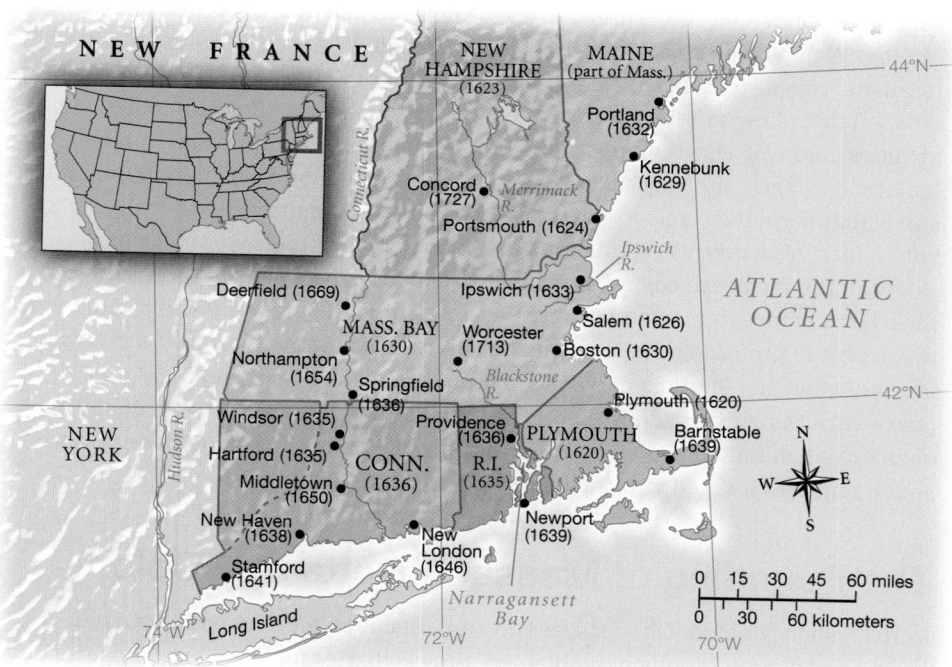

MAP 4.1 ■ New England Colonies in the Seventeenth Century
New Englanders spread across the landscape town by town during the seventeenth century. (For the sake of legibility, only a few of the more important towns are shown on the map.)

And each year from 1630 to 1640, ship after ship followed in the wake of Winthrop's fleet. In all, more than twenty thousand new settlers came, their eyes focused on the Puritans' city on a hill.

Often, when the Church of England cracked down on a Puritan minister in England, he and many of his followers moved together to New England. Smaller groups of English Puritans moved to the Chesapeake, Barbados, and elsewhere in the New World, including New Amsterdam (present-day New York). A few ministers sought to carry the message of Christianity to the Indians, accompanied by instructions replacing what missionary John Eliot termed the Indians' "unfixed, confused, and ungoverned . . . life, uncivilized and unsubdued to labor and order." For the most part, however, the colonists focused less on saving Indians' souls than on saving their own.

On the whole, the immigrants came from the middle ranks of English society. The vast majority were either farmers or tradesmen, including carpenters, tailors, and textile workers. Indentured servants, whose numbers dominated the Chesapeake settlers, accounted for only about a fifth of those headed for New England. Most New England immigrants paid their way to Massachusetts, even though the journey often took their life savings. They were encouraged by the promise of bounty in New England reported in Winthrop's letter to his son: "Here is as good land as I have seen there [in England]. . . . Here can be no want of anything to those who bring means to raise [it] out of the earth and sea."

In contrast to Chesapeake newcomers, New England immigrants usually arrived as families, with women and children making up a solid majority of the region's population. Each family was considered a "little commonwealth" that mirrored the hierarchy among all God's creatures. Just as humankind was subordinate to God, so young people were subordinate to their elders, children to their parents, and wives to their husbands. The immigrants' family ties reinforced their religious beliefs with universally understood notions of hierarchy and mutual dependence. While immigrants to the Chesapeake were disciplined mostly by the coercions of servitude and the caprices of the tobacco market, immigrants to New England entered a social order defined by the interlocking institutions of family, church, and community.

QUICK REVIEW

What was a "little commonwealth," and why was it so important to Puritan settlement in New England?

| What was distinctive about the settlement of New England? | How did New England society change during the seventeenth century? | What was distinctive about the middle colonies? | What was the role of the North American colonies in the English empire? | Conclusion: What made the English colonization of North America distinctive? |

89

How did New England society change during the seventeenth century?

David, Joanna, and Abigail Mason

This 1670 painting depicts the children of Joanna and Anthony Mason, a wealthy Boston baker. The artist lavished attention on the children's elaborate clothing. The portrait is unified not by signs of warm affection, innocent smiles, or familial solidarity, but by the trappings of wealth and sober self-importance. The painting expresses the growing respect for wealth and its worldly rewards in seventeenth-century New England. Fine Arts Museums of San Francisco. Gift of Mr. and Mrs. John D. Rockefeller III.

THE NEW ENGLAND COLONISTS, unlike their counterparts in the Chesapeake, settled in small towns, usually located on the coast or by a river (see Map 4.1, page 88). Massachusetts Bay colonists founded 133 towns during the seventeenth century, each with one or more churches. Church members' fervent piety, buttressed by the institutions of local government, enforced remarkable religious and social conformity in the small settlements. During the century, tensions within the Puritan faith and changes in New England communities splintered religious orthodoxy and weakened Puritan zeal. By 1700, however, Puritanism still maintained a distinctive influence in New England.

Church, Covenant, and Conformity

Puritans believed that the church consisted of men and women who had entered a solemn covenant with one another and with God. Each new member of the covenant had to persuade existing members that she or he had fully experienced conversion.

CHAPTER LOCATOR | How did the English Reformation influence Puritans?

Puritans embraced a distinctive version of Protestantism derived from Calvinism, the doctrines of John Calvin, a sixteenth-century Swiss Protestant theologian. Calvin insisted that Christians strictly discipline their behavior to conform to God's commandments announced in the Bible. Like Calvin, Puritans believed in predestination—the idea that the all-powerful God, before the creation of the world, decided which few human souls would receive eternal life. Only God knows the identity of these fortunate predestined individuals—the "elect" or "saints." Nothing a person did in his or her lifetime could alter God's choice or provide assurance that the person was predestined for salvation or damnation.

Despite the ultimate unknowability of God's choice of the elect, Puritans believed that if a person lived a rigorously godly life, his or her behavior was likely to be a hint, a visible sign, that he or she was one of God's chosen few. Puritans thought that "sainthood" would become visible in individuals' behavior, especially if they were privileged to know God's Word as revealed in the Bible.

The connection between sainthood and saintly behavior, however, was far from certain. The slippery relationship between saintly behavior—observable by anybody—and God's predestined election—invisible and unknowable to anyone—caused Puritans to worry constantly that individuals who acted like saints were fooling themselves and others. Nevertheless, Puritans thought that visible saints—people who passed their demanding tests of conversion and church membership—probably, though not certainly, were among God's elect.

Members of Puritan churches ardently hoped that God had chosen them to receive eternal life and tried to demonstrate saintly behavior. Their covenant bound them to help one another attain salvation and to discipline the entire community by saintly standards. Church members kept an eye on the behavior of everybody in town. Infractions of morality, order, or propriety were reported to Puritan elders, who summoned the wayward to a church inquiry. By overseeing every aspect of life, the visible saints enforced a remarkable degree of righteous conformity in Puritan communities. Total conformity, however, was never achieved. Puritans differed among themselves; non-Puritans shirked orthodox rules. Despite the central importance of religion, churches played no direct role in the civil government of New England communities. Puritans were determined to insulate New England churches from the contaminating influence of the civil state and its merely human laws. Although ministers were the most highly respected figures in New England towns, they were prohibited from holding government office.

Puritans had no qualms, however, about their religious beliefs influencing New England governments. As much as possible, the Puritans tried to bring public life into conformity with their view of God's law. For example, fines were issued for Sabbath-breaking activities such as working, smoking a pipe, and visiting neighbors. Puritans mandated other purifications of what they considered corrupt English practices. They refused to celebrate Christmas or Easter because the Bible did not mention either one. They outlawed religious wedding ceremonies; couples were married by a magistrate in a civil ceremony (the first wedding in Massachusetts performed by a minister occurred in 1686). They prohibited elaborate clothing and finery such as lace trim and short sleeves—"whereby the nakedness of the arm may be discovered." They banned cards, dice, shuffleboard, and

CHRONOLOGY

1636
- Roger Williams is banished from Massachusetts Bay.
- Rhode Island colony is established.

1638
- Anne Hutchinson is excommunicated for heresy.

1642
- Puritan Revolution inflames England.

1649
- English Puritans win civil war and execute Charles I.

1656
- Quakers arrive in Massachusetts and are persecuted there.

1660
- Monarchy is restored in England; Charles II becomes king.

1662
- Many Puritan congregations adopt Halfway Covenant.

1692
- Salem witch trials.

| What was distinctive about the settlement of New England? | **How did New England society change during the seventeenth century?** | What was distinctive about the middle colonies? | What was the role of the North American colonies in the English empire? | Conclusion: What made the English colonization of North America distinctive? |

The World Turn'd Upside Down, a pamphlet printed in London in 1647, satirizes the Puritan notion that the contemporary world was deeply flawed. The pamphlet refers to the "distracted Times" of the Puritan Revolution in England. The drawing on the title page ridicules criticisms of English society that also were common among New England Puritans. By permission of The British Library.

▶ FOR MORE HELP ANALYZING THIS IMAGE, see the visual activity for this chapter in the Online Study Guide at bedfordstmartins.com/roarkunderstanding.

other games of chance, as well as music and dancing. The distinguished minister Increase Mather insisted that "Mixt or Promiscuous Dancing . . . of Men and Women" could not be tolerated since "the unchaste Touches and Gesticulations used by Dancers have a palpable tendency to that which is evil." On special occasions, Puritans proclaimed days of fasting and humiliation, which, as one preacher boasted, amounted to "so many Sabbaths more."

Government by Puritans for Puritanism

It is only a slight exaggeration to say that seventeenth-century New England was governed by Puritans for Puritanism. The charter of the Massachusetts Bay Company empowered the company's stockholders, known as freemen, to meet as a body known as the General Court and make the laws needed to govern the company's affairs. The colonists transformed this arrangement for running a joint-stock company into a structure for governing the colony. Hoping to ensure that godly men would decide government policies, the General Court expanded the number of freemen in 1631 to include all male church members. Only freemen had the right to vote for governor, deputy governor, and other colonial officials. As new settlers were recognized as freemen, the size of the General Court grew too large to meet conveniently. So in 1634, the freemen in each town agreed to send two deputies to the General Court to act as the colony's legislative assembly. All other men were classified as "inhabitants," and they had the right to vote, hold office, and participate fully in town government. A "town meeting," composed of a town's inhabitants and freemen, chose the selectmen and other officials who administered local affairs. Almost every adult man could speak out in town meetings and fortify his voice with a vote. However, all women—even church members—were prohibited from voting, and towns did not permit "contrary-minded" men to become or remain inhabitants. Although town meeting participants wrangled from time to time, widespread political participation tended to reinforce conformity to Puritan ideals.

CHAPTER LOCATOR | How did the English Reformation influence Puritans?

One of the most important functions of New England government was land distribution. Settlers who desired to establish a new town entered a covenant and petitioned the General Court for a grant of land. The court granted town sites to suitably pious petitioners but did not allow settlement until the Indians who inhabited a grant agreed to relinquish their claim to the land, usually in exchange for manufactured goods. For instance, William Pynchon purchased the site of Springfield, Massachusetts, from the Agawam Indians for "eighteen fathams [arm's lengths] of Wampum, eighteen coates, 18 hatchets, 18 hoes, [and] 18 knives."

Having obtained their grant, town founders apportioned land among themselves and any newcomers they permitted to join them. Normally, each family received a house lot large enough for an adjacent garden as well as one or more strips of agricultural land on the perimeter of the town. Although there was a considerable difference between the largest and smallest family plots, most clustered in the middle range—roughly fifty to one hundred acres—resulting in a more nearly equal distribution of land in New England than in the Chesapeake.

The Splintering of Puritanism

Almost from the beginning, John Winthrop and other leaders had difficulty enforcing their views of Puritan orthodoxy. In England, persecution as a dissenting minority had unified Puritan voices in opposition to the Church of England. In New England, the promise of a godly society and the Puritans' emphasis on individual Bible study led New Englanders toward different visions of godliness. Puritan leaders, however, interpreted dissent as an error caused either by a misguided believer or by the malevolent power of Satan. Whatever the cause, errors could not be tolerated.

The case of **Roger Williams** provides an example of division and its consequences. In 1633, Williams became the minister of the church in Salem, Massachusetts. Most New England Puritans believed that churches and governments should enforce both godly belief and behavior according to biblical rules. They claimed that "the Word of God is . . . clear." In contrast, Williams believed that the Bible shrouded the Word of God in "mist and fog." Williams pointed out that devout and pious Christians could and did differ about what the Bible said and what God expected. That observation led him to denounce the emerging New England order as impure, ungodly, and tyrannical.

Williams also disagreed with the New England government's requirement that everyone attend church services. He argued that forcing people who were not Christians to attend church was wrong in four major ways. First, Williams preached, it was akin to requiring "a dead child to suck the breast, or a dead man [to] feast." The only way for any person to become a true Christian was by God's gift of faith revealed to the person's conscience. Second, churches should be reserved exclusively for those already converted, separating "holy from unholy . . . [and] godly from ungodly." He said requiring everybody to attend church was "False Worshipping" that promoted "spiritual drunkenness and whoredom, a soul sleep and a soul sickness." Third, the government had no business ruling on spiritual matters. Williams termed New England's regulation of religious behavior "spiritual rape" that inevitably would lead governments to use coercion and violence to enforce their misguided ways. Finally, Williams believed that governments should tolerate all religious beliefs because only God knows the Truth; no

Roger Williams
▶ Puritan minister who criticized the political and religious order in New England and advocated religious toleration. After his banishment from New England in 1636, Williams went on to found Rhode Island.

| What was distinctive about the settlement of New England? | **How did New England society change during the seventeenth century?** | What was distinctive about the middle colonies? | What was the role of the North American colonies in the English empire? | Conclusion: What made the English colonization of North America distinctive? |

93

person and no religion can understand God with absolute certainty. "I commend that man," Williams wrote, "whether Jew, or Turk, or Papist, or whoever, that steers no otherwise than his conscience dares." In Williams's view, toleration of religious belief and liberty of conscience were the only paths to religious purity and political harmony.

New England's leaders denounced Williams's arguments and banished Williams for his "extreme and dangerous" opinions. He escaped from an attempt to ship him back to England and in 1636 spent fourteen weeks walking south to Narragansett Bay, "exposed to the mercy of an howling Wilderness in Frost and Snow." There he founded the colony of Rhode Island, which enshrined "Liberty of Conscience" as a fundamental ideal and became a refuge for other dissenters.

Shortly after banishing Williams, the Puritan leadership confronted another dissenter, this time a devout Puritan woman steeped in Scripture and absorbed by religious questions: **Anne Hutchinson**. The mother of fourteen children, Hutchinson settled into her new home in Boston in 1634, and neighbors—women and men—gathered there to hear her weekly lectures on recent sermons. As one listener observed, she was a "Woman that Preaches better Gospell then any of your blackcoates [male preachers] . . . [from] the Ninneversity."

Hutchinson expounded on the sermons of John Cotton, her favorite minister. Cotton stressed what he termed the covenant of grace—the idea that individuals could be saved only by God's grace in choosing them to be members of the elect. Cotton contrasted this familiar Puritan doctrine with the covenant of works, the erroneous belief that a person's behavior—one's works—could win God's favor and ultimately earn a person salvation. Belief in the covenant of works and in the possibility of salvation for all was known as Arminianism. Hutchinson's lectures emphasized her opinion that many of the colony's leaders affirmed the Arminian position that a person's behavior could influence their chances for salvation.

Anne Hutchinson

▶ Puritan woman who challenged the Massachusetts Bay colony's position on religious issues, specifically whether a person's works could help earn salvation. Hutchinson began holding mixed-sex discussions at her house, leading the governor of the colony, John Winthrop, to become concerned. She was formally charged with and convicted of heresy in 1638 and banished from the colony.

The meetings at Hutchinson's house alarmed her nearest neighbor, John Winthrop, who believed that she was subverting the good order of the colony. In 1637, Winthrop had formal charges brought against Hutchinson and denounced her lectures as "not tolerable nor comely in the sight of God nor fitting for your sex." He told her, "You have stept out of your place, you have rather bine a Husband than a Wife and a preacher than a Hearer; and a Magistrate than a Subject."

In court, Winthrop interrogated Hutchinson, fishing for a heresy he could pin on her. Winthrop and other Puritan elders referred to Hutchinson and her followers as antinomians, people who believed that Christians could be saved by faith alone and did not need to act in accordance with God's law as set forth in the Bible and as interpreted by the colony's leaders. Hutchinson nimbly defended herself against the accusation of antinomianism. Yes, she acknowledged, she believed that men and women were saved by faith alone; but no, she did not deny the need to obey God's law. "The Lord hath let me see which was the clear ministry and which the wrong," she said. Finally, Winthrop had cornered her. How could she tell which ministry was which? "By an immediate revelation," she replied, "by the voice of [God's] own spirit to my soul." Winthrop spotted in this statement the heresy of prophecy, the view that God revealed his will directly to a believer instead of exclusively through the Bible, as every right-minded Puritan knew.

In 1638, the Boston church formally excommunicated Hutchinson. The minister decreed, "I doe cast you out and . . . deliver you up to Satan that you may learne no more to blaspheme[,] to seduce and to lye. . . . I command you . . . as a Leper to withdraw your selfe out of the Congregation." Banished, Hutchinson and her family moved first to Roger Williams's Rhode Island and then to present-day New York, where she and most of her family were killed by Indians.

The strains within Puritanism exemplified by Anne Hutchinson and Roger Williams caused communities to splinter repeatedly during the seventeenth century. Puritan churches divided and subdivided as acrimony developed over doctrine and church government. Sometimes churches split over the appointment of a controversial minister. Sometimes families who had a long walk to the meetinghouse simply decided to form their own church nearer their houses. These schisms arose from ambiguities and tensions within Puritan belief. As the colonies matured, other tensions developed as well.

Religious Controversies and Economic Changes

A revolutionary transformation in the fortunes of Puritans in England had profound consequences in New England. Disputes between King Charles I and Parliament, dominated by Puritans, escalated in 1642 to civil war in England, a conflict known as the Puritan Revolution. Parliamentary forces led by Oliver Cromwell were victorious, executing Charles I in 1649 and proclaiming England a Puritan republic. From 1649 to 1660, England's rulers were not monarchs who suppressed Puritanism but believers who championed it. In a half century, English Puritans had risen from a harassed group of religious dissenters to a dominant power in English government.

When the Puritan Revolution began, the stream of immigrants to New England dwindled to a trickle, creating hard times for the colonists. When

What was distinctive about the settlement of New England?	How did New England society change during the seventeenth century?	What was distinctive about the middle colonies?	What was the role of the North American colonies in the English empire?	Conclusion: What made the English colonization of North America distinctive?

95

immigrant ships became rare, the colonists faced sky-high prices for scarce English goods and few customers for their own colonial products. As they searched to find new products and markets, they established the enduring patterns of New England's economy.

New England's rocky soil and short growing season ruled out cultivating the southern colonies' crops of tobacco and rice that found ready markets in Atlantic ports. Exports that New Englanders could not get from the soil they took instead from the forest and the sea. During the first decade of settlement, colonists traded with the Indians for animal pelts, which were in demand in Europe. By the 1640s, furbearing animals had become scarce unless traders ventured far beyond the frontiers of English settlement. Trees from the seemingly limitless forests of New England proved a longer-lasting resource. Masts for ships and staves for barrels of Spanish wine and West Indian sugar were crafted from New England timber.

The most important New England export was fish. During the turmoil of the Puritan Revolution, English ships withdrew from the rich North Atlantic fishing grounds, and New England fishermen quickly took their place. Dried, salted codfish found markets in southern Europe and the West Indies. The fish trade also stimulated colonial shipbuilding and trained generations of fishermen, sailors, and merchants, creating a commercial network that endured for more than a century. But this export economy remained peripheral to most New England colonists. Their lives revolved around their farms, their churches, and their families.

Although immigration came to a standstill in the 1640s, the population continued to boom, doubling every twenty years. In New England, almost everyone married, and women often had eight or nine children. Long, cold winters minimized the warm-weather ailments of the southern colonies and reduced New England mortality. The descendants of the immigrants of the 1630s multiplied, boosting the New England population to roughly equal that of the southern colonies (**Figure 4.1**).

FIGURE 4.1 ■ Population of the English North American Colonies in the Seventeenth Century
The colonial population grew at a steadily accelerating rate during the seventeenth century. New England and the southern colonies each accounted for about half the total colonial population until after 1680, when growth in Pennsylvania and New York contributed to a surge in the population of the middle colonies.

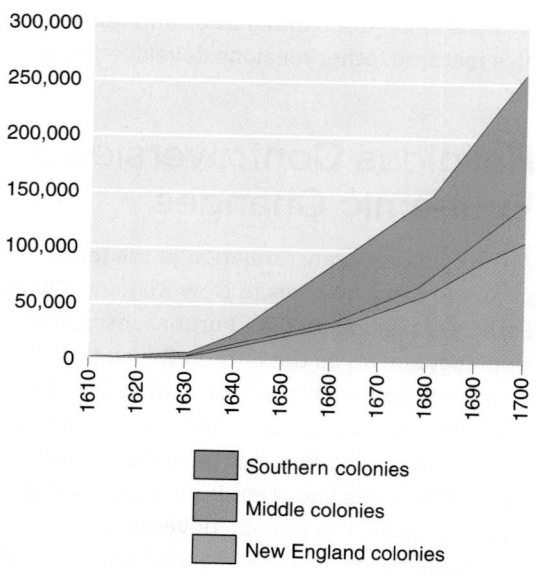

During the second half of the seventeenth century, under the pressures of steady population growth and integration into the Atlantic economy, the red-hot piety of the founders cooled. After 1640, the population grew faster than church membership. In some towns, only 15 percent of the adult men were members. A growing fraction of New Englanders, especially men, embraced what one historian has termed "horse-shed Christianity": They attended sermons but loitered outside near the horse shed, gossiping about the weather, fishing, their crops, or the scandalous behavior of neighbors. Most alarming to Puritan leaders, many of the children of the visible saints of Winthrop's generation failed to experience conversion and attain full church membership. Puritans tended to assume that sainthood was inherited—that the children of visible saints were probably also among the elect. Acting on this premise, churches permitted saints to baptize their infant sons and daughters, symbolically cleansing them of their contamination with original sin. As these children grew up during the 1640s and 1650s, however, they seldom experienced the inward transformation that signaled conversion and qualification for church membership. The problem of declining church membership and the watering-down of Puritan orthodoxy became urgent during the 1650s when the children of saints, who had grown to adulthood in New England but had not experienced conversion, began to have children themselves. Their sons and daughters—the grandchildren of the founders of the colony—could not receive the protection that baptism afforded against the terrors of death because their parents had not experienced conversion.

Puritan churches debated what to do. To allow anyone, even the child of a saint, to become a church member without conversion was an unthinkable retreat from fundamental Puritan doctrine. In 1662, a synod of Massachusetts ministers reached a compromise known as the Halfway Covenant. Unconverted children of saints would be permitted to become "halfway" church members. Like regular church members, they could baptize their infants. But unlike full church members, they could not participate in communion or have the voting privileges of church membership. The Halfway Covenant generated a controversy that sputtered through Puritan churches for the remainder of the century. With the Halfway Covenant, Puritan churches came to terms with the lukewarm piety that had replaced the founders' burning zeal.

Nonetheless, New England communities continued to enforce piety with holy rigor. Beginning in 1656, small bands of **Quakers**—members of the Society of Friends, as they called themselves—began to arrive in Massachusetts. Many of their beliefs were at odds with orthodox Puritanism. Quakers believed that God spoke directly to each individual through an "inner light" and that individuals needed neither a preacher nor the Bible to discover God's Word. Maintaining that all human beings were equal in God's eyes, Quakers refused to conform to mere temporal powers such as laws and governments unless God requested otherwise. Women often took a leading role in Quaker meetings, in contrast to Puritan congregations, where women usually outnumbered men but remained subordinate.

New England communities treated Quakers with ruthless severity. Some Quakers were branded on the face "with a red-hot iron with [an] H. for heresie." When Quakers refused to leave Massachusetts, Boston officials hanged four of them between 1659 and 1661.

Quakers

▶ Religious dissenters who believed that God spoke directly to each individual. Quaker beliefs clashed with those of Puritans and Anglicans, and they were persecuted in both England and Massachusetts.

| What was distinctive about the settlement of New England? | How did New England society change during the seventeenth century? | What was distinctive about the middle colonies? | What was the role of the North American colonies in the English empire? | Conclusion: What made the English colonization of North America distinctive? |

97

Witches Show Their Love for Satan

This seventeenth-century print portrays Satan with clawlike hands and feet, the tail of a rodent, the wings of a bat, and the head of a lustful ram attached to the torso of a man. Notice that women predominate among the witches eager to express their devotion to Satan and to do his bidding.
UCSF Library/Center for Knowledge Management.

New Englanders' partial success in realizing the promise of a godly society ultimately undermined the intense appeal of Puritanism. In the pious Puritan communities of New England, leaders tried to eliminate sin. In the process, they diminished the sense of utter human depravity that was the wellspring of Puritanism. By 1700, New Englanders did not doubt that human beings sinned, but they were more concerned with the sins of others than with their own.

Witch trials held in Salem, Massachusetts, signaled the erosion of religious confidence and assurance. In 1692, the frenzied Salem proceedings accused more than one hundred people of witchcraft, a capital crime. The Salem court executed nineteen accused witches, signaling enduring belief in the supernatural origins of evil and gnawing doubt about the strength of Puritan New Englanders' faith.

> **QUICK REVIEW**

Why did Massachusetts Puritans adopt the Halfway Covenant?

CHAPTER LOCATOR | How did the English Reformation influence Puritans?

What was distinctive about the middle colonies?

New Amsterdam

The settlement on Manhattan Island—complete with a windmill—appears in the background of this 1673 Dutch portrait of New Amsterdam. Wharves connect Manhattan residents to the seaborne commerce of the Atlantic world. In the foreground, the Dutch artist placed native inhabitants of the mainland, drawing them in such a way that they resemble Africans rather than Lenni Lenape (Delaware) Indians. The portrait contrasts orderly, efficient, businesslike New Amsterdam with the exotic natural environment of America. © Collection of the New-York Historical Society.

SOUTH OF NEW ENGLAND and north of the Chesapeake, a group of middle colonies were founded in the last third of the seventeenth century. Before the 1670s, few Europeans settled in the region. For the first two-thirds of the seventeenth century, the most important European outpost in the area was the relatively small Dutch colony of **New Netherland**. By 1700, however, the English monarchy had seized New Netherland, renamed it New York, and encouraged the creation of a Quaker colony in Pennsylvania led by William Penn. Unlike the New England colonies, the middle colonies of New York, New Jersey, and Pennsylvania originated as land grants by the English monarch to one or more proprietors, who then possessed both the land and the extensive, almost monarchical, powers of government (**Map 4.2**). These middle colonies attracted settlers of more diverse European origins and religious faiths than were found in New England.

New Netherland
▶ Dutch colony north of the Chesapeake and south of New England established in the early seventeenth century. Although relatively small, it was an important European outpost. In 1664, England seized the colony and renamed it New York.

From New Netherland to New York

In 1609, the Dutch East India Company dispatched Henry Hudson to search for a Northwest Passage to the Orient. Hudson sailed along the Atlantic coast and ventured up the large river that now bears his name until it dwindled to a stream that obviously did not lead to China. A decade later, the Dutch government granted the West India Company—a group of Dutch merchants and shippers—exclusive rights to trade with the Western Hemisphere. In 1626, Peter Minuit, the resident director of the company, purchased Manhattan Island from the Manhate Indians for trade

| What was distinctive about the settlement of New England? | How did New England society change during the seventeenth century? | **What was distinctive about the middle colonies?** | What was the role of the North American colonies in the English empire? | Conclusion: What made the English colonization of North America distinctive? |

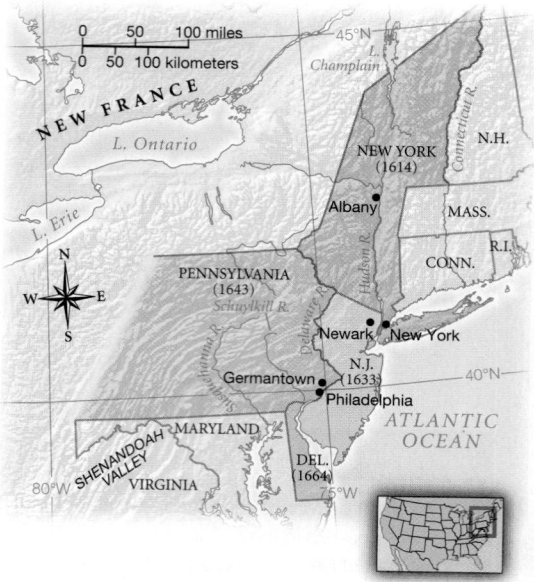

MAP 4.2 ■ Middle Colonies in the Seventeenth Century
For the most part, the middle colonies in the seventeenth century were inhabited by settlers who clustered along the Hudson and Delaware rivers. The vast geographic extent of the colonies shown in this map reflects land grants authorized in England. Most of this area was inhabited by Native Americans rather than settled by colonists.

goods worth the equivalent of a dozen beaver pelts. New Amsterdam, the small settlement established at the southern tip of Manhattan Island, became the principal trading center in New Netherland and the colony's headquarters.

New Netherland did not attract many European immigrants and never realized its sponsors' dreams of great profits. Though few in number, New Netherlanders were remarkably diverse, especially compared with the homogeneous English settlers to the north and south. Religious dissenters and immigrants from Holland, Sweden, France, Germany, and elsewhere made their way to the colony. A minister of the Dutch Reformed Church complained to his superiors in Holland that several groups of Jews had recently arrived, adding to the religious mixture of "Papists, Mennonites and Lutherans among the Dutch [and] many Puritans . . . and many other atheists . . . who conceal themselves under the name of Christians." The West India Company struggled to govern the motley colonists. Peter Stuyvesant, governor from 1647 to 1664, tried to enforce conformity to the Dutch Reformed Church, but the company declared that "the consciences of men should be free and unshackled," making a virtue of New Netherland necessity. The company never permitted the colony's settlers to form a representative government. Instead, the company appointed government officials who established policies, including taxes, that many colonists deeply resented.

CHRONOLOGY

1609
– Henry Hudson searches for Northwest Passage.

1626
– Manhattan Island is purchased; New Amsterdam is founded.

1664
– English seize Dutch colony and rename it New York.
– Colony of New Jersey is created.

1681
– William Penn receives charter for colony of Pennsylvania.

Dutch Patroonships

Allotments of eighteen miles of land along the Hudson River
Given to wealthy stockholders who would bring fifty families to the colony
Only one patroonship succeeded; the others failed to attract permanent settlers

In 1664, New Netherland became New York. Charles II, who became king of England in 1660 when Parliament restored the monarchy, gave his brother James, the Duke of York, an enormous grant of land that included New Netherland. Of course, the Dutch colony did not belong to the king of England, but that did not deter the king or his brother. The duke quickly organized a small fleet of warships, which appeared off Manhattan Island in late summer 1664, and demanded that Stuyvesant surrender. With little choice, he did.

As the new proprietor of the colony, the Duke of York exercised almost the same unlimited authority over the colony as had the West India Company. The duke never set foot in New York, but his governors struggled to impose order on the unruly colonists. Like the Dutch, the duke permitted "all persons of what Religion soever, quietly to inhabit . . . provided they give no disturbance to the publique peace, nor doe molest or disquiet others in the free exercise of their religion." This policy of religious toleration was less an affirmation of liberty of conscience than a recognition of the reality of the most heterogeneous colony in seventeenth-century North America.

New Jersey and Pennsylvania

The creation of New York led indirectly to the founding of two other middle colonies, New Jersey and Pennsylvania (see Map 4.2, page 100). In 1664, the Duke of York subdivided his grant and gave the portion between the Hudson and Delaware rivers to two of his friends. The proprietors of this new colony, New Jersey, quarreled and called in a prominent English Quaker, **William Penn**, to arbitrate their dispute. In the process of working out a settlement, Penn became intensely interested in what he termed a "holy experiment" of establishing a genuinely Quaker colony in America.

Unlike most Quakers, William Penn came from an eminent family. His father had served both Cromwell and Charles II and had been knighted. Born in 1644, the younger Penn trained for a military career, but the ideas of dissenters from the reestablished Church of England appealed to him, and eventually he became a devout Quaker. By 1680, he had published fifty books and pamphlets and spoken at countless public meetings, although he had not won official toleration for Quakers in England.

The Quakers' concept of an open, generous God who made his love equally available to all people manifested itself in behavior that continually brought them into conflict with the English government. Quaker leaders were ordinary men and women, not specially trained preachers. Quakers allowed women to assume positions of religious leadership. "In souls there is no sex," they said. Since all people were equal in the spiritual realm, Quakers considered social hierarchy false and evil. They called everyone "friend" and shook hands instead of curtsying or removing their hats—even when meeting the king. These customs enraged many non-Quakers and provoked innumerable beatings and worse. Penn was jailed four times for such offenses, once for nine months.

Despite his many run-ins with the government, Penn remained on good terms with Charles II. Partly to rid England of the troublesome Quakers, in 1681 Charles made Penn the proprietor of a new colony of some 45,000 square miles called Pennsylvania.

William Penn

▶ Prominent Quaker who was made the proprietor of the new royal colony of Pennsylvania in 1681. Penn established freedom of religion in the colony and was determined to make peace with the colony's Indians.

William Penn

This portrait was drawn about a decade after the founding of Pennsylvania. At a time when extravagant clothing and a fancy wig proclaimed that the wearer was an important person, Penn is portrayed informally, lacking even a coat, his natural hair neat but undressed—all a reflection of his Quaker faith. Historical Society of Pennsylvania.

Toleration and Diversity in Pennsylvania

English Quakers flocked to Pennsylvania in numbers exceeded only by the great Puritan migration to New England fifty years earlier. Quaker missionaries also encouraged immigrants from the European continent, and many came, giving Pennsylvania greater ethnic diversity than any other English colony except New York. The Quaker colony prospered, and the capital city, Philadelphia, soon rivaled New York as a center of commerce. By 1700, the city's five thousand inhabitants participated in a thriving trade exporting flour and other food products to the West Indies and importing English textiles and manufactured goods.

Quaker Immigration to Pennsylvania

1682–1685: Nearly eight thousand Quaker immigrants arrive in Pennsylvania.

Most are from England, Ireland, and Wales.

Artisans, farmers, and laborers predominate.

| What was distinctive about the settlement of New England? | How did New England society change during the seventeenth century? | What was distinctive about the middle colonies? | What was the role of the North American colonies in the English empire? | Conclusion: What made the English colonization of North America distinctive? |

Penn was determined to live in peace with the Indians who inhabited the region. His Indian policy expressed his Quaker ideals and contrasted sharply with the hostile policies of the other English colonies. As he explained to the chief of the Lenni Lenape (Delaware) Indians, "God has written his law in our hearts, by which we are taught and commanded to love and help and do good to one another . . . [and] I desire to enjoy [Pennsylvania lands] with your love and consent." Penn instructed his agents to obtain the Indians' consent by purchasing their land, respecting their claims, and dealing with them fairly.

Penn declared that the first principle of government was that every settler would "enjoy the free possession of his or her faith and exercise of worship towards God." Accordingly, Pennsylvania tolerated Protestant sects of all kinds as well as Roman Catholicism. All voters and officeholders had to be Christians, but the government did not compel settlers to attend religious services, as in Massachusetts, or to pay taxes to maintain a state-supported church, as in Virginia.

Despite its toleration and diversity, Pennsylvania was as much a Quaker colony as New England was a stronghold of Puritanism. Penn had no hesitation about using civil government to enforce religious morality. One of the colony's first laws provided severe punishment for "all such offenses against God, as swearing, cursing, lying, profane talking, drunkenness, drinking of healths, [and] obscene words . . . which excite the people to rudeness, cruelty, looseness, and irreligion."

As proprietor, Penn had extensive powers subject to review only by the king. He appointed a governor, who maintained the proprietor's power to veto any laws passed by the colonial council, which was elected by property owners who possessed at least one hundred acres of land or who paid taxes. The council had the power to originate laws and administer all the affairs of government. A popularly elected assembly served as a check on the council; its members had the authority to reject or approve laws framed by the council.

Penn stressed that the exact form of government mattered less than the men who served in it. In Penn's eyes, "good men" staffed Pennsylvania's government because Quakers dominated elective and appointive offices. Quakers, of course, differed among themselves. Members of the assembly struggled to win the right to debate and amend laws, especially tax laws. They finally won the battle in 1701 when a new Charter of Privileges gave the proprietor the power to appoint the council and in turn stripped the council of all its former powers and gave them to the assembly, which became the only single-house legislature in all the English colonies.

> **QUICK REVIEW**

How did the middle colonies differ from the New England and Chesapeake colonies?

What was the role of the North American colonies in the English empire?

Pine Tree Shilling In violation of English rules that forbade colonies from issuing their own currency, John Hull, a wealthy Boston merchant and shipowner, began to mint coins in 1652. Shown here is one of his pine tree shillings, both sides boldly announcing its origins. *Courtesy of the Museum of the American Numismatic Association.*

PROPRIETARY GRANTS to faraway lands were a cheap way for the king to reward friends. As the colonies grew, however, the grants became more valuable. After 1660, the king took initiatives to channel colonial trade through English hands and to consolidate royal authority over colonial governments. Occasioned by such economic and political considerations and triggered by **King Philip's War** between colonists and Native Americans, these initiatives defined the basic relationship between the colonies and England that endured until the American Revolution (**Map 4.3**).

Royal Regulation of Colonial Trade

English economic policies toward the colonies were designed to yield customs revenues for the monarchy and profitable business for English merchants and shippers. Also, the policies were intended to divert the colonies' trade from England's enemies, especially the Dutch and the French.

The Navigation Acts of 1650, 1651, 1660, and 1663 (see chapter 3) set forth two fundamental rules governing colonial trade. First, goods shipped to and from the colonies had to be transported in English ships using primarily English crews. Second, the Navigation Acts listed colonial products that could be shipped only to England or to other English colonies. While these regulations prevented Chesapeake planters from shipping their tobacco directly to the European continent, they interfered less with the commerce of New England and the middle colonies, whose principal exports—fish, lumber, and flour—were not listed in the regulations and could legally be sent directly to their most important markets in the West Indies.

By the end of the seventeenth century, colonial commerce was defined by regulations that subjected merchants and shippers to royal supervision and gave them access to markets throughout the English empire. In addition, colonial commerce received protection from the English navy. By 1700, colonial goods (including those from the West Indies) accounted for one-fifth of all English imports and for

King Philip's War

▶ Brief but brutal war between New England colonists and Wampanoag, Nipmuck, and Narragansett Indians between 1675 and 1676. Led by the Indian leader Metacomet—known to the English as King Philip—and fighting against encroachment on their lands, the Indians destroyed thirteen English settlements before being defeated.

| What was distinctive about the settlement of New England? | How did New England society change during the seventeenth century? | What was distinctive about the middle colonies? | **What was the role of the North American colonies in the English empire?** | Conclusion: What made the English colonization of North America distinctive? |

103

1660
– English crown begins to intensify efforts to take political and economic control of the colonies.

1675–1676
– King Philip's War.

1686
– Dominion of New England is created.

1688
– England's Glorious Revolution; William III and Mary II become new rulers.

1691
– Massachusetts becomes a royal colony.

1700
– Colonial goods account for one-fifth of all English imports and for two-thirds of all goods reexported from England to the European continent.

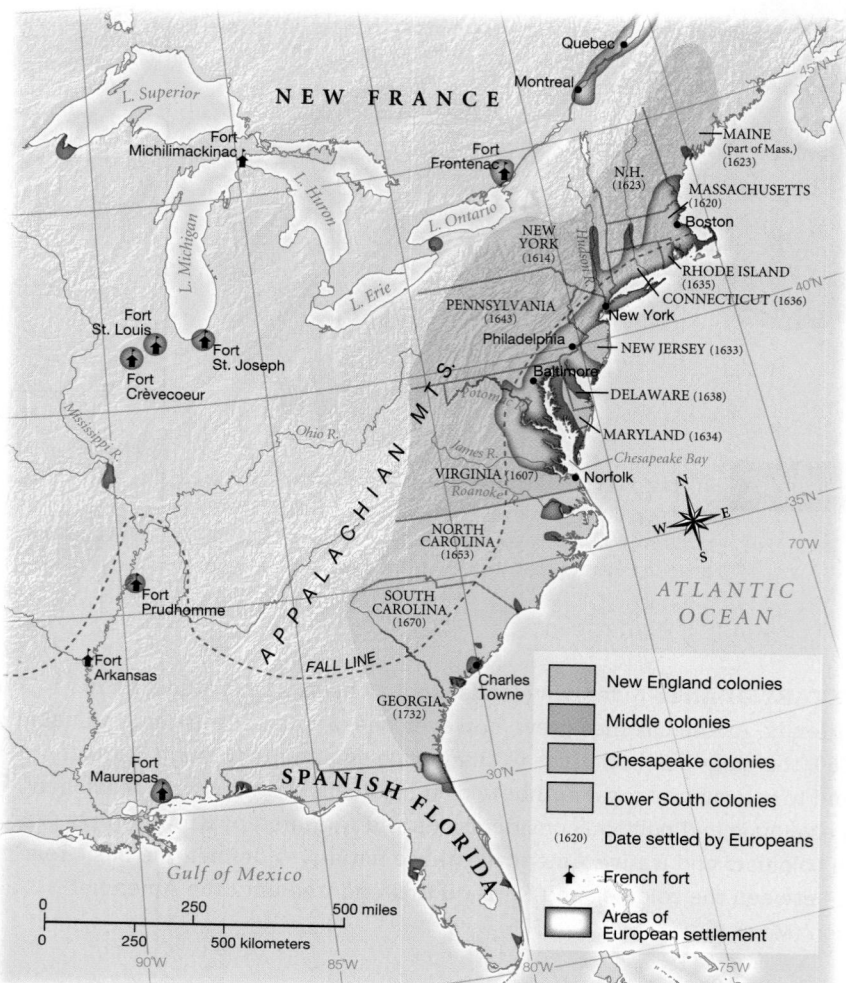

MAP 4.3 ■ American Colonies at the End of the Seventeenth Century

By the end of the seventeenth century, settlers inhabited a narrow band of land that stretched more or less continuously from Boston to Norfolk, with pockets of settlement farther south. The colonies' claims to enormous tracts of land to the west were contested by Native Americans as well as by France and Spain.

> ► FOR MORE HELP ANALYZING THIS MAP, see the map activity for this chapter in the Online Study Guide at bedfordstmartins.com/roarkunderstanding.

two-thirds of all goods reexported from England to the European continent. In turn, the colonies absorbed more than one-tenth of English exports. The commercial regulations gave economic value to England's proprietorship of the American colonies.

King Philip's War and the Consolidation of Royal Authority

The monarchy also took steps to exercise greater control over colonial governments. Virginia had been a royal colony since 1624; Maryland, South Carolina, and the middle colonies were proprietary colonies with close ties to the crown.

CHAPTER LOCATOR | How did the English Reformation influence Puritans?

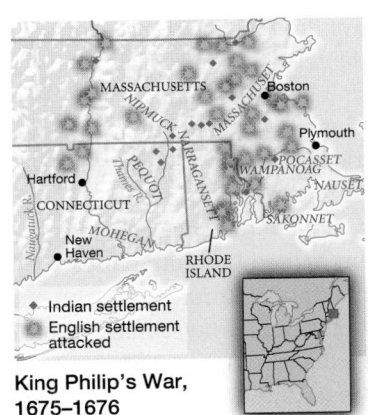

King Philip's War, 1675–1676

- Indian settlement
- English settlement attacked

The New England colonies possessed royal charters, but they had developed their own distinctively Puritan governments. Charles II, whose father, Charles I, had been executed by Puritans in England, took a particular interest in gaining greater royal control of the New England colonies. The occasion was a royal investigation following King Philip's War.

In 1675, warfare between Indians and colonists erupted in the Chesapeake and New England. Massachusetts settlers had massacred hundreds of Pequot Indians in 1637, but they had established relatively peaceful relations with the more powerful Wampanoags. In the decades that followed, New Englanders steadily encroached on Indian land, and in 1675 the Wampanoags struck back with attacks on settlements in western Massachusetts. Metacomet—the chief of the Wampanoags (and son of Massasoit), whom the colonists called King Philip—probably neither planned the attacks nor masterminded a conspiracy with the Nipmucks and the Narragansetts, as the colonists feared. But when militias from Massachusetts and other New England colonies counterattacked all three tribes, a deadly sequence of battles killed more than a thousand colonists and thousands more Indians. The Indians destroyed thirteen English settlements and partially burned another half dozen. By the spring of 1676, Indian warriors ranged freely within seventeen miles of Boston. The colonists finally defeated the Indians, principally with a scorched-earth policy of burning their food supplies. King Philip's War left the New England colonists with an enduring hatred of Indians, a large war debt, and a devastated frontier. And in 1676, an agent of the king arrived to investigate whether New England was abiding by English laws.

Not surprisingly, the king's agent found many deviations from English rules, and the monarchy decided to govern New England more directly. In 1684, an English court revoked the Massachusetts charter. Two years later, royal officials incorporated Massachusetts and the other colonies north of Maryland into the **Dominion of New England**. To govern the dominion, the English sent Sir Edmund Andros to Boston. Some New England merchants cooperated with Andros, but

Dominion of New England

▶ Administrative union established in 1686 of the English colonies north of Maryland. Designed to strengthen royal control over the northern colonies, the Dominion was dissolved in 1689 in the aftermath of the Glorious Revolution.

Wampanoag War Club

This seventeenth-century war club was used to kill King Philip, according to the Anglican missionary who obtained it from Indians early in the eighteenth century. Although the missionary's tale is probably a legend, the club is certainly a seventeenth-century Wampanoag weapon that might well have been used in King Philip's War. Courtesy of the Fruitlands Museums, Harvard, Massachusetts.

| What was distinctive about the settlement of New England? | How did New England society change during the seventeenth century? | What was distinctive about the middle colonies? | **What was the role of the North American colonies in the English empire?** | Conclusion: What made the English colonization of North America distinctive? |

105

most colonists were offended by his open disregard of Puritan traditions. Worst of all, the Dominion of New England invalidated all land titles, confronting every landowner in New England with the prospect of losing his or her land.

Events in England, however, permitted Massachusetts colonists to overthrow Andros and retain title to their property. When Charles II died in 1685, he was succeeded by his brother James II, a zealous Catholic. James's aggressive campaign to appoint Catholics to government posts engendered such unrest that in 1688, a group of Protestant noblemen in Parliament invited the Dutch ruler William III of Orange, James's son-in-law, to claim the English throne.

When William III landed in England at the head of a large army, James fled to France, and William III and his wife, Mary II (James's daughter), became co-rulers in the relatively bloodless "Glorious Revolution," reasserting Protestant influence in England and its empire. Rumors of the revolution raced across the Atlantic and emboldened colonial uprisings against royal authority in Massachusetts, New York, and Maryland.

In Boston in 1689, rebels tossed Andros and other English officials in jail, destroyed the Dominion of New England, and reestablished the former charter government. New Yorkers followed the Massachusetts example. Under the leadership of Jacob Leisler, rebels seized the royal governor in 1689 and ruled the colony for more than a year. That same year in Maryland, the Protestant Association, led by John Coode, overthrew the colony's pro-Catholic government, fearing it would not recognize the new Protestant king.

But these rebel governments did not last. When King William III's governor of New York arrived in 1691, he executed Leisler for treason. Coode's men ruled Maryland until the new royal governor arrived in 1692 and ended both Coode's rebellion and Lord Baltimore's proprietary government. In Massachusetts, John Winthrop's city on a hill became another royal colony in 1691. The new charter said that the governor of the colony would be appointed by the king rather than elected by the colonists' representatives. But perhaps the most unsettling change was the new qualification for voting. Possession of property replaced church membership as a prerequisite for voting in colony-wide elections.

Even though colonists chafed under increasing royal control, they still valued English protection from hostile neighbors. While the northern colonies were distracted by the Glorious Revolution, French forces from the fur-trading regions along the Great Lakes and in Canada attacked villages in New England and New York. Known as King William's War, the conflict with the French was a colonial outgrowth of William's war against France in Europe. The war dragged on until 1697 and ended inconclusively in both Europe and the colonies. But it made clear to many colonists that along with English royal government came a welcome measure of military security.

> QUICK REVIEW

Why did England try to establish greater control of its American colonies in the 1690s?

CHAPTER LOCATOR | How did the English Reformation influence Puritans?

Worcester Art Museum.

Conclusion: What made the English colonization of North America distinctive?

BY 1700, the diverse English colonies in North America had developed along lines quite different from the example New Spain had set in 1600. In the North American colonies, English immigrants and their descendants created societies of settlers unlike the largely Indian societies in New Spain ruled by a tiny group of Spaniards. Although many settlers came to North America from other parts of Europe and a growing number of Africans arrived in bondage, English laws, habits, ideas, and language dominated all the colonies.

Economically, the English colonies thrived on agriculture and trade instead of mining silver and exploiting Indian labor as in New Spain. Although servants and slaves could be found throughout the North American colonies, many settlers depended principally on the labor of family members. Relations between settlers and Native Americans often exploded in warfare, but Indians seldom served as an important source of labor for settlers, as they did in New Spain.

Protestantism prevailed in the North American settlements, relaxed in some colonies and straitlaced in others. Catholics, Quakers, Anglicans (members of the Church of England), Jews, and others settled in the middle and southern colonies, creating considerable religious toleration, especially in Pennsylvania and New York.

Politics and government differed from colony to colony, although English institutions and practices existed everywhere. Local settlers who were free adult white men had an extraordinary degree of political influence, far beyond that of colonists in New Spain or ordinary citizens in England. During the next half century, that English colonial world would undergo surprising new developments built on the achievements of the seventeenth century.

SO NOW YOU KNOW

The Puritans did not celebrate Christmas or Easter because the Bible did not mention either one. Puritans tried to live according to a strict and literal interpretation of the Bible. Puritans' zeal to turn New England into a shining example of Christian piety, into a city on a hill, shaped every feature of New England life.

CHAPTER 4 STUDY GUIDE

Online Study Guide
bedfordstmartins.com/roarkunderstanding

STEP 1
GETTING STARTED

Below are basic terms from this period in American history. Can you identify each term below and explain why it matters? To do this exercise online or to download this chart, visit bedfordstmartins.com/roarkunderstanding.

TERM	WHO OR WHAT & WHEN	WHY IT MATTERS
Puritans, p. 84		
English Reformation, p. 84		
Pilgrims, p. 87		
Massachusetts Bay Company, p. 87		
John Winthrop, p. 88		
Roger Williams, p. 93		
Anne Hutchinson, p. 94		
Quakers, p. 97		
New Netherland, p. 99		
William Penn, p. 101		
King Philip's War, p. 103		
Dominion of New England, p. 105		

STEP 2
MOVING BEYOND THE BASICS

The exercise below represents a more advanced understanding of the chapter material. Compare and contrast the northern colonies: Why was each settled, what kind of political and social structures defined the colony, and what were the bases of its economic organization? To do this exercise online or to download this chart, visit bedfordstmartins.com/roarkunderstanding.

Colony	Reasons for settlement	Social/political structures (religion, family, legal system)	Economics (land use and distribution, industry, income, labor)
Plymouth			
Massachusetts Bay			
Rhode Island			
New Netherland/ New York			
Pennsylvania			

Now that you have reviewed key elements of the chapter, take a step back and try to explain the big picture. Remember to use specific examples from the chapter in your answers. To do this exercise online, visit bedfordsmartins.com/roarkunderstanding.

NEW ENGLAND

▶ What kind of society did the early settlers of New England hope to create?

▶ What forces challenged Puritan domination of New England?

THE MIDDLE COLONIES

▶ How did the settlement of the middle colonies differ from that of New England?

▶ What explains the religious and ethnic diversity of the middle colonies?

LOOKING BACKWARD, LOOKING AHEAD

▶ How did European colonization of the Americas in the seventeenth century differ from Spanish colonization in the previous century?

▶ How did the growth and development of English colonies in the seventeenth century set the stage for conflict between England and its colonies in the eighteenth century?

THE EMPIRE

▶ How did the English crown seek to regulate colonial trade?

▶ How did the colonists respond to the English crown's efforts to assert political authority?

IN YOUR OWN WORDS

Imagine that you must explain chapter 4 to someone who hasn't read it. What would be the most important points to include and why?

5

THE CHANGING WORLD OF COLONIAL AMERICA

1700–1770

> This chapter explores the development of New England, the middle colonies, and the southern colonies between 1700 and 1770. It examines the factors that resulted in regional differences, as well as the common experiences, assumptions, and attitudes that contributed to a growing sense of unity among the colonists. These unifying trends helped prepare the foundation for what would become the United States of America in 1776.

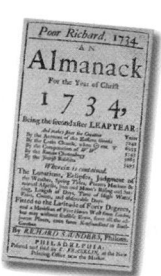

DID YOU KNOW?

In 1776, Philadelphia was the largest city in the British empire except London.

> How and why did British North America change in the eighteenth century?

> What changed in New England life and culture?

> How were the middle colonies distinctive?

> How did slavery become the defining feature of the southern colonies?

> What were the unifying experiences for British American colonists?

> Conclusion: What was the dual identity of British North American colonists?

Chandler Wedding Tapestry. New England, artist unknown, 1756.

How and why did British North America change in the eighteenth century?

New York City Street This painting depicts John Street, a residential neighborhood of New York City, in 1768, as recalled by the artist Joseph B. Smith in the early nineteenth century. Notice that fences separate house yards from the street, rather than houses from one another, hinting of friendly relations among neighbors. Old John Street United Methodist Church.

THE MOST IMPORTANT FACT about eighteenth-century British America is its phenomenal population growth: In 1700, colonists numbered about 250,000; by 1770, they tallied well over 2 million. An index of the emerging significance of colonial North America is that in 1700, there were nineteen people in England for every American colonist; by 1770, there were only three. The eightfold growth of the colonial population signaled the maturation of a distinctive colonial society. That society was by no means homogeneous. Colonists of different ethnic groups, races, and religions lived in varied environments under thirteen different colonial governments, all of them part of the British empire.

In general, the growth and diversity of the eighteenth-century colonial population derived from two sources: immigration and natural increase (growth through reproduction). Natural increase contributed about three-fourths of the population growth, immigration about one-fourth. Immigration shifted the ethnic and racial balance among the colonists, making them by 1770 less English and less white than ever before. In 1670, more than 9 out of 10 colonists were of English ancestry, and only 1 out of 25 was of African ancestry. By 1770, only about half of the colonists were of English descent, while more than 20 percent descended from Africans. Thus, by 1770, the people of the colonies had a distinctive colonial—rather than English—profile (**Map 5.1**).

The booming population of the colonies hints at a second major feature of eighteenth-century colonial society: an expanding economy. In 1700, after almost a century of settlement, nearly all the colonists lived within fifty miles of the Atlantic coast. The almost limitless wilderness stretching westward made land relatively

CHAPTER LOCATOR | How and why did British North America change in the eighteenth century?

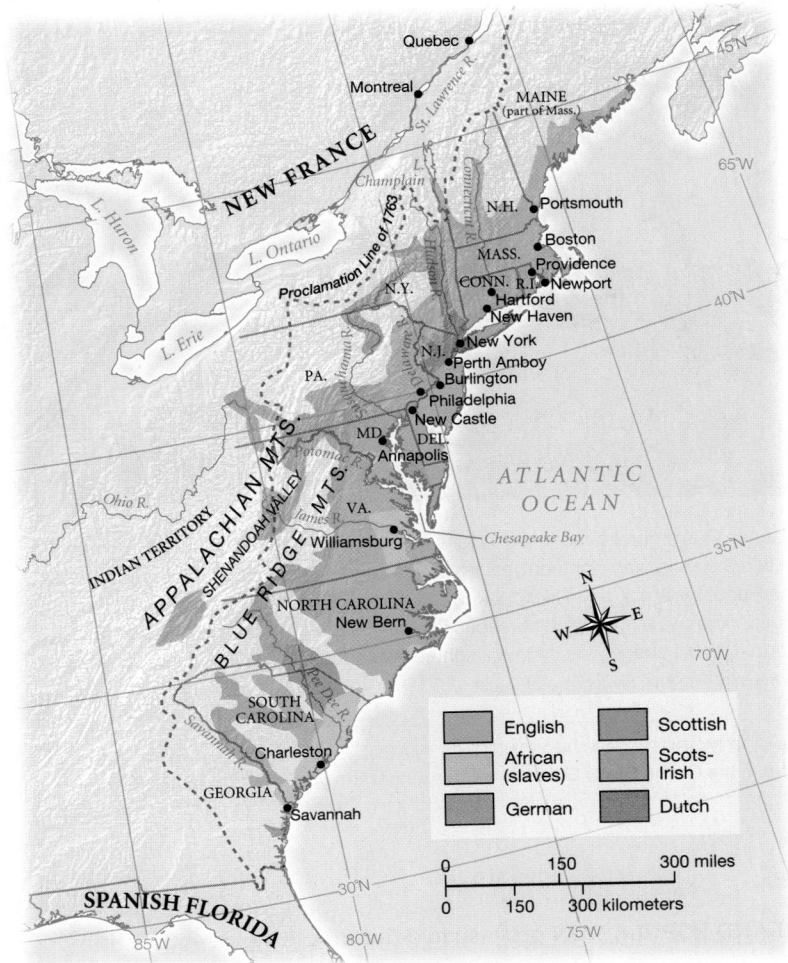

MAP 5.1 ■ **Europeans and Africans in the Eighteenth Century**

This map illustrates regions where Africans and certain immigrant groups clustered. It is important to avoid misreading the map. Predominantly English and German regions, for example, also contained colonists from other places. Likewise, regions where African slaves resided in large numbers also included many whites, slave masters among them. The map suggests the diversity of eighteenth-century colonial society.

cheap. Land in the colonies commonly sold for a fraction of its price in the Old World. The abundance of land in the colonies made labor precious, and the colonists always needed more. The insatiable demand for labor was the fundamental economic environment that sustained the mushrooming population. Economic historians estimate that free colonists (those who were not indentured servants or slaves) had a higher standard of living than the majority of people elsewhere in the Atlantic world. The unique achievement of the eighteenth-century colonial economy was this modest economic welfare of the vast bulk of the free population.

QUICK REVIEW

How did the North American colonies achieve the remarkable population growth of the eighteenth century?

What changed in New England life and culture?	How were the middle colonies distinctive?	How did slavery become the defining feature of the southern colonies?	What were the unifying experiences for British American colonists?	Conclusion: What was the dual identity of British North American colonists?

> What changed in New England life and culture?

Boston Common in Needlework

Hannah Otis embroidered this exquisite needlework portrait of Boston Common in 1750 when she was eighteen years old. The large house (center right) belonged to the Hancock family. John Hancock, who later signed the Declaration of Independence, is shown on horseback in the foreground. What features of this portrait would suggest a city to an eighteenth-century viewer? Photograph © 2008 Museum of Fine Arts, Boston.

▶ FOR MORE HELP ANALYZING THIS IMAGE, see the visual activity for this chapter in the Online Study Guide at bedfordstmartins.com/roarkunderstanding.

THE NEW ENGLAND POPULATION grew sixfold during the eighteenth century but lagged behind the growth in the other colonies. Most immigrants chose other destinations because of New England's relatively densely settled land and because Puritan orthodoxy made these colonies comparatively inhospitable to religious dissenters and those indifferent to religion. As the population grew, many settlers in search of farmland dispersed from towns, and Puritan communities lost much of their cohesion. Nonetheless, networks of economic exchange linked New Englanders to their neighbors, to Boston merchants, and to the broad currents of Atlantic commerce.

Natural Increase and Land Distribution

The New England population grew mostly by natural increase, much as it had during the seventeenth century. Nearly every adult woman married. Most married women had children—often many children, thanks to the relatively low mortality rate in New England. The perils of childbirth gave wives a shorter life expectancy than husbands, but wives often lived to have six, seven, or eight babies.

The growing New England population pressed against a limited amount of land. Compared to colonies farther south, New England had less land for the expansion of settlement (see Map 5.1, page 113). Moreover, as the northernmost group of British colonies, New England had contested northern and western frontiers.

CHAPTER LOCATOR | How and why did British North America change in the eighteenth century?

Powerful Native Americans, especially the Iroquois and Mahican tribes, jealously guarded their territory. The French (and Catholic) colony of New France also menaced the British (and mostly Protestant) New England colonies when provoked by colonial or European disputes.

During the seventeenth century, New England towns parceled out land to individual families. In most cases, the original settlers practiced partible inheritance—that is, they subdivided land more or less equally among sons. By the eighteenth century, repeated subdivisions had left many plots of land too small to support a family. Sons who could not hope to inherit sufficient land to farm had to move away from the town where they were born.

During the eighteenth century, colonial governments in New England abandoned the seventeenth-century policy of granting land to towns. Needing revenue, the governments of both Connecticut and Massachusetts sold land directly to individuals, including speculators. Now money, rather than membership in a community bound by a church covenant, determined whether a person could obtain land. The new land policy eroded the seventeenth-century pattern of settlement. As colonists moved, they tended to settle on individual farms rather than in the towns and villages that characterized the seventeenth century. New Englanders still depended on their relatives and neighbors, but far more than in the seventeenth century, they regulated their behavior in newly settled areas by their own individual choices.

Farms, Fish, and Atlantic Trade

New England farmers grew food for their families, but their fields did not produce huge marketable surpluses. Instead of one big crop, a farmer grew many small ones. If farmers had extra, they sold to or traded with neighbors. By 1770, New Englanders had only one-fourth as much wealth per capita as free colonists in the southern colonies. As consumers, New England farmers participated in a diversified commercial economy that linked remote farms to markets throughout the Atlantic world. Merchants large and small stocked imported goods—British textiles, ceramics, and metal goods; Chinese tea; West Indian sugar; and Chesapeake tobacco. Farmers' needs supported local shoemakers, tailors, wheelwrights, and carpenters. Larger towns, especially Boston, housed skilled tradesmen such as cabinetmakers, silversmiths, and printers. Shipbuilders tended to do better than other artisans because they served the most dynamic sector of the New England economy.

Many New Englanders made their fortunes at sea, as they had since the seventeenth century. Fish accounted for more than a third of New England's eighteenth-century exports; livestock and timber made up another third. The West Indies absorbed two-thirds of all of New England's exports. Slaves on Caribbean sugar plantations ate dried, salted codfish caught by New England fishermen, filled barrels crafted from New England timber with molasses and refined sugar, and loaded those barrels aboard ships bound ultimately for Europe.

| What changed in New England life and culture? | How were the middle colonies distinctive? | How did slavery become the defining feature of the southern colonies? | What were the unifying experiences for British American colonists? | Conclusion: What was the dual identity of British North American colonists? |

Almost all of the rest of New England's exports went to Britain and continental Europe (**Map 5.2**). This Atlantic commerce benefited the entire New England economy, providing jobs for laborers and tradesmen as well as for ship captains, clerks, merchants, and sailors.

Merchants dominated Atlantic commerce. The largest and most successful New England merchants lived in Boston at the hub of trade between local folk and the international market. Merchants not only bought and sold goods, but they also owned and insured the ships that carried merchandise throughout the Atlantic world. Shrewd, diligent, and lucky merchants could make fortunes. The luxurious

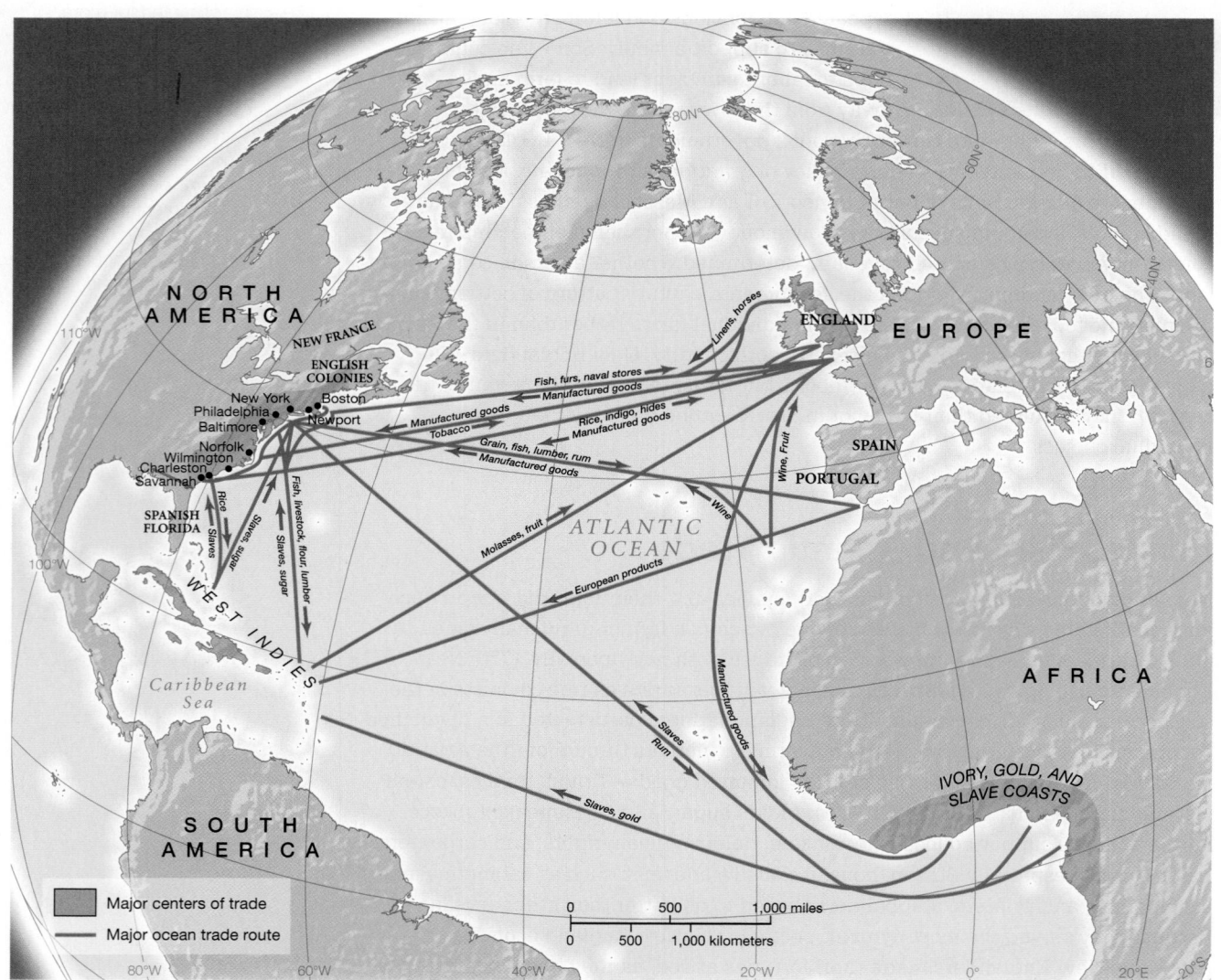

MAP 5.2 ■ North American Atlantic Trade in the Eighteenth Century
This map illustrates the economic outlook of the colonies in the eighteenth century—east toward the Atlantic world rather than west toward the interior of North America. The long distances involved in the Atlantic trade and the uncertainties of ocean travel suggest the difficulties Britain experienced governing the colonies and regulating colonial commerce.

CHAPTER LOCATOR | How and why did British North America change in the eighteenth century?

Boston homes of such men were an indication of the polarization of wealth that developed in Boston and other seaports during the eighteenth century. By 1770, the richest 5 percent of Bostonians owned about half the city's wealth; the poorest two-thirds of the population owned less than one-tenth.

While the rich got richer and everybody else had a smaller share of the total wealth, the incidence of genuine poverty did not change much. About 5 percent of New Englanders qualified for poor relief throughout the eighteenth century. Overall, colonists were better off than most people in England. A Connecticut traveler wrote from England in 1764, "We in New England know nothing of poverty and want, we have no idea of the thing, how much better do our poor people live than 7/8 of the people on this much famed island."

The contrast with English poverty had meaning because the overwhelming majority of New Englanders traced their ancestry to England. New England was more homogeneously English than any other colonial region. People of African ancestry (almost all of them slaves) numbered more than fifteen thousand by 1770, but they barely diversified the region's 97 percent white majority. In the Narragansett region of Rhode Island, large landowners imported numerous slaves to raise livestock. But most New Englanders had little use for slaves on their family farms. Instead, slaves were concentrated in towns, especially Boston, where most of them worked as domestic servants and laborers.

By 1770, the population, wealth, and commercial activity of New England differed from what they had been in 1700. Ministers still enjoyed high status, but Yankee traders had replaced Puritan saints as the symbolic New Englanders. Atlantic commerce competed with religious convictions in ordering New Englanders' daily lives.

QUICK REVIEW

How and why did New England society change in the eighteenth century?

How were the middle colonies distinctive?

Bethlehem, Pennsylvania

This view of the small community of Bethlehem, Pennsylvania, in 1757 dramatizes the profound transformation of the natural landscape wrought in the eighteenth century by highly motivated human labor. By carefully penning their livestock (lower center right) and fencing their fields (lower left), farmers safeguarded their livelihoods from the risks and disorders of untamed nature. Print Collection, Miriam and Ira D. Wallack Division of Art, Prints, and Photographs, The New York Public Library. Astor, Lenox, and Tilden Foundations.

▶ FOR MORE HELP ANALYZING THIS IMAGE, see the visual activity for this chapter in the Online Study Guide at bedfordstmartins.com/roarkunderstanding.

IN 1700, almost twice as many people lived in New England as in the middle colonies of Pennsylvania, New York, New Jersey, and Delaware. But by 1770, the population of the middle colonies had multiplied tenfold, mainly from an influx of German, Irish, Scottish, and other immigrants. Immigrants made the middle colonies a uniquely diverse society. By 1800, barely one-third of Pennsylvanians and less than half the total population of the middle colonies traced their ancestry to England.

German and Scots-Irish Immigrants

Germans made up the largest contingent of migrants from the European continent to the middle colonies. By 1770, about 85,000 Germans had arrived in the colonies. Most German immigrants came from what is now southwestern Germany, where, one observer noted, peasants were "not as well off as cattle elsewhere." German immigrants included numerous artisans and a few merchants, but the great majority were farmers and laborers. Economically, they represented "middling

CHAPTER LOCATOR | How and why did British North America change in the eighteenth century?

folk," neither the poorest (who could not afford the trip) nor the better-off (who did not want to leave). By the 1720s, Germans who had established themselves in the colonies wrote back to their friends and relatives, as one reported, "of the civil and religious liberties [and] privileges, and of all the goodness I have heard and seen." Such letters prompted still more Germans to pull up stakes and embark for America.

Similar motives propelled the Scots-Irish, who considerably outnumbered German immigrants. The "Scots-Irish" actually hailed from northern Ireland, Scotland, and northern England. Like the Germans, the Scots-Irish were Protestants, but with a difference. Most German immigrants worshipped in Lutheran or German Reformed churches; many others belonged to dissenting sects such as the Mennonites, Moravians, and Amish, whose adherents sought relief from the persecution they had suffered in Europe for their refusal to bear arms and to swear oaths, practices they shared with the Quakers. In contrast, the Scots-Irish tended to be militant Presbyterians who seldom hesitated to bear arms or swear oaths. Like German settlers, however, Scots-Irish immigrants were clannish, residing when they could among relatives or neighbors from the old country.

In the eighteenth century, wave after wave of Scots-Irish immigrants arrived, culminating in a flood of immigration in the years just before the American Revolution. Deteriorating economic conditions in northern Ireland, Scotland, and England pushed many toward America. Most of the immigrants were farm laborers or tenant farmers fleeing droughts, crop failures, high food prices, or rising rents. They came, they told inquisitive British officials, because of "poverty," "tyranny of landlords," and their desire to "do better in America."

Ship captains, aware of the hunger for labor in the colonies, eagerly signed up poor emigrants as **redemptioners**, a variant of indentured servants. A captain would agree to provide transportation to Philadelphia, where redemptioners would obtain the money to pay for their passage by borrowing it from a friend or

CHRONOLOGY

1733
- Benjamin Franklin begins publication of *Poor Richard's Almanack*.

1770
- The population of the colonies of Pennsylvania, New York, New Jersey, and Delaware has increased tenfold since 1700, largely the result of immigration.
- Germans make up the largest percentage of migrants from the European continent.
- The middle colonies' per capita consumption of imported goods from Britain has doubled since 1720.

redemptioners
▶ Immigrants who agreed to pay for their passage to America by borrowing from a friend or relative who was already in the colonies or by selling themselves as servants. Many German families came to Pennsylvania as redemptioners in the eighteenth century.

German Hymnal This manuscript hymnal, once owned by Benjamin Franklin, contains works and music created by Johann Conrad Beissel, the founder of the Seventh-Day Baptists and among the earliest musical composers in the colonies. The hymns evoke the Seventh-Day Baptists' vision of "The Bitter good, or . . . the Christian church here on earth, in the valley of sadness." Roger Foley/Library of Congress.

| What changed in New England life and culture? | **How were the middle colonies distinctive?** | How did slavery become the defining feature of the southern colonies? | What were the unifying experiences for British American colonists? | Conclusion: What was the dual identity of British North American colonists? |

relative who was already in the colonies or, as most did, by selling themselves as servants. Many redemptioners traveled in family groups, unlike impoverished Scots-Irish emigrants, who usually traveled alone and paid for their passage by contracting as indentured servants before they sailed to the colonies.

Redemptioners and indentured servants were packed aboard ships "as closely as herring," one migrant observed. Seasickness compounded by exhaustion, poverty, poor food, bad water, inadequate sanitation, and tight quarters encouraged the spread of disease. When one ship finally approached land, a traveler wrote, "everyone crawls from below to the deck . . . and people cry for joy, pray, and sing praises and thanks to God." Unfortunately, their troubles were far from over. Redemptioners and indentured servants had to stay on board until somebody came to purchase their labor. Unlike indentured servants, redemptioners negotiated independently with their purchasers about their period of servitude. Typically, a healthy adult redemptioner agreed to four years of labor. Indentured servants commonly served five, six, or seven years.

Pennsylvania: "The Best Poor [White] Man's Country"

New settlers, whether free or in servitude, poured into the middle colonies because they perceived unparalleled opportunities, particularly in Pennsylvania, "the best poor Man's Country in the World," as an indentured servant wrote in 1743. Although the servant reported that "the Condition of bought Servants is very hard" and masters often failed to live up to their promise to provide decent food and clothing, opportunity abounded because there was more work to be done than workers to do it.

Most servants toiled in Philadelphia, New York City, or one of the smaller towns or villages. From the masters' viewpoint, servants were a bargain. A master could purchase five or six years of a servant's labor for approximately the wages a common laborer would earn in four months. Wageworkers could walk away from their jobs when they pleased, and they did so often enough to be troublesome for employers. Servants, however, could not walk away; they were legally bound to work for their masters until their terms expired.

Since a slave cost at least three times as much as a servant, only affluent colonists could afford the long-term investment in slave labor. Most farmers in the middle colonies used family labor, not slaves. Wheat, the most widely grown crop, did not require more labor than farmers could typically muster from relatives, neighbors, and a hired hand or two. Consequently, although people of African ancestry (almost all slaves) increased to more than thirty thousand in the middle colonies by 1770, they accounted for only about 7 percent of the total population and much less outside the cities.

Most slaves came to the middle colonies and New England after a stopover in the West Indies. Very few came directly from Africa. Enough slaves arrived to prompt colonial assemblies to pass laws that punished slaves much more severely than servants for the same transgressions. But in cases of abuse, servants—unlike slaves—could charge masters with violating the terms of their indenture contracts. Small numbers of slaves managed to obtain their freedom.

CHAPTER LOCATOR | How and why did British North America change in the eighteenth century?

120 CHAPTER 5
THE CHANGING WORLD OF COLONIAL AMERICA

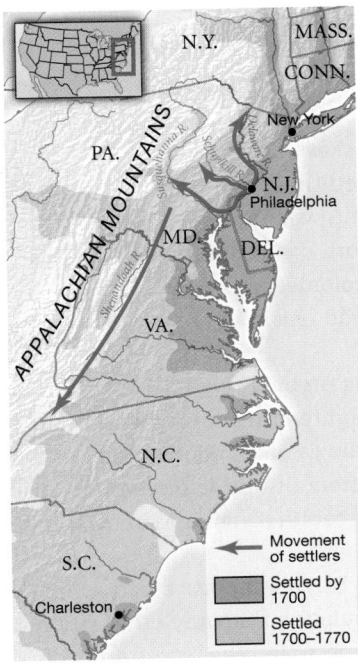

Patterns of Settlement, 1700–1770

But free African Americans did not escape whites' firm convictions about black inferiority and white supremacy.

Whites' racism and blacks' lowly social status made African Americans scapegoats for European Americans' suspicions and anxieties. In 1741, when arson and several unexplained thefts plagued New York City, officials suspected a murderous slave conspiracy and executed thirty-one slaves. Although slaves were certifiably impoverished, they were not among the poor for whom the middle colonies were reputed to be the best country in the world.

Immigrants swarmed to the middle colonies because of the availability of land. The Penn family encouraged immigration to bring in potential buyers for their enormous tracts of land in Pennsylvania. From the beginning, Pennsylvania followed a policy of negotiating with Indian tribes to purchase additional land. This policy reduced the violent frontier clashes more common elsewhere in the colonies.

Few colonists drifted beyond the northern boundaries of Pennsylvania. Owners of the huge estates in New York's Hudson valley preferred to rent rather than sell their land, and therefore they attracted fewer immigrants. The **Iroquois Indians** dominated the lucrative fur trade of the St. Lawrence valley and eastern Great Lakes, and they vigorously defended their territory from colonial encroachment.

The price of farmland depended on soil quality, access to water, distance from a market town, and extent of improvements. Since the cheapest land always lay at the margin of settlement, would-be farmers tended to migrate to promising areas

Iroquois Indians

▶ A confederation of five (and later six) tribes that dominated the fur trade of the St. Lawrence valley and the eastern Great Lakes in the first half of the eighteenth century.

Marten Van Bergen Farm This rare 1730s painting by a local artist depicts the farm of Marten and Catarina Van Bergen, prosperous colonists in New York's Hudson valley. What ideas and attitudes are suggested by the clothing of the people in the painting? What do the design and construction of the house and outbuilding suggest about the influence of different cultures at the farm? Copyright © New York State Historical Association, Cooperstown, NY.

| What changed in New England life and culture? | How were the middle colonies distinctive? | How did slavery become the defining feature of the southern colonies? | What were the unifying experiences for British American colonists? | Conclusion: What was the dual identity of British North American colonists? |

just beyond already improved farms. By midcentury, settlement had reached the eastern slopes of the Appalachian Mountains, and newcomers spilled south down the fertile valley of the Shenandoah River into western Virginia and the Carolinas.

Farmers made the middle colonies the breadbasket of North America. They planted a wide variety of crops to feed their families, but they grew wheat in abundance. Flour milling was the number one industry and flour the number one export, constituting nearly three-fourths of all exports from the middle colonies. For farmers, the grain market in the Atlantic world proved risky but profitable, as grain prices rose steadily after 1720.

The standard of living in rural Pennsylvania was probably higher than in any other agricultural region of the eighteenth-century world. The comparatively widespread prosperity of all the middle colonies allowed the region's per capita consumption of imported goods from Britain to more than double between 1720 and 1770, far outstripping the per capita consumption of British goods in New England and the southern colonies.

At the crossroads of trade in wheat exports and British imports stood Philadelphia. By 1776, Philadelphia had a larger population than any other city in the entire British empire except London. Merchants occupied the top stratum of Philadelphia society. In a city where only 2 percent of the residents owned enough property to qualify to vote, merchants built grand homes and dominated local government. Many of Philadelphia's wealthiest merchants were Quakers, whose traits of industry, thrift, honesty, and sobriety encouraged the accumulation of wealth.

Benjamin Franklin

▶ (1706–1790) American writer, publisher, politician, and diplomat. Franklin published *Poor Richard's Almanack,* which advocated hard work, discipline, and thrift. He was also a deist, believing that God's work was reflected in science and nature.

In 1733, **Benjamin Franklin** began to publish *Poor Richard's Almanack,* which preached the likelihood of long-term rewards for tireless labor. Poor Richard's advice that "God gives all Things to Industry" might be considered the motto for the middle colonies. The promise of a worldly payoff made work a secular faith. Poor Richard advised, "Work as if you were to live 100 years, Pray as if you were to die Tomorrow." William Penn's Quaker utopia had become a center of worldly affluence. Quakers remained influential, but Franklin spoke for most colonists with his aphorisms of work, discipline, and thrift that echoed Quaker rules for outward behavior.

> **QUICK REVIEW**

Why did immigrants flood into Pennsylvania during the eighteenth century?

CHAPTER LOCATOR | How and why did British North America change in the eighteenth century?

122 CHAPTER 5
THE CHANGING WORLD OF COLONIAL AMERICA

Charleston Harbor This 1730s painting of Charleston, South Carolina, depicts the intersecting currents of international trade and local commerce in the variety of vessels conveying goods and people between ship and shore. More African slaves arrived in Charleston than in any other North American port, yet no slaves appear in this painting. Colonial Williamsburg Foundation.

How did slavery become the defining feature of the southern colonies?

BETWEEN 1700 AND 1770, the population of the southern colonies of Virginia, Maryland, North Carolina, South Carolina, and Georgia grew almost ninefold. By 1770, about twice as many people lived in the South as in either the middle colonies or New England. As elsewhere, natural increase and immigration accounted for the rapid population growth. Many Scots-Irish and German immigrants funneled from the middle colonies into the southern backcountry. Other immigrants were indentured servants (mostly English and Scots-Irish) who followed their seventeenth-century predecessors. But slaves made the most striking contribution to the booming southern colonies, transforming the racial composition of the population. Slavery became the defining characteristic of the southern colonies during the eighteenth century, shaping the region's economy, society, and politics.

The Atlantic Slave Trade and the Growth of Slavery

The number of southerners of African ancestry (nearly all of them slaves) rocketed from just over 20,000 in 1700 to well over 400,000 in 1770. The black population increased nearly three times faster than the South's briskly growing white population. Consequently, the proportion of southerners of African ancestry grew from 20 percent in 1700 to 40 percent in 1770.

Southern colonists clustered into two distinct geographic and agricultural zones. The colonies in the upper South, surrounding the Chesapeake Bay, specialized in growing tobacco. Throughout the eighteenth century, nine out of ten southern whites and eight out of ten southern blacks lived in the Chesapeake region. The upper South retained a white majority during the eighteenth century.

In the lower South, a much smaller cluster of colonists inhabited the coastal region and specialized in the production of rice and indigo (a plant used to make blue dye). Lower South colonists made up only 5 percent of the total population of

What changed in New England life and culture? | How were the middle colonies distinctive? | **How did slavery become the defining feature of the southern colonies?** | What were the unifying experiences for British American colonists? | Conclusion: What was the dual identity of British North American colonists?

123

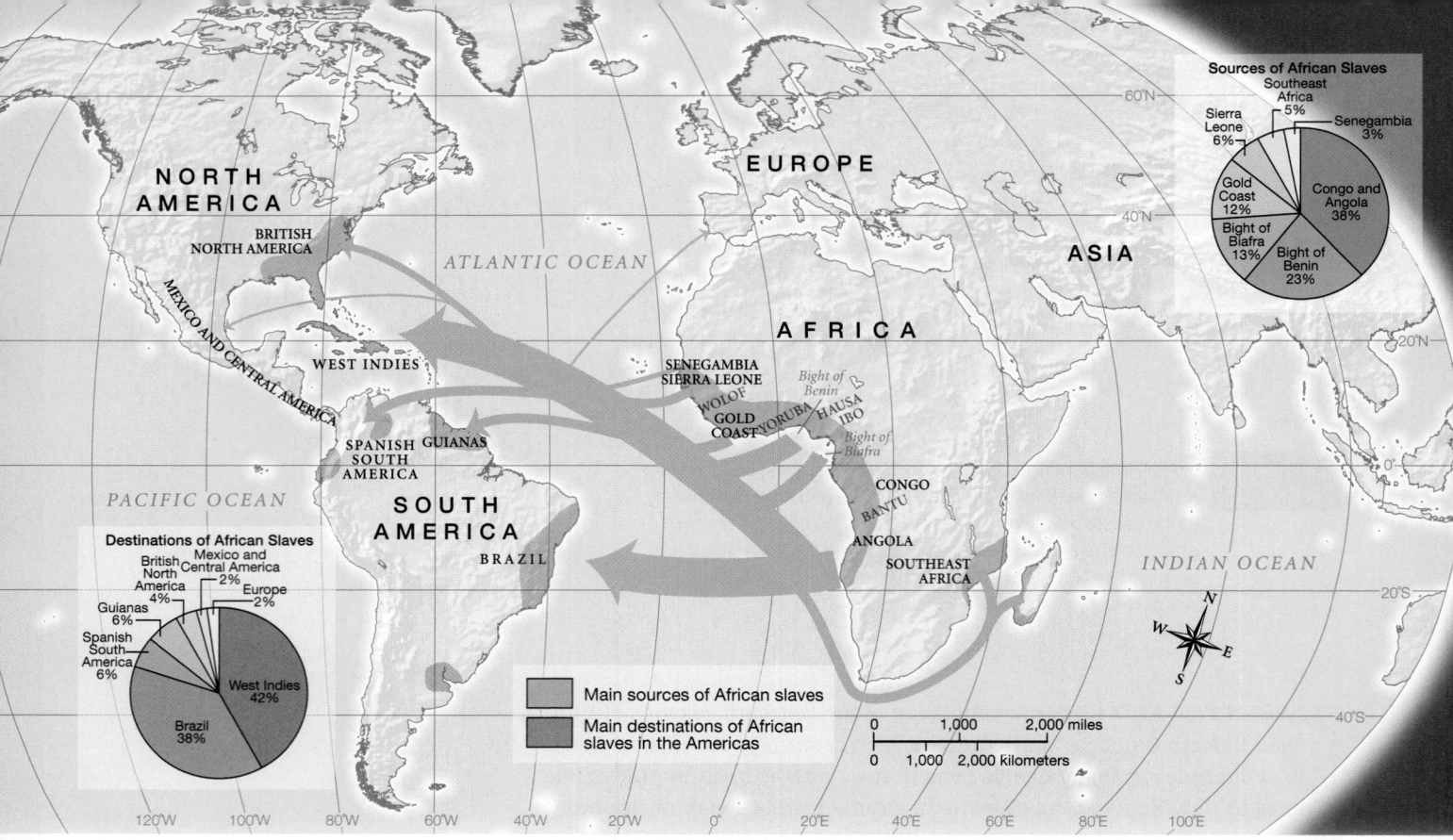

MAP 5.3 ■ The Atlantic Slave Trade

Although the Atlantic slave trade lasted from about 1450 to 1870, it peaked during the eighteenth century, when more than six million African slaves were imported to the New World. Only a small fraction of these slaves were taken to British North America. Most went to sugar plantations in Brazil and the Caribbean.

▶ FOR MORE HELP ANALYZING THIS MAP, see the map activity for this chapter in the Online Study Guide at bedfordstmartins.com/roarkunderstanding.

CHRONOLOGY

1711
– North Carolina is founded.

1732
– Georgia is founded.

1739
– Stono rebellion, an uprising by slaves in South Carolina.

1745
– Olaudah Equiano is born.

1770
– The southern colonies supply 90 percent of all North American exports to Britain.

the southern colonies in 1700 but inched upward to 15 percent by 1770. South Carolina was the sole British colony along the southern Atlantic coast until 1732, when Georgia was founded. (North Carolina, founded in 1711, was largely an extension of the Chesapeake region.) Blacks in South Carolina, in contrast to every other British mainland colony, outnumbered whites almost two to one; in some low-country districts, the ratio of blacks to whites exceeded ten to one.

The enormous growth in the South's slave population occurred through natural increase and the flourishing Atlantic slave trade (**Map 5.3** and **Table 5.1**). Slave ships brought almost 300,000 Africans to British North America between 1619 and 1780. Of these Africans, 95 percent arrived in the South, and 96 percent arrived during the eighteenth century. Most of them had been born into free families in villages located within a few hundred miles of the West African coast.

Although they shared African origins, they came from many different African cultures, including Akan, Angolan, Asante, Bambara, Gambian, Igbo, and Mandinga, among others. They spoke different languages, worshipped different deities, observed different rules of kinship, grew different crops, and recognized different rulers. The most important experience they had in common was enslavement. Captured in war, kidnapped, or sold into slavery by other Africans,

CHAPTER LOCATOR | How and why did British North America change in the eighteenth century?

TABLE 5.1 ■ Slave Imports, 1451–1870

Estimated Slave Imports to the Western Hemisphere	
1451–1600	275,000
1601–1700	1,341,000
1701–1810	6,100,000
1811–1870	1,900,000

they were brought to the coast, sold to African traders who assembled slaves for resale, and sold again to European or colonial slave traders or ship captains, who packed two hundred to three hundred or more aboard ships that carried them on the **Middle Passage** across the Atlantic and then sold them yet again to colonial slave merchants or southern planters.

Olaudah Equiano published an account of his enslavement that hints at the stories that might have been told by the millions of other Africans swept up in the slave trade. Equiano wrote that he was born in 1745 in the interior of what is now Nigeria. "I had never heard of white men or Europeans, nor of the sea," he recalled. One day when he was eleven years old, he was kidnapped by Africans, who sold him to other Africans, who in turn eventually sold him to a slave ship on the coast. Equiano feared that he was "going to be killed" and "eaten by those white men with horrible looks, red faces, and loose hair." Once the ship set sail, many of the slaves, crowded together in suffocating, filthy conditions, died from sickness. "The shrieks of the women and the groans of the dying rendered the whole a scene of horror almost inconceivable," Equiano recalled. Most of the slaves on the ship were sold in Barbados, but Equiano and a few others were shipped off to Virginia, where he "saw few or none of our native Africans and not one soul who could talk to me." Equiano felt isolated and "exceedingly miserable" because he "had no person to speak to that I could understand." Finally, the captain of a tobacco ship bound for England purchased Equiano, and he traveled as a slave between North America, England, and the West Indies for ten years until he succeeded in buying his freedom in 1766.

About 85 percent of the slaves brought into the southern colonies came directly from Africa, and almost all the ships that brought them (roughly 90 percent) belonged to British merchants. Most of the slaves on board were young adults, with men usually outnumbering women two to one. Children under the age of fourteen, like Equiano, typically accounted for no more than 10 to 15 percent of a cargo.

The Deadly Middle Passage

Eighty-five percent of slaves brought into the southern colonies came directly from Africa.

Mortality during the Middle Passage varied considerably from ship to ship.

On average, about 15 percent of the slaves died.

In general, the longer the voyage lasted, the more people died.

Smallpox, dysentery, and acute dehydration were leading causes of death.

Men outnumbered women two to one.

Children usually accounted for no more than 10 to 15 percent of the cargo.

Middle Passage

▶ Name given to the journey across the Atlantic that brought African slaves to the Americas. Slave ships were packed with two hundred to three hundred slaves for their trip across the Atlantic. On average, about 15 percent of the slaves who began the journey died during the Middle Passage.

Olaudah Equiano

▶ Eighteenth-century West African who published an account of his enslavement and transport to North America. After buying his freedom in 1766, Equiano described the horrors of the Middle Passage, which bolstered the arguments of early advocates of the abolition of slavery.

What changed in New England life and culture?	How were the middle colonies distinctive?	How did slavery become the defining feature of the southern colonies?	What were the unifying experiences for British American colonists?	Conclusion: What was the dual identity of British North American colonists?

125

Normally, an individual planter purchased at any one time a relatively small number of newly arrived Africans, or new Negroes, as they were called. New Negroes were often profoundly depressed, demoralized, and disoriented. Planters expected their other slaves—either those born into slavery in the colonies (often called country-born or creole slaves) or Africans who had arrived earlier—to help new Negroes become accustomed to their strange new surroundings. Planters' preferences for slaves from specific regions of Africa aided slaves' acculturation (or seasoning, as it was called) to the routines of bondage in the southern colonies. Chesapeake planters preferred slaves from Senegambia, the Gold Coast, or the Bight of Biafra, which combined accounted for 40 percent of all Africans imported to the Chesapeake. South Carolina planters favored slaves from the central African Congo and Angola regions, the origin of about 40 percent of the African slaves they imported (see Map 5.3, page 124). Although slaves within each of these regions spoke many different languages, enough linguistic and cultural similarities existed that they could usually communicate with other Africans from the same region.

Seasoning acclimated new Africans to the physical as well as the cultural environment of the southern colonies. Slaves who had just endured the Middle Passage were poorly nourished, weak, and sick. In this vulnerable state, they encountered the alien diseases of North America without having acquired immunities. As many as 10 to 15 percent of newly arrived Africans, sometimes more, died during their first year in the southern colonies. Nonetheless, the large number of newly enslaved Africans made the influence of African culture in the South stronger in the eighteenth century than ever before—or since.

While newly enslaved Africans poured into the southern colonies, slave mothers bore children, which caused the slave population in the South to grow rapidly. Slave owners encouraged these births. The growing number of slave babies set the southern colonies apart from other New World slave societies, where mortality rates were so high that deaths exceeded births. The high rate of natural increase in the southern colonies meant that by the 1740s, the majority of southern slaves were country-born.

Slave Labor and African American Culture

Southern planters expected slaves to work from sunup to sundown and beyond. George Washington wrote that his slaves should "be at their work as soon as it is light, work til it is dark, and be diligent while they are at it." The conflict between the masters' desire for maximum labor and the slaves' reluctance to do more than necessary made the threat of physical punishment a constant for eighteenth-century slaves. Masters preferred black slaves to white indentured servants, not just because slaves served for life but also because colonial laws did not limit the force masters could use against slaves. As a traveler observed in 1740, slaves resisted their masters' demands because of their "greatness of soul"—their stubborn unwillingness to conform to their masters' definition of them as merely slaves.

Olaudah Equiano

This portrait shows Equiano more than a decade after he had bought his freedom. The portrait evokes Equiano's successful acculturation to the customs of eighteenth-century England. His clothing and hairstyle reflect the fashions of a respectable young Englishman. Library of Congress.

CHAPTER LOCATOR | How and why did British North America change in the eighteenth century?

CHAPTER 5
126 THE CHANGING WORLD OF COLONIAL AMERICA

Some slaves escalated their acts of resistance to direct physical confrontation with the master, the mistress, or an overseer. But a hoe raised in anger, a punch in the face, or a desperate swipe with a knife led to swift and predictable retaliation by whites. Throughout the southern colonies, the balance of physical power rested securely in the hands of whites.

Rebellion occurred, however, at Stono, South Carolina, in 1739. Before dawn on a September Sunday, a group of about twenty slaves attacked a country store, killed the two storekeepers, and confiscated the store's guns, ammunition, and powder. Enticing other slaves to join, the group plundered and burned more than half a dozen plantations and killed more than twenty white men, women, and children. A mounted force of whites quickly suppressed the rebellion. They placed the rebels' heads atop mileposts along the road, grim reminders of the consequences of rebellion. The **Stono rebellion** illustrated that eighteenth-century slaves had no chance of overturning slavery and very little chance of defending themselves in any bold strike for freedom. After the rebellion, South Carolina legislators enacted repressive laws designed to guarantee that whites would always have the upper hand. No other similar uprisings occurred during the colonial period.

Slaves maneuvered constantly to protect themselves and to gain a measure of autonomy within the boundaries of slavery. In Chesapeake tobacco fields, most slaves were subject to close supervision by whites. In the lower South, the task system gave slaves some control over the pace of their work and some discretion in the use of the rest of their time. A "task" was typically defined as a certain area of ground to be cultivated or a specific job to be completed. A slave who completed the assigned task might use the remainder of the day, if any, to work in a garden, fish, hunt, spin, weave, sew, or cook. When masters sought to boost productivity by increasing tasks, slaves did what they could to defend their customary work assignments.

Eighteenth-century slaves also planted the roots of African American lineages that branch out to the present. Slaves expressed their humanity through the value they placed on family ties, and, as in West African societies, kinship structured slaves' relations with one another. Slave parents often gave a child the name of a grandparent, an aunt, or an uncle. In West Africa, kinship identified a person's place among living relatives and linked the person to ancestors in the past and to descendants in the future. Newly imported African slaves usually arrived alone, like Equiano, without kin. Often slaves who arrived from Africa on the same ship adopted one another as "brothers" and "sisters." Likewise, as new Negroes were seasoned and incorporated into existing slave communities, established families often adopted them as fictive kin.

When possible, slaves expressed many other features of their West African origins in their lives on New World plantations. They gave their children traditional dolls and African names such as Cudjo or Quash, Minda or Fuladi. They grew food crops they had known in Africa, such as yams and okra. They constructed huts with mud walls and thatched roofs similar to African residences. They fashioned banjos, drums, and other musical instruments, held dances, and observed funeral rites that echoed African practices. In these and many other ways, slaves drew upon their African heritages as much as the oppressive circumstances of slavery permitted.

Stono rebellion
▶ Slave uprising in Stono, South Carolina. In September 1739, a small group of slaves attacked a country store, plundered and burned more than half a dozen plantations, and killed more than twenty white colonists. After the uprising, South Carolina passed laws placing further restrictions on the activities and movements of slaves.

Doll Belonging to a Slave Child

This doll, recovered from an archaeological investigation of slaves' housing, was probably a gift from a slave parent or elder to a child, a token of the affection that linked kin groups among slaves. The Stagville Center, Division of Archives and History, North Carolina Department of Archives and History, North Carolina Department of Cultural Resources.

What changed in New England life and culture?

How were the middle colonies distinctive?

How did slavery become the defining feature of the southern colonies?

What were the unifying experiences for British American colonists?

Conclusion: What was the dual identity of British North American colonists?

Tobacco, Rice, and Prosperity

Slaves' labor bestowed prosperity on their masters, British merchants, and the monarchy. The southern colonies supplied 90 percent of all North American exports to Britain. Rice exports from the lower South exploded from less than half a million pounds in 1700 to eighty million pounds in 1770, nearly all of it grown by slaves. Exports of indigo also boomed. Tobacco was by far the most important export from British North America; by 1770, it represented almost one-third of all colonial exports and three-fourths of all Chesapeake exports. Under the provisions of the Navigation Acts (see chapter 4), nearly all of it went to Britain, where the monarchy collected a lucrative tax on each pound. British merchants then reexported more than 80 percent of the tobacco to the European continent, pocketing a nice markup for their troubles.

These products of slave labor made the southern colonies by far the richest in North America. The per capita wealth of free whites in the South was four times greater than that in New England and three times that in the middle colonies. At the top of the wealth pyramid stood the rice grandees of the lower South and the tobacco **gentry** of the Chesapeake. The vast differences in wealth among white southerners engendered envy and occasional tension between rich and poor, but remarkably little open hostility. Although racial slavery made a few whites much richer than others, it also gave those who did not get rich a powerful reason to feel similar (in race) to those who were so different (in wealth).

The slaveholding gentry dominated the politics and economy of the southern colonies. Property requirements prevented about 40 percent of white men in Virginia from voting for representatives to the House of Burgesses. In South Carolina, the property requirement was lower, and therefore most adult white men qualified to vote. In both colonies, voters elected members of the gentry to serve in the colonial legislature. The gentry passed political offices from generation to generation, building a self-perpetuating oligarchy—rule by the elite few—with the votes of their many humble neighbors.

The gentry also set the cultural standard in the southern colonies. They entertained lavishly, gambled regularly, and attended Anglican (Church of England) services more for social than for religious reasons. Above all, they cultivated the leisurely pursuit of happiness. They did not condone idleness, however. Their many pleasures and responsibilities as plantation owners kept them busy. Thomas Jefferson, a phenomenally productive member of the gentry, recalled that his earliest childhood memory was of being carried on a pillow by a family slave—a powerful image of the slave hands supporting the gentry's leisure and achievement.

gentry

▶ The social and political elite of the southern colonies who dominated society and politics. They worked to defuse social and political tensions between rich and poor whites by promoting a sense of solidarity with poor whites along racial lines.

> ## QUICK REVIEW

How did slavery shape the society and economy of the southern colonies?

CHAPTER LOCATOR | How and why did British North America change in the eighteenth century?

128 CHAPTER 5
THE CHANGING WORLD OF COLONIAL AMERICA

What were the unifying experiences for British American colonists?

George Whitefield

An anonymous artist portrayed George Whitefield preaching, emphasizing the power of his sermons to transport his audience to a revived awareness of divine spirituality. The young woman bathed in light below his hands appears transfixed, her focus on some inner realm illuminated by his words. The other people in Whitefield's audience appear not to have achieved this state, failing so far to be ignited by the divine spark. National Portrait Gallery, London.

THE SOCIETIES OF NEW ENGLAND, the middle colonies, and the southern colonies became more sharply differentiated during the eighteenth century, but colonists throughout British North America also shared unifying experiences that eluded settlers in the Spanish and French colonies. The first was economic. All three British colonial regions had their economic roots in agriculture. Colonists sold their distinctive products in markets that, in turn, offered a more or less uniform array of goods to consumers throughout British North America. A second unifying experience was a decline in the importance of religion. Some settlers called for a revival of religious intensity, but most people focused less on religion and more on the affairs of the world than they had in the seventeenth century. Third, white inhabitants throughout British North America became aware that they shared a distinctive identity as *British* colonists. Thirteen different governments presided over these North American colonies, but all of them answered to the British monarchy. British policies governed not only trade but also military and diplomatic relations with the Indians, French, and Spanish arrayed along colonial borderlands. Royal officials who expected loyalty from the colonists often had difficulty obtaining obedience. The British colonists asserted their prerogatives as British subjects to defend their special colonial interests.

1715
- Yamasee War pits Yamasee and Creek Indian allies of the French against British colonists in South Carolina.

1730s
- Jonathan Edwards promotes the religious movement known as the Great Awakening.

1740s
- George Whitefield preaches religious revival in North America.

1754
- Seven Years' War begins.

1769
- American Philosophical Society is founded.
- First Spanish mission in California, San Diego de Alcalá, is established.

1770
- Spanish mission and presidio are established at Monterey, California.

Commerce and Consumption

Colonial products spurred the development of mass markets throughout the Atlantic world. Colonial goods helped make it possible for ordinary people, not just the wealthy elite, to buy the things that they desired in addition to what they absolutely needed. Even news, formerly restricted mostly to a few people through face-to-face conversations or private letters, became an object of public consumption through the innovation of newspapers. With the appropriate stimulus, market demand seemed unlimited.

The Atlantic commerce that took colonial goods to markets in Britain brought consumer products back to the colonies. By midcentury, export-oriented industries in Britain were growing ten times faster than firms attuned to the home market. Most British exports went to the vast European market, where potential customers outnumbered those in the colonies by more than one hundred to one. But as European competition stiffened, colonial markets became increasingly important. British exports to North America multiplied eightfold between 1700 and 1770, outpacing the rate of population growth after midcentury. When the colonists' eagerness to consume exceeded their ability to pay, British exporters willingly extended credit, and colonial debts soared (**Figure 5.1**).

Despite the many differences among the colonists, the consumption of British exports built a certain material uniformity across region, religion, class, and status. Consumption of British exports made the colonists look and feel more British even though they lived at the edge of a wilderness an ocean away from Britain.

The rising tide of colonial consumption had other less visible but no less important consequences. Consumption presented women and men with a novel array of choices. As colonial consumers defined and expressed their desires with greater frequency during the eighteenth century, they became accustomed to thinking of themselves as individuals who had the power to make decisions that influenced the quality of their lives—attitudes of significance in the hierarchical world of eighteenth-century British North America.

Religion, Enlightenment, and Revival

Eighteenth-century colonists could choose from almost as many religions as consumer goods. Virtually all colonial religious denominations represented some form of Christianity, almost all of them Protestant. Slaves made up the largest group of non-Christians. A few slaves converted to Christianity in Africa or after they arrived in North America, but most continued to embrace elements of indigenous African religions. Roman Catholics concentrated in Maryland as they had since the seventeenth century, but even there they were outnumbered by Protestants.

The varieties of Protestant faith and practice ranged across a broad spectrum. The middle colonies and the southern backcountry included militant Baptists and Presbyterians. Huguenots who had fled persecution in Catholic France peopled congregations in several cities. In New England, old-style Puritanism splintered into strands of Congregationalism that differed over fine points of theological doctrine. The Congregational Church was the official established church in New England, and all residents paid taxes for its support. Throughout the plantation South and in urban centers such as Charleston, New York, and Philadelphia,

CHAPTER LOCATOR | How and why did British North America change in the eighteenth century?

130 CHAPTER 5   THE CHANGING WORLD OF COLONIAL AMERICA

FIGURE 5.1 ■ Colonial Exports, 1768–1772

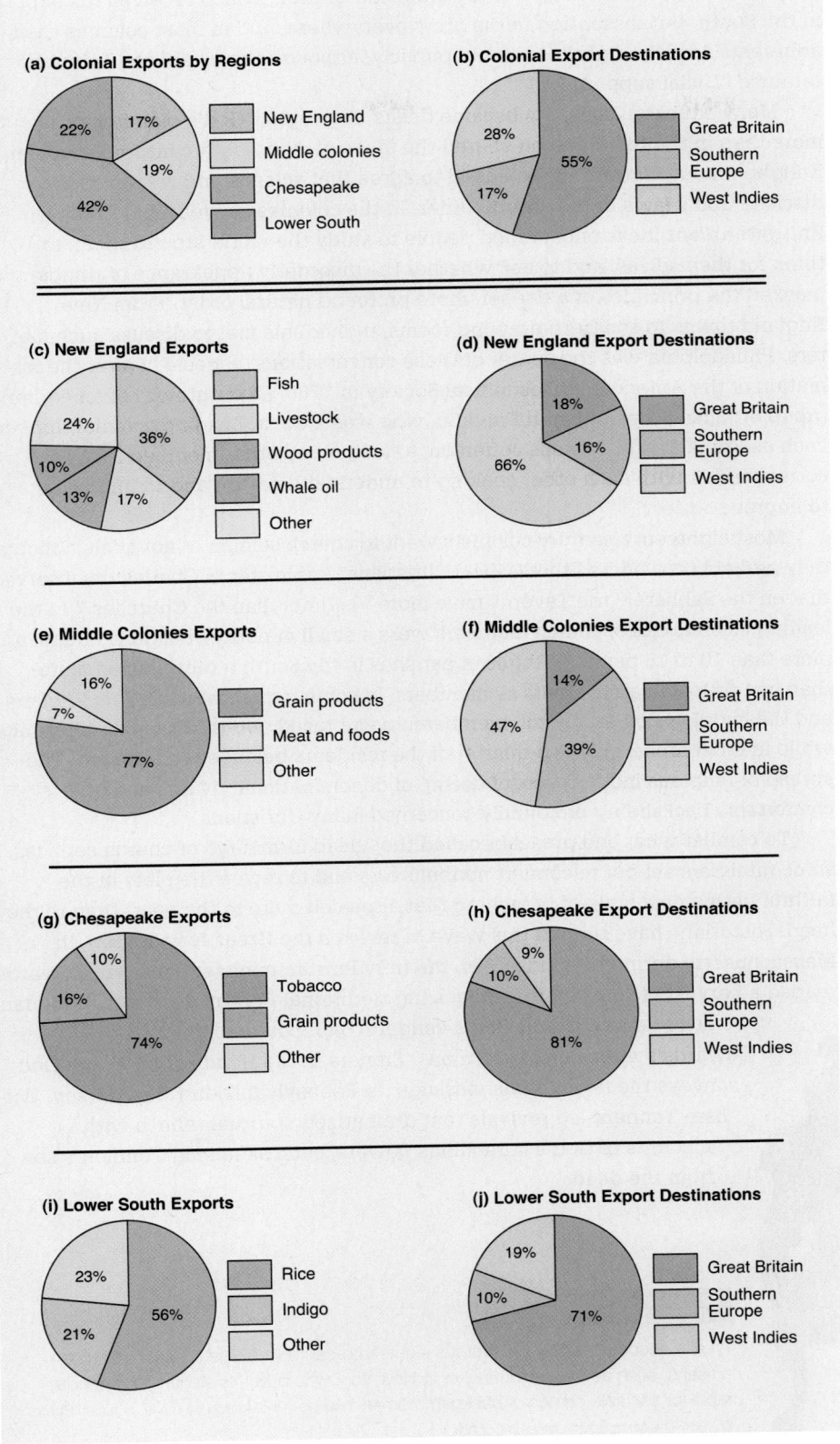

(a) Colonial Exports by Regions

- 17% New England
- 19% Middle colonies
- 42% Chesapeake
- 22% Lower South

(b) Colonial Export Destinations

- 55% Great Britain
- 17% Southern Europe
- 28% West Indies

(c) New England Exports

- 36% Fish
- 17% Livestock
- 13% Wood products
- 10% Whale oil
- 24% Other

(d) New England Export Destinations

- 18% Great Britain
- 16% Southern Europe
- 66% West Indies

(e) Middle Colonies Exports

- 77% Grain products
- 16% Meat and foods
- 7% Other

(f) Middle Colonies Export Destinations

- 14% Great Britain
- 39% Southern Europe
- 47% West Indies

(g) Chesapeake Exports

- 74% Tobacco
- 16% Grain products
- 10% Other

(h) Chesapeake Export Destinations

- 9% Great Britain
- 10% Southern Europe
- 81% West Indies

(i) Lower South Exports

- 56% Rice
- 21% Indigo
- 23% Other

(j) Lower South Export Destinations

- 71% Great Britain
- 10% Southern Europe
- 19% West Indies

FIGURE 5.1 ■ Colonial Exports, 1768–1772

These pie charts provide an overview of the colonial export economy of the 1760s. The first two show that almost two-thirds of colonial exports came from the South and that the majority of the colonies' exports went to Great Britain. The remaining charts illustrate the distinctive patterns of exports in each colonial region. What do these patterns reveal about regional variations in Britain's North American colonies? What do they suggest about Britain's economic interest in the colonies?

What changed in New England life and culture?	How were the middle colonies distinctive?	How did slavery become the defining feature of the southern colonies?	**What were the unifying experiences for British American colonists?**	Conclusion: What was the dual identity of British North American colonists?

deism
▶ Belief that God created a universe governed by natural laws and that those laws could be discovered through the use of reason. Many deists also rejected the possibility of supernatural events and of God's direct intervention in the lives of human beings. Deism was an outgrowth of the eighteenth-century Enlightenment.

Enlightenment
▶ Eighteenth-century cultural and intellectual movement that emphasized the power of reason and focused on improving human life in the here and now. Philadelphia was the center of the discussion of Enlightenment ideas in America, especially after the formation of the American Philosophical Society in 1769.

Great Awakening
▶ Early- to mid-eighteenth-century religious revival that attempted to convert nonbelievers and to revive the piety of the faithful through emotional, as opposed to rational, appeals. The revivals renewed the spiritual energies of thousands of colonists but did not substantially boost the total number of church members.

prominent colonists belonged to the Anglican Church, which received tax support in the South. But dissenting faiths grew everywhere, and in most colonies their adherents won the right to worship publicly, although the established churches retained official support.

Many educated colonists became deists, looking for God's plan in nature more than in the Bible. **Deism** shared the ideas of eighteenth-century European Enlightenment thinkers, who tended to agree that science and reason could disclose God's laws in the natural order. In the colonies as well as in Europe, **Enlightenment** ideas encouraged people to study the world around them, to think for themselves, and to ask whether the disorderly appearance of things masked the principles of a deeper, more profound natural order. From New England towns to southern drawing rooms, individuals met to discuss such matters. Philadelphia was the center of these conversations, especially after the formation of the American Philosophical Society in 1769, an outgrowth of an earlier group organized by Benjamin Franklin, who was a deist. Leading colonial thinkers such as Franklin and Thomas Jefferson, among many other members, corresponded with each other seeking to understand nature and to find ways to improve society.

Most eighteenth-century colonists went to church seldom or not at all, although they probably considered themselves Christians. A minister in Charleston observed that on the Sabbath, "the Taverns have more Visitants than the Churches." In the leading colonial cities, church members were a small minority of eligible adults, no more than 10 to 15 percent. Anglican parishes in the South rarely claimed more than one-fifth of eligible adults as members. In some regions of rural New England and the middle colonies, church membership embraced two-thirds of eligible adults, while in other areas, only one-quarter of the residents belonged to a church. The spread of religious indifference, of deism, of denominational rivalry, and of comfortable backsliding profoundly concerned many Christians.

To combat what one preacher called the "dead formality" of church services, some ministers set out to convert nonbelievers and to revive the piety of the faithful with a new style of preaching that appealed more to the heart than to the head. Historians have termed this wave of revivals the **Great Awakening**. In Massachusetts during the mid-1730s, the fiery Puritan minister Jonathan Edwards reaped a harvest of souls by reemphasizing traditional Puritan doctrines of humanity's utter depravity and God's vengeful omnipotence. The title of Edwards's most famous sermon, "Sinners in the Hands of an Angry God," conveys the flavor of his message. In Pennsylvania and New Jersey, William Tennent led revivals that dramatized spiritual rebirth with accounts of God's miraculous powers, such as raising Tennent's son from the dead.

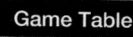
Game Table

Wealth accumulated by prosperous eighteenth-century colonists supported urban artisans, such as the cabinetmaker in New York who built this elegant Chippendale table for sociable games of backgammon and cards. Photograph by Richard Cheek, Photo © 1984 The Metropolitan Museum of Art.

CHAPTER LOCATOR | How and why did British North America change in the eighteenth century?

132 CHAPTER 5
THE CHANGING WORLD OF COLONIAL AMERICA

The most famous revivalist in the eighteenth-century Atlantic world was **George Whitefield**. An Anglican, Whitefield preached to large audiences in England. Whitefield visited the North American colonies seven times, staying for more than three years during the mid-1740s and attracting tens of thousands to his sermons, including Benjamin Franklin and Olaudah Equiano. Whitefield's preaching transported many in his audience to emotion-choked states of religious ecstasy. About one revival he wrote, "The bitter cries and groans were enough to pierce the hardest heart. Some of the people were as pale as death; others were wringing their hands; others lying on the ground; others sinking into the arms of their friends; and most lifting their eyes to heaven, and crying to God for mercy."

Whitefield's successful revivals spawned many lesser imitations. Itinerant preachers, many of them poorly educated, toured the colonial backcountry after midcentury, echoing Whitefield's medium and message as best they could. Bathsheba Kingsley, a member of Jonathan Edwards's flock, preached the revival message informally—as did an unprecedented number of other women throughout the colonies—causing her congregation to brand her a "brawling woman" who had "gone quite out of her place."

The revivals awakened and refreshed the spiritual energies of thousands of colonists struggling with the uncertainties and anxieties of eighteenth-century America. In the end, the conversions at revivals did not substantially boost the total number of church members, but they did communicate the important message that every soul mattered, that men and women could choose to be saved, that individuals had the power to make a decision for everlasting life or death. Colonial revivals expressed in religious terms many of the same democratic and egalitarian values expressed in economic terms by colonists' patterns of consumption. Like consumption, revivals contributed to a set of common experiences that bridged colonial divides of faith, region, class, and status.

Borderlands and Colonial Politics in the British Empire

The plurality of peoples, faiths, and communities that characterized the North American colonies arose from the somewhat haphazard policies of the eighteenth-century British empire. Since the Puritan Revolution of the mid-seventeenth century, British monarchs had valued the colonies' contributions to trade and encouraged their growth and development. Unlike Spain and France—whose policies of excluding Protestants and foreigners kept the population of their North American colonial territories tiny—Britain kept the door to its colonies open to anyone, and tens of thousands of non-British immigrants settled in the North American colonies and raised families. The open door did not extend to trade, however, as the seventeenth-century Navigation Acts restricted colonial trade to British ships and traders. These policies evolved because they served the interests of the monarchy and of influential groups in Britain and the colonies. The policies also gave the colonists a common framework of political expectations and experiences.

At a minimum, British power defended the colonists from Indian, French, and Spanish enemies on their borders—as well as from foreign powers abroad. Each colony organized a militia, and privateers sailed from every port to prey on foreign

George Whitefield

▶ The most famous revivalist of the Great Awakening. Whitefield spoke before enormous audiences in both Britain and the colonies, visiting the North American colonies seven times and staying for more than three years during the mid-1740s. His success inspired numerous lesser imitators to tour the colonies, leading revival meetings of their own.

What changed in New England life and culture? | How were the middle colonies distinctive? | How did slavery become the defining feature of the southern colonies? | What were the unifying experiences for British American colonists? | Conclusion: What was the dual identity of British North American colonists?

133

Large Warships in European Navies, 1660–1760

The large warships in England's navy usually outnumbered those of rival nations from 1660 to 1760. During the eighteenth century, the British fleet grew dramatically, while the fleets of rival nations declined. The British monarchy paid the enormous cost of building, manning, and maintaining the largest European navy because defending commerce and communication with its far-flung colonies was fundamental to the integrity of its empire. Britain's North American colonies benefited from defense by the most powerful navy in the Atlantic. Why do you think British warships outnumbered those of their competitors?

Note: Comparable data does not exist for Spain.

ships. But the British navy and army bore ultimate responsibility for colonial defense. (See "Global Comparison.")

Royal officials warily eyed the small North American settlements of New France and New Spain for signs of threats to the colonies. Alone, neither New France nor New Spain jeopardized British North America, but with Indian allies, they could become a potent force that kept colonists on their guard (**Map 5.4**). Native Americans' impulse to defend their territory from colonial incursions warred with their desire for trade, which tugged them toward the settlers. As a colonial official observed in 1761, "A modern Indian cannot subsist without Europeans. . . . [The European goods that were] only conveniency at first [have] now become necessity." To obtain such necessities as guns, ammunition, clothing, sewing utensils, and much more that was manufactured largely by the British, Indians trapped beavers, deer, and other furbearing animals throughout the interior.

Colonial traders and their respective empires competed to control the fur trade. British, French, Spanish, and Dutch officials monitored the trade to prevent their competitors from deflecting the flow of furs toward their own markets. Indians took advantage of this competition to improve their own prospects, playing one trader and empire off against another. Indian tribes and confederacies also competed among themselves for favored trading rights with one colony or another, a competition colonists encouraged.

The shifting alliances and complex dynamics of the fur trade struck a fragile balance along the frontier. The threat of violence from all sides was ever present, and the threat became reality often enough for all parties to be prepared for the worst. In the Yamasee War of 1715, Yamasee and Creek Indians—with French encouragement—mounted a coordinated attack against colonial settlements in South Carolina and inflicted heavy casualties. The Cherokee Indians, traditional enemies of the Creeks, refused to join the attack. Instead, they protected their access to British trade goods by allying with the colonists and turning the tide of battle.

Relations between Indians and colonists differed from colony to colony and from year to year. But the British colonists' fears kept them continually hoping for

CHAPTER LOCATOR | How and why did British North America change in the eighteenth century?

help from the British to keep the Indians at bay and to maintain the essential flow of trade. In 1754, the British colonists' endemic competition with the French flared into the Seven Years' War, also known as the French and Indian War (see chapter 6). Before the 1760s, neither the British colonists nor the British themselves developed a coherent policy toward the Indians. But both agreed that Indians made deadly enemies, profitable trading partners, and powerful allies. As a result, the British and their colonists kept an eye on the Spanish empire to the west and relations with the Indians there.

Russian hunters in search of seals and sea otters ventured along the Pacific coast from Alaska to California and threatened to become a permanent presence on New Spain's northern frontier. To block Russian access to present-day California, officials in New Spain mounted a campaign to build forts (called *presidios*) and missions there.

In 1769, an expedition headed by a military man, **Gaspar de Portolá**, and a Catholic priest, Junípero Serra, traveled north from Mexico to present-day San Diego, where they founded the first California mission, San Diego de Alcalá. They soon journeyed all the way to Monterey, which became the capital of Spanish California. There Portolá established a presidio in 1770 "to defend us from attacks by the Russians," he wrote. By 1772, Serra had founded other missions along the path from San Diego to Monterey.

One Spanish soldier praised the work of the missionaries, writing that "with flattery and presents [the missionaries] attract the savage Indians and persuade them to adhere to life in society and to receive instruction for a knowledge of the Catholic faith, the cultivation of the land, and the arts necessary for making the instruments most needed for farming." Yet for the Indians, the Spaniards' California missions had horrendous consequences, as they had elsewhere in the Spanish borderlands. European diseases decimated Indian populations, Spanish soldiers raped Indian women, and missionaries beat Indians and subjected them to near slavery. Indian uprisings against the Spaniards occurred repeatedly, but the presidios and missions endured as projections of the Spanish empire along the Pacific coast.

British attempts to exercise political power in their colonial governments met with success so long as British officials were on or very near the sea. Colonists acknowledged British authority to collect customs duties, inspect cargoes, and enforce trade regulations. But when royal officials tried to wield their authority in the internal affairs of the colonies on land, they invariably

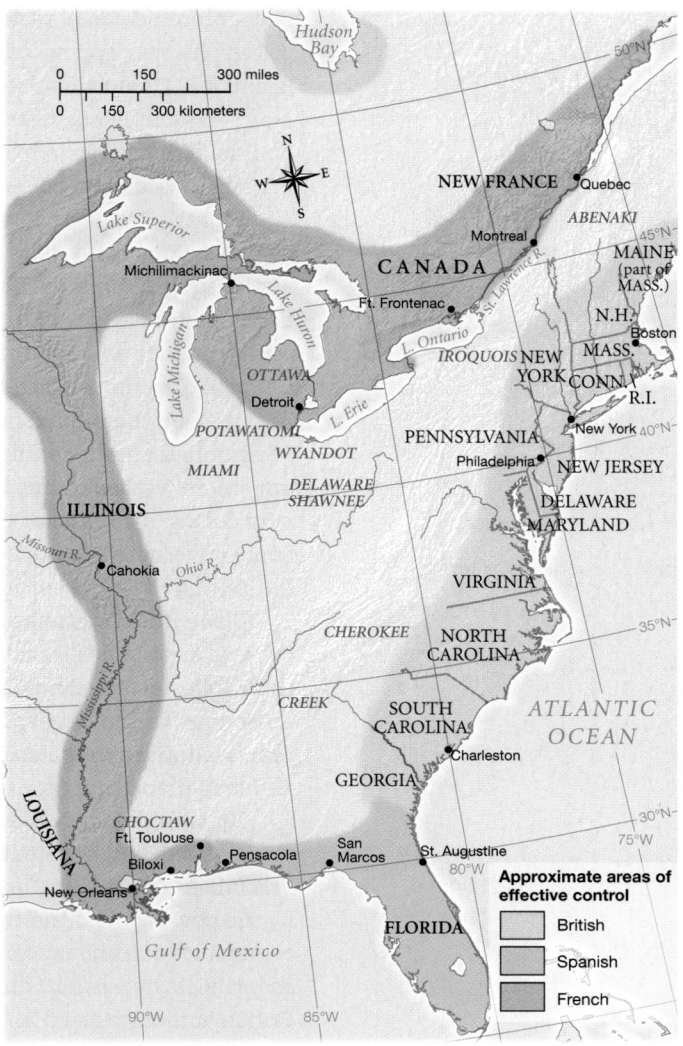

MAP 5.4 ■ **Zones of Empire in Eastern North America**
The British zone, extending west from the Atlantic coast, was much more densely settled than the zones under French, Spanish, and Indian control. The comparatively large number of British colonists made them more secure than the relatively few colonists in the vast regions claimed by France and Spain or the settlers living among the many Indian peoples in the huge area between the Mississippi River and the Appalachian Mountains. Yet the British colonists were not powerful enough to dominate the French, Spaniards, or Indians. Instead, they had to guard against attacks by powerful Indian groups allied with the French or Spaniards.

Gaspar de Portolá
▶ Spanish military leader who, beginning in 1769, began the establishment of Spanish missions in California, ostensibly to defend Spanish interests in the West from Russia. Eventually, these missions extended from San Diego to Monterey.

| What changed in New England life and culture? | How were the middle colonies distinctive? | How did slavery become the defining feature of the southern colonies? | **What were the unifying experiences for British American colonists?** | Conclusion: What was the dual identity of British North American colonists? |

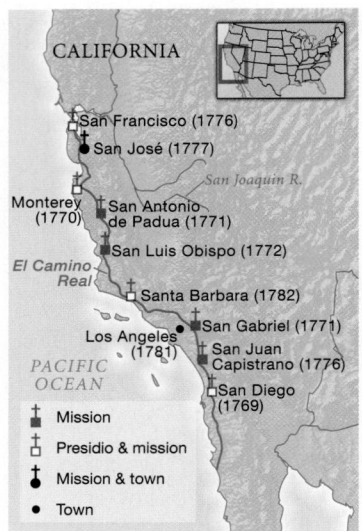

Spanish Missions in California

encountered colonial resistance. A governor headed the government of each colony; he was appointed by the king in each of the nine royal colonies (Rhode Island and Connecticut selected their own governors) or by the proprietors in Maryland and Pennsylvania. The British envisioned colonial governors as mini-monarchs able to exert influence in the colonies much as the king did in Britain. But colonial governors were not kings, and the colonies were not Britain.

Eighty percent of colonial governors had been born in England, not in the colonies. Some governors stayed in England and delegated the details of colonial affairs to subordinates. Even the best-intentioned colonial governors had difficulty developing relations of trust and respect with influential colonists because their terms of office averaged just five years and could be terminated at any time. Colonial governors controlled few patronage positions in the colonies that could have helped them build political alliances. In obedience to Britain, colonial governors fought incessantly with the colonists' assemblies. They battled over governors' vetoes of colonial legislation, removal of colonial judges, creation of new courts, dismissal of the representative assemblies, and other local issues. Some governors developed a working relationship with the colonists' assemblies. But during the eighteenth century, the assemblies gained the upper hand.

Since British policies did not clearly define the colonists' legal powers, colonial assemblies seized the opportunity to make their own rules. Gradually, the assemblies established a strong tradition of representative government analogous, in their eyes, to the British Parliament. Voters often returned the same representatives to the assemblies year after year, building continuity in power and leadership that far exceeded that of the governor.

By 1720, colonial assemblies had won the power to initiate legislation, including tax laws and authorizations to spend public funds. Although all laws passed by the assemblies (except in Maryland, Rhode Island, and Connecticut) had to be approved by the governor and then by the Board of Trade in Britain, the difficulties in communication about complex subjects over long distances effectively ratified the assemblies' decisions. Often years passed before colonial laws were repealed by British authorities, and in the meantime, the assemblies' laws prevailed.

The heated political struggles between royal governors and colonial assemblies that occurred throughout the eighteenth century taught colonists a common set of political lessons. They learned to employ traditionally British ideas of representative government to defend their own colonial interests. They learned that power in the British colonies rarely belonged exclusively to the British government.

> QUICK REVIEW

How did commerce and consumption shape the collective identity of colonists in British North America during the eighteenth century?

CHAPTER LOCATOR | How and why did British North America change in the eighteenth century?

136 CHAPTER 5 THE CHANGING WORLD OF COLONIAL AMERICA

Courtesy, American Antiquarian Society.

Conclusion: What was the dual identity of British North American colonists?

DURING THE EIGHTEENTH CENTURY, a society that was both distinctively colonial and distinctively British emerged in British North America. Tens of thousands of immigrants and slaves gave the colonies an unmistakably colonial complexion and contributed to the colonies' growing population and expanding economy. People of different ethnicities and faiths sought their fortunes in the colonies, where land was cheap, labor was dear, and—as Benjamin Franklin preached—work promised to be rewarding. Indentured servants and redemptioners risked temporary periods of bondage for the potential reward of better opportunities in the colonies than on the Atlantic's eastern shore. Slaves endured lifetime servitude, which they neither chose nor desired but from which their masters greatly benefited.

Identifiably colonial products from New England, the middle colonies, and the southern colonies flowed to the West Indies and across the Atlantic. Back came unquestionably British consumer goods along with fashions in ideas, faith, and politics. The bonds of the British empire required colonists to think of themselves as British subjects and, at the same time, encouraged them to consider their status as colonists.

By 1750, British colonists in North America could not imagine that their distinctively dual identity—as British and as colonists—would soon become a source of intense conflict. But by 1776, colonists in British North America had to choose whether they were British or American.

SO NOW YOU KNOW

All of Britain's North American colonies experienced rapid change and growth over the course of the eighteenth century leading up to the American Revolution. While there were many variations among the colonies, colonial wars and British policies helped foster a growing sense of an *American* identity for many colonists.

| What changed in New England life and culture? | How were the middle colonies distinctive? | How did slavery become the defining feature of the southern colonies? | What were the unifying experiences for British American colonists? | **Conclusion: What was the dual identity of British North American colonists?** |

CHAPTER 5 STUDY GUIDE

Online Study Guide
bedfordstmartins.com/roarkunderstanding

STEP 1 GETTING STARTED

Below are basic terms from this period in American history. Can you identify each term below and explain why it matters? To do this exercise online or to download this chart, visit bedfordstmartins.com/roarkunderstanding.

TERM	WHO OR WHAT & WHEN	WHY IT MATTERS
redemptioners, p. 119		
Iroquois Indians, p. 121		
Benjamin Franklin, p. 122		
Middle Passage, p. 125		
Olaudah Equiano, p. 125		
Stono rebellion , p. 127		
gentry, p. 128		
deism, p. 132		
Enlightenment, p. 132		
Great Awakening, p. 132		
George Whitefield, p. 133		
Gaspar de Portolá, p. 135		

STEP 2 MOVING BEYOND THE BASICS

The exercise below represents a more advanced understanding of the chapter material. In this exercise, identify the changes in colonial society between 1700 and 1770. Use the chart below to describe the economy, society, culture, and politics of the major regions of British North America in 1700 and 1770. What accounts for regional divergence over the course of the eighteenth century? To do this exercise online or to download this chart, visit bedfordstmartins.com/roarkunderstanding.

Region	Economy (imports and exports, jobs, wealth)	Population (ethnicity, race, class)	Culture—ways of life, values (including religious beliefs)	Colonial politics
New England in 1700				
New England in 1770				
Middle colonies in 1700				
Middle colonies in 1770				
Southern colonies in 1700				
Southern colonies in 1770				

Now that you have reviewed key elements of the chapter, take a step back and try to explain the big picture. Remember to use specific examples from the chapter in your answers. To do this exercise online, visit bedfordstmartins.com/roarkunderstanding.

NEW ENGLAND

► How did the economy of New England differ from that of other regions?

► Why did New England not attract as many immigrants as other areas did? How did that affect the social structure of the region?

THE MIDDLE COLONIES

► How did immigration shape the religious and ethnic diversity of the middle colonies? What factors led immigrants to settle in the middle colonies?

► How did Atlantic commerce, particularly colonial consumption, affect the middle colonies?

THE SOUTHERN COLONIES AND SPANISH CALIFORNIA

► What role did slavery play in the social and economic development of the South?

► How did slaves attempt to maintain their own culture and gain some control within the limits of slavery?

► Why did New Spain establish presidios and missions, and what were their consequences for Native Americans?

LOOKING BACKWARD, LOOKING AHEAD

► How did the relationship between the colonies and Britain in the eighteenth century differ from that of the seventeenth century?

► What were the most pressing sources of potential conflict between the colonies and Britain in 1770? What were the most important sources of cooperation and mutual dependence?

IN YOUR OWN WORDS

Imagine that you must explain chapter 5 to someone who hasn't read it. What would be the most important points to include and why?

6
THE MAKING OF AN AMERICAN REVOLUTION

1754–1775

> This chapter explores the efforts of the British government to tax and control the North American colonies in the decade following the Seven Years' War. It examines the resulting deterioration of relations between Britain and its American colonists, tracing the escalating colonial response from political protest, to open resistance, to war.

DID YOU KNOW?

Colonial women were prominent in protesting and resisting British policies.

> How did the Seven Years' War lay the groundwork for colonial crisis?

> Why did the American colonists find offense with the Sugar and Stamp Acts of 1763–1765?

> What were the colonial responses to the Townshend duties?

> What led to the escalation of tensions after 1772?

> What were the varieties of domestic insurrections in 1774–1775?

> Conclusion: What changes did Americans want in 1775?

Resistance to the Stamp Act. This contemporary engraving (ca. 1765) depicts an angry Boston crowd burning a pile of stamps in protest of the Stamp Act.

How did the Seven Years' War lay the groundwork for colonial crisis?

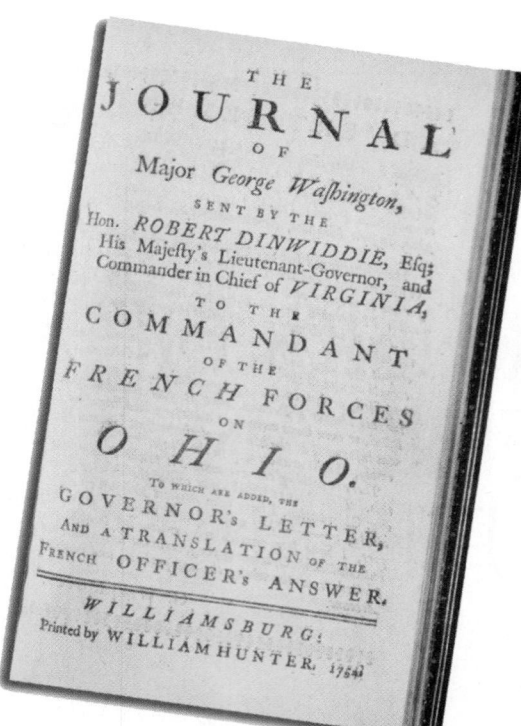

Seven Years' War

▶ War (1754–1762) between Britain and France that ended with British domination of North America. Known in America as the French and Indian War, the war spread in 1756 to encompass much of Europe, the Caribbean, and India. The cost of the war laid the foundation for colonial conflicts that would lead to the American Revolution.

FOR THE FIRST HALF of the eighteenth century, Britain was at war intermittently with France or Spain. In the 1750s, international tensions returned, this time over events originating in America. The conflict began in 1754 over contested land in the Ohio Valley. The result was the costly **Seven Years' War** (its British name—Americans called it the French and Indian War), which spread in 1756 to encompass much of Europe, the Caribbean, and even India. The British and their colonial allies won the war, but the immense costs of the conflict laid the groundwork for the imperial crisis of the 1760s between the British and the Americans.

French-British Rivalry in the Ohio Country

For several decades, French traders had cultivated alliances with the Indian tribes in the Ohio Country, a region they regarded as part of New France, establishing a profitable trade of manufactured goods for beaver furs (**Map 6.1**). But in the 1740s, aggressive Pennsylvania traders began to infringe on their territory. Adding to the tensions, a group of enterprising Virginians formed the Ohio Company in 1747 and advanced on the same land. Their hope for profit lay not in the fur trade but in land speculation, fueled by American population expansion.

In response to these incursions, the French sent soldiers to build a series of military forts to secure their trade routes and to create a western barrier to American expansion. In 1753, the royal governor of Virginia, Robert Dinwiddie,

CHAPTER LOCATOR | How did the Seven Years' War lay the groundwork for colonial crisis?

142 CHAPTER 6
THE MAKING OF AN AMERICAN REVOLUTION, 1754–1775

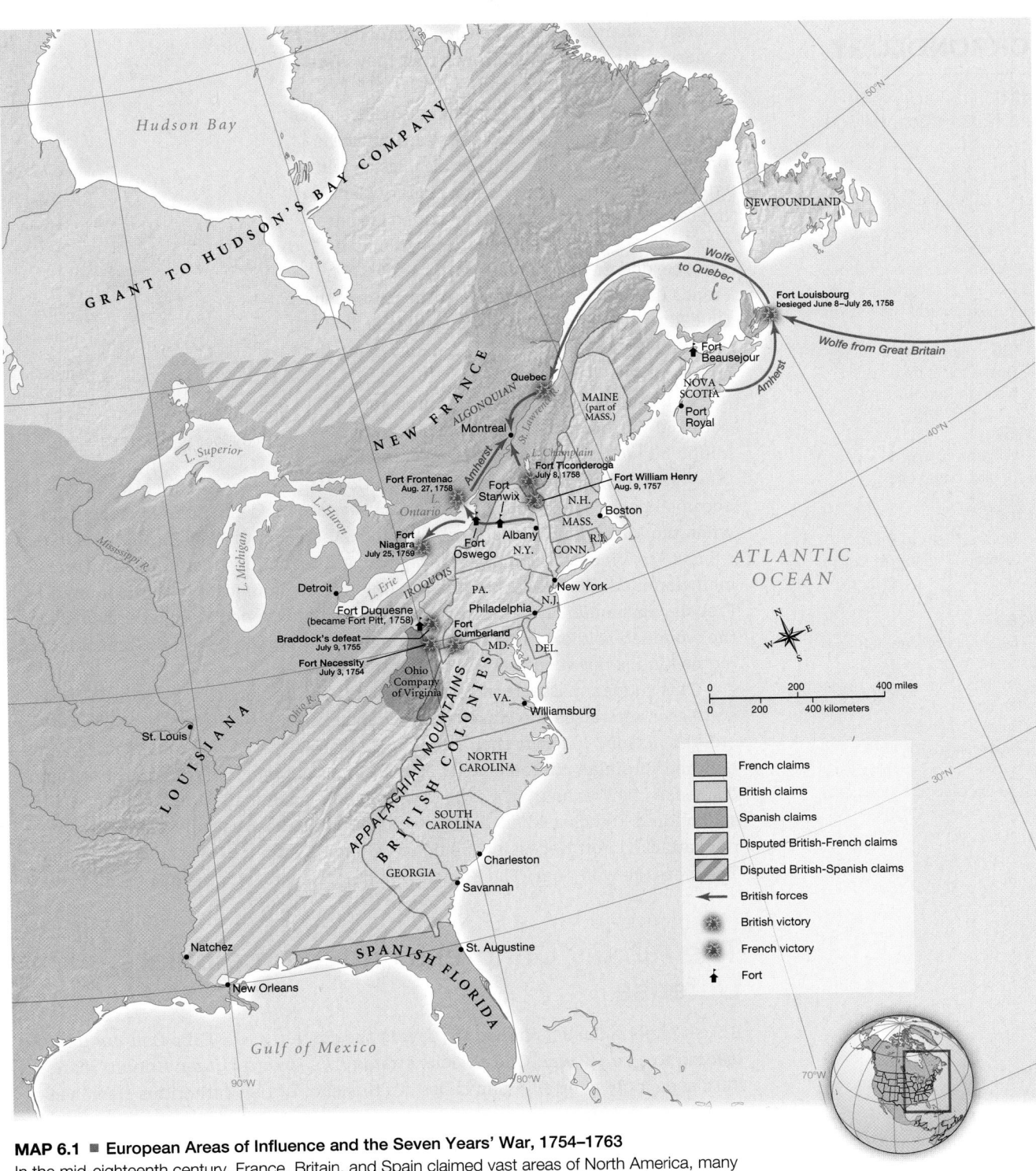

MAP 6.1 ■ European Areas of Influence and the Seven Years' War, 1754–1763
In the mid-eighteenth century, France, Britain, and Spain claimed vast areas of North America, many of them already inhabited by various Indian peoples. The early flash points of the Seven Years' War were in regions of disputed claims where the French had allied with powerful native groups—the Iroquois and the Algonquian tribes—to put pressure on the westward-moving British and Americans.

Why did the American colonists find offense with the Sugar and Stamp Acts of 1763–1765?	What were the colonial responses to the Townshend duties?	What led to the escalation of tensions after 1772?	What were the varieties of domestic insurrections in 1774–1775?	Conclusion: What changes did Americans want in 1775?

CHRONOLOGY

1747
- Ohio Company of Virginia is formed.

1754
- Seven Years' War begins in North America.
- Albany Congress proposes Plan of Union (never implemented).

1755
- Braddock is defeated in western Pennsylvania.

1757
- William Pitt fully commits Britain to war effort.

1760
- Montreal falls to British. George III becomes British king.

1763
- Treaty of Paris ends Seven Years' War.
- Pontiac's uprising increases tensions between Indians and British America.
- Proclamation of 1763 forbids colonists from settling west of the Appalachian Mountains.

himself a shareholder in the Ohio Company, sent a messenger to warn the French that they were trespassing on Virginia land.

The messenger on this dangerous mission was George Washington, twenty-one years old at the time. Washington returned from his mission with crucial intelligence about French military plans. Impressed, Dinwiddie appointed him to lead a small military expedition west to assert and, if need be, defend Virginia's claim. By early 1754, the French had built Fort Duquesne at the forks of the Ohio River; Washington's assignment was to chase the French away without actually being the aggressor.

In the spring of 1754, Washington set out with 160 Virginians and a small contingent of Mingo Indians, who were also concerned about the French military presence in the Ohio Country. The first battle of what would become known as the French and Indian War occurred early one May morning when the Mingo chief Tanaghrisson led a detachment of Washington's soldiers to a small French encampment in the woods. A brief skirmish left fourteen Frenchmen wounded. While Washington struggled to communicate with the injured French commander, Tanaghrisson and his men intervened to kill and then scalp the wounded soldiers, including the commander, probably with the aim of inflaming hostilities between the French and the colonists.

This sudden massacre violated Washington's instructions to avoid being the aggressor and raised the stakes considerably. Fearing retaliation, Washington ordered his men to fortify their position; "Fort Necessity" was the result. Several hundred Virginian reinforcements arrived; but the Mingos, sensing disaster and displeased by Washington's style of command, fled. In early July, more than six hundred French soldiers aided by one hundred Shawnee and Delaware warriors attacked Fort Necessity, killing or wounding a third of Washington's men. The message was clear: The French would not depart from the disputed territory.

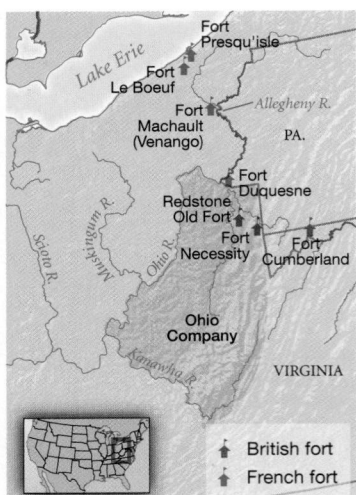

Ohio River Valley, 1753

The Albany Congress and Intercolonial Defense

British imperial leaders hoped to prevent the conflict in the Ohio Country from leading to a larger war. One obvious strategy was to strengthen British alliances with seemingly neutral Indian tribes. To this end, British authorities convened a colonial conference.

In June and July 1754, delegates from seven colonies met in Albany, New York. Also attending were Indians of the Iroquois Confederacy, an alliance of tribes inhabiting the central and western parts of present-day New York. Albany was the traditional meeting place of the Covenant Chain, first created in 1692 as a trade alliance of New York leaders and Mohawk Indians, the most easterly of the Iroquois Confederacy. In 1753, the Mohawk leader Hendrick accused the colonists of breaking the Covenant Chain. A prime goal of the Albany Congress was to

CHAPTER LOCATOR

How did the Seven Years' War lay the groundwork for colonial crisis?

The brave old Hendrick the great SACHEM or Chief of the Mohawk Indians one of the Six Nations now in Alliance with & Subject to the King of Great Britain

▶ FOR MORE HELP ANALYZING THIS IMAGE, see the visual activity for this chapter in the Online Study Guide at bedfordstmartins.com/roarkunderstanding.

repair trade relations with the Mohawks and secure their help—or at least their neutrality—against the French threat.

Benjamin Franklin of Pennsylvania and Thomas Hutchinson of Massachusetts had more ambitious plans. They coauthored the Albany Plan of Union, a proposal for a unified colonial government limited to war, defense policies, and relations with Indians.

Key Features of the Albany Plan of Union

A president general was to be appointed by the crown.

A grand council was to meet annually to consider questions of war, peace, and trade with the Indians.

The plan reaffirmed Parliament's authority and was not a bid for enlarged autonomy of the colonies.

Not a single colony approved the Albany Plan. The Massachusetts assembly feared it was "a Design of gaining power over the Colonies," especially the power of taxation. Others objected that it would be impossible to agree on unified policies toward scores of quite different Indian tribes. The British government never backed the Albany Plan either, and soon after it appointed two superintendents of Indian affairs, one for the northern and another for the southern colonies, each with exclusive powers to negotiate treaties, trade, and land sales with all tribes.

The Albany Congress had very limited success. The Covenant Chain alliance with the Mohawk tribe was reaffirmed, but other Indian nations left without

| Why did the American colonists find offense with the Sugar and Stamp Acts of 1763–1765? | What were the colonial responses to the Townshend duties? | What led to the escalation of tensions after 1772? | What were the varieties of domestic insurrections in 1774–1775? | Conclusion: What changes did Americans want in 1775? |

145

pledging to help the British battle the French. Some of the Iroquois figured that the French military presence around the Great Lakes would discourage the westward push of American colonists and therefore better serve their interests.

The War and Its Consequences

By 1755, Washington's frontier skirmish had turned into a major mobilization of British and American troops against the French. The British expected a quick victory on three fronts. General Edward Braddock marched his army toward Fort Duquesne in western Pennsylvania. Farther north, British troops moved toward Fort Niagara, critically located between Lakes Erie and Ontario. And New Yorker William Johnson led forces north toward Lake Champlain, intending to defend the border against the French in Canada (see Map 6.1, page 143).

Unfortunately for the British, the French were prepared to fight and had cemented alliances with many Indian tribes throughout the region. In July 1755, Braddock's army of 2,000 British soldiers rode west with Washington and Virginia militiamen and were ambushed by 250 French soldiers and 640 Indian warriors. Nearly 1,000 on the British side were killed or wounded, including General Braddock. Washington, who was unhurt, was commended for his bravery and promoted to commander of the Virginia army.

For the next two years, British leaders stumbled badly, deploying inadequate numbers of undersupplied troops. What finally turned the war around was the rise to power in 1757 of William Pitt, Britain's prime minister, a man willing to commit massive resources to fight France and its ally Spain worldwide. In America, British troops aided by American soldiers captured Forts Duquesne, Niagara, and Ticonderoga and then the French cities of Quebec and finally Montreal, all from 1758 to 1760. The American colonists rejoiced, but the war expanded globally, with battles in the Caribbean, Austria, Prussia, and India. By the end of 1762, France and Spain capitulated, and the Treaty of Paris was signed in 1763.

In the complex peace negotiations that followed, Britain gained control of Canada, eliminating the French threat from the north. In addition, British and American title to the eastern half of North America was confirmed. But French territory west of the Mississippi River, including New Orleans, was transferred to Spain as compensation for Spain's assistance during the war. Most significantly, two sugar-producing French islands in the Caribbean were returned to France (**Map 6.2**).

One key group, the Indians, was ignored by the Treaty of Paris. With the French gone, the Indians lost the advantage of having two opponents to play off against each other, and they now had to cope with the westward-moving Americans. Indian policy would soon become a serious point of contention between the British government and the colonists.

The British credited the British army for their victory, while criticizing the inadequate and ungrateful support of the colonists. Fueling resentment, during the war colonial smugglers kept up the trade in beaver pelts with the French as well as an illegal molasses trade in the Caribbean. William Pitt was convinced that these activities "principally, if not alone, enabled France to sustain and protract this long and expensive war."

Colonists read the lessons of the war differently. American soldiers had turned out in force, they claimed, but had been relegated to grunt work by British

CHAPTER LOCATOR

How did the Seven Years' War lay the groundwork for colonial crisis?

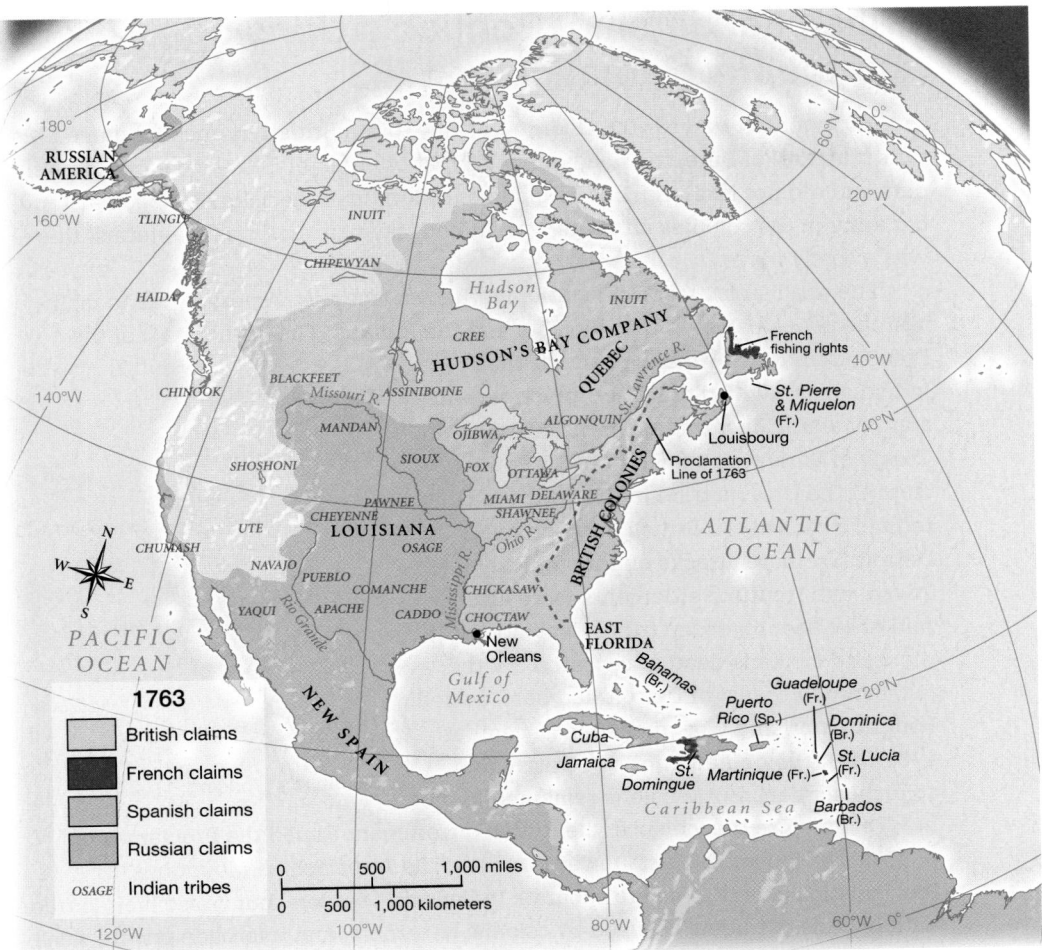

MAP 6.2 ■ North America after the Seven Years' War

In the peace treaty of 1763, France ceded to Britain its interior territory from Quebec to New Orleans, retaining fishing rights in the far north and several sugar islands in the Caribbean. France transferred to Spain its claim to extensive territory west of the Mississippi River.

> ▶ FOR MORE HELP ANALYZING THIS MAP, see the map activity for this chapter in the Online Study Guide at bedfordstmartins.com/roarkunderstanding.

leaders and subjected to unexpectedly harsh military discipline. General Braddock bragged to Benjamin Franklin that "these savages may, indeed, be a formidable enemy to your raw American militia, but upon the king's regular and disciplined troops, sir, it is impossible they should make any impression."

The human costs of the war were etched especially sharply in the minds of New England colonists. About one-third of all Massachusetts men between fifteen and thirty had seen service, and many families lost loved ones.

The enormous expense of the war cast another huge shadow over the victory. By 1763, Britain's national debt, double what it had been when Pitt took office, posed a formidable challenge to the next decade of leadership in Britain.

Why did the American colonists find offense with the Sugar and Stamp Acts of 1763–1765?	What were the colonial responses to the Townshend duties?	What led to the escalation of tensions after 1772?	What were the varieties of domestic insurrections in 1774–1775?	Conclusion: What changes did Americans want in 1775?

British Leadership, Pontiac's Uprising, and the Proclamation of 1763

In 1760, twenty-two-year-old George III came to the British throne and named his tutor, the Earl of Bute, the head of his cabinet of ministers. Bute committed blunders and did not last long, but he made one significant decision—to keep a standing army in the colonies after the war. In both financial and political terms, this was a costly move.

The ostensible reason for stationing British troops in America was to maintain the peace between the colonists and the Indians. The withdrawal of the French from North America had left their Indian allies—who did not accept defeat—in a state of alarm. Just three months after the Treaty of Paris was signed in 1763, Pontiac, chief of the Ottawa tribe in the northern Ohio region, attacked the British garrison near Detroit. Six more attacks on forts quickly followed, and frontier settlements were also raided by about a dozen tribes, leaving two thousand civilians dead or captured. By the fall, every fort west of Detroit had been seized. Pontiac's uprising was quelled in December 1763 by the combined efforts of British and colonial soldiers, but tensions remained high.

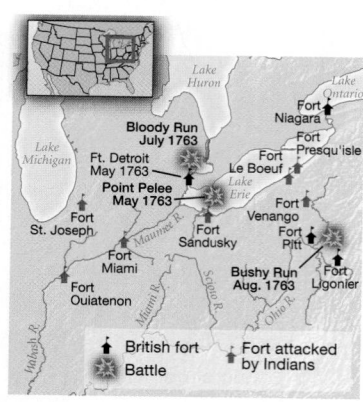

Pontiac's Uprising, 1763

Proclamation of 1763

▶ British proclamation forbidding colonists to settle west of the Appalachian Mountains. The Proclamation chiefly aimed to separate Indians and settlers, but it also limited trade with Indians to traders licensed by colonial governors, and it forbade private sales of Indian land.

To minimize the violence, the British government issued the **Proclamation of 1763**, forbidding colonists to settle west of the Appalachian Mountains. The Proclamation chiefly aimed to separate Indians and settlers, but it also limited trade with Indians to traders licensed by colonial governors, and it forbade private sales of Indian land. The Proclamation's language took care not to identify western lands as belonging to the Indians. And while other parts of the Proclamation of 1763 referred to American and even French colonists in Canada as "our loving subjects," the Indians were not described as British subjects.

The 1763 boundary proved impossible to enforce. Surging population growth had already sent many hundreds of settlers west of the Appalachians, and land speculators, such as those of Virginia's Ohio Company, had no desire to lose opportunities for profitable resale of their land grants. Bute's decision to post a standing army in the colonies was thus a cause for concern among western settlers, eastern speculators, and Indian tribes alike.

> QUICK REVIEW

How did the Seven Years' War erode relations between colonists and British authorities?

CHAPTER LOCATOR | How did the Seven Years' War lay the groundwork for colonial crisis?

148   CHAPTER 6
THE MAKING OF AN AMERICAN REVOLUTION, 1754–1775

Why did the
American colonists
find offense with
the Sugar and
Stamp Acts of
1763–1765?

George Grenville, Prime Minister 1763–1765

George Grenville gained the prime minister's job in 1763 at a point when King George was short of competent alternatives, but the king found him irksome: "When he has wearied me for two hours, he looks at his watch, to see if he may not tire me for an hour more," King George said. The king sacked him in July 1765 for being insolent, not for his controversial colonial policies. The Earl of Halifax, Garrowby, Yorkshire.

LORD BUTE LOST POWER in 1763, and King George turned to a succession of leaders throughout the 1760s, searching for a prime minister he could trust. A half dozen ministers in seven years took turns dealing with one basic, underlying British reality: A huge war debt needed to be serviced, and the colonists, as British subjects, should help pay it off. To many Americans, however, that proposition violated what they perceived to be their rights and liberties as British subjects, and it created resentment that eventually erupted in large-scale protests. The first provocative revenue acts were the work of Sir George Grenville, prime minister from 1763 to 1765.

Grenville's Sugar Act

To find revenue, George Grenville scrutinized the customs service, which monitored the shipping trade and collected all import and export duties. Grenville found that the salaries of customs officers cost the government four times what was collected in revenue. The shortfall was due in part to bribery and smuggling, so Grenville began to insist on rigorous attention to paperwork and a strict accounting of collected duties.

Why did the American colonists find offense with the Sugar and Stamp Acts of 1763–1765?	What were the colonial responses to the Townshend duties?	What led to the escalation of tensions after 1772?	What were the varieties of domestic insurrections in 1774–1775?	Conclusion: What changes did Americans want in 1775?

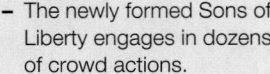
Sugar Act
▶ Officially called the Revenue Act, this 1764 British law lowered the duty on French molasses, making it more attractive for shippers to obey the law, and at the same time raised penalties for smuggling. Conflicts over the Sugar Act foreshadowed later colonial conflicts over taxation.

Stamp Act
▶ 1765 British law imposing a tax on all paper used for official documents and requiring an affixed stamp as proof that the tax had been paid. Unlike the Sugar Act, which regulated trade, the Stamp Act was designed simply to raise money. Widespread resistance to the Stamp Act led to its repeal in 1766.

virtual representation
▶ The theory that all British subjects were represented in Parliament, whether they had elected representatives in that body or not. American colonists rejected the theory of virtual representation, arguing that only direct representatives had the right to tax the colonists.

The hardest duty to enforce was the one imposed by the Molasses Act of 1733—a stiff tax of six pence per gallon on any molasses purchased from non-British sources. Rum-loving Americans, however, were eager to buy molasses from French Caribbean islands, and they had ignored the tax law for decades. Grenville's solution was the Revenue Act of 1764, popularly dubbed the **Sugar Act**. It lowered the duty on French molasses to three pence, making it more attractive for shippers to obey the law, and at the same time raised penalties for smuggling. The act appeared to be in the tradition of navigation acts meant to regulate trade, but Grenville's actual intent was to raise revenue.

The Sugar Act toughened enforcement policies. From now on, all British naval crews could act as impromptu customs officers, boarding suspicious ships and seizing cargoes found to be in violation. Smugglers caught without proper paperwork would be prosecuted, not in a local court with a friendly jury but in a vice admiralty court located in Nova Scotia, where a crown judge presided.

Grenville's hopes for the Sugar Act did not materialize. The small decrease in duty did not offset the attractions of smuggling, while the increased vigilance in enforcement led to several ugly confrontations in port cities. Reaction to the Sugar Act foreshadowed questions about Britain's right to tax Americans, but in 1764 objections to the act came principally from Americans in the shipping trades.

From the British point of view, the Proclamation of 1763 and the Sugar Act seemed to be reasonable efforts to administer the colonies. To the Americans, however, the British supervision appeared to be a disturbing intrusion into colonial practices.

The Stamp Act

In February 1765, Grenville escalated his revenue program with the **Stamp Act**, precipitating a major conflict between Britain and the colonies over Parliament's right to tax. The Stamp Act imposed a tax on all paper used for official documents—newspapers, pamphlets, court documents, licenses, wills, ships' cargo lists—and required an affixed stamp as proof that the tax had been paid. Unlike the Sugar Act, which regulated trade, the Stamp Act was designed simply to raise money. It affected nearly everyone who used any taxed paper but, most of all, users of official documents in the business and legal communities.

Anticipating that the stamp tax would be unpopular, Grenville delegated the administration of the act to Americans to avoid taxpayer hostility toward British enforcers. In each colony, local stamp distributors would be hired at a handsome salary of 8 percent of the revenue collected.

English tradition held that taxes were a gift of the people to their monarch, granted by the people's representatives. The king could not demand money; only the House of Commons could grant it. Grenville agreed with the notion of taxation by consent, but he argued that the colonists were already "virtually" represented in Parliament. The House of Commons, he insisted, represented all British subjects, wherever they were.

Colonial leaders emphatically rejected this view, arguing that **virtual representation** could not withstand the stretch across the Atlantic. The stamp tax itself, levied by a distant Parliament on unwilling colonies, illustrated the problem. In the words of a Maryland lawyer, virtual representation was "a mere cob-web, spread to catch the unwary, and entangle the weak."

CHAPTER LOCATOR | How did the Seven Years' War lay the groundwork for colonial crisis?

CHAPTER 6
150 THE MAKING OF AN AMERICAN REVOLUTION, 1754–1775

Resistance Strategies and Crowd Politics

News of the Stamp Act arrived in the colonies in April 1765, seven months before it was to take effect. There was time, therefore, to object. Governors were unlikely to challenge the law, for most of them owed their office to the king. Instead, the colonial assemblies took the lead; eight of them held discussions on the Stamp Act.

Virginia's assembly, the House of Burgesses, was the first. At the end of its May session, after two-thirds of the members had left, Patrick Henry, a young political newcomer, presented a series of resolutions on the Stamp Act, which were debated and passed, one by one. They became known as the Virginia Resolves. Henry's resolutions inched the assembly toward radical opposition to the Stamp Act. The first three stated the obvious: that Virginians were British citizens, that they enjoyed the same rights and privileges as Britons, and that self-taxation was one of those rights. The fourth resolution noted that Virginians had always taxed themselves, through their representatives in the House of Burgesses. The fifth took a radical leap by pushing the other four unexceptional statements to one logical conclusion—that the Virginia assembly alone had the right to tax Virginians.

Two more resolutions were debated as Henry pressed the logic of his case to the extreme. The sixth resolution denied legitimacy to any tax law originating outside Virginia, and a seventh boldly called anyone who disagreed with these propositions an enemy of Virginia. This was too much for the other representatives. They voted down resolutions six and seven and later rescinded their vote on number five as well.

Their caution hardly mattered, however, because newspapers in other colonies printed all seven Virginia Resolves, creating the impression that a daring first challenge to the Stamp Act had occurred. Consequently, other assemblies were willing to consider even more radical questions, such as this: By what authority could Parliament legislate for the colonies without also taxing them? No one disagreed, in 1765, that Parliament had legislative power over the colonists, who were, after all, British subjects. Several assemblies advanced the argument that there was a distinction between *external* taxes, imposed to regulate trade, and *internal* taxes, such as a stamp tax or a property tax, which could only be self-imposed.

Reaction to the Stamp Act ran far deeper than political debate in assemblies. Every person whose livelihood required official paper had to decide whether to comply with the act. The first organized resistance to the Stamp Act began in Boston in August 1765 under the direction of town leaders, chief among them Samuel Adams, John Hancock, and Ebenezer Mackintosh. Many other artisans, tradesmen, printers, tavern keepers, dockworkers, and sailors—the middling and lower orders—mobilized in resistance to the Stamp Act, taking the name "Sons of Liberty."

The plan hatched in Boston called for a large street demonstration highlighting a mock execution designed to convince Andrew Oliver, the designated stamp distributor, to resign. On August 14, 1765, a crowd of two thousand to three thousand demonstrators, led by the young shoemaker Mackintosh, hung an effigy of Oliver in a tree and then paraded it around town before finally beheading and burning it. In hopes of calming tensions, the royal governor Francis Bernard took no action. The next day Oliver resigned his office in a well-publicized announcement.

The demonstration provided lessons for everyone. Oliver learned that stamp distributors would be very unpopular people. Francis Bernard, the royal governor, learned the limitations of his power to govern, with no police force to call on. The demonstration's leaders learned that street action was effective. And hundreds

Why did the American colonists find offense with the Sugar and Stamp Acts of 1763–1765?	What were the colonial responses to the Townshend duties?	What led to the escalation of tensions after 1772?	What were the varieties of domestic insurrections in 1774–1775?	Conclusion: What changes did Americans want in 1775?

151

of ordinary men not only learned what the Stamp Act was all about but also gained pride in their ability to have a decisive impact on politics.

Twelve days later, a second crowd action showed how well these lessons had been learned. On August 26, a crowd visited the houses of three customs and court officials, breaking windows and raiding wine cellars. A fourth target was the finest dwelling in Massachusetts, owned by Thomas Hutchinson, lieutenant governor of Massachusetts and the chief justice of the colony's highest court. Rumors abounded that Hutchinson had urged Grenville to adopt the Stamp Act. Although he had actually done the opposite, Hutchinson refused to set the record straight, saying, "I am not obliged to give an answer to all the questions that may be put me by every lawless person." The crowd attacked his house, and by daybreak only the exterior walls were standing. Governor Bernard gave orders to call out the militia, but he was told that many militiamen were among the crowd.

The destruction of Hutchinson's house brought a temporary halt to protest activities in Boston. The town meeting issued a statement of sympathy for Hutchinson, but a large reward for the arrest and conviction of rioters failed to produce a single lead. Essentially, the opponents of the Stamp Act in Boston had triumphed; no one replaced Oliver as distributor. When the act took effect on November 1, ships without stamped permits continued to clear the harbor. Since he could not bring the lawbreakers to court, Hutchinson felt obliged to resign his office as chief justice. He remained lieutenant governor, however, and within five years he became the royal governor.

Liberty and Property

Boston's crowd actions of August sparked similar eruptions by groups calling themselves Sons of Liberty in nearly fifty towns throughout the colonies, and stamp distributors everywhere hastened to resign. One Connecticut distributor was forced by a crowd to throw his hat and powdered wig in the air while shouting a cheer for "Liberty and property!" In Charleston, South Carolina, the stamp distributor resigned after crowds burned effigies and chanted "Liberty! Liberty!"

Some colonial leaders, disturbed by the riots, sought a more moderate challenge to parliamentary authority. Twenty-seven delegates representing nine colonial assemblies met in New York City in October 1765 as the Stamp Act

CHAPTER LOCATOR | How did the Seven Years' War lay the groundwork for colonial crisis?

152 CHAPTER 6
THE MAKING OF AN AMERICAN REVOLUTION, 1754–1775

Congress. The result was a petition to the king and Parliament that closely resembled the first five Virginia Resolves, claiming that taxes were "free gifts of the people," which only the people's representatives could give. They dismissed virtual representation: "The people of these colonies are not, and from their local circumstances, cannot be represented in the House of Commons." At the same time, the delegates carefully affirmed their subordination to Parliament and their monarch in deferential language. Nevertheless, the Stamp Act Congress, by the mere fact of its meeting, advanced a radical potential—the notion of intercolonial political action.

The rallying cry of "Liberty and property" made perfect sense to many white Americans of all social ranks, who feared that the Stamp Act threatened their traditional right to liberty as British subjects. The liberty in question was the right to be taxed only by representative government. "Liberty and property" came from a trinity of concepts—"life, liberty, property"—that had come to be regarded as the birthright of freeborn British subjects since at least the seventeenth century. A powerful tradition of British political thought invested representative government with the duty to protect individual lives, liberties, and property against potential abuse by royal authority. Up to 1765, Americans had consented to accept Parliament as a body that represented them. But now, in this matter of taxation via stamps, Parliament seemed a distant body that had failed to protect Americans' liberty and property against royal authority.

Alarmed, some Americans began to speak and write about a plot by British leaders to enslave them. A Maryland writer warned that if the colonies lost "the right of exemption from all taxes without their consent," that loss would "deprive them of every privilege distinguishing freemen from slaves." The opposite meanings of *liberty* and *slavery* were clear to white Americans, but they stopped short of applying similar logic to enslaved black Americans. When a crowd of Charleston blacks paraded with shouts of "Liberty!" just a few months after white Sons of Liberty had done the same, the town militia turned out to break up the demonstration.

Politicians and merchants in Britain reacted with distress to the American demonstrations and petitions. Merchants particularly feared trade disruptions and pressured Parliament to repeal the Stamp Act. By late 1765, yet another new minister, the Marquess of Rockingham, headed the king's cabinet and sought a way to repeal the act without losing face. The solution came in March 1766: The Stamp Act was repealed, but with the repeal came the Declaratory Act, which asserted Parliament's right to legislate for the colonies "in all cases whatsoever." Perhaps the stamp tax had been inexpedient, but the power to tax—one prime case of a legislative power—was upheld.

QUICK REVIEW <

What rights did many Americans feel were challenged by the Sugar Act and the Stamp Act? How did they express their disapproval of the acts?

| Why did the American colonists find offense with the Sugar and Stamp Acts of 1763–1765? | What were the colonial responses to the Townshend duties? | What led to the escalation of tensions after 1772? | What were the varieties of domestic insurrections in 1774–1775? | Conclusion: What changes did Americans want in 1775? |

What were the colonial responses to the Townshend duties?

ROCKINGHAM did not last long as prime minister. By the summer of 1766, George III had persuaded William Pitt to resume that position. Pitt appointed Charles Townshend to be chancellor of the exchequer, the chief financial minister. Facing both the old war debt and the continuing cost of stationing British troops in America, Townshend turned again to taxation. His plan to raise revenue touched off coordinated boycotts of British goods in 1768 and 1769. Boston led the uproar, causing the British to send peacekeeping soldiers to assist the royal governor. The stage was thus set for the first fatalities in the brewing revolution.

The Townshend Duties

Townshend proposed new taxes in the old form of a navigation act. Officially called the Revenue Act of 1767, it established new duties on tea, glass, lead, paper, and painters' colors imported into the colonies, to be paid by the importer but passed on to consumers in the retail price. The **Townshend duties** were not especially burdensome, but the principle they embodied—taxation through trade duties—looked different to the colonists in the wake of the Stamp Act crisis. Although Americans once distinguished between external and internal taxes, accepting external duties as a means to direct the flow of trade, that distinction was wiped out by an external tax meant only to raise money. John Dickinson, a Philadelphia lawyer, articulated this view in a series of articles titled *Letters from a Farmer in Pennsylvania*, widely circulated in late 1767. "We are taxed without our consent. . . . We are therefore—SLAVES," Dickinson wrote, calling for "a total denial of the power of Parliament to lay upon these colonies any 'tax' whatever."

Townshend duties

▶ British law that established new duties on tea, glass, lead, paper, and painters' colors imported into the colonies, to be paid by the importer but passed on to consumers in the retail price. The Townshend duties (officially called the Revenue Act of 1767) led to boycotts and heightened tensions between Britain and the American colonies.

CHAPTER LOCATOR | How did the Seven Years' War lay the groundwork for colonial crisis?

154 CHAPTER 6
THE MAKING OF AN AMERICAN REVOLUTION, 1754–1775

A controversial provision of the Townshend duties directed that some of the revenue generated would pay the salaries of royal governors. Before 1767, local assemblies set the salaries of their own officials, giving them significant influence over crown-appointed officeholders. Townshend wanted to strengthen the governors' position as well as to curb the growing independence of the assemblies.

Massachusetts again took the lead in protesting the Townshend duties. Samuel Adams, now an elected member of the provincial assembly, argued that any form of parliamentary taxation was unjust because Americans were not represented in Parliament. Further, he argued that the new way to pay governors' salaries subverted the proper relationship between the people and their rulers. The assembly circulated a letter with Adams's arguments to other colonial assemblies for their endorsement. As with the Stamp Act Congress of 1765, colonial assemblies were starting to coordinate their protests.

In response to Adams's letter, the new man in charge of colonial affairs in Britain, Lord Hillsborough, instructed Massachusetts governor Bernard to dissolve the assembly if it refused to repudiate the letter. The assembly refused, by a vote of 92 to 17, and Bernard carried out his instruction. In the summer of 1768, Boston was in an uproar.

Nonconsumption and the Daughters of Liberty

The Boston town meeting led the way with nonconsumption agreements calling for a boycott of all British-made goods. Dozens of other towns passed similar resolutions in 1767 and 1768. For example, prohibited purchases in the town of New Haven, Connecticut, included imported carriages, furniture, lace, clocks, and textiles. The idea was to encourage home manufacture and to hurt trade, causing London merchants to pressure Parliament for repeal of the duties.

Nonconsumption agreements were very hard to enforce. With the Stamp Act, there was one hated item, a stamp, and a limited number of official distributors. In contrast, an agreement to boycott all British goods required serious personal sacrifices, sacrifices not everyone was prepared to make. A more direct blow to trade came from nonimportation agreements, but getting merchants to agree to these proved more difficult, because of fears that merchants in other colonies might continue to import goods and make handsome profits. Not until late 1768 could Boston merchants agree to suspend trade through a nonimportation agreement lasting one year starting January 1, 1769. Sixty signed the agreement. New York merchants soon followed suit, as did Philadelphia and Charleston merchants in 1769.

Many of the British products specified in nonconsumption agreements were household goods traditionally under the control of the "ladies." By 1769, male leaders in the patriot cause clearly understood that women's cooperation in nonconsumption and home manufacture was beneficial to their cause. The Townshend duties thus provided an unparalleled opportunity for encouraging female patriotism. During the Stamp Act crisis, Sons of Liberty took to the streets in protest. During the difficulties of 1768 and 1769, the Daughters of Liberty emerged, embodying the new idea that women might play a role in public affairs. Any woman could express affiliation with the colonial protest through conspicuous boycotts of British-made goods. In Boston, more than three hundred women signed a petition to abstain from tea, "sickness excepted," in order to "save this abused Country from Ruin and Slavery."

CHRONOLOGY

1767
- Parliament enacts Townshend duties.

1768
- British station troops in Boston.
- Merchants sign nonimportation agreements.

1770
- Boston Massacre.

Why did the American colonists find offense with the Sugar and Stamp Acts of 1763–1765?

What were the colonial responses to the Townshend duties?

What led to the escalation of tensions after 1772?

What were the varieties of domestic insurrections in 1774–1775?

Conclusion: What changes did Americans want in 1775?

155

Homespun cloth became a prominent symbol of patriotism. A young Boston girl learning to spin called herself "a daughter of liberty," noting that "I chuse to wear as much of our own manufactory as pocible." In the boycott period of 1768 to 1770, newspapers reported on spinning matches, or bees, in some sixty New England towns, in which women came together in public to make yarn. Newspaper accounts variously called the spinners "Daughters of Liberty" or "Daughters of Industry."

This surge of public spinning was related to the politics of the boycott, which infused traditional women's work with new political purpose. But the women spinners were not equivalents of the Sons of Liberty. The Sons marched in streets, burned effigies, threatened officials, and celebrated anniversaries of their successes with drinking in taverns. The Daughters manifested their patriotism quietly, in ways marked by piety, industry, and charity. The difference was due in part to cultural ideals of gender, which prized masculine self-assertion and feminine selflessness. It also was due to class. The Sons were a cross-class alliance, with leaders from the middling orders reliant on members of the lower ranks to fuel their crowds. The Daughters were genteel ladies used to buying British goods. The difference between the Sons and Daughters also speaks to two views of how best to challenge authority: violent threats and street actions, or the self-disciplined, self-sacrificing boycott of goods?

On the whole, the anti-British boycotts were a success. Imports fell by more than 40 percent; British merchants felt the pinch and let Parliament know it. Boston seemed overrun with anti-British sentiment, and both Lieutenant Governor Hutchinson and Governor Bernard concluded that British troops were necessary to restore order.

The Bloody Massacre Perpetrated in King Street, Boston, on March 5, 1770

This mass-produced engraving by Paul Revere sold for six pence per copy. In this patriot version of events, the soldiers fire on an unarmed crowd under orders of their captain. Among the five killed was Crispus Attucks, a black sailor, but Revere shows only whites among the casualties. Anne S. K. Brown Military Collection, Providence, R.I.

▶ FOR MORE HELP ANALYZING THIS IMAGE, see the visual activity for this chapter in the Online Study Guide at bedfordstmartins.com/roarkunderstanding.

CHAPTER LOCATOR

How did the Seven Years' War lay the groundwork for colonial crisis?

156 CHAPTER 6
THE MAKING OF AN AMERICAN REVOLUTION, 1754–1775

Military Occupation and "Massacre" in Boston

In the fall of 1768, three thousand uniformed troops arrived to occupy Boston. Although the situation was frequently tense, no major troubles occurred that winter and through most of 1769. But as January 1, 1770, approached, marking the end of the nonimportation agreement, it was clear that some merchants—such as Thomas Hutchinson's two sons, both importers—were ready to break the boycott.

Trouble began in January, when someone defaced the door of the Hutchinson brothers' shop with manure. In February, a crowd surrounded the house of customs official Ebenezer Richardson, who panicked and fired a musket, accidentally killing a young boy passing on the street. The Sons of Liberty mounted a massive funeral procession to mark this first instance of violent death in the struggle with Britain.

For the next week, tension gripped Boston. The climax came on Monday evening, March 5, 1770, when a crowd taunted eight British soldiers guarding the customs house. Onlookers threw snowballs and rocks and dared the soldiers to fire; finally one did. After a short pause, someone yelled "Fire!" and the other soldiers shot into the crowd, hitting eleven men, killing five of them.

In the immediate aftermath of the **Boston Massacre**, as the event quickly became called, Hutchinson (now acting governor after Bernard's recall to Britain) quickly removed the regiments to an island in the harbor to prevent further bloodshed, and he jailed Captain Thomas Preston and his eight soldiers for their own protection, promising they would be held for trial. Meanwhile, the Sons of Liberty staged elaborate martyrs' funerals for the five victims. Significantly, the one nonwhite victim, Crispus Attucks, shared equally in the public's veneration.

Crispus Attucks, a sailor and rope maker in his forties, was the son of an African man and a Natick Indian woman. A slave in his youth, he was at the time of his death a free laborer at the Boston docks. Attucks was one of the first American partisans to die in the American Revolution, and certainly the first African American.

The trial of the eight soldiers came in the fall of 1770. They were defended by two young Boston attorneys, Samuel Adams's cousin John Adams and Josiah Quincy. Because Adams and Quincy had direct ties to the leadership of the Sons of Liberty, their decision to defend the British soldiers at first seems odd. Beyond Adams's deep commitment to the principle that even unpopular defendants deserved a fair trial, there were strategic reasons to take on their defense. It showed that the Boston leadership was not lawless but could be seen as defenders of British liberty and law. The five-day trial resulted in acquittal for Preston and for all but two of the soldiers, who were convicted of manslaughter, branded on the thumbs, and released.

Boston Massacre

▶ March 1770 incident in Boston in which British soldiers fired on an American crowd, killing five and wounding six others. A five-day trial of the soldiers resulted in acquittal for all but two of them. The Boston Massacre became a rallying point for colonists who increasingly saw the British government as tyrannical and illegitimate.

QUICK REVIEW

Why were Boston's resistance to British policies and British reaction to this resistance so pronounced?

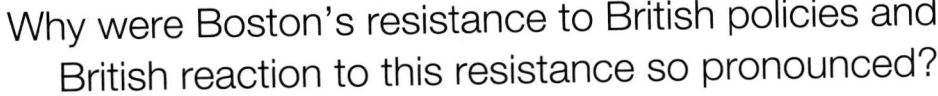

| Why did the American colonists find offense with the Sugar and Stamp Acts of 1763–1765? | **What were the colonial responses to the Townshend duties?** | What led to the escalation of tensions after 1772? | What were the varieties of domestic insurrections in 1774–1775? | Conclusion: What changes did Americans want in 1775? |

What led to the escalation of tensions after 1772?

IN THE SAME WEEK as the Boston Massacre, yet another new British prime minister, Frederick North, acknowledged the harmful impact of the boycott on trade and recommended repeal of the Townshend duties. Seeking peace with the colonies and prosperity for British merchants, North persuaded Parliament to remove all the duties except the tax on tea, kept as a symbol of Parliament's power. For nearly two years following repeal of the Townshend duties, peace seemed possible, but tense incidents in 1772, followed by a renewed struggle over the tea tax in 1773, precipitated a full-scale crisis that by 1775 resulted in war.

The Calm before the Storm

Repeal of the Townshend duties brought an end to nonimportation. Trade boomed in 1770 and 1771, driven by pent-up demand. Then in 1772, new troubles again brought the conflict with Britain into sharp focus. In Rhode Island, suspected smugglers burned the *Gaspée*, a Royal Navy ship. The British investigating commission announced that it would send suspects, if any were found, to Britain for trial on charges of high treason. This ruling seemed to fly in the face of the traditional English right to trial by a jury of one's peers.

When news of the *Gaspée* investigation spread, Patrick Henry, Thomas Jefferson, and Richard Henry Lee in the Virginia House of Burgesses proposed that a network of standing committees be established to link the colonial assemblies and facilitate the spread of alarming news. By mid-1773, every assembly except Pennsylvania's had its own **committees of correspondence**, linking hundreds of towns by express riders. These committees politicized ordinary townspeople, sparking a revolutionary language of rights and constitutional duties. They also bypassed the official flow of power and information through the colony's royal government.

committees of correspondence

▶ Committees first set up in Virginia in 1772 and in Massachusetts in 1773 to provide local forums for debate and to spread news about important political developments. These committees politicized ordinary townspeople, sparking a revolutionary language of rights and constitutional duties.

CHAPTER LOCATOR

How did the Seven Years' War lay the groundwork for colonial crisis?

The paramount incident shattering the relative calm of the early 1770s was the **Tea Act of 1773**. Americans had resumed buying the taxed British tea, but they were also smuggling large quantities of Dutch tea, cutting into the sales of Britain's East India Company. So Lord North proposed legislation giving favored status to the East India Company, allowing it to sell tea directly to government agents rather than through public auction to independent merchants. The hope was to lower the price of the East India tea, including the duty, below that of smuggled Dutch tea, motivating Americans to obey the law.

Tea in Boston Harbor

In the fall of 1773, news of the Tea Act reached the colonies. Parliamentary legislation to make tea inexpensive struck many colonists as a plot to trick Americans into buying the duties tea. The real goal, some argued, was the increased revenue, which would be used to pay the royal governors and judges.

But how to resist the Tea Act? Nonimportation was not viable, because the tea trade was too lucrative to expect merchants to give it up willingly. Consumer boycotts of duties tea seemed ineffective, because it was impossible to distinguish between duties tea and smuggled tea once it was in the teapot. The appointment of tea agents, parallel to the Stamp Act distributors, suggested one solution. In every port city, revived Sons of Liberty pressured tea agents to resign; without agents, governors yielded, and tea cargoes either landed without paperwork or were sent home.

Governor Hutchinson, however, would not bend any rules. Three ships bearing tea arrived in Boston in November 1773. They cleared customs and unloaded their other cargoes, but not the tea. Sensing the town's extreme tension, the captains wished to return to England, but Hutchinson would not grant them clearance to leave without paying the tea duty. He gave them twenty days to pay, after which time the tea would be confiscated.

For the full twenty days, pressure built in Boston. Daily mass meetings energized citizens from Boston and surrounding towns, alerted by the committees of correspondence. On the final day, December 16, a large crowd gathered at Old South Church to debate a course of action. No solution emerged at that meeting, but immediately following it, 100 to 150 men, disguised as Indians, boarded the ships and dumped thousands of pounds of tea into the harbor while a crowd of two thousand watched. In admiration, John Adams wrote: "This Destruction of the Tea is so bold, so daring, so firm, intrepid and inflexible, and it must have so important Consequences."

The Coercive Acts

In response, Lord North persuaded Parliament to issue the **Coercive (Intolerable) Acts**, four laws meant to punish Massachusetts for destroying the tea. A fifth act—the Quebec Act—had nothing to do with the four Coercive Acts, but it fed American fears by confirming the continuation of French civil law and government form, as well as Catholicism, for Quebec and by giving Quebec control of disputed land (and the lucrative fur trade) throughout the Ohio Valley. In America, these laws were soon known as the Intolerable Acts (**Table 6.1**).

The Intolerable Acts spread alarm in all the colonies. If Britain could squelch Massachusetts—change its charter, suspend local government, inaugurate military

Tea Act of 1773
▶ British act that gave favored status to the British East India Company, allowing it to sell tea directly to government agents rather than through public auction to independent merchants. The goal was to lower the price of the East India tea, including the duty, below that of smuggled Dutch tea, motivating Americans to obey the law. Resistance to the Tea Act led to the passage of the Coercive Acts and imposition of military rule in Massachusetts.

Coercive (Intolerable) Acts
▶ British acts of 1774 meant to punish Massachusetts for the destruction of a large amount of tea. Known in America as the Intolerable Acts, they led to open rebellion in the colonies.

| Why did the American colonists find offense with the Sugar and Stamp Acts of 1763–1765? | What were the colonial responses to the Townshend duties? | **What led to the escalation of tensions after 1772?** | What were the varieties of domestic insurrections in 1774–1775? | Conclusion: What changes did Americans want in 1775? |

159

TABLE 6.1 ■ The Coercive (Intolerable) Acts

1. Boston Port Act	Closed Boston harbor to all shipping as of June 1, 1774, until the destroyed tea was paid for. Britain's objective was to halt the commercial life of the city.
2. Massachusetts Government Act	Augmented the royal governor's powers. The governor could appoint the Massachusetts council, which before was elected. He could appoint and remove all judges, sheriffs, and officers of the court. Going forward, town meetings could be held only with the governor's approval.
3. Impartial Administration of Justice Act	Stipulated that any royal official accused of a capital crime would be tried in Britain. The act implied that there would be further violent confrontations between British soldiers and colonists.
4. Quartering Act	Permitted military commanders to lodge soldiers wherever necessary, even in private households, a step toward military rule in Massachusetts.
5. Quebec Act	Not directly related to the Coercive Acts, it gave control of disputed land throughout the Ohio Valley to Quebec.

rule, and on top of that give Ohio to Catholic Quebec—what liberties were secure? Fearful royal governors in half a dozen colonies dismissed the sitting assemblies, adding to the sense of urgency. A few of the assemblies defiantly continued to meet in new locations. Through the committees of correspondence, colonial leaders arranged to convene in Philadelphia in September 1774 to respond to the crisis.

Beyond Boston: Rural Massachusetts

By the time delegates assembled in Philadelphia, all of Massachusetts had arrived at the brink of open insurrection. With Thomas Gage, a British general, occupying the governorship and some three thousand troops controlling Boston, the revolutionary momentum shifted from urban radicals to rural farmers who protested the Massachusetts Government Act in dozens of spontaneous, dramatic showdowns. Some towns found creative ways to get around the prohibition on new town meetings, and others just ignored the law. Gage's call for elections for a new provincial assembly under his control sparked elections for a competing unauthorized assembly. In all counties except one, crowds of armed men converged to prevent the opening of county courts run by crown-appointed jurists. By late August 1774, farmers and artisans all over Massachusetts had effectively taken local control away from the crown.

One incident, the Powder Alarm, nearly provoked violence and showed how close New England farmers were to armed insurrection. Gage sent troops to capture a supply of gunpowder just outside Boston on September 1, and in the surprise and scramble of the attack, false news spread that the troops had fired on men defending the powder, killing six. Within twenty-four hours, several thousand armed men from Massachusetts and Connecticut streamed on foot to Boston seeking revenge. Once the error was corrected and the crisis defused, the men returned home peaceably. But Gage could no longer doubt the strength of rebellious sentiment.

CHAPTER LOCATOR

How did the Seven Years' War lay the groundwork for colonial crisis?

160 CHAPTER 6
THE MAKING OF AN AMERICAN REVOLUTION, 1754–1775

Ordinary Massachusetts citizens began serious planning for the crisis everyone assumed would come. Town militias stockpiled gunpowder "in case of invasion." Judges who had been willing crown appointees reversed their positions or started packing to leave. The new and unauthorized provincial assembly convinced towns to withhold tax money from the royal governor and divert it to military supplies. Gage beefed up fortifications around Boston and sent armed soldiers to stop meetings that quickly dispersed. Bolder action would have to wait until he could acquire a larger army.

The First Continental Congress

Every colony except Georgia sent delegates to Philadelphia in September 1774 to discuss the looming crisis in what was later called the **First Continental Congress**. Delegates sought to articulate their liberties as British subjects and the powers Parliament held over them, and they debated possible responses to the Coercive Acts. Some wanted a total ban on trade with Britain to force repeal, while others, especially southerners dependent on tobacco and rice exports, opposed halting trade. Samuel Adams and Patrick Henry were eager for a ringing denunciation of all parliamentary control. The conservative Joseph Galloway from Pennsylvania proposed a plan (quickly defeated) to create a secondary parliament in America to assist the British Parliament in ruling the colonies.

The congress met for seven weeks and produced a declaration of rights couched in traditional language: "We ask only for peace, liberty and security. We wish no diminution of royal prerogatives, we demand no new rights." But from Britain's point of view, the rights assumed already to exist were radical. Chief among them was the claim that Americans were not represented in Parliament and that therefore each colonial government had the sole right to govern and tax its own people.

To put pressure on Britain, the delegates agreed to a staggered and limited boycott of trade. To enforce the boycott, they called for a Continental Association, with chapters in each town variously called committees of public safety or of inspection, to monitor all commerce and punish suspected violators of the boycott. Its work done in a month, the congress disbanded in October, with agreement to convene the following May.

Britain's severe reaction to Boston's destruction of the tea finally succeeded in making many colonists from New Hampshire to Georgia realize that the problems of British rule went far beyond questions of taxation. The Coercive Acts infringed on liberty and denied self-government; they could not be ignored. With one colony already subordinated to military rule and a British army at the ready in Boston, the threat of a general war was on the doorstep.

First Continental Congress
► September 1774 gathering of colonial delegates in Philadelphia to discuss the crisis precipitated by the Coercive Acts. The congress met for seven weeks and produced a declaration of rights and an agreement to impose a limited boycott of trade with Britain.

QUICK REVIEW

In what ways did colonial responses to British actions change after 1772?

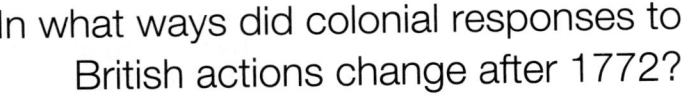

| Why did the American colonists find offense with the Sugar and Stamp Acts of 1763–1765? | What were the colonial responses to the Townshend duties? | What led to the escalation of tensions after 1772? | What were the varieties of domestic insurrections in 1774–1775? | Conclusion: What changes did Americans want in 1775? |

What were the varieties of domestic insurrections in 1774–1775?

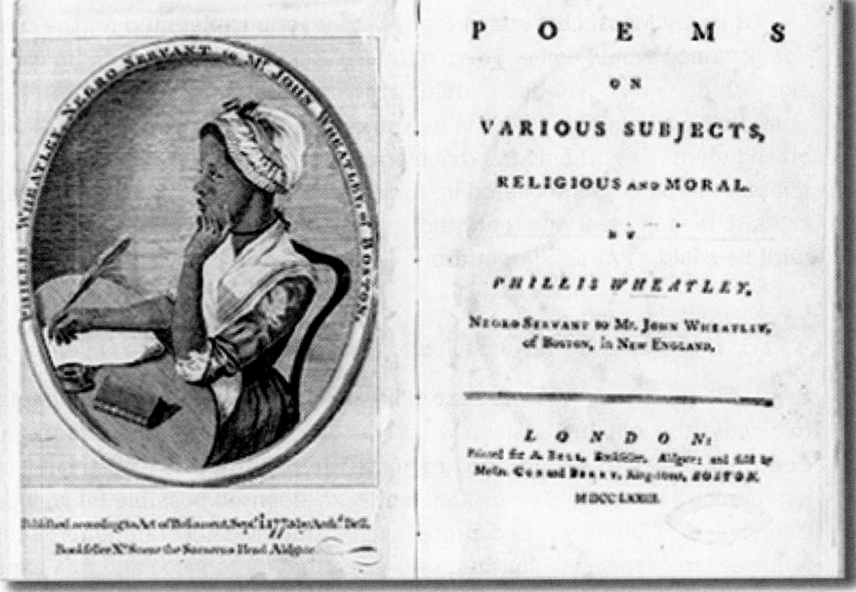

Phillis Wheatley's Title Page

Phillis, born in Africa, was sold into slavery to John Wheatley of Boston at age seven. She published her first poem at age twelve, in 1766. Her master took her to London in 1773, where this book was published, gaining her great literary notice. Library of Congress.

BEFORE THE SECOND CONTINENTAL CONGRESS could meet, violence and bloodshed came to Massachusetts. General Thomas Gage requested more troops from Britain and prepared to subdue rebellion. On the other side, New England farmers prepared to defend their homes against a power they feared was bent on enslaving them. To the south, a different and inverted version of the same story began to unfold, as thousands of enslaved black men and women seized an unprecedented opportunity to mount an insurrection of their own.

Lexington and Concord

During the winter of 1774–75, Americans pressed on with boycotts, hoping to force a repeal of the Coercive Acts, but pessimists stockpiled arms and ammunition. In Massachusetts, militia units known as minutemen prepared to respond at a minute's notice to any threat from the British troops in Boston.

Thomas Gage realized how desperate the British position was. The people, Gage wrote Lord North, were "numerous, worked up to a fury, and not a Boston rabble but the freeholders and farmers of the country." Gage requested twenty thousand reinforcements. He also strongly advised repeal of the Coercive Acts, but leaders in Britain could not admit failure. Instead, in mid-April 1775, they ordered Gage to arrest the troublemakers.

Gage quickly planned a surprise attack on a suspected ammunition storage site at Concord, a village eighteen miles west of Boston (**Map 6.3**). Near midnight

CHAPTER LOCATOR | How did the Seven Years' War lay the groundwork for colonial crisis?

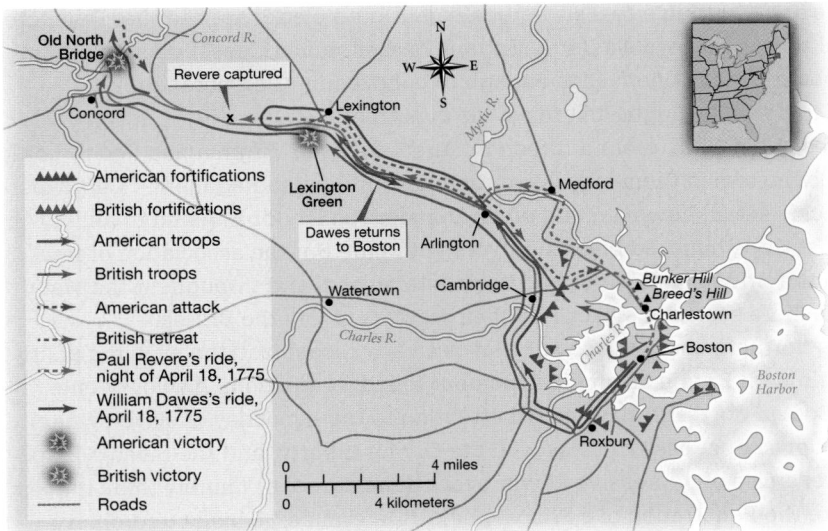

MAP 6.3 ■ Lexington and Concord, April 1775
Under pressure from Britain, some nine hundred British forces at Boston staged a raid on a suspected patriot arms supply in Concord, Massachusetts, starting the first battle of the Revolutionary War. The routes taken by Paul Revere and William Dawes to warn the patriots of the impending raid are marked.

CHRONOLOGY

1773
- Phillis Wheatley's *Poems on Various Subjects, Religious and Moral* is published in London.

1775
- General Gage is ordered to crack down on colonial resistance.

- Battles of Lexington and Concord.
- Lord Dunmore promises freedom to defecting slaves.
- Phillis Wheatley is freed by her master.
- Uprisings by slaves are discovered in New York, Maryland, and North Carolina.

on April 18, 1775, British soldiers moved west across the Charles River. Paul Revere and William Dawes raced ahead to alert the minutemen. When the soldiers got to Lexington, a village five miles east of Concord, they were met by some seventy armed men. The British commander barked out, "Lay down your arms, you damned rebels, and disperse." The militiamen hesitated and began to comply, but then someone—nobody knows who—fired. Within two minutes, eight Americans were dead and ten were wounded.

The British units continued their march to Concord, any pretense of surprise gone. Three companies of minutemen occupied the town center but offered no challenge to the British as they searched in vain for the ammunition. Finally, at Old North Bridge in Concord, troops and minutemen exchanged shots, killing two Americans and three British soldiers. As the British returned to Boston, militia units ambushed them, bringing the bloodiest fighting of the day. In the end, 273 British soldiers were wounded or dead; the toll for the Americans stood at about 95. It was April 19, 1775, and the war had begun.

Rebelling against Slavery

News of the battles of Lexington and Concord spread rapidly. Within eight days, Virginians had heard of the fighting, and, as Thomas Jefferson reflected, "a phrenzy of revenge seems to have seized all ranks of people." The royal governor of Virginia, Lord Dunmore, removed a large quantity of gunpowder from the Williamsburg powder house and put it on a ship, out of reach of the Virginians. Next, he threatened to arm slaves, if necessary, to ward off attacks by colonists.

In November 1775, seeking to frighten Virginia's planters, Dunmore issued an official proclamation promising freedom to defecting able-bodied slaves who would fight for the British. Dunmore had no intention, however, of liberating all

Why did the American colonists find offense with the Sugar and Stamp Acts of 1763–1765?	What were the colonial responses to the Townshend duties?	What led to the escalation of tensions after 1772?	**What were the varieties of domestic insurrections in 1774–1775?**	Conclusion: What changes did Americans want in 1775?

the slaves or of starting a real slave rebellion. Astute blacks noticed that Dunmore neglected to free his own slaves. A Virginia barber named Caesar declared that "he did not know any one foolish enough to believe him [Dunmore], for if he intended to do so, he ought first to set his own free."

By December 1775, around fifteen hundred slaves in Virginia had fled to Lord Dunmore, who armed them and called them his "Ethiopian Regiment." Camp diseases quickly set in, however, and when Dunmore sailed for England in mid-1776, he took just three hundred black survivors with him. But the association of freedom with the British authorities had been established, and throughout the war, thousands more southern slaves fled their masters to join the British.

In the northern colonies as well, slaves clearly recognized the evolving political struggle with Britain as an ideal moment to bid for freedom. A twenty-one-year-old Boston domestic slave called attention to the hypocrisy of slave owners in a 1774 newspaper essay: "How well the Cry for Liberty, and the reverse Disposition for exercise of oppressive Power over others agree,—I humbly think it does not require the Penetration of a Philosopher to Determine." This extraordinary young woman, **Phillis Wheatley**, had already gained international recognition through a book of poems published in London in 1773. Wheatley's poems spoke of "Fair Freedom" as the "Goddess long desir'd" by Africans enslaved in America. At the urging of his wife, Wheatley's master freed the young poet in 1775.

Wheatley's poetic ideas about freedom found concrete expression among other discontented groups. Some slaves in Boston petitioned Thomas Gage, promising to fight for the British if he would liberate them. Gage turned them down. In Ulster County, New York, along the Hudson River, a plot for an armed uprising that involved at least twenty slaves in four villages was discovered.

In Maryland, soon after the news of the Lexington battle arrived, blacks exhibited impatience with their status as slaves, causing one Maryland planter to report that "the insolence of the Negroes in this county is come to such a height, that we are under a necessity of disarming them. . . . We took about eighty guns, some bayonets, swords, etc." In North Carolina, a planned uprising was uncovered, and scores of slaves were arrested.

By 1783, when the Revolutionary War ended, as many as twenty thousand blacks had sought refuge with the British army. Most failed to achieve the liberation they were seeking. The British generally used them for menial labor, and disease, especially smallpox, devastated encampments of runaways. But some eight thousand to ten thousand persisted through the war and later, under the protection of the British army, left America to start new lives of freedom in Canada's Nova Scotia or Africa's Sierra Leone.

Phillis Wheatley

▶ A domestic slave in Boston who was also a published poet. Her writing drew attention to the hypocrisy of Americans' simultaneous embrace of slavery and the ideals of freedom in the years leading up to the American Revolution.

> **QUICK REVIEW**

What was the connection between rebelling against the British and rebelling against slavery?

CHAPTER LOCATOR

How did the Seven Years' War lay the groundwork for colonial crisis?

CHAPTER 6
164 THE MAKING OF AN AMERICAN REVOLUTION, 1754–1775

Conclusion: What changes did Americans want in 1775?

THE SEVEN YEARS' WAR set the stage for the imperial crisis of the 1760s and 1770s by creating distrust between Britain and its colonies and by running up a huge deficit in the British treasury. The years 1763 to 1775 brought repeated attempts by the British government to subordinate the colonies into taxpaying partners in the larger scheme of empire.

American resistance grew slowly but steadily over those years. By 1775, events propelled many Americans to the conclusion that a concerted effort was afoot to deprive them of all their liberties, the most important of which were the right to self-taxation, the right to live free of an occupying army, and the right to self-rule. Hundreds of minutemen converged on Concord, prepared to die for those liberties. April 19 marked the start of their rebellion.

Another rebellion under way in 1775 was doomed to be short-circuited. Black Americans who had experienced actual slavery listened to shouts of "Liberty!" from white crowds and applied the language of revolution to their own circumstances. Defiance of authority was indeed contagious.

The emerging leaders of the patriot cause were mindful of a delicate balance they felt they had to strike. To energize the American public about the crisis with Britain, they had to politicize masses of men—and eventually women, too—and infuse them with a keen sense of their rights and liberties. But in doing so, they became fearful of the unintended consequences of teaching a vocabulary of rights and liberties.

Patriot leaders in 1765 wanted a correction, a restoration of an ancient liberty of self-taxation that Parliament seemed to be ignoring. But events from 1765 to 1775 convinced many that a return to the old ways was impossible. Challenging Parliament's right to tax had led, step-by-step, to challenging Parliament's right to legislate over the colonies in any matter. If Parliament's sovereignty was set aside, who actually had authority over the American colonies? By 1775, with the outbreak of fighting and the specter of slave rebellions, American leaders turned to the king for the answer to that question.

SO NOW YOU KNOW

Colonial women and men showed their opposition to British policies through a variety of collective actions, including boycotts and public demonstrations. By 1775, Britain's relationship with its American colonies reached a crisis point as armed conflict broke out in Lexington and Concord and American patriots began to consider independence as their best option.

CHAPTER 6 STUDY GUIDE

Online Study Guide
bedfordstmartins.com/roarkunderstanding

STEP 1 GETTING STARTED

Below are basic terms from this period in American history. Can you identify each term below and explain why it matters? To do this exercise online or to download this chart, visit bedfordstmartins.com/roarkunderstanding.

TERM	WHO OR WHAT & WHEN	WHY IT MATTERS
Seven Years' War, p. 142		
Proclamation of 1763, p. 148		
Sugar (Revenue) Act, p. 150		
Stamp Act, p. 150		
virtual representation, p. 150		
Townshend duties, p. 154		
Boston Massacre, p. 157		
committees of correspondence, p. 158		
Tea Act of 1773, p. 159		
Coercive (Intolerable) Acts, p. 159		
First Continental Congress, p. 161		
Phillis Wheatley, p. 162		

STEP 2 MOVING BEYOND THE BASICS

The exercise below represents a more advanced understanding of the chapter material. Examine the escalation of tensions between Britain and its North American colonies. Fill in the following chart by describing the key pieces of British legislation aimed at the colonies between 1763 and 1774, the British rationale for each act, and the colonial response. To do this exercise online or to download the chart, visit bedfordstmartins.com/roarkunderstanding.

Legislation	Provisions	British rationale	Colonial response
Proclamation of 1763			
Sugar (Revenue) Act			
Stamp Act			
Townshend duties			
Tea Act of 1773			
Coercive (Intolerable) Acts			

STEP 3

PUTTING IT ALL TOGETHER

Now that you've reviewed various parts of the chapter, take a step back and try to see the big picture by answering these questions. Remember to use specific examples from the chapter in your answers. To do this exercise online, visit bedfordstmartins.com/roarkunderstanding.

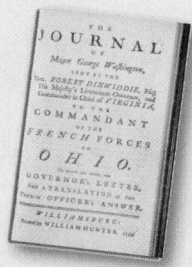

THE SEVEN YEARS' WAR

► How did the outcome of the Seven Years' War change the European balance of power in North America?

► How did British and colonial views of the war and its consequences differ?

TAXING THE COLONIES

► Why did some colonists see British efforts to tax the colonies as illegitimate? How did the British justify their efforts to raise revenue?

► What different groups, both in the colonies and in Great Britain, encouraged Parliament to repeal various taxes? What were their motives?

THE ESCALATION OF THE CONFLICT

► Why was the Tea Act so provocative? How did some colonists protest its passage?

► How did the British response to these protests, and the colonial reaction, help put Britain and the colonies on the path toward war?

LOOKING BACKWARD, LOOKING AHEAD

► How did the relationship between Britain and its North American colonies before 1763 differ from the relationship after 1763?

► Was war between Britain and the colonies inevitable after 1774? Why or why not?

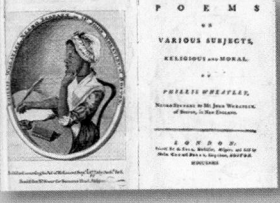

IN YOUR OWN WORDS

Imagine that you must explain chapter 6 to someone who hasn't read it. What would be the most important points to include and why?

7 FIGHTING THE AMERICAN REVOLUTION

1775–1783

> This chapter follows the course of the American Revolution from the Declaration of Independence in 1776 to the signing of the Treaty of Paris in 1783. It examines the events that led up to the Declaration of Independence, the early military strategies of both sides, the experience of war on the home front, the role of Indians and the French in the war, and the events that culminated in a seemingly improbable British defeat.

> Why did the Americans declare their independence?

> What initial challenges did the opposing armies face?

> What role did the home front play in the war?

> How were Native Americans and the French involved in the American Revolution?

> Why did the British southern strategy ultimately fail?

> Conclusion: Why did the British lose the American Revolution?

DID YOU KNOW?

In 1776, about three-fifths of the American colonists either supported the British or were undecided about independence.

A crowd pulls down the statue of King George III in New York City, July 9, 1776, following a formal reading of the Declaration of Independence.

Why did the Americans declare their independence?

Printed copies of the Declaration of Independence were read aloud in public places throughout America in the week after July 4, 1776. Library of Congress.

ON MAY 10, 1775, nearly one month after the fighting at Lexington and Concord, the Second Continental Congress assembled in Philadelphia. The delegates at the congress immediately set to work on two crucial but contradictory tasks: to raise and supply an army and to explore reconciliation with Britain. To do the former, they needed soldiers and a commander, they needed money, and they needed to work out a declaration of war. To do the latter, however, they needed diplomacy to approach the king. But the king was not receptive, and by 1776, as the war progressed and hopes of reconciliation faded, delegates at the congress began to ponder the treasonous act of declaring independence.

Second Continental Congress

▶ Legislative body that governed the United States during the first several years of the Revolutionary War. The Second Continental Congress met for the first time in May 1775 and began preparing for war while pursuing the possibility of reconciliation with Britain. On July 4, 1776, with all hope of peaceful reconciliation with Britain gone, the congress declared independence.

Assuming Political and Military Authority

The delegates to the **Second Continental Congress** had to learn to know and trust one another. Moreover, they did not always agree. The Adams cousins John and Samuel defined the radical end of the spectrum, favoring independence. John Dickinson of Pennsylvania, no longer the eager revolutionary who wrote *Letters from a Farmer* in 1767 (see chapter 6), was now a moderate, seeking reconciliation with Britain. Benjamin Franklin was feared by some to be a British spy. Mutual suspicions flourished easily when the undertaking was so dangerous, opinions were so varied, and a misstep could spell disaster.

Most of the delegates were not yet prepared to break with Britain. Some felt that government without a king was unworkable, while others feared it might be

Abigail Adams

Abigail Smith Adams was twenty-two when she sat for this pastel portrait in 1766. Pearls and a lace collar anchor her femininity, while her facial expression projects a confidence and maturity not often credited to young women of the 1760s. A decade later, she was running the family's Massachusetts farm while her husband, John, attended the Continental Congress in Philadelphia. Her frequent letters gave him the benefit of her sage advice on politics and the war. Courtesy of the Massachusetts Historical Society.

CHRONOLOGY

1775
- Second Continental Congress convenes.
- British win battle of Bunker Hill.
- King George rejects Olive Branch Petition.

1776
- Thomas Paine's *Common Sense*, making the case for independence, is published.
- British evacuate Boston.
- **July 4.** Congress adopts the Declaration of Independence.

suicidal to lose Britain's protection against its traditional enemies, France and Spain. Colonies that traded actively with Britain feared undermining their economies. Probably the vast majority of ordinary Americans were unable to envision complete independence from the monarchy.

The few men at the Continental Congress who did think that independence was desirable were, not surprisingly, from Massachusetts, the target of the Coercive Acts. Even so, those men knew that it was premature to push for a break with Britain. John Adams wrote his wife, Abigail, in June 1775: "America is a great, unwieldy body. Its progress must be slow. It is like a large fleet sailing under convoy. The fleetest sailors must wait for the dullest and slowest."

Yet swift action was needed, for the Massachusetts countryside was under threat of further attack. Even the hesitant moderates in the congress agreed that a military buildup was necessary. Around the country, militia units from New York to Georgia collected arms and drilled on village greens in anticipation. On June 14, the congress voted to create the Continental army, choosing a Virginian, **George Washington**, as commander in chief. Washington's appointment sent the clear message that there was widespread commitment to war beyond New England.

Next the congress drew up a document titled "A Declaration on the Causes and Necessity of Taking Up Arms," which rehearsed familiar arguments about the tyranny of Parliament and the need to defend English liberties. This declaration was first drafted by a young Virginia planter, Thomas Jefferson, a radical on the question of independence. The moderate John Dickinson, fearing that the declaration would offend Britain, was allowed to rewrite it. However, he left intact much of Jefferson's highly charged language about choosing "to die freemen rather than to live slaves."

To pay for the military buildup, the congress authorized a currency issue of $2 million. The Continental dollars were merely paper; they were not backed by gold or silver. The delegates somewhat naively expected that the currency would be accepted as valuable on trust as it spread in the population through the hands of soldiers, farmers, munitions suppliers, and beyond.

In just two months, the Second Continental Congress had created an army, declared war, and issued its own currency. It had taken on the major functions of a

George Washington

▶ Commander in chief of the Continental army. Washington had gained considerable military experience during the French and Indian War. Congress's selection of Washington, a Virginian, as commander in chief in 1775 also sent a clear signal that there was widespread commitment to war beyond New England.

| What initial challenges did the opposing armies face? | What role did the home front play in the war? | How were Native Americans and the French involved in the American Revolution? | Why did the British southern strategy ultimately fail? | Conclusion: Why did the British lose the American Revolution? |

legitimate government, both military and financial, without any legal basis for its authority. It had not yet, however, declared independence from the authority of the king.

Pursuing Both War and Peace

Three days after the congress established the army, one of the bloodiest battles of the Revolution occurred. The British commander in Boston, Thomas Gage, had recently received troop reinforcements, three talented generals (William Howe, John Burgoyne, and Henry Clinton), and new instructions to attack the Massachusetts rebels. But before Gage could take the offensive, the Americans fortified the hilly terrain of Charlestown, a peninsula just north of Boston, on the night of June 16, 1775.

General Howe insisted on a bold frontal assault, sending 2,500 soldiers across the water and up the hill in an intimidating but potentially costly attack. Three bloody assaults were needed before the British took the hill, the third succeeding mainly because the American ammunition supply gave out, and the defenders quickly retreated. The battle of Bunker Hill was thus a British victory, but an expensive one. On the British side, the dead numbered 226, with more than 800 wounded; the Americans suffered 140 dead, 271 wounded, and 30 captured.

Instead of pursuing the fleeing Americans, Howe retreated to Boston, unwilling to risk more raids into the countryside. If the British had had any grasp of the basic instability of the American units around Boston, they might have decisively defeated the Continental army in its infancy. Instead, they lingered in Boston, abandoning it without a fight nine months later.

A week after Bunker Hill, when General Washington arrived to take charge of the new Continental army, he found enthusiastic but undisciplined troops. Sanitation was an unknown concept, with inadequate latrines fouling the campground. Washington attributed the disarray to the New England custom of letting militia units elect their own officers, which he felt undermined deference. Washington quickly imposed more hierarchy and authority. "Discipline is the soul of the army," he stated.

While military plans moved forward, the Second Continental Congress pursued its contradictory objective: reconciliation with Britain. Delegates from the middle colonies (Pennsylvania, Delaware, and New York), whose merchants depended on trade with Britain, urged that channels for negotiation remain open. In July 1775, congressional moderates led by John Dickinson engineered an appeal to the king called the Olive Branch Petition. The petition affirmed loyalty to the monarchy and blamed all the troubles on the king's ministers and on Parliament. It proposed that the American colonial assemblies be recognized as individual parliaments under the umbrella of the monarchy. King George III rejected the Olive Branch Petition and heatedly condemned the Americans as traitors.

Thomas Paine, Abigail Adams, and the Case for Independence

Pressure for independence started to mount in January 1776, when a pamphlet titled *Common Sense* appeared in Philadelphia. Thomas Paine, its author, was an English artisan and coffeehouse intellectual who had come to America in the fall of

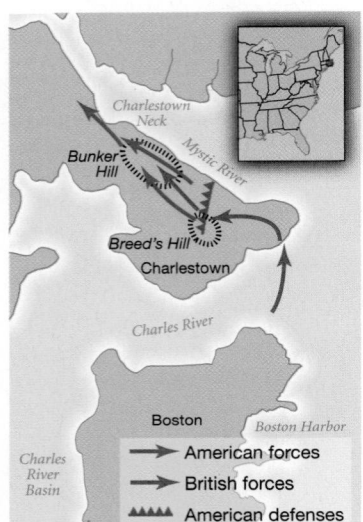

Battle of Bunker Hill, 1775

Common Sense
▶ Pamphlet written by Thomas Paine in 1776 that laid out the case for independence. In it, Paine rejected monarchy, advocating its replacement with republican government based on the consent of the people. The pamphlet sold more than 150,000 copies in a matter of weeks and influenced public opinion throughout the colonies.

1774. With the encouragement of members of the Second Continental Congress, he wrote *Common Sense*.

In simple yet forceful language, Paine elaborated on the absurdities of the British monarchy. Why should one man, by accident of birth, claim extensive power over others? he asked. A king might be foolish or wicked. "One of the strongest natural proofs of the folly of hereditary right in kings," Paine wrote, "is that nature disapproves it; otherwise she would not so frequently turn it into ridicule by giving mankind *an ass for a lion*." To replace monarchy, Paine advocated republican government based on the consent of the people. Rulers, according to Paine, were only representatives of the people, and the best form of government relied on frequent elections to achieve the most direct democracy possible.

Paine's pamphlet sold more than 150,000 copies in a matter of weeks. Newspapers reprinted it; men read it aloud in taverns and coffeehouses; John Adams sent a copy to his wife, Abigail, who passed it around to neighbors in Braintree, Massachusetts. New Englanders desired independence, but other colonies, under no immediate threat of violence, remained cautious.

Abigail Adams was impatient not only for independence but also for other legal changes that would revolutionize the new country. In a series of astute letters to her husband, she outlined obstacles and gave advice. She worried that southern slave owners might shrink from a war in the name of liberty: "I have sometimes been ready to think that the passion for Liberty cannot be Equally strong in the Breasts of those who have been accustomed to deprive their fellow Creatures of theirs." And in March 1776, she expressed her hope that women's legal status would improve under the new government: "In the new Code of Laws which I suppose it will be necessary for you to make I desire you would Remember the Ladies, and be more generous and favourable to them than your ancestors."

John Adams dismissed his wife's concerns. But to a male politician, Adams privately rehearsed the reasons why women (and free black men, propertyless men, and young people) should remain excluded from political participation. Even though he concluded that nothing should change, at least Abigail's letter had forced him to ponder the exclusion, something few men—or women—did in 1776.

The Declaration of Independence

In addition to Paine's *Common Sense*, another factor hastening independence was the prospect of an alliance with France, Britain's archrival. France was willing to provide military supplies and naval power only if assured that the Americans would separate from Britain. By May, all but four colonies were agitating for a declaration.

George Washington's Copy of Thomas Paine's *Common Sense*

Thomas Paine, a recent immigrant to America, wrote *Common Sense* to advance the debate on independence. Although the pamphlet sold more than 150,000 copies, he made no profit on it personally but instead donated proceeds to the Revolutionary cause. Shown here is George Washington's personal copy, with his name inscribed at the top. Boston Athenaeum.

Abigail Adams

▶ Wife of John Adams, Massachusetts delegate to the Second Continental Congress, and advocate for the improvement of women's legal status. In a series of astute letters to her husband, she outlined obstacles to independence and gave advice. She particularly urged John Adams to help end husbands' legal dominion over wives.

| What initial challenges did the opposing armies face? | What role did the home front play in the war? | How were Native Americans and the French involved in the American Revolution? | Why did the British southern strategy ultimately fail? | Conclusion: Why did the British lose the American Revolution? |

The holdouts were Pennsylvania, Maryland, New York, and South Carolina, the latter two containing large loyalist populations. An exasperated Virginian wrote to his friend in the congress, "For God's sake, why do you dawdle in the Congress so strangely? Why do you not at once declare yourself a separate independent state?"

In early June, the Virginia delegation introduced a resolution calling for independence. The moderates still commanded enough support to postpone a vote on the measure until July. In the meantime, the congress appointed a committee, with Thomas Jefferson and others, to draft a longer document setting out the case for independence.

On July 2, after intense politicking, all but one state voted for independence; New York abstained. The congress then turned to the document drafted by Jefferson and his committee. Jefferson began with a preamble that articulated philosophical principles about natural rights, equality, the right of revolution, and the consent of the governed as the only true basis for government. He then listed more than two dozen specific grievances against King George. The congress passed over the preamble with little comment, as though startling ideas about natural rights, the equality of all men, and the consent of the governed were indeed "self-evident truths."

For two days, the congress wrangled over the list of grievances, especially the issue of slavery. Jefferson had included an impassioned statement blaming the king for slavery, which delegates from Georgia and South Carolina struck out. They had no intention of denouncing their labor system as an evil practice. But the congress let stand another of Jefferson's grievances, blaming the king for mobilizing "the merciless Indian Savages" into bloody frontier warfare, a reference to Pontiac's uprising (see chapter 6).

On July 4, the amendments to Jefferson's text were complete, and the congress formally adopted the **Declaration of Independence**. A month later, the delegates gathered to sign the official parchment copy. Four men, including John Dickinson, declined to sign; several others "signed with regret . . . and with many doubts," according to John Adams. The document was then printed, widely distributed, and read aloud in celebrations everywhere. (Printed copies did not include the signers' names, for they had committed treason, a crime punishable by death.) On July 15, the New York delegation switched from abstention to endorsement, making the vote on independence unanimous.

Declaration of Independence

▶ The formal declaration of separation from Britain adopted by the Second Continental Congress on July 4, 1776. A period of intense debate preceded the call for independence, as many moderates still hoped to reconcile with Britain. The document included a statement of philosophical principles and a list of grievances.

> **QUICK REVIEW**

Why were many Americans initially reluctant to pursue independence from Britain? What changed their minds?

What initial challenges did the opposing armies face?

Backcountry Riflemen

A German officer with the British army drew this sketch of two American riflemen, dressed in rustic hunting shirts and leggings. One wears moccasins; the other is barefoot. Their celebrated ability to hit small targets at great distances and their willingness to snipe from behind trees and aim particularly at officers made them a terror to the British. Ten companies of riflemen were recruited in 1775 from western Pennsylvania and Virginia. General Washington worried that they were too undisciplined to make good soldiers, but others suggested that the trademark hunting shirt should become the Continental army uniform for all soldiers, just for the fear it provoked in the enemy. Anne S. K. Brown Military Collection, Brown University Library.

BOTH SIDES APPROACHED the war for America with uneasiness. The Americans, with inexperienced militias, were opposing the mightiest military power in the world. Also, their country was not unified; many people remained loyal to Britain. The British faced serious obstacles as well. Their disdain for the fighting abilities of the Americans required reassessment in light of the Bunker Hill battle. The logistics of supplying an army with food across three thousand miles of water were daunting. And since the British goal was to regain allegiance, not to destroy and conquer, the army was often constrained in its actions.

The American Military Forces

Americans claimed that the initial months of war were purely defensive, triggered by the British invasion. But the war also quickly became a rebellion, an overthrowing of long-established authority. As both defenders and rebels, many Americans were highly motivated to fight, and the potential manpower that could be mobilized was, in theory, very great.

What initial challenges did the opposing armies face?	What role did the home front play in the war?	How were Native Americans and the French involved in the American Revolution?	Why did the British southern strategy ultimately fail?	Conclusion: Why did the British lose the American Revolution?

1775
- Americans lose battle of Quebec.

1776
- British take Manhattan.
- **December 25.** Washington captures German troops stationed along the Delaware River.

Continental army

▶ The army created in June 1775 by the Second Continental Congress to oppose the British. George Washington was selected as its commander in chief and given the task of turning a collection of local militias and untrained volunteers into a disciplined army. British reluctance to follow up early victories allowed the Continental army to develop into an effective fighting force.

Local defense in the colonies had long rested with a militia composed of all able-bodied men over age sixteen. Militias, however, were best suited for limited engagements, such as conflicts with Indians, not for extended wars. In forming the **Continental army**, the congress set enlistment at one year, but leaders soon learned that was inadequate to train and deploy soldiers. A three-year enlistment earned a new soldier a $20 bonus, while men who committed for the duration were promised a postwar land grant of one hundred acres. Over the course of the war, some 230,000 men enlisted, about one-quarter of the white male adult population.

Women also served in the Continental army, cooking, washing, and nursing the wounded. Close to 20,000 "camp followers," as they were called, served during the war. Children also tagged along, and babies were born in the camps.

Black Americans were at first excluded from the Continental army. But as manpower needs increased, northern states welcomed free blacks into service; slaves in some states could serve with their masters' permission. About 5,000 black men served in the Revolutionary War on the rebel side, nearly all from the northern states. Black soldiers sometimes were segregated into separate units, and, while some of these men were draftees, others were clearly inspired by ideals of freedom in a war against tyranny. For example, twenty-three blacks gave "Liberty," "Freedom," and "Freeman" as their surnames at the time of enlistment.

Military service helped politicize Americans during the early stages of the war. But as the war heated up and recruiters demanded commitment, some Americans discovered that apathy had its dangers as well. Anyone who refused to serve ran the risk of being called a traitor to the cause. Military service became a prime way of demonstrating political allegiance.

The American army was at times raw and inexperienced, and often woefully undermanned. It never had the precision and discipline of European professional armies. But it was never as bad as the British continually assumed.

The British Strategy

The American strategy was straightforward—to repulse and defeat an invading army. The British strategy was not as clear. Britain wanted to put down a rebellion and restore monarchical power in the colonies, but the question was how to accomplish this. A decisive defeat of the Continental army was essential but not sufficient to end the rebellion, for the British would still have to contend with an armed and motivated insurgent population. Furthermore, there was no single political nerve center whose capture would spell certain victory. The Continental Congress moved from place to place, staying just out of reach of the British. During the course of the war, the British captured and occupied every major port city, but that brought no serious loss to the Americans, 95 percent of whom lived in the countryside.

Britain's task was to restore the old governments, not to destroy an enemy country. British generals were reluctant to ravage the countryside, confiscate food, or burn villages. With thirteen distinct political entities to capture, pacify, and restore to the crown, stretching from New Hampshire to Georgia, Britain needed a large land army to do the job. Without the willingness to seize food from the locals, the British needed hundreds of supply ships—hence their desire to

CHAPTER LOCATOR | Why did the Americans declare their independence?

capture the ports. The British strategy also assumed that many Americans remained loyal to the king and would come to their aid.

The overall British plan was a divide-and-conquer approach, focusing first on New York, the state judged to have the greatest number of loyal subjects. New York offered a geographic advantage as well: Control of the Hudson River would allow the British to isolate New England. British armies could descend from Canada and move up from New York City along the Hudson River into western Massachusetts. If Massachusetts could be driven to surrender, New Jersey and Pennsylvania would fall in line, the British thought, because of loyalist strength. Virginia was a problem, like Massachusetts, but the British were confident that the Carolinas would help them isolate and subdue Virginia.

Quebec, New York, and New Jersey

In late 1775, an American expedition was launched to capture the cities of Montreal and Quebec before British reinforcements could arrive (**Map 7.1**). This offensive was a clear sign that the war was not purely a reaction to the invasion of Massachusetts. A force of New York Continentals commanded by General

A View of the Attack against Fort Washington and Rebel Redoubts near New York on the 16 of November 1776 by the British and Hessian Brigades. Drawn on the spot by Thos Davies Esqr. R.R. of Artillery.

A View of the Attack on Fort Washington

An eyewitness sketched this scene of Hessian troops attacking Fort Washington in mid-November 1775. The fort, manned by 3,000 American soldiers, sat on well-secured high ground between the Harlem and Hudson rivers. General Washington watched the attack in despair from Fort Lee, on the New Jersey side of the Hudson. The Phelps Stokes Collection, Miriam and Ira D. Wallach Division of Arts, Prints, and Photographs, The New York Public Library. Astor, Lenox, and Tilden Foundations.

| What initial challenges did the opposing armies face? | What role did the home front play in the war? | How were Native Americans and the French involved in the American Revolution? | Why did the British southern strategy ultimately fail? | Conclusion: Why did the British lose the American Revolution? |

MAP 7.1 ■ The War in the North, 1775–1778

After the early battles in Massachusetts in 1775, rebel forces invaded Canada but failed to capture Quebec. A large British army landed in New York in August 1776, turning New Jersey into a continual battle site in 1777 and 1778. Burgoyne arrived from England to secure Canada and attempted to pinch off New England along the Hudson River, but he was stopped at Saratoga in 1777 in the key battle of the early war.

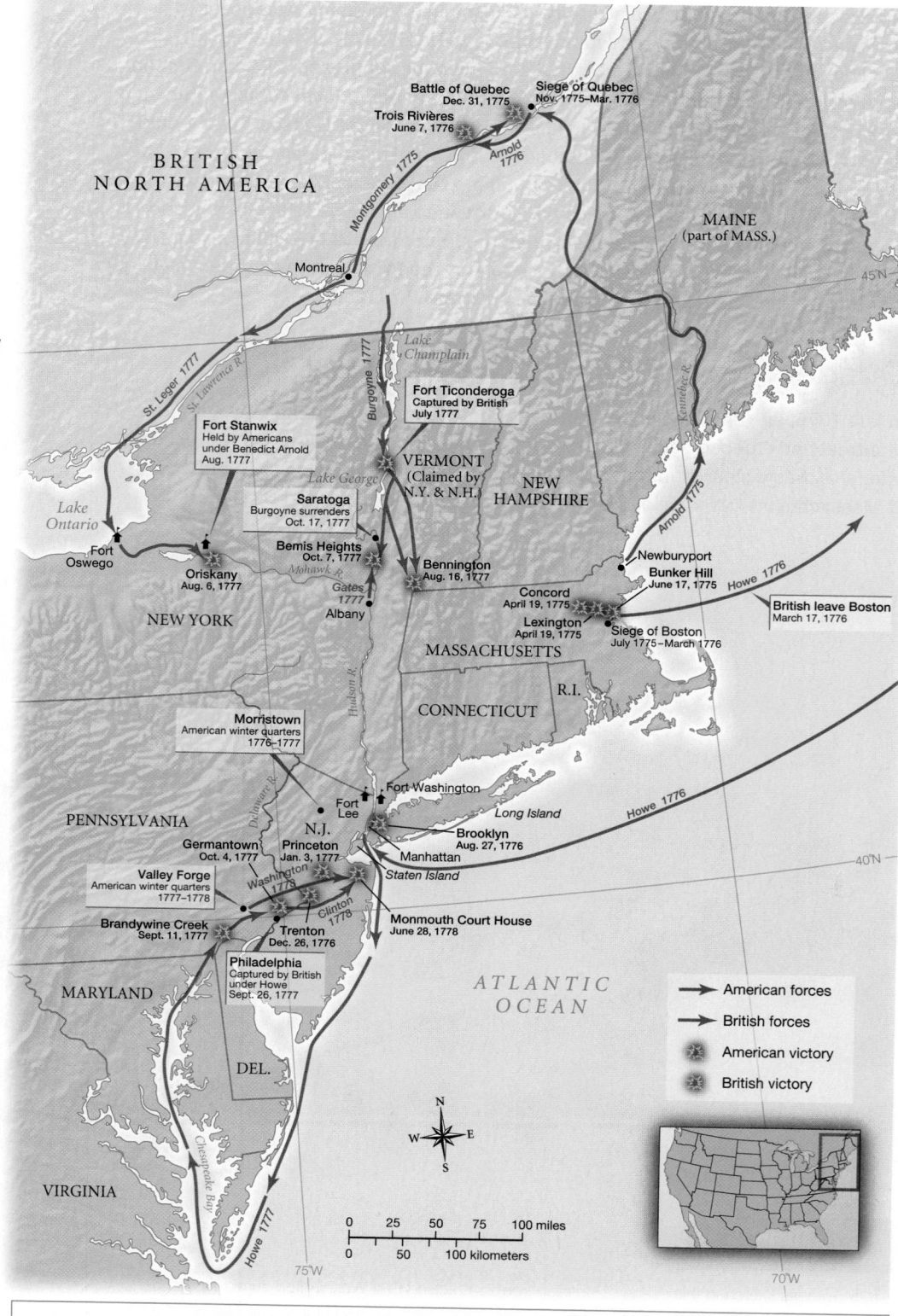

BRITISH NORTH AMERICA

MAINE (part of MASS.)

Battle of Quebec Dec. 31, 1775
Siege of Quebec Nov. 1775–Mar. 1776
Trois Rivières June 7, 1776
Arnold 1776
Montgomery 1775
Montreal
St. Leger 1777
St. Lawrence R.
Burgoyne 1777
Lake Champlain
Fort Ticonderoga Captured by British July 1777
VERMONT (Claimed by N.Y. & N.H.)
NEW HAMPSHIRE
Kennebec R.
Fort Stanwix Held by Americans under Benedict Arnold Aug. 1777
Lake George
Arnold 1775
Lake Ontario
Fort Oswego
Oriskany Aug. 6, 1777
Saratoga Burgoyne surrenders Oct. 17, 1777
Bemis Heights Oct. 7, 1777
Mohawk R.
Gates 1777
Albany
Bennington Aug. 16, 1777
Newburyport
Bunker Hill June 17, 1775
Howe 1776
NEW YORK
Concord April 19, 1775
Lexington April 19, 1775
Siege of Boston July 1775–March 1776
British leave Boston March 17, 1776
MASSACHUSETTS
R.I.
CONNECTICUT
Hudson R.
Morristown American winter quarters 1776–1777
Fort Lee
Fort Washington
Long Island
Howe 1776
PENNSYLVANIA
Germantown Oct. 4, 1777
Valley Forge American winter quarters 1777–1778
N.J.
Princeton Jan. 3, 1777
Washington 1776
Clinton 1778
Brooklyn Aug. 27, 1776
Manhattan
Staten Island
Monmouth Court House June 28, 1778
Brandywine Creek Sept. 11, 1777
Trenton Dec. 26, 1776
Delaware R.
Philadelphia Captured by British under Howe Sept. 26, 1777
MARYLAND
DEL.
Chesapeake Bay
Howe 1777
VIRGINIA

ATLANTIC OCEAN

→ American forces
→ British forces
✳ American victory
✳ British victory

N W E S

0   25   50   75   100 miles
0   50   100 kilometers

75°W   70°W
45°N
40°N

▶ FOR MORE HELP ANALYZING THIS MAP, see the map activity for this chapter in the Online Study Guide at bedfordstmartins.com/roarkunderstanding.

Richard Montgomery took Montreal easily in September 1775 and then advanced on Quebec. Meanwhile, a second contingent of Continentals led by Colonel Benedict Arnold moved north through Maine to Quebec. Arnold and Montgomery jointly attacked Quebec in December but failed to take the city. Worse yet, they encountered smallpox, which killed more men than had battles.

The main action of the first year of the war came not in Canada, however, but in New York. In August 1776, some 45,000 British troops (including 8,000 German mercenaries, called Hessians) under the command of General Howe landed south of New York City. General Washington had anticipated this move and had relocated his army of 20,000 south from Massachusetts. The battle of Long Island, in late August 1776, pitted the well-trained British "redcoats" (slang referring to their red uniforms) against a very green Continental army. Howe attacked, inflicting many casualties. Howe failed to press forward, however, perhaps remembering the costly victory of Bunker Hill, and Washington evacuated his troops to Manhattan Island.

Washington knew it would be hard to hold Manhattan, so he withdrew farther north to two forts on either side of the Hudson River. For two months, the armies engaged in limited skirmishing, but in November, Howe finally captured Fort Washington and Fort Lee, taking nearly 3,000 prisoners. Washington retreated quickly across New Jersey into Pennsylvania. Again Howe unaccountably failed to press his advantage. Instead, he parked his German troops in winter quarters along the Delaware River. Perhaps he knew that many of the Continental soldiers' enlistment periods ended on December 31, making him confident the Americans would not attack him. He was wrong.

On December 25, Washington stealthily moved his army across the Delaware River and at dawn made a quick capture of the unsuspecting German soldiers. This impressive victory lifted the sagging morale of the patriot side. For the next two weeks, Washington remained on the offensive, capturing supplies in a clever attack on British units at Princeton. Soon he was safe in Morristown, in northern New Jersey, where he settled his army for the winter.

All in all, in the first year of declared war, the rebellious Americans had a few proud moments but also many worries. The inexperienced Continental army had barely hung on in the New York campaign. Washington had shown exceptional daring and admirable restraint, but what really saved the Americans was the repeated reluctance of the British to follow through militarily when they had the advantage.

QUICK REVIEW

Why did the British initially exercise restraint in their efforts to defeat the rebellious colonies?

What initial challenges did the opposing armies face?	What role did the home front play in the war?	How were Native Americans and the French involved in the American Revolution?	Why did the British southern strategy ultimately fail?	Conclusion: Why did the British lose the American Revolution?

What role did the home front play in the war?

BATTLEFIELDS ALONE did not determine the outcome of the war. Struggles on the home front were equally important. In 1776, each community contained small numbers of highly committed people on both sides and far larger numbers who were uncertain about whether independence was worth a war. Both persuasion and force were used to gain the allegiance of the many neutrals. The struggle to secure political allegiance was complicated greatly by a shaky wartime economy. The creative financing of the fledgling government brought hardships as well as opportunities, forcing Americans to confront new manifestations of virtue and corruption.

Patriotism at the Local Level

Committees of correspondence, of public safety, and of inspection dominated the political landscape in patriot communities. These committees took on more than customary local governance; they enforced boycotts, picked army draftees, and policed suspected traitors. They sometimes invaded homes to search for contraband goods such as British tea or textiles.

Loyalists were dismayed by the increasing show of power by patriots. A man in Westchester, New York, described his response to intrusions by committees: "Choose your committee or suffer it to be chosen by a half dozen fools in your neighborhood—open your doors to them—let them examine your tea-cannisters and molasses-jugs, and your wives' and daughters' petty coats—bow and cringe and tremble and quake—fall down and worship our sovereign lord the mob. . . . Should any pragmatical committee-gentleman come to my house and give himself airs, I shall show him the door." Oppressive or not, the local committees were rarely challenged. Their persuasive powers convinced many middle-of-the-road citizens that neutrality was not a comfortable option.

Another group new to political life—white women—increasingly demonstrated a capacity for patriotism as wartime hardships dramatically altered their work routines. Many wives whose husbands were away on military or political service took on masculine duties. Their competence to tend farms and make business decisions encouraged some to assert competence in politics as well. Eliza Wilkinson managed a South Carolina plantation and talked revolutionary politics with women friends. "None were greater politicians than the several knots of ladies who met together," she remarked, alert to the unusual turn female conversations had taken. "We commenced perfect statesmen." Women from prominent Philadelphia families took more direct action, forming the Ladies Association in 1780 to collect money for Continental soldiers. A published broadside, "The Sentiments of an American Woman," defended their female patriotism: "The time is arrived to display the same sentiments which animated us at the beginning of the Revolution, when we renounced the use of teas [and] when our republican and laborious hands spun the flax."

The Loyalists

Around one-fifth of the American population remained loyal to the crown in 1776, and another two-fifths tried to stay neutral. In general, **loyalists** had strong cultural and economic ties to England; they thought that social stability depended on a government anchored by monarchy and aristocracy. Perhaps most of all, they feared democratic tyranny. They understood that dissolving the automatic respect that subjects had for their king could lead to a society in which deference to one's social betters might come under challenge. Patriots seemed to them to be unscrupulous, violent, self-interested men who simply wanted power for themselves.

Pockets of loyalism existed everywhere—in New England, in the middle colonies, in the backcountry of the southern colonies, and out beyond the Appalachian Mountains in Indian country (**Map 7.2**). The most visible loyalists (called Tories by their enemies) were royal officials. Wealthy merchants gravitated toward loyalism to maintain the trade protections of navigation acts and the British navy. Conservative urban lawyers admired the stability of British law and order. Some colonists chose loyalism simply to oppose traditional adversaries. Backcountry Carolina farmers leaned toward loyalism out of resentment of the power of the pro-revolution gentry. And, of course, southern slaves had their own resentments and looked to Britain in hope of freedom.

Many Indian tribes hoped to remain neutral at the war's start, seeing the conflict as a civil war between the English and Americans. Eventually, however, most were drawn in, many taking the British side. The powerful Iroquois Confederacy divided: The Mohawk, Cayuga, Seneca, and Onondaga peoples lined up with the British; the Oneida and Tuscarora tribes aided Americans. One young Mohawk leader, **Thayendanegea** (known also by his English name, **Joseph Brant**), traveled to England in 1775 to complain to King George about cheating American settlers. "It is very hard when we have let the King's subjects have so much of our lands for so little value," he wrote, "they should want to

CHRONOLOGY

1775
- **June.** The Second Continental Congress declares all loyalists traitors.
- Mohawk leader Joseph Brant travels to England to pledge support for the British side.

1776
- New York City loyalists circulate a "Declaration of Dependence" in rebuttal to the declaration of the Second Continental Congress.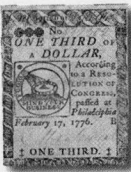

1778
- Colonial committees of public safety fix prices on essential goods.

loyalists
▶ Colonists who remained loyal to Britain during the Revolutionary War. Around one-fifth of the American population remained loyal to the crown in 1776. Colonists remained loyal to Britain for many reasons, and loyalists could be found in every region of the country.

Joseph Brant (Thayendanegea)
▶ Mohawk leader who fought for the British during the Revolutionary War. Brant pledged Indian support for the king in exchange for protection from encroaching settlers. Brant led the Senecas and Mohawks to victory over German settlers living in the Mohawk Valley and Oneida Indians in the battle of Oriskany.

| What initial challenges did the opposing armies face? | **What role did the home front play in the war?** | How were Native Americans and the French involved in the American Revolution? | Why did the British southern strategy ultimately fail? | Conclusion: Why did the British lose the American Revolution? |

181

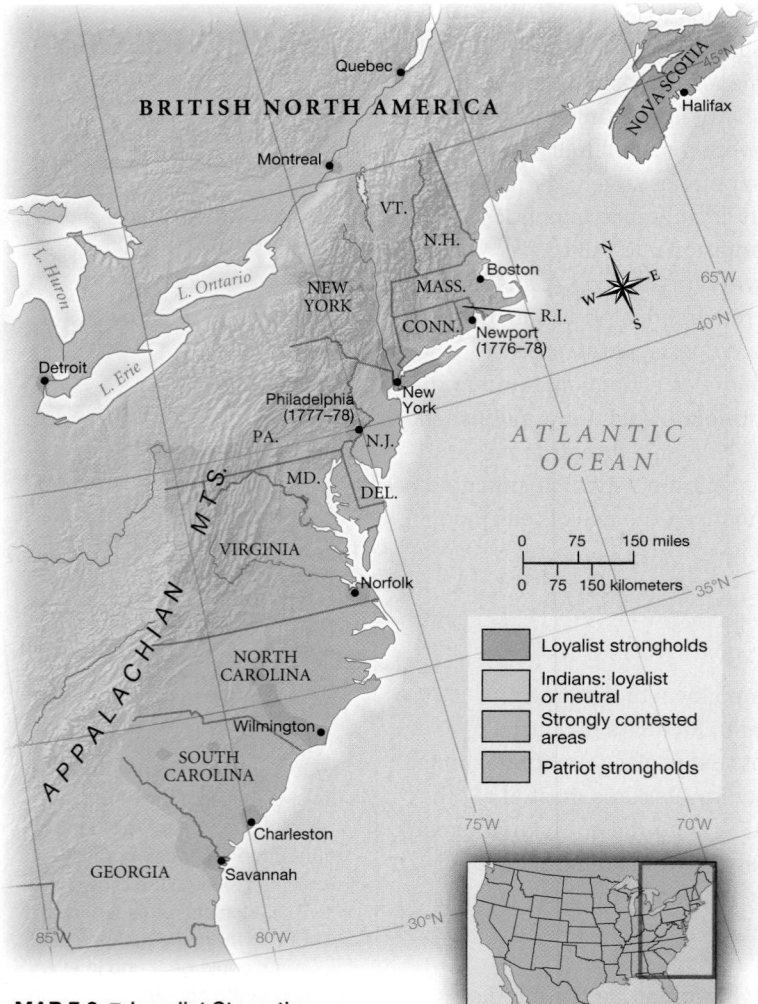

MAP 7.2 ■ Loyalist Strength and Rebel Support

The exact number of loyalists can never be known. No one could have made an accurate count at the time, and political allegiance often shifted with the wind. This map shows the regions of loyalist strength on which the British relied—most significantly, the lower Hudson valley and the Carolina Piedmont.

Map labels: Quebec, BRITISH NORTH AMERICA, Montreal, NOVA SCOTIA, Halifax, VT., N.H., L. Huron, L. Ontario, NEW YORK, MASS., Boston, Detroit, L. Erie, CONN., R.I., Newport (1776–78), Philadelphia (1777–78), New York, PA., N.J., ATLANTIC OCEAN, MD., DEL., VIRGINIA, APPALACHIAN MTS., Norfolk, NORTH CAROLINA, Wilmington, SOUTH CAROLINA, Charleston, GEORGIA, Savannah

Legend: Loyalist strongholds; Indians: loyalist or neutral; Strongly contested areas; Patriot strongholds

Scale: 0 75 150 miles / 0 75 150 kilometers

cheat us in this manner of the small spots we have left for our women and children to live on." Brant pledged Indian support for the king in exchange for protection from encroaching settlers. In the Ohio Country, parts of the Shawnee and Delaware tribes started out pro-American but shifted to the British side by 1779 in the face of repeated betrayals by American settlers and soldiers.

Loyalists were most vocal between 1774 and 1776, when the possibility of a full-scale rebellion against Britain was still uncertain. They challenged the emerging patriot side in pamphlets and newspapers. In New York City, 547 loyalists signed and circulated a broadside titled "A Declaration of Dependence" in rebuttal to the congress's July 4, 1776, declaration, denouncing the "most unnatural, unprovoked Rebellion that ever disgraced the annals of Time."

Who Is a Traitor?

In June 1775, the Second Continental Congress declared all loyalists to be traitors. Over the next year, state laws defined as treason acts such as provisioning the British army, saying anything that undermined patriot morale, and discouraging men from enlisting in the Continental army. Punishments ranged from house arrest and suspension of voting privileges to confiscation of property and deportation. Sometimes self-appointed committees of Tory-hunters bypassed the judicial niceties and terrorized loyalists, raiding their houses or tarring and feathering them.

Were wives of loyalists also traitors? When loyalist families fled the country, their property was typically confiscated. But if the wife stayed, courts usually allowed her to keep one-third of the property, the amount due her if widowed, and confiscated the rest. A wife who fled with her husband might have little choice in the matter. After the Revolution, descendants of refugee loyalists filed several lawsuits to regain property that had entered the family through the mother's inheritance. In 1805, the American son of loyalist refugee Anna Martin recovered her dowry property on the grounds that she had no independent will to be a loyalist.

Tarring and feathering, property confiscation, deportation, terrorism—to the loyalists, such denials of liberty of conscience and of freedom to own private property proved that democratic tyranny was more to be feared than the monarchical variety. A Boston loyalist named Mather Byles aptly expressed this point: "They call me a brainless Tory, but tell me . . . which is better—to be ruled by one tyrant three thousand miles away, or by three thousand tyrants not a mile away?" Byles was soon sentenced to deportation.

CHAPTER LOCATOR | Why did the Americans declare their independence?

Throughout the war, probably 7,000 to 8,000 loyalists fled to England, and 28,000 found haven in Canada. But many chose to remain in the new United States and swing with the changing political winds. In some instances, that proved difficult. In New Jersey, for example, 3,000 Jerseyites felt protected (or scared) enough by the occupying British army in 1776 to swear an oath of allegiance to the king. But then General Howe drew back to New York City, leaving them to the mercy of local patriot committees. British strategy depended on using loyalists to hold occupied territory, but the New Jersey experience showed how poorly that strategy was carried out.

Financial Instability and Corruption

Wars cost money—for arms and ammunition, for food and uniforms, for soldiers' pay. The Continental Congress printed money, but its value quickly deteriorated because the congress held no reserves of gold or silver to back the currency. States began printing paper money to pay for wartime expenses, further complicating the economy.

As the currency depreciated, the congress turned to other means to procure supplies and labor. One method was to borrow hard money (gold or silver coins) from wealthy men in exchange for certificates of debt (public securities) promising repayment with interest. The certificates of debt were similar to present-day government bonds. To pay soldiers, the congress issued land-grant certificates, written promises of acreage usually located in frontier areas such as central Maine or eastern Ohio. Both the public securities and the land-grant certificates quickly became forms of negotiable currency. These certificates soon depreciated, too.

Depreciating currency inevitably led to rising prices, as sellers compensated for the falling value of the money. The wartime economy of the late 1770s, with its unreliable currency and price inflation, was extremely demoralizing to Americans everywhere. In 1778, in an effort to impose stability, local committees of public safety began to fix prices on essential goods such as flour. Inevitably, some turned this unstable situation to their advantage. Money that fell fast in value needed to be spent quickly; being in debt was suddenly advantageous because the debt could be repaid in devalued currency. A brisk black market sprang up in prohibited luxury imports, such as tea, sugar, textiles, and wines, even though these items came from Britain. A New Hampshire delegate to the congress denounced the trade: "We are a crooked and perverse generation, longing for the fineries and follies of those Egyptian task masters from whom we have so lately freed ourselves."

QUICK REVIEW

Why did some colonists promote rebellion while others remained loyal to Britain?

What initial challenges did the opposing armies face?

What role did the home front play in the war?

How were Native Americans and the French involved in the American Revolution?

Why did the British southern strategy ultimately fail?

Conclusion: Why did the British lose the American Revolution?

183

How were Native Americans and the French involved in the American Revolution?

Death of Jane McCrea

This 1804 painting by John Vanderlyn memorializes the martyr legend of Jane McCrea. Daughter of an American patriot family in northern New York, McCrea was in love with a young American loyalist who joined Burgoyne's army. In July 1777, she eloped to join her fiancé, guided by Indians sent by the British to escort her. But she was killed on the short journey—either shot in the crossfire of battle, as the British claimed, or murdered by savage Indians allied with the British, in the patriots' version. Wadsworth Athenaeum, Hartford.

▶ FOR MORE HELP ANALYZING THIS IMAGE, see the visual activity for this chapter in the Online Study Guide at bedfordstmartins.com/roarkunderstanding.

IN EARLY 1777, about the best that could be said was that General Washington had skillfully avoided defeat. The minor victories in New Jersey lent only faint optimism to the American side. Meanwhile, British troops moved south from Quebec in an effort to take control of the Hudson River. Their presence drew the Continental army up into central New York, polarizing Indian tribes of the Iroquois nation and turning the Mohawk Valley into a bloody war zone. By 1779, tribes in western New York and in the Ohio Valley were fully involved in the war. Most sided with the British, and while the Americans had some success in this period, such as the victory at Saratoga, the involvement of Indians and the continuing strength of the British forced the Americans to look to France for help.

Burgoyne's Army and the Battle of Saratoga

In 1777, British general John Burgoyne and a considerable army began the squeeze on the Hudson River valley. His goal was to capture Albany, near the intersection of the Hudson and Mohawk rivers (see Map 7.1, page 178). Accompanied by 1,000 camp followers (cooks, laundresses, musicians) and some 400 Indian warriors, Burgoyne's army of 7,800 men did not travel light. Food had to be packed in, not only for people but also for the 400 horses needed to haul heavy artillery. The British continued to move south, but the large army moved slowly on primitive roads through dense forests. The logical second step in isolating New England should have been to advance troops up the Hudson from New York City to meet Burgoyne. American surveillance indicated that General

CHAPTER LOCATOR | Why did the Americans declare their independence?

Howe in Manhattan was readying his men for a major move in August 1777. But Howe surprised everyone by sailing south to attack Philadelphia.

To reinforce Burgoyne, British troops from Montreal came from the east along the Mohawk River, aided by Mohawks and Senecas of the Iroquois Confederacy. The British were counting on loyalism among the numerous German colonists living in the Mohawk Valley. A hundred miles west of Albany, they encountered American Continental soldiers at Fort Stanwix and laid siege, causing local German militiamen, joined by a few Oneida Indians, to rush to the Continentals' support. Mohawk chief Joseph Brant led the Senecas and Mohawks in an ambush on the Germans and the Oneidas in a narrow ravine called Oriskany, killing nearly 500 out of 840 of them. On Brant's side, some 90 warriors were killed. The defenders of Fort Stanwix ultimately repelled the British and Indians and forced them to retreat (see Map 7.1, page 178). These deadly battles were complexly multiethnic, pitting Indians against Indians, German Americans against German mercenaries, New York patriots against New York loyalists, and English Americans against British soldiers.

The British retreat at Fort Stanwix deprived General Burgoyne of the additional troops he expected. Camped at a small village called Saratoga, he was isolated, with food supplies dwindling and men deserting. The American commander, General Horatio Gates, began moving his army toward him. Burgoyne decided to attack first, and the British prevailed, but at the great cost of 600 dead or wounded. Three weeks later, an American attack on Burgoyne's forces at Saratoga cost the British another 600 men and most of their cannons. Burgoyne finally surrendered on October 17, 1777.

General Howe, meanwhile, had succeeded in occupying Philadelphia in September 1777. Figuring that the Saratoga loss was balanced by the capture of Philadelphia, the British government proposed a negotiated settlement—not including independence—to end the war. The Americans refused.

But supplies of arms and food for the rebel army were precariously low. Washington moved his troops into winter quarters at Valley Forge, just west of Philadelphia. Quartered in drafty huts, the men lacked blankets, boots, stockings, and food. Some 2,000 men at Valley Forge died of disease; another 2,000 deserted over the bitter six-month encampment.

Washington blamed the citizenry for lack of support; indeed, evidence of corruption and profiteering was abundant. Army suppliers too often provided defective food, clothing, and gunpowder. One shipment of bedding arrived with blankets one-quarter their customary size. Food supplies arrived rotten. As one Continental officer said, "The people at home are destroying the Army by their conduct much faster than Howe and all his army can possibly do by fighting us."

The War in Indian Country

Between the fall of 1777 and the summer of 1778, the fighting on the Atlantic coast slowed. But in the interior western areas—the Mohawk Valley, the Ohio Valley, and Kentucky—the war of Indians against the American rebels heated up.

The ambush and slaughter at Oriskany in August 1777 marked the beginning of three years of terror for the inhabitants of the Mohawk Valley. Loyalists and Indians engaged in raids on farms throughout 1778, capturing or killing the residents. In retaliation, American militiamen destroyed Joseph Brant's village but failed to capture any warriors. A month later, Brant's warriors attacked the town of Cherry Valley, killing 16 soldiers and 32 civilians.

CHRONOLOGY

1777
- Ambush at Oriskany.
- British occupy Philadelphia.
- British surrender at Saratoga.
- Continental army endures winter at Valley Forge.

1778
- France enters war on American side.
- Mohawk Valley sees terrorism by both sides.
- White Eyes negotiates treaty with Americans; later dies mysteriously.

1779
- Sullivan's campaign destroys forty Iroquois villages in New York.
- Virginia and Kentucky militiamen take Forts Kaskaskia and Vincennes.

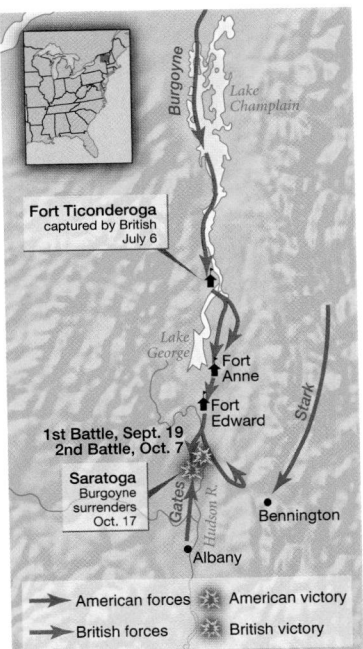

Battle of Saratoga, 1777

| What initial challenges did the opposing armies face? | What role did the home front play in the war? | How were Native Americans and the French involved in the American Revolution? | Why did the British southern strategy ultimately fail? | Conclusion: Why did the British lose the American Revolution? |

The following summer, General Washington authorized a campaign to wreak "total destruction and devastation" on all the Iroquois villages of central New York. Some 4,500 troops commanded by General John Sullivan implemented a campaign of terror in the fall of 1779. Forty Indian towns met with total obliteration; the soldiers looted and torched the dwellings and then burned cornfields and orchards. In a few towns, women and children were slaughtered, but in most, the inhabitants managed to escape, fleeing to the British at Fort Niagara. Thousands of Indian refugees, sick and starving, camped around the fort in one of the most miserable winters on record.

Much farther to the west, beyond Fort Pitt, another complex story of alliances and betrayals between American militiamen and Indians unfolded. Some 150,000 native people lived between the Appalachian Mountains and the Mississippi River. Most sided with the British, but a portion of the Shawnee and Delaware tribes at first sought peace with the Americans. In mid-1778, the Delaware chief White Eyes negotiated a treaty at Fort Pitt, pledging Indian support for the Americans in exchange for supplies and trade goods. But escalating violence undermined the agreement. That fall, when American soldiers killed two friendly Shawnee chiefs, Cornstalk and Red Hawk, the Continental Congress hastened to apologize, as did the governors of Pennsylvania and Virginia, but the soldiers who stood trial for the murders were acquitted. Two months later, White Eyes, nominally an ally of and an informant for the Americans, died under mysterious circumstances, almost certainly murdered by militiamen, who repeatedly had trouble honoring distinctions between allied and enemy Indians.

West of the Appalachian Mountains, Indian raiders from north of the Ohio River, in alliance with the British, repeatedly attacked white settlements such as Boonesborough (in present-day Kentucky) (**Map 7.3**). In retaliation, a young Virginian, George Rogers Clark, led Virginia and Kentucky militiamen into what is now Illinois, attacking and taking the British fort at Kaskaskia in 1779. Clark's men wore native clothing—hunting shirts and breechcloths—but their dress was not a sign of solidarity with the Indians. When they attacked British-held Fort Vincennes in 1779, Clark's troops tomahawked Indian captives and threw their still-live bodies into the river in a gory spectacle witnessed by the redcoats. "To excel them in barbarity is the only way to make war upon Indians," Clark announced.

By 1780, very few Indians remained neutral. Violent raids by Americans drove Indians into the arms of the British at Detroit and Niagara, or into the arms of the Spaniards, who still held much of the land west of the Mississippi River. For those who stayed near their native lands, chaos and confusion prevailed. Rare as it was, Indian support for the American side occasionally emerged out of a strategic sense that the Americans were unstoppable in their westward pressure and that it was better to work out an alliance than to lose in a war. But American treatment of even friendly Indians showed that there was no winning strategy for them.

The French Alliance

On their own, the Americans could not have defeated Britain, especially as pressure from hostile Indians increased. Essential help arrived as a result of the victory at Saratoga, which convinced the French to enter the war; a formal alliance was signed in February 1778. France recognized the United States as an independent nation and promised full military and commercial support. Most

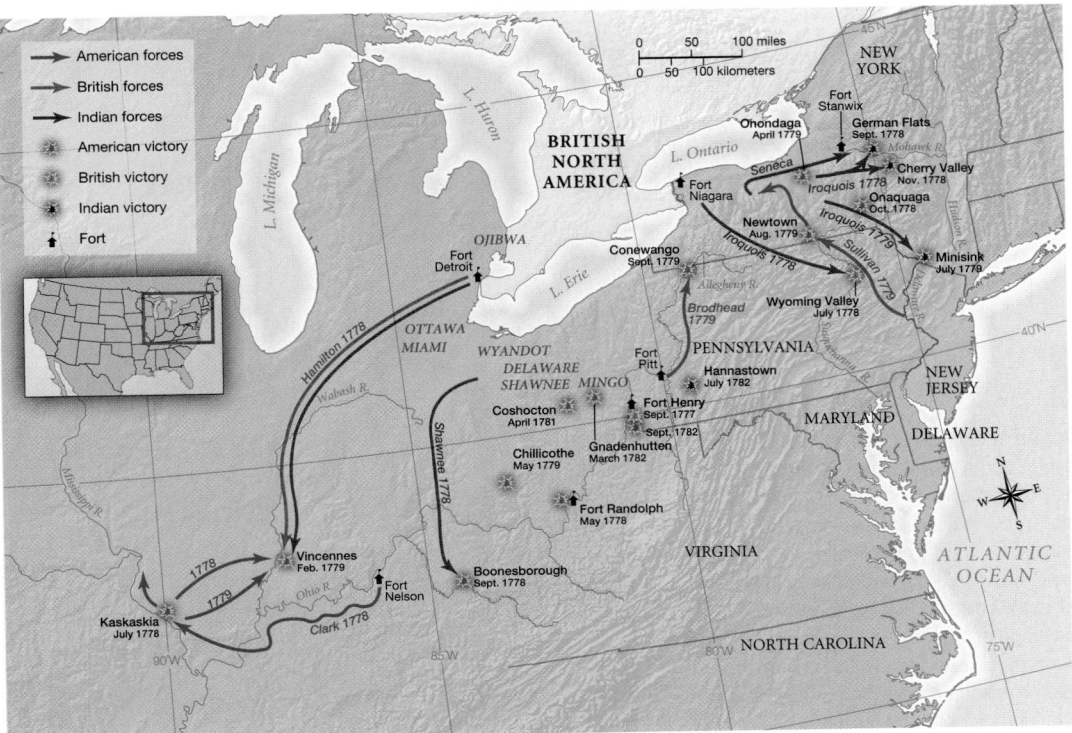

MAP 7.3 ■ **The Indian War in the West, 1777–1782**

The American Revolution involved many Indian tribes, most of them supporting the British. Iroquois Indians, with British aid, attacked American towns in New York's Mohawk Valley throughout 1778. In 1779, the Continental army marched on forty Iroquois villages in central New York and destroyed them. Shawnee and Delaware Indians to the west of Fort Pitt tangled with American militia units in 1779, while tribes supported by the British at Fort Detroit conducted raids on Kentucky settlers, who hit back with raids of their own. George Rogers Clark led Kentucky militiamen against Indians and British in the Illinois region. Sporadic fighting continued in the West through 1782, ending with Indian attacks on Hannastown, Pennsylvania, and Fort Henry on the Ohio River. By the late 1780s, occasional fighting resumed, sparked by American settlers pressing west onto Indian land.

crucial was the French navy, which could challenge British supplies and troops at sea and aid the Americans in taking and holding prisoners of war.

Well before 1778, however, the French had provided cannons, muskets, gunpowder, and highly trained military advisers to the Americans. From the French perspective, the main attraction of an alliance was the opportunity it provided to defeat archrival Britain. A victory would also open pathways to trade and perhaps result in France's acquiring the coveted British West Indies. Even American defeat would not be a disaster for France if the war lasted many years and drained Britain of men and money.

QUICK REVIEW

Why was French assistance so crucial to the American cause?

What initial challenges did the opposing armies face?	What role did the home front play in the war?	**How were Native Americans and the French involved in the American Revolution?**	Why did the British southern strategy ultimately fail?	Conclusion: Why did the British lose the American Revolution?

Why did the British southern strategy ultimately fail?

Lafayette at Yorktown

An enthusiast for American liberty, the young French nobleman Lafayette came to the United States in 1777 at age twenty to volunteer his services to General Washington. After proving his leadership in several northern campaigns, he went to Virginia in 1781 to fight Cornwallis. Near Richmond, he met James, a slave belonging to William Armistead, who loaned him to Lafayette. At the siege of Yorktown, James, pretending to be an escaped slave, infiltrated the British command, giving them misinformation and bringing crucial intelligence back to Lafayette. James obtained his freedom in 1786 after Lafayette wrote a letter on his behalf to the Virginia assembly. Art Gallery, Williams Center, Lafayette College.

WHEN FRANCE JOINED the war, some British officials wondered whether the fight was worth continuing. A troop commander, arguing for an immediate negotiated settlement, shrewdly observed that "we are far from an anticipated peace, because the bitterness of the rebels is too widespread, and in regions where we are masters the rebellious spirit is still in them. The land is too large, and there are too many people. The more land we win, the weaker our army gets in the field." The commander of the British navy argued for abandoning the war, and even Lord North, the prime minister, agreed. But the king was determined to crush the rebellion, and he encouraged a new strategy for victory focusing on the southern colonies, thought to be more persuadably loyalist. It was a brilliant but desperate plan, and ultimately unsuccessful.

Georgia and South Carolina

The new strategy called for British forces to abandon New England and focus on the South, with its valuable crops and its large slave population, a destabilizing factor that might keep rebellious white southerners in line. Georgia and the Carolinas appeared to hold large numbers of loyalists, providing a base for the British to recapture the southern colonies one by one, before moving north to the middle colonies and New England.

Georgia, the first target, fell at the end of December 1778 (**Map 7.4**). A small army of British soldiers occupied Savannah and Augusta, and a new royal governor and loyalist assembly were quickly installed. The British in Georgia

CHAPTER LOCATOR | Why did the Americans declare their independence?

quickly organized twenty loyal militia units, and 1,400 Georgians swore an oath of allegiance to the king. So far, the southern strategy looked as if it might work.

Next came South Carolina. The Continental army put ten regiments into the port city of Charleston to defend it from attack by British troops shipped south from New York under the command of General Henry Clinton, Howe's replacement as commander in chief. For five weeks in early 1780, the British laid siege to the city and took it in May 1780, capturing 3,300 American soldiers.

Clinton returned to New York, leaving the task of pacifying the rest of South Carolina to General Charles Cornwallis and 4,000 troops. A bold commander, Lord Cornwallis quickly chased out the remaining Continentals and established military rule of South Carolina by midsummer. He purged rebels from government office and disarmed rebel militias. Exports of rice, South Carolina's main crop, resumed, and pardons were offered to Carolinians willing to prove their loyalty by taking up arms for the British.

By August, American troops arrived from the North to strike back at Cornwallis. General Gates, the hero of Saratoga, led 3,000 troops, many of them newly recruited militiamen, into battle against Cornwallis at Camden, South Carolina, on August 16. The militiamen panicked at the sight of the approaching British cavalry, however, and fled. When regiment leaders tried to regroup the next day, only 700 soldiers showed up. The battle of Camden was a devastating defeat for the Americans.

Britain's southern strategy succeeded in 1780 in part because of information about American troop movements secretly conveyed by an American officer,

CHRONOLOGY

1780
- British take Charleston, South Carolina.
- French army arrives in Newport, Rhode Island.
- British win battle of Camden.
- Benedict Arnold is exposed as traitor.
- Americans win battle of King's Mountain.

1781
- British forces invade Virginia.
- French fleet blockades Chesapeake Bay.
- Cornwallis surrenders at Yorktown; concedes British defeat.

1783
- Treaty of Paris ends war; United States gains all land to Mississippi River.

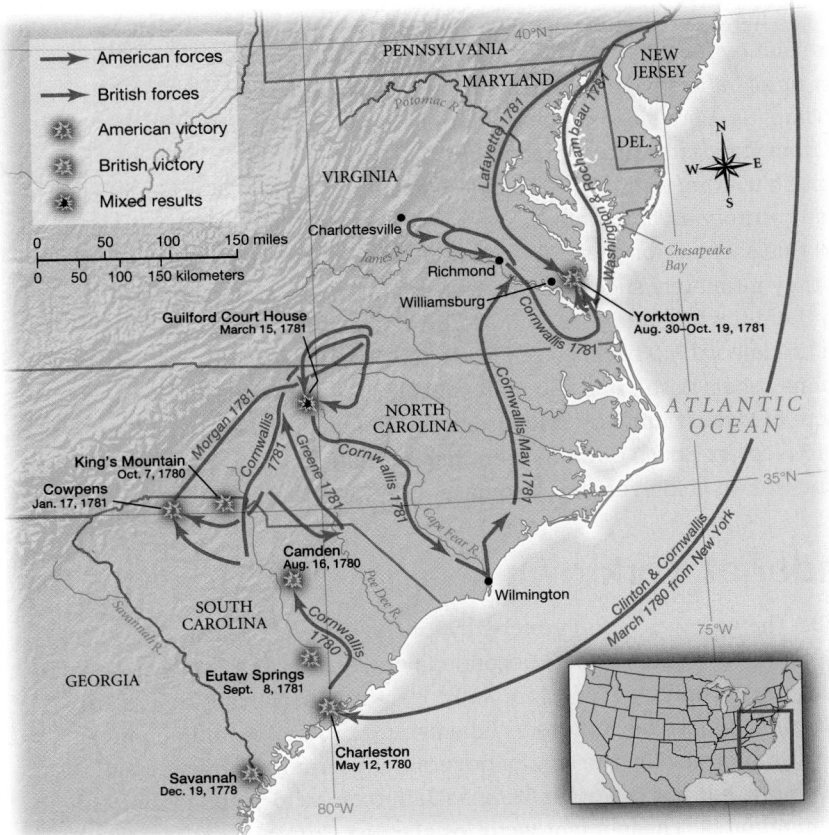

MAP 7.4 ■ **The War in the South, 1780–1781**
After taking Charleston in May 1780, the British advanced into South Carolina and the foothills of North Carolina, leaving a bloody civil war in their wake. When the American general Horatio Gates and his men fled from the humiliating battle of Camden, Gates was replaced by General Nathanael Greene and General Daniel Morgan, who pulled off major victories at King's Mountain and Cowpens. The British general Cornwallis then moved north and invaded Virginia, but he was bottled up and finally overpowered at Yorktown in the fall of 1781.

| What initial challenges did the opposing armies face? | What role did the home front play in the war? | How were Native Americans and the French involved in the American Revolution? | **Why did the British southern strategy ultimately fail?** | Conclusion: Why did the British lose the American Revolution? |

Benedict Arnold. The hero of several American battles, Arnold was a deeply insecure man who never felt he got his due. Sometime in 1779, he opened secret negotiations with General Clinton in New York, trading information for money and hinting that he could deliver far more of value. When General Washington made him commander of West Point, a new fort on the Hudson River sixty miles north of New York City, Arnold's plan crystallized. West Point controlled the Hudson; its capture might well have meant victory for the British.

Arnold's plot to sell a West Point victory to the British was foiled in the fall of 1780 when Americans captured the man carrying plans of the fort's defense from Arnold to Clinton. News of Arnold's treason created shock waves. Arnold represented all of the patriots' worst fears about themselves: greedy self-interest, like that of the war profiteers; the unprincipled abandonment of war aims, like that of turncoat southern Tories; panic, like that of the terrified soldiers at Camden. But instead of demoralizing the Americans, Arnold's treachery revived their commitment to the patriot cause. Vilifying Arnold allowed Americans to stake out a wide distance between themselves and dastardly conduct. It inspired a renewal of patriotism at a particularly low moment.

Guerrilla Warfare in the South

Shock over Gates's defeat at Camden and Arnold's treason revitalized rebel support in western South Carolina, an area that Cornwallis thought was pacified and loyal. The backcountry of the South soon became the site of guerrilla warfare. In hit-and-run attacks, both sides burned and ravaged not only opponents' property but also the property of anyone claiming to be neutral. Loyalist militia units organized by the British were met by fierce rebel militia units. In South Carolina, some 6,000 rebels met loyalist units in bloody engagements. Guerrilla warfare soon spread to Georgia and North Carolina. Both sides committed atrocities and plundered property, clear deviations from standard military practice.

The British southern strategy depended on sufficient loyalist strength to hold reconquered territory as Cornwallis's army moved north. The backcountry civil war proved this assumption false. The Americans won few major battles in the South, but they ultimately succeeded by harassing the British forces and preventing them from foraging for food. Cornwallis moved the war into North Carolina in the fall of 1780 because the North Carolinians were supplying the South Carolina rebels with arms and men (see Map 7.4, page 189). Then news of a massacre of loyalist units by 1,400 frontier riflemen at the battle of King's Mountain, in western South Carolina, sent him hurrying back. The British were stretched too thin to hold even two colonies.

Surrender at Yorktown

By early 1781, the war was going very badly for the British. Their defeat at King's Mountain was quickly followed by a second major defeat at the battle of Cowpens in South Carolina in January 1781. Cornwallis retreated to North Carolina and thence to Virginia, where he captured Williamsburg in June. A raiding party proceeded to Charlottesville, the seat of government, capturing members of the Virginia assembly, but not Governor Thomas Jefferson, who escaped the soldiers by a mere ten minutes. These minor victories allowed Cornwallis to imagine he

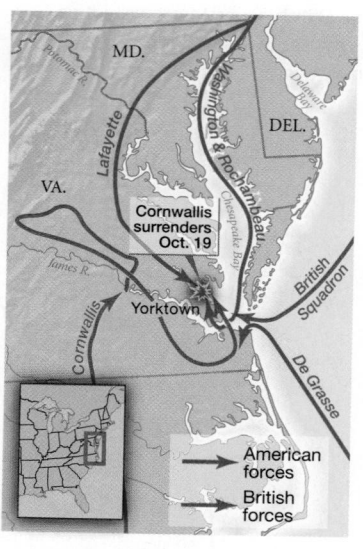

Siege of Yorktown, 1781

was succeeding in Virginia. He next marched to Yorktown, near the Chesapeake Bay, expecting backup troops by ship from British headquarters in New York City.

At this juncture, the French-American alliance came into play. Already, French regiments commanded by the Comte de Rochambeau had joined General Washington in Newport, Rhode Island, in mid-1780, and now in 1781 warships under the Comte de Grasse sailed from France. Washington, Rochambeau, and de Grasse fixed their attention on the Chesapeake Bay. The French fleet got there ahead of the British troop ships from New York; a five-day naval battle left the French navy in control of the Virginia coast. This proved to be the decisive factor in ending the war, because the French ships prevented any rescue of Cornwallis's army.

On land, General Cornwallis and his 7,500 troops faced a combined French and American army of 16,000. For twelve days, the Americans and French bombarded the British fortifications at the **battle of Yorktown**; Cornwallis ran low on food and ammunition. An American observer noted that "the enemy, from want of forage, are killing off their horses in great numbers. Six or seven hundred of these valuable animals have been killed." Realizing that escape was impossible, Cornwallis surrendered on October 19, 1781.

battle of Yorktown

▶ October 1781 battle that sealed American victory in the Revolutionary War. American troops and a French fleet trapped the British army under the command of General Charles Cornwallis at Yorktown, Virginia. The war dragged on for two more years after Cornwallis's surrender on October 19, 1781, but the ultimate outcome was never again in doubt.

"The Ballance of Power," 1780 This cartoon was published in England soon after Spain and the Netherlands declared an alliance with France to support the war in America. On the left, Britannia, a female figure representing Great Britain, cannot be moved by all the lightweights on the right side of the scale. France wears a ruffled shirt, Spain has a feather in his hat, and a Dutch boy has just hopped on, saying, "I'll do anything for Money." The forlorn Indian maiden, the standard icon representing America in the eighteenth century, sits on the scale, wailing, "My Ingratitude is Justly punished." The poem printed below the cartoon predicts, "The Americans too will with Britons Unite." Print Collection, Miriam and Ira D. Wallach Division of Art, Prints, and Photographs, The New York Public Library. Astor, Lenox, and Tilden Foundations.

▶ FOR MORE HELP ANALYZING THIS IMAGE, see the visual activity for this chapter in the Online Study Guide at bedfordstmartins.com/roarkunderstanding.

What initial challenges did the opposing armies face?	What role did the home front play in the war?	How were Native Americans and the French involved in the American Revolution?	**Why did the British southern strategy ultimately fail?**	Conclusion: Why did the British lose the American Revolution?

What began as a promising southern strategy in 1778 turned into a discouraging defeat. British attacks in the South had energized American resistance, as did the timely exposure of Benedict Arnold's treason. The arrival of the French fleet sealed the fate of Cornwallis at the battle of Yorktown, and major military operations came to a halt.

The Losers and the Winners

The surrender at Yorktown spelled the end for the British, but two more years of skirmishes ensued. Frontier areas in Kentucky, Ohio, and Illinois blazed with battles pitting Americans against various Indian tribes. The British army still occupied three coastal cities, including New York City, and an augmented Continental army stayed at the ready.

The peace treaty took six months to negotiate. Commissioners from America, Britain, and France met in Paris and worked out the terms of peace. First and foremost, Britain recognized American independence. Other terms set the western boundary of the new country at the Mississippi River and guaranteed that creditors on both sides could collect debts owed them in sterling money, a provision especially important to British merchants. The **Treaty of Paris** was signed on September 3, 1783.

Like the treaty ending the Seven Years' War, this treaty ignored the Indians as players in the conflict. As one American told the Shawnee people, "Your Fathers the English have made Peace with us for themselves, but forgot you their Children, who Fought with them, and neglected you like Bastards." Indian lands were assigned to the victors as though they were uninhabited. Some Indian refugees fled west into present-day Missouri and Arkansas; others, such as Joseph Brant's Mohawks, relocated to Canada. But significant numbers remained within the new United States, occupying their traditional homelands in areas west and north of the Ohio River. For them, the Treaty of Paris brought no peace at all; their longer war against the Americans would extend at least until 1795 and for some until 1813. Their ally, Britain, conceded defeat, but the Indians did not.

With the treaty finally signed, the British began their evacuation of New York, Charleston, and Savannah, a process complicated by the sheer numbers involved—soldiers, fearful loyalists, and runaway slaves by the thousands. In New York City, more than 27,000 soldiers and 30,000 loyalists sailed on hundreds of ships for England in the late fall of 1783.

Treaty of Paris

▶ September 3, 1783, treaty that ended the Revolutionary War. The treaty acknowledged America's independence, set the western boundary of the new country, guaranteed that creditors on both sides could collect debts owed them in sterling money, and promised the quick withdrawal of British troops from American soil. Like the treaty ending the Seven Years' War, the Treaty of Paris failed to recognize Indians as players in the conflict.

> ## QUICK REVIEW

Why did the British southern strategy ultimately fail?

CHAPTER LOCATOR | Why did the Americans declare their independence?

Picture Research Consultants & Archives.

Conclusion: Why did the British lose the American Revolution?

THE BRITISH BEGAN the war for America convinced that they could not lose. They had the best-trained army and navy in the world; they were familiar with the landscape from the Seven Years' War; they had the support of most of the native tribes of the backcountry; and they easily captured every port city of consequence in America. Probably one-fifth of the population was loyalist, and another two-fifths were undecided. Why, then, did the British lose?

One continuing problem the British faced was the uncertainty of supplies. The army depended on a steady stream of supply ships from home, and insecurity about food helps explain their reluctance to pursue the Continental army aggressively. A further obstacle was their continual misuse of loyalist energies. Any plan to repacify the colonies required the cooperation of the loyalists, but the British repeatedly left them to the mercy of vengeful rebels. French aid also helps explain the British defeat. Even before the formal alliance, French artillery and ammunition proved vital to the Continental army. After 1780, the French army fought alongside the Americans, and the French navy made the Yorktown victory possible. Finally, the British abdicated civil power in the colonies in 1775 and 1776, when royal officials fled to safety, and they never really regained it. The basic British goal—to turn back the clock to imperial rule—receded into impossibility as the war dragged on.

The Revolution profoundly disrupted the lives of Americans everywhere. It was a war for independence from Britain, but it was more. It was a war that required men and women to think about politics and the legitimacy of authority. The rhetoric employed to justify the revolution against Britain put words such as *liberty, tyranny, slavery, independence*, and *equality* into common usage. These words carried far deeper meanings than a mere complaint over taxation without representation. The Revolution unleashed a dynamic of equality and liberty that was largely unintended and unwanted by many of the American leaders of 1776. But that dynamic emerged as a potent force in American life in the decades to come.

SO NOW YOU KNOW

Only two-fifths of the colonists fully supported the idea of American independence in 1776. But by 1783, that minority became a majority that created new government structures, defeated the British army and its allies, and revolutionized the ways most Americans thought about politics and the ideas of liberty and equality.

CHAPTER 7 STUDY GUIDE

Online Study Guide
bedfordstmartins.com/roarkunderstanding

STEP 1 GETTING STARTED

Below are basic terms from this period in American history. Can you identify each term below and explain why it matters? To do this exercise online or to download this chart, visit bedfordstmartins.com/roarkunderstanding.

TERM	WHO OR WHAT & WHEN	WHY IT MATTERS
Second Continental Congress, p. 170		
George Washington, p. 171		
Common Sense, p. 172		
Abigail Adams, p. 173		
Declaration of Independence, p. 174		
Continental army, p. 176		
loyalists, p. 181		
Joseph Brant (Thayendanegea), p. 181		
Benedict Arnold, p. 190		
battle of Yorktown, p. 191		
Treaty of Paris (1783), p. 192		

STEP 2 MOVING BEYOND THE BASICS

The exercise below represents a more advanced understanding of the chapter material. The following chart divides the war into three periods. Fill in the chart by providing details of the American strategy, the British strategy, key events, and major battles for each of the periods. When you are finished, ask yourself how and why each side's strategy shifted or changed. Why were the Americans ultimately victorious? To do this exercise online or to download this chart, visit bedfordstmartins.com/roarkunderstanding.

Period	American strategy	British strategy	Key events	Major battles/ victor
June 1775– December 1776				
January 1777– February 1778				
March 1778– September 1783				

Now that you have reviewed key elements of the chapter, take a step back and try to explain the big picture by answering these questions. Remember to use specific examples from the chapter in your answers. To do this exercise online, visit bedfordstmartins.com/roarkunderstanding.

DECLARING INDEPENDENCE

► Why were so many Americans divided about the question of independence from Britain?
► What factors contributed to the decision by the Continental Congress to declare independence in July 1776?

THE FIRST TWO YEARS OF WAR

► What challenges did the Americans face in the first year of the war? How successful were they in meeting them?
► What impact did other European powers and Indian peoples have on the course of the war?

LOOKING BACKWARD, LOOKING AHEAD

► When did the chain of events that culminated in the establishment of an independent United States begin? In 1763? In 1776? In 1783? At another date? Present evidence to support your answer.
► What challenges did the United States face as it emerged victorious from the Revolutionary War?

AMERICAN VICTORY

► Why did the British switch to the southern strategy? Why did it fail?
► Is it more accurate to say that the Americans won the Revolutionary War or that the British lost it? Why?

IN YOUR OWN WORDS

Imagine that you must explain chapter 7 to someone who hasn't read it. What would be the most important points to include and why?

8
BUILDING A REPUBLIC

1775–1789

> This chapter explores the events and debates that led to the formulation and ratification of the Constitution, the legal foundation of American government after 1788. It examines the challenges the country faced in the 1780s, the efforts of the states to define freedom and citizenship, and the process that led to the abandonment of the Articles of Confederation and the ratification of the United States Constitution.

> What kind of government did the Articles of Confederation create?

> How did the states define freedom and citizenship?

> Why did the Articles of Confederation fail?

> How did the U.S. Constitution increase federal power?

> What were the obstacles to ratification of the Constitution?

> Conclusion: What was the "republican remedy"?

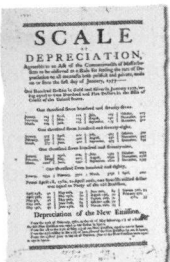

DID YOU KNOW?

Immediately after the American Revolution, the first federal government had no power of taxation.

> What kind of government did the Articles of Confederation create?

Articles of Confederation Delegates to the Second Continental Congress hammered out the Articles of Confederation over many months in 1776 and 1777. Once the congress agreed on it, the plan was printed and distributed to state legislatures for ratification, a process that took nearly five years because it required the assent of all thirteen. National Archives.

BEGINNING IN 1775 and continuing for five years after declaring independence, the Second Continental Congress lacked a formal constitutional basis for its governance. Delegates first had to work out a plan of government that embodied Revolutionary principles. With monarchy gone, where would sovereignty lie? What would be the nature of representation? Who would hold the power of taxation? Who should vote? Who should rule? The resulting plan, called the **Articles of Confederation**, proved to be surprisingly difficult to implement, mainly because the thirteen states had serious disagreements about how to manage areas to the west whose political ownership was contested. Once the Articles were finally ratified, the confederation government seemed to many to be far less relevant or interesting than the state governments.

Articles of Confederation

▶ The constitutional basis for national government from 1781 to 1788. The Articles defined the Union as a loose confederation of states existing mainly to foster a common defense. The Articles provided for no executive and limited congress's authority to tax, leaving the preponderance of political power in the hands of the states.

Congress, Confederation, and the Problem of Western Lands

Only after declaring independence did the Continental Congress turn its attention to creating a written document that would specify what powers the congress had and by what authority it existed. There was widespread agreement on key government powers: pursuing war and peace, conducting foreign relations, regulating trade, and running a postal service. But there was serious disagreement about the powers of the congress over the western boundaries of the states. Virginia and Connecticut, for example, had old colonial charters that located their western boundaries at the Mississippi River. States without extensive land claims insisted on redrawing those colonial boundaries.

CHAPTER LOCATOR | What kind of government did the Articles of Confederation create?

198 CHAPTER 8
BUILDING A REPUBLIC, 1775–1789

This was no mere quarrel over lines on a map. In the 1780s, more than 100,000 Americans had moved west of the Appalachian Mountains, and another 100,000 were moving from eastern towns to newly opened land in northern Vermont and western New York and Pennsylvania, as well as to Kentucky, Georgia, and beyond. Who owned the land, who protected it, and who governed it? These were major and pressing questions.

Congress reached agreement on a proposal for the Articles of Confederation in November 1777. The Articles defined the union as a loose confederation of states, characterized as "a firm league of friendship" existing mainly to foster a common defense. The structure of the government paralleled that of the existing Continental Congress. There was no national executive (that is, no president) and no national judiciary. Each state delegation cast a single vote in congress. Routine decisions in the congress required a simple majority of seven states; for momentous decisions, such as declaring war, nine states needed to agree. To approve or amend the Articles required the unanimous consent both of the thirteen state delegations and of the thirteen state legislatures.

On the delicate question of taxes, necessary to finance the war, the Articles provided an ingenious but troublesome solution. Each state was to contribute in proportion to the property value of the state's land. Large and populous states would give more than small or sparsely populated states. The actual taxes would be levied by the state legislatures, not by the congress, to preserve the Revolution's principle of taxation only by direct representation. However, no mechanism compelled states to pay.

The lack of centralized authority in the confederation government was exactly what many state leaders wanted in the late 1770s. A league of states with rotating personnel, no executive branch, no power of taxation, and a requirement of unanimity for any major change seemed to be a good way to keep government in check. Yet there were problems. The requirement for unanimous approval stalled the acceptance of the Articles for four additional years. The key dispute involved lands west of the existing states (**Map 8.1**). Five states, all lacking land claims, insisted that the congress preserve western lands as a national domain that would eventually constitute new states. The other eight states refused to yield their colonial-era claims and opposed giving the congress power to alter boundaries.

The eight land-claiming states were ready to sign the Articles of Confederation in 1777. Three states without claims, Rhode Island, Pennsylvania, and New Jersey, eventually capitulated and signed, "not from a Conviction of the Equality and Justness of it," said a New Jersey delegate, "but merely from an absolute Necessity there was of complying to save the Continent." But Delaware and Maryland continued to hold out. In 1779, the disputants finally compromised: Any land a state volunteered to relinquish would become the national domain. When James Madison and Thomas Jefferson ceded Virginia's huge land claim in 1781, the Articles were at last unanimously approved.

The western lands issue demonstrated that powerful interests divided the thirteen new states. The apparent unity of purpose inspired by fighting the war against Britain papered over sizable cracks in the new confederation.

Running the New Government

No fanfare greeted the long-awaited inauguration of the new government. The congress continued to sputter along, its problems far from solved by the signing of the

CHRONOLOGY

1775
– Second Continental Congress begins to meet.

1777
– Articles of Confederation are sent to states.

1781
– Articles of Confederation are ratified.
– Creation of executive departments.

How did the states define freedom and citizenship?

Why did the Articles of Confederation fail?

How did the U.S. Constitution increase federal power?

What were the obstacles to ratification of the Constitution?

Conclusion: What was the "republican remedy"?

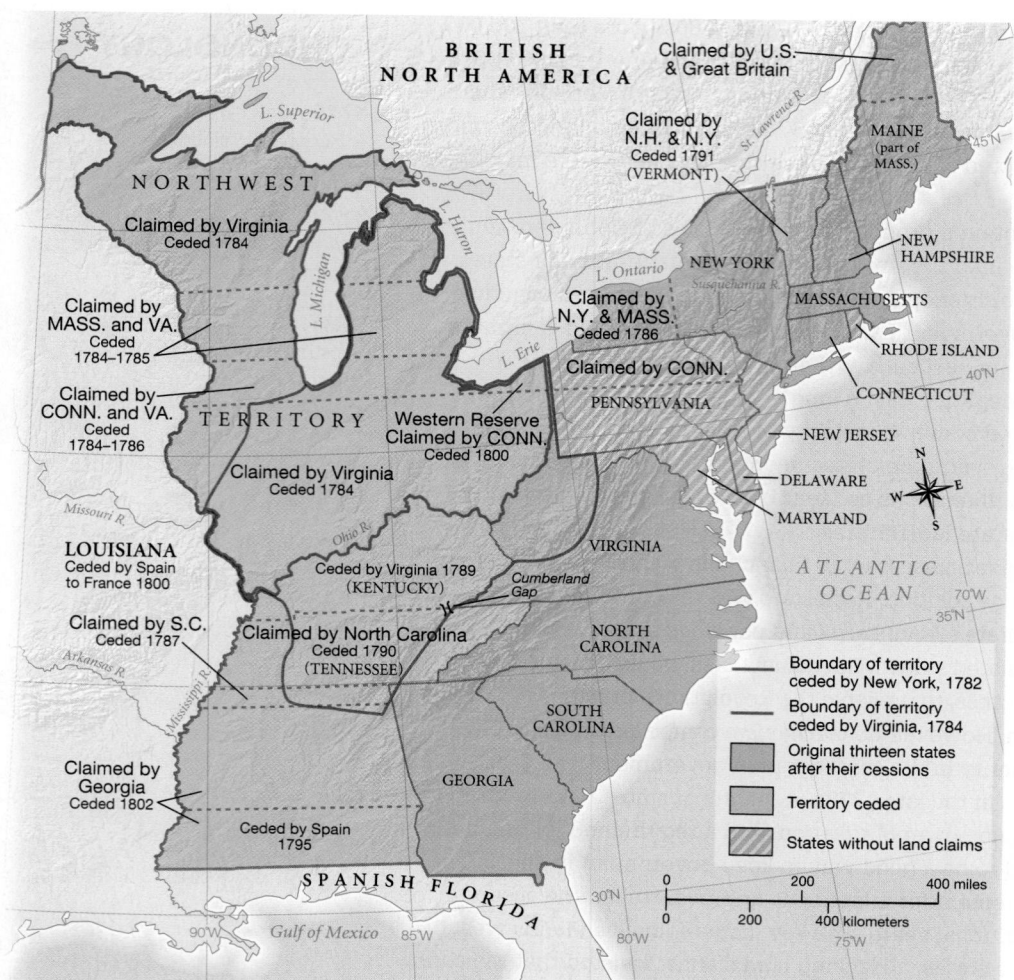

MAP 8.1 ■ Cession of Western Lands, 1782–1802
The thirteen new states found it hard to ratify the Articles of Confederation without settling their conflicting land claims in the West, an area larger than the original states and occupied by Indian tribes. The five states objecting to the Articles' silence over western lands policy were Maryland, Delaware, New Jersey, Rhode Island, and Pennsylvania.

Articles. Lack of a quorum often hampered day-to-day activities. Many politicians preferred to devote their energies to state governments, especially when the congress seemed deadlocked or, worse, irrelevant. It also did not help that the congress had no permanent home. During the war, when the British army threatened Philadelphia, the congress relocated to small Pennsylvania towns such as Lancaster and York and then to Baltimore. After hostilities ceased, the congress moved from Trenton to Princeton to Annapolis to New York City.

To address the difficulties of an inefficient congress, executive departments of war, finance, and foreign affairs were created in 1781 to handle purely administrative functions. When the department heads were ambitious, they could exercise considerable executive power. The Articles of Confederation had deliberately refrained from setting up an executive branch, but a modest one was being invented by necessity.

> ## QUICK REVIEW

Why was the confederation government's authority so limited?

CHAPTER LOCATOR | What kind of government did the Articles of Confederation create?

How did the states define freedom and citizenship?

Widow from Essex County

Mrs. Elizabeth Alexander Stevens was married to John Stevens, a New Jersey delegate to the Continental Congress in 1783. Widowed in 1792, she would have then been eligible to vote in state elections according to New Jersey's unique enfranchisement of property-holding women. The widow Stevens died in 1799, before suffrage was redefined to be the exclusive right of males. New Jersey Historical Society.

IN THE FIRST DECADE of independence, the states were sovereign and all-powerful. Relatively few functions, such as declaring war and peace, had been transferred to the confederation government. As Americans discarded their British identity, they thought of themselves instead as Virginians or New Yorkers or Rhode Islanders. Familiar and close to home, state governments claimed the allegiance of citizens and became the arena in which the Revolution's innovations would first be tried.

The State Constitutions

In May 1776, the congress recommended that all states draw up constitutions based on "the authority of the people." By 1778, ten states had done so, and three more (Connecticut, Massachusetts, and Rhode Island) had adopted and updated their original colonial charters. A shared feature of all the state constitutions was the conviction that government ultimately rests on the consent of the governed. Political writers in the late 1770s embraced the concept of republicanism as the underpinning of the new governments. Republicanism meant more than popular elections and representative institutions. For some, republicanism invoked a way of thinking about who leaders should be: autonomous, virtuous citizens who placed civic values above private interests. For others, it suggested direct

| How did the states define freedom and citizenship? | Why did the Articles of Confederation fail? | How did the U.S. Constitution increase federal power? | What were the obstacles to ratification of the Constitution? | Conclusion: What was the "republican remedy"? |

201

bills of rights
▶ Lists of basic individual liberties that governments could not violate. Virginia debated and passed the first bill of rights in June 1776, and other states borrowed from its language. These lists usually included general rights to life, liberty, and property, and specific rights to freedom of speech, freedom of the press, and trial by jury.

democracy, with nothing standing in the way of the will of the people. For all, it meant government that promoted the people's welfare.

Widespread agreement about the virtues of republicanism went hand in hand with the idea that republics could succeed only in relatively small units so that the people could make sure their interests were being served. Nearly every state continued the colonial practice of a two-chamber assembly but greatly augmented the powers of the lower house. Two states, Pennsylvania and Georgia, abolished the more elite upper house altogether, and most states severely limited the term and powers of the governor.

Six of the state constitutions included **bills of rights**—lists of basic individual liberties that government could not abridge. Virginia debated and passed the first bill of rights in June 1776, and many of the other states borrowed from it. Along with inherent rights, closely resembling the inalienable rights to "life, liberty, and the pursuit of happiness" claimed in the Declaration of Independence, these documents included more specific rights to freedom of speech, freedom of the press, and trial by jury.

Who Are "the People"?

When the Continental Congress called for state constitutions based on "the authority of the people," and when the Virginia bill of rights granted "all men" certain rights, who was meant by "the people"? Who exactly were the citizens of this new country, and how far would the principle of democratic government extend? Different people answered these questions differently, but in the 1770s certain limits to full political participation by all Americans were widely agreed upon.

One limit was defined by property. In nearly every state, voters and political candidates had to meet varying property qualifications. Only property owners were presumed to possess the necessary independence of mind to make wise political choices. Are not propertyless men, asked John Adams, "too little acquainted with public affairs to form a right judgment, and too dependent upon other men to have a will of their own?"

Property qualifications probably disfranchised from one-quarter to one-half of adult white males in all the states. Not all of them took their nonvoter status quietly. One Maryland man wondered what was so special about being worth £30, the property threshold for voting in that state: "Every poor man has a life, a personal liberty, and a right to his earnings; and is in danger of being injured by government in a variety of ways." Why then restrict such a man from voting? Others pointed out that propertyless men were fighting and dying in the Revolutionary War; surely they were expressing an active concern about politics. Finally, a few radical voices challenged the notion that wealth was correlated with good citizenship; maybe the opposite was true. But ideas like this were outside the mainstream. The writers of the new constitutions, themselves men of property, viewed the right to own and preserve property as a central principle of the Revolution.

Another exclusion from voting—women—was so ingrained that few stopped to question it. Yet the logic of allowing propertied females to vote did occur to a handful of well-placed women. Abigail Adams wrote to her husband, John, in 1782, "Even in the freest countrys our property is subject to the controul and disposal of our partners, to whom the Laws have given a sovereign Authority.

CHAPTER LOCATOR | What kind of government did the Articles of Confederation create?

Deprived of a voice in Legislation, obliged to submit to those Laws which are imposed upon us, is it not sufficient to make us indifferent to the publick Welfare?"

Only three states specified that voters had to be male, so powerful was the unspoken assumption that only men could vote. Still, in one state, small numbers of women began to turn out at the polls in the 1780s. New Jersey's constitution of 1776 enfranchised all free inhabitants worth more than £50, language that in theory opened the door to free blacks as well as unmarried women who met the property requirement. (Married women owned no property, for by law their husbands held title to everything.) In 1790, only about 1,000 free black adults of both sexes lived in New Jersey, a state with a population of 184,000. The number of unmarried adult white women was probably also small and comprised mainly widows. In view of the property requirement, the voter blocs enfranchised under this law were minuscule. Still, this highly unusual situation lasted until 1807, when a new state law specifically disfranchised both blacks and women. Henceforth, independence of mind, that essential precondition of voting, was redefined to be sex- and race-specific.

In the 1780s, voting everywhere was class-specific because of the property restrictions. John Adams urged the framers of the Massachusetts constitution not even to discuss the scope of suffrage but simply to adopt the traditional colonial property qualifications. If suffrage is brought up for debate, he warned, "there will be no end of it. New claims will arise; women will demand a vote; lads from twelve to twenty-one will think their rights not enough attended to; and every man who has not a farthing, will demand an equal voice with any other."

Equality and Slavery

Restrictions on political participation did not mean that propertyless people enjoyed no civil rights and liberties. The various state bills of rights applied to all free individuals. No matter how poor, a free person was entitled to life, liberty, property, and freedom of conscience. Unfree people, however, were another matter.

The author of the Virginia bill of rights was George Mason, a plantation owner with 118 slaves. When drafting the right that "All men are by nature equally free and independent," Mason did not have slaves in mind; he instead was asserting that white Americans were the equals of the British and could not be denied the liberties of British citizens. Other Virginia legislators, worried about misinterpretations, added a qualifying phrase: that all men "when they enter into a state of society" have inherent rights. As one legislator wrote, with relief, "Slaves, not being constituent members of our society, could never pretend to any benefit from such a maxim."

One month later, the Declaration of Independence used essentially the same phrase about equality, this time without the modifying clause about entering society. Two state constitutions, for Pennsylvania and Massachusetts, also picked it up. In Massachusetts, one town suggested rewording the draft constitution to read "All men, whites and blacks, are born free and equal." The suggestion was not implemented.

Nevertheless, after 1776, the ideals of the Revolution about natural equality and liberty began to erode the institution of slavery. Often, enslaved blacks led the challenge. In 1777, several Massachusetts slaves petitioned the state

| How did the states define freedom and citizenship? | Why did the Articles of Confederation fail? | How did the U.S. Constitution increase federal power? | What were the obstacles to ratification of the Constitution? | Conclusion: What was the "republican remedy"? |

203

Paul Cuffe's Silhouette

Paul Cuffe of Martha's Vineyard, off the Massachusetts coast, was the son of a Wampanoag Indian woman and an African man named Kofi, who had purchased his own freedom from a Quaker owner. Cuffe went to sea at age sixteen during the American Revolution and endured several months of imprisonment by the British. After the war, he and his brother John protested that Massachusetts taxed free blacks who lacked the privilege of voting—in other words, taxation without representation. Library of Congress.

legislature, claiming a "natural & unalienable right to that freedom which the great Parent of the Universe hath bestowed equally on all mankind." They modestly asked for freedom for their children at age twenty-one and were turned down. In 1779, similar petitions in Connecticut and New Hampshire met with no success. Seven Massachusetts freemen, including the mariner brothers Paul and John Cuffe, refused to pay taxes for three years on the grounds that they could not vote and so were not represented. The Cuffe brothers landed in jail in 1780 for tax evasion, but their petition to the Massachusetts legislature spurred the extension of suffrage to taxpaying free blacks in 1783.

Another way to bring the issue before lawmakers was to sue in court. In 1781, a woman called Elizabeth Freeman (Mum Bett) was the first to win freedom in a Massachusetts court, basing her case on the just-passed state constitution that declared "all men are born free and equal." Later that year, another Massachusetts slave, Quok Walker, charged his master with assault and battery, arguing that he was a free man under that same constitutional phrase. Walker won and was set free, a decision confirmed in an appeal to the state's superior court in 1783. Several similar cases followed, and by 1789 slavery had been effectively abolished by a series of judicial decisions in Massachusetts.

State legislatures acted more slowly. Pennsylvania enacted a gradual emancipation law in 1780. Only infants born to a slave mother on or after March 1, 1780, would be freed, but not until age twenty-eight. Thus no current slave in Pennsylvania could gain freedom until 1808, while those born before 1780 remained slaves. Not until 1847 did Pennsylvania fully abolish slavery. But slaves did not wait for such slow implementation. Untold numbers in Pennsylvania simply

CHAPTER LOCATOR | What kind of government did the Articles of Confederation create?

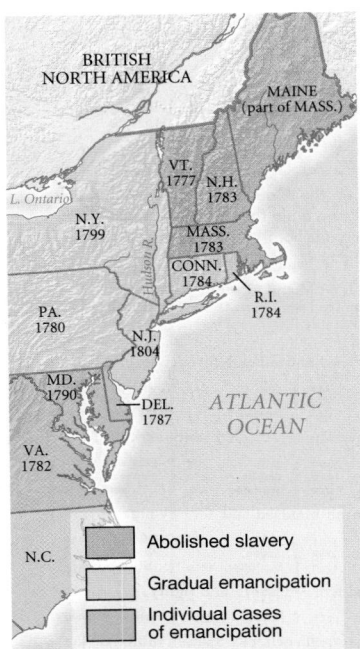

Legal Changes to Slavery, 1777–1804

ran away and asserted their freedom, sometimes with the help of sympathetic whites. One estimate holds that more than half of young slave men in Philadelphia joined the ranks of free blacks, and by 1790, free blacks outnumbered slaves in Pennsylvania two to one.

Between 1784 and 1804, Rhode Island, Connecticut, New York, and New Jersey followed Pennsylvania's lead and adopted gradual emancipation laws. Gradual emancipation illustrates the tension between radical and conservative implications of republican ideology. Republican government protected people's liberties and property, yet slaves were both people and property. Gradual emancipation balanced the civil rights of blacks and the property rights of their owners by delaying the promise of freedom.

South of Pennsylvania, in Delaware, Maryland, and Virginia, where slavery was so important to the economy, emancipation bills were rejected. All three states, however, eased legal restrictions and allowed individual acts of emancipation for adult slaves below the age of forty-five under new manumission laws. By 1790, close to 10,000 newly freed Virginia slaves had formed local free black communities complete with schools and churches.

In the deep South—the Carolinas and Georgia—freedom for slaves was unthinkable among whites. Yet several thousand slaves had defected to the British during the war, and between 3,000 and 4,000 left with the British at the war's conclusion. Adding northern blacks evacuated from New York City in 1783, the probable total of emancipated blacks who left the United States was between 8,000 and 10,000. Some went to Canada, some to England, and some to Sierra Leone on the west coast of Africa. Many hundreds took refuge with the Seminole and Creek Indians, becoming permanent members of their communities in Spanish Florida and western Georgia.

Although all these instances of emancipation were gradual, small, and certainly incomplete, their symbolic importance was enormous. Every state from Pennsylvania north acknowledged that slavery was fundamentally inconsistent with Revolutionary ideology; "all men are created equal" was beginning to acquire real force as a basic principle.

Slave Populations of Pennsylvania, New York, and New Jersey in 1800

Pennsylvania: 1,700
New York: 20,000
New Jersey: 12,000

QUICK REVIEW

What were the limits of rights and freedom within the various states?

| How did the states define freedom and citizenship? | Why did the Articles of Confederation fail? | How did the U.S. Constitution increase federal power? | What were the obstacles to ratification of the Constitution? | Conclusion: What was the "republican remedy"? |

Why did the Articles of Confederation fail?

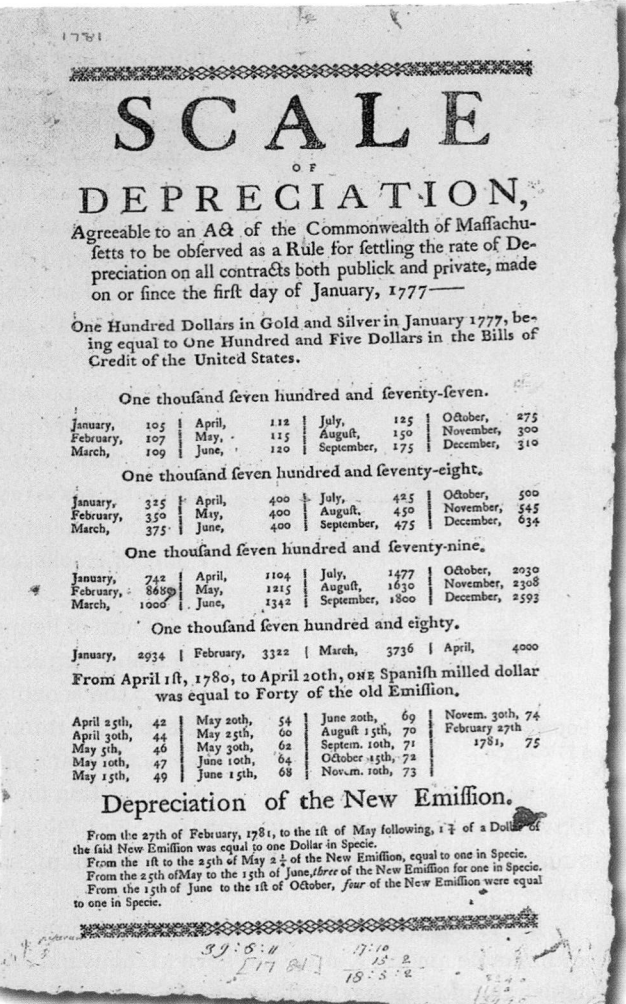

Scale of Depreciation

This chart shows the declining monthly value of two emissions of paper dollars from January 1777 to October 1781 as stipulated by the government of Massachusetts. In January 1777, 105 paper dollars were equal in buying power to $100 in silver or gold. In April 1780, 4,000 paper dollars were needed to equal the buying power of $100 in gold or silver. Such a chart was needed when debtors and creditors settled accounts contracted at one time and paid off later in greatly depreciated dollars. Courtesy, American Antiquarian Society.

▶ FOR MORE HELP ANALYZING THIS IMAGE, see the visual activity for this chapter in the Online Study Guide at bedfordstmartins.com/roarkunderstanding.

IN 1783, the confederation government faced three interrelated concerns: paying down the large war debt, making formal peace with the Indians, and dealing with western settlement. From 1784 to 1786, the congress struggled mightily with these three issues. Some leaders were gripped by a sense of crisis, fearing that the Articles of Confederation were too weak. Others defended the Articles as the best guarantee of liberty because real governance occurred at the state level, closer to the people. A major outbreak of civil disorder in western Massachusetts quickly crystallized the debate and propelled the critics of the Articles into decisive and far-reaching action.

Financial Chaos and Paper Money

Seven years of war produced a chaotic economy in the 1780s. The confederation and the individual states had run up huge war debts financed by printing paper money and borrowing from private sources. Some $400 million to $500 million in paper currency had been injected into the economy, and prices and wages fluctuated wildly. Private debt and rapid expenditure flourished, and as Massachusetts

CHAPTER LOCATOR | What kind of government did the Articles of Confederation create?

laborer William Manning described, "jails were crowded with debtors." A serious postwar depression settled in by the mid-1780s and did not lift until the 1790s.

The confederation government itself was in a terrible financial fix. Continental dollars had lost almost all value. Desperate times required desperate measures. The congress chose Robert Morris, Philadelphia merchant and newly reelected delegate, to be superintendent of finance. From 1781 to 1784, he took charge of the confederation's economic problems.

To augment the government's revenue, Morris first proposed a 5 percent impost (an import tax). Since the Articles of Confederation did not authorize taxation, an amendment was needed, but unanimous agreement proved impossible. Rhode Island and New York, whose bustling ports provided ample state revenue, preferred to keep their money for themselves.

Morris's next idea was the creation of the Bank of North America. This private bank would enjoy a special relationship with the confederation, holding the government's hard money (gold and silver coins), as well as private deposits, and providing it with short-term loans. The bank's contribution to economic stability came in the form of banknotes, pieces of paper inscribed with a dollar value. Unlike paper money, banknotes were backed by hard money in the bank's vaults and thus would not depreciate. Congress voted to approve the bank in 1781. But the bank had limited success in curing the confederation's economic woes because it issued very little currency, and its charter was allowed to expire in 1786.

The government formed by the Articles of Confederation tried but failed to resuscitate the economy in the 1780s. Because the Articles reserved most economic functions to the states, the congress was helpless to tax trade, control inflation, curb the flow of state-issued paper money, or pay the mounting public debt. However, the confederation had one source of enormous potential wealth: the huge western territories, attractive to the fast-growing white population but inhabited by Indians.

The Treaty of Fort Stanwix

Since the Indians had not participated in the Treaty of Paris of 1783, the confederation government hoped to formalize treaties ending ongoing hostilities between Indians and settlers and securing land cessions. The most pressing problem was the land inhabited by the Iroquois Confederacy, a league of six tribes, now claimed by the states of New York and Massachusetts based on their colonial charters.

At issue was the revenue stream that land sales would generate: which government would get it? The congress summoned the Iroquois to a meeting in October 1784 at Fort Stanwix, on the upper reaches of the Mohawk River. The Articles of Confederation gave the congress (as opposed to individual states) the right to manage diplomacy, war, and "all affairs with the Indians, not members of any of the States." But New York's governor seized on this ambiguous language to claim that the Iroquois were in fact "members" of his state, and called his own meeting with the Iroquois at Fort Stanwix in September. Suspecting that New York might be superseded by the congress, the most important chiefs declined to come and instead sent deputies without authority to negotiate. The Mohawk leader Joseph Brant shrewdly identified the problem of divided authority that afflicted the confederation government: "Here lies some Difficulty in our Minds, that there should be two separate bodies to manage these Affairs." No deal was struck with New York.

| How did the states define freedom and citizenship? | **Why did the Articles of Confederation fail?** | How did the U.S. Constitution increase federal power? | What were the obstacles to ratification of the Constitution? | Conclusion: What was the "republican remedy"? |

CHRONOLOGY

1781
– Bank of North America is chartered.

1784
– Treaty of Fort Stanwix with Iroquois Confederacy.

1785
– Ordinance of 1785 maps western lands into squares.

1786-1787
– Shays's Rebellion protesting taxes in Massachusetts leads to call for a constitutional convention.

1787
– Northwest Ordinance establishes a three-step process for new states to enter the Union.

Treaty of Fort Stanwix

Treaty of Fort Stanwix
► October 1784 treaty between the United States and the Iroquois Confederacy. The Americans demanded a return of prisoners of war, recognition of the confederation's authority to negotiate, and cession of a strip of land from Fort Niagara due south. The Americans took hostages until the terms of the treaty were met. This act, combined with the fact that many affected tribes were not present at the negotiations, led some Indians to later disavow the treaty.

Three weeks later, U.S. commissioners opened proceedings at Fort Stanwix with the Seneca chief Cornplanter and Captain Aaron Hill, a Mohawk leader, accompanied by six hundred Indians from the six tribes. The U.S. commissioners arrived with a security detail of one hundred New Jersey militiamen. The Americans demanded a return of prisoners of war; recognition of the confederation's authority to negotiate, rather than that of individual states; and an all-important cession of a strip of land from Fort Niagara due south, which established U.S.-held territory adjacent to the border with Canada. This crucial change enclosed the Iroquois land within the United States and made it impossible for the Indians to claim to be *between* the United States and Canada. When the tribal leaders balked, one of the commissioners sternly replied, "You are mistaken in supposing that, having been excluded from the treaty *between* the United States and the King of England, you are become a free and independent nation and may make what terms you please. It is not so. You are a subdued people."

In the end, the treaty was signed, gifts were given, and six high-level Indian hostages were kept at the fort awaiting the release of the American prisoners taken during the Revolutionary War, mostly women and children. In addition, a significant side deal sealed the release of much of the Seneca tribe's claim to the Ohio Valley to the United States. This move was a major surprise and disappointment to the Delaware, Mingo, and Shawnee Indians who lived there. In the months to come, tribes not at the meeting tried to disavow the **Treaty of Fort Stanwix** as a document signed under coercion by virtual hostages. But the confederation government ignored those complaints and made plans to survey and develop the Ohio Territory.

New York's governor shrewdly figured that the congress's power to implement the treaty terms was limited. The confederation had little money, and its leadership was stretched. So New York began surveying and then selling the very land it had failed to secure by individual treaty with the Iroquois. As that fact became generally known, it pointed up the weakness of the confederation government. One Connecticut leader wondered, "What is to defend us from the ambition and rapacity of New-York, when she has spread over that vast territory, which she claims and holds? Do we not already see in her the seeds of an over-bearing ambition?"

Land Ordinances and the Northwest Territory

The congress ignored western New York and turned instead to the Ohio Valley to make good on the promise of western expansion. Delegate Thomas Jefferson, charged with drafting a policy, proposed dividing the territory north of the Ohio River and east of the Mississippi—called the Northwest Territory—into nine new states with evenly spaced east-west boundaries and townships ten miles square. He advocated giving the land to settlers, rather than selling it, arguing that future property taxes on the improved land would be payment enough. Jefferson's aim was to encourage rapid and democratic settlement, to build a nation of freeholders (as opposed to renters), and to discourage land speculation. Jefferson also insisted on representative governments in the new states; they would not become colonies of the older states. Finally, Jefferson's draft prohibited slavery in the nine new states.

The congress adopted parts of Jefferson's plan in the Ordinance of 1784: the rectangular grid, the nine new states, and the guarantee of self-government and eventual statehood. What the congress found too radical was the proposal to give

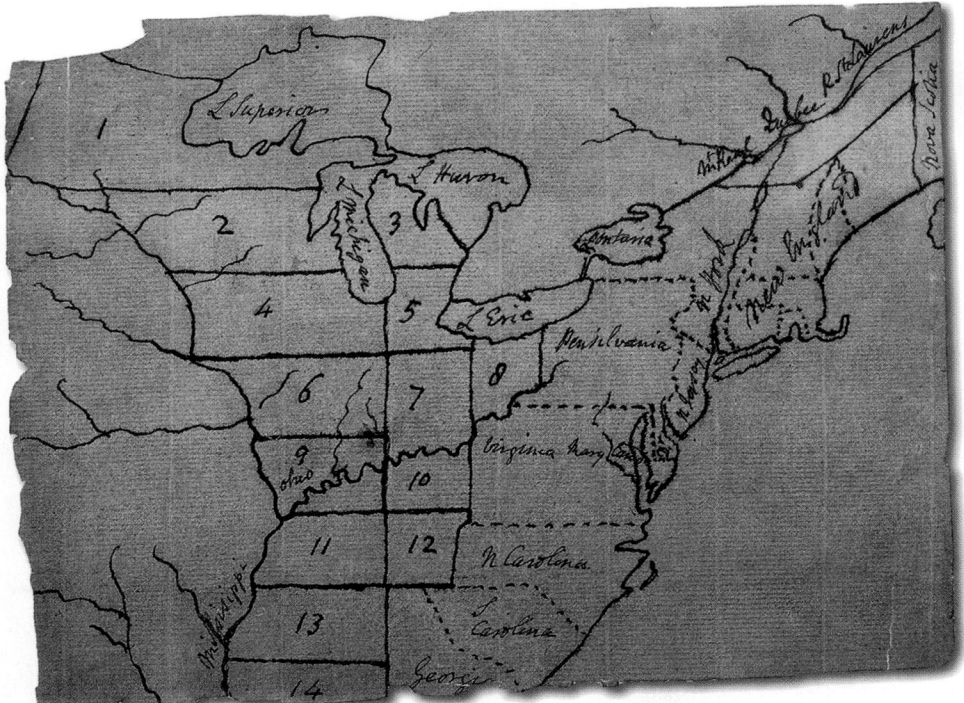

Jefferson's Map of the Northwest Territory

Thomas Jefferson sketched out borders for nine new states in his initial plan for the Northwest Territory in 1784 and additional anticipated states south of the Ohio River. Straight lines and right angles held a strong appeal for him. But such regularity ignored inconvenient geographic features such as rivers and even more inconvenient political facts such as Indian territorial claims. William L. Clements Library.

▶ FOR MORE HELP ANALYZING THIS IMAGE, see the visual activity for this chapter in the Online Study Guide at bedfordstmartins.com/roarkunderstanding.

away the land; the national domain was the confederation's only source of independent wealth. The slavery prohibition also failed, by a vote of seven to six states.

A year later, the congress revised the legislation with procedures for mapping and selling the land. The Ordinance of 1785 called for three to five states, divided into townships six miles square, further divided into thirty-six sections of 640 acres, each section enough for four family farms (**Map 8.2**). Property was thus reduced to easily mappable squares. Land would be sold by public auction at a minimum price of one dollar an acre, with highly desirable land bid up for more. Two further restrictions applied: The minimum purchase was 640 acres, and payment must be in hard money or in certificates of debt from Revolutionary days. This effectively meant that the land's first purchasers would be prosperous speculators. The grid of invariant squares further enhanced speculation, allowing buyers and sellers to operate without ever setting foot on the acreage. The commodification of land had been taken to a new level.

Speculators usually held the land for resale rather than inhabiting it. Thus they avoided direct contact with the most serious obstacle to settlement: the dozens of Indian tribes that claimed the land as their own. The treaty signed at Fort Stanwix in 1784 was followed by the Treaty of Fort McIntosh in 1785, which similarly coerced partial cessions of land from the Delaware, Huron, and Miami tribes. Finally, in 1786, a united Indian meeting near Detroit issued an ultimatum: No cession would be valid without the unanimous consent of the tribes. The Indians advised the United States to "prevent your surveyors and other people from coming upon our side of the Ohio river." For two more decades, violent Indian wars in Ohio and Indiana would continue to impede white settlement (see chapter 9).

| How did the states define freedom and citizenship? | **Why did the Articles of Confederation fail?** | How did the U.S. Constitution increase federal power? | What were the obstacles to ratification of the Constitution? | Conclusion: What was the "republican remedy"? |

209

MAP 8.2 ■ The Northwest Territory and the Ordinance of 1785

Surveyors mapping the eastern edge of the Northwest Territory followed the Ordinance of 1785, using the stars as well as poles and chains (standard surveying equipment) to run boundary lines. The result was a blanket of six-mile-square townships, subdivided into one-mile squares each containing sixteen 40-acre farms.

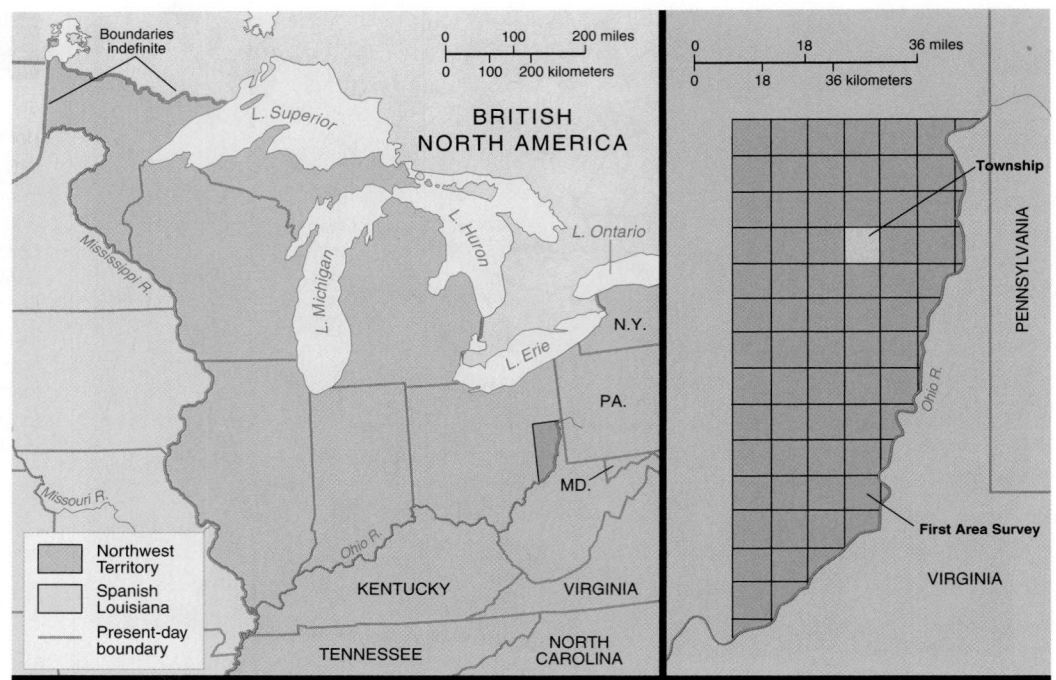

Northwest Ordinance

▶ Land act of 1787 that set forth the process by which settled territories would become states. The law stipulated that as the population of a territory increased, it would move step-by-step closer to full statehood. It also banned slavery in the Northwest Territory. The Northwest Ordinance was intended to guarantee that the United States would not become a colonial power over western lands.

In 1787, a third land act, called the **Northwest Ordinance**, set forth a three-stage process by which settled territories would advance to statehood. As the population of a territory increased, it would move step-by-step closer to full statehood. At all three territorial stages, the inhabitants were subject to taxation to support the Union, in the same manner as were the original states.

The Northwest Ordinance of 1787 and the Path to Statehood

Phase One	Congress appoints officials for a sparsely populated territory who adopt a legal code and appoint local magistrates to administer justice.
Phase Two	When the free male population of voting age and landowning status (fifty acres) reaches 5,000, the territory elects its own legislature and sends a nonvoting delegate to the congress.
Phase Three	When the population of voting citizens reaches 60,000, the territory writes a state constitution and applies for full admission to the Union.

The Northwest Ordinance of 1787 was perhaps the most important legislation passed by the confederation government. It ensured that the new United States, so recently released from colonial dependency, would not itself become a colonial power—at least not with respect to white citizens. The mechanism it established allowed for the successful and orderly expansion of the United States across the continent in the next century.

Nonwhites were not forgotten or neglected in the 1787 ordinance. The brief document acknowledged the Indian presence in the Northwest Territory and promised that "the utmost good faith shall always be observed towards the Indians; their lands and property shall never be taken from them without their consent; and, in their property, rights, and liberty, they shall never be invaded or

CHAPTER LOCATOR | What kind of government did the Articles of Confederation create?

disturbed, unless in just and lawful wars authorized by Congress." The 1787 ordinance further pledged that "laws founded in justice and humanity, shall from time to time be made for preventing wrongs being done to them, and for preserving peace and friendship with them." Such promises were full of noble intentions, but they were not generally honored in the decades to come.

Jefferson's original and remarkable suggestion to prohibit slavery in the Northwest Territory resurfaced in the 1787 ordinance, passing this time without any debate. Probably the addition of a fugitive slave provision in the act set southern congressmen at ease: Escaped slaves caught north of the Ohio River would be returned south. The ordinance thus acknowledged and supported slavery even as it prohibited it in one region. Further, abundant territory south of the Ohio remained available for the spread of slavery. Still, the prohibition of slavery in the Northwest Territory perpetuated the dynamic of gradual emancipation in the North. North-South sectionalism based on slavery was slowly taking shape.

Shays's Rebellion, 1786–1787

Without an impost amendment, and with public land sales projected but not yet realized, the confederation turned to the states in the 1780s to contribute revenue voluntarily. Struggling with their own war debts, most state legislatures were reluctant to tax their constituents too heavily. Massachusetts, however, had a fiscally conservative legislature dominated by the coastal commercial centers. For four years, the legislature passed tough tax laws that called for payment in hard money, not cheap paper. Farmers in the western two-thirds of the state found it increasingly difficult to comply and repeatedly petitioned against what they called oppressive taxation. In July 1786, when the legislature adjourned, having yet again ignored their complaints, dissidents held a series of conventions and called for revisions to the state constitution to promote democracy, eliminate the elite upper house, and move the capital farther west in the state.

Still unheard in Boston, the dissidents targeted the county courts, the local symbol of state authority. In the fall of 1786, several thousand armed men marched on courthouses in six Massachusetts counties and forced judges to close their courts until the state constitution was revised. Sympathetic local militias did not intervene. The insurgents were not predominantly poor or debt-ridden farmers; they included veteran soldiers and officers in the Continental army as well as town leaders. One was a farmer and onetime army captain, Daniel Shays.

The governor of Massachusetts, James Bowdoin, once a protester against British taxes, now characterized the western dissidents as illegal rebels. He vilified Shays as the chief leader, and a Boston newspaper claimed that Shays planned to burn Boston to the ground and overthrow the government. Another former radical, Samuel Adams, took the extreme position that "the man who dares rebel against the laws of a republic ought to suffer death." The dissidents challenged the aging revolutionaries' assumption that popularly elected governments would always be fair and just.

Members of the Continental Congress worried that the Massachusetts insurgency was spinning out of control. In October, the congress attempted to triple the size of the federal army, but fewer than 100 men enlisted. So Governor Bowdoin raised a private army, gaining the services of some 3,000 men, with pay provided by wealthy and fearful Boston merchants.

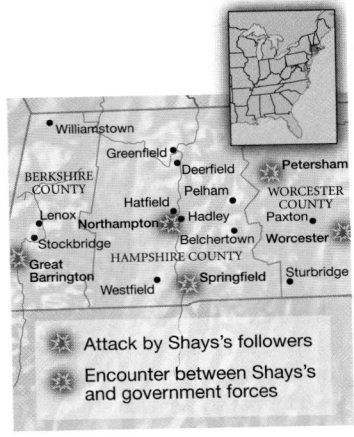

Shays's Rebellion, 1786–1787

| How did the states define freedom and citizenship? | **Why did the Articles of Confederation fail?** | How did the U.S. Constitution increase federal power? | What were the obstacles to ratification of the Constitution? | Conclusion: What was the "republican remedy"? |

211

Daniel Shays and Job Shattuck

A Boston almanac of 1787 yields the only rough depiction of Daniel Shays in existence. Shays is standing with another rebel leader, Job Shattuck, from the town of Groton. This particular almanac series was quite pro-Constitution in 1788, so very likely this picture was intended to mock the rebels by showing them in fancy uniforms and armed with swords, trappings beyond their presumed lowly means. National Portrait Gallery, Smithsonian Institution/Art Resource, NY.

In January 1787, the insurgents learned of the private army marching their way, and 1,500 of them moved to capture a federal armory in Springfield to obtain weapons. But a militia band loyal to the state government beat them to the weapons facility and met their attack with gunfire; 4 rebels were killed and another 20 wounded. The final and bloodless encounter came in February at Petersham, where Bowdoin's army surprised the rebels and took 150 prisoners; the others fled into the woods but were soon rounded up and jailed.

In the end, 2 men were executed for rebellion; 16 more sentenced to hang were reprieved at the last moment on the gallows. Some 4,000 men gained leniency by confessing their misconduct and swearing an oath of allegiance to the state. A special Disqualification Act prohibited the penitent rebels from voting, holding public office, serving on juries, working as schoolmasters, or operating taverns for up to three years.

Shays's Rebellion caused leaders throughout the country to worry about the confederation's ability to handle civil disorder. Inflammatory Massachusetts newspapers wrote about bloody mob rule and the possibility of similar uprisings in other states. New York lawyer John Jay wrote to George Washington, "Our affairs seem to lead to some crisis, some revolution—something I cannot foresee or conjecture. I am uneasy and apprehensive; more so than during the war." Benjamin Franklin, in his eighties, shrewdly observed that in 1776, Americans had feared "an excess of power in the rulers" but now the problem was perhaps "a defect of obedience" in the subjects. Among such leaders, the sense of crisis in the confederation had greatly deepened.

Shays's Rebellion

▶ Uprising (1786–1787) led by Massachusetts farmer and former soldier Daniel Shays. Centered in western Massachusetts, the uprising was sparked by what dissidents considered the oppressive policies of the eastern elites who controlled the state's government. Shays's Rebellion caused leaders throughout the country to worry about the confederation's ability to handle civil disorder.

> **QUICK REVIEW**

How were the issues of war debt, Indian policy, and western land settlement interconnected in the 1780s?

CHAPTER LOCATOR | What kind of government did the Articles of Confederation create?

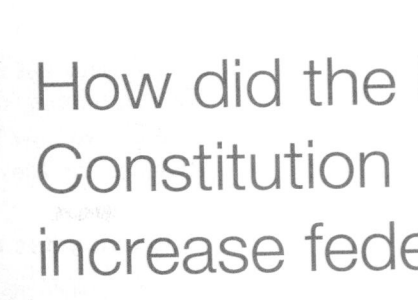

The constitutional convention assembled at the Pennsylvania statehouse in the summer of 1787. Despite the heat, the delegates nailed the windows shut to eliminate the chance of being heard by eavesdroppers, so intent were they on secrecy. The building is now called Independence Hall in honor of the signing of the Declaration of Independence there in 1776. Historical Society of Pennsylvania.

How did the U. S. Constitution increase federal power?

SHAYS'S REBELLION PROVOKED an odd mixture of fear and hope that the government under the Articles of Confederation was losing its grip on power. A small circle of Virginians decided to try one last time to augment the powers granted to the government by the Articles. Their call for a meeting to discuss trade regulation led to a total reworking of the national government.

From Annapolis to Philadelphia

The Virginians, led by James Madison, convinced the confederation congress to allow a meeting of delegates at Annapolis, Maryland, in September 1786, to try again to revise the trade regulation powers of the Articles. Only five states participated, and they rescheduled the meeting for Philadelphia in May 1787. The congress reluctantly endorsed the Philadelphia meeting and limited its scope to "the sole and express purpose of revising the Articles of Confederation." But at least one representative at the Annapolis meeting had more ambitious plans. Alexander Hamilton of New York hoped the Philadelphia meeting would do whatever was necessary to strengthen the federal government.

The fifty-five men who assembled at Philadelphia in May 1787 for the **constitutional convention** were generally those who had already concluded that there were weaknesses in the Articles of Confederation. Patrick Henry, author of

constitutional convention
▶ May 1787 meeting in Philadelphia to revise the Articles of Confederation. Going well beyond their original mandate, the delegates at the convention crafted a new basis for the government of the United States, the Constitution. The Constitution greatly enhanced the power of the federal government.

| How did the states define freedom and citizenship? | Why did the Articles of Confederation fail? | How did the U.S. Constitution increase federal power? | What were the obstacles to ratification of the Constitution? | Conclusion: What was the "republican remedy"? |

- **May.** Constitutional convention convenes in Philadelphia. Virginia Plan proposes a two-house legislature and three branches of government.
- **June.** New Jersey plan proposes a single-house legislature and a three-man presidency.
- **July.** Great Compromise breaks a stalemate at the constitutional convention, and the basic features of the Constitution emerge.
- **September.** Constitutional convention approves the U.S. Constitution and sends it to the states for ratification.

Virginia Plan

▶ Plan presented at the constitutional convention by James Madison that set out a three-branch government composed of a two-chamber legislature, a powerful executive, and a judiciary. Under Madison's plan, representation in both houses of the congress would be tied to population, all but eliminating the voice of small states in national government.

New Jersey Plan

▶ Alternative plan presented by New Jersey delegates of the constitutional convention. The plan retained the confederation principle that the national government was an assembly of states, maintained the existing single-house congress of the Articles of Confederation in which each state had one vote, and created a plural presidency to be shared by three men elected by the congress from its membership. This proposal gave the new congress sweeping powers, including the right to tax, regulate trade, and use force on unruly state governments.

the Virginia Resolves in 1765 and more recently state governor, refused to go to the convention, saying he "smelled a rat." Rhode Island refused to send delegates. Two New York representatives left in dismay in the middle of the convention, leaving Alexander Hamilton as the sole delegate from New York.

The Delegates to the Constitutional Convention

All were white men.
None were artisans or day laborers, or even farmers of middling wealth.
Two-thirds of the delegates were lawyers.
The majority had served in the confederation congress.
Half had been officers in the Continental army.
Seven had been governors of their states.

The Virginia and New Jersey Plans

The convention worked in secrecy so that the men could freely explore alternatives without fear that their honest opinions would come back to haunt them. The Virginia delegation first laid out a fifteen-point plan for a complete restructuring of the government. This **Virginia Plan** was a total repudiation of the principle of a confederation of states. Largely the work of Madison, the plan set out a three-branch government composed of a two-chamber legislature, a powerful executive, and a judiciary. It practically eliminated the voices of the smaller states by pegging representation in both houses of the congress to population. The theory was that government operated directly on people, not on states. Among the breathtaking powers assigned to the congress were the rights to veto state legislation and to coerce states militarily to obey national laws. To prevent the congress from having absolute power, the executive and judiciary could jointly veto its actions.

In mid-June, a delegate from New Jersey, after caucusing with delegates from other small states, unveiled an alternative proposal. The **New Jersey Plan**, as it was called, maintained the existing single-house congress of the Articles of Confederation in which each state had one vote. Acknowledging the need for an executive, it created a plural presidency to be shared by three men elected by the congress from among its membership. Where it sharply departed from the existing government was in the sweeping powers it gave to the new congress: the right to tax, regulate trade, and use force on unruly state governments. In favoring national power over states' rights, it aligned itself with the Virginia Plan. But the New Jersey Plan retained the confederation principle that the national government was to be an assembly of states, not of people.

For two weeks, delegates debated the two plans, focusing on the key issue of representation. The small-state delegates conceded that one house in a two-house legislature could be apportioned by population, but they would never agree that both houses could be. Madison was equally vehement about bypassing representation by state, which he viewed as the fundamental flaw in the Articles.

The debate seemed deadlocked, and for a while the convention was "on the verge of dissolution, scarce held together by the strength of a hair," according to

CHAPTER LOCATOR | What kind of government did the Articles of Confederation create?

one delegate. Only in mid-July did the so-called Great Compromise break the stalemate and produce the basic structural features of the emerging United States Constitution. Proponents of the competing plans agreed on a bicameral legislature.

Representation in the lower house, the House of Representatives, would be apportioned by population, and representation in the upper house, the Senate, would come from all the states equally, with each state represented by two independently voting senators. Representation by population turned out to be an ambiguous concept once it was subjected to rigorous discussion. Who counted? Were slaves, for example, people or property? As people, they would add weight to the southern delegations in the House of Representatives, but as property they would add to the tax burdens of those states. What emerged was the compromise known as the **three-fifths clause**: All free persons plus "three-fifths of all other Persons" constituted the numerical base for the apportionment of representatives.

Using "all other Persons" as a substitute for "slaves" indicates the discomfort delegates felt in acknowledging in the Constitution the existence of slavery. But though slavery was nowhere named, nonetheless it was recognized, guaranteed, and thereby perpetuated by the U.S. Constitution.

Democracy versus Republicanism

The delegates in Philadelphia made a distinction between *democracy* and *republicanism* new to the American political vocabulary. Pure democracy was now taken to be a dangerous thing. As a Massachusetts delegate put it, "The evils we experience flow from the excess of democracy." The delegates still favored republican institutions, but they created a government that gave direct voice to the people only in the House and that granted a check on that voice to the Senate, a body of men elected not by direct popular vote but by the state legislatures. Senators served for six years, with no limit on reelection; they were protected from the whims of democratic majorities, and their long terms fostered experience and maturity in office.

Similarly, the presidency evolved into a powerful office out of the reach of direct democracy. The delegates devised an electoral college whose only function was to elect the president and vice president. Each state's legislature would choose the electors, whose number was the sum of representatives and senators for the state. The president thus would owe his office not to the Congress, the

City Tavern

Philadelphia's City Tavern, built in 1773, became a favorite gathering place for the delegates to the Constitutional Convention in the summer of 1787. The men who wrote the Constitution took meals and drinks at the tavern. Rare Book Department, The Free Library of Philadelphia.

three-fifths clause

▶ Clause in the Constitution that stipulated that all free persons plus "three-fifths of all other persons" would constitute the numerical base for the apportionment of representatives. The clause was a compromise designed to resolve the issue of how slaves would be counted for purposes of representation and taxation. The clause tacitly acknowledged the existence of slavery in the United States.

How did the states define freedom and citizenship? | Why did the Articles of Confederation fail? | **How did the U.S. Constitution increase federal power?** | What were the obstacles to ratification of the Constitution? | Conclusion: What was the "republican remedy"?

215

states, or the people, but to a temporary assemblage of distinguished citizens who could vote their own judgment on the candidates.

The framers had developed a far more complex form of federal government than that provided by the Articles of Confederation. To curb the excesses of democracy, they devised a government with limits and checks on all three of its branches. They set forth a powerful president who could veto legislation passed in Congress, but they gave Congress power to override presidential vetoes. They set up a national judiciary to settle disputes between states and citizens of different states. They separated the branches of government not only by functions and by reciprocal checks but also by deliberately basing the election of each branch on different universes of voters—voting citizens (the House), state legislators (the Senate), and the electoral college (the presidency). The convention carefully listed the powers of the president and of Congress. The president could initiate policy, propose legislation, and veto acts of Congress; he could command the military and direct foreign policy; and he could appoint the entire judiciary, subject to Senate approval. Congress held the purse strings: the power to levy taxes, to regulate trade, and to coin money and control the currency. States were expressly forbidden to issue paper money. Two more powers of Congress—to "provide for the common defence and general Welfare" of the country and "to make all laws which shall be necessary and proper" for carrying out its powers—provided elastic language that came closest to Madison's wish to grant sweeping powers to the new government.

While no one was entirely satisfied with every line of the Constitution, only three dissenters refused to sign the document. The Constitution specified a mechanism for ratification that avoided the dilemma faced earlier by the confederation government: Nine states, not all thirteen, had to ratify it, and special ratifying conventions elected only for that purpose, not state legislatures, would make the crucial decision. On September 17, the convention passed the Constitution and sent it to the states for ratification.

> **QUICK REVIEW**

What problems with the Articles of Confederation did the delegates to the constitutional convention seek to rectify?

CHAPTER LOCATOR | What kind of government did the Articles of Confederation create?

216 CHAPTER 8
BUILDING A REPUBLIC, 1775–1789

What were the obstacles to ratification of the Constitution?

This pro-Federalist cartoon depicts the debate over the ratification of the Constitution. On the left, Federalists pull a stuck cart toward the shining sun. To the right, anti-Federalists pull it toward stormy skies. Library of Congress.

THE PROCESS of ratifying the Constitution was highly contentious. In the three most populous states—Virginia, Massachusetts, and New York—substantial majorities opposed a powerful new national government. North Carolina and Rhode Island refused to call ratifying conventions. Seven of the eight remaining states were easy victories for the Constitution, but securing the approval of the ninth proved difficult. Pro-Constitution forces, called Federalists, had to strategize very shrewdly to defeat anti-Constitution forces, called Antifederalists.

The Federalists

Proponents of the Constitution moved into action swiftly. To silence the criticism that they had gone beyond their charge, they sent the document to the congress. The congress withheld explicit approval but resolved to send the Constitution to the states for their consideration. The pro-Constitution forces shrewdly secured another advantage by calling themselves **Federalists**. Their opponents became known as **Antifederalists**, a label that made them sound defensive and negative, lacking a program of their own.

To gain momentum, the Federalists targeted the states most likely to ratify quickly. Delaware ratified the Constitution in early December, and Pennsylvania, New Jersey, and Georgia followed within a month (**Map 8.3**). Delaware and New Jersey were small states surrounded by more powerful neighbors; a government that would regulate trade and set taxes according to population was an attractive

Federalists

▶ Supporters of ratification of the Constitution. Federalists believed that a stronger national government was vital to the country's survival. Leading Federalists included John Adams, Alexander Hamilton, and George Washington.

Antifederalists

▶ Opponents of ratification of the Constitution. Antifederalists feared that the Constitution would create a potentially tyrannical government, out of touch with the needs of the citizens of individual states and localities. One widespread objection to the Constitution was its omission of any guarantees of individual liberties in a bill of rights like those contained in many state constitutions.

How did the states define freedom and citizenship?	Why did the Articles of Confederation fail?	How did the U.S. Constitution increase federal power?	**What were the obstacles to ratification of the Constitution?**	Conclusion: What was the "republican remedy"?

CHRONOLOGY

1787
- Constitutional convention meets in Philadelphia.
- **October.** Publication of *The Federalist Papers* begins.
- **December.** Delaware is the first state to ratify Constitution.

1788
- New Hampshire and Virginia ratify Constitution, with New Hampshire providing the ninth and decisive vote.
- **July.** New York ratifies Constitution.

1789
- **November.** North Carolina ratifies Constitution.

1790
- **May.** Rhode Island ratifies Constitution.

proposition. Georgia sought the protection that a stronger national government would afford against hostile Indians and Spanish Florida to the south.

Another three easy victories came in Connecticut, Maryland, and South Carolina. As in Pennsylvania, merchants, lawyers, and urban artisans in general favored the new Constitution, as did large landowners and slaveholders. This tendency for the established political elite to be Federalist enhanced the prospects of victory. Antifederalists in these states tended to be rural, western, and noncommercial, men whose access to news was limited and whose participation in state government was tenuous.

Massachusetts was the only early state that gave the Federalists difficulty. The vote to select the ratification delegates decidedly favored the Antifederalists, whose strength lay in the western areas of the state, home to Shays's Rebellion. One rural delegate from Worcester County voiced widely shared suspicions: "These lawyers and men of learning and money men that talk so finely, and gloss over matters so smoothly, to make us poor illiterate people swallow down the pill, expect to get into Congress themselves; they expect to be the managers of the Constitution and get all the power and all the money into their own hands, and then they will swallow up all us little folks." Nevertheless, the Antifederalists' lead was slowly eroded by a vigorous newspaper campaign. In the end, the Federalists won by a very slim margin and only with promises that amendments to the Constitution would be taken up in the first Congress.

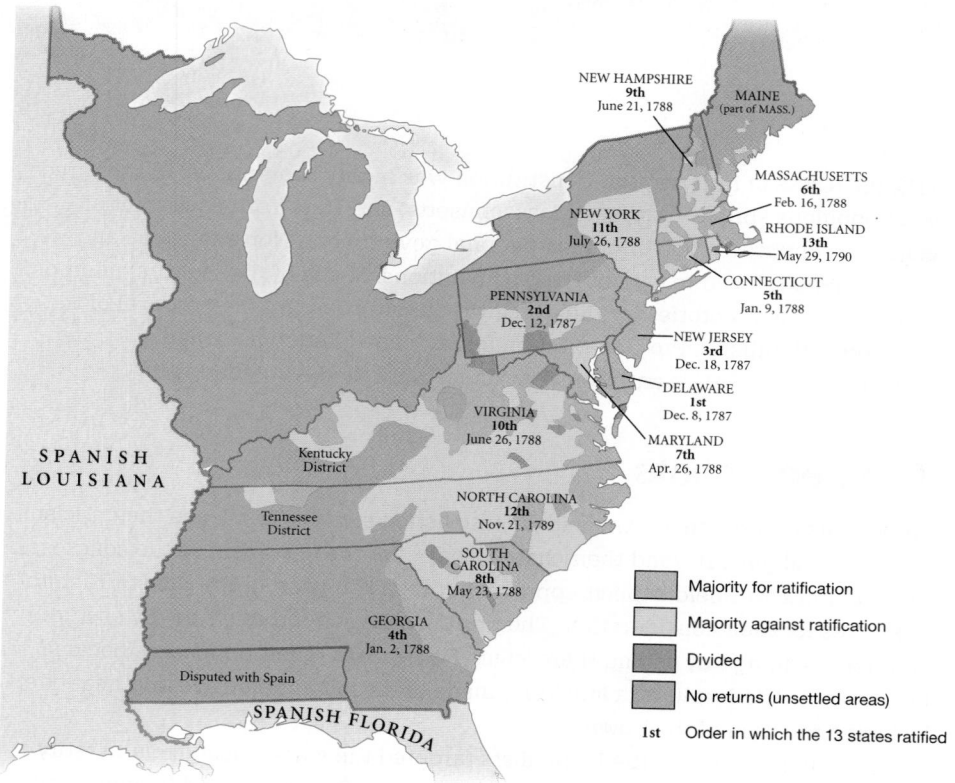

MAP 8.3 ■ Ratification of the Constitution, 1788–1790
Populated areas cast votes for delegates to state ratification conventions. This map shows Antifederalist strength generally concentrated in backcountry, noncoastal, and non-urban areas, but with significant exceptions (for example, Rhode Island).

► FOR MORE HELP ANALYZING THIS MAP, see the map activity for this chapter in the Online Study Guide at bedfordstmartins.com/roarkunderstanding.

218 CHAPTER 8 BUILDING A REPUBLIC, 1775–1789

CHAPTER LOCATOR | What kind of government did the Articles of Confederation create?

By May 1788, eight states had ratified; only one more was needed. North Carolina and Rhode Island were hopeless for the Federalist cause, and New Hampshire seemed nearly as bleak. More worrisome was the failure to win over the largest and most important states, Virginia and New York.

The Antifederalists

The Antifederalists were a composite group, united mainly in their desire to block the Constitution. Although much of their strength came from backcountry areas long suspicious of eastern elites, many Antifederalist leaders came from the same social background as Federalist leaders. The Antifederalists also drew strength in states already on sure economic footing, such as New York, which could afford to remain independent. Probably the biggest appeal of the Antifederalists' position lay in the long-nurtured fear that distant power might infringe on people's liberties.

But by the time eight states had ratified the Constitution, the Antifederalists faced a difficult task. First, they were no longer defending the status quo now that the momentum lay with the Federalists. Second, it was difficult to defend the confederation government with its admitted flaws. Even so, they remained genuinely fearful that the new government would be too distant from the people and could thus become corrupt or tyrannical. "The difficulty, if not impracticability, of exercising the equal and equitable powers of government by a single legislature over an extent of territory that reaches from the Mississippi to the western lakes, and from them to the Atlantic ocean, is an insuperable objection to the adoption of the new system," wrote Mercy Otis Warren, an Antifederalist woman writing under the alias "A Columbia Patriot."

The new government was indeed distant. In the proposed House of Representatives, the only directly democratic element of the Constitution, one member represented some 30,000 people. How could that member really know or communicate with his whole constituency, Antifederalists worried. They also worried that representatives would always be elites and thus "ignorant of the sentiments of the middling and much more of the lower class of citizens, strangers to their ability, unacquainted with their wants, difficulties, and distress," as one Maryland man said.

The Federalists generally agreed that the elite would be favored for national elections. Indeed, they did not envision a government constituted of every class of people. "Fools and knaves have voice enough in government already," argued one Federalist, without being guaranteed representation in proportion to their total population. Alexander Hamilton claimed that mechanics and laborers preferred to have their social betters represent them. Antifederalists disagreed: "In reality, there will be no part of the people represented, but the rich. . . . It will literally be a government in the hands of the few to oppress and plunder the many."

Antifederalists fretted over many specific features of the Constitution. The most widespread objection, however, was the Constitution's glaring omission of any guarantees of individual liberties in a bill of rights like those contained in many state constitutions.

Despite Federalist campaigns in the large states, it was a small state—New Hampshire—that provided the decisive ninth vote for ratification on June 21, 1788. Federalists there succeeded in getting the convention postponed from February to June and conducted an intense and successful lobbying effort on specific delegates in the interim.

How did the states define freedom and citizenship? | Why did the Articles of Confederation fail? | How did the U.S. Constitution increase federal power? | **What were the obstacles to ratification of the Constitution?** | Conclusion: What was the "republican remedy"?

219

The Big Holdouts: Virginia and New York

Four states still remained outside the new union, and a glance at a map demonstrated the necessity of pressing the Federalist case in the two largest, Virginia and New York (see Map 8.3, page 218). In Virginia, an influential Antifederalist group led by Patrick Henry and George Mason made the outcome uncertain. The Federalists finally won ratification by proposing twenty specific amendments that the new government would promise to consider.

New York voters tilted toward the Antifederalists out of a sense that a state so large and powerful need not relinquish so much authority to the new federal government. But New York was also home to some of the most persuasive Federalists. Starting in October 1787, Alexander Hamilton collaborated with James Madison and New York lawyer John Jay on a series of eighty-five essays on the political philosophy of the new Constitution published in New York newspapers and later republished as *The Federalist Papers*. The essays set out the failures of the Articles of Confederation and offered an analysis of the complex nature of the Federalist position. In one of the most compelling essays, number 10, Madison challenged the Antifederalists' conviction that republican government had to be small-scale. Madison argued that a large and diverse population was itself a guarantee of liberty. In a national government, no single faction could ever be large enough to subvert the freedom of other groups. "Extend the sphere, and you take in a greater variety of parties and interests; you make it less probable that a majority of the whole will have a common motive to invade the rights of other citizens," Madison asserted. He called it "a republican remedy for the diseases most incident to republican government."

At New York's ratifying convention, Antifederalists predominated, but impassioned debate and lobbying—plus the dramatic news of Virginia's ratification—finally tipped the balance to the Federalists. New York's ratification ensured the legitimacy of the new government. It took another year and a half for Antifederalists in North Carolina to come around. Rhode Island held out until May 1790, and even then it ratified by only a two-vote margin.

In less than twelve months, the U.S. Constitution was both written and ratified. The Federalists had faced a formidable task, but by building momentum and assuring consideration of a bill of rights, they carried the day.

> QUICK REVIEW

Why did Antifederalists oppose the Constitution?

CHAPTER LOCATOR | What kind of government did the Articles of Confederation create?

220 CHAPTER 8
BUILDING A REPUBLIC, 1775–1789

The Granger Collection, New York.

Conclusion: What was the "republican remedy"?

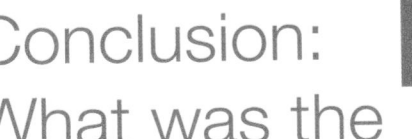

THE PERIOD DISCUSSED in this chapter began in 1775 with a confederation government that could barely be ratified because of its requirement of unanimity, but there was no reaching unanimity on the western lands, an impost, or the proper way to respond to unfair taxation in a republican state. The new Constitution offered a different approach to these problems by loosening the grip of impossible unanimity and by embracing the ideas of a heterogeneous public life and a carefully balanced government that together would prevent any one part of the public from tyrannizing another. The genius of James Madison was to anticipate that diversity of opinion was not only an unavoidable reality but also a hidden strength of the new society beginning to take shape. This is what he meant in *Federalist* essay number 10 when he spoke of the "republican remedy" for the troubles most likely to befall a government in which the people are the source of authority.

Despite Madison's optimism, political differences remained keen and worrisome to many. The Federalists still hoped for a society in which leaders of exceptional wisdom would discern the best path for public policy. They looked backward to a society of hierarchy, rank, and benevolent rule by an aristocracy of talent, but they created a government with forward-looking checks and balances as a guard against corruption, which they figured would most likely emanate from the people. The Antifederalists also looked backward, but to an old order of small-scale direct democracy and local control, in which virtuous people kept a close eye on potentially corruptible rulers. The Antifederalists feared a national government led by distant, self-interested leaders who needed to be held in check. In the 1790s, these two conceptions of republicanism and of leadership would be tested in real life.

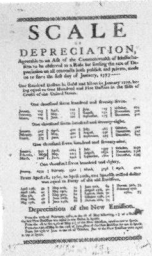

SO NOW YOU KNOW

In the aftermath of the American Revolution, the new United States faced mounting conflicts over western settlement and taxation, questions that the government under the Articles of Confederation could not resolve. The result was the constitutional convention, which hammered out the Constitution of the United States. This document shaped a new federal government that was both more balanced and more powerful.

How did the states define freedom and citizenship?

Why did the Articles of Confederation fail?

How did the U.S. Constitution increase federal power?

What were the obstacles to ratification of the Constitution?

Conclusion: What was the "republican remedy"?

221

CHAPTER 8 STUDY GUIDE

Online Study Guide
bedfordstmartins.com/roarkunderstanding

STEP 1 GETTING STARTED

Below are basic terms from this period in American history. Can you identify each term below and explain why it matters? To do this exercise online or to download this chart, visit bedfordstmartins.com/roarkunderstanding.

TERM	WHO OR WHAT & WHEN	WHY IT MATTERS
Articles of Confederation, p. 198		
bills of rights, p. 202		
Treaty of Fort Stanwix, p. 208		
Northwest Ordinance, p. 210		
Shays's Rebellion, p. 212		
constitutional convention, p. 213		
Virginia Plan, p. 214		
New Jersey Plan, p. 214		
three-fifths clause, p. 215		
Federalists, p. 217		
Antifederalists, p. 217		

STEP 2 MOVING BEYOND THE BASICS

The exercise below represents a more advanced understanding of the chapter material. Compare the government established by the Articles of Confederation with the government established by the U.S. Constitution. Fill in the chart below with the powers and responsibilities of Congress, the executive branch, the judiciary, and the states under the Articles of Confederation and under the Constitution. What were the important differences between the two documents? What weaknesses in the Articles were corrected? What groups were most in favor of creating a stronger central government and why? To do this exercise online or to download this chart, visit bedfordstmartins.com/roarkunderstanding.

	Powers and responsibilities under Articles of Confederation	Powers and responsibilities under U.S. Constitution
Congress		
Executive branch		
Federal judiciary		
States		

STEP

3

PUTTING IT ALL TOGETHER

THE ARTICLES OF CONFEDERATION

► How did the confederation government deal with the problem of western lands?

► What do the state constitutions drawn up during the confederation period tell us about the range of political opinion during the Revolutionary War and the years immediately following?

THE CREATION OF A NEW CONSTITUTION

► What forces and events combined to produce momentum for the creation of a new constitution?

► What political compromises were embodied in the Constitution?

THE FIGHT FOR RATIFICATION

► Where was support for the Constitution strongest? Where was it weakest? Why?

► Why did the Federalists ultimately prevail over the Antifederalists? What were the Federalists' most important weapons in the debate over the Constitution?

LOOKING BACKWARD, LOOKING AHEAD

► How did pre-revolutionary experiences with colonial legislatures and the British government shape the Articles of Confederation? The United States Constitution?

► What issues were left unresolved by the framers of the Constitution? Why?

IN YOUR OWN WORDS

Imagine that you must explain chapter 8 to someone who hasn't read it. What would be the most important points to include and why?

Peter Lacour delin.   A. Doolittle Sculp.

FEDERAL HALL

The Seat of Congress

Printed & Sold by A. Doolittle New-Haven 1790

9
FORMING THE NEW NATION
1789–1800

> This chapter explores the early attempts to translate the rules and guidelines established by the Constitution into a functioning government and political system. It examines the efforts to achieve political stability in the wake of the ratification of the Constitution, Alexander Hamilton's plans to bring economic stability to the federal government, and the external threats and internal rivalries that led to the emergence of party politics.

> What were the sources of political stability in Federalist America?

> What was Hamilton's plan to solidify the government's fiscal position?

> What external threats did the United States face in the 1790s?

> How did partisan rivalries shape the politics of the late 1790s?

> Conclusion: Why did the new nation ultimately form political parties?

DID YOU KNOW?

George Washington proposed that he, and future presidents, should be addressed as "His High Mightiness."

George Washington takes the oath of office. Federal Hall, Philadelphia, April 30, 1789.

> What were the sources of political stability in Federalist America?

> ► FOR MORE HELP ANALYZING THIS IMAGE, see the visual activity for this chapter in the Online Study Guide at bedfordstmartins.com/roarkunderstanding.

AFTER THE STRUGGLES of the 1780s, the most urgent task in establishing the new government was to secure stability. Leaders sought ways to heal old divisions, and the first presidential election offered the means to do that in the person of George Washington, who enjoyed widespread veneration. People trusted him to exercise the untested and perhaps elastic powers of the presidency.

Congress had important work as well in initiating the new government. Congress quickly agreed on the Bill of Rights, which answered the concerns of many Antifederalists. Beyond politics, cultural change in the area of gender also enhanced political stability. The private virtue of women was mobilized to bolster the public virtue of male citizens; republicanism was forcing a rethinking of women's relation to the state.

Washington Inaugurates the Government

George Washington was elected president in February 1789 by a unanimous vote of the electoral college. Washington perfectly embodied the republican ideal of disinterested, public-spirited leadership. Indeed, he cultivated that image through astute ceremonies such as the dramatic surrender of his sword to the Continental Congress at the end of the war, symbolizing the subservience of military power to the law.

CHAPTER LOCATOR   What were the sources of political stability in Federalist America?

226   CHAPTER 9
FORMING THE NEW NATION, 1789–1800

Once in office, Washington calculated his moves, knowing that every step set a precedent and that any misstep could be dangerous for the fragile government. Congress debated a title for Washington, such as "His Highness, the President of the United States of America and Protector of Their Liberties" and "His Majesty, the President"; Washington favored "His High Mightiness." But in the end, republican simplicity prevailed. The final title was simply "President of the United States of America," and the established form of address became "Mr. President."

Washington's genius in establishing the presidency lay in his capacity for implanting his own reputation for integrity into the office itself. In the political language of the day, he was "virtuous," meaning that he took pains to elevate the public good over private interest and projected honesty and honor over ambition. At all times, he remained aloof, resolute, and dignified. He encouraged pomp and ceremony to create respect for the office, traveling with six horses to pull his coach, hosting formal balls, and surrounding himself with uniformed servants. He even held weekly "levees," as European monarchs did, hour-long audiences granted to distinguished visitors (including women), at which Washington appeared attired in black velvet, with a feathered hat and a polished sword. The president and his guests bowed, avoiding the egalitarian familiarity of a handshake. But he always managed, perhaps just barely, to avoid the extreme of royal splendor.

Washington chose talented and experienced men to preside over the newly created Departments of War, Treasury, and State.

Washington's cabinet

Secretary of state	Thomas Jefferson
Secretary of the treasury	Alexander Hamilton
Secretary of war	Henry Knox
Attorney general	Edmund Randolph
Chief justice of the Supreme Court	John Jay

Soon Washington began to hold regular meetings with these men, thereby establishing the precedent of a presidential cabinet. No one anticipated that two decades of party turbulence would emerge from the brilliant but explosive mix of Washington's first cabinet.

The Bill of Rights

An important piece of business for the First Congress, meeting in 1789, was the passage of the **Bill of Rights**. Seven states had ratified the Constitution on the condition that guarantees of individual liberties and limitations to federal power be swiftly incorporated. The Federalists of 1787 had thought an enumeration of rights unnecessary, but in 1789 Congressman James Madison understood that healing the divisions of the 1780s was of prime importance. "It will be a desirable thing to extinguish from the bosom of every member of the community, any apprehensions that there are those among his countrymen who wish to deprive them of the liberty for which they valiantly fought and honorably bled."

CHRONOLOGY

1789
- George Washington is inaugurated first president.
- First Congress meets.

1790
- Judith Sargent Murray publishes "On the Equality of the Sexes."

1791
- States ratify the Bill of Rights.

Bill of Rights
▶ The first ten amendments to the Constitution, ratified between 1789 and 1791. The First through Eighth Amendments dealt with individual liberties, and the Ninth and Tenth concerned the boundary between federal and state authority. Passage of the Bill of Rights was critical to healing the political divisions of the 1780s.

| What was Hamilton's plan to solidify the government's fiscal position? | What external threats did the United States face in the 1790s? | How did partisan rivalries shape the politics of the late 1790s? | Conclusion: Why did the new nation ultimately form political parties? |

227

Drawing on existing state constitutions with bills of rights, Madison enumerated guarantees of freedom of speech, press, and religion; the right to petition and assemble; and the right to be free from unwarranted searches and seizures. One amendment asserted the right to keep and bear arms in support of a "well-regulated militia," to which Madison added, "but no person religiously scrupulous of bearing arms, shall be compelled to render military service in person." That provision for what a later century would call "conscientious objector" status failed to gain acceptance in Congress.

In September 1789, Congress approved a set of twelve amendments and sent them to the states for approval; by 1791, ten were eventually ratified. The First through Eighth Amendments dealt with individual liberties, and the Ninth and Tenth concerned the boundary between federal and state authority.

Still, not everyone was entirely satisfied. State ratifying conventions had submitted some eighty proposed amendments. Congress never considered proposals to change structural features of the new government, and Madison had no intention of reopening debates about the length of the president's term or the power to levy excise taxes.

Significantly, no one complained about one striking omission in the Bill of Rights: the right to vote. Only much later was voting seen as a fundamental liberty requiring protection by constitutional amendment—indeed, by four amendments. The Constitution deliberately left the definition of voters to the states because of the existing wide variation in local voting practices. Most of these practices were based on property qualifications, but some touched on religion and, in one unusual case (New Jersey), on sex and race (see chapter 8).

The Republican Wife and Mother

The exclusion of women from political activity did not mean they had no civic role or responsibility. A flood of periodical articles in the 1790s by both male and female writers reevaluated courtship, marriage, and motherhood in light of republican ideals. Tyrannical power in the ruler, whether king or husband, was declared a thing of the past. Affection, not duty, bound wives to their husbands and citizens to their government. In republican marriages, the writers claimed, women had the capacity to reform the morals and manners of men. One male author promised women that "the solidity and stability of the liberties of your country rest with you; since Liberty is never sure, 'till Virtue reigns triumphant. . . . While you thus keep our country virtuous, you maintain its independence."

Until the 1790s, public virtue was strictly a masculine quality. But another sort of virtue enlarged in importance: sexual chastity, a private asset prized as a feminine quality. Essayists of the 1790s explicitly advised young women to use sexual virtue to increase public virtue in men. "Love and courtship . . . invest a lady with more authority than in any other situation that falls to the lot of human beings," one male essayist proclaimed. If women spurned selfish suitors, they could promote good morals more than any social institution could, essayists promised.

Republican ideals also cast motherhood in a new light. Throughout the 1790s, advocates for female education, still a controversial proposition, argued that education would produce better mothers, who in turn would produce better citizens, a concept historians call republican motherhood. Benjamin Rush, a Pennsylvania physician and educator, called for female education because "our

CHAPTER LOCATOR | What were the sources of political stability in Federalist America?

CHAPTER 9
228 FORMING THE NEW NATION, 1789–1800

ladies should be qualified . . . in instructing their sons in the principles of liberty and government." A series of essays by Judith Sargent Murray of Massachusetts favored education that would remake women into self-confident, rational beings. Her first essay, published in 1790, was boldly titled "On the Equality of the Sexes." In a subsequent essay on education, she reassured readers that educated women "will not be assuming; the characteristic trait [sweetness] will still remain." Even Murray had to justify female education in the context of family duty.

Although women's obligations as wives and mothers were now infused with political meaning, traditional gender relations remained unaltered. The analogy between marriage and civil society worked precisely because of the self-subordination inherent in the term *virtue*. Men should put the public good first, before selfish desires, just as women must put their husbands and families first, before themselves. Women might gain literacy and knowledge, but only in the service of improved domestic duty. In Federalist America, wives and citizens alike should feel affection for and trust in their rulers; neither should ever rebel.

QUICK REVIEW

How did political leaders in the 1790s attempt to overcome the divisions of the 1780s?

What was Hamilton's plan to solidify the government's fiscal position?

What external threats did the United States face in the 1790s?

How did partisan rivalries shape the politics of the late 1790s?

Conclusion: Why did the new nation ultimately form political parties?

What was Hamilton's plan to solidify the government's fiscal position?

Alexander Hamilton, by John Trumbull Hamilton was confident, handsome, audacious, brilliant, and very hardworking. Ever slender, in marked contrast to the more corpulent leaders of his day, he posed for this portrait in 1792, at the age of thirty-seven and at the height of his power. Yale University Art Gallery.

Alexander Hamilton

▶ Secretary of the Treasury during the presidency of George Washington. Starting in 1790, Hamilton embarked on an innovative and controversial plan to solidify the government's economic base. His proposals for the creation of a national bank, dealing with the national debt, and the promotion of domestic manufacturing all met with considerable opposition and contributed to the rise of partisan politics in the 1790s.

COMPARED TO THE severe financial instability of the 1780s, the 1790s brimmed with opportunity, as seen in increased agricultural trade and improvements in transportation and banking. In 1790, the federal government moved from New York City to Philadelphia, a more central location with a substantial mercantile class. There, Secretary of the Treasury **Alexander Hamilton** embarked on his innovative and controversial plan to solidify the government's economic base.

Agriculture, Transportation, and Banking

Dramatic increases in international grain prices motivated American farmers to boost agricultural production for the export trade. Europe's rising population needed grain, and the French Revolutionary and Napoleonic Wars, which engulfed Europe for a dozen years after 1793, severely compromised production there. From the Connecticut River valley to the Chesapeake, farmers planted more wheat, generating new jobs for millers, coopers, dockworkers, and ship and wagon builders.

Cotton production also underwent a boom, spurred by market demand and a mechanical invention. Limited amounts of smooth-seed cotton had long been grown in the coastal areas of the South, but this variety of cotton did not prosper in the drier inland regions. Greenseed cotton grew well inland, but its rough seeds stuck to the cotton fibers and were labor-intensive to remove. In 1793, Yale graduate Eli Whitney devised a machine called a gin that easily separated out the seeds; cotton production soared.

A surge of road building also stimulated the economy. Before 1790, one road connected Maine to Georgia, but with the establishment of the U.S. Post Office in 1792,

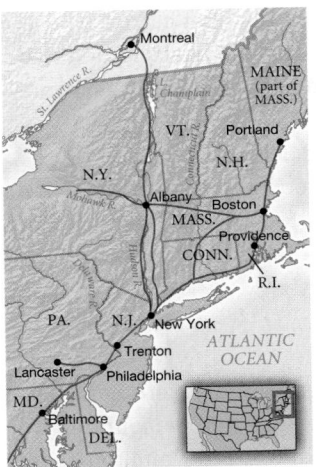

Major Roads in the 1790s

road mileage sextupled to facilitate the transport of mail. Private companies also built toll roads, the first of which was the Lancaster Turnpike of 1794, connecting Philadelphia with Lancaster, Pennsylvania. Another turnpike linked Boston with Albany, New York. Farther inland, a major road extended southwest down the Shenandoah Valley, while another joined Richmond, Virginia, with the Tennessee towns of Knoxville and Nashville.

By 1800, a dense network of dirt, gravel, and plank roadways connected towns in southern New England and the Middle Atlantic states, spurring commercial stage companies to regularize and speed up passenger traffic. A trip from New York to Boston took four days; from New York to Philadelphia, less than two (**Map 9.1**). In 1790, Boston had only three stagecoach companies; by 1800, there were twenty-four.

A third development signaling economic resurgence was the growth of commercial banking. During the 1790s, the number of banks nationwide multiplied tenfold, from three to twenty-nine in 1800. Banks drew in money chiefly through the

CHRONOLOGY

1790
- Hamilton issues his *Report on Public Credit*.
- Congress approves Hamilton's debt plan.

1791
- Congress and president charter Bank of the United States.
- Hamilton issues his *Report on Manufactures*.
- Congress passes whiskey tax.

1792
- U.S. Post Office is established.

1793
- War breaks out between France and Britain.
- Eli Whitney patents the cotton gin.

1794
- Whiskey Rebellion.

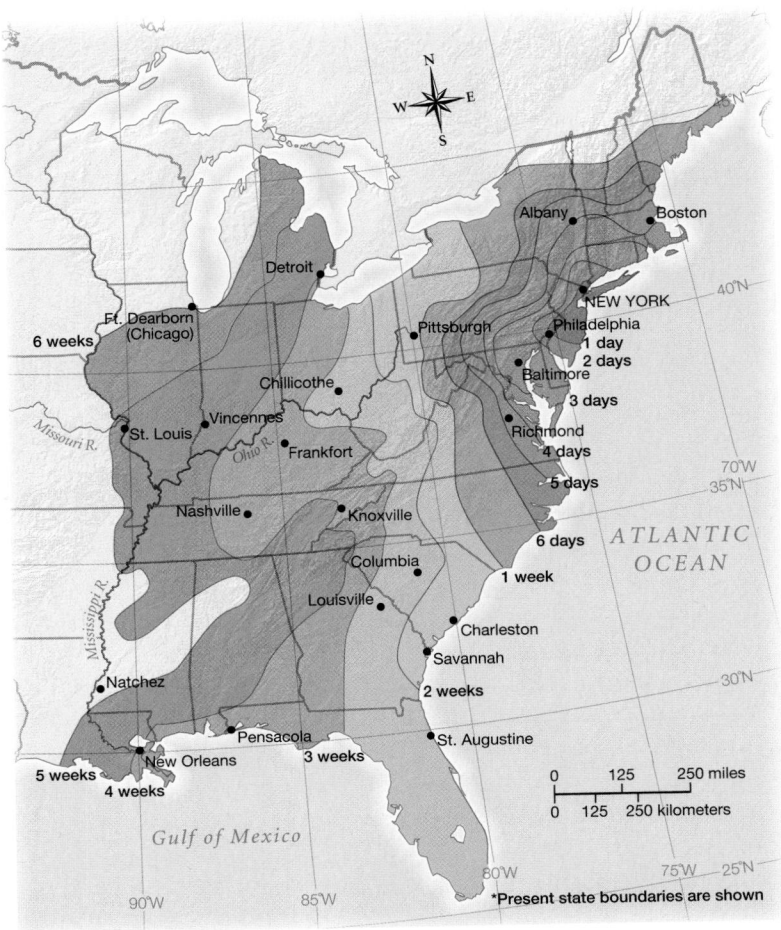

MAP 9.1 ■ Travel Times from New York City in 1800

Notice that travel out of New York extends over a much greater distance in the first week than in subsequent weeks. In one week, a traveler could get to Pittsburgh, but it would take another four weeks to go a comparable distance west of that city. River corridors in the West and East speeded up travel—but only if one were going downriver. Also notice that travel by sea (north and south along the coast) was much faster than land travel.

| What was Hamilton's plan to solidify the government's fiscal position? | What external threats did the United States face in the 1790s? | How did partisan rivalries shape the politics of the late 1790s? | Conclusion: Why did the new nation ultimately form political parties? |

sale of stock. They then made loans in the form of banknotes, paper currency backed by the gold and silver that stockholders paid in. Because banks issued two or three times as much money in banknotes as they held in hard money, they were creating new money for the economy.

The U.S. population expanded along with economic development, propelled by large average family size and better than adequate food and land resources. As measured by the first two federal censuses in 1790 and 1800, the population grew from 3.9 million to 5.3 million, an increase of 35 percent.

The Public Debt and Taxes

The upturn in the economy, plus the new taxation powers of the government, suggested that the government might soon repay its wartime debt, amounting to more than $52 million owed to foreign and domestic creditors. But Hamilton had a different plan. He issued a ***Report on Public Credit*** in January 1790, recommending that the debt be funded—but not repaid immediately—at full value. This meant that old certificates of debt would be rolled over into new bonds, which would earn interest until they were retired several years later. There would still be a public debt, but it would be secure, giving its holders a direct financial stake in the

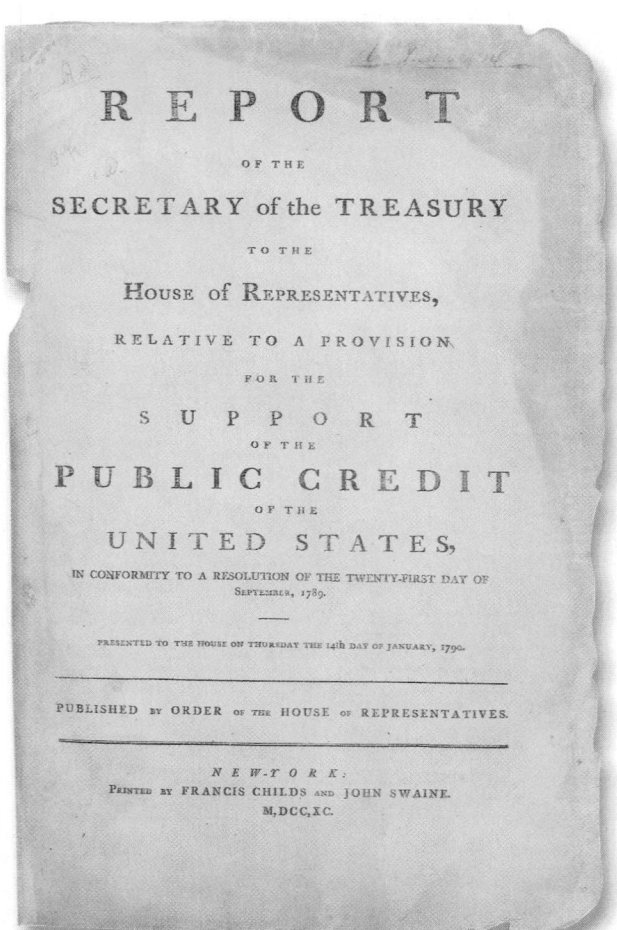

Hamilton's *Report on Public Credit*

Hamilton wrote this report in just over three months, in response to a resolution by Congress. He proposed funding the debt, rolling it over into a new debt instead of paying it off. The Gilder Lehrman Collection, Pierpont Morgan Library.

new government. The bonds would circulate, injecting millions of dollars of new money into the economy. "A national debt if not excessive will be to us a national blessing; it will be a powerfull cement of our union," Hamilton wrote to a financier. Hamilton's goal was to make the new country creditworthy, not debt-free.

Funding the debt in full was controversial because speculators had already bought up debt certificates cheaply, and Hamilton's report touched off further speculation. Philadelphia and New York speculators sent agents into backcountry regions looking for certificates of debt whose unwary owners were ignorant about the proposed face-value funding.

Hamilton compounded controversy with his proposal to add to the federal debt another $25 million that some state governments still owed to individuals. During the war, states had obtained supplies by issuing IOUs to farmers, merchants, and moneylenders. Some states, such as Virginia and New York, had paid off these debts entirely. Others, such as Massachusetts, had partially paid them off through heavy taxation of the people. About half the states had made little headway. Hamilton called for the federal government to assume these state debts and combine them with the federal debt, in effect consolidating federal power over the states.

Congressman James Madison strenuously objected to putting windfall profits in the pockets of speculators. He instead proposed a complex scheme to pay both the original holders of the federal debt and the speculators, each at fair fractions of the face value. He also strongly objected to assumption of all the states' debts. A large debt was dangerous, Madison warned, especially because it would lead to high taxation. Secretary of State Jefferson also was fearful of Hamilton's proposals. "No man is more ardently intent to see the public debt soon and sacredly paid off than I am. This exactly marks the difference between Colonel Hamilton's views and mine, that I would wish the debt paid tomorrow; he wishes it never to be paid, but always to be a thing where with to corrupt and manage the legislature." A solution to this impasse arrived when Jefferson invited Hamilton and Madison to dinner. Hamilton secured the reluctant Madison's promise to restrain his opposition. In return, Hamilton pledged to back efforts to locate the nation's new capital city in the South, along the Potomac River, an outcome that was sure to please Virginians. In early July 1790, Congress voted for the Potomac site, and in late July, Congress passed Hamilton's debt proposal without significant modification.

The First Bank of the United States and the *Report on Manufactures*

The second and third major elements of Hamilton's economic plan were his proposal to create a national Bank of the United States and his program to encourage domestic manufacturing. Arguing that banks were the "nurseries of national wealth," Hamilton modeled his bank plan on European central banks, such as the Bank of England, a private corporation that used its government's money to invigorate the British economy. According to Hamilton's plan, the central bank was to be capitalized at $10 million, a sum larger than all the hard money in the entire nation. The federal government would hold 20 percent of the bank's stock, making the bank in effect the government's fiscal agent, holding its revenues derived from import duties, land sales, and various other taxes. The other 80 percent of the bank's capital would come from private investors, who could buy stock in the bank with either

| What was Hamilton's plan to solidify the government's fiscal position? | What external threats did the United States face in the 1790s? | How did partisan rivalries shape the politics of the late 1790s? | Conclusion: Why did the new nation ultimately form political parties? |

233

hard money (silver or gold) or federal securities. Because of its size and the privilege of being the only national bank, the central bank would help stabilize the economy by exerting control over credit, interest rates, and the value of the currency.

Concerned that a few rich bankers might have undue influence over the economy, Madison tried but failed to stop the plan in Congress. Jefferson advised President Washington that the Constitution did not permit Congress to charter banks. Hamilton, however, pointed out that the Constitution gave Congress specific powers to regulate commerce and a broad right "to make all laws which shall be necessary and proper for carrying into execution the foregoing powers." Washington sided with Hamilton and signed the Bank of the United States into law in February 1791, with a charter allowing it to operate for twenty years.

When the bank's privately held stock went on sale in Philadelphia, Boston, and New York City in July, it sold out in a few hours, touching off a period of speculation in resale that lasted a month and drew in many hundreds of urban merchants and artisans. A discouraged Madison reported that in New York, "the Coffee House is an eternal buzz with the gamblers," some of them self-interested congressmen intent on "public plunder." Stock prices shot upward but then crashed in mid-August. Hamilton shrewdly managed to cushion the crash to an extent, but Jefferson worried about the risk to morality inherent in gambling in stocks: "The spirit of gaming, once it has seized a subject, is incurable. The tailor who has made thousands in one day, tho' he has lost them the next, can never again be content with the slow and moderate earnings of his needle."

The third component of Hamilton's plan was issued in December 1791 in the *Report on Manufactures*, a proposal to encourage the production of American-made goods. Domestic manufacturing was in its infancy, and Hamilton aimed to mobilize the new powers of the federal government to grant subsidies to manufacturers and to impose moderate tariffs on those same products from overseas. Hamilton's plan targeted manufacturing of iron goods, arms and ammunition, coal, textiles, wood products, and glass. Among the blessings of manufacturing, he counted the new employment opportunities that would open to children and unmarried young women, who he assumed were underutilized in agricultural societies. The *Report on Manufactures*, however, was never approved by Congress. Many confirmed agriculturalists in Congress feared that manufacturing was a curse rather than a blessing. Madison and Jefferson in particular were alarmed by stretching the "general welfare" clause of the Constitution to include public subsidies to private businesses.

The Whiskey Rebellion

Hamilton's plan to restore public credit required new taxation to pay the interest on the large national debt. In deference to the merchant class, Hamilton did not propose a general increase in import duties, nor did he propose land taxes, which would have fallen hardest on the nation's wealthiest landowners. Instead, he convinced Congress in 1791 to pass a 25 percent excise tax on whiskey, to be paid by farmers when they brought their grain to the distillery, then passed on to individual whiskey consumers in the form of higher prices.

Not surprisingly, the new excise tax proved unpopular with grain farmers in the western regions and whiskey drinkers everywhere. In 1791, farmers in Kentucky and the western parts of Pennsylvania, Virginia, Maryland, and the

CHAPTER LOCATOR | What were the sources of political stability in Federalist America?

234 CHAPTER 9
FORMING THE NEW NATION, 1789–1800

Carolinas forcefully conveyed to Congress their resentment of Hamilton's tax. One farmer complained that he already paid half his grain to the local distillery for distilling his rye, and now the distiller was taking the new whiskey tax out of the farmer's remaining half. This "reduces the balance to less than one-third of the original quantity. If this is not an oppressive tax, I am at a loss to describe what is so," the farmer wrote. Congress responded with modest modifications to the tax in 1792, but even so, discontent was rampant. Simple evasion of the law was the most common response. In some places, crowds threatened to tar and feather federal tax collectors, and distilleries underreported their production. Four counties in Pennsylvania established committees of correspondence and held assemblies to carry their message to Congress. Hamilton admitted to Congress that the revenue was far less than anticipated. But rather than abandon the law, he tightened up the prosecution of tax evaders.

In western Pennsylvania, Hamilton had one ally, a stubborn tax collector named John Neville, who refused to quit even after a group of spirited farmers burned him in effigy. In May 1794, Neville filed charges against seventy-five farmers and distillers for tax evasion. His action touched off the **Whiskey Rebellion.** In July, he and a federal marshal were ambushed in Allegheny County by a group of forty men. Neville's house was then burned to the ground by a crowd estimated at five hundred, and one man in the crowd was killed. At the end of July, seven thousand Pennsylvania farmers planned a march—or perhaps an attack, some thought—on Pittsburgh to protest the hated tax.

In response, President Washington nationalized the Pennsylvania militia and set out, with Hamilton at his side, at the head of thirteen thousand soldiers. A worried Philadelphia newspaper criticized the show of force: "Shall Pennsylvania be converted into a human slaughter house because the dignity of the United States will not admit of conciliatory measures? Shall torrents of blood be spilled to support an odious excise system?" But in the end, no blood was spilled. By the time the army arrived in late September, the demonstrators had dispersed. Twenty men were rounded up as rebels and charged with high treason, but only two were convicted, and both were soon pardoned by Washington.

Had the federal government overreacted? Thomas Jefferson thought so; he saw the event as a replay of Shays's Rebellion of 1786, when a protest against government taxation had been met with unreasonable government force (see chapter 8). The rebel farmers agreed; they felt entitled to protest oppressive taxation. Hamilton and Washington, however, thought that laws passed by a republican government must be obeyed. The Whiskey Rebellion presented an opportunity for the new federal government to flex its muscles and stand up to civil disorder.

Whiskey Rebellion

▶ July 1794 uprising by farmers and distillers in western Pennsylvania in response to efforts to enforce an unpopular excise tax on whiskey. When angry farmers gathered to march on Pittsburgh to protest the tax, George Washington led an army of thirteen thousand soldiers to Pennsylvania to suppress the rebellion. Some thought that Washington overreacted, but Washington defended his actions as necessary to preserve the rule of law. No battle was fought; the dissidents dispersed.

QUICK REVIEW

Why were Hamilton's economic policies controversial?

What was Hamilton's plan to solidify the government's fiscal position?

What external threats did the United States face in the 1790s?

How did partisan rivalries shape the politics of the late 1790s?

Conclusion: Why did the new nation ultimately form political parties?

235

> What external threats did the United States face in the 1790s?

Treaty of Greenville, 1795

This painting by an unknown artist of the 1790s purports to depict the signing of the Treaty of Greenville in 1795. The treaty was signed by General Anthony Wayne, Chief Little Turtle of the Miami tribe, and Chief Tarhe the Crane of the Wyandot tribe. One Indian of the three pictured seems to be gesturing with emphasis, as if to dictate terms to the Americans, but in fact the treaty was most favorable to the United States. Chicago Historical Society.

WHILE THE WHISKEY REBELS challenged federal leadership from within the country, disorder threatened the United States from external sources as well. From 1790 onward, serious trouble brewed in three directions. To the west, a powerful confederation of Indian tribes in the Ohio Country resisted white encroachment, resulting in a brutal war. At the same time, conflicts between the major European powers forced Americans to take sides and nearly pulled the country into another war. And to the south, a Caribbean slave rebellion raised fears that racial war would be imported to the United States.

To the West: The Indians

In the 1783 Treaty of Paris, Britain had yielded all land east of the Mississippi River to the United States without regard to the resident Indian population. The 1784 Treaty of Fort Stanwix (see chapter 8) had attempted to solve that omission by establishing terms between the new confederation government and native peoples, but the key tribes of the Ohio Valley—the Shawnee, Delaware, and Miami—had not been involved in those negotiations. To confuse matters further, British troops still occupied half a dozen forts in the northwest, protecting an

236 CHAPTER 9
FORMING THE NEW NATION, 1789–1800

CHAPTER LOCATOR | What were the sources of political stability in Federalist America?

ongoing fur trade between British traders and Indians and thereby sustaining Indians' claims to that land.

The doubling of the American population from two million in 1770 to nearly four million in 1790 greatly intensified the pressure for western land. Several thousand settlers a year moved down the Ohio River in the mid-1780s. Most headed for Kentucky on the south bank of the river, but some looked north to Indian country. By the late 1780s, government land sales in eastern Ohio had commenced, although actual settlement lagged.

Meanwhile, the U.S. Army entered the western half of Ohio, where white settlers did not dare to go. Fort Washington, built on the Ohio River in 1789 at the site of present-day Cincinnati, became the command post for three major invasions of Indian country (**Map 9.2**). General Josiah Harmar, under orders to subdue the Indians of western Ohio, marched with 1,400 men into Ohio's northwest region in the fall of 1790, burning Indian villages. His inexperienced troops were ambushed by Miami and Shawnee Indians led by their chiefs, Little Turtle and Blue Jacket. Harmar lost one-eighth of his soldiers.

Harmar's defeat spurred efforts to clear Ohio for permanent American settlement. General Arthur St. Clair, the military governor of the Northwest Territory, had pursued peaceful tactics in the 1780s, signing treaties with Indians for land in eastern Ohio. In the fall of 1791, in the wake of Harmar's bungled operation, St. Clair led two thousand men north from Fort Washington to claim Ohio territory from the Miami and Shawnee tribes. Along the route, St. Clair's men quickly built two forts, named for Hamilton and Jefferson. However, when the Indians attacked at daybreak on November 4 at the headwaters of the Wabash River, St. Clair's army was not protected by fortifications.

Before noon, 55 percent of the Americans were dead or wounded. "The savages seemed not to fear anything we could do," wrote an officer afterward. "The ground was literally covered with the dead." The Indians captured valuable weaponry, scalped and dismembered the dying, and pursued fleeing survivors for miles. With more than nine hundred lives lost, this was the most stunning American loss in the history of the U.S.-Indian wars. Grisly tales of St. Clair's defeat increased the level of terror that Americans brought to their confrontations with the Indians.

Washington doubled the U.S. military presence in Ohio and appointed a new commander, General Anthony Wayne of Pennsylvania. About the Ohio natives, Wayne wrote, "I have always been of the opinion that we never should have a permanent peace with those Indians until they were made to experience our superiority." Throughout 1794, Wayne's army engaged in skirmishes with Shawnee,

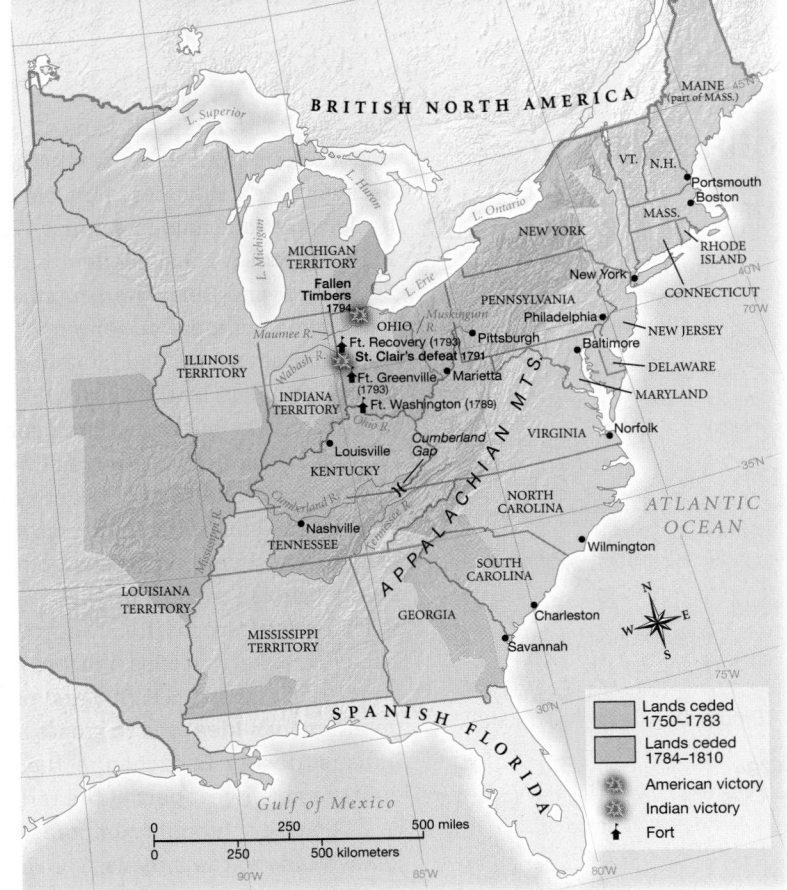

MAP 9.2 ■ Western Expansion and Indian Land Cessions to 1810
By the first decade of the nineteenth century, intense Indian wars had resulted in significant cessions of land to the U.S. government by treaty.

▶ FOR MORE HELP ANALYZING THIS MAP, see the map activity for this chapter in the Online Study Guide at bedfordstmartins.com/roarkunderstanding.

What was Hamilton's plan to solidify the government's fiscal position?	What external threats did the United States face in the 1790s?	How did partisan rivalries shape the politics of the late 1790s?	Conclusion: Why did the new nation ultimately form political parties?

CHRONOLOGY

1789
- Fort Washington is erected in western Ohio.
- French Revolution begins.

1790
- Shawnee and Miami Indians in Ohio defeat General Josiah Harmar.

1791
- Ohio Indians defeat General Arthur St. Clair.
- Haitian Revolution begins.

1793
- War breaks out between France and Britain.
- Washington issues Neutrality Proclamation.

1794
- Ohio Valley Indians suffer major defeat in battle of Fallen Timbers.

1795
- Treaty of Greenville settles conflict with Ohio Valley Indians.
- Jay Treaty settles conflict with Great Britain.

Treaty of Greenville

▶ 1795 treaty between the United States and various Indian tribes. The United States gave the tribes treaty goods valued at $25,000 and promised additional annual shipments of goods. In exchange, the Indians ceded most of Ohio to the Americans. The treaty brought only temporary peace to the region.

Delaware, and Miami Indians. Chief Little Turtle of the Miami tribe advised negotiation; in his view, Wayne's large army looked overpowering. But Blue Jacket of the Shawnees counseled continued warfare, and his view prevailed. The decisive action came in August 1794 at the battle of Fallen Timbers, near the Maumee River. The confederated Indians—mainly Ottawas, Potawatomis, Shawnees, and Delawares, numbering around eight hundred—ambushed the Americans but were underarmed, and Wayne's troops made effective use of their guns and bayonets. The Indians withdrew and sought refuge at nearby Fort Miami, still held by the British. Their former allies locked the gate and refused protection. The surviving Indians fled to the woods, their ranks decimated.

Fallen Timbers was a major defeat for the Indians. The Americans had destroyed cornfields and villages on the march north, and with winter approaching, the Indians' confidence was sapped. They reentered negotiations in a much less powerful bargaining position. In 1795, about a thousand Indians representing nearly a dozen tribes met with Wayne and other American emissaries to work out the **Treaty of Greenville**. The Americans offered treaty goods (calico shirts, axes, knives, blankets, kettles, mirrors, ribbons, thimbles, and abundant wine and liquor casks) worth $25,000 and promised additional shipments every year. The government's idea was to create a dependency on American goods to keep the Indians friendly. In exchange, the Indians ceded most of Ohio to the Americans; only the northwest part of the territory was reserved solely for the Indians.

The treaty brought temporary peace to the region, but it did not restore a peaceful life to the Indians. The annual allowance from the United States too often came in the form of liquor. "More of us have died since the Treaty of Greenville than we lost by the years of war before, and it is all owing to the introduction of liquor among us," said Chief Little Turtle in 1800. "This liquor that they introduce into our country is more to be feared than the gun and tomahawk."

Across the Atlantic: France and Britain

While Indian battles engaged the American military in the west, another war overseas to the east was also closely watched. Since 1789, revolution had been raging in France. At first, the general American reaction was positive. As monarchy and privilege were overthrown in France, towns throughout America celebrated the victory of the French people with civic feasts and public festivities. Dozens of pro-French political clubs, called democratic or republican societies, sprang up around the country.

Many American women exhibited solidarity with revolutionary France by donning sashes and cockades made with ribbons of red, white, and blue. Pro-French headgear for committed women included an elaborate turban, leading one horrified Federalist newspaper editor to chastise the "fiery frenchified dames" thronging Philadelphia's streets. In Charleston, South Carolina, a pro-French pageant in 1793 united two women as partners, one representing France and the other America. The women repudiated their husbands "on account of ill treatment" and pledged mutual "union and friendship," while a gun salute sealed the pledge. Most likely, this ceremony was not the country's first civil union but instead a richly metaphorical piece of street theater in which the spurned husbands represented Britain.

Anti–French Revolution sentiments also ran deep. Vice President John Adams, who lived in France in the 1780s, trembled to think of radicals in France

CHAPTER LOCATOR | What were the sources of political stability in Federalist America?

238 CHAPTER 9 FORMING THE NEW NATION, 1789–1800

or America. "Too many Frenchmen, after the example of too many Americans, pant for the equality of persons and property," Adams said. "The impracticability of this, God Almighty has decreed, and the advocates for liberty, who attempt it, will surely suffer for it."

Support for the French Revolution remained a matter of personal conviction until 1793, when Britain and France went to war and French versus British loyalty became a critical foreign policy debate. France had helped America substantially during the American Revolution, and the confederation government had signed an alliance in 1778 promising aid if France were ever under attack. Americans optimistic about the eventual outcome of the French Revolution wanted to deliver on that promise. Others, including those shaken by the report of the guillotining of thousands of French people, as well as those with strong commercial ties to Britain, sought ways to stay neutral.

In May 1793, President Washington issued the Neutrality Proclamation, which contained friendly assurances to both sides, in an effort to stay out of European wars. Yet American ships continued to trade between the French West Indies and France. In late 1793 and early 1794, the British expressed their displeasure by capturing more than three hundred of these vessels near the West Indies. Clearly, something had to be done to assert American power.

President Washington sent John Jay, the chief justice of the Supreme Court and a man of strong pro-British sentiments, to England to negotiate commercial relations in the British West Indies and secure compensation for the seizure of American ships. In addition, Jay was supposed to resolve several long-standing problems. Southern planters wanted reimbursement for the slaves liberated by the British army during the war, and western settlers wanted Britain to vacate the frontier forts still occupied because of their proximity to the Indian fur trade.

Jay returned from his diplomatic mission in 1795 with a treaty that no one could love. First, the **Jay Treaty** failed to address the captured cargoes or the lost property in slaves. Second, it granted the British a lenient eighteen months to withdraw from the frontier forts, as well as continued rights in the fur trade. (The provision disheartened the Indians just then negotiating the Treaty of Greenville in Ohio. It was a significant factor in their decision to make peace.) Finally, the treaty called for repayment with interest of the debts that some American planters still owed to British firms dating from the Revolutionary War. In exchange for such generous terms, Jay secured limited trading rights in the West Indies and agreement that some issues—boundary disputes with Canada and the damage and loss claims of shipowners—would be decided later by arbitration commissions.

When newspapers published the terms of the treaty, powerful opposition quickly emerged. In Massachusetts, this graffito appeared on a wall: "Damn John Jay! Damn everyone who won't damn John Jay! Damn everyone who won't stay up all night damning John Jay!" Bonfires in many places burned effigies of Jay and copies of the treaty. Nevertheless, the treaty passed the Senate in 1795 by a vote of 20 to 10. Some representatives in the House, led by Madison, tried to undermine the Senate's approval by insisting on a separate vote on the funding provisions of the treaty, on the grounds that the House controlled all money bills. Finally, in 1796, the House approved funds to implement the various commissions mandated by the treaty, but by only a three-vote margin. The bitter vote in both houses of Congress divided along the same lines as the Hamilton-Jefferson split on economic policy.

French Dress Style: Woman with Cockade

In the early 1790s, some Americans showed enthusiasm for the French Revolution by wearing a tricolor cockade—a distinctive bow made from red, white, and blue ribbons. Bibliothèque Nationale de France.

Jay Treaty

▶ 1795 treaty between the United States and England. John Jay was sent by President Washington to negotiate commercial relations in the British West Indies and secure compensation for the seizure of American ships. In addition, Jay was supposed to press for the reimbursement of southern planters for the slaves set free by the British army during the war and for the removal of British soldiers from frontier forts still occupied because of their proximity to the Indian fur trade. The resulting treaty was seen as too favorable to the British and was widely unpopular.

What was Hamilton's plan to solidify the government's fiscal position?

What external threats did the United States face in the 1790s?

How did partisan rivalries shape the politics of the late 1790s?

Conclusion: Why did the new nation ultimately form political parties?

239

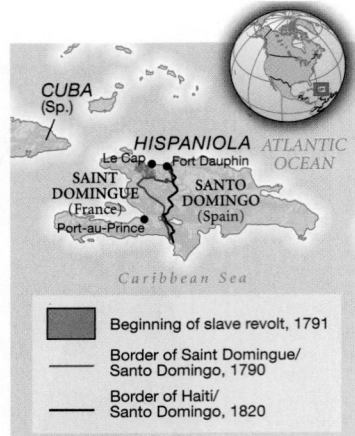

CUBA (Sp.)

HISPANIOLA *ATLANTIC OCEAN*

Le Cap • • Fort Dauphin

SAINT DOMINGUE (France)
Port-au-Prince

SANTO DOMINGO (Spain)

Caribbean Sea

■ Beginning of slave revolt, 1791

— Border of Saint Domingue/ Santo Domingo, 1790

— Border of Haiti/ Santo Domingo, 1820

Haitian Revolution, 1791–1804

Haitian Revolution

▶ A complex conflict lasting from 1791 to 1804 and involving many participants, including the diverse population of Haiti and, eventually, three European countries. As a result of the revolution, Haiti became an independent country, and slavery was outlawed within its borders. The Haitian Revolution fueled fears among white southerners that their own slaves might rise to ignite a bloody race war.

To the South: The Haitian Revolution

In addition to the Indian wars in Ohio and the European wars across the Atlantic, a third bloody conflict to the south polarized and even terrorized many Americans in the 1790s. The western third of the large Caribbean island of Hispaniola, just to the east of Cuba, became engulfed in revolution starting in 1791. The eastern portion of the island was a Spanish colony called Santo Domingo; the western part was the French Saint Domingue. War raged in Saint Domingue for more than a decade, resulting in 1804 in the birth of the Republic of Haiti, the first and only independent black state to arise out of a successful slave revolution.

The **Haitian Revolution** was a complex event involving many participants, including the diverse local population and, eventually, three European countries. Some 30,000 whites ruled the island in 1790, running sugar and coffee plantations with close to half a million enslaved blacks, two-thirds of them of African birth. The white French colonists were not the only plantation owners, however. About 28,000 free mixed-race people (*gens de couleur*) also lived in Saint Domingue; they owned one-third of the island's plantations and nearly a quarter of the slave labor force. Despite their economic status, these mixed-race planters were barred from political power, but they aspired to it.

The French Revolution of 1789 was the immediate catalyst for rebellion in this already tense society. First, white colonists challenged the white royalist government in an effort to link Saint Domingue with the new revolutionary government in France. Next, the mixed-race planters rebelled in 1791, demanding equal civil rights with the whites. No sooner was this revolt viciously suppressed than another part of the island exploded as thousands of enslaved blacks armed with machetes and torches wreaked devastation and slaughter. In 1793, the civil war escalated to include French, Spanish, and British troops fighting the inhabitants and also one another. Slaves led by Toussaint L'Ouverture in alliance with Spain occupied the northern regions of the island, leaving a thousand plantations in ruins and tens of thousands of people dead. Thousands of white and mixed-race planters, along with some of their slaves, fled to Spanish Louisiana and southern cities in the United States.

White Americans followed the revolution in horror through newspapers and refugees' accounts. A few sympathized with the impulse for liberty, but many more feared that violent black insurrection might spread to the United States. Many black American slaves also followed the revolution, for the news of the success of a first-ever massive revolution by slaves traveled quickly in this oral culture.

The Haitian Revolution provoked naked fear of a race war in white southerners. Jefferson, agonizing over the contagion of liberty in 1797, wrote another Virginia slaveholder that "if something is not done, and soon done, we shall be the murderers of our own children . . . ; the revolutionary storm, now sweeping the globe, will be upon us, and happy if we make timely provision to give it an easy passage over our land. From the present state of things in Europe and America, the day which brings our combustion must be near at hand; and only a single spark is wanting to make that day to-morrow."

> ## QUICK REVIEW

What connections did Americans make between events overseas and domestic stability in the 1790s?

CHAPTER LOCATOR | What were the sources of political stability in Federalist America?

How did partisan rivalries shape the politics of the late 1790s?

Cartoon of the Matthew Lyon Fight in Congress

The political tensions of 1798 were not merely intellectual. A February session in Congress degenerated from name-calling to a brawl. Roger Griswold, a Connecticut Federalist, called Matthew Lyon, a Vermont Republican, a coward. Lyon responded with some well-aimed spit, the first departure from the gentleman's code of honor. Griswold responded by raising his cane to Lyon, whereupon Lyon grabbed nearby fire tongs to beat back his assailant. Library of Congress.

► FOR MORE HELP ANALYZING THIS IMAGE, see the visual activity for this chapter in the Online Study Guide at bedfordstmartins.com/roarkunderstanding.

BY THE MID-1790s, polarization over the French Revolution, Haiti, the Jay Treaty, and Hamilton's economic plans had led to two distinct and consistent rival political groups: **Federalists** and **Republicans**. Federalist leaders supported Britain in foreign policy and commercial interests at home, while Republicans rooted for liberty in France and worried about monarchical Federalists at home. The labels did not yet describe full-fledged political parties, which were still thought to be a sign of failure of the experiment in government. Washington's decision not to seek a third term led to serious partisan electioneering in the presidential and congressional elections of 1796. Federalist John Adams won the presidency, but party strife accelerated over failed diplomacy in France, bringing the United States to the brink of war. Pro-war and antiwar antagonism created a major crisis over political free speech, militarism, and fears of sedition and treason.

The Election of 1796

Washington struggled to appear to be above party politics, and in his farewell address, he stressed the need to maintain a "unity of government" reflecting a unified body politic. He also urged the country to "steer clear of permanent alliances with any portion of the foreign world." The leading contenders for his position, John Adams of

Federalists
► One of the two dominant political groups that emerged in the 1790s. Federalist leaders supported Britain in foreign policy and commercial interests at home. Prominent Federalists included George Washington, Alexander Hamilton, and John Adams.

Republicans
► One of the two dominant political groups that emerged in the 1790s. Republicans supported the revolutionaries in France and worried about monarchical Federalists at home. Prominent Republicans included Thomas Jefferson and James Madison.

What was Hamilton's plan to solidify the government's fiscal position?

What external threats did the United States face in the 1790s?

How did partisan rivalries shape the politics of the late 1790s?

Conclusion: Why did the new nation ultimately form political parties?

241

Massachusetts and Thomas Jefferson of Virginia, in theory agreed with him, but around them raged a party contest split along pro-British versus pro-French lines.

The leading Federalists informally caucused and chose Adams as their candidate, with Thomas Pinckney of South Carolina to run with him. The Republicans settled on Aaron Burr of New York to pair with Jefferson. The Constitution did not anticipate parties and tickets. Instead, each electoral college voter could cast two votes for any two candidates, but on only one ballot. The top vote-getter became president, and the next-highest assumed the vice presidency. (This procedural flaw was corrected by the Twelfth Amendment, adopted in 1804.) With only one ballot, careful maneuvering was required to make sure that the chief rivals for the presidency did not land in the top two spots.

A failed effort by Alexander Hamilton to influence the outcome of the election landed the country in just such a position. Hamilton did not trust Adams; he preferred Pinckney, and he tried to influence electors to throw their support to the South Carolinian. But his plan backfired: Adams was elected president with 71 electoral votes; Jefferson came in second with 68 and thus became vice president. Pinckney got 59 votes, while Burr trailed with 30.

Adams's inaugural speech pledged neutrality in foreign affairs and respect for the French people, which made Republicans hopeful. To please Federalists, Adams retained three cabinet members from Washington's administration—the secretaries of state, treasury, and war. But the three were Hamilton loyalists, passing off Hamilton's judgments and advice as their own to the unwitting Adams. Vice President Jefferson extended a conciliatory hand to Adams, but the Hamiltonian cabinet ruined the honeymoon. Jefferson's advice was spurned, and he withdrew from active counsel of the president.

The XYZ Affair

From the start, Adams's presidency was in crisis. France retaliated for the British-friendly Jay Treaty by abandoning its 1778 alliance with the United States. French

John Adams

In 1793, a year after painting a portrait of the youthful secretary of the treasury Alexander Hamilton (see page 230), John Trumbull painted Vice President John Adams, then age fifty-eight. National Portrait Gallery, Smithsonian Institution/ Art Resources, NY.

CHAPTER LOCATOR | What were the sources of political stability in Federalist America?

242 CHAPTER 9 FORMING THE NEW NATION, 1789–1800

privateers—armed private vessels—started detaining American ships carrying British goods; by March 1797, more than three hundred American vessels had been seized. To avenge these insults, Federalists started murmuring openly about war with France. Adams preferred negotiations and dispatched a three-man commission to France in the fall of 1797. When the three commissioners arrived in Paris, French officials would not receive them. Finally, the French minister of foreign affairs, Talleyrand, sent three French agents—unnamed and later known to the American public as X, Y, and Z—to the American commissioners with the information that $250,000 might grease the wheels of diplomacy and that a $12 million loan to the French government would be the price of a peace treaty. Incensed, the commissioners brought news of the bribery attempt to the president.

Americans reacted to the **XYZ affair** with shock and anger. Even staunch pro-French Republicans began to reevaluate their allegiance. The Federalist-dominated Congress appropriated money for an army of ten thousand soldiers and repealed all prior treaties with France. In 1798, twenty naval warships launched the United States into its first undeclared war, called the Quasi-War by historians to underscore its uncertain legal status. The main scene of action was the Caribbean, where more than one hundred French ships were captured.

There was no home-front unity in this time of undeclared war; antagonism only intensified between Federalists and Republicans. Republican newspapers heaped abuse on Adams. Pro-French mobs roamed the capital, and Adams, fearing for his personal safety, stocked weapons in his presidential quarters. Federalists, too, went on the offensive. In Newburyport, Massachusetts, they lit a huge bonfire and burned issues of the state's Republican newspapers. One Federalist editor ominously declared that "he who is not for us is against us."

XYZ affair

▶ 1797 scandal in which an American commission sent to negotiate with France was rebuffed for refusing to pay a substantial bribe. When the incident became public, the United States entered into an undeclared war with France, known as the Quasi-War. The Quasi-War led to intensified antagonism between Federalists and Republicans.

The Alien and Sedition Acts

With tempers so dangerously high and fears that political dissent was perhaps akin to treason, Federalist leaders moved to muffle the opposition. In mid-1798, Congress passed the Sedition Act, which not only made conspiracy and revolt illegal but also penalized speaking or writing anything that defamed the president or Congress. Criticizing government leaders became a criminal offense. One Federalist warned of the threat that existed "to overturn and ruin the government by publishing the most shameless falsehoods against the representatives of the people." In all, twenty-five men, almost all Republican newspaper editors, were charged with sedition; twelve were convicted.

Congress also passed two Alien Acts. The first extended the waiting period for an alien to achieve citizenship from five to fourteen years and required all aliens to register with the federal government. The second empowered the president in time of war to deport or imprison without trial any foreigner suspected of being a danger to the United States. The clear intent of these laws was to harass French immigrants already in the United States and to discourage others from coming.

Republicans strongly opposed the **Alien and Sedition Acts** on the grounds that they were in conflict with the Bill of Rights, but they did not have the votes to revoke the acts in Congress, nor could the federal judiciary, dominated by Federalist judges, be counted on to challenge them. Jefferson and Madison turned to the state legislatures, the only other competing political arena, to press their opposition. Each man drafted a set of resolutions condemning the acts and had the

Alien and Sedition Acts

▶ 1798 acts passed by the Federalist Congress to suppress political dissent. The Sedition Act not only made conspiracy and revolt illegal but also penalized speaking or writing anything that defamed the president or Congress. The two Alien Acts extended the waiting period for an alien to achieve citizenship from five to fourteen years, required all aliens to register with the federal government, and empowered the president in time of war to deport or imprison without trial any foreigner suspected of being a danger to the United States. The Alien and Sedition Acts reflected the highly partisan politics and war hysteria of the late 1790s.

What was Hamilton's plan to solidify the government's fiscal position?	What external threats did the United States face in the 1790s?	How did partisan rivalries shape the politics of the late 1790s?	Conclusion: Why did the new nation ultimately form political parties?

legislatures of Virginia and Kentucky present them to the federal government in late fall 1798. The Virginia and Kentucky Resolutions tested the novel argument that state legislatures have the right to judge the constitutionality of federal laws and to nullify laws that infringe on the liberties of the people as defined in the Bill of Rights. The resolutions made little dent in the Alien and Sedition Acts, but the idea of a state's right to nullify federal law did not disappear. It would resurface several times in decades to come, most notably in a major tariff dispute in 1832 and in the sectional arguments that led to the Civil War.

Amid all the war hysteria and sedition fears in 1798, President Adams regained his balance. He was uncharacteristically restrained in pursuing opponents under the Sedition Act, and he finally refused to declare war on France, as extreme Federalists wished. He also shrewdly realized that France was not eager for war and that a peaceful settlement might be close at hand. In January 1799, a peace initiative from France arrived in the form of a letter assuring Adams that diplomatic channels were open again and that new commissioners would be welcomed in France.

Adams accepted this overture and appointed new negotiators. By late 1799, the Quasi-War with France had subsided, and in 1800 the negotiations resulted in a treaty declaring "a true and sincere friendship" between the United States and France. But Federalists were not pleased; Adams lost the support of a significant part of his own party and sealed his fate as the first one-term president of the United States.

The election of 1800 was openly organized along party lines. The self-designated national leaders of each group met to handpick their candidates for president and vice president. Adams's chief opponent was Thomas Jefferson. When the election was finally over, President Jefferson mounted the inaugural platform to announce, "We are all republicans, we are all federalists," an appealing rhetoric of harmony appropriate to an inaugural address. But his formulation perpetuated a denial of the validity of party politics, a denial that ran deep in the founding generation of political leaders.

> **QUICK REVIEW**

How did war between Britain and France intensify political division in the United States?

CHAPTER LOCATOR | What were the sources of political stability in Federalist America?

244 CHAPTER 9
FORMING THE NEW NATION, 1789–1800

Courtesy, The Henry Francis du Pont Winterthur Museum.

Conclusion: Why did the new nation ultimately form political parties?

AMERICAN POLITICAL LEADERS began operating the new government in 1789 with great hopes of unifying the country and overcoming selfish factionalism. The enormous trust in President Washington was the central foundation for those hopes, and Washington did not disappoint, becoming a model Mr. President with a blend of integrity and authority. Stability was further aided by easy passage of the Bill of Rights (to appease Antifederalists) and by attention to cultivating a virtuous citizenry of upright men supported and rewarded by republican womanhood. Yet the hopes of the honeymoon period soon turned to worries and then fears as major political disagreements flared up.

At the core of the conflict was a group of talented men—Hamilton, Madison, Jefferson, and Adams—so recently allies but now opponents. They diverged over Hamilton's economic program, over relations with the British and the Jay Treaty, over the French and Haitian revolutions, and over preparedness for war abroad and free speech at home. Hamilton was perhaps the driving force in these conflicts, but the antagonism was not about mere personality. Parties were taking shape not around individuals, but around principles, such as ideas about what constituted enlightened leadership, how powerful the federal government should be, who was the best ally in Europe, and when oppositional political speech turned into treason.

In his inaugural address of 1800, Jefferson offered his conciliatory assurance that Americans were at the same time "all republicans" and "all federalists," suggesting that both groups shared two basic ideas—the value of republican government, in which power derived from the people, and the value of the unique federal system of shared governance structured by the Constitution. But by 1800, *Federalist* and *Republican* defined competing philosophies of government. For the next two decades, these two groups would battle each other, each fearing that the success of the other might bring the demise of the country.

SO NOW YOU KNOW

Even though Washington had originally favored "His High Mightiness" as the title by which the president should be addressed, ultimately the established form of address became "Mr. President." Washington, a "virtuous" man in the language of the day, maintained dignity and even encouraged ceremonialism, but in the end he helped shape the presidency in a way that signaled new republican ideals.

| What was Hamilton's plan to solidify the government's fiscal position? | What external threats did the United States face in the 1790s? | How did partisan rivalries shape the politics of the late 1790s? | Conclusion: Why did the new nation ultimately form political parties? |

245

CHAPTER 9 STUDY GUIDE

Online Study Guide
bedfordstmartins.com/roarkunderstanding

STEP 1 GETTING STARTED

Below are basic terms from this period in American history. Can you identify each term below and explain why it matters? To do this exercise online or to download this chart, visit bedfordstmartins.com/roarkunderstanding.

TERM	WHO OR WHAT & WHEN	WHY IT MATTERS
Bill of Rights, p. 227		
Alexander Hamilton, p. 230		
Report on Public Credit, p. 232		
Whiskey Rebellion, p. 235		
Treaty of Greenville, p. 238		
Jay Treaty, p. 239		
Haitian Revolution, p. 240		
Federalists, p. 241		
Republicans, p. 241		
XYZ affair, p. 243		
Alien and Sedition Acts, p. 243		

STEP 2 MOVING BEYOND THE BASICS

The exercise below represents a more advanced understanding of the chapter material. Assess the growing split between the Federalists and the Republicans in the late eighteenth century. Fill in the chart below by describing the Federalist and Republican positions and opinions on the key issues of the period. What core assumptions and beliefs informed the policies and positions of each group? Is it accurate to describe the two groups as political parties? Why or why not? To do this exercise online or to download this chart, visit bedfordstmartins.com/roarkunderstanding.

	Federalists	Republicans
States' rights		
Government influence on economy		
Social and political hierarchy		
Relations with Britain		
Relations with France		

Now that you've reviewed various parts of the chapter, take a step back and try to see the big picture by answering these questions. Remember to use specific examples from the chapter in your answers. To do this exercise online, visit bedfordsmartins.com/roarkunderstanding.

DOMESTIC AFFAIRS

▶ What important precedents did George Washington set? How did he use the presidency to bring political stability to the country?

▶ How did Hamilton imagine the future of the United States? How did his vision conflict with that of Jefferson?

NATIONAL SECURITY

▶ What were the most important threats to America's national security in the 1790s? How did the Washington and Adams administrations respond to those threats?

▶ How did the French Revolution contribute to the split between Federalists and Republicans in the United States?

FEDERALISTS AND REPUBLICANS

▶ What led to the factionalizing of American politics in the 1790s?

▶ How did the development of political factions affect the country domestically? In its external affairs?

LOOKING BACKWARD, LOOKING AHEAD

▶ How did the government Washington headed differ from the government created by the Articles of Confederation?

▶ What steps had been taken toward the creation of national political parties by 1800? What steps were still required before a true party system was in place?

IN YOUR OWN WORDS

Imagine that you must explain chapter 9 to someone who hasn't read it. What would be the most important points to include and why?

E OWE ALLEGIANCE TO NO CRO

10
A MATURING REPUBLIC

1800–1824

> This chapter explores the changing political landscape in America from the election of Thomas Jefferson in 1800 to the election of John Quincy Adams in 1824. It examines the foreign and domestic challenges and opportunities that shaped American politics in the early nineteenth century, as well the shifting political culture that resulted in the expansion of suffrage for white men, the disfranchisement of most of their black counterparts, and new educational opportunities for American women.

> How did Thomas Jefferson radically transform the presidency?

> What were the challenges and successes of the Madison presidency?

> To what extent did women's status change in the early Republic?

> Why did partisan conflict increase during the administrations of Monroe and Adams?

> Conclusion: How did republican simplicity become complex?

DID YOU KNOW?

The Department of State had a grand total of eight employees during Thomas Jefferson's first term as president.

"We Owe Allegiance to No Crown," by American sailor John A. Woodside, ca. 1815–1820.

How did Thomas Jefferson radically transform the presidency?

When the young widower Thomas Jefferson lived in Paris in the late 1780s, he distributed three copies of this miniature portrait as affectionate gifts, one to his daughter Martha, another to a very attractive (but married) American woman in London, and the third to a British woman, also married. A much younger fourth woman in Paris shared his residence: his slave Sally Hemings, attendant to Jefferson's two daughters. Early in Jefferson's presidency, a scandal erupted when a journalist charged that Jefferson had fathered several children by Sally Hemings. DNA evidence, when combined with historical evidence about Jefferson's whereabouts at the start of each of Hemings's six pregnancies, makes a powerful case that Jefferson fathered some and probably all of her children. Monticello/Thomas Jefferson Memorial Foundation, Inc.

Thomas Jefferson

▶ Republican president of the United States from 1801 to 1809 who presided over the Louisiana Purchase, Lewis and Clark's exploration of the West, and precarious relations with Britain and France. He brought the presidency more in line with his own republican values by limiting the size of the federal government and displaying modest simplicity in affairs of state.

THE ELECTION OF 1800, decided in the House of Representatives, stoked fears that party divisions would ruin the country. A panicky Federalist newspaper in Connecticut predicted that **Thomas Jefferson's** victory would produce a civil war and usher in a reign of "murder, robbery, rape, adultery and incest." Similar fears were expressed in the South, where a slave uprising seemed a possible outcome of Jefferson's victory.

Although nothing so dramatic occurred, Jefferson did radically transform the presidency, away from the Federalists' vision of a powerful executive branch and toward republican simplicity and limited government. Yet even Jefferson found that circumstances sometimes required him to draw on the expansive powers of the presidency. The rise of Napoleon in France brought France and Britain into open warfare again in 1803, creating unexpected opportunities and challenges for Jefferson. One major opportunity arrived in the spectacular purchase from

CHAPTER LOCATOR | How did Thomas Jefferson radically transform the presidency?

France of the Louisiana Territory; a significant challenge arose when pirates threatened American ships off the north coast of Africa and when British and French naval forces nipped at American ships—and American honor—in the Atlantic Ocean.

Turbulent Times: Election and Rebellion

The result of the election of 1800 remained uncertain from polling time in November to repeated roll call votes in the House of Representatives in February 1801. Federalist John Adams was no longer in the presidential race once it got to the House. Instead, the contest was between Thomas Jefferson and his running mate, Senator Aaron Burr of New York. Republican voters in the electoral college slipped up, giving Jefferson and Burr an equal number of votes, an outcome possible because of the single balloting to choose both president and vice president. (To fix this problem, the Twelfth Amendment to the Constitution, adopted in 1804, provided for distinct ballots for the two offices.) The vain and ambitious Burr declined to concede, so the sitting Federalist-dominated House of Representatives got to choose the president (**Map 10.1**).

Some Federalists preferred Burr, believing that he was susceptible to Federalist pressure. But the influential Alexander Hamilton, though no friend of Jefferson, recognized that Burr would be more dangerous in the presidency. Jefferson was a "contemptible hypocrite" in Hamilton's opinion, but at least he was not corrupt. (In 1804, Burr shot and killed Hamilton in a formal but illegal duel.) Thirty-six ballots and six days later, Jefferson got the votes he needed to win the presidency. This election demonstrated a remarkable feature of the new government: No matter how hard fought the campaign, the leadership of the nation could shift from one group to its rivals in a peaceful transfer of power.

As the country struggled over its white leadership crisis, a twenty-four-year-old blacksmith named Gabriel, the slave of Thomas Prossor, plotted rebellion in Virginia. Inspired by the Haitian Revolution (see chapter 9), Gabriel was said to be organizing a thousand slaves to march on the state capital of Richmond and take the governor, James Monroe, hostage. On the appointed day, however, a few nervous slaves went to the authorities with news of Gabriel's rebellion, and within days, scores of implicated conspirators were jailed and brought to trial.

CHRONOLOGY

1800
- Republicans Thomas Jefferson and Aaron Burr tie in electoral college.
- Fears of slave rebellion led by Gabriel in Virginia result in twenty-seven executions.

1801
- House of Representatives elects Thomas Jefferson president after thirty-six ballots.

1803
- In *Marbury v. Madison*, the U.S. Supreme Court rules that it can declare laws unconstitutional.
- Rivals Britain and France warn United States not to ship war-related goods to the other.
- United States purchases the Louisiana Territory from France.

1804–1806
- Lewis and Clark expedition to the Louisiana Territory travels to the Pacific Ocean.

1807
- British attack and search the American ship *Chesapeake*.
- Embargo Act bans importation of British goods.

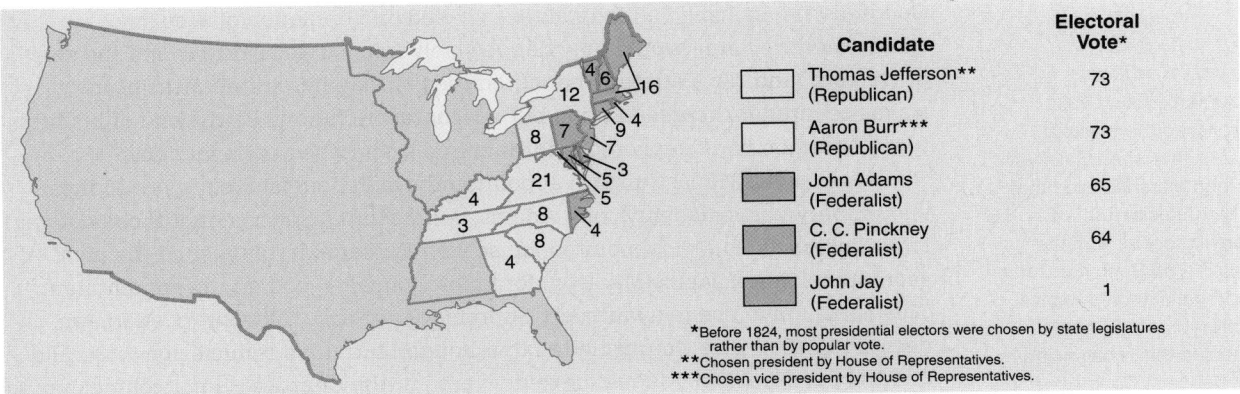

Candidate	Electoral Vote*
Thomas Jefferson** (Republican)	73
Aaron Burr*** (Republican)	73
John Adams (Federalist)	65
C. C. Pinckney (Federalist)	64
John Jay (Federalist)	1

*Before 1824, most presidential electors were chosen by state legislatures rather than by popular vote.
**Chosen president by House of Representatives.
***Chosen vice president by House of Representatives.

MAP 10.1 ■ The Election of 1800

What were the challenges and successes of the Madison presidency?	To what extent did women's status change in the early Republic?	Why did partisan conflict increase during the administrations of Monroe and Adams?	Conclusion: How did republican simplicity become complex?

One of the jailed rebels compared himself to the most venerated icon of the early Republic: "I have nothing more to offer than what General Washington would have had to offer, had he been taken by the British and put to trial by them." Such talk worried white Virginians, and in fall of 1800, twenty-seven black men were hanged for allegedly contemplating rebellion. Finally, Jefferson advised Governor Monroe to halt the hangings. "The world at large will forever condemn us if we indulge a principle of revenge," Jefferson wrote.

The Jeffersonian Vision of Republican Simplicity

Once elected, Thomas Jefferson turned his attention to establishing his administration in clear contrast to the Federalists. For his inauguration, he dressed in everyday clothing to strike a tone of republican simplicity, and he walked to the Capitol for the modest swearing-in ceremony. As president, he scaled back Federalist building plans for Washington and cut the government budget.

Martha Washington and Abigail Adams had received the wives of government officials at weekly teas, thereby cementing social relations in the governing class. But Jefferson, a longtime widower, disdained female gatherings and avoided the women of Washington City. He abandoned George Washington's practice of holding weekly formal receptions. He preferred small dinner parties with carefully chosen politicos, either all Republicans or all Federalists (and all male). At these intimate dinners, the president exercised influence and strengthened informal relationships that would help him govern.

Jefferson was no Antifederalist. He had supported the Constitution in 1788. But events of the 1790s had caused him to worry about the stretching of powers in the executive branch. Jefferson had watched with distrust as Hamiltonian policies refinanced the public debt, established a national bank, and secured commercial ties with Britain (see chapter 9). These policies seemed to Jefferson to promote the interests of greedy speculators and profiteers at the expense of the rest of the country. In Jefferson's vision, the source of true liberty in America was the independent farmer, someone who owned and worked his land both for himself and for the market.

Jefferson set out to dismantle Federalist innovations. He reduced the size of the army by a third, and he limited the navy to six ships. With the consent of Congress, he abolished all federal taxes based on population or whiskey. Government revenue would now derive solely from customs duties and the sale of western land. This strategy benefited the South, where three-fifths of the slaves counted for representation but not for taxation now. By the end of his first term, Jefferson had deeply reduced Hamilton's cherished national debt.

Faced with 217 last-minute appointments of Federalists to various judicial and military posts made by John Adams, Jefferson refused to honor those not yet fully processed. One disappointed job seeker, William Marbury, sued the new secretary of state, James Madison, for failure to make good on the appointment. This action gave rise to a landmark Supreme Court case, *Marbury v. Madison*, decided in 1803. The Court ruled that although Marbury's commission was valid and the new president should have delivered it, the Court could not compel him to do so. The Court found that the grounds of Marbury's suit, resting in the Judiciary

Marbury v. Madison
▶ 1803 Supreme Court case that established the concept of judicial review when Chief Justice John Marshall ruled that parts of the Judiciary Act of 1789 were in conflict with the Constitution. The Supreme Court assumed legal authority to nullify acts of other branches of the government in this rebalancing of power between Congress and the judiciary.

CHAPTER LOCATOR | How did Thomas Jefferson radically transform the presidency?

252 CHAPTER 10
A MATURING REPUBLIC, 1800–1824

Act of 1789, were in conflict with the Constitution. Thus, for the first time, the Court acted to disallow a law on the grounds that it was unconstitutional.

A properly limited federal government, according to Jefferson, was responsible merely for running a postal system, maintaining the federal courts, staffing lighthouses, collecting customs duties, and conducting a census once every ten years. Government jobs were kept to a minimum. The president had one private secretary, a young man named Meriwether Lewis, to help with his correspondence, and Jefferson paid him out of his own pocket. The Department of State employed only 8 people: Secretary James Madison, 6 clerks, and a messenger. The Treasury Department was by far the largest unit, with 73 revenue commissioners, auditors, and clerks, plus 2 watchmen. The entire payroll of the executive branch amounted to a mere 130 people in 1801.

The Promise of the West: The Louisiana Purchase and the Lewis and Clark Expedition

Jefferson's government was small, but his ambitions for the trans-Mississippi West were great. A large expanse of the Great Plains had been transferred from France to Spain under the 1763 Treaty of Paris. Spain never controlled or settled it, and Spanish power in North America remained precarious everywhere outside New Orleans. In an effort to augment population, Spain encouraged American farmers to move west across the Mississippi River, and by 1801, Americans made up a sizable minority of the population around New Orleans. Publicly, Jefferson protested the luring of Americans to Spanish territory, but privately he welcomed it: "I wish a hundred thousand of our inhabitants would accept the invitation; it will be the means of delivering to us peaceably, what may otherwise cost us a war."

In 1802, rumors reached Jefferson that Spain had struck a secret bargain with far more powerful France to transfer all of Spain's trans-Mississippi territory to Napoleon in exchange for land in Italy. Jefferson was so alarmed that he instructed Robert R. Livingston, America's minister in France, to try to buy New Orleans. When Livingston hinted that the United States might seize it if buying was not an option, the French negotiator asked him to name his price for the entire Louisiana Territory from the Gulf of Mexico north to Canada. Livingston shrewdly stalled and within days accepted the bargain price of $15 million (**Map 10.2**). In late 1803, the American army took formal control of the Louisiana Territory, and the United States nearly doubled in size.

Even before the **Louisiana Purchase**, Jefferson had his eye on the trans-Mississippi West. In early 1803, he had arranged congressional funding for a secret scientific and military mission into Indian territory. Jefferson appointed twenty-eight-year-old Meriwether Lewis, his secretary, to head the expedition, instructing him to investigate Indian cultures, to collect plant and animal specimens, and to chart the geography of the West. Congress wanted the expedition to scout locations for military posts, negotiate fur trade agreements, and identify river routes to the West.

For his co-leader, Lewis chose Kentuckian William Clark, a veteran of the 1790s Indian wars. Lewis and Clark, along with their crew of forty-five, left St. Louis in the spring of 1804, working their way northwest up the Missouri River. They camped for the winter at a Mandan village in what is now central North Dakota.

Louisiana Purchase

▶ 1803 purchase of French territory in the United States that stretched from the Gulf of Mexico to Canada. The Louisiana Purchase nearly doubled the size of the United States and opened the way for future American expansion west.

What were the challenges and successes of the Madison presidency?

To what extent did women's status change in the early Republic?

Why did partisan conflict increase during the administrations of Monroe and Adams?

Conclusion: How did republican simplicity become complex?

253

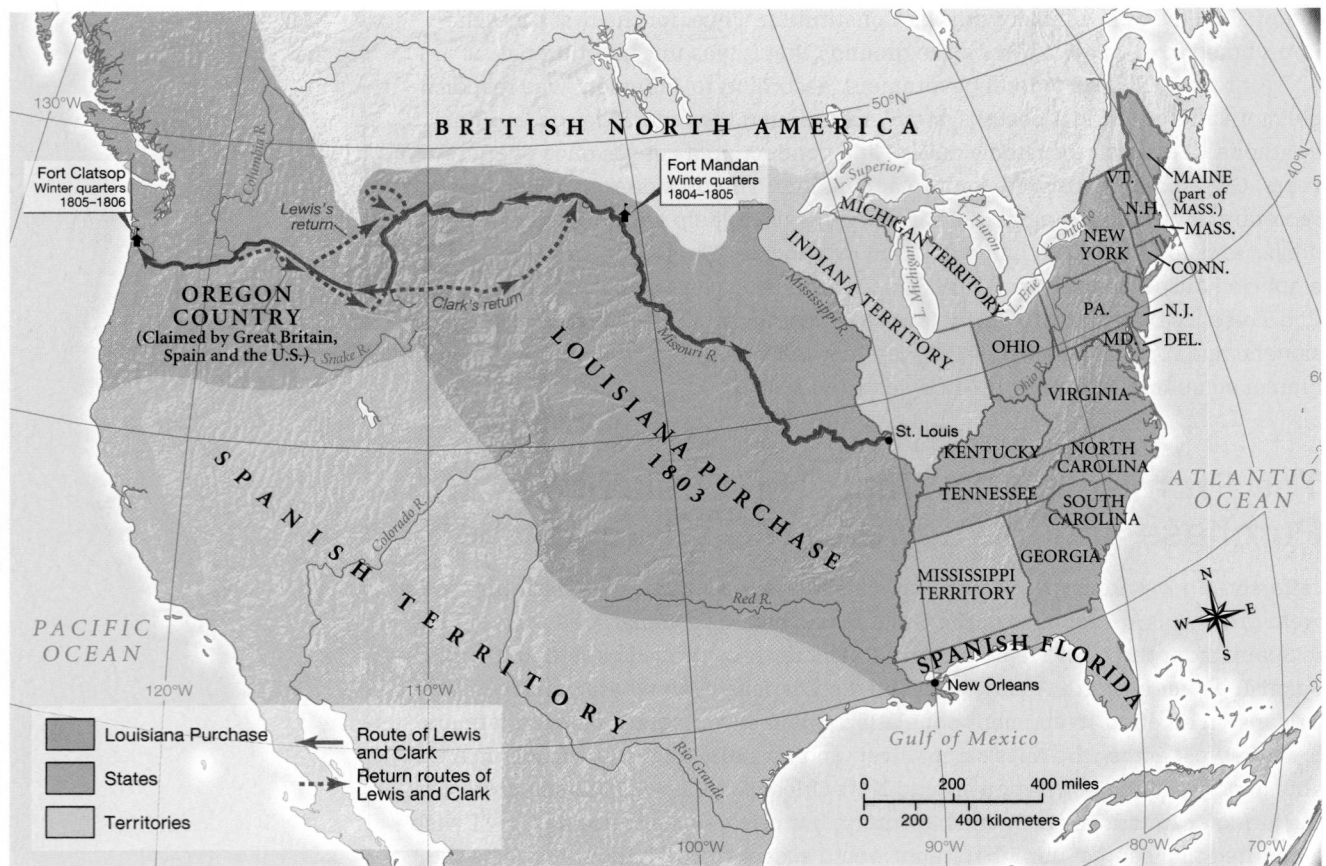

MAP 10.2 ■ The Louisiana Purchase and the Lewis and Clark Expedition
Robert Livingston's bargain buy of 1803 far exceeded his initial assignment to acquire the city of New Orleans. New England Federalists, worried that their geographically based power in the federal government would someday be eclipsed by the West, voted against the purchase. The Indians who inhabited the vast region, unaware that their land had been claimed by either the French or the Americans, got their first look at Anglo-American and African American men when the Lewis and Clark expedition explored the territory in 1804–1806.

▶ FOR MORE HELP ANALYZING THIS MAP, see the map activity for this chapter in the Online Study Guide at bedfordstmartins.com/roarkunderstanding.

Lewis and Clark expedition
▶ 1804–1806 expedition led by Meriwether Lewis and William Clark that explored the trans-Mississippi West on behalf of the U.S. government. The expedition's mission was to scout locations for military posts, negotiate fur trade agreements, and identify river routes to the West. The expedition made Lewis and Clark heroes and focused the nation's attention on the potential of western expansion.

The following spring, they headed west, accompanied by a sixteen-year-old Shoshoni woman named Sacajawea. Kidnapped by Mandans at about age ten, she had been sold to a French trapper as a slave/wife. Hers was not a unique story among Indian women; such women knew several languages, making them valuable translators and mediators. Further, Sacajawea and her new baby allowed the American expedition to appear peaceful to suspicious tribes. As Lewis wrote in his journal, "No woman ever accompanies a war party of Indians in this quarter."

The **Lewis and Clark expedition** reached the Pacific Ocean at the mouth of the Columbia River in November 1805. When Lewis and Clark returned home the following year, they were greeted as national heroes. They had established favorable relations with dozens of Indian tribes; they had collected invaluable informa-

Grizzly Bear Claw Necklace

Lewis and Clark collected hundreds of Indian artifacts on their expedition, including this bear claw necklace presented by Shoshoni warriors in the Rocky Mountains. The thirty-eight impressive claws, each three to four inches long, are strung together by rawhide thongs: At least two grizzly bears were killed to create the necklace. This was no simple task: Male grizzlies are large—six to seven feet tall and five hundred to nine hundred pounds—and aggressive. It seems certain that a sense of the bears' power would be bestowed on the wearer. Peabody Museum of Archaeology and Ethnology, Harvard University.

tion on the peoples, soils, plants, animals, and geography of the West; and they had inspired a nation of restless explorers and solitary imitators.

Challenges Overseas: The Barbary Wars

Around the same time, events in the western Mediterranean led to the first declaration of war against the United States by a foreign power. For well over a century, four Muslim states on the northern coast of Africa—Morocco, Algiers, Tunis, and Tripoli, called the Barbary States by Americans—controlled all Mediterranean shipping traffic by demanding large annual payments (called "tribute") for safe passage. Countries electing not to pay found their ships at risk for seizure. By the mid-1790s, the United States was paying $50,000 a year.

American Commerce in the Mediterranean

Mediterranean trade involved about a hundred American merchant ships annually.

Exports to the region included lumber, tobacco, sugar, and rum.

Imports from the region included raisins, figs, capers, and opium for medicinal use.

Some 20 percent of all American exports went to the Middle East.

In May 1801, when the pasha (military head) of Tripoli failed to secure a large increase in his tribute, he declared war on the United States. Jefferson had long considered such payments extortion, and he sent four warships to the Mediterranean to protect U.S. shipping. From 1801 to 1803, U.S. frigates engaged in skirmishes with Barbary privateers.

Then, in late 1803, the USS *Philadelphia* ran aground near Tripoli harbor and was captured along with its crew. In retaliation, a U.S. naval ship commanded by navy lieutenant Stephen Decatur sailed into the harbor after dark and set the *Philadelphia* on fire, making Decatur an instant hero in America. A later foray into the harbor to try to blow up the entire Tripoli fleet with a bomb-laden boat failed when the explosives detonated prematurely, killing eleven Americans.

In 1804, William Eaton, an American officer stationed in Tunis, felt the humiliation of his country's ineffectiveness. He wrote to Secretary of State James

| What were the challenges and successes of the Madison presidency? | To what extent did women's status change in the early Republic? | Why did partisan conflict increase during the administrations of Monroe and Adams? | Conclusion: How did republican simplicity become complex? |

255

Madison to ask for a thousand marines to invade Tripoli. Madison rejected the plan and another scheme to ally with the pasha's exiled brother to effect a regime change. On his own, Eaton contacted the brother, assembled a force of four hundred men (most of them Egyptian mercenaries), and marched them over five hundred miles of desert for a surprise attack on Tripoli's second-largest city. Amazingly, he succeeded. The pasha of Tripoli yielded, released the prisoners taken from the *Philadelphia*, and negotiated a treaty with the United States. Peace with the other Barbary States came in a second treaty in 1812.

More Transatlantic Troubles: Impressment and Embargo

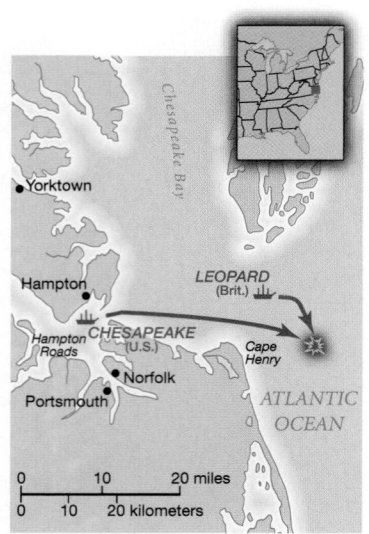

The *Chesapeake* Incident, June 22, 1807

Jefferson easily retained the presidency in the election of 1804, winning 162 electoral votes to the 14 won by Federalist Charles Cotesworth Pinckney of South Carolina. But governing in his second term was not easy, because of seriously escalating tensions between the United States and both France and Britain. Beginning in 1803, both European rivals, embroiled in a war with each other, repeatedly warned the United States not to ship arms to the other. Britain acted on these threats in 1806, stopping U.S. ships to inspect cargoes for military aid to France and seizing suspected deserters from the British navy, along with many Americans. Ultimately, 2,500 U.S. sailors were "impressed" (taken by force) by the British. In retaliation against the impressment of U.S. sailors, Jefferson convinced Congress to pass nonimportation laws banning certain British-made goods.

Jefferson found one event particularly provoking. In June 1807, the American ship *Chesapeake*, harboring some British deserters, was ordered to stop by the British frigate *Leopard*. The *Chesapeake* refused, and the *Leopard* opened fire, killing three Americans—right at the mouth of the Chesapeake Bay, well within U.S. territory. In response, Congress passed the Embargo Act of 1807, banning all importation of British goods into the country. All foreign ports were declared off-limits to American merchants to discourage illegal trading through secondary ports. Though a drastic measure, the embargo was meant to forestall war by forcing concessions from the British through economic pressure.

The Embargo Act of 1807 was a disaster. From 1790 to 1807, U.S. exports had increased fivefold, but the embargo brought commerce to a standstill. In New England, the heart of the shipping industry, unemployment rose. Grain plummeted in value, river traffic halted, tobacco rotted in the South, and cotton went unpicked. Protest petitions flooded Washington. The federal government suffered, too, for import duties were a significant source of revenue. Jefferson paid political costs as well. The Federalist Party, weakened by its poor showing in the election of 1804, began to revive.

> **QUICK REVIEW**

How did Jefferson attempt to undo the Federalist innovations of earlier administrations?

CHAPTER LOCATOR | How did Thomas Jefferson radically transform the presidency?

256 CHAPTER 10
A MATURING REPUBLIC, 1800–1824

Dolley Madison, by Gilbert Stuart

The "presidentress" of the Madison administration sat for this official portrait in 1804. She wears an empire-style dress, at the height of French fashion in 1804 and a style worn by many women at the coronation of the emperor Napoleon in Paris. The hallmarks of such a dress were a light fabric (muslin or chiffon), short sleeves, a high waistline from which the fabric fell straight to the ground, and usually a low, open neckline, as shown here. © White House Historical Association.

What were the challenges and successes of the Madison presidency?

IN MID-1808, Jefferson indicated that he would not run for a third term. Secretary of State James Madison was chosen by the Republican caucuses—informal political groups that orchestrated the selection of candidates. The Federalist caucuses again chose Charles Cotesworth Pinckney. Madison won, but Pinckney received 47 electoral votes, nearly half of Madison's total. Support for the Federalists remained centered in New England, and Republicans still held the balance of power nationwide.

Women in Washington City

Although women could not vote and supposedly left politics to men, the female relatives of Washington politicians took on several overtly political functions that greased the wheels of the affairs of state. They networked through dinners, balls, receptions, and the intricate custom of "calling," in which men and women paid brief visits at each other's homes. Webs of friendship and influence in turn facilitated female political lobbying. It was not uncommon for women in this social set to write letters of recommendation for men seeking government work.

When James Madison became president, **Dolley Madison**, called by some the "presidentress," struck a balance between queenliness and republican openness. She dressed the part in resplendent clothes, opening three elegant rooms in the executive mansion for a weekly party called "Mrs. Madison's crush" or "squeeze." In contrast to George and Martha Washington's stiff, brief receptions, the Madisons' parties went on for hours, with scores or even hundreds of guests milling about, talking, and eating. Members of Congress, cabinet officers, distinguished guests, envoys from foreign countries, and their womenfolk attended with regularity. Mrs. Madison's squeeze was an essential event for gaining political access, trading information, and establishing informal channels that would smooth the governing process.

Dolley Madison
► Wife of President James Madison and center of Washington's social scene during his presidency. She was called by some the "presidentress." Her social gatherings were important political events at which the Washington elite would gather to gain political access, trade information, and establish informal channels that would smooth the governing process.

What were the challenges and successes of the Madison presidency?

To what extent did women's status change in the early Republic?

Why did partisan conflict increase during the administrations of Monroe and Adams?

Conclusion: How did republican simplicity become complex?

1808
- Republican James Madison is elected president; Dolley Madison is soon dubbed "presidentress."

1811
- Battle of Tippecanoe ends uprising by Native Americans in the old Northwest.

1812
- United States declares war on Great Britain.

1813
- Tecumseh dies at battle of the Thames.

1814
- British attack Washington, D.C.
- New England Federalists meet at Hartford Convention.

1815
- U.S. troops led by Andrew Jackson defeat British at the battle of New Orleans.

Tecumseh

▶ Shawnee chief who, along with this brother Tenskwatawa (known as the Prophet), built a pan-Indian confederacy in the first decade of the nineteenth century to resist further white encroachment on Indian lands. The two promoted a potent blend of spiritual regeneration and political unity that attracted thousands of followers. Tecumseh was killed in 1813 while fighting on the British side in the War of 1812.

In 1810–1811, the Madisons' house acquired its present name, the White House. The many guests at the weekly parties experienced simultaneously the splendor of the executive mansion and the atmosphere of republicanism that made it accessible to so many. Dolley Madison, ever an enormous political asset to her rather shy husband, understood well the symbolic function of the White House to enhance the power and legitimacy of the presidency.

Indian Troubles in the West

While the Madisons cemented alliances at home, difficulties with Britain and France overseas and with Indians in the old Northwest continued to increase. In the Ohio Country, the Shawnee chief **Tecumseh** and his brother Tenskwatawa (known as the Prophet) actively solidified a pan-Indian confederacy to resist further white encroachment on Indian lands. The two promoted a potent blend of spiritual regeneration and political unity that attracted thousands of followers. At the same time, the more northern tribes renewed their ties with supportive British agents and fur traders in Canada, a potential source of food and weapons. If the United States went to war with Britain, there would clearly be serious repercussions on the frontier.

Shifting demographics put the Indians under pressure. The 1810 census counted some 230,000 Americans in Ohio, while another 40,000 inhabited the territories of Indiana, Illinois, and Michigan. The Indian population of the same area was much smaller, probably about 70,000.

Up to 1805, Indiana's territorial governor, William Henry Harrison, had negotiated a series of treaties in a divide-and-conquer strategy aimed at extracting Indian lands for paltry payments. But with the rise to power of Tecumseh and his brother Tenskwatawa, the Prophet, Harrison's strategy faltered. A fundamental part of Tecumseh's message was the assertion that all Indian lands were held in common by all the tribes. "No tribe has the right to sell [these lands], even to each

Tenskwatawa, by George Catlin

Tenskwatawa, the Prophet, and his brother Tecumseh led the spiritual and political efforts of a number of Indian tribes to resist land-hungry Americans moving west in the decade before the War of 1812. Artist George Catlin portrays the Prophet wearing beaded necklaces, metal arm- and wristbands, and earrings. National Museum of American Art, Washington, D.C./ Art Resource, NY.

CHAPTER LOCATOR | How did Thomas Jefferson radically transform the presidency?

other, much less to strangers . . . ," Tecumseh said. "Sell a country! Why not sell the air, the great sea, as well as the earth? Didn't the Great Spirit make them all for the use of his children?" In 1809, while Tecumseh was away on a recruiting trip, Harrison assembled the leaders of the Potawatomi, Miami, and Delaware tribes to negotiate the Treaty of Fort Wayne. After promising (falsely) that this was the last cession of land the United States would seek, Harrison secured three million acres at about two cents per acre.

When he returned, Tecumseh was furious with both Harrison and the tribal leaders. Leaving his brother in charge at his headquarters of Prophetstown on Tippecanoe River, the Shawnee chief left to seek alliances with tribes in the South. In November 1811, Harrison decided to attack Prophetstown with a thousand men. The two-hour battle resulted in the deaths of sixty-two Americans and forty Indians before the Prophet's forces fled. The Americans won the battle of Tippecanoe, but Tecumseh was now more ready than ever to make war on the United States.

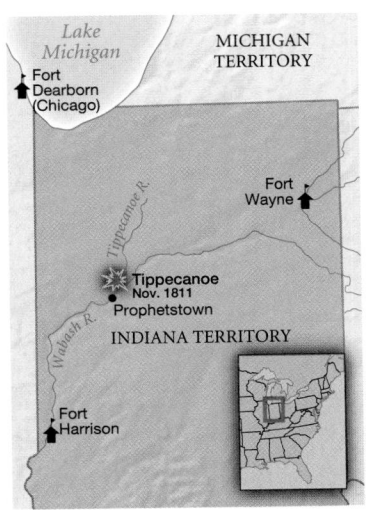

Battle of Tippecanoe, 1811

The War of 1812

The Indian conflicts in the old Northwest soon merged into the wider conflict with Britain now known as the **War of 1812**. Between 1809 and 1812, President Madison teetered between declaring either Britain or France America's primary enemy, as attacks by both countries on U.S. ships continued. In 1809, Congress replaced Jefferson's embargo with the Non-Intercourse Act, which prohibited trade only with Britain and France and their colonies, thus opening up other trade routes to alleviate somewhat the anguish of shippers, farmers, and planters. By 1811, the country was seriously divided and on the verge of war.

The new Congress seated in March 1811 contained several dozen young Republicans from the West and South who would come to be known as the War Hawks. Led by thirty-four-year-old Henry Clay from Kentucky and twenty-nine-year-old John C. Calhoun from South Carolina, they welcomed a war with Britain both to justify attacks on the Indians and to bring an end to impressment. Many were also expansionists, looking to occupy Florida and threaten Canada. Clay was elected Speaker of the House. Calhoun won a seat on the Foreign Relations Committee. The War Hawks approved major defense expenditures, and the army soon quadrupled in size.

In June 1812, Congress declared war on Great Britain in a vote divided along sectional lines: New England and some Middle Atlantic states opposed the war, fearing its effect on commerce, while the South and West were strongly for it. Ironically, Britain had just announced that it would stop the search and seizure of American ships, but the war momentum would not be slowed. The Foreign Relations Committee issued an elaborate justification titled *Report on the Causes and Reasons for War*, written mainly by Calhoun and containing extravagant language about Britain's "lust for power," "unbounded tyranny," and "mad ambition." These were fighting words in a war that was in large measure about insult and honor.

The War Hawks proposed an invasion of Canada, confidently predicting victory in four weeks. Instead, the war lasted two and a half years, and Canada never fell. The northern invasion turned out to be one of a series of blunders that revealed America's grave unpreparedness for war against the unexpectedly powerful British and Indian forces (**Map 10.3**). By the fall of 1812, the outlook was grim.

War of 1812

▶ War between the United States and Great Britain. After years of attacks on American vessels abroad, the War Hawks pushed for the United States to declare war on Britain to end impressment of Americans, legitimize attacks on Indians in the West, and pursue expansionist impulses. In June 1812, Congress declared war on Great Britain. The War Hawks proposed an invasion of Canada and expected quick success; instead, the conflict dragged on for two and a half years. The Treaty of Ghent ended the war in late 1814, although the final battle in New Orleans occurred in early 1815: Americans yielded on impressment and relinquished any claims to Canada, and the British stopped giving aid to Indians.

What were the challenges and successes of the Madison presidency?	To what extent did women's status change in the early Republic?	Why did partisan conflict increase during the administrations of Monroe and Adams?	Conclusion: How did republican simplicity become complex?

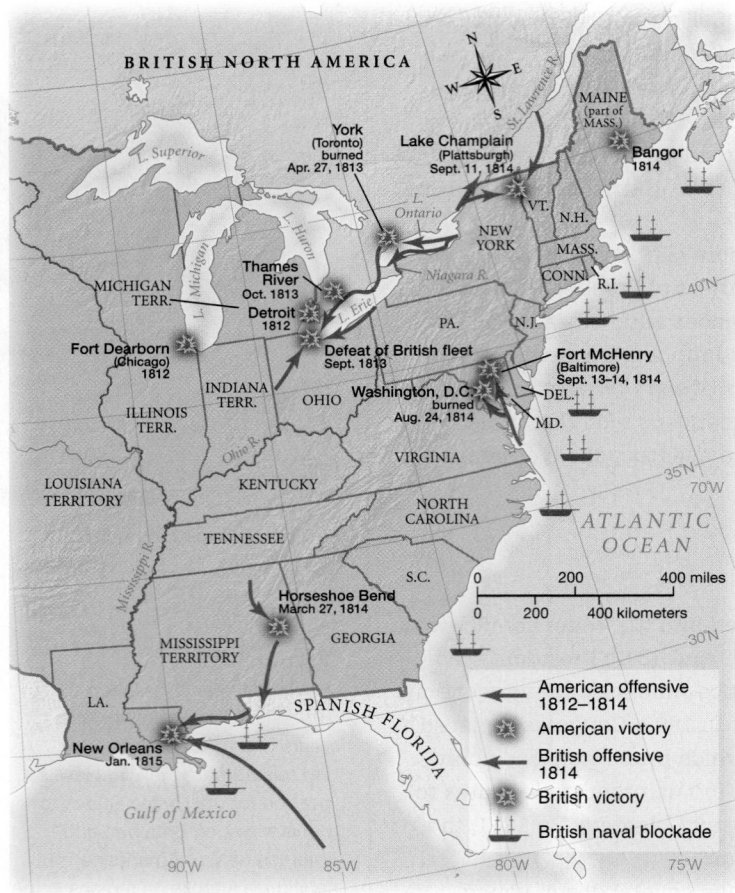

MAP 10.3 ■ The War of 1812
During the War of 1812, battles were fought along the Canadian border and in the Chesapeake region. The most important American victory came in New Orleans two weeks after a peace agreement had been signed in Europe.

Worse, the New England states were slow to raise troops, and some New England merchants carried on illegal trade with Britain. The fall presidential election pitted Madison against DeWitt Clinton of New York, nominally a Republican but able to attract the Federalist vote. Clinton picked up all of New England's electoral votes, with the exception of Vermont's, and also took New York, New Jersey, and part of Maryland. Madison won in the electoral college, 128 to 89, but his margin of victory was considerably smaller than in 1808.

In late 1812 and early 1813, the tide began to turn in the Americans' favor. First came some reassuring victories at sea. Then the Americans attacked York (now Toronto) and burned it in April 1813. A few months later, Commodore Oliver Hazard Perry defeated the British fleet at the western end of Lake Erie. Emboldened, General Harrison drove an army into Canada from Detroit and in October 1813 defeated the British and Indians at the battle of the Thames, where Tecumseh was killed.

Creek Indians in the South who had allied with Tecumseh's confederacy were also plunged into war. Some 10,000 living in the Mississippi Territory put up a spirited fight against U.S. forces for ten months. But the Creek War ended suddenly in March 1814 when a general named Andrew Jackson led 2,500 Tennessee militiamen in a bloody attack called the Battle of Horseshoe Bend. More than 550 Indians were killed, and several hundred more died trying to escape across a river. Later that year, General Jackson extracted a treaty relinquishing thousands of square miles of Creek land to the United States.

Washington City Burns: The British Offensive

In August 1814, British ships sailed into the Chesapeake Bay, landing five thousand troops and throwing the capital into a panic. The British troops entered the city and burned the White House, the Capitol, a newspaper office, and a well-stocked arsenal. Instead of trying to hold the city, the British headed north and attacked Baltimore, but a fierce defense by the Maryland militia thwarted that effort.

In another powerful offensive that same month, British troops marched from Canada into New York State, but a series of mistakes cost them a naval skirmish at Plattsburgh on Lake Champlain, and they retreated to Canada. Five months later, another large British army landed in lower Louisiana and, in early January 1815, encountered General Andrew Jackson and his militia just outside New Orleans. Jackson's forces carried the day, and Jackson instantly became known as the hero

CHAPTER LOCATOR | How did Thomas Jefferson radically transform the presidency?

of the battle of New Orleans. No one in the United States knew that negotiators in Europe had signed a peace agreement two weeks earlier.

The Treaty of Ghent, signed in December 1814, settled few of the surface issues that had led to war. Neither country could claim victory, and no land changed hands. Instead, the treaty reflected a mutual agreement to give up certain goals. The Americans dropped their plea for an end to impressments, which in any case subsided as soon as Britain and France ended their war in 1815. They also gave up any claim to Canada. The British agreed to stop all aid to the Indians. Nothing was said about shipping rights.

Antiwar Federalists in New England could not gloat over the war's ambiguous conclusion because of an ill-timed and seemingly unpatriotic move on their part. The region's leaders had convened a secret meeting in Hartford, Connecticut, in December 1814 to discuss a series of proposals aimed at reducing the South's political power and breaking Virginia's lock on the presidency. The Federalists at Hartford even discussed secession from the Union but rejected that path. Coming just as peace was achieved, however, the Hartford Convention looked very unpatriotic. The Federalist Party never recovered, and within a few years, it was reduced to a shadow of its former self, even in New England.

Proposals Supported at the Hartford Convention

Abolition of the Constitution's three-fifths clause as a basis of representation.

Requirement of a two-thirds vote instead of a simple majority for imposing embargoes, admitting states, or declaring war.

Limit of one term for presidents.

Prohibition of the election of successive presidents from the same state.

No one really won the War of 1812. The war did, however, give rise to a new spirit of American nationalism. The paranoia over British tyranny that contributed to the outbreak of war was replaced by pride in a more equal relationship with the old mother country. Indeed, in 1817 the two countries signed the Rush-Bagot disarmament treaty (named after its two negotiators), which limited each country to a total of four naval vessels, each with just a single cannon, to patrol the vast watery border between them.

The biggest winners in the War of 1812 were the War Hawks, who took up the banner of the Republican Party and carried it in new, expansive directions. These young politicians favored trade, western expansion, internal improvements, and the energetic development of new economic markets. The biggest losers of the war were the Indians. Tecumseh was dead, his brother the Prophet was discredited, the prospects of an Indian confederacy were dashed, the Creeks' large homeland was seized, and the British protectors were gone.

QUICK REVIEW

Why did Congress declare war on Great Britain in 1812?

| What were the challenges and successes of the Madison presidency? | To what extent did women's status change in the early Republic? | Why did partisan conflict increase during the administrations of Monroe and Adams? | Conclusion: How did republican simplicity become complex? |

To what extent did women's status change in the early Republic?

DOLLEY MADISON'S pioneering role as "presidentress" showed that elite women could assume an active presence in civic affairs. But, as with the 1790s cultural compromise that endorsed female education to make women into better wives and mothers (see chapter 9), Mrs. Madison and her female circle practiced politics to further their husbands' careers. There was little talk of the "rights of woman." Indeed, from 1800 to 1825, key institutions central to the shaping of women's lives—the legal system, marriage, and religion—proved fairly resistant to change. Nonetheless, the trend toward increased commitment to female education that began in the 1780s and 1790s, continued in the first decades of the nineteenth century.

Women and the Law

feme covert

▶ Legal doctrine grounded in British common law that held that a wife's civic life was completely subsumed by her husband's. This meant that a married woman could not own property, make contracts, sue or be sued, or keep her own wages; even her children legally belonged to her husband. The doctrine shaped women's social and legal status in the early Republic despite a few departures from British law, such as limited provisions for divorce.

In English common law, wives had no independent legal or political personhood. The legal doctrine of **feme covert** (covered woman) held that a wife's civic life was completely subsumed by her husband's. A wife had to obey her husband; her property was his, her domestic and sexual services were his, and even their children were legally his. Wives had no right to keep their wages or to make contracts. State legislatures passed up the opportunity to rewrite the laws of domestic relations even though they redrafted other British laws in light of republican principles.

The one aspect of family law that changed in the early Republic was divorce. Before the Revolution, only New England jurisdictions recognized a limited right to divorce; by 1820, every state except South Carolina did so. However, divorce was uncommon and in many states could be obtained only by petition to the

CHAPTER LOCATOR | How did Thomas Jefferson radically transform the presidency?

262 CHAPTER 10
A MATURING REPUBLIC, 1800–1824

state's legislature, a daunting obstacle for many ordinary people. A mutual wish to terminate a marriage was never sufficient grounds for a legal divorce. A New York judge affirmed that "it would be aiming a deadly blow at public morals to decree a dissolution of the marriage contract merely because the parties requested it. Divorces should never be allowed, except for the protection of the innocent party, and for the punishment of the guilty." States upheld the institution of marriage both to protect persons they thought of as naturally dependent (women and children) and to regulate the use and inheritance of property. Legal enforcement of marriage as an unequal relationship played a major role in maintaining gender inequality in the nineteenth century.

Single adult women could own and convey property, make contracts, initiate lawsuits, and pay taxes. They could not vote (except in New Jersey before 1807), serve on juries, or practice law, so their civil status was limited. Single women's economic status was often limited as well, by custom as much as by law. Unless they had inherited adequate property or could live with married siblings, single adult women in the early Republic were very often poor.

None of the legal institutions that structured white gender relations applied to black slaves. Treated as property, they could not freely consent to any contractual obligations, including marriage. The protective features of state-sponsored unions were thus denied to black men and women in slavery. But this also meant that slave unions did not establish unequal power relations between partners backed by the force of law, as did marriages among the free.

Women and Church Governance

In most Protestant denominations around 1800, white women made up the majority of congregants. Yet church leadership generally rested in men's hands. There were some exceptions, however. In Baptist congregations in New England, women joined men on church governance committees that hired ministers, admitted members, and debated doctrinal points. Quakers, too, had a history of recognizing women's spiritual talents. Some were accorded the status of minister, capable of leading and speaking in Quaker meetings.

Between 1790 and 1820, a small and highly unusual set of women actively engaged in open preaching. Most were from Freewill Baptist groups centered in New England and upstate New York. Others came from small Methodist sects, and yet others rejected any formal religious affiliation. Probably fewer than a hundred such women existed, but several dozen traveled beyond their local communities, creating converts and controversy.

The best-known such woman was Jemima Wilkinson, who called herself "the Publick Universal Friend." After a near-death experience from a high fever, Wilkinson proclaimed her body no longer female or male but the incarnation of the "Spirit of Light." She dressed in men's clothes, wore her hair in a masculine style, shunned gender-specific pronouns, and preached openly in Rhode Island and Philadelphia. In the early nineteenth century, Wilkinson established a town called New Jerusalem in western New York with some 250 followers.

The decades from 1790 to the 1820s marked a period of unusual confusion, ferment, and creativity in American religion. New denominations blossomed, new styles of religiosity gripped adherents, and an extensive periodical press devoted to religion popularized all manner of theological and institutional innovations.

CHRONOLOGY

1790–1820
- In an era of religious ferment, a small number of women engage in open preaching.

1821
- Emma Willard founds the Troy Female Seminary in New York.

1822
- Catharine Beecher founds the Hartford Seminary in Connecticut for female students.

1830
- By this time, nearly two hundred female academies are operating in the United States.

What were the challenges and successes of the Madison presidency?

To what extent did women's status change in the early Republic?

Why did partisan conflict increase during the administrations of Monroe and Adams?

Conclusion: How did republican simplicity become complex?

263

Congregations increasingly attracted female participation, often eclipsing the number of male congregants. In such a climate, gender subordination came into question here and there among the most radically democratic of the churches. But the presumption of male authority over women was deeply entrenched in American culture. Even denominations that had allowed women to participate in church governance began to pull back, and most churches reinstated patterns of hierarchy along gender lines.

Female Education

First in the North and then in the South, states and localities began investing in public schools to create the educated citizenry thought necessary in a republic. Young girls attended district schools, sometimes along with boys or, in rural areas, more often in separate summer sessions. By 1830, girls had made rapid gains, in many places approaching male literacy rates.

More advanced female education came from a growing number of private academies. Judith Sargent Murray, the Massachusetts author who had called for equality of the sexes around 1790 (see chapter 9), predicted in 1800 that "a new era in female history" would emerge because "**female academies** are everywhere establishing." Some dozen female academies were established in the 1790s, and by 1830 that number had grown to nearly two hundred.

The three-year curriculum included both ornamental arts and solid academics. The former strengthened female gentility: drawing, needlework, music, and French conversation. The academic subjects included English grammar, literature, history, the natural sciences, geography, and elocution (the art of effective public speaking). Academy catalogs show that, by the 1820s, the courses and reading lists at the top female academies equaled those at male colleges such as Harvard, Yale, Dartmouth, and Princeton. The girls at these academies studied Latin, rhetoric, logic, theology, moral philosophy, algebra, geometry, and even chemistry and physics.

Two of the best-known female academies were the Troy Female Seminary in New York, founded by Emma Willard in 1821, and the Hartford Seminary in Connecticut, founded by Catharine Beecher in 1822. Both prepared their students to teach, on the grounds that women made better teachers than men did. Author Harriet Beecher Stowe, educated at her sister's school and then a teacher there, agreed: "If men have more knowledge they have less talent at communicating it. Nor have they the patience, the long-suffering, and gentleness necessary to superintend the formation of character."

The most immediate value of advanced female education lay in the self-cultivation and confidence it provided. Female graduation exercises showcased speeches and recitations performed in front of a mixed-sex audience of family, friends, and local notables. Academies also took care to promote a pleasing female modesty. Female pedantry or intellectual immodesty triggered the stereotype of the "bluestocking," a British term of hostility for a too-learned woman doomed to fail in the marriage market.

By the mid-1820s, the total annual enrollment at the female academies and seminaries equaled male enrollment at the five dozen male colleges in the United States. Both groups accounted for only about 1 percent of their age cohorts in the country at large, indicating that advanced education was clearly limited to a privileged few. Most female graduates in time married and raised families, but

female academies

▶ Private schools that began providing advanced education to teenage girls in the late 1700s. A dozen or so female academies were formed in the 1790s, and by 1830 there were almost two hundred such schools. The girls at these academies were primarily daughters of elite families and received instruction in ornamental arts (drawing, needlework, music, dancing) as well as in academic subjects such as English grammar, literature, history, geography, and the natural sciences.

CHAPTER LOCATOR | How did Thomas Jefferson radically transform the presidency?

264 CHAPTER 10
A MATURING REPUBLIC, 1800–1824

first many of them became teachers at academies and district schools. A large number also became authors, contributing essays and poetry to newspapers, editing periodicals, and publishing novels. The new attention to the training of female minds laid the foundation for major changes in the gender system as girl students of the 1810s matured into adult women of the 1830s.

Home and Away: The New Boarding School

These two engravings show "before" and "after" pictures of a young woman around 1820 whose family enrolled her in one of the new female academies. The artist, Philadelphia painter John Lewis Krimmel, worked as a drawing master at such an academy. Library Company of Philadelphia.

▶ FOR MORE HELP ANALYZING THIS IMAGE, see the visual activity for this chapter in the Online Study Guide at bedfordstmartins.com/roarkunderstanding.

QUICK REVIEW ❮

How did the civil status of American women and men differ in the early Republic?

| What were the challenges and successes of the Madison presidency? | To what extent did women's status change in the early Republic? | Why did partisan conflict increase during the administrations of Monroe and Adams? | Conclusion: How did republican simplicity become complex? |

> Why did partisan conflict increase during the administrations of Monroe and Adams?

Election Sewing Box Everyday household objects could become vehicles for the expression of political partisanship. Here a sewing box sporting John Quincy Adams's face allowed its owner—almost certainly a woman—to proclaim her sympathy for the Adams Republicans. On the top of the Adams box sits a velvet pincushion (not visible here) printed with the slogan "Be Firm for Adams." Collection of Janice L. and David J. Frent.

IN 1816, JAMES MONROE beat Federalist Rufus King of New York, garnering 183 electoral votes to King's 34. In 1820, Republican Monroe was reelected with all but one electoral vote. At the state level, increasing voter engagement sparked a drive for universal white male suffrage. The collapse of the Federalist Party ushered in an apparent period of one-party rule, but politics remained highly contentious, with many factors promoting increased partisanship. Put to the test of practical circumstances, the one-party political system failed and then fractured.

From Property to Democracy

Up to 1820, presidential elections occurred in the electoral college, at a remove from ordinary voters. The excitement generated by state elections, however, created pressure for greater democratization of presidential elections.

In the 1780s, twelve of the original thirteen states enacted property qualifications based on the theory that only male freeholders—landowners, as distinct from tenants or servants—had sufficient independence of mind to be entrusted with the vote. Of course, not everyone accepted that restricted idea of the people's role in government (see chapter 8). In the 1790s, Vermont became the first state to enfranchise all adult males, and four other states soon broadened suffrage considerably by allowing all taxpayers to vote. Between 1800 and 1830, greater democratization became a lively issue both in established states and in new states emerging in the West.

In new states, small populations together with yet smaller numbers of large property owners meant that few men could vote under typical restrictive property qualifications. Congress initially set a fifty-acre freehold as the threshold for voting, but in Illinois, fewer than three hundred men met that test at the time of

CHAPTER LOCATOR | How did Thomas Jefferson radically transform the presidency?

statehood. When Indiana, Illinois, and Mississippi became states, their constitutions granted suffrage to all taxpayers. Five additional new western states abandoned property and taxpayer qualifications altogether.

The most heated battles over suffrage occurred in eastern states, where expanding numbers of commercial men, renters, and mortgage holders of all classes contended with entrenched landed elites who, not surprisingly, favored the status quo. Still, by 1820, a half dozen states passed suffrage reform. Some stopped short of complete manhood suffrage, instead tying the vote to tax status or militia service. In the remainder of the states, the defenders of landed property qualifications managed to delay expanded suffrage for two more decades. But it was increasingly hard to persuade the disfranchised that landowners alone had a stake in government. Proponents of the status quo began to argue instead that the "industry and good habits" necessary to achieve a propertied status in life were what gave landowners the right character to vote. Rejecting that position, one delegate to New York's constitutional convention said, "More integrity and more patriotism are generally found in the labouring class of the community than in the higher orders." Owning land was no more predictive of wisdom and good character than it was of a person's height or strength, said another.

Both sides of the debate generally agreed that character mattered, and many ideas for ensuring an electorate of proper wisdom came up for discussion. The exclusion of paupers and felons convicted of "infamous crimes" found favor in legislation in many states. Literacy tests and raising the voting age to a figure in the thirties were debated but ultimately discarded. In one exceptional moment, at the Virginia convention in 1829, a delegate wondered aloud why unmarried women over the age of twenty-one could not vote; he was quickly silenced with the argument that all women lacked the "free agency and intelligence" necessary for wise voting.

Free black men's enfranchisement generated much discussion at all the conventions. Under existing freehold qualifications, a small number of propertied black men could vote; universal or taxpayer suffrage would inevitably enfranchise many more. Many delegates at the various state conventions spoke against that extension, claiming that blacks as a race lacked prudence, independence, and knowledge. With the exception of New York, which retained the existing property qualification for black voters as it removed it for whites, the general pattern was one of expanded suffrage for whites and a total eclipse of suffrage for blacks.

The Missouri Compromise

The politics of race produced perhaps the most divisive issue during Monroe's term. In February 1819, Missouri applied for statehood. Since 1815, four other states had joined the Union (Indiana, Mississippi, Illinois, and Alabama) following the blueprint laid out by the Northwest Ordinance of 1787. But Missouri posed a problem. Although much of its area was on the same latitude as the free state of Illinois, its territorial population included ten thousand slaves brought there by southern planters.

The problem led a New York congressman, James Tallmadge Jr., to propose two amendments to the statehood bill. The first stipulated that slaves born in Missouri after statehood would be free at age twenty-five, and the second declared that no new slaves could be imported into the state. Tallmadge's model was New York's gradual emancipation law of 1799. It did not strip slave owners of their

CHRONOLOGY

1816
– Republican James Monroe is elected president.

1820
– Missouri Compromise allows Missouri to enter the Union as a slave state and Maine to enter as a free state and sets a boundary for future slave states.

1823
– Monroe Doctrine asserts that the Western Hemisphere should be free from European interference.

1825
– John Quincy Adams is elected president by House of Representatives in a bitterly contested election.

What were the challenges and successes of the Madison presidency?

To what extent did women's status change in the early Republic?

Why did partisan conflict increase during the administrations of Monroe and Adams?

Conclusion: How did republican simplicity become complex?

267

current property, and it allowed them full use of the labor of newborn slaves well into their prime productive years. Still, southern congressmen objected because in the long run the amendments would make Missouri a free state, presumably no longer allied with southern economic and political interests. Just as southern economic power rested on slave labor, southern political power drew extra strength from the slave population because of the three-fifths rule. In 1820, the South owed seventeen of its seats in the House of Representatives to its slave population.

Tallmadge's amendments passed in the House by a close and sharply sectional vote of North against South. The ferocious debate led a Georgia representative to observe that the question had started "a fire which all the waters of the ocean could not extinguish. It can be extinguished only in blood." The Senate, with an even number of slave and free states, voted down the amendments, and Missouri statehood was postponed until the next congressional term.

In 1820, a compromise emerged. Maine, once part of Massachusetts, applied for statehood as a free state, balancing against Missouri as a slave state. The Senate further agreed that the southern boundary of Missouri—latitude 36°30'—extended west, would become the permanent line dividing slave from free states, guaranteeing the North a large area where slavery was banned (**Map 10.4**). The House also approved the **Missouri Compromise**, thanks to expert deal brokering by Kentucky's Henry Clay. The whole package passed because seventeen northern congressmen decided that minimizing sectional conflict was the best course and voted with the South.

President Monroe and former president Jefferson at first worried that the Missouri crisis would reinvigorate the Federalist Party as the party of the North. But even ex-Federalists agreed that the split between free and slave states was too danger-

Missouri Compromise

▶ 1820 congressional compromise engineered by Henry Clay that allowed Missouri to enter the Union as a slave state and Maine to enter as a free state. The compromise also established Missouri's southern border as the permanent line dividing slave from free states. The Missouri Compromise calmed tensions in the short run but did nothing to resolve the underlying issue of the future of slavery in the United States.

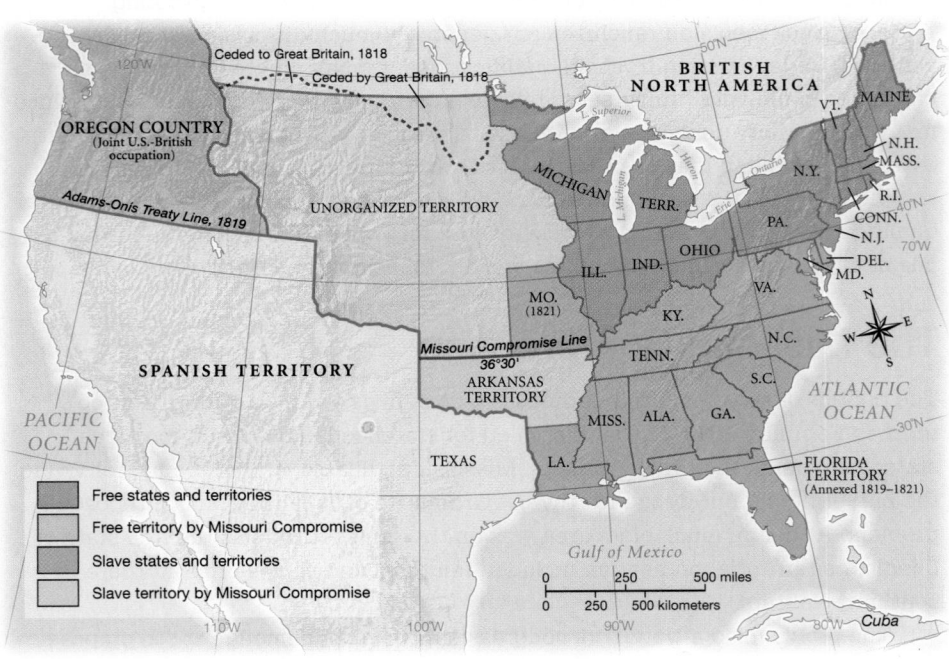

MAP 10.4 ■ The Missouri Compromise, 1820
After a difficult battle in Congress, Missouri entered the Union in 1821 as part of a package of compromises. Maine was admitted as a free state to balance slavery in Missouri, and a line drawn at latitude 36°30' put most of the rest of the Louisiana Territory off-limits to slavery in the future.

CHAPTER LOCATOR | How did Thomas Jefferson radically transform the presidency?

A View of St. Louis from an Illinois Town, 1835

Just fifteen years after the Missouri Compromise, St. Louis was already a booming city, having gotten its start in the eighteenth century as a French fur-trading village. In this 1835 view, commercial buildings and steamships line the riverfront; a ferry on the Illinois shore prepares to transport travelers across the Mississippi River. Black laborers (in the foreground) handle loading tasks. Illinois was a free state; Missouri, where the ferry will land, was a slave state. *A View of St. Louis from an Illinois Town*, 1835: Private collection.

> ▶ FOR MORE HELP ANALYZING THIS IMAGE, see the visual activity for this chapter in the Online Study Guide at bedfordstmartins.com/roarkunderstanding.

ous a fault line to be permitted to become a shaper of national politics. When new parties did develop in the 1830s, they took pains to bridge geography, each party developing a presence in both North and South. Monroe and Jefferson also worried about the future of slavery. Both understood slavery to be deeply problematic, but, as Jefferson said, "we have the wolf by the ears, and we can neither hold him, nor safely let him go. Justice is in one scale, and self-preservation in the other."

The Monroe Doctrine

New foreign policy challenges arose even as Congress struggled with the slavery issue. In 1816, U.S. troops led by General Andrew Jackson invaded Spanish Florida in search of Seminole Indians harboring escaped slaves. Once there, Jackson declared himself the commander of northern Florida, demonstrating his power in

| What were the challenges and successes of the Madison presidency? | To what extent did women's status change in the early Republic? | Why did partisan conflict increase during the administrations of Monroe and Adams? | Conclusion: How did republican simplicity become complex? |

269

1818 by executing two British men who he claimed were dangerous enemies. In asserting rule over the territory, and in executing the two British subjects on Spanish land, Jackson had gone too far. Privately, President Monroe was distressed and pondered court-martialing Jackson, prevented only by Jackson's immense popularity as the hero of the battle of New Orleans. Instead, John Quincy Adams, the secretary of state, negotiated with Spain the Adams-Onís Treaty, which delivered Florida to the United States in 1819. In exchange, the Americans agreed to abandon any claim to Texas or Cuba. Southerners viewed this as a large concession, having eyed both places as potential acquisitions for future slave states.

Spain at that moment was preoccupied with its colonies in South America. One after another, Chile, Colombia, Peru, and finally Mexico declared themselves independent in the early 1820s. To discourage Spain or France from reconquering these colonies, Monroe in 1823 formulated a declaration of principles on South America, known in later years as the **Monroe Doctrine**. The president warned that "the American Continents, by the free and independent condition which they have assumed and maintain, are henceforth not to be considered as subjects for future colonization by any European power." Any attempt to interfere in the Western Hemisphere would be regarded as "the manifestation of an unfriendly disposition towards the United States." In exchange for noninterference by Europeans, Monroe pledged that the United States would stay out of European struggles.

The Election of 1824

Monroe's nonpartisan administration was the last of its kind, a throwback to eighteenth-century ideals, as was Monroe, with his powdered wig and knee breeches. Monroe's cabinet contained men of sharply different philosophies, all calling themselves Republicans. Secretary of State **John Quincy Adams** represented the urban Northeast; South Carolinian John C. Calhoun spoke for the planter aristocracy as secretary of war; and William H. Crawford of Georgia, secretary of the treasury, was a proponent of Jeffersonian states' rights and limited federal power. Even before the end of Monroe's first term, these men and others began to maneuver for the election of 1824.

Crucially helping them to maneuver were their wives, who accomplished some of the work of modern campaign managers by courting men—and women—of influence. Louisa Catherine Adams had a weekly party for guests numbering in the hundreds. The somber Adams lacked charm—"I am a man of reserved, cold, austere, and forbidding manners," he once wrote—but his abundantly charming (and hardworking) wife made up for that. She attended to the etiquette of social calls, sometimes making two dozen in a morning, and counted sixty-eight members of Congress as her regular guests.

John Quincy Adams (and Louisa Catherine) were ambitious for the presidency, but so were others. Candidate Henry Clay, Speaker of the House and negotiator of the Treaty of Ghent with Britain in 1814, promoted a new "American System," a package of protective tariffs to encourage manufacturing and federal expenditures for internal improvements such as roads and canals. Treasurer William Crawford was a favorite of Republicans from Virginia and New York, even after he suffered an incapacitating stroke in mid-1824. Calhoun was another serious contender, having served in Congress and in several cabinets. A southern

Monroe Doctrine

▶ 1823 declaration by President James Monroe that the United States would regard any attempt by an external power to interfere in the Western Hemisphere as a hostile act. In exchange for noninterference by Europeans, Monroe pledged that the United States would stay out of European struggles. The Monroe Doctrine became the foundation of U.S. foreign policy with respect to the Western Hemisphere.

John Quincy Adams

▶ Secretary of state during James Monroe's administration. In 1819, he negotiated the Adams-Onís Treaty with Spain, which gave the United States control over Florida in exchange for relinquishing U.S. claims to Texas and Cuba. Adams also served as president from 1825 to 1829, at which time it became clear that he lacked the political skills necessary to manage the fractures in his cabinet or to advance his legislative goals.

CHAPTER LOCATOR | How did Thomas Jefferson radically transform the presidency?

270 CHAPTER 10
A MATURING REPUBLIC, 1800–1824

planter, he attracted northern support for his backing of internal improvements and protective tariffs.

The final candidate was an outsider and a latecomer: General Andrew Jackson of Tennessee. Jackson had far less national political experience than the others, but he enjoyed great celebrity from his military career. When Jackson's supporters put his name forward for the presidency, voters in the West and South reacted with enthusiasm. Adams was dismayed, while Calhoun dropped out of the race.

Along with democratizing the vote, eighteen states had put the power to choose members of the electoral college directly in the hands of voters, making the 1824 election the first one to have a popular vote tally for the presidency. Jackson proved by far to be the most popular candidate, winning 153,544 votes. Adams was second with 108,740, Clay won 47,136 votes, and Crawford garnered 46,618.

In the electoral college, Jackson received 99 votes, Adams 84, Crawford 41, and Clay 37 (**Map 10.5**). Jackson lacked a majority, so the House of Representatives stepped in for the second time in U.S. history. Each congressional delegation had one vote; according to the Constitution's Twelfth Amendment, only the top three candidates joined the runoff. Thus Henry Clay was out of the race and in a position to bestow his support on another candidate.

Jackson's supporters later characterized the election of 1824 as the "corrupt bargain." Clay backed Adams, and Adams won by one vote in the House in February 1825. Clay's support made sense on several levels. Despite strong mutual dislike, he and Adams agreed on issues such as federal support to build roads and canals. Moreover, Clay was uneasy with Jackson's volatile temperament and unstated political views and with Crawford's diminished capacity. What made

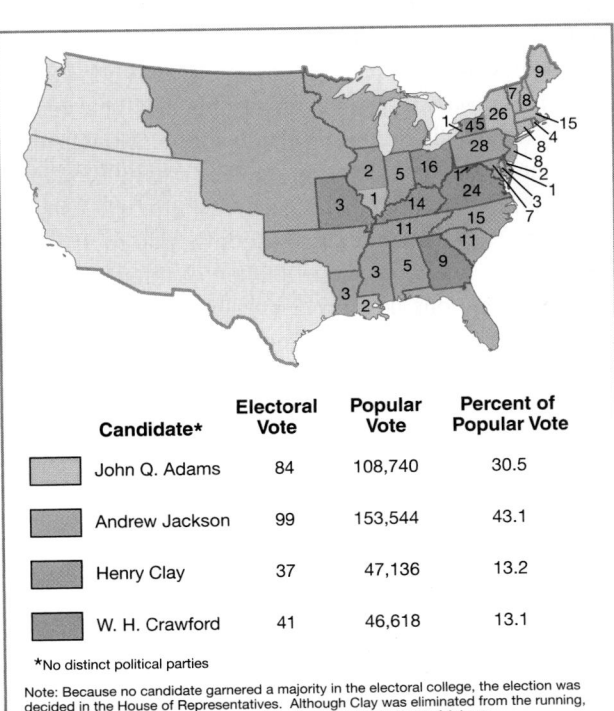

MAP 10.5 ■ The Election of 1824

Candidate*	Electoral Vote	Popular Vote	Percent of Popular Vote
John Q. Adams	84	108,740	30.5
Andrew Jackson	99	153,544	43.1
Henry Clay	37	47,136	13.2
W. H. Crawford	41	46,618	13.1

*No distinct political parties

Note: Because no candidate garnered a majority in the electoral college, the election was decided in the House of Representatives. Although Clay was eliminated from the running, as Speaker of the House he influenced the final decision in favor of Adams.

| What were the challenges and successes of the Madison presidency? | To what extent did women's status change in the early Republic? | **Why did partisan conflict increase during the administrations of Monroe and Adams?** | Conclusion: How did republican simplicity become complex? |

271

Clay's decision look "corrupt" was that immediately after the election, Adams offered to appoint Clay secretary of state—and Clay accepted.

In fact, there probably was no concrete bargain; Adams's subsequent cabinet appointments demonstrated his lack of political astuteness. But Andrew Jackson felt that the election had been stolen from him, and he wrote bitterly that "the Judas of the West [Clay] has closed the contract and will receive the thirty pieces of silver."

The Adams Administration

John Quincy Adams, like his father, was a one-term president. His career had been built on diplomacy, not electoral politics, and his political horse sense was not well developed. With his cabinet choices, he welcomed his opposition into his inner circle. He asked Crawford to stay on in the Treasury. He retained an openly pro-Jackson postmaster general even though that position controlled thousands of nationwide patronage appointments. He even asked Jackson to become secretary of war. With Calhoun as vice president (elected without opposition by the electoral college) and Clay at the State Department, the whole argumentative crew would have been thrust into the executive branch. Crawford and Jackson had the good sense to decline the appointments.

Adams had lofty ideas for federal action during his presidency, and the plan he put before Congress was sweeping. Adams called for federally built roads, canals, and harbors. He proposed a national university in Washington as well as government-sponsored scientific research. He wanted to build observatories to advance astronomical knowledge and to promote precision in timekeeping, and he backed a decimal-based system of weights and measures. In all these endeavors, Adams believed he was continuing the legacy of Jefferson and Madison, using the powers of government to advance knowledge. But his opponents feared he was too Hamiltonian, using federal power inappropriately to advance commercial interests.

Lacking the give-and-take political skills required to gain congressional support, Adams was unable to implement much of his program. He scorned the idea of courting voters to gain support and using the patronage system to enhance his power. He often made appointments to placate enemies rather than to reward friends. A story of a toast offered to the president may well have been mythical, but it came to summarize Adams's precarious hold on leadership. A dignitary raised a glass and said, "May he strike confusion to his foes," to which another voice scornfully chimed in, "as he has already done to his friends."

> **QUICK REVIEW**

How did the collapse of the Federalist Party influence the administrations of James Monroe and John Quincy Adams?

CHAPTER LOCATOR | How did Thomas Jefferson radically transform the presidency?

272 CHAPTER 10
A MATURING REPUBLIC, 1800–1824

Picture Research Consultants & Archives.

Conclusion: How did republican simplicity become complex?

THE JEFFERSONIAN REPUBLICANS tried at first to undo much of what the Federalists had created in the 1790s, but their promise of a simpler government gave way to the complexities of domestic and foreign issues. The sudden acquisition of the Louisiana Purchase promised land and opportunity to settlers but also complicated the country's political future with the issues central to the Missouri Compromise. Antagonism from both foreign and Indian nations led to complex and costly policies, culminating in the War of 1812.

The war elevated to national prominence General Andrew Jackson, whose popularity with voters in the 1824 election surprised traditional politicians and threw the one-party rule of Republicans into a tailspin. John Quincy Adams had barely assumed office in 1825 before the election campaign of 1828 was off and running. Appeals to the people—the mass of white male voters—would be the hallmark of all elections after 1824. It was a game Adams could not easily play.

Politics in this entire period was a game that women could not play either. Except for the political wives of Washington, women, whether white or free black, had no place in government. Male legislatures maintained women's feme covert status, keeping wives dependent on husbands. A few women found a pathway to greater personal autonomy through religion. Meanwhile, the routine inclusion of girls in public schools and the steady spread of female academies planted seeds that would blossom into a major transformation of gender in the 1830s and 1840s.

The War of 1812 started another chain of events that would prove momentous in later decades. Jefferson's long embargo and Madison's wartime trade stoppages gave strong encouragement to American manufacturing, momentarily protected from competition with British factories. When peace returned in 1815, the years of independent development burst forth into a period of sustained economic growth that continued nearly unabated into the mid-nineteenth century.

SO NOW YOU KNOW

When he took office in 1801, Thomas Jefferson promised to counter the influence of the Federalists and to restore smaller, simpler government. But the increasing complexity of domestic and international issues in the early 1800s actually required Jefferson and his Republican successors to expand the federal government's size and influence.

What were the challenges and successes of the Madison presidency?

To what extent did women's status change in the early Republic?

Why did partisan conflict increase during the administrations of Monroe and Adams?

Conclusion: How did republican simplicity become complex?

CHAPTER 10 STUDY GUIDE

Online Study Guide
bedfordstmartins.com/roarkunderstanding

STEP 1 GETTING STARTED

Below are basic terms from this period in American history. Can you identify each term below and explain why it matters? To do this exercise online or to download this chart, visit bedfordstmartins.com/roarkunderstanding.

TERM	WHO OR WHAT & WHEN	WHY IT MATTERS
Thomas Jefferson, p. 250		
Marbury v. Madison, p. 252		
Louisiana Purchase, p. 253		
Lewis and Clark expedition, p. 254		
Dolley Madison, p. 257		
Tecumseh, p. 258		
War of 1812, p. 259		
feme covert, p. 262		
female academies, p. 264		
Missouri Compromise, p. 268		
Monroe Doctrine, p. 270		
John Quincy Adams, p. 270		

STEP 2 MOVING BEYOND THE BASICS

The exercise below represents a more advanced understanding of the chapter material. Explore the key events of the presidents in the early nineteenth century, using the results to formulate an accurate and insightful overview of their administrations. Fill in the chart below by describing the important aspects and developments of each administration, and the results those policies produced. What core assumptions and beliefs informed each president's policies and positions? How did each successive president change the presidency? To do this exercise online or to download this chart, visit bedfordstmartins.com/roarkunderstanding.

Aspects and developments	Jefferson	Madison	Monroe	J. Q. Adams
Power of the presidency				
Expansion of the nation				
Domestic affairs				
Foreign affairs				
Difficulties				
Successes				

Now that you have reviewed key elements of the chapter, take a step back and try to explain the big picture by answering these questions. Remember to use specific examples from the chapter in your answers. To do this exercise online, visit bedfordstmartins.com/roarkunderstanding.

JEFFERSON AND REPUBLICANISM

▶ Why did Jefferson believe that western expansion was so important? How did he encourage expansion?

▶ How did foreign policy issues shape the Jefferson presidency?

MADISON AND THE WAR OF 1812

▶ Where was support for the War of 1812 strongest? Where was it weakest? Why?

▶ How did the status of women change in the early decades of the nineteenth century? In what ways did some women exert political influence?

MONROE, ADAMS, AND PARTISANSHIP

▶ What forces led to the expansion of the franchise in the early nineteenth century?

▶ In what ways did the election of 1824 mark a turning point in American politics?

LOOKING BACKWARD, LOOKING AHEAD

▶ How did the partisanship of the 1820s differ from the partisanship of the 1790s? What explains the changes you note?

▶ What problems were solved by the Missouri Compromise? What tensions and conflicts were left unresolved?

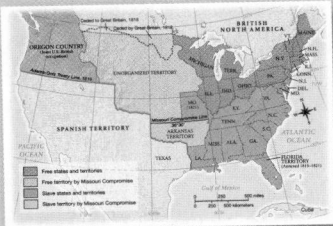

IN YOUR OWN WORDS

Imagine that you must explain chapter 10 to someone who hasn't read it. What would be the most important points to include and why?

11
THE EXPANDING REPUBLIC

1815–1840

> This chapter explores the causes and consequences of the market revolution, examining its impact on American social and cultural life. It also traces the political development of the United States between 1828 and 1840, noting the connections between political events and their larger social, cultural, and economic context.

> What caused the market revolution?

> What changes in national politics were reflected in the election of 1828?

> What was Andrew Jackson's impact on the presidency?

> How did the market revolution transform social and cultural life?

> Why was Martin Van Buren a one-term president?

> Conclusion: Age of Jackson or era of reform?

DID YOU KNOW?

Before 1815, it cost as much to ship a crate over thirty miles of domestic roads in the United States as it did to send it across the Atlantic Ocean.

The Clermont. Robert Fulton's steamboat travels up the Hudson River from New York City.

What caused the market revolution?

When the Erie Canal was completed in 1825, it was impressive not only for its length of 350 miles but also for its elevation. Eighty-three locks were required to move canal boats over the combined ascent and descent of 680 feet. The biggest challenge came at Lockport, 20 miles northeast of Buffalo, where the canal traversed a steep slate escarpment by means of five double locks, which slowed traffic considerably. The village of Lockport grew up here to service waiting passengers and crews. Library of Congress.

THE RETURN OF PEACE in 1815 unleashed powerful forces that revolutionized the organization of the economy. Spectacular changes in transportation facilitated the movement of commodities, information, and people, while textile mills and other factories created many new jobs, especially for young unmarried women. Innovations in banking, legal practices, and tariff policies promoted swift economic growth.

This was not yet an industrial revolution, as was beginning in Britain, but rather a market revolution fueled by traditional sources—water, wood, beasts of burden, and human muscle. What was new was the accelerated pace of economic activity and the scale of the distribution of goods. The new nature and scale of production and consumption changed Americans' economic behavior, attitudes, and expectations.

Improvements in Transportation

Before 1815, transportation in the United States was slow and expensive; it cost as much to ship a crate over thirty miles of domestic roads as it did to send it across

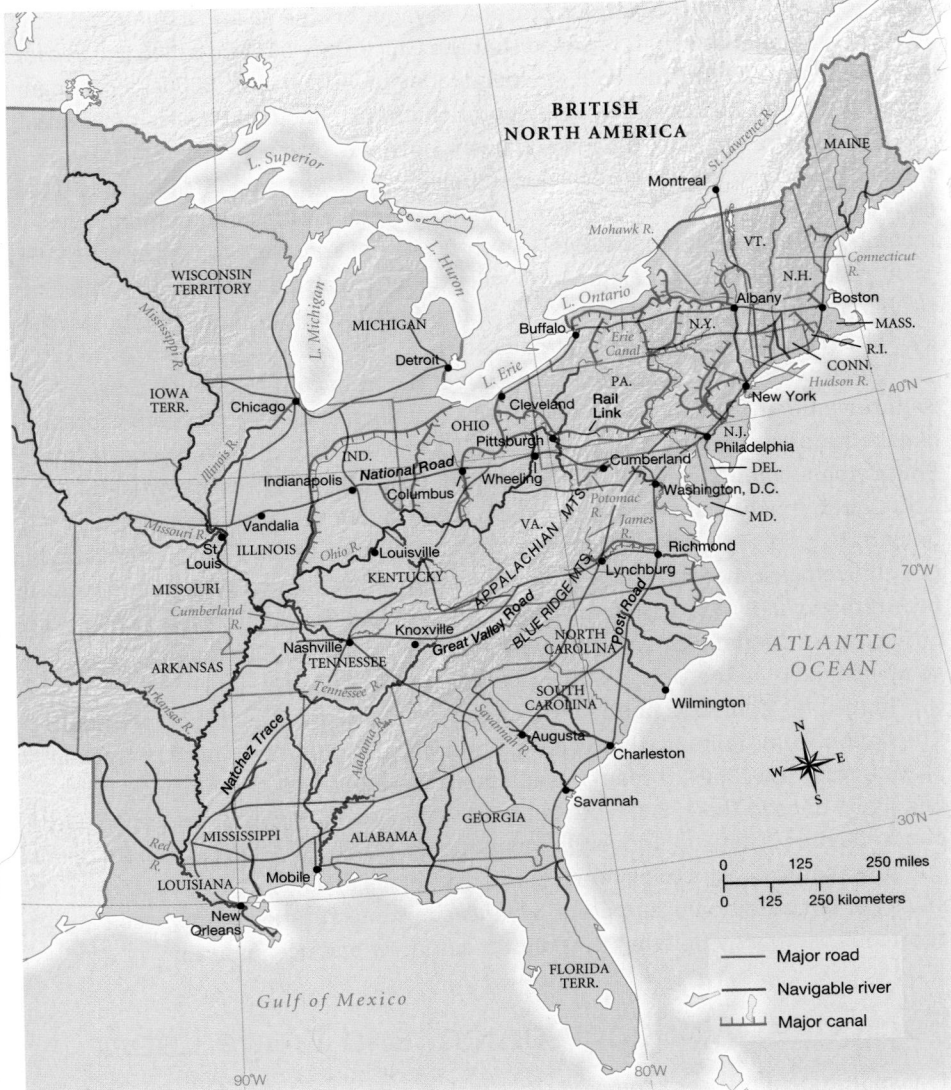

MAP 11.1 ■ **Routes of Transportation in 1840**
By the 1830s, transportation advances had cut travel times significantly. By way of the Erie Canal, goods and people could move from New York City to Buffalo in four days, a trip that had taken two weeks by road in 1800. Similarly, the trip from New York to New Orleans, which had taken four weeks in 1800, could now be accomplished in less than half that time on steamboats plying the western rivers.

CHRONOLOGY

1807
- Robert Fulton's *Clermont* sets off steamboat craze.

1816
- Second Bank of the United States is chartered.

1819
- Economic panic leads to the loss of property and jobs for thousands.

1821
- Mill town of Lowell, Massachusetts, is founded.

1825
- Erie Canal is completed in New York, extending 350 miles between Albany and Buffalo.

1829
- Baltimore and Ohio Railroad starts laying track.

1834
- Female mill workers strike in Lowell, Massachusetts, and again in 1836.

the Atlantic Ocean. A stagecoach trip from Boston to New York took four days. But between 1815 and 1840, networks of roads, canals, steamboats, and finally railroads dramatically raised the speed and lowered the cost of travel (**Map 11.1**).

Improved transportation moved goods into wider markets. It moved passengers, too, broadening their horizons and allowing young people as well as adults to take up new employment in cities or factory towns. Transportation also facilitated the flow of political information via the U.S. mail. Enhanced public transport was expensive and produced uneven economic benefits, so presidents from Jefferson to Monroe were reluctant to fund it with federal dollars. Instead, private investors pooled resources and chartered transport companies, receiving significant subsidies and monopoly rights from state governments. Turnpike and roadway mileage increased dramatically after 1815, reducing shipping costs. Stagecoach companies proliferated, and travel time on main routes was cut in half.

Water travel was similarly transformed. In 1807, Robert Fulton's steam-propelled boat, the *Clermont*, churned up the Hudson River from New York City to

| What changes in national politics were reflected in the election of 1828? | What was Andrew Jackson's impact on the presidency? | How did the market revolution transform social and cultural life? | Why was Martin Van Buren a one-term president? | Conclusion: Age of Jackson or era of reform? |

Albany, touching off a steamboat craze. A voyager on one of the first steamboats to go down the Mississippi reported that the Chickasaw Indians called the vessel a "fire canoe" and considered it "an omen of evil." By the early 1830s, more than seven hundred steamboats were in operation on the Ohio and Mississippi rivers.

Steamboats were not benign advances, however. The urgency to cut travel time led to overstoked furnaces, sudden boiler explosions, and terrible mass fatalities. Another huge cost, to the environment, was the deforestation brought by steamboats, which had to load fuel—"wood up"—every twenty miles or so. By the 1830s, the banks of many main rivers were denuded of trees, and forests miles back from the rivers fell to the ax. The smoke from wood-burning steamboats created America's first significant air pollution.

Canals were another major innovation of the transportation revolution. Pennsylvania in 1815 and New York in 1817 commenced major state-sponsored canal enterprises. Pennsylvania's Schuylkill Canal stretched 108 miles west from Philadelphia when it was completed in 1826. Much more impressive was the **Erie Canal**, finished in 1825, covering 350 miles between Albany and Buffalo and linking the port of New York City with the entire Great Lakes region. Wheat and flour moved east, household goods and tools moved west, and passengers went in both directions. By the 1830s, the cost of shipping by canal fell to less than a tenth of the cost of overland transport, and New York City quickly became the premier commercial city in the United States.

In the 1830s, private railroad companies began to give canals competition. The nation's first railroad, the Baltimore and Ohio, laid thirteen miles of track in 1829. During the 1830s, three thousand more miles of track materialized nationwide. Rail lines in the 1830s were generally short, on the order of twenty to one hundred miles. They did not yet provide an efficient distribution system for goods, but passengers flocked to experience the marvelous speeds of fifteen to twenty miles per hour. Railroads and other advances in transportation made possible enormous change by unifying the country culturally and economically.

Factories, Workingwomen, and Wage Labor

Transportation advances promoted the expansion of manufacturing after 1815, creating an ever-expanding market for goods. The two leading industries, textiles and shoes, altered methods of production and labor relations. Textile production was greatly spurred by the development of water-driven machinery built near fast-coursing rivers. Shoe manufacturing, still using the power and skill of human hands, involved only a reorganization of production. Shoes and textiles pulled young women into wage-earning labor for the first time.

The earliest textile factory was built by English immigrant Samuel Slater in Pawtucket, Rhode Island, in the 1790s. By 1815, nearly 170 spinning mills had been built along New England rivers. In British manufacturing cities, entire families worked in low-wage, health-threatening factories. In contrast, American factories targeted young women as employees; they were cheap to hire because of their limited employment options. "Mill girls" would retire to marriage, replaced by fresh recruits earning beginners' wages.

In 1821, a group of Boston entrepreneurs founded the town of Lowell on the Merrimack River, centralizing all aspects of cloth production: combing, shrinking, spinning, weaving, and dyeing. By 1836, the eight Lowell mills employed more

Erie Canal
▶ Canal finished in 1825, covering 350 miles between Albany and Buffalo and linking the port of New York City with the entire Great Lakes region. Aided by the canal, New York City quickly became the premier commercial city in the United States. The Erie Canal was a powerful example of the economic impact of the transportation revolution.

than five thousand young women, who lived in carefully managed company-owned boardinghouses.

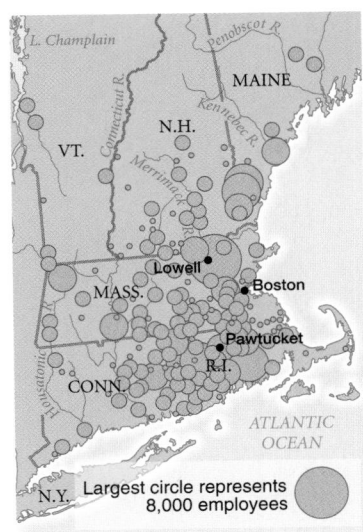

Cotton Textile Industry, ca. 1840

Life in the Lowell Mills

Rules: church attendance mandatory, drinking and unsupervised courtship prohibited, dorms locked at 10 p.m.

Wages: typically $2 to $3 for a seventy-hour week.

Work: tending noisy power looms in hot and humid rooms.

Young women embraced factory work as a means to earn spending money and build savings before marriage. Also welcome was the unprecedented, though still limited, personal freedom of living in an all-female social space, away from parents and domestic tasks. In the evening, the women could engage in self-improvement activities, such as attending lectures or writing for the company's periodical, the *Lowell Offering*.

In the mid-1830s, worldwide changes in the cotton market impelled mill owners to speed up work and decrease wages. The workers protested, emboldened by their communal living arrangement and by their relative independence as temporary employees. In 1834 and again in 1836, hundreds of women at the Lowell mills went out on strike. All over New England, female mill workers led strikes and formed unions. In 1834, mill women in Dover, New Hampshire, denounced their owners for trying to turn them into "slaves": "However freely the epithet of 'factory slaves' may be bestowed upon us, we will never deserve it by a base and cringing submission to proud wealth or haughty insolence." Their assertiveness surprised many, but ultimately the ease of replacing them undermined their bargaining power, and owners in the 1840s began to shift to immigrant families as their primary labor source.

Mill Worker Tending a Power Loom, 1850

This daguerreotype (the earliest form of photograph) shows a young woman tending a power loom in a textile mill. In the 1830s, women weavers generally tended two machines at a time. In the 1840s, some companies increased the workload to four. American Textile History Museum.

| What changes in national politics were reflected in the election of 1828? | What was Andrew Jackson's impact on the presidency? | How did the market revolution transform social and cultural life? | Why was Martin Van Buren a one-term president? | Conclusion: Age of Jackson or era of reform? |

281

The shoe manufacturing industry centered in eastern New England reorganized production and hired women, including wives, as shoebinders. Male shoemakers still cut the leather and made the soles in shops, but female shoebinders working from home now stitched the upper parts of the shoes. Working from home meant that wives could still perform their domestic chores. But they earned money to contribute to family income, which was unusual for most wives in that period.

In the economically turbulent 1830s, shoebinder wages fell. Unlike mill workers, female shoebinders worked in isolation, a serious hindrance to organized protest. In Lynn, Massachusetts, a major shoemaking center, women used female church networks to organize resistance. The Lynn shoebinders who demanded higher wages in 1834 built on a collective sense of themselves as women. "Equal rights should be extended to all—to the weaker sex as well as the stronger," they wrote in a document establishing the Female Society of Lynn.

In the end, the Lynn shoebinders' protests failed to achieve wage increases. At-home workers all over New England continued to accept low wages, and even in Lynn, many women shied away from organized protest, preferring to situate their work in the context of family duty (helping their husbands to finish the shoes) instead of market relations.

Bankers and Lawyers

Entrepreneurs like the Lowell factory owners relied on innovations in the banking system to finance their ventures. Between 1814 and 1816, the number of state-chartered banks in the United States more than doubled from fewer than 90 to 208. By 1830, there were 330, and by 1840 hundreds more. Banks stimulated the economy by making loans to merchants and manufacturers and by enlarging the money supply. Borrowers were issued loans in the form of banknotes—certificates unique to each bank—that were used as money for all transactions. Neither federal nor state governments issued paper money, so banknotes became the country's currency.

second Bank of the United States

▶ National bank chartered in 1816. The rechartering of the bank was a major issue in Andrew Jackson's reelection campaign in 1832. Efforts by Daniel Webster and Henry Clay to use Jackson's opposition to the bank against him backfired, helping Jackson win the election and put an end to the bank.

Bankers exercised great power over the economy, and the most powerful bankers sat on the board of directors for the **second Bank of the United States**, headquartered in Philadelphia. The twenty-year charter of the first Bank of the United States had expired in 1811. The second Bank of the United States, with eighteen branches throughout the country, opened for business in 1816 under another twenty-year charter. The rechartering of this bank would become a major issue in the 1832 presidential campaign.

Lawyer-politicians too exercised economic power, by refashioning commercial law to enhance the prospects of private investment. In 1811, states started to rewrite their laws of incorporation (allowing the chartering of businesses by states), and the number of corporations expanded rapidly, from about twenty in 1800 to eighteen hundred by 1817. Incorporation protected individual investors from being held liable for corporate debts. State lawmakers also wrote laws of eminent domain, empowering states to buy land for roads and canals even from unwilling sellers. In such ways, entrepreneurial lawyers of the 1820s and 1830s created the legal foundation for an economy that favored ambitious individuals interested in maximizing their own wealth.

Not everyone applauded these developments. **Andrew Jackson**, himself a skillful lawyer turned politician, spoke for a large and mistrustful segment of the population when he warned about the potential abuses of power "which the moneyed interest derives from a paper currency which they are able to control, from the multitude of corporations with exclusive privileges which they have succeeded in obtaining in the different states, and which are employed altogether for their benefit." Jacksonians believed that ending government-granted privileges was the way to maximize individual liberty and economic opportunity.

Booms and Busts

One aspect of the economy that the lawyer-politicians could not control was the threat of financial collapse. In 1819 and again in the 1830s, boom times of high inflation and speculative investment were punctured by sharp economic recessions called "panics." Some blamed the panic of 1819 on the second Bank of the United States for failing to control state banks that had suspended specie payments—the exchange of gold or silver for banknotes—in their eagerness to expand the economic bubble. By mid-1818, when the Bank of the United States called in its loans and insisted that the state banks do likewise, the contracting of the money supply sent tremors throughout the economy. The crunch was made worse by a financial crisis in Europe in the spring of 1819. Overseas, prices for American cotton, tobacco, and wheat plummeted by more than 50 percent. Thus, when the banks began to call in their outstanding loans, American debtors involved in the commodities trade could not come up with the money. The intricate web of credit and debt relationships meant that almost everyone with even a toehold in the new commercial economy was affected by the panic. Thousands of Americans lost their savings and property, and unemployment estimates suggest that half a million people lost their jobs.

Recovery took several years. Unemployment declined, but bitterness lingered, ready to be stirred up by politicians in the decades to come. The dangers of a system dependent on extensive credit were now clear. In one folksy formulation that circulated around 1820, a farmer compared credit to "a man pissing in his breeches on a cold day to keep his arse warm—very comfortable at first but I dare say . . . you know how it feels afterwards."

By the mid-1820s, the economy was back on track, driven by increases in productivity, consumer demand for goods, and international trade. Despite the panic of 1819, credit financing continued to fuel the system. A network of credit and debt relations grew dense by the 1830s in a system that encouraged speculation and risk taking. A pervasive optimism about continued growth supported the elaborate system, but a single business failure could produce many innocent victims. Well after the panic of 1819, an undercurrent of anxiety about rapid economic change continued to shape the political views of many Americans.

Andrew Jackson

▶ U.S. president from 1829 to 1837 whose tough, unrefined frontier image helped define the age. His presidency coincided with the democratization of American politics. He presided over the removal of Indians from most of the eastern states and the destruction of the second Bank of the United States.

QUICK REVIEW

What role did state governments play in stimulating the market revolution?

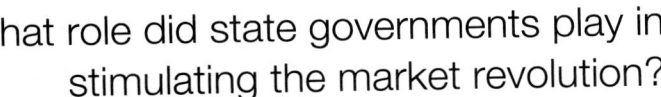

What changes in national politics were reflected in the election of 1828?

Jackson Forever!
The Hero of Two Wars and of Orleans!
The Man of the People!
HE WHO COULD NOT BARTER NOR BARGAIN FOR THE
PRESIDENCY!
Who, although "*A Military Chieftain*," valued the purity of Elections and of the Electors, MORE than the Office of PRESIDENT itself! Although the greatest in the gift of his countrymen, and the highest in point of dignity of any in the world,

BECAUSE
It should be derived from the
PEOPLE!

No Gag Laws! No Black Cockades! No Reign of Terror! No Standing Army or Navy Officers, when under the pay of Government, to browbeat, or

KNOCK DOWN
Old Revolutionary Characters, or our Representatives while in the discharge of their duty. To the Polls then, and vote for those who will support

OLD HICKORY
AND THE ELECTORAL LAW.

Campaign Poster for 1828 Election

This poster praises Andrew Jackson as a war hero and a "man of the people" and reminds readers that Jackson, who won the largest popular vote in 1824, did not stoop to "bargain for the presidency," as John Quincy Adams presumably had in his dealings with Henry Clay. © Collection of the New-York Historical Society.

JUST AS THE MARKET REVOLUTION held out the promise, if not the reality, of economic opportunity for all who worked, the political transformation of the 1830s held out the promise of political opportunity for hundreds of thousands of new voters. During Andrew Jackson's presidency (1829–1837), the second American party system took shape. Not until 1836, however, would the parties have distinct names and consistent programs transcending the particular personalities running for office. Over those years, more men could and did vote, responding to new methods of arousing voter interest.

Popular Politics and Partisan Identity

The election of 1828, pitting Andrew Jackson against John Quincy Adams, was the first presidential contest in which the popular vote determined the outcome. In twenty-two out of twenty-four states, voters—not state legislatures—designated the number of electors committed to a particular candidate. More than a million voters participated, three times the number in 1824 and nearly half the free male population. Throughout the 1830s, voter turnout continued to rise and reached 70 percent in some localities, partly because of the disappearance of property qualifications in all but three states and partly because of heightened political interest.

The 1828 election inaugurated new campaign styles. State-level candidates routinely gave speeches at rallies, picnics, and banquets. Adams and Jackson still declined such appearances as undignified, but Henry Clay of Kentucky, campaigning for Adams, earned the nickname "the Barbecue Orator." Campaign rhetoric became more informal and even blunt. The Jackson camp established many

TABLE 11.1 ■ The Growth of Newspapers, 1820–1840

	1820	1830	1835	1840
U.S. population (in millions)	9.6	12.8	15.0	17.1
Number of newspapers published	500	800	1,200	1,400
Daily newspapers	42	65	—	138

KEY FACTORS

The Election of 1828
- It was the first presidential race in which the popular vote determined the outcome.
- Nearly half the free male population voted, three times as many as voted in the 1824 election.
- It was the first national election to be dominated by character issues.

Hickory Clubs, trading on Jackson's popular nickname, "Old Hickory," from a common Tennessee tree suggesting resilience and toughness.

Partisan newspapers in ever-larger numbers defined issues and publicized political personalities as never before (**Table 11.1**). Party leaders dispensed subsidies and other favors to secure the support of papers, even in remote towns and villages. In New York State, where party development was most advanced, a pro-Jackson group called the Bucktails controlled fifty weekly publications.

Politicians at first identified themselves as Jackson or Adams men, honoring the fiction of Republican Party unity. By 1832, however, the terminology had evolved to National Republicans, favoring federal action to promote commercial development, and Democratic Republicans, who promised to be responsive to the will of the majority. Between 1834 and 1836, National Republicans came to be called Whigs, while those in Jackson's party became simply the Democrats.

The Election of 1828 and the Character Issue

The campaign of 1828 was the first national election dominated by scandal and character questions. They became central issues because voters used them to comprehend the kind of public official each man would make. Character issues conveyed in shorthand larger questions about morality, honor, and discipline. Jackson and Adams presented two radically different styles of manhood.

John Quincy Adams was vilified by his opponents as an elitist, a bookish academic, and even a monarchist. They attacked his "corrupt bargain" of 1824—the alleged election deal between Adams and Henry Clay (see chapter 10). Adams's supporters countered by playing on Jackson's fatherless childhood to portray him as the bastard son of a prostitute. Worse, the circumstances around his marriage to Rachel Donelson Robards in 1791 gave rise to the story that Jackson was a seducer and an adulterer, having married a woman whose divorce from her first husband was not entirely legal. Pro-Adams newspapers howled that Jackson was sinful and impulsive, while portraying Adams as pious, learned, and virtuous.

Editors in favor of Adams played up Jackson's violent temper, as evidenced by his participation in many duels, brawls, and canings. Jackson's supporters used the same stories to project Old Hickory as a tough frontier hero who knew how to command obedience. As for learning, Jackson's rough frontier education gave him a "natural sense," wrote a Boston editor, that "can never be acquired by reading books—it can only be acquired, in perfection, by reading men."

Jackson won a sweeping victory, with 56 percent of the popular vote and 178 electoral votes to Adams's 83 (**Map 11.2**). Old Hickory took most of the South and West and carried Pennsylvania and New York as well; Adams carried the remainder of the East. Jackson's vice president was **John C. Calhoun**, who had just served as vice president under Adams but had broken with Adams's policies.

John C. Calhoun
▶ Vice president under John Quincy Adams and Andrew Jackson. Calhoun was a leading advocate of South Carolina's statement of nullification. When Jackson ignored Calhoun's views on the subject, Calhoun resigned and became a senator to better serve the interests of his state.

| What changes in national politics were reflected in the election of 1828? | What was Andrew Jackson's impact on the presidency? | How did the market revolution transform social and cultural life? | Why was Martin Van Buren a one-term president? | Conclusion: Age of Jackson or era of reform? |

285

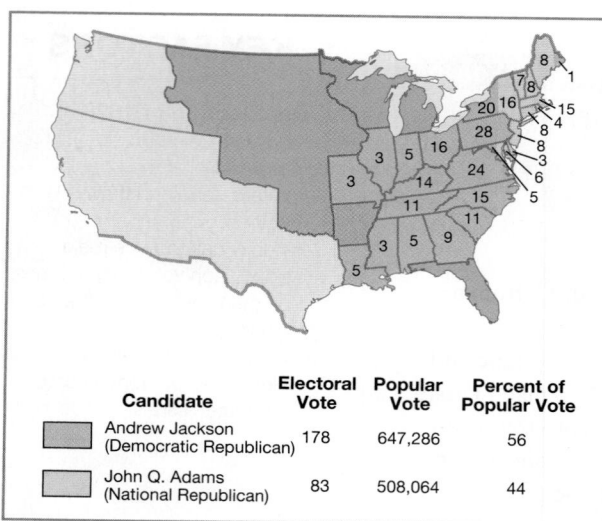

Candidate	Electoral Vote	Popular Vote	Percent of Popular Vote
Andrew Jackson (Democratic Republican)	178	647,286	56
John Q. Adams (National Republican)	83	508,064	44

MAP 11.2 ■ The Election of 1828

Whigs

▶ Political party that evolved out of the National Republicans between 1834 and 1836. The Whigs' power base was in the Northeast. They supported federal action to promote commercial development and generally looked favorably on the reform movements associated with the Second Great Awakening.

Democrats

▶ Political party that evolved out of the Democratic Republicans between 1834 and 1836. The Democrats were strongest in the South and West. Closely associated with Andrew Jackson, the Democrats embraced Jackson's vision of limited government, expanded political participation for white men, and the promotion of an ethic of individualism.

After 1828, national politicians no longer deplored the existence of political parties. They were coming to see that parties mobilized and delivered voters, sharpened candidates' differences, and created party loyalty that surpassed loyalty to individual candidates and elections. Adams and Jackson clearly symbolized the competing ideas of the emerging parties: a moralistic, top-down party (the **Whigs**) ready to make major decisions to promote economic growth competing against a contentious, energetic party (the **Democrats**) ready to embrace liberty-loving individualism.

Jackson's Democratic Agenda

Jackson's supporters went wild at his March 1829 inauguration. Thousands cheered his ten-minute inaugural address, the shortest in history. An open reception at the White House turned into a near riot as well-wishers jammed the premises, used windows as doors, stood on furniture for a better view of the great man, and broke thousands of dollars' worth of china and glasses. During his presidency, Jackson continued to offer unprecedented hospitality to the public. The courteous Jackson, committed to his image as president of the "common man," held audiences with unannounced visitors throughout his two terms.

Past presidents had tried to lessen party conflict by including men of different factions in their cabinets, but Jackson would have only loyalists. For secretary of state, the key job, he tapped New Yorker Martin Van Buren, one of the shrewdest politicians of the day. Throughout the federal government, from postal clerks to ambassadors, Jackson replaced competent civil servants with party loyalists. Jackson's appointment practices came to be known as the spoils system.

Jackson's agenda quickly emerged. He favored a Jeffersonian limited federal government, fearing that intervention in the economy inevitably favored some groups at the expense of others. He therefore opposed federal support of transportation and grants of monopolies and charters that privileged wealthy investors. Like Jefferson, he anticipated the rapid settlement of the country's interior, where land sales would spread economic democracy to settlers. Thus, establishing a federal policy to remove the Indians had high priority. Jackson was freer than previous presidents with the use of the presidential veto power over Congress. In 1830, he vetoed a Congress-backed highway project in Maysville, Kentucky, Henry Clay's home state. The Maysville Road veto articulated Jackson's principled stand that citizens' tax dollars could be spent only on projects of a "general, not local" character.

 QUICK REVIEW

What role did character play in the 1828 presidential campaign?

What was Andrew Jackson's impact on the presidency?

Andrew Jackson as "the Great Father"

In 1828, a new process of cheap commercial lithography found immediate application in a colorful presidential campaign aimed at capturing popular votes, and with it, a rich tradition of political cartoons was born. Jackson inspired at least five dozen satirical cartoons centering on caricatures of him. Strikingly, only one of them featured his Indian policy, controversial as it was, and only a single copy still exists. William L. Clements Library.

▶ FOR MORE HELP ANALYZING THIS IMAGE, see the visual activity for this chapter in the Online Study Guide at bedfordstmartins.com/ roarkunderstanding.

IN HIS TWO TERMS AS PRESIDENT, Andrew Jackson worked to implement his vision of a politics of opportunity for all white men. To open land for white settlement, he favored the relocation of all eastern Indian tribes. He confronted John C. Calhoun and South Carolina when that state tried to nullify the tariff of 1828. Disapproving of all government-granted privilege, Jackson challenged and defeated the Bank of the United States. In all this, he greatly enhanced the power of the presidency.

Indian Policy and the Trail of Tears

Probably nothing defined Jackson's presidency more than his efforts to solve what he saw as the Indian problem. Thousands of Indians lived in the South and the old Northwest, and many remained in New England and New York. In his first message to Congress in 1829, Jackson declared that removing the Indians to territory west of the Mississippi was the only way to save them. White civilization destroyed Indian resources and thus doomed the Indians, he claimed: "That this fate surely awaits them if they remain within the limits of the states does not admit of a doubt. Humanity and national honor demand that every effort should be made to avert so great a calamity." Jackson never publicly wavered from this seemingly noble theme, returning to it in his next seven annual messages.

Prior administrations had experimented with different Indian policies. Starting in 1819, Congress funded missionary associations eager to "civilize" native

| What changes in national politics were reflected in the election of 1828? | **What was Andrew Jackson's impact on the presidency?** | How did the market revolution transform social and cultural life? | Why was Martin Van Buren a one-term president? | Conclusion: Age of Jackson or era of reform? |

287

1828
- Congress passes Tariff of Abominations.
- Democrat Andrew Jackson is elected president.

1830
- Indian Removal Act establishes process for relocating eastern Indian tribes west of the Mississippi River.

1832
- Sauk and Fox Indians led by Chief Black Hawk are massacred by state militias.
- Supreme Court rules in *Worcester v. Georgia* that the Cherokee nation is a distinct community not subject to Georgia state law.
- Jackson vetoes charter renewal of Bank of the United States.

1833
- South Carolina leaders declare nullification of federal tariffs.

1838
- Trail of Tears: Cherokees are forced to relocate.

Indian Removal Act of 1830
▶ Act that provided funds for relocating eastern tribes west of the Mississippi. The act embodied Jackson's preferred solution to the "Indian problem," the mandatory expulsion of all Indians from the then-existing states. Indians resisted in numerous ways, but, in the end, most were forced to comply with the terms of the act.

peoples by converting them to Christianity and to whites' agricultural practices. The federal government had pursued aggressive treaty making with many tribes, dealing with the Indians as foreign nations (see chapter 10). In contrast, Jackson saw Indians as subjects of the United States, and he did not approve of assimilation. In his 1833 message to Congress, he wrote, "They have neither the intelligence, the industry, the moral habits, nor the desire of improvement which are essential. . . . Established in the midst of a superior race . . . they must necessarily yield to the force of circumstances and ere long disappear." Congress backed Jackson's goal of relocating eastern tribes west of the Mississippi and passed the **Indian Removal Act of 1830**. About 100 million acres of eastern land would be vacated for eventual white settlement under this act authorizing ethnic expulsion (**Map 11.3**).

The Indian Removal Act generated widespread controversy. Newspapers, public lecturers, and local clubs debated the expulsion law. In an unprecedented move, thousands of northern white women signed anti-removal petitions, directly challenging the prevailing assumption that women could not be political actors.

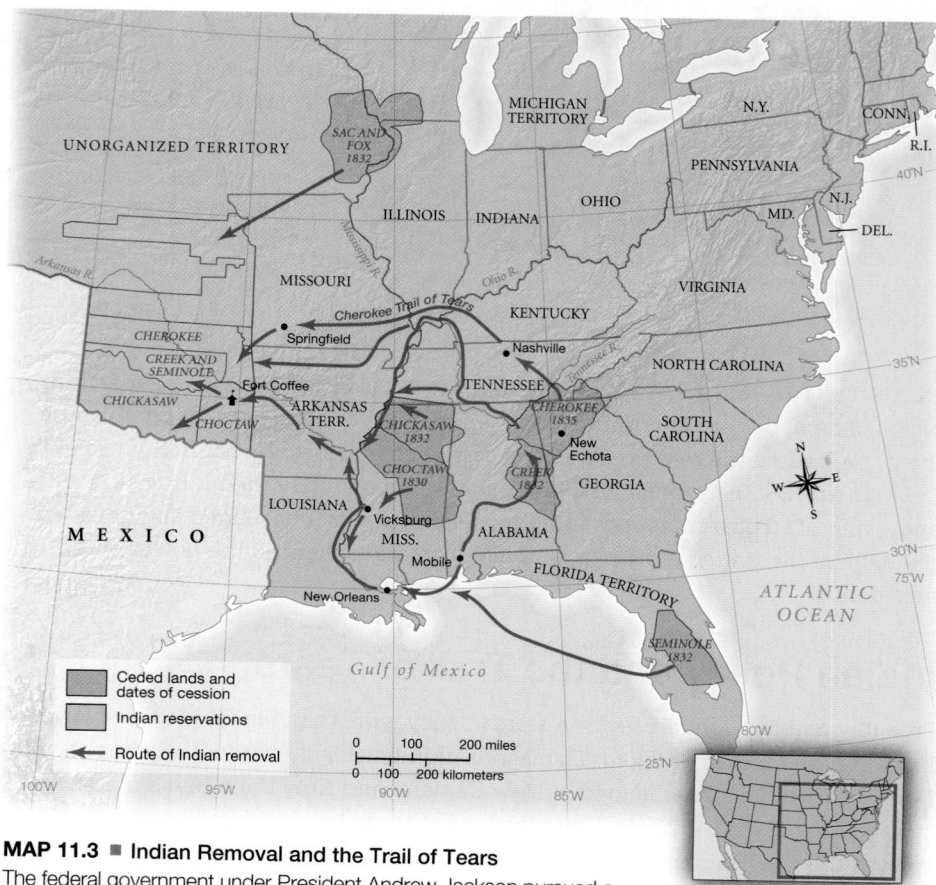

MAP 11.3 ■ Indian Removal and the Trail of Tears
The federal government under President Andrew Jackson pursued a vigorous policy of Indian removal in the 1830s. Tribes were forcibly moved west to land known as Indian Territory (present-day Oklahoma). As many as a quarter of the Cherokee Indians died on the route known as the Trail of Tears in 1838.

▶ FOR MORE HELP ANALYZING THIS MAP, see the map activity for this chapter in the Online Study Guide at bedfordstmartins.com/roarkunderstanding.

Between 1830 and 1832, women's petitions rolled into Washington, arguing specifically that the Cherokee Indians of Georgia were a sovereign people on the road to Christianity and entitled to stay on their land. Jackson ignored the petitions.

For the northern tribes, their numbers diminished by years of war, gradual removal was already well under way. But not all the Indians went quietly. In 1832 in western Illinois, Black Hawk, a leader of the Sauk and Fox Indians who had fought in alliance with Tecumseh in the War of 1812 (see chapter 10, page 257), resisted removal. Volunteer militias attacked and chased the Indians into southern Wisconsin, where, after several skirmishes and a deadly battle (later called the Black Hawk War), Black Hawk was captured and four hundred of his people were massacred.

The large southern tribes—the Creek, Chickasaw, Choctaw, and Cherokee—proved even more resistant to removal. Georgia Cherokees had already taken several assimilationist steps. Aided by dedicated missionaries, these leaders had adopted written laws, including, in 1827, a constitution modeled on the U.S. Constitution. Two hundred of the wealthiest Cherokee men had intermarried with whites, adopting white styles of housing, dress, and cotton agriculture, including the ownership of slaves. They developed a written alphabet and published a newspaper and Christian prayer books in their language. These features helped make their cause attractive to the northern white women who petitioned the government on their behalf. Yet most of the seventeen thousand Cherokees maintained cultural continuity with past traditions.

In 1831, when Georgia announced its plans to seize all Cherokee property, the tribal leadership took their case to the U.S. Supreme Court. In *Worcester v. Georgia* (1832), the Supreme Court upheld the territorial sovereignty of the Cherokee people, recognizing their existence as "a distinct community, occupying its own territory, in which the laws of Georgia can have no force." An angry President Jackson ignored the Court and pressed the Cherokee tribe to move west: "If they now refuse to accept the liberal terms offered, they can only be liable for whatever evils and difficulties may arise. I feel conscious of having done my duty to my red children."

The Cherokee tribe remained in Georgia for two more years without significant violence. Then, in 1835, a small, unauthorized faction of the acculturated leaders signed a treaty selling all the tribal lands to the state, which rapidly resold the land to whites. Most Cherokees refused to move, so in May 1838, the deadline for voluntary evacuation, federal troops arrived to remove them. Under armed guard, the Cherokees embarked on a 1,200-mile journey west that came to be called the **Trail of Tears**. Nearly a quarter of the Cherokees died en route from the hardship. Survivors joined the fifteen thousand Creek, twelve thousand Choctaw, five thousand Chickasaw, and several thousand Seminole Indians also forcibly relocated to Indian Territory (which became the state of Oklahoma in 1907).

In his farewell address to the nation in 1837, Jackson professed his belief in the benefit of Indian removal: "This unhappy race . . . are now placed in a situation where we may well hope that they will share in the blessings of civilization and be saved from the degradation and destruction to which they were rapidly hastening while they remained in the states." Perhaps Jackson genuinely believed that removal was necessary, but for the forcibly removed tribes, the costs of relocation were high.

Trail of Tears

▶ Forced westward journey of Cherokees from their homes in Georgia. After the Cherokees resisted Georgia's efforts to remove them for almost a decade, federal troops in 1838 forced them to leave after a small, unauthorized faction of the tribe signed away all of the Cherokee lands. Nearly a quarter of the Cherokees died during the 1,200-mile trip; the survivors joined other Indian groups forcibly relocated to Indian Territory in present-day Oklahoma.

| What changes in national politics were reflected in the election of 1828? | **What was Andrew Jackson's impact on the presidency?** | How did the market revolution transform social and cultural life? | Why was Martin Van Buren a one-term president? | Conclusion: Age of Jackson or era of reform? |

289

The Tariff of Abominations and Nullification

Because it advanced his Indian policy, Jackson supported Georgia's right to ignore the Supreme Court's decision in *Worcester v. Georgia*. But in another pressing question of states' rights, Jackson contested South Carolina's attempt to ignore federal tariff policy.

Federal tariffs as high as 33 percent on imports such as textiles and iron goods had been passed in 1816 and again in 1824 in an effort to shelter new American manufacturers from foreign competition. Some southern congressmen opposed the steep tariffs, fearing they would decrease overseas shipping and thereby hurt cotton exports. In 1828, Congress passed a revised tariff that came to be known as the Tariff of Abominations. A bundle of conflicting duties, some as high as 50 percent, the legislation contained provisions that both pleased and angered every economic and sectional interest.

South Carolina in particular suffered from the Tariff of Abominations. Worldwide prices for cotton had declined in the late 1820s, and the falloff in shipping caused by the high tariffs further hurt the South. In 1828, a group of South Carolina politicians headed by John C. Calhoun advanced a doctrine called **nullification**. They argued that when Congress overstepped its powers, states had the right to nullify Congress's acts. As precedents, they pointed to the Virginia and Kentucky Resolutions of 1798, intended to invalidate the Alien and Sedition Acts (see chapter 9). Congress had erred in using tariff policy to benefit specific industries, they claimed; tariffs should be used only to raise revenue.

On assuming the presidency in 1829, Jackson ignored the South Carolina statement of nullification and shut out Calhoun, his new vice president, from influence or power. Tariff revisions in early 1832 brought little relief to the South. Calhoun resigned the vice presidency and became a senator to better serve his state. Finally, strained to their limit, South Carolina leaders declared federal tariffs null and void in their state as of February 1, 1833.

In response, Jackson sent armed ships to Charleston harbor and threatened to invade the state. He pushed through Congress the Force Bill, defining the Carolina stance as treason and authorizing military action to collect federal tariffs. At the same time, Congress moved quickly to pass a revised tariff that was more acceptable to the South. On March 1, 1833, Congress passed both the new tariff and the Force Bill. South Carolina then withdrew its nullification of the old tariff—and then nullified the Force Bill. It was a symbolic gesture, since Jackson's show of muscle was no longer necessary.

Yet the question of federal power versus states' rights was far from settled. The implied threat behind nullification was secession, a position articulated in 1832 by some South Carolinians whose concerns went beyond tariff policy. In the 1830s, the political moratorium on discussions of slavery agreed on at the time of the Missouri Compromise (see chapter 10) was coming unglued, and new northern voices opposed to slavery gained increasing attention. If and when a northern-dominated federal government decided to end slavery, the South Carolinians thought, the South should nullify such laws, or remove itself from the Union.

The Bank War and Economic Boom

Along with the tariff and nullification, President Jackson fought another political battle, over the Bank of the United States. With twenty-nine branches, the bank

nullification

▶ The doctrine that when Congress overstepped its powers, states had the right to nullify Congress's acts. South Carolina advanced the doctrine of nullification in 1828 in response to passage of the Tariff of Abominations. A show of force by Andrew Jackson, combined with revision of the objectionable tariff, prompted South Carolina to withdraw its nullification.

handled the federal government's deposits, extended credit and loans, and issued banknotes. Jackson, however, thought the bank concentrated undue economic power in the hands of a few.

National Republican (Whig) senators Daniel Webster and Henry Clay, the National Republican candidate for president in 1832, decided to force the issue. They convinced the bank to apply for charter renewal in 1832, well before the fall election, even though the existing charter ran until 1836. They fully expected that Congress's renewal would be vetoed by Jackson, that the unpopular veto would cause Jackson to lose the election, and that the bank would survive on an override vote by a new Congress swept into power on the anti-Jackson tide.

At first, the plan seemed to work. The bank applied for rechartering, Congress voted to renew, and Jackson issued his veto. But it was a brilliantly written veto, presenting Jackson as the champion of the democratic masses. "Many of our rich men have not been content with equal protection and equal benefits, but have besought us to make them richer by act of Congress," Jackson wrote.

Fistfight between Andrew Jackson and Nicholas Biddle

This 1834 cartoon represents President Andrew Jackson squaring off against Nicholas Biddle, the director of the Bank of the United States. To Biddle's left are his seconds, Daniel Webster and Henry Clay. Behind the president is Vice President Martin Van Buren. Whiskey and port wine lubricate the action. The Library Company of Philadelphia.

What changes in national politics were reflected in the election of 1828?

What was Andrew Jackson's impact on the presidency?

How did the market revolution transform social and cultural life?

Why was Martin Van Buren a one-term president?

Conclusion: Age of Jackson or era of reform?

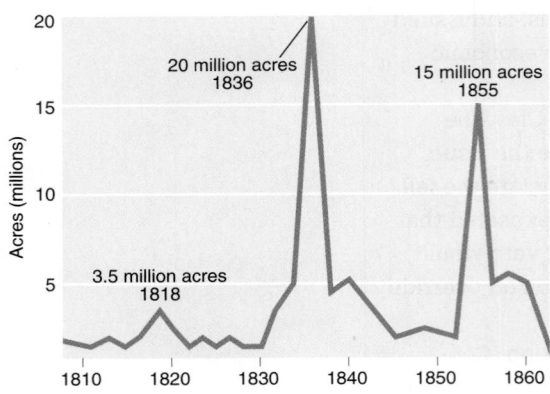

FIGURE 11.1 ■ Western Land Sales, 1810–1860
Land sales peaked in the 1810s, 1830s, and 1850s as Americans rushed to speculate in western land sold by the federal government. The surges in 1818 and 1836 demonstrate the volatile, speculative economy that suddenly collapsed in the panics of 1819 and 1837.

Jackson's translation of the bank controversy into a language of class antagonism and egalitarian ideals resonated with many Americans. Jackson won 55 percent of the popular vote and 219 electoral votes to Clay's 49. Jackson's party still controlled Congress, so no override was possible. The second Bank of the United States would cease to exist after 1836.

Jackson, however, wanted to destroy the bank sooner. Calling it a "monster," he ordered the sizable federal deposits to be removed from its vaults and redeposited into Democratic-inclined state banks. In retaliation, the Bank of the United States raised interest rates and called in loans. This action caused a brief decline in the economy in 1833 and actually enhanced Jackson's claim that the bank was too powerful for the good of the country.

Unleashed and unregulated, the economy went into high gear in 1834. Just at this moment, an excess of silver from Mexican mines made its way into American banks, giving bankers license to print ever more banknotes. From 1834 to 1837, inflation soared; prices of basic goods rose more than 50 percent. States quickly chartered hundreds of new private banks, each issuing its own banknotes. Entrepreneurs borrowed and invested money, and the webs of credit and debt relationships that were the hallmark of the American economy grew denser yet. The market in western land sales also heated up. In 1834, about 4.5 million acres of the public domain had been sold, the highest annual volume since 1818. By 1836, the total reached an astonishing 20 million acres.

In one respect, the economy attained an admirable goal: The national debt disappeared, and from 1835 to 1837, for the only time in American history, the government had a monetary surplus. But much of that surplus consisted of questionable bank currencies—"bloated, diseased" currencies, in Jackson's vivid terminology. While the boom was on, however, few stopped to worry about the consequences if and when the bubble burst.

> QUICK REVIEW

What were the most significant policies of Andrew Jackson's presidency?

How did the market revolution transform social and cultural life?

| The Talcott Family at Home, 1832 | Folk art depicting family life became popular and affordable in the early Republic. Samuel Talcott, twenty-eight, a farmer in Madison County, New York, poses with his wife, Betsey, twenty; his recently widowed mother, Mary, seventy; and daughters Clarissa, three, and Emily, three months. The couple wear quite fashionable clothes: Betsey's enormous sleeves are a hallmark of the 1830s, as is Samuel's "cutaway" waistcoat with its stiff, high collar. Abby Aldrich Rockefeller Folk Art Center, Williamsburg, Va. |

THE GROWING ECONOMY, booming by the mid-1830s, transformed social and cultural life. For many families, especially in the commercialized Northeast, standards of living rose, consumption patterns changed, and the nature and location of work were altered. All this had a direct impact on the duties of men and women and on the training of youths for the economy of the future.

Along with economic change came an unprecedented revival of evangelical religion known as the Second Great Awakening. Among the most serious adherents of evangelical Protestantism were men and women of the new merchant classes. Not content with individual perfection, many of these people sought to perfect society as well, by defining excessive alcohol consumption, nonmarital sex, and slavery as three major evils of modern life in need of correction.

The Family and Separate Spheres

The centerpiece of new ideas about gender relations was the notion that husbands found their status and authority in the new world of work, leaving wives to tend the hearth and home. Sermons, advice books, periodicals, and novels reinforced the idea that men and women inhabited separate spheres and had separate duties. "To woman it belongs . . . to elevate the intellectual character of her household [and] to kindle the fires of mental activity in childhood," wrote Mrs. A. J. Graves in a popular book titled *Advice to American Women*. For men, in

| What changes in national politics were reflected in the election of 1828? | What was Andrew Jackson's impact on the presidency? | **How did the market revolution transform social and cultural life?** | Why was Martin Van Buren a one-term president? | Conclusion: Age of Jackson or era of reform? |

293

Changing Trends in Age at First Marriage for Women

Average age at first marriage is a remarkably sensitive indicator of social, economic, and cultural factors in all societies. In general, conditions favoring low age at marriage for women are those that provide young couples with early financial support: abundant affordable farmland, co-residence with parents, or steady employment for men at a wage that can support a family. Factors that postpone marriage include a lack of farmland, deterioration in male employment prospects, a changed economy requiring more years of pre-job education and training, or enhanced employment for women, which makes the job market more attractive than the marriage market. The low mean ages in this table reflect abundant farmland (1800, United States), factory wage labor (1800, England), and serfdom (1850, Russia). In Europe and the United States, age of first marriage for women rose steeply in the nineteenth century. The northeastern United States led the way in the 1820s and 1830s. Can you suggest reasons why? One immediate consequence of later marriage was a decline in completed family size, since brides shaved two years off their exposure to the risk of pregnancy. Finally, demographers note that in some cases, rising age at first marriage is accompanied by rising rates of nonmarriage, sometimes as high as 20 percent. How might these two trends be connected?

	Nineteenth Century		Twentieth Century		
	1800	*1850*	*1900*	*1960*	*2000*
United States	21	23	23	20	25
England	20	24	24	22	28
Netherlands	—	28	26	25	28
Russia	—	19	—	25	22

Note: Dates are approximate. Dashes indicate a lack of reliable information.

contrast, "the absorbing passion for gain, and the pressing demands of business, engross their whole attention." In particular, the home, now the exclusive domain of women, was sentimentalized as the source of intimacy, love, and safety, a refuge from the cruel and competitive world of market relations.

Some new aspects of society gave substance to this formulation of separate spheres. Men's work was undergoing profound change after 1815 and increasingly brought cash to the household, especially in the manufacturing and urban Northeast. Farmers and tradesmen sold products in a market, and bankers, bookkeepers, shoemakers, and canal diggers got pay envelopes. Furthermore, many men now worked away from the home, at an office or a store.

A woman's domestic role was more complicated than the cultural prescriptions indicated. (See "Global Comparison.") Although the vast majority of married white women did not hold paying jobs, their homes required time-consuming labor. But the advice books treated housework as a loving familial duty, thus rendering it invisible in an economy that evaluated work by how much cash it generated. In reality, many wives contributed to family income by taking in boarders or sewing for cash. Wives in the poorest classes, including most free black wives, did not have the luxury of husbands earning adequate wages; for them, work as servants or laundry workers helped augment family income.

Idealized notions about the feminine home and the masculine workplace gained acceptance in the 1830s because of the cultural ascendancy of the commercialized Northeast, with its domination of book and periodical publication. Beyond white families of the middle and upper classes, however, these new gender ideals had limited applicability. Despite their apparent authority in printed material of the period, they were never all-pervasive.

The Education and Training of Youths

The market economy required expanded opportunities for training youths of both sexes. By the 1830s, in both the North and the South, state-supported public school systems were the norm, designed to produce pupils of both sexes able, by age twelve to fourteen, to read, write, and participate in marketplace calculations. Literacy rates for white females climbed dramatically, rivaling the rates for white males for the first time. The fact that taxpayers paid for children's education created an incentive to seek an inexpensive teaching force. By the 1830s, school districts replaced male teachers with young female teachers, for, as a Massachusetts report on education put it, "females can be educated cheaper, quicker, and better, and will teach cheaper after they are qualified."

Advanced education continued to expand in the 1830s, with an additional two dozen colleges for men and several more female seminaries offering education on a par with the male colleges. Still, only a very small percentage of young people attended institutions of higher learning. The vast majority of male youths left public school at age fourteen to apprentice in specific trades or to embark on business careers by seeking entry-level clerkships. Young girls headed for mill towns or cities in unprecedented numbers, seeking work in the expanding service sector as seamstresses and domestic servants. Changes in patterns of youth employment meant that large numbers of youngsters escaped the watchful eyes of their parents, a cause of great concern for the moralists of the era.

The Second Great Awakening

A newly invigorated version of Protestantism gained momentum in the 1820s and 1830s as the economy reshaped gender and age relations. The earliest manifestations of this fervent piety appeared in 1801 in Kentucky, when a crowd of ten thousand people camped out on a hillside at Cane Ridge for a revival meeting that lasted several weeks. By the 1810s and 1820s, "camp meetings" had spread to the Atlantic seaboard states.

The gatherings attracted women and men hungry for a more immediate access to spiritual peace, one not requiring years of soul-searching. One eyewitness reported that "some of the people were singing, others praying, some crying for mercy. . . . At one time I saw at least five hundred swept down in a moment as if a battery of a thousand guns had been opened upon them, and then immediately followed shrieks and shouts that rent the very heavens."

From 1800 to 1820, church membership doubled in the United States, much of it among the evangelical groups. Methodists, Baptists, and Presbyterians formed the core of the new movement. Women more than men were attracted to the evangelical movement, and wives and mothers typically recruited husbands and sons to join them.

The ministry of Charles Grandison Finney embodied the **Second Great Awakening**. Finney lived in western New York, where the completion of the Erie

CHRONOLOGY

1817
– American Colonization Society is founded.

1826
– American Temperance Society is founded.

1829
– David Walker's *Appeal . . . to the Coloured Citizens of the World* is published.

1830–1831
– Charles Grandison Finney preaches in Rochester, New York.

1831
– William Lloyd Garrison starts *Liberator*.

1832
– New England Anti-Slavery Society is founded.

1833
– New York and Philadelphia antislavery societies are founded.
– New York Female Moral Reform Society is founded.

1836
– American Temperance Union is founded.

Second Great Awakening
▶ Unprecedented revival of evangelical religion in the 1820s and 1830s. The revival attracted men and women who, in the face of the changes wrought by the market revolution, sought new and immediate sources of spiritual solace. The Second Great Awakening was also a major force behind the reform movements of the era, inspiring efforts to combat drinking, sexual sin, and slavery.

| What changes in national politics were reflected in the election of 1828? | What was Andrew Jackson's impact on the presidency? | **How did the market revolution transform social and cultural life?** | Why was Martin Van Buren a one-term president? | Conclusion: Age of Jackson or era of reform? |

295

► FOR MORE HELP ANALYZING THIS IMAGE, see the visual activity for this chapter in the Online Study Guide at bedfordstmartins.com/roarkunderstanding.

Charles G. Finney and His Broadway Tabernacle

The Reverend Charles Grandison Finney took his evangelical movement to New York City in the early 1830s, operating first out of a renovated theater. In 1836, the Broadway Tabernacle was built for his pastorate. In its use of space, the tabernacle resembled a theater more than a traditional church.
Oberlin College Archives, Oberlin, Ohio.

American Temperance Society

► Organization founded in 1826 by Lyman Beecher that warned that drinking led to poverty, idleness, crime, and family violence. Adopting the methods of evangelical ministers, temperance lecturers traveled the country expounding the damage of drink. The temperance movement had considerable success, contributing to a sharp drop in American alcohol consumption.

Canal in 1825 fundamentally altered the social and economic landscape overnight. Growth and prosperity came with less admirable side effects, such as prostitution, drinking, and gaming. Finney saw New York canal towns as ripe for evangelical awakening. In Rochester, he sustained a six-month revival through the winter of 1830–31, generating thousands of converts.

Finney's message was directed primarily at the business classes and pressed for public-spirited outreach to the less-than-perfect to foster their salvation. Evangelicals promoted Sunday schools to bring piety to children; they battled to end mail delivery, stop public transport, and close shops on Sundays to honor the Sabbath. Many women formed missionary societies that distributed millions of Bibles and religious tracts. Through such avenues, evangelical religion offered women expanded spheres of influence. Finney adopted the tactics of Jacksonian-era politicians—publicity, argumentation, rallies, and speeches—to sell his cause. His object, he said, was to get Americans to "vote in the Lord Jesus Christ as the governor of the Universe."

The Temperance Movement and the Campaign for Moral Reform

Evangelical fervor animated vigorous campaigns to eliminate alcohol abuse and eradicate sexual sin. Millions of Americans took the temperance pledge to abstain from strong drink, and thousands became involved in efforts to end prostitution.

Alcohol consumption had risen steadily in the decades up to 1830. All classes imbibed. A lively saloon culture fostered masculine camaraderie along with extensive alcohol consumption among laborers, while in elite homes, the after-dinner whiskey or sherry was commonplace. Colleges before 1820 routinely served students a pint of ale with meals, and the military included rum in the daily ration.

Average Annual Alcohol Consumption in 1830

Nine gallons of hard liquor.
Thirty gallons of hard cider, beer, and wine.

Organized opposition to drinking first surfaced in the 1810s among health and religious reformers. In 1826, Lyman Beecher, a Connecticut minister of an "awakened" church, founded the **American Temperance Society**, which warned that drinking led to poverty, idleness, crime, and family violence. Adopting the methods of evangelical ministers, temperance lecturers traveled the country expounding the damage of drink. By 1833, some six thousand local affiliates of the American Temperance Society boasted more than a million members.

In 1836, leaders of the temperance movement regrouped into a new society, the American Temperance Union, which demanded total abstinence from its adherents. The intensified war against alcohol moved beyond individual moral suasion into the realm of politics as reformers sought to deny taverns liquor licenses. By 1845, temperance advocates had put an impressive dent in alcohol consumption, which diminished to one-quarter of the per capita consumption of 1830.

More controversial than temperance was a social movement called "moral reform," which first aimed at public morals in general but quickly narrowed to a campaign to eradicate sexual sin. In 1833, a group of Finneyite women started the New York Female Moral Reform Society. Its members insisted that uncontrolled male sexual expression posed a serious threat to society in general and to women in particular. Within five years, more than four thousand auxiliary groups of women had sprung up, mostly in New England, New York, Pennsylvania, and Ohio.

In its analysis of sexual sin and its conviction that women had a duty to speak out about unspeakable things, the Moral Reform Society pushed the limits of what even the men in the evangelical movement could tolerate. Yet these women did not regard themselves as radicals. They were simply pursuing the logic of a gender system that defined home protection and morality as women's special sphere and a religious conviction that called for the eradication of sin.

Organizing against Slavery

More radical still was the movement in the 1830s to abolish the sin of slavery. Previously, the American Colonization Society, founded in 1817 by Maryland and Virginia planters, aimed to promote gradual individual emancipation of slaves followed by colonization in Africa. By the early 1820s, several thousand ex-slaves had been transported to Liberia on the West African coast. But not surprisingly, newly freed men and women were often not eager to emigrate; their African roots were three or more generations in the past. Colonization was too gradual (and expensive) to have much impact on American slavery.

Around 1830, northern challenges to slavery intensified, beginning in free black communities. In 1829, a Boston printer named David Walker published *An Appeal . . . to the Coloured Citizens of the World*, which condemned racism, invoked the egalitarian language of the Declaration of Independence, and hinted at racial violence if whites did not change their prejudiced ways. In 1830, at the inaugural National Negro Convention meeting in Philadelphia, forty blacks from nine states discussed the racism of American society and proposed emigration to Canada. In 1832 and 1833, a twenty-eight-year-old black woman named Maria Stewart delivered public lectures on slavery and racial prejudice to black audiences in Boston. Her lectures gained wider circulation when they were published in a national publication called the *Liberator*.

The *Liberator*, founded in 1831 in Boston, took antislavery agitation to new heights. Its founder and editor, **William Lloyd Garrison**, advocated immediate abolition: "On this subject, I do not wish to think, or speak, or write, with moderation. No! No! Tell a man whose house is on fire to give a moderate alarm; tell him to moderately rescue his wife from the hands of the ravisher; tell the mother to gradually extricate her babe from the fire into which it has fallen;—but urge me not to use moderation in a cause like the present." In 1832, Garrison's supporters started the New England Anti-Slavery Society.

William Lloyd Garrison

▶ Leading advocate of the immediate abolition of slavery. Garrison founded his abolitionist newspaper, the *Liberator*, in 1831 and, along with his supporters, started the New England Anti-Slavery Society in 1832. Garrison played a key role in the growing antislavery movement of the 1830s and 1840s.

What changes in national politics were reflected in the election of 1828? | What was Andrew Jackson's impact on the presidency? | **How did the market revolution transform social and cultural life?** | Why was Martin Van Buren a one-term president? | Conclusion: Age of Jackson or era of reform?

297

Garrison, Thompson, and Phillips

George Thompson (middle) was a leading figure in the successful campaign to abolish slavery in Britain and its West Indies colonies in 1833. William Lloyd Garrison (left) welcomed Thompson to the United States in 1835 and promoted his speaking tour in Garrison's antislavery newspaper, the *Liberator*. Boston lawyer Wendell Phillips (right) heard Thompson speak and was inspired to make abolition his lifework. This picture dates from 1850, when Thompson returned to the United States. Historical Library of Swarthmore College.

Similar groups were organized in Philadelphia and New York in 1833. Soon a dozen antislavery newspapers and scores of antislavery lecturers were spreading the word and inspiring the formation of new local societies, which numbered thirteen hundred by 1837. Confined entirely to the North, their membership totaled a quarter of a million men and women.

Many white northerners, even those who opposed slavery, were not prepared to embrace the abolitionist call for emancipation. From 1834 to 1838, there were more than a hundred eruptions of serious mob violence against abolitionists and free blacks.

Women played a prominent role in abolition, just as they did in moral reform and evangelical religion. They formed women's auxiliaries and held fairs to sell handmade crafts to support male lecturers in the field. They circulated antislavery petitions, presented to the U.S. Congress with tens of thousands of signatures. Up to 1835, women's petitions were framed as respectful memorials to Congress about the evils of slavery, but by mid-decade these petitions used urgent language to call for political action.

When a southern planter's daughter named Angelina Grimké wrote to Garrison about her personal repugnance for slavery, he published the letter in the *Liberator* and brought her overnight fame. In 1837, Grimké and her older sister, Sarah, became antislavery lecturers targeting women, but their powerful eyewitness speeches attracted male audiences as well. This caused leaders of the Congregational Church in Massachusetts to ban the Grimkés from their pulpits, because women should not presume to instruct men.

In the late 1830s, the cause of abolition divided the nation as no other issue did. Even among abolitionists, significant divisions emerged. Angelina and Sarah Grimké, radicalized by the controversy over their speaking tour, began to write and speak about woman's rights. They were opposed by moderate abolitionists who were unwilling to mix the new and contentious issue of woman's rights with their first cause, the rights of blacks.

The many men and women active in reform movements in the 1830s found their initial inspiration in evangelical Protestantism's dual message: Salvation was open to all, and society needed to be perfected. Their activist mentality squared well with the interventionist tendencies of the Whig Party forming in opposition to Andrew Jackson's Democrats.

> **QUICK REVIEW**

How did idealized roles for men and women change in the 1830s? What impact did these have on the rise of evangelical Protestantism and social reform movements?

Panic of 1837 Cartoon A sad family with an unemployed father faces sudden privation in this cartoon showing the consequences of the panic of 1837. The wife and children complain of hunger, the house is stripped nearly bare, and rent collectors loom in the doorway. Faint pictures on the wall show Andrew Jackson and Martin Van Buren presiding over the economic devastation of the family. Library of Congress.

BY THE MID-1830s, a vibrant and tumultuous political culture occupied center stage of American life. Andrew Jackson's vice president and successor, the northerner Martin Van Buren, inherited a strong Democratic organization, but he faced doubts from slave-owning Jacksonians and outright opposition from increasingly combative Whigs. Van Buren was a skilled politician, but there was little he could do in the face of economic collapse. A shattering panic in 1837, followed by another panic in 1839, brought the country its worst economic depression yet.

CHRONOLOGY

1835
- Abolitionist literature is burned in Charleston, South Carolina.

1836
- Democrat Martin Van Buren is elected president.
- Congress adopts "gag rule" forbidding antislavery petitions from being entered into the public record.

1837–1839
- Economic panics lead to runs on banks, business failures, and a deflated economy.

1840
- Whig William Henry Harrison is elected president.

The Politics of Slavery

Sophisticated party organization was the specialty of Martin Van Buren. He earned the nickname "the Little Magician" for his consummate political skills. First a senator and then a governor, he became Jackson's secretary of state and then his running mate in 1832.

Jackson clearly favored Van Buren for the nomination in 1836, but starting in 1832, the major political parties had developed nominating conventions to choose their candidates. In 1835, Van Buren got the convention nod unanimously, to the dismay of his archrival, Calhoun, who then worked to discredit Van Buren among southern proslavery Democrats. Van Buren spent months assuring them that he was a "northern man with southern principles."

Calhoun was able to stir up trouble for Van Buren because, in 1835, southerners were increasingly alarmed by the rise of northern antislavery sentiment. When, in late 1835, abolitionists prepared to circulate in the South a million pamphlets condemning slavery, a mailbag of their literature was hijacked at the post office in Charleston, South Carolina, and ceremoniously burned along with effigies of leading abolitionists.

The petitioning tactics of abolitionists escalated sectional tensions. When the number of antislavery petitions presented to Congress grew into the hundreds, proslavery congressmen responded by passing a "gag rule" in 1836. The gag rule prohibited entering the documents into the public record on the grounds that what the abolitionists prayed for was unconstitutional and, further, an assault on the rights of white southerners, as one South Carolina representative put it.

Van Buren shrewdly seized on the conflict between abolitionists and their opponents to express his prosouthern sympathies. Abolitionists were "fanatics," he repeatedly claimed, possibly under the influence of "foreign agents" (British abolitionists). He promised that if he was elected president, he would not allow any interference in southern "domestic institutions."

Elections and Panics

Although the elections of 1824, 1828, and 1832 clearly bore the stamp of Jackson's personality, by 1836 the party apparatus was sufficiently developed to give Van Buren, a backroom politician, a shot at the presidency. Local and state committees existed throughout the country, and more than four hundred newspapers were Democratic partisans.

The Whigs had also built state-level organizations and cultivated newspaper loyalty. They had no top contender with nationwide support, so three regional candidates opposed Van Buren: Senator Daniel Webster of Massachusetts, Senator Hugh Lawson White of Tennessee, and the aging General William Henry Harrison, now residing in Ohio. Not one of the three candidates had the ability to win the presidency, but together they came close to denying Van Buren a majority vote and throwing the election into the House of Representatives.

In the end, Van Buren won with 170 electoral votes, while the other three received a total of 113. Although Van Buren had pulled together a national Democratic Party with wins in both the North and the South, he had done it at the cost of committing northern Democrats to the proslavery agenda. And running three candidates had maximized the Whigs' success by drawing Whigs into office at the state level.

When Van Buren took office in March 1837, the financial markets were already quaking; by April, the country was plunged into crisis. The causes of the panic of 1837 were multiple and far-ranging. Bad harvests in Europe and a large trade imbalance between Britain and the United States caused the Bank of England to start calling in loans to American merchants. Failures in various crop markets and a 30 percent downturn in international cotton prices fed the growing disaster. Frightened citizens thronged the banks to try to get their money out, and businesses rushed to liquefy their remaining assets to pay off debts. Prices of stocks, bonds, and real estate fell 30 to 40 percent. The credit market tumbled like a house of cards.

Some Whig leaders were certain that Jackson's antibank and hard-money policies were responsible for the ruin. New Yorker Philip Hone, a wealthy Whig, called the Jackson administration "the most disastrous in the annals of the country" for its "wicked interference" in banking and monetary matters. Others framed the devastation as retribution for the frenzy of speculation that had gripped the nation. A religious periodical in Boston hoped that Americans would now moderate their greed: "We were getting to think that there was no end to the wealth, and could be no check to the progress of our country; that economy was not needed, that prudence was weakness." Others identified the competitive, profit-maximizing capitalist system as the cause and looked to Britain and France for new socialist ideas calling for the common ownership of the means of production.

The panic of 1837 subsided by 1838, but in 1839, another run on the banks and ripples of business failures deflated the economy, creating a second panic. President Van Buren called a special session of Congress to consider creating an independent treasury system to perform some of the functions of the defunct Bank of the United States. Such a system, funded by government deposits, would deal only in hard money and would exert a powerful moderating influence on inflation and the credit market. But Van Buren encountered strong resistance in Congress, even among Democrats. The treasury system finally won approval in 1840, but by then Van Buren's chances of winning a second term in office were virtually nil.

In 1840, the Whigs settled on William Henry Harrison to oppose Van Buren. The campaign drew on voter involvement as no presidential campaign ever had. The Whigs borrowed tricks from the Democrats: Harrison was touted as a common man born in a log cabin (in reality, he was born on a Virginia plantation), and his Indian-fighting days, now thirty years behind him, were played up to give him a Jacksonian aura. Whigs staged festive rallies around the country, drumming up mass appeal with candlelight parades and song shows, and women participated in rallies as never before. Some 78 percent of eligible voters cast ballots, the highest percentage ever in American history. Harrison took 53 percent of the popular vote and won 234 electoral college votes to Van Buren's 60. A Democratic editor lamented, "We have taught them how to conquer us!"

QUICK REVIEW

What impact did the economy have on national life in the late 1830s?

> Conclusion: Age of Jackson or era of reform?

ECONOMIC TRANSFORMATIONS loom large in explaining the fast-paced changes of the 1830s. Transportation advances put goods and people in circulation, augmenting urban growth and helping to create a national culture, and water-powered manufacturing began to change the face of wage labor. Trade and banking mushroomed, and western land once occupied by Indians was auctioned off in a landslide of sales. Two periods of economic downturn—including the panic of 1819 and the panics of 1837 and 1839—offered sobering lessons about speculative fever.

Andrew Jackson symbolized this age of opportunity for many. His fame as an aggressive general, an Indian fighter, a champion of the common man, and a defender of slavery attracted growing numbers of voters to the emergent Democratic Party, which championed personal liberty, free competition, and egalitarian opportunity for all white men.

Jackson's constituency was challenged by a small but vocal segment of the population troubled by serious moral problems that Jacksonians preferred to ignore. Inspired by the Second Great Awakening, reformers targeted personal vices (illicit sex and intemperance) and social problems (prostitution, poverty, and slavery) and joined forces with evangelicals and wealthy lawyers and merchants (from the North and South) who appreciated a national bank and protective tariffs. The Whig Party was the party of activist moralism and state-sponsored entrepreneurship. Whig voters were, of course, male, but thousands of reform-minded women broke new ground by signing political petitions on the issues of Indian removal and slavery.

National politics in the 1830s were more divisive than at any time since the 1790s. The new party system of Democrats and Whigs reached far deeper into the electorate than had the Federalists and Republicans. Politics acquired immediacy and excitement, causing nearly four out of five white men to cast ballots in 1840.

High rates of voter participation would continue into the 1840s and 1850s. Unprecedented urban growth, westward expansion, and early industrialism marked those decades, sustaining the Democrat-Whig split in the electorate. But critiques of slavery, concerns for free labor, and an emerging protest against women's second-class citizenship complicated the political scene of the 1840s, leading to third-party political movements. One of these third parties, called the Republican Party, would achieve dominance in 1860 with the election of an Illinois lawyer, Abraham Lincoln, to the presidency.

The Granger Collection, New York.

SO NOW YOU KNOW

Before 1815, transportation in the United States was slow and expensive, but by 1840, networks of roads, canals, and even railroads began to unify the country culturally and economically. Improved transportation also brought improved communication, which energized new voters, created new party loyalties, and brought new issues such as temperance, moral reform, and abolition into American politics.

| What changes in national politics were reflected in the election of 1828? | What was Andrew Jackson's impact on the presidency? | How did the market revolution transform social and cultural life? | Why was Martin Van Buren a one-term president? | Conclusion: Age of Jackson or era of reform? |

303

CHAPTER 11 STUDY GUIDE

Online Study Guide
bedfordstmartins.com/roarkunderstanding

STEP 1 GETTING STARTED

Below are basic terms from this period in American history. Can you identify each term below and explain why it matters? To do this exercise online or to download this chart, visit bedfordstmartins.com/roarkunderstanding.

TERM	WHO OR WHAT & WHEN	WHY IT MATTERS
Erie Canal, p. 280		
second Bank of the United States, p. 282		
Andrew Jackson, p. 283		
John C. Calhoun, p. 285		
Whigs, p. 286		
Democrats, p. 286		
Indian Removal Act of 1830, p. 288		
Trail of Tears, p. 289		
nullification, p. 290		
Second Great Awakening, p. 295		
American Temperance Society, p. 296		
William Lloyd Garrison, p. 297		

STEP 2 MOVING BEYOND THE BASICS

The exercise below represents a more advanced understanding of the chapter material. Fill in the following chart by describing the key developments that combined to create the market revolution and by assessing the impact of each development. When you are finished, consider the relationship between each of the developments. How did improved transportation facilitate industrialization? How did the advent of factories alter labor relations? How did financial innovations contribute to economic volatility? To do this exercise online or to download this chart, visit bedfordstmartins.com/roarkunderstanding.

	Key developments	Societal and political effects
Improvements in transportation		
New methods of production		
Changes in the workforce and in labor relations		
Financial innovations		
Changes in commercial law		
Increased economic volatility		

Now that you have reviewed key elements of the chapter, take a step back and try to explain the big picture by answering these questions. Remember to use specific examples from the chapter in your answers. To do this exercise online, visit bedfordstmartins.com/roarkunderstanding.

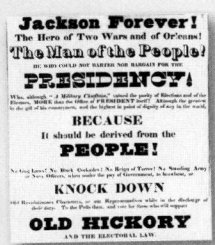

THE MARKET REVOLUTION

▶ Why were improvements in transportation so crucial to America's economic growth and development in the early nineteenth century?

▶ What changes in workers' lives and status accompanied industrialization?

THE AGE OF JACKSON

▶ What does Andrew Jackson's rise to the presidency tell us about popular politics in the 1820s?

▶ How did Andrew Jackson change the presidency? How did he see and manipulate the relationship among the president, Congress, and the courts?

THE ERA OF REFORM

▶ How did the Second Great Awakening lead to a variety of social reform movements? What impact did these various reform movements have on politics and society in the 1830s?

▶ What role did women play in the reform movements of the early nineteenth century?

LOOKING BACKWARD, LOOKING AHEAD

▶ How did the second American party system differ from the first party system? How did it differ from the partisanship of the 1790s?

▶ How do the reform movements of the 1820s and 1830s shed light on the causes of the sectional tensions that would dominate the 1840s and 1850s?

IN YOUR OWN WORDS

Imagine that you must explain chapter 11 to someone who hasn't read it. What would be the most important points to include and why?

12

THE NEW WEST AND FREE NORTH

1840–1860

> This chapter explores the factors that propelled American economic growth and territorial expansion in the mid-nineteenth-century West and North. Rapid growth shaped the nation's economy and geographic boundaries as well as political debates and movements for social reform. This era of growth contributed to emerging tensions between the free-labor economy and slavery.

> What factors contributed to America's "industrial evolution"?

> Who benefited from America's economic growth?

> What factors spurred westward expansion?

> Why did the United States go to war with Mexico?

> How did reform efforts change after 1840?

> Conclusion: How was white freedom in the West and North defined?

DID YOU KNOW?

In 1860, the United States had about as many miles of railroad track as the rest of the world combined.

War news from Mexico. In 1848, artist Richard Caton Woodville imagined this scene of a man reading of the war.

What factors contributed to America's "industrial evolution"?

This painting by Andrew Melrose depicts the mid-nineteenth-century landscape of agricultural and technological progress. Museum of the American West, Autry National Center, 92.147.1.

▶ FOR MORE HELP ANALYZING THIS IMAGE, see the visual activity for this chapter in the Online Study Guide at bedfordstmartins.com/roarkunderstanding.

DURING THE 1840s AND 1850s, Americans experienced a profound economic transformation that had been under way since the start of the nineteenth century. Since 1800, the total output of the U.S. economy had multiplied twelvefold. Four fundamental changes in American society fueled this remarkable economic growth.

First, millions of Americans moved from farms to towns and cities. Second, the number of Americans who worked in factories, mainly in urban centers, grew to about 20 percent of the labor force by 1860. This trend contributed to the nation's economic growth because, in general, factory workers produced twice as much (per unit of labor) as agricultural workers.

Third, a shift from water power to steam as a source of energy raised productivity, especially in factories and transportation. Between 1840 and 1860, coal production multiplied eightfold, cutting prices in half and permitting coal-fired steam engines to power ever more factories, railroads, and ships.

A fourth fundamental change propelling America's economic development was the rise in agricultural productivity, which nearly doubled between 1800 and 1860. More than any other single factor, agricultural productivity spurred the nation's economic growth.

Historians often refer to this cascade of changes in farms, cities, factories, power, and transportation as an industrial revolution. However, these changes did not cause an abrupt discontinuity in America's economy or society. The United States remained overwhelmingly rural and agricultural. Old methods of production continued alongside new ones. By 1860, the muscles of people and

CHAPTER LOCATOR | What factors contributed to America's "industrial evolution"?

308 CHAPTER 12 THE NEW WEST AND FREE NORTH, 1840–1860

work animals still provided thirty times more energy for manufacturing than did steam power. The changes in the American economy during the 1840s and 1850s might better be termed "industrial evolution."

Agriculture and Land Policy

As farmers pushed westward in their quest for cheap land, they encountered the Midwest's comparatively treeless prairie. Rich prairie soils yielded bumper crops, enticing farmers to migrate to the Midwest by the tens of thousands between 1830 and 1860. The populations of Indiana, Illinois, Michigan, Wisconsin, and Iowa exploded tenfold between 1830 and 1860, four times faster than the growth of the nation as a whole.

Labor-saving improvements in farm implements also hiked agricultural productivity. In 1837, John Deere patented a strong, smooth steel plow that sliced through prairie soil so cleanly that farmers called it the "singing plow." Deere's company became the leading plow manufacturer in the Midwest, turning out more than ten thousand plows a year by the late 1850s.

Improvements in wheat harvesting also multiplied farmers' productivity. In 1850, most farmers harvested wheat by hand, cutting two or three acres a day with backbreaking labor. In the 1840s, Cyrus McCormick and others experimented with designs for mechanical reapers, and by the 1850s, an inexpensive McCormick reaper allowed a farmer to harvest twelve acres a day. Most continued to cut their grain by hand, but improved reapers and plows, usually powered by horses or oxen, allowed farmers to cultivate more land, doubling the corn and wheat harvests between 1840 and 1860.

Federal land policy made possible the agricultural productivity that fueled the nation's economy. Up to 1860, the United States continued to be land-rich and labor-poor. Territorial acquisitions made the nation a great deal richer in land, adding more than a billion acres with the Louisiana Purchase (see chapter 10) and the annexation of Florida, Oregon, and vast territories following the Mexican-American War (see page 323). The federal government made most of this land available for purchase to attract settlers and to generate revenue. Speculators found ways to claim large tracts of the most desirable plots and sell them to settlers at a profit. But millions of ordinary farmers bought federal land for just $1.25 an acre, or $50 for a forty-acre farm, which could support a family. Millions of other farmers squatted on unclaimed federal land. By making land available to millions of Americans on relatively easy terms, the federal government achieved the goal of attracting settlers to the new territories in the West, which in due course joined the Union as new states. Above all, federal land policy fueled the increase in agricultural productivity that underlay the nation's impressive economic growth.

Manufacturing and Mechanization

In contrast to the United States, Britain and other European countries had land-poor, labor-rich economies; there, meager opportunities in agriculture kept factory laborers plentiful and wages low. In the United States, western expansion and government land policies buoyed agriculture, keeping millions of people on

CHRONOLOGY

1800–1860
- American agricultural productivity nearly doubles.

1837
- John Deere patents steel plow.

1840s
- Practical mechanical reapers are created.

1840–1860
- American coal production multiplies eightfold.
- American corn and wheat harvests double.

1844
- Samuel F. B. Morse demonstrates telegraph.

| Who benefited from America's economic growth? | What factors spurred westward expansion? | Why did the United States go to war with Mexico? | How did reform efforts change after 1840? | Conclusion: How was white freedom in the West and North defined? |

309

the farm and thereby limiting the supply of workers for manufacturing and elevating wages. Because of this relative shortage of workers, manufacturers searched constantly for ways to save labor.

Mechanization allowed manufacturers to produce more with less labor. The practice of manufacturing and then assembling interchangeable parts spread from gun making to other industries and became known as the **American system**. Standardized parts produced by machine allowed manufacturers to employ unskilled workers, who were much cheaper and more readily available than highly trained craftsmen. A visitor to a Springfield, Massachusetts, gun factory in 1842 noted, for example, that standardized parts made the trained gunsmith's "skill of the eye and the hand, [previously] acquired by practice alone . . . no longer indispensable." Even in heavily mechanized industries, factories remained fairly small; few had more than twenty or thirty employees.

Manufacturing and agriculture meshed into a dynamic national economy. New England led the nation in manufacturing, shipping goods such as guns, clocks, plows, and axes west and south, while southern and western states sent commodities such as wheat, pork, whiskey, tobacco, and cotton north and east. Manufacturers produced for the huge domestic market rather than for export. To protect their access to domestic consumers, manufacturers supported tariffs on goods imported from foreign countries. The burgeoning national economy was further fueled by the growth of the railroads, which linked farms and factories in new ways.

Railroads: Breaking the Bonds of Nature

Railroads seemed to break the bonds of nature. When canals and rivers froze in winter or became impassable during summer droughts, trains steamed ahead. When becalmed sailing ships went nowhere, locomotives kept on chugging, averaging more than twenty miles an hour during the 1850s. Above all, railroads gave cities not blessed with canals or navigable rivers a way to compete for rural trade. The massive expansion of American railroads helped catapult the nation into position as the world's second-greatest industrial power, after Great Britain (**Map 12.1**).

In addition to speeding transportation, railroads propelled the growth of other industries, such as iron and communications. Iron production grew five times faster than the population during the decades up to 1860, in part to meet railroads' demand. Railroads also stimulated the fledgling telegraph industry. In 1844, Samuel F. B. Morse demonstrated the potential of his telegraph by transmitting an electronic message along forty miles of wire strung between Washington, D.C., and Baltimore. By 1861, more than fifty thousand miles of wire stretched

The Telegraph

Samuel F. B. Morse is credited with inventing the telegraph because of his patent in June 1840, but, as one contemporary observed, Morse's talent consisted of "combining and applying the discoveries of others in the invention of a particular instrument and process for telegraphic purposes." Morse sent the first message in 1844 on this telegraph using a code he devised that represented each letter and number with dots and dashes.
Division of Political History, Smithsonian Institution, Washington, D.C.

The Railroad Boom of the 1850s

1850: 9,000 miles of railroad track in the United States, almost two-thirds of it in New England.

1860: 30,000 miles of railroad track in the United States, with several railroads spanning the Mississippi River.

By 1860, the United States has approximately as much railroad track as the rest of the world combined.

CHAPTER LOCATOR | What factors contributed to America's "industrial evolution"?

310 CHAPTER 12
THE NEW WEST AND FREE NORTH, 1840–1860

MAP 12.1 ■ Railroads in 1860
Railroads were a crucial component of the revolutions in transportation and communications that transformed nineteenth-century America. The railroad system reflected the differences in the economies of the North and South.

across the continent to the Pacific Ocean, often alongside railroad tracks, making trains safer and more efficient and accelerating communications of all sorts.

Private corporations built and owned almost all railroads, in contrast to government ownership of railroads common in other industrial nations. But privately owned American railroads received massive government aid, especially federal land grants. By 1860, Congress had granted railroads more than twenty million acres of federal land, thereby underwriting construction costs and promoting the expansion of the rail network, the settlement of federal land, and the integration of the domestic market.

The railroad boom of the 1850s signaled the growing industrial might of the American economy. But railroads, like other industries, succeeded because they served both farms and cities. Despite this growth, in 1860, most Americans were far more familiar with horses than with locomotives.

QUICK REVIEW

How did the United States become a leading industrial power in the nineteenth century?

| Who benefited from America's economic growth? | What factors spurred westward expansion? | Why did the United States go to war with Mexico? | How did reform efforts change after 1840? | Conclusion: How was white freedom in the West and North defined? |

Who benefited from America's economic growth?

Miner with Pick, Pan, and Shovel This young man exhibits the spirit of individual effort that was the foundation of free-labor ideals. Hard work with these tools, the picture suggests, promised rewards and maybe riches. Collection of Matthew Isenburg.

THE NATION'S IMPRESSIVE economic performance did not reward all Americans equally. Native-born white men tended to do better than immigrants. With few exceptions, women were excluded from opportunities open to men. In the North and West, slavery was slowly eliminated in the half century after the American Revolution, but most free African Americans were relegated to dead-end jobs as laborers and servants. Discrimination against immigrants, women, and free blacks did not trouble most white men. With certain notable exceptions, they considered it proper and just.

The Free-Labor Ideal: Freedom Plus Labor

During the 1840s and 1850s, leaders throughout the North and West emphasized a set of ideas that seemed to explain why the changes under way in their society benefited some people more than others. They referred again and again to the advantages of what they termed free labor, that is to say, laborers who were not slaves. By the 1850s, free-labor ideas described a social and economic ideal that accounted for both the successes and the shortcomings of the economy and society taking shape in the North and the West.

CHAPTER LOCATOR

What factors contributed to America's "industrial evolution"?

Spokesmen for the **free-labor ideal** celebrated hard work, self-reliance, and independence. They proclaimed that the door to success was open not just to those who inherited wealth or status but also to self-made men. Free labor, Abraham Lincoln argued, was "the just and generous, and prosperous system, which opens the way for all—gives hope to all, and energy, and progress, and improvement of condition to all." Free labor permitted farmers and artisans to enjoy the products of their own labor, and it also benefited wageworkers. "The prudent, penniless beginner in the world," Lincoln asserted, "labors for wages awhile, saves a surplus with which to buy tools or land, for himself; then labors on his own account another while, and at length hires another new beginner to help him."

The free-labor ideal affirmed an egalitarian vision of human potential. Advocates stressed the importance of universal education. (See "Global Comparison," page 314.) By 1860, many cities and towns had public schools that boasted that up to 80 percent of children ages seven to thirteen attended school for at least a few weeks each year. In rural areas, where the labor of children was more difficult to spare, schools typically enrolled no more than half the school-age children. Lessons included more than arithmetic, penmanship, and a smattering of other subjects. Textbooks and teachers—most of whom were young women—drummed into students the lessons of the free-labor system: self-reliance, discipline, and, above all else, hard work. "Remember that all the ignorance, degradation, and misery in the world is the result of indolence and vice," one textbook intoned. In school and out, free-labor ideology emphasized labor as much as freedom.

Economic Inequality

The opportunities presented by the expanding economy made a few men rich. Most Americans, however, measured success in more modest terms. The average wealth of adult white men in the North in 1860 barely topped $2,000. Nearly half of American men had no wealth at all; about 60 percent owned no land. Because property possessed by married women was normally considered to belong to their husbands, women had less wealth than men. Free African Americans had still less; 90 percent of them were propertyless.

Free-labor spokesmen considered these economic inequalities a natural outgrowth of freedom—the inevitable result of some individuals being more able and willing to work and luckier. These inequalities also demonstrate the gap between the promise and the performance of the free-labor ideal. Economic growth permitted many men to move from being landless squatters to landowning farmers and from being hired laborers to independent, self-employed producers. But many more Americans remained behind, landless and working for wages.

Seeking out new opportunities in pursuit of free-labor ideals created restless social and geographic mobility. While fortunate people rose far beyond their social origins, others shared the misfortune of a merchant who, an observer noted, "has been on the sinking list all his life." In search of better prospects, roughly two-thirds of the rural population moved every decade, and population turnover in cities was even greater. This constant coming and going weakened community ties to neighbors and friends and threw individuals even more on their own resources in times of trouble.

CHRONOLOGY

1840s–1850s
- Free-labor ideal develops to describe the economic and social successes and shortcomings in the North and the West.

1840–1860
- Almost 4.5 million immigrants arrive in the United States, three-fourths of them from Ireland and Germany.

free-labor ideal
▶ Social and economic ideal popular in the 1840s and 1850s that attributed success to the hard work and self-reliance of free laborers working in a democratic society. The free-labor ideal affirmed an egalitarian vision of human potential. Most free-labor advocates, however, did not include women and racial minorities in their vision of American individualism.

| Who benefited from America's economic growth? | What factors spurred westward expansion? | Why did the United States go to war with Mexico? | How did reform efforts change after 1840? | Conclusion: How was white freedom in the West and North defined? |

313

Nineteenth-Century School Enrollment and Literacy Rates

In the first half of the nineteenth century, school enrollment and literacy rates in northern and western Europe and the United States were high compared with those in the rest of the world. U.S. figures would be even higher but for the South, where fewer than 10 percent of black slaves were literate and whites were less likely to attend school than in the North. The ability to read and write facilitates communication, business transactions, acquisition of skills, and perhaps even greater openness to change, all building blocks of rapid economic growth. But mass literacy has not always been a prerequisite for economic development. When England underwent industrialization between 1780 and 1830, fewer than half of the nation's children attended school. By 1850, England was the world's greatest industrial power, but where did it rank in literacy? Literacy levels may actually have fallen in Lancashire, a region of England that experienced great industrial growth, as children went to work in factories rather than attend school.

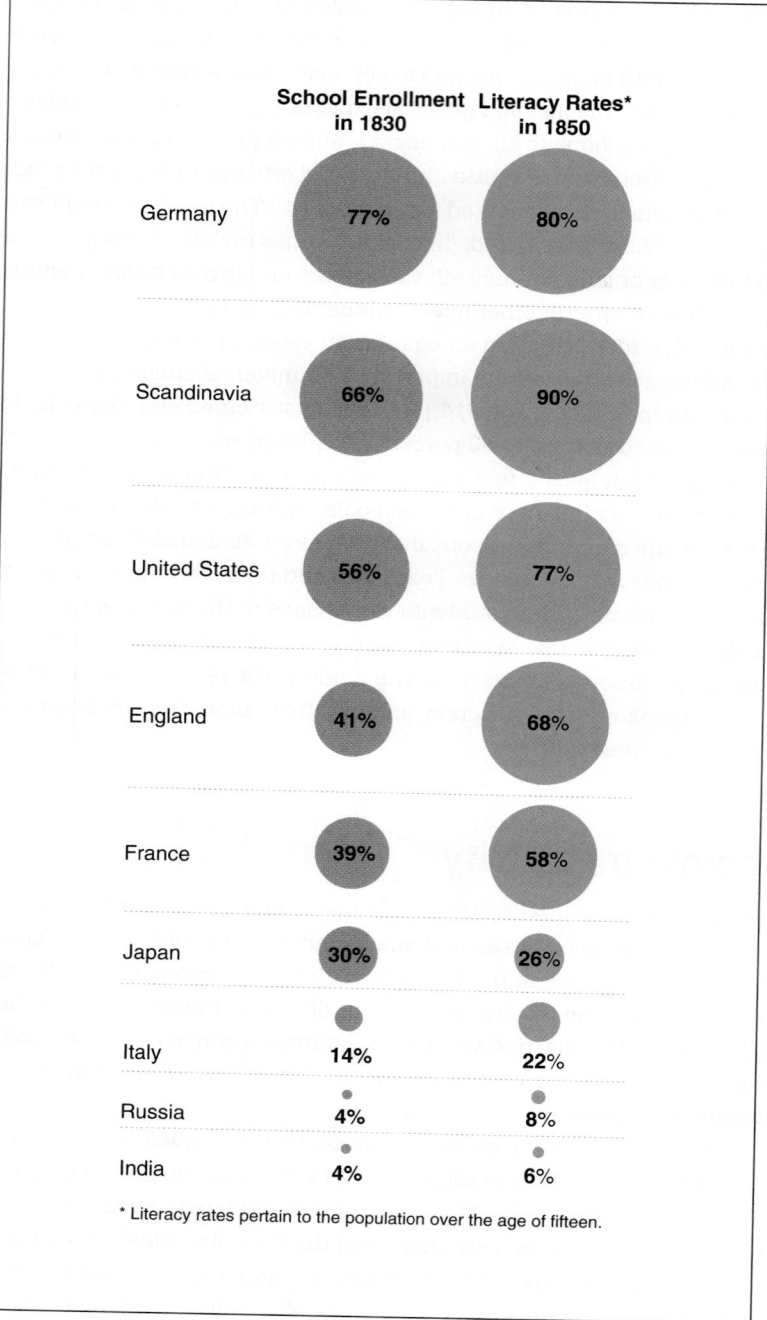

	School Enrollment in 1830	Literacy Rates* in 1850
Germany	77%	80%
Scandinavia	66%	90%
United States	56%	77%
England	41%	68%
France	39%	58%
Japan	30%	26%
Italy	14%	22%
Russia	4%	8%
India	4%	6%

* Literacy rates pertain to the population over the age of fifteen.

Immigrants and the Free-Labor Ladder

The risks and uncertainties of free labor did not deter millions of immigrants from entering the United States during the 1840s and 1850s. Almost 4.5 million immigrants arrived between 1840 and 1860, six times more than had come during the previous two decades. By 1860, foreign-born residents made up about one-eighth of the U.S. population.

CHAPTER LOCATOR

What factors contributed to America's "industrial evolution"?

Nearly three out of four immigrants who arrived in the United States between 1840 and 1860 came from Germany and Ireland. The vast majority of the 1.4 million Germans who entered during these years were skilled tradesmen and their families. German tradesmen settled mostly in the Midwest, often congregating in cities. Roughly a quarter of German immigrants were farmers, some of whom settled in Texas. On the whole, German Americans occupied the middle stratum of independent producers celebrated by free-labor spokesmen.

Irish immigrants, in contrast, entered at the bottom of the free-labor ladder and struggled to climb up. Nearly 1.7 million Irish immigrants arrived between 1840 and 1860, nearly all of them desperately poor and often weakened by hunger and disease. Potato blight struck Ireland in 1845 and returned repeatedly in subsequent years, spreading a catastrophic famine throughout the island. Many of the lucky ones crowded into the holds of ships and set out for America, where they congregated in northeastern cities. As one immigrant group declared, "All we want is to get out of Ireland; we must be better anywhere than here." Roughly three out of four Irish immigrants worked as laborers or domestic servants. Almost all Irish immigrants were Catholic, a fact that set them apart from the overwhelmingly Protestant native-born residents. Many natives regarded the Irish as hard-drinking, obstreperous, half-civilized folk. Such views lay behind the discrimination reflected in job announcements that commonly stated, "No Irish need apply."

In America's labor-poor economy, Irish laborers could earn more in one day than in several weeks in Ireland, if they could find work there. In America, one immigrant explained in 1853, there was "plenty of work and plenty of wages plenty to eat and no land lords thats enough what more does a man want." But some immigrants wanted more, especially respect and decent working conditions. One immigrant complained that he was "a slave for the Americans as the generality of the Irish . . . are."

Such testimony illustrates that the free-labor system, whether for immigrants or native-born laborers, often did not live up to its optimistic promise. Many wage laborers could not realistically aspire to become independent, self-sufficient property holders, despite the claims of free-labor proponents.

QUICK REVIEW

What values underlay the free-labor ideal?

| Who benefited from America's economic growth? | What factors spurred westward expansion? | Why did the United States go to war with Mexico? | How did reform efforts change after 1840? | Conclusion: How was white freedom in the West and North defined? |

315

What factors spurred westward expansion?

▶ FOR MORE HELP ANALYZING THIS IMAGE, see the visual activity for this chapter in the Online Study Guide at bedfordstmartins.com/roarkunderstanding.

UNTIL THE 1840s, the overwhelming majority of Americans lived east of the Mississippi River. Native Americans inhabited the plains, deserts, and rugged coasts to the west. The British claimed the Oregon Country, and the Mexican flag flew over the vast expanse of the Southwest. But by 1850, the boundaries of the United States stretched to the Pacific, and the nation had more than doubled in size. By 1860, the great migration had carried four million Americans west of the Mississippi River.

Manifest Destiny

Most Americans believed that the superiority of their institutions and white culture bestowed on them a God-given right to spread their civilization across the continent. They imagined the West as a wilderness, empty and undeveloped. If they recognized Indians and Mexicans at all, they dismissed them as mere obstacles to American progress. The West provided young men especially an arena in which to "show their manhood." Americans' belief in their own superiority had been bolstered by the United States' amazing success. Most Americans believed that the West could only be improved by the spread of their civilization.

In 1845, a New York political journal edited by John L. O'Sullivan coined the term **manifest destiny** as the latest justification for American expansionism. O'Sullivan called on Americans to resist any foreign power—British, French, or Mexican—that attempted to thwart "the fulfillment of our manifest destiny to overspread the continent allotted by Providence for the free development of our yearly multiplying millions . . . [and] for the development of the great experiment of liberty and federative self-government entrusted to us." Almost overnight, the phrase *manifest destiny* swept the nation, framing the conquest of the West as part of a divine plan.

manifest destiny
▶ Term coined in 1845 by John L. O'Sullivan to justify American expansion. O'Sullivan claimed that it was Americans' "manifest destiny" to move westward, bringing with them their values and civilization. Manifest destiny framed the American conquest of the West as part of a divine plan.

CHAPTER LOCATOR

What factors contributed to America's "industrial evolution"?

As important as national pride and racial arrogance were to manifest destiny, economic gain made up its core. Land hunger drew hundreds of thousands of average Americans westward. Some politicians, moreover, had become convinced that national prosperity depended on capturing the rich trade of the Far East. To trade with Asia, the United States needed Pacific coast ports. "The sun of civilization must shine across the sea: socially and commercially," Missouri senator Thomas Hart Benton declared. The United States and Asia must "talk together, and trade together. Commerce is a great civilizer." In the 1840s, American economic expansion came wrapped in the rhetoric of uplift and civilization.

Oregon and the Overland Trail

The Oregon Country—a vast region bounded on the west by the Pacific Ocean, on the east by the Rocky Mountains, on the south by the forty-second parallel, and on the north by Russian Alaska—was claimed by both the United States and Britain. Unable to agree which country had the stronger claim, the United States and Great Britain decided in 1818 on a "joint occupation" that would leave Oregon "free and open" to settlement by both countries. A handful of American fur traders and "mountain men" roamed the region in the 1820s.

By the late 1830s, settlers began to trickle along the **Oregon Trail** (**Map 12.2,** page 318). The first wagon trains headed west in 1841, and by 1843 about 1,000 emigrants a year set out from Independence, Missouri. By 1869, when the first transcontinental railroad was completed, approximately 350,000 migrants had traveled west to the Pacific in wagon trains.

Emigrants encountered a quarter of a million Plains Indians. Some Native Americans were farmers who lived peaceful, sedentary lives, but a majority were horse-mounted, nomadic, nonagricultural peoples whose warriors symbolized the "savage Indian" in the minds of whites.

Horse Cultures of the Great Plains

Central plains: Sioux, Cheyenne, Shoshoni, and Arapaho

Southern plains: Kiowa, Wichita, and Comanche

Horses, which had been brought to North America by Spaniards in the sixteenth century, permitted the Plains tribes to become highly mobile hunters of buffalo. They came to depend on buffalo for nearly everything—food, clothing, shelter, and fuel. Competition for buffalo led to war between the tribes. Young men were introduced to warfare early, learning to ride ponies at breakneck speed while firing off arrows and, later, rifles with astounding accuracy. "A Comanche on his feet is out of his element," observed western artist George Catlin, "but the moment he lays his hands upon his horse, his *face* even becomes handsome, and he gracefully flies away like a different being."

The Plains Indians struck fear in the hearts of whites on the wagon trains. But Native Americans had far more to fear from whites. Indians killed fewer than four hundred emigrants on the trail between 1840 and 1860, while whites brought alcohol and deadly epidemics of smallpox, measles, cholera, and scarlet fever. Moreover, whites killed the buffalo, often slaughtering them for sport. The buffalo

CHRONOLOGY

1836
- Texas declares independence from Mexico.

1841
- First wagon trains head west on Oregon Trail.

1845
- Term *manifest destiny* is coined.

1846
- Bear Flag Revolt in California.

1847
- Mormons settle in Utah.

1850
- Mormon community is annexed to United States as Utah Territory.

1851
- Conference in Laramie, Wyoming, marks the beginning of government policy of concentration for Plains Indians.

1857
- U.S. troops invade Salt Lake City in Mormon War.

Oregon Trail
▶ Route from Independence, Missouri, to Oregon traveled by American settlers starting in the late 1830s. Despite the fears of American migrants, disease and accidents caused many more deaths along the trail than did Indian attacks. By 1869, approximately 350,000 migrants had traveled west along the Oregon Trail to the Pacific in wagon trains.

| Who benefited from America's economic growth? | **What factors spurred westward expansion?** | Why did the United States go to war with Mexico? | How did reform efforts change after 1840? | Conclusion: How was white freedom in the West and North defined? |

317

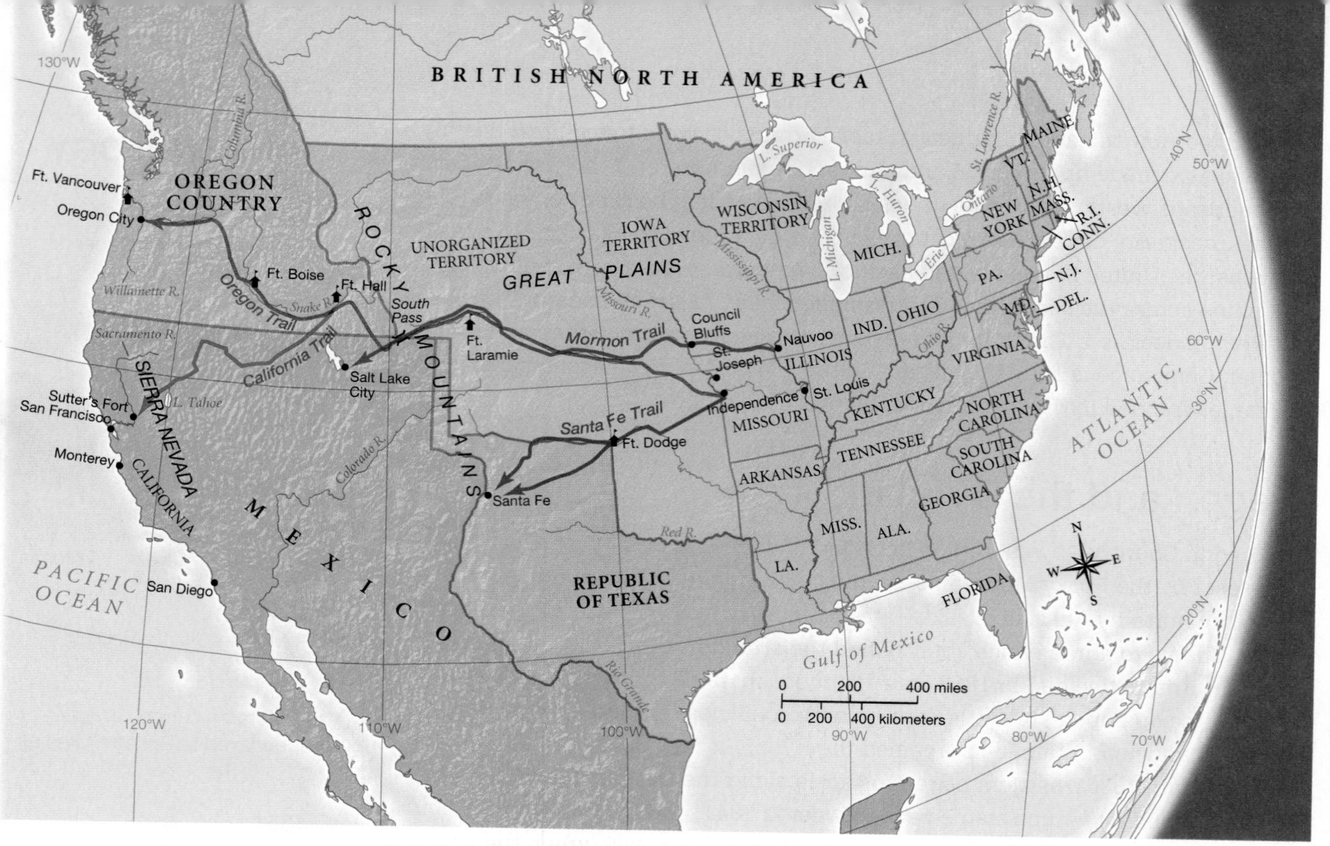

MAP 12.2 ■ Major Trails West
In the 1830s, wagon trains began snaking their way to the Southwest and the Pacific coast. Deep ruts, some of which can still be seen today, soon marked the most popular routes.

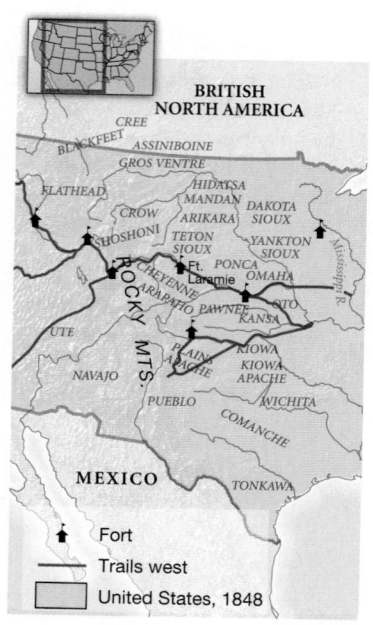

Plains Indians and Trails West in the 1840s and 1850s

still numbered some twelve million in 1860, but the herds were shrinking rapidly, intensifying conflict among the Plains tribes.

Emigrants insisted that the federal government provide them with more protection. The government constructed a chain of forts along the Oregon Trail (see Map 12.2). More important, it adopted a new Indian policy: "concentration." In 1851, the government called the Plains tribes to a conference at Fort Laramie, Wyoming. Government negotiators persuaded the chiefs to sign agreements that cleared a wide corridor for wagon trains by restricting Native Americans to specific areas that whites promised they would never violate. This policy of concentration became the seedbed for the subsequent policy of reservations. But whites would not keep out of Indian territory, and Indians would not easily give up their traditional ways of life. Struggle for control of the West meant warfare for decades to come.

Still, Indians threatened emigrants less than life on the trail did. The men, women, and children who headed west each spring could count on at least six months of grueling travel. The pioneers endured parching heat, drought, treacherous rivers, disease, physical and emotional exhaustion, and, if the snows closed the mountain passes before they got through, freezing and starvation. Such tribulations led one miserable woman, trying to keep her children dry in a rainstorm and to calm them as they listened to Indian shouts, to wonder "what had possessed my husband, anyway, that he should have thought of bringing us away out through this God forsaken country."

Men usually found Oregon "one of the greatest countries in the world." From "the Cascade mountains to the Pacific, the whole country can be cultivated," exclaimed one eager settler. When women reached Oregon, they found that

CHAPTER LOCATOR

What factors contributed to America's "industrial evolution"?

neighbors were scarce and things were in a "primitive state." Necessity blurred the traditional division between men's and women's work. "I am maid of all traids," one busy woman remarked in 1853. Work seemed unending. "I am a very old woman," declared twenty-nine-year-old Sarah Everett. "My face is thin sunken and wrinkled, my hands bony withered and hard." Another settler observed, "A woman that can not endure almost as much as a horse has no business here." Yet despite the ordeal of the trail and the difficulties of starting from scratch, emigrants kept coming.

The Mormon Exodus

Not every wagon train heading west was bound for the Pacific Slope. One remarkable group of religious emigrants halted near the Great Salt Lake in what was then Mexican territory. The Mormons deliberately chose the remote site as a refuge. After years of persecution in the East, they fled west to find religious freedom and communal security.

In 1830, Joseph Smith Jr., who was only twenty-four, published *The Book of Mormon* and founded the Church of Jesus Christ of Latter-Day Saints (the Mormons). A decade earlier, the upstate New York farm boy had begun to experience revelations that were followed, he said, by a visit from an angel who led him to golden tablets buried near his home. *The Book of Mormon*, as the tablets' text came to be known, told the story of an ancient Hebrew civilization in the New World and predicted the appearance of an American prophet who would reestablish Jesus Christ's kingdom in America. Converts, repulsed by antebellum America's social turmoil and rampant materialism, flocked to the new church.

Neighbors branded Mormons heretics and drove Smith and his followers from New York to Ohio, then to Missouri, and finally in 1839 to Nauvoo, Illinois, where they built a prosperous community. But a rift in the church developed after Smith sanctioned "plural marriage" (polygamy). Non-Mormons caught wind of the controversy and eventually arrested Smith and his brother. On June 27, 1844, a mob stormed the jail and shot both men dead.

The embattled church turned to an extraordinary new leader, Brigham Young, who oversaw a great exodus. In 1846, traveling in 3,700 wagons, 12,000 Mormons made their way to eastern Iowa, then the following year to their new home beside the Great Salt Lake. Young described the region as a barren waste, "the paradise of the lizard, the cricket and the rattlesnake." Within ten years, however, the Mormons developed an irrigation system that made the desert bloom and, under Young's stern leadership, built a thriving community.

In 1850, the Mormon kingdom was annexed to the United States as Utah Territory. The nation's attention focused on Utah in 1852 when Brigham Young announced that many Mormons practiced polygamy. Young's statement caused a popular outcry that forced the U.S. government to establish its authority in Utah. In 1857, 2,500 U.S. troops invaded Salt Lake City in a bloodless occupation that was known as the Mormon War. The invasion did not, however, dislodge the Mormon Church from its central place in Utah.

The Mexican Borderlands

In the Mexican Southwest, westward-moving Anglo-American pioneers confronted northern-moving Spanish-speaking frontiersmen, resulting in a collision of national cultures, interests, and aspirations. Independent from Spain since 1821,

Who benefited from America's economic growth? | **What factors spurred westward expansion?** | Why did the United States go to war with Mexico? | How did reform efforts change after 1840? | Conclusion: How was white freedom in the West and North defined?

319

MAP 12.3 ■ Texas and Mexico in the 1830s

As Americans spilled into lightly populated and loosely governed northern Mexico, Texas and then other Mexican provinces became contested territory.

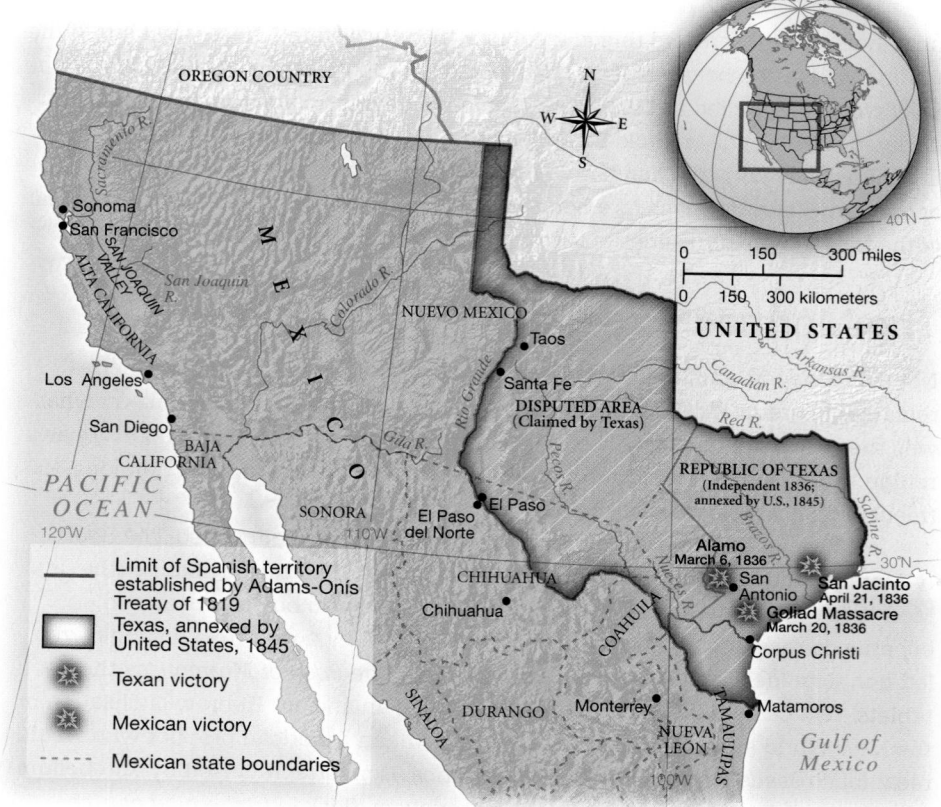

Mexico was a vast country that stretched from the Gulf of Mexico to the Pacific and from the Oregon Country to Guatemala (**Map 12.3**). But Mexico's northern provinces were sparsely populated, and the young nation found it increasingly difficult to defend its borderlands, especially when faced with a northern neighbor convinced of its superiority and bent on territorial acquisition.

The American assault began quietly. In the 1820s, Anglo-American trappers, traders, and settlers drifted into Mexico's far northern provinces. Santa Fe, a remote outpost in the province of New Mexico, became a magnet for American enterprise. Each spring, American traders gathered at Independence, Missouri, for the long trek southwest along the Santa Fe Trail (see Map 12.2, page 318). They crammed their wagons with inexpensive American manufactured goods and returned home with Mexican silver, furs, and mules.

The Mexican province of Texas attracted a flood of Americans who had settlement, not long-distance trade, on their minds (see Map 12.3). Wanting to populate and develop its northern territory, the Mexican government granted the American Stephen F. Austin a huge tract of land along the Brazos River. In the 1820s, Austin became the first Anglo-American *empresario* (colonization agent) in Texas, offering land at only ten cents an acre. Thousands of Americans poured across the border. Most were Southerners who brought cotton and slaves with them.

By the 1830s, the settlers had established a thriving plantation economy in Texas. Americans numbered 35,000, while the *Tejano* (Spanish-speaking) population was less than 8,000. Few Anglo-American settlers were Roman Catholic, spoke Spanish, or cared about assimilating into Mexican culture. Afraid of losing

Texas to the new arrivals, the Mexican government in 1830 banned further immigration to Texas from the United States and outlawed the introduction of additional slaves. The Anglo-Americans made it clear that they wanted to be rid of the "despotism of the sword and the priesthood" and to govern themselves. In Mexico City, however, General Antonio López de Santa Anna seized political power and set about restoring order to the northern frontier.

When the Texan settlers rebelled, Santa Anna ordered the Mexican army northward. In February 1836, the army arrived at the outskirts of San Antonio, where a small band of rebels had taken refuge in a former Franciscan mission known as the Alamo. Santa Anna sent wave after wave of his 2,000-man army crashing against the walls until the attackers finally broke through and killed all 187 rebels. A few weeks later, outside the small town of Goliad, Mexican forces captured a garrison of Texans and proceeded to execute almost 400 of the men as "pirates and outlaws." In April 1836, at San Jacinto, General Sam Houston's army adopted the massacre of Goliad as a battle cry and crushed Santa Anna's troops. The Texans had succeeded in establishing the Lone Star Republic, and the following year, the United States recognized the independence of Texas from Mexico.

Earlier, in 1824, in an effort to increase Mexican migration to the province of California, the Mexican government granted *ranchos*—huge estates devoted to cattle raising—to new settlers. *Rancheros* ruled over near-feudal empires worked by Indians whose condition sometimes approached that of slaves. Not satisfied, the rancheros coveted the vast lands controlled by the Franciscan missions. In 1834, they persuaded the Mexican government to confiscate the missions and make their lands available to new settlement, a development that accelerated the decline of the California Indians.

Despite the efforts of the Mexican government, California in 1840 had a population of only 7,000 Mexican settlers and 380 non-Mexican settlers. Among the non-Mexicans were Americans who championed manifest destiny and sought to woo American emigrants to California. In the 1840s, wagon after wagon left the Oregon Trail to head southwest on the California Trail, alarming Mexican officials (see Map 12.2, page 318). Many Americans hoped California would someday become part of the United States. As a New York newspaper put it in 1845, "Let the tide of emigration flow toward California and the American population will soon be sufficiently numerous to play the Texas game."

In 1846, American settlers in the Sacramento Valley took matters into their own hands. Prodded by John C. Frémont, a former army captain and explorer who had arrived with a party of sixty buckskin-clad frontiersmen spoiling for a fight, the Californians raised an independence movement known as the Bear Flag Revolt. By then, James K. Polk, a champion of aggressive expansion, sat in the White House.

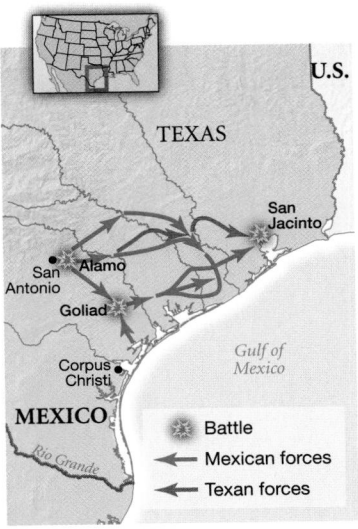

Texas War for Independence, 1836

QUICK REVIEW <

Why did westward migration expand dramatically in the mid-nineteenth century?

| Who benefited from America's economic growth? | **What factors spurred westward expansion?** | Why did the United States go to war with Mexico? | How did reform efforts change after 1840? | Conclusion: How was white freedom in the West and North defined? |

321

> Why did the United States go to war with Mexico?

Polk and Dallas Banner, 1844 In 1844, Democratic presidential nominee James K. Polk and vice presidential nominee George M. Dallas campaigned under this cotton banner. The extra star spilling over into the red and white stripes symbolizes Polk's vigorous support for annexing the huge slave republic of Texas, which had declared its independence from Mexico eight years earlier. Collection of Janice L. and David J. Frent.

ALTHOUGH EMIGRANTS acted as the advance guard of American empire, acquiring territory in the West required political action. In the 1840s, the politics of expansion became entangled with sectionalism and the slavery question. Texas, Oregon, and the Mexican borderlands thrust the United States into a dangerous diplomatic crisis with Great Britain and a full-scale war with Mexico.

The Politics of Expansion

Texans had sought admission to the Union almost since winning their independence from Mexico in 1836. But any suggestion of adding another slave state to the Union outraged most Northerners. Moreover, annexing Texas risked precipitating war, because Mexico had never relinquished its claim to its lost province.

President John Tyler, who became president in April 1841 when William Henry Harrison died one month after taking office, understood that Texas was a dangerous issue but decided to risk annexing the Lone Star Republic. In April 1844, when he laid an annexation treaty before the Senate, howls of protest erupted across the North. Future Massachusetts senator Charles Sumner deplored the "insidious" plan to annex Texas and to carve from it "great slaveholding states." The Senate soundly rejected the treaty, and it appeared that Tyler had succeeded only in inflaming sectional conflict.

The issue of Texas had not died down by the 1844 election. In an effort to appeal to northern voters, the Whig nominee for president, Henry Clay, came out against the annexation of Texas. "Annexation and war with Mexico are identical," he declared. The Democrats chose Tennessean **James K. Polk**, who was strongly in favor of annexation. To make annexation palatable to Northerners, the Democrats shrewdly yoked Texas to Oregon, thus tapping the desire for expansion in the free states of the North as well as in the slave states of the South. The Democratic platform called for the "reannexation of Texas" and the "reoccupation of Oregon," suggesting erroneously that the United States was merely reasserting

James K. Polk

► The tenth president of the United States. The Democrat Polk was elected in 1844. His support for the annexation of Texas was the key issue in the election against Whig nominee Henry Clay. Polk made the annexation of Texas more acceptable to northern voters by tying it to the acquisition of the vast Oregon territory from the British.

CHAPTER LOCATOR What factors contributed to America's "industrial evolution"?

existing rights. When Clay waffled, hinting that he might accept the annexation of Texas, his retreat succeeded only in alienating antislavery opinion in the North. In the November election, Polk received 170 electoral votes and Clay 105.

One month after the election, President Tyler announced that the triumph of the Democratic Party provided a mandate for the annexation of Texas "promptly and immediately." In February 1845, after a fierce debate between antislavery and proslavery forces, Congress approved a joint resolution offering the Republic of Texas admission to the United States. Texas entered as the fifteenth slave state.

Tyler delivered Texas, but Polk had promised Oregon, too. Westerners particularly demanded that the new president make good on the Democrats' pledge "Fifty-four Forty or Fight"—that is, all of Oregon, right up to Alaska (54°40' was the southern latitude of Russian Alaska). But Polk was close to war with Mexico and could not afford a war with Britain over U.S. claims in Canada. He renewed an old offer to divide Oregon along the forty-ninth parallel. When Britain accepted the compromise, some Americans cried betrayal, but most celebrated the agreement, which gave the nation an enormous territory peacefully. When the Senate finally approved the treaty in June 1846, the United States and Mexico were already at war.

The Mexican-American War, 1846–1848

From the day he entered the White House, Polk craved Mexico's remaining northern provinces: California and New Mexico, land that today makes up California, Nevada, Utah, most of New Mexico and Arizona, and parts of Wyoming and Colorado. Polk hoped to buy the territory, but when the Mexicans refused to sell, he concluded that military force would be needed to realize the United States' manifest destiny.

Polk had already ordered General **Zachary Taylor** to march his 4,000-man army 150 miles south from its position on the Nueces River, the southern boundary of Texas according to the Mexicans, to the banks of the Rio Grande, the boundary claimed by Texans (**Map 12.4**). The Mexicans saw the American advance as aggression, and on April 25, Mexican cavalry attacked a party of American soldiers, killing or wounding sixteen and capturing the rest. Even before news of the battle arrived in Washington, Polk had obtained his cabinet's approval of a war message.

On May 11, 1846, the president told Congress, "Mexico has passed the boundary of the United States, has invaded our territory, and shed American blood upon American soil." Thus "war exists, and, notwithstanding all our efforts to avoid it, exists by the act of Mexico herself." Congress passed a declaration of war and began raising an army. Faced with the nation's first foreign war, Polk called for volunteers. Eventually, more than 112,000 white Americans (blacks were banned) joined the army to fight in Mexico.

Despite the flood of volunteers, the war divided the nation. Northern Whigs in particular condemned the war. The Massachusetts legislature claimed that the war was being fought for the "triple object of extending slavery, of strengthening the slave power, and of obtaining control of the free states." Antislavery, antiwar Whigs kept up the attack throughout the conflict.

Polk planned a short war in which U.S. armies would occupy Mexico's northern provinces and defeat the Mexican army in a decisive battle or two, after which Mexico would sue for peace and the United States would keep the territory its

CHRONOLOGY

1841
- Vice President John Tyler becomes president when William Henry Harrison dies.

1844
- Democrat James K. Polk is elected president.

1845
- United States annexes Texas, which enters Union as slave state.

1846
- Congress declares war on Mexico.
- United States and Great Britain agree to divide Oregon Country.

1848
- Treaty of Guadalupe Hidalgo ends Mexican-American War.

1849
- California gold rush begins.

Zachary Taylor
▶ U.S. general who led the American fight in northern Mexico in the Mexican-American War (1846–1848). His aggression on the battlefield played a major role in crushing Mexico. In 1849, Taylor succeeded James K. Polk as the president of the United States.

Who benefited from America's economic growth?

What factors spurred westward expansion?

Why did the United States go to war with Mexico?

How did reform efforts change after 1840?

Conclusion: How was white freedom in the West and North defined?

323

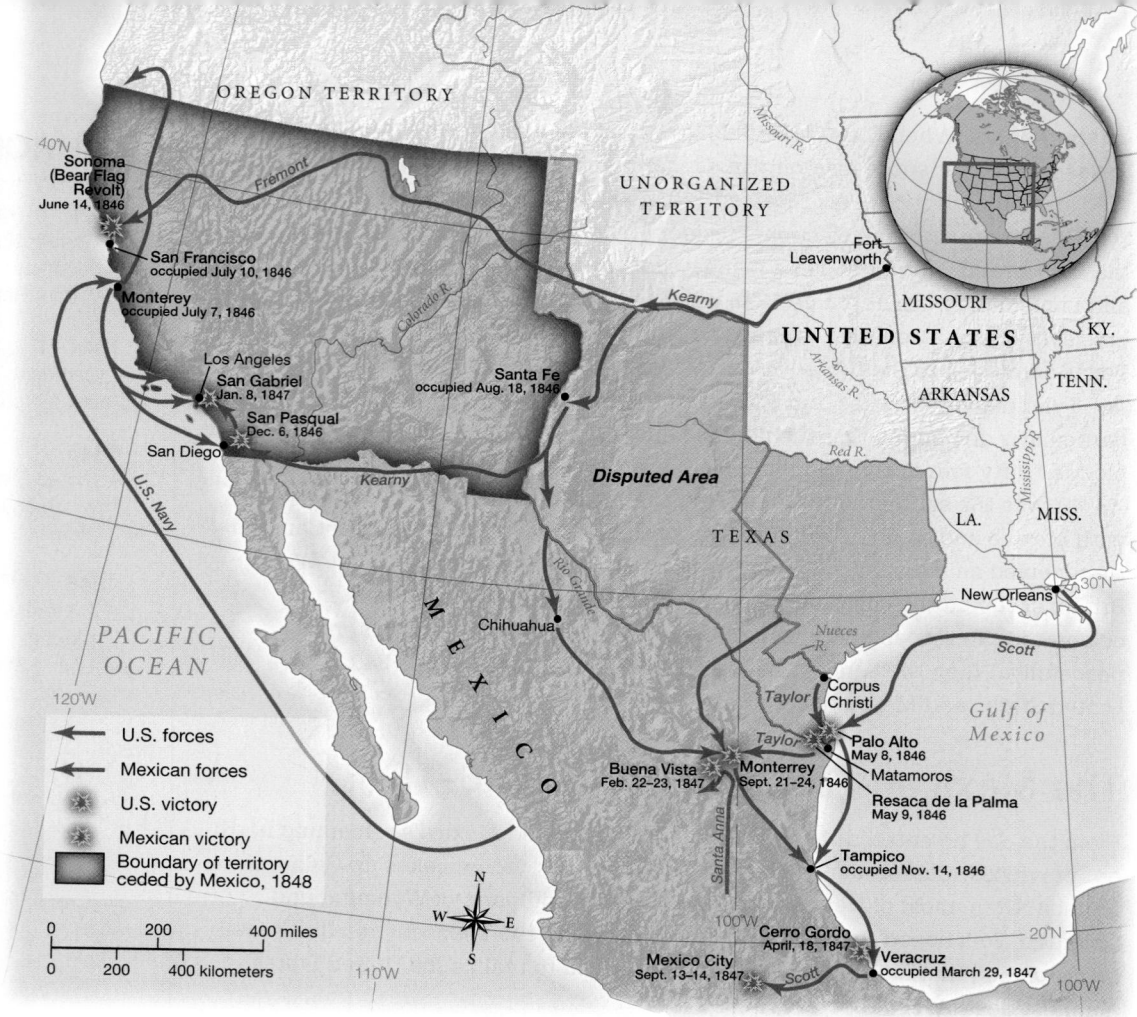

MAP 12.4 ■ The Mexican-American War, 1846–1848 American and Mexican soldiers skirmished across much of northern Mexico, but the major battles took place between the Rio Grande and Mexico City.

armies occupied. At first, Polk's strategy seemed to work. In May 1846, Zachary Taylor's troops drove south from the Rio Grande and routed the Mexican army, first at Palo Alto, then at Resaca de la Palma (see Map 12.4). Polk rewarded Taylor for his victories by making him commander of the Mexican campaign.

A second prong of the campaign centered on Colonel Stephen Watts Kearny, who led a 1,700-man army from Missouri into New Mexico. Without firing a shot, U.S. forces took Santa Fe in August 1846. Kearny then marched into San Diego three months later, encountering a major Mexican rebellion against American rule. In January 1847, after several clashes and severe losses, the U.S. forces occupied Los Angeles. California and New Mexico were in American hands.

By then, Taylor had driven deep into the interior of Mexico. In September 1846, he took the city of Monterrey. Taylor then pushed his 5,000 troops southwest, where the Mexican hero of the Alamo, General Antonio López de Santa Anna, was concentrating an army of 21,000. On February 23, 1847, Santa Anna's troops attacked Taylor at Buena Vista. The Americans suffered heavy casualties, but the Mexicans suffered even greater losses (some 3,400 dead, wounded, and missing, compared with 650 Americans). During the night, Santa Anna withdrew his battered army, much to the "profound disgust of the troops," one Mexican officer remembered. "They are filled with grief that they were going to lose the benefit of all the sacrifices that they had made; that the conquered field would be abandoned, and that the victory would be given to the enemy."

CHAPTER LOCATOR

What factors contributed to America's "industrial evolution"?

This family had its portrait taken in 1847, in the middle of the war. Mexican civilians were vulnerable to atrocities committed by the invading army. Volunteers, a large portion of the American troops, received little training and resisted discipline. The "lawless Volunteers stop at no outrage," Brigadier General William Worth declared. "Innocent blood has been basely, cowardly, and barbarously shed in cold blood."

Mexican Family, unknown, ca. 1847, Daguerreotype, Amon Carter Museum, Fort Worth, Texas.

Victory in Mexico

Although the Americans won battle after battle, President Polk's strategy misfired. Despite heavy losses on the battlefield, Mexico refused to trade land for peace. One American soldier captured the Mexican mood: "They cannot submit to be deprived of California after the loss of Texas, and nothing but the conquest of their Capital will force them to such a humiliation." Polk had arrived at the same conclusion. While Taylor occupied the north, General Winfield Scott would land an army on the Gulf coast of Mexico and march 250 miles inland to Mexico City. Polk's plan entailed enormous risk because Scott would have to cut himself off from supplies and lead his men deep into enemy country against a much larger army.

An amphibious landing on March 9, 1847, near Veracruz put some 10,000 American troops ashore, and the city surrendered two weeks later. In early April 1847, the U.S. Army moved westward. After the defeat at Buena Vista, Santa Anna had returned to Mexico City, where he rallied his troops and marched them east to set a trap for Scott in the mountain pass at Cerro Gordo. The American victory in the ensuing battle was so complete that Scott gloated to Taylor, "Mexico no longer has an army." But Santa Anna, ever resilient, again rallied the Mexican army. Some 30,000 troops took up defensive positions on the outskirts of Mexico City and began melting down church bells to cast new cannons.

In August, Scott began his assault on the Mexican capital. The fighting proved the most brutal of the war. Santa Anna backed his army into the city, fighting each step of the way. At the battle of Churubusco, the Mexicans took 4,000 casualties in a single day and the Americans more than 1,000. At the castle of Chapultepec, American troops scaled the walls and fought the Mexican defenders hand to hand. After Chapultepec, Mexico City officials persuaded Santa Anna to evacuate the city to save it from destruction, and on September 14, 1847, General Winfield Scott rode in triumphantly.

On February 2, 1848, American and Mexican officials signed the **Treaty of Guadalupe Hidalgo** in Mexico City. Mexico agreed to give up all claims to Texas

Treaty of Guadalupe Hidalgo

▶ February 1848 treaty that brought the Mexican-American War to an end. Mexico agreed to give up all claims to Texas north of the Rio Grande and to cede the provinces of New Mexico and California to the United States. The United States agreed to pay Mexico $15 million and to assume $3.25 million in claims that American citizens had against Mexico.

| Who benefited from America's economic growth? | What factors spurred westward expansion? | Why did the United States go to war with Mexico? | How did reform efforts change after 1840? | Conclusion: How was white freedom in the West and North defined? |

325

north of the Rio Grande and to cede the provinces of New Mexico and California—more than 500,000 square miles—to the United States (see Map 12.4, page 324). The United States agreed to pay Mexico $15 million and to assume $3.25 million in claims that American citizens had against Mexico.

The American triumph had enormous consequences. Less than three-quarters of a century after its founding, the United States had achieved its self-proclaimed manifest destiny to stretch from the Atlantic to the Pacific (**Map 12.5**). It would enter the industrial age with vast new natural resources and a two-ocean economy, while Mexico faced a sharply diminished economic future.

Golden California

Another consequence of the Mexican defeat was that California gold poured into American, not Mexican, pockets. In January 1848, James Marshall discovered gold in the American River in the foothills of the Sierra Nevada. Marshall's discovery set off the **California gold rush**. Between 1849 and 1852, more than 250,000 "forty-niners," as the would-be miners were known, descended on the Golden State.

California gold rush

▶ Gold rush set off by James Marshall's discovery of gold in the foothills of the Sierra Nevada in January 1848. Between 1849 and 1852, more than 250,000 "forty-niners," as the would-be miners were known, descended on California. As a result of the gold rush, California quickly attracted sufficient population to apply for statehood.

MAP 12.5 ■ Territorial Expansion by 1860

Less than a century after its founding, the United States spread from the Atlantic seaboard to the Pacific coast. War, purchase, and diplomacy had gained a continent.

▶ FOR MORE HELP ANALYZING THIS MAP, see the map activity for this chapter in the Online Study Guide at bedfordstmartins.com/roarkunderstanding.

News of the gold strike quickly spread around the world. Soon, a stream of men of various races and nationalities, all bent on getting rich, arrived in California. Only a few struck it rich. Men faced miserable living conditions, sometimes sheltering in holes and brush lean-tos. They also faced cholera and scurvy, exorbitant prices for food (eggs cost a dollar apiece), deadly encounters with claim jumpers, and endless backbreaking labor. Miners could find only temporary relief in the saloons, gambling dens, and brothels that flourished in the mining camps.

By 1853, San Francisco had grown into a raw, booming city of 50,000 that depended as much on gold as did the mining camps inland. Like all the towns that dotted the San Joaquin and Sacramento valleys, it suffered from overcrowding, fire, crime, and violence. But enterprising individuals had learned that there was money to be made tending to the needs of the miners. Hotels, saloons, restaurants, laundries, and stores of all kinds exchanged services and goods for miners' gold.

In 1851, the Committee of Vigilance determined to bring order to the city. Members pledged that "no thief, burglar, incendiary or assassin shall escape punishment, either by the quibbles of the law, the insecurity of prisons, the carelessness or corruption of the police, or a laxity of those who pretended to administer justice." Lynchings proved that the committee meant business. Gunfights declined, but many years would pass before anyone pacified San Francisco.

Establishing civic order was made more difficult by California's diversity and Anglo bigotry. The Chinese attracted special scrutiny. By 1851, 25,000 Chinese lived in California, and many Anglos were convinced that they were not fit citizens of the Golden State. As early as 1852, opponents demanded a halt to Chinese immigration. Chinese leaders in San Francisco fought back. Admitting deep cultural differences, they insisted that "in the important matters we are good men. We honor our parents; we take care of our children; we are industrious and peaceable; we trade much; we are trusted for small and large sums; we pay our debts; and are honest, and of course must tell the truth." Their protestations offered little protection, however, and racial violence persisted.

Chinese Man

This daguerreotype of an unidentified Chinese man was made by Isaac Wallace Baker, a photographer who traveled through California's mining camps in his wagon studio. One of the earliest known portraits of an Asian in California, the portrait shows a proud man boldly displaying his queue (long braid). This was almost certainly an act of defiance, for Anglos ridiculed Chinese cultural traditions, and vigilantes chased down men who wore queues. Copyright the Dorothea Lange Collection, Oakland Museum of California, City of Oakland. Gift of Paul S. Taylor.

QUICK REVIEW

What were the consequences of the U.S. victory in the war with Mexico?

| Who benefited from America's economic growth? | What factors spurred westward expansion? | Why did the United States go to war with Mexico? | How did reform efforts change after 1840? | Conclusion: How was white freedom in the West and North defined? |

327

How did reform efforts change after 1840?

Abolitionist Meeting This rare daguerreotype was made by Ezra Greenleaf Weld in August 1850 at an abolitionist meeting in Cazenovia, New York. Frederick Douglass, who had escaped from slavery in Maryland twelve years earlier, is seated on the platform next to the woman at the table. One of the nation's most brilliant and eloquent abolitionists, Douglass also supported equal rights for women. Collection of the J. Paul Getty Museum, Malibu, Calif.

WHILE MANIFEST DESTINY, the Mexican-American War, and the California gold rush transformed the nation's geography, many Americans sought personal and social reform. The emphasis on self-discipline and individual effort at the core of the free-labor ideal led Americans to believe that insufficient self-control caused the major social problems of the era. The evangelical temperament—a conviction of righteousness coupled with energy, self-discipline, and faith that the world could be improved—animated most reformers.

A few activists pointed out that certain fundamental injustices lay beyond the reach of individual self-control. Transcendentalists and utopians believed that perfection could be attained only by rejecting the competitive, individualistic

CHAPTER LOCATOR | What factors contributed to America's "industrial evolution"?

values of mainstream society. Woman's rights activists and abolitionists sought to reverse the subordination of women and to eliminate the enslavement of blacks by changing laws and social institutions as well as attitudes and customs.

The Pursuit of Perfection: Transcendentalists and Utopians

A group of New England writers who came to be known as transcendentalists believed that individuals should conform neither to the dictates of the materialistic world nor to the dogma of formal religion. Instead, people should look within themselves for truth and guidance. Ralph Waldo Emerson, the leading transcendentalist, proclaimed that the power of the solitary individual was nearly limitless. Henry David Thoreau, Margaret Fuller, and other transcendentalists agreed with Emerson that "if the single man plant himself indomitably on his instincts, and there abide, the huge world will come round to him." In many ways, the confident egoism of transcendentalism represented less an alternative to mainstream values than an exaggerated form of the rampant individualism of the age.

Unlike transcendentalists who sought to turn inward, a few reformers tried to change the world by organizing utopian communities as alternatives to prevailing social arrangements. Some communities set out to become models of perfection whose success would point the way toward a better life for everyone. During the 1840s, more than two dozen communities organized around the ideas of Charles Fourier, a French critic of contemporary society. Members of Fourierist phalanxes, as these communities were called, believed that individualism and competition were evils that denied the basic truth that "men . . . are brothers and not competitors." Phalanxes aspired to replace competition with harmonious cooperation based on the communal ownership of property. But Fourierist communities failed to realize their lofty goals, and few survived more than two or three years.

The Oneida community went beyond the Fourierist notion of communalism. John Humphrey Noyes, the charismatic leader of Oneida, believed that American society's commitment to private property made people greedy and selfish. Noyes claimed that the root of private property lay in marriage, in men's conviction that their wives were their exclusive property. Drawing from a substantial inheritance, Noyes organized the Oneida community in New York in 1848 to abolish marital property rights through the practice of what he called "complex marriage." Sexual intercourse was not restricted to married couples but was permitted between any consenting man and woman in the community. Noyes also required all members to relinquish their economic property to the community. Oneida's sexual and economic communalism attracted several hundred members, but most of their neighbors considered Oneidans adulterers, blasphemers, and worse. Yet the practices that set Oneida apart from its mainstream neighbors strengthened the community, and it survived long after the Civil War.

Woman's Rights Activists

Women participated in the many reform activities that grew out of evangelical churches. Women church members outnumbered men two to one and worked to

CHRONOLOGY

1840s
- More than two dozen communities organize around the ideas of Charles Fourier.

1843
- Henry Highland Garnet calls for slaves to rise in insurrection in "Liberty or Death."

1848
- Oneida community is organized in New York.
- First U.S. woman's rights convention takes place at Seneca Falls, New York.

1849
- Harriet Tubman escapes from slavery.

1848–1860
- Nearly two dozen other woman's rights conventions call for suffrage and an end to discrimination against women.

| Who benefited from America's economic growth? | What factors spurred westward expansion? | Why did the United States go to war with Mexico? | How did reform efforts change after 1840? | Conclusion: How was white freedom in the West and North defined? |

329

Elizabeth Cady Stanton Women's rights leader Elizabeth Cady Stanton, pictured here with two of her sons, knew firsthand the joys and frustrations of domestic life as she sought to expand women's political, moral, and social responsibilities beyond the confines of the home. Collection of Rhoda Jenkins.

Elizabeth Cady Stanton

▶ Activist and reformer who played a key role in the first national woman's rights convention in the United States at Seneca Falls, New York. Stanton and other reformers sought fair pay and expanded employment opportunities for women by appealing to free-labor ideology. While the efforts of woman's rights activists produced little tangible gain in the short run, they inspired many women to challenge the barriers that limited their opportunities.

put their religious ideas into practice by joining peace, temperance, antislavery, and other societies. Involvement in reform organizations gave a few women activists practical experience in such political arts as speaking in public, running meetings, drafting resolutions, and circulating petitions. Along with such experience came confidence. The abolitionist Lydia Maria Child pointed out in 1841 that "those who urged women to become missionaries and form tract societies . . . have changed the household utensil to a living energetic being and they have no spell to turn it into a broom again."

In 1848, about three hundred reformers led by **Elizabeth Cady Stanton** and Lucretia Mott gathered at Seneca Falls, New York, for the first national woman's rights convention in the United States. As Stanton recalled, "The general discontent I felt with women's portion as wife, mother, housekeeper, physician, and spiritual guide, [and] the wearied anxious look of the majority of women impressed me with a strong feeling that some active measure should be taken

CHAPTER LOCATOR | What factors contributed to America's "industrial evolution"?

330 CHAPTER 12 THE NEW WEST AND FREE NORTH, 1840–1860

to right the wrongs of society in general, and of women in particular." The **Seneca Falls Declaration of Sentiments** proclaimed that "the history of mankind is a history of repeated injuries and usurpations on the part of man toward woman, having in direct object the establishment of an absolute tyranny over her." In the style of the Declaration of Independence (see appendix I, page A-1), the Seneca Falls declaration demanded that women "have immediate admission to all the rights and privileges which belong to them as citizens of the United States," particularly the "inalienable right to the elective franchise."

Nearly two dozen other woman's rights conventions assembled before 1860, repeatedly calling for suffrage and an end to discrimination against women. But women had difficulty receiving a respectful hearing, much less achieving legislative action. Even so, the Seneca Falls declaration served as a pathbreaking manifesto of dissent against male supremacy and of support for woman suffrage, and it inspired many women to challenge the barriers that limited their opportunities.

Stanton and other activists sought fair pay and expanded employment opportunities for women by appealing to free-labor ideology. Woman's rights advocate Paula Wright Davis urged Americans to stop discriminating against able and enterprising women: "Let [women] . . . open a Store, . . . plant and tend an Orchard, . . . learn any of the lighter mechanical Trades, . . . study for a Profession, . . . be called to the lecture-room, [and] . . . the Temperance rostrum . . . [and] let her be appointed [to serve in the Post Office]." Some women pioneered in these and many other occupations during the 1840s and 1850s. Woman's rights activists also succeeded in protecting married women's rights to their own wages and property in New York in 1860. But discrimination against women persisted, as most men believed that free-labor ideology required no compromise of male supremacy.

Abolitionists and the American Ideal

During the 1840s and 1850s, abolitionists continued to struggle to draw the nation's attention to the plight of slaves and the need for emancipation. Former slaves **Frederick Douglass**, Henry Bibb, and Sojourner Truth lectured to reform audiences throughout the North about the cruelties of slavery. Abolitionists published newspapers, held conventions, and petitioned Congress, but they never attracted a mass following among white Americans. Many white Northerners became convinced that slavery was wrong, but they still believed that blacks were inferior. Many other white Northerners shared the common view of white Southerners that slavery was necessary and even desirable. The geographic expansion of the nation during the 1840s offered abolitionists an opportunity to link their unpopular ideal to a goal that many white Northerners found much more attractive—limiting the geographic expansion of slavery, an issue that moved to the center of national politics during the 1850s (see chapter 14).

Black leaders rose to prominence in the abolitionist movement during the 1840s and 1850s. Frederick Douglass, Henry Highland Garnet, William Wells Brown, Martin R. Delany, and others became impatient with white abolitionists' appeals to the conscience of the white majority. In 1843, Garnet urged slaves to choose "Liberty or Death" and rise in insurrection against their masters, an idea that alienated almost all white people and carried little influence among slaves.

Seneca Falls Declaration of Sentiments

▶ Declaration issued in 1848 at the first national woman's rights convention in the United States. The declaration described the history of mankind as the history of the oppression of women and demanded that women receive all the same rights and privileges of American citizenship as men. Nearly two dozen other woman's rights conventions assembled between 1848 and 1860, repeatedly calling for suffrage and an end to discrimination against women.

Frederick Douglass

▶ Former slave and a leader in the abolitionist movement. During the 1840s and 1850s, Douglass and other black abolitionists lectured to reform audiences throughout the North about the cruelties of slavery. In time, Douglass became impatient with the slow and cautious approach of white abolitionists and began to advocate a more aggressive assault on the institution of slavery.

| Who benefited from America's economic growth? | What factors spurred westward expansion? | Why did the United States go to war with Mexico? | How did reform efforts change after 1840? | Conclusion: How was white freedom in the West and North defined? |

331

To express their own uncompromising ideas, black abolitionists founded their own newspapers and held their own antislavery conventions, although they still cooperated with sympathetic whites.

The commitment of black abolitionists to battling slavery grew out of their own experiences with white supremacy. The 250,000 free African Americans in the North and West constituted less than 2 percent of the total population in 1860. Pervasive racial discrimination both handicapped and energized black abolitionists. Some cooperated with the efforts of the American Colonization Society to send freed slaves and other black Americans to Liberia in West Africa. Others sought to move to Canada, Haiti, or someplace else, convinced that, as an African American from Michigan wrote, "it is impracticable, not to say impossible, for the whites and blacks to live together, and upon terms of social and civil equality, under the same government." Most black American leaders refused to embrace emigration and worked against racial prejudice in their own communities, organizing campaigns against segregation, particularly in transportation and education.

Outside the public spotlight, free African Americans in the North and West contributed to the antislavery cause by quietly aiding fugitive slaves. **Harriet Tubman** escaped from slavery in Maryland in 1849 and repeatedly risked her freedom and her life to return to the South to escort slaves to freedom. When the opportunity arose, free blacks in the North provided fugitive slaves with food, a safe place to rest, and a helping hand. An outgrowth of the antislavery sentiment, this "underground railroad" ran mainly through black neighborhoods, black churches, and black homes.

Harriet Tubman

▶ Former slave who contributed to the antislavery cause by aiding fugitive slaves. Tubman escaped from slavery in Maryland in 1849 and repeatedly risked her freedom and her life to return to the South to escort slaves to freedom. The "underground railroad" she worked on ran mainly through black neighborhoods, black churches, and black homes.

> ## QUICK REVIEW

Why were women especially prominent in many nineteenth-century reform efforts?

National Gallery of Art, Washington, D.C.

DURING THE 1840s AND 1850s, a cluster of interrelated developments—steam power, railroads, and the growing mechanization of agriculture and manufacturing—meant greater economic productivity, a burst of output from farms and factories, and prosperity for many. Diplomacy and war handed the United States 1.2 million square miles and more than 1,000 miles of Pacific coastline. One prize of manifest destiny, California, almost immediately rewarded its new owners with tons of gold. To most Americans, new territory and vast riches were appropriate accompaniments to the nation's stunning economic progress.

To those in the West and North, industrial evolution confirmed the choice they had made to eliminate slavery and to promote free labor as the key to independence, equality, and prosperity. Like Abraham Lincoln, millions of Americans could point to their personal experiences as evidence of the practical truth of the free-labor ideal. But millions of others had different stories to tell. They knew that in the free-labor system, poverty and wealth continued to rub shoulders. By 1860, more than half of the nation's free-labor workforce still toiled for someone else. Free-labor enthusiasts denied that the problems were inherent in the country's social and economic systems. Instead, they argued, most social ills—including poverty and dependency—sprang from individual deficiencies. Consequently, many reformers focused on self-control and discipline, on avoiding sin and alcohol. Other reformers focused on woman's rights and slavery. They challenged widespread conceptions of male supremacy and black inferiority, but neither group managed to overcome the prevailing free-labor ideology based on individualism, racial prejudice, and notions of male superiority.

By midcentury, the nation was half slave and half free, and each region was animated by different economic interests, cultural values, and political aims. Not even the victory over Mexico could bridge the deepening divide between North and South.

SO NOW YOU KNOW

The United States experienced an amazing railroad boom in the first half of the nineteenth century. Railroads were at the heart of America's economic growth before the Civil War. They stimulated old industries and helped to create new ones, aided westward expansion, and connected communities across the United States to expanding national and international markets.

CHAPTER 12 STUDY GUIDE

Online Study Guide
bedfordstmartins.com/roarkunderstanding

STEP 1 GETTING STARTED

Below are basic terms from this period in American history. Can you identify each term below and explain why it matters? To do this exercise online or to download this chart, visit bedfordstmartins.com/roarkunderstanding.

TERM	WHO OR WHAT & WHEN	WHY IT MATTERS
American system, p. 310		
free-labor ideal, p. 313		
manifest destiny, p. 316		
Oregon Trail, p. 317		
James K. Polk, p. 322		
Zachary Taylor, p. 323		
Treaty of Guadalupe Hidalgo, p. 325		
California gold rush, p. 326		
Elizabeth Cady Stanton, p. 330		
Seneca Falls Declaration of Sentiments, p. 331		
Frederick Douglass, p. 331		
Harriet Tubman, p. 332		

STEP 2 MOVING BEYOND THE BASICS

The exercise below represents a more advanced understanding of the chapter material. Fill in the following chart by describing key economic developments and their contributions to industrialization. When you have finished filling in the chart, ask yourself how each development was influenced by the others. How, for example, did increases in agricultural production contribute to the growth of manufacturing? How, in turn, did new industrial processes and products aid agricultural production? To do this exercise online or to download this chart, visit bedfordstmartins.com/roarkunderstanding.

	Key developments	Consequences/who benefited
Agricultural technology		
Federal land policy		
Mechanization and energy sources		
Railroads		

Now that you've reviewed various parts of the chapter, take a step back and try to see the big picture by answering these questions. Remember to use specific examples from the chapter in your answers. To do this exercise online, visit bedfordstmartins.com/roarkunderstanding.

INDUSTRIAL DEVELOPMENT AND WESTWARD EXPANSION

▶ What were the social consequences of American industrial development in the first half of the nineteenth century?

▶ What role did American nationalism and economic opportunity play in promoting westward expansion?

THE MEXICAN-AMERICAN WAR

▶ Where was support for war with Mexico strongest? Where was there the least support? Why?

▶ How did victory in the Mexican-American War contribute to rising tensions over slavery?

REFORM

▶ What common concerns linked the reform movements of the 1840s and 1850s?

▶ What role did women play in reform movements in the decades before the Civil War?

LOOKING BACKWARD, LOOKING AHEAD

▶ How had America's economy and society changed between 1800 and 1860?

▶ How did American expansion and industrial development contribute to the sectional conflicts that culminated in the Civil War?

IN YOUR OWN WORDS

Imagine that you must explain chapter 12 to someone who hasn't read it. What would be the most important points to include and why?

13
UNDERSTANDING THE SLAVE SOUTH

1820–1860

> This chapter explores the emergence and development of a distinctive slave society in the American South. It examines the causes and consequences of the divergence of the North and the South, the social world of the slave South, and the impact of slavery on internal southern politics.

DID YOU KNOW?

By 1860, the South contained more slaves than all the other slave societies in the New World combined.

> Why and how did the South become so different from the North?

> What was plantation life like for masters and mistresses?

> What was plantation life like for slaves?

> What place did free blacks occupy in southern society?

> How did nonslaveholding southern whites work and live?

> How did slavery shape southern politics?

> Conclusion: How did slavery come to define the South?

Slave quarters. This early photograph depicts a slave family in Savannah, Georgia, ca. 1860.

Why and how did the South become so different from the North?

The steamboat *Henry Frank* sits dangerously overloaded with cotton bales at the New Orleans levee in 1854. The magnitude of the cotton trade in the South's largest city and major port is difficult to capture. Six years earlier, a visitor, Solon Robinson, had expressed awe: "It must be seen to be believed; and even then, it will require an active mind to comprehend acres of cotton bales standing upon the levee, while miles of drays [carts] are constantly taking it off to the cotton presses. . . . Boats are constantly arriving, so piled up with cotton, that the lower tier of bales on deck are in the water." Amid the mountains of cotton, few Southerners doubted that cotton was king. Historic New Orleans Collection.

> ▶ FOR MORE HELP ANALYZING THIS IMAGE, see the visual activity for this chapter in the Online Study Guide at bedfordstmartins.com/roarkunderstanding.

FROM THE EARLIEST SETTLEMENTS, inhabitants of the southern colonies had shared a great deal with northern colonists. Most whites in both sections were British and Protestant, spoke a common language, and shared pride in their victorious revolution against British rule. The creation of the new nation under the Constitution in 1789 forged political ties that bound all Americans. The beginnings of a national economy fostered economic interdependence and communication across regional boundaries. White Americans everywhere celebrated the achievements of the prosperous young nation, and they looked forward to its seemingly boundless future.

Despite these national similarities, Southerners and Northerners grew increasingly different. The French political observer Alexis de Tocqueville believed he knew why. "I could easily prove," he asserted in 1831, "that almost all the differences which may be noticed between the character of the Americans in the Southern and Northern states have originated in slavery." Slavery made the South different, and it was the differences between the North and the South, not the similarities, that increasingly shaped antebellum American history.

CHAPTER LOCATOR | Why and how did the South become so different from the North? | What was plantation life like for masters and mistresses?

Cotton Kingdom, Slave Empire

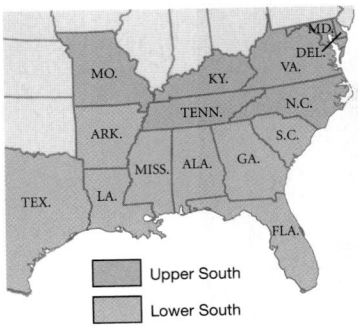

The Upper and Lower South

In the first half of the nineteenth century, millions of Americans migrated west. In the South, the stampede began after the Creek War of 1813–1814, which divested the Creek Indians of 24 million acres and initiated the government campaign to remove Indian people living east of the Mississippi River to the West (see chapters 10 and 11). Southerners—planters, small farmers, and herders and drovers—pushed westward relentlessly, until by midcentury the South encompassed nearly a million square miles. Contemporaries spoke of this vast region as the Lower South, those states where cotton was dominant, and the Upper South, where cotton was less important.

The South's climate and geography were ideally suited for the cultivation of cotton. By the 1830s, cotton fields stretched from southern Virginia to central Texas. Heavy migration led to statehood for Arkansas in 1836 and for Texas and Florida in 1845. Production soared from 300,000 bales in 1830 to nearly 5 million in 1860, when the South produced three-fourths of the world's supply. The

CHRONOLOGY

1813–1814
- Creek War opens Indian land to white settlement.

1820s–1830s
- Southern legislatures enact slave codes to strengthen slavery.
- Southern intellectuals fashion systematic defense of slavery.

1830
- Southern slaves number approximately two million.

1836
- Arkansas is admitted to Union as slave state.

1840
- Cotton accounts for more than 60 percent of American exports.

1845
- Texas and Florida are admitted to Union as slave states.

1860
- Southern slaves number nearly four million, one-third of the South's population.

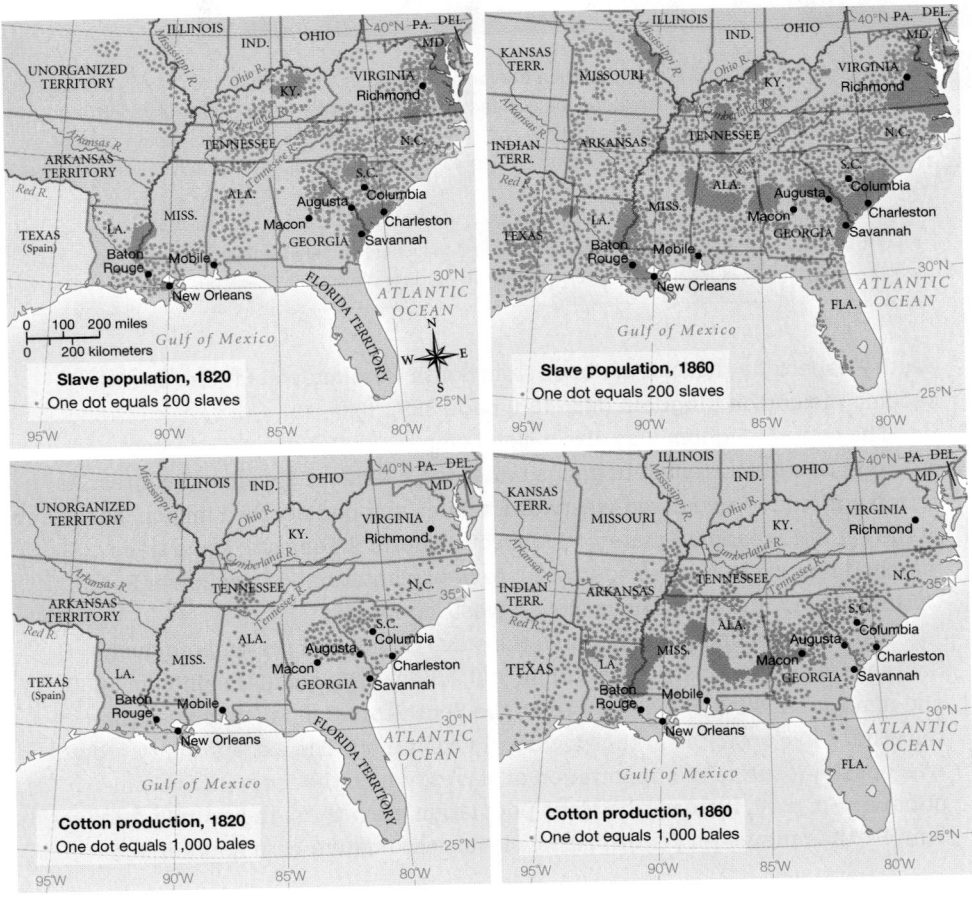

MAP 13.1 ■ Cotton Kingdom, Slave Empire: 1820 and 1860 As the production of cotton soared, the slave population increased dramatically. Slaves continued to toil in tobacco and rice fields along the Atlantic seaboard, but increasingly they worked on cotton plantations in Alabama, Mississippi, and Louisiana.

What was plantation life like for slaves? | What place did free blacks occupy in southern society? | How did nonslaveholding southern whites work and live? | How did slavery shape southern politics? | Conclusion: How did slavery come to define the South?

The Price of Blood This 1868 painting by T. S. Noble depicts a transaction between a slave trader and a rich planter. The trader nervously pretends to study the contract, while the planter waits impatiently for the completion of the sale. The planter's mulatto son, who is being sold, looks away. The children of white men and slave women were property and could be sold by the father/master. Morris Museum of Art, Augusta, Ga.

▶ FOR MORE HELP ANALYZING THIS IMAGE, see the visual activity for this chapter in the Online Study Guide at bedfordstmartins.com/roarkunderstanding.

cotton kingdom
▶ Term for the South that reflected the dominance of cotton in the southern economy. Cotton was particularly important in the tier of states from South Carolina west to Texas. The spread of cotton cultivation in the first half of the nineteenth century was the key factor in the growth of slavery.

South—especially that tier of states from South Carolina west to Texas—had become the **cotton kingdom** (**Map 13.1,** page 339).

The cotton kingdom was also a slave empire. Slaves grew 75 percent of the crop on plantations, toiling in gangs under the direct supervision of whites. As cotton agriculture expanded westward, whites shipped nearly a million slaves out of the Atlantic seaboard states. Victims of this brutal domestic slave trade marched hundreds of miles southwest to new plantations in the Lower South. Cotton, slaves, and plantations moved west together.

As cotton production expanded, the slave population grew enormously. Southern slaves numbered fewer than 700,000 in 1790, about 2 million in 1830, and almost 4 million by 1860. By 1860, the South contained more slaves than all the other slave societies in the New World combined. The extraordinary growth was not the result of the importation of slaves, which the federal government outlawed in 1808. Instead, the slave population grew through natural reproduction. By the nineteenth century, most slaves were native-born Southerners.

CHAPTER LOCATOR | Why and how did the South become so different from the North? | What was plantation life like for masters and mistresses?

340 CHAPTER 13
UNDERSTANDING THE SLAVE SOUTH, 1820–1860

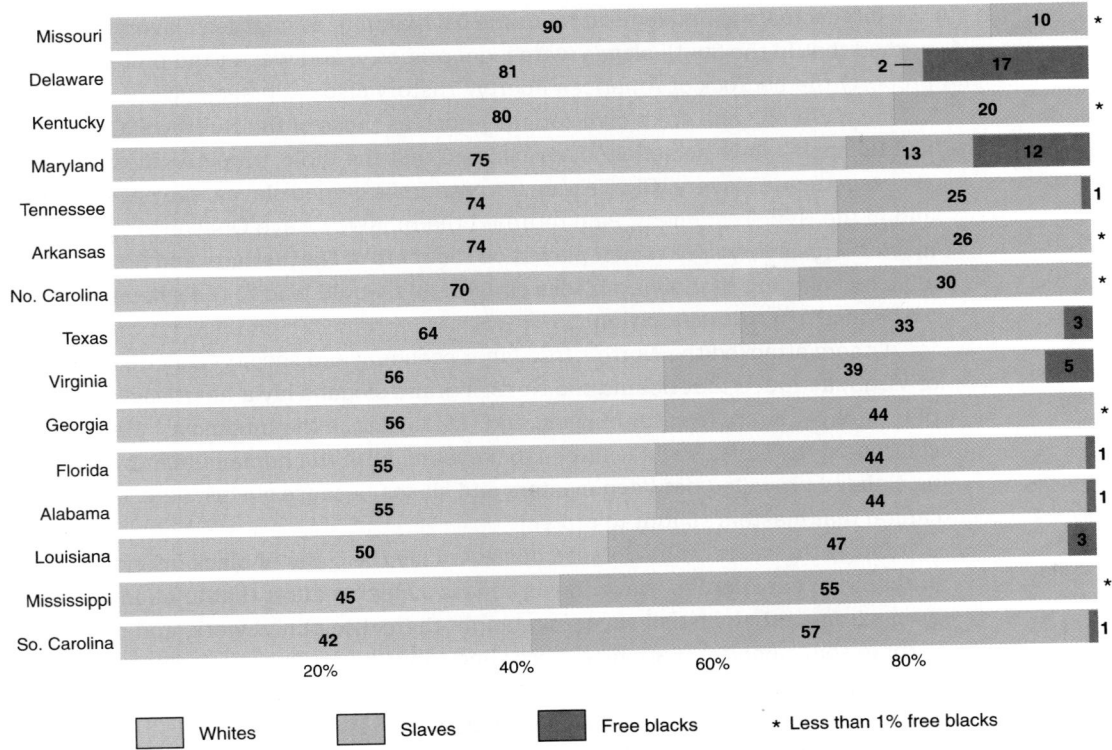

FIGURE 13.1 ■ **Black and White Population in the South, 1860**

Blacks represented a much larger fraction of the population in the South than in the North, but considerable variation existed from state to state. Only one Missourian in ten, for example, was black, while Mississippi and South Carolina had black majorities. States in the Upper South were "whiter" than states in the Lower South, despite the Upper South's greater number of free blacks.

The South in Black and White

By 1860, one in every three Southerners was black (approximately 4 million blacks and 8 million whites) **(Figure 13.1)**. The presence of large numbers of African Americans had profound consequences for the South. Southern culture—language, food, music, religion, and even accents—was in part shaped by blacks. But the most direct consequence of the South's biracialism was southern whites' commitment to white supremacy. Northern whites believed in racial superiority, too, but their dedication to white supremacy lacked the intensity and urgency increasingly felt by white Southerners who lived among millions of blacks who had every reason to hate them and to strike back.

Attacks on slavery after 1820 jolted southern slaveholders into an awareness that they lived in a dangerous world. As the only slave society embedded in an egalitarian, democratic republic, the South made extraordinary efforts to strengthen slavery. State legislatures constructed **slave codes** (laws) that required the total submission of slaves. As the Louisiana code stated, a slave "owes his master . . . a respect without bounds, and an absolute obedience." The laws also underlined the authority of all whites, not just masters. Any white could "correct" slaves who did not stay "in their place."

slave codes

▶ Laws enacted in southern states that required the total submission of slaves. Attacks by antislavery activists convinced southern legislators that they had to do everything in their power to strengthen the institution. They were joined in their efforts by intellectuals who argued that slavery was a just and beneficial practice.

| What was plantation life like for slaves? | What place did free blacks occupy in southern society? | How did nonslaveholding southern whites work and live? | How did slavery shape southern politics? | Conclusion: How did slavery come to define the South? |

Intellectuals joined legislators in the campaign to strengthen slavery. They argued that in the South slaves were legal property, and wasn't the protection of property the bedrock of American liberty? History also endorsed slavery, they claimed. Weren't the great civilizations—such as those of the Hebrews, Greeks, and Romans—slave societies? They claimed that the Bible, properly interpreted, also sanctioned slavery. Old Testament patriarchs owned slaves, they observed, and in the New Testament, Paul returned the runaway slave Onesimus to his master. Proslavery spokesmen played on the fears of Northerners and Southerners alike by charging that giving blacks equal rights would lead to the sexual mixing of the races, or **miscegenation**.

Others attacked the North's free-labor economy and society. George Fitzhugh of Virginia argued that behind the North's grand slogans lay a heartless philosophy: "Every man for himself, and the devil take the hindmost." He contrasted the North's vicious free-labor system with the humane relations that he claimed prevailed between masters and slaves because slaves were valuable capital that masters sought to protect.

But at the heart of the defense of slavery lay the claim of black inferiority. Rather than exploitative, slavery was a mass civilizing effort that lifted lowly blacks from barbarism and savagery, taught them disciplined work, and converted them to soul-saving Christianity. According to Virginian Thomas R. Dew, most slaves were grateful. He declared that "the slaves of a good master are his warmest, most constant, and most devoted friends."

Whites gradually moved away from defending slavery as a "necessary evil"—the halfhearted argument popular in Jefferson's day—and toward an aggressive defense of slavery as a "positive good." John C. Calhoun, an influential southern politician, declared that in the states where slavery had been abolished, "the condition of the African, instead of being improved, has become worse," while in the slave states, the Africans "have improved greatly in every respect."

Black slavery encouraged southern whites to unify around race rather than to divide by class. Because of racial slavery, Georgia attorney Thomas R. R. Cobb observed, every white Southerner "feels that he belongs to an elevated class. It matters not that he is no slaveholder; he is not of the inferior race; he is a free-born citizen." Consequently, the "poorest meets the richest as an equal; sits at his table with him; salutes him as a neighbor; meets him in every public assembly, and stands on the same social platform." In the South, Cobb boasted, "there is no war of classes." In reality, slavery did not create perfect harmony among whites or ease every strain along class lines. But by providing every white Southerner membership in the ruling race, slavery helped whites bridge differences in wealth, education, and culture.

The Plantation Economy

As important as slavery was in unifying white Southerners, only about a quarter of the white population lived in slaveholding families. Most slaveholders owned fewer than five slaves. Only about 12 percent of slave owners owned twenty or more, the number of slaves that historians consider necessary to distinguish a **planter** from a farmer. Nevertheless, planters dominated the southern economy. In 1860, 52 percent of the South's slaves lived and worked on plantations. Plantation slaves produced more than 75 percent of the South's export crops, the backbone of the region's economy.

miscegenation

▶ The sexual mixing of the races. Proslavery spokesmen played on the fears of whites when they suggested that giving blacks equal rights would lead to miscegenation. In reality, the power dynamics of slavery led to considerable sexual abuse of black women by their white masters.

planter

▶ A substantial landowner who tilled his estate with twenty or more slaves. Planters dominated the social and political world of the South. Their values and ideology influenced the values and ideology of all southern whites, slaveholders and nonslaveholders alike.

CHAPTER LOCATOR | Why and how did the South become so different from the North? | What was plantation life like for masters and mistresses?

342 CHAPTER 13 UNDERSTANDING THE SLAVE SOUTH, 1820–1860

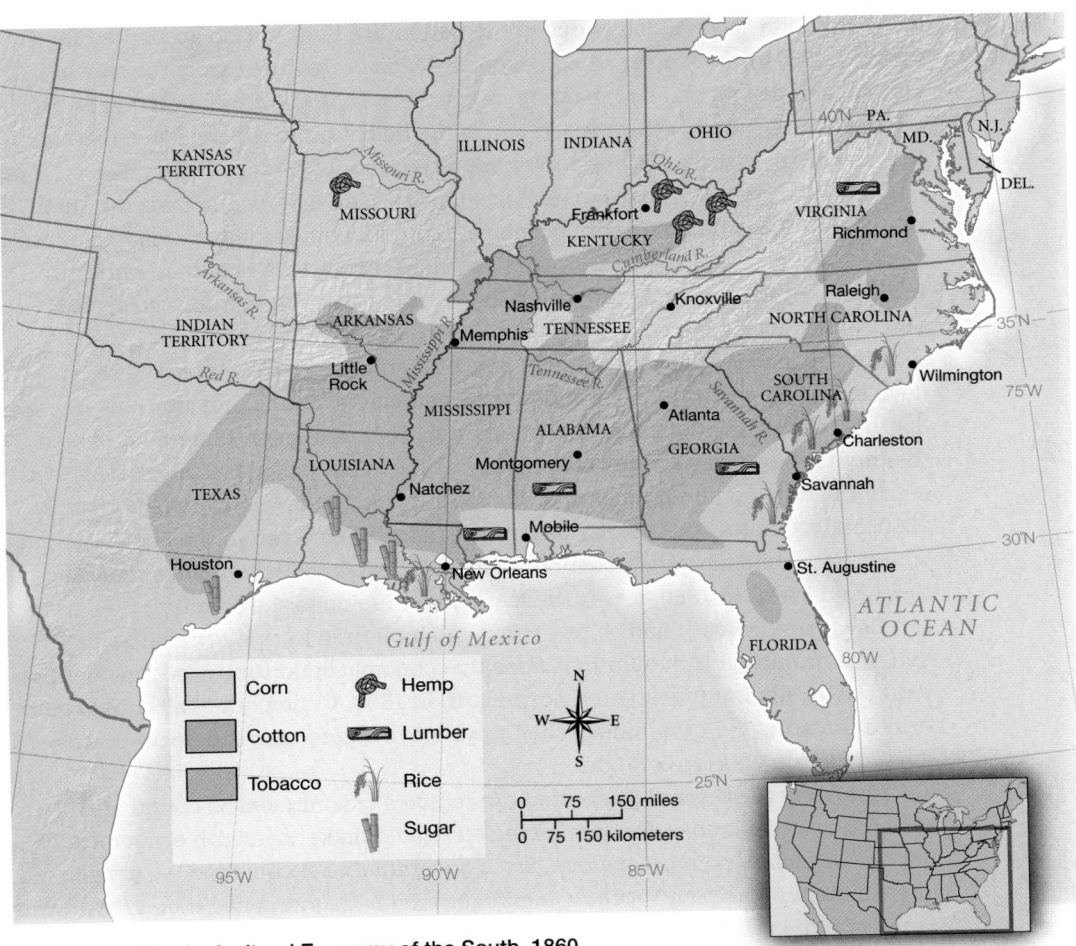

MAP 13.2 ■ The Agricultural Economy of the South, 1860
Cotton dominated the South's agricultural economy, but the region grew a variety of crops and was largely self-sufficient in foodstuffs.

> ► FOR MORE HELP ANALYZING THIS MAP, see the map activity for this chapter in the Online Study Guide at bedfordstmartins.com/roarkunderstanding.

The South's major cash crops—tobacco, sugar, rice, and cotton—grew on plantations (**Map 13.2**). Tobacco, the original plantation crop in North America, had shifted westward in the nineteenth century from the Chesapeake to Tennessee and Kentucky. Large-scale sugar production began in 1795, when Étienne de Boré built a modern sugar mill in what is today New Orleans, and sugar plantations were confined almost entirely to Louisiana. Commercial rice production began in the seventeenth century, and like sugar, rice was confined to a small geographic area, a narrow strip of coast stretching from the Carolinas into Georgia.

By the nineteenth century, cotton was king of the South's plantation crops. Cotton became commercially significant in the 1790s after the invention of a new cotton gin by Eli Whitney dramatically increased the production of raw cotton. Cotton was relatively easy to grow and took little capital to get started. Thus small farmers as well as planters grew cotton. But planters, whose fields were worked by slaves, produced three-quarters of the South's cotton, and cotton made planters rich.

What was plantation life like for slaves?	What place did free blacks occupy in southern society?	How did nonslaveholding southern whites work and live?	How did slavery shape southern politics?	Conclusion: How did slavery come to define the South?

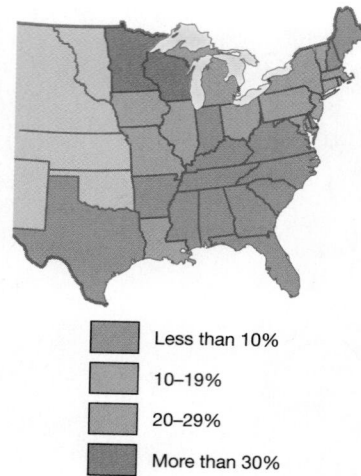

▨	Less than 10%
▨	10–19%
▨	20–29%
▨	More than 30%

Immigrants as a Percent of State Populations, 1860

Plantation slavery also enriched the nation. By 1840, cotton accounted for more than 60 percent of American exports. Much of the profit from the sale of cotton overseas returned to planters, but some went to northern middlemen who bought, sold, insured, warehoused, and shipped cotton to the mills in Great Britain and elsewhere. As one New York merchant observed, "Cotton has enriched all through whose hands it has passed." As middlemen invested their profits in the booming northern economy, industrial development received a burst of much-needed capital. Furthermore, southern plantations benefited northern industry by providing an important market for textiles, agricultural tools, and other manufactured goods.

The economies of the North and South steadily diverged. While the North developed a mixed economy—agriculture, commerce, and manufacturing—the South remained overwhelmingly agricultural. Year after year, planters funneled the profits they earned from land and slaves back into more land and slaves. With its capital flowing into agriculture, the South did not develop many factories. By 1860, only 10 percent of the nation's industrial workers lived in the South. Without significant economic diversification, the South developed fewer cities than the North and West. In 1860, it was the least urban region in the country.

Because the South had so few cities and industrial jobs, it attracted small numbers of European immigrants. Seeking economic opportunity, not competition with slaves, immigrants steered northward. In 1860, 13 percent of all Americans were born abroad. But in nine of the fifteen slave states, only 2 percent or less of the population was foreign-born.

Not every Southerner celebrated the region's commitment to cotton and slaves. Diversification, reformers promised, would make the South economically independent and more prosperous. State governments encouraged economic development by helping to create banking systems that supplied credit for a wide range of projects and by constructing railroads, but they failed to create some of the essential services modern economies required. By the mid-nineteenth century, for example, no southern legislature had created a statewide public school system.

Northerners claimed that slavery was a backward labor system, and compared with Northerners, Southerners invested less of their capital in industry, transportation, and public education. But plantations were profitable, and planters' decisions to reinvest in agriculture ensured the momentum of the plantation economy and the political and social relationships rooted in it.

> QUICK REVIEW

Why did the nineteenth-century southern economy remain primarily agricultural?

CHAPTER LOCATOR | Why and how did the South become so different from the North? | What was plantation life like for masters and mistresses?

344 CHAPTER 13
UNDERSTANDING THE SLAVE SOUTH, 1820–1860

What was plantation life like for masters and mistresses?

Southern Man with Children and Their Mammy Obviously prosperous and looking like a man accustomed to giving orders and being obeyed, this patriarch poses around 1848 with his young daughters and their nurse. Collection of the J. Paul Getty Museum, Malibu, Calif.

NOWHERE WAS THE CONTRAST between northern and southern life more vivid than on the plantations of the South. The plantation was the home of masters, mistresses, and slaves (**Figure 13.2,** page 347). Slavery shaped the lives of all the plantation's inhabitants, from work to leisure activities, but it affected each group differently. A hierarchy of rigid roles and duties governed relationships. Presiding was the master, who ruled his wife, children, and slaves, none of whom had many legal rights, and all of whom were designated by the state as dependents under his dominion and protection.

A Typical Plantation

Located on a patchwork of cleared fields and dense forests.

Included several structures:

- "Big house": The residence of the master and his family.
- Slave quarter: The cluster of cabins where slaves lived.
- Outbuildings: Scattered buildings such as storehouses, barns, and specialized buildings for crop processing.
  - Infirmary and chapel for slaves, sometimes found on large plantations.

What was plantation life like for slaves?	What place did free blacks occupy in southern society?	How did nonslaveholding southern whites work and live?	How did slavery shape southern politics?	Conclusion: How did slavery come to define the South?

KEY FACTORS

Plantation Masters
- Often characterized their roles in terms of paternalism.
- On larger plantations, hired overseers to supervise slaves in the field.
- Were increasingly interested in extending the lives of slave property.

Plantation Mistresses
- Were expected to conform to gender norms for white women.
- Lived within a system that both glorified and subordinated them.
- Lived privileged lives but also experienced discontent.

overseer
▶ Person hired by a planter to supervise the labor of slaves. The use of overseers allowed planters to concentrate on marketing, finance, and general affairs of the plantation.

paternalism
▶ The theory of slavery that emphasized reciprocal duties and obligations between planters and their slaves. Southern planters denied that slavery was brutal and exploitative; instead, they argued that they were Christian guardians who had the responsibility of caring for a childlike, dependent people.

Plantation Masters

Whereas smaller planters supervised the labor of their slaves themselves, larger planters hired **overseers** who went to the fields with the slaves, leaving the planters free to concentrate on marketing, finance, and general affairs of the plantation. Planters also found time to escape to town to discuss cotton prices, to the courthouse and legislature to debate politics, and to the woods to hunt and fish.

Increasingly, planters characterized their mastery in terms of what they called "Christian guardianship" and what historians have called **paternalism**. As owners of blacks, masters argued, they had the responsibility of caring for a childlike, dependent people. In 1814, Thomas Jefferson captured the essence of the advancing ideal: "We should endeavor, with those whom fortune has thrown on our hands, to feed & clothe them well, protect them from ill usage, require such reasonable labor only as is performed voluntarily by freemen, and be led by no repugnancies to abdicate them, and our duties to them." A South Carolina rice planter insisted, "I manage them as my children."

Paternalism was part propaganda and part self-delusion. But it was also economically shrewd. Masters increasingly recognized slaves as valuable assets. As one planter declared in 1849, "It behooves those who own them to make them last as long as possible." One consequence of this paternalism and economic self-interest was a small improvement in slaves' welfare. Diet improved, although nineteenth-century slaves still ate mainly fatty pork and cornmeal. Housing improved, although slave cabins were still small and in poor condition. Clothing improved, although slaves seldom received much more than two crude outfits a year and perhaps a pair of cheap shoes. In the fields, workdays remained sunup to sundown, but planters often provided a rest period in the heat of the day. And most owners ceased the colonial practice of punishing slaves by branding and mutilation.

Paternalism should not be mistaken for kindness and goodwill. It encouraged better treatment because it made economic sense to provide at least minimal care for valuable slaves. Nor did paternalism require that planters put aside their whips. State laws gave masters nearly "uncontrolled authority over the body" of the slave, according to one North Carolina judge. With its notion that slavery imposed on masters a burden and a duty, paternalism provided slaveholders with a means of rationalizing their rule. But it also provided some slaves with leverage in controlling the conditions of their lives. Slaves learned to manipulate the slaveholder's need to see himself as a good master. To avoid a reputation as a cruel tyrant, planters sometimes negotiated with slaves, rather than just resorting to the whip. Masters sometimes granted slaves small garden plots in which they could work for themselves after working all day in the fields, or they gave slaves a few days off and a dance when they had gathered the last of the cotton.

Virginia statesman Edmund Randolph argued that slavery created in white southern men a "quick and acute sense of personal liberty" and a "disdain for every abridgement of personal independence." Indeed, prickly individualism and aggressive independence became crucial features of the southern concept of honor. Defending honor became a male passion. Andrew Jackson's mother reportedly told her son, "Never tell a lie, nor take what is not your own, nor sue anybody for slander or assault and battery. *Always settle them cases yourself.*"

Southerners also expected an honorable gentleman to be a proper patriarch. Nowhere in America was masculine power more accentuated. Planters brooked

CHAPTER LOCATOR | Why and how did the South become so different from the North? | What was plantation life like for masters and mistresses?

CHAPTER 13
346 UNDERSTANDING THE SLAVE SOUTH, 1820–1860

no opposition from any of their dependents, black or white. The master's absolute dominion sometimes led to miscegenation. As long as slavery gave white men extraordinary power, slave women were forced to submit to the sexual appetites of the men who owned them.

In time, as the children of one elite family married the children of another, ties of blood and kinship, as well as economic interest and ideology, linked planters to one another. Conscious of what they shared as slaveholders, planters worked together to defend their common interests. The values of the big house—slavery, honor, male domination—washed over the boundaries of plantations and flooded all of southern life.

Plantation Mistresses

Like their northern counterparts, southern ladies were expected to possess the feminine virtues of piety, purity, chastity, and obedience within the context of marriage, motherhood, and domesticity. The ideal southern lady was the perfect complement to her husband, the commanding patriarch. For women, this image of the southern lady was no blessing. **Chivalry**—the South's romantic ideal of male-female relationships—glorified the lady while it subordinated her. Chivalry's underlying assumptions about the weakness of women and the protective authority of men resembled the paternalistic defense of slavery.

Indeed, the most articulate spokesmen for slavery also vigorously defended the subordination of women. George Fitzhugh insisted that "a woman, like children, has but one right and that is the right to protection. The right to protection involves the obligation to obey. A husband, a lord and master, nature designed for every woman. . . . If she be obedient she stands little danger of maltreatment." Just as the slaveholder's mastery was written into law, so too were the paramount rights of husbands. Married women lost almost all their property rights to their husbands. Women throughout the nation found divorce difficult, but southern women found it almost impossible.

Daughters of planters confronted chivalry's demands at an early age. Their education aimed at fitting them to become southern ladies. Elite women began courting at a young age and married early. Kate Carney exaggerated only slightly when she despaired in her diary: "Today, I am seventeen, getting quite old, and am not married." Yet marriage meant turning their fates over to their husbands and making enormous efforts to live up to their region's lofty ideal.

Proslavery advocates claimed that slavery freed white women from drudgery. Surrounded "by her domestics," declared Thomas R. Dew, "she ceases to be a mere beast of burden" and "becomes the cheering and animating center of the family circle." In reality, however, having servants required the plantation mistress to work long hours. She managed the big house, directly supervising as many as a dozen slaves. She assigned them tasks each morning, directed their work throughout the day, and punished them when she found fault.

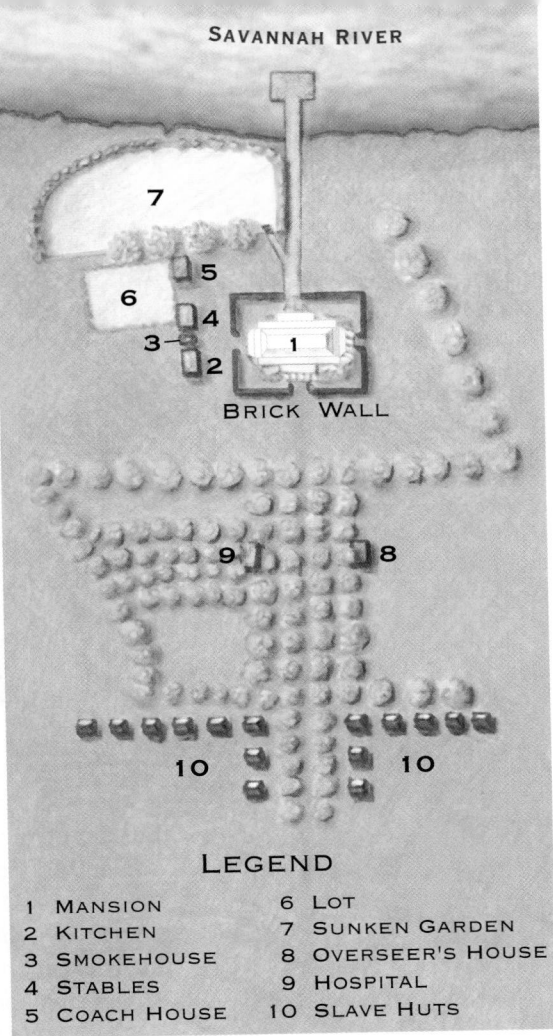

SAVANNAH RIVER

BRICK WALL

LEGEND

1	MANSION	6	LOT
2	KITCHEN	7	SUNKEN GARDEN
3	SMOKEHOUSE	8	OVERSEER'S HOUSE
4	STABLES	9	HOSPITAL
5	COACH HOUSE	10	SLAVE HUTS

FIGURE 13.2 ■ A Southern Plantation

Slavery determined how masters laid out their plantations, where they situated their "big houses" and slave quarters, and what kinds of buildings they constructed. This model of a plantation shows the overseer's house poised in a grove of oak trees halfway between the owner's mansion and the slave huts. The placement of the mansion at the end of an extended road leading up from the river underscored the owner's affluence and authority. Adapted from *Back of the Big House: The Architecture of Plantation Slavery* by John Michael Vlach. Copyright © 1993 by the University of North Carolina Press. Reprinted with permission of the University of North Carolina Press. Original illustration property of the Historical American Buildings Survey, a division of the National Park Service.

chivalry

▶ The South's romantic ideal of male-female relationships. The ideal southern lady was the perfect complement to her husband, the commanding patriarch. Chivalry's underlying assumptions about the weakness of women and the protective authority of men resembled the paternalistic defense of slavery.

What was plantation life like for slaves?	What place did free blacks occupy in southern society?	How did nonslaveholding southern whites work and live?	How did slavery shape southern politics?	Conclusion: How did slavery come to define the South?

Bird Store, New Orleans

Most elite women in the antebellum South lived isolated existences on rural plantations. But when they visited cities, they liked to shop. Here a wealthy mother and daughter shop for a pet in a New Orleans bird store. Elite white women themselves were, in a way, like birds kept in golden cages. Could it be that they were attracted to the thought of owning birds of their own, something they could care for, train, and control? Historic New Orleans Collection.

Whereas masters used their status as slaveholders as a springboard into public affairs, mistresses' lives were circumscribed by the plantation. Masters left the plantation when they pleased, but mistresses needed chaperones to travel. Women spent most days at home, where they often became lonely. In 1853, Mary Kendall wrote how much she enjoyed her sister's letter: "For about three weeks I did not have the pleasure of seeing one white female face, there being no white family except our own upon the plantation."

As members of slaveholding families, mistresses lived privileged lives. But they also had significant grounds for discontent. No feature of plantation life generated more anguish among mistresses than miscegenation. Mary Boykin Chesnut of Camden, South Carolina, confided in her diary, "Ours is a monstrous system, a wrong and iniquity. Like the patriarchs of old, our men live all in one house with their wives and their concubines; and the mulattos one sees in every family partly resemble the white children. Any lady is ready to tell you who is the father of all the mulatto children in everybody's household but her own. Those, she seems to think drop from the clouds."

Most planters' wives, including Chesnut, accepted slavery. After all, the mistress's world rested on slave labor, just as the master's did. By acknowledging the realities of male power, mistresses enjoyed the rewards of their class and race. But these rewards came at a price. Still, the heaviest burdens of slavery fell not on those who lived in the big house, but on those who toiled to support them.

> QUICK REVIEW

Why did the ideology of paternalism gain currency among planters in the nineteenth century?

CHAPTER LOCATOR | Why and how did the South become so different from the North? | What was plantation life like for masters and mistresses?

348 CHAPTER 13 UNDERSTANDING THE SLAVE SOUTH, 1820–1860

What was plantation life like for slaves?

Slave Quarter, South Carolina

On large plantations, several score of African Americans lived in cabins that were often arranged along what slaves called "the street." The dwellings in this picture were better built than the typical rickety, one-room, dirt-floored slave cabin. During the daylight hours of the workweek, when most men and women labored in the fields, the quarter was mostly empty. At night and on Sundays, it was a busy place. Collection of the New-York Historical Society.

ON MOST PLANTATIONS, only a few hundred yards separated the big house and the slave quarter. There, slaves drew together and built lives of their own. They created families, worshipped God, and developed an African American community and culture. Individually and collectively, slaves found subtle and not so subtle ways to resist their bondage.

Despite the rise of plantations, a substantial minority of slaves lived and worked elsewhere. Most labored on small farms. But by 1860, almost half a million slaves (one in eight) did not work in agriculture at all. Some were employed in towns and cities as domestics, day laborers, bakers, barbers, tailors, and more. Others, far from urban centers, toiled as fishermen, lumbermen, and railroad workers. Slaves could also be found in most of the South's factories. Nevertheless, a majority of slaves (52 percent) counted plantations as their workplaces and homes.

Work

Ex-slave Albert Todd recalled, "Work was a religion that we were taught." Whites enslaved blacks for their labor, and all slaves who were capable of productive labor worked. Former slave Carrie Hudson recalled that children who were "knee high to a duck" were sent to the fields to carry water to thirsty workers or to protect ripening crops from hungry birds. Others helped in the slave nursery, caring for children even younger than themselves, or in the big house, where they swept

| What was plantation life like for slaves? | What place did free blacks occupy in southern society? | How did nonslaveholding southern whites work and live? | How did slavery shape southern politics? | Conclusion: How did slavery come to define the South? |

349

1822
- Denmark Vesey, a free black man in Charleston, South Carolina, is accused of planning a slave revolt.

1831
- Nat Turner's rebellion in Virginia.

In 1860:
- One in eight slaves does not work in agriculture.
- The majority of slaves (52 percent) live on plantations.
- An overwhelming majority of plantation slaves work as field hands.
- One in ten slaves is a house servant.

slave driver

▶ Slave who was a kind of foreman whose primary task was driving other slaves to work harder in the fields. Probably no more than one male slave in a hundred worked in this capacity. Some drivers were harsh, but others showed restraint when they could.

floors or shooed flies in the dining room. When slave boys and girls reached the age of eleven or twelve, masters sent most of them to the fields, where they learned farmwork by laboring alongside their parents. After a lifetime of labor, old women left the fields to care for the small children and spin yarn, and old men moved on to mind livestock and clean stables.

The overwhelming majority of plantation slaves worked as field hands. Planters sometimes assigned men and women to separate gangs, the women working at lighter tasks and the men doing the heavy work of clearing and breaking the land. But women also did heavy work. "I had to work hard," Nancy Boudry remembered, and "plow and go and split wood just like a man." The backbreaking labor and the monotonous routines caused one ex-slave to observe that the "history of one day is the history of every day."

A few slaves (about one in ten) became house servants. Nearly all of those (nine out of ten) were women. House servants enjoyed somewhat less physically demanding work than field hands, but they were constantly on call, with no time that was entirely their own. Since no servant could please constantly, most bore the brunt of white frustration and rage. Ex-slave Jacob Branch of Texas remembered, "My poor mama! Every washday old Missy give her a beating."

Even rarer than house servants were skilled artisans. In the cotton South, no more than one slave in twenty (almost all men) worked in a skilled trade. Most were carpenters or blacksmiths. Slave craftsmen took pride in their skills and often exhibited the independence of spirit that caused slaveholder James H. Hammond of South Carolina to declare in disgust that when a slave became a skilled artisan, "he is more than half freed." Skilled slave fathers took pride in teaching their crafts to their sons. "My pappy was one of the black smiths and worked in the shop," John Mathews remembered. "I had to help my pappy in the shop when I was a child and I learnt how to beat out the iron and make wagon tires, and make plows."

Rarest of all slave occupations was that of **slave driver**. Probably no more than one male slave in a hundred worked in this capacity. Their primary task was driving other slaves to work harder in the fields. In some drivers' hands, the whip never rested. Ex-slave Jane Johnson of South Carolina called her driver the "meanest man, white or black, I ever see." But other drivers showed all the

Isaac Jefferson

In this 1845 daguerreotype, seventy-year-old Isaac Jefferson proudly poses in the apron he wore while practicing his crafts as a tinsmith and nail maker. Slaves of Thomas Jefferson, he, his wife, and their two children were deeded to Jefferson's daughter Mary when she married in 1797. Isaac worked at Jefferson's home, Monticello, until 1820, when he moved to Petersburg, Virginia. Special Collections Department, University of Virginia Library.

CHAPTER LOCATOR | Why and how did the South become so different from the North? | What was plantation life like for masters and mistresses?

350 CHAPTER 13 UNDERSTANDING THE SLAVE SOUTH, 1820–1860

restraint they could. "Ole Gabe didn't like that whippin' business," West Turner of Virginia remembered. "When Marsa was there, he would lay it on 'cause he had to. But when old Marsa wasn't lookin', he never would beat them slaves."

Normally, slaves worked from what they called "can to can't," from "can see" in the morning to "can't see" at night. Even with a break at noon for a meal and rest, it made for a long day. For slaves, Lewis Young recalled, "work, work, work, 'twas all they do."

Family, Religion, and Community

From dawn to dusk, slaves worked for the master, but at night, when the labor was done, and all day Sunday and usually Saturday afternoon, slaves were left largely to themselves. They used this limited time to develop and enjoy what mattered most: family, religion, and community. One of the most important consequences of slaves' limited autonomy was the preservation of the family. No laws recognized slave marriage, and therefore no master or slave was legally obligated to honor the bond. Nevertheless, plantation records show that slave marriages were often long-lasting. The primary cause of the ending of slave marriages was death, just as it was in white families. But the second most frequent cause was the sale of the husband or wife, something no white family ever had to fear.

In 1858, a South Carolina slave named Abream Scriven wrote a letter to his wife, who lived on a neighboring plantation. "My dear wife," he began, "I take the pleasure of writing you . . . with much regret to inform you I am Sold to man by the name of Peterson, a Treader and Stays in New Orleans." Scriven promised to send some things when he got to his new home in Louisiana, but he admitted that he was not sure how he would "get them to you and my children." He asked his wife to "give my love to my father and mother and tell them good Bye for me. And if we do not meet in this world I hope to meet in heaven. . . . My dear wife for you and my children my pen cannot express the griffe I feel to be parted from you all." He closed with words no master would have permitted in a slave's marriage vows: "I remain your truly husband until Death." The letter makes clear Scriven's love for his family; it also demonstrates slavery's massive assault on family life in the quarter.

Religion also provided slaves with a refuge and a reason for living. Evangelical Baptists and Methodists had great success in converting slaves from their African beliefs. By the mid-nineteenth century, perhaps as many as one-quarter of all slaves claimed church membership, and many of the rest would not have objected to being called Christians. Planters promoted Christianity in the quarter because they believed that the slaves' salvation was part of their obligation and that religion made slaves more obedient. But slaves had little use for the religion offered them by their masters. "That old white preacher just was telling us slaves to be good to our masters," one ex-slave said with a chuckle. "We ain't cared a bit about that stuff he was telling us 'cause we wanted to sing, pray, and serve God in our own way."

Meeting in their cabins or secretly in the woods, slaves created an African American Christianity that served their needs, not the masters'. Laws prohibited teaching slaves to read, but a few could read enough to struggle with the Bible. They interpreted the Christian message themselves. Rather than obedience, their faith emphasized justice. Slaves believed that the injustices of this world would

| What was plantation life like for slaves? | What place did free blacks occupy in southern society? | How did nonslaveholding southern whites work and live? | How did slavery shape southern politics? | Conclusion: How did slavery come to define the South? |

351

be settled in the next. "The idea of a revolution in the conditions of the whites and blacks is the corner-stone" of the slaves' religion, recalled one ex-slave. But the slaves' faith also spoke to their experiences in this world. In the Old Testament, they discovered Moses, who delivered his people from slavery, and in the New Testament, they found Jesus, who offered a message of equality and of salvation to all.

Christianity did not entirely drive out traditional African beliefs. Even slaves who were Christians sometimes continued to believe that conjurers, witches, and spirits possessed the power to injure and protect. Moreover, slaves' Christian music, preaching, and rituals reflected the influence of Africa, as did many of their secular activities, such as wood carving, quilt making, and storytelling. But by the mid-nineteenth century, black Christianity had assumed a central place in slaves' quest for freedom. In the words of one spiritual, "O my Lord delivered Daniel / O why not deliver me too?"

Resistance and Rebellion

Slaves did not suffer slavery passively. They were, as whites said, "troublesome property." Slaves understood that accommodation to what they could not change was the price of survival, but in a hundred ways, they protested their bondage. Theoretically, the master was all-powerful and the slave powerless. But sustained by their families, religion, and community, slaves engaged in day-to-day resistance against their enslavers.

The spectrum of slave resistance ranged from mild to extreme. Protest in the fields included putting rocks in their cotton bags before having them weighed and feigning illness. Slaves broke so many hoes that owners outfitted the tools with oversized handles. Slaves so mistreated the work animals that masters switched from horses to mules, which could absorb more abuse. Although slaves worked hard in the master's fields, they also sabotaged his interests.

Running away was a common form of protest. Except along the borders with northern states and with Mexico, escape to freedom was almost impossible. Most runaways could hope to escape only for a few days. Seeking temporary respite from hard labor or avoiding punishment, they usually stayed close to their plantations, keeping to the deep woods or swamps and slipping back into the quarter at night to get food.

Although resistance was common, outright rebellion—a violent assault on slavery by large numbers of slaves—was very rare. The scarcity of revolts in the South reflected the fact that conditions gave rebels almost no chance of success. By 1860, whites in the South outnumbered blacks two to one and were heavily armed. Moreover, communication between plantations was difficult, and the South provided little protective wilderness into which rebels could retreat and defend themselves.

Nat Turner

▶ Leader of an 1831 slave uprising in Virginia. Turner and his followers killed fifty-seven whites before the rebellion was suppressed. The ferocity of the white counterattack that put down the uprising illustrates the futility of slave revolts and helps explain their rarity.

Nat Turner's rebellion illustrates the inevitable consequences of even the most ferocious uprising. **Nat Turner** was born a slave in Southampton County, Virginia. In the early morning of August 22, 1831, Turner set out with six trusted friends to punish slave owners. The rebels killed all of the white men, women, and children they encountered. By noon, they had visited eleven farms and slaughtered fifty-seven whites. Along the way, they had added fifty or sixty men to their army. Word spread quickly, and soon the militia and hundreds of local

CHAPTER LOCATOR | Why and how did the South become so different from the North? | What was plantation life like for masters and mistresses?

352 CHAPTER 13
UNDERSTANDING THE SLAVE SOUTH, 1820–1860

whites gathered. By the next day, whites had captured or killed all of the rebels except Turner, who hid out for about ten weeks before being captured in nearby woods. Within a week, he was tried, convicted, and executed. By then, forty-five slaves had stood trial, twenty had been convicted and hanged, and another ten had been banished from Virginia. Frenzied whites had killed another hundred or more blacks—insurgents and innocent bystanders—in their counterattack against the rebellion.

Despite the rarity of slave revolts, whites believed that they were surrounded by conspiracies to rebel. In 1822, whites in Charleston accused **Denmark Vesey**, a free black carpenter, of conspiring with plantation slaves to slaughter Charleston's white inhabitants. The authorities rounded up scores of suspects, who, prodded by torture and the threat of death, implicated others in the plot "to riot in blood, outrage, and rapine." Although the city fathers never found any weapons and Vesey and most of the accused steadfastly denied the charges of conspiracy, officials hanged thirty-five black men, including Vesey, and banished another thirty-seven blacks from the state.

Despite steady resistance and occasional rebellion, slaves did not have the power to end their bondage. Nonetheless, slaves fought back physically, cultur- ally, and spiritually. They not only survived bondage but also created a vibrant African American culture that buoyed them up during long hours in the fields and brought them joy and hope in the few hours they had to themselves.

Denmark Vesey

▶ A free black carpenter who, in 1822, was accused of planning a slave uprising in Charleston, South Carolina. Although no weapons were found and Vesey and most of the accused denied the charges, thirty-five black men were hanged, including Vesey, and another thirty-seven blacks were banished from the state. The event illustrates the deep fear southern whites had of slave conspiracies.

QUICK REVIEW

What types of resistance did slaves participate in, and why did slave resistance rarely take the form of rebellion?

| What was plantation life like for slaves? | What place did free blacks occupy in southern society? | How did nonslaveholding southern whites work and live? | How did slavery shape southern politics? | Conclusion: How did slavery come to define the South? |

353

> What place did free blacks occupy in southern society?

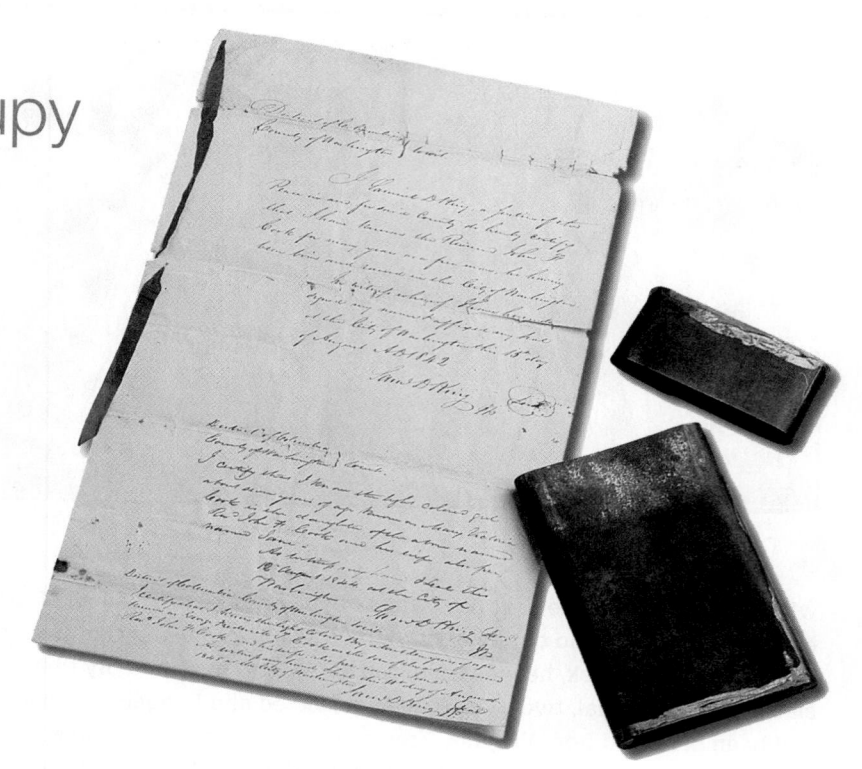

Freedom Paper

This legal document attests to the free status of the Reverend John F. Cook of Washington, D.C., his daughter Mary, and his son George. Cook was a free black man who kept his "freedom paper" in this watertight tin, which he probably carried with him at all times. Free blacks had to be prepared to prove their free status anytime a white man challenged them, for southern law presumed that a black person was a slave unless he or she could prove otherwise. Moorland-Spingarn Research Center, Howard University, Washington, D.C.

NOT EVERY BLACK SOUTHERNER was a slave. In 1860, some 260,000 (approximately 6 percent) of the region's 4.1 million African Americans were free (see Figure 13.1, page 341). What is surprising is not that their numbers were small but that they existed at all. According to the emerging racial thinking, blacks were supposed to be slaves. Blacks who were free stood out, and whites made them more and more the targets of oppression. Free blacks stood precariously between slavery and full freedom, on what a free black artisan in Charleston characterized in 1848 as "a middle ground." But they made the most of their freedom, and a few found success despite the restrictions placed on them by white Southerners.

Precarious Freedom

The population of free blacks swelled after the Revolution, when the natural rights philosophy of the Declaration of Independence and the egalitarian message of evangelical Protestantism joined to challenge slavery. A brief flurry of **emancipation**—the act of freeing from slavery—visited the Upper South, where the ideological assault on slavery coincided with a deep depression in the tobacco economy. By 1810, free blacks in the South numbered more than 100,000.

In the 1820s and 1830s, state legislatures acted to stem the growth of the free black population and to shrink the liberty of those blacks who had gained their freedom. Laws denied masters the right to free their slaves. Other laws humiliated and restricted free blacks, increasingly subjecting free blacks to the same laws as slaves. They could not testify under oath in a court of law or serve on

emancipation

▶ The act of freeing slaves. Emancipation occurred in significant numbers in the Upper South after the American Revolution, and by 1810 there were more than 100,000 free blacks in the South.

CHAPTER LOCATOR | Why and how did the South become so different from the North? | What was plantation life like for masters and mistresses?

354 CHAPTER 13
UNDERSTANDING THE SLAVE SOUTH, 1820–1860

juries. Like slaves, they were liable to whipping. Free blacks were forbidden to strike whites, even to defend themselves. "Free negroes belong to a degraded caste of society," a South Carolina judge said in 1848. "They are in no respect on a perfect equality with the white man. . . . They ought, by law, to be compelled to demean themselves as inferiors."

Limits on Free Blacks

Subjected to special taxes.
Prohibited from interstate travel.
Denied the right to have schools.
Denied the right to participate in politics.
Required to carry "freedom papers" to prove they were not slaves.

Laws confined most free African Americans to a constricted life of poverty and dependence. Typically, free blacks were rural, uneducated, unskilled agricultural laborers and domestic servants. Opportunities of all kinds—for work, education, or community—were slim.

Achievement despite Restrictions

Despite increasingly harsh laws and stepped-up persecution, free African Americans made the most of the advantages their status offered. Unlike slaves, free blacks could legally marry. They could protect their families from arbitrary disruption and pass on their heritage of freedom to their children. Freedom also meant that they could choose occupations and own property. For most, however, these economic rights proved only theoretical, for a majority of the South's free blacks remained propertyless.

Still, some free blacks escaped the poverty and degradation whites thrust on them. Particularly in the cities of Charleston, Savannah, Mobile, and New Orleans, a small elite of free blacks emerged. Urban whites enforced restrictive laws only sporadically, allowing free blacks room to maneuver. The free black elite, which consisted overwhelmingly of light-skinned African Americans who worked at skilled trades, operated schools for their children and traveled in and out of their states, despite laws forbidding both activities. They worshipped with whites (in separate seating) in the finest churches and lived scattered about in white neighborhoods, not in ghettos. And like elite whites, some owned slaves.

Most free blacks neither became slaveholders nor sought to raise a slave rebellion, as whites accused Denmark Vesey of doing. Rather, most free blacks simply tried to preserve their freedom, which was under increasing attack. Unlike blacks in the North whose freedom was secure, free blacks in the South clung to a precarious freedom by seeking to impress whites with their reliability, economic contributions, and good behavior.

CHRONOLOGY

1810
– More than 100,000 free blacks are living in the South.

1820s–1830s
– Southern state legislatures pass laws to limit the number of free blacks and the rights accorded to them.

1860
– 260,000 (6 percent of total) southern blacks are free.

QUICK REVIEW

In what ways did the South's free black population stand on a "middle ground"?

| What was plantation life like for slaves? | What place did free blacks occupy in southern society? | How did nonslaveholding southern whites work and live? | How did slavery shape southern politics? | Conclusion: How did slavery come to define the South? |

355

How did nonslaveholding southern whites work and live?

Gathering Corn in Virginia

In this romanticized agricultural scene, painter Felix O. C. Darley depicts members of a white farm family gathering its harvest by hand. In reality, growing corn was hard work. The artist, however, is less concerned with realism than with extolling rural family labor as virtuous and noble. Darley surrounds the southern yeomen with an aura of republican independence, dignity, and freedom. Warner Collection of Gulf States Paper Corporation.

MOST WHITES IN THE SOUTH did not own slaves. In 1860, more than six million of the South's eight million whites lived in slaveless households. Some slaveless whites lived in cities and worked as artisans, mechanics, and traders. Others lived in the country and worked as storekeepers, parsons, and schoolteachers. But most "plain folk" were small farmers. Perhaps three out of four were **yeomen**, small farmers who owned their own land. In an important sense, the South had more than one white yeomanry. The huge southern landscape provided space enough for two yeoman societies, separated roughly along geographic lines: plantation belt yeomen and upcountry yeomen. And some rural slaveless whites were not yeomen; they owned no land at all and were sometimes desperately poor.

yeomen

▶ Small farmers who owned their own land. Perhaps three out of four nonslaveholding southern farmers were yeomen. The South contained two distinct yeoman societies, separated roughly along geographic lines: plantation belt yeomen and upcountry yeomen. Planters took great pains to win the loyalty and support of the region's yeomen.

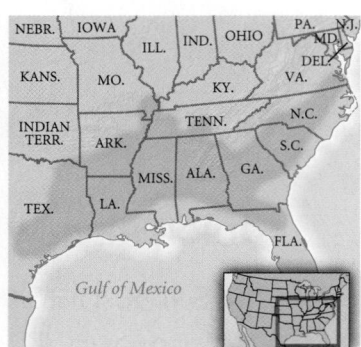

The Cotton Belt

Plantation Belt Yeomen

Plantation belt yeomen lived within the orbit of the planter class. Small farmers grew mainly food crops, particularly corn, but they also devoted a portion of their land to cotton. The small farmers' cotton tied them to planters. Unable to afford cotton gins or baling presses of their own, they relied on slave owners to gin and bale their cotton. With no link to merchants in the port cities, plantation belt yeomen also turned to better-connected planters to ship and sell their cotton. A network of relationships laced small farmers and planters together. Planters hired out surplus slaves to ambitious yeomen who wanted to expand cotton production. They sometimes chose overseers from among the sons of local farm families. Plantation mistresses occasionally nursed ailing neighbors. Male yeomen helped police slaves by riding in slave patrols, which nightly scoured country roads to make certain that no slaves were moving about without permission. On Sundays,

CHAPTER LOCATOR | Why and how did the South become so different from the North? | What was plantation life like for masters and mistresses?

356 CHAPTER 13 UNDERSTANDING THE SLAVE SOUTH, 1820–1860

plantation dwellers and plain folk came together in church to worship and afterward lingered to gossip and to transact small business.

Plantation belt yeomen may have envied, and at times even resented, wealthy slaveholders, but small farmers learned to accommodate. Planters made accommodation easier by going out of their way to behave as good neighbors and avoid direct exploitation of slaveless whites in their community. As a consequence, rather than raging at the oppression of the planter regime, the typical plantation belt yeoman sought entry into it.

Upcountry Yeomen

By contrast, the hills and mountains of the South resisted the spread of slavery and plantations. In the western parts of Virginia, North Carolina, and South Carolina; in northern Georgia and Alabama; and in eastern Tennessee and Kentucky, the higher elevation, colder climate, rugged terrain, and poor transportation made it difficult for commercial agriculture to make headway. As a result, yeomen dominated these isolated areas, and planters and slaves were scarce.

At the core of this upcountry society was the sturdy farm family working its own patch of land; raising hogs, cattle, and sheep; and seeking self-sufficiency and independence. Toward that end, all members of the family worked, their tasks depending on their sex and age. Husbands labored in the fields, and with their sons, they cleared, plowed, planted, and cultivated primarily food crops. Women and their daughters labored primarily in and about the cabin. Male and female tasks were equally crucial to the farm's success, but as in other white southern households, the domestic sphere was subordinated to the will of the male patriarch.

The typical upcountry yeoman also grew a little cotton or tobacco, but food production was more important than cash crops. Not much currency changed hands in the upcountry, and barter was common. Farm families also joined together in log-rolling, house and barn raising, and cornhusking.

The few upcountry folks who owned slaves usually had only two or three. As a result, slaveholders had much less social and economic power, and yeomen had more. But the upcountry did not oppose slavery. As long as upcountry plain folk were free to lead their own lives, they defended slavery and white supremacy just as staunchly as other white Southerners.

Poor Whites

Although hardworking, landholding small farmers made up the majority of white Southerners, Northerners had a different image of southern society. They believed that slavery had condemned most whites to poverty and backwardness. One anti-slavery advocate charged that the South harbored three classes: "the slaves on whom devolves all the regular industry, the slaveholders who reap all the fruits, and an idle and lawless rabble who live dispersed over vast plains little removed from absolute barbarism."

Contrary to northern opinion, only about one in four nonslaveholding rural white men was landless and very poor. Some worked as tenants, renting land and struggling to make a go of it. Others survived by herding pigs and cattle. And still others worked for meager wages, ditching, mining, logging, and laying track for railroads. A Georgian remembered that his "father worked by the day when ever he could get work."

Although they sat at the bottom of the white pecking order, poor whites were ambitious people eager to climb into the yeomanry. The Lipscomb family illustrates

KEY FACTORS

- More than six million of the South's eight million whites owned no slaves.
- Approximately three out of four nonslaveholding southern whites were small farmers who owned their own land (yeomen).
- In the southern upcountry, slaves and plantations were rare.

Upcountry of the South

| What was plantation life like for slaves? | What place did free blacks occupy in southern society? | How did nonslaveholding southern whites work and live? | How did slavery shape southern politics? | Conclusion: How did slavery come to define the South? |

the possibility of upward mobility. In 1845, Smith and Sally Lipscomb and their children abandoned their worn-out land in South Carolina for Benton County, Alabama. "Benton is a mountainous country but ther is a heep of good levil land to tend in it," Smith wrote back to his brother. Alabama, Smith said, "will be better for the rising generation if not for ourselves but I think it will be the best for us all that live any length of time."

Because the Lipscombs had no money to buy land, they squatted on seven unoccupied acres. With the help of neighbors, they built a 22-by-24-foot cabin, a detached kitchen, and two stables. From daylight to dark, Smith and his sons worked the land, and the first year they produced enough food for the table and several bales of cotton. Sally contributed to the family's income by selling homemade shirts and socks. In time, the Lipscombs bought land and joined the Baptist church, completing their transformation to respectable yeomen.

Many poor whites succeeded in climbing the economic ladder, but in the 1850s upward mobility slowed. The cotton boom of that decade caused planters to expand their operations, driving the price of land beyond the reach of poor families.

The Culture of the Plain Folk

Situated on scattered farms and in tiny villages, rural plain folk lived isolated lives. Life revolved around family, neighbors, the local church, and perhaps a country store. Work occupied most hours, but plain folk still found time for pleasure. "Dancing they are all fond of," a visitor to North Carolina discovered, "especially when they can get a fiddle, or bagpipe." The most popular pastimes of men and boys were fishing and hunting. A traveler in Mississippi recalled that his host sent "two of his sons, little fellows that looked almost too small to shoulder a gun," for food. "In a few hours we were feasting on delicious venison, trout and turtle."

Plain folk did not usually associate "book learning" with the basic needs of life. A northern woman visiting the South in the 1850s observed, "Education is not extended to the masses here as at the North." Private academies charged fees that yeomen could not afford, and public schools were scarce. Although most people managed to pick up the "three R's," approximately one southern white man in five was illiterate in 1860, and the rate for white women was even higher. "People here prefer talking to reading," a Virginian remarked. Telling stories, reciting ballads, and singing hymns were important activities in yeoman culture.

Plain folk spent more hours in revival tents than in classrooms. Not all rural whites were religious, but many were, and the most characteristic feature of their evangelical Christian faith was the revival. Revivalism crossed denominational lines, but Baptists and Methodists adopted it most readily and by midcentury had become the South's largest religious groups. By emphasizing free choice and individual worth, the plain folk's religion was hopeful and affirming. Hymns and spirituals provided guides to right and wrong. Above all, hymns spoke of the eventual release from worldly sorrows and the assurance of eternal salvation.

> ## QUICK REVIEW

How did the lives of plantation belt and upcountry yeomen differ?

CHAPTER LOCATOR | Why and how did the South become so different from the North? | What was plantation life like for masters and mistresses?

358 CHAPTER 13 UNDERSTANDING THE SLAVE SOUTH, 1820–1860

How did slavery shape southern politics?

Gen. James Chesnut, Jr., C.S.A.

James Chesnut

James Chesnut came from a family with a large number of slaves and thus represents the power of slaveholders in southern politics. He served in the South Carolina state legislature for years before becoming a U.S. senator in 1858. He resigned in 1860 and became a colonel in the Confederate army during the Civil War. Courtesy of South Carolina Library, University of South Carolina, Columbia.

BY THE MID-NINETEENTH CENTURY, all southern white men—planters and plain folk alike—had gained the vote. Nonetheless, political power remained unevenly distributed. The nonslaveholding white majority wielded less political power than their numbers indicated. The slaveholding white minority wielded more. Self-conscious, cohesive, and with a well-developed sense of class interest, slaveholders were active in politics and made demands of state governments. As a result, they received significant benefits. Nonslaveholding whites were concerned mainly with preserving their liberties and keeping their taxes low. Collectively, they asked government for little of an economic nature, and they received little.

Slaveholders sometimes worried about nonslaveholders' loyalty to slavery, but the majority of whites accepted the planters' argument that the existing social order served all Southerners' interests. White men in the South fought furiously about many things, but they agreed that they should take land from Indians, promote agriculture, uphold white supremacy and masculine privilege, and defend slavery from its enemies.

The Democratization of the Political Arena

The political reforms that swept the nation in the first half of the nineteenth century reached deeply into the South. Southerners eliminated the wealth and property requirements that had once restricted political participation. Most southern states also removed the property requirements for holding state offices. To be sure, undemocratic features lingered. Plantation districts still wielded disproportionate power in several state legislatures. Nevertheless, southern politics took place within an increasingly democratic political structure.

White male suffrage ushered in an era of vigorous electoral competition in the South. As politics became aggressively democratic, it also grew fiercely partisan. From the 1830s to the 1850s, Whigs and Democrats battled for the electorate's favor. Both parties presented themselves as the plain white folk's best friend.

In 1860:
- All southern white men can vote.
- Slaveholding white men are most active in politics and are far more likely to hold political office than those without slaves.

Planter Power

Whether Whig or Democrat, southern officeholders were likely to be slave owners, often owning large numbers of slaves. The democratization of politics in the nineteenth century meant that more ordinary citizens participated in elections, but yeomen did not throw the planters out.

Upper-class dominance of southern politics reflected the elite's success in persuading the yeoman majority that what was good for slaveholders was also good for them. In reality, the South had, on the whole, done well by the plain folk. Most had farms of their own. They participated as equals in a democratic political system. They enjoyed an elevated social status, above all blacks and in theory equal to all other whites. They commanded patriarchal authority over their households. And as long as slavery existed, they could dream of joining the planter class.

Most slaveholders took pains to win the plain folk's trust and to nurture their respect. One South Carolinian told his wealthy neighbor that he had a bright political future because he never thought himself "too good to sit down & talk to a poor man." Mary Boykin Chesnut complained about the fawning attention her husband, U.S. senator from South Carolina, showed to poor men, including one who had "mud sticking up through his toes."

Georgia politics illustrate how well planters protected their interests in state legislatures. In 1850, about half of the state's revenues came from taxes on slaves, the characteristic form of planter wealth. However, the tax rate on slaves was only about one-fifth the rate on land. Moreover, planters benefited far more than other groups from public spending. Financing railroads—which carried cotton to market—was the largest state expenditure. The legislature also established low tax rates on land, the characteristic form of yeoman wealth, which meant that the typical yeoman's annual tax bill was small. Still, relative to their wealth, large slaveholders paid less than did other whites. Relative to their numbers, they got more in return. Slaveholding legislators protected planters' interests while giving the impression of protecting the small farmers' interests as well.

The South's elite defended slavery in other ways. In the 1830s, whites decided that slavery was too important to debate. To end free speech on the slavery question, powerful whites dismissed slavery's critics from college faculties, drove them from pulpits, and hounded them from political life. Sometimes antislavery Southerners fell victim to vigilantes and mob violence.

In the South, therefore, the rise of the common man occurred alongside the continuing, even growing, power of the planter class. Rather than pitting slaveholders against nonslaveholders, elections remained an effective means of binding the region's whites together. Elections affirmed the sovereignty of white men, whether planter or plain folk, and the subordination of African Americans. Those twin themes played well among white women as well. Though unable to vote, white women supported equality for whites and slavery for blacks. In the antebellum South, the politics of slavery helped knit together all of white society.

> **QUICK REVIEW**

How did planters benefit from their control of state legislatures?

CHAPTER LOCATOR | Why and how did the South become so different from the North? | What was plantation life like for masters and mistresses?

360 CHAPTER 13 UNDERSTANDING THE SLAVE SOUTH, 1820–1860

Collection of the New-York Historical Society.

Conclusion: How did slavery come to define the South?

<

BY THE EARLY NINETEENTH CENTURY, northern states had either abolished slavery or put it on the road to extinction, while southern states were building the largest slave society in the New World. Regional differences increased over time, not merely because the South became more and more dominated by slavery, but also because developments in the North rapidly propelled it in a very different direction.

One-third of the South's population was enslaved by 1860. Bondage saddled blacks with enormous physical and spiritual burdens: hard labor, harsh treatment, broken families, and, most important, the denial of freedom itself. Although degraded and exploited, they were not defeated. Out of African memories and New World realities, blacks created a life-affirming African American culture that sustained and strengthened them. Defined as property, they refused to be reduced to things. Perceived as inferior beings, they rejected the notion that they were natural slaves.

Slavery was crucial to the South's distinctiveness and to the loyalty and regional identification of its whites. The South was not merely a society with slaves; it had become a slave society. Slavery shaped the region's economy, culture, social structure, and politics. Whites south of the Mason-Dixon line believed that racial slavery was necessary and just. By making all blacks a pariah class, all whites gained a measure of equality and harmony.

Racism did not erase all stress along class lines. Anxious slaveholders continued to worry that yeomen would defect from the proslavery consensus. But during the 1850s, a far more ominous division emerged—that between "slave states" and "free states."

SO NOW YOU KNOW

By 1860, slaves made up one-third of the South's population. Slaves were degraded and exploited by their owners, but they also created their own African American culture, which strengthened and sustained them. Slavery shaped the South's economy, culture, social structure, and politics and made it very different from the North.

What was plantation life like for slaves?	What place did free blacks occupy in southern society?	How did nonslaveholding southern whites work and live?	How did slavery shape southern politics?	Conclusion: How did slavery come to define the South?

CHAPTER 13 STUDY GUIDE

Online Study Guide
bedfordstmartins.com/roarkunderstanding

STEP 1 GETTING STARTED

Below are basic terms from this period in American history. Can you identify each term below and explain why it matters? To do this exercise online or to download this chart, visit bedfordstmartins.com/roarkunderstanding.

TERM	WHO OR WHAT & WHEN	WHY IT MATTERS
cotton kingdom, p. 340		
slave codes, p. 341		
miscegenation, p. 342		
planter, p. 342		
overseer, p. 346		
paternalism, p. 346		
chivalry, p. 347		
slave driver, p. 350		
Nat Turner, p. 352		
Denmark Vesey, p. 353		
emancipation, p. 354		
yeomen, p. 356		

STEP 2 MOVING BEYOND THE BASICS

The exercise below represents a more advanced understanding of the chapter material. Fill in the following chart by describing key characteristics and trends in the North (see chapter 12) and the South in the nineteenth century. When you have finished filling in your chart, ask yourself what role slavery played in creating the split between North and South. How did slavery shape white racial attitudes in both the North and the South? To do this exercise online or to download this chart, visit bedfordstmartins.com/roarkunderstanding.

Key characteristics and trends	North	South
Agriculture		
Urbanization/industrialization		
White racial attitudes		
Economic diversity/labor		
Population/immigration		

Now that you've reviewed various parts of the chapter, take a step back and try to see the big picture by answering these questions. Remember to use specific examples from the chapter in your answers. To do this exercise online, visit bedfordstmartins.com/roarkunderstanding.

REGIONAL DIVERGENCE

▶ How and why did the economies of the North and South steadily diverge over the course of the first half of the nineteenth century?

▶ How did the presence of large numbers of African Americans shape southern culture?

PLANTATION LIFE

▶ How did plantation owners see the relationship between master and slave? How did slavery shape other social relationships in the antebellum South?

▶ In what ways did slaves create communities for themselves and develop methods to resist their bondage?

SOUTHERN SOCIETY AND POLITICS

▶ How did southern yeomen see themselves and their place in southern society? How was slavery a part of that place?

▶ How did slavery shape southern politics?

Gen. James Chesnut, Jr., C.S.A.

LOOKING BACKWARD, LOOKING AHEAD

▶ How did southern slave society change from the eighteenth to nineteenth centuries?

▶ Why did many white Southerners come to believe that slavery had to be preserved at any cost? How might that have influenced national politics?

IN YOUR OWN WORDS

Imagine that you must explain chapter 13 to someone who hasn't read it. What would be the most important points to include and why?

THE EAGLE'S NEST.

"THE UNION: IT MUST AND SHALL BE PRESERVED"

14
THE HOUSE DIVIDED
1846–1861

> This chapter explores the politics of slavery in the tumultuous decades before the Civil War. It examines the ways the recurring issue of the expansion of slavery into newly acquired territory deepened sectional divisions, undermined old political parties, made room for new parties, and, ultimately, led to secession and civil war.

> How did the acquisition of land from Mexico contribute to sectional tensions?

> What factors helped unravel the balance between slave and free states?

> How did the party system change in the 1850s?

> Why did northern fear of the "Slave Power" intensify in the 1850s?

> What caused some southern states to secede after the election of 1860?

> Conclusion: Why did political compromise fail?

DID YOU KNOW?

Uncle Tom's Cabin was the first American novel to sell a million copies.

The Eagle's Nest. This 1861 cartoon by E.B. Kellogg of Hartford, Connecticut, makes his position clear in the subtitle: "The Union! It Must and Shall Be Preserved."

How did the acquisition of land from Mexico contribute to sectional tensions?

Oak Home Farm, San Joaquin County, California The discovery of gold in California initiated a stampede west, but not everyone wanted to be a prospector. In 1860, an unknown artist painted this idyllic view of the farm of W. I. Overhiser in California's fertile San Joaquin Valley. Thousands of miles away, farmers compared farmsteads like Overhiser's with their own. Many judged life more bountiful in the West and trekked across the country to try to strike it rich in western agriculture. University of California at Berkeley, Bancroft Library.

BETWEEN 1846 AND 1848, the nation grew by 1.2 million square miles, an incredible two-thirds. Victory in the Mexican-American War brought vast new territories in the West into the United States. The gold rush of 1849 transformed California into a booming economy (see chapter 12). The 1850s witnessed new "rushes," for gold in Colorado and silver in Nevada's Comstock Lode, and people from around the world flocked to the West. But it quickly became clear that Northerners and Southerners had very different visions of the West, particularly the place of slavery in its future. Still, Congress in 1850 patched together a settlement that Americans hoped would be permanent.

The Wilmot Proviso and the Expansion of Slavery

Most Americans agreed that the Constitution left the issue of slavery to the individual states to decide. Northern states had done away with slavery, while southern states had retained it. But what about slavery in the nation's territories? The Constitution states that "Congress shall have power to . . . make all needful rules and regulations respecting the territory . . . belonging to the United States." The debate about slavery, then, turned toward Congress.

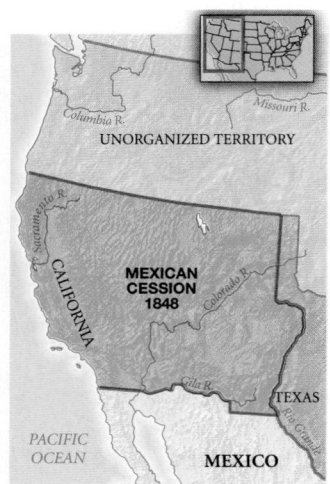

Mexican Cession, 1848

CHAPTER LOCATOR | How did the acquisition of land from Mexico contribute to sectional tensions?

366 CHAPTER 14
THE HOUSE DIVIDED, 1846–1861

Slavery in the Territories: Contradictory Precedents

1787: Northwest Ordinance bans slavery north of the Ohio River.

1803: Congress allows slavery to remain in the newly acquired Louisiana Territory.

1820: The Missouri Compromise prohibits slavery in part of the Louisiana Territory but allows it in the rest.

The spark for the national debate was provided in August 1846 by a Democratic representative from Pennsylvania, David Wilmot, who proposed that Congress bar slavery from all lands acquired in the war with Mexico. Regardless of party affiliation, Northerners lined up behind the **Wilmot Proviso**. Many supported free soil, by which they meant territory in which slavery would be prohibited, because they wanted to preserve the West for free labor, for hardworking, self-reliant free men, not for slaveholders and slaves. But support also came from those who were simply anti-South. New slave territories would eventually mean new slave states, and they opposed magnifying the political power of Southerners. Wilmot himself said his proposal would blunt "the *power* of slaveholders" in the national government.

Additional support for free soil came from Northerners who were hostile to blacks and wanted to reserve new land for whites. Wilmot himself declared, "I would preserve for free white labor a fair country, a rich inheritance, where the sons of toil, of my own race and own color, can live without the disgrace which association with negro slavery brings upon free labor." It is no wonder that some called the Wilmot Proviso the "White Man's Proviso."

The thought that slavery might be excluded outraged white Southerners. Like Northerners, they regarded the West as a ladder for economic and social opportunity. They also believed that the exclusion of slavery was a slap in the face to southern veterans of the Mexican-American War. "When the war-worn soldier returns home," one Alabaman asked, "is he to be told that he cannot carry his property to the country won by his blood?"

Southern leaders also sought to maintain political parity with the North to protect the South's interests, especially slavery. The need seemed especially urgent in the 1840s, when the North's population and wealth were booming. James Henry Hammond of South Carolina predicted that ten new states would be carved from the acquired Mexican land. If free soil won, the North would "ride over us roughshod" in Congress, he claimed. "Our only safety is in *equality* of POWER."

Because Northerners had a majority in the House, they easily passed the Wilmot Proviso. In the Senate, however, where slave states outnumbered free states fifteen to fourteen, Southerners defeated it. Senator John C. Calhoun of South Carolina denied that Congress had the constitutional authority to exclude slavery from the nation's territories. Whereas Wilmot demanded that Congress slam shut the door to slavery, Calhoun called on Congress to hold the door wide open.

In 1847, Senator Lewis Cass of Michigan offered a compromise through the doctrine of **popular sovereignty**, by which the people who settled the territories would decide for themselves slavery's fate. This solution, Cass argued, sat squarely in the American tradition of democracy and local self-government. Popular sovereignty's most attractive feature was its ambiguity about the precise moment when

CHRONOLOGY

1846
- Wilmot Proviso prohibiting the expansion of slavery into territory acquired from Mexico is introduced in Congress.

1847
- Wilmot Proviso is defeated in Senate.
- Compromise of "popular sovereignty" is offered allowing the people of the territories to decide the issue of slavery.

1848
- Free-Soil Party is founded.
- Whig Zachary Taylor is elected president.

1849
- California gold rush begins.

1850
- Taylor dies; Vice President Millard Fillmore becomes president.
- Compromise of 1850 becomes law.

Wilmot Proviso

▶ Proposal put forward by Representative David Wilmot of Pennsylvania in August 1846 to ban slavery in territory acquired as a result of the Mexican-American War. The proviso enjoyed widespread support in the North, but many Southerners saw it as an attack on their economic and political interests.

| What factors helped unravel the balance between slave and free states? | How did the party system change in the 1850s? | Why did northern fear of the "Slave Power" intensify in the 1850s? | What caused some southern states to secede after the election of 1860? | Conclusion: Why did political compromise fail? |

popular sovereignty

▶ The principle that the people of a given territory should resolve the issue of slavery in the territory themselves by a popular vote. First advanced by Senator Lewis Cass of Michigan in 1847, popular sovereignty initially appeared to offer a compromise on the slavery question. In the end, popular sovereignty did little to resolve sectional tensions, and its application in Kansas in 1856 actually led to violence.

settlers could determine slavery's fate. Northern advocates believed that the decision on slavery could be made as soon as the first territorial legislature assembled. With free-soil majorities likely because of the North's greater population, they would shut the door to slavery almost before the first slave arrived. Southern supporters believed that popular sovereignty guaranteed that slavery would be unrestricted throughout the entire territorial period. Only at the very end, when settlers in a territory drew up a constitution and applied for statehood, could they decide the issue of slavery. By then, slavery would have sunk deep roots. As long as the matter of timing remained vague, popular sovereignty gave hope to both sides.

When Congress ended its session in 1848, no plan had won a majority in both houses. Northerners who demanded no new slave territory anywhere, ever, and Southerners who demanded entry for their slave property into all territories, or else, staked out their extreme positions. Unresolved in Congress, the territorial question naturally became an issue in the presidential election of 1848.

The Election of 1848

When President Polk chose not to seek reelection, the Democratic convention nominated Lewis Cass of Michigan, the man most closely associated with popular sovereignty. The Whigs nominated a Mexican-American War hero, General Zachary Taylor. The Whigs declined to adopt a party platform, betting that the combination of a military hero and total silence on the slavery issue would unite their divided party. Taylor, who owned more than one hundred slaves on plantations in Mississippi and Louisiana, was hailed by Georgia politician Robert Toombs as a "Southern man, a slaveholder, a cotton planter."

Antislavery Whigs balked and looked for an alternative. Senator Charles Sumner called for a major political realignment, "one grand Northern party of Freedom." In the summer of 1848, antislavery Whigs and antislavery Democrats founded the Free-Soil Party, nominating a Democrat, Martin Van Buren, for president and a Whig, Charles Francis Adams, for vice president. The platform boldly proclaimed, "Free soil, free speech, free labor, and free men."

The November election dashed the hopes of the Free-Soilers. They did not carry a single state. Taylor won the all-important electoral college vote 163 to 127, carrying eight of the fifteen slave states and seven of the fifteen free states (**Map 14.1**).

General Taylor Cigar Case

This papier-mâché cigar case portrays General Zachary Taylor, Whig presidential candidate in 1848, in a colorful scene from the Mexican-American War. Shown here as a dashing, elegant officer, Taylor was in fact a short, thickset, and roughly dressed Indian fighter who had spent his career commanding small frontier garrisons. The inscription reminds voters that Taylor was a victor in the first four battles fought in the war and directs attention away from the fact that in politics, he was a rank amateur. Collection of Janice L. and David Frent.

CHAPTER LOCATOR | How did the acquisition of land from Mexico contribute to sectional tensions?

(Wisconsin had entered the Union earlier in 1848 as the fifteenth free state.) Northern voters were not yet ready for Sumner's "one grand Northern party of Freedom," but the struggle over slavery in the territories had shaken the major parties badly.

Debate and Compromise

Believing that he could avoid further sectional strife if California and New Mexico skipped the territorial stage, new president Zachary Taylor in 1849 encouraged the settlers to apply for admission to the Union as states. Predominantly antislavery, the settlers began writing free-state constitutions. "For the first time," Mississippian Jefferson Davis lamented, "we are about permanently to destroy the balance of power between the sections."

Congress convened in December 1849, beginning one of the most contentious and most significant sessions in its history. President Taylor urged Congress to admit California as a free state immediately and to admit New Mexico, which lagged behind a few months, as soon as it applied. Southerners exploded. A North Carolinian declared that Southerners who would "consent to be thus degraded and enslaved, ought to be whipped through their fields by their own negroes."

At this juncture, Senator Henry Clay of Kentucky stepped in to offer a series of resolutions meant to answer and balance "all questions in controversy between the free and slave states, growing out of the subject of slavery." Admit California as a free state, he proposed, but organize the rest of the Southwest without restrictions on slavery. Require Texas to abandon its claim to parts of New Mexico, but compensate it by assuming its preannexation debt. Abolish the domestic slave trade in Washington, D.C., but confirm slavery itself in the nation's capital. Reassert Congress's lack of authority to interfere with the interstate slave trade, and enact a more effective fugitive slave law.

Both antislavery advocates and "fire-eaters" (as radical Southerners who urged secession from the Union were called) savaged Clay's plan. Senator Salmon P. Chase of Ohio ridiculed it as "sentiment for the North, substance for the South." Senator Henry S. Foote of Mississippi denounced it as more offensive to the South than the speeches of abolitionists William Lloyd Garrison, Wendell Phillips, and Frederick Douglass combined. The most ominous response came from John C. Calhoun, who argued that the fragile political unity of North and South depended on continued equal representation in the Senate, which Clay's plan for a free California destroyed. "As things now stand," he said in February 1850, the South "cannot with safety remain in the Union."

Senator Daniel Webster of Massachusetts then addressed the Senate. Like Clay, Webster defended compromise. He told Northerners that the South had legitimate complaints, but he told Southerners that secession from the Union would mean civil war. Referring to the Wilmot Proviso, he argued that a legal ban on slavery in the territories was unnecessary because the harsh climate effectively prohibited the expansion of cotton and slaves into the new American Southwest.

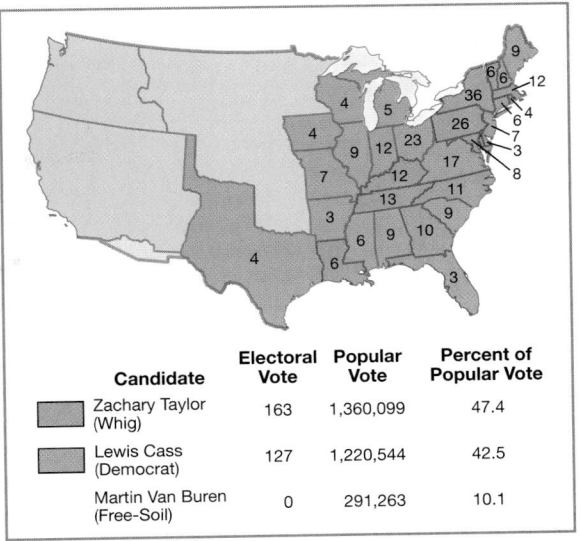

Candidate	Electoral Vote	Popular Vote	Percent of Popular Vote
Zachary Taylor (Whig)	163	1,360,099	47.4
Lewis Cass (Democrat)	127	1,220,544	42.5
Martin Van Buren (Free-Soil)	0	291,263	10.1

MAP 14.1 ■ The Election of 1848

[handwritten margin note: Compromise of 1850 CA entry spells end of 50/50 split in Senate]

| What factors helped unravel the balance between slave and free states? | How did the party system change in the 1850s? | Why did northern fear of the "Slave Power" intensify in the 1850s? | What caused some southern states to secede after the election of 1860? | Conclusion: Why did political compromise fail? |

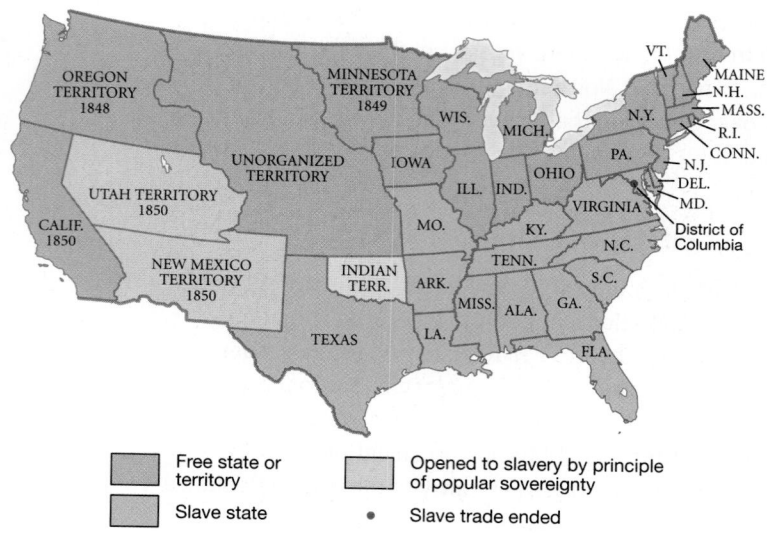

Free state or territory

Slave state

Opened to slavery by principle of popular sovereignty

• Slave trade ended

MAP 14.2 ■ The Compromise of 1850
The patched-together sectional agreement was both clumsy and unstable. Few Americans—in either North or South—supported all five parts of the Compromise.

Free-Soil forces recoiled from what they saw as Webster's desertion. Senator William H. Seward of New York responded that Webster's and Clay's compromise with slavery was "radically wrong and essentially vicious." He rejected Calhoun's argument that Congress lacked the constitutional authority to exclude slavery from the territories. In any case, Seward said, there was a "higher law than the Constitution"—the law of God—to ensure freedom in all the public domain. Claiming that God was a Free-Soiler did nothing to cool the superheated political atmosphere.

In May, the Senate considered a bill that joined Clay's resolutions into a single comprehensive package. Clay bet that a majority of Congress wanted compromise and that the members would vote for the package. But the strategy backfired. Free-Soilers and proslavery Southerners voted down the comprehensive plan.

Fortunately for those who favored a settlement, Senator Stephen A. Douglas, a rising Democratic star from Illinois, broke the bill into its parts and skillfully ushered each through Congress. The agreement Douglas won in September 1850 was very much the one Clay had proposed in January. California entered the Union as a free state. New Mexico and Utah became territories where slavery would be decided by popular sovereignty. Texas accepted its boundary with New Mexico and received $10 million from the federal government. Congress ended the slave trade in the District of Columbia but enacted a more stringent fugitive slave law. In September, Millard Fillmore, who had become president when Zachary Taylor died in July, signed into law each bill, collectively known as the **Compromise of 1850 (Map 14.2)**. The nation breathed a sigh of relief. The Compromise preserved the Union and peace for the moment.

Compromise of 1850
▶ Collection of laws passed in 1850 meant to resolve the dispute over the spread of slavery in the territories. Key elements of the Compromise of 1850 included the admission of California as a free state and the passage of the Fugitive Slave Act. The Compromise of 1850 began to unravel almost immediately after its passage, as sectional tensions continued to rise.

> QUICK REVIEW

What provisions of the Compromise of 1850 might have eased sectional tensions and why?

CHAPTER LOCATOR | How did the acquisition of land from Mexico contribute to sectional tensions?

What factors helped unravel the balance between slave and free states?

The Modern Medea In 1855, a slave family—Robert Garner; his twenty-two-year-old wife, Margaret; their four children; and his parents—fled Kentucky. Margaret's owner tracked them to a cabin in Ohio. Thinking that her children would be returned to slavery, Margaret seized a butcher knife and cut the throat of her two-year-old daughter. She was turning on her other children when slave catchers burst in and captured her. Abolitionists claimed that the act revealed the horror of slavery; defenders of slavery argued that the deed proved that slaves were savages. This 1867 painting shows Margaret standing over the bodies of two boys. Artist Thomas Satterwhite Noble departed from history in order to allude to the Greek myth of Medea, who killed her two children to spite her husband. *Harper's Weekly*, May 18, 1867/Picture Research Consultants & Archives.

> ▶ FOR MORE HELP ANALYZING THIS IMAGE, see the visual activity for this chapter in the Online Study Guide at bedfordstmartins.com/roarkunderstanding.

THE COMPROMISE OF 1850 began to come apart almost immediately. The implementation of the Fugitive Slave Act and the publication of Harriet Beecher Stowe's *Uncle Tom's Cabin* combined to inflame antislavery feeling in the North. Congress did its part to undo the Compromise as well. In 1854, Congress passed the Kansas-Nebraska Act, once again opening up the question of slavery in the territories, the deadliest of all sectional issues.

The Fugitive Slave Act

The issue of runaway slaves was as old as the Constitution, which contained a provision for the return of any "person held to service or labor in one state" who escaped to another. In 1793, a federal law authorized slave owners to enter other states to recapture their slave property. Proclaiming the 1793 law a license to kidnap free blacks, northern states in the 1830s began passing "personal liberty laws" that provided fugitives with some protection.

What factors helped unravel the balance between slave and free states?	How did the party system change in the 1850s?	Why did northern fear of the "Slave Power" intensify in the 1850s?	What caused some southern states to secede after the election of 1860?	Conclusion: Why did political compromise fail?

Some northern communities also formed vigilance committees to help runaways. Each year, a few hundred slaves escaped into free states and found friendly northern "conductors" who put them on board the underground railroad, which was not a railroad at all but a series of secret "stations" (hideouts) on the way to Canada (see chapter 12).

Furious about northern interference, Southerners in 1850 insisted on the stricter fugitive slave law that was passed as part of the Compromise. According to the **Fugitive Slave Act**, to seize an alleged slave, a slaveholder simply had to appear before a commissioner and swear that the runaway was his. The commissioner earned $10 for every individual returned to slavery but only $5 for those set free. Most galling to Northerners, the law stipulated that all citizens were expected to assist officials in apprehending runaways.

In Boston in February 1851, an angry crowd overpowered federal marshals and snatched a runaway named Shadrach from a courtroom, put him on the underground railroad, and whisked him off to Canada. Three years later, when another Boston crowd rushed the courthouse in a failed attempt to rescue Anthony Burns, who had recently fled slavery in Richmond, a guard was shot dead. To white Southerners, it seemed that antislavery fanatics had whipped Northerners into a frenzy of massive resistance.

Actually, the overwhelming majority of fugitives claimed by slaveholders were reenslaved peacefully. But brutal enforcement of the unpopular law had a radicalizing effect in the North, particularly in New England. To Southerners, it seemed that Northerners had betrayed the Compromise. "The continued existence of the United States as one nation," warned the *Southern Literary Messenger*, "depends upon the full and faithful execution of the Fugitive Slave Bill."

Uncle Tom's Cabin

As unsettling as the Fugitive Slave Act was, even more Northerners were turned against slavery by a novel. Harriet Beecher Stowe, a Northerner who had never set foot on a plantation, made the South's slaves into flesh-and-blood human beings for many of her readers. A member of a famous clan of preachers, teachers, and reformers, Stowe despised the slave catchers and wrote to expose the sin of slavery. Published as a book in 1852, **Uncle Tom's Cabin, or Life among the Lowly** sold 300,000 copies in its first year and more than 2 million copies within ten years. Stowe's characters leaped from the page. Here was the gentle slave Uncle Tom, a Christian saint who forgave those who beat him to death; the courageous slave Eliza, who fled with her child across the frozen Ohio River; and the fiendish overseer Simon Legree, whose Louisiana plantation was a nightmare of torture and death. Northerners shed tears and sang praises to *Uncle Tom's Cabin*.

What Northerners accepted as truth, however, Southerners denounced as slander. Virginian George F. Holmes proclaimed Stowe a member of the "Woman's Rights" and "Higher Law" schools and dismissed the novel as a work of "intense fanaticism." Although it is impossible to measure precisely the impact of a novel on public opinion, *Uncle Tom's Cabin* clearly helped to crystallize northern sentiment against slavery and to confirm white Southerners' suspicion that they no longer received any sympathy in the free states. Other writers—

ex-slaves who knew life in slave cabins firsthand—also produced stinging indictments of slavery. Solomon Northup's compelling *Twelve Years a Slave* (1853) sold 27,000 copies in two years, and the powerful *Narrative of the Life of Frederick Douglass, as Told by Himself* (1845) eventually sold more than 30,000 copies. But no work touched the North's conscience like Stowe's novel.

The Kansas-Nebraska Act

As the 1852 election approached, the Democrats and Whigs sought to close the sectional rifts that had opened within their parties. For their presidential nominee, the Democrats turned to Franklin Pierce of New Hampshire. Pierce's well-known sympathy with southern views on public issues caused his northern critics to include him among the "doughfaces," northern men malleable enough to champion southern causes. Adopting the formula that had worked in 1848, the Whigs chose another Mexican-American War hero, General Winfield Scott of Virginia. But the Whigs' northern and southern factions were hopelessly divided, and the party suffered a humiliating defeat. The Democrat Pierce carried twenty-seven states to Scott's four and won the electoral college vote 254 to 42 (Map 14.4, page 376). The Free-Soil Party lost almost half of the voters who had turned to it in the tumultuous political atmosphere of 1848.

Eager to leave the sectional controversy behind, the new president turned swiftly to foreign expansion. Pierce's major objective was Cuba, but when antislavery Northerners blocked Cuba's acquisition to keep more slave territory from entering the Union, he turned his attention to Mexico. In 1853, diplomat James Gadsden negotiated a $15 million purchase of some 30,000 square miles of land in present-day Arizona and New Mexico. The Gadsden Purchase stemmed from Pierce's desire for a southern transcontinental railroad to California. Inevitably in the 1850s, the contest for a transcontinental railroad route evolved into a sectional contest over slavery.

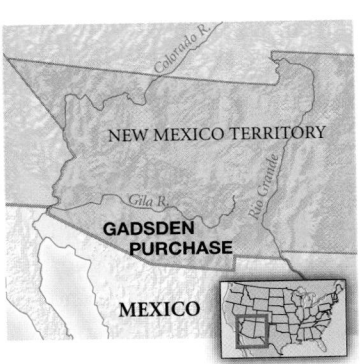

Gadsden Purchase, 1853

Illinois's Democratic senator Stephen A. Douglas badly wanted the transcontinental railroad for Chicago, and he was the chair of the Senate Committee on Territories. Any railroad that ran west from Chicago would pass through a region that Congress in 1830 had designated a "permanent" Indian reserve. Douglas proposed giving this vast area between the Missouri River and the Rocky Mountains an Indian name, Nebraska, and then throwing the Indians out. Once the region achieved territorial status, whites could survey and sell the land, establish a civil government, and build a railroad.

Nebraska lay within the Louisiana Purchase and, according to the Missouri Compromise of 1820, was closed to slavery (see chapter 10). Douglas needed southern votes to pass his Nebraska legislation, but Southerners had no incentive to create another free territory or to help a northern city win the transcontinental railroad. Southerners, however, agreed to help if Congress organized Nebraska

CHRONOLOGY

1830s
– Northern states begin passing "personal liberty laws" to protect fugitive slaves.

1851
– Boston crowd overpowers federal marshals to liberate a runaway slave named Shadrach.

1852
– *Uncle Tom's Cabin* is published.
– Democrat Franklin Pierce is elected president.

1854
– Congress passes Kansas-Nebraska Act, allowing popular sovereignty to decide the issue of slavery in the Nebraska and Kansas territories.

What factors helped unravel the balance between slave and free states?	How did the party system change in the 1850s?	Why did northern fear of the "Slave Power" intensify in the 1850s?	What caused some southern states to secede after the election of 1860?	Conclusion: Why did political compromise fail?

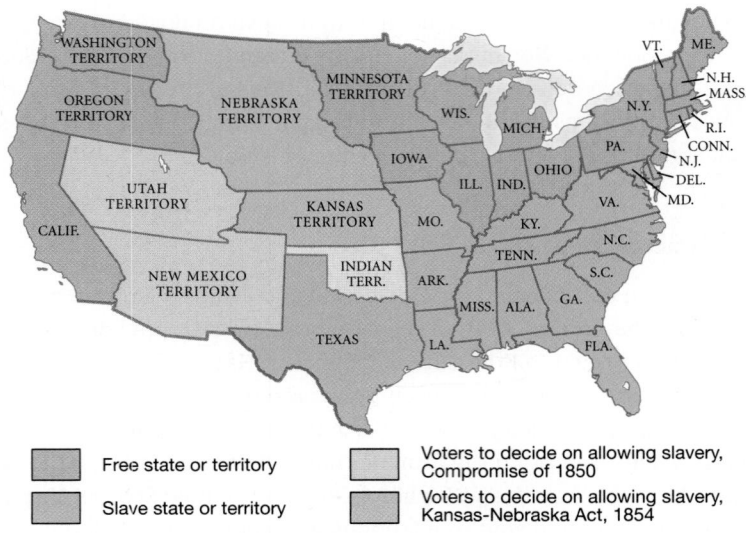

MAP 14.3 ■ The Kansas-Nebraska Act, 1854

Americans hardly thought twice about dispossessing the Indians of land guaranteed them by treaty, but many worried about the outcome of repealing the Missouri Compromise and opening up the region to slavery.

Free state or territory

Slave state or territory

Voters to decide on allowing slavery, Compromise of 1850

Voters to decide on allowing slavery, Kansas-Nebraska Act, 1854

Kansas-Nebraska Act

▶ 1854 law championed by Stephen A. Douglas that removed Indians from Nebraska Territory, divided the territory into Kansas and Nebraska, and stipulated that the issue of slavery in each of the new territories would be decided on the basis of popular sovereignty. Implementation of the measure led to bloody fighting between pro- and antislavery forces in Kansas.

according to popular sovereignty. That meant giving slavery a chance in Nebraska Territory and reopening the dangerous issue of the expansion of slavery.

In January 1854, Douglas introduced his bill to organize Nebraska Territory, leaving to the settlers themselves the decision about slavery. At southern insistence, Douglas added an explicit repeal of the Missouri Compromise. Free-Soilers branded Douglas's plan "a gross violation of a sacred pledge" and an "atrocious plot" to transform free land into a "dreary region of despotism, inhabited by masters and slaves."

Undaunted, Douglas skillfully shepherded the explosive bill through Congress in May 1854. Nine-tenths of the southern members (Whigs and Democrats) and half of the northern Democrats cast votes in favor of the bill. Like Douglas, most northern supporters believed that popular sovereignty would make Nebraska free territory. In its final form, the **Kansas-Nebraska Act** divided the huge territory in two: Nebraska and Kansas (**Map 14.3**). With this act, the government pushed the Plains Indians farther west, making way for farmers and railroads.

> **QUICK REVIEW**

Why did the desire for a transcontinental railroad turn into a debate over slavery in the 1850s?

CHAPTER LOCATOR | How did the acquisition of land from Mexico contribute to sectional tensions?

How did the party system change in the 1850s?

John and Jessie Frémont Poster

The election of 1856 marked the first time a candidate's wife appeared on campaign items. In this poster, Jessie Frémont and her husband, John, the Republican Party's presidential nominee, ride spirited horses. The scene emphasizes their youth (John was forty-three; Jessie, thirty-one), their vigor, and their outdoor exuberance. Smart and ambitious, Jessie helped plan her husband's campaign, coauthored his election biography, and drew northern women into political activity as never before. Museum of American Political Life.

[handwritten margin note: KS Nebraska shattered party system]

SINCE THE RISE of the Whig Party in the early 1830s, Whigs and Democrats had organized and channeled political conflict in the nation. This party system dampened sectionalism and strengthened the Union. To achieve national political power, the Whigs and Democrats had to retain their strength in both the North and the South. And strength in both regions required that parties compromise and find positions acceptable to both wings. But the Kansas-Nebraska controversy shattered this stabilizing political system. In place of two national parties with bisectional strength, the mid-1850s witnessed the development of one party heavily dominated by one section and another party entirely limited to the other section. The new party system thwarted political compromise and promoted political polarization.

The Old Parties: Whigs and Democrats

As early as the Mexican-American War, members of the Whig Party had clashed over the future of slavery in annexed Mexican lands. By 1852, the Whig Party could please its proslavery southern wing or its antislavery northern wing but not both. The Whigs' miserable showing in the election of 1852 made clear that they were no longer a strong national party. By 1856, after more than two decades of contesting the Democrats, they were hardly a party at all (**Map 14.4**).

What factors helped unravel the balance between slave and free states?	How did the party system change in the 1850s?	Why did northern fear of the "Slave Power" intensify in the 1850s?	What caused some southern states to secede after the election of 1860?	Conclusion: Why did political compromise fail?

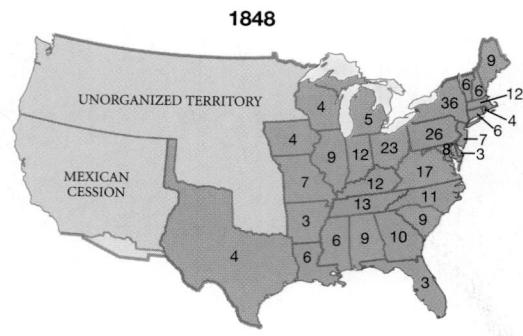

1848

Candidate	Electoral Vote	Popular Vote	Percent of Popular Vote
Zachary Taylor (Whig)	163	1,360,099	47.4
Lewis Cass (Democrat)	127	1,220,544	42.5
Martin Van Buren (Free-Soil)	0	291,263	10.1

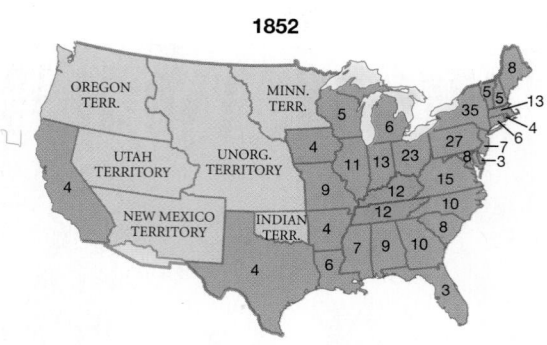

1852

Candidate	Electoral Vote	Popular Vote	Percent of Popular Vote
Franklin Pierce (Democrat)	254	1,601,274	50.9
Winfield Scott (Whig)	42	1,386,580	44.1
John P. Hale (Free-Soil)	5	155,825	5.0

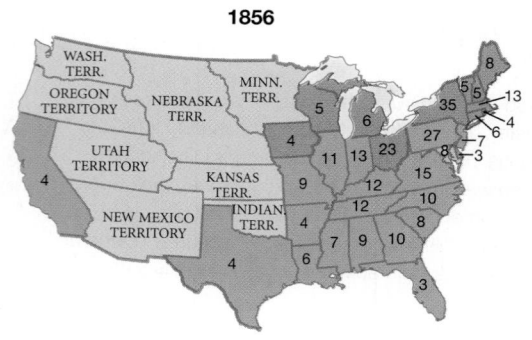

1856

Candidate	Electoral Vote	Popular Vote	Percent of Popular Vote
James Buchanan (Democrat)	174	1,838,169	45.3
John C. Frémont (Republican)	114	1,341,264	33.1
Millard Fillmore (American)	8	874,534	21.6

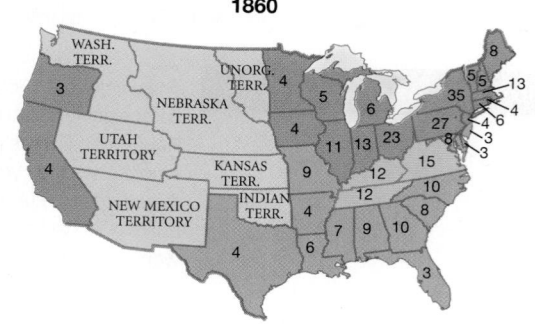

1860

Candidate	Electoral Vote	Popular Vote	Percent of Popular Vote
Abraham Lincoln (Republican)	180	1,866,452	39.9
John C. Breckinridge (Southern Democrat)	72	847,953	18.1
Stephen A. Douglas (Northern Democrat)	12	1,375,157	29.4
John Bell (Constitutional Union)	39	590,631	12.6

MAP 14.4 ■ **Political Realignment, 1848–1860**

In 1848, slavery and sectionalism began taking their toll on the country's party system. The Whig Party was an early casualty. By 1860, national parties—those that contended for votes in both North and South—had been replaced by regional parties.

▶ FOR MORE HELP ANALYZING THIS MAP, see the map activity for this chapter in the Online Study Guide at bedfordstmartins.com/roarkunderstanding.

CHAPTER LOCATOR | How did the acquisition of land from Mexico contribute to sectional tensions?

The collapse of the Whig Party left the Democrats as the country's only national party. Although the Democrats were not immune to the disruptive pressures of the territorial question, they discovered in popular sovereignty a doctrine that many Democrats could support. Even so, popular sovereignty very nearly undid the party. When Stephen Douglas applied the doctrine to the part of the Louisiana Purchase where slavery had been barred, he divided northern Democrats and destroyed the dominance of the Democratic Party in the free states. After 1854, even though the Democrats were a southern-dominated party, they remained a national political organization. Gains in the South more than balanced Democratic losses in the North. During the 1850s, Democrats elected two presidents and won majorities in Congress in almost every election.

The breakup of the Whigs and the disaffection of significant numbers of northern Democrats set many Americans politically adrift. As they searched for new political harbors, Americans found that the death of the old party system created a multitude of fresh political alternatives.

The New Parties: Know-Nothings and Republicans

Out of the confusion, two parties emerged as true contenders for national prominence. One grew out of the slavery controversy, a coalition of indignant anti-slavery Northerners. The other arose from an entirely different split in American society, between Roman Catholic immigrants and native Protestants.

The wave of immigrants that arrived in America from 1845 to 1855 led some Protestant Americans to believe that the Republic would soon be dominated by Roman Catholics from Ireland and Germany. In the 1850s, nativists (individuals who were anti-immigrant) began to organize, first into secret fraternal societies and then in 1854 into a political party. Recruits swore never to vote for either foreign-born or Roman Catholic candidates and not to reveal any information about the organization. When questioned, they said, "I know nothing." Officially, they were the American Party, but most Americans called them Know-Nothings.

CHRONOLOGY

1854
- American (Know-Nothing) Party emerges.
- Republican Party is founded.

1855
- Height of Know-Nothings' political success.

1856
- Democrat James Buchanan is elected president.

Campaign Flag of the Know-Nothing Party

Convinced that the incendiary issue of slavery had blinded Americans to the greater dangers of uncontrolled immigration and foreign influence, the Know-Nothings nominated Millard Fillmore for president in 1856. Milwaukee County Historical Society.

What factors helped unravel the balance between slave and free states?	How did the party system change in the 1850s?	Why did northern fear of the "Slave Power" intensify in the 1850s?	What caused some southern states to secede after the election of 1860?	Conclusion: Why did political compromise fail?

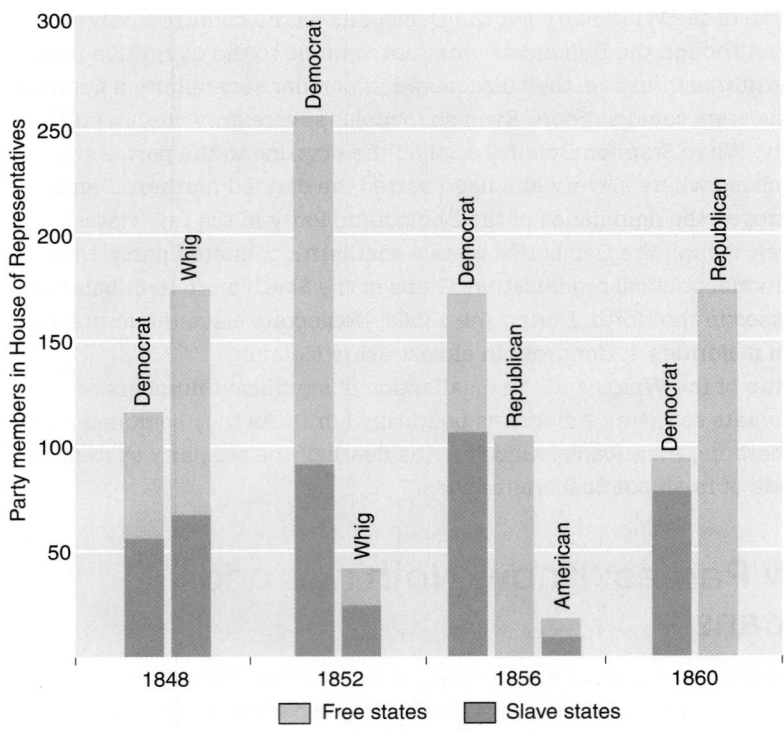

FIGURE 14.1 ■ Changing Political Landscape, 1848–1860
The polarization of American politics between free states and slave states occurred in little more than a decade.

The Know-Nothings exploded onto the political stage in 1854 and 1855 with a series of dazzling successes. They captured state legislatures in the Northeast, West, and South and claimed dozens of seats in Congress. By 1855, an observer might reasonably have concluded that the Know-Nothings had emerged as the successor to the Whigs.

The Know-Nothings were not the only new party making noise, however. One of the new antislavery organizations provoked by the Kansas-Nebraska Act called itself the **Republican Party**. The Republicans attempted to unite all those who opposed the extension of slavery into any territory of the United States (see **Figure 14.1**).

The Republican creed tapped into the basic beliefs and values of the northern public. Slavery, the Republicans believed, degraded the dignity of white labor by associating work with blacks and servility. They warned that the insatiable slave-holders of the South, whom antislavery Northerners called the "Slave Power," were conspiring through their control of the Democratic Party to expand slavery, subvert liberty, and undermine the Constitution.

Only if slavery was restricted to the South, Republicans believed, could the system of free labor flourish elsewhere. In the North, one Republican declared in 1854, "every man holds his fortune in his own right arm; and his position in society, in life, is to be tested by his own individual character" (see chapter 12). Powerful images of liberty and opportunity attracted a wide range of Northerners to the Republican cause.

Republican Party
▶ Antislavery party formed in 1854 in the wake of the passage of the Kansas-Nebraska Act. The Republicans attempted to unite all those who opposed the extension of slavery into any territory of the United States. In 1860, Abraham Lincoln won the presidency running as the Republican candidate.

CHAPTER LOCATOR | How did the acquisition of land from Mexico contribute to sectional tensions?

378 CHAPTER 14
THE HOUSE DIVIDED, 1846–1861

Women as well as men rushed to the new Republican Party. Indeed, three women helped found the party in Ripon, Wisconsin, in 1854. Although they could not vote before the Civil War and suffered from a raft of other legal handicaps, women nevertheless participated in partisan politics by writing campaign literature, marching in parades, giving speeches, and lobbying voters. Women's antislavery fervor attracted them to the Republican Party, and participation in party politics in turn nurtured the woman's rights movement. Susan B. Anthony, who attended Republican meetings throughout the 1850s, found that her political activity made her disfranchisement all the more galling. She and other women in the North worked on behalf of antislavery and to secure both woman suffrage and the right of married women to control their own property.

The Election of 1856

The election of 1856 revealed that the Republicans had become the Democrats' main challenger, and slavery in the territories, not nativism, was the election's principal issue. When the Know-Nothings insisted on a platform that endorsed the Kansas-Nebraska Act, most of the Northerners walked out, and the party came apart. The few Know-Nothings who remained nominated ex-president Millard Fillmore.

The Republicans adopted a platform that focused almost exclusively on "making every territory free." For president, they nominated the soldier and California adventurer John C. Frémont. Frémont lacked political credentials, but his wife, Jessie Frémont, the daughter of Senator Thomas Hart Benton of Missouri, knew the political map as well as her husband knew the western trails. Though careful to maintain a proper public image, the young mother and antislavery zealot helped attract voters and draw women into politics.

The Democrats, successful in 1852 in bridging sectional differences by nominating a northern man with southern principles, chose another "doughface," James Buchanan of Pennsylvania. They took refuge in the ambiguity of popular sovereignty and portrayed the Republicans as extremists ("Black Republican Abolitionists") whose support for the Wilmot Proviso risked pushing the South out of the Union.

The Democratic strategy carried the day for Buchanan. Buchanan won 174 electoral college votes against Frémont's 114 and Fillmore's 8 (see Map 14.4, page 376). But the big news was what the press called the "glorious defeat" of the Republicans. Despite being a brand-new party and purely sectional, Frémont and the Republicans had seriously challenged the Democrats for national power. Sectionalism had fashioned a new party system, one that spelled danger for the Republic. Indeed, war had already broken out between proslavery and antislavery forces in distant Kansas Territory.

QUICK REVIEW <

Why did the Whig Party disintegrate in the 1850s?

| What factors helped unravel the balance between slave and free states? | How did the party system change in the 1850s? | Why did northern fear of the "Slave Power" intensify in the 1850s? | What caused some southern states to secede after the election of 1860? | Conclusion: Why did political compromise fail? |

Why did northern fear of the "Slave Power" intensify in the 1850s?

Armed Settlers near Lawrence, Kansas Armed with rifles, knives, swords, and pistols, these tough antislavery men gathered for a photograph near Lawrence in 1856. Kansas State Historical Society.

EVENTS IN KANSAS TERRITORY provided the young Republican organization with an enormous boost and help explain its strong showing in the election of 1856. Republicans organized around the premise that the slaveholding South provided a profound threat to "free soil, free labor, and free men," and now Kansas reeled with violence that Republicans argued was southern in origin. In fact, everywhere Republicans looked in the 1850s, they saw what they believed was evidence of the South's drive toward tyranny and minority rule.

"Bleeding Kansas"

Three days after the House of Representatives approved the Kansas-Nebraska Act in 1854, Senator William H. Seward of New York boldly challenged the South. "Come on then, Gentlemen of the Slave States," he cried, "since there is no escaping your challenge, I accept it in behalf of the cause of freedom. We will engage in competition for the virgin soil of Kansas, and God give the victory to the side which is stronger in numbers as it is in right."

In both North and South, emigrant aid societies sprang up to promote settlement from free states or slave states. Missourians, already bordered on the east by the free state of Illinois and on the north by the free state of Iowa, especially thought it important to secure Kansas for slavery. Thousands of rough frontiersmen, egged on by Missouri senator David Rice Atchison, invaded Kansas. "There are eleven hundred coming over from Platte County to vote," Atchison reported, "and if that ain't

CHAPTER LOCATOR | How did the acquisition of land from Mexico contribute to sectional tensions?

enough we can send five thousand—enough to kill every God-damned abolitionist in the Territory." Not surprisingly, proslavery candidates swept the territorial elections in November 1854. When Kansas's first territorial legislature met, it enacted a raft of proslavery laws. Ever-pliant President Pierce endorsed the work of the fraudulently elected legislature. Free-soil Kansans did not. They elected their own legislature, which promptly banned both slaves and free blacks from the territory. Organized into two rival governments and armed to the teeth, Kansans verged on civil war.

Fighting broke out on the morning of May 21, 1856, when several hundred proslavery men raided the town of Lawrence, the center of free-state settlement. The "Sack of Lawrence," as free-soil forces called it, inflamed northern opinion. Elsewhere in Kansas, news of the events in Lawrence provoked **John Brown**, a free-soil settler, to announce that "it was better that a score of bad men should die than that one man who came here to make Kansas a Free State should be driven out" and to lead the posse that massacred five allegedly proslavery settlers along Pottawatomie Creek. After that, guerrilla war engulfed the territory.

Just as "Bleeding Kansas" gave the fledgling Republican Party fresh ammunition for its battle against the Slave Power, so too did an event that occurred in the national capital. In May 1856, Senator Charles Sumner of Massachusetts delivered a speech titled "The Crime against Kansas," which included a scalding personal attack on South Carolina senator Andrew P. Butler. Sumner described Butler as a "Don Quixote" who had taken as his mistress "the harlot, slavery."

Preston Brooks, a young South Carolina member of the House and a kinsman of Butler, felt compelled to defend the honor of both his relative and his state. On May 22, Brooks entered the Senate, where he found Sumner working at his desk. He beat Sumner over the head with his cane until Sumner lay bleeding and unconscious on the floor. Brooks resigned his seat in the House, only to be promptly reelected. In the North, the southern hero became an arch-villain. Like "Bleeding Kansas," "Bleeding Sumner" provided the Republican Party with a potent symbol of the South's "twisted and violent civilization."

The *Dred Scott* Decision

Political debate over slavery in the territories became so heated in part because the Constitution lacked precision on the issue. In 1857, in the case of *Dred Scott v. Sandford*, the Supreme Court announced its understanding of the meaning of the Constitution regarding slavery in the territories. The Court's decision demonstrated that it was not immune from the sectional and partisan passions that convulsed the land.

In 1833, an army doctor bought the slave *Dred Scott* in St. Louis, Missouri, and took him as his personal servant to Fort Armstrong, Illinois, and then to Fort

"Bleeding Kansas," 1850s

CHRONOLOGY

1856
- "Bleeding Kansas."
- Congressman Preston Brooks canes Senator Charles Sumner in the Senate chambers.
- Pottawatomie massacre.

1857
- In the *Dred Scott* decision, the U.S. Supreme Court rules the Missouri Compromise unconstitutional and declares that blacks are not U.S. citizens.

1858
- Abraham Lincoln and Stephen A. Douglas debate slavery during the Illinois Senate race.

John Brown
▶ Militant abolitionist who led the Pottawatomie massacre in "Bleeding Kansas" in 1856 and the October 16, 1859, raid on Harpers Ferry, Virginia. Brown hoped his raid would spark a general slave uprising, but his invasion failed, and he was captured. His subsequent execution made him a martyr and a hero to many in the North.

| What factors helped unravel the balance between slave and free states? | How did the party system change in the 1850s? | Why did northern fear of the "Slave Power" intensify in the 1850s? | What caused some southern states to secede after the election of 1860? | Conclusion: Why did political compromise fail? |

Dred Scott

This portrait of Dred Scott was painted in 1857, the year of the Supreme Court's decision. Although the Court rejected his suit, Scott gained his freedom in May 1857 when a white man purchased and freed Scott and his family. Collection of the New-York Historical Society.

Dred Scott decision

▶ 1857 Supreme Court decision that ruled the Missouri Compromise of 1820 unconstitutional. The case centered on Dred Scott, a slave who claimed that his travels with his master into free states made him and his family free. Ruling against Scott, the Court denied the federal government the right to exclude slavery in the territories and declared that African Americans were not citizens. The decision infuriated many in the North and contributed to the growing strength of the Republican Party.

Snelling in Wisconsin Territory. Back in St. Louis in 1846, Scott, with the help of white friends, sued to prove that he and his family were legally entitled to their freedom. Scott argued that living in Illinois, a free state, and Wisconsin, a free territory, had made his family free, and that they remained free even after returning to Missouri, a slave state.

In 1857, the U.S. Supreme Court ruled seven to two against Scott. Chief Justice Roger B. Taney, who hated Republicans and detested racial equality, wrote the Court's majority opinion. First, the Court ruled in the *Dred Scott* decision that Scott could not legally claim violation of his constitutional rights because he was not a citizen of the United States. When the Constitution was written, Taney said, blacks "were regarded as beings of an inferior order . . . so far inferior, that they had no rights which the white man was bound to respect." Second, the laws of Dred Scott's home state, Missouri, determined his status, and thus his travels in free areas did not make him free. Third, Congress's power to make "all needful rules and regulations" for the territories did not include the right to prohibit slavery. The Court explicitly declared the Missouri Compromise unconstitutional, even though it had already been voided by the Kansas-Nebraska Act.

The Taney Court's extreme proslavery decision outraged Republicans. By denying the federal government the right to exclude slavery in the territories, it cut the legs out from under the Republican Party. Moreover, as the *New York Tribune* lamented, the decision cleared the way for "all our Territories . . . to be ripened into Slave States." Particularly frightening to African Americans in the North was the Court's declaration that free blacks were not citizens and had no rights.

In essence, the Court's decision validated an extreme statement of the South's territorial rights. John C. Calhoun's claim that Congress had no authority to exclude slavery became the law of the land. White Southerners cheered, but the *Dred Scott* decision actually strengthened the young Republican Party.

CHAPTER LOCATOR | How did the acquisition of land from Mexico contribute to sectional tensions?

Indeed, that "outrageous" decision, one Republican argued, was "the best thing that could have happened." It provided dramatic evidence of the Republicans' claim that a hostile Slave Power conspired against northern liberties.

Prairie Republican: Abraham Lincoln

The *Dred Scott* case provided Republican politicians with fresh challenges and fresh opportunities. Abraham Lincoln had long since put behind him his log-cabin beginnings in Kentucky and Indiana. Now living in Springfield, Illinois, Lincoln earned good money as a lawyer, but politics was his life. "His ambition was a little engine that knew no rest," observed his law partner William Herndon. Lincoln had served as a Whig in the Illinois state legislature and in the House of Representatives, but he had not held public office since 1849.

Convinced that slavery was a "great moral wrong" and an "unqualified evil to the negro, the white man, and the State," Lincoln condemned Douglas's Kansas-Nebraska Act of 1854 for giving slavery a new life, and in 1856 he joined the Republican Party. He accepted that the Constitution permitted slavery in those states where it existed, but he believed that Congress could contain its spread. In time, Lincoln believed, plantation slavery would wither and Southerners would end slavery themselves.

Lincoln held what were, for his times, moderate racial views. Although he denounced slavery and defended black humanity, he also viewed black equality as impractical and unachievable. "Negroes have natural rights . . . as other men have," he said, "although they cannot enjoy them here." Insurmountable white prejudice made it impossible to extend full citizenship to blacks in America, he believed. Freeing blacks and allowing them to remain in this country would lead to a race war. In Lincoln's mind, social stability and black progress required that slavery end and that blacks leave the country.

Lincoln envisioned the western territories as "places for poor people to go to, and better their conditions." But slavery's expansion threatened free men's basic right to succeed. The Kansas-Nebraska Act and the *Dred Scott* decision persuaded him that slaveholders were engaged in a dangerous conspiracy to nationalize slavery. The next step, Lincoln warned, would be "another Supreme Court decision, declaring that the Constitution of the United States does not permit a State to exclude slavery from its limits." Unless the citizens of Illinois woke up, he warned, the Supreme Court would make "Illinois a slave State."

In Lincoln's view, the nation could not "endure, permanently half slave and half free." Either opponents of slavery would arrest its spread and place it on the "course of ultimate extinction," or its advocates would see that it became legal in "*all* the States, *old* as well as *new*—*North* as well as *South*." Lincoln's convictions that slavery was wrong and that Congress must stop its spread formed the core of the Republican ideology. Lincoln so impressed his fellow Republicans in Illinois that in 1858 they chose him to challenge the nation's premier Democrat, who was seeking reelection to the U.S. Senate.

The Lincoln-Douglas Debates

When Stephen Douglas learned that the Republican Abraham Lincoln would be his opponent for the Senate, he observed: "He is the strong man of the party—full of wit, facts, dates—and the best stump speaker, with his droll ways and dry jokes, in

Abraham Lincoln

► Successful lawyer who served as a Whig politician in Illinois in the 1840s and rose to national prominence in the newly formed Republican Party. Lincoln denounced slavery and defended black humanity, but he also accepted that the Constitution permitted slavery in the states where it already existed. His election as U.S. president in 1860 caused seven states to secede from the Union by February 1861 and spurred the creation of the Confederate States of America.

| What factors helped unravel the balance between slave and free states? | How did the party system change in the 1850s? | Why did northern fear of the "Slave Power" intensify in the 1850s? | What caused some southern states to secede after the election of 1860? | Conclusion: Why did political compromise fail? |

383

the West. He is as honest as he is shrewd, and if I beat him my victory will be hardly won."

Not only did Douglas have to contend with a formidable foe, but he also carried the weight of a burden not of his own making. The previous year, the nation's economy had experienced a sharp downturn. As a Democrat, Douglas had to go before the voters as a member of the party whose policies stood accused of causing the panic of 1857.

Douglas's response to another crisis in 1857, however, helped shore up his standing in Illinois. Proslavery forces in Kansas met in the town of Lecompton, drafted a proslavery constitution, and applied for statehood. Everyone knew that free-soilers outnumbered proslavery settlers, but President Buchanan instructed Congress to admit Kansas as the sixteenth slave state. Senator Douglas broke with the Democratic administration and denounced the Lecompton constitution; Congress killed the Lecompton bill. (When Kansans reconsidered the Lecompton constitution in an honest election, they rejected it six to one. Kansas entered the Union in 1861 as a free state.) By denouncing the fraudulent proslavery constitution, Douglas declared his independence from the South and, he hoped, made himself acceptable at home.

A relative unknown and a decided underdog in the Illinois election, Lincoln challenged Douglas to debate him face-to-face. The two met seven times for what would become a legendary series of debates. Thousands stood straining to see and hear as the two candidates debated the crucial issues of the age—slavery and freedom.

Lincoln badgered Douglas with the question of whether he favored the spread of slavery. He tried to force Douglas into the damaging admission that the Supreme Court had repudiated Douglas's own territorial solution, popular sovereignty. At Freeport, Illinois, Douglas admitted that settlers could not now pass legislation barring slavery, but he argued that they could ban slavery just as effectively by not passing protective laws, such as those found in slave states. Southerners condemned Douglas's "Freeport Doctrine" and charged him with trying to steal the victory they had gained with the *Dred Scott* decision. Lincoln chastised his opponent for his "don't care" attitude about slavery, for "blowing out the moral lights around us."

Douglas worked the racial issue. He called Lincoln an abolitionist and an egalitarian enamored of "our colored brethren." Put on the defensive, Lincoln reaffirmed his faith in white rule: "I will say, then, that I am not, nor ever have been, in favor of bringing about in any way the social and political equality of the white and black race." But Lincoln was no negrophobe, and he tried to steer the debate back to what he considered the true issue: the morality and future of slavery. "Slavery is wrong," Lincoln repeated, because "a man has the right to the fruits of his own labor."

As Douglas predicted, the election was hard-fought and closely contested, with Douglas pulling out a narrow victory. But the **Lincoln-Douglas debates** thrust Lincoln, the prairie Republican, into the national spotlight.

Lincoln-Douglas debates
► Series of debates on the issue of slavery and freedom between Democrat Stephen Douglas and Republican Abraham Lincoln, held as part of the 1858 Illinois senatorial race. Douglas won the election, but the debates helped catapult Lincoln to national attention.

> **QUICK REVIEW**

Why did the *Dred Scott* decision strengthen northern suspicions of a "Slave Power" conspiracy?

CHAPTER LOCATOR | How did the acquisition of land from Mexico contribute to sectional tensions?

What caused some southern states to secede after the election of 1860?

Abraham Lincoln

Lincoln actively sought the Republican presidential nomination in 1860. While in New York City to give a political address, he had his photograph taken by Mathew Brady. "While I was there I was taken to one of the places where they get up such things," Lincoln explained, sounding more innocent than he was, "and I suppose they got my shadow, and can multiply copies indefinitely." The Lincoln Museum, Fort Wayne, Indiana, #0-17.

LINCOLN'S THESIS that the "slavocracy" conspired to make slavery a national institution now seems exaggerated. But from the northern perspective, the Kansas-Nebraska Act, the Brooks-Sumner affair, the *Dred Scott* decision, and the Lecompton constitution amounted to irrefutable evidence of the South's aggressiveness. White Southerners, of course, saw things differently. They were the ones who were under siege, they declared. Signs were everywhere that the North planned to use its numerical advantage to attack slavery, and not just in the territories. Republicans had made it clear that they were unwilling to accept the *Dred Scott* ruling as the last word on the issue of slavery expansion. And John Brown's attempt to incite a slave insurrection in Virginia in 1859 proved that Northerners would stop at nothing to achieve their aims.

Talk of leaving the Union had been heard for years, but until the final crisis, Southerners had used secession as a ploy to gain concessions within the Union, not to destroy it. Then the 1850s delivered powerful blows to Southerners'

| What factors helped unravel the balance between slave and free states? | How did the party system change in the 1850s? | Why did northern fear of the "Slave Power" intensify in the 1850s? | **What caused some southern states to secede after the election of 1860?** | Conclusion: Why did political compromise fail? |

confidence that they could remain Americans and protect slavery. When the Republican Party won the White House in 1860, many Southerners concluded that they would have to leave.

John Brown's Raid and Its Aftermath

After his participation in the Pottawatomie Creek massacre, John Brown slipped out of Kansas and reemerged in the East. More than ever, he was a man on fire for abolition. He spent thirty months begging money to support his vague plan for military operations against slavery, raising enough money to gather a small band of antislavery warriors.

On the night of October 16, 1859, Brown took his war against slavery into the South. With only twenty-one men, including five African Americans, he invaded Harpers Ferry, Virginia, believing his attack would spark a general slave uprising. It did not. His band seized the town's armory and rifle works, but the invaders were immediately surrounded, first by local militia and then by Colonel Robert E. Lee, who commanded the U.S. troops in the area. When Brown refused to surrender, federal soldiers charged with bayonets. Seventeen men, two of whom were slaves, lost their lives. Although a few of Brown's raiders escaped, federal forces killed ten (including two of his sons) and captured seven, among them Brown.

For his attack on Harpers Ferry, John Brown stood trial for treason, murder, and incitement of slave insurrection. On December 2, 1859, Virginia executed Brown. In life, he was a ne'er-do-well, but he died with courage and dignity. He told his wife that he was "determined to make the utmost possible out of a defeat." He told the court: "If it is deemed necessary that I should forfeit my life for the furtherance of the ends of justice, and mingle my blood further with the blood of . . . millions in this slave country whose rights are disregarded by wicked, cruel, and unjust enactments, I say, let it be done."

After Brown's death, northern denunciation of Brown as a dangerous fanatic gave way to grudging respect. Some even celebrated his "splendid martyrdom." Abolitionist Lydia Maria Child likened Brown to Christ and declared that he made "the scaffold . . . as glorious as the Cross of Calvary." Some abolitionists explicitly endorsed Brown's resort to violence. Abolitionist William Lloyd Garrison, who usually professed pacifism, announced, "I am prepared to say 'success to every slave insurrection at the South and in every country.'"

Most Northerners did not advocate bloody rebellion, however. Still, when northern churches marked John Brown's execution with tolling bells, hymns, and prayer vigils, white Southerners contemplated what they had in common with Northerners. With the presidential election only months away, Georgia senator Robert Toombs announced solemnly that Southerners must "never permit this Federal government to pass into the traitorous hands of the black Republican party."

Republican Victory in 1860

At the Democratic convention in Charleston in April 1860, fire-eating Southerners denounced Stephen Douglas and demanded a platform that included federal protection of slavery in the territories. When the delegates, led by northern Democrats, approved a platform with popular sovereignty, representatives from the

CHAPTER LOCATOR | How did the acquisition of land from Mexico contribute to sectional tensions?

John Brown Going to His Hanging, by Horace Pippin, 1942 The grandparents of Horace Pippin, a Pennsylvania artist, were slaves. His grandmother witnessed the hanging of John Brown, and this painting recalls the scene she so often described to him. Pennsylvania Academy of Fine Arts, Philadelphia. John Lambert Fund.

▶ FOR MORE HELP ANALYZING THIS IMAGE, see the visual activity for this chapter in the Online Study Guide at bedfordstmartins.com/roarkunderstanding.

entire Lower South and Arkansas left the convention. The remaining Democrats adjourned to meet a few weeks later in Baltimore, where they nominated Douglas for president.

When southern Democrats met, they nominated Vice President John C. Breckinridge of Kentucky and approved a platform with a federal slave code. Southern moderates, however, refused to support Breckinridge. They formed the Constitutional Union Party to provide voters with a Unionist choice. Instead of adopting a platform and confronting the slavery question, the Constitutional Union Party merely approved a vague resolution pledging "to recognize no political principle other than *the Constitution . . . the Union . . . and the Enforcement of the Laws.*" For president, they picked former senator John Bell of Tennessee.

| What factors helped unravel the balance between slave and free states? | How did the party system change in the 1850s? | Why did northern fear of the "Slave Power" intensify in the 1850s? | What caused some southern states to secede after the election of 1860? | Conclusion: Why did political compromise fail? |

The Republicans smelled victory, but they estimated that they needed to carry nearly all the free states to win. To make their party more appealing, they expanded their platform beyond antislavery. They hoped that free homesteads, a protective tariff, a transcontinental railroad, and a guarantee of immigrant political rights would provide an economic and social agenda broad enough to unify the North. While reasserting their commitment to stop the spread of slavery, they also denounced John Brown's raid as "among the gravest of crimes" and confirmed the security of slavery in the South.

The foremost Republican, William H. Seward, was a poor match for this even-handed platform. He had made enemies with his radical statements, including the claims that there was a "higher law" than the Constitution (God's law) and that there was an "irrepressible conflict" between slavery and freedom. Lincoln, however, since bursting onto the national scene in 1858, had demonstrated his clear purpose, good judgment, and moderate opinions. That, and his residence in Illinois, a crucial state, made him attractive to the party. On the third ballot, the delegates at the nominating convention chose Lincoln. Defeated by Douglas in a state contest less than two years earlier, Lincoln now stood ready to take him on for the presidency.

The election of 1860 was like none other in American politics. It took place in the midst of the nation's severest crisis. Four major candidates crowded the presidential field. Rather than a four-cornered contest, however, the election broke into two contests, each with two candidates. In the North, Lincoln faced Douglas; in the South, Breckinridge confronted Bell.

On November 6, 1860, Lincoln swept all of the eighteen free states except New Jersey, which split its electoral votes between him and Douglas. Although Lincoln received only 39 percent of the popular vote, he won easily in the electoral college with 180 votes, 28 more than he needed for victory (**Map 14.5**). The reason Lincoln won was not because his opposition was splintered. Even if the votes of his three

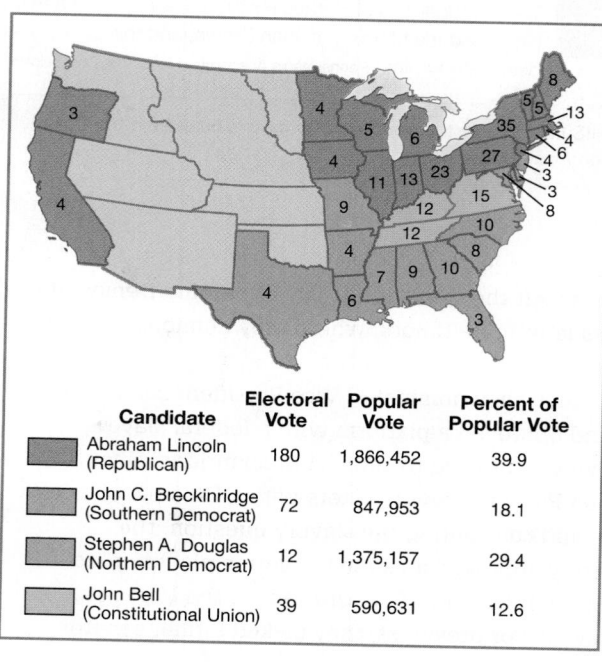

Candidate	Electoral Vote	Popular Vote	Percent of Popular Vote
Abraham Lincoln (Republican)	180	1,866,452	39.9
John C. Breckinridge (Southern Democrat)	72	847,953	18.1
Stephen A. Douglas (Northern Democrat)	12	1,375,157	29.4
John Bell (Constitutional Union)	39	590,631	12.6

MAP 14.5 ■ The Election of 1860

CHAPTER LOCATOR | How did the acquisition of land from Mexico contribute to sectional tensions?

388 CHAPTER 14
THE HOUSE DIVIDED, 1846–1861

opponents had been combined, Lincoln still would have won. He won because his votes were concentrated in the free states, which contained a majority of electoral votes. Ominously, however, Breckinridge, running on a southern-rights platform, won the entire Lower South, plus Delaware, Maryland, and North Carolina.

Secession Winter

Anxious Southerners immediately began debating their next step. Although Breckinridge had carried the South, a vote for "southern rights" was not necessarily a vote for secession. Besides, slightly more than half of the Southerners who had voted had cast ballots for Douglas and Bell, two stout defenders of the Union.

Southern Unionists tried to calm the fears that Lincoln's election triggered. Former congressman Alexander Stephens of Georgia asked what Lincoln had done to justify something as extreme as secession. Had he not promised to respect slavery where it existed? Moreover, secession might lead to war, which would loosen the hinges of southern society and possibly even open the door to slave insurrection. "Revolutions are much easier started than controlled," he warned. "I consider slavery much more secure in the Union than out of it."

Secessionists emphasized the dangers of delay. "Mr. Lincoln and his party assert that this doctrine of equality applies to the negro," former Georgia governor Howell Cobb declared, "and necessarily there can exist no such thing as property in our equals." Lincoln's election without a single electoral vote from the South meant that Southerners were no longer able to defend themselves within the Union, Cobb argued. Why wait, he asked, for the abolitionists to attack? As for war, there would be none. The Union was a voluntary compact, and Lincoln would not coerce patriotism. If Northerners did resist with force, secessionists argued, one southern woodsman could whip five of Lincoln's greasy mechanics.

For all their differences, southern whites agreed that they had to defend slavery. John Smith Preston of South Carolina spoke for the overwhelming majority when he declared, "The South cannot exist without slavery." They disagreed about whether the mere presence of a Republican in the White House made it necessary to exercise what they considered a legitimate right to secede.

The debate about what to do was briefest in South Carolina; it seceded from the Union on December 20, 1860. By February 1861, the six other Lower South states had followed suit. In February, representatives from South Carolina, Georgia, Florida, Alabama, Mississippi, Louisiana, and Texas met in Montgomery, Alabama, where they celebrated the birth of the Confederate States of America. **Jefferson Davis** became president, and Alexander Stephens, who had spoken so eloquently about the dangers of revolution, became vice president.

Lincoln's election had split the Union. Now secession split the South. Seven slave states seceded during the winter, but the eight slave states of the Upper South rejected secession, at least for the moment. The Upper South had a smaller stake in slavery. Barely half as many white families in the Upper South held slaves (21 percent) as in the Lower South (37 percent). Slaves represented twice as large a percentage of the population in the Lower South (48 percent) as in the Upper South (23 percent). Consequently, whites in the Upper South had fewer fears that Republican ascendancy meant economic catastrophe, social chaos, and racial war.

Jefferson Davis
▶ Member of the U.S. Senate from Mississippi who became president of the Confederate States of America in 1861.

| What factors helped unravel the balance between slave and free states? | How did the party system change in the 1850s? | Why did northern fear of the "Slave Power" intensify in the 1850s? | What caused some southern states to secede after the election of 1860? | Conclusion: Why did political compromise fail? |

389

Secession of the Lower South, December 1860–February 1861

Lincoln would need to do more than just be elected to provoke them into secession.

The nation had to wait until March 4, 1861, when Lincoln took office, to see what he would do. After his election, Lincoln chose to stay in Springfield and to say nothing. "Lame-duck" president James Buchanan sat in Washington and did nothing. In Congress, efforts at cobbling together a peace-saving compromise came to nothing.

At his swearing-in ceremony, Lincoln began his inaugural address with reassurances to the South. He had "no lawful right" to interfere with slavery where it existed, he declared again, adding for emphasis that he had "no inclination to do so." Conciliatory about slavery, Lincoln proved inflexible about the Union. The Union, he declared, was "perpetual." Secession was "anarchy" and "legally void." The Constitution required him to execute the law "in all the States."

The decision for civil war or peace rested in the South's hands, Lincoln said. "You can have no conflict, without being yourselves the aggressors. *You* have no oath registered in Heaven to destroy the government, while *I* shall have the most solemn one to 'preserve, protect, and defend' it."

> ## QUICK REVIEW

Why did some southern states secede immediately after Lincoln's election?

CHAPTER LOCATOR | How did the acquisition of land from Mexico contribute to sectional tensions?

Library of Congress.

Conclusion: Why did political compromise fail?

AS THEIR ECONOMIES, societies, and cultures diverged in the nineteenth century, Northerners and Southerners expressed different concepts of the American promise and the place of slavery within it. Their differences crystallized into political form in 1846 when David Wilmot proposed banning slavery in any territory won in the Mexican-American War. Discovery of gold and other precious metals in the West added urgency to the controversy over slavery in the territories. Although Congress addressed the issue with the Compromise of 1850, the consequences of the Fugitive Slave Act and the publication of *Uncle Tom's Cabin* hardened northern sentiments against slavery and confirmed southern suspicions of northern ill will. The bloody violence that erupted in Kansas in 1856 and the incendiary *Dred Scott* decision in 1857 further eroded hope for a solution to this momentous question.

During the extended crisis of the Union that stretched from 1846 to 1861, the slavery question was interwoven with national politics. The traditional Whig and Democratic parties struggled to hold together, while new parties, most notably the Republican Party, emerged. Politicians fixed their attention on the expansion of slavery, but from the beginning, the nation recognized that the controversy had less to do with slavery in the territories than with the future of slavery in America.

For more than seventy years, statesmen had found compromises that accepted slavery and preserved the Union. But as each section grew increasingly committed to its labor system and the promise it offered, Americans discovered that accommodation had limits. In 1859, John Brown's militant antislavery pushed white Southerners to the edge. In 1860, Lincoln's election convinced whites in the Lower South that slavery and the society they had built on it were at risk in the Union, and they seceded. It remained to be seen whether disunion would mean war.

SO NOW YOU KNOW

Uncle Tom's Cabin was America's first million-selling book, but it was by no means the only antislavery book. Other writers, such as Solomon Northup and Frederick Douglass, both of whom had firsthand knowledge of being enslaved, also made impassioned cases against slavery. The sectional tensions that the debate over slavery created threatened civil war.

CHAPTER 14 STUDY GUIDE

Online Study Guide
bedfordstmartins.com/roarkunderstanding

STEP 1 GETTING STARTED

Below are basic terms from this period in American history. Can you identify each term below and explain why it matters? To do this exercise online or to download this chart, visit bedfordstmartins.com/roarkunderstanding.

TERM	WHO OR WHAT & WHEN	WHY IT MATTERS
Wilmot Proviso, p. 367		
popular sovereignty, p. 368		
Compromise of 1850, p. 370		
Fugitive Slave Act, p. 372		
Uncle Tom's Cabin, p. 372		
Kansas-Nebraska Act, p. 374		
Republican Party, p. 378		
John Brown, p. 381		
Dred Scott decision, p. 382		
Abraham Lincoln, p. 383		
Lincoln-Douglas debates, p. 384		
Jefferson Davis, p. 389		

STEP 2 MOVING BEYOND THE BASICS

The exercise below represents a more advanced understanding of the chapter material. Use the following chart to sketch the political landscape of the 1850s. First, describe the groups and regions where the Democratic, Whig, Republican, and American parties found their greatest support. Then describe each party's position on slavery, expansion, and immigration. When you are finished, see if you can make connections between each party's supporters and the positions the party took on important issues. How did slavery help transform the American political landscape? To do this exercise online or to download this chart, visit bedfordstmartins.com/roarkunderstanding.

Party	Who supported this party?	Position on slavery	Views on expansion	Perspectives on immigration
Democratic Party				
Whig Party				
Republican Party				
American (Know-Nothing) Party				

Now that you've reviewed various parts of the chapter, take a step back and try to see the big picture by answering these questions. Remember to use specific examples from the chapter in your answers. To do this exercise online, visit bedfordstmartins.com/roarkunderstanding.

EXPANSION AND SECTIONALISM

▶ Why was the Wilmot Proviso so controversial? What did the response to the Proviso reveal about the diverging visions of America in the North and in the South?

▶ Why was the expansion of slavery not only a moral issue for abolitionists but also an economic concern to both Northerners and Southerners?

POLITICAL INSTABILITY

▶ Why did the Compromise of 1850 ultimately fail?

▶ What were the consequences of the events of the 1840s and 1850s for America's political parties? How did the party system change under the pressure of the sectional divide?

THE ROAD TO SECESSION

▶ If most Northerners and Southerners wanted to avoid war, why did war come?

▶ Why did so many Southerners see the election of Abraham Lincoln as a threat to their way of life? Why did more than half of the southern electorate vote for pro-Union candidates?

LOOKING BACKWARD, LOOKING AHEAD

▶ Why, in the early nineteenth century, was compromise on the issue of slavery possible? Why did so many reject compromise in the 1840s and 1850s?

▶ What consequences might Southerners have imagined would follow from secession? What might have led them to underestimate Lincoln's determination to fight for the Union?

IN YOUR OWN WORDS

Imagine that you must explain chapter 14 to someone who hasn't read it. What would be the most important points to include and why?

1865.
FEB. 13.

15
THE CRUCIBLE OF WAR

1861–1865

> This chapter traces the course of the Civil War. It explores the connections between events on the battlefield and political, social, and economic developments on the home fronts, explains how the war became a fight for black freedom, and examines why the North ultimately prevailed.

> How did the war begin?

> Why did each side expect to win?

> How did each side fare in the early years of the war?

> Why did the war for union become a fight for black freedom?

> What problems did the Confederacy face at home?

> How did the war affect the economy and politics of the North?

> How did the Union finally win the war?

> Conclusion: In what ways was the Civil War a "Second American Revolution"?

DID YOU KNOW?

During the Civil War, 71 percent of northern African American men of military age served in the Union army.

"Price Raid," October 1864. This 1865 illustration by Samuel J. Reader shows a regiment of Kansas Militia captured by Confederate soldiers in Texas. Reader was one of the captives.

> How did the war begin?

Fort Sumter Bombardment Located on an artificial island inside the entrance to Charleston harbor, Fort Sumter had walls eight to twelve feet thick. The fort was so undermanned that when Confederate shells began raining down on April 12, U.S. troops could answer back with only a few of the fort's forty-eight guns. Minnesota Historical Society.

ABRAHAM LINCOLN faced the worst crisis in the history of the nation: disunion. He revealed his strategy on March 4, 1861, in his inaugural address, which was firm yet conciliatory. First, he tried to avoid any act that would push the skittish Upper South (North Carolina, Virginia, Maryland, Delaware, Kentucky, Tennessee, Missouri, and Arkansas) out of the Union. Second, he sought to reassure the seceding Lower South (South Carolina, Georgia, Florida, Alabama, Mississippi, Louisiana, and Texas) that the Republicans would not abolish slavery. Lincoln believed that Unionists there would assert themselves and overturn the secession decision.

His counterpart, Jefferson Davis, fully intended to establish the Confederate States of America as an independent republic. Without additional states, however, the Confederacy would have little hope of long-term survival. Davis watched for opportunities to add new stars to the Confederate flag.

Neither man sought war; both wanted to achieve their objectives peacefully. As Lincoln later observed, "Both parties deprecated war, but one of them would

CHAPTER LOCATOR | How did the war begin? | Why did each side expect to win? | How did each side fare in the early years of the war?

396 CHAPTER 15 THE CRUCIBLE OF WAR, 1861–1865

make war rather than let the nation survive, and the other would *accept* war rather than let it perish. And the war came."

Attack on Fort Sumter

Major Robert Anderson and some eighty U.S. soldiers occupied **Fort Sumter**, which was perched on a tiny island at the entrance to Charleston harbor. By the end of March 1861, Anderson and his men were running dangerously short of food. In the first week of April, Lincoln authorized a peaceful expedition to bring supplies, but not military reinforcements, to the fort. The president understood that he risked war, but his plan honored his inaugural promises to defend federal property and to avoid using military force unless first attacked. Masterfully, Lincoln had shifted the fateful decision of war or peace to Jefferson Davis.

On April 9, Davis and his cabinet met to consider the situation in Charleston harbor. After sharp debate, Davis sent word to Confederate troops in Charleston to take the fort before the relief expedition arrived. Thirty-three hours of bombardment on April 12 and 13 reduced the fort to rubble. On April 14, Major Anderson offered his surrender. The Confederates had Fort Sumter, but they also had war.

On April 15, when Lincoln called for 75,000 militiamen to serve for ninety days to put down the rebellion, several times that number enlisted. Stephen A. Douglas, the recently defeated Democratic candidate for president, pledged his support. "There are only two sides to the question," he said. "Every man must be for the United States or against it. There can be no neutrals in this war, *only patriots—or traitors*." But the people of the Upper South found themselves torn.

The Upper South Chooses Sides

In the Upper South, many who only months earlier had rejected secession now embraced the Confederacy. To vote against southern independence was one thing, to fight fellow Southerners another. Thousands felt betrayed, believing that Lincoln had promised to achieve a peaceful reunion by waiting patiently for Unionists to retake power in the seceding states. One man furiously denounced the conflict as a "politician's war," conceding that "this is no time now to discuss the causes, but it is the duty of all who regard Southern institutions of value to side with the South, make common cause with the Confederate States and sink or swim with them."

In the end, Virginia, Arkansas, Tennessee, and North Carolina joined the Confederacy (**Map 15.1**). But in the border states of Delaware, Maryland, Kentucky, and Missouri, Unionism triumphed. Only in Delaware, where slaves accounted for less than 2 percent of the population, was the victory easy. In Maryland, Lincoln suspended the writ of habeas corpus, essentially setting aside constitutional guarantees that protect citizens from arbitrary arrest and detention, and he ordered U.S. troops into Baltimore. Maryland's legislature rejected secession.

The struggle turned violent in the West. In Missouri, Unionists won a narrow victory, but southern-sympathizing guerrilla bands roamed the state for the duration of the war, terrorizing civilians and soldiers alike. In Kentucky, Unionists

CHRONOLOGY

1861
- **March**. Lincoln's inauguration.
- Fort Sumter begins to run low on supplies.
- **April**. Lincoln authorizes resupply of Fort Sumter.
- Attack on Fort Sumter.
- Lincoln calls up 75,000 militiamen to put down rebellion.
- **April–May**. Virginia, North Carolina, Arkansas, and Tennessee join the Confederacy.

Fort Sumter
▶ Union fort on an island at the entrance to Charleston harbor in South Carolina. When, in early April 1861, President Lincoln made clear his intention to resupply Fort Sumter, the Confederates responded by attacking and capturing the fort. The attack on Fort Sumter marked the beginning of the Civil War.

| Why did the war for union become a fight for black freedom? | What problems did the Confederacy face at home? | How did the war affect the economy and politics of the North? | How did the Union finally win the war? | Conclusion: In what ways was the Civil War a "Second American Revolution"? |

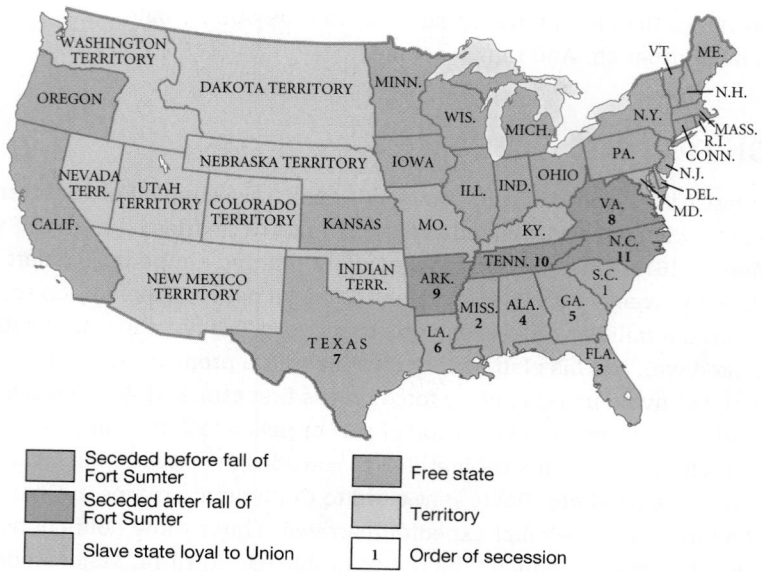

MAP 15.1 ■ Secession, 1860–1861

After Lincoln's election, the fifteen slave states debated what to do. Seven states quickly left the Union, four left after the firing on Fort Sumter, and four remained loyal to the Union.

also narrowly defeated secession, but the prosouthern minority claimed otherwise.

Lincoln understood that the border states—particularly Kentucky—contained indispensable resources, population, and wealth and also controlled major rivers and railroads. "I think to lose Kentucky is nearly the same as to lose the whole game," Lincoln said. "Kentucky gone, we can not hold Missouri, nor, as I think, Maryland. These all against us, . . . we would as well consent to separation at once."

In the end, only eleven of the fifteen slave states joined the Confederate States of America. Moreover, the four seceding Upper South states contained significant numbers of people who felt little affection for the Confederacy. Dissatisfaction was so rife in the western counties of Virginia that in 1863, citizens there voted to create the separate state of West Virginia, loyal to the Union. Still, the acquisition of four new states greatly strengthened the Confederacy's drive for national independence.

> ## QUICK REVIEW

Why did the attack on Fort Sumter force the Upper South to choose sides?

CHAPTER LOCATOR | How did the war begin? | **Why did each side expect to win?** | How did each side fare in the early years of the war?

CHAPTER 15
398 THE CRUCIBLE OF WAR, 1861–1865

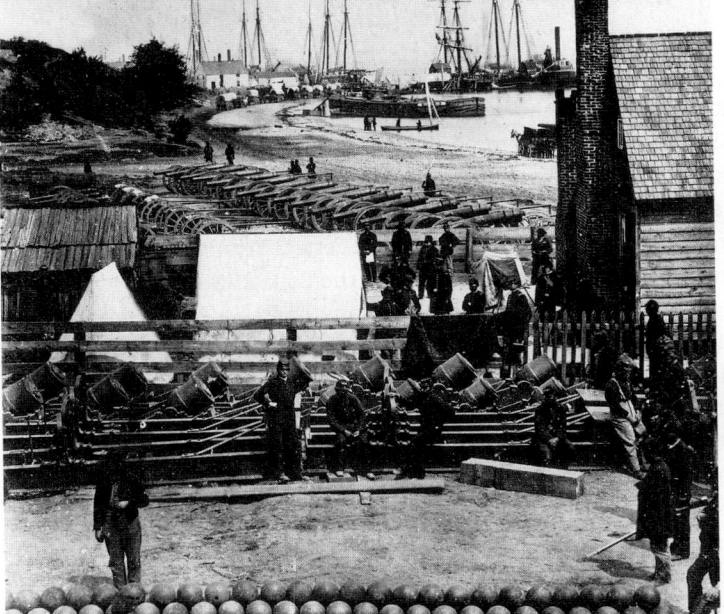

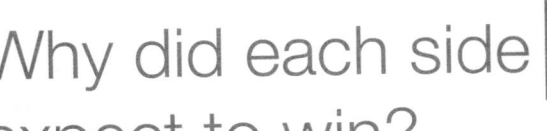
Why did each side expect to win?

Union Ordnance, Yorktown, Virginia

As the North successfully harnessed its enormous industrial capacity to meet the needs of the war, cannons, mortars, and shells poured out of its factories. A fraction of that abundance is seen here at Yorktown in 1862, ready for transportation to Union troops in the field. Library of Congress.

▶ FOR MORE HELP ANALYZING THIS IMAGE, see the visual activity for this chapter in the Online Study Guide at bedfordstmartins.com/roarkunderstanding.

ONLY SLAVEHOLDERS had a direct economic stake in preserving slavery, but most whites in the Confederacy defended the institution, the way of life built on it, and the Confederate nation. The degraded and subjugated status of blacks elevated the status of the poorest whites. One Southerner declared, "It is enough that one simply belongs to the superior and ruling race, to secure consideration and respect." Moreover, Yankee "aggression" was no longer a mere threat; it was real and at the South's door.

For Northerners, the South's failure to accept the democratic election of a president and its firing on the nation's flag challenged the rule of law, the authority of the Constitution, and the ability of the people to govern themselves. As an Indiana soldier told his wife, a "good government is the best thing on earth. Property is nothing without it, because it is not protected."

At the outset of the war, Yankees took heart from their superior numbers and resources, but the rebels believed they had advantages that nullified every northern strength. Both sides mobilized swiftly in 1861, and each devised what it believed would be a winning military and diplomatic strategy.

How They Expected to Win

The Union had overwhelming advantages in population, wealth, resources, and industrial capacity (**Figure 15.1**, page 400). Southerners knew they bucked the military odds, but hadn't the liberty-loving colonists in 1776 also done so? "Britain could not conquer three million," a Louisianan proclaimed, and "the world cannot conquer the South." The justice of their cause and the toughness of their people would overcome their material deficits.

The South's confidence also rested on its belief that northern prosperity depended on the South's cotton. Without cotton, New England textile mills would

Why did the war for union become a fight for black freedom?	What problems did the Confederacy face at home?	How did the war affect the economy and politics of the North?	How did the Union finally win the war?	Conclusion: In what ways was the Civil War a "Second American Revolution"?

stand idle. Without planters purchasing northern manufactured goods, northern factories would fail. And without the foreign exchange earned by the overseas sales of cotton, the financial structure of the entire Yankee nation would collapse.

Cotton would also make Europe a powerful ally of the Confederacy, Southerners reasoned. Of the 900 million pounds of cotton Britain imported annually, more than 700 million pounds came from the South. If the supply was interrupted, sheer economic need would make Britain (and perhaps France) a Confederate ally. And because the British navy ruled the seas, the North would find Britain a formidable foe.

The Confederacy devised a military strategy to exploit its advantages and minimize its liabilities. It recognized that a Union victory required the North to defeat and subjugate the South, but a Confederate victory required only that the South stay at home, blunt invasions, avoid battles that risked annihilating its army, and outlast the North's will to fight. When an opportunity presented itself, the South would strike the invaders.

The Lincoln administration countered with a strategy designed to take advantage of its superior resources. Lincoln declared a naval blockade of the Confederacy to deny it the ability to sell cotton abroad, giving the South far fewer dollars to pay for war goods. Lincoln also ordered the Union army into Virginia, at the same time planning a march through the Mississippi valley that would cut the Confederacy in two.

Lincoln and Davis Mobilize

Mobilization required effective political leadership, and at first glance, the South appeared to have the advantage. Jefferson Davis brought to the Confederate presidency a distinguished political career, including experience in the U.S.

FIGURE 15.1 ■ Resources of the Union and Confederacy
The Union's enormous statistical advantages failed to convince Confederates that their cause was doomed.

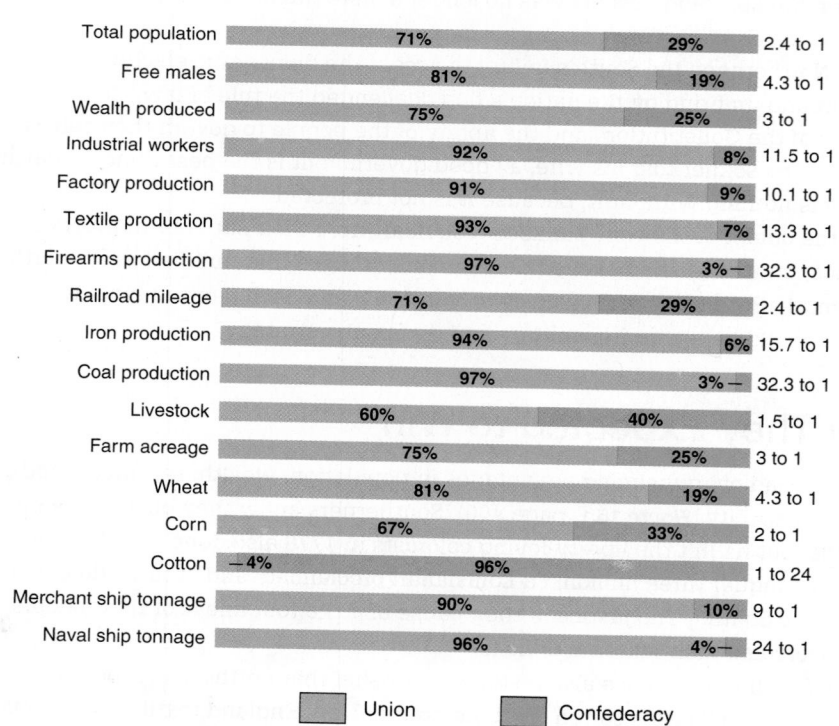

	Union	Confederacy	Ratio
Total population	71%	29%	2.4 to 1
Free males	81%	19%	4.3 to 1
Wealth produced	75%	25%	3 to 1
Industrial workers	92%	8%	11.5 to 1
Factory production	91%	9%	10.1 to 1
Textile production	93%	7%	13.3 to 1
Firearms production	97%	3%	32.3 to 1
Railroad mileage	71%	29%	2.4 to 1
Iron production	94%	6%	15.7 to 1
Coal production	97%	3%	32.3 to 1
Livestock	60%	40%	1.5 to 1
Farm acreage	75%	25%	3 to 1
Wheat	81%	19%	4.3 to 1
Corn	67%	33%	2 to 1
Cotton	4%	96%	1 to 24
Merchant ship tonnage	90%	10%	9 to 1
Naval ship tonnage	96%	4%	24 to 1

CHAPTER LOCATOR | How did the war begin? | Why did each side expect to win? | How did each side fare in the early years of the war?

400 CHAPTER 15 THE CRUCIBLE OF WAR, 1861–1865

Senate. He was also a West Point graduate, a combat veteran of the Mexican-American War, and a former secretary of war.

In contrast, Abraham Lincoln brought to the White House one term in the House of Representatives and almost no administrative experience. His sole brush with anything military was as a captain in the militia in the Black Hawk War, a brief struggle in Illinois in 1832 in which whites expelled the last Indians from the state.

Davis, however, proved to be less than he appeared. Although he worked hard, he had no gift for military strategy yet intervened often in military affairs. He was an even less able political leader. Quarrelsome and proud, he had an acid tongue that made enemies the Confederacy could ill afford.

With Lincoln, the North got far more than met the eye. He proved himself a master politician and a superb leader. When forming his cabinet, Lincoln appointed the ablest men, no matter that they were often his chief rivals and critics. He appointed Salmon P. Chase secretary of the treasury knowing that Chase had presidential ambitions. As secretary of state, he chose his chief opponent for the Republican nomination in 1860, William H. Seward. Despite his civilian background, Lincoln displayed an innate understanding of military strategy.

As Lincoln and Davis began gathering their armies, Confederates had to build almost everything from scratch, and Northerners had to channel their superior numbers and industrial resources to the war. On the eve of the war, the federal army numbered only 16,000 men. One-third of the officers followed the example of the Virginian Robert E. Lee, resigning their commissions and heading south. The U.S. Navy was in better shape. Forty-two ships were in service, and a large merchant marine would in time provide more ships and sailors for the Union cause.

The Confederacy made prodigious efforts to build new factories to supply its armies, but with only limited success. Even when factories managed to produce what the soldiers needed, southern railroads often could not deliver the goods. And each year, more railroads were captured, destroyed, or left in disrepair. Food production proved less of a problem, but food sometimes rotted before it reached the soldiers. The one bright spot was the Confederacy's Ordnance Bureau, headed by Josiah Gorgas, a near miracle worker when it came to manufacturing gunpowder, cannons, and rifles.

Recruiting and supplying huge armies required enormous new revenues. At first, the Union and the Confederacy sold war bonds, which essentially were loans from patriotic citizens. In addition, both sides turned to taxes. Eventually, both began printing paper money. Inflation soared, but the Confederacy suffered more because it financed a greater part of its wartime costs through the printing press. Prices in the Union rose by about 80 percent during the war, while inflation in the Confederacy topped 9,000 percent.

Within months of the bombardment of Fort Sumter, both sides found men to fight and ways to supply them. But the underlying strength of the northern economy gave the Union the decided advantage, and Northerners became itchy for action that would smash the rebellion. Horace Greeley's *New York Tribune* began to chant: "Forward to Richmond! Forward to Richmond!"

QUICK REVIEW

Why did the South believe it could win the war despite its material disadvantages?

| Why did the war for union become a fight for black freedom? | What problems did the Confederacy face at home? | How did the war affect the economy and politics of the North? | How did the Union finally win the war? | Conclusion: In what ways was the Civil War a "Second American Revolution"? |

How did each side fare in the early years of the war?

The Battle of Savage's Station, by Robert Knox Sneden, 1862 Artist Robert Sneden captured an early Confederate assault in what became known as the Seven Days Battle. Over the next three years, Sneden produced hundreds of vivid drawings and eventually thousands of pages of remembrance, providing one of the most complete accounts of a Union soldier's Civil War experience. 1996, Lora Robbins Collection of Virginia Art, Virginia Historical Society.

▶ FOR MORE HELP ANALYZING THIS IMAGE, see the visual activity for this chapter in the Online Study Guide at bedfordstmartins.com/roarkunderstanding.

DURING THE FIRST YEAR AND A HALF of the war, armies fought major campaigns in both the East and the West. As Yankee and rebel armies pounded each other on land, the navies fought on the seas and on the rivers of the South. In Europe, Confederate and U.S. diplomats competed for advantage in the corridors of power. All the while, casualties on both sides mounted.

Stalemate in the Eastern Theater

In the summer of 1861, Lincoln ordered the Union army assembling outside Washington to attack the Confederates defending Manassas, a railroad junction in Virginia about thirty miles southwest of Washington. On July 21, the army forded Bull Run, a branch of the Potomac River, and engaged the southern forces (**Map 15.2**). But southern reinforcements blunted the Union attack and then counterattacked. What began as an orderly Union retreat turned into a panicky stampede.

The significance of the **battle of Bull Run** (or **Manassas**, as Southerners called the battle) lay in the lessons Northerners and Southerners drew from it. For Southerners, it confirmed the superiority of rebel fighting men and the inevitability of Confederate nationhood. While victory fed southern pride, defeat sobered Northerners. It was a major setback, admitted the *New York Tribune*, but "let us go to work, then, with a will." Within four days of the disaster, President Lincoln authorized the enlistment of 1 million men for three years.

battle of Bull Run (Manassas)

▶ The first major engagement of the Civil War. Union and Confederate troops met on July 21, 1861, at Manassas, Virginia, thirty miles southwest of Washington, D.C. The Confederate victory over a larger Union force convinced many in the South that they would win the war, at the same time as it demonstrated to Northerners that victory would not be quick or easy.

CHAPTER LOCATOR | How did the war begin? | Why did each side expect to win? | How did each side fare in the early years of the war?

CHAPTER 15
402 THE CRUCIBLE OF WAR, 1861–1865

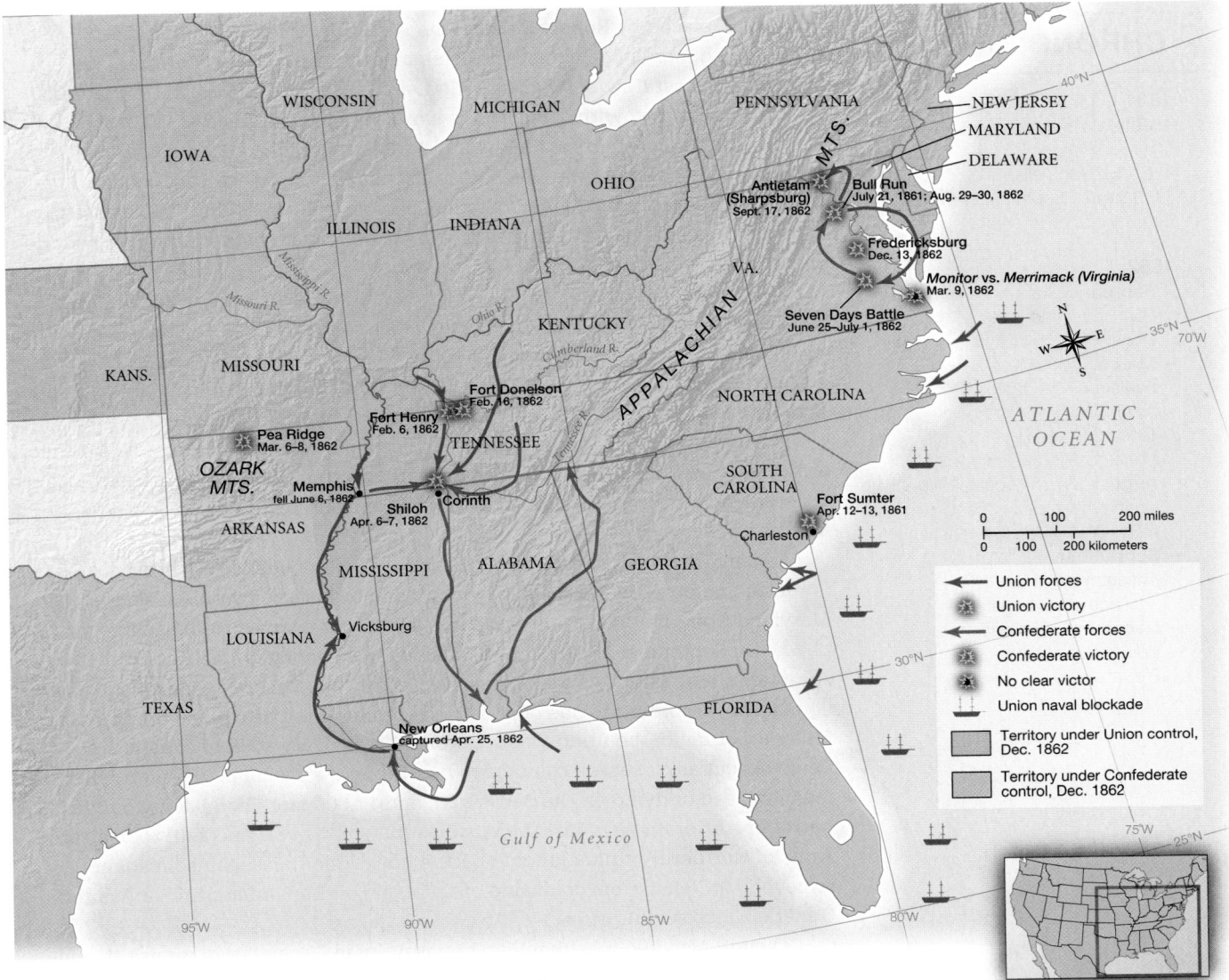

MAP 15.2 ■ The Civil War, 1861–1862
While most eyes were focused on the eastern theater, especially the ninety-mile stretch of land between Washington, D.C., and the Confederate capital of Richmond, Virginia, Union troops were winning strategic victories in the West.

Lincoln also appointed **George B. McClellan** commander of the newly named Army of the Potomac. A superb administrator and organizer, McClellan whipped his dispirited soldiers into shape, but he was reluctant to send them into battle. For all his energy, McClellan lacked decisiveness. Lincoln wanted a general who would advance, take risks, and fight, but McClellan went into winter quarters. "If General McClellan does not want to use the army I would like to *borrow* it," Lincoln declared in frustration.

Finally, in May 1862, McClellan launched his long-awaited offensive. He transported his highly polished army, now 130,000 strong, to the mouth of the James River and began slowly moving up the Yorktown peninsula toward Richmond. When he was within six miles of the Confederate capital, General Joseph Johnston hit him like a hammer. In the assault, Johnston was wounded

George B. McClellan

► General appointed to the command of the Army of the Potomac following the Union defeat at the battle of Bull Run in July 1861. McClellan was an able administrator and organizer, but he was indecisive and reluctant to take risks. Lincoln relieved him of his command twice. In 1864, McClellan ran against Lincoln for the presidency as a Democratic candidate.

Why did the war for union become a fight for black freedom?	What problems did the Confederacy face at home?	How did the war affect the economy and politics of the North?	How did the Union finally win the war?	Conclusion: In what ways was the Civil War a "Second American Revolution"?

CHRONOLOGY

1861
- **July**. Union forces are routed at Bull Run.
- George McClellan is appointed commander of the Army of the Potomac.

1862
- **February**. Grant captures Fort Henry and Fort Donelson.
- **March**. Union victory at battle of Pea Ridge.
- **April**. Battle of Shiloh in Tennessee ends Confederate bid to control Mississippi valley.
- **August**. Union forces are again defeated at second battle of Bull Run (Manassas).
- **September**. Battle of Antietam stops Lee's advance into Maryland.
- **December**. Confederate victory at battle of Fredericksburg

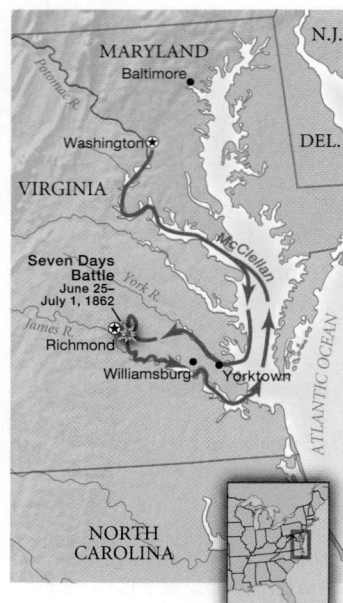

Peninsula Campaign, 1862

and was replaced by **Robert E. Lee**, who would become the South's most celebrated general. Lee named his command the Army of Northern Virginia.

The contrast between Lee and McClellan could hardly have been greater. McClellan brimmed with conceit; Lee was courteous and reserved. On the battlefield, McClellan grew timid, and Lee became audaciously, even recklessly, aggressive. And Lee had at his side military men of real talent: Thomas J. Jackson, nicknamed "Stonewall" for holding the line at Manassas, and James E. B. ("Jeb") Stuart, a twenty-nine-year-old cavalry commander who rode circles around Yankee troops.

Lee's assault initiated the Seven Days Battle (June 25–July 1) and began McClellan's retreat down the peninsula. By the time McClellan reached safety, 30,000 men from both sides had died or been wounded. Although Southerners suffered twice as many casualties as Northerners did, Lee had saved Richmond. Lincoln fired McClellan and replaced him with General John Pope.

In August, north of Richmond, at the second battle of Bull Run, Lee's smaller army battered Pope's forces and sent them scurrying back to Washington. Lincoln ordered Pope to Minnesota to pacify the Indians and restored McClellan to command.

Sensing that he had the enemy on the ropes, Lee pushed his army across the Potomac and invaded Maryland. A victory on northern soil would dislodge Maryland from the Union, Lee reasoned, and might even cause Lincoln to sue for peace. On September 17, 1862, McClellan's forces engaged Lee's army at Antietam Creek (see Map 15.2, page 403). With "solid shot . . . cracking skulls like eggshells," according to one observer, the armies went after each other. At Miller's Cornfield, the firing was so intense that "every stalk of corn in the . . . field was cut as closely as could have been done with a knife." By nightfall, 6,000 men lay dead or dying on the battlefield, and 17,000 more had been wounded. The **battle of Antietam** would be the bloodiest day of the war and sent the battered Army of Northern Virginia limping back home. Nonetheless, Lincoln again removed McClellan from command of the Army of the Potomac and appointed General Ambrose Burnside.

Though bloodied, Lee found an opportunity in December to punish the enemy at Fredericksburg, Virginia, where Burnside's 122,000 Union troops faced 78,500 Confederates dug in behind a stone wall on the heights above the Rappahannock River. Half a mile of open ground separated the armies. "A chicken could not live on that field when we open on it," a Confederate artillery officer predicted. Yet Burnside ordered a disastrous frontal assault. The battle of Fredericksburg was one of the Union's worst defeats. As 1862 ended, the North seemed no nearer to ending the rebellion than it had been when the war began.

Union Victories in the Western Theater

While most eyes focused on events in the East, the decisive early encounters of the war were taking place between the Appalachian Mountains and the Ozarks (see Map 15.2, page 403). Confederates wanted Missouri and Kentucky, states they claimed but did not control. Federals wanted to split Arkansas, Louisiana, and Texas from the Confederacy by taking control of the Mississippi River and to occupy Tennessee, one of the Confederacy's main producers of food, mules, and iron—all vital resources.

CHAPTER LOCATOR | How did the war begin? | Why did each side expect to win? | How did each side fare in the early years of the war?

CHAPTER 15
404 THE CRUCIBLE OF WAR, 1861–1865

Before Union forces could march on Tennessee, they needed to secure Missouri to the west. Union troops swept across Missouri to the border of Arkansas, where in March 1862 they encountered a 16,000-man Confederate army, which included three regiments of Indians from the Five Civilized Tribes in Indian Territory. The Union victory at the battle of Pea Ridge left Missouri free of Confederate troops, but guerrilla bands led by the notorious William Clarke Quantrill and "Bloody Bill" Anderson burned, tortured, scalped, and murdered Union civilians and soldiers until the final year of the war.

Even farther west, Confederate armies sought to fulfill Jefferson Davis's vision of a slaveholding empire stretching all the way to the Pacific. Both sides recognized the immense value of the gold and silver mines of California, Nevada, and Colorado. A quick strike by Texas troops took Santa Fe, New Mexico, in the winter of 1861–62. Then in March 1862, a band of Colorado miners ambushed and crushed southern forces at Glorieta Pass, outside Santa Fe, effectively ending the Confederate campaign in the far West.

The principal western battles took place in Tennessee, where General **Ulysses S. Grant** emerged as the key northern commander. "The art of war is simple," Grant said. "Find out where your enemy is, get at him as soon as you can and strike him as hard as you can, and keep moving on." Grant's philosophy of war as attrition would take a huge toll in human life, but it played to the North's superiority in manpower.

In February 1862, operating in tandem with U.S. Navy gunboats, Grant captured Fort Henry on the Tennessee River and Fort Donelson on the Cumberland (see Map 15.2, page 403). Defeat forced the Confederates to withdraw from all of Kentucky and most of Tennessee, but Grant followed.

On April 6, Confederate general Albert Sidney Johnston's army surprised him at Shiloh Church in Tennessee. Grant's troops were badly mauled the first day, but Grant remained cool and brought up reinforcements throughout the night.

Battle of Glorieta Pass, 1862

Robert E. Lee

▶ Commander of the Army of Northern Virginia. Lee was the South's most renowned general, and his skill played a key role in the Confederacy's successes against the much larger Union army.

battle of Antietam

▶ Battle fought in Maryland on September 17, 1862, between Union forces led by George McClellan and Confederate troops under the command of Robert E. Lee. The battle, a Union victory that left 6,000 dead and 17,000 wounded, was the bloodiest day of the war.

Ulysses S. Grant

▶ General in chief of all Union armies from March 1864 until the end of the war. Grant was a veteran of the Mexican-American War and made his name in the western theater in the early years of the Civil War. His strategy of waging a relentless war of attrition resulted in high casualties on both sides, but also in Union victory.

Major Battles of the Civil War, 1861–1862

April 12–13, 1861	Attack on Fort Sumter
July 21, 1861	First battle of Bull Run (Manassas)
February 6, 1862	Battle of Fort Henry
February 16, 1862	Battle of Fort Donelson
March 6–8, 1862	Battle of Pea Ridge
March 9, 1862	Battle of the *Merrimack* (the *Virginia*) and the *Monitor*
March 26, 1862	Battle of Glorieta Pass
April 6–7, 1862	Battle of Shiloh
May–July 1862	McClellan's peninsula campaign
June 6, 1862	Fall of Memphis
June 25–July 1, 1862	Seven Days Battle
August 29–30, 1862	Second battle of Bull Run (Manassas)
September 17, 1862	Battle of Antietam
December 13, 1862	Battle of Fredericksburg

Why did the war for union become a fight for black freedom?	What problems did the Confederacy face at home?	How did the war affect the economy and politics of the North?	How did the Union finally win the war?	Conclusion: In what ways was the Civil War a "Second American Revolution"?

The next morning, the Union army counterattacked, driving the Confederates before it. The battle of Shiloh was terribly costly to both sides; there were 20,000 casualties, among them General Johnston. Grant later said that after Shiloh, he "gave up all idea of saving the Union except by complete conquest."

Although no one knew it at the time, Shiloh ruined the Confederacy's bid to control the theater of operations in the West. The Yankees quickly captured the strategic town of Corinth, Mississippi; the river city of Memphis; and the South's largest city, New Orleans. By the end of 1862, the far West and most—but not all—of the Mississippi valley lay in Union hands. At the same time, the outcome of the struggle in another theater of war was also becoming clearer.

The Atlantic Theater

When the war began, the U.S. Navy's blockade fleet was much too small for the task and was thus ineffective. But as the Union built more ships and the size of the fleet increased, the Union navy dramatically improved its score. Despite its best efforts, the Confederacy never found a way to break the Union blockade. Each month, the Union fleet tightened its noose. By 1865, the blockaders were intercepting about half of the southern ships attempting to break through. The Confederacy was sealed off, with devastating results.

War at Sea

Unable to match the growth of the U.S. fleet, the Confederates experiment with ironclad warships.

The wooden Confederate warship *Merrimack* is refitted with armor plate and rechristened *Virginia*.

March 8, 1862: The *Virginia* sinks two wooden federal ships, killing at least 240 Union sailors.

March 9, 1862: The battle between the *Virginia* and the federal ironclad *Monitor* ends in a draw.

International Diplomacy

What the Confederates could not achieve on the seas, they sought to achieve through international diplomacy. The Confederates based their hope for European support on King Cotton. In theory, cotton-starved European nations would have no choice but to break the Union blockade and recognize the Confederacy. Southern hopes were not unreasonable, for at the height of the "cotton famine" in 1862, when 2 million British workers were unemployed, Britain tilted toward recognition. Along with several other European nations, Britain granted the Confederacy "belligerent" status, which enabled it to buy goods and build ships in European ports. But no country challenged the blockade or recognized the Confederate States of America as a nation.

King Cotton diplomacy failed for several reasons. A bumper cotton crop in 1860 meant that British textile manufacturers had plenty of cotton throughout 1861. In 1862, when a cotton shortage did occur, European manufacturers found new sources in India, Egypt, and elsewhere. (See "Global Comparison.")

King Cotton diplomacy
▶ Confederate diplomatic strategy centered on starving Britain and France of cotton and forcing them to side with the Confederacy. A bumper cotton crop in 1860, the emergence of new sources of cotton outside the South, and the issuing of the Emancipation Proclamation all contributed to the failure of King Cotton diplomacy.

CHAPTER LOCATOR | How did the war begin? | Why did each side expect to win? | How did each side fare in the early years of the war?

CHAPTER 15
406 THE CRUCIBLE OF WAR, 1861–1865

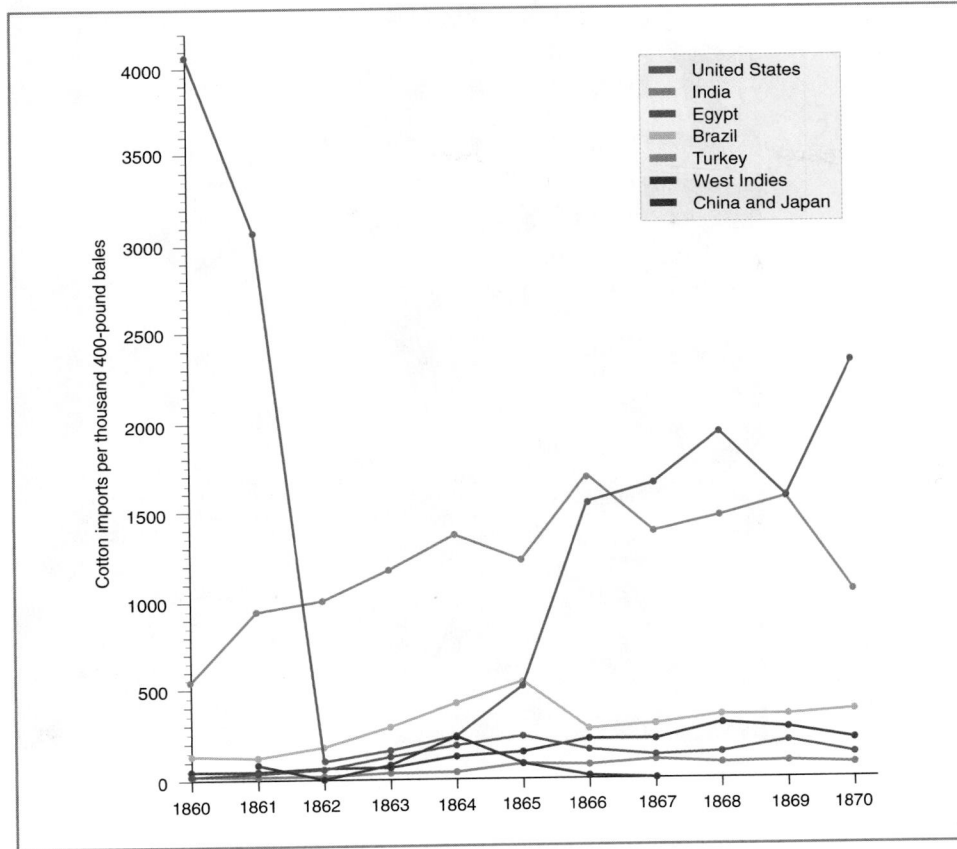

GLOBAL COMPARISON

European Cotton Imports, 1860–1870

In 1860, the South enjoyed a near monopoly in supplying cotton to Europe's textile mills, but the Civil War almost entirely halted its exports. Figures for Europe's importation of cotton for 1861 to 1865 reveal one of the reasons the Confederacy's King Cotton diplomacy failed: Europeans found other sources of cotton. Which countries were most important in filling the void? When the war ended in 1865, cotton production resumed in the South, and exports to Europe again soared. Did the South regain its near monopoly? How would you characterize the United States' competitive position five years after the war?

In addition, the development of a brisk trade between the Union and Britain—British war materiel for American grain and flour—helped offset the decline in textiles and encouraged Britain to remain neutral.

Europe's temptation to intervene disappeared for good in 1862. Union military successes in the West made Britain and France think twice about linking their fates to the struggling Confederacy. Moreover, in September 1862, Lincoln announced a new policy that made an alliance with the Confederacy an alliance with slavery—a commitment the French and British, who had outlawed slavery in their empires and looked forward to its eradication worldwide, were not willing to make. After 1862, the South's cause was linked irrevocably with slavery and reaction, and the Union's cause was linked with freedom and democracy.

QUICK REVIEW

What successes and failures did the Union and the Confederacy experience in 1861 and 1862?

| Why did the war for union become a fight for black freedom? | What problems did the Confederacy face at home? | How did the war affect the economy and politics of the North? | How did the Union finally win the war? | Conclusion: In what ways was the Civil War a "Second American Revolution"? |

Why did the war for union become a fight for black freedom?

FOR A YEAR AND A HALF, Lincoln insisted that the North fought strictly to save the Union and not to abolish slavery. Despite Lincoln's repeated pronouncements, however, the war for union became a war for African American freedom. Each month the conflict dragged on, it became clearer that the Confederate war machine depended heavily on slavery. Rebel armies used slaves to build fortifications, haul materiel, tend horses, and perform camp chores. On the home front, slaves labored in ironworks and shipyards, and they grew the food that fed both soldiers and civilians. Union military commanders and politicians alike gradually realized that to defeat the Confederacy, the North would have to destroy slavery.

From Slaves to Contraband

Lincoln detested human bondage, but as president he felt compelled to act prudently in the interests of the Union. He doubted his right under the Constitution to tamper with the "domestic institutions" of any state, even states in rebellion. An astute politician, Lincoln also worked within the tight limits of public opinion. The issue of black freedom was particularly explosive in the loyal border states, where slaveholders threatened to jump into the arms of the Confederacy at even the hint of emancipation.

Black freedom also raised alarms in the free states. The Democratic Party gave notice that emancipation would make the war strictly a Republican affair. Moreover, many white Northerners were not about to risk their lives to satisfy what they

CHAPTER LOCATOR | How did the war begin? | Why did each side expect to win? | How did each side fare in the early years of the war?

408 CHAPTER 15
THE CRUCIBLE OF WAR, 1861–1865

considered abolitionist "fanaticism." "We Won't Fight to Free the Nigger," one popular banner read. They feared that emancipation would propel "two or three million semi-savages" northward, where they would crowd into white neighborhoods, compete for white jobs, and mix with white "sons and daughters."

Yet proponents of emancipation pressed Lincoln as relentlessly as the anti-emancipation forces. The Republican-dominated Congress declined to leave slavery policy entirely in President Lincoln's hands. In August 1861, Congress approved the Confiscation Act, which allowed the seizure of any slave employed directly by the Confederate military. It also prohibited slavery in the territories and abolished slavery in Washington, D.C. Democrats and border-state representatives voted against even these mild measures.

Slaves, not politicians, became the most insistent force for emancipation. By escaping their masters by the tens of thousands and running away to Union lines, they put slavery on the North's wartime agenda. Runaways forced Northerners to answer a crucial question: Were the runaways now free, or were they still slaves who, according to the fugitive slave law, had to be returned to their masters? At first, Yankee military officers sent the fugitives back. But Union armies needed laborers, and some officers accepted the runaways and put them to work. At Fort Monroe, Virginia, General Benjamin F. Butler refused to turn them over to their owners, calling them contraband of war, meaning "confiscated property." Congress made Butler's practice national policy in March 1862 when it forbade the return of fugitive slaves to their masters. Slaves were still not legally free, but there was a tilt toward emancipation.

Lincoln's policy of noninterference with slavery gradually crumbled. To calm Northerners' racial fears, Lincoln offered colonization, the deportation of African Americans from the United States to Haiti, Panama, or elsewhere. Congress voted a small amount of money to underwrite colonization, but after one miserable experiment on a small island in the Caribbean, practical limitations and stiff black opposition sank further efforts.

While Lincoln was developing his own antislavery initiatives, he snuffed out actions that he believed would jeopardize northern unity. He was particularly alert to Union commanders who tried to dictate slavery policy from the field. In August 1861, when John C. Frémont, former Republican presidential nominee and now commander of federal troops in Missouri, freed the slaves belonging to Missouri rebels, Lincoln forced the general to revoke his edict. The following May, when General David Hunter freed the slaves in Georgia, South Carolina, and Florida, Lincoln countermanded his order. Increasingly, Lincoln found it impossible to control federal policy on slavery.

From Contraband to Free People

On August 22, 1862, Lincoln replied to an angry abolitionist who demanded that he attack slavery. "My paramount objective in this struggle *is* to save the Union," Lincoln said deliberately, "and is *not* either to save or destroy slavery. If I could save the Union without freeing *any* slave I would do it, and if I could save it by freeing *all* the slaves I would do it; and if I could save it by freeing some and leaving others alone I would also do that." Thus, Lincoln announced that he would emancipate every slave if doing so would preserve the Union.

CHRONOLOGY

1861
– **August**. First Confiscation Act.

1862
– **March**. Congress forbids the return of fugitive slaves to their masters.
– **July**. Second Confiscation Act.
– Militia Act.
– **September**. Preliminary Emancipation Proclamation.
– **November**. Democrats gain thirty-four congressional seats in midterm election.

1863
– **January**. Emancipation Proclamation becomes law.

Why did the war for union become a fight for black freedom?	What problems did the Confederacy face at home?	How did the war affect the economy and politics of the North?	How did the Union finally win the war?	Conclusion: In what ways was the Civil War a "Second American Revolution"?

By the summer of 1862, events were tumbling rapidly toward emancipation. On July 17, Congress adopted the second Confiscation Act. The first had confiscated slaves employed by the Confederate military; the second declared all slaves of rebel masters "forever free of their servitude." In theory, this breathtaking measure freed most Confederate slaves, for slaveholders formed the backbone of the rebellion. Congress had traveled far since the war began.

Lincoln had, too. He now saw emancipation as a "military necessity, absolutely essential to the preservation of the Union." On September 22, Lincoln issued his preliminary **Emancipation Proclamation** promising freedom to slaves in areas still in rebellion on January 1, 1863. The limitations of the proclamation—it exempted the loyal border states and the Union-occupied areas of the Confederacy—caused some to ridicule the act. The *Times* (London) observed cynically, "Where he has no power Mr. Lincoln will set the negroes free, where he retains power he will consider them as slaves." But Lincoln had no power to free slaves in loyal states, and invading Union armies would liberate slaves in the Confederacy as they advanced.

By presenting emancipation as a "military necessity," Lincoln hoped he had disarmed his conservative critics. Emancipation would deprive the Confederacy of valuable slave laborers, shorten the war, and thus save lives. Democrats, however, fumed that the "shrieking and howling abolitionist faction" had captured the White House. In the November 1862 elections, the Democrats gained thirty-four congressional seats. House Democrats quickly proposed a resolution branding emancipation "a high crime against the Constitution." The Republicans, who maintained narrow majorities in both houses of Congress, barely beat it back.

As promised, on New Year's Day 1863, Lincoln issued the final Emancipation Proclamation. In addition to freeing the slaves in the rebel states, the edict also committed the federal government to the fullest use of African Americans to defeat the Confederate enemy.

War of Black Liberation

Even before Lincoln proclaimed emancipation a Union war aim, African Americans in the North had volunteered to fight. But the War Department, doubtful of their abilities and fearful of white reaction to serving side by side with them, refused to make black men soldiers. Instead, the army employed black men as manual laborers; black women sometimes found employment as laundry workers and cooks.

As Union casualty lists lengthened, Northerners gradually and reluctantly turned to African Americans. With the Militia Act of July 1862, Congress authorized enrolling blacks in "any military or naval service for which they may be found competent." After the Emancipation Proclamation, whites were fighting and dying for black freedom, and few insisted that blacks remain out of harm's way behind the lines. Indeed, whites insisted that blacks share the danger, especially after March 1863, when Congress resorted to the draft to fill the Union army.

The military was far from color-blind, and black soldiers suffered discrimination and abuse. Still, when the war ended, 179,000 African American men had served in the Union army, and, in time, whites allowed blacks to put down their shovels and to shoulder rifles. At the battles of Port Hudson and Milliken's Bend on the Mississippi River and at Fort Wagner in Charleston harbor, black courage

Emancipation Proclamation

▶ Presidential proclamation issued on January 1, 1863, declaring all slaves in Confederate-controlled territory free. The limitations of the proclamation—it exempted the loyal border states and the Union-occupied areas of the Confederacy—caused some to ridicule the act. Nonetheless, the Emancipation Proclamation made the Civil War a war to free slaves.

CHAPTER LOCATOR | How did the war begin? | Why did each side expect to win? | How did each side fare in the early years of the war?

CHAPTER 15
410 THE CRUCIBLE OF WAR, 1861–1865

under fire finally dispelled notions that African Americans could not fight. More than 38,000 black soldiers died in the Civil War, a mortality rate that was higher than that of white troops. Blacks played a crucial role in the triumph of the Union and the destruction of slavery in the South.

African Americans in Uniform

African American soldiers were:

  Segregated into black regiments.

  Paid substantially less than whites.

  Denied the opportunity to become commissioned officers.

  Punished by the army as if they were slaves.

  Often assigned to labor battalions rather than to combat units.

African Americans comprised 10 percent of all Union soldiers.

In the free states, 71 percent of black men ages eighteen to forty-five fought for the Union.

More than 130,000 black soldiers came from the slave states.

Approximately 100,000 ex-slaves fought for the Union.

QUICK REVIEW

Why did Lincoln feel compelled to issue the Emancipation Proclamation?

Why did the war for union become a fight for black freedom?	What problems did the Confederacy face at home?	How did the war affect the economy and politics of the North?	How did the Union finally win the war?	Conclusion: In what ways was the Civil War a "Second American Revolution"?

What problems did the Confederacy face at home?

Southern Women Women such as these North Carolinians were expected to shift their energies from family to the southern cause. Most served by sewing uniforms, knitting socks, and rolling bandages at home. Some worked in newly founded hospitals nursing the sick and wounded. As the war ground on, southern women had their hands full trying to keep their families fed and safe. Museum of the Confederacy, Richmond, Virginia.

MONSTROUS LOSSES ON THE BATTLEFIELD nearly bled the Confederacy to death. White Southerners on the home front also suffered, even at the hands of their own government. Efforts by the Davis administration in Richmond to centralize power in order to fight the war effectively convinced some men and women that the Confederacy had betrayed them. Wartime economic changes hurt everyone, some more than others. By 1863, planters and yeomen who had stood together began to drift apart. Most disturbing of all, slaves became open participants in the destruction of slavery and the Confederacy.

Revolution from Above

Jefferson Davis faced the task of building an army and a navy from almost nothing, supplying them from inadequate factories, and paying for the war from a nonexistent treasury. Finding eager soldiers proved easiest. Hundreds of officers defected from the U.S. Army, and hundreds of thousands of eager young rebels volunteered to follow them.

The Confederacy's economy and finances proved tougher problems. Because of the Union blockade, the government had no choice but to build an industrial sector itself. The government also harnessed private companies, such as the huge

CHAPTER LOCATOR | How did the war begin? | Why did each side expect to win? | How did each side fare in the early years of the war?

CHAPTER 15
412 THE CRUCIBLE OF WAR, 1861–1865

Tredegar Iron Works in Richmond, to the war effort. Paying for the war became the most difficult task. A flood of paper money caused debilitating inflation. By 1863, people in Charleston paid ten times more for food than they had paid at the start of the war. The Confederacy manufactured much more than most people imagined possible, but it never produced all that the South needed.

Richmond's war-making effort brought unprecedented government intrusion into the private lives of Confederate citizens. In April 1862, the Confederate Congress passed the first conscription (draft) law in American history. All able-bodied white males between the ages of eighteen and thirty-five (later seventeen and fifty) were liable to serve in the rebel army. The government adopted a policy of impressment, which allowed officials to confiscate food, horses, and wagons from private citizens and to pay for them at below-market rates. After March 1863, the Confederacy legally impressed slaves, employing them as military laborers.

Richmond's centralizing efforts ran head-on into the South's traditional values of states' rights and unfettered individualism. The states lashed out at what Georgia governor Joseph E. Brown denounced as the "dangerous usurpation by Congress of the reserved right of the States." Richmond and the states struggled for control of money, supplies, and soldiers, with damaging consequences for the war effort.

Hardship Below

Hardships on the home front fell most heavily on the poor. The draft stripped yeoman farms of men, leaving the women and children to grow what they ate. Inflation and shortages afflicted the entire population, but the rich lost luxuries while the poor lost necessities. In the spring of 1863, bread riots broke out in a dozen cities and villages across the South. "Men cannot be expected to fight for the Government that permits their wives & children to starve," one Southerner observed. Although a few wealthy individuals shared their bounty and the Confederate and state governments made efforts at social welfare, every attempt fell short. When the war ended, one-third of the soldiers had already gone home. A Mississippi deserter explained, "We are poor men and are willing to defend our country but our families [come] first."

Yeomen perceived a profound inequality of sacrifice. The draft law permitted a man who had money to hire a substitute to take his place. Moreover, the "twenty-Negro law" exempted one white man on every plantation with twenty or more slaves. The government intended this law to provide protection for white women and to see that slaves tended the crops, but yeomen perceived it as rich men's evasion of military service. A Mississippian complained that stay-at-home planters sent their slaves into the fields to grow cotton while in plain view "poor soldiers' wives are plowing with *their own* hands to make a subsistence for themselves and children—while their husbands are suffering, bleeding and dying for their country." In fact, most slaveholders went off to war, but the extreme suffering of common folk and the relative immunity of planters increased class friction.

The Richmond government hoped that the crucible of war would mold a region into a nation. Officials promoted a southern nationalism to "excite in our citizens an ardent and enduring attachment to our Government and its institutions." Clergymen assured their congregations that God had blessed slavery and

CHRONOLOGY

1862
- The South faces various war-related problems: inadequate manufacturing, inflation, shortages of food and other necessities, and government impressment of civilian goods.
- Confederate Congress passes the first conscription (draft) law in American history.

1863
- Riots break out in a dozen southern cities and villages because of the high cost of food.

Why did the war for union become a fight for black freedom?	What problems did the Confederacy face at home?	How did the war affect the economy and politics of the North?	How did the Union finally win the war?	Conclusion: In what ways was the Civil War a "Second American Revolution"?

the new nation. Patriotic songwriters, poets, authors, and artists extolled southern culture. Jefferson Davis asked citizens to observe national days of fasting and prayer. But these efforts failed to win over thousands of die-hard Unionists, and animosity between yeomen and planters increased rather than decreased. The war also threatened to rip the southern social fabric along its racial seam.

The Disintegration of Slavery

Slaves took advantage of the upheaval of war to reach for freedom. Some half a million of the South's 4 million slaves ran away to Union military lines. More than 100,000 runaways took up arms as federal soldiers and sailors and attacked slavery directly. Other men and women stayed in the slave quarter, where they staked their claim to more freedom.

War disrupted slavery in many ways. Almost immediately, it called the master away, leaving the mistress to assume responsibility for the plantation. But mistresses could not maintain traditional standards of slave discipline in wartime, and the balance of power shifted. Slaves got to the fields late, worked indifferently, and quit early. Some slaveholders responded violently; most saw no alternative but to strike bargains—offering gifts or part of the crop—to keep slaves at home and at work. Slaveholders had believed that they "knew" their slaves, but they learned that they did not. When the war began, a North Carolina woman praised her slaves as "diligent and respectful." When it ended, she said, "As to the idea of a *faithful servant, it is all a fiction.*"

> **QUICK REVIEW**

How did wartime hardship in the South contribute to class animosity?

CHAPTER LOCATOR | How did the war begin? | Why did each side expect to win? | How did each side fare in the early years of the war?

414 CHAPTER 15
THE CRUCIBLE OF WAR, 1861–1865

U.S. Sanitary Commission, Brandy Station, Virginia, 1863 The burden of caring for millions of Union soldiers was more than the government could shoulder. Private initiative in the form of the U.S. Sanitary Commission brought additional medical attention to the Union wounded and boosted the comfort and morale of soldiers in the camps. National Archives.

ALTHOUGH THE NORTH was largely untouched by the fighting, Northerners could not avoid being touched by the war. Almost every family had a son, husband, father, or brother in uniform. Moreover, total war blurred the distinction between home front and battlefield. As in the South, men marched off to fight, but preserving the country was also women's work. For civilians as well as soldiers, for women as well as men, war was transforming.

The need to build and fuel the Union war machine boosted the economy. The Union sent nearly 2 million men into the military and still increased production in almost every area. But because the rewards and burdens of patriotism were distributed unevenly, the North experienced sharp, even violent, divisions. Workers confronted employers, whites confronted blacks, and Democrats confronted Republicans. Still, Northerners on the home front remained fervently attached to the Union.

The Government and the Economy

When the war began, the United States had no national banking system, no national currency, and no federal income tax. But the secession of eleven slave states cut the Democrats' strength in Congress in half, allowing the Republicans to put all of these things in place. By revolutionizing the country's banking, monetary, and tax structures, the Republicans generated enormous economic power.

The Republican Economic Program

The Legal Tender Act (February 1862) creates a national currency.

The National Banking Act (February 1863) establishes a system of national banks.

Congress also enacts a series of sweeping tax laws, including the first income tax.

The Republicans' wartime legislation also aimed at integrating the West more thoroughly into the Union. In May 1862, Congress approved the Homestead Act, which offered 160 acres of public land to settlers who would live and labor on it. The Homestead Act bolstered western loyalty and in time resulted in more than a million new farms. The Pacific Railroad Act in July 1862 provided massive federal assistance for building a transcontinental railroad that ran from Omaha to San Francisco when completed in 1869. Congress further bound East and West by subsidizing the Pony Express mail service and a transcontinental telegraph.

Two additional initiatives had long-term economic consequences. Congress created the Department of Agriculture and passed the Land-Grant College Act (also known as the Morrill Act after its sponsor, Representative Justin Morrill of Vermont), which set aside public land to support universities that emphasized "agriculture and mechanical arts." The Lincoln administration immeasurably strengthened the North's effort to win the war, but its ideas also permanently changed the nation.

Women and Work on the Home Front

More than a million farm men were called to the military, placing additional burdens on farm women. "I met more women driving teams on the road and saw more at work in the fields than men," a visitor to Iowa reported in the fall of 1862. Rising production testified to their success in plowing, planting, and harvesting. Rapid mechanization assisted farm women in their new roles. Cyrus McCormick sold 165,000 of his reapers during the war years. The combination of high prices for farm products and increased production ensured that war brought prosperity to the rural North.

In cities, women stepped into jobs vacated by men, particularly in manufacturing, and also into essentially new occupations such as government secretaries and clerks. Women made up about one-quarter of the manufacturing workforce when the war began and one-third when it ended. As more and more women entered the workforce, employers cut wages. In 1864, New York seamstresses working fourteen-hour days earned only $1.54 a week. Urban workers resorted increasingly to strikes, but their protests rarely succeeded.

Most middle-class white women stayed home and contributed to the war effort in traditional ways. They sewed, wrapped bandages, and sold homemade goods at local fairs to raise money to aid the soldiers. Other women expressed their patriotism in an untraditional way, defying prejudices about female delicacy by volunteering to nurse the wounded. Many northern female volunteers worked through the U.S. Sanitary Commission, a civilian organization that bought and distributed clothing, food, and medicine and recruited doctors and nurses.

CHAPTER LOCATOR | How did the war begin? | Why did each side expect to win? | How did each side fare in the early years of the war?

416 CHAPTER 15 THE CRUCIBLE OF WAR, 1861–1865

Some volunteers went on to become paid military nurses. Dorothea Dix, well known for her efforts to reform insane asylums, was named superintendent of female nurses in April 1861. Eventually, some 3,000 women served under her. Most nurses worked in hospitals behind the battle lines, but some, like Clara Barton, who later founded the American Red Cross, worked in battlefield units. Women who served in the war went on to lead the postwar movement to establish training schools for female nurses.

Politics and Dissent

At first, the bustle of economic and military mobilization seemed to silence politics, but bipartisan unity did not last. Within a year, Democrats were labeling the Republican administration a "reign of terror," and Republicans were calling Democrats the party of "Dixie, Davis, and the Devil."

In September 1862, in an effort to stifle opposition to the war, Lincoln placed under military arrest any person who discouraged enlistments, resisted the draft, or engaged in "disloyal" practices. Before the war ended, his administration imprisoned nearly 14,000 individuals, most in the border states. The majority of the prisoners were not northern Democratic opponents but Confederates, blockade runners, and citizens of foreign countries, and most of those arrested gained quick release. Still, the administration's heavy-handed tactics did suppress free speech.

When the Republican-dominated Congress enacted the draft law in March 1863, Democrats had another grievance. The law required that all men between the ages of twenty and forty-five enroll and make themselves available for a lottery that would decide who went to war. It also allowed a draftee to hire a substitute or simply to pay a $300 fee and get out of his military obligation. As in the South, common folk could be heard chanting, "A rich man's war and a poor man's fight."

Linking the draft and emancipation, Democrats argued that Republicans employed an unconstitutional means (the draft) to achieve an unconstitutional end (emancipation). In the summer of 1863, antidraft, antiblack mobs went on rampages in northern cities. In July in New York City, Democratic Irish workingmen erupted in four days of rioting. The **New York City draft riots** killed at least 105 people, most of them black.

Racist mobs failed to subordinate African Americans, however. Free black leaders had lobbied aggressively for emancipation, and after Lincoln's proclamation, they pushed for equality in the North. They won a few small victories, but significant progress toward black equality would have to wait until the war ended.

New York City draft riots

▶ Four days of rioting in July 1863 triggered by efforts to enforce the military draft. The antidraft, antiblack mob was dominated by Democratic Irish workingmen. Some 105 people were killed, most of them black. The riots reflected growing northern discontent with the war.

QUICK REVIEW

What were the most important changes that occurred in the North during the war?

Why did the war for union become a fight for black freedom?

What problems did the Confederacy face at home?

How did the war affect the economy and politics of the North?

How did the Union finally win the war?

Conclusion: In what ways was the Civil War a "Second American Revolution"?

How did the Union finally win the war?

Ruins of Richmond As the Confederate government evacuated Richmond during the evening of April 2, 1865, demolition squads set fire to everything that had military or industrial value. Huge explosions devastated the arsenal, the ruins of which are shown here. As one witness observed, "The old war-scarred city seemed to prefer annihilation to conquest." Library of Congress.

siege of Vicksburg

▶ A six-week siege by General Grant that came to an end on July 4, 1863, when the 30,000 Confederate troops holding the city surrendered. Victory at Vicksburg gave the Union control of the entire Mississippi River. Together with Gettysburg, Vicksburg marked a major turning point in the war.

IN THE EARLY MONTHS OF 1863, the Union's prospects looked bleak, and the Confederate cause stood at high tide. Then, in July 1863, the tide began to turn. The military man most responsible for this shift was Ulysses S. Grant. Elevated to supreme command, Grant knit together a powerful war machine that integrated a sophisticated command structure, modern technology, and complex logistics and supply systems. Grant's plan was simple: Killing more of the enemy than he kills of you equaled "the complete overthrow of the rebellion."

The North ground out the victory battle by bloody battle. Still, Southerners were not deterred. The fighting escalated in the last two years of the war. As national elections approached in the fall of 1864, Lincoln expected a war-weary North to reject him. Instead, northern voters declared their willingness to continue the war in the defense of the ideals of union and freedom.

Vicksburg and Gettysburg

Vicksburg, Mississippi, situated on the eastern bank of the Mississippi River, stood between Union forces and complete control of the river. Union forces under Grant lay siege to the city in an effort to starve out the enemy. The **siege of Vicksburg** lasted six weeks, coming to an end on July 4, 1863, when nearly 30,000 rebels marched out of Vicksburg, stacked their arms, and surrendered unconditionally. A Yankee captain wrote home to his wife: "The backbone of the Rebellion is this day broken. The Confederacy is divided. . . . Vicksburg is ours. The Mississippi River is opened, and Gen. Grant is to be our next President."

Vicksburg Campaign, 1863

- Union advance
- Confederate advance
- Confederate retreat
- Union victory

CHAPTER LOCATOR | How did the war begin? | Why did each side expect to win? | How did each side fare in the early years of the war?

418 CHAPTER 15 THE CRUCIBLE OF WAR, 1861–1865

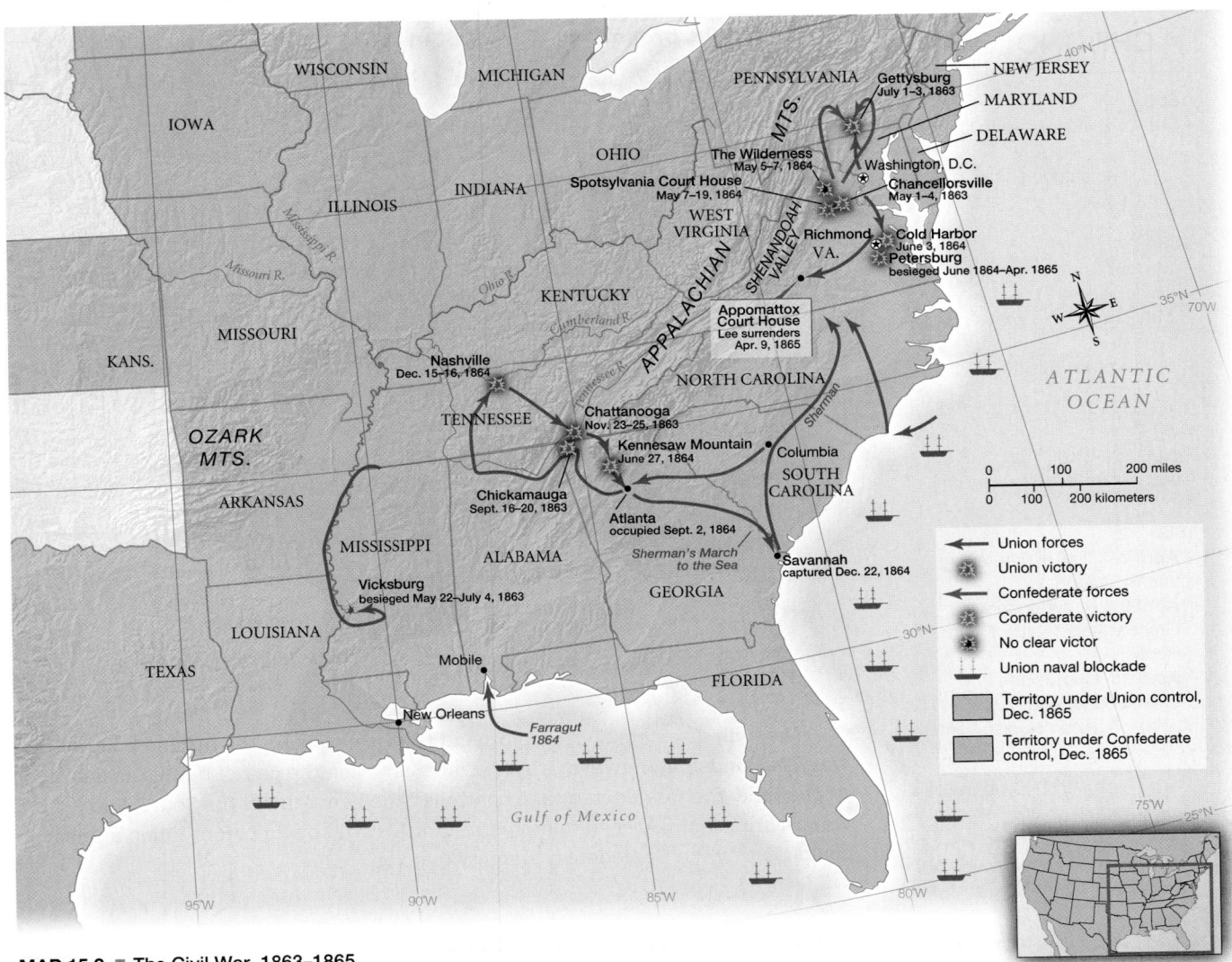

MAP 15.3 ■ The Civil War, 1863–1865
Ulysses S. Grant's victory at Vicksburg divided the Confederacy at the Mississippi River. William Tecumseh Sherman's march from Chattanooga to Savannah divided it again. In northern Virginia, Robert E. Lee fought fiercely, but Grant's larger, better-supplied armies prevailed.

▶ FOR MORE HELP ANALYZING THIS MAP, see the map activity for this chapter in the Online Study Guide at bedfordstmartins.com/roarkunderstanding.

On the same Fourth of July, word arrived that Union forces had defeated General Lee at Gettysburg, Pennsylvania (**Map 15.3**). Emboldened by his victory at Chancellorsville in May, Lee and his 75,000-man army had invaded Pennsylvania. On June 28, Union forces under General George G. Meade intercepted the Confederates at the small town of Gettysburg, where Union soldiers occupied the high ground. In three days of furious fighting from July 1 to July 3, the Confederates failed to dislodge the Yankees. The **battle of Gettysburg** cost Lee more than one-third of his army—28,000 casualties. On the night of July 4, 1863, he marched his battered army back to Virginia.

battle of Gettysburg
▶ Battle fought at Gettysburg, Pennsylvania (July 1–3, 1863), between Union forces under General Meade and Confederate forces under General Lee. The Union emerged victorious, and Lee lost more than one-third of his men. Together with Vicksburg, Gettysburg marked a major turning point in the war.

| Why did the war for union become a fight for black freedom? | What problems did the Confederacy face at home? | How did the war affect the economy and politics of the North? | **How did the Union finally win the war?** | Conclusion: In what ways was the Civil War a "Second American Revolution"? |

CHRONOLOGY

1863
- **July**. Vicksburg falls to Union forces.
- Lee is defeated at battle of Gettysburg.

1864
- **March**. Grant is appointed Union general in chief.
- **May–June**. Wilderness campaign.
- **September**. Atlanta falls to Sherman.
- **November**. Lincoln is reelected.
- **December**. Savannah falls to Sherman.

1865
- **April 2–3**. Fall of Petersburg and Richmond.
- **April 9**. Lee surrenders to Grant at Appomattox Court House.
- **April 15**. Lincoln dies from bullet wound; Andrew Johnson becomes president.

Major Battles of the Civil War, 1863–1865

May 1–4, 1863	Battle of Chancellorsville
July 1–3, 1863	Battle of Gettysburg
July 4, 1863	Fall of Vicksburg
September 16–20, 1863	Battle of Chickamauga
November 23–25, 1863	Battle of Chattanooga
May 5–7, 1864	Battle of the Wilderness
May 7–19, 1864	Battle of Spotsylvania Court House
June 3, 1864	Battle of Cold Harbor
June 27, 1864	Battle of Kennesaw Mountain
September 2, 1864	Fall of Atlanta
November–December 1864	Sheridan sacks Shenandoah Valley Sherman's March to the Sea
December 15–16, 1864	Battle of Nashville
December 22, 1864	Fall of Savannah
April 2–3, 1865	Fall of Petersburg and Richmond
April 9, 1865	Lee surrenders at Appomattox Court House

The twin disasters at Vicksburg and Gettysburg were the turning point of the war. It is hindsight, however, that permits us to see the pair of battles as decisive. At the time, the Confederacy still controlled the heartland of the South, and war-weariness threatened to erode the North's will to win before Union armies could destroy the Confederacy's ability to go on.

Grant Takes Command

In September 1863, Union general William Rosecrans placed his army in a dangerous situation in Chattanooga, Tennessee, where he had retreated after defeat at the battle of Chickamauga (see Map 15.3, page 419). Rebels surrounded the disorganized bluecoats and threatened to starve them into submission. Grant, now commander of Union forces between the Mississippi River and the Appalachians, arrived in Chattanooga in October. Within weeks, he opened an effective supply line, broke the siege, and routed the Confederate army. The victory at Chattanooga on November 25 opened the door to Georgia. In March 1864, Lincoln asked Grant to come east to become the general in chief of all Union armies.

In Washington, General Grant implemented his grand strategy for a war of attrition. He ordered a series of simultaneous assaults from Virginia all the way to Louisiana. Two actions proved particularly significant. In one, General William Tecumseh Sherman, Grant's successor in the West, plunged southeast toward Atlanta. In the other, Grant, commanding the Army of the Potomac, went head-to-head with Lee in Virginia for almost four straight weeks.

Twice as many Union soldiers as rebel soldiers died in four weeks of fighting in Virginia in May and June, but because Lee had only half as many troops as Grant,

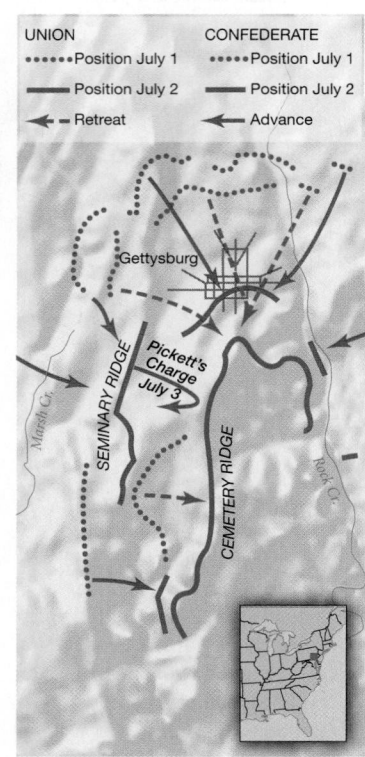

UNION	CONFEDERATE
•••••Position July 1	•••••Position July 1
——Position July 2	——Position July 2
◄— Retreat	◄— Advance

Battle of Gettysburg, July 1–3, 1863

CHAPTER LOCATOR | How did the war begin? | Why did each side expect to win? | How did each side fare in the early years of the war?

420 CHAPTER 15
THE CRUCIBLE OF WAR, 1861–1865

his losses were equivalent to Grant's. Grant knew that the South could not replace the losses. Moreover, the campaign carried Grant to the outskirts of Petersburg, just south of Richmond, where he abandoned the costly tactic of the frontal assault and began a siege that immobilized both armies and dragged on for nine months.

Grant's War of Attrition in Virginia (May–June 1864)

Battle of the Wilderness 18,000 Union dead, 11,000 Confederate dead.
Battle of Spotsylvania 18,000 Union dead, 10,000 Confederate dead.
Battle of Cold Harbor 13,000 Union dead, 5,000 Confederate dead.

Simultaneously, Sherman invaded Georgia. Grant instructed Sherman to "get into the interior of the enemy's country as far as you can, inflicting all the damage you can against their War resources." Skillful maneuvering, constant skirmishing, and one pitched battle, at Kennesaw Mountain, brought Sherman to Atlanta, which fell on September 2.

Intending to "make Georgia howl," Sherman marched out of Atlanta on November 15, heading for Savannah, 285 miles away on the Atlantic coast. One veteran remembered, "[We] destroyed all we could not eat, stole their niggers, burned their cotton & gins, spilled their sorghum, burned & twisted their R. Roads and raised Hell generally." **Sherman's March to the Sea** aimed at destroying white Southerners' will to continue the war. When Sherman's troops entered an undefended Savannah in mid-December, the general telegraphed Lincoln that he had "a Christmas gift" for him. A month earlier, Union voters had bestowed on the president an even greater gift.

The Election of 1864

In the summer of 1864, with Sherman temporarily checked outside Atlanta and Grant bogged down in the siege of Petersburg, the Democratic Party smelled victory in the fall elections. Lincoln himself concluded, "It seems exceedingly probable that this administration will not be re-elected."

The Democrats were badly divided, however. "Peace" Democrats insisted on an armistice, while "war" Democrats supported the conflict but opposed Republican means of fighting it. The party tried to paper over the chasm by nominating a war candidate, General George McClellan, but adopting a peace platform that demanded that "immediate efforts be made for a cessation of hostilities." Republicans denounced the peace plank as a plan that "virtually proposed to surrender the country to the rebels in arms against us."

The capture of Atlanta in September turned the political tide in favor of the Republicans. Lincoln received 55 percent of the popular vote, but his electoral margin was a whopping 212 to McClellan's 21. Lincoln's party won a resounding victory, one that gave him a mandate to continue the war until slavery and the Confederacy were dead.

The Confederacy Collapses

As 1865 dawned, military disaster littered the Confederate landscape. With the destruction of John B. Hood's army at Nashville in December 1864, the interior of

Sherman's March to the Sea

▶ Military campaign from September through December 1864 in which Union forces under General Sherman marched from Atlanta, Georgia, to the coast at Savannah. Carving a path of destruction as it progressed, Sherman's army aimed at destroying white Southerners' will to continue the war.

Why did the war for union become a fight for black freedom?	What problems did the Confederacy face at home?	How did the war affect the economy and politics of the North?	How did the Union finally win the war?	Conclusion: In what ways was the Civil War a "Second American Revolution"?

the Confederacy lay in Yankee hands (see Map 15.3, page 419). Sherman's troops, resting momentarily in Savannah, eyed South Carolina hungrily. Farther north, Grant had Lee's army pinned down in Petersburg, a few miles from Richmond.

Some Confederates turned their backs on the rebellion. News from the battlefield made it difficult not to conclude that the Yankees had beaten them. Soldiers' wives begged their husbands to return home to keep their families from starving, and the stream of deserters grew dramatically. Still, white Southerners had demonstrated a remarkable endurance for their cause. Half of the 900,000 Confederate soldiers had been killed or wounded, and ragged, hungry women and children had sacrificed throughout one of the bloodiest wars then known to history.

The end came with a rush. On February 1, 1865, Sherman's troops stormed out of Savannah into South Carolina, the "cradle of the Confederacy." In Virginia, Lee abandoned Petersburg on April 2, and Richmond fell on April 3. Grant pursued Lee until he surrendered on April 9, 1865, at Appomattox Court House, Virginia. Grant offered generous peace terms. He allowed Lee's men to return home and to keep their horses to help "put in a crop to carry themselves and their families through the next winter." With Lee gone, the remaining Confederate armies lost hope and gave up within two weeks. After four years, the war was over.

No one was more relieved than Lincoln, but his celebration was restrained. He told his cabinet that his postwar burdens would weigh almost as heavily as those of wartime. Seeking a distraction, Lincoln attended Ford's Theatre on the evening of Good Friday, April 14, 1865. John Wilkes Booth, an actor with southern sympathies, slipped into the president's box and shot Lincoln, who died the next morning. Vice President Andrew Johnson became president. The man who had led the nation through the war would not lead it during the postwar search for a just peace.

> **QUICK REVIEW**

Why were the siege of Vicksburg and the battle of Gettysburg critical turning points in the war?

CHAPTER LOCATOR | How did the war begin? | Why did each side expect to win? | How did each side fare in the early years of the war?

CHAPTER 15
422 THE CRUCIBLE OF WAR, 1861–1865

Kansas State Historical Society.

Conclusion: In what ways was the Civil War a "Second American Revolution"?

A TRANSFORMED NATION emerged from the crucible of war. Antebellum America was decentralized politically and loosely integrated economically. To bend the resources of the country to a Union victory, Congress enacted legislation that reshaped the nation's political and economic character. It created a transcontinental railroad and miles of telegraph lines to bind the West to the rest of the nation. The massive changes brought about by the war—the creation of a national government, a national economy, and a national spirit—led one historian to call the American Civil War the "Second American Revolution."

The Civil War also had a profound effect on individual lives. Men in uniform fought and suffered for what they passionately believed was right. The war disrupted families, leaving women at home with additional responsibilities while offering new opportunities to others for wartime work in factories, offices, and hospitals. It offered blacks new and more effective ways to resist slavery and agitate for equality.

The war devastated the South. Three-fourths of southern white men of military age served in the Confederate army, and at least half of them were captured, wounded, or killed or died of disease. The war destroyed two-fifths of the South's livestock, wrecked half of the farm machinery, and blackened dozens of cities and towns. The struggle also cost the North a heavy price: 360,000 lives. But rather than devastating the land, the war stimulated the economy. The radical shift in power from the South to the North signaled a new direction in American development: the long decline of agriculture and the rise of industrial capitalism.

Most revolutionary of all, the war ended slavery. Nearly 200,000 black men dedicated their wartime service to its eradication. Because slavery was both a labor and a racial system, the institution was entangled in almost every aspect of southern life. Slavery's uprooting inevitably meant fundamental change. But the full meaning of abolition remained unclear in 1865 and the status of ex-slaves would be the principal task of reconstruction.

SO NOW YOU KNOW

By 1863, the war had evolved from one to preserve the Union to a war to preserve the Union *and* to end slavery. African Americans were able to participate by enlisting and fighting at a rate substantially higher than that of white men, playing a decisive role in the Union victory that ended slavery.

Why did the war for union become a fight for black freedom?	What problems did the Confederacy face at home?	How did the war affect the economy and politics of the North?	How did the Union finally win the war?	Conclusion: In what ways was the Civil War a "Second American Revolution"?

CHAPTER 15 STUDY GUIDE

Online Study Guide
bedfordstmartins.com/roarkunderstanding

STEP 1 GETTING STARTED

Below are basic terms from this period in American history. Can you identify each term and explain why it matters? To do this exercise online or to download this chart, visit bedfordstmartins.com/roarkunderstanding.

TERM	WHO OR WHAT & WHEN	WHY IT MATTERS
Fort Sumter, p. 397		
battle of Bull Run (Manassas), p. 402		
George B. McClellan, p. 403		
Robert E. Lee, p. 405		
battle of Antietam, p. 405		
Ulysses S. Grant, p. 405		
King Cotton diplomacy, p. 406		
Emancipation Proclamation, p. 410		
New York City draft riots, p. 417		
siege of Vicksburg, p. 418		
battle of Gettysburg, p. 419		
Sherman's March to the Sea, p. 421		

STEP 2 MOVING BEYOND THE BASICS

The exercise below represents a more advanced understanding of the chapter material. Assess the strengths and weaknesses of the North and South at the outset of the Civil War. First, use the chart below to describe the two sides' strengths and weaknesses in four categories: population, industry, financial resources, and leadership. Then describe the initial war strategy of the North and South. When you are finished, see if you can make connections between each side's assets and its strategy. Why did the war take much longer than most people imagined at the outset? To do this exercise online or to download this chart, visit bedfordstmartins.com/roarkunderstanding.

Category	South	North
Population		
Industry		
Financial resources		
Leadership		
War strategy		

STEP

3

**PUTTING
IT ALL
TOGETHER**

Now that you've reviewed various parts of the chapter, take a step back and try to see the big picture by answering these questions. Remember to use specific examples from the chapter in your answers. To do this exercise online, visit bedfordstmartins.com/roarkunderstanding.

THE EARLY YEARS OF THE WAR

▶ Why did the North, with all its advantages, fail to achieve a rapid victory over the South?

▶ Why did the South fail to attract international support for its cause?

THE HOME FRONT

▶ Why did Lincoln decide to issue the Emancipation Proclamation? How did Northerners respond to this decision?

▶ Why did conditions in the South deteriorate as the war went on? How did problems on the home front undermine the South's war effort?

UNION VICTORY

▶ What was Grant's strategy? How did it turn the tide of the war?

▶ Is it possible to identify a point at which Union victory became inevitable? Explain your reasoning.

LOOKING BACKWARD, LOOKING AHEAD

▶ Argue for or against the following statement: "The root cause of the Civil War was the failure of the architects of the Constitution to resolve the issue of slavery once and for all."

▶ What changes that occurred during the Civil War might have forecast what a northern victory would mean for the nation?

IN YOUR OWN WORDS

Imagine that you must explain chapter 15 to someone who hasn't read it. What would be the most important points to include and why?

16
RECONSTRUCTING A NATION

1863–1877

> This chapter explores the period known as Reconstruction, in which the nation struggled to define the defeated South's status within the Union and the meaning of freedom for ex-slaves. Despite the end of the Civil War, the nation entered one of its most violent eras, as victorious Northerners, defeated white Southerners, and newly freed African Americans battled to shape the postwar South.

> What were Lincoln's plans for wartime reconstruction?

> What vision did Andrew Johnson have for presidential reconstruction?

> How radical was congressional reconstruction?

> How was the battle over reconstruction fought in the South?

> Why did reconstruction collapse?

> Conclusion: What were the achievements and failures of reconstruction?

S AML. DOVE wishes to know of the whereabouts of his mother, Areno, his sisters Maria, Neziah, and Peggy; and his brother Edmond, who were owned by Geo. Dove, of Rockingham county, Shenandoah Valley, Va. Sold in Richmond, after which Saml. and Edmond were taken to Nashville, Tenn., by Joe Mick; Areno was left at the Eagle Tavern, Richmond
Respectfully yours,
SAML. DOVE.
Utica, New York, Aug. 5, 1865–3m
U. S. CHRISTIAN COMMISSION,
NASHVILLE, TENN., July 19, 1865.

DID YOU KNOW?

The priorities for newly freed African Americans were to locate family members, acquire land, and worship in their own churches.

Voting day, June 5, 1867. Black freedmen line up to vote in Washington, D.C.

What were Lincoln's plans for wartime reconstruction?

Military Auction of Condemned Property, Beaufort, South Carolina, 1865

During the war, thousands of acres of land in the South came into federal hands as abandoned property or as a result of seizures because of nonpayment of taxes. The government authorized the sale of some of this land at public auction. This rare photograph shows expectant blacks (and a few whites) gathered in Beaufort, South Carolina, for a sale. The Huntington Library, San Marino, California.

RECONSTRUCTION OF THE SOUTH did not wait for the end of war. As the odds of a northern victory increased, thinking about reunification quickened. Both President Abraham Lincoln, believing that reconstruction was an executive responsibility, and Congress, believing that reconstruction lay in its jurisdiction, developed plans. Fueling the argument about who had the authority to set the terms of reconstruction were significant differences about the terms themselves. In their eagerness to formulate a plan for political reunification, neither Lincoln nor Congress gave much attention to the South's land and labor problems. But as the war eroded slavery and traditional plantation agriculture, Yankee military commanders in the Union-occupied areas of the Confederacy had no choice but to oversee the emergence of a new labor system.

"To Bind Up the Nation's Wounds"

As early as 1863, Lincoln contemplated how "to bind up the nation's wounds" and achieve "a just, and a lasting peace." While compassion for the defeated enemy guided his thinking, his plan for reconstruction aimed primarily at shortening the war and ending slavery.

Lincoln's Proclamation of Amnesty and Reconstruction in December 1863 set out easy terms for the reintegration of Confederate states into the Union. Lincoln's plan did not require ex-rebels to extend social or political rights to ex-slaves, nor did it anticipate a program of long-term federal assistance to freedmen. Clearly, the president looked forward to the speedy, forgiving restoration of the broken Union.

CHAPTER LOCATOR | What were Lincoln's plans for wartime reconstruction?

428 CHAPTER 16
RECONSTRUCTING A NATION, 1863–1877

Lincoln's Plan for Reconstruction

All property and political rights were to be restored to rebels willing to renounce secession and to accept the emancipation of slaves.

High-ranking Confederate military and political officers and a few other groups were to be excluded from this offer.

When 10 percent of a state's voting population had taken an oath of allegiance, the state could organize a new government.

Lincoln's plan enraged abolitionists such as Wendell Phillips of Boston, who charged that the president "makes the negro's freedom a mere sham." He "is willing that the negro should be free but seeks nothing else for him." Phillips and other northern radicals called instead for a thorough overhaul of southern society. Their ideas proved to be too drastic for most Republicans during the war years, but Congress agreed that Lincoln's plan was inadequate. It wanted greater assurances of white loyalty and greater guarantees of black rights.

In July 1864, Congressman Henry Winter Davis of Maryland and Senator Benjamin Wade of Ohio jointly sponsored a bill that demanded that at least half of the voters in a conquered rebel state take the oath of allegiance before reconstruction could begin. The Wade-Davis bill also banned all ex-Confederates from participating in the drafting of new state constitutions. Finally, the bill guaranteed the equality of freedmen before the law. When Lincoln refused to sign the bill and let it die, Wade and Davis charged the president with usurpation of power.

Undeterred, Lincoln continued to nurture the formation of loyal state governments under his own plan. Four states—Louisiana, Arkansas, Tennessee, and Virginia—fulfilled the president's requirements, but Congress refused to seat representatives from the "Lincoln states." In his last public address in April 1865, Lincoln defended his plan but for the first time expressed publicly his endorsement of suffrage for southern blacks, at least "the very intelligent, and . . . those who serve our cause as soldiers." The announcement demonstrated that Lincoln's thinking about reconstruction was still evolving. Four days later, he was dead.

Land and Labor

Of all the problems raised by the North's victory in the war, none proved more critical than the South's transition from slavery to free labor. As federal armies invaded and occupied the Confederacy, hundreds of thousands of slaves became free workers. In addition, Union armies controlled vast territories in the South where legal title to land had become unclear. The Confiscation Acts punished "traitors" by taking away their property. The question of what to do with federally occupied land and how to organize labor on it engaged former slaves, former slaveholders, Union military commanders, and federal government officials long before the war ended.

In the Mississippi valley, occupying federal troops announced a new labor code. It required slaveholders to sign contracts with ex-slaves and to pay wages. It also required black laborers to enter into contracts, work diligently, and remain subordinate and obedient. Military leaders clearly had no intention of promoting a social or economic revolution. Instead, they sought to restore plantation agriculture with wage labor.

CHRONOLOGY

1863
- President Lincoln issues Proclamation of Amnesty and Reconstruction.

1864
- Lincoln vetoes Wade-Davis bill imposing more severe restrictions on former Confederates.

1865
- General Sherman sets aside part of the coast south of Charleston for black settlement.
- Freedmen's Bureau is established and places 10,000 black families on half a million acres abandoned by planters.

What vision did Andrew Johnson have for presidential reconstruction?

How radical was congressional reconstruction?

How was the battle over reconstruction fought in the South?

Why did reconstruction collapse?

Conclusion: What were the achievements and failures of reconstruction?

The system pleased no one. Planters complained because the new system fell short of slavery. Without the right to whip, ex-masters argued, the new labor system did not have a chance. African Americans found the new regime too reminiscent of slavery to be called free labor. Its chief deficiency, they believed, was the failure to provide them with land of their own. "What's the use of being free if you don't own land enough to be buried in?" one man asked. Several wartime developments led freedmen to believe that the federal government planned to undergird black freedom with landownership.

In January 1865, General William Tecumseh Sherman set aside part of the coast south of Charleston for black settlement. By June 1865, some 40,000 freedmen sat on 400,000 acres of "Sherman land." In March 1865, Congress passed a bill establishing the Bureau of Refugees, Freedmen, and Abandoned Lands. The **Freedmen's Bureau**, as it was called, distributed food and clothing to destitute Southerners and eased the transition of blacks from slaves to free persons. Congress also authorized the agency to divide abandoned and confiscated land into 40-acre plots, to rent them to freedmen, and eventually to sell them "with such title as the United States can convey." By June 1865, the bureau had situated nearly 10,000 black families on half a million acres abandoned by fleeing planters. Other ex-slaves eagerly anticipated farms of their own.

Freedmen's Bureau

▶ Government organization created in March 1865 to distribute food and clothing to destitute Southerners and to ease the transition of blacks from slaves to free persons. Early efforts by the Freedmen's Bureau to distribute land to newly freed blacks were later overturned by President Johnson.

Harry Stephens and Family, 1866 Dressed in their Sunday best, this Virginia family sits proudly for a photograph. Many black families were not as fortunate as the Stephens family and spent years seeking missing family members. The Metropolitan Museum of Art, Gilman Collection, Purchase, The Horace W. Goldsmith Foundation Gift, 2005 (2005.100.277).

CHAPTER LOCATOR | What were Lincoln's plans for wartime reconstruction?

The African American Quest for Autonomy

Ex-slaves never had any doubt about what they wanted from freedom. They had only to contemplate what they had been denied as slaves. Slaves had to remain on their plantations; freedom allowed blacks to see what was on the other side of the hill. Slaves had to be at work in the fields by dawn; freedom permitted blacks to sleep through a sunrise. Freedmen also tested the etiquette of racial subordination. "Lizzie's maid passed me today when I was coming from church *without speaking to me*," huffed one plantation mistress.

To whites, emancipation looked like pure anarchy. Blacks, they said, had reverted to their natural condition: lazy, irresponsible, and wild. Actually, former slaves were experimenting with freedom, but they could not long afford to roam the countryside, neglect work, and casually provoke whites. Soon, most were back at work in whites' kitchens and fields.

But they continued to dream of land and economic independence. "The way we can best take care of ourselves is to have land," one former slave declared in 1865, "and turn it and till it by our own labor." Freedmen also wanted to learn to read and write. "I wishes the Childern all in School," one black veteran asserted. "It is beter for them then to be their Surveing a mistes [mistress]."

The restoration of broken families was another persistent black aspiration. Thousands of freedmen took to the roads in 1865 to look for kin who had been sold away or to free those who were being held illegally as slaves. A black soldier from Missouri wrote his daughters that he was coming for them. "I will have you if it cost me my life," he declared. "Your Miss Kitty said that I tried to steal you," he told them. "But I'll let her know that god never intended for a man to steal his own flesh and blood." And he swore that "if she meets me with ten thousand soldiers, she [will] meet her enemy."

Independent worship was another continuing aspiration. Some African Americans joined the newly established southern branches of all-black northern churches, such as the African Methodist Episcopal Church. Others formed black versions of the major southern denominations, Baptists and Methodists.

QUICK REVIEW

What were the goals of Lincoln's wartime plans for reconstruction? To what extent did these goals reflect the concerns of the newly freed slaves?

What vision did Andrew Johnson have for presidential reconstruction?

The Black Codes

Titled "Selling a Freeman to Pay His Fine at Monticello, Florida," this 1867 drawing from a northern magazine equates black codes with the reinstitution of slavery. The ascension of Andrew Johnson to the presidency emboldened many southern states to pass laws severely restricting blacks' freedom. Granger Collection.

WITH ABRAHAM LINCOLN'S death on April 15, 1865, Vice President Andrew Johnson of Tennessee became the new president. Congress had adjourned in March and would not reconvene until December. Thus, throughout the summer and fall, Johnson drew up and executed a plan of reconstruction without congressional advice.

Congress reconvened in December to find that, as far as the president and former Confederates were concerned, reconstruction was completed. Most Republicans, however, thought Johnson's puny demands of ex-rebels encouraged the rebirth of the Old South at the expense of black liberty. They proceeded to dismantle Johnson's program and substitute a program of their own.

Johnson's Program of Reconciliation

Andrew Johnson

► President of the United States from 1865 to 1869, Vice President Johnson became president after the assassination of Abraham Lincoln. Like Lincoln, Johnson sought the quick restoration of civil government in the South and pardoned most ex-Confederates. Johnson battled with Congress over the course of Reconstruction and was the first president in U.S. history to be impeached by the House of Representatives. He barely escaped removal from office by the Senate.

Born in 1808 in Raleigh, North Carolina, **Andrew Johnson** was the son of illiterate parents. Self-educated and ambitious, Johnson moved to Tennessee, where he built a career in politics championing the South's common white people and assailing its "illegitimate, swaggering, bastard, scrub aristocracy." The only senator from a Confederate state to remain loyal to the Union, Johnson held the planter class responsible for secession.

A Democrat all his life, Johnson occupied the White House only because the Republican Party in 1864 had needed a vice presidential candidate who would appeal to loyal, Union-supporting Democrats. Johnson vigorously defended states' rights (but not secession) and opposed Republican efforts to expand the power of the federal government. A steadfast supporter of slavery, Johnson grudgingly accepted emancipation more because he hated planters than because he sympathized with slaves. "Damn the negroes," he said. "I am fighting those traitorous aristocrats, their masters." The new president harbored unshakable racist convictions. Africans, Johnson said, were "inferior to the white man in point of intellect—better calculated in physical structure to undergo drudgery and hardship."

CHAPTER LOCATOR | What were Lincoln's plans for wartime reconstruction?

Like Lincoln, Johnson stressed the rapid restoration of civil government in the South. Like Lincoln, he promised to pardon most, but not all, ex-rebels. Johnson recognized the state governments created by Lincoln but set out his own requirements for restoring the other rebel states to the Union. All that the citizens of a state had to do was to renounce the right of secession, deny that the debts of the Confederacy were legal and binding, and ratify the Thirteenth Amendment, abolishing slavery, which became part of the Constitution in December 1865.

Johnson also returned to pardoned ex-Confederates all confiscated and abandoned land, even if it was in the hands of freedmen. Reformers were shocked. Instead of punishing planters as Republicans expected, his instructions canceled the promising beginnings made by General Sherman and the Freedmen's Bureau to settle blacks on land of their own. As one freedman observed, "Things was hurt by Mr. Lincoln getting killed."

White Southern Resistance and Black Codes

In the summer of 1865, delegates across the South gathered to draw up the new state constitutions required by Johnson's plan of reconstruction. Rather than accept Johnson's plan, delegates balked at even the president's mild requirements to renounce secession, disown their war debts, and ratify the Thirteenth Amendment. Despite this defiance, Johnson did nothing. White Southerners began to think that by standing up for themselves they could define the terms of reconstruction.

State governments across the South adopted a series of laws known as **black codes**, which made a travesty of black freedom. The codes sought to keep ex-slaves subordinate to whites by subjecting them to every sort of discrimination.

Black Codes

Several states made it illegal for blacks to own a gun.

Mississippi made insulting gestures and language by blacks a criminal offense.

The codes barred blacks from jury duty.

Not a single southern state granted any black the right to vote.

At the core of the black codes, however, lay the matter of labor and the desire to force freedmen back to the plantations. South Carolina attempted to limit blacks to either farmwork or domestic service by requiring them to pay annual taxes of $10 to $100 to work in any other occupation. Mississippi declared that blacks who did not possess written evidence of employment could be declared vagrants and be subject to involuntary plantation labor. Under so-called apprenticeship laws, courts bound thousands of black children—orphans and others whose parents they deemed unable to support them—to work for planter "guardians."

Johnson, a staunch defender of states' rights and white supremacy, refused to intervene. His stance was politically advantageous. A conservative Tennessee Democrat at the head of a northern Republican Party, he had begun to look southward for political allies. By pardoning powerful whites, by accepting governments even when they failed to satisfy his minimal demands, and by acquiescing in the black codes, he won useful southern friends.

In the fall elections of 1865, white Southerners dramatically expressed their mood. To represent them in Congress, they chose former Confederates, many of whom had

CHRONOLOGY

1865
- President Abraham Lincoln is shot; dies on April 15; is succeeded by Andrew Johnson.
- Johnson carries out rapid restoration of civil government in the South.
- Johnson returns confiscated and abandoned land to pardoned ex-Confederates.
- Southern states enact black codes.
- The Thirteenth Amendment, abolishing slavery, becomes part of Constitution.

1866
- Civil Rights Act nullifies black codes and extends civil rights to blacks.

black codes
▶ Laws passed by state governments in the South in 1865 that sought to keep ex-slaves subordinate to whites. At the core of the black codes lay the desire to force freedmen back to the plantations.

What vision did Andrew Johnson have for presidential reconstruction?

How radical was congressional reconstruction?

How was the battle over reconstruction fought in the South?

Why did reconstruction collapse?

Conclusion: What were the achievements and failures of reconstruction?

433

been high-ranking military and government officials in the Confederacy. As one Georgian remarked, "It looked as though Richmond had moved to Washington."

Expansion of Federal Authority and Black Rights

Southerners had assumed that what Andrew Johnson was willing to accept, Republicans would accept as well. But southern intransigence compelled even moderate Republicans to conclude that ex-rebels were still untrustworthy and dangerous. The black codes became a symbol of southern intentions to "restore all of slavery but its name." "We tell the white men of Mississippi," the *Chicago Tribune* roared, "that the men of the North will convert the State of Mississippi into a frog pond before they will allow such laws to disgrace one foot of the soil in which the bones of our soldiers sleep and over which the flag of freedom waves."

The moderate majority of the Republican Party did not champion black equality, the confiscation of plantations, or black voting, as did the radicals. But southern obstinacy had succeeded in forging temporary unity among Republican factions. In December 1865, Republicans refused to seat the southern representatives elected in the fall elections. Rather than accept Johnson's claim that the "work of restoration" was done, Congress challenged his executive power.

Republican senator Lyman Trumbull declared that the president's policy meant that ex-slaves would "be tyrannized over, abused, and virtually reenslaved without some legislation by the nation for [their] protection." Early in 1866, the moderates produced two bills that strengthened the federal shield. The first, the Freedmen's Bureau bill, prolonged the life of the agency established by the previous Congress. Arguing that the Constitution never contemplated a "system for the support of indigent persons," President Andrew Johnson vetoed the bill. Congress failed by a narrow margin to override the president's veto.

The moderates designed their second measure, the Civil Rights Act, to nullify the black codes by affirming African Americans' rights to "full and equal benefit of all laws and proceedings for the security of person and property as is enjoyed by white citizens." The act required the end of racial discrimination in state laws and represented an extraordinary expansion of black rights and federal authority. The president argued that the civil rights bill amounted to "unconstitutional invasion of states' rights" and vetoed it.

In April 1866, an incensed Republican Congress passed the civil rights bill again and overrode the presidential veto. In July, it passed another Freedmen's Bureau bill and overrode Johnson's veto. For the first time in American history, Congress had overridden presidential vetoes of major legislation. As a worried South Carolinian observed, Johnson had succeeded in uniting the Republicans and probably touched off "a fight this fall such as has never been seen."

> **QUICK REVIEW**

When the southern states passed the black codes, how did President Andrew Johnson respond? How did congressional Republicans respond?

CHAPTER LOCATOR | What were Lincoln's plans for wartime reconstruction?

434 CHAPTER 16 RECONSTRUCTING A NATION, 1863–1877

State Convention at Richmond, Virginia

Between 1867 and 1869, every southern state except Tennessee held a convention to draft a new constitution. In Virginia, where blacks were more than 40 percent of the population, they made up about 20 percent of the convention. Richmond History Center.

BY THE SUMMER OF 1866, President Andrew Johnson and Congress were locked in a battle unprecedented in American history. Johnson made it clear that he would not budge on either constitutional issues or policy. Moderate Republicans responded by amending the Constitution. But the obstinacy of Johnson and white Southerners pushed Republican moderates ever closer to the radicals and to acceptance of additional federal intervention in the South. Congress also voted to impeach the president. In time, Congress debated whether to make voting rights color-blind, while women sought to make voting sex-blind as well.

The Fourteenth Amendment and Escalating Violence

In June 1866, Congress passed the **Fourteenth Amendment** to the Constitution, and two years later the states ratified it. The most important provisions of this complex amendment made all native-born or naturalized persons American citizens and prohibited states from abridging the "privileges and immunities" of citizens, depriving them of "life, liberty, or property without due process of law," and denying them "equal protection of the laws." By making blacks national citizens, the amendment provided a national guarantee of equality before the law. In essence, it protected blacks against violation by southern state governments.

Fourteenth Amendment

▶ Constitutional amendment ratified in 1868 that made all native-born or naturalized persons U.S. citizens and prohibited states from abridging the rights of national citizens. The amendment hoped to provide a guarantee of equality before the law for black citizens.

1866
- Congress approves Fourteenth Amendment, granting citizenship and equal rights to former slaves.
- Elizabeth Cady Stanton and Susan B. Anthony found the American Equal Rights Association to support woman suffrage.

1867
- Military Reconstruction Act initiates military occupation of the South and, with black suffrage and the disfranchisement of many ex-rebels, guarantees Republican governments in the South.

1868
- Impeachment trial of President Andrew Johnson.

1869
- Congress approves Fifteenth Amendment, making it illegal to deny voting rights on the basis of race.

The Fourteenth Amendment also dealt with voting rights. It gave Congress the right to reduce the congressional representation of states that withheld suffrage from some of its adult male population. In other words, white Southerners could either allow black men to vote or see their representation in Washington slashed.

The Fourteenth Amendment's suffrage provisions ignored the small band of women who had emerged from the war demanding "the ballot for the two disenfranchised classes, negroes and women." Founding the American Equal Rights Association in 1866, Susan B. Anthony and Elizabeth Cady Stanton lobbied for "a government by the people, and the whole people; for the people and the whole people." They felt betrayed when their old antislavery allies refused to work for their goals. "It was the Negro's hour," Frederick Douglass explained. Senator Charles Sumner suggested that woman suffrage could be "the great question of the future."

The Fourteenth Amendment provided for punishment of any state that excluded voters on the basis of race but not on the basis of sex. The amendment also introduced the word *male* into the Constitution when it referred to a citizen's right to vote. Stanton predicted that "if that word 'male' be inserted, it will take us a century at least to get it out."

Tennessee approved the Fourteenth Amendment in July, and Congress promptly welcomed the state's representatives and senators back. Had President Johnson counseled other southern states to ratify this relatively mild amendment, they might have listened. Instead, Johnson advised Southerners to reject the Fourteenth Amendment and to rely on him to trounce the Republicans in the fall congressional elections.

Johnson had decided to make the Fourteenth Amendment the overriding issue of the 1866 elections and to gather its white opponents into a new conservative party, the National Union Party. The president's strategy suffered a setback

Andrew Johnson Cartoon

Appearing in 1868 during President Andrew Johnson's impeachment trial, this cartoon includes captions that read: "This little boy would persist in handling books above his capacity" and "And this was the disastrous result."
The cartoonist's portrait of Johnson being crushed by the Constitution refers to the president's flouting of the Tenure of Office Act, which caused Republicans to vote for his impeachment.
Granger Collection.

THIS LITTLE BOY WOULD PERSIST IN HANDLING BOOKS ABOVE HIS CAPACITY.

AND THIS WAS THE DISASTROUS RESULT.

CHAPTER LOCATOR | What were Lincoln's plans for wartime reconstruction?

when whites in several southern cities went on rampages against blacks. The mob violence shocked Northerners and renewed skepticism about Johnson's claim that southern whites could be trusted. "Who doubts that the Freedmen's Bureau ought to be abolished forthwith," a New Yorker observed sarcastically, "and the blacks remitted to the paternal care of their old masters, who 'understand the nigger, you know, a great deal better than the Yankees can.'"

The 1866 elections resulted in an overwhelming Republican victory. Johnson had bet that Northerners would not support federal protection of black rights and that a racist backlash would blast the Republican Party. But the war was still fresh in northern minds, and as one Republican explained, southern whites "with all their intelligence were traitors, the blacks with all their ignorance were loyal."

Radical Reconstruction and Military Rule

When Johnson continued to urge Southerners to reject the Fourteenth Amendment, every southern state except Tennessee voted it down. "The last one of the sinful ten," thundered Representative James A. Garfield of Ohio, "has flung back into our teeth the magnanimous offer of a generous nation." After the South rejected the moderates' program, the radicals seized the initiative.

Each act of defiance by southern whites had boosted the standing of the radicals within the Republican Party. Radicals such as Massachusetts senator Charles Sumner and Pennsylvania representative Thaddeus Stevens did not speak with a single voice, but they united in demanding civil and political equality for ex-slaves. Southern states were "like clay in the hands of the potter," Stevens declared in January 1867, and he called on Congress to begin reconstruction all over again.

In March 1867, Congress overturned the Johnson state governments and initiated military rule of the South. The **Military Reconstruction Act** (and three subsequent acts) divided the ten unreconstructed Confederate states into five military districts. Congress placed a Union general in charge of each district and instructed him to "suppress insurrection, disorder, and violence" and to begin political reform. After the military had completed voter registration, which would include black men, voters in each state would elect delegates to conventions that would draw up new state constitutions. Each constitution would guarantee black suffrage. When the voters of each state had approved the constitution and the state legislature had ratified the Fourteenth Amendment, the state could submit its work to Congress. If Congress approved, the state's senators and representatives could be seated, and political reunification would be accomplished.

Radicals proclaimed the provision for black suffrage "a prodigious triumph," for it extended far beyond the limited suffrage provisions of the Fourteenth Amendment. When combined with the disfranchisement of thousands of ex-rebels, it promised to cripple any neo-Confederate resurgence and guarantee Republican state governments in the South.

Despite its bold suffrage provision, the Military Reconstruction Act of 1867 disappointed those who also advocated the confiscation and redistribution of southern plantations to ex-slaves. Thaddeus Stevens agreed with the freedman who said, "Give us our own land and we take care of ourselves, but without land, the old masters can hire us or starve us, as they please." But most Republicans

Reconstruction Military Districts, 1867

Military Reconstruction Act

▶ Congressional act of March 1867 that initiated military rule of the South. Congressional reconstruction divided the ten unreconstructed Confederate states into five military districts, each under the direction of a Union general. It also established the procedure by which unreconstructed states could reenter the Union.

What vision did Andrew Johnson have for presidential reconstruction?

How radical was congressional reconstruction?

How was the battle over reconstruction fought in the South?

Why did reconstruction collapse?

Conclusion: What were the achievements and failures of reconstruction?

believed they had provided blacks with what they needed: equal legal rights and the ballot. If blacks were to get land, they would have to gain it themselves.

Declaring that he would rather sever his right arm than sign such a formula for "anarchy and chaos," Andrew Johnson vetoed the Military Reconstruction Act, but Congress quickly overrode his veto. With the passage of the Reconstruction Acts of 1867, congressional reconstruction was virtually completed. Congress left whites owning most of the South's land but, in a departure that justified the term "radical reconstruction," had given black men the ballot.

Impeaching a President

Despite his defeats, Andrew Johnson had no intention of yielding control of reconstruction. In a dozen ways, he sabotaged Congress's will and encouraged southern whites to resist. He issued a flood of pardons, waged war against the Freedmen's Bureau, and replaced Union generals eager to enforce Congress's Reconstruction Acts with conservative men eager to defeat them. Johnson claimed that he was merely defending the "violated Constitution." At bottom, however, the president subverted congressional reconstruction to protect southern whites from what he considered the horrors of "Negro domination."

Radicals argued that Johnson's abuse of constitutional powers and his failure to fulfill constitutional obligations to enforce the law were impeachable offenses. But moderates disagreed, arguing that only actual violations of criminal statutes were impeachable offenses. As long as Johnson refrained from breaking the law, impeachment (the process of formal charges of wrongdoing against the president or other federal official) remained stalled.

Then in August 1867, Johnson suspended Secretary of War Edwin M. Stanton from office. As required by the Tenure of Office Act, which demanded the approval of the Senate for the removal of any government official who had been appointed with Senate approval, the president requested the Senate to consent to the dismissal. When the Senate balked, Johnson removed Stanton anyway. "Is the President crazy, or only drunk?" asked a dumbfounded Republican moderate. "I'm afraid his doings will make us all favor impeachment."

News of Johnson's open defiance of the law convinced every Republican in the House to vote for a resolution impeaching the president. Supreme Court chief justice Salmon Chase presided over the Senate trial, which lasted from March until May 1868. When the critical vote came, thirty-five senators voted guilty and nineteen not guilty. The impeachment forces fell one vote short of the two-thirds needed to convict.

After his trial, Johnson called a truce, and for the remaining ten months of his term, congressional reconstruction proceeded unhindered by presidential interference. Without interference from Johnson, Congress revisited the suffrage issue.

The Fifteenth Amendment and Women's Demands

In February 1869, Republicans passed the **Fifteenth Amendment** to the Constitution, which prohibited states from depriving any citizen of the right to vote

Fifteenth Amendment
▶ Constitutional amendment ratified in 1870 prohibiting states from depriving any citizen of the right to vote because of "race, color, or previous condition of servitude." The Reconstruction Acts of 1867 already required black suffrage in the South; the Fifteenth Amendment extended black suffrage nationwide. Woman suffrage advocates, in particular Susan B. Anthony and Elizabeth Cady Stanton, were disappointed with the Fifteenth Amendment's failure to extend voting rights to women.

CHAPTER LOCATOR | What were Lincoln's plans for wartime reconstruction?

438 CHAPTER 16
RECONSTRUCTING A NATION, 1863–1877

because of "race, color, or previous condition of servitude." The Reconstruction Acts of 1867 already required black suffrage in the South; the Fifteenth Amendment extended black voting nationwide.

Some Republicans, however, found the final wording of the Fifteenth Amendment "lame and halting." Rather than absolutely guaranteeing the right to vote, the amendment merely prohibited exclusion on the grounds of race. The distinction would prove to be significant. In time, white Southerners would devise tests of literacy and property and other apparently nonracial measures that would effectively disfranchise blacks yet not violate the Fifteenth Amendment. But an amendment that fully guaranteed the right to vote courted defeat outside the South. Rising antiforeign sentiment—against the Chinese in California and European immigrants in the Northeast—caused states to resist giving up total control of suffrage requirements. In March 1870, after three-fourths of the states had ratified it, the Fifteenth Amendment became part of the Constitution. Republicans generally breathed a sigh of relief, confident that black suffrage was "the last great point that remained to be settled of the issues of the war."

Woman suffrage advocates, however, were sorely disappointed with the Fifteenth Amendment's failure to extend voting rights to women. Elizabeth Cady Stanton and Susan B. Anthony condemned the Republicans' "negro first" strategy and pointed out that women remained "the only class of citizens wholly unrepresented in the government." Stanton wondered aloud why ignorant black men should legislate for educated and cultured white women. The Fifteenth Amendment severed the early feminist movement from its abolitionist roots. Over the next several decades, feminists established an independent suffrage crusade that drew millions of women into political life.

Republicans took enough satisfaction in the Fifteenth Amendment to promptly scratch the "Negro question" from the agenda of national politics. Even that steadfast crusader for equality Wendell Phillips concluded that the black man now held "sufficient shield in his own hands. . . . Whatever he suffers will be largely now, and in future, his own fault." Northerners had no idea of the violent struggles that lay ahead.

QUICK REVIEW

Why and how did the aims of Congress and the president diverge? What specifically were the issues over which they clashed?

> How was the battle over reconstruction fought in the South?

Black Woman in Cotton Fields, Thomasville, Georgia

Few images of everyday black women during the Reconstruction era survive. This photograph was taken in 1895, but it nevertheless goes to the heart of the labor struggle after the Civil War. Before emancipation, black women worked in the fields; after emancipation, white landlords wanted them to continue working there. Freedom allowed some women to escape field labor, but not this Georgian, who probably worked to survive. Courtesy, Georgia Department of Archives and History, Atlanta, Georgia.

NORTHERNERS BELIEVED THEY HAD discharged their responsibilities with the Reconstruction Acts and the amendments to the Constitution, but Southerners knew that the battle had just begun. Black suffrage established the foundation for the rise of the Republican Party in the South. Gathering together outsiders and outcasts, southern Republicans won elections, wrote new state constitutions, and formed new state governments.

Challenging the established class for political control was dangerous business. Equally dangerous were the confrontations that took place on southern farms and plantations, where blacks sought to give economic meaning to their newly won legal and political equality. Freedom remained contested territory, and Southerners fought pitched battles with one another to determine the contours of their new world.

Freedmen, Yankees, and Yeomen

African Americans made up the majority of southern Republicans. After gaining voting rights in 1867, nearly all eligible black men registered to vote as Republicans. Southern blacks did not have identical political priorities, but they united in their desire for education and equal treatment before the law.

Northern whites who made the South their home after the war were a second element of the South's Republican Party. Conservative white Southerners called

CHAPTER LOCATOR | What were Lincoln's plans for wartime reconstruction?

them carpetbaggers, opportunistic men who put all their belongings in a single carpet-sided suitcase and headed south to "fatten on our misfortunes." But most Northerners who moved south were young men who looked upon the South as they did the West—as a promising place to make a living. Northerners in the southern Republican Party consistently supported programs that encouraged vigorous economic development along the lines of the northern free-labor model.

Southern whites made up the third element of the South's Republican Party. Approximately one out of four white Southerners voted Republican. The other three condemned the one who did as a traitor to his region and his race and called him a scalawag, a term for runty horses and low-down, good-for-nothing rascals. Yeoman farmers accounted for the majority of southern white Republicans. Some were Unionists who emerged from the war with bitter memories of Confederate persecution. Others were small farmers who wanted to end state governments' favoritism toward plantation owners. Yeomen supported initiatives for public schools and for expanding economic opportunity in the South.

The South's Republican Party, then, was made up of freedmen, Yankees, and yeomen—an improbable coalition. The mix of races, regions, and classes inevitably meant friction as each group maneuvered to define the party. But Reconstruction represents an extraordinary moment in American politics: Blacks and whites joined together in the Republican Party to pursue political change. Formally, of course, only men participated in politics—casting ballots and holding offices—but white and black women also played a part in the political struggle by joining in parades and rallies, attending stump speeches, and even campaigning.

Most whites in the South condemned southern Republicans as illegitimate and felt justified in doing whatever they could to stamp them out. Violence against blacks—the "white terror"—took brutal institutional form in 1866 with the formation in Tennessee of the **Ku Klux Klan**, a social club of Confederate veterans that quickly developed into a paramilitary organization supporting Democrats. The Klan went on a rampage of murder and mayhem to defeat Republicans and restore white supremacy. Rapid demobilization of the Union army after the war left only twenty thousand troops to patrol the entire South. Without effective military protection, southern Republicans had to take care of themselves.

Republican Rule

In the fall of 1867, southern states held elections for delegates to state constitutional conventions, as required by the Reconstruction Acts. About 40 percent of the white electorate stayed home because they had been disfranchised or because they had decided to boycott politics. Republicans won three-fourths of the seats. About 15 percent of the Republican delegates to the conventions were Northerners who had moved south, 25 percent were African Americans, and 60 percent were white Southerners. As a British visitor observed, the delegate elections reflected "the mighty revolution that had taken place in America."

The reconstruction constitutions introduced two broad categories of changes in the South: those that reduced aristocratic privilege and increased democratic equality and those that expanded the state's responsibility for the general welfare. In the first category, the constitutions adopted universal male suffrage, abolished property qualifications for holding office, and made more offices elective and fewer appointed. In the second category, they enacted prison reform; made

CHRONOLOGY

1866
– Ku Klux Klan is founded.

1867
– Southern African Americans gain voting rights under the Military Reconstruction Act.
– In elections for state constitutional convention delegates, Republicans win three-fourths of the seats.

1875
– One-half of South Carolina's and Mississippi's children, the majority of whom are black, are attending school.
– Sharecropping is the dominant labor system for rural southern blacks.

Ku Klux Klan
▶ A paramilitary organization formed in Tennessee in 1866 that supported Democrats. With too few Union troops in the South to control the region, the Klan went on a rampage of murder and mayhem to defeat Republicans and restore white supremacy. Legislative efforts by Congress to suppress violence in the South were undermined by failures of enforcement.

| What vision did Andrew Johnson have for presidential reconstruction? | How radical was congressional reconstruction? | How was the battle over reconstruction fought in the South? | Why did reconstruction collapse? | Conclusion: What were the achievements and failures of reconstruction? |

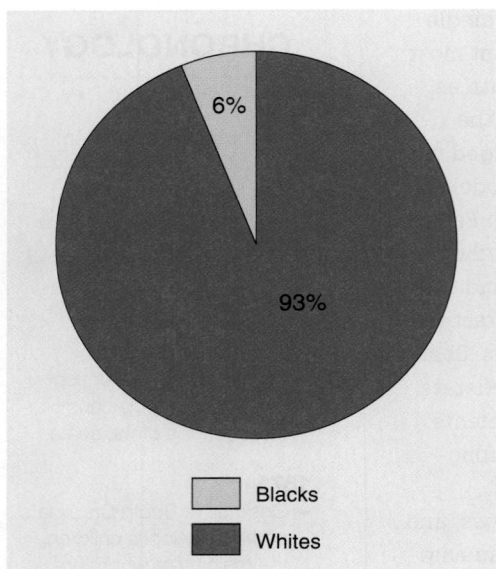

FIGURE 16.1 ■ Southern Congressional Delegations, 1865–1877
The statistics contradict the myth of black domination of congressional representation during Reconstruction.

the state responsible for caring for orphans, the insane, and the deaf and mute; and exempted debtors' homes from seizure.

To Democrats, however, these forward-looking state constitutions looked like wild revolution. Democrats were blind to the fact that no constitution confiscated and redistributed land, as virtually every former slave wished, or disfranchised ex-rebels wholesale, as most southern Unionists advocated. And they were convinced that the new constitutions initiated "Negro domination" in politics. In fact, although 80 percent of Republican voters were black men, only 6 percent of Southerners in Congress during Reconstruction were black (**Figure 16.1**). And no state legislature experienced "Negro rule," despite black majorities in the populations of some states.

Southern voters ratified the new constitutions and swept Republicans into power. When the former Confederate states ratified the Fourteenth Amendment, Congress readmitted them. Southern Republicans then turned to the staggering array of problems that faced them. The southern landscape and economy lay in ruins. Making matters worse, racial harassment and reactionary violence dogged Southerners who sought reform. It was in this context that Republicans struggled to reform and rebuild the region.

Activity focused on three areas—education, civil rights, and economic development. Every state inaugurated a system of public education. Before the Civil War, whites had deliberately kept slaves illiterate, and planter-dominated governments rarely spent tax money to educate the children of yeomen. By 1875, half of Mississippi's and South Carolina's eligible children (the majority of whom were black) were attending school. Although schools were underfunded, literacy rates rose sharply. Public schools were racially segregated, but education remained for many blacks a tangible, deeply satisfying benefit of freedom and Republican rule.

State legislatures also attacked racial discrimination and defended civil rights. Republicans especially resisted efforts to segregate blacks from whites in public transportation. Mississippi levied fines of up to $1,000 and three years in jail for railroads and steamboats that pushed blacks into "smoking cars" or to lower decks. A Mississippian complained: "Money cannot buy for a colored man or woman decent treatment and the comforts that white people claim and can obtain." But passing color-blind laws was one thing; enforcing them was another. Despite the laws, segregation—later called Jim Crow—developed at white insistence and became a feature of southern life long before the end of the Reconstruction era.

Republican governments also launched ambitious programs of economic development. They envisioned a South of diversified agriculture, roaring factories, and booming towns. State legislatures chartered scores of banks and industrial companies, appropriated funds to fix ruined levees and drain swamps, and went on a railroad-building binge. These efforts fell far short of solving the South's economic troubles, however. Republican spending to stimulate economic growth also meant rising taxes and enormous debt, which drained funds from schools and other programs.

The southern Republicans' record, then, was mixed. To their credit, the biracial party took up an ambitious agenda to change the South. Their agenda, however, faced difficult obstacles. Money was scarce, the Democrats continued their harassment, and factionalism and corruption threatened the Republican Party from within. Despite shortcomings, however, the Republican Party made headway in its efforts to purge the South of aristocratic privilege and racist oppression. Republican governments had less success in overthrowing the long-established white oppression of black farm laborers in the rural South.

White Landlords, Black Sharecroppers

Ex-slaves who wished to escape slave labor and ex-masters who wanted to reinstitute old ways clashed repeatedly. Except for having to pay subsistence wages, planters had not been required to offer many concessions to emancipation. They continued to believe that African Americans would not work without coercion. Whites moved quickly to restore work regimes that were as close to those of slavery as possible.

Ex-slaves resisted every effort to turn back the clock. They argued that if any class could be described as "lazy," it was the planters, who, as one ex-slave noted, "lived in idleness all their lives on stolen labor." Land of their own would anchor their economic independence, they believed, and end planters' interference in their personal lives. They could then, for example, make their own decisions about whether women and children would labor in the fields. Indeed, within months after the war, perhaps one-third of black women abandoned field labor to work on chores in their own cabins just as poor white women did. Hundreds of thousands of black children enrolled in school. But without their own land, ex-slaves had little choice but to work on plantations.

Although forced to return to the planters' fields, freedmen resisted efforts to restore slavelike conditions. Instead of working for wages, a South Carolinian observed, "the negroes all seem disposed to rent land," which increased their independence from whites. Out of this tug-of-war between white landlords and black laborers emerged a new system of southern agriculture.

Sharecropping was a compromise that offered both ex-masters and ex-slaves something but satisfied neither. Under the new system, planters divided their cotton plantations into small farms that freedmen rented, paying with a share of each year's crop, usually half. Sharecropping gave blacks more freedom than did the system of wages and labor gangs and released them from the day-to-day supervision of whites. Black families abandoned the old slave quarters and scattered over plantations, building separate cabins for themselves on the patches of land they rented (**Map 16.1**). Still, most blacks remained dependent on white landlords, who had the power to expel them at the end of each growing season. For planters, sharecropping offered a way to resume agricultural production, but it did not restore the old slave plantation.

Sharecropping introduced a new figure—the country merchant—into the agricultural equation. Landlords supplied sharecroppers with land, mules, seeds, and tools, but blacks also needed credit to obtain essential food and clothing before they harvested their crops. Thousands of small crossroads stores sprang up to offer credit. Under an arrangement called a crop lien, a merchant would advance goods to a sharecropper in exchange for a lien, or legal claim, on the farmer's future crop. Some merchants charged exorbitant rates of interest, as much as 60 percent, on the goods they sold. At the end of the growing season, after the landlord had taken half of the farmer's crop for rent, the merchant took most of the

sharecropping

▶ System of southern agriculture that emerged in the decade following the Civil War. Under the system, planters divided their cotton plantations into small farms that freedmen rented, paying with a share of each year's crop. Sharecropping gave blacks more freedom than did the system of wages and labor gangs and released them from the day-to-day supervision of whites. White landowners, however, used a variety of tactics, particularly debt, to restrict the freedom of sharecroppers.

| What vision did Andrew Johnson have for presidential reconstruction? | How radical was congressional reconstruction? | How was the battle over reconstruction fought in the South? | Why did reconstruction collapse? | Conclusion: What were the achievements and failures of reconstruction? |

443

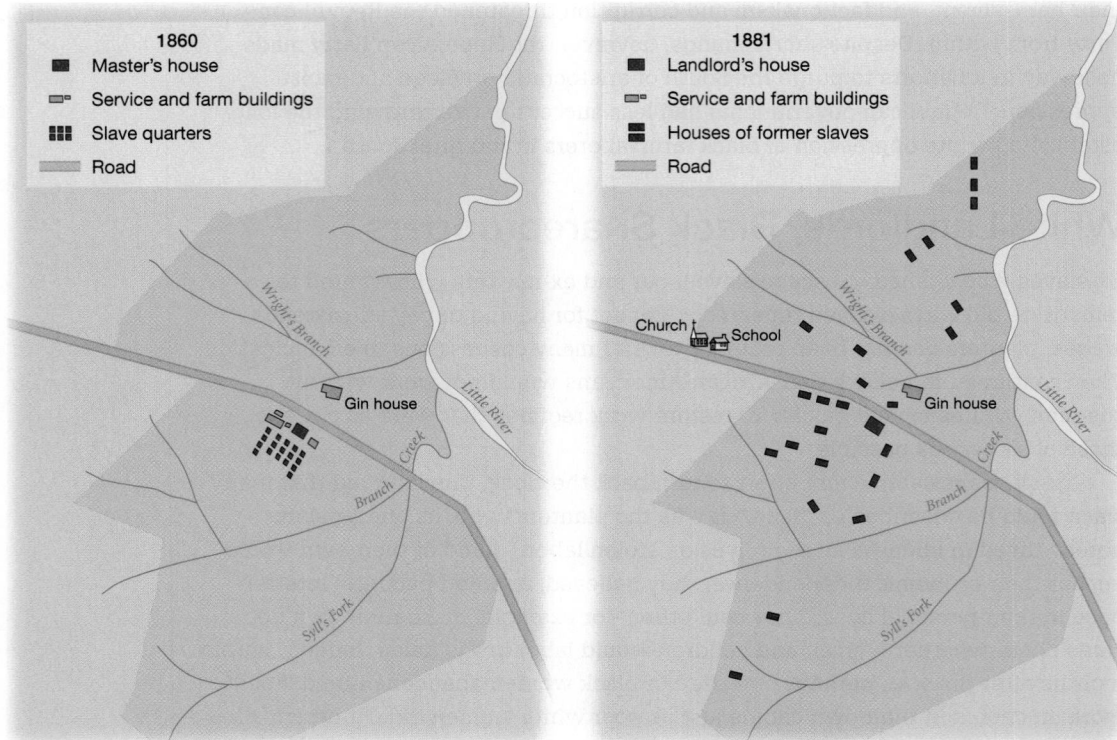

MAP 16.1 ■ A Southern Plantation in 1860 and 1881
These maps of the Barrow plantation in Georgia illustrate some of the ways in which ex-slaves expressed their freedom. Freedmen and freedwomen deserted the clustered living quarters behind the master's house, scattered over the plantation, built family cabins, and farmed rented land. The former Barrow slaves also worked together to build a school and a church.

> ▶ FOR MORE HELP ANALYZING THIS MAP, see the map activity for this chapter in the Online Study Guide at bedfordstmartins.com/roarkunderstanding.

rest. Sometimes, the farmer's debt to the merchant exceeded the income he received from his remaining half of the crop, and the farmer would have no choice but to borrow more from the merchant and begin the cycle all over again.

An experiment at first, sharecropping spread quickly and soon dominated the cotton South. Lien merchants forced tenants to plant cotton, which was easy to sell, instead of food crops. The result was excessive production of cotton and falling cotton prices, developments that cost thousands of small white farmers their land and pushed them into the ranks of sharecroppers. The new sharecropping system of agriculture took shape just as the political power of Republicans in the South began to buckle under Democratic pressure.

> ## QUICK REVIEW

How did politics and economics shape the lives of postwar blacks in the South?

CHAPTER LOCATOR | What were Lincoln's plans for wartime reconstruction?

This Republican cartoon from the October 21, 1876, issue of *Harper's Weekly* comments sarcastically on the possibility of honest elections in the South. The caption reads, "You're free as air, ain't you? Say you are or I'll blow yer black head off." Granger Collection.

▶ FOR MORE HELP ANALYZING THIS IMAGE, see the visual activity for this chapter in the Online Study Guide at bedfordstmartins.com/roarkunderstanding.

Why did reconstruction collapse?

BY 1870, after a decade of war and reconstruction, Northerners wanted to put "the southern problem" behind them. While northern commitment to defend black freedom eroded, southern commitment to white supremacy intensified. Without northern protection, southern Republicans were no match for the Democrats' economic coercion, political corruption, and bloody violence. The election of 1876 both confirmed and completed the collapse of reconstruction.

Grant's Troubled Presidency

In 1868, the Republican nominee for president was Ulysses S. Grant. Hero of the Civil War and a supporter of congressional reconstruction, Grant was the obvious choice. His Democratic opponent, Horatio Seymour of New York, ran on a platform that blasted congressional reconstruction as "a flagrant usurpation of power . . . unconstitutional, revolutionary, and void." The Republicans answered by waving the bloody shirt—that is, they reminded voters that the Democrats were "the party of rebellion." Grant won a narrow 309,000-vote margin in the popular vote and a substantial victory (214 votes to 80) in the electoral college (**Map 16.2**).

The talents Grant had demonstrated on the battlefield— decisiveness, clarity, and resolution—were less obvious in the White House. He surrounded himself with friends and family

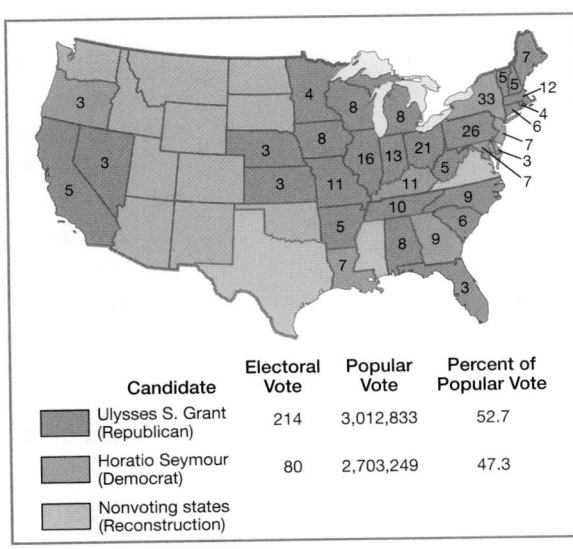

Candidate	Electoral Vote	Popular Vote	Percent of Popular Vote
Ulysses S. Grant (Republican)	214	3,012,833	52.7
Horatio Seymour (Democrat)	80	2,703,249	47.3
Nonvoting states (Reconstruction)			

MAP 16.2 ■ The Election of 1868

What vision did Andrew Johnson have for presidential reconstruction?	How radical was congressional reconstruction?	How was the battle over reconstruction fought in the South?	**Why did reconstruction collapse?**	Conclusion: What were the achievements and failures of reconstruction?

1868
– Republican Ulysses S. Grant is elected president.

1871
– Ku Klux Klan Act makes interference with voting rights a felony.

1872
– Liberal Party is formed; calls for end of government corruption and the end of reconstruction.
– President Grant is reelected.

1873
– Economic depression sets in for the remainder of the decade.
– In the *Slaughterhouse* cases, the U.S. Supreme Court rules that the Fourteenth Amendment protects only those rights that stem from the federal government.

1874
– Democrats win majority in House of Representatives.

1875
– Civil Rights Act outlaws racial discrimination in transportation, public accommodations, and juries.

1876
– In *United States v. Cruikshank*, the U.S. Supreme Court rules that the reconstruction amendments give Congress the power to legislate against discrimination by states but not by individuals.

1877
– Republican Rutherford B. Hayes assumes presidency; Reconstruction era ends.

"I BEG TO REPEAT THAT THESE FRAUDS ON THE GOVERNMENT SHALL BE PROBED TO THE VERY BOTTOM."

Grant and Scandal

This anti-Grant cartoon by Thomas Nast, the nation's most celebrated political cartoonist, shows the president falling headfirst into the barrel of fraud and corruption that tainted his administration. Library of Congress.

▶ FOR MORE HELP ANALYZING THIS IMAGE, see the visual activity for this chapter in the Online Study Guide at bedfordstmartins.com/roarkunderstanding.

and made a string of dubious appointments that led to a series of damaging scandals. Charges of corruption tainted his vice president, Schuyler Colfax, and brought down two of his cabinet officers. Though never personally implicated in any scandal, Grant was seemingly blind to the rot that filled his administration.

In 1872, anti-Grant Republicans bolted and launched the Liberal Party. To clean up the graft and corruption, Liberals proposed the creation of a nonpartisan civil service commission that would oversee competitive examinations for appointment to government offices. Liberals also demanded that the federal government remove its troops from the South and restore "home rule" (southern white control). Democrats liked the Liberals' southern policy and endorsed the Liberal presidential candidate, Horace Greeley, the longtime editor of the *New York Tribune*. The nation, however, still felt enormous affection for the man who had saved the Union and reelected Grant with 56 percent of the popular vote.

Northern Resolve Withers

Although Grant genuinely wanted to see blacks' civil and political rights protected, he understood that most Northerners had grown weary of reconstruction

CHAPTER LOCATOR | What were Lincoln's plans for wartime reconstruction?

446 CHAPTER 16 RECONSTRUCTING A NATION, 1863–1877

and were increasingly willing to let southern whites manage their own affairs. Citizens wanted to shift their attention to other issues, especially after the nation slipped into a devastating economic depression in 1873. More than eighteen thousand businesses collapsed, leaving more than a million workers on the streets. Northern businessmen wanted to invest in the South but believed that recurrent federal intrusion was itself a major cause of instability in the region. Republican leaders began to question the wisdom of their party's alliance with the South's lower classes—its small farmers and sharecroppers. One member of Grant's administration proposed allying with the "thinking and influential native southerners . . . the intelligent, well-to-do, and controlling class."

Congress, too, wanted to leave reconstruction behind, but southern Republicans made that difficult. When the South's Republicans begged for federal protection from Klan violence, Congress enacted three laws in 1870 and 1871 that were intended to break the back of white terrorism. The severest of the three, the Ku Klux Klan Act (1871), made interference with voting rights a felony. Federal marshals arrested thousands of Klansmen and came close to destroying the Klan, but they did not end all terrorism against blacks. Congress also passed the Civil Rights Act of 1875, which boldly outlawed racial discrimination in transportation, public accommodations, and juries. But federal authorities never enforced the law aggressively, and segregated facilities remained the rule throughout the South.

By the early 1870s, the Republican Party had lost its leading champions of African American rights to death or defeat at the polls. Other Republicans concluded that the quest for black equality was mistaken or hopelessly naive. In May 1872, Congress restored the right of officeholding to all but three hundred ex-rebels. Many Republicans had come to believe that traditional white leaders offered the best hope for honesty, order, and prosperity in the South.

Underlying the North's abandonment of reconstruction was unyielding racial prejudice. Northerners had learned to accept black freedom during the war, but deep-seated prejudice prevented many from accepting black equality. Even the actions they took on behalf of blacks often served partisan political advantage. Northerners generally supported Indiana senator Thomas A. Hendricks's harsh declaration that "this is a white man's Government, made by the white man for the white man."

The U.S. Supreme Court also did its part to undermine reconstruction. The Court issued a series of decisions that significantly weakened the federal government's ability to protect black Southerners. In the *Slaughterhouse* cases (1873), the Court distinguished between national and state citizenship and ruled that the Fourteenth Amendment protected only those rights that stemmed from the federal government, such as voting in federal elections and interstate travel. Since the Court decided that most rights derived from the states, it sharply curtailed the federal government's authority to defend black citizens. Even more devastating, the *United States v. Cruikshank* ruling (1876) said that the reconstruction amendments gave Congress the power to legislate against discrimination only by states, not by individuals. The "suppression of ordinary crime," such as assault, remained a state responsibility. The Supreme Court did not declare reconstruction unconstitutional but eroded its legal foundation.

The mood of the North found political expression in the election of 1874, when for the first time in eighteen years the Democrats gained control of the House of Representatives. As one Republican observed, the people had grown

| What vision did Andrew Johnson have for presidential reconstruction? | How radical was congressional reconstruction? | How was the battle over reconstruction fought in the South? | **Why did reconstruction collapse?** | Conclusion: What were the achievements and failures of reconstruction? |

447

tired of the "negro question, with all its complications, and the reconstruction of Southern States, with all its interminable embroilments." Reconstruction had come apart. Rather than defend reconstruction from its southern enemies, Northerners steadily backed away from the challenge. By the early 1870s, southern Republicans faced the forces of reaction largely on their own.

White Supremacy Triumphs

Republican governments in the South attracted more hatred than any other political regimes in American history. To most whites, Republican rule meant an intolerable reversal of what they saw as the natural racial hierarchy. The northern retreat from reconstruction permitted southern Democrats to set things right.

Taking the name Redeemers, they promised to replace "bayonet rule" (a few federal troops continued to be stationed in the South) with "home rule." They promised that honest, thrifty Democrats would supplant the corrupt and irresponsible tax-and-spend Republicans. Above all, Redeemers swore to save southern civilization from a descent into "African barbarism." As one man put it, "We must render this either a white man's government, or convert the land into a Negro man's cemetery."

Southern Democrats adopted a multipronged strategy to overthrow Republican governments. First, they sought to polarize the parties around color. They went about gathering all the South's white voters into the Democratic Party, leaving the Republicans to depend on blacks, who made up a minority of population in almost every southern state. To dislodge whites from the Republican Party, Democrats fanned the flames of racial prejudice. A South Carolina Democrat crowed that his party appealed to the "proud Caucasian race, whose sovereignty on earth God has proclaimed." Local newspapers published the names of whites who kept company with blacks, and neighbors ostracized offenders.

Democrats also exploited the severe economic plight of small white farmers by blaming it on Republican financial policy. Government spending soared during reconstruction, and small farmers saw their tax burden skyrocket. "This is tax time," a South Carolinian reported. "We are nearly all on our head about them. They are so high & so little money to pay with" that farmers were "selling every egg and chicken they can get." In 1871, Mississippi reported that one-seventh of the state's land—3.3 million acres—had been forfeited for nonpayment of taxes. The small farmers' economic distress had a racial dimension. Because few freedmen succeeded in acquiring land, they rarely paid taxes. In Georgia in 1874, blacks made up 45 percent of the population but paid only 2 percent of the taxes. From the perspective of a small white farmer, Republican rule meant that he was paying more taxes and paying them to aid blacks.

If racial pride, social isolation, and financial hardship proved insufficient to drive yeomen from the Republican Party, Democrats turned to terrorism. "Night riders" targeted white Republicans as well as blacks for murder and assassination. Whether white or black, a "dead Radical is very harmless," South Carolina Democratic leader Martin Gary told his followers.

But the primary victims of white violence were black Republicans. The object was to "kill out the leading men of the republican party," a black Republican from Florida declared. But violence targeted all black voters, not just leaders. And it escalated to unprecedented levels. In 1873, a clash between black militiamen and

CHAPTER LOCATOR | What were Lincoln's plans for wartime reconstruction?

448 CHAPTER 16
RECONSTRUCTING A NATION, 1863–1877

whites in Louisiana killed two white men and an estimated seventy black men. The whites slaughtered half of the black men after they surrendered. Although the federal government indicted more than one hundred of the white men, local juries failed to convict even one.

Even before adopting the all-out white supremacist tactics of the 1870s, Democrats had taken control of the governments of Virginia, Tennessee, and North Carolina. The new campaign brought fresh gains. The Redeemers retook Georgia in 1871, Texas in 1873, and Arkansas and Alabama in 1874. As the state election in Mississippi approached in 1876, Governor Adelbert Ames appealed to Washington for federal troops to control Democratic violence, only to hear from the attorney general that the "whole public are tired of these annual autumnal outbreaks in the South." Abandoned, Mississippi Republicans succumbed to the Democratic onslaught in the fall elections. By 1877, only three Republican state governments survived in the South (**Map 16.3**).

An Election and a Compromise

The year 1876 witnessed one of the most tumultuous elections in American history. The election took place in November, but not until March 2 of the following year did the nation know who would be inaugurated president on March 4. The Democrats nominated New York's governor, Samuel J. Tilden, who immediately targeted the corruption of the Grant administration and the "despotism" of Republican reconstruction. The Republicans put forward Rutherford B. Hayes, governor of Ohio. Privately, Hayes considered "bayonet rule" a mistake but concluded that waving the bloody shirt remained the Republicans' best political strategy.

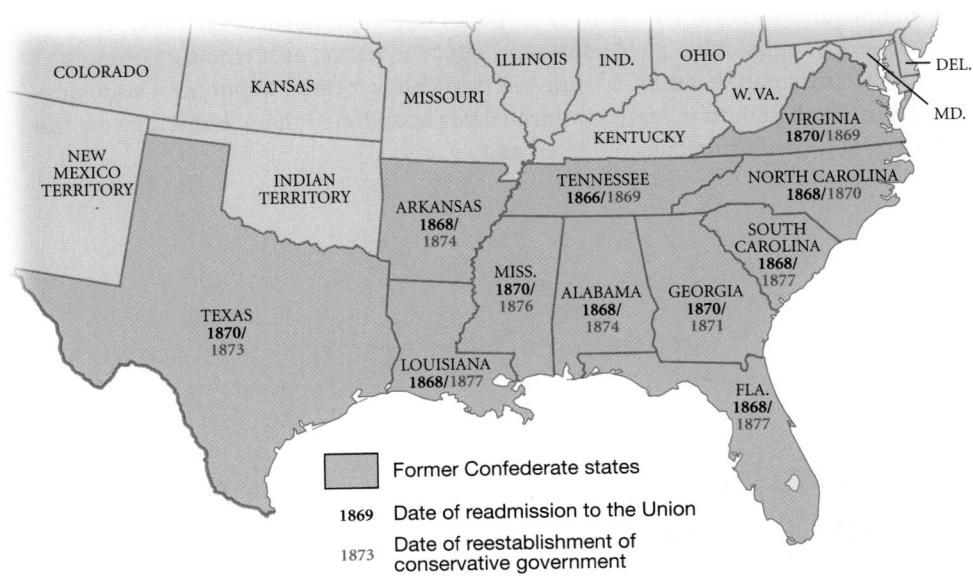

MAP 16.3 ■ The Reconstruction of the South
Myth has it that Republican rule of the former Confederacy was not only harsh but long. In most states, however, conservative southern whites stormed back into power in months or just a few years. By the election of 1876, Republican governments could be found in only three states, and they soon fell.

What vision did Andrew Johnson have for presidential reconstruction?	How radical was congressional reconstruction?	How was the battle over reconstruction fought in the South?	**Why did reconstruction collapse?**	Conclusion: What were the achievements and failures of reconstruction?

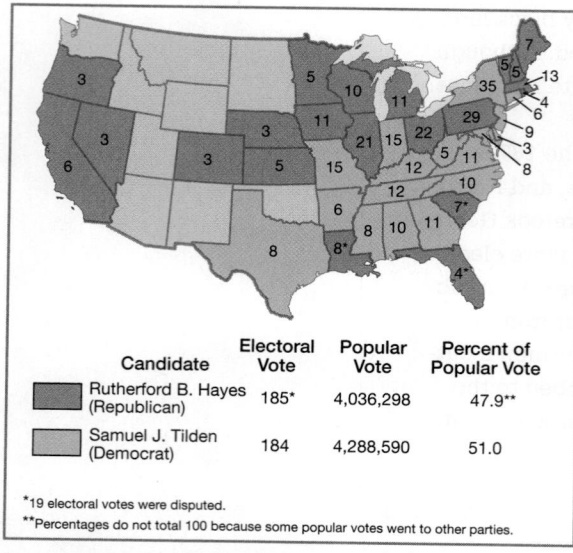

Candidate	Electoral Vote	Popular Vote	Percent of Popular Vote
Rutherford B. Hayes (Republican)	185*	4,036,298	47.9**
Samuel J. Tilden (Democrat)	184	4,288,590	51.0

*19 electoral votes were disputed.

**Percentages do not total 100 because some popular votes went to other parties.

MAP 16.4 ■ The Election of 1876

On election day, Tilden tallied 4,288,590 votes to Hayes's 4,036,000. But in the all-important electoral college, Tilden fell one vote short of the majority required for victory. The electoral votes of three states—South Carolina, Louisiana, and Florida, the only remaining Republican governments in the South— remained in doubt because both Republicans and Democrats in those states claimed victory. To win, Tilden needed only one of the nineteen contested votes. Hayes had to have all of them.

Congress had to decide who had actually won the elections in the three southern states and thus who would be president. The Constitution provided no guidance for this situation. Moreover, Democrats controlled the House, and Republicans controlled the Senate. Congress created a special electoral commission to arbitrate the disputed returns. All of the commissioners voted their party affiliation, giving every state to the Republican Hayes and putting him over the top in electoral votes (**Map 16.4**).

Some outraged Democrats vowed to resist Hayes's victory. Rumors flew of an impending coup and renewed civil war. But the impasse was broken when negotiations behind the scenes resulted in an informal understanding known as the **Compromise of 1877**. In exchange for a Democratic promise not to block Hayes's inauguration and to deal fairly with the freedmen, Hayes vowed to refrain from using the army to uphold the remaining Republican regimes in the South and to provide the South with substantial federal subsidies for internal improvements.

Stubborn Tilden supporters bemoaned the "stolen election" and damned "His Fraudulency," Rutherford B. Hayes. Old-guard radicals such as William Lloyd Garrison denounced Hayes's bargain as a "policy of compromise, of credulity, of weakness, of subserviency, of surrender." But the nation as a whole celebrated, for the country had weathered a grave crisis. The last three Republican state governments in the South fell quickly once Hayes abandoned them and withdrew the U.S. Army. Reconstruction came to an end.

Compromise of 1877

▶ Political compromise that delivered the presidency to Rutherford B. Hayes. In exchange for a Democratic promise not to block Hayes's inauguration and to deal fairly with the freedmen, Hayes vowed to refrain from using the army to uphold the remaining Republican regimes in the South and to provide the South with substantial federal subsidies for internal improvements. The Compromise of 1877 effectively brought Reconstruction to an end.

> QUICK REVIEW

How did the decline of northern support for reconstruction help southern Democrats "redeem" the South?

CHAPTER LOCATOR | What were Lincoln's plans for wartime reconstruction?

450 CHAPTER 16 RECONSTRUCTING A NATION, 1863–1877

The Granger Collection, New York.

Conclusion: What were the achievements and failures of reconstruction?

MOST WHITE SOUTHERNERS resisted the passage from slavery to free labor, from white racial despotism to equal justice, and from white political monopoly to biracial democracy. The old elite wanted as little change as possible, while African Americans and some whites were eager to exploit the revolutionary implications of emancipation.

The northern-dominated Republican Congress pushed the revolution along. Congress employed constitutional amendments to require ex-Confederates to accept legal equality and share political power with black men. Conservative southern whites fought ferociously to recover their power and privilege. When Democrats regained control of politics, whites used both state power and private violence to wipe out many of the gains of Reconstruction.

Yet Northern victory in the Civil War ensured that ex-slaves no longer faced the auction block and could send their children to school, worship in their own churches, and work independently on their own rented farms. Sharecropping, with all its hardships, provided more autonomy and economic welfare than bondage had.

The Civil War and emancipation set in motion the most profound upheaval in the nation's history. War destroyed the largest slave society in the New World and gave birth to a modern nation-state. Washington increased its role in national affairs, and the victorious North set the nation's compass toward the expansion of industrial capitalism and the final conquest of the West.

Despite massive changes, however, the Civil War remained only a "half accomplished" revolution. By not fulfilling the promises the nation seemed to hold out to black Americans at war's end, reconstruction represents a tragedy of enormous proportions. The failure to protect blacks and guarantee their rights had enduring consequences. It was the failure of the first reconstruction that made the modern civil rights movement necessary.

> ⌐AML. DOVE wishes to know of the
> whereabouts of his mother, Areno, his
> sisters Maria, Neziah, and Peggy, and his
> brother Edmond, who were owned by Geo.
> Dove, of Rockingham county, Shenandoah
> Valley, Va. Sold in Richmond, after which
> Saml. and Edmond were taken to Nashville,
> Tenn., by Joe Mick; Areno was left at the
> Eagle Tavern, Richmond
> Respectfully yours,
> SAML. DOVE.
> Utica, New York, Aug. 5, 1865–3m
>
> U. S. Christian Commission,
> Nashville, Tenn., July 19, 1865.

SO NOW YOU KNOW

Even though newly freed African Americans had their own ideas of freedom— family, land, and independence—the politics of Reconstruction in both the North and South and the violent reaction of many white Southerners undermined these hopes. By the end of the era, political rights for most southern blacks were restricted, and economic independence was rare.

What vision did Andrew Johnson have for presidential reconstruction?	How radical was congressional reconstruction?	How was the battle over reconstruction fought in the South?	Why did reconstruction collapse?	Conclusion: What were the achievements and failures of reconstruction?

Online Study Guide
bedfordstmartins.com/roarkunderstanding

STEP 1

GETTING STARTED

Below are basic terms from this period in American history. Can you identify each term below and explain why it matters? To do this exercise online or to download this chart, visit bedfordstmartins.com/roarkunderstanding.

TERM	WHO OR WHAT & WHEN	WHY IT MATTERS
Freedmen's Bureau, p. 430		
Andrew Johnson, p. 432		
black codes, p. 433		
Fourteenth Amendment, p. 435		
Military Reconstruction Act, p. 437		
Fifteenth Amendment, p. 438		
Ku Klux Klan, p. 441		
sharecropping, p. 443		
Compromise of 1877, p. 450		

STEP 2

MOVING BEYOND THE BASICS

The exercise below represents a more advanced understanding of the chapter material. Indicate how each phase of reconstruction addressed the key issues involved. When assessing the achievements and failures of each plan, consider the unintended or indirect consequences. To do this exercise online or to download this chart, visit bedfordstmartins.com/roarkunderstanding.

Phase of reconstruction	Requirements for readmission	Role/rights of freedmen	Achievements	Failures
Wartime reconstruction (Lincoln)				
Presidential reconstruction (Johnson)				
Congressional reconstruction				

Now that you've reviewed various parts of the chapter, take a step back and try to see the big picture by answering these questions. Remember to use specific examples from the chapter in your answers. To do this exercise online, visit bedfordsmartins.com/roarkunderstanding.

PRESIDENTIAL AND CONGRESSIONAL RECONSTRUCTION

▶ What role did the black codes play in shaping the course of reconstruction?

▶ What steps did Congress take between 1865 and 1869 to assist ex-slaves in their lives as freedmen? How effective were these actions?

SOUTHERN RECONSTRUCTION IN ACTION

▶ How did white Southerners respond during Reconstruction? Consider both Democrats and Republicans in your response.

▶ How did southern African Americans attempt to shape their own lives during Reconstruction?

LOOKING BACKWARD, LOOKING AHEAD

▶ How did long-held racial views among whites, in both the South and the North, shape Reconstruction?

▶ What were the lasting accomplishments of Reconstruction? What were its most important failures?

THE END OF RECONSTRUCTION

▶ How and why did the decline of northern support for Reconstruction help southern Democrats "redeem" the South?

▶ Why did white supremacy become the foundation of southern politics in the 1870s?

IN YOUR OWN WORDS

Imagine that you must explain chapter 16 to someone who hasn't read it. What would be the most important points to include and why?

17
CONTESTING THE WEST

1870–1900

> This chapter explores the westward expansion of the late nineteenth century. It examines the impact of expansion on Native Americans, the role mining played in the creation of the American West, and Americans' settlement and exploitation of western lands. Finally, it considers the enduring power of the mythic West in American memory.

> What did American expansion mean for Native Americans?

> How did mining motivate and shape American expansion?

> Who fought for control of the land and resources of the American West?

> Conclusion: What is the meaning of the mythic West?

DID YOU KNOW?

It took the United States less than 40 years to gain control of the western half of the country.

Cliffs of the Upper Colorado, 1882. When artist Thomas Moran arrived in Wyoming Territory in 1871, these towering buttes were his first sight.

What did American expansion mean for Native Americans?

WHILE THE EUROPEAN POWERS expanded their authority and wealth through imperialism and colonialism, establishing far-flung empires abroad, the United States focused its attention on the West. Expansion in the American West involved the conquest, displacement, and rule over native peoples. Removed to Indian Territory or confined on reservations, Indians became wards of the federal government, their culture assaulted by policies designed to force assimilation (**Map 17.1**). Through the lens of colonialism, we can see how the United States' commitment to an imperialist, expansionist ideology resulted in the displacement of Native Americans and the establishment of new territories and eventually states. The colonizing of the West was a dynamic process in which Native Americans actively resisted, contested, and adapted to colonial rule.

Indian Removal and the Reservation System

Manifest destiny—the belief that the United States had a "God-given" right to aggressively spread the values of white civilization and expand the nation from ocean to ocean—dictated U.S. policy. In the name of manifest destiny, Americans forced the removal of the Five Civilized Tribes to Oklahoma; colonized Texas and won its independence from Mexico in 1836; conquered California, Arizona, New Mexico, and parts of Utah and Colorado in the Mexican-American War of 1846–1848; and invaded Oregon in the 1840s.

By midcentury, settlers in unprecedented numbers crossed the Great Plains on their way to the goldfields of California or the rich farmland of Washington and Oregon. In their path stood a solid wall of Indian land, stretching from Minnesota

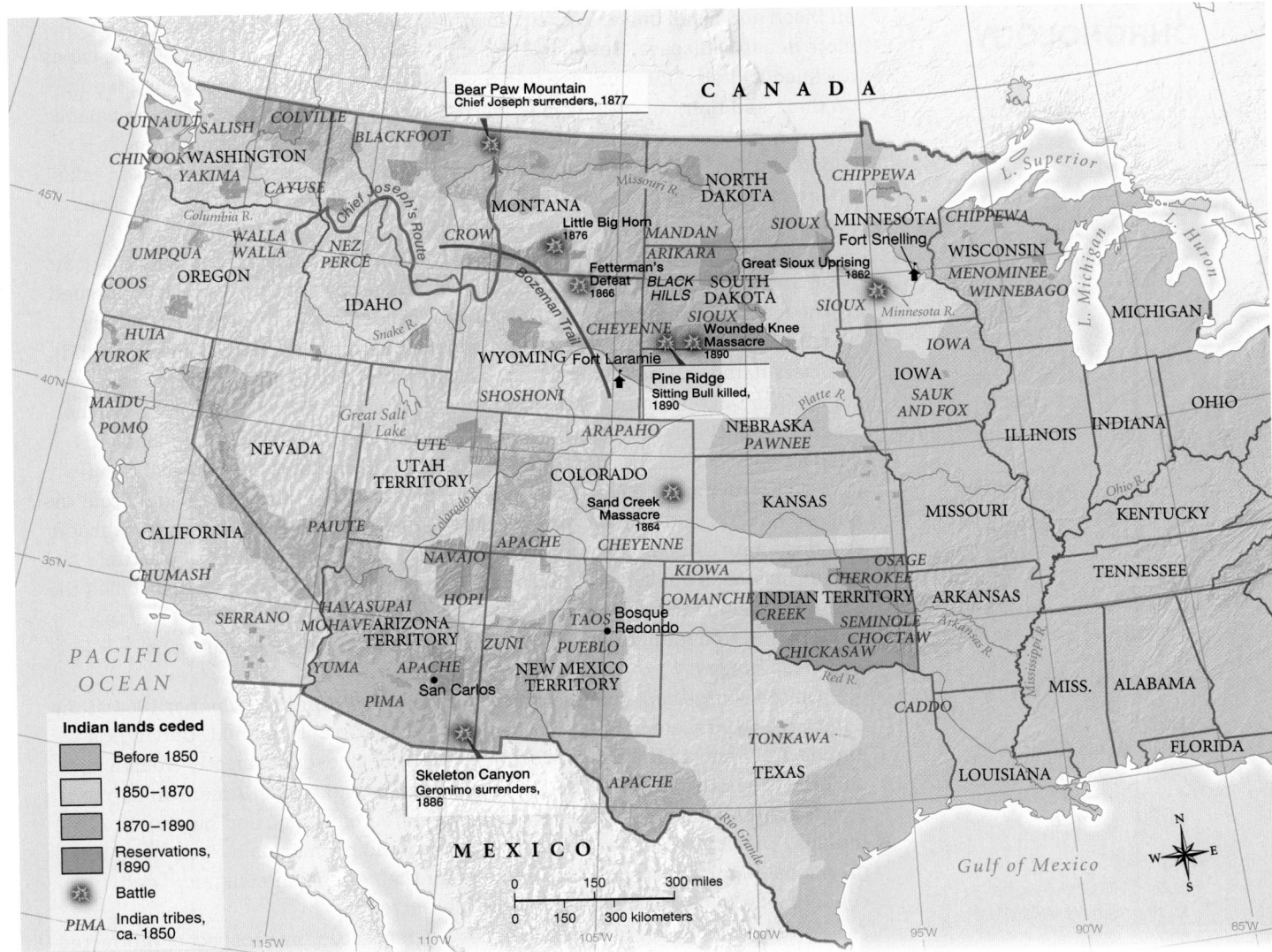

MAP 17.1 ■ The Loss of Indian Lands, 1850–1890
By 1890, western Indians were isolated on small, scattered reservations. Native Americans had struggled to retain their land in major battles, from the Great Sioux Uprising in Minnesota in 1862 to the massacre at Wounded Knee, South Dakota, in 1890.

▶ FOR MORE HELP ANALYZING THIS MAP, see the map activity for this chapter in the Online Study Guide at bedfordstmartins.com/roarkunderstanding.

to Texas, much of it granted through the policy of Indian removal. The "Indian problem" needed to be solved—through treaties if possible or coercion if necessary. In 1851, some ten thousand Plains Indians came together at Fort Laramie in Wyoming to negotiate a treaty that ceded a wide swath of their land to allow passage of the wagon trains. In return, the government promised that the rest of the Indian land would remain inviolate.

The Indians who "touched the pen" to the 1851 Treaty of Fort Laramie hoped to preserve their culture in the face of the white onslaught on their people and land. White invaders cut down trees, miners polluted streams, and hunters killed

CHAPTER LOCATOR | What did American expansion mean for Native Americans? | How did mining motivate and shape American expansion? | Who fought for control of the land and resources of the American West? | Conclusion: What is the meaning of the mythic West?

457

1862
– Great Sioux Uprising leads to the largest mass execution in American history.

1864
– Sand Creek Massacre, in which Colorado militiamen kill 270 Cheyenne Indians.

1867
– Treaty of Medicine Lodge negotiates peace with southern Plains Indians.

1868
– Sioux victories on the northern plains lead to U.S. concessions at the second Treaty of Fort Laramie.

1876
– At the Battle of the Little Big Horn, Sioux forces decimate the U.S. cavalry led by George Armstrong Custer.

1882
– Indian Rights Association, composed of whites sympathetic to the Indian cause, is formed.

1883
– Buffalo Bill Cody begins touring with his Wild West show.

1887
– Dawes Allotment Act provides for the breakup of reservation lands.

1889
– The Ghost Dance movement, a spiritual revival, spreads among Indians across the West.

1890
– At Wounded Knee, South Dakota, U.S. cavalry massacre more than two hundred Sioux followers of the Ghost Dance.

off bison and small game. Whites brought alcohol, guns, and something even more deadly—disease. Between 1780 and 1870, the population of the Plains tribes declined by half. "If I could see this thing, if I knew where it came from, I would go there and fight it," a Cheyenne warrior anguished. Disease shifted the balance of power on the plains from Woodland agrarian tribes like the Mandan and Hidatsa to the Lakota (Western) Sioux, who fled the contagion of villages to take up life as equestrian (horse-riding) nomads on the western plains. As the Sioux pushed west, they displaced weaker tribes.

The Indian wars in the West marked the last resistance of a Native American population devastated by disease and demoralized by the removal policy pursued by the federal government. More accurately called "settlers' wars" (since they began with "peaceful settlers," often miners, overrunning Native American land), the wars flared up again only a few years after the signing of the Fort Laramie treaty. The Dakota Sioux in Minnesota went to war in 1862. For years, under the leadership of Chief Little Crow, the Dakota, also known as the Santee, had pursued a policy of accommodation, ceding land in return for the promise of annuities. But with his people on the verge of starvation (the local Indian agent told the hungry Dakota, "Go and eat grass"), Little Crow reluctantly led his angry warriors in a desperate campaign against the intruders, killing more than 1,000 settlers. American troops quelled what was called the Great Sioux Uprising (also called the Santee Uprising) and marched 1,700 Sioux to Fort Snelling, where 400 Indians were put on trial for murder and 38 died in the largest mass execution in American history.

On the southern plains, the conflict reached its nadir in November 1864 at the Sand Creek Massacre in Colorado Territory. There Colonel John M. Chivington and his Colorado militia descended on a village of Cheyenne, mostly women and children. Their leader, Black Kettle, raised a white flag and an American flag to signal surrender, but the charging cavalry ignored his signal and butchered 270 Indians. The city of Denver treated Chivington and his men as heroes, but a congressional inquiry castigated the soldiers for their "fiendish malignity" and condemned the "savage cruelty" of the massacre.

After the Civil War, President Ulysses S. Grant faced the prospect of protracted Indian war on the Great Plains. Reluctant to spend more money and sacrifice more lives in battle, Grant adopted a "peace policy" designed to segregate and control the Indians while opening up land to white settlers. The government sought control of Indian lands and promised in return to pay annuities and put the Indians on lands reserved for their use—reservations. This policy won the support of both friends of the Indians, who feared for their survival, and Indian haters, who coveted their land and wished to confine them to the least desirable areas in the West. General William Tecumseh Sherman summed up the new Indian policy succinctly: "Remove all to a safe place and then reduce them to a helpless condition."

Poverty and starvation stalked the reservations (see Map 17.1, page 457). Confined by armed force, the Indians eked out an existence on stingy government rations. They found themselves dependent on government handouts and the assistance of Indian agents who, in the words of Paiute Sarah Winnemucca, did "nothing but fill their pockets." Winnemucca launched a lecture campaign in the United States and Europe denouncing the government's reservation policy.

Indian reservations soon became cultural battlegrounds. Reservations closely resembled colonial societies where native populations, ruled by outside bureau-

crats, saw their culture assaulted, their religious practices outlawed, their children sent away to school, and their way of life attacked in the name of progress and civilization. Self-styled "friends of the Indians," many of them easterners with little experience in the West, maintained that reservations would provide a classroom of civilization where Indians could be taught to speak English, to worship a Christian god, to give up hunting for farming, and to reject tribal ways.

The white reformers also proposed that Indian children be sent to off-reservation boarding schools. At these schools, children as young as seven were forced to adopt white dress, manners, culture, and language. While many boarding schools were in the West, a few—including the famous Carlisle Indian School in Pennsylvania—were hundreds of miles from the reservations. To a large extent, the plan, in the words of Carlisle founder Richard Henry Pratt, to "kill the Indian and save the man" failed. Instead, Indian children from different tribes formed bonds and a new sense of pan-Indian identity. In the face of this assault on their cultures, Indians found ways to resist, adapt, and hold on to their cultural identity.

The Decimation of the Great Bison Herds and the Fight for the Black Hills

By the nineteenth century, more than two hundred years of contact with whites had utterly transformed Native American societies. Indians had been pushed off their lands east of the Mississippi and moved west. Through trade with the Spaniards and French, Indians had acquired horses and guns. The Sioux, hunting on horseback, staked their survival on the buffalo (American bison). But the great herds, once numbering as many as thirty million, fell into decline. A host of environmental and human factors contributed to the destruction of the bison. By the 1850s, a combination of drought and buffalo hunting had driven the great herds onto the far western plains.

After the Civil War, the accelerating pace of industrial expansion brought about the near extinction of the bison. Industrial demand for heavy leather belting

CHAPTER LOCATOR | What did American expansion mean for Native Americans? | How did mining motivate and shape American expansion? | Who fought for control of the land and resources of the American West? | Conclusion: What is the meaning of the mythic West?

459

used in machinery and the development of larger, more accurate rifles combined to hasten the slaughter of the bison. At the same time, the nation's growing transcontinental rail system cut the range in two and divided the herds. "It will not be long before all the buffaloes are extinct near and between the railroads," Ohio senator John Sherman predicted in 1868. The army took credit for the conquest of the Plains Indians, but victory came about largely as a result of the decimation of the great bison herds. General Philip Sheridan acknowledged as much when he applauded white hide hunters for "destroying the Indians' commissary." With their food supply gone, Indians had to choose between starvation and the reservation. "A cold wind blew across the prairie when the last buffalo fell," the great Sioux leader **Sitting Bull** lamented, "a death wind for my people."

On the southern plains in 1867, more than five thousand warring Comanches, Kiowas, and Southern Arapahos gathered at Medicine Lodge Creek in Kansas to negotiate a treaty. Satak, or Sitting Bear, a prominent Kiowa chief and medicine man, explained why the Indians sought peace: "In the far-distant past . . . the world seemed large enough for both the red man and the white man." But, he observed, "its broad plains seem now to contract, and the white man grows jealous of his red brother." To preserve their land from white encroachment, the Indians signed the Treaty of Medicine Lodge, agreeing to move to a reservation. But after 1870, hide hunters poured into the region, and within a decade, they had nearly exterminated the southern bison herds. Luther Standing Bear recounted the sight and stench: "I saw the bodies of hundreds of dead buffalo lying about, just wasting, and the odor was terrible. . . . They were letting our food lie on the plains to rot."

On the northern plains, gold sparked the conflict between Indians and Euro-Americans. In 1866, the Cheyenne united with the Sioux in Wyoming to protect their hunting grounds in the Powder River valley, which were threatened by the construction of the Bozeman Trail connecting Fort Laramie with the goldfields in Montana. Impressive Sioux victories led to the **1868 Treaty of Fort Laramie**, in which the United States agreed to abandon the Bozeman Trail and guaranteed the Indians control of the Black Hills, land sacred to the Lakota Sioux. The treaty was vague and full of contradictions. Nonetheless, some tribes accepted it. The great Sioux chief Red Cloud led many of his people onto the reservation. Red Cloud soon regretted his decision. "Think of it!" he told a visitor to the Pine Ridge Reservation. "I, who used to own . . . country so extensive that I could not ride through it in a week . . . must tell Washington when I am hungry. I must beg for that which I own." Several Sioux chiefs, among them Crazy Horse of the Oglala band and Sitting Bull of the Hunkpapa, refused to sign the treaty. Crazy Horse said that he wanted no part of the "piecemeal penning" of his people.

In 1874, the discovery of gold in the Black Hills of the Dakotas led the government to break its promise to Red Cloud. At first, the government offered to purchase the Black Hills. But to the Lakota Sioux, the Black Hills were sacred—"the heart of everything that is." They refused to sell. The army responded by issuing an ultimatum ordering all Lakota Sioux and Northern Cheyenne bands onto the Pine Ridge Reservation and threatening to hunt down those who refused.

In the summer of 1876, the army launched a three-pronged attack led by Lieutenant Colonel George Armstrong Custer, General George Crook, and Colonel John Gibbon. Crazy Horse stopped Crook at the Battle of the Rosebud. Custer,

Sitting Bull

▶ Great Sioux leader of the second half of the nineteenth century. Sitting Bull was among those who refused to sign the two Treaties of Fort Laramie (1851 and 1868). Along with Crazy Horse, he led Indian forces at the Battle of Little Big Horn. Sitting Bull surrendered in 1881. When, in 1890, Sitting Bull joined the Ghost Dance, he was killed by Indian police as they tried to arrest him.

1868 Treaty of Fort Laramie

▶ Treaty with the Sioux in which the United States agreed to abandon the Bozeman Trail and guarantee Sioux control of the Black Hills. The treaty was signed following a brief war with the Sioux on the northern plains.

leading the second prong of the army's offensive, divided his troops and ordered an attack. On June 25, he spotted signs of the Indians' camp and, crying "Hurrah Boys, we've got them," led 265 men of the Seventh Cavalry into the largest Indian camp ever assembled on the Great Plains. Indian warriors led by Sitting Bull and Crazy Horse set upon Custer and his men and quickly annihilated them. "It took us about as long as a hungry man to eat his dinner," the Cheyenne chief Two Moons recalled.

"Custer's Last Stand," as the **Battle of the Little Big Horn** was styled in myth, turned out to be the last stand for the Sioux. The bands that had massed at the Little Big Horn scattered, and the army hunted them down. "Wherever we went," wrote the Oglala holy man Black Elk, "the soldiers came to kill us." In 1877, Crazy Horse was captured and killed. Four years later, in 1881, Sitting Bull surrendered. The government took the Black Hills and confined the Lakota to the Great Sioux Reservation. The Sioux never accepted the loss of the Black Hills. In 1923, they filed suit, demanding the return of the land taken illegally from them. After a protracted court battle lasting nearly sixty years, the U.S. Supreme Court ruled in 1980 that the government had illegally abrogated the Treaty of Fort Laramie and upheld an award of $122.5 million in compensation to the tribes. The Sioux refused the settlement and continue to press for the return of the Black Hills.

Battle of the Little Big Horn

▶ Battle between Sioux warriors led by Crazy Horse and Sitting Bull and American cavalry led by George Armstrong Custer. When Custer charged into a Sioux encampment, he and his men were killed. The Battle of Little Big Horn was a major military victory for the Sioux, but their success was shortlived.

The Dawes Act and Indian Land Allotment

In the 1880s, the practice of rounding up Indians and herding them onto reservations lost momentum in favor of allotment—a new policy designed to encourage assimilation through farming and the ownership of private property. Pressure for this shift in policy came both from white Americans who coveted reservation lands and from those who were appalled at the desperate poverty on the reservations and feared for the Indians' survival. Helen Hunt Jackson, in her classic work *A Century of Dishonor* (1881), convinced many readers that the Indians had been treated unfairly. "Our Indian policy," *the New York Times* concluded, "is usually spoliation behind the mask of benevolence."

The Indian Rights Association, a group of mainly white easterners formed in 1882, campaigned for the dismantling of the reservations, now viewed as obstacles to progress. To "cease to treat the Indian as a red man and treat him as a man" meant putting an end to tribal communalism and fostering individualism. "Selfishness," declared Senator Henry Dawes of Massachusetts, "is at the bottom of civilization." Dawes called for "allotment in severalty"—the institution of private property.

In 1887, Congress passed the **Dawes Allotment Act**, dividing up reservations and allotting parcels of land to individual Indians as private property.

Provisions of the Dawes Allotment Act

Indian heads of household received an allotment of 160 acres from reservation lands.

Single persons over eighteen and orphans under eighteen received 80 acres.

Indians who took allotments earned U.S. citizenship.

The government reserved the right to sell "surplus" reservation lands to white settlers.

Dawes Allotment Act

▶ 1887 law that divided up reservations and allotted parcels of land to individual Indians as private property. In the end, the American government sold almost two-thirds of Indian land to white settlers. The Dawes Act dealt a crippling blow to traditional tribal culture.

CHAPTER LOCATOR | What did American expansion mean for Native Americans? | How did mining motivate and shape American expansion? | Who fought for control of the land and resources of the American West? | Conclusion: What is the meaning of the mythic West?

461

As a result of the Dawes Act, Indian land dropped from 138 million acres in 1887 to a scant 48 million in 1934. The legislation, in the words of one critic, worked "to despoil the Indians of their lands and to make them vagabonds on the face of the earth." The Dawes Act completed the dispossession of the western Indian peoples and dealt a crippling blow to traditional tribal culture. It remained in effect until 1934, when the United States restored the right of Native Americans to own land communally (see chapter 24).

Indian Resistance and Survival

Faced with the extinction of their entire way of life, different groups of Indians responded in different ways in the waning decades of the nineteenth century. Some tribes, including the Crow, Arikara, Pawnee, and Shoshoni, fought alongside the U.S. Army against their old enemies, the Sioux. The Crow chief Plenty Coups explained why he allied with the United States: "Not because we loved the white man . . . or because we hated the Sioux . . . but because we plainly saw that this course was the only one which might save our beautiful country for us." The Crow and Shoshoni got to stay in their homelands and avoided the fate of other tribes shipped to reservations far away.

Indians who refused to stay on reservations risked being hunted down. The Nez Percé war of 1877 is perhaps the most harrowing example of the army's policy. In 1863, the government dictated a treaty drastically reducing Nez Percé land. Most of the chiefs refused to sign the treaty and did not move to the reservation. In 1877, the army issued an ultimatum—come in to the reservation or be hunted down. Some eight hundred Nez Percé people, many of them women and children, fled across the mountains of Idaho, Wyoming, and Montana, heading for the safety of Canada. Only 50 miles from the border, after a 1,300-mile journey, the army caught up with them and attacked. Yellow Wolf recalled their plight: "Children crying with cold. No fire. There could be no light. Everywhere the crying, the death wail." After a five-day siege, the Nez Percé leader, Chief Joseph, surrendered. His speech, reported by a white soldier, would become famous. "I am tired of fighting," he said as he surrendered his rifle. "Our chiefs are killed. It is cold and we have no blankets. The little children are freezing to death. . . . I am tired. My heart is sick and sad. From where the sun now stands, I will fight no more forever."

In the Southwest, the Apaches resorted to armed resistance. They roamed the Sonoran Desert of southern Arizona and northern Mexico, perfecting a hit-and-run guerrilla warfare in the 1870s and 1880s. General George Crook combined a policy of dogged pursuit with judicious diplomacy. Crook relied on Indian scouts to track the raiding parties, recruiting nearly two hundred, including Apaches along with Navajos and Paiutes. By 1882, Crook had succeeded in persuading most of the Apaches to settle on the San Carlos Reservation in Arizona Territory. A desolate piece of desert inhabited by scorpions and rattlesnakes, San Carlos, in the words of one Apache, was "the worst place in all the great territory stolen from the Apaches."

Geronimo, a respected shaman (medicine man) of the Chiricahua Apache, refused to stay at San Carlos and repeatedly led raiding parties in the early 1880s. His warriors attacked ranches to obtain ammunition and horses. In the

Geronimo

▶ Chiricahua Apache shaman (medicine man) who refused to stay at the San Carlos Reservation and repeatedly led raiding parties in the early 1880s. Geronimo and his band were captured in September 1886. Although fewer than three dozen Apaches had been identified as "hostiles," the government rounded up nearly five hundred Apaches, including the scouts who had helped track Geronimo, and sent them as prisoners to Florida.

Ghost Dancers

Arapaho women at the Darlington Agency in Indian Territory (Oklahoma) participate in the Ghost Dance. Different tribes performed variations of the dance, but generally dancers formed a circle and danced until they reached the trancelike state shown here. National Anthropological Archives, Smithsonian Institution, Washington, D.C. (#81-9626).

spring of 1885, Geronimo and his followers went on a ten-month offensive, moving from the Apache sanctuary in the Sierra Madre to raid and burn ranches and towns on both sides of the Mexican border. General Crook caught up with Geronimo in the fall and persuaded him to return to San Carlos, only to have him slip away on the way back to the reservation. Chagrined, Crook resigned his post. General Nelson Miles, Crook's replacement, adopted a policy of hunt and destroy.

Geronimo's band of thirty-three Apaches, including women and children, managed to elude Miles's troops for more than five months. Eventually, Miles's scouts cornered Geronimo in 1886 at Skeleton Canyon. Caught between Mexican regulars and the U.S. Army, Geronimo agreed to march north with the soldiers and negotiate a settlement. "We have not slept for six months," he admitted, "and we are worn out." Although fewer than three dozen Apaches had been considered "hostile," when General Miles induced them to surrender, the government rounded up nearly five hundred Apaches, including the scouts who had helped track Geronimo, and sent them as prisoners to Florida.

On the plains, many tribes turned to a nonviolent form of resistance—a new religion called the **Ghost Dance**. The Paiute shaman Wovoka, drawing on a cult that had developed in the 1870s, combined elements of Christianity and traditional Indian religion to found the Ghost Dance religion in 1889. Wovoka claimed that he had received a vision in which the Great Spirit spoke through him to all

Ghost Dance

▶ New religion that served as a nonviolent form of resistance for Indians in the late nineteenth century. The Paiute shaman Wovoka combined elements of Christianity and traditional Indian religion to found the Ghost Dance religion in 1889. The Ghost Dance frightened whites and was violently suppressed.

CHAPTER LOCATOR | What did American expansion mean for Native Americans? | How did mining motivate and shape American expansion? | Who fought for control of the land and resources of the American West? | Conclusion: What is the meaning of the mythic West?

463

Indians, prophesying that if they would unite in the Ghost Dance ritual, whites would be destroyed in an apocalypse. This religion, born of despair and carrying a message of hope, spread like wildfire over the plains. The Ghost Dance was performed in Idaho, Montana, Utah, Wyoming, Colorado, Nebraska, Kansas, the Dakotas, and Indian Territory by tribes as diverse as the Sioux, Arapaho, Cheyenne, Pawnee, and Shoshoni.

The Ghost Dance was nonviolent, but it frightened whites, especially when the Sioux taught that wearing a white ghost shirt made Indians immune to soldiers' bullets. Soon whites began to fear an uprising. "Indians are dancing in the snow and are wild and crazy," wrote the Bureau of Indian Affairs agent at the Pine Ridge Reservation in South Dakota. Frantic, he pleaded for reinforcements. "We are at the mercy of these dancers. We need protection, and we need it now." President Benjamin Harrison dispatched several thousand federal troops to Sioux country.

In December 1890, when Sitting Bull joined the Ghost Dance, he was killed by Indian police as they tried to arrest him at his cabin on the Standing Rock Reservation. His people, fleeing the scene, joined with a larger group of Miniconjou Sioux, who were apprehended by the Seventh Cavalry near Wounded Knee Creek, South Dakota. As the Indians laid down their arms, a shot rang out, and the soldiers opened fire. In the ensuing melee, more than two hundred Sioux men, women, and children were killed. Settler Jules Sandoz surveyed the scene the day after the massacre at **Wounded Knee**. "Here in ten minutes an entire community was as the buffalo that bleached on the plains," he wrote. "There was something loose in the world that hated joy and happiness as it hated brightness and color, reducing everything to drab agony and gray." It had taken Euro-Americans 250 years to wrest control of the eastern half of the United States from the Indians. It took them less than 40 years to take the western half. The subjugation of the Native Americans marked the first chapter in a national mission of empire that would later lead to overseas imperialistic adventures in Asia, Latin America, the Caribbean, and the Pacific Islands.

Wounded Knee

▶ December 1890 massacre of Sioux Indians by American cavalry at Wounded Knee Creek, South Dakota. Sent to suppress the Ghost Dance, the soldiers opened fire on a group of Sioux as they attempted to surrender. More than two hundred Sioux men, women, and children were killed.

> **QUICK REVIEW**

How did U.S. policy toward Native Americans change between 1870 and 1900?

| "Mining on the Comstock" | This illustration, made at Gold Hill, Nevada, in 1876, shows a sectional view of a mine, including the tunnels, incline, cooling-off room, blower, and air shaft, along with a collection of miner's tools. University of California at Berkeley, Bancroft Library. |

How did mining motivate and shape American expansion?

▶ FOR MORE HELP ANALYZING THIS IMAGE, see the visual activity for this chapter in the Online Study Guide at bedfordstmartins.com/roarkunderstanding.

MINING STOOD AT THE CENTER of the United States' quest for empire in the West. The California gold rush of 1849 touched off the frenzy. The four decades following witnessed equally frenetic rushes for gold and other metals, most notably on the Comstock Lode in Nevada and later in New Mexico, Colorado, the Dakotas, Montana, Idaho, Arizona, and Utah. The diverse peoples drawn to the West by the promise of mining riches made the region the most cosmopolitan in the nation. A close look at mining on the Comstock Lode indicates some of the patterns and paradoxes of western mining. And a look at territorial government uncovers striking parallels with corruption and cupidity in politics east of the Mississippi (**Map 17.2**).

Mining on the Comstock Lode

By 1859, refugees from California's played-out goldfields flocked to the Washoe basin in Nevada. While searching for gold, Washoe miners stumbled on the richest vein of silver ore on the continent—the legendary **Comstock Lode**, named for prospector Henry Comstock. To exploit even potentially valuable silver claims required capital and expensive technology well beyond the means of the prospector. An active San Francisco stock market sprang up to finance operations on the Comstock. Shrewd businessmen soon recognized that the easiest way to get rich was not to mine at all but to sell their claims or to form mining companies and sell shares of stock. Speculation, misrepresentation, and outright thievery ran rampant. In twenty years, more than $300 million poured from the earth in Nevada alone, most of it going to speculators in California.

Comstock Lode

▶ Silver ore deposit discovered in 1859 in the Washoe basin in Nevada. Discovery of the Comstock Lode touched off an influx of people into the region and led to the establishment of a number of boomtowns, including Virginia City, Nevada. By 1875, Virginia City had a diverse population of about 25,000 people.

CHAPTER LOCATOR | What did American expansion mean for Native Americans? | **How did mining motivate and shape American expansion?** | Who fought for control of the land and resources of the American West? | Conclusion: What is the meaning of the mythic West?

465

1859
- Initial discovery of Comstock Lode in Nevada.

1870
- Women constitute 30 percent of the population of Virginia City, Nevada.

1873
- Miners uncover "Big Bonanza" on Comstock Lode.

1875
- Population of Virginia City, Nevada, reaches 25,000.

1882
- Chinese Exclusion Act effectively bars Chinese immigration.

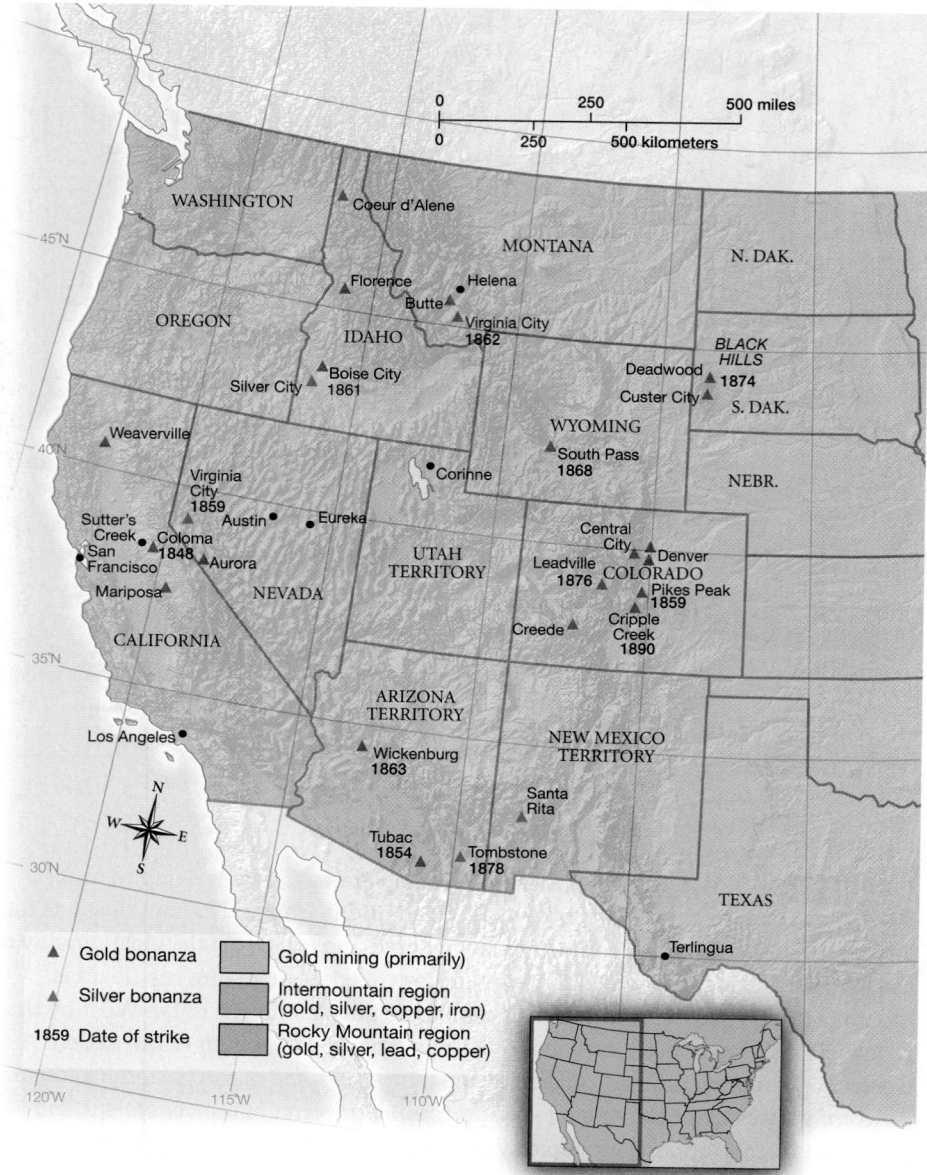

MAP 17.2 ■ Western Mining, 1848–1890

Rich deposits of gold, silver, copper, lead, and iron larded the mountains of the West, from the Sierra Nevada of California to the Rockies of Colorado and the Black Hills of South Dakota. Miners from all over the world flocked to the West. Few struck it rich, but many stayed on as paid workers in the increasingly mechanized corporate mines. Source: After Francaviglia.

The promise of gold and silver drew thousands to the mines of the West. As Mark Twain observed, the Comstock attracted an international array of immigrants. "All the peoples of the earth had representative adventures in the Silverland," he wrote. Irish, Chinese, Germans, English, Scots, Welsh, Canadians, Mexicans, Italians, Scandinavians, French, Swiss, Chileans, and other South and Central Americans came to share in the bonanza. With them came a sprinkling of Russians, Poles, Greeks, Japanese, Spaniards, Hungarians, Portuguese, Turks, Pacific Islanders, and Moroccans, as well as other North Americans, African Americans, and American Indians. This polyglot population, typical of mining boomtowns, made Virginia City, Nevada (a boomtown created by the Comstock Lode), in the 1870s more cosmopolitan than New York or Boston. In the part of

Utah Territory that eventually became Nevada, as many as 30 percent of the people came from outside the United States, compared with 25 percent in New York and 21 percent in Massachusetts.

Irish immigrants formed the largest ethnic group in the mining district. In Virginia City, fully one-third of the population claimed at least one parent from Ireland. Irish and Irish American women constituted the largest group of women on the Comstock. As servants, boardinghouse owners, and washerwomen, they made up a significant part of the workforce. In contrast, the Chinese community, numbering 642 in 1870, remained overwhelmingly male. Virulent anti-Chinese sentiment barred the men from work in the mines, but despite the violent anti-Asian rhetoric, the mining community came to depend on Chinese domestic labor.

The discovery of precious metals on the Comstock spelled disaster for the Indians. No sooner had the miners struck pay dirt than they demanded army troops to "hunt Indians" and establish forts to protect transportation to and from the diggings. This sudden and dramatic intrusion left Nevada's native tribes—the Northern Paiute and Bannock Shoshoni—exiles in their own land. At first they resisted, but over time they made peace with the invaders and proved resourceful in finding ways to adapt and preserve their culture and identity.

In 1873, Comstock miners uncovered a new vein of ore. This "Big Bonanza" speeded the transition from small-scale industry to corporate oligopoly, creating a radically new social and economic environment. The Comstock became a laboratory for new mining technology. Huge stamping mills pulverized rock with piston-like hammers driven by steam engines. Enormous Cornish pumps sucked water from the mine shafts, and huge ventilators circulated air in the underground chambers. Virginia City quickly grew into an industrial center with more than 1,200 stamping mills working on average a ton of ore every day. Almost 400 men worked in milling, nearly 300 labored in manufacturing industries, and roughly 3,000 toiled in the mines. Most of the miners who came to the Comstock ended up as laborers for the big companies.

New technology eliminated some of the dangers of mining but often created new ones. In the hard-rock mines of the West, accidents in the 1870s disabled 1 out of every 30 miners and killed 1 in 80. Ross Moudy, who worked as a miner in Cripple Creek, Colorado, recalled how a stockholder visiting the mine nearly fell to his death. The terrified visitor told the miner next to him that "instead of being paid $3 a day, they ought to have all the gold they could take out." On the Comstock Lode, because of the difficulty of obtaining skilled labor, the richness of the ore, and the need for a stable workforce, labor unions formed early and held considerable bargaining power. Comstock miners commanded $4 a day, the highest wage in the mining West.

The mining towns of the "Wild West" are often portrayed as lawless outposts, filled with saloons and rough gambling dens and populated almost exclusively by men. The truth is more complex, as Virginia City's development attests. An established urban community built to serve an industrial giant, Virginia City in its first decade boasted churches, schools, theaters, an opera house, and hundreds of families. By 1870, women composed 30 percent of the population, and 75 percent of the women listed their occupation in the census as housekeeper. Mary McNair Mathews, a widow from Buffalo, New York, who lived on the Comstock in the 1870s, worked as a teacher, nurse, seamstress, laundress, and

CHAPTER LOCATOR | What did American expansion mean for Native Americans? | **How did mining motivate and shape American expansion?** | Who fought for control of the land and resources of the American West? | Conclusion: What is the meaning of the mythic West?

467

lodging-house operator. She later published a book on her adventures. By 1875, Virginia City boasted a population of 25,000 people, making it one of the largest cities between St. Louis and San Francisco.

The Diverse Peoples of the West

The West of the late nineteenth century was a polyglot place, as much so as the big cities of the East. The sheer number of peoples who mingled in the West produced a complex blend of racism and prejudice. One historian has noted, not entirely facetiously, that the West was home to at least eight oppressed "races"—Indians, Latinos, Chinese, Japanese, blacks, Mormons, strikers, and radicals.

African Americans who ventured out to the territories faced hostile settlers determined to keep the West "for whites only." In response, they formed all-black communities such as Nicodemus, Kansas. That settlement, founded by thirty black Kentuckians in 1877, grew to a community of seven hundred by 1880. Isolated and often separated by great distances, small black settlements grew up throughout the West, in Nevada, Utah, and the Pacific Northwest as well as in Kansas. Black soldiers who served in the West during the Indian wars often stayed on as settlers. Called buffalo soldiers because Native Americans thought their hair resembled that of the buffalo, these black troops numbered up to 25,000. In the face of discrimination, poor treatment, and harsh conditions, the buffalo soldiers served with distinction and boasted the lowest desertion rate in the army.

Hispanic peoples had lived in Texas and the Southwest since Juan de Oñate led pioneer settlers up the Rio Grande in 1598. Hispanics had occupied the Pacific coast since San Diego was founded in 1769. Overnight, they were reduced to a "minority" after the United States annexed Texas in 1845 and took land stretching to California after the Mexican-American War ended in 1848. At first, the Hispanic owners of large *ranchos* in California, New Mexico, and Texas greeted conquest as an economic opportunity. But racial prejudice soon ended their optimism. Californios (Mexican residents of California), who had been granted American citizenship by the Treaty of Guadalupe Hidalgo (1848), faced discrimination by Anglos who sought to keep them out of California's mines and commerce. Whites illegally squatted on *rancho* land while protracted litigation over Spanish and Mexican land grants forced the Californios into court. Although the U.S. Supreme Court eventually validated most of their claims, it took so long—seventeen years on average—that many Californios sold their property to pay taxes and legal bills.

Swindles, chicanery, and intimidation dispossessed scores of Californios. Many ended up segregated in urban barrios (neighborhoods) in their own homeland. Their percentage of California's population declined from 82 percent in 1850 to 19 percent in 1880 as Anglos migrated to the state. In New Mexico and Texas, Mexicans remained a majority of the population but became increasingly impoverished as Anglos dominated business and took the best jobs. Skirmishes between Hispanics and whites in northern New Mexico over the fencing of the open range lasted for decades. In Texas, violence along the Rio Grande pitted Tejanos (Mexican residents of Texas) against the Texas Rangers, who saw their role as "keeping Mexicans in their place."

Like the Mexicans, the Mormons faced prejudice and hostility. The followers of Joseph Smith, the founder and prophet of the Church of Jesus Christ of Latter-Day Saints, fled west to avoid religious persecution. They believed that they had a divine right to the land, and their messianic militancy contributed to making them outcasts. The Mormon practice of polygamy (a man taking more than one wife) became a convenient point of attack for those who hated and feared the group. After Smith was killed by an Illinois mob in 1844, Brigham Young led more than 20,000 Mormons over the Rockies to the valley of the Great Salt Lake in Utah Territory. The Mormons quickly set to work irrigating the desert. They relied on cooperation and communalism, a strategy that excluded competition from those outside the faith. By 1882, the Mormons had built Salt Lake City, a thriving metropolis of more than 150,000 residents.

The Mormon practice of polygamy (Brigham Young had twenty-seven wives) had come under attack as early as 1857, when U.S. troops occupied Salt Lake City (see chapter 12). To counter criticism of polygamy, the Utah territorial legislature gave women the right to vote in 1870, the first universal woman suffrage act in the nation. (Wyoming had granted suffrage to white women in 1869.) Although women's rights advocates argued that the newly enfranchised women would "do away with the horrible institution of polygamy," it remained in force. Not until 1890 did the church hierarchy give in to pressure to renounce polygamy. The fierce controversy over polygamy postponed statehood for Utah until 1896.

The Chinese suffered brutal treatment at the hands of employers and other laborers. Drawn by the promise of gold, more than 20,000 Chinese had joined the rush to California by 1852. Miners determined to keep "California for Americans" succeeded in passing prohibitive foreign license laws to keep the Chinese out of the mines. But Chinese immigration continued. In the 1860s, when white workers moved on to find riches in the mines of Nevada, Chinese laborers took jobs abandoned by the whites. Railroad magnate Charles Crocker hired Chinese gangs to work on the Central Pacific, reasoning that the race that built the Great Wall could lay tracks across the treacherous Sierra Nevada. Some 12,000 Chinese, representing 90 percent of Crocker's workforce, completed America's first transcontinental railroad in 1869.

Chinese Workers

Chinese section hands are shown here in 1898 shoveling dirt for the North Pacific Coast Railroad in Corte Madera, California. California Historical Society, FN-25345.

CHAPTER LOCATOR | What did American expansion mean for Native Americans? | How did mining motivate and shape American expansion? | Who fought for control of the land and resources of the American West? | Conclusion: What is the meaning of the mythic West?

469

By 1870, more than 63,000 Chinese immigrants lived in America, 77 percent of them in California. A 1790 federal statute that limited naturalization to "white persons" was modified after the Civil War to extend naturalization to blacks ("persons of African descent"). But the Chinese and other Asians continued to be denied access to citizenship. As perpetual aliens, they constituted a reserve army of transnational laborers that many saw as a threat to American labor. For the most part, the Chinese did not displace white workers but instead found work as railroad laborers, cooks, servants, and farmhands while white workers sought out more lucrative fields. In the 1870s, when California and the rest of the nation weathered a major economic depression, the Chinese became easy scapegoats. California workingmen rioted and fought to keep Chinese workers out of the state.

In 1876, the Workingmen's Party formed to fight for Chinese exclusion. Racial and cultural animosities stood at the heart of anti-Chinese agitation. Denis Kearney, the fiery San Francisco leader of the movement, made clear this racist bent when he urged legislation to "expel every one of the moon-eyed lepers." Nor was California alone in its anti-immigrant nativism. As the country confronted growing ethnic and racial diversity with the rising tide of global immigration in the decades following the Civil War, many questioned the principle of racial equality at the same time they argued against the assimilation of "nonwhite" groups. In this climate, Congress passed the **Chinese Exclusion Act** in 1882, effectively barring Chinese immigration and setting a precedent for further immigration restrictions. The Chinese Exclusion Act led to a sharp drop in the Chinese population—from 105,465 in 1880 to 89,863 in 1900—because Chinese immigrants, overwhelmingly male, did not have families to sustain their population. Eventually, Japanese immigrants, including women as well as men, replaced the Chinese, particularly in agriculture. As "nonwhite" immigrants, they could not become naturalized citizens, but their children born in the United States claimed the rights of citizenship. Japanese parents, seeking to own land, purchased it in their children's names. Although anti-Asian prejudice remained strong in California and elsewhere in the West, Asian immigrants formed an important part of the economic fabric of the western United States.

The American West in the nineteenth century witnessed more than its share of conflict and bloodshed. Violent prejudice against the Chinese and other Asian immigrants remained common. But violence also broke out between cattle ranchers and sheep ranchers, between ranchers and farmers, between striking miners and their bosses, among rival Indian groups, and between whites and Indians. At issue was who would control the vast resources of the emerging region.

Chinese Exclusion Act

▶ 1882 law that effectively barred Chinese immigration and set a precedent for further immigration restrictions. Racial and cultural animosities stood at the heart of the anti-Chinese agitation that led to the passage of the Exclusion Act. The Chinese Exclusion Act led to a sharp drop in the Chinese population in America.

> **QUICK REVIEW**

What role did mining play in shaping the society and economy of the American West?

Who fought for control of the land and resources of the American West?

Railroad Locomotive In the years following the Civil War, the locomotive replaced the covered wagon, enabling settlers to travel from Chicago or St. Louis to the West Coast in two days. The first transcontinental railroad, completed in 1869, soon led to the creation of competing systems, so that by the 1880s, travelers going west could choose from four railroad lines. Library of Congress.

IN THE THREE DECADES following 1870, more land was settled than in all the previous history of the country. Americans by the hundreds of thousands packed up and moved west, many drawn by the promise of owning land. The agrarian West shared with the mining West a persistent restlessness, an equally pervasive addiction to speculation, and a penchant for exploiting natural resources and labor.

Two factors stimulated the land rush in the trans-Mississippi West. The **Homestead Act of 1862** promised 160 acres free to any citizen or prospective citizen, male or female, who settled on the land for five years. Even more important, transcontinental railroads opened up new areas and actively recruited settlers. After the completion of the first transcontinental railroad in 1869, homesteaders abandoned the covered wagon, making the trip west in a matter of days.

Although the country was rich in land and resources, not all who wanted to own land achieved their goal. During the transition from the family farm to large commercial farming, small farms gave way to vast spreads worked by migrant labor or paid farmworkers. Just as industry corporatized and consolidated in the East, the period from 1870 to 1900 witnessed corporate consolidation in mining, ranching, and agriculture.

Homestead Act of 1862

▶ Act that promised 160 acres in the trans-Mississippi West free to any citizen or prospective citizen who settled on the land for five years. Between 1870 and 1900, hundreds of thousands of Americans moved west, many drawn by the promise of free land.

Homesteaders and Speculators

A Missouri homesteader remembered packing as her family pulled up stakes and headed west to Oklahoma in 1890. "We were going to God's Country," she wrote.

CHAPTER LOCATOR | What did American expansion mean for Native Americans? | How did mining motivate and shape American expansion? | **Who fought for control of the land and resources of the American West?** | Conclusion: What is the meaning of the mythic West?

471

1862
- Homestead Act promises free land in the West to American settlers.

1869
- First transcontinental railroad is completed.

1879
- More than fifteen thousand black Exodusters move to Kansas from the South.

1886–1888
- Severe blizzards decimate cattle herds.

1889
- Two million acres in Oklahoma are opened for settlement.

1893
- Last land rush takes place in Oklahoma Territory.

Midwestern Settlement before 1862

"You had to work hard on that rocky country in Missouri. I was glad to be leaving it. . . . We were going to a new land and get rich."

People who ventured west searching for "God's Country" faced hardship, loneliness, and deprivation. Hard work was no guarantee of success. Blizzards, tornadoes, grasshoppers, hailstorms, drought, prairie fires, accidental death, and disease were only a few of the catastrophes that could befall even the best farmer. Homesteaders on free land still needed as much as $1,000 for a house, a team of farm animals, a well, fencing, and seed. Poor farmers called "sodbusters" did without even these basics, living in dugouts carved into hillsides.

"Father made a dugout and covered it with willows and grass," one Kansas girl recounted. When it rained, the dugout flooded, and "we carried the water out in buckets, then waded around in the mud until it dried." Rain wasn't the only problem. "Sometimes the bull snakes would get in the roof and now and then one would lose his hold and fall down on the bed. . . . Mother would grab the hoe . . . and after the fight was over Mr. Bull Snake was dragged outside."

For women on the frontier, obtaining simple daily necessities such as water and fuel meant backbreaking labor. "A yoke was made to place across [Mother's] shoulders, so as to carry at each end a bucket of water," one daughter recollected, "and then water was brought a half mile from spring to house." Gathering fuel was another heavy chore. Without ready sources of coal or firewood, the most prevalent fuel was "chips"—chunks of dried cattle and buffalo dung, found in abundance on the plains.

Despite the hardships, some homesteaders succeeded in building comfortable lives. The sod hut made way for a more substantial house; the log cabin yielded to a white clapboard home with a porch and a rocking chair. For others, the promise of the West failed to materialize. Already by the 1870s, much of the best land had been taken. "There is plenty of land for sale in California," one migrant complained in 1870, but "the majority of the available lands are held by speculators, at prices far beyond the reach of a poor man." The railroads, flush from land grants provided by the state and federal governments, owned huge swaths of land in the West and actively recruited settlers. Altogether, the land grants totaled approximately 180 million acres—an area almost one-tenth the size of the United States (**Map 17.3**). Of the 2.5 million farms established between 1860 and 1900, homesteading accounted for only one in five; the vast majority of farmland sold for a profit.

As land grew scarce on the prairie in the 1870s, farmers began to push farther west, moving into western Kansas, Nebraska, and eastern Colorado—the region called the Great American Desert by settlers who had passed over it on their way to California and Oregon. Words of caution about insufficient rain were drowned out by the extravagant claims of western promoters, many employed by the railroads to sell off their land grants. "Rain follows the plow" became the slogan of western boosters, who insisted that cultivation would alter the climate of the region and bring more rainfall. Instead, drought followed the plow. Droughts were a cyclical fact of life on the Great Plains. Plowed up, the dry topsoil blew away in the wind. A protracted drought in the late 1880s and early 1890s sent starving farmers reeling back from the plains. Thousands left, some in wagons carrying the slogan "In God we trusted, in Kansas we busted."

Fever for fertile land set off a series of spectacular land runs in Oklahoma. When two million acres of land in former Indian Territory opened for settlement in 1889, thousands of homesteaders massed on the border. At the opening pistol shot, "with a shout and a yell the swift riders shot out, then followed the light buggies or wagons," a reporter wrote. "Above all, a great cloud of dust hover[ed]

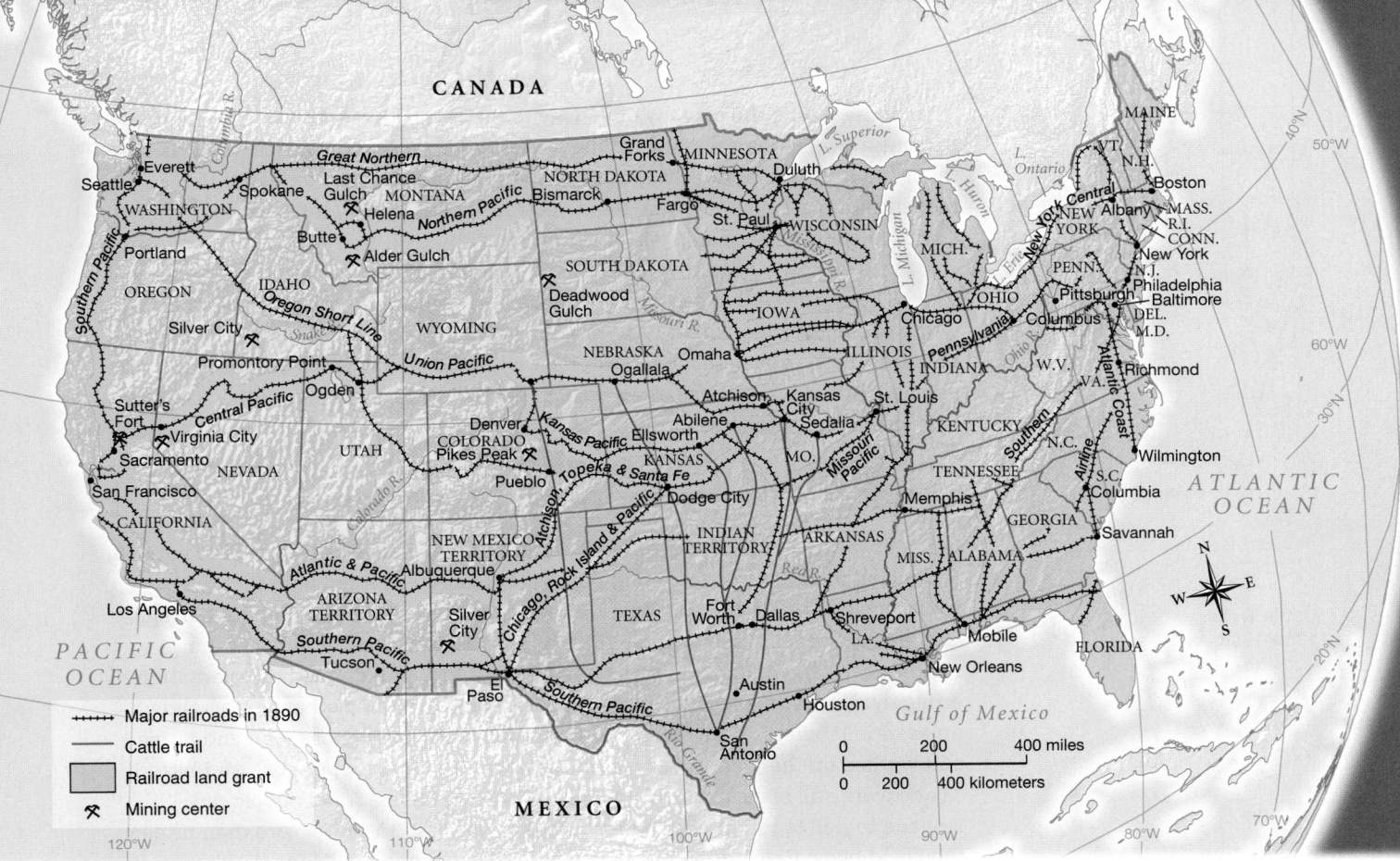

MAP 17.3 ■ Federal Land Grants to Railroads and the Development of the West, 1850–1900
Generous federal land grants meant that railroads could sell the desirable land next to the track at a profit or hold it for speculation. Railroads received more than 180 million acres, an area as large as Texas. Notice how the railroads connect with major cattle trailheads in Dodge City, Abilene, and Kansas City and to mining towns in Montana, Nevada, Colorado, and New Mexico.

like smoke over a battlefield." By nightfall, Oklahoma boasted two tent cities with more than ten thousand residents. As public land grew scarce, the hunger for land grew fiercer for both farmers and ranchers.

Ranchers and Cowboys

Cattle ranchers followed the railroads onto the plains, establishing a cattle kingdom from Texas to Wyoming between 1865 and 1885. Cowboys drove huge herds, as many as three thousand head of cattle that grazed on public lands as they followed cattle tracks like the Chisholm Trail from Texas to railheads in Kansas.

Barbed wire, invented in 1874, revolutionized the cattle business and sounded the death knell for the open range. As the largest ranches in Texas began to fence, fights broke out between big ranchers and "fence cutters," who resented the end of the free range. One old-timer observed, "Those persons, Mexicans and Americans, without land but who had cattle were put out of business by fencing." Fencing forced small-time ranchers who owned land but could not afford to buy barbed wire or sink wells to sell out for the best price they could get. The displaced ranchers, many of them Mexicans, ended up as wageworkers on the huge spreads owned by Anglos or by European syndicates.

CHAPTER LOCATOR | What did American expansion mean for Native Americans? | How did mining motivate and shape American expansion? | Who fought for control of the land and resources of the American West? | Conclusion: What is the meaning of the mythic West?

473

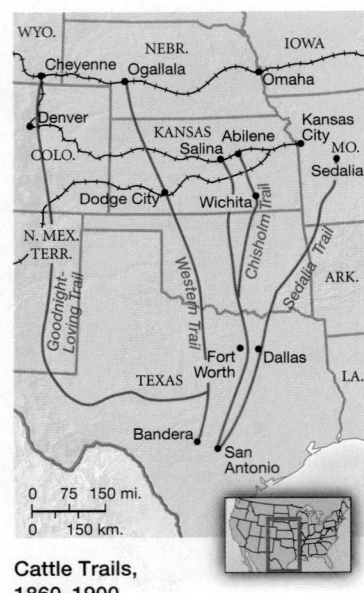

Cattle Trails, 1860–1900

Exodusters

▶ A group of former slaves from Mississippi and Louisiana who moved west to Kansas in 1879 so that they could own land and escape the sharecropping system.

On the range, the cowboy gave way to the cattle king and, like the miner, became a wage laborer. Many cowboys were African Americans (as many as five thousand in Texas alone). Writers of western literature chose to ignore the presence of black cowboys like Deadwood Dick (Nat Love), who was portrayed as a white man in the dime novels of the era.

By 1886, cattle overcrowded the range. Severe blizzards during the winters of 1886–87 and 1887–88 decimated the herds. "A whole generation of cowmen," wrote one chronicler, "went dead broke." Fencing worsened the situation. During blizzards, cattle stayed alive by keeping on the move. But when they ran up against barbed-wire fences, they froze to death. In the aftermath of the "Great Die Up," new labor-intensive forms of cattle ranching replaced the open-range model.

Tenants, Sharecroppers, and Migrants

In the post–Civil War period, as agriculture became a big business tied to national and global markets, an increasing number of laborers worked land that they would never own. In the southern United States, farmers labored under particularly heavy burdens (see chapter 16). The Civil War wiped out much of the region's capital, which had been invested in slaves, and crippled the plantation economy. Newly freed slaves rarely obtained land of their own and often ended up as farm laborers. "The colored folks stayed with the old boss man and farmed and worked on the plantations," a black Alabama sharecropper observed bitterly. "They were still slaves, but they were free slaves." Some freed people did manage to pull together enough resources to go west. In 1879, more than fifteen thousand black **Exodusters** moved from Mississippi and Louisiana to take up land in Kansas.

California's highly skilled Mexican cowboys, or *vaqueros*, commanded decent wages throughout the Southwest. But by 1880, as the coming of the railroads ended the long cattle drives and large feedlots began to replace the open range, the value of their skills declined. Many vaqueros ended up as migrant laborers, often on land their families had once owned. Similarly, in Texas, Tejanos found themselves displaced. After the heyday of cattle ranching ended in the late 1880s, cotton production rose in the southeastern regions of the state. Ranchers turned their pastures into sharecroppers' plots and hired displaced cowboys, most of them Mexicans, as seasonal laborers for as little as seventy-five cents a day, thereby creating a growing army of agricultural wageworkers.

Land monopoly and large-scale farming fostered tenancy and migratory labor on the West Coast. By the 1870s, less than 1 percent of California's population owned half the state's available agricultural land. The rigid economics of large-scale commercial agriculture and the seasonal nature of the crops spawned an army of migratory agricultural laborers. Most farm laborers were Chinese immigrants. After passage of the Chinese Exclusion Act of 1882, Mexicans, Filipinos, and Japanese immigrants filled the demand for migratory workers.

Commercial Farming and Industrial Cowboys

In the late nineteenth century, America's population remained overwhelmingly rural. The 1870 census showed that nearly 80 percent of the nation's people lived on farms and in villages of fewer than 8,000 inhabitants. By 1900, the figure had dropped to 66 percent (**Figure 17.1**). At the same time, the number of farms rose. Rapid growth in the West increased the number of the nation's farms from 2 million in 1860 to more than 5.7 million in 1900.

Despite the hardships individual farmers experienced, new technology and farming techniques revolutionized American farm life. Mechanized plows and reapers halved the time and labor cost of production and made it possible to cultivate vast tracts of land. Urbanization provided farmers with expanding markets for their produce, and railroads carried crops to markets thousands of miles away. Even before the start of the twentieth century, American agriculture had entered the era of what would come to be called agribusiness—farming as a big business—with the advent of huge commercial farms.

As farming moved onto the prairies and plains, mechanization took command. Horse-drawn implements gave way to steam-powered machinery. By 1880, a single combine could do the work of twenty men, vastly increasing the acreage a farmer could cultivate. This agricultural revolution meant that Americans raised more than four times the corn, five times the hay, and seven times the wheat and oats they had before the Civil War.

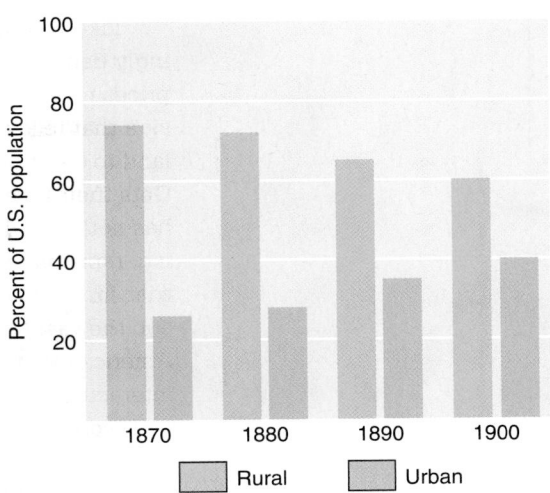

FIGURE 17.1 ■ Changes in Rural and Urban Populations, 1870–1900

Between 1870 and 1900, not only did the number of urban dwellers increase, but, even as the number of rural inhabitants fell, the number of farms increased. Mechanization made it possible to farm with fewer hands, fueling the exodus from farm to city throughout the second half of the nineteenth century.

Mechanical Corn Planter

Mechanical planters came into use in the 1860s. The Farmers Friend Manufacturing Company of Dayton, Ohio, advertised its lever and treadle corn planter in the early 1880s. Ohio History Society

▶ FOR MORE HELP ANALYZING THIS IMAGE, see the visual activity for this chapter in the Online Study Guide at bedfordstmartins.com/roarkunderstanding.

CHAPTER LOCATOR | What did American expansion mean for Native Americans? | How did mining motivate and shape American expansion? | **Who fought for control of the land and resources of the American West?** | Conclusion: What is the meaning of the mythic West?

475

Like cotton farmers in the South, western grain and livestock farmers increasingly depended on foreign markets for their livelihood. A fall in global market prices meant that a farmer's entire harvest went to pay off debts. In the depression that followed the panic of 1893, many heavily mortgaged farmers lost their land to creditors. As a Texas cotton farmer complained, "By the time the World Gets their Liveing out of the Farmer as we have to Feed the World, we the Farmer has nothing Left but a Bear Hard Liveing." Commercial farming, along with mining, represented another way in which the West developed its own brand of industrialism. The far West's industrial economy sprang initially from California gold and the vast territory that came under American control following the Mexican-American War. In the ensuing rush on land and resources, environmental factors interacted with economic and social forces to produce enterprises as vast in scale and scope as anything found in the East.

Two Alsatian immigrants, Henry Miller and Charles Lux, pioneered the West's mix of agriculture and industrialism. Beginning as meat wholesalers, Miller and Lux quickly expanded their business to encompass cattle, land, and land reclamation projects such as dams and irrigation systems. With a labor force of migrant workers, a highly coordinated corporate system, and large sums of investment capital, the firm of Miller & Lux became one of America's industrial behemoths. Eventually, these "industrial cowboys" grazed a herd of 100,000 cattle on 1.25 million acres of company land in California, Oregon, and Nevada and employed more than 1,200 migrant laborers on their corporate ranches. Miller & Lux attracted labor by offering free meals to migratory workers. When the company's Chinese cooks rebelled at washing the dishes resulting from the free meals, the migrant laborers were forced to eat after the ranch hands and use their dirty plates. By the 1890s, more than eight hundred migrants a year followed what came to be known as the "Dirty Plate Route" on Miller & Lux ranches throughout California.

Since the days of Thomas Jefferson, agrarian life had been linked with the highest ideals of a democratic society. Now agrarianism itself had been transformed. The farmer was no longer a self-sufficient yeoman but often a businessman or a wage laborer tied to a global market. And even as farm production soared, industrialization outstripped it. More and more farmers left the fields for urban factories or found work in the "factories in the fields" of the new industrialized agribusiness. Now that the future seemed to lie not with the small farmer but with industrial enterprises, was democracy itself at risk? This question would ignite a farmers' revolt in the 1880s and dominate political debate in the 1890s.

> **QUICK REVIEW**

Why did many homesteaders find it difficult to acquire good land in the West?

Smithsonian American Art Museum, Washington, D.C./Art Resource, NY.

Conclusion: What is the meaning of the mythic West? ‹

EVEN AS THE OLD WEST was changing, the mythic West was being born. Buffalo Bill became its icon. Born William F. Cody, the masterful showman formed a touring Wild West company in 1883. Part circus, part theater, the Wild West extravaganza featured exhibitions of riding, shooting, and roping and presented dramatic reenactments of great moments in western lore. Highly dubious as history, as spectacle the Wild West show was unbeatable. At the World's Columbian Exposition in 1893, crowds numbering tens of thousands packed the bleachers to cheer. By the turn of the twentieth century, the high drama of the struggle for the West had become little more than a thrilling but harmless entertainment.

Across the fairgrounds historian Frederick Jackson Turner addressed the American Historical Association on "The Significance of the Frontier in American History." Turner noted that by 1890, the census could no longer discern a clear frontier line. His tone was elegiac: "The existence of an area of free land, its continuous recession, and the advance of settlement westward," he observed, "explained American development" and was inextricably linked to what was best and unique in America. Of course, land in the West had never been empty or free. And the pastoral agrarianism Turner celebrated belied the urban, industrial West found on the Comstock and in the commercial farms of California. Nevertheless, Turner's frontier thesis became one of the most enduring myths of the American West.

The real West was no less dramatic than the mythic West. In the decades following the Civil War, as the United States pursued empire in the American West, new problems replaced the old issues of slavery and sectionalism. The growing power of big business, the exploitation of labor and natural resources, corruption in politics, and ethnic and racial tensions exacerbated by colonial expansion and unparalleled immigration dominated the debates of the day in both the East and the West. As the nineteenth century ended, Americans had more questions than answers. Could the American promise survive in the new world of corporations, wage labor, and mushrooming cities? Neither out of place nor out of time, the West contributed its share to both the promise and the problems of the era Mark Twain would brand the Gilded Age.

SO NOW YOU KNOW

It took Euro-Americans 250 years to conquer the eastern half of what became the United States. In the second half of the nineteenth century, using new technology in both transportation and warfare, the United States was able to gain relatively quick possession of western lands.

CHAPTER LOCATOR | What did American expansion mean for Native Americans? | How did mining motivate and shape American expansion? | Who fought for control of the land and resources of the American West? | Conclusion: What is the meaning of the mythic West?

477

CHAPTER 17 STUDY GUIDE

Online Study Guide
bedfordstmartins.com/roarkunderstanding

STEP 1 GETTING STARTED

Below are basic terms from this period in American history. Can you identify each term below and explain why it matters? To do this exercise online or to download this chart, visit bedfordstmartins.com/roarkunderstanding.

TERM	WHO OR WHAT & WHEN	WHY IT MATTERS
Sitting Bull, p. 460		
1868 Treaty of Fort Laramie, p. 460		
Battle of the Little Big Horn, p. 461		
Dawes Allotment Act, p. 461		
Geronimo, p. 462		
Ghost Dance, p. 463		
Wounded Knee, p. 464		
Comstock Lode, p. 465		
Chinese Exclusion Act, p. 470		
Homestead Act of 1862, p. 471		
Exodusters, p. 474		

STEP 2 MOVING BEYOND THE BASICS

The exercise below represents a more advanced understanding of the chapter material. Fill in the chart below by describing the policies and goals of the federal government with respect to Indian peoples, natural resources, land, and the flow of migrants into the West. What connections were there among the policies in each of these four areas? To do this exercise online or to download this chart, visit bedfordstmartins.com/roarkunderstanding.

	Federal policies and legislation	Goals
Indian peoples		
Natural resources		
Land		
Migrants		

Now that you've reviewed the chapter, take a step back and try to see the big picture. Remember to use specific examples from the chapter in your answers. To do this exercise online, visit bedfordstmartins.com/roarkunderstanding.

INDIAN POLICY

► How did Indians respond to the flood of westward migration after the Civil War?

► How did federal Indian policy change over the course of the late nineteenth century, and what was the Indian reaction?

MINING AND THE WEST

► Why was mining such an important factor in promoting western expansion?

► How did mining affect the economy and society of the West and the nation?

WESTERNERS

► Who went west and why?

► How did racial and ethnic prejudice affect relations among westerners?

LOOKING BACKWARD, LOOKING AHEAD

► How did western expansion before the Civil War differ from western expansion after the Civil War?

► What new political issues and tensions did American expansion raise? What was the relationship between the East and the West in 1900?

IN YOUR OWN WORDS

Imagine that you must explain chapter 17 to someone who hasn't read it. What would be the most important points to include and why?

18

DEFINING THE GILDED AGE OF BUSINESS AND POLITICS

1870–1895

> This chapter examines the acceleration of industrialization and the growing interplay of business and politics in the era known as the Gilded Age. It details the practices of business pioneers from 1870 to 1895 and explores the impact of economic change on the political and cultural landscape of late-nineteenth-century America.

> How did the railroads stimulate big business?

> How did big business change at the end of the nineteenth century?

> What factors influenced political life in the late nineteenth century?

> What issues shaped presidential politics in the late nineteenth century?

> What role did the economy play in the politics of the 1880s and 1890s?

> Conclusion: Why was business so dominant in the Gilded Age?

DID YOU KNOW?

Author Mark Twain labeled the Gilded Age as an age of gaudy excess in a best-selling novel he wrote in 1873.

The Lost Bet, **1893.** Artist Joseph Klir painted the scene of a Chicago parade after a local Republican agreed to pull his Democratic friend if Grover Cleveland won the 1892 presidential election.

How did the railroads stimulate big business?

The power wielded by John D. Rockefeller and the Standard Oil Company is captured in this political cartoon by Horace Taylor, which appeared in the January 22, 1900, issue of the *Verdict*. Rockefeller is pictured holding the White House and the Treasury Department in the palm of his hand, while in the background the U.S. Capitol has been converted into an oil refinery. Collection of the New-York Historical Society.

► FOR MORE HELP ANALYZING THIS IMAGE, see the visual activity for this chapter in the Online Study Guide at bedfordstmartins.com/roarkunderstanding.

IN THE YEARS following the Civil War, the scale and scope of American industry expanded dramatically. Old industries transformed into modern corporations typified by the behemoth U.S. Steel. Discovery and invention stimulated new industries, from oil refining to electric light and power. The expansion of the nation's rail system in the decades after the Civil War played the key role in the transformation of the American economy. New rail lines created a national market that enabled businesses to expand from a regional to a nationwide scale. The railroads became America's first big business. Jay Gould, Andrew Carnegie, John D. Rockefeller, and other business leaders pioneered new strategies to seize markets and consolidate power in the rising railroad, steel, and oil industries and set the tone in the get-rich-quick era of freewheeling capitalism that Mark Twain labeled the Gilded Age.

Railroads: America's First Big Business

In the decades following the Civil War, the United States built the greatest railroad network in the world. The first transcontinental railroad was completed in 1869, linking new markets in the West to the nation's economy. Between 1870 and 1880, the amount of track in the country doubled, and it nearly doubled again in the following decade. By 1900, the nation boasted more than 193,000 miles of railroad track—more than in all of Europe and Russia combined (see **Map 18.1**, page 484, and "Global Comparison," page 486). To understand how the railroads developed and came to dominate American life, there is no better place to start than with the career of Jay Gould, who pioneered the expansion of America's railway system and became the era's most notorious speculator.

CHAPTER LOCATOR | How did the railroads stimulate big business?

Gould, by his own admission, knew little about railroads and cared less about their operation. Instead he operated in the stock market like a shark, looking for vulnerable railroads, buying enough stock to take control, and threatening to undercut his competitors until they bought him out at a high profit. In the 1880s, he moved to put together a second transcontinental railroad. To defend their interests, his competitors had little choice but to adopt his strategy of expansion and consolidation, which in turn encouraged railroad building and stimulated a national market.

The dramatic growth of the railroads created the country's first big business. Before the Civil War, even the largest textile mill in New England employed no more than 800 workers. In contrast, the Pennsylvania Railroad by the 1870s boasted a payroll of more than 55,000 workers, making it the largest private enterprise in the world.

The Republican Party, firmly entrenched in Washington, worked closely with business interests, subsidizing the transcontinental railroad system with land grants of 100 million acres of public land and $64 million in tax incentives and direct aid. States and local communities joined the railroad boom, with the combined federal and state giveaway amounting to more than 180 million acres, an area larger than Texas.

A revolution in communication accompanied and supported the growth of the railroads. Developed by Samuel F. B. Morse, the telegraph formed the "nervous system" of the new industrial order. Telegraph service transformed business by providing instantaneous communication. Again Jay Gould took the lead. In 1879, through stock manipulation, he seized control of Western Union, the company that monopolized the telegraph industry.

The railroads soon fell on hard times. Already by the 1870s, lack of planning led to overbuilding. On the eastern seaboard, railroads competed fiercely for business. A manufacturer in an area served by competing railroads could get substantially reduced shipping rates in return for promises of steady business. Because railroad owners lost money through this kind of competition, they tried to set up agreements to end competition by dividing up territory and setting rates. But these informal agreements invariably failed because men like Jay Gould, intent on undercutting all competitors, refused to play by the rules.

The public's alarm at the control wielded by the new railroad magnates provided a barometer of attitudes toward big business itself. When Gould died in 1892, he was, as he himself admitted shortly before his death, "the most hated man in America."

Andrew Carnegie, Steel, and Vertical Integration

If Jay Gould was the man Americans loved to hate, **Andrew Carnegie** became one of America's heroes. Unlike Gould, Carnegie turned his back on speculation and worked to build something enduring—Carnegie Steel, the biggest steel business in the world during the Gilded Age.

The growth of the steel industry proceeded directly from railroad building. The first railroads ran on iron rails. Steel, both stronger and more flexible than iron, remained too expensive for use in rails until Englishman Henry Bessemer

CHRONOLOGY

1869
- First transcontinental railroad is completed.

1870
- John D. Rockefeller incorporates Standard Oil Company.

1872
- Andrew Carnegie opens his steel mill outside of Pittsburgh and pioneers vertical integration.

1876
- Alexander Graham Bell demonstrates the telephone.

1882
- John D. Rockefeller develops the trust.

1880s
- Thomas Edison pioneers the use of electricity as an energy source.

Andrew Carnegie
▶ Investor and philanthropist who built Carnegie Steel, the biggest steel business in the world during the Gilded Age. Carnegie pioneered a system of business organization called vertical integration. Famed as a philanthropist, Carnegie espoused the gospel of wealth, calling on the rich to use their riches for the good of the people.

| How did big business change at the end of the nineteenth century? | What factors influenced political life in the late nineteenth century? | What issues shaped presidential politics in the late nineteenth century? | What role did the economy play in the politics of the 1880s and 1890s? | Conclusion: Why was business so dominant in the Gilded Age? |

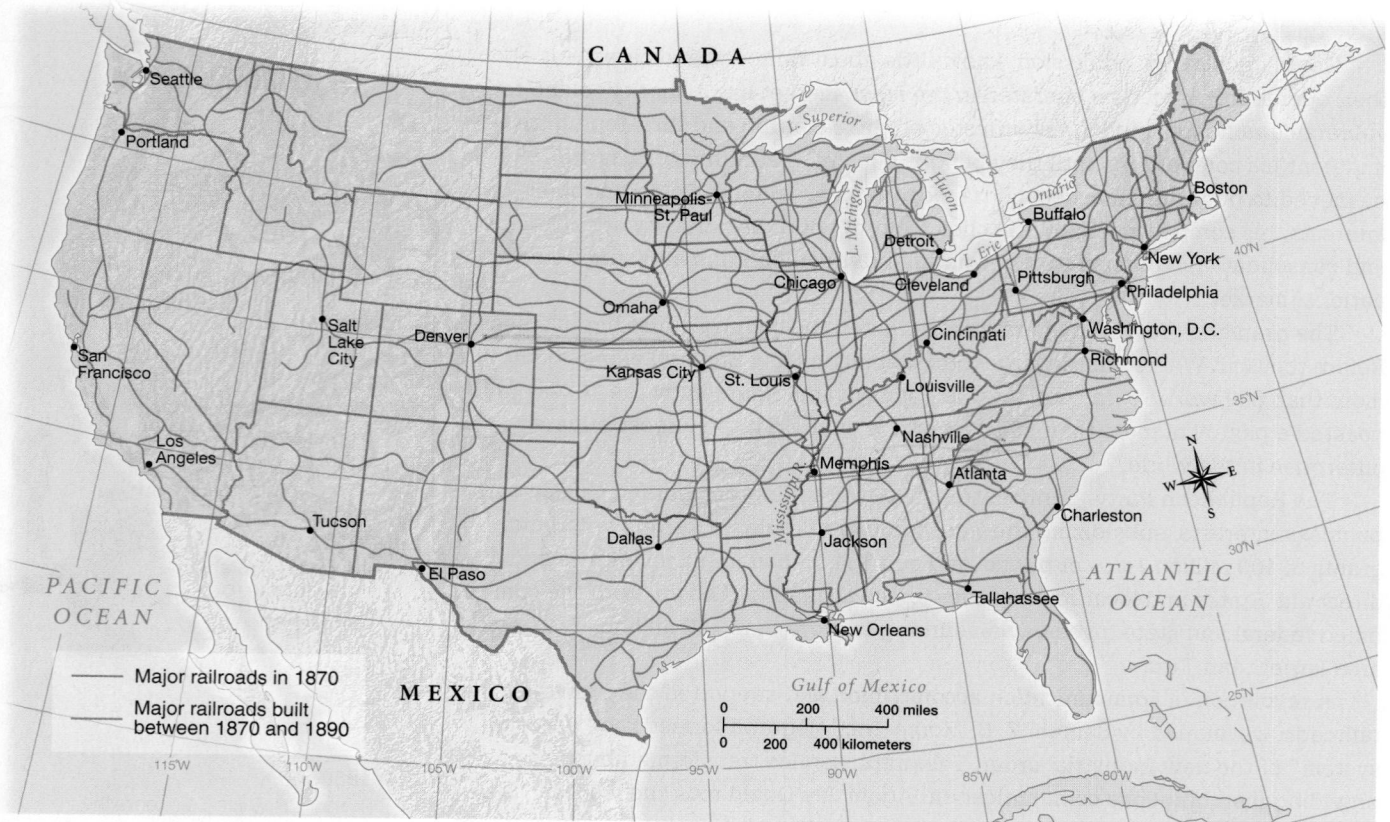

MAP 18.1 ■ Railroad Expansion, 1870–1890

Railroad mileage nearly quadrupled between 1870 and 1890, with the greatest growth occurring in the trans-Mississippi West. New transcontinental lines—the Great Northern, Northern Pacific, Southern Pacific, and Atlantic and Pacific—were completed in the 1880s. Small feeder lines such as the Oregon Short Line and the Atchison, Topeka, and Santa Fe fed into the great transcontinental systems, knitting the nation together.

► FOR MORE HELP ANALYZING THIS MAP, see the map activity for this chapter in the Online Study Guide at bedfordstmartins.com/roarkunderstanding.

developed a way to make steel more cheaply from pig iron. Andrew Carnegie came to dominate the emerging industry.

Carnegie, a Scottish immigrant, landed in New York in 1848 at the age of twelve. He rose from poverty to become one of the richest men in America. Before he died, he gave away more than $300 million, most notably to public libraries. His generosity, combined with his humble beginnings, burnished his public image.

When Carnegie was a teenager, his skill as a telegraph operator caught the attention of Tom Scott, superintendent of the Pennsylvania Railroad. Scott hired Carnegie and lent him the money for his first investments. A millionaire before his thirtieth birthday, Carnegie turned away from speculation and set out to reshape the iron and steel industry. "My preference was always manufacturing," he wrote. "I wished to make something tangible." By applying the lessons of cost accounting and efficiency that he had learned working for the Pennsylvania Railroad, Carnegie turned steel into the nation's first manufacturing big business. In 1872 he built the the most up-to-date steel plant in the nation outside of Pittsburgh (**Figure 18.1**).

Carnegie's formula for success was simple: "Cut the prices, scoop the market, run the mills full; watch the costs and profits will take care of themselves." To guarantee the lowest costs and the maximum output, Carnegie pioneered a system of business organization called vertical integration. All aspects of the business were under Carnegie's control—from the mining of iron ore, to its transport

CHAPTER LOCATOR | How did the railroads stimulate big business?

on the Great Lakes, to the production of steel. Vertical integration, in the words of one observer, meant that "from the moment these crude stuffs were dug out of the earth until they flowed in a stream of liquid steel in the ladles, there was never a price, profit, or royalty paid to any outsider."

The great productivity Carnegie encouraged came at a high price. He deliberately pitted his managers against one another, firing the losers and rewarding the winners with a share in the company. Workers achieved the output Carnegie demanded by enduring low wages, dangerous working conditions, and twelve-hour days six days a week. One worker, commenting on the contradiction between Carnegie's endowments to public libraries and his labor policies, observed, "After working twelve hours, how can a man go to a library?"

By 1900, Andrew Carnegie had become the best-known manufacturer in the nation, and the age of iron had yielded to an age of steel. As a captain of industry, Carnegie's only rival was the titan of the oil industry, John D. Rockefeller.

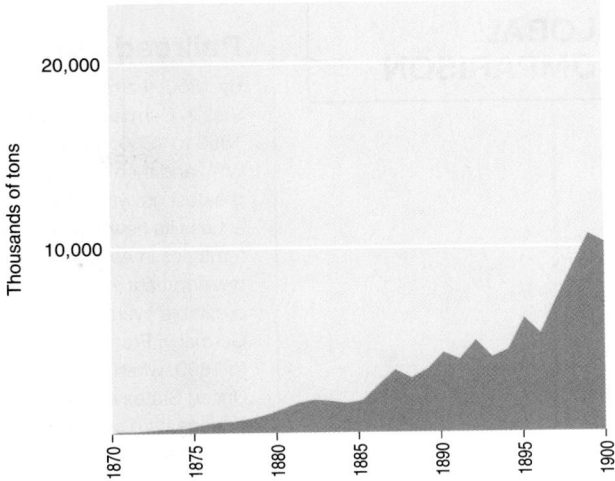

FIGURE 18.1 ■ Iron and Steel Production, 1870–1900
Iron and steel production in the United States grew from nearly none in 1870 to 10 million tons a year by 1900. The secrets to the great increase in steel production were the use of the Bessemer process and vertical integration, pioneered by Andrew Carnegie. By 1900, Carnegie's mills alone produced more steel than all of Great Britain. With corporate consolidation after 1900, the rate of growth in steel proved even more spectacular.

John D. Rockefeller, Standard Oil, and the Trust

In the days before the automobile and gasoline, crude oil was refined into lubricating oil for machinery and kerosene for lamps. The amount of capital needed to buy or build an oil refinery in the 1860s and 1870s remained relatively low. As a result, the new petroleum industry experienced riotous competition among many small refineries. Ultimately, **John D. Rockefeller** and his Standard Oil Company succeeded in controlling nine-tenths of the oil-refining business.

Rockefeller was the son of a peddler who taught him to drive a hard bargain. Rockefeller learned his lessons well. In 1865, at the age of twenty-five, he controlled the largest oil refinery in Cleveland. Like a growing number of business owners, Rockefeller abandoned partnership or single proprietorship to embrace the corporation as the business structure best suited to maximize profit and minimize personal liability. In 1870, he incorporated his oil business, founding the Standard Oil Company.

As the largest refiner in Cleveland, Rockefeller demanded secret rebates from the railroads in exchange for his steady business. Rebates enabled Rockefeller to drive out his competitors through predatory pricing. The railroads needed Rockefeller's business so badly that they gave him a share of the rates that his competitors paid. Secret deals, predatory pricing, and rebates enabled Rockefeller to undercut his competitors and pressure competing refiners to sell out or face ruin.

To gain legal standing for Standard Oil's secret deals, Rockefeller in 1882 pioneered a new form of corporate structure—the trust. The trust differed markedly from Carnegie's vertical approach in steel. Instead of attempting to control all

John D. Rockefeller
▶ Oil tycoon whose Standard Oil Company came to control 90 percent of the oil-refining business. Rockefeller used trusts, and later holding companies, to stifle competition and force railroads to offer him secret rebates. His business tactics were the subject of a scathing exposé written by Ida M. Tarbell.

How did big business change at the end of the nineteenth century?

What factors influenced political life in the late nineteenth century?

What issues shaped presidential politics in the late nineteenth century?

What role did the economy play in the politics of the 1880s and 1890s?

Conclusion: Why was business so dominant in the Gilded Age?

485

Railroad Track Mileage, 1890

By 1850, the railway network in Great Britain was already well established, and most of the main lines in Germany had been built. France was slower to invest in railroads, but during the period 1850 to 1860, the government invested heavily in laying track, and the French soon caught up with, and then bypassed, their European neighbors. Russia's railway development experienced its greatest growth in the late nineteenth century. This growth was driven by the country's need to access its newly developing industrial regions and the vast natural resources of its far-flung territories in Asia. Like Russia, most of India's railroad growth occurred late in the century. This development was financed by the British, who were eager to tap the economic potential of their profitable overseas colony. By 1890, the United States had laid more railroad track than Britain, Germany, France, Russia, and India combined. Most of this growth occurred in the period 1870 to 1890, when railroad mileage in the United States nearly quadrupled. The vast area of the United States and its western territories accounted for some of the disparity between railroad mileage here and in Europe. England, France, and Germany combined contained less land than the states east of the Mississippi River.

	Completed Track in Miles
India	16,918
Great Britain	17,291
Russia	19,012
France	20,679
Germany	26,638
United States	208,152

Completed Track in Miles

aspects of the oil business, Rockefeller used horizontal integration to control the refining process. Several trustees held stock in various refinery companies "in trust" for Standard's stockholders. This elaborate stock swap allowed the trustees to coordinate policy among the refineries, giving Rockefeller a virtual monopoly on the oil-refining business. The Standard Oil trust, valued at more than $70 million, paved the way for trusts in sugar, whiskey, matches, and many other products.

When the federal government responded to public pressure to outlaw the trust as a violation of free trade, Standard Oil changed tactics and reorganized as a holding company. Instead of stockholders in competing companies acting through trustees to set prices and determine territories, the holding company simply brought competing companies under one central administration. No longer technically separate businesses, they could act in concert without violating antitrust laws that forbade companies from forming "combinations in restraint of trade." By the 1890s, Standard Oil ruled more than 90 percent of the oil business, employed 100,000 people, and was the biggest, richest, most feared, and most admired business organization in the world.

John D. Rockefeller enjoyed enormous success in business, but he was not well liked by the public. Editor and journalist Ida M. Tarbell's "History of the Standard Oil Company," which ran for three years (1902–1905) in serial form in *McClure's*

CHAPTER LOCATOR | How did the railroads stimulate big business?

Magazine, largely shaped the public's harsh view of Rockefeller. Her history chronicled the methods Rockefeller had used to take over the oil industry. Publicly, Rockefeller refused to respond to her allegations. "If I step on that worm I will call attention to it," he explained. "If I ignore it, it will disappear." Yet by the time Tarbell finished publishing her story, Standard Oil and the man who created it had become the symbol of heartless monopoly.

New Inventions: The Telephone and Electricity

The second half of the nineteenth century was an age of invention (**Table 18.1**). Men like Thomas Alva Edison and Alexander Graham Bell became folk heroes. But no matter how dramatic the inventors or the inventions, the new electric and telephone industries pioneered by Edison and Bell soon eclipsed their inventors and fell under the control of bankers and industrialists.

Alexander Graham Bell came to America from Scotland at the age of twenty-four with a passion to find a way to teach the deaf to speak (his wife and mother were deaf). Instead, he developed a way to transmit voice over wire—the telephone. His invention astounded the world when he demonstrated it at the Philadelphia Bicentennial Exposition in 1876. In 1880, Bell's company, American Bell, pioneered "long lines" (long-distance telephone service), creating American Telephone and Telegraph (AT&T) as a subsidiary. Bell's invention proved a boon to business, contributing to speed and efficiency. The number of telephones soared, reaching 310,000 in 1895 and more than 1.5 million in 1900.

Even more than Alexander Graham Bell, inventor **Thomas Alva Edison** embodied the ingenuity and rugged individualism that Americans most admired. Self-educated, he worked twenty hours a day in his laboratory in Menlo Park, New Jersey, vowing to turn out "a minor invention every ten days and a big thing every six months or so." At the height of his career, he averaged a patent every eleven days and invented such "big things" as the phonograph, the motion picture camera, and the filament for the incandescent lightbulb.

Edison, in competition with George W. Westinghouse, pioneered the use of electricity as an energy source. By the late nineteenth century, electricity had become a part of American urban life. It powered trolley cars and lighted factories, homes, and office buildings. Indeed, electricity became so prevalent in urban life that it symbolized the city, whose bright lights contrasted with rural America, left largely in the dark because private enterprise judged it not profitable enough to run electric lines to outlying farms and ranches.

The day of the inventor quietly yielded to the heyday of the corporation. In 1892, the electric industry consolidated. Reflecting a nationwide trend in business, Edison General Electric dropped the name of its inventor, becoming simply General Electric (GE). For years, an embittered Edison refused to set foot inside a GE building. General Electric could afford to overlook the slight. A prime example of the trend toward business consolidation taking place in the 1890s, GE soon dominated the market.

TABLE 18.1 ■ Notable American Inventions 1865–1899

Year	Invention
1865	Railroad sleeping car
1867	Typewriter
1868	Railroad refrigerator car
1870	Stock ticker
1874	Barbed wire
1876	Telephone
1877	Phonograph
1879	Electric lightbulb
1882	Electric fan
1885	Adding machine
1886	Coca-Cola
1888	Kodak camera
1890	Electric chair
1891	Zipper
1895	Safety razor
1896	Electric stove
1899	Tape recorder

Thomas Alva Edison

▶ Self-educated American inventor who in the 1880s pioneered the use of electricity. Other inventions included the phonograph, the motion picture camera, and the filament for incandescent lightbulbs.

QUICK REVIEW

What tactics and strategies did America's business owners employ during the early years of the Gilded Age?

How did big business change at the end of the nineteenth century?

Homestead Steelworks

The Homestead steelworks, outside Pittsburgh, is pictured shortly after J. P. Morgan bought out Andrew Carnegie and created U.S. Steel. Hagley Museum & Library.

EVEN AS ROCKEFELLER and Carnegie built their empires, the era of the "robber barons," as they were dubbed by their detractors, was drawing to a close. Increasingly, businesses replaced partnerships and sole proprietorships with the anonymous corporate structure that would come to dominate the twentieth century. At the same time, mergers led to the creation of huge new corporations.

Banks and financiers played a key role in this consolidation, so much so that the decades at the turn of the twentieth century can be characterized as a period of finance capitalism—investment sponsored by banks and bankers. During these years, a new social philosophy based on the theories of naturalist Charles Darwin helped to justify consolidation and to inhibit state or federal regulation of business. A conservative Supreme Court further frustrated attempts to control business by consistently declaring that legislation designed to regulate railroads or to outlaw trusts and monopolies was unconstitutional.

J. P. Morgan and Finance Capitalism

John Pierpont Morgan, the preeminent finance capitalist of the late nineteenth century, sought whenever possible to eliminate competition by substituting consolidation and central control. **J. P. Morgan**'s passion for order made him the architect of business mergers. At the turn of the twentieth century, he dominated American banking, exerting an influence so powerful that his critics charged he controlled a vast "money trust."

J. P. Morgan

▶ The preeminent finance capitalist of the late nineteenth century. Morgan acted as a power broker in the reorganization of the railroads and the creation of industrial giants such as General Electric and U.S. Steel. His efforts formed the model for corporate consolidation that would characterize the modern economy.

the powerbroker

Morgan acted as a power broker in the reorganization of the railroads and the creation of industrial giants such as General Electric and U.S. Steel. When the railroads fell on hard times in the 1890s, Morgan quickly took over struggling railroads and moved to eliminate competition by creating what he called "a community of interest" among handpicked managers. By the time he finished reorganizing the railroads, Morgan had concentrated the nation's rail lines in the hands of a few directors who controlled two-thirds of the nation's track.

Banker control of the railroads rationalized, or coordinated, the industry. But stability came at a high price. To keep investors happy and to guarantee huge profits from the sale of stock, Morgan issued more shares than the assets of the company warranted. Overcapitalization hurt the railroads in the long run, saddling them with enormous debt. Equally harmful was the management style of the Morgan directors, who aimed at short-term profit and discouraged the continued technological and organizational innovation needed to run the railroads effectively.

In 1898, Morgan moved into the steel industry and, in 1901, purchased Carnegie Steel for $480 million (the equivalent of about $10 billion in today's currency). Morgan's acquisition of Carnegie Steel signaled the passing of the old entrepreneurial order personified by Andrew Carnegie and the arrival of a new, anonymous corporate world. Morgan quickly moved to pull together Carnegie's chief competitors to form a huge new corporation, United States Steel. Created in 1901 and capitalized at $1.4 billion, U.S. Steel was the largest corporation in the world.

Even more than Carnegie or Rockefeller, Morgan left his stamp on the twentieth century. His efforts formed the model for corporate consolidation that would characterize the modern economy. Economists and social scientists soon justified such consolidation with a new social theory known as social Darwinism.

Social Darwinism, Laissez-Faire, and the Supreme Court

John D. Rockefeller Jr., the son of the founder of Standard Oil, once remarked to his Baptist Bible class that the Standard Oil Company, like the American Beauty rose, resulted from "pruning the early buds that grew up around it." The elimination of smaller, inefficient units, he said, was "merely the working out of a law of nature and a law of God." The comparison of the business world to the natural world gave rise to a theory of society based on the law of evolution formulated by British naturalist Charles Darwin. In *On the Origin of Species* (1859), Darwin theorized that in the struggle for survival, adaptation to the environment triggered among species a natural selection process that led to evolution. Herbert Spencer in Britain and William Graham Sumner in the United States developed the theory of **social Darwinism**, which became popular in the 1880s. The social

CHRONOLOGY

1880s
– Herbert Spencer and William Graham Sumner espouse social Darwinism.

1889
– Andrew Carnegie publishes "Gospel of Wealth."

1901
– J. P. Morgan purchases Carnegie Steel for $480 million and creates U.S. Steel, America's first billion-dollar corporation.

social Darwinism
▶ Developed by Herbert Spencer and William Graham Sumner, social Darwinism gained favor in the late nineteenth century. Social Darwinists believed that wealth was a sign of "fitness" and poverty a sign of "unfitness" for survival. They argued that efforts to alleviate inequality were counterproductive and even destructive.

| How did big business change at the end of the nineteenth century? | What factors influenced political life in the late nineteenth century? | What issues shaped presidential politics in the late nineteenth century? | What role did the economy play in the politics of the 1880s and 1890s? | Conclusion: Why was business so dominant in the Gilded Age? |

489

Darwinists concluded that progress came about as a result of relentless competition in which the strong survived and the weak died out.

In social terms, the idea of the "survival of the fittest" had profound significance, as Sumner, a professor of political economy at Yale University, made clear in his book *What Social Classes Owe to Each Other* (1883). "The drunkard in the gutter is just where he ought to be, according to the fitness and tendency of things," Sumner insisted. Conversely, "millionaires are the product of natural selection," and although "they get high wages and live in luxury," Sumner claimed, "the bargain is a good one for society."

Social Darwinists equated wealth and power with "fitness" and believed that the unfit should be allowed to die off to advance the progress of humanity. Any efforts by the rich to aid the poor would only tamper with the rigid laws of nature and slow down evolution. Social Darwinism acted to curb social reform while at the same time glorifying great wealth and justifying economic inequality.

Andrew Carnegie softened some of the harshness of social Darwinism in his essay "The Gospel of Wealth," published in 1889. The millionaire, Carnegie wrote, acted as a "mere trustee and agent for his poorer brethren, bringing to their service his superior wisdom, experience, and ability to administer, doing for them better than they could or would do for themselves." Carnegie urged the rich to "live unostentatious lives" and "administer surplus wealth for the good of the people." His gospel of wealth earned much praise but won few converts.

Social Darwinism suited an age in which the gross inequalities accompanying industrialization seemed to cry out for action. Assuaging the nation's conscience, social Darwinism justified neglect of the poor in the name of "race progress." With so many of the poor coming from different races and ethnicities, social Darwinism fueled racism. A new "scientific racism" purported to prove "Anglo-Saxons" superior to all other groups. Social Darwinism buttressed the status quo and reassured comfortable, white Americans that all was as it should be.

Social Darwinism, with its emphasis on the free play of competition and the survival of the fittest, encouraged the economic theory of laissez-faire (French for "let it alone"). Business argued that government should not meddle in economic affairs, while ignoring the huge land grants and protective tariffs that benefited industry. During the 1880s and 1890s, a conservative Supreme Court in a series of landmark decisions used the Fourteenth Amendment—originally intended to protect freed slaves from state laws violating their rights—to protect corporations from taxation, regulation, labor organization, and antitrust legislation. Only in the arena of politics did Americans attempt to tackle the power of corporate capitalism.

> QUICK REVIEW

How did social Darwinism shape American society and business in the late nineteenth century?

This political cartoon styles the temperance campaign as "Woman's Holy War." Women's activism against alcohol in the 1870s led to the creation of the Woman's Christian Temperance Union in 1874. Picture Research Consultants & Archives.

▶ FOR MORE HELP ANALYZING THIS IMAGE, see the visual activity for this chapter in the Online Study Guide at bedfordstmartins.com/roarkunderstanding.

What factors influenced political life in the late nineteenth century?

FOR MANY AMERICANS, politics provided a source of identity, a livelihood, and a form of entertainment. A variety of factors contributed to the complicated interplay of politics and culture. Patronage provided an economic incentive for voter participation (see **Figure 18.2**, page 492), but ethnicity, religion, sectional loyalty, race, and gender all influenced the political life of the period.

Political Participation and Party Loyalty

Patronage proved a strong motivation for party loyalty among many voters. Political parties in power doled out hundreds of thousands of federal, state, and local government jobs to their loyal supporters. Money greased the wheels of this system of patronage, dubbed the **spoils system** from the adage "to the victor go the spoils." With their livelihoods tied to their party identity, government employees in particular had an incentive to vote in great numbers.

Political affiliation provided a powerful sense of group identity for many voters. Democrats, who traced the party's roots back to Thomas Jefferson, called theirs "the party of the fathers." The Republican Party still claimed strong loyalties as a result of its alignment with the Union during the Civil War.

Religion and ethnicity also played a significant role in politics. In the North, Protestants from the old-line denominations, particularly Presbyterians and Methodists, flocked to the Republican Party, which championed a series of moral

spoils system
▶ The system in which government positions were distributed to the supporters of successful political candidates. Under this system, the political parties in power doled out hundreds of thousands of federal, state, and local government jobs to their loyal supporters. The assassination of President James Garfield in 1881 led to civil service reform.

| How did big business change at the end of the nineteenth century? | **What factors influenced political life in the late nineteenth century?** | What issues shaped presidential politics in the late nineteenth century? | What role did the economy play in the politics of the 1880s and 1890s? | Conclusion: Why was business so dominant in the Gilded Age? |

1869
– National Woman Suffrage Association is founded.

1874
– Woman's Christian Temperance Union, an all-women reform organization, is founded.

1886
– *Atlanta Constitution* editor Henry Grady calls for a New South modeled on the industrial North.

1890
– General Federation of Women's Clubs is founded.

1892
– Ida B. Wells launches antilynching campaign.

reforms, including local laws requiring businesses to close in observance of the Sabbath. In the cities, the Democratic Party courted immigrants and working-class Catholic and Jewish voters and charged, rightly, that Republican moral crusades often masked attacks on immigrant culture.

Sectionalism and the New South

After the end of Reconstruction, most white voters in the former Confederate states remained loyal Democrats. Labeling the Republican Party the agent of "Negro rule," Democrats urged white southerners to "vote the way you shot." Yet the so-called solid South proved far from solid on the state and local levels. The economic plight of the South led to shifting political alliances and to third-party movements that challenged Democratic attempts to define politics along race lines and maintain the Democratic Party as the white man's party.

The South's economy, devastated by the war, foundered at the same time the North experienced an unprecedented industrial boom. Soon an influential group of southerners called for a **New South** modeled on the industrial North. Henry Grady, the editor of the *Atlanta Constitution*, used his paper's influence to exhort the South to use its natural advantages—cheap labor and abundant natural resources—to go head-to-head in competition with northern industry. Many southerners, men and women, black and white, joined the national migration from farm to city. And even as southern Democrats took back control of state governments (see chapter 16), they embraced northern promoters who promised prosperity and profits.

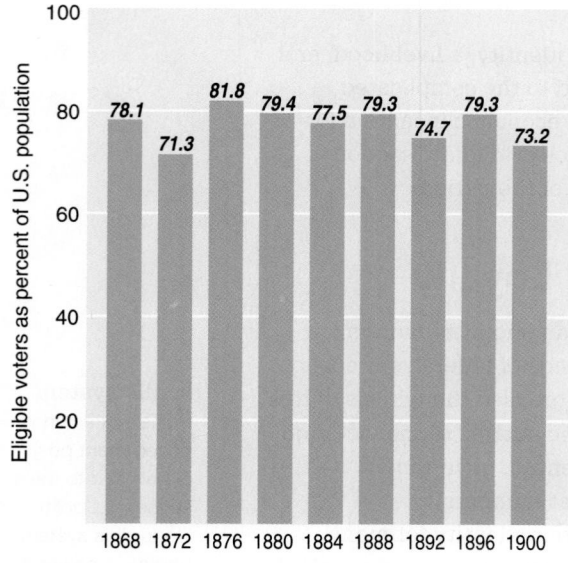

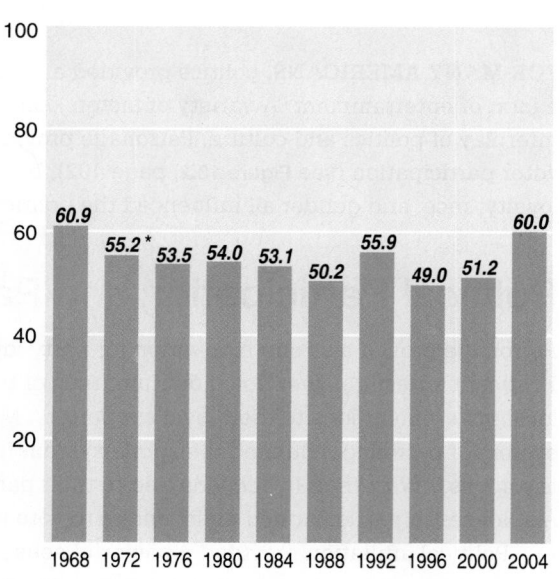

*Decrease because of expansion of eligibility with the enfranchisement of 18- to 21-year-olds.

FIGURE 18.2 ■ **Voter Turnout, 1868–1900 and 1968–2004**
Despite the weakness of the presidency and the largely undistinguished men who filled the office, people turned out in record numbers to vote in late-nineteenth-century elections. Compare the rate of voter participation to that of the late twentieth century. What factors do you think account for the differences?

CHAPTER LOCATOR | How did the railroads stimulate big business?

The railroads came first, opening up the region for industrial development. Southern railroad mileage grew fourfold from 1865 to 1890. The number of cotton spindles also soared as textile mill owners abandoned New England in search of the cheap labor and proximity to raw materials promised in the South. By 1900, the South had become the nation's leading producer of cloth, and more than 100,000 southerners, many of them women and children, worked in the region's textile mills.

The New South prided itself most on its iron and steel industry, which grew up in the area surrounding Birmingham, Alabama. Andrew Carnegie toured the region in 1889 and observed, "The South is Pennsylvania's most formidable industrial enemy." But southern industry remained controlled by northern investors. Elaborate mechanisms rigged the price of southern steel, inflating it, as one northern insider confessed, "for the purpose of protecting the Pittsburgh mills and in turn the Pittsburgh steel users." Similar policies also prevailed in the lumber and mining industries.

In practical terms, the industrialized New South proved an illusion. Much of the South remained agricultural, caught in the grip of the insidious crop lien system (see chapter 16). White southern farmers, desperate to get out of debt, sometimes joined with African Americans to pursue their goals politically. Between 1865 and 1900, voters in every southern state experimented with political alliances that crossed the color line. In Virginia, the "Readjusters," a coalition of blacks and whites determined to "readjust" (lower) the state debt and spend more money on public education, captured state offices from 1879 to 1883. In southern politics, the interplay of race and gender made coalitions like the Readjusters a potent threat to the status quo.

Gender, Race, and Politics

Gender—society's notion of what constitutes acceptable masculine or feminine behavior—influenced politics throughout the nineteenth century. From the early days of the Republic, citizenship had been defined in male terms. Citizenship and its prerogatives (voting and officeholding) served as a badge of manliness and rested on its corollary, patriarchy—the power and authority men exerted over their wives and families. With the advent of universal (white) male suffrage in the early nineteenth century, gender eclipsed class as the defining feature of citizenship. Once the public sphere of political participation became equated with manhood, women found themselves increasingly restricted to the private sphere of home and hearth.

Gender permeated politics in other ways, especially in the New South. Cross-racial alliances rested on the belief that universal political rights (voting, officeholding, patronage) could be extended to black males in the public sphere without eliminating racial barriers in the private sphere. Democrats fought back by trying to convince voters that black voting would inevitably lead to miscegenation (racial mixing). Black male political power and sexual power, they warned, went hand in hand. Ultimately their arguments prevailed, and many whites returned to the Democratic fold to protect "white womanhood" and with it white supremacy.

The notion that black men threatened white southern womanhood reached its most vicious form in the practice of lynching—the killing and mutilation of black men by white mobs. By 1892, the practice had become so prevalent that a

New South

▶ Vision of economic development of the South to mirror the industrial North. In the aftermath of the Civil War, Henry Grady, among others, promoted the virtues of a new industrial South. Despite some achievements, the industrialized New South, in practical terms, proved an illusion.

How did big business change at the end of the nineteenth century?

What factors influenced political life in the late nineteenth century?

What issues shaped presidential politics in the late nineteenth century?

What role did the economy play in the politics of the 1880s and 1890s?

Conclusion: Why was business so dominant in the Gilded Age?

493

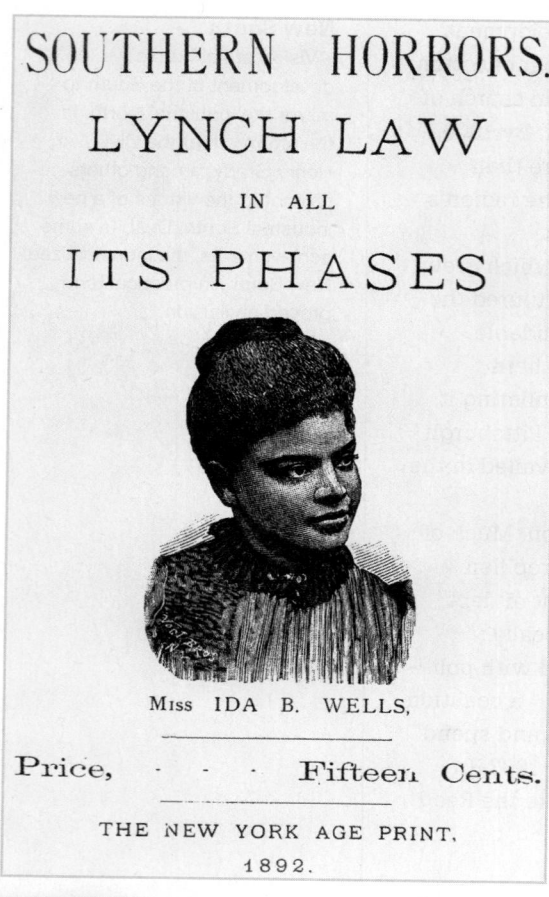

SOUTHERN HORRORS.

LYNCH LAW

IN ALL

ITS PHASES

Miss IDA B. WELLS,

Price, - - - Fifteen Cents.

THE NEW YORK AGE PRINT.
1892.

Ida B. Wells

Ida B. Wells began her antilynching campaign in 1892 after a friend's murder led her to examine the problem of lynching in the South. She spread her message in lectures and pamphlets like this one, distributed for fifteen cents. Manuscript, Archives and Rare Books Division, Schomburg Center for Research in Black Culture, The New York Public Library, Astor, Lenox, and Tilden Foundations.

Ida B. Wells

▶ Black female journalist who launched an antilynching crusade in the 1890s. Wells saw lynching as part of an effort by whites to protect the racial and economic status quo. Despite reprisals and death threats, Wells worked all her life to end lynching.

courageous black woman, **Ida B. Wells**, launched an antilynching movement. That year, a white mob lynched a friend of Wells's whose grocery store competed too successfully with a white-owned store. Wells shrewdly concluded that lynching served "as an excuse to get rid of Negroes who were acquiring wealth and property and thus keep the race terrorized." She began to collect data on lynching and discovered that in the decade between 1882 and 1892, lynching rose in the South by an overwhelming 200 percent, with more than 241 people killed. The vast increase in lynching testified to the retreat of the federal government following Reconstruction and to white southerners' determination to maintain supremacy through terrorism and intimidation.

Wells articulated lynching as a problem of race and gender. She insisted that the myth of black attacks on white southern women masked the reality that mob violence had more to do with economics and the shifting social structure of the South than with rape. She demonstrated in a sophisticated way how the southern patriarchal system, having lost its control over blacks with the end of slavery, used its control over women to circumscribe the liberty of black men.

Wells's strong stance immediately resulted in reprisal. While she was traveling in the North, vandals ransacked her office in Tennessee and destroyed her printing equipment. Yet the warning that she would be killed on sight if she ever returned to Memphis only stiffened her resolve. As she wrote in her autobiography, *Crusade for Justice* (1928), "Having lost my paper, had a price put on my life and been made an exile . . . , I felt that I owed it to myself and to my race to tell the whole truth now that I was where I could do so freely."

Lynching did not end during Wells's lifetime, but her forceful voice brought the issue to national and international prominence. At her funeral in 1931, black leader W. E. B. Du Bois eulogized Wells as the woman who "began the awakening of the conscience of the nation." Wells's determined campaign against lynching provided just one example of women's political activism during the Gilded Age. The suffrage and temperance movements, along with the growing popularity of women's clubs, dramatized how women refused to be kept out of politics.

Women's Activism

In 1869, Elizabeth Cady Stanton along with Susan B. Anthony formed the National Woman Suffrage Association (NWSA), the first independent women's rights organization in the United States. Although it would be many years before women gained suffrage, they found ways to act politically long before they voted and cleverly used their moral authority as wives and mothers to move from the domestic sphere into the realm of politics.

The extraordinary activity of women's clubs in the period following the Civil War provides just one example. Women's clubs proliferated from the 1860s to the 1890s, often in response to the exclusionary policies of men's organizations. In 1868, newspaper reporter Jane Cunningham Croly founded the Sorosis Club in

New York City after the New York Press Club denied entry to women journalists wishing to attend a banquet honoring the British author Charles Dickens. In 1890, Croly brought state and local clubs together under the umbrella of the General Federation of Women's Clubs (GFWC). Not wanting to alienate southern women, the GFWC barred black women's clubs from joining, despite their vehement objections. Women's clubs soon turned from literary pursuits to politics and reform, endorsing an end to child labor, supporting the eight-hour workday, and helping pass pure food and drug legislation.

The temperance movement (the movement to end drunkenness) attracted by far the largest number of organized women in the late nineteenth century. During the winter of 1873–74, temperance women adopted a radical new tactic. Armed with Bibles and singing hymns, they marched on taverns and saloons and refused to leave until the proprietors signed a pledge to quit selling liquor. Known as the Woman's Crusade, the movement spread through small towns in Ohio, Indiana, Michigan, and Illinois and soon moved east into New York, New England, and Pennsylvania. Before it was over, more than 100,000 women had marched in more than 450 cities and towns.

The women's tactics may have been new, but the temperance movement dated back to the 1820s. Originally, the movement was led by Protestant men who organized clubs to pledge voluntary abstinence from liquor. By the 1850s, temperance advocates won significant victories when states, starting with Maine, passed laws to prohibit the sale of liquor. The Woman's Crusade dramatically brought the issue of temperance back into the national spotlight and led to the formation of a new organization, the **Woman's Christian Temperance Union (WCTU)**, in 1874. Composed entirely of women, the WCTU advocated total abstinence from alcohol.

Temperance provided women with a respectable outlet for their increasing resentment of women's inferior status and their growing recognition of women's capabilities. In its first five years, the WCTU relied on education and moral suasion, but when Frances Willard became president in 1879, she politicized the organization (see chapter 20). When the women of the WCTU joined with the Prohibition Party (formed in 1869 by a group of evangelical clergymen), one wag observed, "Politics is a man's game, an' women, childhern, and prohyibitionists do well to keep out iv it." By sharing power with women, the Prohibitionist men violated the old political rules and risked attacks on their honor and manhood.

Even though they could not yet vote, women found ways to affect the political process. Like men, they displayed strong party loyalties and rallied around traditional Republican and Democratic candidates. Third parties courted women, recognizing that their volunteer labor and support could be key assets in party building. Nevertheless, despite growing political awareness among women, politics, particularly presidential politics, remained an exclusively male prerogative.

Woman's Christian Temperance Union (WCTU)

► All-women organization founded in 1874 to advocate for total abstinence from alcohol. The WCTU became an important way for women to express their political views.

QUICK REVIEW ◄

How did race and gender influence politics in the late nineteenth century?

> What issues shaped presidential politics in the late nineteenth century?

Civil Service Exam In the 1890s, prospective police officers in Chicago take the written civil service exam. Civil service meant that politicians and party bosses could no longer use jobs to reward their supporters. Chicago Historical Society.

patronage
v
civil service

U**NTIL THE 1890s,** few Americans thought the president or the national government had any role to play in addressing the problems accompanying the nation's industrial transformation. The dominant creed of laissez-faire, coupled with the dictates of social Darwinism, warned government to leave business alone. Still, presidents in the Gilded Age grappled with corruption and party strife and struggled toward the creation of new political ethics designed to replace patronage with a civil service system that promised to award jobs on the basis of merit, not party loyalty.

Corruption and Party Strife

The political corruption and party factionalism that characterized the administration of Ulysses S. Grant (1869–1877) (see chapter 16) continued to trouble the nation in the 1880s. The spoils system remained the driving force in party politics at all levels of government in the Gilded Age. Pro-business Republicans generally held a firm grip on the White House, while Democrats had better luck in Congress. Both parties relied on patronage to cement party loyalty.

A small but determined group of reformers championed a new ethics that would preclude politicians from getting rich from public office. The selection of U.S. senators particularly concerned them. Under the Constitution, senators were selected by state legislatures, not directly elected by the voters. Powerful business interests often controlled state legislatures and through them U.S. senators.

CHAPTER LOCATOR | How did the railroads stimulate big business?

As journalist Henry Demarest Lloyd quipped, Standard Oil "had done everything to the Pennsylvania legislature except to refine it." In this climate, a constitutional amendment calling for the direct election of senators faced stiff opposition from entrenched interests.

Republican president Rutherford B. Hayes, whose disputed election in 1876 signaled the end of Reconstruction in the South, tried to steer a middle course between spoilsmen and reformers. Hayes was a hardworking, well-informed executive who wanted peace, prosperity, and an end to party strife. Yet the Republican Party remained divided into three factions led by strong party bosses who boasted that they could make or break any president.

Republican Factions in 1880

Stalwarts	Supporters of the patronage system, led by master spoilsman Senator Roscoe Conkling of New York.
Half Breeds	Less openly corrupt than the Stalwarts, led by Conkling's archrival, Senator James G. Blaine of Maine.
Mugwumps	Reform-minded Republicans from Massachusetts and New York who deplored the spoils system and advocated civil service reform.

President Hayes's middle course pleased no one, and he soon managed to alienate all factions of his party. No one was surprised when he announced that he would not seek reelection in 1880. To avoid choosing among its factions, the Republican Party in 1880 nominated a dark-horse candidate, Representative James A. Garfield from Ohio. To appease Senator Roscoe Conkling (leader of the "Stalwart" faction), they picked Stalwart Chester A. Arthur as the vice presidential candidate. The Democrats made an attempt to overcome sectionalism and establish a national party by selecting an old Union general, Winfield Scott Hancock. But as one observer noted, "It is a peculiarly constituted party that sends rebel brigadiers to Congress because of their rebellion, and then nominates a Union General as its candidate for president because of his loyalty." Hancock received 155 electoral votes to Garfield's 214, although the popular vote was less lopsided.

Garfield's Assassination and Civil Service Reform

"My God," Garfield swore after only a few months in office, "what is there in this place that a man should ever want to get into it?" Garfield, like Hayes, faced the difficult task of remaining independent while pacifying the party bosses and placating the reformers. On July 2, 1881, less than four months after taking office, Garfield was shot and died two months later. His assailant, Charles Guiteau, though clearly insane, turned out to be a disappointed office seeker who claimed to be motivated by political partisanship. He told the police officer who arrested him, "I did it; I will go to jail for it; Arthur is president, and I am a Stalwart." The press almost universally condemned Republican factionalism for creating the political climate that produced Guiteau and led to the second political assassination in a generation.

After Garfield's assassination, attacks on the spoils system increased, and the public joined the chorus calling for reform. Both parties claimed credit for passage

CHRONOLOGY

1880
- Republican compromise candidate James A. Garfield is elected president.

1881
- Garfield is assassinated; Vice President Chester A. Arthur becomes president.

1883
- Pendleton Civil Service Act establishes a merit system for thousands of federal jobs to replace the spoils system.

1884
- Grover Cleveland becomes the first Democrat to be elected president since 1856.

How did big business change at the end of the nineteenth century?	What factors influenced political life in the late nineteenth century?	**What issues shaped presidential politics in the late nineteenth century?**	What role did the economy play in the politics of the 1880s and 1890s?	Conclusion: Why was business so dominant in the Gilded Age?

of the Pendleton Civil Service Act of 1883, which established a permanent Civil Service Commission consisting of three members appointed by the president. Some fourteen thousand jobs came under a merit system that required examinations for office and made it impossible to remove jobholders for political reasons. The new law also prohibited federal jobholders from contributing to political campaigns, thus drying up the major source of the party bosses' revenue. Soon, business interests stepped in to replace officeholders as the nation's chief political contributors. Ironically, **civil service reform** thus gave business an even greater influence in political life.

civil service reform

▶ Effort in the 1880s to do away with the spoils system. The assassination of President James Garfield in 1881 led to the passage of the Pendleton Civil Service Act of 1883, which established a permanent Civil Service Commission. Some fourteen thousand jobs came under a merit system that required examinations for office and made it impossible to remove jobholders for political reasons.

Reform and Scandal: The Campaign of 1884

When Conkling's political star fell after Garfield's assassination, James G. Blaine assumed leadership of the Republican Party and at long last captured the presidential nomination in 1884. But Mugwumps like editor Carl Schurz insisted that Blaine "wallowed in spoils like a rhinoceros in an African pool." They bolted the party and embraced the Democrats' presidential nominee, Grover Cleveland, reform governor of New York. Cleveland distinguished himself from an entire generation of politicians by the simple motto "A public office is a public trust." First

Campaign Pins, 1884

These gilt campaign pins from the election of 1884 show Republican candidate James G. Blaine, on the right, thumbing his nose at Democratic candidate Grover Cleveland. The gilt pins are a symbol for Gilded Age politics, an era characterized by corruption and party strife. Collection of Janice L. and David J. Frent.

CHAPTER LOCATOR | How did the railroads stimulate big business?

as mayor of Buffalo and later as governor of New York, he built a reputation for honesty, economy, and administrative efficiency. The Democrats, who had not won the presidency since 1856, had high hopes for his candidacy, especially after the Mugwumps threw their support to Cleveland, insisting that "the paramount issue this year is moral rather than political."

The Mugwumps soon regretted their words. The 1884 contest degenerated so far into scandal and nasty mudslinging that one disgusted journalist styled it "the vilest campaign ever waged." In July, Cleveland's hometown paper, the *Buffalo Telegraph*, revealed that the candidate had fathered an illegitimate child in an affair with a local widow. Cleveland, a bachelor, accepted responsibility for the child. Crushed by the scandal, the Mugwumps lost much of their enthusiasm. At public rallies, Blaine's partisans taunted Cleveland, chanting, "Ma, Ma, where's my Pa?"

Blaine set a new campaign style by launching a whirlwind national tour. On a last-minute stop in New York City, Blaine committed a misstep that may have cost him the election. He overlooked a remark by a supporter, a local clergyman who cast a slur on Catholic voters by styling the Democrats as the party of "Rum, Romanism, and Rebellion." Linking drinking (rum) and Catholicism (Romanism) offended Irish Catholic voters, whom Blaine had counted on to desert the Democratic Party and support him because of his Irish background.

With less than a week to go until the election, Blaine had no chance to recover from the negative publicity. He lost New York State by fewer than 1,200 votes and with it the election ending twenty-five years of Republican control of the presidency (**Map 18.2**). Cleveland's followers had the last word. To the chorus of "Ma, Ma, where's my Pa?" they retorted, "Going to the White House, ha, ha, ha."

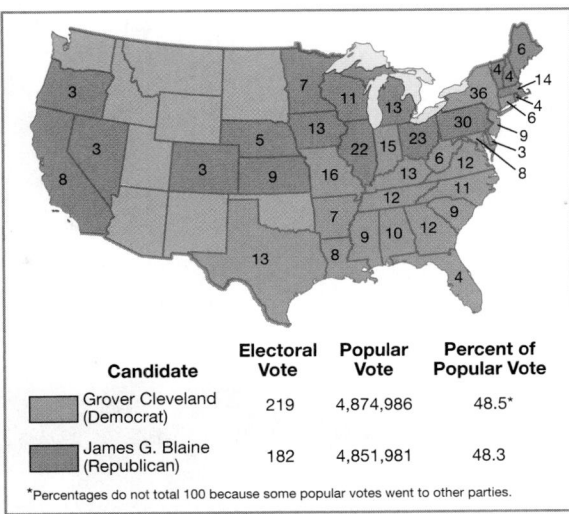

Candidate	Electoral Vote	Popular Vote	Percent of Popular Vote
Grover Cleveland (Democrat)	219	4,874,986	48.5*
James G. Blaine (Republican)	182	4,851,981	48.3

*Percentages do not total 100 because some popular votes went to other parties.

MAP 18.2 ■ The Election of 1884

QUICK REVIEW <

How did the divisions within the Republican Party contribute to the outcome of the 1884 presidential election?

How did big business change at the end of the nineteenth century?

What factors influenced political life in the late nineteenth century?

What issues shaped presidential politics in the late nineteenth century?

What role did the economy play in the politics of the 1880s and 1890s?

Conclusion: Why was business so dominant in the Gilded Age?

What role did the economy play in the politics of the 1880s and 1890s?

FOUR YEARS LATER, in the election of 1888, voters turned Cleveland out, electing Republican Benjamin Harrison. Then, in the only instance in America's history when a president once defeated at the polls returned to office, the voters brought Cleveland back in the election of 1892. What factors account for such a surprising turnaround? The 1880s witnessed a remarkable political realignment as a set of economic concerns replaced appeals to Civil War sectional loyalties. The tariff, federal regulation of the railroads and trusts, and the campaign for free silver restructured American politics.

The Tariff and the Politics of Protection

The tariff became a potent political issue in the 1880s. The concept of a protective tariff to raise the price of imported goods and stimulate American industry dated back to Alexander Hamilton in the founding days of the Republic. The Republicans turned the tariff to political ends in 1861 by enacting a measure that both

CHAPTER LOCATOR | How did the railroads stimulate big business?

raised revenues for the Civil War and rewarded their industrial supporters, who wanted protection from foreign competition. After the war, the pro-business Republicans continued to revise and enlarge the tariff. By the 1880s, the tariff produced more than $2.1 billion in revenue and had created a huge surplus that sat idly in the Treasury's vaults while the government argued about how (or even whether) to spend it.

To many Americans, particularly southern and midwestern farmers who sold their crops in a world market but had to buy goods priced artificially high because of the protective tariff, the answer was simple: Reduce the tariff. Advocates of free trade and moderates agitated for tariff reform. But those who benefited from the tariff—industrialists insisting that America's "infant industries" needed protection and some westerners producing protected raw materials such as wool, hides, and lumber—firmly opposed lowering the tariff. Many argued that workers, too, benefited from high tariffs that protected American wages by giving American products an edge over imported goods.

The Republican Party seized on the tariff question to forge a new national coalition. "Fold up the bloody shirt and lay it away," Blaine advised a colleague in 1880. "It's of no use to us. You want to shift the main issue to protection." By encouraging an alliance among industrialists, labor, and western producers of raw materials—groups seen to benefit from the tariff—Blaine hoped to solidify the North, Midwest, and West against the solidly Democratic South. Although the tactic failed for Blaine in the presidential election of 1884, it worked for the Republicans four years later.

Cleveland, who had straddled the tariff issue in the election of 1884, startled the nation in 1887 by calling for tariff reform. Cleveland attacked the tariff as a tax levied on American consumers by powerful industries. And he pointed out that high tariffs impeded the expansion of American markets abroad at a time when American industries needed to expand if they were to keep growing. The Republicans countered by arguing that "tariff tinkering" would only unsettle prosperous industries, drive down wages, and shrink the farmers' home market. Republican Benjamin Harrison, who supported the high tariff, ousted Cleveland from the White House in 1888, carrying all the western and northern states except Connecticut and New Jersey.

Back in power, the Republicans passed the highest tariff in the nation's history in 1890. The new tariff, sponsored by Republican representative William McKinley of Ohio and signed into law by Harrison, stirred up protests across the United States. The American people had elected Harrison to preserve protection but not to enact a higher tariff. Democrats condemned the McKinley tariff and labeled the Republican Congress that passed it the "Billion Dollar Congress" for its spending, which depleted the nation's surplus by enacting a series of pork barrel programs designed to bring federal money to congressmen's own constituents. In the congressional election of 1890, angry voters swept the Republicans, including tariff sponsor McKinley, out of office. Two years later, Harrison himself was defeated, and Grover Cleveland returned to the White House.

Controversy over the tariff masked deeper divisions in American society. Conflict between workers and farmers on the one side and bankers and corporate giants on the other erupted throughout the 1880s and came to a head in the 1890s. Both sides in the tariff debate spoke to concern over class conflict when

CHRONOLOGY

1873
- Wall Street panic leads to major economic depression.

1887
- Interstate Commerce Act establishes the nation's first regulatory agency.

1890
- Congress passes the McKinley tariff, the highest in U.S. history.
- Sherman Antitrust Act forbids businesses from entering into agreements to restrict competition.

1893
- Wall Street panic touches off national depression.

1895
- Banker J. P. Morgan bails out U.S. Treasury.

| How did big business change at the end of the nineteenth century? | What factors influenced political life in the late nineteenth century? | What issues shaped presidential politics in the late nineteenth century? | What role did the economy play in the politics of the 1880s and 1890s? | Conclusion: Why was business so dominant in the Gilded Age? |

501

they insisted that their respective plans, whether McKinley's high tariff or Cleveland's tariff reform, would bring prosperity and harmony. For their part, many working people shared the sentiment voiced by one labor leader that the tariff was "only a scheme devised by the old parties to throw dust in the eyes of laboring men."

Railroads, Trusts, and the Federal Government

American voters may have divided on the tariff, but increasingly they agreed on the need for federal regulation of the railroads and federal legislation to curb the power of the "trusts" (a term loosely applied to all large business combinations). As early as the 1870s, angry farmers in the Midwest who suffered from the unfair shipping practices of the railroads organized to fight for railroad regulation. The Patrons of Husbandry, or the Grange, founded in 1867 as a social and educational organization for farmers, soon became an independent political movement. By electing Grangers to state office, farmers made it possible for several midwestern states to pass laws in the 1870s and 1880s regulating the railroads. At first, the Supreme Court ruled in favor of state regulation (*Munn v. Illinois*, 1877). But in 1886, the Court reversed itself, ruling that because railroads crossed state boundaries, they fell outside state jurisdiction (*Wabash v. Illinois*). With more than three-fourths of railroads crossing state lines, the Supreme Court's decision effectively quashed the states' attempts at railroad regulation.

Anger at the *Wabash* decision finally led to the first federal law regulating the railroads, the Interstate Commerce Act, passed in 1887 during Cleveland's first administration. The act established the nation's first federal regulatory agency, the Interstate Commerce Commission (ICC), to oversee the railroad industry. In its early years, however, the ICC was never strong enough to pose a serious threat to the railroads and was more important as a precedent than effective as a watchdog.

Concern over the growing power of the trusts led Congress to pass the **Sherman Antitrust Act** in 1890. The act outlawed pools and trusts, ruling that businesses could no longer enter into agreements to restrict competition. It did nothing to restrict huge holding companies such as Standard Oil, however, and proved to be a weak sword against the trusts. In the following decade, the government successfully struck down only six trusts but used the law four times against labor by outlawing unions as a "conspiracy in restraint of trade." In 1895, the conservative Supreme Court dealt the antitrust law a crippling blow in *United States v. E. C. Knight Company*. In its decision, the Court ruled that "manufacture" did not constitute "trade." The ruling drastically narrowed the law, in this case allowing the American Sugar Refining Company, which had bought out a number of other sugar companies (including E. C. Knight) and controlled 98 percent of the production of sugar, to continue its virtual monopoly.

Both the ICC and the Sherman Antitrust Act testified to the nation's concern about corporate abuses of power and to a growing willingness to use federal measures to intervene on behalf of the public interest. As corporate capitalism became more and more powerful, public pressure toward government intervention grew. Yet not until the twentieth century would more active presidents sharpen and use these weapons effectively against the large corporations.

Sherman Antitrust Act
▶ 1890 act that outlawed pools and trusts, ruling that businesses could no longer enter into agreements to restrict competition. Government inaction, combined with the Supreme Court's narrow reading of the act in the *United States v. E. C. Knight Company* decision, undermined the law's effectiveness.

The Fight for Free Silver

While the tariff and regulation of the trusts gained many backers, the silver issue stirred passions like no other issue of the day. On one side stood those who believed that gold constituted the only honest money. The government's support of the gold standard meant that anyone could redeem paper money for gold. Many who supported the gold standard were eastern creditors who did not wish to be paid in devalued dollars. On the opposite side stood a coalition of western silver barons and poor farmers from the West and South who called for **free silver**. The mining interests, who had seen the silver bonanza in the West drive down the price of the precious metal, wanted the government to buy silver and mint silver dollars. Farmers from the West and South who had suffered from deflation during the 1870s and 1880s hoped that increasing the money supply with silver dollars, thus causing inflation, would give them some debt relief by enabling them to pay off their creditors with cheaper dollars.

During the depression following the panic of 1873, critics of hard money organized the Greenback Labor Party, an alliance of farmers and urban wage laborers. The Greenbackers favored issuing paper currency not tied to the gold supply, citing the precedent of the greenbacks issued during the Civil War. The government had the right to define what constituted legal tender, the Greenbackers reasoned: "Paper is equally money, when . . . issued according to law." They proposed that the nation's currency be based on its wealth—land, labor, and capital—and not simply on its reserves of gold. The Greenback Labor Party captured more than a million votes and elected fourteen members to Congress in 1878. Although conservatives considered the Greenbackers dangerous cranks, their views eventually prevailed in the 1930s, when the country abandoned the gold standard.

After the Greenback Labor Party collapsed, proponents of free silver came to dominate the monetary debate in the 1890s. Advocates of free silver pointed out that until 1873, the country had enjoyed a system of bimetallism—the minting of both silver and gold into coins. In that year, at the behest of those who favored gold, the Republican Congress had voted to stop buying and minting silver, an act silver supporters denounced as the "crime of '73." By sharply contracting the money supply at a time when the nation's economy was burgeoning, the Republicans had enriched bankers and investors at the expense of cotton and wheat farmers and industrial wageworkers. In 1878 and again in 1890, with the Sherman Silver Purchase Act, Congress took steps to ease the tight money policy and appease advocates of silver by passing legislation requiring the government to buy silver and issue silver certificates. Though good for the mining interests, the laws did little to promote the inflation desired by farmers. Soon monetary reformers began to call for "the free and unlimited coinage of silver," a plan whereby nearly all the silver mined in the West would be minted into coins circulated at the rate of sixteen ounces of silver to one ounce of gold.

By the 1890s, the silver issue crossed party lines. The Democrats hoped to use it to achieve a union between western and southern voters. Unfortunately for them, Democratic president Grover Cleveland supported the gold standard as vehemently as any Republican. After a panic on Wall Street in the spring of 1893, Cleveland called a special session of Congress and bullied the legislature into repealing the

free silver

▶ Term used by opponents of the gold standard for their proposal that the government buy silver and use it to mint currency. Western silver barons and poor farmers from the West and South were the primary advocates of free silver. The latter hoped that such a policy would result in inflation, effectively providing them with debt relief.

How did big business change at the end of the nineteenth century?	What factors influenced political life in the late nineteenth century?	What issues shaped presidential politics in the late nineteenth century?	**What role did the economy play in the politics of the 1880s and 1890s?**	Conclusion: Why was business so dominant in the Gilded Age?

503

Silver Purchase Act because he believed it threatened economic confidence. Repeal proved disastrous for Cleveland, not only economically but also politically. It did nothing to bring prosperity and dangerously divided the country.

Panic and Depression

President Cleveland had scarcely begun his second term in office in 1893 when the country faced the worst depression it had yet seen. In the face of economic disaster, Cleveland clung to the gold standard. In the winter of 1894–95, the president walked the floor of the White House, sleepless over the prospect that the United States might go bankrupt. Individuals and investors, rushing to trade in their banknotes for gold, strained the country's monetary system. The Treasury's gold reserves dipped so low that the government faced a real risk of going bankrupt.

At this juncture, J. P. Morgan stepped in to purchase gold abroad and supply it to the Treasury. A storm of controversy erupted over the deal. The press claimed that Cleveland had lined his own pockets and rumored that Morgan had made $8.9 million. Neither allegation was true. Cleveland had not profited a penny, and Morgan made far less than the millions his critics claimed.

But if President Cleveland's action managed to salvage the gold standard, it did not save the country from hardship. The winter of 1894–95 was one of the worst times in American history. People faced unemployment, cold, and hunger. A firm believer in limited government, Cleveland insisted that nothing could be done to help. "I do not believe that the power and duty of the General Government ought to be extended to the relief of individual suffering which is in no manner properly related to the public service or benefit." Nor did it occur to Cleveland that his great faith in the gold standard prolonged the depression, favored creditors over debtors, and caused immense hardship for millions of Americans.

> **QUICK REVIEW**

What role did the gold standard play in the economic crisis of the 1890s?

Library of Congress.

Conclusion: Why was business so dominant in the Gilded Age?

THE GOLD DEAL between J. P. Morgan and Grover Cleveland underscored a dangerous reality: The federal government was so weak that its solvency depended on a private banker. This lopsided power relationship signaled the dominance of business in the era author Mark Twain satirically but accurately characterized as the Gilded Age. Perhaps no other era in American history spawned greed, corruption, and vulgarity on so grand a scale.

Nevertheless, the Gilded Age was not without its share of achievements. In these years, America made the leap into the industrial age. Factories and refineries poured out American steel and oil at unprecedented rates. Businessmen developed new strategies to consolidate American industry. New inventions, including the telephone and electric light and power, changed Americans' everyday lives. By the end of the nineteenth century, the country had achieved industrial maturity. It boasted the largest, most innovative, most productive economy in the world.

Yet the changes that came with these developments worried many Americans and gave rise to the era's political turmoil. Race and gender profoundly influenced American politics, leading to new political alliances. Ida B. Wells fought racism in its most brutal form—lynching. Women's organizations championed causes, notably suffrage and temperance, and challenged prevailing views of woman's proper place. Reformers fought corruption by instituting civil service. And new issues—the tariff, the regulation of the trusts, and currency reform—restructured the nation's politics.

The Gilded Age witnessed a nation transformed. Where dusty roads and cattle trails once sprawled across the continent, steel rails now bound the country together. Cities grew exponentially, not only with new inhabitants from around the globe but also with new bridges, subways, and skyscrapers. The nation's workers and the great cities they labored to build are the focus of chapter 19.

SO NOW YOU KNOW

Mark Twain accurately labeled the late nineteenth century the Gilded Age, but not everyone shared in the gaudy excess of the period. The gap between the rich and the poor grew ever larger.

CHAPTER 18 STUDY GUIDE

Online Study Guide
bedfordstmartins.com/roarkunderstanding

STEP 1 GETTING STARTED

Below are basic terms from this period in American history. Can you identify each term below and explain why it matters? To do this exercise online or to download this chart, visit bedfordstmartins.com/roarkunderstanding.

TERM	WHO OR WHAT & WHEN	WHY IT MATTERS
Andrew Carnegie, p. 483		
John D. Rockefeller, p. 485		
Thomas Alva Edison, p. 487		
J. P. Morgan, p. 488		
social Darwinism, p. 489		
spoils system, p. 491		
New South, p. 493		
Ida B. Wells, p. 494		
Woman's Christian Temperance Union, p. 495		
civil service reform, p. 498		
Sherman Antitrust Act, p. 502		
free silver, p. 503		

STEP 2 MOVING BEYOND THE BASICS

The exercise below represents a more advanced understanding of the chapter material. Fill in the following chart by describing the positions that various political parties held on the key economic issues of the period and the regional differences in viewpoint on these issues. How did people in different parts of the country see these issues? To do this exercise online or to download this chart, visit bedfordstmartins.com/roarkunderstanding.

Key economic issues	Democrats	Republicans	Third parties	Regional differences
Tariffs				
Railroads				
Trusts				
Free silver				

Now that you've reviewed various parts of the chapter, take a step back and try to see the big picture by answering these questions. Remember to use specific examples from the chapter in your answers. To do this exercise online, visit bedfordstmartins.com/roarkunderstanding.

THE RISE OF BIG BUSINESS

▶ What role did railroads and new technologies play in the rise of American big business?

▶ How did the business pioneers of the late nineteenth century organize and grow their businesses?

LATE-NINETEENTH-CENTURY POLITICS

▶ How did ideas about gender and race shape late-nineteenth-century politics?

▶ How did new social philosophical theories justify business and political practices in the late nineteenth century?

ECONOMIC ISSUES AND POLITICAL CONFLICT

▶ How did each Gilded Age president react to economic issues? How did Supreme Court decisions affect economic issues?

▶ What made free silver such a powerful and emotional issue in the late nineteenth century?

LOOKING BACKWARD, LOOKING AHEAD

▶ How did the role of business in politics in the late nineteenth century differ from its role in the first half of the century?

▶ How did the rise of big business affect the economic and political landscape of early-twentieth-century America? In what ways did Americans try to deal with the excesses of big business?

IN YOUR OWN WORDS

Imagine that you must explain chapter 18 to someone who hasn't read it. What would be the most important points to include and why?

PRICE 25¢

NEW YORK
ILLUSTRATED

19

THE GROWTH OF AMERICA'S CITIES

1870–1900

> This chapter explores the rise of urban, industrial America. It examines urban growth and its consequences, focusing on the nature of industrial labor, tensions between workers and employers, the impact of urbanization on daily life, and the cities' efforts to respond to the demands of their fast-growing populations.

> Why did American cities grow so fast in the late nineteenth century?

> What kinds of work did people do in industrial America?

> What steps did workers take to organize in the 1870s and 1880s?

> How did industrialization transform home life and leisure?

> How did cities respond to the challenges of growth?

> Conclusion: Who built the cities?

DID YOU KNOW?

More than 40 percent of Americans have ancestors who came through Ellis Island.

Brooklyn Bridge. Completed in 1883, the Brooklyn Bridge realized John Roebling's dream of creating "a great work of art" as well as a superbly engineered bridge.

Why did American cities grow so fast in the late nineteenth century?

Russian Immigrant Family

A Russian immigrant family is shown leaving Ellis Island in 1900. Notice the white slips of paper pinned to their coats indicating that they have been processed. An immigration official in uniform stands on the left. The original wooden structure burned down and was replaced with an elaborate stone building the year this photo was taken.
Keystone-Mast Collection, UCR/California Museum of Photography, University of California, Riverside.

"WE CANNOT ALL LIVE IN CITIES, yet nearly all seem determined to do so," New York editor Horace Greeley complained. The last three decades of the nineteenth century witnessed an urban explosion. Cities and towns grew more than twice as rapidly as the total population. Most of the nation's largest cities were east of the Mississippi, although St. Louis and San Francisco both ranked among the top ten urban areas in 1900. Patterns of global migration contributed to the surge in urban population. In the port cities of the East Coast, more than fourteen million people arrived, many from southern and eastern Europe.

The Urban Explosion, a Global Migration

Between 1870 and 1900, eleven million people moved into cities. Industrial centers such as Pittsburgh, Chicago, New York, and Cleveland acted as giant magnets, attracting workers from the countryside. But migrants to the cities were by no means only rural Americans. Worldwide in scope, the movement from rural areas to urban industrial centers attracted millions of immigrants to American shores.

By the 1870s, the world could be conceptualized as three interconnected geographic regions (**Map 19.1**). At the center stood an industrial core that included parts of North America and Europe. This core was surrounded by a vast agricultural domain. Capitalist development in the late nineteenth century shattered traditional patterns of economic activity in this rural periphery. As old patterns broke down, these rural areas exported, along with other raw materials, new recruits for the industrial labor force.

CHAPTER LOCATOR | Why did American cities grow so fast in the late nineteenth century?

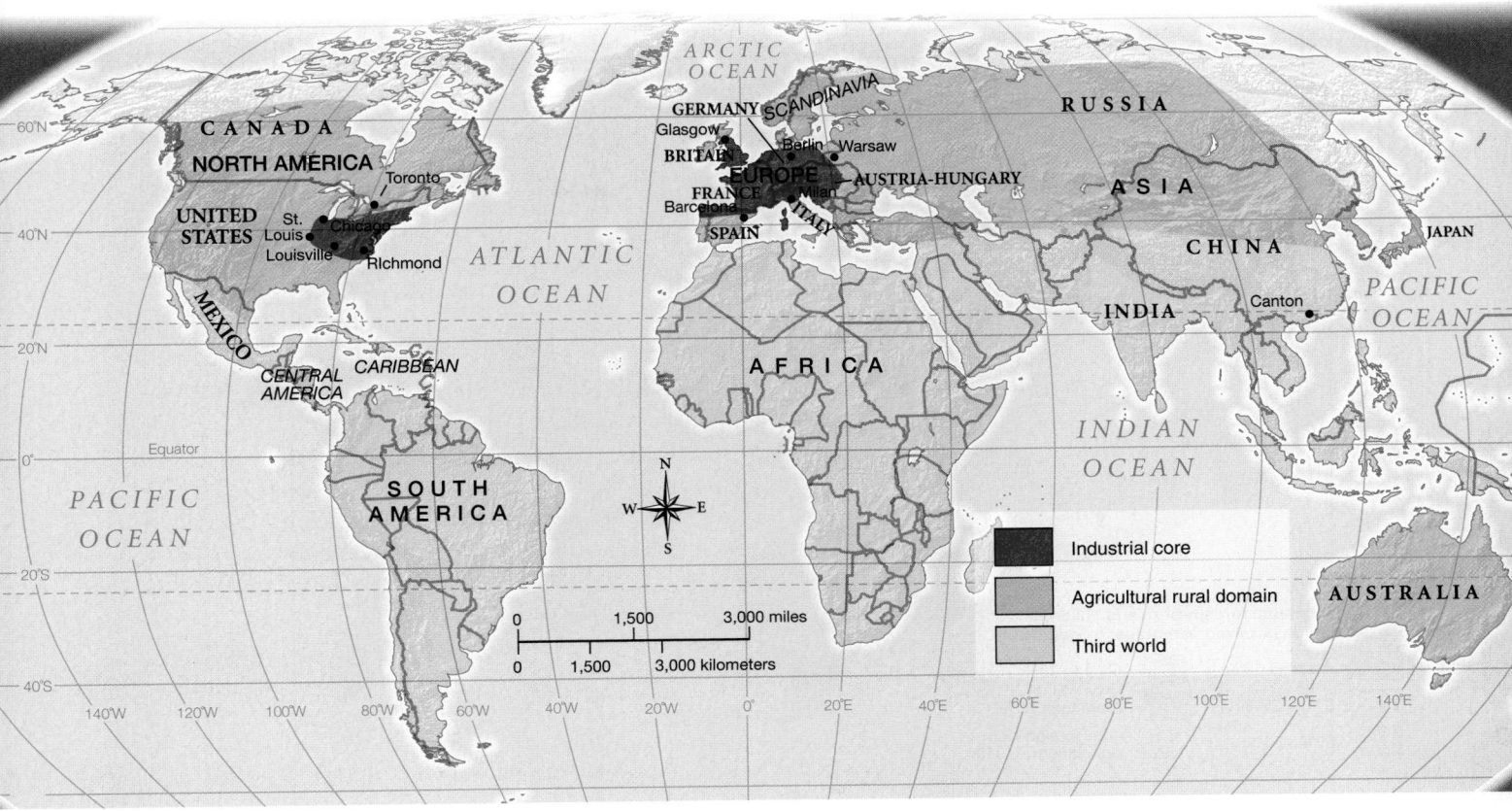

MAP 19.1 ■ **Economic Regions of the World, 1890s**
The global nature of the world economy at the turn of the twentieth century is indicated by three interconnected geographic regions. At the center stands the industrial core—western Europe and the northeastern United States. The second region—the agricultural periphery—supplied immigrant laborers to the industries in the core. Beyond these two regions lay a vast area tied economically to the industrial core by colonialism.

Beyond this second circle lay an even larger third world. Ties between this part of the world and the industrial core strengthened in the late nineteenth century, but most of the people living there stayed put. They worked on plantations and railroads, in mines and ports, as part of a huge export network managed by foreign powers that staked out spheres of influence and colonies.

In the 1870s, railroad expansion and low steamship fares gave the world's peoples a newfound mobility that enabled industrialists to draw on a global population for cheap labor. When Andrew Carnegie opened his first steel mill in 1872, his superintendent hired workers he called "buckwheats"—young American boys just off the farm. By the 1890s, however, Carnegie's workforce included rural Hungarians and Slavs who had migrated to the United States, willing to work for low wages.

Altogether, more than 25 million immigrants came to the United States between 1850 and 1920 (**Map 19.2**, page 512). Part of a worldwide migration, immigrants traveled to South America and Australia as well as to the United States. Yet more than 70 percent of all European immigrants chose North America as their destination. (See "Global Comparison," page 513.)

At first, the largest number of immigrants to the United States came from the British Isles and from German-speaking lands. The vast majority of immigrants were white; Asians accounted for fewer than one million immigrants, and other people of color numbered even fewer. Yet ingrained racial prejudices increasingly influenced the country's perception of immigration patterns. One of the classic formulations of the history of European immigration divided immigrants into two distinct waves that have been called the "old" and the "new" immigration. According to this theory, before 1880 the majority of immigrants came from northern and western Europe. After 1880, the pattern shifted, with more and more

What kinds of work did people do in industrial America?	What steps did workers take to organize in the 1870s and 1880s?	How did industrialization transform home life and leisure?	How did cities respond to the challenges of growth?	Conclusion: Who built the cities?

Immigrants: foreign-born and children of foreign or mixed parentage; by county

- Less than 10%
- 10% to 25%
- 25% to 50%
- 50% to 75%
- More than 75%
- N.Y. 2,748,011 Total foreign-born population in 1910

MAP 19.2 ■ The Impact of Immigration, to 1910
Immigration flowed in all directions—south from Canada, north from Mexico and Latin America, east from Asia to Seattle and San Francisco, and west from Europe to East Coast port cities, including Boston and New York.

▶ FOR MORE HELP ANALYZING THIS MAP, see the map activity for this chapter in the Online Study Guide at bedfordstmartins.com/roarkunderstanding.

ships carrying passengers from southern and eastern Europe. Implicit in the distinction was an invidious comparison between "old" pioneer settlers and "new" unskilled proletarians. Yet this sweeping generalization spoke more to perception than to reality. In fact, many of the earlier immigrants from Ireland, Germany, and Scandinavia came not as settlers or farmers, but as wage laborers, much like the Italians and Slavs who followed them.

The "new" immigration resulted from a number of factors. Improved economic conditions in western Europe coupled with increased immigration to Australia and Canada slowed the flow of immigrants coming into the United States from northern and western Europe. At the same time, economic depression in southern Italy, the persecution of Jews in eastern Europe, and a general desire to avoid conscription into the Russian army led many people from southern and eastern Europe to move to the United States. The need of America's industries for cheap, unskilled labor during prosperous years also stimulated immigration.

Steamship companies courted immigrants with low fares. By the 1880s, the price of a ticket from Liverpool had dropped to less than $25. Would-be immigrants eager for information about the United States relied on letters from friends and relatives, advertisements, and word of mouth—sources that were not always dependable or truthful. No wonder people left for the United States believing, as one Italian immigrant observed, "that if they were ever fortunate enough to reach America, they would fall into a pile of manure and get up brushing the diamonds out of their hair."

CHAPTER LOCATOR | Why did American cities grow so fast in the late nineteenth century?

512 CHAPTER 19
THE GROWTH OF AMERICA'S CITIES, 1870–1900

European Emigration, 1870–1890

A comparison of European emigrants and their destinations between 1870 and 1890 shows that emigrants from Germany and the British Isles (including England, Ireland, Scotland, and Wales) formed the largest group of out-migrants. The United States, which took in 63 percent of these emigrants, was by far the most popular destination. After 1890, the origin of European emigrants would tilt south and east, with Italians and eastern Europeans growing in number. Argentina proved a particularly popular destination for Italian emigrants, who found the climate and geography to their liking. What factors might account for why Europeans immigrated to the port cities of the eastern United States rather than to South America or Australia?

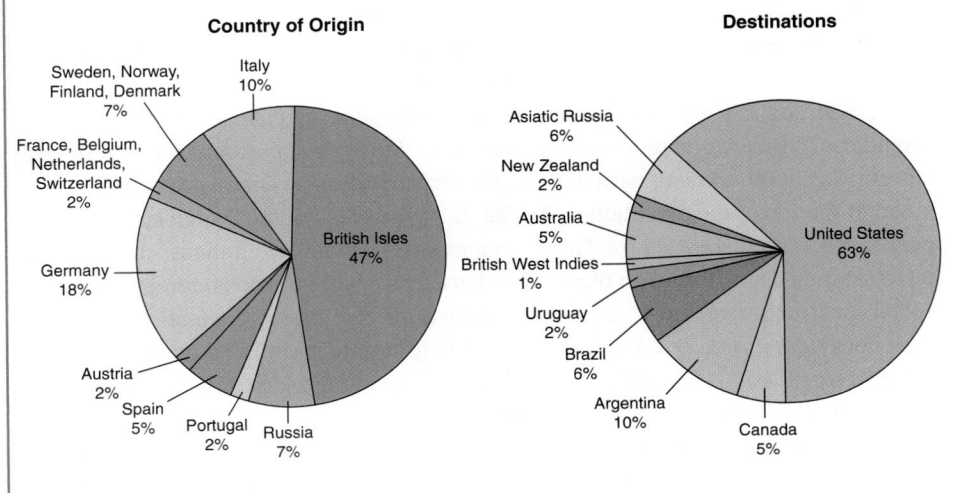

Most of the newcomers stayed in the nation's cities. By 1900, almost two-thirds of the country's immigrant population resided in cities, many of the immigrants being too poor to move on. Although the foreign-born population rarely outnumbered the native-born population, taken together immigrants and their American-born children did constitute a majority, particularly in the nation's largest cities: Philadelphia, 55 percent; Boston, 66 percent; Chicago, 75 percent; and New York City, an amazing 80 percent in 1900.

Not all the newcomers came to stay. Perhaps eight million European immigrants—most of them young men—worked for a year or a season and then returned to their homelands. Immigration officers called these immigrants, many of them Italians, "birds of passage" because they followed a regular pattern of migration to and from the United States. By 1900, almost 75 percent of the new immigrants were young, single men. Women generally had less access to funds for travel and faced tighter family control. For these reasons, women most often came to the United States as wives, mothers, or daughters, not as single wage laborers. Only among the Irish did women immigrants outnumber men by a small margin.

Jews from eastern Europe most often came with their families and came to stay. Beginning in the 1880s, a wave of violent pogroms, or persecutions, in Russia and Poland prompted the departure of more than a million Jews in the next two decades. Most of the Jewish immigrants settled in the port cities of the East, creating distinct ethnic enclaves.

| What kinds of work did people do in industrial America? | What steps did workers take to organize in the 1870s and 1880s? | How did industrialization transform home life and leisure? | How did cities respond to the challenges of growth? | Conclusion: Who built the cities? |

CHRONOLOGY

1880s
- Immigration from southern and eastern Europe rises.

1890
- Jacob Riis publishes *How the Other Half Lives*, documenting in photographs the lives of tenement dwellers.

1890s
- African American migration from the South begins.

1892
- Ellis Island, a facility for processing new immigrants arriving in New York City, opens.

1896
- President Grover Cleveland vetoes immigrant literacy test.

Racism and the Cry for Immigration Restriction

Ethnic diversity and racism played a role in dividing skilled workers (those with a craft or specialized ability) from unskilled workers (those who supplied muscle or tended machines). As industrialists mechanized to replace skilled workers with lower-paid unskilled labor, they drew on immigrants, particularly those from southern and eastern Europe, who had come to the United States in the hope of bettering their lives. Skilled workers, frequently members of older immigrant groups, criticized the newcomers. Throughout the nineteenth century and into the twentieth, many Americans viewed ethnic and even religious differences as racial characteristics, referring to the Polish or the Jewish "race." Americans judged "new" immigrants of southern and eastern European "races" as inferior to those of Anglo-Teutonic "stock." Each wave of newcomers was deemed somehow inferior to the established residents.

In addition, the new immigrants brought their own religious and racial prejudices to the United States and also absorbed the popular prejudices of American culture. Social Darwinism, with its strongly racist overtones, decreed that whites stood at the top of the evolutionary ladder. But who was "white"? Skin color supposedly served as a marker for the "new" immigrants—"swarthy" Italians; dark-haired, olive-skinned Jews. But even blond, blue-eyed Poles were not considered white. The social construction of "race" is nowhere more apparent than in the testimony of an Irish dockworker who boasted that he hired only "white men," a category that he insisted excluded "Poles and Italians." For the new immigrants, Americanization and assimilation would prove inextricably part of becoming "white."

For African Americans, the cities of the North promised not just economic opportunity but also an end to institutionalized segregation and persecution. Jim Crow laws—restrictions that segregated blacks—became common throughout the South in the decades following Reconstruction. Intimidation and lynching terrorized blacks throughout the South (see chapter 18). "To die from the bite of frost is far more glorious than at the hands of a mob," proclaimed the *Defender*, Chicago's largest African American newspaper. In the 1890s, many blacks moved north, settling for the most part in the growing cities. Racism relegated them to poor jobs and substandard living conditions, but by 1900 New York, Philadelphia, and Chicago had the largest black communities in the nation.

On the West Coast, Asian immigrants became scapegoats of the changing economy. After California's gold rush, many Chinese who had come to work "on the gold mountain" found jobs on the country's transcontinental railroads. When the railroad work ended, they took work other groups shunned, including domestic service. But hard times in the 1870s made them a target for disgruntled workers. Prohibited from owning land, the Chinese migrated to the cities. The Chinese population of San Francisco continued to grow until passage of the Chinese Exclusion Act in 1882 (see chapter 17). For the first time in the nation's history, U.S. law excluded an immigrant group on the basis of race. In contrast, the nation's small Japanese community of about 3,000 expanded rapidly after 1890, until pressures to keep out all Asians led in 1910 to the creation of an immigration station at Angel Island in San Francisco Bay. Asian immigrants were detained there, sometimes for months, and many were deported as "undesirables."

On the East Coast, the volume of immigration from Europe in the last two decades of the century proved unprecedented. In 1888 alone, more than half a million Europeans landed in America, 75 percent of them in New York City. The Statue of Liberty, a gift from the people of France erected in 1886, stood sentinel

CHAPTER LOCATOR | Why did American cities grow so fast in the late nineteenth century?

514 CHAPTER 19 THE GROWTH OF AMERICA'S CITIES, 1870–1900

in the harbor. The tide of immigrants to New York City soon swamped the immigration office at Castle Garden in lower Manhattan. A new facility opened on **Ellis Island** in New York harbor in 1892. Its overcrowded halls became the gateway to the United States for millions.

To many Americans, the "new" immigrants seemed impossible to assimilate. "These people are not Americans," editorialized the popular journal *Public Opinion*, "they are the very scum and offal of Europe." Terence V. Powderly, head of the broadly inclusive Knights of Labor, complained that the newcomers "herded together like animals and lived like beasts." Blue-blooded Yankees led by Senator Henry Cabot Lodge of Massachusetts formed an unlikely alliance with organized labor to press for immigration restrictions. In 1896, Congress approved a literacy test for immigrants, but President Grover Cleveland promptly vetoed it. "It is said," the president reminded Congress, "that the quality of recent immigration is undesirable. The time is quite within recent memory when the same thing was said of immigrants, who, with their descendants, are now numbered among our best citizens." Cleveland's veto forestalled immigration restriction but did not stop anti-immigrant forces from pressing for restrictions until they achieved their goal in the 1920s (see chapter 23).

The Social Geography of the City

During the Gilded Age, cities experienced demographic and technological changes that greatly altered the social geography of the city. Cleveland, Ohio, provides a good example. In the 1870s, Cleveland was a small city in both population and area. Oil magnate John D. Rockefeller could, and often did, walk from his large brick house to his office downtown. On his way, he passed the small homes of his clerks and other middle-class families. Behind these homes ran alleys crowded with the dwellings of Cleveland's working class. Farther out, on the shores of Lake Erie, close to the factories and foundries, clustered the shanties of the city's poorest laborers.

Within two decades, the coming of mass transit had transformed this walking city. In its place emerged a central business district surrounded by concentric rings of residences organized by ethnicity and income. First the horsecar in the 1870s and then the electric streetcar in the 1880s made it possible for those who could afford the fare to work downtown and live in the "cool green rim" of the city, with its single-family homes, lawns, gardens, and trees. Social segregation—the separation of rich and poor, and of ethnic and old-stock Americans—was one of the major social changes engendered by the rise of the industrial metropolis, evident not only in Cleveland but in cities across the nation.

Race and ethnicity affected the way cities evolved. Newcomers to the nation's cities faced hostility and not surprisingly sought out their kin and country folk as they struggled to survive. Distinct ethnic neighborhoods often formed around a synagogue or church. Blacks typically experienced the greatest residential segregation, but every large city had its ethnic enclaves where English was rarely spoken.

Poverty, crowding, dirt, and disease constituted the daily reality of New York City's immigrant poor—a plight documented by photojournalist Jacob Riis in his best-selling book *How the Other Half Lives* (1890). Riis's photographs opened the nation's eyes to conditions in the city's slums. Many middle-class Americans worried equally about the excesses of the wealthy. They feared the class antagonism fueled by the growing inequality so visible in the nation's cities and shared

Ellis Island

▶ Immigration facility opened in 1892 in New York harbor that processed new immigrants coming into New York City. In the late nineteenth century, some 75 percent of European immigrants to America came through New York.

What kinds of work did people do in industrial America?

What steps did workers take to organize in the 1870s and 1880s?

How did industrialization transform home life and leisure?

How did cities respond to the challenges of growth?

Conclusion: Who built the cities?

515

The gap between the rich and the poor documented in Jacob Riis's best seller, *How the Other Half Lives*, is underscored here by juxtaposing the photographs of two women. Riis took the photograph of a "scrub" or washerwoman (left) in one of the notorious Police Station lodging houses, the shelters of last resort for the city's poor. On the right is Alice Vanderbilt costumed as the "Spirit of Electricity" for her sister-in-law Alva Vanderbilt's costume ball in 1883. Washerwoman: Museum of the City of New York; Vanderbilt: Collection of the New-York Historical Society.

▶ FOR MORE HELP ANALYZING THIS IMAGE, see the visual activity for this chapter in the Online Study Guide at bedfordstmartins.com/roarkunderstanding.

Riis's view that "the real danger to society comes not only from the tenements, but from the ill-spent wealth which reared them."

Such excesses were nowhere more visible than in the lifestyle of the Vanderbilts. With a fortune amassed in the railroads, the Vanderbilts spent their money on residences that sought to rival the palaces of Europe. In 1883, Alva (Mrs. William) Vanderbilt launched herself into New York society by throwing a costume party so lavish that not even old New York society, which turned up its nose at the nouveau riche, could resist an invitation. Her sister-in-law Alice Vanderbilt stole the show by appearing as that miraculous new invention, the electric light, in a white satin evening dress studded with diamonds (see photo). The *New York World* speculated that Alva Vanderbilt's party cost more than a quarter of a million dollars (more than $4 million today).

Such ostentatious displays of wealth became especially alarming when they were coupled with disdain for the well-being of ordinary people. When a reporter in 1882 asked William Vanderbilt whether he considered the public good when running his railroads, he shot back, "The public be damned." The fear that America had become a society ruled by the rich gained credence from the fact that the wealthiest 1 percent of the population owned more than half the real and personal property in the country.

> ## QUICK REVIEW

What global trends were reflected in the growth of American cities in the late nineteenth century?

CHAPTER LOCATOR | Why did American cities grow so fast in the late nineteenth century?

516 CHAPTER 19
THE GROWTH OF AMERICA'S CITIES, 1870–1900

Sweatshop Worker Sweatshop workers endured crowded and often dangerous conditions. Young working girls earned low wages but prided themselves on their independence. Notice the young woman's stylish hairdo, white shirtwaist, and necklace. George Eastman House.

What kinds of work did people do in industrial America?

THE NUMBER OF INDUSTRIAL WAGEWORKERS in the United States exploded in the second half of the nineteenth century, more than tripling from 5.3 million in 1860 to 17.4 million in 1900. These workers toiled in a variety of settings. Many skilled workers and artisans still earned a living in small workshops. But with the rise of corporate capitalism, large factories, mills, and mines increasingly dotted the landscape. The best way to get a sense of the diversity of workers and workplaces is to look at the industrial nation at work.

America's Diverse Workers

Common laborers formed the backbone of the American labor force. These "human machines" stood at the bottom of the country's economic ladder and generally came from the most recent immigrant groups. Initially, the Irish wielded the picks and shovels that built American cities, but by the turn of the twentieth century, as the Irish bettered their lot, Slavs and Italians took their place.

At the opposite end of labor's hierarchy stood skilled craftsmen like iron puddler James J. Davis, a Welsh immigrant who worked in the Pennsylvania mills. The job of iron puddler required intelligence and experience, and Davis drew good wages, up to $7 a day, when there was work. But most industry and manufacturing

| What kinds of work did people do in industrial America? | What steps did workers take to organize in the 1870s and 1880s? | How did industrialization transform home life and leisure? | How did cities respond to the challenges of growth? | Conclusion: Who built the cities? |

CHRONOLOGY

1860
- There are 5.3 million industrial workers in the United States.

1880s
- The number of foreign-born mill workers doubles.
- Mill workers in Fall River, Massachusetts, work twelve hours a day, six days a week, for about $1 a day.

1890
- Typical male worker earns $500 a year, equivalent to about $12,000 a year today.
- Twenty-five percent of married African American women work outside the home.
- Three percent of married white women work outside the home.

1900
- There are 17.4 million industrial workers in the United States.

work in the nineteenth century remained seasonal; few workers could count on year-round pay. In addition, two major depressions only twenty years apart, beginning in 1873 and 1893, spelled unemployment and hardship. In an era before unemployment insurance, workers' compensation, or old-age pensions, even the best worker could not guarantee security for his family. "The fear of ending in the poorhouse is one of the terrors that dog a man through life," Davis confessed.

Skilled workers like Davis wielded power on the shop floor. Employers attempted to limit workers' control by replacing people with machines, breaking down skilled work into ever-smaller tasks that could be performed by unskilled factory operatives. New England's textile mills provide a classic example of the effects of mechanized factory labor in the nineteenth century. Mary, a weaver at the mills in Fall River, Massachusetts, went to work in the 1880s at the age of twelve. By then, mechanization of the looms had reduced the job of the weaver to watching for breaks in the thread. "At first the noise is fierce, and you have to breathe the cotton all the time, but you get used to it," Mary told a reporter from the *Independent* magazine. "When the bobbin flies out and a girl gets hurt, you can't hear her shout—not if she just screams, you can't. She's got to wait, 'till you see her. . . . Lots of us is deaf."

During the 1880s, the number of foreign-born mill workers almost doubled. At Fall River, Mary and her Scots-Irish family resented the new immigrants. "The Polaks learn weavin' quick," she remarked. "They just as soon live on nothin' and work like that. But it won't do 'em much good for all they'll make out of it." Employers encouraged racial and ethnic antagonism because it inhibited labor organization.

The majority of factory operatives in the textile mills were young, unmarried women like Mary. They worked from six in the morning to six at night six days a week, and they took home about $1 a day. The seasonal nature of the work also drove wages down. "Like as not your mill will 'shut down' three months," and "some weeks you only get two or three days' work," Mary recounted.

Mechanization transformed the garment industry as well. With the introduction of the foot-pedaled sewing machine in the 1850s and the use of mechanical cloth-cutting knives in the 1870s, independent tailors were replaced with workers hired by contractors to sew pieces of cloth into suits and dresses. Working in sweatshops, small rooms hired for the season or even in the contractor's own tenement, women and children formed an important segment of garment workers. Discriminated against in the marketplace, where they earned less than men, women generally worked for wages only eight to ten years, until they married.

The Family Economy: Women and Children

In 1890, the typical male worker earned $500 a year, about $12,000 in today's dollars. Many working-class families, whether native-born or immigrant, lived in or near poverty, their economic survival dependent on the contributions of all family members, regardless of sex or age. The paid and unpaid work of women and children proved essential for family survival and economic advancement.

In the cities, boys as young as six years old plied their trades as bootblacks and newsboys. Often working under an adult contractor, these children earned as little as fifty cents a day. Many of them were homeless—orphaned or cast off by their families. "We wuz six, and we ain't got no father," a child of twelve told reporter Jacob Riis. "Some of us had to go."

CHAPTER LOCATOR | Why did American cities grow so fast in the late nineteenth century?

518 CHAPTER 19
THE GROWTH OF AMERICA'S CITIES, 1870–1900

Bootblacks

The faces and hands of the two bootblacks shown here with a third boy on a New York City street in 1896 testify to their grimy trade. Boys as young as six worked on city streets as bootblacks and newsboys. For these child workers, education was a luxury they could not afford. Alice Austin photo, Staten Island Historical Society.

Child labor increased decade by decade after 1870. The percentage of children under fifteen engaged in paid labor did not drop until after World War I. The number of women workers also rose sharply, with their most common occupation changing slowly from domestic service to factory work and then to office work. Between 1870 and 1890, the number of women working for wages in nonagricultural occupations more than doubled (**Figure 19.1**, page 520). Women's working patterns varied considerably according to race and ethnicity. White married women, even among the working class, rarely worked for wages outside the home. In 1890, only 3 percent were employed. Black women, married and unmarried, worked for wages in much greater numbers. The 1890 census showed that 25 percent of married African American women were employed, often as domestics in the houses of white families.

White-Collar Workers: Managers, "Typewriters," and Salesclerks

In the late nineteenth century, business expansion and consolidation led to a managerial revolution, creating a new class of white-collar workers who worked in offices and stores. As skilled workers saw their crafts replaced by mechanization, some moved into management positions. "The middle class is becoming a salaried class," a writer for the *Independent* magazine observed, "and is rapidly losing the economic and moral independence of former days." As large business organizations consolidated, corporate development separated management from

| What kinds of work did people do in industrial America? | What steps did workers take to organize in the 1870s and 1880s? | How did industrialization transform home life and leisure? | How did cities respond to the challenges of growth? | Conclusion: Who built the cities? |

519

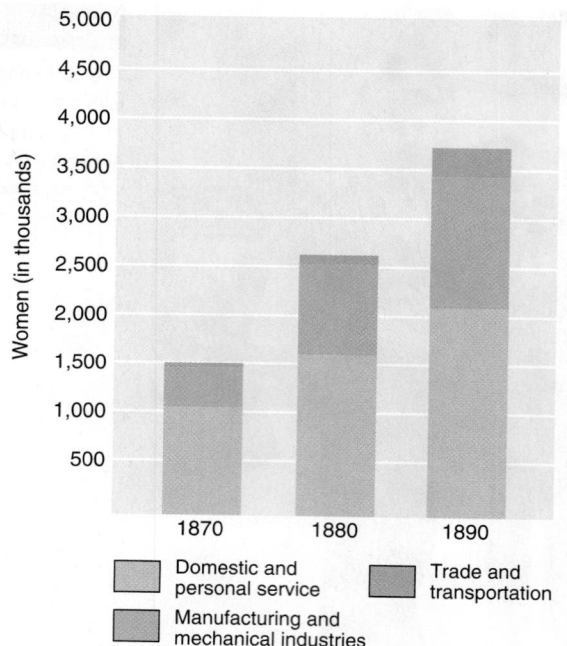

FIGURE 19.1 ■ Women and Work, 1870–1890

In 1870, close to 1.5 million women worked in nonagricultural occupations. By 1890, that number had more than doubled to 3.7 million. More and more women sought work in manufacturing and mechanical industries, although domestic service still constituted the largest employment arena for women.

ownership, and the job of directing the firm became the province of salaried executives and managers, the majority of whom were white men drawn from the 8 percent of Americans who held high school diplomas.

Until late in the century, when engineering schools began to supply recruits, many skilled workers moved from the shop floor to positions of considerable responsibility. William "Billy" Jones, the son of a Welsh immigrant, was one such worker. Beginning as an apprentice at the age of ten, Jones rose through the ranks to become plant superintendent at Andrew Carnegie's Pittsburgh steelworks in 1872.

The new white-collar workforce also included women "typewriters" and salesclerks. In the decades after the Civil War, as businesses became larger and more far-flung, the need for more elaborate and exact records, as well as the greater volume of correspondence, led to the hiring of more office workers. Mechanization transformed business as it had industry and manufacturing. The adding machine, the cash register, and the typewriter came into general use in the 1880s. Employers seeking literate workers soon turned to women. Educated men had many other career choices, but for middle-class white women, secretarial work constituted one of very few areas where they could put their literacy to use for wages.

Sylvie Thygeson was typical of the young women who went to work as secretaries. When her father died in 1884, Thygeson went to work as a country schoolteacher at the age of sixteen, after graduating high school. Realizing that teaching school did not pay a living wage, she mastered typing and stenography and found

CHAPTER LOCATOR | Why did American cities grow so fast in the late nineteenth century?

520 CHAPTER 19
THE GROWTH OF AMERICA'S CITIES, 1870–1900

work as a secretary to help support her family. According to her account, she made "a fabulous sum of money." Nevertheless, she gave up her job after a few years when she met and married her husband.

By the 1890s, secretarial work was the overwhelming choice of native-born white women, who constituted more than 90 percent of the female clerical force. Not only considered more genteel than factory work or domestic labor, office work also meant more money for shorter hours. Boston's clerical workers made more than $6 a week in 1883, compared with less than $5 for women working in manufacturing.

As a new consumer culture came to dominate American urban life in the late nineteenth century, department stores offered another employment opportunity for women in the cities. Stores such as Macy's in New York, Wanamaker's in Philadelphia, and Marshall Field in Chicago stood as monuments to the material promise of the era. Within these palaces of consumption, cash girls, stock clerks, and wrappers earned as little as $3 a week, while at the top of the scale, buyers like Belle Cushman of the fancy goods department at Macy's earned $25 a week. Salesclerks counted themselves a cut above factory workers. Their work was neither dirty nor dangerous, and even when they earned less than factory workers, they felt a sense of superiority.

Clerical Worker

A stenographer takes dictation in an 1890s office. In the 1880s, with the invention of the typewriter, many women put their literacy skills to use in the nation's offices. Brown Brothers.

QUICK REVIEW

How did business expansion and consolidation change workers' occupations in the late nineteenth century?

| What kinds of work did people do in industrial America? | What steps did workers take to organize in the 1870s and 1880s? | How did industrialization transform home life and leisure? | How did cities respond to the challenges of growth? | Conclusion: Who built the cities? |

Pictures of the devastation caused in Pittsburgh during the strike shocked many Americans. When militiamen fired on striking workers, killing more than twenty strikers, the mob retaliated by destroying a two-mile area along the track. Carnegie Library of Pittsburgh.

What steps did workers take to organize in the 1870s and 1880s?

BY THE LATE NINETEENTH CENTURY, industrial workers were losing ground in the workplace. In the fierce competition to reduce prices and cut costs, industrialists like Andrew Carnegie invested heavily in new machinery that enabled them to replace skilled workers with unskilled labor. The erosion of skills and the redefinition of labor as mere "machine tending" left the worker with a growing sense of individual helplessness that served as a spur to collective action. In the 1870s and 1880s, labor organizations grew, and the Knights of Labor and the American Federation of Labor attracted workers. Convinced of the inequity of the wage-labor system, labor organizers spoke eloquently of abolishing class privileges and monopoly.

The Great Railroad Strike of 1877

Great Railroad Strike
▶ Strike that began in 1877 with a strike of West Virginia railroad brakemen and quickly spread to include roughly 600,000 workers. Responding to pressure from railroad owners and managers, President Rutherford B. Hayes used federal troops to break the strike. Despite the strike's failure, it led to a surge in union membership.

Economic depression following the panic of 1873 threw as many as three million people out of work. Those who were lucky enough to keep their jobs watched as pay cuts eroded their wages until they could no longer feed their families. In the summer of 1877, the Baltimore and Ohio (B&O) Railroad announced a 10 percent wage cut at the same time it declared a 10 percent dividend to its stockholders. Angry brakemen in West Virginia, whose wages had already fallen from $70 to $30 a month, walked out on strike.

The West Virginia brakemen's strike touched off the **Great Railroad Strike** of 1877, a nationwide uprising that spread rapidly to Pittsburgh and Chicago, St. Louis and San Francisco (**Map 19.3**). Within a few days, nearly 100,000 railroad workers walked off the job. An estimated 500,000 laborers soon joined the train workers. In Reading, Pennsylvania, militiamen refused to fire on the strikers,

CHAPTER LOCATOR | Why did American cities grow so fast in the late nineteenth century?

Strike activity

MAP 19.3 ■ The Great Railroad Strike of 1877
Starting in West Virginia and Pennsylvania, the strike spread as far north as Albany, New York, and as far west as San Francisco, bringing rail traffic to a standstill. Called the Great Uprising, the strike heralded the beginning of a new era of working-class protest and trade union organization.

CHRONOLOGY

1869
– Knights of Labor is founded.

1873
– Panic on Wall Street touches off depression.

1877
– In Great Railroad Strike, more than 600,000 workers across the country go on strike.

1878
– Knights of Labor launches a campaign to organize all workers.

1886
– American Federation of Labor (AFL) is founded to represent skilled workers.
– Haymarket bombing in Chicago deals a death blow to the Knights of Labor.

saying, "We may be militiamen, but we are workmen first." Rail traffic ground to a halt; the nation lay paralyzed.

Violence erupted as the strike spread. In Pittsburgh, militia brought in from Philadelphia opened fire on a crowd, killing twenty people. Angry workers retaliated by reducing an area two miles long beside the tracks to rubble. Before the day ended, twenty more workers had been shot, and the railroad had sustained property damage totaling $2 million.

Within eight days, the governors of nine states, acting at the prompting of the railroad owners and managers, defined the strike as an "insurrection" and called for federal troops. President Rutherford B. Hayes, after hesitating briefly, called out the army. By the time the troops arrived, the violence had run its course. Federal troops did not shoot a single striker in 1877. But they struck a blow against labor by acting as strikebreakers—opening rail traffic, protecting nonstriking "scab" train crews, and maintaining peace along the line. In three weeks, the strike was over.

Although many middle-class Americans initially sympathized with the conditions that led to the strike, they condemned the strikers for the violence and property damage that occurred. The *Independent* magazine offered the following advice on how to deal with "rioters": "If the club of a policeman, knocking out the brains of the rioter, will answer then well and good; but if it does not promptly meet the exigency, then bullets and bayonets . . . constitutes [*sic*] the one remedy and one duty of the hour."

"The strikes have been put down by force," President Hayes noted in his diary on August 5. "But now for the real remedy. Can't something be done by education of the strikers, by judicious control of the capitalists, by wise general policy to end or diminish the evil? The railroad strikers, as a rule, are good men,

| What kinds of work did people do in industrial America? | **What steps did workers take to organize in the 1870s and 1880s?** | How did industrialization transform home life and leisure? | How did cities respond to the challenges of growth? | Conclusion: Who built the cities? |

523

sober, intelligent, and industrious." While Hayes acknowledged the workers' grievances, most businessmen and industrialists did not and fought the idea of labor unions. For their part, workers quickly recognized that they held little power individually and flocked to join unions. As labor leader Samuel Gompers noted, the strike served as an alarm bell to labor "that sounded a ringing message of hope to us all."

The Knights of Labor and the American Federation of Labor

The **Knights of Labor**, the first mass organization of America's working class, proved the chief beneficiary of labor's newfound consciousness. Founded in 1869, the Knights were a secret society that envisioned a "universal brotherhood" of all workers, from common laborers to master craftsmen. Secrecy and ritual served to bind Knights together at the same time that it discouraged company spies and protected members from reprisals.

Although the Knights played no active role in the 1877 railroad strike, membership swelled as a result of the growing interest in labor organizing that followed the strike. In 1878, the Knights abandoned secrecy and launched an ambitious campaign to organize workers regardless of skill, sex, race, or nationality. The Knights attempted to bridge the boundaries of ethnicity, gender, ideology, race, and occupation. Leonora Barry served as general investigator for women's work from 1886 to 1890, helping the Knights recruit teachers, waitresses, housewives, and domestics along with factory and sweatshop workers. Women comprised perhaps 20 percent of the membership. The Knights also included African Americans, organizing more than 95,000 black workers. That the Knights of Labor often fell short of its goals to unify the working class proved less surprising than the scope of its efforts.

Under the direction of Grand Master Workman **Terence V. Powderly**, the Knights became the dominant force in labor during the 1880s. The organization advocated a kind of workers' democracy that embraced reforms including public ownership of the railroads, an income tax, equal pay for women workers, and the abolition of child labor. The Knights called for one big union to create a cooperative commonwealth that would supplant the wage system and remove class distinctions. Only the "parasitic" members of society—gamblers, stockbrokers, lawyers, bankers, and liquor dealers—were denied membership.

In theory, the Knights of Labor opposed strikes. Powderly championed arbitration and preferred to use boycotts. But in practice, much of the organization's appeal came from a successful strike the Knights mounted in 1885 against railroads controlled by Jay Gould. Despite the reservations of its leadership, the Knights became a militant labor organization that won support from working people with the slogan "An injury to one is the concern of all."

The Knights of Labor was not without rivals. Many skilled workers belonged to craft unions organized by trade. Trade unionists spurned the broad reform goals of the Knights and focused on workplace issues such as higher pay and better working conditions. **Samuel Gompers** promoted what he called "pure and simple" unionism. Gompers founded the Organized Trades and Labor Unions in 1881 and reorganized it in 1886 into the **American Federation of Labor (AFL)**, which coordinated the activities of craft unions throughout the United States.

Knights of Labor
▶ The first mass organization of America's working class. Founded in 1869, the Knights of Labor attempted to bridge the boundaries of ethnicity, gender, ideology, race, and occupation to build a brotherhood of all workers. The 1886 Haymarket bombing contributed to the Knights' decline and the ascendancy of trade unionism.

Terence V. Powderly
▶ Leader of the Knights of Labor during the 1880s. Under his leadership, the Knights became the dominant force in labor during the decade. Powderly's Knights called for one big union to create a cooperative commonwealth that would supplant the wage system and remove class distinctions.

Samuel Gompers
▶ Labor organizer who founded the Organized Trades and Labor Unions in 1881 and reorganized it in 1886 into the American Federation of Labor (AFL). Gompers organized skilled workers and focused on workplace issues such as wages and working conditions.

American Federation of Labor (AFL)
▶ Organization created by Samuel Gompers in 1886 that coordinated the activities of craft unions throughout the United States. Under Gompers's leadership, the AFL worked to achieve immediate benefits for skilled workers. In its early days, the AFL attracted fewer members than the Knights of Labor, but in time its approach to unionism came to prevail.

CHAPTER LOCATOR | Why did American cities grow so fast in the late nineteenth century?

524 CHAPTER 19
THE GROWTH OF AMERICA'S CITIES, 1870–1900

Gompers at first drew few converts. The AFL had only 138,000 members in 1886, compared with 730,000 for the Knights of Labor. But events soon brought down the Knights, and Gompers's brand of unionism came to prevail.

Haymarket and the Specter of Labor Radicalism

While the AFL and the Knights of Labor competed for members, more-radical labor groups, including socialists and anarchists, believed that reform was futile and called instead for social revolution. Both groups, sensitive to criticism that they preferred revolution in theory to improvements here and now, rallied around the popular issue of the eight-hour day.

Since the 1840s, labor had sought to end the twelve-hour workday, which was standard in industry and manufacturing. By the mid-1880s, it seemed clear to many workers that labor shared too little in the new prosperity of the decade, and pressure mounted for the eight-hour day. Labor rallied to the popular issue and launched major rallies in cities across the nation. Supporters of the movement set May 1, 1886, as the date for a nationwide general strike in support of the eight-hour workday.

All factions of the labor movement came together in Chicago on May Day. A group of labor radicals led by anarchist Albert Parsons, a *Mayflower* descendant, and August Spies, a German socialist, spearheaded the eight-hour movement in Chicago. Chicago's Knights of Labor rallied to the cause even though Terence Powderly and the union's national leadership refused to endorse the movement for shorter hours. Samuel Gompers was on hand, too, to lead the city's trade unionists, although he privately urged the AFL assemblies not to participate in the general strike.

Gompers's skilled workers were labor's elite. Many still worked in small shops where negotiations between workers and employers took place in an environment tempered by personal relationships. The AFL's skilled workers stood in sharp contrast to the dispossessed workers out on strike across town at Chicago's McCormick reaper works. There strikers watched helplessly as the company brought in strikebreakers to take their jobs and marched the "scabs" to work under the protection of the Chicago police and private security guards.

During the May Day rally, 45,000 workers paraded peacefully down Michigan Avenue in support of the eight-hour day. Trouble came two days later, when strikers attacked strikebreakers outside the McCormick works and police opened fire, killing or wounding six men. Angry radicals called on workers to "arm yourselves and appear in full force" at a rally in Haymarket Square.

"The Chicago Riot"

Inflammatory pamphlets like this one published in the wake of the Haymarket bombing presented a one-sided view of the incident and stirred public passion. Chicago Historical Society.

> ▶ FOR MORE HELP ANALYZING THIS IMAGE, see the visual activity for this chapter in the Online Study Guide at bedfordstmartins.com/roarkunderstanding.

| What kinds of work did people do in industrial America? | **What steps did workers take to organize in the 1870s and 1880s?** | How did industrialization transform home life and leisure? | How did cities respond to the challenges of growth? | Conclusion: Who built the cities? |

525

On the evening of May 4, the turnout at Haymarket was disappointing. No more than two or three thousand gathered to hear Spies, Parsons, and the other speakers. Mayor Carter Harrison, known as a friend of labor, mingled conspicuously in the crowd, pronounced the meeting peaceable, and went home. A short time later, police captain John "Blackjack" Bonfield marched his men into the crowd, by now fewer than three hundred people, and demanded that it disperse. Suddenly, someone threw a bomb into the police ranks. After a moment of stunned silence, the police drew their revolvers. "Fire and kill all you can," shouted a police lieutenant. When the melee ended, seven policemen and an unknown number of other people lay dead. An additional sixty policemen and thirty or forty civilians suffered injuries.

News of the "Haymarket riot" provoked a nationwide convulsion of fear and rage directed at anarchists, labor unions, strikers, immigrants, and the working class in general. Eight men, including Parsons and Spies, went on trial in Chicago. "Convict these men," thundered the state's attorney, Julius S. Grinnell, "make examples of them, hang them, and you save our institutions." Although the state could not link any of the defendants to the **Haymarket bombing**, the jury nevertheless found them all guilty. Four were executed, one committed suicide, and three received prison sentences.

The bomb blast at Haymarket had lasting repercussions. To commemorate the death of the Haymarket martyrs, labor made May 1 an annual international celebration of the worker. But the Haymarket bomb, in the eyes of one observer, proved "a godsend to all enemies of the labor movement." It effectively scotched the eight-hour day movement and dealt a blow to the Knights of Labor, already wracked by internal divisions. With the labor movement under attack, many skilled workers turned to the American Federation of Labor. Gompers's narrow economic strategy made sense at the time and enabled one segment of the workforce—the skilled—to organize effectively and achieve tangible gains. But the nation's unskilled workers remained untouched by the AFL's brand of trade unionism.

Haymarket bombing

▶ May 4, 1886, conflict between labor protesters and police in which both workers and policemen were killed or wounded. The violence began when an unknown person threw a bomb into the ranks of the police assigned to the labor gathering. The incident created a powerful backlash against labor activism.

> ## QUICK REVIEW

What were the long-term effects of the Great Railroad Strike of 1877 and the Haymarket bombing in 1886?

CHAPTER LOCATOR | Why did American cities grow so fast in the late nineteenth century?

526 CHAPTER 19
THE GROWTH OF AMERICA'S CITIES, 1870–1900

How did industrialization transform home life and leisure?

Beach Scene at Coney Island Opened in the 1870s, Coney Island came into its own at the turn of the twentieth century with the development of elaborate amusement parks. It became a symbol of commercialized leisure and mechanical excitement. This fanciful rendering captures the frenetic goings-on. Weekend crowds on the island reportedly reached one million. Library of Congress.

THE GROWTH OF URBAN INDUSTRIALISM not only dramatically altered the workplace but also transformed home and family life and gave rise to new forms of commercialized leisure. Industrialization redefined the very concepts of work and home. Increasingly, men went out to work for wages, while most white married women stayed home, either working in the home without pay—cleaning, cooking, and rearing children—or supervising paid domestic servants who did the housework.

Domesticity and "Domestics"

The separation of the workplace and the home that marked the shift to industrial society led to a new ideology, one that sentimentalized the home and women's role in it. The cultural ideology that dictated woman's place in the home has been called the cult of domesticity, a phrase used to prescribe an ideal of middle-class, white womanhood that dominated the period from 1820 to the end of the nineteenth century (see chapter 11).

The cult of domesticity and the elaboration of the middle-class home led to a major change in patterns of hiring household help. The live-in servant, or domestic, became a fixture in the North, replacing the hired girl of the previous century. (The South continued to rely on black female labor, first slave and later free.) In American cities by 1870, 15 to 30 percent of all households included live-in domestic servants, more than 90 percent of them women. By the mid-nineteenth century, native-born women increasingly took up other work and left domestic service to immigrants.

Servants by all accounts resented the long hours and lack of privacy. "She is liable to be rung up at all hours," one study reported. "Her very meals are not secure from interruption, and even her sleep is not sacred." Domestic service

| What kinds of work did people do in industrial America? | What steps did workers take to organize in the 1870s and 1880s? | **How did industrialization transform home life and leisure?** | How did cities respond to the challenges of growth? | Conclusion: Who built the cities? |

527

1869
– Cincinnati Red Stockings becomes the first professional baseball team. By the 1870s, baseball is the "national pastime" for men.

1870
– Between 15 and 30 percent of urban households employ live-in domestic servants, some 90 percent of them women.

1890s
– Coney Island, New York, becomes one of the largest and most elaborate amusement parks in the country, attracting as many as one million visitors a weekend.

Coney Island
▶ Popular leisure destination for New York City's residents, particularly its working class. In the 1890s, Coney Island became the site of some of the largest and most elaborate amusement parks in the country. Coney Island embodied the commercialization of entertainment in the late nineteenth century.

became the occupation of last resort, a "hard and lonely life" in the words of one servant girl.

For women of the white middle class, domestics were a boon, freeing them from household drudgery and giving them more time to spend with their children or to pursue club work or reform. Thus, while domestic service supported the cult of domesticity, it created, for those women who could afford it, opportunities to expand their horizons outside the home in areas such as women's clubs and the temperance and suffrage movements.

Cheap Amusements

Growing class divisions manifested themselves in patterns of leisure as well as in work and home life. The poor and working class took their leisure, not in the crowded tenements that housed their families, but increasingly in the cities' new dance halls, music houses, ballparks, and amusement arcades, which by the 1890s formed a familiar part of the urban landscape.

The growing anonymity of urban industrial society posed a challenge to traditional rituals of courtship. Adolescent working girls no longer met prospective husbands only through their families. Fleeing crowded tenements, the young sought each other's company in dance halls and other commercial retreats. Young workingwomen, who rarely could afford more than trolley fare when they went out, counted on being "treated" by men, a transaction that often implied sexual payback. Young women's need to negotiate sexual encounters if they wished to participate in commercial amusements blurred the line between respectability and promiscuity and made the dance halls a favorite target of reformers who feared they lured girls into prostitution.

For men, baseball became a national pastime in the 1870s, one force in urban life capable of uniting a city across class lines. Cincinnati mounted the first entirely paid team, the Red Stockings, in 1869. Soon professional teams proliferated in cities across the nation, and Mark Twain hailed baseball as "the very symbol, the outward and visible expression, of the drive and push and rush and struggle of the raging, tearing, booming nineteenth century."

The increasing commercialization of entertainment in the late nineteenth century can best be seen at **Coney Island**, New York. Long a center for popular amusements, in the 1890s Coney Island was transformed into the site of some of the largest and most elaborate amusement parks in the country. Promoter George Tilyou built Steeplechase Park in 1897, advertising "10 hours of fun for 10 cents." With its mechanical thrills and fun-house laughs, the amusement park encouraged behavior that one schoolteacher aptly described as "everyone with the brakes off." By 1900, as many as a million New Yorkers flocked to Coney Island on any given weekend, making the amusement park the unofficial capital of a new mass culture.

> **QUICK REVIEW**

How did urban industrialism shape the world of leisure?

CHAPTER LOCATOR | Why did American cities grow so fast in the late nineteenth century?

528 CHAPTER 19
THE GROWTH OF AMERICA'S CITIES, 1870–1900

Central Park Lake

Looking south across Central Park Lake, this photograph shows boaters and well-dressed New Yorkers taking their leisure on Bethesda Terrace. The bronze figure in the center of the photograph, *Angel of the Waters*, was the work of sculptor Emma Stebbins. Calvert Vaux, who along with Frederick Law Olmsted designed the landscaping, considered Bethesda Terrace the "drawing room of the park." People of all ages, from children floating toy sailboats (inset) to grandparents out for a stroll, found something to enjoy in the park.
Photo: Culver Pictures; Boat: Picture Research Consultants & Archives.

PRIVATE ENTERPRISE, not planners, built the cities of the United States. With a few notable exceptions, cities simply mushroomed, formed by the dictates of private enterprise and the exigencies of local politics. With the rise of the city came the need for public facilities, transportation, and services that would tax the imaginations of America's architects and engineers and set the scene for the rough-and-tumble of big-city government, politics, and politicians.

Building Cities of Stone and Steel

In the late nineteenth century, Americans rushed to embrace new technology of all kinds, making their cities the most modern in the world. Structural steel made enormous advances in building possible. The Brooklyn Bridge, a soaring monument to the New York City, opened in 1883. As the age of steel supplanted the age of stone and iron, skyscrapers and mighty bridges dominated the imagination and the urban landscape.

Chicago, not New York, gave birth to the modern skyscraper. Rising from the ashes of the Great Fire of 1871, which destroyed three square miles and left eighteen thousand people homeless, Chicago offered a generation of skilled architects and engineers the chance to experiment. A group of architects known as the "Chicago school," whose members included Louis Sullivan and John Wellborn Root, gave Chicago some of the world's finest commercial buildings. Employing the dictum "Form follows function," they built startlingly modern structures.

Frederick Law Olmsted

▶ Landscape architect who designed numerous urban parks in the late nineteenth century. Olmsted is best known for New York's Central Park, completed in 1873. His parks were meant to provide city residents with a place where they could retreat from crowded, noisy city streets.

William Marcy "Boss" Tweed

▶ The most notorious city boss. In the mid-nineteenth century, Tweed was the leader of New York's Democratic machine, Tammany Hall. Through the use of bribery and graft, Tweed kept the Democratic Party in power and ran New York City. Tweed's excesses produced demands for reform and led to his fall from power in 1871.

Across the United States, municipal governments undertook public works on a scale never before seen. They paved streets, built sewers and water mains, installed electric lights, ran trolley tracks, and dug underground to build subways. Cities became more beautiful with the creation of urban public parks. Much of the credit for America's greatest parks goes to one man—landscape architect **Frederick Law Olmsted**. Olmsted designed parks for many cities, but he is best remembered for the creation of New York City's Central Park. Completed in 1873, it became the first landscaped public park in the United States. Olmsted's goal for the eight hundred acres between 59th and 110th streets was to create a place where people "may stroll for an hour, seeing, hearing, and feeling nothing of the bustle and jar of the streets."

American cities did not overlook the mind in their efforts at improvement. In the late nineteenth century, American cities created the most extensive free public library system in the world. In 1895, the Boston Public Library opened with more than 700,000 books available to the reading public. Cities also created a comprehensive free public school system that educated everyone from the children of the middle class to the sons and daughters of immigrant workers. The exploding urban population strained the system and led to crowded and inadequate facilities. In 1899, more than 544,000 pupils attended school in New York's five boroughs.

The parks, the libraries, and even the subways and sewers benefited some city dwellers more than others. Few library cards were held by Boston's laborers, who worked six days a week and found the library closed on Sunday. And in the 1890s, there was nothing central about New York's Central Park. It was a four-mile walk from the tenements of Hester Street to the park's entrance at 59th Street and Fifth Avenue.

Any story of the American city, it seems, must be a tale of two cities—or, given the cities' great diversity, a tale of many cities within each metropolis. At the turn of the twentieth century, a central paradox emerged: The enduring monuments of America's cities—the bridges, skyscrapers, parks, and libraries—stood as the undeniable achievements of the same system of municipal government that reformers dismissed as boss-ridden, criminal, and corrupt.

City Government and the "Bosses"

The physical growth of the cities required the expansion of public services and the creation of entirely new facilities: streets, subways, elevated trains, bridges, docks, sewers, and public utilities. With work to be done and money to be made, the professional politician—the colorful big-city boss—became a phenomenon of urban growth. Though corrupt and often criminal, the boss saw to the building of the city and provided needed social services for the new residents. Yet not even the big-city boss could be said to rule the city. The governing of America's cities resembled more a tug-of-war than boss rule.

The most notorious of all the city bosses was **William Marcy "Boss" Tweed** of New York. At midcentury, Boss Tweed's Democratic Party "machine" held sway. A machine was really no more than a political party organized at the grassroots level. Its purpose was to win elections and reward its followers, often with jobs on the city's payroll. New York's citywide Democratic machine, Tammany Hall, commanded an army of party functionaries. They formed a shadow government more powerful than the city's elected officials.

The only elected office Tweed ever held was alderman. But as chairman of the Tammany general committee, he wielded more power than the mayor. Through the use

CHAPTER LOCATOR | Why did American cities grow so fast in the late nineteenth century?

CHAPTER 19
530 THE GROWTH OF AMERICA'S CITIES, 1870–1900

of bribery and graft, he kept the Democratic Party together and ran the city. "As long as I count the votes," he shamelessly boasted, "what are you going to do about it?"

The excesses of the Tweed ring soon led to a clamor for reform. Cartoonist Thomas Nast pilloried Tweed in the pages of *Harper's Weekly*. His cartoons, easily understood even by those who could not read, did the boss more harm than hundreds of outraged editorials. Tweed's rule ended in 1871. Eventually, he was tried and convicted and later died in jail.

New York was not the only city to experience bossism and corruption. More than 80 percent of the nation's thirty largest cities experienced some form of boss rule in the decades around the turn of the twentieth century. However, infighting among powerful ward bosses often meant that no single boss enjoyed exclusive power in the big cities.

Urban reformers and proponents of good government (derisively called "goo goos" by their rivals) challenged machine rule and sometimes succeeded in electing reform mayors, but they rarely managed to stay in office for long. The bosses enjoyed continued success largely because the urban political machines helped the cities' immigrants and poor, who remained machine rule's staunchest allies. "What tells in holding your district," a Tammany ward boss observed, "is to go right down among the poor and help them in the different ways they need help. It's philanthropy, but it's politics, too—mighty good politics."

The big-city boss, through the skillful orchestration of rewards, exerted powerful leverage and lined up support for his party from a broad range of constituents, from the urban poor to wealthy industrialists. In 1902, when journalist Lincoln Steffens began "The Shame of the Cities," a series of articles exposing city corruption, he found that business leaders who refused to mingle socially with the bosses nevertheless struck deals with them. "He is a self-righteous fraud, this big businessman," Steffens concluded. "I found him buying boodlers [bribers] in St. Louis, defending grafters in Minneapolis, originating corruption in Pittsburgh, sharing with bosses in Philadelphia, deploring reform in Chicago, and beating good government with corruption funds in New York."

For all the color and flamboyance of the big-city boss, he was simply one of many players in municipal government. Old-stock aristocrats, new professionals, saloonkeepers, pushcart peddlers, and politicians all fought for their interests. They didn't much like each other, and they sometimes fought savagely. But they learned to live with one another. Compromise and accommodation—not boss rule—best characterized big-city government by the turn of the twentieth century, although the cities' reputation for corruption left an indelible mark on the consciousness of the American public.

Tammany Bank

This cast-iron bank, a campaign novelty, bears the name of the New York City Democratic machine. It conveys its political reform message graphically: When you put a penny in the politician's hand, he puts it in his pocket. Collection of Janice L. and David J. Frent.

| What kinds of work did people do in industrial America? | What steps did workers take to organize in the 1870s and 1880s? | How did industrialization transform home life and leisure? | **How did cities respond to the challenges of growth?** | Conclusion: Who built the cities? |

White City or City of Sin?

World's Columbian Exposition

▶ World's fair held in Chicago in 1893. Millions of fairgoers visited the fabulous grounds that came to be known as the White City. The White City embodied the American urban ideal and offered a stark contrast to the realities of Chicago life.

Americans have always been of two minds about the city. They like to boast of its skyscrapers and bridges, its culture and sophistication, and they pride themselves on its bigness and bustle. At the same time, they fear it as the city of sin, the home of immigrant slums, the center of vice and crime. Nowhere did the divided view of the American city take form more graphically than in Chicago in 1893.

In that year, Chicago hosted the **World's Columbian Exposition**, the grandest world's fair in the nation's history. The fairground, called the White City and built on the shores of Lake Michigan, offered a lesson in what Americans on the eve of the twentieth century imagined a city might be. Only five miles down the shore from downtown Chicago, the White City seemed light-years away. Its very name celebrated a harmony and pristine beauty unknown in Chicago, with its stock-yards, slums, and bustling terminals. Frederick Law Olmsted and architect Daniel Burnham supervised the creation of a paradise of lagoons, fountains, wooded islands, gardens, and imposing buildings.

Visitors from home and abroad strolled the elaborate grounds and visited the exhibits—everything from a model of the Brooklyn Bridge carved in soap to the latest goods and inventions. Half carnival, half culture, the great fair offered something for everyone. On the Midway Plaisance, crowds thrilled to the massive wheel built by Mr. Ferris and watched agog as Little Egypt danced the hootchy-kootchy.

In October, the fair closed its doors in the midst of the worst depression the country had yet seen. During the winter of 1894, Chicago's unemployed and homeless took over the grounds, vandalized the buildings, and frightened the city's comfortable citizens. When reporters asked Daniel Burnham what should be done with the moldering remains of the White City, he responded, "It should be torched." And it was. In July 1894, in a clash between federal troops and striking railway workers, incendiaries set fires that leveled the fairgrounds.

In the end, the White City remained what it had always been, a dreamscape. Perhaps it was not so strange, after all, that the legacy of the White City could be found on Coney Island, where two new amusement parks, Luna and Dreamland, sought to combine, albeit in a more tawdry form, the beauty of the White City and the thrill of the Midway Plaisance. More enduring than the White City itself was what it represented: the emergent industrial might of the United States, at home and abroad, with its inventions, manufactured goods, and growing consumer culture.

> **QUICK REVIEW**

How did American cities change in the late nineteenth century?

CHAPTER LOCATOR | Why did American cities grow so fast in the late nineteenth century?

532 CHAPTER 19
THE GROWTH OF AMERICA'S CITIES, 1870–1900

Picture Research Consultants & Archives

AS MUCH AS THE GREAT INDUSTRIALISTS and financiers, common workers, most of them immigrants, built the nation's cities. The unprecedented growth of urban, industrial America resulted from the labor of millions of men, women, and children who toiled in workshops and factories, in sweatshops and mines, on railroads and construction sites across America.

America's cities in the late nineteenth century teemed with life. Americans from all walks of life lived in the cities and contributed to their growth. Town houses and tenements jostled for space with skyscrapers and great department stores, while parks, ball fields, amusement arcades, and public libraries provided the city masses with recreation and entertainment. Municipal governments, straining to build the new cities, experienced the rough-and-tumble of machine politics as bosses and their constituents looked to profit from city growth.

For America's workers, urban industrialism, along with the rise of big business and corporate consolidation, drastically changed the workplace. Industrialists replaced skilled workers with new machines that could be operated by cheaper unskilled labor. And during hard times, employers did not hesitate to cut workers' already meager wages. Organization held out the best hope for the workers; first the Knights of Labor and later the American Federation of Labor won converts among the nation's working class.

The rise of urban industrialism challenged the American promise, which for decades had been dominated by Jeffersonian agrarian ideals. Could such a promise exist in the changing world of cities, tenements, immigrants, and huge corporations? In the great depression that came in the 1890s, mounting anger and frustration would lead workers and farmers to join forces and create a grassroots movement to fight for change under the banner of a new People's Party.

SO NOW YOU KNOW

The late nineteenth century witnessed an influx of "new" immigrants into the United States, most of them from Southern and Eastern Europe. Ellis Island, the destination of many new immigrants to the East Coast, was just the first stop for the newcomers who would provide critical labor in building America's growing cities.

| What kinds of work did people do in industrial America? | What steps did workers take to organize in the 1870s and 1880s? | How did industrialization transform home life and leisure? | How did cities respond to the challenges of growth? | Conclusion: Who built the cities? |

STEP 1

GETTING STARTED

Below are basic terms from this period in American history. Can you identify each term below and explain why it matters? To do this exercise online or to download this chart, visit bedfordstmartins.com/roarkunderstanding.

TERM	WHO OR WHAT & WHEN	WHY IT MATTERS
Ellis Island, p. 515		
Great Railroad Strike, p. 522		
Knights of Labor, p. 524		
Terrence V. Powderly, p. 524		
Samuel Gompers, p. 524		
American Federation of Labor, p. 524		
Haymarket bombing, p. 526		
Coney Island, p. 528		
Frederick Law Olmsted, p. 530		
William Marcy "Boss" Tweed, p. 530		
World's Columbian Exposition, p. 532		

STEP 2

MOVING BEYOND THE BASICS

The exercise below represents a more advanced understanding of the chapter material. Describe the key characteristics of American cities at the turn of the twentieth century and the impact that these characteristics had on city life. How did growth contribute to changes in work and social relationships? How did the influx of immigrants in the late nineteenth century shape city politics? How did the relationship among work, domestic life, and leisure activities change over the course of the late nineteenth and early twentieth centuries? To do this exercise online or to download this chart, visit bedfordstmartins.com/roarkunderstanding.

Characteristic	The American city, ca. 1900	Impact on city life
Population		
Diversity		
Social structure		
Work and labor relations		
Politics		
Domestic life		
Leisure		

Now that you have reviewed key elements of the chapter, take a step back and try to explain the big picture by answering these questions. Remember to use specific examples from the chapter in your answers. To do this exercise online, visit bedfordstmartins.com/roarkunderstanding.

URBANIZATION

▶ What factors led immigrants to American cities in the late nineteenth century? How did their arrival change the cities in which they settled?

▶ How and why did the social geography of the American city change in the late nineteenth century?

INDUSTRY AND LABOR

▶ What new social divisions accompanied business expansion and industrialization?

▶ What kinds of organizations did workers form in the late nineteenth century, and why did they start them? How successful were they?

CITY LIFE

▶ How did urban industrialism transform home and family life?

▶ What led to the rise of the big-city boss? Whose interests did late-nineteenth-century city governments serve?

LOOKING BACKWARD, LOOKING AHEAD

▶ How did early-twentieth-century American cities differ from their early-nineteenth-century counterparts?

▶ How did the rise of urban industrialism change Americans' sense of themselves as a people?

IN YOUR OWN WORDS

Imagine that you must explain chapter 19 to someone who hasn't read it. What would be the most important points to include and why?

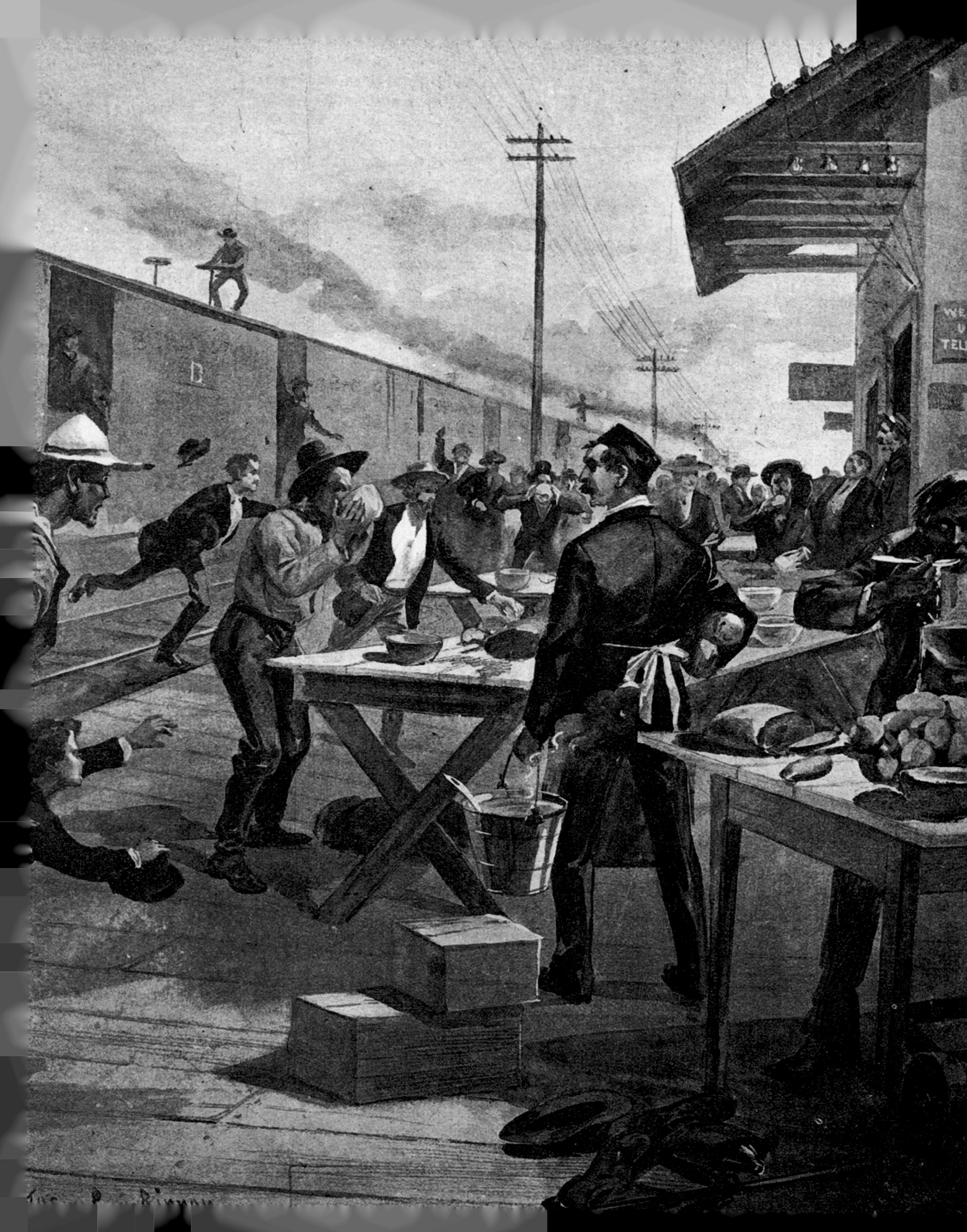

20
A DECADE OF DISSENT, DEPRESSION, AND WAR

1890–1900

> This chapter explores the political and economic conflicts of the 1890s. It looks at the responses of a variety of Americans to the challenges of the 1880s and 1890s, concluding with an examination of the shift in American foreign policy at the end of the nineteenth century.

> What were the reasons behind the farmers' revolt?

> What led to the "labor wars" of the 1890s?

> How were women involved in late-nineteenth-century politics?

> How did economic problems shape American politics in the 1890s?

> Why did the United States move away from isolationism?

> Why did America go to war with Spain in 1898?

> Conclusion: What was the connection between domestic tensions and U.S. foreign policy?

DID YOU KNOW?

The first march on Washington took place in 1894 when thousands of unemployed Americans demanded that the government take action to find them work.

The Unemployed—Scene at Country Railway Station. *The Graphic*, Chicago, September 9, 1893.

What were the reasons behind the farmers' revolt?

Nebraska Farm Family A Nebraska farm family posed in front of their sod hut in Custer County, Nebraska, in 1889. The house is formed of blocks of sod cut from the prairie. The photo testifies to the hard, lonely life of farmers on the Great Plains. Nebraska State Historical Society.

HARD TIMES in the 1880s and 1890s created a groundswell of agrarian revolt. A bitter farmer wrote from Minnesota, "I settled on this Land in good Faith Built House and Barn. Broken up Part of the Land. Spent years of hard Labor in grubbing fencing and Improving." About to lose his farm to foreclosure, he lamented, "Are they going to drive us out like trespassers . . . and give us away to the Corporations?"

Farm prices fell decade after decade, even as American farmers' share of the world market grew. In parts of Kansas, corn sold for as little as ten cents a bushel, and angry farmers burned it for fuel rather than market it at that price. At the same time, consumer prices soared. In Kansas alone, almost half the farms had fallen into the hands of the banks by 1894 because poor farmers could no longer afford to pay their mortgages (**Figure 20.1**).

At the heart of the problem stood a banking system dominated by eastern commercial banks committed to the gold standard, a railroad rate system that was capricious and unfair, and rampant speculation that drove up the price of land. In the West, farmers rankled under a system that allowed railroads to charge them exorbitant freight rates while granting rebates to large shippers like grain elevator companies (see chapter 18). In the South, lack of currency and credit drove farmers to the stopgap credit system of the crop lien. To pay for seed and supplies, farmers had to pledge their crops to local creditors, called "furnishing merchants," whose exorbitant prices meant chronic debt and destitution for southern farmers. Determined to do something, farmers banded together to fight for change.

The Farmers' Alliance

Farm protest was not new. In the 1870s, farmers had supported the Grange and the Greenback Labor Party. As the farmers' situation grew more desperate, they

CHAPTER LOCATOR | What were the reasons behind the farmers' revolt? | What led to the "labor wars" of the 1890s?

CHAPTER 20
538 A DECADE OF DISSENT, DEPRESSION, AND WAR , 1890–1900

organized, forming regional alliances. The first of the **Farmers' Alliances** came together in Lampasas County, Texas, to fight "landsharks and horse thieves." During the 1880s, the movement spread rapidly. Across the country, separate groups of farmers formed similar alliances for self-help.

As the movement grew, farmers' groups consolidated into two regional alliances. The Northwestern Farmers' Alliance was active in Kansas, Nebraska, and other midwestern Granger states. The more radical Southern Farmers' Alliance got its start in Texas and spread rapidly. In the 1880s, traveling lecturers preached the Alliance message. Overnight, scores of local alliances sprang up, each with its own lecturer, who in turn carried the word throughout the South. By 1887, the Southern Farmers' Alliance had grown to more than 200,000 members, and by 1890, it counted more than 3 million members.

Radical in its inclusiveness, the Southern Alliance reached out to African Americans, women, and industrial workers. Through cooperation with the Colored Farmers' Alliance, an African American group founded in Texas in the 1880s, blacks and whites attempted to make common cause. As Georgia's Tom Watson, a Southern Alliance stalwart, pointed out, "The colored tenant is in the same boat as the white tenant, . . . and . . . the accident of color can make no difference in the interests of farmers, croppers, and laborers." The political culture of the Alliance encouraged the inclusion of women and children and used the family as its defining symbol. Women rallied to the Alliance banner. "I am going to work for prohibition, the Alliance, and for Jesus as long as I live," swore one woman.

CHRONOLOGY

1876
- First Farmers' Alliance forms in Lampasas County, Texas.

1886
- Colored Farmers' Alliance is founded.

1890
- Southern Farmers' Alliance numbers three million members.

1892
- People's (Populist) Party is founded.

1894
- Almost half of Kansas farms are in the hands of banks.

Farmers' Alliance

▶ Movement to form local organizations to advance farmers' collective interests that gained popularity in the 1880s. Over time, farmers' groups consolidated into two regional alliances: the Northwestern Farmers' Alliance and the Southern Farmers' Alliance. In 1892, the Farmers' Alliance gave birth to the People's Party and launched the Populist movement.

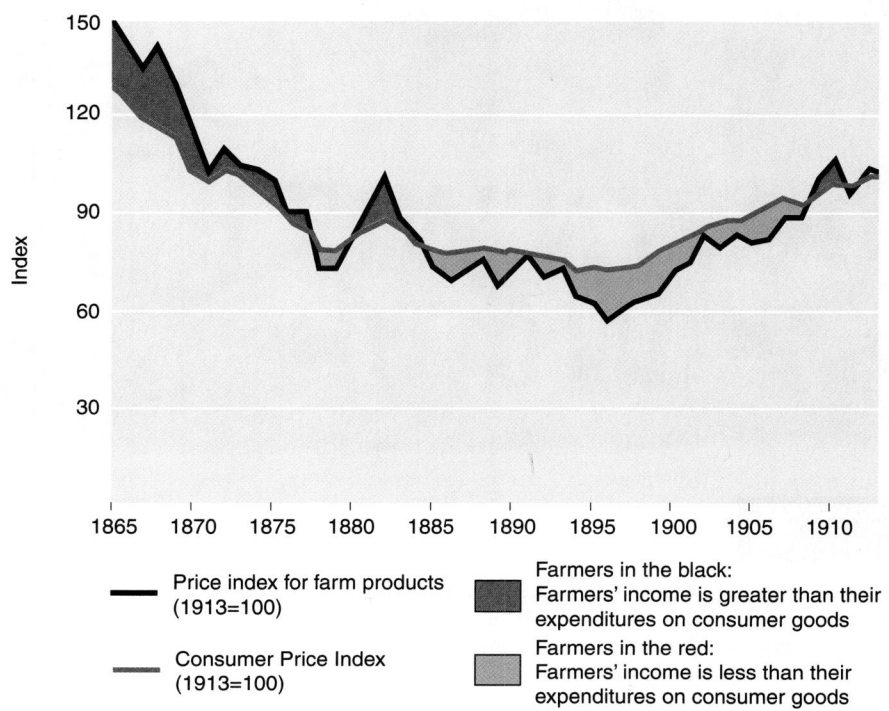

Price index for farm products (1913=100)

Consumer Price Index (1913=100)

Farmers in the black: Farmers' income is greater than their expenditures on consumer goods

Farmers in the red: Farmers' income is less than their expenditures on consumer goods

FIGURE 20.1 ■ Consumer Prices and Farm Income, 1865–1910

Around 1870, consumer prices and farm income were about equal. During the 1880s and 1890s, however, farmers suffered great hardships as prices for their crops steadily declined and the cost of consumer goods continued to rise.

| How were women involved in late-nineteenth-century politics? | How did economic problems shape American politics in the 1890s? | Why did the United States move away from isolationism? | Why did America go to war with Spain in 1898? | Conclusion: What was the connection between domestic tensions and U.S. foreign policy? |

At the heart of the Alliance movement stood a series of farmers' cooperatives. By selling their cotton together, farmers could negotiate a better price. And by setting up trade stores and exchanges, they sought to escape the grasp of the merchant/creditor. Through the cooperatives, the Farmers' Alliance promised to change the way farmers lived. "We are going to get out of debt and be free and independent people once more," exulted one Georgia farmer. But the Alliance faced insurmountable difficulties in running successful cooperatives. Opposition by merchants, bankers, wholesalers, and manufacturers made it impossible for the cooperatives to get credit. As the cooperative movement died, the Farmers' Alliance moved, often reluctantly, toward direct political action and the creation of a third political party.

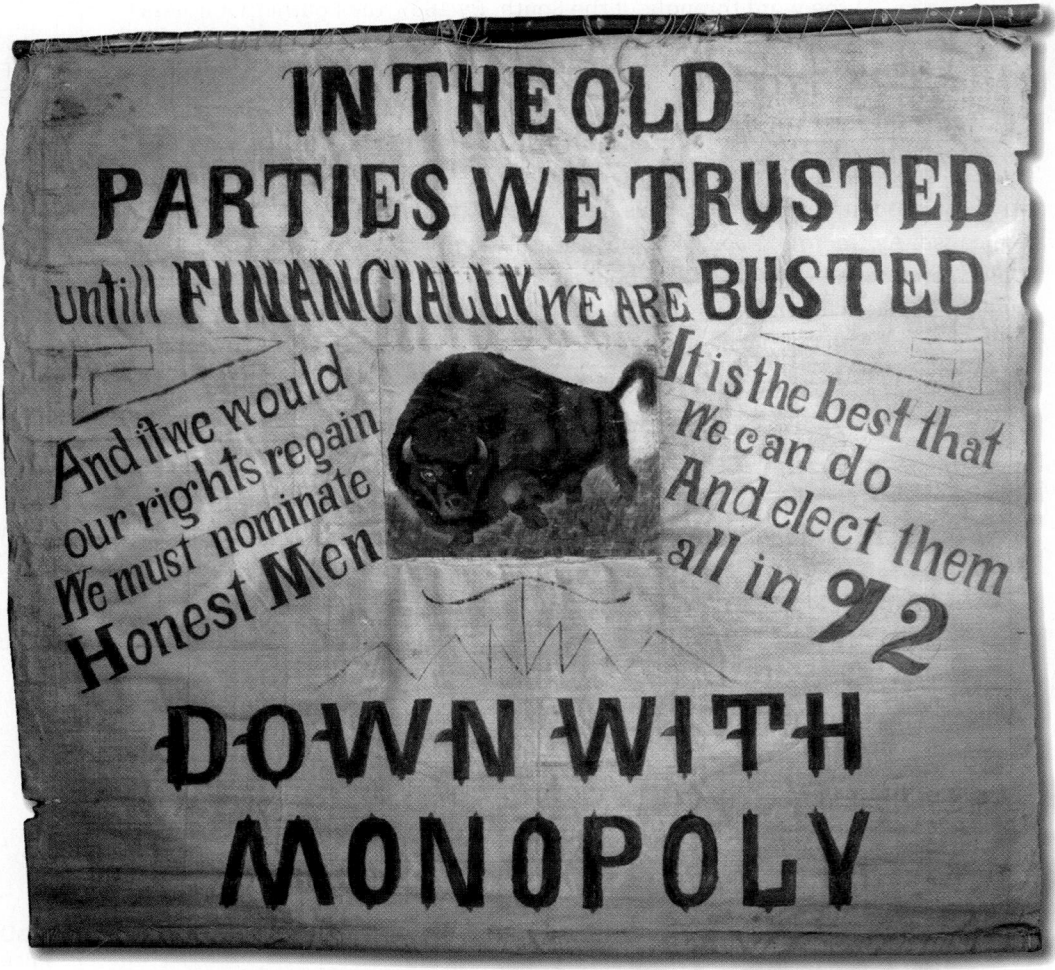

Buffalo Banner from the 1892 Populist Convention

This flag graphically declares the frustration with the Democratic and Republican parties that led angry Americans, particularly farmers, to gather in St. Louis in 1892 to create a new People's Party. Featuring the buffalo (American bison) as a symbol, the flag urged the election of "honest men" and proclaimed as its motto "Down with Monopoly." Nebraska State Historical Society.

CHAPTER LOCATOR   What were the reasons behind the farmers' revolt?   What led to the "labor wars" of the 1890s?

CHAPTER 20
540   A DECADE OF DISSENT, DEPRESSION, AND WAR , 1890–1900

The Populist Movement

Although there was resistance to the farmers' move into politics, by 1892 they had formed a third party at a convention of laborers, farmers, and common folk in St. Louis. There, the Farmers' Alliance gave birth to the **People's Party** and launched the Populist movement. The same spirit of religious revival that animated the Farmers' Alliance infused the People's Party. Convinced that the money and banking systems worked to the advantage of the wealthy few, the Populists demanded economic democracy. To help farmers get the credit they needed at reasonable rates, southern farmers hit on the idea of a subtreasury—a plan that would allow farmers to store their nonperishable crops and receive commodity credit from the federal government. The subtreasury promised to get rid of the crop lien system once and for all. To the western farmer, the Populists promised land reform, championing a plan that would claim excessive land granted to railroads or sold to foreign investors. The Populists' boldest proposal called for government ownership of the railroads and the telegraph system to put an end to discriminatory rates.

The Populists also demanded currency reform, calling for free silver and greenbacks—attempts to increase the nation's tight money supply and thus make credit easier to obtain. And to empower the common people, the Populist platform called for the direct election of senators and for other electoral reforms, including the secret ballot and the right to initiate legislation, to recall elected officials, and to submit issues to the people by means of a referendum. Because the Populists shared common cause with labor against corporate interests, they also supported the eight-hour workday and an end to contract labor.

The sweeping array of Populist reforms enacted in the Populist platform changed the agenda of politics for decades to come. More than just a response to hard times, Populism presented an alternative vision of American economic democracy.

People's Party (Populist Party)

▶ Political party formed in 1892 by the Farmers' Alliance to advance the goals of the Populist movement. Populists sought economic democracy, promoting land, electoral, banking, and monetary reform. Republican victory in the presidential election of 1896 effectively destroyed the People's Party.

QUICK REVIEW

Why did the Farmers' Alliance decide to form a third political party in 1892?

| How were women involved in late-nineteenth-century politics? | How did economic problems shape American politics in the 1890s? | Why did the United States move away from isolationism? | Why did America go to war with Spain in 1898? | Conclusion: What was the connection between domestic tensions and U.S. foreign policy? |

541

What led to the "labor wars" of the 1890s?

National Guard Occupying Pullman, Illinois

After President Grover Cleveland called out troops to put down the Pullman strike in 1894, the National Guard occupied the town of Pullman. The intervention enabled owner George M. Pullman to bring in strikebreakers and defeat the unions. Chicago Historical Society.

WHILE FARMERS UNITED to fight for change, industrial laborers fought their own battles in a series of bloody strikes so fiercely waged on both sides that historians have called them the "labor wars." Industrial workers felt increasingly threatened as businesses combined into huge corporations, and in the 1890s labor took a stand. At issue was the right of workers to organize and to speak through unions to bargain collectively for better working conditions, higher wages, shorter hours, and greater worker control in the face of increased mechanization. Three major conflicts of the period—the lockout of steelworkers in Homestead, Pennsylvania, in 1892; the miners' strike in Cripple Creek, Colorado, in 1894; and the Pullman strike in Illinois that same year—raised fundamental questions about the rights of labor and the sanctity of private property.

The Homestead Lockout

In 1892, steelworkers in Pennsylvania squared off against Andrew Carnegie in a decisive struggle over the right to organize in the Homestead steel mills. In 1892, Carnegie resolved to crush the Amalgamated Iron and Steel Workers, one of the largest and richest craft unions in the American Federation of Labor (AFL). When the Amalgamated attempted to renew its contract at Carnegie's Homestead mill, its leaders were told that since "the vast majority of our employees are Non union, the Firm has decided that the minority must give place to the majority." While it was true that only 800 skilled workers belonged to the elite Amalgamated, the union had long enjoyed the support of the plant's 3,000 nonunion workers. Slavs, who did much of the unskilled work, made common cause with the Welsh, Scots, and Irish skilled workers who belonged to the union.

CHAPTER LOCATOR | What were the reasons behind the farmers' revolt? | What led to the "labor wars" of the 1890s?

In anticipation of the coming conflict, Carnegie put Henry Clay Frick, the toughest antilabor man in the industry, in charge of the Homestead plant. By summer, a strike looked inevitable. Frick prepared by erecting a fifteen-foot fence around the plant and topping it with barbed wire. To defend the plant and protect strikebreakers, Frick hired 316 mercenaries from the Pinkerton National Detective Agency at the rate of $5 per day, more than double the wage of the average Homestead worker.

On June 28, the Homestead lockout began when Frick locked the workers out of the mills and prepared to bring in strikebreakers. Hugh O'Donnell, the young Irishman who led the union, vowed to prevent the "scabs" from entering the plant. On July 6 at four in the morning, a lookout spotted two barges moving up the Monongahela River. Frick was attempting to smuggle Pinkertons into Homestead.

Workers sounded the alarm, and within minutes a crowd of more than a thousand, hastily armed with rifles, hoes, and fence posts, rushed to the riverbank. For twelve hours, the workers, joined by their family members, threw everything they had at the barges, from fireworks to dynamite. Finally, the Pinkertons hoisted a white flag and arranged with O'Donnell to surrender. With three workers already dead and scores wounded, the crowd, numbering perhaps ten thousand, was in no mood for conciliation. As the hated "Pinks" came up the hill, they were forced to run a gantlet of screaming, cursing men, women, and children. When a young guard dropped to his knees, weeping for mercy, a woman used her umbrella to poke out his eye. One Pinkerton had been killed in the siege on the barges. In the grim rout that followed their surrender, not one avoided injury. In the aftermath of the battle, the workers took control of the plant and elected a council to run the community. At first, public opinion favored their cause. Newspapers urged Frick to negotiate or submit to arbitration. Populists, meeting in St. Louis, condemned the use of "hireling armies."

The action of the Homestead workers struck at the heart of the capitalist system, pitting the workers' right to their jobs against the rights of private property. The workers' insistence that "we are not destroying the property of the company—merely protecting our rights" did not prove as compelling to the courts and the state as the property rights of the mill owners. Four days after the confrontation, Pennsylvania's governor, who sympathized with the workers, nonetheless yielded to pressure from Frick and ordered eight thousand National Guard troops into Homestead. The strikers, thinking they had nothing to fear from the militia, welcomed the troops with a brass band. But the troops' occupation not only protected Carnegie's property but also enabled Frick to reopen the mills and bring in strikebreakers. "We have been deceived," one worker complained bitterly. "We have stood idly by and let the town be occupied by soldiers who come here, not as our protectors, but as the protectors of non-union men. . . . If we undertake to resist the seizure of our jobs, we will be shot down like dogs."

Then, in a misguided effort to ignite a general uprising, Alexander Berkman, a Russian immigrant and anarchist, attempted to assassinate Frick. Berkman bungled his attempt. Shot twice and stabbed with a dagger, Frick survived. "I do not think that I shall die," Frick remarked coolly, "but whether I do or not, the Company will pursue the same policy and it will win."

After the assassination attempt, public opinion turned against the workers. Berkman was quickly tried and sentenced to prison. Although the Amalgamated and the AFL denounced his action, the incident linked anarchism and unionism,

CHRONOLOGY

1890
- George Pullman establishes model company town outside of Chicago.

1892
- Unionized steelworkers in Homestead, Pennsylvania, are locked out by management.

1893
- Stock market crash touches off severe economic depression.

1894
- Miners' strike in Cripple Creek, Colorado.
- Federal troops and court injunction crush Pullman strike.

How were women involved in late-nineteenth-century politics?

How did economic problems shape American politics in the 1890s?

Why did the United States move away from isolationism?

Why did America go to war with Spain in 1898?

Conclusion: What was the connection between domestic tensions and U.S. foreign policy?

Homestead Workers Attack the Pinkertons

The nation's attention was riveted on labor strife at the Homestead steel mill in the summer of 1892. Frank Leslie's *Illustrated Weekly* ran a cover story on the violence that Pinkerton agents faced from a crowd of men, women, and children armed with clubs, guns, and ax handles. The workers were enraged that Henry Clay Frick had hired the Pinkertons to bring in strikebreakers. The illustration shows a boy with a gun in the foreground. Although the mob was armed, not one of the Pinkertons was shot as they ran the gantlet. All, however, were beaten. The New-York Society Library.

FRANK LESLIE'S ILLUSTRATED WEEKLY

HOMESTEAD TROUBLES.

NEW YORK, JULY 16, 1892. [Price, 10 Cents.

THE LABOR TROUBLES AT HOMESTEAD, PENNSYLVANIA—ATTACK OF THE STRIKERS AND THEIR SYMPATHIZERS ON THE SURRENDERED PINKERTON MEN.—Drawn by Miss G. A. Davis, from a Sketch by C. Upham.—[See Page 41.]

▶ FOR MORE HELP ANALYZING THIS IMAGE, see the visual activity for this chapter in the Online Study Guide at bedfordstmartins.com/roarkunderstanding.

already associated in the public mind as a result of the Haymarket bombing in 1886 (see chapter 19). In the end, the workers capitulated. The Homestead mill reopened in November, and the men returned to work, except for the union leaders, now blacklisted in every steel mill in the country. With the owners firmly in charge, the company slashed wages, reinstated the twelve-hour day, and eliminated five hundred jobs.

The workers at Homestead had been taught a significant lesson. They would never again, in the words of the National Guard commander, "believe the works are their's [*sic*] quite as much as Carnegie's." Another forty-five years would pass before steelworkers, unskilled as well as skilled, successfully unionized. In the meantime, Carnegie's production tripled, even in the midst of a depression.

CHAPTER LOCATOR | What were the reasons behind the farmers' revolt? | What led to the "labor wars" of the 1890s?

544 CHAPTER 20 A DECADE OF DISSENT, DEPRESSION, AND WAR , 1890–1900

"Ashamed to tell you profits these days," Carnegie wrote a friend in 1899. And no wonder: Carnegie's profits had grown from $4 million in 1892 to $40 million in 1900.

The Cripple Creek Miners' Strike of 1894

Less than a year after the Homestead lockout, a panic on Wall Street in the spring of 1893 touched off an economic depression. In the West, silver mines fell on hard times, touching off the Cripple Creek miners' strike of 1894. When mine owners moved to lengthen the workday from eight to ten hours, the newly formed Western Federation of Miners (WFM) vowed to hold the line in Cripple Creek, Colorado. In February 1894, the WFM threatened to strike all mines working more than eight-hour shifts. The mine owners divided: Some quickly settled with the WFM; others continued to demand ten-hour workdays, provoking a strike.

The striking miners received help from many quarters. Working miners paid $15 a month to a strike fund, and miners in neighboring districts sent substantial contributions. The miners enjoyed the support and assistance of local businesses and grocers, who provided credit to the strikers. With these advantages, the Cripple Creek strikers could afford to hold out for their demands.

Even more significant, Governor Davis H. Waite, a Populist elected in 1892, had strong ties to the miners and refused to use the power of the state against the strikers. Governor Waite asked the strikers to lay down their arms and demanded that the mine owners disperse their hired deputies. The miners agreed to arbitration and selected Waite as their sole arbitrator. By May, the recalcitrant mine owners capitulated, and the union won an eight-hour day.

Governor Waite's intervention demonstrated the pivotal power of the state in the nation's labor wars. A decade later, in 1904, with Waite out of office, mine owners relied on state troops to take back control of the mines, defeating the WFM and blacklisting all of its members. In retrospect, the Cripple Creek miners' strike of 1894 proved the exception to the rule of state intervention on the side of private property.

Eugene V. Debs and the Pullman Strike

The economic depression that began in 1893 swelled the ranks of the unemployed to three million, almost half of the working population. "A fearful crisis is upon us," wrote a labor publication. Nowhere were workers more demoralized than in the model town of Pullman, on the outskirts of Chicago.

In the wake of the Great Railroad Strike of 1877, George M. Pullman, who built Pullman railroad cars, moved his plant and workers nine miles south of Chicago to a model town boasting parks, fountains, playgrounds, an auditorium, a library, a hotel, shops, and markets, along with 1,800 units of housing. Noticeably absent was a saloon.

The housing in Pullman was superior to that in neighboring areas, but workers paid a high price to live there. Pullman's rents ran 10 to 20 percent higher than housing costs in nearby communities. In addition, George Pullman refused to "sell an acre under any circumstances." As long as he had the power of eviction over his employees, he could quickly get rid of "troublemakers." Although observers at

| How were women involved in late-nineteenth-century politics? | How did economic problems shape American politics in the 1890s? | Why did the United States move away from isolationism? | Why did America go to war with Spain in 1898? | Conclusion: What was the connection between domestic tensions and U.S. foreign policy? |

545

first praised the beauty and orderliness of the town, critics by the 1890s compared Pullman's model town to a "gilded cage" for workers.

The depression brought hard times to Pullman. Workers saw their wages slashed five times between May and December 1893, with cuts totaling at least 28 percent. At the same time, Pullman refused to lower the rents in his model town, insisting that "the renting of the dwellings and the employment of workmen at Pullman are in no way tied together." When workers went to the bank to cash their paychecks, they found the rent had been taken out. One worker discovered only forty-seven cents in his pay envelope for two weeks' work. At the same time, Pullman continued to pay his stockholders an 8 percent dividend, and the company accumulated a $25 million surplus.

At the heart of the labor problems at Pullman lay not only economic inequity but also the company's attempt to control the work process, substituting piecework for day wages and undermining skilled craftsworkers. During the spring of 1894, Pullman's desperate workers, seeking help, flocked to the ranks of the American Railway Union (ARU), led by the charismatic **Eugene V. Debs**. The ARU, unlike the skilled craft unions of the AFL, pledged to organize all railway workers—from engineers to engine wipers.

George Pullman responded to union organization at his plant by firing three of the union's leaders the day after they led a delegation to protest wage cuts. Angry men and women walked off the job in disgust. What began as a spontaneous protest in May 1894 quickly blossomed into a strike that involved more than 90 percent of Pullman's 3,300 workers. Pullman countered by shutting down the plant. In June, the Pullman strikers appealed to the ARU for aid. Debs hesitated and pleaded with the workers to find another solution. When George Pullman adamantly refused arbitration, the ARU membership voted to boycott all Pullman cars. Beginning on June 29, switchmen across the United States refused to handle any train that carried Pullman cars.

The conflict escalated quickly. The General Managers Association (GMA), an organization of managers from twenty-four different railroads, acted in concert to quash the Pullman boycott. They recruited strikebreakers and fired all the protesting switchmen. Their tactics set off a chain reaction. Entire train crews walked off the job in a show of solidarity with the Pullman workers. By July 2, rail lines from New York to California lay paralyzed. Even the GMA was forced to concede that the railroads had been "fought to a standstill."

The boycott remained surprisingly peaceful. In contrast to the Great Railroad Strike of 1877, no major riots broke out, and no serious property damage occurred.

A Pullman Craftsworker

Pullman Palace cars were known for their luxurious details. Here, a painter working in the 1890s applies elaborate decoration to the exterior of a Pullman car. The Pullman workers' strike in 1894 stemmed in part from the company's efforts to undermine the status of craftsworkers by reducing them to low-paid piecework. *Chicago Historical Society.*

CHAPTER LOCATOR | What were the reasons behind the farmers' revolt? | What led to the "labor wars" of the 1890s?

546 CHAPTER 20
A DECADE OF DISSENT, DEPRESSION, AND WAR , 1890–1900

Debs fired off telegrams to all parts of the country advising his followers to avoid violence and respect law and order. But the nation's newspapers, fed press releases by the GMA, distorted the issues and misrepresented the strike. Across the country, papers ran headlines like "Wild Riot in Chicago" and "Mob Is in Control."

In Washington, Attorney General Richard B. Olney, a lawyer with strong ties to the railroads, determined to put down the strike. In his way stood the governor of Illinois, John Peter Altgeld, who refused to call out troops. To get around Altgeld, Olney convinced President Grover Cleveland that federal troops had to intervene to protect the mails. To further cripple the boycott, two conservative Chicago judges issued an injunction so sweeping that it prohibited Debs from speaking in public. By issuing the injunction, the court made the boycott a crime punishable by a jail sentence for contempt of court, a civil process that did not require a jury trial. Even the conservative *Chicago Tribune* judged the injunction "a menace to liberty . . . a weapon ever ready for the capitalist."

Olney's strategy worked. With the strikers violating a federal injunction and with the mails in jeopardy (the GMA made sure that Pullman cars were put on every mail train), Cleveland called out the army. On July 5, nearly 8,000 troops marched into Chicago. Violence immediately erupted. In one day, troops killed 25 workers and wounded more than 60. Nonetheless, the strikers held firm. "Troops cannot move trains," Debs reminded his followers, a fact borne out as the railroads remained paralyzed despite the military intervention. But if the army could not put down the boycott, the injunction could and did. Debs was arrested and imprisoned for contempt of court. With its leader in jail, the ARU was defeated. Pullman reopened his factory, hiring new workers to replace many of the strikers and leaving 1,600 workers without jobs.

In the aftermath of the strike, a special commission investigated the events at Pullman, taking testimony from 107 witnesses, including Pullman himself. Stubborn and self-righteous, Pullman steadfastly affirmed the right of business to safeguard its interests through confederacies such as the GMA and at the same time denied labor's right to organize. "If we were to receive these men as representatives of the union," he stated, "they could probably force us to pay any wages which they saw fit."

With the courts and the government ready to side with industrialists in the interest of defending private property, Debs realized that labor had little recourse. Strikes seemed futile, and unions remained helpless; workers would have to take control of the state itself. Debs went into jail a trade unionist and came out six months later a socialist. At first, he turned to the People's Party, but after its demise, he formed the Socialist Party in 1900 and ran for president five times. Debs's dissatisfaction with the status quo was shared by another group even more alienated from the political process—women.

Eugene V. Debs

▶ Charismatic leader of the American Railroad Union (ARU). In 1894, Debs and the ARU came to the aid of striking Pullman workers by organizing a boycott of Pullman cars. Debs's skillful orchestration of the peaceful boycott was to no avail, as railroad and government officials collaborated, using propaganda, troops, and a dubious injunction to bring an end to the boycott and to imprison Debs.

QUICK REVIEW

Why were the labor conflicts of the 1890s so often marked by violence?

How were women involved in late-nineteenth-century politics?

Frances Willard

Frances Willard, the forward-thinking leader of the Woman's Christian Temperance Union, learned to ride a bicycle at age fifty-three. The bicycle became hugely popular in the 1890s, even though traditionalists fulminated that it was unladylike for women to straddle a bike and immodest for them to wear the divided skirts that allowed them to pedal. Willard, shown here in 1895, declared bicycling a "harmless pleasure" that encouraged "clear heads and steady hands." Courtesy of the Frances E. Willard Memorial Library and Archives (WCTU).

"**DO EVERYTHING,**" Frances Willard urged her followers in 1881. The new president of the Woman's Christian Temperance Union (WCTU) meant what she said. The WCTU followed a trajectory that was common for women in the late nineteenth century. As women organized to deal with issues that touched their homes and families, they moved into politics, lending new urgency to the cause of woman suffrage. Like men, women sought political change and organized to promote issues central to their lives, campaigning for temperance and woman suffrage.

Frances Willard and the Woman's Christian Temperance Union

Frances Willard
▶ Visionary leader of the Woman's Christian Temperance Union (WCTU). When Willard became president of the WCTU in 1879, she radically changed the direction of the organization. Viewing alcoholism as a disease rather than a sin, the organization became involved in political and labor issues, urging the vote for women.

Frances Willard, the visionary leader of the WCTU, spoke for a group left almost entirely out of the U.S. electoral process—women. In 1890, only one state, Wyoming, allowed women to vote in national elections. But lack of the franchise did not mean that women were apolitical. The WCTU demonstrated the breadth of women's political activity in the late nineteenth century.

When Frances Willard became president of the WCTU in 1879, she radically changed the direction of the organization. Viewing alcoholism as a disease rather than a sin and poverty as a cause rather than a result of drink, the WCTU became involved in labor issues, joining with the Knights of Labor to press for better working conditions for women workers. Describing workers in a textile mill, a WCTU member wrote in the *Union Signal*, "It is dreadful to see these girls, stripped almost to the skin . . . and running like racehorses from the beginning to the end of the day." She concluded, "The hard slavish work is drawing the girls into the saloon."

CHAPTER LOCATOR | What were the reasons behind the farmers' revolt? | What led to the "labor wars" of the 1890s?

Willard capitalized on the cult of domesticity as a shrewd political tactic. Using "home protection" as her watchword, she argued as early as 1884 that women needed the vote to protect home and family. By the 1890s, the WCTU was a formidable group with more than 200,000 dues-paying members and a grassroots network of local unions that had spread to all but the most isolated rural areas of the country.

Willard worked to create a broad reform coalition in the 1890s, embracing the Knights of Labor, the People's Party, and the Prohibition Party. Until her death in 1898, she led the first organized mass movement of women united around a women's issue. By 1900, thanks largely to the WCTU, women could claim a generation of experience in political action. As Willard observed, "All this work has tended more toward the liberation of women than it has toward the extinction of the saloon."

Elizabeth Cady Stanton, Susan B. Anthony, and the Movement for Woman Suffrage

Unlike the WCTU, the organized movement for woman suffrage remained small and relatively weak in the late nineteenth century. In 1869, Elizabeth Cady Stanton and her ally, **Susan B. Anthony**, launched the National Woman Suffrage Association (NWSA), demanding the vote for women (see chapter 18). A more conservative group, the American Woman Suffrage Association (AWSA), formed the same year. Composed of men as well as women, the AWSA believed that women should vote in local but not national elections.

By 1890, the split had healed, and the new National American Woman Suffrage Association (NAWSA) launched campaigns on the state level to gain the vote for women. Twenty years had made a great change. Woman suffrage, though not yet generally supported, was no longer considered a crackpot idea, thanks in part to the WCTU's support of the "home protection" ballot. The NAWSA elected Elizabeth Cady Stanton as its first president, but Susan B. Anthony, who took the helm in 1892, emerged as the leading figure in the new united organization.

Stanton and Anthony, both in their seventies, were coming to the end of their public careers. Since the days of the Seneca Falls woman's rights convention, they had worked for reforms for their sex, including property rights, custody rights, and the right to education and gainful employment. But the prize of woman suffrage still eluded them. Never losing faith, Susan B. Anthony remarked in her last public appearance, in 1906, "Failure is impossible." Although it would take until 1920 for all women to gain the vote with the ratification of the Nineteenth Amendment, the unification of the woman suffrage movement in 1890 signaled a new era in women's fight for the vote.

CHRONOLOGY

1879
– Frances Willard becomes president of the Woman's Christian Temperance Union (WCTU).

1884
– The WCTU calls for woman suffrage.

1890
– National American Woman Suffrage Association is formed.

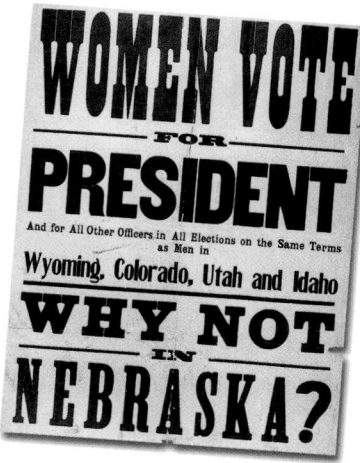

Susan B. Anthony
▶ Women's rights activist, who, along with Elizabeth Cady Stanton, spearheaded the movement in 1848. While in her seventies, Anthony emerged as the leader of the newly united National American Woman Suffrage Association, a move that began a new era in women's fight for voting rights.

QUICK REVIEW

How did the Woman's Christian Temperance Union contribute to the cause of woman suffrage?

How did economic problems shape American politics in the 1890s?

Coxey's Army A contingent of Coxey's army stops to rest on its way to Washington, D.C. A "petition in boots," Coxey's followers were well dressed, as evidenced by the men in this photo wearing white shirts, vests, neckties, and bowler hats. Music was an important component of the march; band members are pictured on the right with their instruments. Ohio Historical Society.

THE DEPRESSION that began in the spring of 1893 and lasted for more than four years put nearly half of the labor force out of work, a higher percentage than during the Great Depression of the 1930s. The human cost of the depression was staggering. "I Take my pen in hand to let you know that we are Starving to death," a Kansas farm woman wrote to the governor in 1894. "Last cent gone," wrote a young widow in her diary. "Children went to work without their breakfasts." Following the harsh dictates of social Darwinism and laissez-faire, the majority of America's elected officials believed that it was inappropriate for the government to intervene. But the scope of the depression made it impossible for local agencies to supply sufficient relief, and increasingly Americans called on the federal government to take action. Armies of the unemployed marched on Washington to demand relief, and the Populist Party experienced a surge of support as the election of 1896 approached.

Coxey's Army

Masses of unemployed Americans marched to Washington, D.C., in the spring of 1894 to call attention to their plight and to urge Congress to enact a public works

CHAPTER LOCATOR | What were the reasons behind the farmers' revolt? | What led to the "labor wars" of the 1890s?

CHAPTER 20
550 A DECADE OF DISSENT, DEPRESSION, AND WAR , 1890–1900

program to end unemployment. Jacob S. Coxey of Massillon, Ohio, led the most publicized contingent. Convinced that men could be put to work building badly needed roads for the nation, Coxey proposed a scheme to finance public works through non-interest-bearing bonds. "What I am after," he maintained, "is to try to put this country in a condition so that no man who wants work shall be obliged to remain idle." His plan won support from the AFL and the Populists.

Starting out from Ohio with one hundred men, **Coxey's army**, as it was dubbed, swelled as it marched east. In Pennsylvania, Coxey recruited several hundred from the ranks of those left unemployed by the Homestead lockout. On May 1, Coxey's army arrived in Washington. When Coxey defiantly marched his men onto the Capitol grounds, police set upon the demonstrators with nightsticks, arresting Coxey and his lieutenants for walking on the grass. But other armies of the unemployed, totaling possibly as many as five thousand people, were still on their way. The more daring contingents commandeered entire trains, stirring fears of revolution. Journalists who covered the march did little to quiet the nation's fears. Describing themselves as "war correspondents," they gave the episode a tone of urgency and heightened the sense of a nation imperiled.

By August, the leaderless armies dissolved. Although the "On to Washington" movement proved ineffective in forcing federal relief legislation, Coxey's army dramatized the plight of the unemployed and acted, in the words of one participant, as a "living, moving object lesson." Like the Populists, Coxey's army called into question the underlying values of the new industrial order and demonstrated how ordinary citizens turned to means outside the regular party system to influence politics in the 1890s.

The People's Party and the Election of 1896

Even before the depression of 1893, the Populists had railed against the status quo. "We meet in the midst of a nation brought to the verge of moral, political, and material ruin," Ignatius Donnelly had declared in his keynote address at the creation of the People's Party in St. Louis in 1892. "The fruits of the toil of millions are boldly stolen to build up colossal fortunes for a few. . . . From the same prolific womb of governmental injustice we breed the two great classes—tramps and millionaires."

The fiery rhetoric frightened many who saw in the People's Party a call not to reform but to revolution. Throughout the country, the press denounced the Populists as "cranks, lunatics, and idiots." When one self-righteous editor dismissed them as "calamity howlers," Populist governor Lorenzo Lewelling of Kansas shot back, "If that is so I want to continue to howl until those conditions are improved."

The People's Party captured more than a million votes in the presidential election of 1892, a respectable showing for a new party (**Map 20.1**). But increasingly, sectional and racial animosities threatened its unity. Realizing that race prejudice obscured the common economic interests of black and white farmers, Populist Tom

CHRONOLOGY

1894
- Coxey's army marches to Washington, D.C.

1896
- Democrats and Populists support William Jennings Bryan for president.
- Republican William McKinley is elected president.

Coxey's army
▶ Unemployed men who marched to Washington, D.C., in 1894 to protest economic conditions in the wake of the panic of 1893. The leader of the march, Jacob S. Coxey, advocated public works programs to alleviate unemployment. Coxey's army inspired many other groups of unemployed Americans to head to Washington.

| How were women involved in late-nineteenth-century politics? | **How did economic problems shape American politics in the 1890s?** | Why did the United States move away from isolationism? | Why did America go to war with Spain in 1898? | Conclusion: What was the connection between domestic tensions and U.S. foreign policy? |

551

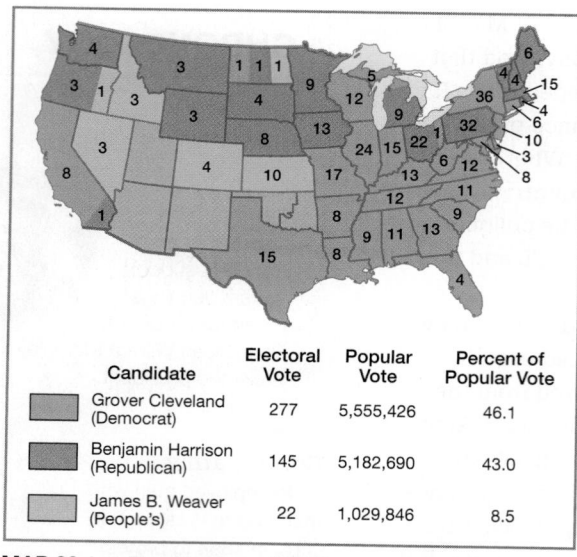

Candidate	Electoral Vote	Popular Vote	Percent of Popular Vote
Grover Cleveland (Democrat)	277	5,555,426	46.1
Benjamin Harrison (Republican)	145	5,182,690	43.0
James B. Weaver (People's)	22	1,029,846	8.5

MAP 20.1 ■ The Election of 1892

William Jennings Bryan

► Democratic candidate for president in 1896. Bryan was famed for his oratorical skills and his passionate support of free silver. He was nominated in 1896 by both the Democrats and the Populists but lost by a narrow margin to Republican William McKinley.

Watson of Georgia openly courted African Americans, appearing on platforms with black speakers and promising "to wipe out the color line." When angry Georgia whites threatened to lynch a black Populist preacher, Watson rallied two thousand gun-toting Populists to the man's defense. Although many Populists remained racist in their attitudes toward African Americans, the spectacle of white Georgians riding to protect a black man from lynching was symbolic of the enormous changes the Populist Party promised in the South.

As the presidential election of 1896 approached, the depression intensified cries for reform not only from the Populists but also throughout the electorate. Depression worsened the tight money problem caused by the deflationary pressures of the gold standard. Once again, proponents of free silver (the unlimited coinage of silver in addition to gold) stirred rebellion in the ranks of both the Democratic and the Republican parties. When the Republicans nominated Ohio governor William McKinley on a platform pledging the preservation of the gold standard, western advocates of free silver representing miners and farmers walked out of the convention. Open rebellion also split the Democratic Party as vast segments in the West and South repudiated President Grover Cleveland because of his support for gold.

At the 1896 Democratic National Convention in Chicago, thirty-six-year-old **William Jennings Bryan** of Nebraska whipped the convention into a frenzy with his passionate call for free silver, closing his dramatic keynote speech with a ringing exhortation: "Do not crucify mankind upon a cross of gold." Pandemonium broke loose as delegates stampeded to nominate Bryan, the youngest candidate ever to run for the presidency.

When the People's Party met in St. Louis, a week after the Democrats adjourned, many western Populists urged the party to ally with the Democrats and endorse Bryan. A major obstacle in the path of fusion, however, was Bryan's running mate, Arthur M. Sewall. A Maine railway director and bank president, Sewall, who had been placed on the ticket to appease conservative Democrats, embodied everything the Populists detested. Moreover, die-hard southern Populists wanted no part of fusion. Southern Democrats had resorted to fraud and violence to steal elections from the Populists in 1892 and 1894, and support for a Democratic ticket proved hard to swallow.

Populists struggled to work out a compromise. To show that they remained true to their principles, delegates first voted to support all the planks of the 1892 platform, adding to it a call for public works projects for the unemployed. To deal with the problem of fusion, the convention selected the vice presidential candidate first. The nomination of Tom Watson undercut opposition to Bryan's candidacy. And although Bryan quickly sent a telegram to protest that he would not drop Sewall as his running mate, mysteriously his message never reached the convention floor. Watson's vice presidential nomination paved the way for the selection of Bryan. The Populists did not know it, but their cheers for Bryan signaled the death knell of the People's Party.

Few contests in the nation's history have been as fiercely fought as the presidential election of 1896. On one side stood Republican William McKinley, backed

CHAPTER LOCATOR | What were the reasons behind the farmers' revolt? | What led to the "labor wars" of the 1890s?

552 CHAPTER 20 A DECADE OF DISSENT, DEPRESSION, AND WAR , 1890–1900

by the wealthy industrialist and party boss Mark Hanna. Hanna played on the business community's fears of Populism to raise a Republican war chest more than double the amount of any previous campaign. On the other side, William Jennings Bryan struggled to make up in energy and eloquence what his party lacked in campaign funds, crisscrossing the country in a whirlwind tour. According to his own reckoning, he visited twenty-seven states and spoke to more than five million Americans.

On election day, four out of five voters went to the polls in an unprecedented turnout. In the critical midwestern swing states, as many as 95 percent of the eligible voters cast their ballots. In the end, the election hinged on between 100 and 1,000 votes in several key states, including Wisconsin, Iowa, and Minnesota. Although McKinley won twenty-three states to Bryan's twenty-two, the electoral vote showed a lopsided 271 to 176 in McKinley's favor (**Map 20.2**).

The biggest losers in 1896 turned out to be the Populists. On the national level, they polled fewer than 300,000 votes, a million less than in 1894. In the clamor to support Bryan, Populists in the South had drifted back to the Democratic Party. The People's Party was crushed, and with it the agrarian revolt.

But if Populism proved unsuccessful at the polls, it nevertheless set the domestic political agenda for the United States in the next decades, highlighting issues such as banking and currency reform, electoral reforms, and an enlarged role for the federal government in the economy. Meanwhile, as the decade ended, America's attention turned to foreign affairs. The struggle for social justice gave way to a war for empire as the United States asserted its power on the world stage.

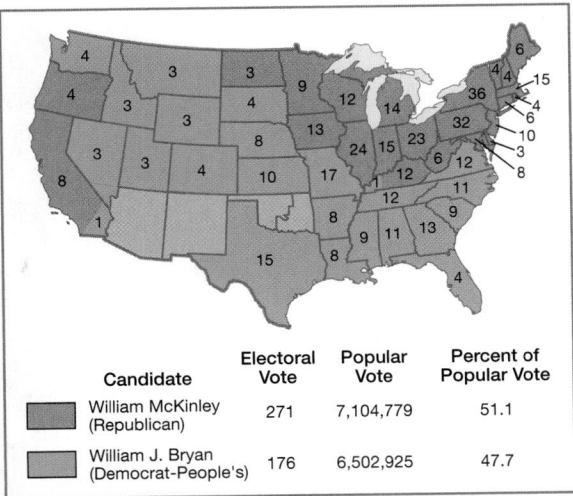

Candidate	Electoral Vote	Popular Vote	Percent of Popular Vote
William McKinley (Republican)	271	7,104,779	51.1
William J. Bryan (Democrat-People's)	176	6,502,925	47.7

MAP 20.2 ■ The Election of 1896

QUICK REVIEW

Why was the People's Party unable to translate national support into victory in the 1896 election?

| How were women involved in late-nineteenth-century politics? | How did economic problems shape American politics in the 1890s? | Why did the United States move away from isolationism? | Why did America go to war with Spain in 1898? | Conclusion: What was the connection between domestic tensions and U.S. foreign policy? |

Why did the United States move away from isolationism?

The Open Door The trade advantage gained by the United States through the Open Door policy, enunciated by Secretary of State John Hay in 1900, is portrayed graphically in this political cartoon. Uncle Sam stands prominently in the "open door," while representatives of the other great powers seek admittance to the "Flowery Kingdom" of China. In fact, the Open Door policy promised equal access for all powers to the China trade, not U.S. preeminence as the cartoon implies. Culver Pictures.

▶ FOR MORE HELP ANALYZING THIS IMAGE, see the visual activity for this chapter in the Online Study Guide at bedfordstmartins.com/roarkunderstanding.

THROUGHOUT MUCH OF THE SECOND HALF of the nineteenth century, U.S. interest in foreign policy took a backseat to territorial expansion in the American West. The United States fought the Indian wars while European nations, along with the increasingly powerful Japan, competed for empires in Asia, Africa, Latin America, and the Pacific.

At the turn of the twentieth century, American foreign policy consisted of two currents—isolationism and expansionism. Although the determination to remain aloof from European politics had been a hallmark of U.S. foreign policy since the nation's founding, Americans simultaneously believed in manifest destiny—the "obvious" right to expand the nation from ocean to ocean. The United States' determination to protect its sphere of influence in the Western Hemisphere at the same time it expanded its trading in Asia moved the nation away from isolationism and toward a more active role on the world stage.

Markets and Missionaries

The depression of the 1890s provided a powerful impetus to American commercial expansion. As markets weakened at home, American businesses looked abroad for profits. As the depression deepened, one diplomat warned that

CHAPTER LOCATOR | What were the reasons behind the farmers' revolt? | What led to the "labor wars" of the 1890s?

CHAPTER 20
554 A DECADE OF DISSENT, DEPRESSION, AND WAR , 1890–1900

Americans "must turn [their] eyes abroad, or they will soon look inward upon discontent."

Exports constituted a small but significant percentage of the profits of American business in the 1890s (**Figure 20.2**). And where American interests led, businessmen expected the government's power and influence to follow to protect their investments. Companies like Standard Oil actively sought to use the U.S. government as their agent, often putting foreign service employees on the payroll. "Our ambassadors and ministers and consuls," wrote John D. Rockefeller appreciatively, "have aided to push our way into new markets and to the utmost corners of the world." Whether "our" referred to the United States or to Standard Oil remained ambiguous.

America's foreign policy often appeared to be little more than a sidelight to business development. In Hawaii (first called the Sandwich Islands), American sugar interests toppled the increasingly independent Queen Liliuokalani in 1893. They pushed Congress to annex the islands, which would allow planters to avoid the high McKinley tariff on sugar. When President Cleveland learned that Hawaiians opposed annexation, he withdrew the proposal from Congress. But expansionists still coveted the islands and continued to look for an excuse to push through annexation.

Business interests alone, however, did not account for the new expansionism that seized the nation during the 1890s. As Captain Alfred Thayer Mahan, leader of a growing group of American expansionists, confessed, "Even when material interests are the original exciting cause, it is the sentiment to which they give rise, the moral tone which emotion takes that constitutes the greater force." Much

CHRONOLOGY

1893
– President Grover Cleveland rejects attempt to annex Hawaii.

1899–1900
– Secretary of State John Hay enunciates Open Door policy in China.
– Boxer uprising in China.

FIGURE 20.2 ■ **Expansion in U.S. Trade, 1870–1910**

Between 1870 and 1910, American exports more than tripled. Imports generally rose, but they were held in check by the high protective tariffs championed by Republican presidents from Ulysses S. Grant to William Howard Taft. A decline in imports is particularly noticeable after the passage of the prohibitive McKinley tariff in 1890.

(Line graph: vertical axis "Millions of dollars" ranging 500 to 2,000; horizontal axis years 1870 to 1910. Two lines: Exports and Imports.)

| How were women involved in late-nineteenth-century politics? | How did economic problems shape American politics in the 1890s? | **Why did the United States move away from isolationism?** | Why did America go to war with Spain in 1898? | Conclusion: What was the connection between domestic tensions and U.S. foreign policy? |

Women Missionaries

Methodist women missionaries in China's Szechuan province relied on traditional means of transportation, in this case "back chairs." Women constituted 60 percent of America's foreign missionaries by 1890.
Special Collections, Yale Divinity School Library.

of that moral tone was set by American missionaries, many of whom set their sights on China.

The 1858 Tientsin treaty admitted foreign missionaries to China. Although Christians converted only 100,000 in a population of 400 million, the Chinese nevertheless resented the interference of missionaries in village life. Opposition to foreign missionaries took the form of antiforeign secret societies, most notably the Boxers, whose Chinese name translated to "Righteous Harmonious Fist." In 1899, the Boxers began to hunt down and kill Chinese Christians and missionaries in northwestern Shandong Province. With the tacit support of China's Dowager Empress, the Boxers became bolder. Under the slogan "Uphold the Ch'ing Dynasty, Exterminate the Foreigners," they marched on the cities. Their rampage eventually led to the massacre of some 30,000 Chinese converts and 250 foreign nuns, priests, and missionaries along with their families. In August 1900, 2,500 U.S. troops joined an international force sent to rescue the foreigners besieged in Beijing. The European powers imposed the humiliating Boxer Protocol in 1901, giving them the right to maintain military forces in the Chinese capital and requiring the Chinese government to pay an indemnity of $333 million for the loss of life and property resulting from the Boxer uprising.

In the aftermath of the uprising, missionaries voiced no concern at the paradox of bringing Christianity to China at gunpoint. "It is worth any cost in money, worth any cost in bloodshed," argued one bishop, "if we can make millions of Chinese true and intelligent Christians." Merchants and missionaries alike shared such reasoning. Indeed, trade and Christianity marched into Asia together. "Missionaries," admitted the American clergyman Charles Denby, "are the pioneers of trade and commerce. . . . The missionary, inspired by holy zeal, goes everywhere and by degrees foreign commerce and trade follow."

CHAPTER LOCATOR | What were the reasons behind the farmers' revolt? | What led to the "labor wars" of the 1890s?

CHAPTER 20
556 A DECADE OF DISSENT, DEPRESSION, AND WAR , 1890–1900

The Monroe Doctrine and the Open Door Policy

The emergence of the United States as a world power pitted the nation against other colonial powers, particularly Germany and Japan, which posed a threat to the twin pillars of America's expansionist foreign policy. The first, the Monroe Doctrine, came to be interpreted as establishing the Western Hemisphere as an American "sphere of influence" and warned European powers to stay away or risk war. The second, the Open Door, dealt with maintaining market access to China.

American diplomacy actively worked to buttress the Monroe Doctrine, with its assertion of American hegemony (domination) in the Western Hemisphere. In the 1880s, Republican secretary of state James G. Blaine promoted hemispheric peace and trade through Pan-American cooperation but at the same time used American troops to intervene in Latin American border disputes. In 1895, Americans risked war with Great Britain to enforce the Monroe Doctrine when a conflict developed between Venezuela and British Guiana.

In Central America, American business triumphed in a bloodless takeover that saw French and British interests routed. The United Fruit Company of Boston virtually dominated the Central American nations of Costa Rica and Guatemala, while an importer from New Orleans turned Honduras into a "banana republic" (a country run by U.S. business interests). Thus, by 1895, the United States, through business as well as diplomacy, had successfully achieved hegemony in Latin America and the Caribbean.

At the same time that American foreign policy warned European powers to stay out of the Western Hemisphere, the United States competed for trade in the Eastern Hemisphere. As American interests in China grew, the United States became more aggressive in defending its presence in Asia and the Pacific.

In the 1890s, China, weakened by years of internal warfare, was beginning to be partitioned into spheres of influence by Britain, Japan, Germany, France, and Russia. Concerned about the integrity of China and no less about American trade, Secretary of State John Hay in 1899–1900 wrote a series of notes calling for an "open door" policy that would ensure trade access to all and maintain Chinese sovereignty. The notes were greeted by the major powers with polite evasion. Nevertheless, Hay skillfully managed to maneuver the major powers into doing his bidding, and in 1900 he boldly announced the Open Door as international policy. The United States, by insisting on the **Open Door policy**, managed to secure access to Chinese markets, expanding its economic power while avoiding the problems of maintaining a far-flung colonial empire on the Asian mainland. But as the Spanish-American War soon demonstrated, Americans found it hard to resist the temptations of overseas empire.

Open Door policy

▶ Proposal first put forward by Secretary of State John Hay in 1899–1900 recommending that all major powers share access to trade with China and that Chinese sovereignty be maintained. The proposal was made against a backdrop of intensifying efforts by the other major powers to establish spheres of influence in China. Through skillful diplomacy, Hay was able to establish the Open Door as international policy.

QUICK REVIEW

What roles did business and Christianity play in American foreign policy in the 1890s?

How were women involved in late-nineteenth-century politics?	How did economic problems shape American politics in the 1890s?	**Why did the United States move away from isolationism?**	Why did America go to war with Spain in 1898?	Conclusion: What was the connection between domestic tensions and U.S. foreign policy?

Why did America go to war with Spain in 1898?

VOL. XLIX. No. 1257.   PUCK BUILDING, New York, April 6th, 1901.   PRICE TEN CENTS.

Puck

COLUMBIA'S EASTER BONNET.

Columbia's Easter Bonnet

The United States, symbolized by the female figure of Columbia, tries on "World Power" in this cartoon from *Puck* that appeared in 1901 after the Spanish-American War left the United States in control of Spain's former colonies in Guam, the Philippines, and Puerto Rico. "Expansion," spelled out in the smoke from the ship's smokestack, points to a new overseas direction for American foreign policy at the turn of the twentieth century. Library of Congress.

THE SPANISH-AMERICAN WAR began as an effort to free Cuba from Spain's colonial grasp and ended with the United States itself acquiring territory overseas and fighting a guerrilla war with Filipino nationalists, who, like the Cubans, sought independence. Behind the contradiction stood the twin pillars of American foreign policy: The Monroe Doctrine made Spain's presence in Cuba unacceptable, and U.S. determination to keep open the door to Asia made the Philippines attractive as a stepping-stone to China.

"A Splendid Little War"

Looking back on the **Spanish-American War** of 1898, Secretary of State John Hay judged it "a splendid little war; begun with the highest motives, carried on with magnificent intelligence and spirit, favored by that fortune which loves the brave." At the close of a decade marred by bitter depression, social unrest, and political upheaval, the war offered Americans a chance to wave the flag and march in unison. Few argued the merits of the conflict until it was over and the time came to divide the spoils.

Spanish-American War

▶ 1898 war between Spain and the United States that began as an effort to free Cuba from Spain's colonial rule. It ended with the United States acquiring control of Cuba and colonies in Puerto Rico, Guam, and the Philippines. The war itself was both popular and brief. When it was over, the United States stood as an imperial power.

CHAPTER LOCATOR | What were the reasons behind the farmers' revolt? | What led to the "labor wars" of the 1890s?

The war began with moral outrage over the treatment of Cuban revolutionaries, who had launched a fight for independence against the Spanish colonial regime in 1895. In an attempt to isolate the guerrillas, the Spanish general Valeriano Weyler herded Cubans into concentration camps, where thousands died of hunger, disease, and exposure. Starvation soon spread to the cities. Tens of thousands of Cubans died, and countless others were left without food, clothing, or shelter. By 1898, fully a quarter of the island's population had perished in the Cuban revolution.

As the Cuban rebellion dragged on, pressure for American intervention mounted. American newspapers fueled public outrage at Spain. A fierce circulation war raged in New York City between William Randolph Hearst's *Journal* and Joseph Pulitzer's *World*. Their competition provoked what came to be called **yellow journalism**. Practitioners of yellow journalism pandered to the public's appetite for sensationalism. The Cuban war provided a wealth of dramatic copy. Hearst sent artist Frederic Remington to document the horror, and when Remington wired home, "There is no trouble here. There will be no war," Hearst shot back, "You furnish the pictures and I'll furnish the war."

American interests in Cuba were, in the words of the U.S. minister to Spain, more than "merely theoretical or sentimental." American business had more than $50 million invested in Cuban sugar, and, as a result of the rebellion, American trade with Cuba had dropped to near zero. Nevertheless, the business community balked, wary of a war with Spain. When industrialist Mark Hanna, the Republican kingmaker and senator from Ohio, urged restraint, Theodore Roosevelt exploded, "We will have this war for the freedom of Cuba, Senator Hanna, in spite of the timidity of commercial interests."

To expansionists like Roosevelt, more than Cuban independence was at stake. Appointed assistant secretary of the navy in April 1897, Roosevelt took the helm in the absence of his boss and audaciously ordered the U.S. fleet to Manila in the Philippines. In the event of conflict with Spain, Roosevelt put the navy in a position to capture the islands and gain an entry point to China.

President McKinley slowly moved toward intervention. In a show of American force, he dispatched the battleship *Maine* to Cuba. On the night of February 15, 1898, a mysterious explosion destroyed the *Maine*, killing 267 crew members. The source of the explosion remained unclear, but inflammatory stories in the press enraged Americans, who immediately blamed the Spanish government. Rallying to the cry "Remember the *Maine*," Congress declared war on Spain in April. In a surge of patriotism, more than a million men rushed to enlist. War brought with it a unity of purpose and national harmony that ended a decade of political dissent and strife. "In April, everywhere over this good fair land, flags were flying," wrote Kansas editor William Allen White. "At the stations, crowds gathered to hurrah for the soldiers, and to throw hats into the air, and to unfurl flags."

Five days after McKinley signed the war resolution, a U.S. navy squadron commanded by Admiral George Dewey destroyed the Spanish fleet in Manila Bay (**Map 20.3**, page 560). Dewey's stunning victory caught the United States by surprise. Although naval strategists including Theodore Roosevelt had been orchestrating the move for some time, few Americans had ever heard of the Philippines. Even McKinley confessed that he could not immediately locate the archipelago on the map. Nevertheless, he dispatched U.S. troops to secure the islands.

CHRONOLOGY

1898
- U.S. battleship *Maine* explodes in Havana harbor.
- Congress declares war on Spain.
- Admiral George Dewey destroys Spanish fleet in Manila Bay, the Philippines.
- U.S. troops defeat Spanish forces in Cuba.
- Treaty of Paris ends war with Spain and cedes the Philippines, Puerto Rico, and Guam to the United States.
- United States annexes Hawaii.

yellow journalism

▶ Term given to sensationalistic newspaper reporting and cartoon images rendered in yellow to promote U.S. entry into war with Spain. A fierce circulation war between two New York City papers provoked the journalistic tactics that helped fuel popular support for the war.

| How were women involved in late-nineteenth-century politics? | How did economic problems shape American politics in the 1890s? | Why did the United States move away from isolationism? | Why did America go to war with Spain in 1898? | Conclusion: What was the connection between domestic tensions and U.S. foreign policy? |

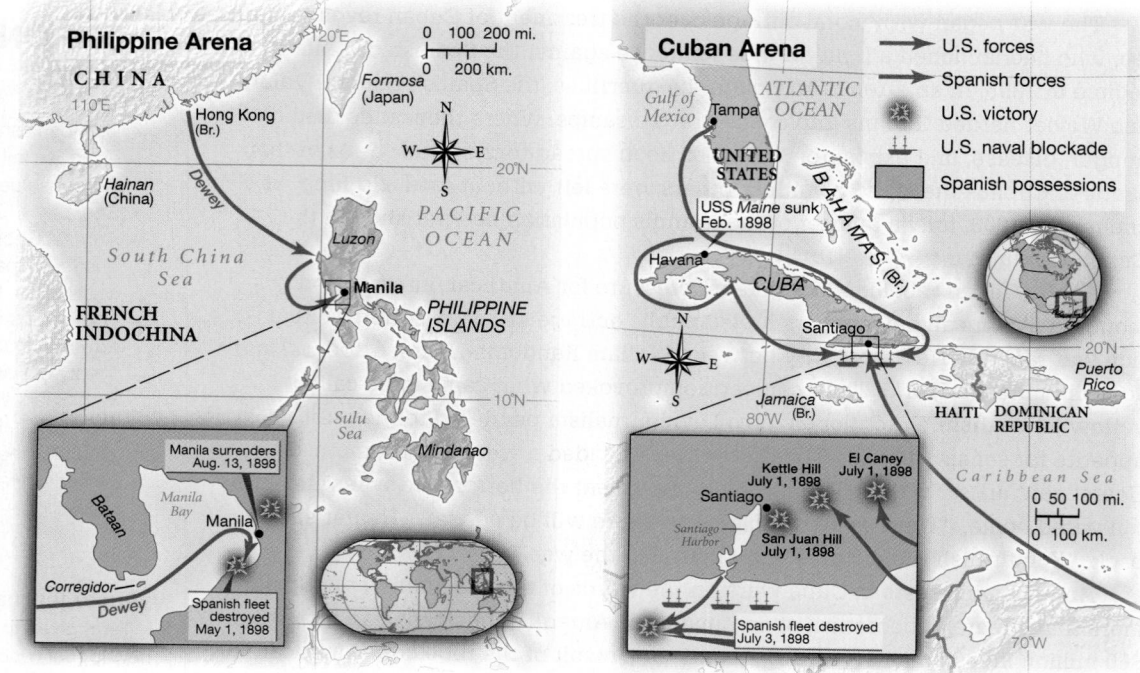

MAP 20.3 ■ The Spanish-American War, 1898

The Spanish-American War was fought in two theaters, the Philippine Islands and Cuba. Five days after President William McKinley called for a declaration of war, Admiral George Dewey captured Manila without the loss of a single American sailor. The war lasted only eight months. Troops landed in Cuba in mid-June and by mid-July had taken Santiago and Havana and had destroyed the Spanish fleet.

> ▶ FOR MORE HELP ANALYZING THIS MAP, see the map activity for this chapter in the Online Study Guide at bedfordstmartins.com/roarkunderstanding.

The war in Cuba ended almost as quickly as it began. The first U.S. troops landed on June 22, and after a handful of battles, the Spanish surrendered on July 17. The war lasted just long enough to elevate Theodore Roosevelt to the status of war hero. Roosevelt resigned his navy post and formed the Rough Riders, a regiment composed of Ivy League polo players and cowboys Roosevelt learned to respect during his stint as a cattle rancher in the Dakotas. The Rough Riders' charge up Kettle Hill and Roosevelt's role in the decisive battle of San Juan Hill made front-page news. Overnight, Roosevelt became the most famous man in America. By the time he sailed home from Cuba, a coalition of independent Republicans was already plotting his political future.

The Debate over American Imperialism

After a few brief campaigns in Cuba and Puerto Rico brought the Spanish-American War to an end, America gained possession of an empire that stretched halfway around the globe. As part of the spoils of war, the United States acquired Cuba, Puerto Rico, Guam, and the Philippines. Yielding to pressure from American sugar

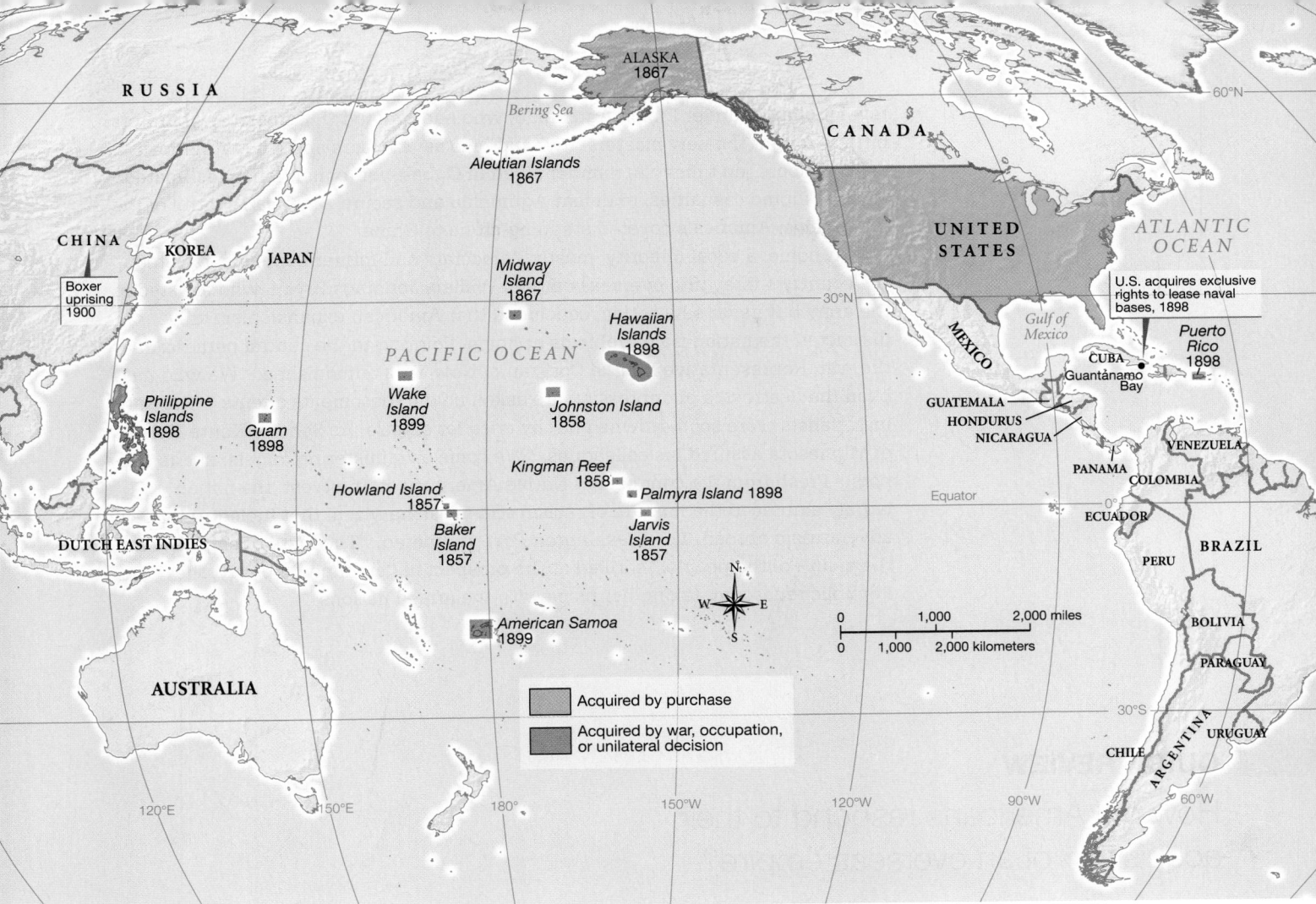

MAP 20.4 ■ U.S. Overseas Expansion through 1900

The United States extended its interests abroad with a series of territorial acquisitions. Although Cuba was granted independence, the Platt Amendment kept the new nation firmly under U.S. control. In the wake of the Spanish-American War, the United States woke up to find that it held an empire extending halfway around the globe.

planters, President McKinley expanded the empire further, annexing Hawaii in July 1898.

Contemptuous of the Cubans, the U.S. government dictated a Cuban constitution in 1898. It included the so-called Platt Amendment—a series of provisions that granted the United States the right to intervene to protect Cuba's "independence," as well as the power to oversee Cuban debt so that European creditors would not find an excuse for intervention. The United States also gave itself a ninety-nine-year lease on a naval base at Guantánamo. In return, McKinley promised to implement an extensive sanitation program to clean up the island, making it more attractive to American investors.

In the formal Treaty of Paris (1898), Spain ceded the Philippines to the United States along with its former colonies of Puerto Rico and Guam (**Map 20.4**). Filipino

| How were women involved in late-nineteenth-century politics? | How did economic problems shape American politics in the 1890s? | Why did the United States move away from isolationism? | **Why did America go to war with Spain in 1898?** | Conclusion: What was the connection between domestic tensions and U.S. foreign policy? |

561

revolutionaries under Emilio Aguinaldo, who had greeted U.S. troops as liberators, bitterly fought the new masters. It would take seven years and 4,000 American dead—almost ten times the number killed in Cuba—not to mention an estimated 20,000 Filipino casualties, to defeat Aguinaldo and secure American control of the Philippines, America's coveted stepping-stone to China.

At home, a vocal minority, mostly Democrats and former Populists, resisted the country's foray into overseas empire. William Jennings Bryan, who enlisted in the army but never saw action, concluded that American expansionism only distracted the nation from problems at home. Pointing to the central paradox of the war, Representative Bourke Cockran of New York admonished, "We who have been the destroyers of oppression are asked now to become its agents." The anti-imperialists were soon drowned out by cries for empire. As Senator Knute Nelson of Minnesota assured his colleagues, "We come as ministering angels, not as despots." Fresh from the conquest of Native Americans in the West, the nation largely embraced the mixture of racism and missionary zeal that fueled American adventurism abroad. The *Washington Post* trumpeted, "The taste of empire is in the mouth of the people," thrilled at the prospect of "an imperial policy, the Republic renascent, taking her place with the armed nations."

> **QUICK REVIEW**

How did Americans respond to their acquisition of an overseas empire?

CHAPTER LOCATOR | What were the reasons behind the farmers' revolt? | What led to the "labor wars" of the 1890s?

CHAPTER 20
562 A DECADE OF DISSENT, DEPRESSION, AND WAR , 1890–1900

Chicago History Museum.

Conclusion: What was the connection between domestic tensions and U.S. foreign policy?

A DECADE OF DOMESTIC STRIFE ended amid the blare of martial music and the waving of flags. The Spanish-American War drowned out the calls for social reform that had fueled the Populist politics of the 1890s. During that decade, angry farmers facing hard times looked to the Farmers' Alliance to fight for their vision of economic democracy, workers staged bloody strikes across the country to assert their rights, and women attacked drunkenness and the conditions that fostered it and mounted a suffrage movement to secure their basic political rights. In St. Louis in 1892, disaffected Americans formed a new People's Party to fight for change.

The bitter depression that began in 1893 led to increased labor strife. The Pullman boycott brutally dramatized the power of property and the conservatism of the laissez-faire state. But workers' willingness to confront capitalism on the streets of Chicago, Homestead, Cripple Creek, and a host of other sites across America eloquently testified to labor's growing determination, unity, and strength.

As the depression deepened, the sight of Coxey's army of unemployed men marching on Washington to demand federal intervention in the economy signaled a growing shift in the public mind against the stand-pat politics of laissez-faire. The call for the government to take action to better the lives of workers, farmers, and the dispossessed manifested itself in the fiercely fought presidential campaign of William Jennings Bryan in 1896. With the outbreak of the Spanish-American War in 1898, the decade ended on a harmonious note with patriotic Americans rallying around the flag. But even though Americans basked in patriotism and contemplated empire, old grievances had not been laid to rest. The People's Party had been beaten, but the Populists' call for greater government involvement in the economy, expanded opportunities for direct democracy, and a more equitable balance of profits and power between the people and the big corporations sounded the themes that would be taken up by a new generation of progressive reformers in the first decades of the twentieth century.

SO NOW YOU KNOW

The first march on Washington by Coxey's army in 1894 signified the frustration of America's working people with the economic collapse of the 1890s and the failure of political leaders to ameliorate the most basic hardships of American citizens.

> CHAPTER 20 STUDY GUIDE

Online Study Guide
bedfordstmartins.com/roarkunderstanding

STEP 1 GETTING STARTED

Below are basic terms from this period in American history. Can you identify each term below and explain why it matters? To do this exercise online or to download this chart, visit bedfordstmartins.com/roarkunderstanding.

TERM	WHO OR WHAT & WHEN	WHY IT MATTERS
Farmers' Alliance, p. 539		
People's Party, p. 541		
Eugene V. Debs, p. 547		
Frances Willard, p. 548		
Susan B. Anthony, p. 549		
Coxey's army, p. 551		
William Jennings Bryan, p. 552		
Open Door policy, p. 557		
Spanish-American War, p. 558		
yellow journalism, p. 559		

STEP 2 MOVING BEYOND THE BASICS

The exercise below represents a more advanced understanding of the chapter material. Begin by identifying the key issues in each of four major focal points of conflict: agriculture, labor, temperance, and women's rights. Then describe the goals and actions of activists and reformers in each area. When you are finished, look for connections among activists and reformers in all four areas. Then assess the success or failure of each movement. To do this exercise online or to download this chart, visit bedfordstmartins.com/roarkunderstanding.

Point of conflict	Key issues	Goals and actions of activists and reformers	How successful?
Agriculture			
Labor			
Temperance			
Women's rights			

Now that you have reviewed key elements of the chapter, take a step back and try to explain the big picture by answering these questions. Remember to use specific examples from the chapter in your answers. To do this exercise online, visit bedfordstmartins.com/roarkunderstanding.

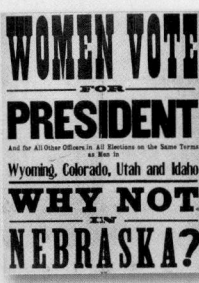

ECONOMICS

▶ What key issues fueled farm protest in the late nineteenth century? How did the Farmers' Alliance attempt to address these issues?

▶ What strategies and tactics did unions employ in the late nineteenth century? How did companies fight back?

POLITICS

▶ How did reform movements provide a vehicle for women's involvement in public political life?

▶ How did the depression of the mid-1890s shape the politics of the decade?

EMPIRE

▶ How did U.S. foreign policy reflect the tension between American tendencies toward isolationism and expansionism?

▶ How did the Spanish-American War change the place of the United States in global politics?

LOOKING BACKWARD, LOOKING AHEAD

▶ What were the United States' most important strengths and weaknesses in 1900? How had the nation's place in the world changed since 1800?

▶ Defend or refute the following statement: "With its victory in the Spanish-American War in 1898, the United States became an imperial power."

IN YOUR OWN WORDS

Imagine that you must explain chapter 20 to someone who hasn't read it. What would be the most important points to include and why?

21
PROGRESSIVISM FROM THE GRASS ROOTS UP

1890–1916

> This chapter examines the efforts of progressives to combat the ills of industrial America. It explores the grassroots initiatives of progressive activists, their core values and beliefs, and the impact of the progressive agenda on local, state, and national politics. Finally, it looks at the limits of progressive reform.

> How did grassroots progressives attack the problems of industrial America?

> What were the key tenets of progressive theory?

> How did Theodore Roosevelt advance the progressive agenda?

> How did progressivism fare during the Taft administration?

> What was Woodrow Wilson's progressive agenda and how did it change during his administration?

> What were the limits of progressive reform?

> Conclusion: How did the liberal state transform during the Progressive Era?

DID YOU KNOW?

The NAACP, an integrated organization, was founded more than 100 years ago.

Progressive social work. An Infant Welfare Society nurse instructs an immigrant mother on clean home care in 1910.

How did grassroots progressives attack the problems of industrial America?

Jane Addams

Jane Addams's desire to live among the poor and her insistence that settlement house work benefited educated women such as herself as well as her immigrant neighbors separated her from the charity workers who had come before her and marked the distance from philanthropy to progressive reform. Her autobiographical *Twenty Years at Hull-House*, published in 1910, is shown in the inset. Photo: Jane Addams Memorial Collection (JAMC neg. 14) Special Collections, University of Illinois at Chicago, photographer: Max Platz; book: Newberry Library.

MUCH OF PROGRESSIVE REFORM began at the grassroots level and percolated upward into local, state, and eventually national politics as reformers attacked the social problems fostered by urban industrialism. Although reform flourished in many different settings across the country, urban problems inspired the progressives' greatest efforts. In their zeal to "civilize the city," reformers founded settlement houses, professed a new Christian social gospel, and campaigned against vice and crime in the name of "social purity."

Civilizing the City

Progressives attacked the problems of the city on many fronts. The **settlement house** movement attempted to bridge the distance between the classes. The movement began in England and came to the United States in 1886 with the opening of the University Settlement House in New York City. The needs of poor urban neighborhoods provided the impetus for these social settlements. In 1889, Jane Addams leased a house in an immigrant neighborhood in Chicago. Throwing open

settlement houses
▶ Settlements established in poor neighborhoods beginning in the 1880s by reformers attempting to bridge the distance between the classes. Reformers like Jane Addams and Lillian Wald believed that only by living among the poor could they help bridge the growing class divide. College-educated women formed the backbone of the settlement house movement.

CHAPTER LOCATOR	How did grassroots progressives attack the problems of industrial America?	What were the key tenets of progressive theory?

the doors of Hull House, she invited her neighbors to share their interests and problems. And she invited young college graduates like herself to come and offer their expertise. Within a decade, Hull House had expanded from one rented floor to some thirteen buildings housing a remarkable variety of activities, including public baths, a nursery and kindergarten, a labor museum, manual training workshops, and the first public playground in Chicago.

The Progressives and Urban Reform

Settlement house movement	Effort by reformers to bridge the social divide by living and working among the poor
Social gospel	Call for churches and their members to play an active role in social reformation
Social purity movement	Campaign to clean up vice, particularly prostitution

Women, particularly college-educated women, formed the backbone of the settlement house movement and stood in the vanguard of the progressive movement. Settlement houses gave college-educated women eager to use their knowledge a place to put their talents to work in the service of society and to champion progressive reform. Largely due to women's efforts, settlements like Jane Addams's Hull House in Chicago and Lillian Wald's Henry Street in New York City grew in number from six in 1891 to more than four hundred in 1911. In the process, settlement house women created a new profession—social work—and stimulated a new reform movement—progressivism.

For their part, churches confronted urban social problems by enunciating a new **social gospel**, one that saw its mission not simply to reform individuals but to reform society. The social gospel offered a powerful corrective to social Darwinism and the gospel of wealth, which fostered the belief that riches signaled divine favor. In place of the gospel of wealth, progressive clergy exhorted their congregations to put Christ's teachings to work in their daily lives. Charles M. Sheldon's popular book *In His Steps* (1898) called on men and women to Christianize capitalism by asking the question "What would Jesus do?"

Ministers also played an active role in the social purity movement, the campaign to attack vice. To end the "social evil," as reformers euphemistically called prostitution, the social purity movement brought together clergymen who wished to stamp out sin, doctors concerned about the spread of venereal disease, and women reformers determined to fight the double standard that tolerated male promiscuity but demanded chastity of women. Advanced progressive reformers linked prostitution to poverty and championed higher wages for women. "Is it any wonder," asked the Chicago vice commission, "that a tempted girl who receives only six dollars per week working with her hands sells her body for twenty-five dollars per week when she learns there is a demand for it and men are willing to pay the price?"

Attacks on alcohol went hand in hand with the push for social purity. Reformers pointed to links between drinking, prostitution, wife and child abuse, unemployment, and industrial accidents. The powerful liquor lobby fought back, spending liberally in election campaigns, fueling the charge that liquor corrupted the political process.

CHRONOLOGY

1889
- Jane Addams opens Hull House settlement in Chicago.

1903
- Women's Trade Union League, an alliance of women workers and middle-class "allies," is founded.

1908
- In *Muller v. Oregon*, U.S. Supreme Court upholds an Oregon law limiting the number of hours women can work.

1909
- Some 20,000 garment workers, most of them women, strike in New York City for better working conditions.

1911
- Triangle fire in New York City kills 146 workers.

social gospel
▶ A vision of Christianity that saw its mission not simply to reform individuals but to reform society. The social gospel offered a powerful corrective to social Darwinism and the gospel of wealth. In place of the gospel of wealth, progressive clergy exhorted their congregations to put Christ's teachings to work in their daily lives.

How did Theodore Roosevelt advance the progressive agenda?	How did progressivism fare during the Taft administration?	What was Woodrow Wilson's progressive agenda and how did it change during his administration?	What were the limits of progressive reform?	Conclusion: How did the liberal state transform during the Progressive Era?

An element of nativism (dislike of foreigners) ran through the movement for prohibition, as it did in a number of progressive reforms. The Irish, the Italians, and the Germans were among the groups stigmatized by temperance reformers for their drinking. To deny the working class access to alcohol, these progressives pushed for state legislation to outlaw the sale of liquor. By 1912, seven states were "dry."

Core Progressive Attitudes

A willingness to take action
The belief that environment, not heredity alone, determined human behavior
Optimism that reform could be achieved through government action without radically altering America's economy or institutions

Progressives and the Working Class

Day-to-day contact with their neighbors made settlement house workers particularly sympathetic to labor unions. When Mary Kenney O'Sullivan complained that her bookbinders' union met in a dirty, noisy saloon, Jane Addams invited the union to meet at Hull House. And during the Pullman strike in 1894, Hull House residents organized strike relief. "Hull-House has been so unionized," grumbled one Chicago businessman, "that it has lost its usefulness and become a detriment and harm to the community." But to the working class, the support of middle-class reformers marked a significant gain.

Attempts to forge a cross-class alliance became institutionalized in 1903 with the creation of the **Women's Trade Union League (WTUL)**. The WTUL brought together women workers and middle-class "allies." Its goal was to organize workingwomen into unions under the auspices of the American Federation of Labor (AFL).

Although the alliance between workingwomen, primarily immigrants and daughters of immigrants, and their middle-class allies was not without tension, the WTUL helped workingwomen achieve significant gains. Its most notable success came in 1909 in the "uprising of the twenty thousand," when women employees of the Triangle Shirtwaist Company in New York City went on strike to protest low wages, dangerous working conditions, and management's refusal to recognize their union, the International Ladies' Garment Workers Union (ILGWU). By the time the strike ended in February 1910, the workers had won important demands in many shops. The solidarity shown by the women workers proved to be the strike's greatest achievement. As Clara Lemlich, one of the strike's leaders, exclaimed, "They used to say that you couldn't even organize women. They wouldn't come to union meetings. They were 'temporary' workers. Well we showed them!"

The WTUL made enormous contributions to the strike. It provided volunteers for the picket lines, posted more than $29,000 in bail, protested police brutality, organized a parade of ten thousand strikers, took part in the arbitration conference, appealed for funds, and generated publicity for the strike. Under the leadership of the WTUL, women from every class of society, from J. P. Morgan's

Women's Trade Union League (WTUL)

▶ A cross-class alliance created in 1903 that brought together women workers and middle-class "allies." Its goal was to organize workingwomen into unions. The WTUL helped workingwomen achieve significant gains. Its most notable success came in 1909 in the "uprising of the twenty thousand," in New York City.

CHAPTER LOCATOR | How did grassroots progressives attack the problems of industrial America? | What were the key tenets of progressive theory?

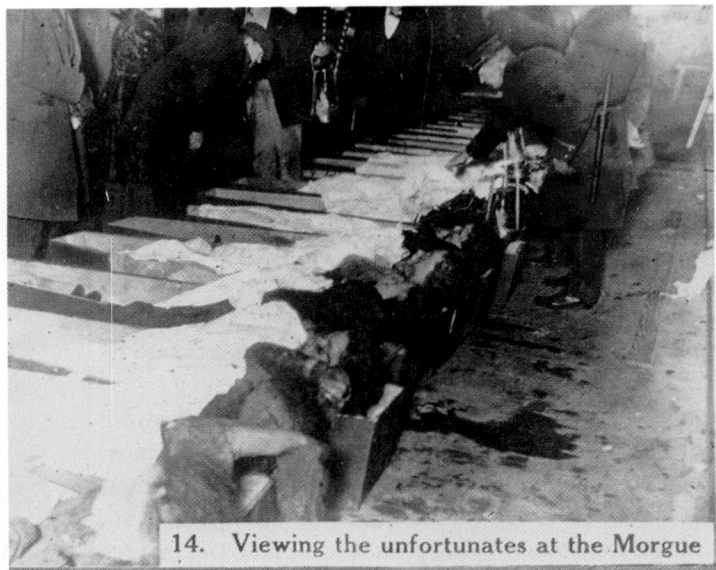

14. Viewing the unfortunates at the Morgue

Triangle Fire Morgue

After the Triangle fire on March 26, 1911, New York City set up a makeshift morgue where the remains of more than a hundred young women and two dozen young men were laid out in coffins for their friends and relatives to identify. Artist John Sloan created this striking illustration to commemorate those who died in the fire—a businessman weeps over his lost profits while a young woman worker lies burning on the pavement and a leering skeleton poses on the left. Photo: United Archives, Kheel Center, Cornell University, Ithaca, N.Y.; Illustration: Granger Collection.

▶ FOR MORE HELP ANALYZING THIS IMAGE, see the visual activity for this chapter in the Online Study Guide at bedfordstmartins.com/roarkunderstanding.

daughter Anne to socialists on New York's Lower East Side, joined the strikers in a dramatic display of cross-class alliance.

But for all its success, the uprising of the twenty thousand failed fundamentally to change conditions for women workers, as a tragic fire at the Triangle factory dramatized in 1911. A WTUL member described the scene on the street as the factory burned: "Two young girls whom I knew to be working in the vicinity came rushing toward me, tears were running from their eyes and they were white and shaking as they caught me by the arm. 'Oh,' shrieked one of them, 'they are jumping. Jumping from ten stories up! They are going through the air like bundles of clothes.'"

The terrified Triangle workers had little choice but to jump. Flames blocked one exit, and the other door had been locked to prevent workers from pilfering. The flimsy, rusted fire escape collapsed under the weight of fleeing workers, killing dozens. Trapped, 54 workers jumped to their deaths from the ninth-floor window. Of 500 workers, 146 died and scores of others were injured. The owners of the Triangle firm went to trial for negligence, but they avoided conviction when authorities determined that the fire had been started by a careless smoker. The Triangle Shirtwaist Company reopened in another firetrap within a matter of weeks.

How did Theodore Roosevelt advance the progressive agenda?	How did progressivism fare during the Taft administration?	What was Woodrow Wilson's progressive agenda and how did it change during his administration?	What were the limits of progressive reform?	Conclusion: How did the liberal state transform during the Progressive Era?

Outrage and frustration overwhelmed Rose Schneiderman, a leading WTUL organizer, who spoke at the memorial service for the dead Triangle workers. "I would be a traitor to those poor burned bodies if I came here to talk good fellowship," she told her audience. "We have tried you good people of the public and we have found you wanting. . . . I know from my experience it is up to the working people to save themselves . . . by a strong working class movement." The Triangle fire severely tested the bonds of the cross-class alliance. Along with Rose Schneiderman, WTUL leaders experienced a growing sense of futility. It seemed not enough to organize and to strike. Increasingly, the WTUL turned its efforts to lobbying for protective legislation—laws that would limit hours and regulate working conditions for women workers.

Advocates of protective legislation won a major victory in 1908 when the U.S. Supreme Court, in *Muller v. Oregon*, reversed its previous rulings and upheld an Oregon law that limited to ten the number of hours women could work in a day. A mass of sociological evidence put together by Florence Kelley of the National Consumers' League and Josephine Goldmark of the WTUL convinced the Court that long hours endangered women and therefore the entire human race. The Court's ruling set a precedent, but one that separated the well-being of women workers from that of men by arguing that women's reproductive role justified special treatment. Later generations of women fighting for equality would question the effectiveness of this strategy and argue that it ultimately closed good jobs to women.

The National Consumers' League, like the WTUL, fostered cross-class alliance. And, like the WTUL, the National Consumers' League increasingly promoted protective legislation to improve working conditions for working women. Frustrated by the reluctance of the private sector to respond to the need for reform, progressives turned to government at all levels.

Reform also fueled the fight for woman suffrage. For women like Jane Addams and Florence Kelley, involvement in social reform led inevitably to support for woman suffrage. Emphasizing the reforms that could be accomplished if women had the vote, these new suffragists argued that in an urban, industrial society, a good housekeeper could not protect her family unless she became involved in politics and wielded the ballot—and not just the broom—in the service of "municipal housekeeping."

> QUICK REVIEW

How did progressives work to "civilize" the city?

CHAPTER LOCATOR | How did grassroots progressives attack the problems of industrial America? | What were the key tenets of progressive theory?

CHAPTER 21
572 PROGRESSIVISM FROM THE GRASS ROOTS UP, 1890–1916

What were the key tenets of progressive theory?

Tom Johnson

The reform mayor of Cleveland from 1901 to 1909, Tom Johnson is shown here campaigning in Cleveland's Wade Park in 1908. To get a three-cent streetcar fare and win the support of the working classes, Johnson instituted municipal ownership of the transit system. The Western Reserve Historical Society, Cleveland, Ohio.

THE PROGRESSIVES EMPHASIZED action and experimentation. Dismissing the view that humans should leave progress to the dictates of natural selection, progressive reform Darwinists argued that human intelligence could shape change and improve society. Progressive theory found practical application in state and local politics, where reformers challenged traditional laissez-faire government.

Reform Darwinism and Social Engineering

Without abandoning the evolutionary framework of Darwinism, a new group of sociologists argued that evolution could be advanced more rapidly if men and women used their intellects to alter the environment. Sociologist Lester Frank Ward put it clearly in his book *Dynamic Sociology* (1883). "I insist that the time must soon come," he wrote, "when control of blind natural forces in society must give way to human foresight." Dubbed **reform Darwinism**, the new sociological theory condemned the laissez-faire approach, insisting that the liberal state should play a more active role in solving social problems.

Efficiency and *expertise* became watchwords in the progressive vocabulary. In *Drift and Mastery* (1914), journalist and critic Walter Lippmann called for "technocrats" to use scientific techniques to control and direct social change. At its extreme, the application of expertise and social engineering took the form of scientific management. Frederick Winslow Taylor pioneered "systematized shop management." Obsessed with making humans and machines produce more and faster, Taylor carefully timed workers and attempted to break down their work into its simplest components. An advocate of piecework, quotas, and pay incentives for productivity, he insisted that unions were unnecessary. Taylor won many converts among corporate managers, but workers hated the monotony of

reform Darwinism
▶ Sociological theory developed in the 1880s that condemned the laissez-faire approach to government, insisting that the liberal state should play a more active role in solving social problems. Reform Darwinists believed that the human intellect could shape and speed up the process of human evolution. This belief was reflected in a variety of progressive initiatives.

1883
- Lester Frank Ward publishes *Dynamic Sociology*, championing reform Darwinism.

1900
- Progressive Tom Loftin Johnson is elected mayor of Cleveland for the first of four terms.
- Robert M. La Follette capitalizes on grassroots progressivism and is elected governor of Wisconsin.

1906
- Robert M. La Follette is elected to the U.S. Senate.

1910
- Progressive Hiram Johnson of California is elected governor of California.

1914
- Walter Lippmann's *Drift and Mastery* calls for "technocrats" to control social change.

systematized shop management and argued that it led to the speedup—pushing workers to produce more in less time and for less pay. Yet many progressives applauded the increased productivity and efficiency of Taylor's system.

Progressive Government: City and State

Progressivism burst forth at every level of government in 1900, but nowhere more forcefully than in Cleveland with the election of Tom Loftin Johnson as mayor. A self-made millionaire, Johnson moved in 1899 to Cleveland, where he began his career in politics. During his mayoral campaign, he pledged to reduce the streetcar fare from five cents to three cents. His election touched off a seven-year war between Johnson and the streetcar moguls, who argued that they couldn't meet costs with the lower fare. Serving as mayor for four terms, Johnson fought for fair taxation and championed greater democracy through the use of the initiative, referendum, and recall—devices that allowed voters to have a direct say in legislative and judicial matters. Under Johnson's administration, Cleveland became, in the words of journalist Lincoln Steffens, the "best governed city in America."

In Wisconsin, Robert M. La Follette converted to the progressive cause early in the 1900s. La Follette capitalized on the grassroots movement for reform to launch his long political career as governor (1901–1906) and U.S. senator (1906–1925). La Follette brought scientists and professors into his administration and used the University of Wisconsin as a resource in drafting legislation. As governor, he lowered railroad rates, raised railroad taxes, improved education, preached conservation, established factory regulation and workers' compensation, instituted the first direct primary in the country, and inaugurated the first state income tax. Under his leadership, Wisconsin earned the title "laboratory of democracy." A fiery orator, "Fighting Bob" La Follette united his supporters around issues that transcended party loyalties. This emphasis on reform characterized progressivism, which attracted followers from both major parties. Democrats like Tom Johnson and Republicans like Robert La Follette could lay equal claim to the label "progressive."

West of the Rockies, progressivism found a champion in Hiram Johnson of California, who served as governor from 1911 to 1917 and later as a U.S. senator. Since the 1870s, California politics had been dominated by the Southern Pacific Railroad. Johnson ran for governor in 1910 on the promise to "kick the Southern Pacific out of politics." With the support of the reform wing of the Republican Party and the promise "to return the government to the people," he won. As governor, he introduced the direct primary; supported the initiative, referendum, and recall; strengthened the state's railroad commission; supported conservation; and signed an employer's liability law.

> **QUICK REVIEW**

How did state and local politicians apply progressive theory?

CHAPTER LOCATOR | How did grassroots progressives attack the problems of industrial America? | What were the key tenets of progressive theory?

CHAPTER 21
574 PROGRESSIVISM FROM THE GRASS ROOTS UP, 1890–1916

Theodore Roosevelt Described aptly by a contemporary observer as "a steam engine in trousers," Theodore Roosevelt brought to the presidency energy, intellect, and activism in equal measure. Roosevelt boasted that he used the presidency as a "bully pulpit"—a forum from which he advocated reforms ranging from trust-busting to conservation. Library of Congress.

How did Theodore Roosevelt advance the progressive agenda?

ON SEPTEMBER 6, 1901, President William McKinley was shot by Leon Czolgosz, an anarchist, while attending the Pan-American Exposition in Buffalo, New York. Eight days later, McKinley died, and Vice President Theodore Roosevelt became president.

An activist and a moralist, imbued with the progressive spirit, Roosevelt would turn the White House into a "bully pulpit," advocating reforms like conservation and championing the nation's emergence as a world power. In the process, Roosevelt would work to shift the nation's center of power from Wall Street to Washington.

The Square Deal

At age forty-two, Theodore Roosevelt became the youngest man ever to move into the White House. Roosevelt went from the New York assembly at the age of twenty-three to the presidency in less than twenty years, with time out as a cowboy in the Dakotas, police commissioner of New York City, assistant secretary of the navy, colonel of the Rough Riders, and governor of New York.

A patrician by birth and an activist by temperament, Roosevelt brought to the presidency enormous talent and energy. As president, Roosevelt would harness his explosive energy to strengthen the power of the federal government, putting business on notice that it could no longer count on a laissez-faire government to give it free rein. The "absolutely vital question" facing the country, Roosevelt wrote to a friend in 1901, was "whether or not the government has the power to

CHRONOLOGY

1901
– William McKinley is assassinated; Theodore Roosevelt becomes president.

1902
– Federal government files antitrust lawsuit against Northern Securities Company.
– Roosevelt mediates anthracite coal strike.

1903
– United States begins construction of Panama Canal.

1904
– Roosevelt Corollary to Monroe Doctrine.

1906
– Pure Food and Drug Act and Meat Inspection Act.

1907
– Panic on Wall Street.
– Roosevelt signs "Gentlemen's Agreement" with Japan, restricting immigration.

control the trusts." The Sherman Antitrust Act of 1890 had been badly weakened by a conservative Supreme Court and by attorneys general more willing to use it against labor unions than against monopolies. In one of his first acts as president, Roosevelt ordered his attorney general to begin a secret antitrust investigation of the Northern Securities Company that led to an antitrust suit filed by the government in February 1902. Northern Securities was a giant company that linked three competing railroads under one management and monopolized railroad traffic in the Northwest.

The news of the antitrust suit against Northern Securities rocked Wall Street. As one newspaper editor sarcastically observed, "Wall Street is paralyzed at the thought that a President of the United States would sink so low as to try to enforce the law." Roosevelt's thunderbolt put Wall Street on notice that the new president expected to be treated as an equal and was willing to use government as a weapon to curb business excesses. The Supreme Court, in a significant turnaround, upheld the Sherman Act and called for the dissolution of Northern Securities in 1904.

"Hurrah for Teddy the Trustbuster," cheered the papers. Roosevelt went on to use the Sherman Act against forty-three trusts, including such giants as American Tobacco, Du Pont, and Standard Oil. While willing to use the Sherman Act, he preferred regulation to antitrust suits. In 1903, he pressured Congress to pass the Elkins Act, outlawing railroad rebates. And he created the new cabinet-level Department of Commerce and Labor, with the subsidiary Bureau of Corporations to act as a corporate watchdog.

In his handling of the anthracite coal strike in 1902, Roosevelt again demonstrated his willingness to assert the authority of the presidency, this time to mediate between labor and management. In May, 147,000 coal miners in Pennsylvania went on strike. The United Mine Workers (UMW) demanded a reduction in the workday from twelve to ten hours, an equitable system of weighing each miner's output, and a 10 percent wage increase, along with recognition of the union.

The strike dragged on through the summer and into the fall. Hoarding and profiteering drove the price of coal from $2.50 to $6.00 a ton. As winter approached, coal shortages touched off near riots in the nation's big cities. At this juncture, Roosevelt stepped in to mediate, inviting representatives from both sides to meet in Washington in October. His unprecedented intervention served notice that government counted itself an independent force in business and labor disputes. At the same time, it gave unionism a boost by granting the UMW a place at the table.

At the meeting, the mine owners refused to talk with the union representative—a move that angered the attorney general and insulted the president. The meeting ended in an impasse. Beside himself with anger over the "wooden-headed obstinacy and stupidity" of management, Roosevelt threatened to seize the mines and run them with federal troops. It was a powerful bluff, one that called into question not only the supremacy of private property but also the rule of law. But it brought management around. In the end, the miners won a reduction in hours and a wage increase, but the owners succeeded in preventing formal recognition of the UMW.

Taken together, Roosevelt's actions in the Northern Securities case and the anthracite coal strike marked a dramatic departure from the passivity of Gilded

CHAPTER LOCATOR | How did grassroots progressives attack the problems of industrial America? | What were the key tenets of progressive theory?

576   CHAPTER 21   PROGRESSIVISM FROM THE GRASS ROOTS UP, 1890–1916

Age presidents. Roosevelt's actions demonstrated conclusively that government intended to act as a countervailing force to the power of the big corporations. Pleased with his role in the anthracite strike, he announced that all he had tried to do was give labor and capital a "square deal."

The phrase "Square Deal" became Roosevelt's campaign slogan in the 1904 election. Roosevelt easily defeated the Democrats, who abandoned their candidate, William Jennings Bryan, to support Judge Alton B. Parker, a "safe" candidate they hoped would lure business votes away from Roosevelt. In the months before the election, the president prudently toned down his criticism of big business. Roosevelt swept into office with the largest popular majority—57.9 percent—any candidate had polled up to that time.

Breaker Boys

Child labor in America's mines and mills was common at the turn of the twentieth century, despite state laws that tried to restrict it. Here, "breaker boys," some as young as seven years old, pick over coal in a Pennsylvania mine.
Brown Brothers.

Roosevelt the Reformer

"Tomorrow I shall come into my office in my own right," Roosevelt is said to have remarked on the eve of his election. "Then watch out for me!" Roosevelt's stunning victory gave him a mandate for reform. The Senate, however, remained controlled by a conservative Republican "old guard," with many senators on the payrolls of the corporations Roosevelt sought to curb. Roosevelt's pet project remained railroad regulation. The Elkins Act prohibiting rebates had not worked. No one could stop big shippers like Standard Oil from wringing concessions from the railroads. Roosevelt determined that the only solution lay in giving the Interstate Commerce Commission (ICC) real power to set rates and prevent discriminatory practices.

The result of Roosevelt's efforts was the Hepburn Act, passed in May 1906, which gave the ICC the power to set rates subject to court review. The law left the courts too much power and failed to provide adequate means for the ICC to determine rates, but its passage proved a landmark in federal control of private industry. For the first time, a government commission had the power to investigate private business records and to set rates.

Passage of the Hepburn Act marked the high point of Roosevelt's presidency. In a serious political blunder, Roosevelt had announced on the eve of his election in 1904 that he would not run again. By 1906, he had become a "lame duck" at the very moment he enjoyed his greatest public popularity.

Always an apt reader of the public temper, Roosevelt witnessed a growing appetite for reform fed by newspaper and magazine revelations of corporate and political wrongdoing and social injustice. Roosevelt counted many of the new investigative journalists among his friends. But he warned them against going too far, citing the allegorical character in *Pilgrim's Progress* who was so busy raking muck that he took no notice of higher things. Roosevelt's criticism gave the American vocabulary a new word, *muckraker*, which journalists soon appropriated as a title of honor.

| How did Theodore Roosevelt advance the progressive agenda? | How did progressivism fare during the Taft administration? | What was Woodrow Wilson's progressive agenda and how did it change during his administration? | What were the limits of progressive reform? | Conclusion: How did the liberal state transform during the Progressive Era? |

The Jungle

Novelist Upton Sinclair, a lifelong socialist, wrote *The Jungle* to expose the evils of capitalism. But readers were more horrified by his descriptions of the unsanitary conditions in the meatpacking industry, where the novel's hapless hero sees rats, filth, and diseased animals processed into meat products. The public outcry surrounding *The Jungle* contributed to the enactment of pure food and drug legislation and a federal meat inspection law. Picture Research Consultants, Inc.

Muckraking, as Roosevelt well knew, provided enormous help in securing progressive legislation. In the spring of 1906, publicity generated by the muckrakers about poisons in patent medicines goaded the Senate, with Roosevelt's backing, into passing a pure food and drug bill. Opponents in the House of Representatives hoped to keep the legislation locked up in committee. There it would have died, were it not for the publication of Upton Sinclair's novel *The Jungle* (1906), with its sensational account of filthy conditions in meatpacking plants. A massive public outcry led to the passage of the Pure Food and Drug Act and the Meat Inspection Act in 1906.

In the waning years of his administration, Roosevelt allied with the more progressive elements of the Republican Party. Styling himself a "radical," he claimed credit for leading the "ultra conservative" party of McKinley to a position of "progressive conservatism and conservative radicalism."

When an economic panic developed in the fall of 1907, business interests quickly blamed the president. Once again, J. P. Morgan stepped in to avert disaster, this time switching funds from one bank to another to prop up weak institutions. For his services, he claimed the Tennessee Coal and Iron Company, an independent steel business that had long been coveted by the U.S. Steel Corporation. Persuaded that the sale of the company would aid the economy "but little benefit" U.S. Steel, Roosevelt tacitly agreed not to institute antitrust proceedings against U.S. Steel over the acquisition. In fact, U.S. Steel acquired Tennessee Coal and Iron for a price well below market value, doing away with a competitor and undercutting the economy of the Southeast. Roosevelt's promise not to institute antitrust proceedings against U.S. Steel would give rise to the charge that he acted as a tool of the Morgan interests.

The charge of collusion between business and government underscored the extent to which corporate leaders like Morgan found federal regulation preferable to unbridled competition or harsher state measures. During the Progressive Era, enlightened business leaders cooperated with government in the hope of avoiding antitrust prosecution. Convinced that regulation and not trust-busting offered the best way to deal with big business, Roosevelt never acknowledged that his regulatory policies fostered an alliance between business and government that today is called corporate liberalism.

Roosevelt and Conservation

In the area of conservation, Roosevelt proved indisputably ahead of his time. When he took office, some 45 million acres of land remained as government reserves. By the time he left office, he had saved more than 230 million acres of wild America for posterity.

As the first president to have lived and worked in the West, Roosevelt came to the White House convinced of the need for better management of the nation's rivers and forests. During his presidency, he placed the nation's conservation

CHAPTER LOCATOR | How did grassroots progressives attack the problems of industrial America? | What were the key tenets of progressive theory?

CHAPTER 21

578 PROGRESSIVISM FROM THE GRASS ROOTS UP, 1890–1916

policy in the hands of experts like his chief forester, Gifford Pinchot. Pinchot preached conservation—the efficient use of natural resources. Willing to permit grazing, lumbering, and the development of hydroelectric power, conservationists fought private interests only when they felt business acted irresponsibly or threatened to monopolize water and electric power. Preservationists like John Muir, founder of the Sierra Club, believed the wilderness needed to be protected. Roosevelt, ever the pragmatist, believed in both conservation and preservation and worked for both throughout his lifetime.

In 1907, Congress put the brakes on Roosevelt's conservation program by passing a law limiting his power to create forest reserves in six western states. In the days leading up to the law's enactment, Roosevelt created twenty-one new reserves and enlarged eleven more, saving sixteen million acres. "Opponents of the forest service turned handsprings in their wrath," he wrote, "but the threats . . . were really only a tribute to the efficiency of our action." Today, the six national parks, sixteen national monuments, and fifty-one wildlife refuges that he created bear witness to his substantial accomplishments as a conservationist (**Map 21.1**).

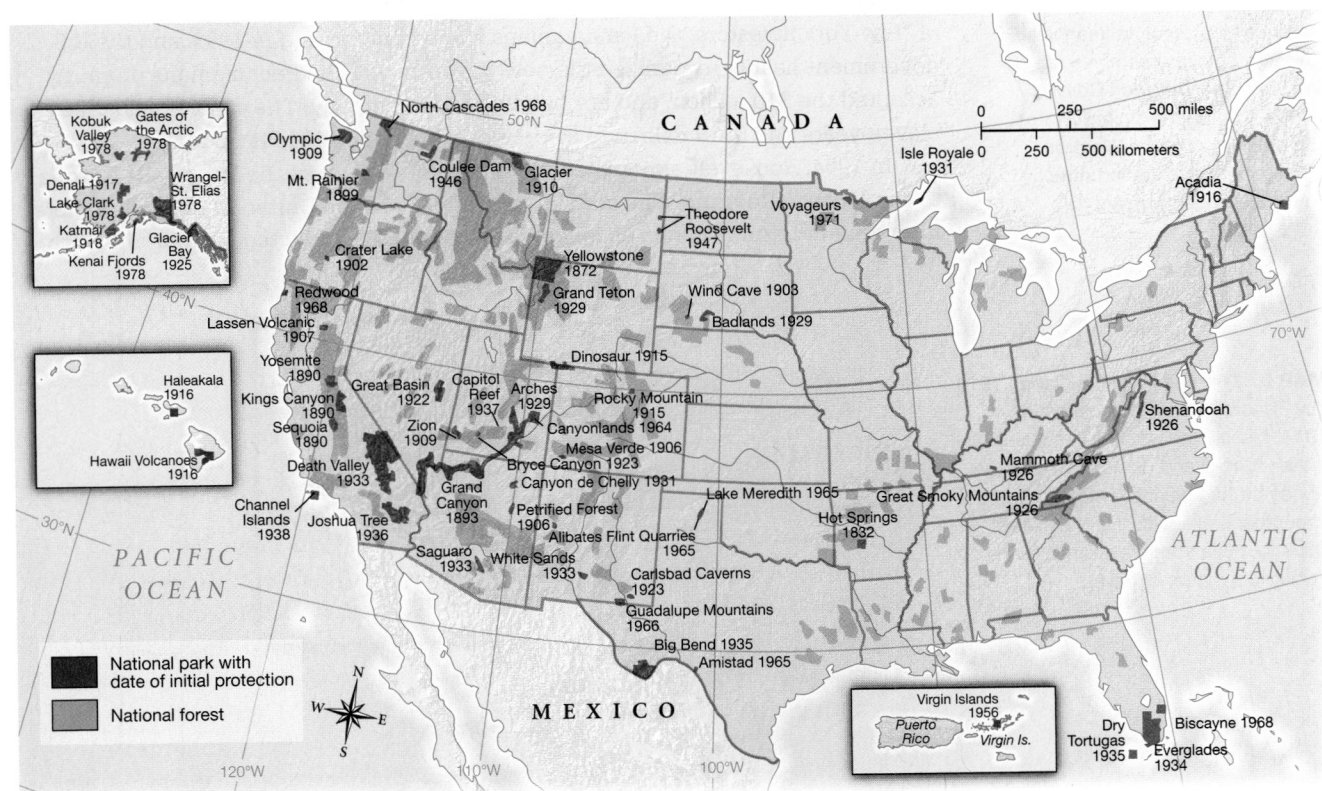

MAP 21.1 ■ National Parks and Forests
The national park system in the West began with Yellowstone in 1872. Grand Canyon, Yosemite, Kings Canyon, and Sequoia followed in the 1890s. During his presidency, Theodore Roosevelt added six parks—Crater Lake, Wind Cave, Petrified Forest, Lassen Volcanic, Mesa Verde, and Zion.

▶ FOR MORE HELP ANALYZING THIS MAP, see the map activity for this chapter in the Online Study Guide at bedfordstmartins.com/roarkunderstanding.

| How did Theodore Roosevelt advance the progressive agenda? | How did progressivism fare during the Taft administration? | What was Woodrow Wilson's progressive agenda and how did it change during his administration? | What were the limits of progressive reform? | Conclusion: How did the liberal state transform during the Progressive Era? |

The Big Stick

Roosevelt's activism extended to his foreign policy. A fierce proponent of America's interests abroad, he relied on executive power to pursue a vigorous foreign policy, sometimes stretching the powers of the presidency beyond legal limits. In his relations with the European powers, he relied on military strength and diplomacy, a combination he aptly described with the aphorism "Speak softly but carry a big stick."

A strong supporter of the Monroe Doctrine, Roosevelt's proprietary attitude toward the Western Hemisphere became evident in the case of the Panama Canal. Roosevelt had long advocated a canal linking the Caribbean and the Pacific. By enabling ships to move quickly from the Atlantic to the Pacific, a canal could effectively double the U.S. Navy's power. Having decided on a route across the Panamanian isthmus (a narrow strip of land connecting North and South America), then part of Colombia, Roosevelt in 1902 offered the Colombian government a one-time sum of $10 million and an annual rent of $250,000. When Colombia turned down the deal, Roosevelt became incensed at what he called the "homicidal corruptionists" in Colombia for trying to "blackmail" the United States. At the prompting of a group of New York investors, the Panamanians staged an uprising in 1903, and the U.S. government hastily recognized the new government. The Panamanians promptly accepted the $10 million, and the building got under way. The canal would take eleven years and $375 million to complete; it opened in 1914 (**Map 21.2**).

In 1904, Roosevelt announced what became known as the **Roosevelt Corollary** to the Monroe Doctrine. The corollary declared that the United States would not intervene in Latin America as long as nations there conducted their affairs with

MAP 21.2 ■ The Panama Canal, 1914
The Panama Canal, completed in 1914, bisects the isthmus in a series of massive locks and dams. As Theodore Roosevelt had planned, the canal greatly strengthened the U.S. Navy by allowing ships to move from the Atlantic to the Pacific in a matter of days.

CHAPTER LOCATOR | How did grassroots progressives attack the problems of industrial America? | What were the key tenets of progressive theory?

580 CHAPTER 21
PROGRESSIVISM FROM THE GRASS ROOTS UP, 1890–1916

"decency." But the United States would step in if any Latin American nation proved guilty of "brutal wrongdoing." The Roosevelt Corollary in effect made the United States the policeman of the Western Hemisphere and served notice to the European powers to keep out.

In Asia, Roosevelt inherited the Open Door policy initiated by Secretary of State John Hay in 1899, designed to ensure U.S. commercial entry into China. As Britain, France, Russia, Japan, and Germany raced to secure Chinese trade and territory, Roosevelt was tempted to use force to enter the fray and gain economic or possibly territorial concessions. Realizing that Americans would not support an aggressive Asian policy, Roosevelt sensibly held back.

In his relations with Europe, Roosevelt sought to establish the United States as a rising force in world affairs. When tensions flared between France and Germany in Morocco in 1905, Roosevelt mediated at a conference in Algeciras, Spain, where he worked to maintain a balance of power that helped neutralize German ambitions. His skillful mediation gained him a reputation as an astute player on the world stage and demonstrated the nation's new presence in world affairs.

Roosevelt earned the Nobel Peace Prize in 1906 for his role in negotiating an end to the Russo-Japanese War, which had broken out when the Japanese invaded Chinese Manchuria, threatening Russia's sphere of influence. Once again, Roosevelt sought to maintain a balance of power, in this case working to curb Japanese expansionism. Roosevelt admired the Japanese, judging them "the most dashing fighters in the world," but he did not want Japan to become too strong in Asia.

When good relations with Japan were jeopardized by discriminatory legislation in California calling for segregated public schools for "Orientals," Roosevelt smoothed over the incident and negotiated the "Gentlemen's Agreement" in 1907, which allowed the Japanese to save face by voluntarily restricting immigration to the United States. To demonstrate America's naval power and counter Japan's growing bellicosity, Roosevelt dispatched the Great White Fleet, sixteen of the navy's most up-to-date battleships, on a "goodwill mission" around the world. U.S. relations with Japan improved, and in the 1908 Root-Takahira agreement, the two nations pledged to maintain the Open Door and support the status quo in the Pacific.

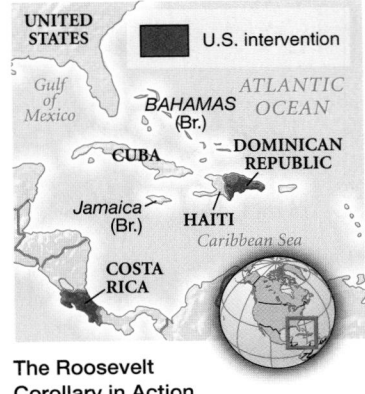

The Roosevelt Corollary in Action

QUICK REVIEW

How did Roosevelt change the relationship between big business and the federal government?

| How did Theodore Roosevelt advance the progressive agenda? | How did progressivism fare during the Taft administration? | What was Woodrow Wilson's progressive agenda and how did it change during his administration? | What were the limits of progressive reform? | Conclusion: How did the liberal state transform during the Progressive Era? |

How did progressivism fare during the Taft administration?

IN THE PRESIDENTIAL ELECTION OF 1908, Roosevelt's handpicked successor, William Howard Taft, a lawyer who had served as governor-general of the Philippines, soundly defeated the Democratic candidate, William Jennings Bryan. Any man would have found it difficult to follow in Roosevelt's footsteps, but Taft proved hopelessly ill suited to the task. A genial man with a talent for law, Taft had no experience in elective office, no feel for politics, and no nerve for controversy.

The Troubled Presidency of William Howard Taft

Once in office, Taft proved a perfect tool in the hands of Republicans who yearned for a return to the days of a less active executive. A lawyer by training and instinct, Taft believed that it was up to the courts, not the president, to arbitrate social issues. Wary of the progressive insurgents in Congress, Taft relied increasingly on conservatives in the Republican Party. As a progressive senator lamented, "Taft is a ponderous and amiable man completely surrounded by men who know exactly what they want."

Taft's troubles began on the eve of his inaugural, when he called a special session of Congress to deal with the tariff, which had grown inordinately high under Republican rule. Roosevelt had been too politically astute to tackle the troublesome tariff issue, even though he knew that rates needed to be lowered. Taft blundered into the fray. Shaped by the conservative Senate, the Payne-Aldrich bill that emerged from Congress actually raised the tariff, benefiting big business and

CHAPTER LOCATOR | How did grassroots progressives attack the problems of industrial America? | What were the key tenets of progressive theory?

582 CHAPTER 21
PROGRESSIVISM FROM THE GRASS ROOTS UP, 1890–1916

the trusts at the expense of consumers. As if paralyzed, Taft neither fought for changes nor vetoed the measure. On a tour of the Midwest in 1909, he was greeted with jeers when he claimed, "I think the Payne bill is the best bill that the Republican Party ever passed." In the eyes of a growing number of Americans, Taft's praise of the tariff made him either a fool or a liar.

Taft's legalism soon got him into hot water in the area of conservation. He undid Roosevelt's work to preserve hydroelectric power sites when he learned that they had been improperly designated as ranger stations. And when Gifford Pinchot publicly denounced Taft's secretary of the interior as a tool of western land-grabbers, Taft fired Pinchot, touching off a storm of controversy that damaged Taft and alienated Roosevelt.

When Roosevelt returned to the United States from a safari in Africa in June 1910, he received a hero's welcome. Hurt, Taft kept his distance. By late summer, Roosevelt had taken sides with the progressive insurgents in his party. "Taft is utterly hopeless as a leader," Roosevelt confided to his son. Reading the mood of the country, Roosevelt began to sound more and more like a candidate.

With the Republican Party divided, the Democrats swept the congressional elections of 1910. Branding the Payne-Aldrich tariff "the mother of trusts," they captured a majority in the House of Representatives and won several key governorships. The revitalized Democratic Party could look to new leaders, among them the progressive governor of New Jersey, Woodrow Wilson.

The new Democratic majority in the House, working with progressive Republicans in the Senate, achieved a number of key reforms. Two significant constitutional amendments—the Sixteenth Amendment, which provided for a modest graduated income tax, and the Seventeenth Amendment, which called for the direct election of senators (formerly chosen by state legislatures)—went to the states, where they would win ratification in 1913. While Congress rode the high tide of progressive reform, Taft sat on the sidelines.

Achievements of the New Democratic Majority

Regulation of mine and railroad safety
Sixteenth and Seventeenth Amendments
The creation of the Children's Bureau in the Department of Labor
The establishment of an eight-hour day for federal workers

In foreign policy, Taft continued Roosevelt's policy of extending U.S. influence abroad, but here, too, Taft had a difficult time following in Roosevelt's footsteps. His policy of dollar diplomacy championed commercial goals rather than the strategic aims Roosevelt had pursued. Taft naively assumed he could substitute "dollars for bullets." In the Caribbean, he provoked anti-American feeling by attempting to force commercial treaties on Nicaragua and Honduras and by dispatching U.S. Marines to Nicaragua and the Dominican Republic in 1912. In Asia, he openly avowed his intent to promote in China "active intervention to secure for . . . our capitalists opportunity for profitable investment." Taft never recognized that an aggressive commercial policy could not exist without the willingness to use military might to back it up.

CHRONOLOGY

1908
- Republican William Howard Taft is elected president.

1909
- Payne-Aldrich tariff.

1910
- Democrats gain majority in the House of Representatives in midterm elections.
- Congress sends Sixteenth and Seventeenth Amendments to the states for ratification.

1911
- Taft launches antitrust suit against U.S. Steel.

1912
- Taft sends U.S. Marines to Nicaragua and the Dominican Republic.
- Roosevelt runs for president on Progressive Party ticket.

| How did Theodore Roosevelt advance the progressive agenda? | **How did progressivism fare during the Taft administration?** | What was Woodrow Wilson's progressive agenda and how did it change during his administration? | What were the limits of progressive reform? | Conclusion: How did the liberal state transform during the Progressive Era? |

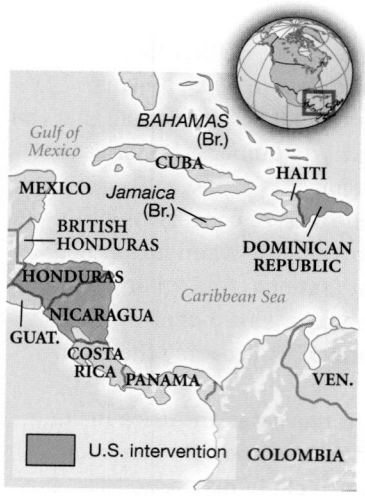

Taft's "Dollar Diplomacy"

Taft faced the limits of dollar diplomacy when revolution broke out in Mexico in 1911. Under pressure to protect American investments, he mobilized troops along the border. In the end, however, with no popular support for a war with Mexico, he had to fall back on diplomatic pressure to salvage American interests.

Taft hoped to encourage world peace through the use of a world court and arbitration. He unsuccessfully sponsored a series of arbitration treaties that Roosevelt vehemently opposed as weak and cowardly. By 1910, Roosevelt had become a vocal critic of Taft's foreign policy, which he dismissed as "maudlin folly."

The final breach between Taft and Roosevelt came in 1911, when Taft's attorney general filed an antitrust suit against U.S. Steel. In its brief against the corporation, the government cited Roosevelt's agreement with the Morgan interests in the 1907 acquisition of Tennessee Coal and Iron. Thoroughly enraged, Roosevelt lambasted Taft's "archaic" antitrust policy and hinted that he might be persuaded to run for president again.

Progressive Insurgency and the Election of 1912

In February 1912, Roosevelt challenged Taft for the Republican nomination, announcing, "My hat is in the ring." Roosevelt took advantage of newly passed primary election laws and ran in thirteen states, winning 278 delegates to Taft's 48. But at the Chicago convention, Taft's party bosses refused to seat the Roosevelt delegates. Fistfights broke out on the convention floor as Taft won the nomination on the first ballot. Crying robbery, Roosevelt's supporters bolted the party.

Progressive Party Platform

Woman suffrage
Presidential primaries
Conservation of natural resources
An end to child labor
Workers' compensation
A minimum wage that would include women workers
Social security
A federal income tax

CHAPTER LOCATOR | How did grassroots progressives attack the problems of industrial America? | What were the key tenets of progressive theory?

584 CHAPTER 21
PROGRESSIVISM FROM THE GRASS ROOTS UP, 1890–1916

Seven weeks later, the hastily organized Progressive Party met in Chicago to nominate Roosevelt. The delegates chose Roosevelt and Hiram Johnson to head the new party and approved the most ambitious platform since that of the Populists. Roosevelt arrived in Chicago to accept the nomination and announced that he felt "as strong as a bull moose," giving the new party a nickname and a mascot. But for all the excitement and the cheering, the new Progressive Party was doomed, and the candidate knew it. The people may have supported the party, but the politicians, even progressives like La Follette, stayed within the Republican fold. "I am under no illusion about it," Roosevelt confessed to a friend. "It is a forlorn hope."

The Democrats, delighted at the split in the Republican ranks, nominated Woodrow Wilson. Wilson's career in politics was nothing short of meteoric. He was elected governor of New Jersey in 1910, and after only eighteen months in office, the former professor of political science and president of Princeton University found himself running for president of the United States.

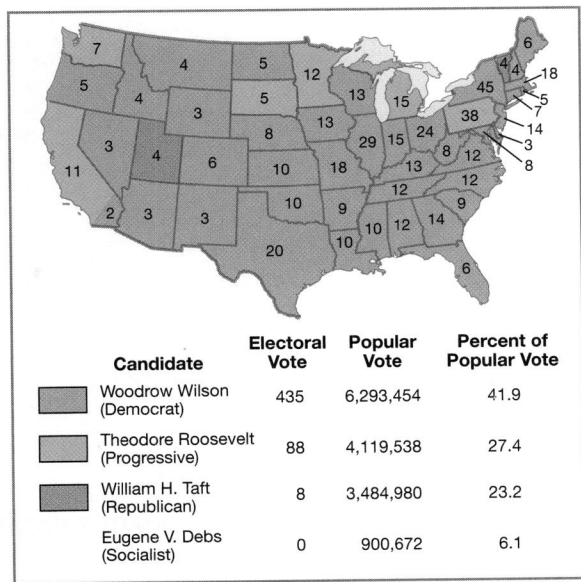

Candidate	Electoral Vote	Popular Vote	Percent of Popular Vote
Woodrow Wilson (Democrat)	435	6,293,454	41.9
Theodore Roosevelt (Progressive)	88	4,119,538	27.4
William H. Taft (Republican)	8	3,484,980	23.2
Eugene V. Debs (Socialist)	0	900,672	6.1

MAP 21.3 ■ The Election of 1912

Voters in 1912 could choose among four candidates who claimed to be progressives. Taft, Roosevelt, and Wilson each embraced the label, and even the Socialist Party candidate, Eugene V. Debs, styled himself a progressive. That the term progressive could stretch to cover these diverse candidates underscored major disagreements in progressive thinking about the relationship between business and government. Taft was generally viewed as the candidate of the old guard. The real contest for the presidency was between Roosevelt and Wilson and between the two political philosophies summed up in their respective campaign slogans: the New Nationalism and the New Freedom.

The New Nationalism expressed Roosevelt's belief in federal planning and regulation. He accepted the inevitability of big business but demanded that government act as "a steward of the people" to regulate the giant corporations. Wilson set a markedly different course with his New Freedom. Wilson promised to use antitrust legislation to get rid of big corporations and to give small businesses and farmers better opportunities in the marketplace.

In the end, the Republican vote split, while the Democrats remained united. No candidate claimed a majority of the popular vote. In the electoral college, however, Wilson won a decisive 435 votes, with 88 going to Roosevelt and only 8 to Taft (**Map 21.3**). The Progressive Party essentially collapsed after Roosevelt's defeat. It had always been, in the words of one astute observer, "a house divided against itself and already mortgaged."

QUICK REVIEW

Why did the Republican Party split in 1912?

How did Theodore Roosevelt advance the progressive agenda?

How did progressivism fare during the Taft administration?

What was Woodrow Wilson's progressive agenda and how did it change during his administration?

What were the limits of progressive reform?

Conclusion: How did the liberal state transform during the Progressive Era?

What was Woodrow Wilson's progressive agenda and how did it change during his administration?

Wilson Ribbon

The Democrats turned to Woodrow Wilson to lead the party in 1912, nominating him on the forty-sixth ballot. The ribbon in this photograph belonged to a member of the Democratic National Committee, who traveled to Wilson's summer home in Sea Girt, New Jersey, to inform Wilson officially of his nomination. Collection of Janice L. and David J. Frent.

BORN IN VIRGINIA and raised in Georgia, Woodrow Wilson became the first southerner to be elected president since 1844 and only the second Democrat to occupy the White House since Reconstruction. Although he opposed big government in his campaign, Wilson was prepared to work on the base built by Roosevelt to strengthen presidential power, exerting leadership to achieve banking reform and working through his party in Congress to accomplish the Democratic agenda. Before he was finished, Wilson presided over progressivism at high tide and lent his support not only to the platform of the Democratic Party but also to many of the Progressive Party's social reforms.

Wilson's Reforms: Tariff, Banking, and the Trusts

With the Democratic Party firmly in control, Wilson called for tariff reform. "The object of the tariff," Wilson told Congress, "must be effective competition." The Democratic House of Representatives passed the Underwood tariff, which lowered rates by 15 percent. To compensate for lost revenue, the House approved a moderate federal income tax, made possible by ratification of the Sixteenth Amendment a month earlier. In the Senate, lobbyists for industries went to work to get the tariff raised, but Wilson rallied public opinion by attacking the "industrious and insidious lobby." In the harsh glare of publicity, the Senate passed the Underwood tariff, which earned praise as "the most honest tariff since the Civil War."

Wilson next turned his attention to banking. In 1913, a Senate committee investigated the "money trust," calling J. P. Morgan himself to testify. The committee uncovered an alarming concentration of banking power. J. P. Morgan and Company and its affiliates held 341 directorships in 112 corporations, controlling assets of more than $22 billion ($457 billion in today's dollars). The sensational findings created a mandate for banking reform.

The Federal Reserve Act of 1913 marked the most significant piece of domestic legislation of Wilson's presidency. It established a national banking system composed of twelve regional banks, privately controlled but regulated and supervised by the

CHAPTER LOCATOR | How did grassroots progressives attack the problems of industrial America? | What were the key tenets of progressive theory?

Federal Reserve Board, appointed by the president. It gave the United States its first efficient banking and currency system and, at the same time, provided for a greater degree of government control over banking. The new system made currency more elastic and credit adequate for the needs of business and agriculture.

Wilson tackled the trust issue next. When Congress reconvened in January 1914, he supported the introduction of the Clayton Antitrust Act to outlaw "unfair competition"—practices such as price discrimination and interlocking directorates (directors from one corporation sitting on the board of another). In the midst of the fight for the Clayton Act, Wilson changed course and threw his support behind the creation of the **Federal Trade Commission (FTC)**, precisely the kind of federal regulatory agency that Roosevelt had advocated in his New Nationalism platform. The FTC, created in 1914, had wide investigatory powers as well as the authority to prosecute corporations for "unfair trade practices" and to enforce its judgments by issuing "cease and desist" orders. Despite his campaign promises, Wilson's antitrust program worked to regulate rather than to break up big business.

Wilson, Reluctant Progressive

By the fall of 1914, Wilson declared that the progressive movement had fulfilled its mission and that the country needed "a time of healing." Progressives watched in dismay as Wilson repeatedly obstructed or refused to endorse further progressive reforms. He failed to support labor's demand for an end to court injunctions against labor unions. He threatened to veto legislation providing farm credits for nonperishable crops. He refused to support child labor legislation or woman suffrage. Wilson used the rhetoric of the New Freedom to justify his actions, claiming that his administration would condone "special privileges to none." But, in fact, his stance often reflected the interests of his small-business constituency.

In the face of Wilson's obstinacy, reform might have ended in 1913 had not politics intruded. In the congressional elections of 1914, the Republican Party, no longer split by Roosevelt's Bull Moose faction, won substantial gains. Democratic strategists, with their eyes on the 1916 presidential race, recognized that Wilson needed to pick up support in the Midwest and the West by capturing votes from former Bull Moose progressives. Wilson responded by lending his support to reform in the months leading up to the election of 1916, cultivating union labor, farmers, and social reformers. To please labor, he appointed progressive Louis Brandeis to the Supreme Court. To woo farmers, he threw his support behind legislation to obtain rural credits. And he won praise from labor by supporting workers' compensation and the Keating-Owen child labor law (1916), which outlawed the regular employment of children younger than sixteen. Wilson boasted that the Democrats had "opened their hearts to the demands of social justice" and had "come very near to carrying out the platform of the Progressive Party." Wilson's shift toward reform, along with his claim that he had kept the United States out of the war in Europe (see chapter 22), helped him win reelection in 1916.

(see chapter 22)

CHRONOLOGY

1912
- Democrat Woodrow Wilson is elected president.

1913
- Federal Reserve Act.

1914
- Federal Trade Commission is created.
- Clayton Antitrust Act passed.

1916
- Keating-Owen child labor law.

Federal Trade Commission (FTC)

▶ Federal regulatory agency created in 1914 that had wide investigatory powers, the authority to prosecute corporations for "unfair trade practices," and the power to enforce its judgments by issuing "cease and desist" orders. Woodrow Wilson supported the creation of the FTC, despite his campaign promises to break up big business rather than to regulate it.

QUICK REVIEW

How and why did Wilson's reform program evolve during his first term?

How did Theodore Roosevelt advance the progressive agenda?	How did progressivism fare during the Taft administration?	**What was Woodrow Wilson's progressive agenda and how did it change during his administration?**	What were the limits of progressive reform?	Conclusion: How did the liberal state transform during the Progressive Era?

What were the limits of progressive reform?

Booker T. Washington and Theodore Roosevelt Dine at the White House

When Theodore Roosevelt invited Booker T. Washington to the White House in 1901, he stirred up a hornet's nest of controversy that continued into the election of 1904. This Republican campaign piece gives the meeting a positive slant, showing Roosevelt and a light-skinned Washington sitting under a portrait of Abraham Lincoln, a symbol of the party's historic commitment to African Americans. Democrats, in contrast, pictured Washington with darker skin and implied that Roosevelt favored "race mingling" and had "painted the White House black." Collection of Janice L. and David J. Frent.

WHILE PROGRESSIVISM CALLED for a more active role for the liberal state, at heart it was a movement that sought reforms designed to preserve American institutions and stem the tide of more radical change. Its basic conservatism can be seen by comparing it to the more radical movements of socialism, radical labor, and birth control—and by looking at the groups progressive reform left behind, including women and African Americans.

Radical Alternatives

The year 1900 marked the birth of the Social Democratic Party in America, later called simply the Socialist Party. Like the progressives, the socialists were middle-class and native-born. They had broken with the older, more militant Socialist Labor Party precisely because of its dogmatic approach and immigrant constituency.

The Socialist Party chose as its presidential standard-bearer Eugene V. Debs. Debs would run for president five times, in every election (except the one in 1916) from 1900 to 1920. The socialism Debs advocated preached cooperation over competition and urged men and women to liberate themselves from "the barbarism of private ownership and wage slavery." In the 1912 election, Debs indicted

CHAPTER LOCATOR

How did grassroots progressives attack the problems of industrial America?

What were the key tenets of progressive theory?

588 CHAPTER 21
PROGRESSIVISM FROM THE GRASS ROOTS UP, 1890–1916

both old parties as "Tweedledee and Tweedledum," each dedicated to the preservation of capitalism and the continuation of the wage system. Only through socialism, he argued, could democracy exist. Debs's best showing came in 1912, when he polled 6 percent of the popular vote, capturing more than 900,000 votes.

Farther to the left of the socialists stood the Industrial Workers of the World (IWW), nicknamed the Wobblies. In 1905, Debs, along with Western Federation of Miners leader William Dudley "Big Bill" Haywood, created the IWW, "one big union" dedicated to organizing the most destitute segment of the workforce, the unskilled workers. Seeing workers on the lowest rung of the social ladder as the victims of violent repression, the IWW advocated direct action, sabotage, and the general strike—tactics designed to trigger a workers' uprising. The IWW never had more than 10,000 members at any one time. Nevertheless, the IWW's influence on the country extended far beyond its numbers.

Margaret Sanger's Brownsville Birth Control Clinic

Margaret Sanger opened the first birth control clinic in the United States in the Brownsville section of Brooklyn in 1916. During the nine days it operated before police shut it down, more than four hundred women visited the clinic. Her clinic was located in the heart of an immigrant neighborhood, so Sanger published her fliers in English, Yiddish, and Italian. Sophia Smith Collection, Smith College.

▶ FOR MORE HELP ANALYZING THIS IMAGE, see the visual activity for this chapter in the Online Study Guide at bedfordstmartins.com/roarkunderstanding.

| How did Theodore Roosevelt advance the progressive agenda? | How did progressivism fare during the Taft administration? | What was Woodrow Wilson's progressive agenda and how did it change during his administration? | **What were the limits of progressive reform?** | Conclusion: How did the liberal state transform during the Progressive Era? |

Margaret Sanger

▶ Leader of the movement to promote birth control as a means for producing social change. A nurse who worked among New York City's poor, Sanger opened the nation's first birth control clinic in October 1916. Under her leadership, birth control gained legitimacy, if not legality.

In contrast to political radicals like Debs and Haywood, **Margaret Sanger** promoted birth control as a movement for social change. Sanger, a nurse who had worked among the poor on New York's Lower East Side, coined the term *birth control* in 1915 and launched a movement with broad social implications. Sanger and her followers saw birth control not only as a sexual and medical reform but also as a means to alter social and political power relationships and to alleviate human misery.

The desire for family limitation was widespread, and in this sense, birth control was nothing new. But the open advocacy of *contraception*, the use of artificial means to prevent pregnancy, struck many people as shocking. And it was illegal. Anthony Comstock, New York City's commissioner of vice, promoted laws in the 1870s making it a felony not only to sell contraceptive devices but also to publish information on how to prevent pregnancy.

When Margaret Sanger used her militant feminist newspaper, the *Woman Rebel*, to promote birth control, the Post Office confiscated Sanger's publication and brought charges against her. Facing arrest, she fled to Europe, only to return in 1916 as something of a national celebrity. In her absence, birth control had become linked with free speech and had been taken up as a liberal cause. Under public pressure, the government dropped the charges against Sanger, who undertook a nationwide tour to publicize the birth control cause.

Sanger then turned to direct action, opening the nation's first birth control clinic in October 1916. Located in the heart of a Jewish and Italian immigrant neighborhood in Brooklyn, the clinic attracted 464 clients. On the tenth day, police shut down the clinic and threw Sanger in jail. By then, she had become a national figure, and the cause she championed had gained legitimacy, if not legality.

Progressivism for White Men Only

The day before President Woodrow Wilson's inauguration in March 1913, the largest mass march to date in the nation's history took place as more than five thousand demonstrators took to the streets in Washington to demand the vote for women. A rowdy crowd on hand to celebrate the Democrats' triumph attacked the marchers. "If my wife were where you are," a burly cop told one suffragist, "I'd break her head." Wilson, who didn't believe that a "lady" should vote, pointedly ignored woman suffrage in his inaugural address the next day.

The march served as a reminder that the political gains of progressivism were not spread equally throughout the population. Increasingly, however, woman suffrage had become an international movement. In Great Britain, Emmeline Pankhurst and her daughters Cristabel and Sylvia promoted a new, militant suffragism. They seized the spotlight in a series of marches, mass meetings, and acts of civil disobedience that sometimes escalated into riots, violence, and arson.

Alice Paul, a Quaker social worker who had visited England and participated in suffrage activism there, returned to the United States in 1910 in time to plan the mass march on the eve of Wilson's inauguration. Paul's tactics alienated many in the National American Woman Suffrage Association. In 1916, Paul founded the militant National Woman's Party, which became the radical voice of the suffrage movement.

CHAPTER LOCATOR | How did grassroots progressives attack the problems of industrial America? | What were the key tenets of progressive theory?

590   CHAPTER 21   PROGRESSIVISM FROM THE GRASS ROOTS UP, 1890–1916

Women weren't the only group left out in progressive reform. Progressivism, as it was practiced in the West and South, was tainted with racism and sought to limit the rights of African and Asian Americans. Anti-Asian bigotry in the West led to a renewal of the Chinese Exclusion Act in 1902. In 1913, California governor Hiram Johnson caved in to popular pressure and signed the Alien Land Law, which barred Japanese immigrants from purchasing land in California.

In the South, the progressives' racism targeted African Americans. Progressives preached the disfranchisement of black voters as a "reform." During the bitter electoral fights that had pitted Populists against Democrats in the 1890s, the Democratic Party held its power by votes purchased or coerced from African Americans. Southern progressives proposed to "reform" the electoral system by eliminating black voters. Beginning in 1890 with Mississippi, southern states curtailed the African American vote through devices such as poll taxes (fees required for voting) and literacy tests. The racist intent of southern voting legislation became especially clear after 1900, when states resorted to the grandfather clause, a legal provision that allowed men who failed a literacy test to vote if their grandfathers had cast a ballot. Grandfathering permitted southern white men to vote while excluding blacks.

The Progressive Era also witnessed the rise of Jim Crow laws to segregate public facilities. Soon, separate railcars, separate waiting rooms, separate bathrooms, and separate dining facilities for blacks sprang up across the South. In courtrooms in Mississippi, blacks were required to swear on a separate Bible.

In the face of this growing repression, **Booker T. Washington**, the preeminent black leader of the day, urged caution and restraint. A former slave, Washington had opened the Tuskegee Institute in Alabama in 1881 to teach vocational skills to African Americans. He emphasized education and economic progress for his race and urged African Americans to put aside issues of political and social equality. In an 1895 speech in Atlanta that came to be known as the Atlanta Compromise, he stated, "In all things that are purely social we can be as separate as the fingers, yet one as the hand in all things essential to mutual progress." Washington's accommodationist policy appealed to whites and elevated him to the role of national spokesman for African Americans.

The year after Washington proclaimed the Atlanta Compromise, the Supreme Court upheld the legality of racial segregation, affirming in *Plessy v. Ferguson* (1896) the constitutionality of the doctrine of "separate but equal." Blacks could be segregated in separate schools, restrooms, and other facilities as long as the facilities were "equal" to those provided for whites. Of course, facilities for blacks rarely proved equal.

Woodrow Wilson brought to the White House southern attitudes toward race and racial segregation. He instituted segregation in the federal workforce, especially the Post Office, and approved segregated drinking fountains and restrooms in the nation's capital. When critics attacked the policy, Wilson insisted that segregation was "in the interest of the Negro."

In 1906, a major race riot in Atlanta called into question Booker T. Washington's strategy of uplift and accommodation. For three days in September, angry white mobs chased and cornered any blacks they happened upon, pulling passengers from streetcars and invading black neighborhoods to kill and loot.

Booker T. Washington
▶ Preeminent black leader of the late nineteenth century. A former slave, Washington opened the Tuskegee Institute in Alabama in 1881 to teach vocational skills to African Americans. He emphasized education and economic progress for his race and urged African Americans to put aside issues of political and social equality.

Plessy v. Ferguson
▶ 1896 Supreme Court ruling that upheld the legality of racial segregation. According to the ruling, blacks could be segregated in separate schools, restrooms, and other facilities as long as the facilities were "equal" to those provided for whites. *Plessy v. Ferguson* gave official sanction to the proliferation of Jim Crow legislation.

How did Theodore Roosevelt advance the progressive agenda?

How did progressivism fare during the Taft administration?

What was Woodrow Wilson's progressive agenda and how did it change during his administration?

What were the limits of progressive reform?

Conclusion: How did the liberal state transform during the Progressive Era?

W. E. B. Du Bois

In 1895, W. E. B. Du Bois became the first African American to earn a doctorate from Harvard. Throughout his lifetime, he urged African Americans to work for political and racial equality. He wrote in *The Souls of Black Folk* in 1903 that he wished "to make it possible for a man to be both a Negro and an American, without being cursed and spit upon by his fellows." Special Collections Department, W. E. B. Du Bois Library, University of Massachusetts, Amherst.

W. E. B. Du Bois

▶ Black intellectual and opponent of Booker T. Washington's accommodationist position. Du Bois founded the Niagara movement in 1905, calling for universal male suffrage, civil rights, and leadership of a black intellectual elite. In 1909, the Niagara movement helped found the National Association for the Advancement of Colored People (NAACP).

An estimated 250 African Americans died in the riots—members of Atlanta's black middle class along with the poor and derelict. Professor William Crogman of Clark College noted the central irony of the riot: "Here we have worked and prayed and tried to make good men and women of our colored population," he observed, "and at our very doorstep the whites kill these good men." The riot caused many African Americans to question Washington's strategy of gradualism and accommodation.

Foremost among Washington's critics stood **W. E. B. Du Bois**, a Harvard graduate who urged African Americans to fight for civil rights and racial justice. In *The Souls of Black Folk* (1903), Du Bois attacked the "Tuskegee Machine," comparing Washington to a political boss who used his influence to silence his critics and reward his followers. Du Bois founded the Niagara movement in 1905, calling for universal male suffrage, civil rights, and leadership of a black intellectual elite. In 1909, the Niagara movement helped found the National Association for the Advancement of Colored People (NAACP), a coalition of blacks and whites that sought legal and political rights for African Americans through the courts.

> **QUICK REVIEW**

How did race, class, and gender shape the limits of progressive reform?

CHAPTER LOCATOR | How did grassroots progressives attack the problems of industrial America? | What were the key tenets of progressive theory?

592 CHAPTER 21
PROGRESSIVISM FROM THE GRASS ROOTS UP, 1890–1916

Chicago History Museum.

Conclusion: How did the liberal state transform during the Progressive Era?

PROGRESSIVISM'S GOAL WAS TO REFORM the existing system—by government intervention if necessary, but without uprooting any of the traditional American political, economic, or social institutions. As Theodore Roosevelt, the bellwether of the movement, insisted, "The only true conservative is the man who resolutely sets his face toward the future." Roosevelt was such a man, and progressivism was such a movement. But although progressivism was never radical, progressives' willingness to use the power of government to regulate business and achieve a measure of social justice redefined liberalism in the twentieth century, tying it to the expanded power of the state.

Progressivism contained many paradoxes. A diverse coalition of individuals and interests, the progressive movement began at the grass roots but left as its legacy a stronger presidency and unprecedented federal involvement in the economy and social welfare. A movement that believed in social justice, progressivism often promoted social control. And while progressives called for greater democracy, they fostered elitism with their worship of experts and efficiency.

Whatever its inconsistencies and limitations, progressivism took action to deal with the problems posed by urban industrialism. Progressivism saw grassroots activists address social problems on the local and state levels and search for national solutions. By increasing the power of the presidency and expanding the power of the state, progressives worked to bring about greater social justice and to achieve a better balance between government and business. Jane Addams and Theodore Roosevelt could lay equal claim to the movement that redefined liberalism and launched the liberal state of the twentieth century. War on a global scale would provide progressivism with yet another challenge even before it had completed its ambitious agenda.

SO NOW YOU KNOW

Despite the advances of social and political reform and the increased regulation of business and industry during the Progressive Era, blacks and other minorities remained marginalized, workers continued to fight for union recognition, and women continued their struggle for suffrage.

How did Theodore Roosevelt advance the progressive agenda?

How did progressivism fare during the Taft administration?

What was Woodrow Wilson's progressive agenda and how did it change during his administration?

What were the limits of progressive reform?

Conclusion: How did the liberal state transform during the Progressive Era?

STEP 1

GETTING STARTED

Below are basic terms from this period in American history. Can you identify each term below and explain why it matters? To do this exercise online or to download this chart, visit bedfordstmartins.com/roarkunderstanding.

TERM	WHO OR WHAT & WHEN	WHY IT MATTERS
settlement houses, p. 568		
social gospel, p. 569		
Women's Trade Union League (WTUL), p. 570		
reform Darwinism, p. 573		
Roosevelt Corollary, p. 580		
Federal Trade Commission (FTC), p. 587		
Margaret Sanger, p. 590		
Booker T. Washington, p. 591		
Plessy v. Ferguson, p. 591		
W. E. B. Du Bois, p. 592		

STEP 2

MOVING BEYOND THE BASICS

The exercise below represents a more advanced understanding of the chapter material. First, describe the actions and proposals of the progressives at the local, state, and national levels in the 1890s and during the administrations of three Progressive Era presidents. Then describe the progressive successes during each period. When you are finished, consider the following questions. How did progressive reforms at the grassroots level influence progressive politics at the state and national levels? In what areas and during what times were the progressives most successful? To do this exercise online or to download this chart, visit bedfordstmartins.com/roarkunderstanding.

Period	Actions and proposals at local, state, and national levels	Reforms implemented
1890s		
Theodore Roosevelt administration		
William H. Taft administration		
Woodrow Wilson administration		

STEP

3

PUTTING IT ALL TOGETHER

Now that you've reviewed various parts of the chapter, take a step back and try to see the big picture by answering these questions. Remember to use specific examples from the chapter in your answers. To do this exercise online, visit bedfordstmartins.com/roarkunderstanding.

PROGRESSIVES AND PROGRESSIVISM

▶ What core principles underlay progressivism? How was progressivism different from earlier reform movements?

▶ Why was grassroots activism so important to the progressive movement?

THEODORE ROOSEVELT AND PROGRESSIVISM

▶ What progressive ideals were embodied in Roosevelt's Square Deal?

▶ What were the limits of Roosevelt's reform activities? Was he a true progressive? Why or why not?

WOODROW WILSON AND PROGRESSIVISM

▶ How did Wilson's progressivism differ from that of Roosevelt?

▶ How did Wilson's progressive agenda change during his presidency? What evidence can you produce to support your answer?

LOOKING BACKWARD, LOOKING AHEAD

▶ Defend or refute the following statement: "The progressive movement enacted the Populist platform."

▶ What progressive ideas and policies continue to influence American social and political life today?

IN YOUR OWN WORDS

Imagine that you must explain chapter 21 to someone who hasn't read it. What would be the most important points to include and why?

22

THE UNITED STATES IN WORLD WAR I

1914–1920

> This chapter explores the nature and impact of America's involvement in World War I. It examines Woodrow Wilson's role in taking the country to war and in shaping the peace that followed, the contribution of American armed forces to the Allied victory, the impact of the war on Americans at home, and the uneasy years that followed the return of peace.

> What was Woodrow Wilson's foreign policy agenda?

> What role did the United States play in World War I?

> What impact did the war have on the home front?

> What part did Woodrow Wilson play in the Paris peace conference?

> Why was America's transition from war to peace so turbulent?

> Conclusion: What was the domestic cost of foreign victory?

Beat back the HUN with LIBERTY BONDS

DID YOU KNOW?

During World War I, Americans across the nation changed the name of German toast to French toast.

Writing home. A Salvation Army worker writes a letter for a wounded American soldier, 1918.

What was Woodrow Wilson's foreign policy agenda?

"Enlist"

This poster depicting a young mother and her baby sinking beneath the cold waters of the Atlantic Ocean brought home the terrible cost of Germany's sinking of the British passenger liner *Lusitania* in 1915. Burned into American memory, the *Lusitania* remained a compelling reason to enlist in the armed forces after the United States entered the war in 1917.

Library of Congress.

> ► FOR MORE HELP ANALYZING THIS IMAGE, see the visual activity for this chapter in the Online Study Guide at bedfordstmartins.com/roarkunderstanding.

SHORTLY AFTER WINNING election to the presidency in 1912, Woodrow Wilson confided to a friend: "It would be an irony of fate if my administration had to deal with foreign affairs." Indeed, Wilson had focused his life and career on domestic concerns, seldom venturing far from home and traveling abroad only on brief vacations.

But Wilson could not avoid the world and its problems. Economic interests compelled the nation outward. Moreover, Wilson was drawn abroad by his own progressive political principles. He believed that the United States had a moral duty to champion national self-determination, peaceful free trade, and political democracy. "We have no selfish ends to serve," he proclaimed. "We desire no conquest, no dominion. . . . We are but one of the champions of the rights of mankind." Yet as president, Wilson revealed he was as ready as any American president to apply military solutions to problems of foreign policy.

Taming the Americas

When he took office, Wilson sought to distinguish his foreign policy from what he saw as the belligerent policies of his Republican predecessors, Roosevelt and Taft.

CHAPTER LOCATOR | What was Woodrow Wilson's foreign policy agenda?

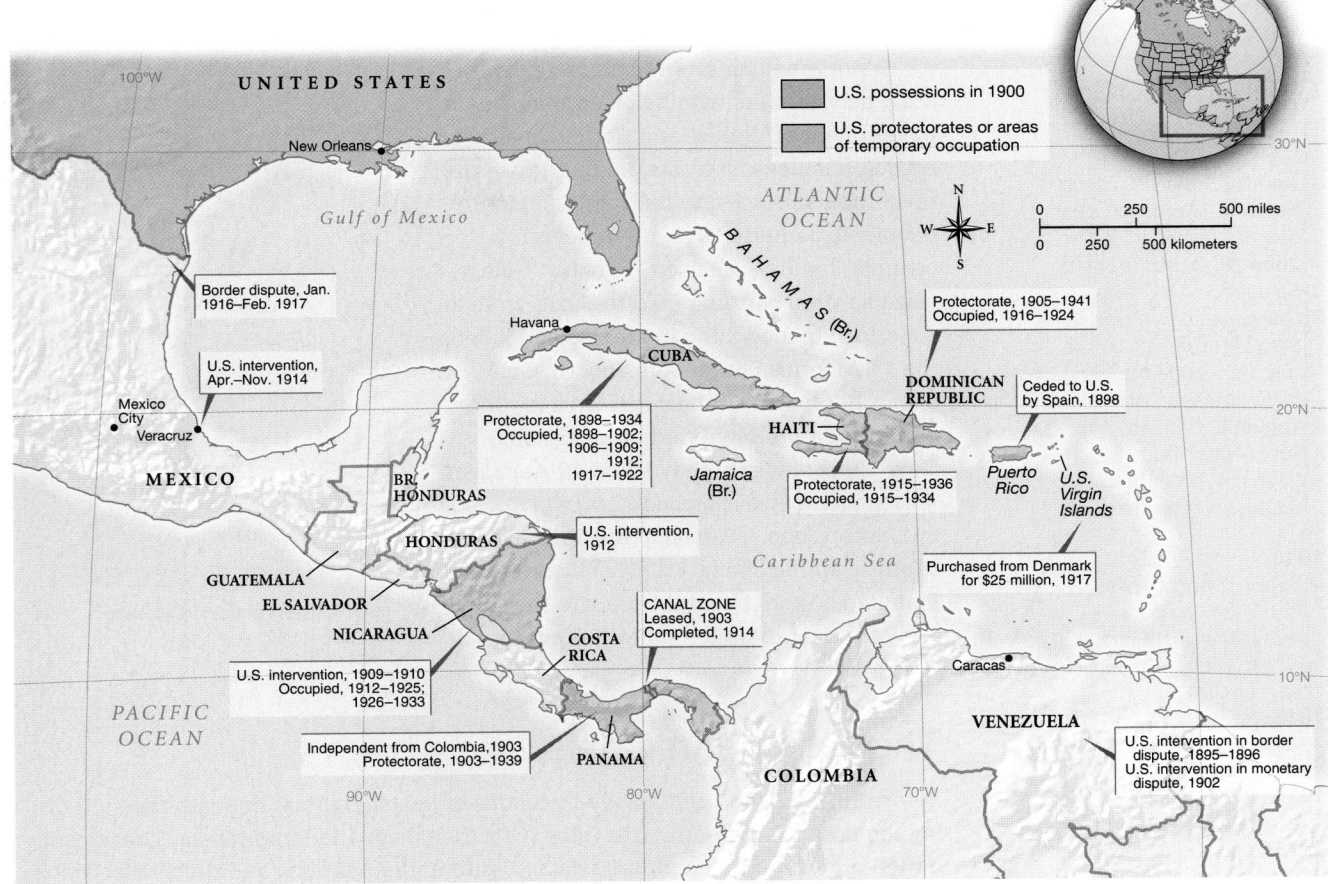

MAP 22.1 ■ **U.S. Involvement in Latin America and the Caribbean, 1895–1941**
Victory against Spain in 1898 made Puerto Rico an American possession and Cuba a protectorate. The United States later gained control of the Panama Canal Zone. The nation was quick to protect expanding economic interests with military force by propping up friendly, though not necessarily democratic, governments.

To signal a new direction, Wilson appointed William Jennings Bryan as secretary of state. A pacifist on religious grounds, Bryan immediately turned his attention to making agreements with thirty nations for the peaceful settlement of disputes.

But Wilson and Bryan, like Roosevelt and Taft, also believed that the Monroe Doctrine gave the United States special rights and responsibilities in the Western Hemisphere. Wilson thus authorized U.S. military intervention in Nicaragua, Haiti, and the Dominican Republic, paving the way for U.S. banks and corporations to take financial control. All the while, Wilson believed that U.S. actions were promoting order and democracy. "I am going to teach the South American Republics to elect good men!" he declared (**Map 22.1**).

Wilson's most serious involvement in Latin America came in Mexico. When General Victoriano Huerta seized power by violent means, most European nations promptly recognized Mexico's new government, but Wilson refused, declaring that he would not support a "government of butchers." In April 1914, Wilson sent 800 marines to seize the port of Veracruz to prevent the unloading of a large shipment of arms for Huerta, who was by then involved in a civil war of his own. Huerta fled to Spain, and the United States welcomed a more compliant government.

| What role did the United States play in World War I? | What impact did the war have on the home front? | What part did Woodrow Wilson play in the Paris peace conference? | Why was America's transition from war to peace so turbulent? | Conclusion: What was the domestic cost of foreign victory? |

1914
- **April.** U.S. Marines occupy Veracruz, Mexico, during the Mexican revolution.
- **June 28.** Archduke Franz Ferdinand of Austria is assassinated by a Bosnian Serb terrorist.
- **July 18.** Austria-Hungary declares war on Serbia.
- **August 3.** Germany attacks Russia and France.
- **August 4.** Great Britain declares war on Germany.

1915
- German U-boat sinks the British passenger liner *Lusitania*, killing 128 Americans.

1916
- Wilson is reelected.

1916–1917
- General John Pershing pursues Mexican revolutionary leader Pancho Villa.

1917
- **January.** Germany resumes unrestricted submarine warfare.
- **February.** Zimmermann telegram between Germany and Mexico is intercepted.
- **April.** United States declares war on Germany.

But a rebellion erupted among desperately poor farmers who believed that the new government of Venustiano Carranza, aided by U.S. business interests, had betrayed the revolution's promise to help the common people. In January 1916, the rebel army, commanded by Francisco "Pancho" Villa, seized a train carrying gold to Texas from an American-owned mine in Mexico and killed the 17 American engineers aboard. On March 9, another band of Villa's men crossed the border for a predawn raid on Columbus, New Mexico, where they killed 18 Americans. Wilson promptly dispatched 12,000 troops, led by General John J. Pershing. But Villa avoided capture, and in January 1917, Wilson recalled Pershing so that he might prepare the army for the possibility of fighting in the Great War.

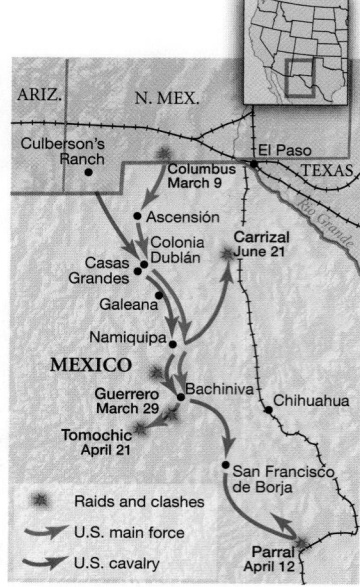

U.S. Intervention in Mexico, 1916–1917

The European Crisis

Before 1914, Europe had enjoyed decades of peace, but just beneath the surface lay the potentially destructive forces of nationalism and imperialism. The consolidation of the German and Italian states into unified nations and the similar ambition of Russia to create a Pan-Slavic union initiated new rivalries throughout Europe. As the conviction spread that colonial possessions were a mark of national greatness, competition expanded onto the world stage. Most ominously, Germany's efforts under Kaiser Wilhelm II to challenge Great Britain's world supremacy by creating industrial muscle at home, an empire abroad, and a mighty navy threatened the balance of power and thus the peace.

European nations sought to avoid an explosion with a complex web of military and diplomatic alliances. By 1914, Germany, Austria-Hungary, and Italy (the Triple Alliance) stood opposed to Great Britain, France, and Russia (the Triple Entente, also known as "the Allies"). But in their effort to prevent war through a balance of power, Europeans had actually magnified the possibility of large-scale conflict (**Map 22.2**). Treaties, some of them secret, obligated members of the alliances to come to the aid of another member if attacked.

The fatal sequence began on June 28, 1914, in the Bosnian city of Sarajevo, when a Bosnian-Serb terrorist assassinated Archduke Franz Ferdinand, heir to the Austro-Hungarian throne. On July 18, Austria-Hungary declared war on Serbia. The elaborate alliance system meant that the war could not remain local. Russia announced that it would back the Serbs. Compelled by treaty to support Austria-Hungary, Germany on August 3 attacked Russia and France. In response, on August 4, Great Britain, upholding its pact with France, declared war on Germany. Within weeks, Europe was engulfed in war. The conflict became a world war when Japan, seeing an opportunity to rid itself of European competition in China, joined the cause against Germany.

CHAPTER LOCATOR | What was Woodrow Wilson's foreign policy agenda?

600 CHAPTER 22 THE UNITED STATES IN WORLD WAR I, 1914–1920

MAP 22.2 ■ European Alliances after the Outbreak of World War I
With Germany and Austria-Hungary wedged between their Entente rivals and all parties fully armed, Europe was poised for war when Archduke Franz Ferdinand of Austria-Hungary was assassinated in Sarajevo in June 1914.

The Ordeal of American Neutrality

Woodrow Wilson promptly announced that because the war engaged no vital American interest and involved no significant principle, the United States would remain neutral. Neutrality entitled the United States to trade safely with all nations at war, he declared. Unfettered trade with Europe, Wilson believed, was not only a right under international law but also a necessity because the U.S. economy had in 1913 slipped into a recession, which wartime disruption of trade could drastically worsen.

Although Wilson proclaimed neutrality, his sympathies, like those of many Americans, lay with Great Britain and France. Americans gratefully remembered crucial French assistance in the American Revolution and shared with the British a language, a culture, and a commitment to liberty. Germany, in contrast, was a monarchy with strong militaristic traditions. Still, Wilson insisted on neutrality, in

| What role did the United States play in World War I? | What impact did the war have on the home front? | What part did Woodrow Wilson play in the Paris peace conference? | Why was America's transition from war to peace so turbulent? | Conclusion: What was the domestic cost of foreign victory? |

601

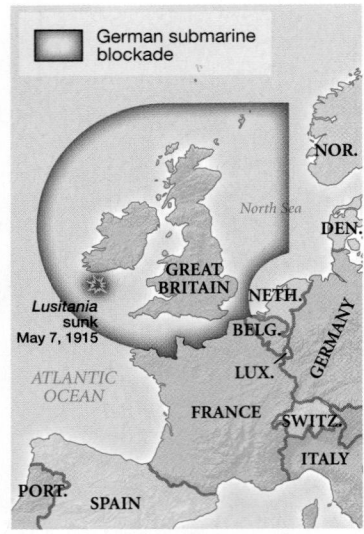

Sinking of the *Lusitania*, 1915

U-boats

▶ *Unterseebooten*, or German submarines. Germany used U-boats to try to halt international trade with Britain. In the process, they sank a number of ships with Americans on board, most famously the *Lusitania* in 1915. Germany's resumption of unrestricted submarine warfare in January 1917 directly contributed to America's entry into the war.

part because he feared the conflict's effects on the United States as a nation of immigrants. As he told the German ambassador, "We definitely have to be neutral, since otherwise our mixed populations would wage war on each other."

Britain's powerful fleet controlled the seas and quickly set up an economic blockade of Germany. The United States vigorously protested, but Britain refused to give up its naval advantage. The blockade actually had little economic impact on the United States. Between 1914 and the spring of 1917, while trade with Germany evaporated, war-related exports to Britain—food, clothing, steel, and munitions—escalated by some 400 percent. Although the British blockade violated American neutrality, the Wilson administration gradually acquiesced, thus beginning the fateful process of alienation from Germany.

Germany retaliated with a submarine blockade of British ports. German *Unterseebooten*, or **U-boats**, threatened traditional rules of war. Unlike surface warships that could harmlessly stop freighters and prevent them from entering a war zone, submarines relied on sinking their quarry. And once they sank a ship, the U-boats could not pick up survivors. Britain portrayed the submarine as an outlaw weapon that violated notions of "civilized" warfare. Nevertheless, in February 1915, Germany announced that it intended to sink on sight enemy ships en route to the British Isles. On May 7, 1915, a German U-boat torpedoed the British passenger liner *Lusitania*, killing 1,198 passengers, 128 of them U.S. citizens.

American newspapers featured drawings of drowning women and children, and some demanded war. Others pointed out that Germany had warned prospective passengers and that the *Lusitania* carried millions of rounds of ammunition and so was a legitimate target. Secretary of State Bryan resisted the hysteria and declared that a ship carrying war materiel "should not rely on passengers to protect her from attack—it would be like putting women and children in front of an army." He counseled Wilson to warn American citizens that they traveled on ships of belligerent countries at their own risk.

Wilson sought a middle course that would retain his commitment to peace and neutrality without condoning German attacks on passenger ships. On May 10, 1915, Wilson declared that any further destruction of ships would be regarded as "deliberately unfriendly" and might lead the United States to break diplomatic relations with Germany. Wilson essentially demanded that Germany abandon unrestricted submarine warfare. Bryan resigned, predicting that the president had placed the United States on a collision course with Germany. Wilson's replacement for Bryan, Robert Lansing, was far from neutral. He believed that Germany's antidemocratic character and goal of "world dominance" meant that it "must not be permitted to win this war or even to break even."

After Germany apologized for the civilian deaths on the *Lusitania*, tensions subsided. But in 1916, Germany went further, promising no more submarine attacks without warning and without provisions for the safety of civilians. Wilson's supporters celebrated the success of his middle-of-the-road strategy.

Wilson's diplomacy proved helpful in his bid for reelection in 1916. In the contest against Republican Charles Evans Hughes, the Democratic Party ran Wilson under the slogan "He kept us out of war." The Democrats' case for Wilson's neutrality appealed to enough of those in favor of peace to eke out a majority. Wilson won, but only by the razor-thin margins of 600,000 popular and 23 electoral votes.

CHAPTER LOCATOR | What was Woodrow Wilson's foreign policy agenda?

The United States Enters the War

Step-by-step, the United States backed away from "absolute neutrality." The consequence of protesting the German blockade of Great Britain but accepting the British blockade of Germany was that by 1916 the United States was supplying the Allies with 40 percent of their war materiel. When France and Britain ran short of money to pay for U.S. goods and asked for loans, Wilson argued that "loans by American bankers to any foreign government which is at war are inconsistent with the true spirit of neutrality." But rather than jeopardize America's wartime prosperity, Wilson relaxed his objections, and billions of dollars in loans kept American goods flowing to Britain and France.

In January 1917, Germany decided that it could no longer afford to allow neutral shipping to reach Great Britain and announced that it would resume unrestricted submarine warfare and sink without warning any ship, enemy or neutral, found in the waters off Great Britain. Germany understood that the decision would probably bring the United States into the war but gambled that the submarines would strangle the British economy and allow German armies to win a military victory in France before American troops arrived in Europe.

Resisting demands for war, Wilson continued to hope for a negotiated peace and only broke off diplomatic relations with Germany. Then on February 25, 1917, British authorities informed Wilson of a secret telegram sent by the German foreign secretary, Arthur Zimmermann, to the German minister in Mexico. It promised that in the event of war between Germany and the United States, Germany would see that Mexico regained its "lost provinces" of Texas, New Mexico, and Arizona if Mexico would declare war against the United States. Wilson angrily responded to the **Zimmermann telegram** by asking Congress to approve a policy of "armed neutrality" that would allow merchant ships to fight back against any attackers.

In March, German submarines sank five American vessels off Britain, killing 66 Americans. On April 2, the president asked Congress to issue a declaration of war. Wilson called for a "war without hate" and insisted that the destruction of Germany was not the goal of the United States. Rather, America fought to "vindicate the principles of peace and justice." He promised a world made "safe for democracy." On April 6, 1917, Congress voted to declare war.

Wilson feared what war would do at home. He said despairingly, "Once lead this people into war, and they'll forget there ever was such a thing as tolerance. To fight you must be brutal and ruthless, and the spirit of ruthless brutality will infect Congress, the courts, the policeman on the beat, the man in the street."

Zimmermann telegram

▶ February 1917 telegram sent by the German foreign secretary, Arthur Zimmermann, to the German minister in Mexico. The telegram suggested that in the event that Germany and the United States went to war, Mexico would regain "lost territories" in the Southwest if it declared war on the United States. The British intercepted the telegram and passed it on to the United States, leading to an escalation of tensions between the United States and Germany.

QUICK REVIEW ◁

How was the United States drawn into the conflict in Europe?

What role did the United States play in World War I?

What impact did the war have on the home front?

What part did Woodrow Wilson play in the Paris peace conference?

Why was America's transition from war to peace so turbulent?

Conclusion: What was the domestic cost of foreign victory?

What role did the United States play in World War I?

Life in the Trenches One U.S. soldier in a rat-infested trench tensely looks out for danger, another slumps in exhausted sleep, and a third lies flat on his stomach. Nothing could make living in such holes anything better than miserable. Photo: Imperial War Museum.

TWO MILLION AMERICAN TROOPS eventually reached Europe. Filled with a sense of democratic mission and trained to be morally upright as well as fiercely effective, some doughboys found the adventure exhilarating and maintained their idealism to the end. The majority, however, saw little that was gallant in rats, lice, and poison gas, and—despite the progressives' hopes—little to elevate the human soul in a landscape of utter destruction and death.

The Call to Arms

When America entered the war, Britain and France were nearly exhausted after almost three years of conflict. Another Allied power, Russia, was in turmoil. In March 1917, a revolution had forced Czar Nicholas II to abdicate, and eight months later, in a separate peace with Germany, the Bolshevik revolutionary government withdrew Russia from the war.

On May 18, 1917, Wilson signed a sweeping Selective Service Act, authorizing a draft of all young men into the armed forces. Conscription soon transformed a tiny volunteer armed force of 80,000 men into a vast army and navy. Draft boards eventually inducted 2.8 million men into the armed services, in addition to the 2 million who volunteered.

"Follow the Flag"

This heroic navy recruiting poster helped attract thousands of volunteers into the U.S. military, but President Wilson was unwilling to trust voluntary enlistments. He included in his war message to Congress an endorsement of "the principle of universal liability to service"—in other words, a draft. When the war ended, 2 million men had volunteered for military service, and 2.8 million had been drafted. Image by © Swim Ink 2, LLC/Corbis.

CHAPTER LOCATOR | What was Woodrow Wilson's foreign policy agenda?

604 CHAPTER 22
THE UNITED STATES IN WORLD WAR I, 1914–1920

Pershing Button

General John J. Pershing, surrounded by the flags of the Allied nations, stares out at the viewer. The words circling the button declare that the Allies are "united in the cause of liberty," echoing President Woodrow Wilson's insistence that American democratic ideals were universal and could be achieved internationally through U.S. participation in the war. Collection of Janice L. and David J. Frent.

CHRONOLOGY

1917
- **May.** Congress passes Selective Service Act, first draft since Civil War.

1918
- **March.** Treaty of Brest-Litovsk ends the war between Germany and Russia.
- **May–June.** U.S. Marines see first major combat at Cantigny and Château-Thierry.

- Allies launch summer counterattack that leads to Germany's defeat.
- **November 11.** Armistice ending World War I is signed.

Among the 4.8 million men under arms, 370,000 were black Americans. Although African Americans remained understandably skeptical about President Wilson's war for democracy, most followed W. E. B. Du Bois's advice to "close ranks" and to temporarily "forget our special grievances" until the nation had won the war. During training, black recruits suffered the same prejudices that they encountered in civilian life. Rigidly segregated, they faced abuse and miserable conditions, and they were usually assigned to labor battalions, rather than combat units.

Training camps sought to transform white recruits into fighting men. Progressives in the government were also determined that the camps turn out soldiers with the highest moral and civic values. Secretary of War Newton D. Baker created the Commission on Training Camp Activities, staffed by YMCA workers and veterans of the settlement house and playground movements. Military training included games, singing, and college extension courses. The army asked soldiers to stop thinking about sex, explaining that a "man who is thinking below the belt is not efficient." The Military Draft Act of 1917 prohibited prostitution and alcohol near training camps. Wilson's choice to command the American Expeditionary Force (AEF), Major General **John "Black Jack" Pershing,** was as morally upright as he was militarily uncompromising. Described by one observer as "lean, clean, keen," he gave progressives perfect confidence.

The War in France

At the front, the AEF discovered a desperate situation. The war had degenerated into a stalemate of armies dug defensively into hundreds of miles of trenches across France. When ordered "over the top," troops raced desperately toward the enemy's trenches, only to be entangled in barbed wire, enveloped in poison gas, and mowed down by machine guns. The three-day battle of the Somme in 1916 cost the French and British forces 600,000 dead and wounded and the Germans 500,000. The deadliest battle of the war allowed the Allies to advance their trenches only a few meaningless miles.

Still, U.S. troops saw almost no combat in 1917. The only exception was the 92nd Division of black troops. When Pershing received an urgent call for troops from the French, he sent the 92nd to the front to be integrated into the French army because he did not want to lose command over the white troops he valued more. In the 191 days they spent in battle—longer than any other American outfit—the 369th Regiment of the 92nd Division won more medals than any other American combat unit. Black soldiers recognized the irony of having to serve with the French to gain respect.

John "Black Jack" Pershing

▶ Commander of the American Expeditionary Force. Pershing led the American forces that went to France in 1917 to fight in World War I. Known to be as morally upright as he was militarily uncompromising, Pershing expected his troops to conform to a high standard of behavior on and off the battlefield.

| What role did the United States play in World War I? | What impact did the war have on the home front? | What part did Woodrow Wilson play in the Paris peace conference? | Why was America's transition from war to peace so turbulent? | Conclusion: What was the domestic cost of foreign victory? |

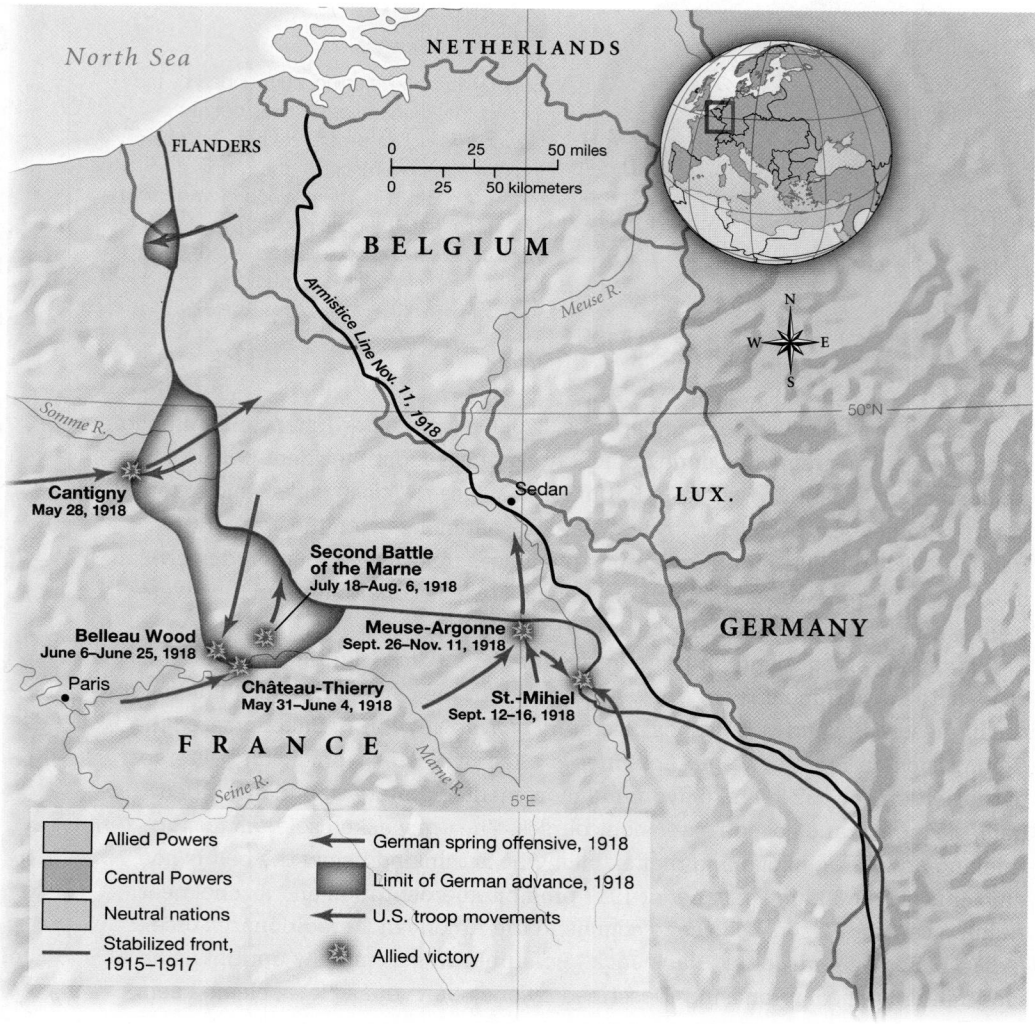

MAP 22.3 ■ The American Expeditionary Force, 1918
In the last year of the war, the AEF joined the French army on the western front to respond to the final German offensive and pursue the retreating enemy until surrender.

Map labels:
North Sea
NETHERLANDS
FLANDERS
BELGIUM
Armistice Line Nov. 11, 1918
Meuse R.
Somme R.
50°N
Sedan
LUX.
Cantigny
May 28, 1918
GERMANY
Second Battle
of the Marne
July 18–Aug. 6, 1918
Belleau Wood
June 6–June 25, 1918
Meuse-Argonne
Sept. 26–Nov. 11, 1918
Paris
Château-Thierry
May 31–June 4, 1918
St.-Mihiel
Sept. 12–16, 1918
F R A N C E
Seine R.
Marne R.
5°E

Scale: 0 25 50 miles / 0 25 50 kilometers

Legend:
- Allied Powers
- Central Powers
- Neutral nations
- Stabilized front, 1915–1917
- German spring offensive, 1918
- Limit of German advance, 1918
- U.S. troop movements
- Allied victory

▶ FOR MORE HELP ANALYZING THIS MAP, see the map activity for this chapter in the Online Study Guide at bedfordstmartins.com/roarkunderstanding.

White troops continued to train and used their free time to explore places that most of them otherwise could never have hoped to see. The sightseeing ended abruptly in March 1918. The Brest-Litovsk treaty signed that month by Germany and the Bolsheviks officially took Russia out of the war, and the Germans launched a massive offensive aimed at French ports on the Atlantic. After a million German soldiers punched a hole in the Allied lines, Pershing decided that the right moment for U.S. action had finally come.

In May and June, at Cantigny and then at Château-Thierry, the Americans checked the German advance with a series of assaults (**Map 22.3**). Then they headed toward the forest stronghold of Belleau Wood, moving against streams of retreating Allied soldiers who cried defeat: "La guerre est finie!" (The war is over!). A French officer commanded American soldiers to retreat with them, but the American commander replied sharply, "Retreat, hell. We just got here." After charging through a wheat field against withering machine-gun fire, the marines plunged into hand-to-hand combat. Victory came hard, but a German report praised the enemy's spirit,

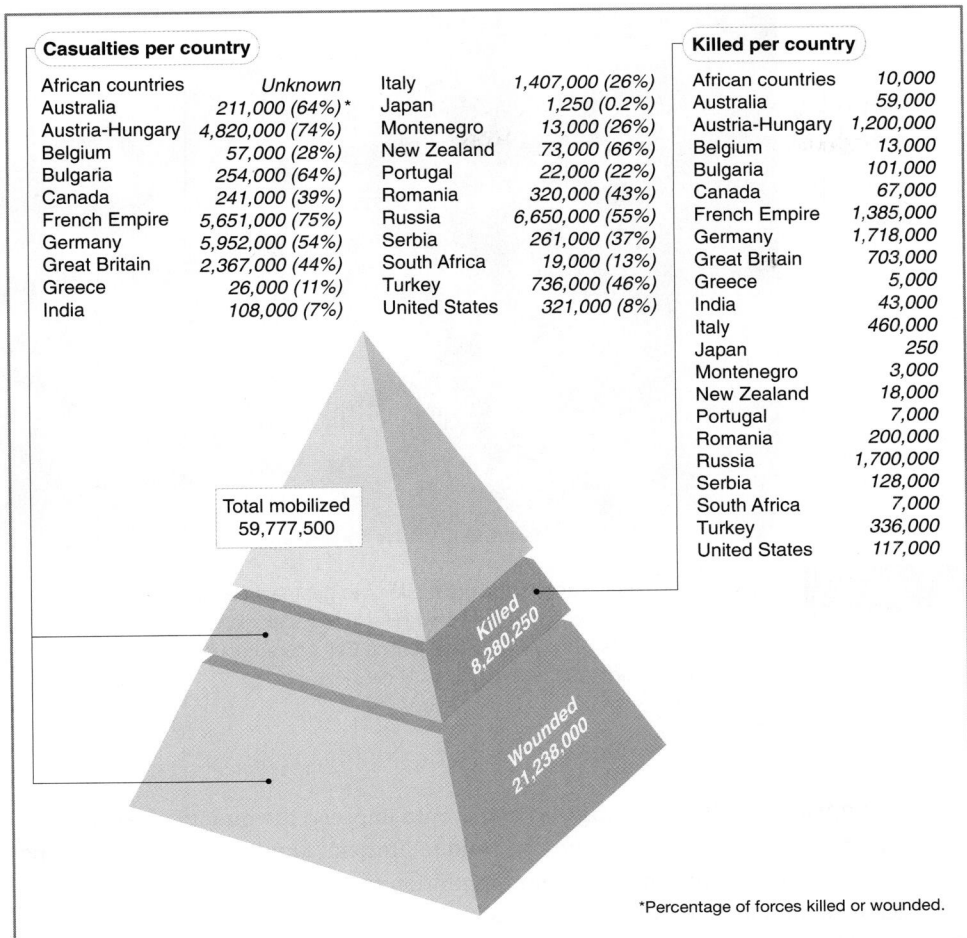

Casualties per country

African countries	Unknown	Italy	1,407,000 (26%)
Australia	211,000 (64%)*	Japan	1,250 (0.2%)
Austria-Hungary	4,820,000 (74%)	Montenegro	13,000 (26%)
Belgium	57,000 (28%)	New Zealand	73,000 (66%)
Bulgaria	254,000 (64%)	Portugal	22,000 (22%)
Canada	241,000 (39%)	Romania	320,000 (43%)
French Empire	5,651,000 (75%)	Russia	6,650,000 (55%)
Germany	5,952,000 (54%)	Serbia	261,000 (37%)
Great Britain	2,367,000 (44%)	South Africa	19,000 (13%)
Greece	26,000 (11%)	Turkey	736,000 (46%)
India	108,000 (7%)	United States	321,000 (8%)

Killed per country

African countries	10,000
Australia	59,000
Austria-Hungary	1,200,000
Belgium	13,000
Bulgaria	101,000
Canada	67,000
French Empire	1,385,000
Germany	1,718,000
Great Britain	703,000
Greece	5,000
India	43,000
Italy	460,000
Japan	250
Montenegro	3,000
New Zealand	18,000
Portugal	7,000
Romania	200,000
Russia	1,700,000
Serbia	128,000
South Africa	7,000
Turkey	336,000
United States	117,000

Total mobilized 59,777,500

Killed 8,280,250

Wounded 21,238,000

*Percentage of forces killed or wounded.

Casualties of the First World War

There is no agreement about the number of casualties in World War I. Record keeping in many countries was only rudimentary. Moreover, the destructive nature of the war meant that countless soldiers were wholly obliterated or instantly buried. However approximate, these figures make clear that the conflict that raged from 1914 to 1918 was a truly catastrophic world war. Although soldiers came from almost every part of the globe, the human devastation was not evenly distributed. Which country suffered the most casualties? Which country lost the greatest percentage of its soldiers? What do you think was the principal reason that the United States lost a smaller percentage of its soldiers than most other nations lost?

noting that "the Americans' nerves are not yet worn out." Indeed, it was German morale that was on the verge of cracking.

In the summer of 1918, the Allies launched a massive counteroffensive that would end the war. A quarter of a million U.S. troops joined in the rout of German forces along the Marne River. In September, more than a million Americans took part in the assault that threw the Germans back from positions along the Meuse River. In November, a revolt against the German government sent Kaiser Wilhelm II fleeing to Holland. On November 11, 1918, a delegation from the newly established German republic met with the French high command to sign an armistice that brought the fighting to an end.

By the end, 112,000 AEF soldiers perished from wounds and disease, while another 230,000 Americans suffered casualties but survived. European nations, however, suffered much greater losses. (See "Global Comparison.") Where they had fought, the landscape was as blasted and barren as the moon.

QUICK REVIEW

How did the American Expeditionary Force contribute to the defeat of Germany?

| What role did the United States play in World War I? | What impact did the war have on the home front? | What part did Woodrow Wilson play in the Paris peace conference? | Why was America's transition from war to peace so turbulent? | Conclusion: What was the domestic cost of foreign victory? |

What impact did the war have on the home front?

Women's Liberty Bell

Suffragists in Pennsylvania made great efforts to get their message out to rural people. This life-size replica of the Liberty Bell in Philadelphia, which suffragists called the Women's Liberty Bell or the Justice Bell, toured country roads on a specially reinforced truck. Historical Society of Pennsylvania.

MANY PROGRESSIVES HOPED that war would improve the quality of American life as well as free Europe from tyranny and militarism. Mobilization helped propel the crusades for woman suffrage and prohibition to success. Progressives enthusiastically channeled industrial and agricultural production into the war effort. Labor shortages caused by workers' entering the military provided new opportunities for women in the booming wartime economy. With labor at a premium, unionized workers gained higher pay and shorter hours. To instill loyalty in Americans whose ancestry was rooted in the belligerent nations, Wilson launched a campaign to foster patriotism. But boosting patriotism led to suppressing dissent. When the government launched a harsh assault on civil liberties, mobs gained license to attack those whom they considered disloyal. Democracy took a beating at home when the nation undertook its foreign crusade for democracy.

The Progressive Stake in the War

The idea of the war as an agent of national improvement fanned the zeal of the progressive movement. The Wilson administration, realizing that the federal government would have to assert greater control to mobilize the nation's human and physical resources, created new agencies charged with managing the war effort. Bernard Baruch headed the War Industries Board, created to stimulate and direct industrial production. Baruch brought industrial management and labor together into a team that produced everything from boots to bullets and made U.S. troops the best-equipped soldiers in the world.

Herbert Hoover headed the Food Administration. He led remarkably successful "Hooverizing" campaigns for "meatless" Mondays and "wheatless"

CHAPTER LOCATOR | What was Woodrow Wilson's foreign policy agenda?

CHAPTER 22
608 THE UNITED STATES IN WORLD WAR I, 1914–1920

Wednesdays and other ways of conserving resources. Guaranteed high prices, the American heartland not only supplied the needs of U.S. citizens and armed forces but also became the breadbasket of America's allies. As the war went on, wartime agencies multiplied.

Wartime Agencies

Railroad Administration	Directed railroad traffic
Fuel Administration	Coordinated the coal industry and other fuel suppliers
Shipping Board	Organized the merchant marine
National War Labor Policies Board	Resolved labor disputes

Some progressives, however, refused to accept the argument that war and reform marched together. Wisconsin senator Robert La Follette attacked the war unrelentingly, claiming that Wilson's promises of peace and democracy were a case of "the blind leading the blind" at home and abroad.

Industrial leaders found that wartime agencies enforced efficiency and helped corporate profits triple. Some working people also had cause to celebrate. Mobilization meant high prices for farmers and plentiful jobs at high wages in the new war industries. Because increased industrial production required peaceful labor relations, the National War Labor Policies Board enacted the eight-hour day, a living minimum wage, and collective bargaining rights in some industries. Wages rose sharply during the war (as did prices), and the American Federation of Labor (AFL) saw its membership soar from 2.7 million to more than 5 million.

The war also provided a huge boost to the crusade to ban alcohol. By 1917, prohibitionists had convinced nineteen states to go dry. Liquor's opponents now argued that banning alcohol would make the cause of democracy powerful and pure. At the same time, shutting down the distilleries would save millions of bushels of grain that could feed the United States and its allies. "Shall the many have food or the few drink?" the drys asked. In December 1917, Congress passed the **Eighteenth Amendment**, which banned the manufacture, transportation, and sale of alcohol. After swift ratification by the states, the amendment went into effect on January 1, 1920.

Women, War, and the Battle for Suffrage

Women had made real strides during the Progressive Era, but war presented new opportunities. More than 25,000 women served in France. About half were nurses. The others drove ambulances; ran canteens for the Salvation Army, Red Cross, and YMCA; worked with French civilians in devastated areas; and acted as telephone operators and war correspondents. Like men who joined the war effort, they believed that they were taking part in a great national venture. "I am more than willing to live as a soldier and know of the hardships I would have to undergo," one canteen worker declared when applying to go overseas, "but I want to help my country. . . . I want . . . to do the *real* work." And like men, women struggled against disillusionment in France. One woman explained: "Over in America, we thought we knew something about the war . . . but when you get

CHRONOLOGY

1915
- Women's Peace Party is formed.

1917
- War Industries Board is formed.
- Committee on Public Information is created.
- Congress passes Eighteenth Amendment, banning the manufacture and sale of alcohol in the United States.

1917–1918
- The Espionage Act, the Trading with the Enemy Act, and the Sedition Act give the government sweeping powers to suppress opposition to the war.

1918
- Republicans gain majority in House and Senate.

1919
- Congress passes Nineteenth Amendment, extending suffrage to women.

1920
- **January 1.** Prohibition begins.
- **August.** Nineteenth Amendment is ratified.

Eighteenth Amendment
▶ Amendment banning the manufacture, transportation, and sale of alcohol. Congress passed the amendment in December 1917, and it was ratified in January 1920. The war provided a huge boost to the crusade to ban alcohol and was key to the passage of the amendment.

| What role did the United States play in World War I? | What impact did the war have on the home front? | What part did Woodrow Wilson play in the Paris peace conference? | Why was America's transition from war to peace so turbulent? | Conclusion: What was the domestic cost of foreign victory? |

609

here the difference is [like the one between] studying the laws of electricity and being struck by lightning."

At home, long-standing barriers against hiring women fell when millions of workingmen became soldiers and few new immigrant workers crossed the Atlantic. Tens of thousands of women found work in defense plants as welders, metalworkers, and heavy machine operators and with the railroads. A black woman, a domestic before the war, celebrated her job as a laborer in a railroad yard: "We are making more money at this than any work we can get, and we do not have to work as hard as at housework which requires us to be on duty from six o'clock in the morning until nine or ten at night, with might[y] little time off and at very poor wages." Other women found white-collar work. Between 1910 and 1920, the number of women clerks doubled. Before the war ended, more than a million women had found work in war industries.

The most dramatic advance for women came in the political arena. Adopting a state-by-state approach, suffragists had achieved some success, but before 1910 only four small western states had adopted woman suffrage (**Map 22.4**). Elsewhere, voting rights for women met strong hostility and defeat. After 1910, suffrage leaders added a federal campaign to amend the Constitution, targeting Congress and the president, to the traditional state-by-state strategy for suffrage.

The radical wing of the suffragists, led by Alice Paul, picketed the White House, where the marchers unfurled banners that proclaimed "America Is Not a Democracy. Twenty Million Women Are Denied the Right to Vote." They chained themselves to fences and went to jail, where many engaged in hunger strikes. "They seem bent on making their cause as obnoxious as possible," Woodrow Wilson declared. But membership in the mainstream organization, the National American Woman Suffrage Association (NAWSA), led by Carrie Chapman Catt, soared to some two million members. The NAWSA even accepted African American

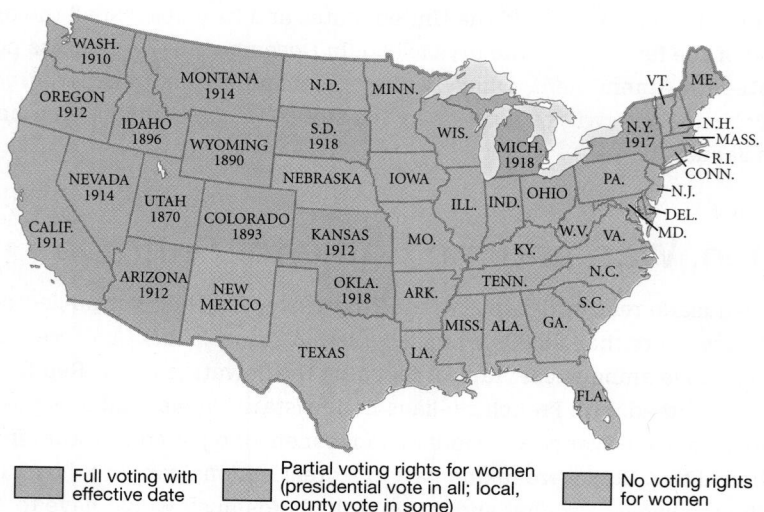

Full voting with effective date	Partial voting rights for women (presidential vote in all; local, county vote in some)	No voting rights for women

MAP 22.4 ■ Women's Voting Rights before the Nineteenth Amendment
The long campaign for women's voting rights reversed the pioneer epic that moved from east to west. From its first successes in the new democratic West, suffrage rolled eastward toward the entrenched, male-dominated public life of the Northeast and South.

CHAPTER LOCATOR | What was Woodrow Wilson's foreign policy agenda?

CHAPTER 22
610 THE UNITED STATES IN WORLD WAR I, 1914–1920

women into its ranks, though not on an equal basis. Seeing the handwriting on the wall, the Republican and Progressive parties endorsed woman suffrage in 1916.

In 1918, Wilson gave his support to suffrage, calling the amendment "vital to the winning of the war." He conceded that it would be wrong not to reward the wartime "partnership of suffering and sacrifice" with a "partnership of privilege and right." By linking their cause to the wartime emphasis on national unity, the advocates of woman suffrage finally triumphed. In 1919, Congress passed the **Nineteenth Amendment**, granting women the vote, and by August 1920, the required two-thirds of the states had ratified it.

Rally around the Flag—or Else

When Congress committed the nation to war, most peace advocates rallied around the flag. The Carnegie Endowment for International Peace adopted new stationery with the heading "Peace through Victory" and issued a resolution saying that "the most effectual means of promoting peace is to prosecute the war against the Imperial German Government."

Only a handful of reformers resisted the tide of patriotism. A group of professional women, led by settlement house leader Jane Addams and economics professor Emily Greene Balch, denounced what Addams described as "the pathetic belief in the regenerative results of war." The Women's Peace Party that emerged in 1915 and its foreign affiliates in the Women's International League for Peace and Freedom led the struggle to persuade governments to negotiate peace and spare dissenters from harsh punishment. After America entered the conflict, advocates for peace were routinely labeled cowards and traitors.

To suppress criticism of the war, Wilson stirred up patriotic fervor. In 1917, the president created the Committee on Public Information under the direction of George Creel. Creel sent "Four-Minute Men," a squad of 75,000 volunteers, around the country to give brief pep talks that celebrated successes on the battlefields and in the factories. Posters, pamphlets, and cartoons depicted brave American soldiers and sailors defending freedom and democracy against the evil "Huns," the derogatory nickname applied to German soldiers. America rallied around Creel's campaign. The film industry produced pro-war movies and taught audiences to hiss at the German kaiser. A musical, *The Kaiser: The Beast of Berlin*, opened on Broadway in 1918. Colleges and universities generated war propaganda in the guise of scholarship. When Professor James McKeen Cattell of Columbia University urged that America seek peace with Germany short of victory, university president Nicholas Murray Butler fired him on the grounds that "what had been folly is now treason."

Across the nation, "100% American" campaigns enlisted ordinary people to sniff out disloyalty. German, the most widely taught foreign language in 1914, practically disappeared from the nation's schools. Targeting German-born Americans, the *Saturday Evening Post* declared that it was time to rid the country of

Nineteenth Amendment

▶ Amendment granting women the vote. Congress passed the amendment in 1919, and it was ratified in August 1920. Like proponents of prohibition, the advocates of woman suffrage triumphed by linking their cause to the war.

D. W. Griffith's *Hearts of the World*

Hollywood joined the government's efforts to stir up rage against the Germans. In a 1918 film made by D. W. Griffith for the British and French governments, a hulking German is about to whip a defenseless farm woman. Library of Congress.

What role did the United States play in World War I?

What impact did the war have on the home front?

What part did Woodrow Wilson play in the Paris peace conference?

Why was America's transition from war to peace so turbulent?

Conclusion: What was the domestic cost of foreign victory?

"the scum of the melting pot." Anti-German action reached its extreme with the lynching of Robert Prager, a German-born baker with socialist leanings. Persuaded by the defense lawyer who praised what he called a "patriotic murder," the jury at the trial of the killers took only twenty-five minutes to acquit.

As hysteria increased, the campaign reached absurd levels. In Montana, a school board barred a history text that had good things to say about medieval Germany. Menus across the nation changed German toast to French toast and sauerkraut to liberty cabbage. In Milwaukee, vigilantes mounted a machine gun outside the Pabst Theater to prevent the staging of Schiller's *Wilhelm Tell*, a powerful protest against tyranny.

The Wilson administration's zeal in suppressing dissent contrasted sharply with its war aims of defending democracy. In the name of self-defense, the Espionage Act (June 1917), the Trading with the Enemy Act (October 1917), and the Sedition Act (May 1918) gave the government sweeping powers to punish any opinion or activity it considered "disloyal, profane, scurrilous, or abusive." When Postmaster General Albert Burleson blocked mailing privileges for dissenting publications, dozens of journals were forced to close down. Of the fifteen hundred individuals eventually charged with sedition, all but a dozen had merely spoken words the government found objectionable. One of them was Eugene V. Debs, the leader of the Socialist Party, who was convicted under the Espionage Act for speeches condemning the war as a capitalist plot and was sent to the Atlanta penitentiary.

The president hoped that national commitment to the war would silence partisan politics, but his Republican rivals used the war as a weapon against the Democrats. Republicans outshouted Wilson on the nation's need to mobilize for war but then complained that Wilson's War Industries Board crushed free enterprise. Such attacks appealed to widely diverse business, labor, and patriotic groups. As the war progressed, Republicans gathered power against the Democrats, who had narrowly reelected Wilson in 1916.

In 1918, Republicans gained a narrow majority in both the House and Senate. The end of Democratic control of Congress not only halted further domestic reform but also meant that the United States would advance toward military victory in Europe with political power divided between a Democratic president and a Republican Congress likely to challenge Wilson's plans for international cooperation.

> **QUICK REVIEW**

How did progressive ideals fare during wartime?

CHAPTER LOCATOR | What was Woodrow Wilson's foreign policy agenda?

612 CHAPTER 22
THE UNITED STATES IN WORLD WAR I, 1914–1920

What part did Woodrow Wilson play in the Paris peace conference?

Leaders of the Paris Peace Conference

The three leaders in charge of putting the world back together after the Great War—from left to right, David Lloyd George, prime minister of Great Britain; Georges Clemenceau, premier of France; and U.S. president Woodrow Wilson—amiably and confidently stride toward the peace conference at the Versailles palace. Gamma Liaison.

WILSON DECIDED TO REAFFIRM his noble war ideals by announcing his peace aims before the end of hostilities. He hoped the victorious Allies would adopt his plan for international democracy, but he was sorely disappointed. America's allies understood that Wilson's principles jeopardized their own postwar plans for the acquisition of enemy territory, new colonial empires, and reparations. Wilson also faced strong opposition at home from those who feared that his enthusiasm for international cooperation would undermine American sovereignty.

Wilson's Fourteen Points

On January 8, 1918, President Wilson revealed to Congress his **Fourteen Points**, his blueprint for a new democratic world order. The first five points affirmed basic liberal ideals: an end to secret treaties; freedom of the seas; removal of economic barriers to free trade; reduction of weapons of war; and recognition of the rights of colonized peoples. The next eight points supported the right to self-determination of European peoples who had been dominated by Germany or its allies. Wilson's fourteenth point called for a "general association of nations"—a **League of Nations**—to provide "mutual guarantees of political independence and territorial integrity to great and small states alike." Only such an organization of "peace-loving nations," he believed, could justify the war and secure a lasting peace. During the final year of the war, he pressured the Allies to accept the Fourteen Points as the basis of the postwar settlement.

Fourteen Points

▶ Woodrow Wilson's plan, first put forward in January 1918, for achieving a lasting postwar peace. Wilson's plan affirmed basic liberal ideals, supported the right to self-determination, and called for the creation of a League of Nations. Wilson was forced to compromise on his plan at the 1919 Paris peace conference, and the U.S. Senate refused to ratify the resulting treaty.

League of Nations

▶ Woodrow Wilson's vision of an international association of nations that would support democracy around the world and maintain the peace. The League of Nations was the key element in Wilson's Fourteen Points, put forward in 1918. Wilson, however, was unable to overcome opposition to the league in the Senate, and the United States never became a member.

| What role did the United States play in World War I? | What impact did the war have on the home front? | **What part did Woodrow Wilson play in the Paris peace conference?** | Why was America's transition from war to peace so turbulent? | Conclusion: What was the domestic cost of foreign victory? |

613

CHRONOLOGY

1918
- **January 8.** President Wilson gives Fourteen Points speech, outlining his plans for lasting peace in the world.

1919
- **January.** Paris peace conference begins.
- **June.** Treaty of Versailles is signed.
- **September.** Wilson undertakes speaking tour to urge Americans to support the Treaty of Versailles.

1920
- **March.** Senate votes against ratification of the Treaty of Versailles.

The Paris Peace Conference

From January 18 to June 28, 1919, the eyes of the world focused on the Paris peace conference. Wilson, inspired by his mission, decided to head the U.S. delegation. He said he owed it to the American soldiers. "It is now my duty," he announced, "to play my full part in making good what they gave their life's blood to obtain." A dubious British diplomat retorted that Wilson was drawn to Paris "as a debutante is entranced by the prospect of her first ball." The decision to leave the country at a time when his political opponents were challenging his leadership was risky enough, but his refusal to include prominent Republicans in the delegation proved foolhardy and eventually cost him his dream of a new world order.

After four terrible years of war, the common people of Europe almost worshipped Wilson, believing that he would create a safer, more decent world. When the peace conference convened at Louis XIV's magnificent palace at Versailles, however, Wilson encountered a different reception. To the Allied leaders, Wilson appeared a naive and impractical moralist. His desire to gather former enemies within a new international democratic order showed how little he understood European realities. Georges Clemenceau, premier of France, claimed that Wilson "believed you could do everything by formulas" and "empty theory." Disparaging the Fourteen Points, he added, "God himself was content with ten commandments."

Allied Leaders at the Paris Peace Conference

United States	Woodrow Wilson
Great Britain	David Lloyd George
France	Georges Clemenceau
Italy	Vittorio Orlando

The Allies wanted to fasten blame for the war on Germany, totally disarm it, and make it pay so dearly that it would never threaten its neighbors again. The French demanded retribution in the form of territory containing Germany's richest mineral resources. The British made it clear that they were not about to give up the powerful weapon of naval blockade for the vague principle of freedom of the seas.

The Allies forced Wilson to make drastic compromises. In return for France's moderating its territorial claims, he agreed to support Article 231 of the peace treaty, assigning war guilt to Germany. Though saved from permanently losing Rhineland territory to the French, Germany was outraged at being singled out as the instigator of the war and saddled with more than $33 billion in damages. Many Germans felt that their nation had been betrayed. After agreeing to an armistice in the belief that peace terms would be based on Wilson's Fourteen Points, they faced hardship and humiliation instead.

Wilson had better success in establishing the principle of self-determination. But from the beginning, Secretary of State Robert Lansing knew that the president's concept of self-determination was "simply loaded with dynamite." Lansing wondered, "What unit has he in mind? Does he mean a race, a territorial area, or a community?" Even Wilson was vague about what self-determination actually meant. "When I gave utterance to those words," he admitted, "I said them without the knowledge that nationalities existed, which are coming to us day after day."

CHAPTER LOCATOR | What was Woodrow Wilson's foreign policy agenda?

614 CHAPTER 22
THE UNITED STATES IN WORLD WAR I, 1914–1920

Lansing suspected that the notion "will raise hopes which can never be realized. It will, I fear, cost thousands of lives. In the end it is bound to be discredited, to be called the dream of an idealist who failed to realize the danger until it was too late."

Yet partly on the basis of self-determination, the conference redrew the map of Europe and parts of the rest of the world. Portions of Austria-Hungary were ceded to Italy, Poland, and Romania, and the remainder was reassembled into Austria, Hungary, Czechoslovakia, and Yugoslavia—independent republics whose boundaries were drawn with attention to concentrations of major ethnic groups. More arbitrarily, the Ottoman empire was carved up into small mandates (including Palestine) run by local leaders but under the control of France and Great Britain. The conference reserved the mandate system for those regions it deemed insufficiently "civilized" to have full independence. Thus, the reconstructed nations—each beset with ethnic and nationalist rivalries—faced the challenge of making a new democratic government work (**Map 22.5**). Many of today's bitterest disputes—in the Balkans and Iraq, between Greece and Turkey, between Arabs and Jews—have roots in the decisions made in Paris in 1919.

Wilson hoped that self-determination would also dictate the fate of Germany's colonies in Asia and Africa. But the Allies, which had taken over the colonies during the war, only allowed the League of Nations a mandate to administer them.

MAP 22.5 ■ **Europe after World War I**

The post–World War I settlement redrew boundaries to create new nations based on ethnic groupings. This outcome left within defeated Germany and Russia bitter peoples who resolved to recover the territory taken from them.

What role did the United States play in World War I?

What impact did the war have on the home front?

What part did Woodrow Wilson play in the Paris peace conference?

Why was America's transition from war to peace so turbulent?

Conclusion: What was the domestic cost of foreign victory?

615

Technically, the mandate system rejected imperialism, but in reality it allowed the Allies to maintain control. Thus, while denying Germany its colonies, the Allies retained and added to their own empires.

The cause of democratic equality suffered another setback when the peace conference rejected Japan's call for a statement of racial equality in the treaty. Wilson's belief in the superiority of whites, as well as his apprehension about how white Americans would respond to such a declaration, led him to oppose the clause. To soothe hurt feelings, Wilson agreed to grant Japan a mandate over the Shantung Peninsula in northern China, which had formerly been controlled by Germany. The gesture mollified Japan's moderate leaders, but the military faction preparing to take over the country used bitterness toward racist Western colonialism to build support for expanding Japanese power throughout Asia.

Closest to Wilson's heart was finding a new way to manage international relations. In Wilson's view, war had discredited the old strategy of balance of power. Instead, he proposed a League of Nations that would provide collective security. The league would establish rules of international conduct and resolve conflicts between nations through rational and peaceful means. When the Allies agreed to the league, Wilson was overjoyed. He believed that the league would rectify the errors his colleagues had forced on him in Paris.

To some Europeans and Americans, the **Versailles treaty** came as a bitter disappointment. Wilson's admirers were shocked that the president dealt in compromise like any other politician. But without Wilson's presence, the treaty that was signed on June 28, 1919, surely would have been more vindictive. Wilson returned home in July 1919 consoled that, despite his frustrations, he had gained what he most wanted—a League of Nations.

The Fight for the Treaty

The tumultuous reception Wilson received when he arrived home persuaded him, probably correctly, that the American people supported the treaty. When the president submitted the treaty to the Senate in July 1919, he warned that failure to ratify it would "break the heart of the world." By then, however, criticism of the treaty was mounting, especially from Americans convinced that their countries of ethnic origin had not been given fair treatment. Irish Americans, Italian Americans, and German Americans launched especially sharp attacks. Others worried that the president's concessions at Versailles had jeopardized the treaty's capacity to provide a generous plan for rebuilding Europe and to guarantee world peace.

In the Senate, a group of Republican "irreconcilables" condemned the treaty for entangling the United States in world affairs. A larger group of Republicans did not object to American participation in world politics but feared that membership in the League of Nations would jeopardize the nation's ability to act independently. No Republican, in any case, was eager to hand Wilson and the Democrats a foreign policy victory.

At the center of Republican opposition was Wilson's archenemy, Senator **Henry Cabot Lodge** of Massachusetts. Lodge was no isolationist, but he thought that much of the Fourteen Points was a "general bleat about virtue being better than vice." Lodge expected the United States' economic and military power to propel the nation into a major role in world affairs. But he insisted that membership in the League of Nations, which would require collective action to maintain

Versailles treaty

▶ Treaty signed on June 28, 1919, that brought World War I to a formal conclusion. The treaty assigned Germany sole responsibility for the war and saddled it with a debt of $33 billion in war damages. Most Germans felt the terms of the treaty were unduly harsh, and resentment of the treaty laid the foundation for future conflict between Germany and the Allied nations of France and England.

Henry Cabot Lodge

▶ Senator from Massachusetts who in 1919 and 1920 led the opposition to America's membership in the League of Nations. Lodge had a strong personal dislike of Wilson, but he also thought the league would compromise American independence. When Wilson refused to go along with Lodge's amendments to the Versailles treaty, the treaty was doomed to go down to defeat.

CHAPTER LOCATOR | What was Woodrow Wilson's foreign policy agenda?

CHAPTER 22
616 THE UNITED STATES IN WORLD WAR I, 1914–1920

peace, threatened the nation's independence in foreign relations.

With Lodge as its chairman, the Senate Foreign Relations Committee crafted several amendments, or "reservations," that sought to limit the consequences of American membership in the league. For example, several reservations required approval of both the House and Senate before the United States could participate in league-sponsored economic sanctions or military action.

It gradually became clear that ratification of the treaty depended on acceptance of the Lodge reservations. Democratic senators, who overwhelmingly supported the treaty, urged Wilson to accept Lodge's terms, arguing that they left the essentials of the treaty intact. Wilson, however, insisted that the reservations cut "the very heart out of the treaty."

Wilson decided to take his case directly to the people. On September 3, 1919, he set out by train on the most ambitious speaking tour ever undertaken by a president. On September 25 in Pueblo, Colorado, Wilson collapsed and had to return to Washington. There, he suffered a massive stroke that partially paralyzed him. From his bedroom, Wilson sent messages instructing Democrats in the Senate to hold firm against any and all reservations. Wilson commanded enough loyalty to ensure a vote against the Lodge reservations. But when the treaty without reservations came before the Senate in March 1920, the combined opposition of the Republican irreconcilables and reservationists left Wilson six votes short of the two-thirds majority needed for passage.

The nations of Europe organized the League of Nations at Geneva, Switzerland, but the United States never became a member. Whether American membership could have prevented the world war that would begin in Europe in 1939 is highly unlikely, but the United States' failure to join certainly weakened the league from the start. In refusing to accept relatively minor compromises with Senate moderates, Wilson lost his treaty and American membership in the league.

"Refusing to Give the Lady a Seat"

When stiff opposition to American membership in the League of Nations developed in the United States, friends of the league mounted a counterattack. This cartoon skewers the three leading Republican opponents of the league—Senators William Borah of Idaho, Henry Cabot Lodge of Massachusetts, and Hiram Johnson of California—who stubbornly refuse to budge an inch for the angel of peace. Picture Research Consultants & Archives.

QUICK REVIEW

Why did the Senate fail to ratify the Versailles treaty?

What role did the United States play in World War I?

What impact did the war have on the home front?

What part did Woodrow Wilson play in the Paris peace conference?

Why was America's transition from war to peace so turbulent?

Conclusion: What was the domestic cost of foreign victory?

Why was America's transition from war to peace so turbulent?

This southern family arrived in a new home in an unnamed northern city in 1912. Wearing their Sunday best, family members carried the rest of what they owned in two suitcases. In Chicago, the League on Urban Conditions among Negroes, which eventually became the Urban League, sought to ease the transition of southern blacks to life in the North. Photographs and Prints Division, Schomburg Center for Research in Black Culture, New York Public Library, Astor, Lenox, and Tilden Foundations.

> ▶ FOR MORE HELP ANALYZING THIS IMAGE, see the visual activity for this chapter in the Online Study Guide at bedfordstmartins.com/roarkunderstanding.

THE DEFEAT OF WILSON'S plan for international democracy proved the crowning blow to progressives who had hoped that the war would boost reform at home. When the war ended, Americans wanted to demobilize swiftly. In the process, servicemen, defense workers, and farmers lost their war-related jobs. The volatile combination—of unemployed veterans returning home, a stalled economy, and leftover wartime patriotism looking for a new cause—threatened to explode.

Economic Hardship and Labor Upheaval

Americans greeted peace with a demand that the United States return to a peacetime economy. The government abruptly abandoned its wartime economic controls and canceled war contracts worth millions of dollars. In a matter of months, more than three million soldiers were mustered out of the military and flooded the job market just as war production ceased. Unemployment soared. At the same time, consumers went on a postwar spending spree that drove inflation skyward. In 1919, prices rose 75 percent over prewar levels, and in 1920 prices rose another 28 percent.

Most of the gains workers had made during the war evaporated. Freed from wartime controls, business turned against the eight-hour day and attacked labor

CHAPTER LOCATOR | What was Woodrow Wilson's foreign policy agenda?

618 CHAPTER 22
THE UNITED STATES IN WORLD WAR I, 1914–1920

unions. With inflation eating up their paychecks, workers fought back. The year 1919 witnessed nearly 3,600 strikes involving 4 million workers. The most spectacular strike occurred in February 1919 in Seattle, where shipyard workers had been put out of work by demobilization. When a coalition of the radical Industrial Workers of the World (IWW, known as Wobblies) and the moderate American Federation of Labor called a general strike, the largest work stoppage in American history shut down the city. Newspapers claimed that the walkout was "a Bolshevik effort to start a revolution." The suppression of the Seattle general strike by officials cost the AFL many of its wartime gains and contributed to the destruction of the IWW soon afterward.

A strike by Boston policemen in the fall of 1919 underscored postwar hostility toward labor militancy. Although the police were paid less than pick-and-shovel laborers, they won little sympathy. Once the officers stopped walking their beats, looters sacked the city. Massachusetts governor Calvin Coolidge called in the National Guard to restore order. The public, yearning for peace and security in the wake of war, welcomed Coolidge's anti-union assurance that "there is no right to strike against the public safety by anybody, anywhere, any time."

Labor strife climaxed in the steel strike of 1919. Faced with the industry's plan to revert to seven-day weeks, twelve-hour days, and weekly wages of about $20, Samuel Gompers, head of the AFL, called for a strike. In response, 350,000 workers in fifteen states walked out in September 1919. The steel industry hired 30,000 strikebreakers (many of them African Americans) and convinced the public that the strikers were radicals and subversives. In January 1920, after eighteen striking workers were killed, the strike collapsed. That defeat initiated a sharp decline in the fortunes of the labor movement, a trend that would continue for almost twenty years.

The Red Scare

Suppression of labor strikes was one response to the widespread fear of internal subversion that swept the nation in 1919. The **Red scare** ("Red" referred to the color of the Bolshevik flag) had homegrown causes: the postwar recession, labor unrest, and the difficulties of reintegrating millions of returning veterans. But unsettling events abroad also added to Americans' anxieties.

Russian bolshevism became even more menacing in March 1919, when the new Soviet leaders created the Comintern, a worldwide association of Communist leaders intent on fomenting revolution in capitalist countries. A Communist revolution in the United States was extremely unlikely, but edgy Americans faced with a flurry of terrorist acts, most notably thirty-eight bombs mailed to prominent individuals, believed otherwise. Attorney General A. Mitchell Palmer launched a hunt to find terrorists. Targeting men and women who harbored ideas that Palmer believed could lead to violence, even though the individuals may not have done anything illegal, the Justice Department sought to purge the supposed enemies of America.

In January 1920, Palmer ordered a series of raids that netted 6,000 alleged subversives. Finding no revolutionary conspiracies, Palmer nevertheless ordered 500 noncitizen suspects deported. His action came in the wake of a campaign against the most notorious radical alien, Russian-born Emma Goldman. Before the war, Goldman's support of labor strikes, women's rights, and birth control had made her a symbol of radicalism. Finally, after a stay in prison for attacking military conscription, she was ordered deported by J. Edgar Hoover, the director of

CHRONOLOGY

1910–1920
- Mexican-born population in the United States more than doubles.

1915–1920
- Ten percent of the South's black population migrates north.

1919
- Prices rise 75 percent over prewar levels.
- Wave of labor strikes sweeps the country.
- The Red scare—fear of internal subversion and Russian bolshevism—engulfs the country.
- *Schenck v. United States* establishes a "clear and present danger" test for war resisters.

1920
- **November.** Republican Warren G. Harding is elected president.

Red scare

▶ The widespread fear of internal subversion that swept the nation in 1919. The Red scare had many domestic causes: the postwar recession, labor unrest, and the difficulties of reintegrating millions of returning veterans. It was also stimulated by the creation of the Comintern by Soviet leaders in March 1919. The Red scare resulted in widespread suppression of dissent, carried out by both private citizens and government officials.

| What role did the United States play in World War I? | What impact did the war have on the home front? | What part did Woodrow Wilson play in the Paris peace conference? | Why was America's transition from war to peace so turbulent? | Conclusion: What was the domestic cost of foreign victory? |

Emma Goldman Is Deported

In the fall of 1919, federal agents arrested hundreds of "Bolsheviks" whom they considered a "menace to law and order." In December 1919, anarchist Emma Goldman and some 250 others were deported to Soviet Russia.
© Bettmann/Corbis.

the Justice Department's Radical Division. In December 1919, Goldman and some 250 others boarded a ship for exile in Russia.

The effort to rid the country of alien radicals was matched by efforts to crush troublesome citizens. Law enforcement officials and vigilante groups joined hands against so-called Reds. In November 1919 in the lumber town of Centralia, Washington, a menacing crowd gathered in front of the IWW hall. Nervous Wobblies inside opened fire, killing three people. Three IWW members were arrested and later convicted of murder, but another, ex-soldier Wesley Everett, was carried off by the mob, which castrated him, hung him from a bridge, and then riddled his body with bullets. His death was officially ruled a suicide.

Public institutions joined the attack on civil liberties. Local libraries removed dissenting books. Schools fired unorthodox teachers. Police shut down radical newspapers. State legislatures refused to seat elected representatives who professed socialist ideas. And in 1919, Congress removed its lone socialist representative, Victor Berger, on the pretext that he was a threat to national safety.

That same year, the Supreme Court provided a formula for restricting free speech. In upholding the conviction of socialist Charles Schenck for publishing a pamphlet urging resistance to the draft during wartime (*Schenck v. United States*), the Court established a "clear and present danger" test. Such utterances as Schenck's during a time of national peril, Justice Oliver Wendell Holmes wrote, were equivalent to shouting "Fire!" in a crowded theater.

In time, the Red scare lost credibility, especially after Attorney General Palmer warned in 1920 that radicals were planning to celebrate the Bolshevik Revolution with a nationwide wave of violence. Officials called out state militias, mobilized bomb squads, and even placed machine-gun nests at major city intersections. When May 1 came and went without a single disturbance, the public mood turned from fear to scorn. The Red scare collapsed as a result of its excesses.

The Great Migrations of African Americans and Mexicans

Before the Red scare lost steam, the government raised alarms about the loyalty of African Americans. A Justice Department investigation concluded that Reds were fomenting racial unrest among blacks. Although the report was wrong about Bolshevik influence, it was correct in noticing a new assertiveness among African Americans.

In 1900, nine of every ten blacks still lived in the South, where poverty, disfranchisement, segregation, and violence dominated their lives. Whites remained committed to keeping blacks down. "If we own a good farm or horse, or cow, or bird-dog, or yoke of oxen," a black sharecropper in Mississippi observed in 1913, "we are harassed until we are bound to sell, give away, or run away, before we can have any peace in our lives."

The First World War provided African Americans with new opportunities. War channeled almost five million American workers into military service and all

CHAPTER LOCATOR | What was Woodrow Wilson's foreign policy agenda?

620 CHAPTER 22
THE UNITED STATES IN WORLD WAR I, 1914–1920

but ended European immigration. Deprived of their traditional sources of laborers just as production demands were increasing, northern industrialists turned to black labor. From 1915 to 1920, half a million blacks (approximately 10 percent of the South's black population) boarded trains bound for Philadelphia, Detroit, Cleveland, Chicago, St. Louis, and other industrial cities.

Thousands of migrants wrote home to tell family and friends about their experiences in the North. One man announced proudly that he had recently been promoted to "first assistant to the head carpenter." He added, "I should have been here twenty years ago. I just begin to feel like a man. . . . My children are going to the same school with the whites and I don't have to [h]umble to no one. I have registered—will vote the next election and there ain't any 'yes sir'—it's all yes and no and Sam and Bill."

But the North was not the promised land. Black men stood on the lowest rungs of the labor ladder. Jobs of any kind proved scarce for black women, and most worked as domestic servants as they did in the South. The existing black middle class sometimes shunned the less educated, less sophisticated rural southerners crowding into northern cities. Many whites, fearful of losing jobs and status, lashed out against the new migrants. Savage race riots ripped through two dozen northern cities. In 1918, the nation witnessed ninety-six lynchings of blacks, some of them returning war veterans still in uniform.

Still, most black migrants stayed in the North and encouraged friends and family to follow. By 1940, more than one million blacks had left the South, profoundly changing their own lives and the course of the nation's history. Black enclaves such as Harlem in New York and the South Side of Chicago emerged in the North. These assertive communities provided a foundation for black protest and political organization in the years ahead.

At nearly the same time, another migration was under way in the American Southwest. Between 1910 and 1920, the Mexican-born population in the United States soared from 222,000 to 478,000. Mexican immigration resulted from developments on both sides of the border. When Mexicans revolted against dictator Porfirio Díaz in 1910, initiating a ten-year civil war, migrants flooded northward. In the United States, the Chinese Exclusion Act of 1882 and later the disruption of World War I cut off the supply of cheap foreign labor and caused western employers in the expanding rail, mining, construction, and agricultural industries to look south to Mexico for workers. By 1920, ethnic Mexicans made up about three-fourths of California's farm laborers. They were also crucial to the Texas economy, accounting for three-fourths of laborers in the cotton fields and in construction there.

Like immigrants from Europe and black migrants from the South, Mexicans in the American Southwest dreamed of a better life. And like the others, they found both opportunity and disappointment. Wages were better than in Mexico, but life in the fields, mines, and factories was hard, and living conditions often were dismal. Signs warning "No Mexicans Allowed" increased rather than declined. Among Mexican Americans, some of whom had lived in the Southwest for a

Mexican Women Arriving in El Paso, 1911

These Mexican women, carrying bundles and wearing traditional shawls, try to get their bearings upon arriving in El Paso, Texas— the Ellis Island for Mexican immigrants. Women like them found work in the cotton and sugar beet fields, canneries, and restaurants of the Southwest, as well as at home taking in sewing, laundry, and boarders. *Courtesy of the Rio Grande Historical Collections, New Mexico State University, Las Cruces, New Mexico.*

What role did the United States play in World War I?

What impact did the war have on the home front?

What part did Woodrow Wilson play in the Paris peace conference?

Why was America's transition from war to peace so turbulent?

Conclusion: What was the domestic cost of foreign victory?

621

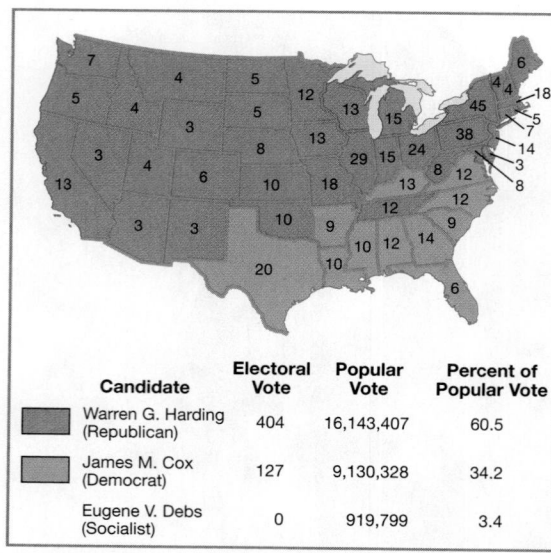

Candidate	Electoral Vote	Popular Vote	Percent of Popular Vote
Warren G. Harding (Republican)	404	16,143,407	60.5
James M. Cox (Democrat)	127	9,130,328	34.2
Eugene V. Debs (Socialist)	0	919,799	3.4

MAP 22.6 ■ The Election of 1920

century or more, *los recien llegados* (the recent arrivals) encountered mixed reactions. One Mexican American expressed this ambivalence: "We are all Mexicans anyway because the *gueros* [Anglos] treat us all alike." But he also called for immigration quotas because the recent arrivals drove down wages and incited white prejudice that affected all ethnic Mexicans.

Despite friction, large-scale immigration into the Southwest meant a resurgence of the Mexican cultural presence, which became the basis for greater solidarity and political action for the ethnic Mexican population. In 1929, Mexican Americans formed the League of United Latin American Citizens in Texas.

Postwar Politics and the Election of 1920

A thousand miles away in Washington, D.C., President Woodrow Wilson, bedridden and paralyzed, ignored the country's many domestic troubles and insisted that the 1920 election would be a "solemn referendum" on the League of Nations. Dutifully, the Democratic nominees for president, James M. Cox of Ohio, and for vice president, Franklin Delano Roosevelt of New York, campaigned on Wilson's international ideals. The Republican Party chose the handsome, gregarious Warren Gamaliel Harding, senator from Ohio. Harding's rise in Ohio politics was a tribute to his amiability, not his mastery of the issues.

Harding found the winning formula when he declared that "America's present need is not heroics, but healing; not nostrums [questionable remedies] but normalcy." But what was "normalcy"? Harding explained: "By 'normalcy' I don't mean the old order but a regular steady order of things. I mean normal procedure, the natural way, without excess." Eager to put wartime crusades and postwar strife behind them, voters responded by giving Harding the largest presidential victory ever: 60.5 percent of the popular vote and 404 out of 531 electoral votes (**MAP 22.6**). Once in office, Harding and his wife, Florence, threw open the White House gates, which had been closed since the declaration of war in 1917. Their welcome brought throngs of visitors and lifted the national pall, signaling a new, more easygoing era.

> **QUICK REVIEW**

How did the Red scare contribute to the erosion of civil liberties after the war?

CHAPTER LOCATOR | What was Woodrow Wilson's foreign policy agenda?

622 CHAPTER 22 THE UNITED STATES IN WORLD WAR I, 1914–1920

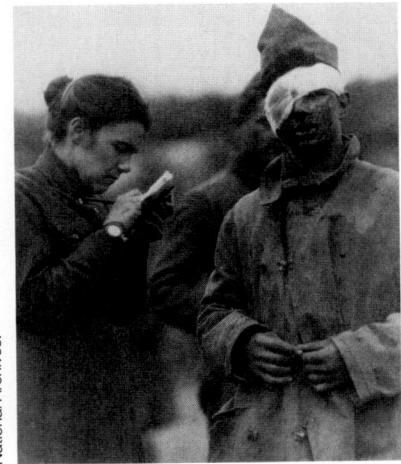

National Archives.

Conclusion: What was the domestic cost of foreign victory?

AMERICA'S EXPERIENCE IN WORLD WAR I was exceptional. For much of the world, the Great War produced great destruction, acres of blackened fields, ruined factories, and millions of casualties. But in the United States, war and prosperity marched hand in hand. America emerged from the war with the strongest economy in the world and a position of international preeminence.

Still, the nation paid a heavy price both at home and abroad. American soldiers and sailors encountered unprecedented horrors—submarines, poison gas, machine guns—and more than 100,000 died. On Memorial Day 1919, at the Argonne Cemetery, where 14,200 Americans lie, General John J. Pershing said: "It is not for us to proclaim what they did, their silence speaks more eloquently than words, but it is for us to uphold the conception of duty, honor and country for which they fought and for which they died. It is for the living to carry forward their purpose and make fruitful their sacrifice." Rather than redeeming their sacrifice, however, as Wilson promised, the peace that followed the armistice tarnished it. At home, rather than permanently improving working conditions, advancing public health, and spreading educational opportunity, as progressives had hoped, the war threatened to undermine the achievements of the previous two decades. Moreover, rather than promoting democracy in the United States, the war bred fear, intolerance, and repression that led to a crackdown on dissent and a demand for conformity. Reformers could count only woman suffrage as a permanent victory.

Woodrow Wilson had promised more than anyone could deliver. Progressive hopes of extending democracy and liberal reform nationally and internationally were dashed. In 1920, a bruised and disillusioned society stumbled into a new decade. The era coming to an end had called on Americans to crusade and to sacrifice. The new era promised peace, prosperity, and a good time.

Beat back the HUN
with
LIBERTY BONDS

SO NOW YOU KNOW

Not only did menus across the United States change the name of German toast to French toast, but some people also expressed their anger toward Germany and political dissidents in ways that at times included violence. Rather than promoting democracy and freedom at home, World War I bred fear, intolerance, and repression and justified demands for conformity and the erosion of civil liberties.

> CHAPTER 22 STUDY GUIDE

Online Study Guide
bedfordstmartins.com/roarkunderstanding

STEP 1 GETTING STARTED

Below are basic terms from this period in American history. Can you identify each term below and explain why it matters? To do this exercise online or to download this chart, visit bedfordstmartins.com/roarkunderstanding.

TERM	WHO OR WHAT & WHEN	WHY IT MATTERS
U-boats, p. 602		
Zimmermann telegram, p. 603		
John "Black Jack" Pershing, p. 605		
Eighteenth Amendment, p. 609		
Nineteenth Amendment, p. 611		
Fourteen Points, p. 613		
League of Nations, p. 613		
Versailles treaty, p. 616		
Henry Cabot Lodge, p. 616		
Red scare, p. 619		

STEP 2 MOVING BEYOND THE BASICS

The exercise below represents a more advanced understanding of the chapter material. Use the following chart to describe the United States' entry into the war and to list government initiatives in three areas: wartime agencies, legislation, and propaganda. When you are finished, assess the overall effects of the government's efforts. Was the government able to harness the economy to the war effort? Did the public come to support the war? How did the various tools at the government's disposal contribute to the war effort? Finally, reflect on the costs of the government's domestic war policies. How much damage was done to civil liberties? To do this exercise online or to download this chart, visit bedfordstmartins.com/roarkunderstanding.

	Description or list	Reasons for	Effects of
U.S. entry into World War I			
Wartime agencies			
Legislation			
Propaganda			

Now that you have reviewed key elements of the chapter, take a step back and try to explain the big picture. Remember to use specific examples from the chapter in your answers. To do this exercise online, visit bedfordstmartins.com/roarkunderstanding.

THE PATH TO WAR

▶ Describe Woodrow Wilson's foreign policy during his first term in office. How did Wilson see the relationship between the United States and the rest of the world?

▶ Is it fair to describe the American people as "isolationist" prior to America's entry into World War I? Why or why not?

THE HOME FRONT

▶ How did the war affect the progressive agenda? How did progressives use the war to achieve their goals?

▶ To what extent did U.S. participation in World War I involve the domestic efforts of the American people?

A TROUBLED PEACE

▶ What vision did Wilson have of the postwar world? Why did the Senate refuse to endorse his vision, as embodied in the Treaty of Versailles?

▶ What led to the Red scare, and why did it eventually subside?

LOOKING BACKWARD, LOOKING AHEAD

▶ Why did a majority of Americans initially oppose the country's entry into World War I? What events and experiences in the country's past helped shape prewar public opinion?

▶ How did World War I change the place of the United States in the world? What role in world affairs was America poised to take as it entered the 1920s?

IN YOUR OWN WORDS

Imagine that you must explain chapter 22 to someone who hasn't read it. What would be the most important points to include and why?

23
FROM NEW ERA TO GREAT DEPRESSION

1920–1932

> This chapter examines the central place of business in 1920s society, the policies of the Republican administrations, the key cultural trends and conflicts of the decade, and the events that led to the collapse of the American economy. Finally, this chapter addresses the failure of government to adequately respond to the human toll of economic catastrophe.

> How did big business shape the New Era of the 1920s?

> In what ways did the Roaring Twenties challenge traditional values?

> Why did the divide between rural and urban America grow in the 1920s?

> What caused the crash of 1929?

> What was life like in the early years of the depression?

> Conclusion: Why did the hope of the 1920s turn to despair?

DID YOU KNOW?

By 1929, more than 80 million people went to the movies every week, as many as lived in the entire United States.

"Sheik with Sheba." Cover of *Judge* magazine, by A. John Held, Jr.

How did big business shape the New Era of the 1920s?

Henry and Edsel Ford

In this 1924 photograph, Henry Ford looks fondly at his first car while his son, Edsel, stands next to the ten millionth Model T. Henry Ford Museum and Greenfield Village.

ONCE WOODROW WILSON left the White House, energy flowed away from civic reform and toward private economic endeavor. The rise of a freewheeling economy and a heightened sense of individualism caused Secretary of Commerce Herbert Hoover to declare that America had entered a "New Era," one of many labels used to describe the complex 1920s.

America in the twenties was many things, but President Calvin Coolidge got at an essential truth when he declared, "The business of America is business." Politicians and diplomats proclaimed business the heart of American civilization. Average men and women bought into the idea that business and its products were what made America great, as they snatched up the flood of new consumer items American factories sent forth.

A Business Government

Republicans controlled the White House from 1921 to 1933. The first of the three Republican presidents was Warren Gamaliel Harding, the Ohio senator who in his 1920 campaign called for a "return to normalcy," by which he meant the end of public crusades and a return to private pursuits. Harding promised a government run by the best minds, and he appointed a few men of real stature to his cabinet, including Herbert Hoover, who became secretary of commerce. But wealth and friendship also counted. Andrew Mellon, one of the richest men in

CHAPTER LOCATOR | How did big business shape the New Era of the 1920s?

CHAPTER 23
628 FROM NEW ERA TO GREAT DEPRESSION, 1920–1932

America, became secretary of the treasury, and Harding handed out jobs to members of his old "Ohio gang," whose only qualification was their friendship. This curious combination of merit and cronyism made for a disjointed administration.

When Harding was elected in 1920 (see chapter 22, Map 22.6), the unemployment rate hit 20 percent, the highest ever up to that point. Farmers fared the worst; their bankruptcy rate increased tenfold. Harding pushed measures to regain national prosperity—high tariffs to protect American businesses, price supports for agriculture, and the dismantling of wartime government control over industry in favor of unregulated private business. "Never before, here or anywhere else," the U.S. Chamber of Commerce said proudly, "has a government been so completely fused with business."

Harding's policies to boost American enterprise made him very popular, but ultimately his small-town congeniality and trusting ways did him in. Some of his friends in the Ohio gang were up to their necks in lawbreaking. Three of Harding's appointees would go to jail. Interior Secretary Albert Fall was convicted of accepting bribes of more than $400,000 for leasing oil reserves on public land in Teapot Dome, Wyoming, and "Teapot Dome" became a synonym for political corruption.

On August 2, 1923, when the fifty-eight-year-old Harding died from a heart attack, Vice President Calvin Coolidge became president. Coolidge once expressed his belief that "the man who builds a factory builds a temple, the man who works there worships there." Reverence for free enterprise meant that Coolidge continued and extended Harding's policies of promoting business and limiting government. Secretary of the Treasury Andrew Mellon reduced the government's control over the economy and cut taxes for corporations and wealthy individuals. New rules for the Federal Trade Commission severely limited its power to regulate business. Secretary of Commerce Herbert Hoover limited government authority by encouraging trade associations that ideally would keep business honest and efficient through voluntary cooperation.

Coolidge found an ally in the Supreme Court. The Court ruled against closed shops—businesses where only union members could be employed—while confirming the right of owners to form exclusive trade associations. In 1923, the Court declared unconstitutional the District of Columbia's minimum-wage law for women, asserting that the law interfered with the freedom of employer and employee to make labor contracts. The Court and the president attacked government intrusion in the free market, even when the prohibition of government regulation threatened the welfare of workers.

The election of 1924 confirmed the defeat of the progressive principle that the state should take a leading role in ensuring the general welfare. To oppose Coolidge, the Democrats nominated John W. Davis, a corporate lawyer whose conservative views differed little from Republican principles. Only the Progressive Party and its presidential nominee, Senator Robert La Follette of Wisconsin, offered a genuine alternative. When La Follette championed labor unions, regulation of business, and protection of civil liberties, Republicans coined the slogan "Coolidge or Chaos." Turning their backs on what they considered labor radicalism and reckless reform, voters chose Coolidge in a landslide. Coolidge was right when he declared, "This is a business country, and it wants a business

CHRONOLOGY

1920
- Republican Warren G. Harding is elected president.

1922
- Teapot Dome scandal shakes Harding's administration.
- Five-Power Naval Treaty reduces the naval forces of Britain, France, Japan, Italy, and the United States.

1923
- Harding dies; Vice President Calvin Coolidge becomes president.

1924
- Coolidge is elected president.
- Dawes Plan lowers reparation payments and provides for loans for Germany.

1928
- In the Kellogg-Briand pact, nearly fifty nations pledge to renounce war.

1929
- One in four American jobs is linked to the automobile industry.

In what ways did the Roaring Twenties challenge traditional values?

Why did the divide between rural and urban America grow in the 1920s?

What caused the crash of 1929?

What was life like in the early years of the depression?

Conclusion: Why did the hope of the 1920s turn to despair?

government." What was true of the government's relationship to business at home was also true abroad.

Promoting Prosperity and Peace Abroad

After orchestrating the Senate's successful effort to block U.S. membership in the League of Nations, Henry Cabot Lodge boasted, "We have torn Wilsonism up by the roots." But repudiation of Wilsonian internationalism and rejection of collective security through the League of Nations did not mean that the United States retreated into isolationism. The United States emerged from World War I with its economy intact and enjoyed a decade of stunning growth. Economic involvement in the world and the continuing chaos in Europe made an American retreat into isolationism impossible. New York replaced London as the center of world finance, and the United States became the world's chief creditor.

One of the Republicans' most ambitious foreign policy initiatives was the Washington Disarmament Conference, which convened to establish a global balance of naval power. Secretary of State Charles Evans Hughes shaped the Five-Power Naval Treaty of 1922 committing Britain, France, Japan, Italy, and the United States to a proportional reduction of naval forces. The treaty led to the scrapping of more than two million tons of warships, by far the world's greatest success in disarmament. By fostering international peace, Harding helped make the world a safer place for American trade.

A second major effort on behalf of world peace came in 1928, when Secretary of State Frank Kellogg joined French foreign minister Aristide Briand to produce the Kellogg-Briand pact. Nearly fifty nations signed the solemn pledge to renounce war and settle international disputes peacefully.

But Republican administrations preferred private sector diplomacy to state action. With the blessing of the White House, a team of American financiers led by Chicago banker Charles Dawes swung into action when Germany suspended its war reparation payments in 1923. Impoverished, Germany was staggering under the massive bill of $33 billion presented by the victorious Allies in the Versailles treaty. When Germany failed to meet its annual payment, France occupied Germany's industrial Ruhr Valley, creating the worst international crisis since the war. In 1924, American corporate leaders produced the Dawes Plan, which halved Germany's annual reparation payments, initiated fresh American loans to Germany, and caused the French to retreat from the Ruhr. Although the United States failed to join the League of Nations, it continued to exercise significant economic and diplomatic influence abroad. These Republican successes overseas helped fuel prosperity at home.

Automobiles, Mass Production, and Assembly-Line Progress

Henry Ford
▶ Founder of the Ford Motor Company and pioneer of the mass production of automobiles. Affordable cars like those Ford produced transformed America.

The automobile industry emerged as the largest single manufacturing industry in the nation. **Henry Ford**, pioneer of the mass production of automobiles, shrewdly located his company in Detroit, knowing that key materials for his automobiles were manufactured in nearby states (**Map 23.1**). Keystone of the American

CHAPTER LOCATOR | How did big business shape the New Era of the 1920s?

economy, the automobile industry not only employed hundreds of thousands of workers directly but also brought whole industries into being—filling stations, garages, fast-food restaurants, and "guest cottages" (motels). The need for tires, glass, steel, highways, oil, and refined gasoline for automobiles provided millions of related jobs. By 1929, one American in four found employment directly or indirectly in the automobile industry. "Give us our daily bread" was no longer addressed to the Almighty, one commentator quipped, but to Detroit.

The Ford Motor Company in the 1920s

1920–1927	Nine million cars are sold.
1920–1925	Speed of production increases sixfold.
1920–1928	Cost of a Ford car falls from $845 to less than $300.

Cars changed where people lived, what work they did, how they spent their leisure, even how they thought. Hundreds of small towns decayed because the automobile enabled rural people to bypass them in favor of more distant cities and towns. In cities, streetcars began to disappear as workers moved to the suburbs and commuted to work along crowded highways. Nothing shaped modern America more than the automobile, and efficient mass production made the automobile revolution possible.

Mass production by the assembly-line technique had become standard in almost every factory, from automobiles to meatpacking to cigarettes. To improve efficiency, corporations reduced assembly-line work to the simplest, most repetitive tasks. They also established specialized divisions—procurement,

mass production

▶ The production of large quantities of a given product through efficient production methods. During the 1920s, mass production by the assembly-line technique became standard in almost every American factory. Mass production resulted in greater productivity and profits for American businesses but also removed skilled jobs from the economy.

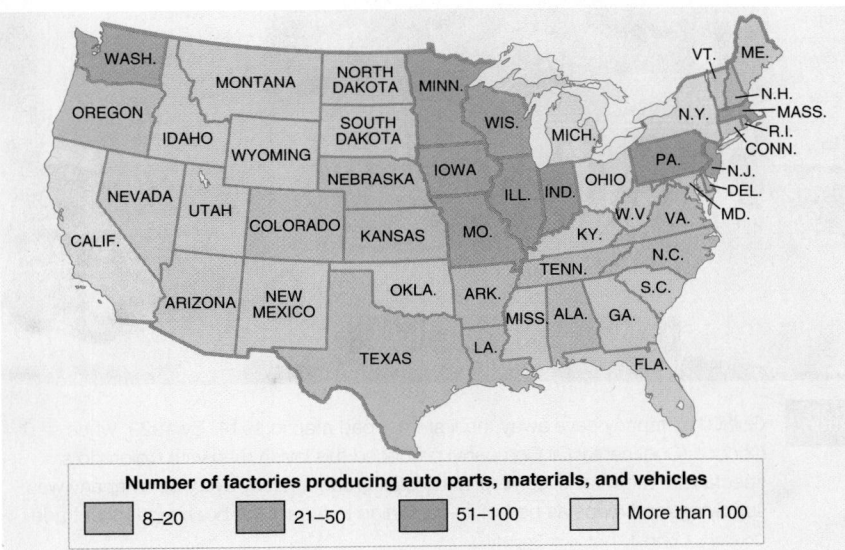

Number of factories producing auto parts, materials, and vehicles

| 8–20 | 21–50 | 51–100 | More than 100 |

MAP 23.1 ■ Auto Manufacturing
By the mid-1920s, the massive coal and steel industries of the Midwest had made that region the center of the new automobile industry. A major road-building program by the federal government carried the thousands of new cars produced each day to every corner of the country.

| In what ways did the Roaring Twenties challenge traditional values? | Why did the divide between rural and urban America grow in the 1920s? | What caused the crash of 1929? | What was life like in the early years of the depression? | Conclusion: Why did the hope of the 1920s turn to despair? |

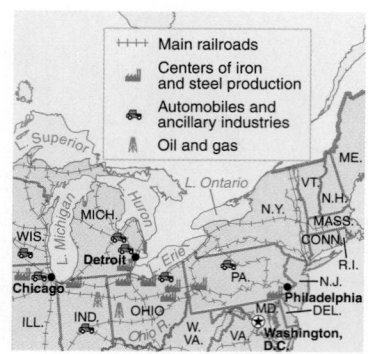

Detroit and the Automobile Industry in the 1920s

production, marketing, and employee relations—each with its own team of professionally trained managers. Changes on the assembly line and in management, along with technological advances, significantly boosted overall efficiency. Between 1922 and 1929, productivity in manufacturing increased 32 percent. Average wages, however, increased only 8 percent.

Industries also developed programs for workers that came to be called welfare capitalism. Some businesses improved safety and sanitation inside factories and instituted paid vacations and pension plans. Welfare capitalism encouraged loyalty to the company and discouraged traditional labor unions. One labor organizer in the steel industry bemoaned the success of welfare capitalism. "So many workmen here had been lulled to sleep by the company union, the welfare plans, the social organizations fostered by the employer," he declared, "that they had come to look upon the employer as their protector, and had believed vigorous trade union organization unnecessary for their welfare."

Colorado Filling Station Gulf Oil Company gave away the first free road map in 1914. By 1929, when Conoco (Continental Oil Company) produced this lavish map with Colorado's spectacular mountains looming in the background, nearly every oil company was supplying road maps as part of its campaign to attract the booming tourist trade. Courtesy, Colorado Historical Society.

▶ FOR MORE HELP ANALYZING THIS IMAGE, see the visual activity for this chapter in the Online Study Guide at bedfordstmartins.com/roarkunderstanding.

CHAPTER LOCATOR | How did big business shape the New Era of the 1920s?

Consumer Culture

Mass production fueled corporate profits and national economic prosperity. During the 1920s, per capita income increased by a third, the cost of living stayed the same, and unemployment remained low. But the rewards of the economic boom were not evenly distributed. Americans who labored with their hands inched ahead, while white-collar workers enjoyed significantly more spending money and more leisure time to spend it. Mass production of a broad range of new products—automobiles, radios, refrigerators, electric irons, washing machines—produced a consumer-goods revolution.

In this new era of abundance, more people than ever conceived of the American dream in terms of the things they could acquire. *Middletown* (1929), a study of the lives of the inhabitants of Muncie, Indiana, revealed that Muncie had become, above all, "a culture in which everything hinges on money." Moreover, faced with technological and organizational change beyond their comprehension, many citizens had lost confidence in their ability to play an effective role in civic affairs. More and more they became passive consumers, deferring to leaders in politics and economics.

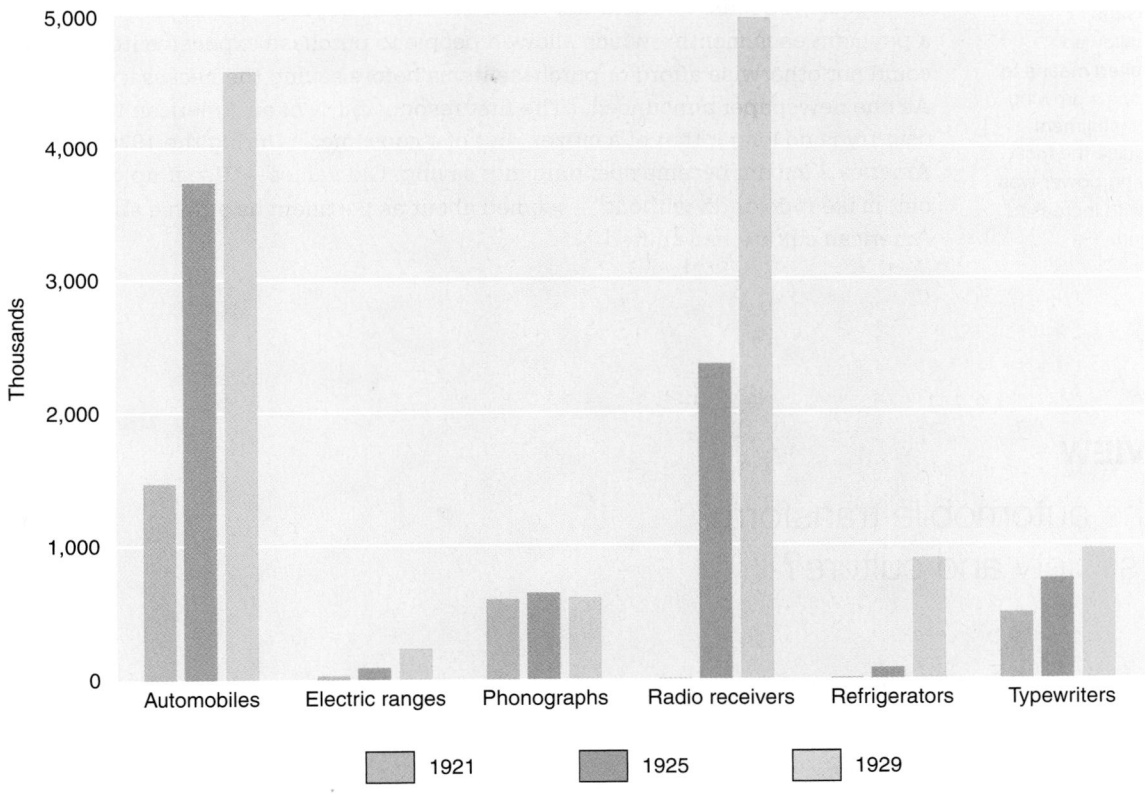

FIGURE 23.1 ■ Production of Consumer Goods, 1920–1930
Transportation, communications, and entertainment changed the lives of consumers in the 1920s. Laborsaving devices for the home were popular, but the vastly greater sales of automobiles and radios showed that consumerism was powerful in moving people's attention beyond their homes.

In what ways did the Roaring Twenties challenge traditional values?	Why did the divide between rural and urban America grow in the 1920s?	What caused the crash of 1929?	What was life like in the early years of the depression?	Conclusion: Why did the hope of the 1920s turn to despair?

The rapidly expanding business of advertising stimulated the desire for new products and undermined the traditional values of thrift and saving. Advertising linked material goods to the fulfillment of every spiritual and emotional need. Americans increasingly defined and measured their social status, and indeed their personal worth, on the yardstick of material possessions. Happiness itself rode on owning a car and choosing the right cigarettes and toothpaste.

By the 1920s, the United States had achieved the physical capacity to satisfy Americans' material wants (**Figure 23.1**, page 633). The economic problem shifted from production to consumption: Who would buy the goods flying off American assembly lines? One solution was to expand America's markets in foreign countries, and government and business joined in that effort. Another solution to the problem of consumption was to expand the market at home.

Henry Ford realized early on that "mass production requires mass consumption." He understood that automobile workers not only produced cars but would also buy them if they made enough money. "One's own employees ought to be one's own best customers," Ford said. In 1914, he raised wages in his factories to $5 a day, more than twice the going rate. High wages made for workers who were more loyal and more exploitable, and high wages returned as profits when workers bought Fords.

Many people's incomes, however, were too puny to satisfy the growing desire for consumer goods. The solution was **installment buying**—a little money down, a payment each month—which allowed people to purchase expensive items they could not otherwise afford or purchase items before saving the necessary money. As one newspaper announced, "The first responsibility of an American to his country is no longer that of a citizen, but of a consumer." During the 1920s, America's maxim became spending, not saving. Old values—"Use it up, wear it out, make it do or do without"—seemed about as pertinent as a horse and buggy. American culture had shifted.

installment buying

▶ Purchasing on credit with little money down and monthly payments. In the 1920s, installment buying allowed consumers with limited means to participate in America's growing consumer culture. Installment buying helped disguise the fact that consumer buying power was not keeping pace with increased American production.

> **QUICK REVIEW**

How did the automobile transform American society and culture?

CHAPTER LOCATOR | How did big business shape the New Era of the 1920s?

In what ways did the Roaring Twenties challenge traditional values?

A NEW ETHIC OF PERSONAL FREEDOM excited many Americans to seek pleasure without guilt in a whirl of activity that earned the decade the name "Roaring Twenties." Prohibition made lawbreakers of millions of otherwise decent folk. Flappers and "new women" challenged traditional gender boundaries. Other Americans enjoyed the Roaring Twenties through the words and images of vastly expanded mass communication. In America's big cities, particularly New York, a burst of creativity produced the "New Negro," who confounded and disturbed white Americans. The "Lost Generation" of writers, profoundly disillusioned with mainstream America's cultural direction, fled the country.

Prohibition

Republicans generally sought to curb the powers of government, but the twenties witnessed a great exception to this rule when the federal government implemented one of the last reforms of the Progressive Era: the Eighteenth Amendment, which banned the manufacture and sale of alcohol and took effect in January 1920 (see chapter 22) and made the United States the world's only society ever to outlaw alcohol. Supporters of **prohibition** believed that stopping consumption would boost productivity, eliminate crime, and lift the nation's morality.

The Treasury Department agents charged with enforcing prohibition faced a staggering task. In 1929, an agent in Indiana reported, "Conditions in most important cities very bad. Lax and corrupt public officials great handicap . . . prevalence of drinking among minor boys and the . . . middle or better class of adults." The "speakeasy," a place where men (and, increasingly, women) drank publicly, became a common feature of the urban landscape. One dealer, trading on common knowledge that whiskey still flowed in the White House, distributed cards advertising himself as the "President's Bootlegger."

prohibition
▶ The ban on the manufacture and sale of alcohol that went into effect in January 1920. Enforcement of prohibition proved almost impossible. By the end of the 1920s, most Americans had concluded that the social and political costs of prohibition outweighed the benefits. In 1933, the Eighteenth Amendment, which had created prohibition, was repealed.

| In what ways did the Roaring Twenties challenge traditional values? | Why did the divide between rural and urban America grow in the 1920s? | What caused the crash of 1929? | What was life like in the early years of the depression? | Conclusion: Why did the hope of the 1920s turn to despair? |

635

1917
- Marcus Garvey forms the Universal Negro Improvement Association.

1920
- Eighteenth Amendment, banning alcohol, goes into effect.
- Nineteenth Amendment, guaranteeing women's right to vote, is ratified.
- Nation's first licensed radio station, KDKA in Pittsburgh, begins broadcasting.

1921
- Sheppard-Towner Act.

1923
- Equal Rights Amendment is defeated in Congress.

1927
- Charles Lindbergh flies nonstop across the Atlantic.

1933
- Eighteenth Amendment is repealed.

new woman
► Alternative image of womanhood that came into the American mainstream in the 1920s. After the ratification of the Nineteenth Amendment, which granted women the right to vote, the mass media frequently portrayed young, college-educated women who drank cocktails, smoked cigarettes, bobbed their hair, and wore makeup and skimpy dresses. New women defied old notions about acceptable appearances for women, and they also challenged American convictions about separate spheres for women and men and the sexual double standard.

Eventually, serious criminals took over the liquor trade. During the first four years of prohibition, Chicago witnessed more than two hundred gang-related killings as rival mobs struggled for control of the lucrative liquor trade. The most notorious event came on St. Valentine's Day 1929, when Al Capone's Italian-dominated mob machine-gunned seven members of a rival Irish gang. Federal authorities finally sent Capone to prison for income tax evasion. "I give the public what the public wants," Capone told a reporter, "and all I get is abuse."

Gang-war slayings prompted demands for the repeal of the Eighteenth Amendment. In 1931, a panel of distinguished experts reported that prohibition, which supporters had defended as "a great social and economic experiment," had failed. The social and political costs of prohibition outweighed the benefits. Prohibition caused ordinary citizens to disrespect the law, corrupted the police, and demoralized the judiciary. In 1933, after thirteen years, the nation ended prohibition, making the Eighteenth Amendment the only constitutional amendment to be repealed.

The New Woman

Of all the changes in American life in the 1920s, none sparked more heated debate than the alternatives offered to the traditional roles of women. Increasing numbers of women worked and went to college, defying older gender hierarchies and norms. Even mainstream magazines such as the *Saturday Evening Post* began publishing stories about young, college-educated women who drank gin cocktails, smoked cigarettes, and wore skimpy dresses and dangly necklaces. Before the Great War, the **new woman** dwelt in New York City's bohemian Greenwich Village, but afterward the mass media brought her into middle-class America's living rooms.

When the Nineteenth Amendment, ratified in 1920, granted women the vote, feminists felt liberated and expected women to reshape the political landscape. A Kansas woman declared, "I went to bed last night a *slave*[;] I awoke this morning a *free woman*." Women began pressuring Congress to pass laws that especially concerned women, including measures to protect women in factories and grant federal aid to schools. Black women lobbied particularly for federal courts to assume jurisdiction over the crime of lynching. But women's only significant legislative success came in 1921 when Congress enacted the Sheppard-Towner Act, which extended federal assistance to states seeking to reduce high infant mortality rates.

A number of factors helped thwart women's political influence. Male domination of both political parties, the rarity of female candidates, and lack of experience in voting, especially among recent immigrants, kept many women away from the polls. In the South, poll taxes, literacy tests, and outright terrorism continued to decimate the vote of African Americans, men and women alike.

Most important, rather than forming a solid voting bloc, feminists divided. Some argued for women's right to special protection; others demanded equal protection. The radical National Woman's Party fought for an Equal Rights Amendment that stated flatly: "Men and women shall have equal rights through-out the United States." The more moderate League of Women Voters feared that the amendment's wording threatened state laws that provided women special protection, such as preventing them from working on certain machines. Put before Congress in 1923, the Equal Rights Amendment went down to defeat,

CHAPTER LOCATOR | How did big business shape the New Era of the 1920s?

and radical women were forced to work for the causes of birth control, legal equality for minorities, and the end of child labor through other means.

Economically, more women worked for pay—approximately one in four by 1930—but they clustered in "women's jobs." The proportion of women working as secretaries, stenographers, and typists skyrocketed. Women almost monopolized the occupations of librarian, nurse, elementary school teacher, and telephone operator. Women also represented 40 percent of salesclerks by 1930. More female white-collar workers meant that fewer women were interested in protective legislation for women; new women wanted salaries and opportunities equal to men's.

Increased earnings gave working women more buying power in the new consumer culture. A stereotype soon emerged of the flapper, so called because of the short-lived fad of wearing unbuckled galoshes. The flapper had short "bobbed" hair and wore lipstick and rouge. She dressed in the latest styles—short skirts, drop waists, bare arms, and no petticoats—and she danced all night to wild jazz.

The new woman both reflected and propelled the modern birth control movement. Margaret Sanger, the crusading pioneer for contraception during the Progressive Era, restated her principal conviction in 1920: "No woman can call herself free until she can choose consciously whether she will or will not be a mother." By shifting strategy in the twenties, Sanger courted the conservative American Medical Association; linked birth control with the eugenics movement, which advocated limiting reproduction among "undesirable" groups; and thus made contraception a respectable subject for discussion.

New women challenged American convictions about separate spheres for women and men, the double standard of sexual conduct, and Victorian ideas of proper female appearance and behavior. Although only a minority of American women became flappers, all women, even those who remained at home, felt the great changes of the era.

The New Negro

The 1920s witnessed the emergence not only of the new woman but also of the New Negro. African Americans who challenged the caste system that confined dark-skinned Americans to the lowest levels of society confronted whites who insisted that race relations would not change.

The prominent African American intellectual W. E. B. Du Bois and the National Association for the Advancement of Colored People (NAACP) aggressively pursued the passage of a federal antilynching law to counter mob violence against blacks in the South. At the same time, the Jamaican-born visionary Marcus Garvey urged African Americans to rediscover the heritage of Africa, take pride in their own achievements, and maintain racial purity by avoiding miscegenation. In 1917, Garvey launched the Universal Negro Improvement Association to help African Americans gain economic and political independence entirely outside white society. In 1927 the federal government pinned charges of illegal practices on Garvey and deported him to Jamaica. Nevertheless, the issues Garvey raised about racial pride, black identity, and the search for equality persisted, and his legacy remains at the center of black nationalist thought.

Still, most African Americans maintained hope in the American promise. In New York City, hope and talent came together. Black artists, sculptors, novelists, musicians, and poets poured into Harlem in uptown Manhattan, where they set

| In what ways did the Roaring Twenties challenge traditional values? | Why did the divide between rural and urban America grow in the 1920s? | What caused the crash of 1929? | What was life like in the early years of the depression? | Conclusion: Why did the hope of the 1920s turn to despair? |

637

Noah's Ark

Kansas-born painter Aaron Douglas expressed the Harlem Renaissance visually. Douglas sought ways of integrating the African cultural heritage with American experience. This depiction of an African Noah commanding the loading of the ark displays a technique that became closely associated with African American art: strong silhouetted figures awash in misty color, indicating a connection between Christian faith and the vital, colorful origins of black Americans in a distant, mythologized African past. Fisk University Art Galleries.

Harlem Renaissance

▶ African American cultural flowering that took place in Harlem in the 1920s. The Harlem Renaissance produced dazzling literary, musical, and artistic talent. The vigor of the Harlem Renaissance left a powerful legacy for black Americans, but the creative burst did little in the short run to dissolve the prejudice of white society.

out to create a distinctive African American culture that drew on their identities as Americans and Africans. As scholar Alain Locke put it in 1925, they introduced to the world the "New Negro," who rose from the ashes of slavery and segregation to proclaim African Americans' creative genius.

The emergence of the New Negro came to be known as the **Harlem Renaissance**. "We younger Negro artists . . . intend to express our individual dark-skinned selves without fear or shame," poet Langston Hughes said of the Harlem Renaissance. "If white people are pleased, we are glad. If they are not, it doesn't matter. We know we are beautiful. And ugly, too."

The Harlem Renaissance produced dazzling literary, musical, and artistic talent. Despite such vibrancy, Harlem for most whites remained a separate black ghetto known only for its lively nightlife. Fashionable whites crowded into Harlem's nightclubs, where they believed they could hear "real" jazz, a relatively new musical form, in its "natural" surroundings. The vigor of the Harlem Renaissance left a powerful legacy for black Americans, but the creative burst did little in the short run to dissolve the prejudice of white society.

Leaders of the Harlem Renaissance

James Weldon Johnson	writer, civil rights leader
Langston Hughes, Claude McKay, Countee Cullen	poets
Zora Neale Hurston	novelist
Aaron Douglas	artist

Mass Culture

In the twenties, popular culture, like consumer goods, was mass-produced and mass-consumed. The proliferation of movies, radios, music, and sports meant that Americans found plenty to do, and in doing the same things, they helped create a national culture.

Nothing offered escapist delights like the movies (**Figure 23.2**). Hollywood, California, discovered the successful formula of combining opulence, sex, and adventure. By 1929, the movies were drawing more than 80 million people in a single week, as many as lived in the entire country. Rudolph Valentino, described as "catnip to women," and Clara Bow, the "It Girl" (everyone knew what *it* was), became household names. Most loved of all was the comic Charlie Chaplin, whose famous character, the Little Tramp, showed an endearing inability to cope with the rules and complexities of modern life.

Americans also found heroes in sports. Baseball solidified its place as the national pastime in the 1920s. It remained essentially a game played by and for the working class. In George Herman "Babe" Ruth, baseball had the most cherished free spirit of the time. The rowdy escapades of the "Sultan of Swat" demonstrated to fans that sports offered a way to break out of the ordinariness of everyday life. By "his sheer exuberance," one sportswriter declared, Ruth "has lightened the cares of the world."

CHAPTER LOCATOR | How did big business shape the New Era of the 1920s?

The public also fell in love with a young boxer from the grim mining districts of Colorado, Jack Dempsey. When he took the heavyweight crown just after World War I, he was revered as the people's champ, a stand-in for the average American who felt increasingly confined by bureaucracy and machine-made culture.

Football, essentially a college sport, held greater sway with the upper classes. But in keeping with the times, football moved toward a more commercial spectacle. Harold "Red" Grange, "the Galloping Ghost," led the way by going from stardom at the University of Illinois to the Chicago Bears in the new professional football league.

The decade's hero worship reached its zenith in the celebration of Charles Lindbergh, a young pilot who set out on May 20, 1927, to become the first person to fly nonstop across the Atlantic. Lindbergh was the perfect hero for an age that celebrated individual accomplishment. "Charles Lindbergh," one journalist proclaimed, "is the stuff out of which have been made the pioneers that opened up the wilderness. His are the qualities which we, as a people, must nourish." Lindbergh realized, however, that technical and organizational complexity was fast reducing chances for solitary achievement. Consequently, he titled his book about the flight *We* (1927) to include the machine that had made it all possible.

Another machine—the radio—became important to mass culture in the 1920s. The nation's first licensed radio station, KDKA in Pittsburgh, began broadcasting in 1920, and soon American airwaves buzzed with news, sermons, soap operas, sports, comedy, and music. Because they could now reach prospective customers in their own homes, advertisers bankrolled radio's rapid growth. Between 1922 and 1929, the number of radio stations in the United States increased from 30 to 606. In just seven years, homes with radios jumped from 60,000 to a staggering 10.25 million.

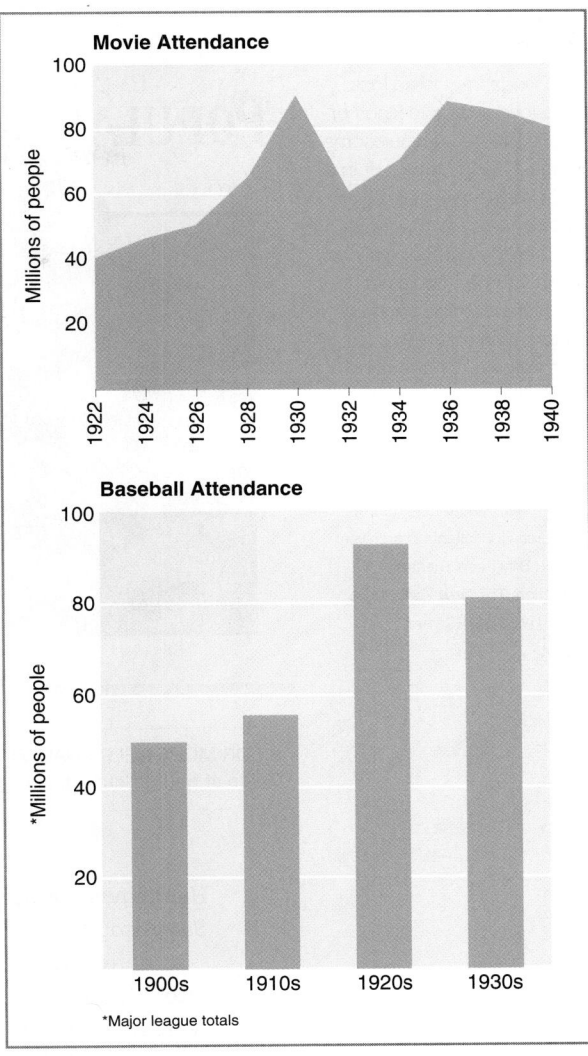

FIGURE 23.2 ■ **Movie and Baseball Attendance**
America's favorite pastimes, movies and baseball, tracked the economy. The rise and fall of weekly movie attendance and seasonal baseball attendance shown here mirrored the rise and fall of prosperity.

The Lost Generation

Some writers and artists felt alienated from America's mass-culture society, which they found shallow, anti-intellectual, and materialistic. Young, white, and mostly college educated, these expatriates, as they came to be called, felt embittered by the war and renounced the progressives who had promoted it as a crusade. For them, Europe—not Hollywood or Harlem—seemed the place to seek their renaissance.

The American-born writer Gertrude Stein, long established in Paris, remarked famously as the young exiles gathered around her, "They are the lost generation." Most of the expatriates, however, believed to the contrary that they had finally found themselves. The **Lost Generation** helped launch the most creative period in American art and literature in the twentieth century. The novelist whose spare, clean style best exemplified the expatriate efforts to make art mirror basic reality was Ernest

Lost Generation
▶ Generation of young Americans who were disillusioned with American society and sought inspiration in Europe. Young, white, and mostly college educated, the Lost Generation felt alienated from America's mass-culture society, which they found shallow, anti-intellectual, and materialistic. The Lost Generation helped launch the most creative period in American art and literature in the twentieth century.

| In what ways did the Roaring Twenties challenge traditional values? | Why did the divide between rural and urban America grow in the 1920s? | What caused the crash of 1929? | What was life like in the early years of the depression? | Conclusion: Why did the hope of the 1920s turn to despair? |

639

> ▶ FOR MORE HELP ANALYZING THIS IMAGE, see the visual activity for this chapter in the Online Study Guide at bedfordstmartins.com/roarkunderstanding.

Hemingway. Admirers found the terse language and hard lessons of his novel *The Sun Also Rises* (1926) to be perfect expressions of a world stripped of illusions.

Many writers who remained in America were exiles in spirit. Before the war, intellectuals had eagerly joined progressive reform movements. Afterward, they were more likely critics of American cultural vulgarity. Novelist Sinclair Lewis in *Main Street* (1920) and *Babbitt* (1922) satirized his native Midwest as a cultural wasteland. Humorists such as James Thurber created outlandish characters to poke fun at American stupidity and inhibitions. And southern writers, led by William Faulkner, explored the South's grim class and race heritage. Worries about alienation surfaced as well. F. Scott Fitzgerald spoke sadly in *This Side of Paradise* (1920) of a disillusioned generation "grown up to find all Gods dead, all wars fought, all faiths in man shaken."

> QUICK REVIEW

How did the cultural change in the 1920s affect older conceptions of gender and race?

CHAPTER LOCATOR | How did big business shape the New Era of the 1920s?

Why did the divide between rural and urban America grow in the 1920s?

WKKK Badge

Some half a million women were members of the Women of the Ku Klux Klan (WKKK). Klanswomen fit perfectly within the KKK because the organization proclaimed itself the defender of the traditional virtues of pure womanhood and decent homes. This badge from Harrisburg, Pennsylvania, advertises the local WKKK's support for a home for "orphan and dependent children." Klanswomen also joined in boycotts of businesses owned by Jews and others whom they did not consider "100% American." Collection of Janice L. and David J. Frent.

LARGE AREAS OF THE COUNTRY did not share in the wealth of the 1920s and had little confidence that they would anytime soon. By the end of the decade, 40 percent of the nation's farmers were landless, and 90 percent of rural homes had no indoor plumbing, gas, or electricity. By the 1920s, the census reported that the majority of the population had shifted from the country to the city (**Map 23.2**, page 642).

Cities seemed to stand for everything rural areas stood against. Rural America imagined itself as solidly Anglo-Saxon (despite the presence of millions of African Americans in the South and Mexican Americans, Native Americans, and Asian Americans in the West), and the cities seemed to be filled with undesirable immigrants. Rural America was the home of old-time Protestant religion, and the cities teemed with Catholics, Jews, liberal Protestants, and atheists. Rural America championed old-fashioned moral standards—abstinence and self-denial—while the cities spawned every imaginable vice. Once the "backbone of the Republic," rural Americans had become poor country cousins. Urban domination over the nation's political and cultural life and sharply rising economic disparity drove rural Americans in often ugly, reactionary directions.

Rejecting the Undesirables

Before the war, when about a million immigrants arrived each year, some Americans warned that unassimilable foreigners were smothering the nation. War

| In what ways did the Roaring Twenties challenge traditional values? | **Why did the divide between rural and urban America grow in the 1920s?** | What caused the crash of 1929? | What was life like in the early years of the depression? | Conclusion: Why did the hope of the 1920s turn to despair? |

641

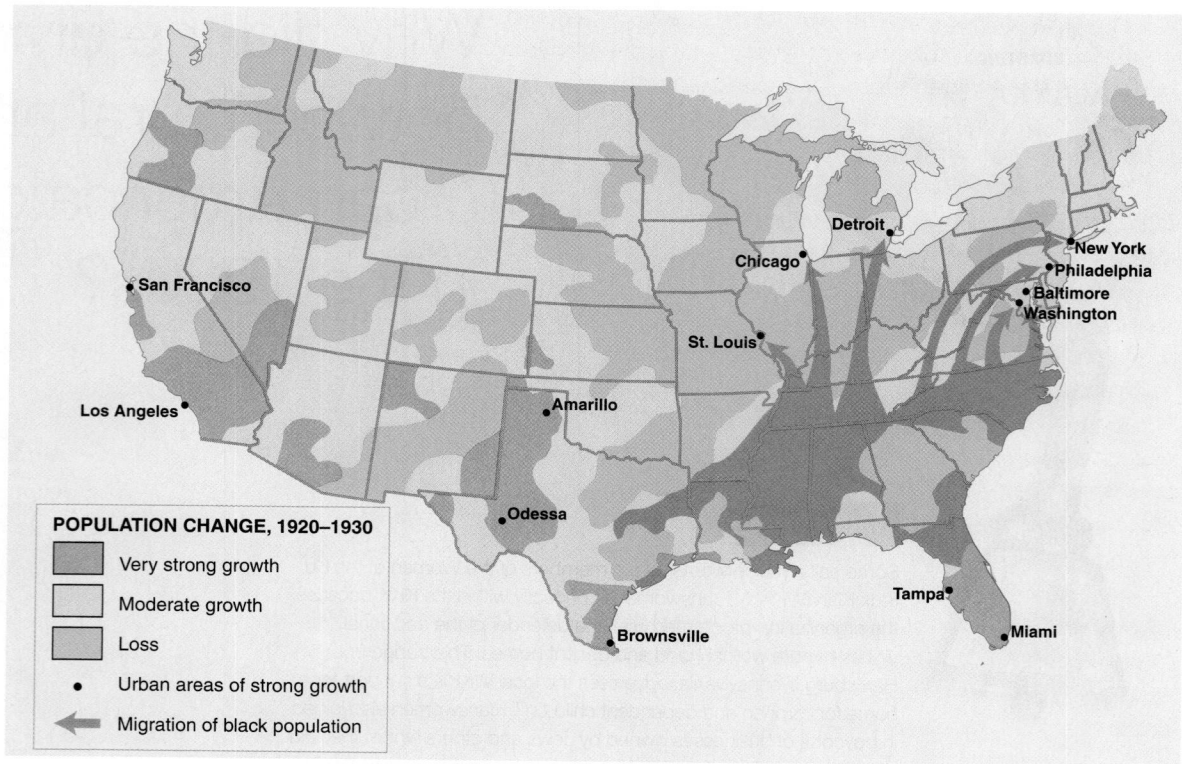

MAP 23.2 ■ **The Shift from Rural to Urban Population, 1920–1930**
The movement of whites and Hispanics toward urban and agricultural opportunity made Florida, the West, and the Southwest the regions of fastest population growth. In contrast, large numbers of blacks left the rural South to find a better life in the North. Because almost all migrating blacks went from the countryside to cities in distant parts of the nation, while white and Hispanic migrants tended to move shorter distances toward familiar places, the population shift brought more drastic overall change to blacks than to whites and Hispanics.

> ▶ FOR MORE HELP ANALYZING THIS MAP, see the map activity for this chapter in the Online Study Guide at bedfordstmartins.com/roarkunderstanding.

against Germany and its allies expanded nativist and antiradical sentiment. After the war, large-scale immigration resumed (another 800,000 immigrants arrived in 1921) at a moment when industrialists no longer needed new factory laborers. African American and Mexican migration had relieved labor shortages. Moreover, union leaders feared that millions of poor immigrants would undercut their efforts to organize American workers. Rural American Protestants were particularly alarmed that most of the immigrants were Catholic or Jewish. In 1921, Congress responded by severely restricting immigration.

In 1924, Congress went further. The **Johnson-Reid Act** limited the number of immigrants to no more than 161,000 a year and established quotas for each European nation. The act revealed the fear and bigotry that fueled anti-immigration legislation. While it cut immigration by more than 80 percent, it squeezed some nationalities far more than others. Backers of Johnson-Reid openly

Johnson-Reid Act
▶ 1924 law that severely restricted immigration to the United States. The law limited the number of immigrants to no more than 161,000 a year and established quotas for each European nation. Racist by design, the new restrictions were intended to staunch the flow of immigrants from southern and eastern Europe and Asia.

declared that America had become the "garbage can and the dumping ground of the world," and they manipulated quotas to ensure entry only to "good" immigrants from western Europe. The law effectively reversed the trend toward immigration from southern and eastern Europe, which by 1914 had amounted to 75 percent of the yearly total.

The 1924 law reaffirmed the 1880s legislation barring Chinese immigrants and added Japanese and other Asians to the list of the excluded. But it left open immigration from the Western Hemisphere, and during the 1920s, some 500,000 Mexicans crossed the border. Farm interests preserved Mexican immigration because of Mexicans' value in southwestern agriculture. Rural Americans strongly supported the law, as did industrialists and labor leaders.

Antiforeign hysteria climaxed in the trial of two anarchist immigrants from Italy, Nicola Sacco and Bartolomeo Vanzetti. Arrested in 1920 for robbery and murder in South Braintree, Massachusetts, the men were sentenced to death by a judge who openly referred to them as "anarchist bastards." In response to doubts about the fairness of the verdict, a review committee found the trial judge guilty of a "grave breach of official decorum" but refused to recommend a motion for retrial. When Massachusetts executed Sacco and Vanzetti on August 23, 1927, fifty thousand mourners followed their caskets, convinced that the men had died because they were immigrants and radicals, not because they were murderers.

The Rebirth of the Ku Klux Klan

The nation's antiforeign mood struck a responsive chord in members of the **Ku Klux Klan**. The Klan first appeared in the South during Reconstruction to thwart black freedom and expired with the reestablishment of white supremacy. In 1915, the Klan was reborn at Stone Mountain, Georgia, but when the new Klan extended its targets beyond black Americans, it quickly spread beyond the South. Under a banner proclaiming "100 percent Americanism," the Klan promised to defend family, morality, and traditional American values against the threats posed by blacks, immigrants, radicals, feminists, Catholics, and Jews.

Building on the frustrations of rural America, the Klan attracted three million to four million members—women as well as men. By the mid-1920s, the Klan had spread throughout the nation, almost controlling Indiana and influencing politics in Illinois, California, Oregon, Texas, Louisiana, Oklahoma, and Kansas. In 1926, Klan imperial wizard Hiram Wesley Evans described the assault of modernity: "One by one all our traditional moral standards went by the boards or were so disregarded that they ceased to be binding," he explained. "The sacredness of our Sabbath, of our homes, of chastity, and finally even of our right to teach our own children in schools [were] fundamental facts and truth torn away from us."

Eventually, social changes, along with lawless excess, crippled the Klan. Immigration restrictions eased the worry about invading foreigners, and sensational wrongdoing by Klan leaders cost it the support of traditional moralists. Grand Dragon David Stephenson of Indiana, for example, went to jail for the kidnapping and rape of a woman who subsequently committed suicide. Yet the social grievances, economic problems, and religious anxieties of the countryside and small towns remained unresolved.

CHRONOLOGY

1915
– Ku Klux Klan is reborn at Stone Mountain, Georgia.

1921
– Congress restricts immigration.

1924
– Johnson-Reid Act restricts immigration further.

1925
– Scopes trial challenges the right to prohibit teaching evolution in public schools.

1927
– Nicola Sacco and Bartolomeo Vanzetti are executed amid the Red scare.

1928
– Republican Herbert Hoover is elected president.

Ku Klux Klan

▶ Racist organization that, in the 1920s, fought against perceived threats posed by blacks, immigrants, radicals, feminists, Catholics, and Jews. The Klan first emerged after the Civil War to thwart black freedom but was reborn in 1915 with a broader agenda. The new Klan spread well beyond the South, attracting some three million to four million members in the 1920s.

In what ways did the Roaring Twenties challenge traditional values?

Why did the divide between rural and urban America grow in the 1920s?

What caused the crash of 1929?

What was life like in the early years of the depression?

Conclusion: Why did the hope of the 1920s turn to despair?

The Scopes Trial

In 1925 in a Tennessee courtroom, old-time religion and the new spirit of science went head-to-head. The confrontation occurred after several southern states passed legislation barring the teaching of Charles Darwin's theory of evolution in the public schools. At the urging of scientists and civil liberties organizations, John Scopes, a young biology teacher in Dayton, Tennessee, offered to test his state's ban on teaching evolution. When Scopes came to trial, Clarence Darrow, a brilliant defense lawyer from Chicago, volunteered to defend him. Darrow, an avowed agnostic, took on the prosecution's William Jennings Bryan, three-time Democratic nominee for president, symbol of rural America, and fervent fundamentalist.

The **Scopes trial** quickly degenerated into a media circus. The first trial to be covered live on radio, it attracted a nationwide audience. Most of the reporters from big-city newspapers were hostile to Bryan. When, under relentless questioning by Darrow, Bryan declared on the witness stand that he did indeed believe that the world had been created in six days and that Jonah had lived in the belly of a whale, his humiliation in the eyes of most urban observers was complete. Nevertheless, the Tennessee court upheld the law and punished Scopes with a $100 fine. Although fundamentalism won the battle, it lost the war. The journalist H. L. Mencken had the last word in a merciless obituary for Bryan, who died just a week after the trial ended. Portraying the "monkey trial" as a battle between the country and the city, Mencken flayed Bryan as a "charlatan, a mountebank, a zany without shame or dignity," motivated solely by "hatred of the city men who had laughed at him for so long."

As Mencken's acid prose indicated, Bryan's humiliation was not purely a victory of reason and science. It also revealed the disdain urban people felt for country people and the values they clung to. The Ku Klux Klan revival and the Scopes trial dramatized and inflamed divisions between city and country, intellectuals and the uneducated, the privileged and the poor, the scoffers and the faithful.

Al Smith and the Election of 1928

The presidential election of 1928 brought many of the developments of the 1920s—prohibition, immigration, religion, and the clash of rural and urban values—into sharp focus. Republicans emphasized the economic success of their party's pro-business government and turned to Herbert Hoover, the energetic secretary of commerce and leading public symbol of 1920s prosperity. But because both parties generally agreed that the American economy was basically sound, the campaign turned on social issues that divided Americans.

The Democrats nominated four-time governor of New York Alfred E. Smith. Smith seemed to represent all that rural Americans feared and resented. A child of immigrants, Smith got his start in politics with the help of New York's Tammany Hall political machine, to many the epitome of big-city corruption. He denounced immigration quotas, signed New York State's anti-Klan bill, and opposed prohibition, believing that it was a nativist attack on immigrant customs.

CHAPTER LOCATOR | How did big business shape the New Era of the 1920s?

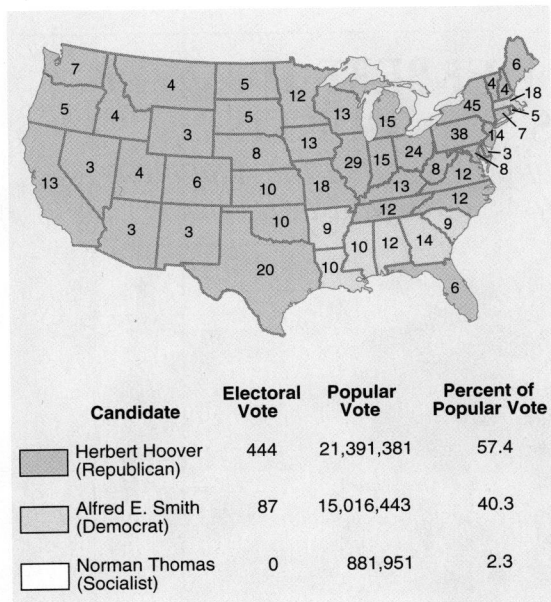

Candidate	Electoral Vote	Popular Vote	Percent of Popular Vote
Herbert Hoover (Republican)	444	21,391,381	57.4
Alfred E. Smith (Democrat)	87	15,016,443	40.3
Norman Thomas (Socialist)	0	881,951	2.3

MAP 23.3 ■ The Election of 1928

Prohibition forces dubbed him "Alcohol Al." Smith's greatest vulnerability in the heartland, however, was his religion. He was the first Catholic to run for president. A Methodist bishop in Virginia denounced Roman Catholicism as "the Mother of ignorance, superstition, intolerance and sin" and begged Protestants not to vote for a candidate who represented "the kind of dirty people that you find today on the sidewalks of New York."

Hoover, who neatly combined the images of morality, efficiency, service, and prosperity, won the election by a landslide (**Map 23.3**). He received nearly 58 percent of the vote and gained 444 electoral votes to Smith's 87. The only bright spot for Democrats was the nation's cities, which voted Democratic, indicating the rising strength of ethnic minorities, including Smith's fellow Catholics.

QUICK REVIEW

Why did rural Americans increasingly fear and mistrust urban America?

| In what ways did the Roaring Twenties challenge traditional values? | Why did the divide between rural and urban America grow in the 1920s? | What caused the crash of 1929? | What was life like in the early years of the depression? | Conclusion: Why did the hope of the 1920s turn to despair? |

What caused the crash of 1929?

Hoover Campaign Poster

This poster effectively illustrates Herbert Hoover's 1928 campaign message: Republican administrations in the 1920s had produced middle-class prosperity, complete with a house in the suburbs and the latest automobile. To remind voters that Hoover as secretary of commerce had promoted industry that made the suburban dream possible, the poster portrays smoking chimneys at a discreet distance. Collection of Janice L. and David J. Frent.

Herbert Hoover

▶ Engineer and progressive Republican who made his name as secretary of commerce in the Harding and Coolidge administrations and won the presidential election in 1928. As president after the stock market crash in 1929, Hoover relied primarily on private enterprise as the solution to the economic crisis; his decision to limit government intervention in the economy contributed to the downward spiral that created the Great Depression.

AT HIS INAUGURATION in 1929, Herbert Hoover told the American people, "Given a chance to go forward with the policies of the last eight years, we shall soon with the help of God be in sight of the day when poverty will be banished from this nation." Within eight months, the prosperity Hoover touted collapsed with the stock market, and the nation ended nearly three decades of barely interrupted economic growth. Like much of the world, the United States fell into the most serious economic depression of all time.

Herbert Hoover: The Great Engineer

When **Herbert Hoover** became president in 1929, he seemed the perfect choice to lead a prosperous business nation. His rise from poverty to become one of the world's most celebrated mining engineers personified America's rags-to-riches

CHAPTER LOCATOR | How did big business shape the New Era of the 1920s?

ideal. His success in managing efforts to feed civilian victims of the fighting during World War I won him acclaim as the "Great Humanitarian" and led Woodrow Wilson to name him head of the Food Administration once the United States entered the war. Hoover's reputation soared even higher as secretary of commerce in the Harding and Coolidge administrations.

Hoover belonged to the progressive wing of his party, and as early as 1909, he declared, "The time when the employer could ride roughshod over his labor is disappearing with the doctrine of 'laissez-faire' on which it is founded." He urged a limited business-government partnership that would manage the sweeping changes Americans were experiencing. When Hoover entered the White House, he brought a reform agenda: "We want to see a nation built of home owners and farm owners. We want to see their savings protected. We want to see them in steady jobs. We want to see more and more of them insured against death and accident, unemployment and old age. We want them all secure."

But Hoover also had ideological and political liabilities. Principles that appeared strengths in the prosperous 1920s—individual self-reliance, industrial self-management, and a limited federal government—became straitjackets when economic catastrophe struck. Moreover, Hoover had never held an elected public office, had a poor political touch, and was too thin-skinned to be an effective politician. Prophetically, he confided to a friend his fear that "if some unprecedented calamity should come upon the nation . . . I would be sacrificed to the unreasoning disappointment of a people who expected too much." The distorted national economy set the stage for the calamity Hoover so feared.

The Distorted Economy

In the spring of 1929, the United States enjoyed a fragile prosperity. Although America had become the world's leading economy, it had done little to help rebuild Europe's shattered economy after World War I. Instead, the Republican administrations demanded that Allied nations repay their war loans, creating a tangled web of debts and reparations that sapped Europe's economic vitality. Moreover, to boost American business, the United States enacted tariffs that prevented other nations from selling their goods to Americans. Fewer sales meant that foreign nations had less money to buy American goods. American banks propped up the nation's export trade by extending credit to foreign customers, deepening their debt.

The domestic economy was also in trouble. Wealth was badly distributed. Farmers continued to suffer from low prices and chronic indebtedness; the average income of families working the land amounted to only $240 per year. The wages of industrial workers, though rising during the decade, failed to keep up with productivity and corporate profits. Overall, nearly two-thirds of all American families lived on less than the $2,000 per year that economists estimated would "supply only basic necessities." In sharp contrast, the top 1 percent received 15 percent of the nation's income, an amount equal to that received by the bottom 42 percent of the population. The Coolidge administration worsened the deepening inequality by cutting taxes on the wealthy.

By 1929, the inequality of wealth produced a serious problem in consumption. The rich spent lavishly, but they could absorb only a tiny fraction of the nation's output. For a time, the new device of installment buying—buying on credit—kept

CHRONOLOGY

1929
- Farm Board is created to buy up surplus agricultural products and keep food prices from falling.
- **October.** Stock market collapses.

1930
- Congress authorizes $420 million for public works projects.
- Hawley-Smoot tariff establishes the highest rates in history.

1932
- Reconstruction Finance Corporation is established to lend government funds to banks and corporations.

In what ways did the Roaring Twenties challenge traditional values?

Why did the divide between rural and urban America grow in the 1920s?

What caused the crash of 1929?

What was life like in the early years of the depression?

Conclusion: Why did the hope of the 1920s turn to despair?

647

consumer demand up. By the end of the decade, four out of five cars and two out of three radios were bought on credit.

Signs of economic trouble began to appear at mid-decade. New construction slowed down. Automobile sales faltered. Companies began cutting back production and laying off workers. Between 1921 and 1928, as investment and loan opportunities faded, five thousand banks failed, wiping out the life savings of thousands.

The Crash of 1929

Even as the economy faltered, America's faith in it remained unshaken. Hoping for even bigger slices of the economic pie, Americans speculated wildly in the stock market on Wall Street. Between 1924 and 1929, the values of stocks listed on the New York Stock Exchange increased by more than 400 percent. Buying stocks on margin—that is, putting up only part of the money at the time of purchase—accelerated. Many people got rich this way, but those who bought on credit could finance their loans only if their stocks increased in value.

Finally, in the autumn of 1929, the market hesitated. Investors nervously began to sell their overvalued stocks. The dip quickly became a panic on October 24, the day that came to be known as Black Thursday. More panic selling came on Black Tuesday, October 29, the day the market suffered a greater fall than ever before. In the next six months, the stock market lost six-sevenths of its total value.

It was once thought that the crash alone caused the Great Depression. It did not. In 1929, the national and international economies were already riddled with severe problems. But the dramatic losses in the stock market crash and the fear of risking what was left acted as a great brake on economic activity. The collapse on Wall Street shattered the New Era's confidence that America would enjoy perpetually expanding prosperity.

Hoover and the Limits of Individualism

In November 1929, to keep the stock market collapse from ravaging the entire economy, Herbert Hoover called a White House conference of business and labor leaders and urged them to join in a voluntary plan for recovery: Businesses would maintain production and keep their workers on the job; labor would accept existing wages, hours, and conditions. Within a few months, however, the bargain fell apart. As demand for their products declined, industrialists cut production, sliced wages, and laid off workers. Poorly paid or unemployed workers could not buy much, and their decreased spending led to further cuts in production and further loss of jobs. Thus began the terrible spiral of economic decline.

To deal with the problems of rural America, Hoover got Congress to pass the Agricultural Marketing Act in 1929. The act created the Farm Board, which used its budget of $500 million to buy up agricultural surpluses and thus, it was hoped, raise prices. But prices declined. To help end the decline, Hoover joined conservatives in urging protective tariffs on agricultural goods, and the Hawley-Smoot tariff of 1930 established the highest rates in history. The same year, Congress also authorized $420 million for public works projects to give the unemployed jobs and

CHAPTER LOCATOR | How did big business shape the New Era of the 1920s?

648 CHAPTER 23
FROM NEW ERA TO GREAT DEPRESSION, 1920–1932

create more purchasing power. In three years, the Hoover administration nearly doubled federal public works expenditures.

But with each year of Hoover's term, the economy weakened. Tariffs did not end the suffering of farmers because foreign nations retaliated with increased tariffs of their own that crippled American farmers' ability to sell abroad. In 1932, Hoover hoped to help hard-pressed industry with the Reconstruction Finance Corporation (RFC), a federal agency empowered to lend government funds to endangered banks and corporations. The theory was trickle-down economics: Pump money into the economy at the top, and in the long run, the people at the bottom would benefit. In the end, very little of what critics of the RFC called a "millionaires' dole" trickled down to the poor.

Meanwhile, hundreds of thousands of workers lost their jobs each month. By 1932, an astounding one-quarter of the American workforce—more than twelve million people—were unemployed. There was no direct federal assistance, and state services and private charities were swamped. The depression that began in 1929 devastated much of the world, but no other modern nation provided such feeble support to the jobless. Cries grew louder for the federal government to give hurting people relief.

In responding, Hoover revealed the limits of his conception of government's proper role. He compared direct federal aid to the needy to the "dole" in Britain, which he thought destroyed the moral fiber of the chronically unemployed. In 1931, he allowed the Red Cross to distribute government-owned agricultural surpluses to the hungry. In 1932, he relaxed his principles further to offer small federal loans, not gifts, to the states to help them in their relief efforts. But Hoover's circumscribed notions of legitimate government action proved vastly inadequate to address the problems of restarting the economy and ending human suffering.

QUICK REVIEW

Why and how did the American economy collapse in 1929?

> What was life like in the early years of the depression?

An Unemployed Youth Joblessness was frightening and humiliating. Brought up to believe that if you worked hard, you got ahead, the unemployed had difficulty seeing failure to find work as anything other than personal failure. Many slipped into despair and depression. Library of Congress.

IN 1930, SUFFERING on a massive scale set in as unemployment increased and poverty spread and deepened. The gap between the American people and leaders who failed to resolve these contradictions widened as the depression deepened. By 1932, America's economic problems had created a dangerous social and political crisis.

The Human Toll

Statistics only hint at the human tragedy of the Great Depression. When Herbert Hoover took office in 1929, the American economy stood at its peak. When he left in 1933, it had reached its twentieth-century low (**FIGURE 23.3**). In 1929, national income was $88 billion. By 1933, it had declined to $40 billion. In 1929, unemployment was 3.1 percent, or 1.5 million workers. By 1933, unemployment stood at 25 percent, or 12.5 million workers. By 1932, more than 9,000 banks had shut their doors, and depositors had lost more than $2.5 billion.

Jobless, homeless victims wandered in search of work, and the tramp, or hobo, became one of the most visible figures of the 1930s. Riding the rails or hitchhiking, a million vagabonds moved southward and westward looking for seasonal agricultural work. Other unemployed men and women, sick or less hopeful, huddled in doorways, overcome, one man remembered, by "helpless despair and submission." Scavengers haunted alleys behind restaurants in search

CHAPTER LOCATOR | How did big business shape the New Era of the 1920s?

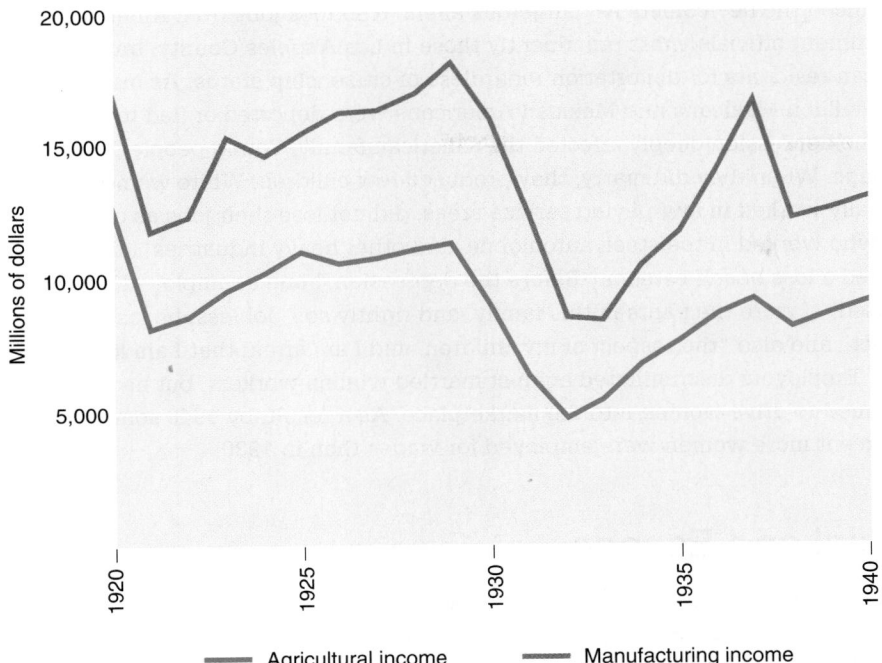

FIGURE 23.3 ■ **Manufacturing and Agricultural Income, 1920–1940**
After economic collapse, recovery in the 1930s began under New Deal auspices. The sharp declines in 1937–1938, when federal spending was reduced, indicated that New Deal stimuli were still needed to restore manufacturing and agricultural income.

CHRONOLOGY

1931
– Scottsboro Boys, nine young black men in Alabama, are arrested on trumped-up rape charges.
– The American Communist Party supports the Harlan County, Kentucky, coal strike.

1932
– Unemployed workers demonstrate at Henry Ford's River Rouge factory in Dearborn, Michigan.
– Farmers form the National Farmers' Holiday Association to take a "holiday" from shipping crops to market.

of food. "I don't want to steal," a Pennsylvania man wrote to the governor in 1931, "but I won't let my wife and boy cry for something to eat. . . . How long is this going to keep up? I cannot stand it any longer."

Rural poverty was most acute. Tenant farmers and sharecroppers, mainly in the South, came to symbolize how poverty crushed the human spirit. Eight and a half million people, three million of them black, crowded into cabins without plumbing, electricity, or running water. They subsisted—just barely—on salt pork, cornmeal, molasses, beans, peas, and whatever they could hunt or fish. When economist John Maynard Keynes was asked whether anything like this degradation had existed before, he replied, "Yes, it was called the Dark Ages and it lasted four hundred years."

There was no federal assistance to meet this human catastrophe, only a patchwork of charities and destitute state and local agencies. For a family of four without any income, the best the city of Philadelphia could do was provide $5.50 per week. That was not enough to live on but was still comparatively generous. New York City provided only $2.39 per week; and Detroit, devastated by the auto industry's failure, allotted 60 cents a week before the city ran out of money altogether.

The deepening crisis roused old fears and caused some Americans to look for scapegoats. Among the most thoroughly scapegoated were Mexican Americans. During the 1920s, cheap agricultural labor from Mexico flowed legally across the U.S. border, welcomed by the large farmers. In the 1930s, however, the public

| In what ways did the Roaring Twenties challenge traditional values? | Why did the divide between rural and urban America grow in the 1920s? | What caused the crash of 1929? | **What was life like in the early years of the depression?** | Conclusion: Why did the hope of the 1920s turn to despair? |

denounced the newcomers as dangerous aliens who took jobs from Americans. Government officials, most prominently those in Los Angeles County, targeted Mexican residents for deportation regardless of citizenship status. As many as half a million Mexicans and Mexican Americans were deported or fled to Mexico.

The depression deeply affected the American family. Young people postponed marriage. When they did marry, they produced few children. White women, who generally worked in low-paying service areas, did not lose their jobs as often as men who worked in the steel, automobile, and other heavy industries. Idle men suffered a loss of self-esteem. "Before the depression," one unemployed father reported, "I wore the pants in this family, and rightly so." Jobless, he lost "self-respect" and also "the respect of my children, and I am afraid that I am losing my wife." Employers discriminated against married women workers, but necessity continued to drive women into the marketplace. As a result, by 1940 some 25 percent more women were employed for wages than in 1930.

Denial and Escape

President Hoover assured the American people that economic recovery was on its way. Contradicting the president's optimism were makeshift shantytowns, called "Hoover-villes," that sprang up on the edges of America's cities. Bitter jokes circulated about the increasingly unpopular president. One told of Hoover asking for a nickel to telephone a friend. Flipping him a dime, an aide said, "Here, call them both."

While Hoover practiced denial, other Americans sought refuge from reality at the movies. Throughout the depression, between 60 million and 75 million people (nearly two-thirds of the nation) scraped together enough change to fill the movie palaces every week. Box office hits such as *Forty-second Street* and *Gold Diggers of 1933* capitalized on the hope that prosperity lay just around the corner. But a few filmmakers grappled with hard realities rather than escape them. *The Public Enemy* (1931) taught hard lessons about gangsters' ill-gotten gains. Indeed, under the new production code of 1930, designed to protect public morals, all movies had to find some way to show that crime did not pay.

Despite Hollywood's efforts to keep Americans on the right side of the law, crime increased. Out in the countryside, the plight of people who had lost their farms to bank foreclosures led to the romantic idea that bank robbers were only getting back what banks had stolen from the poor. Woody Guthrie, the populist folksinger from Oklahoma, captured the public's tolerance for outlaws in his tribute to a murderous bank robber with a choirboy face, "The Ballad of Pretty Boy Floyd":

> Yes, as through this world I ramble,
> I see lots of funny men,
> Some will rob you with a six-gun,
> Some will rob you with a pen.
> But as through your life you'll travel,
> Wherever you may roam,
> You won't never see an outlaw drive
> A family from their home.

CHAPTER LOCATOR | How did big business shape the New Era of the 1920s?

652 CHAPTER 23 FROM NEW ERA TO GREAT DEPRESSION, 1920–1932

Working-Class Militancy

Members of the nation's working class bore the brunt of the economic collapse. By 1931, William Green, head of the American Federation of Labor (AFL), had turned militant. "I warn the people who are exploiting the workers," he shouted, "that they can drive them only so far before they will turn on them and destroy them. They are taking no account of the history of nations in which governments have been overturned. Revolutions grow out of the depths of hunger."

The American people were slow to anger, but on March 7, 1932, several thousand unemployed autoworkers massed at the gates of Henry Ford's River Rouge factory in Dearborn, Michigan, to demand work. Pelted with rocks, Ford's private security forces responded with gunfire, killing four demonstrators. Forty thousand outraged citizens turned out for the unemployed men's funerals.

Farmers mounted uprisings of their own. When Congress refused to guarantee farm prices, several thousand farmers created the National Farmers' Holiday

"Scottsboro Boys" Nine black youths stand in front of rifle-bearing National Guard troops called up by Alabama governor B. M. Miller, who feared a mob lynching after two white women accused the nine of rape in March 1931. Despite a lack of evidence, an all-white jury convicted the nine of rape and sentenced them to death. Although none was executed, all nine spent years in jail. Eventually, the state dropped the charges against the youngest four and granted paroles to the others. The last "Scottsboro Boy" left jail in 1950. © Bettmann/Corbis.

| In what ways did the Roaring Twenties challenge traditional values? | Why did the divide between rural and urban America grow in the 1920s? | What caused the crash of 1929? | **What was life like in the early years of the depression?** | Conclusion: Why did the hope of the 1920s turn to despair? |

Harlan County Coal Strike, 1931

Scottsboro Boys

▶ Nine African American youths, ranging in age from thirteen to twenty-one, who were arrested for the alleged rape of two white women in Scottsboro, Alabama, in 1931. After an all-white jury sentenced the young men to death, the Communist Party took action that saved them from the electric chair.

Association in 1932, so named because its members planned to take a "holiday" from shipping crops to market. Farm militants also resorted to what they called "penny sales." When banks foreclosed and put farms up for auction, neighbors warned others not to bid, bought the foreclosed property for a few pennies, and returned it to the bankrupt owners. Militancy won farmers little in the way of long-term solutions, but one individual observed that "the biggest and finest crop of revolutions you ever saw is sprouting all over the country right now."

In 1932, thousands of unemployed World War I veterans traveled to Washington, D.C., to petition Congress for the immediate payment of the pension (known as a "bonus") that Congress had promised in 1924. Hoover feared that the veterans would spark a riot and ordered the U.S. Army to evict the Bonus Marchers from the city. The spectacle of the army driving peaceful, petitioning veterans from the nation's capital further undermined public support for the beleaguered Hoover.

The Great Depression—the massive failure of capitalism—catapulted the Communist Party to its greatest size and influence in American history. Some 100,000 Americans—workers, intellectuals, college students—joined the Communist Party in the belief that only an overthrow of the capitalist system could save the victims of the depression. In 1931, the party, through its National Miners Union, moved into Harlan County, Kentucky, to support a strike by brutalized coal miners. The mine owners unleashed thugs against the strikers and eventually beat the miners down. But the Communist Party gained a reputation as the most dedicated and fearless champion of the union cause.

The left also led the fight against racism. While both major parties refused to challenge segregation in the South, the Socialist Party, led by Norman Thomas, attacked the system of sharecropping that left many African Americans in near servitude. The Communist Party also took action. When nine young black men in Scottsboro, Alabama (the **Scottsboro Boys**), were arrested on trumped-up rape charges in 1931, a team of lawyers sent by the party saved the defendants from the electric chair.

Radicals on the left often sparked action, but protests by moderate workers and farmers occurred on a far greater scale. Breadlines, soup kitchens, foreclosures, unemployment, and cold despair drove patriotic men and women to question American capitalism. "I am as conservative as any man could be," a Wisconsin farmer explained, "but any economic system that has in its power to set me and my wife in the streets, at my age—what can I see but red?"

> **QUICK REVIEW**

How did the depression reshape American life and politics?

CHAPTER LOCATOR | How did big business shape the New Era of the 1920s?

The Granger Collection, New York.

Conclusion: Why did the hope of the 1920s turn to despair?

IN THE AFTERMATH of World War I, America turned its back on progressive crusades and embraced conservative Republican politics, the growing influence of corporate leaders, and business values. Changes in the nation's economy propelled fundamental change throughout society. Living standards rose, economic opportunity increased, and Americans threw themselves into private pleasures. At home in Harlem and abroad in Paris, American literature, art, and music flourished.

For many Americans, however, none of the glamour and vitality had much meaning. The vast majority struggled to earn a decent living. Blue-collar America did not participate fully in white-collar prosperity. Country folk, deeply suspicious and profoundly discontented, championed prohibition, revived the Klan, attacked immigration, and defended old-time Protestant religion.

The crash of 1929 and the depression that followed starkly revealed the economy's crises of international trade and consumption. The depression hurt everyone, but the poor were hurt most. As farmers and workers sank into aching hardship, businessmen rallied around Herbert Hoover to proclaim that private enterprise would get the country moving again. But things fell apart, and Hoover faced increasingly more radical opposition. Membership in the Socialist and Communist parties surged, and more and more Americans contemplated desperate measures. By 1932, the depression had nearly brought the nation to its knees. America faced its greatest crisis since the Civil War, and citizens demanded new leaders who would save them from the "Hoover Depression."

SO NOW YOU KNOW

The economic changes of the 1920s led to higher incomes and better standards of living for many Americans, who eagerly consumed new products and amusements such as automobiles, washing machines, baseball games, and movies.

> CHAPTER 23 STUDY GUIDE

Online Study Guide
bedfordstmartins.com/roarkunderstanding

STEP 1 GETTING STARTED

Below are basic terms from this period in American history. Can you identify each term below and explain why it matters? To do this exercise online or to download this chart, visit bedfordstmartins.com/roarkunderstanding.

TERM	WHO OR WHAT & WHEN	WHY IT MATTERS
Henry Ford, p. 630		
mass production, p. 631		
installment buying, p. 634		
prohibition, p. 635		
new woman, p. 636		
Harlem Renaissance, p. 638		
Lost Generation, p. 639		
Johnson-Reid Act, p. 642		
Ku Klux Klan, p. 643		
Scopes trial, p. 644		
Herbert Hoover, p. 646		
Scottsboro Boys, p. 654		

STEP 2 MOVING BEYOND THE BASICS

The exercise below represents a more advanced understanding of the chapter material. Examine the social, cultural, and economic trends that marked the 1920s as a "New Era" and the changes that occurred as the nation entered the Great Depression. Fill in the chart below by providing details of each development. When you are finished, ask yourself how change in each area affected the others. How, for example, did changes in manufacturing lead to new patterns of consumer behavior? What role did consumption play in changing gender roles? To do this exercise online or to download this chart, visit bedfordstmartins.com/roarkunderstanding.

	Characteristics/developments in the 1920s	Changes from 1929 to 1932
Business and manufacturing/ urban life		
Agriculture/rural life		
Society: consumerism, religion, mass culture		
Population: gender, race relations, immigrants		
Government and politics		
The economy		

STEP 3

PUTTING IT ALL TOGETHER

Now that you have reviewed key elements of the chapter, take a step back and try to explain the big picture by answering these questions. Remember to use specific examples from the chapter in your answers. To do this exercise online, visit bedfordstmartins.com/roarkunderstanding.

POSTWAR DEVELOPMENTS

▶ What place did big business hold in the politics and culture of the 1920s?

▶ How did the economic changes of the 1920s contribute to challenges to social, cultural, and ethical norms?

RESISTANCE TO CHANGE

▶ What explains the rising anti-immigrant mood of America in the 1920s?

▶ What cultural divisions between rural and urban America were highlighted by the election of 1928?

THE CRASH AND THE GREAT DEPRESSION

▶ What underlying weaknesses in the American and world economies led to the Great Depression?

▶ How did Herbert Hoover respond to the economic crisis that engulfed his presidency? Why were his efforts unsuccessful?

▶ What was the "human toll" of the Great Depression?

LOOKING BACKWARD, LOOKING AHEAD

▶ In your opinion, were the 1920s truly a New Era? Why or why not?

▶ How were American life and culture challenged by the economic collapse of 1929? How did economic disaster make political change possible?

IN YOUR OWN WORDS

Imagine that you must explain chapter 23 to someone who hasn't read it. What would the most important points to include and why?

24
FORGING THE NEW DEAL

1932–1939

> This chapter traces the efforts of President Franklin D. Roosevelt's administration to respond to the Great Depression. It also explores the principles and political factors that shaped the development and implementation of New Deal policies and examines the impact of those policies on 1930s America.

> How did Franklin D. Roosevelt and the Democrats win the 1932 election?

> What were the goals and achievements of the first New Deal?

> Who opposed the New Deal and why?

> How did the second phase of the New Deal differ from the first?

> Why did support for the New Deal decline in the late 1930s?

> Conclusion: What were the achievements and limitations of the New Deal?

DID YOU KNOW?

Congress established Social Security as part of the New Deal.

"Work Pays America!" Poster from the New Deal's Works Progress Administration.

How did Franklin D. Roosevelt and the Democrats win the 1932 election?

Roosevelt's Common Touch

Sensing that his presentation of himself as a good neighbor was responsible for much of his popularity, Roosevelt arranged to have a friendly chat outside the polls in his hometown of Hyde Park with working-class voter Ruben Appel. In this photograph, Appel seems unaware that Roosevelt's standing was itself a feat of stagecraft. Franklin D. Roosevelt Library.

▶ FOR MORE HELP ANALYZING THIS IMAGE, see the visual activity for this chapter in the Online Study Guide at bedfordstmartins.com/roarkunderstanding.

Franklin Delano Roosevelt
▶ The thirty-second president of the United States. Roosevelt was elected in 1932 and reelected three times. He proposed a set of policies and legislation during the Great Depression that he called the "New Deal." He died in office shortly after beginning his fourth term.

UNLIKE MILLIONS of impoverished Americans, Franklin Roosevelt came from a wealthy and privileged background that contributed to his optimism, self-confidence, and vitality. He drew on these personal qualities in his political career to bridge the chasm that separated him from the struggles of ordinary people. During the twelve years he served as president (1933–1945), many elites came to hate him as a traitor to his class, while millions more Americans, especially the hardworking poor and dispossessed, revered him because he cared about them and their problems.

The Making of a Politician

Born in 1882, **Franklin Delano Roosevelt** was steeped at home and school in high-minded doctrines of public service and Christian duty to help the poor and

CHAPTER LOCATOR

weak. He prepared for a career in politics, hoping to follow in the footsteps of his fifth cousin, Theodore Roosevelt. Unlike Teddy, Franklin Roosevelt sought his political fortune in the Democratic Party. In 1920, he catapulted to the second spot on the national Democratic ticket as the vice presidential candidate of presidential nominee James M. Cox. Although Cox lost the election (see chapter 22), Roosevelt's performance convinced Democratic leaders that he had a future in national politics.

In the summer of 1921, Roosevelt became infected with polio. For the rest of his life, he wore heavy steel braces, and he could only walk a few steps by leaning on another person. Tireless physical therapy helped him regain his vitality and intense desire for high political office. After his polio attack, Roosevelt frequented a polio therapy facility at Warm Springs, Georgia. There, he made overtures to southern Democrats, forging relationships that would prove valuable for the rest of his political career.

By 1928, Roosevelt had recovered sufficiently to campaign successfully for governor of New York. His activist policies as governor foreshadowed his presidency. Governor Roosevelt believed that government should intervene to protect citizens from the economic hardships that came with the **Great Depression**. In contrast, many conservatives believed that government help for the needy sapped individual initiative and impeded the self-correcting forces of the market by rewarding people for losing the economic struggle to survive. Roosevelt lacked a full-fledged counterargument to these conservative claims, but he sympathized with the plight of poor people. "To these unfortunate citizens," he proclaimed, "aid must be extended by governments. . . . [No one should go] unfed, unclothed, or unsheltered." His many supporters appreciated his energy, activism, and conviction that government should do something to help Americans climb out of the economic abyss.

The Election of 1932

Democrats knew that President Herbert Hoover's unpopularity gave them a historic opportunity to recapture the White House in 1932. To do so, however, Democrats had to overcome warring factions within their party. Southern Democrats chaired powerful committees in Congress thanks to their continual reelection in the one-party South devoted to white supremacy. This southern, native-born, white, rural, Protestant, conservative wing of the Democratic Party found little common ground with the northern, immigrant, urban, disproportionately Catholic, liberal wing. Eastern-establishment Democrats shared few goals with angry farmers and factory workers. Still, this unruly coalition managed to agree to nominate Franklin Roosevelt as their presidential candidate.

In his acceptance speech, Roosevelt vowed to help "the forgotten man at the bottom of the pyramid" with "bold, persistent experimentation." Highlighting his differences with Hoover and the Republicans, he pledged "a new deal for the American people." Although few details about what Roosevelt meant by "a new deal" emerged during the presidential campaign, voters decided that whatever his new deal might be, it was better than reelecting Hoover.

Roosevelt won the 1932 presidential election in a historic landslide (**Map 24.1,** page 662). He received 57 percent of the nation's votes, the first time a Democrat

CHRONOLOGY

1882
– Franklin D. Roosevelt is born.

1920
– Roosevelt campaigns for vice president with Democratic presidential nominee James M. Cox.

1921
– Roosevelt contracts polio.

1928
– Roosevelt is elected governor of New York.

1932
– Roosevelt is elected president of the United States.

Great Depression
▶ Massive economic crisis that began in the late 1920s and continued until the United States entered World War II in 1941. The depression was a worldwide phenomenon, affecting not only the United States but most other nations as well.

What were the goals and achievements of the first New Deal?	Who opposed the New Deal and why?	How did the second phase of the New Deal differ from the first?	Why did support for the New Deal decline in the late 1930s?	Conclusion: What were the achievements and limitations of the New Deal?

Candidate	Electoral Vote	Popular Vote	Percent of Popular Vote
Franklin D. Roosevelt (Democrat)	472	22,821,857	57.4
Herbert C. Hoover (Republican)	59	15,761,841	39.7
Norman Thomas (Socialist)	0	881,951	2.2
William Z. Foster (Communist)	0	102,991	0.3

MAP 24.1 ■ **The Election of 1932**

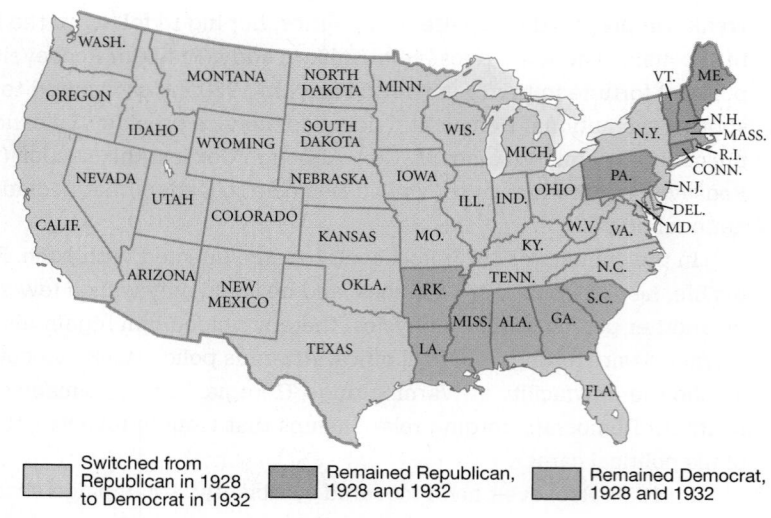

Switched from Republican in 1928 to Democrat in 1932 ▪ Remained Republican, 1928 and 1932 ▪ Remained Democrat, 1928 and 1932

MAP 24.2 ■ **Electoral Shift, 1928–1932**
The Democratic victory in 1932 signaled the rise of a New Deal coalition within which women and minorities, many of them new voters, made the Democrats the majority party for the first time in the twentieth century.

had won a majority of the popular vote since 1852 (**Map 24.2**). Roosevelt's coattails swept Democrats into control of Congress by large margins.

Roosevelt's victory represented the emergence of what came to be known as the New Deal coalition. Attracting support from farmers, factory workers, immigrants, city folk, African Americans, women, progressive intellectuals, and traditional Democratic strongholds in the South, Roosevelt launched a realignment of the nation's political loyalties. The New Deal coalition dominated American politics throughout Roosevelt's presidency and remained powerful long after his death in 1945. United less by ideology or support for specific policies, voters in the New Deal coalition instead expressed faith in Roosevelt's promise of a government that would, somehow, change things for the better.

> ## QUICK REVIEW

Why did Franklin D. Roosevelt win the 1932 presidential election by such a large margin?

CHAPTER LOCATOR | How did Franklin D. Roosevelt and the Democrats win the 1932 election?

662 CHAPTER 24 FORGING THE NEW DEAL, 1932–1939

What were the goals and achievements of the first New Deal?

Eleanor Roosevelt Serving Unemployed Women

A tireless ambassador of the New Deal, Eleanor Roosevelt used her status as First Lady to highlight New Dealers' sympathy for the plight of poor, unemployed, and neglected working people. Said one North Carolina woman about her, "One of my great pleasures was meeting Mrs. Roosevelt . . . she was so free of prejudice . . . she was always willing to take a stand." © Bettmann/Corbis.

AT NOON ON MARCH 4, 1933, Americans gathered around their radios to hear the inaugural address of the newly elected president. Roosevelt began by asserting his "firm belief that the only thing we have to fear is fear itself—nameless, unreasoning, unjustified terror which paralyzes needed efforts to convert retreat into advance." He promised "direct, vigorous action," and the first months of his administration, termed "the Hundred Days," fulfilled that promise in a whirlwind of government initiatives that launched the **New Deal**.

Roosevelt and his advisers had three interrelated objectives: relief, recovery, and reform. The New Deal never fully achieved these goals, but by aiming for them, Roosevelt's experimental programs enormously expanded government's role in the nation's economy and society.

New Deal
► The legislation, policies, and initiatives launched during Franklin Roosevelt's presidency that were aimed at easing the crisis of the Great Depression. Although the New Deal never fully achieved its goals, Roosevelt and his advisers had three interrelated objectives: relief, recovery, and reform.

What were the goals and achievements of the first New Deal?	Who opposed the New Deal and why?	How did the second phase of the New Deal differ from the first?	What were the varieties of domestic insurrections in 1774–1775?	Conclusion: What changes did Americans want in 1775?

1933
March
- In his inaugural address, Roosevelt promises government action.
- Emergency Banking Act and the Glass-Steagall Banking Act
- Roosevelt gives first fireside chat.
- Civilian Conservation Corps is established.

May
- Federal Emergency Relief Administration is established.
- Agricultural Adjustment Act
- Tennessee Valley Authority is created.

June
- National Relief Administration is established.

1934
June
- Securities and Exchange Commission is established.

Eleanor Roosevelt

▶ Wife of Franklin Roosevelt and First Lady of the United States from 1933 to 1945. Eleanor Roosevelt was a champion of her husband's New Deal policies. She traveled throughout the United States to meet with ordinary Americans and hear their concerns.

Goals of the New Deal

Relief	Provide help to the millions of poor and unemployed Americans victimized by the depression.
Recovery	Foster economic recovery of farms and businesses, thereby creating jobs and reducing the need for relief.
Reform	Reshape government and the economy to protect citizens against future economic downturns.

The New Dealers

To design and implement the New Deal, Roosevelt convened a "Brains Trust" of economists and other leaders to offer suggestions and advise him about the problems facing the nation. Among the most important reformers to join the Roosevelt administration were two veterans of Roosevelt's New York governorship: Harry Hopkins and Frances Perkins. Hopkins, a social worker, administered New Deal relief efforts and served as one of the president's loyal confidants. Perkins, who had extensive experience trying to improve working conditions in shops and factories, served as secretary of labor, making her the first woman cabinet member in American history.

No New Dealers were more important than the president and his wife, Eleanor. The gregarious president radiated charm and good cheer, giving the New Deal a benevolent human face. **Eleanor Roosevelt** became the New Deal's unofficial ambassador, traveling throughout the nation meeting Americans of all colors and creeds in church basements, town halls, and front parlors.

As Roosevelt and his advisers developed plans to meet the economic emergency, their watchwords were *action*, *experiment*, and *improvise*. Without a sharply defined template for how to provide relief, recovery, and reform, they moved from ideas to policies as quickly as possible, hoping to identify ways to help people and to boost the economy. Four guiding ideas shaped their policies.

First, Roosevelt and his advisers sought capitalist solutions to the economic crisis. They believed that the depression had resulted from basic imbalances in the nation's capitalist economy—imbalances they wanted to correct. They had no desire to end capitalism. Instead, they hoped to save the capitalist economy by remedying its flaws.

Second, they believed that underconsumption was the root cause of the current economic paralysis. Factories and farms produced more than they could sell to consumers, causing factories to lay off workers and farmers to lose money on bumper crops. Workers without wages and farmers without profits shrank consumption and choked the economy. Somehow, the balance between consumption and production needed to be restored.

Third, New Dealers believed that the immense size and economic power of American corporations needed to be counterbalanced by government and by organization among workers and small producers. Unlike progressive trust-busters, New Dealers did not seek to splinter big businesses. Instead, Roosevelt and his advisers hoped to counterbalance big economic institutions with government programs focused on protecting individuals and the public interest.

CHAPTER LOCATOR

How did Franklin D. Roosevelt and the Democrats win the 1932 election?

Fourth, New Dealers felt that government must somehow moderate the imbalance of wealth created by American capitalism. Wealth concentrated in a few hands reduced consumption by most Americans and thereby contributed to the current economic gridlock. In the long run, government needed to find a way to permit ordinary working people to share more fully in the fruits of the economy. In the short term, New Dealers sought to lend a helping hand to poor people who suffered from the maldistribution of wealth.

Banking and Finance Reform

As Roosevelt took the oath of office on March 4, 1933, the nation's banking system was on the brink of collapse (**Figure 24.1**). New Dealers rushed to draft the Emergency Banking Act, which gave the secretary of the treasury the power to decide which banks could be safely reopened and to release funds from the Reconstruction Finance Corporation to bolster banks' assets. To secure the confidence of depositors, Congress passed the Glass-Steagall Banking Act, setting up the Federal Deposit Insurance Corporation (FDIC), which guaranteed bank customers that the federal government would reimburse them for deposits if their banks failed.

On Sunday night, March 12, while the banks were still closed, Roosevelt broadcast the first of a series of "fireside chats." Speaking in a friendly, informal manner, he explained the new banking legislation. This and subsequent fireside chats forged a direct connection between Roosevelt and millions of Americans, a connection felt by a man from Paris, Texas, who wrote to Roosevelt, "You are the one & only President that ever helped a Working Class of People. . . . Please help us some way[.] I Pray to God for relief." The banking legislation and fireside chat

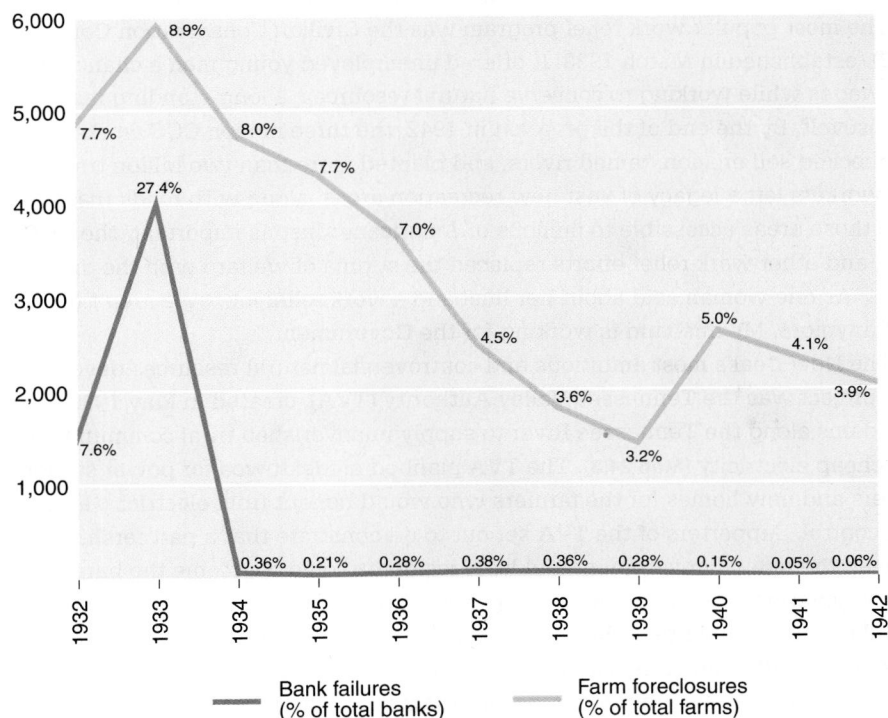

FIGURE 24.1 ■ **Bank Failures and Farm Foreclosures, 1932–1942**
New Deal legislation to stabilize the economy had its most immediate and striking effect in preventing banks, along with their depositors, from failing and farmers from losing their land.

Bank failures (% of total banks) — Farm foreclosures (% of total farms)

| What were the goals and achievements of the first New Deal? | Who opposed the New Deal and why? | How did the second phase of the New Deal differ from the first? | Why did support for the New Deal decline in the late 1930s? | Conclusion: What were the achievements and limitations of the New Deal? |

worked. Within a few days, most of the nation's major banks reopened, and they remained solvent as reassured depositors returned funds to their bank accounts.

To prevent the fraud, corruption, and insider trading that had tainted Wall Street and contributed to the crash of 1929, Roosevelt pressed Congress to regulate the stock market. Legislation in 1934 created the Securities and Exchange Commission (SEC) to oversee financial markets by licensing investment dealers, monitoring all stock transactions, and requiring corporate officers to make full disclosures about their companies.

Relief and Conservation Programs

Patching the nation's financial structure provided little relief for the hungry and unemployed. A poor man from Nebraska asked Eleanor Roosevelt, "if the folk who was borned here in America . . . are this Forgotten Man, the President had in mind, [and] if we are this Forgotten Man[,] then we are still Forgotten." Since its founding, the federal government had never assumed responsibility for needy people, except in moments of natural disaster or emergencies such as the Civil War. Instead, churches, private charities, county and municipal governments, and occasionally states provided poor relief, usually with meager payments. The depression necessitated unprecedented federal relief efforts, according to Harry Hopkins and other New Dealers. As one New Yorker who still had a job wrote the government, "We work, ten hours a day for six days. In the grime and dirt of a nation [for] . . . low pay [making us] . . . slaves—slaves of the depression!"

Hopkins galvanized support for the Federal Emergency Relief Administration (FERA), which supported four million to five million households with $20 or $30 a month. FERA also created jobs for the unemployed on thousands of public works projects, organized by Hopkins into the Civil Works Administration (CWA), which put paychecks worth more than $800 million into the hands of previously jobless workers. CWA laborers renovated schools, dug sewers, and rebuilt roads and bridges.

The most popular work relief program was the Civilian Conservation Corps (CCC), established in March 1933. It offered unemployed young men a chance to earn wages while working to conserve natural resources, a long-standing interest of Roosevelt. By the end of the program in 1942, the three million CCC workers had checked soil erosion, tamed rivers, and planted more than two billion trees. CCC workers left a legacy of vast new recreation areas, along with roads that made those areas accessible to millions of Americans. Just as important, the CCC, CWA, and other work relief efforts replaced the stigma of welfare with the dignity of jobs. As one woman said about her husband's work relief job, "We aren't on relief anymore. My husband is working for the Government."

The New Deal's most ambitious and controversial natural resources development project was the Tennessee Valley Authority (TVA), created in May 1933 to build dams along the Tennessee River to supply impoverished rural communities with cheap electricity (**Map 24.3**). The TVA planned model towns for power station workers and new homes for the farmers who would benefit from electricity and flood control. Supporters of the TVA set out to demonstrate that a partnership between the federal government and local residents could overcome the barriers of state governments and private enterprises to make efficient use of abundant natural resources and break the ancient cycle of poverty. The TVA never fully realized these utopian ends, but it improved the lives of millions in the region with electric power, flood protection, soil reclamation, and jobs.

CHAPTER LOCATOR

How did Franklin D. Roosevelt and the Democrats win the 1932 election?

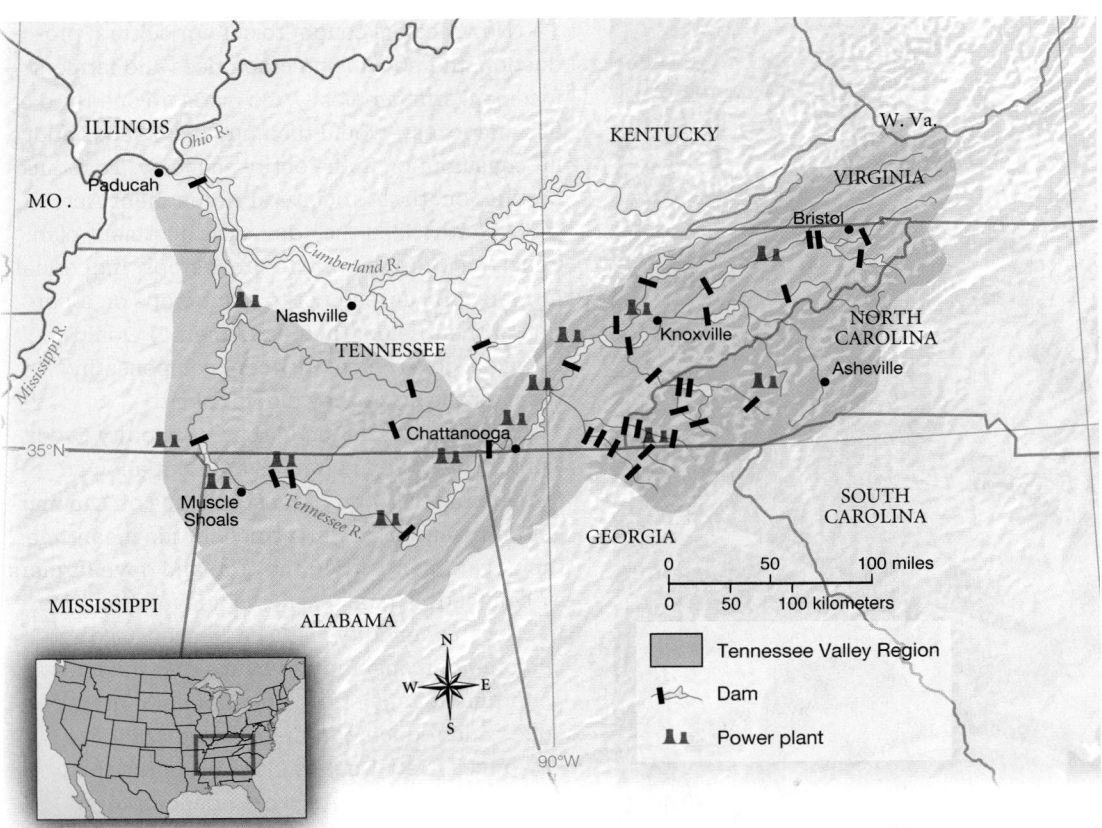

MAP 24.3 ■ The Tennessee Valley Authority
The New Deal created the Tennessee Valley Authority to modernize a vast impoverished region with hydroelectric power dams and, at the same time, to reclaim eroded land and preserve old folkways.

> ▶ FOR MORE HELP ANALYZING THIS MAP, see the map activity for this chapter in the Online Study Guide at bedfordstmartins.com/roarkunderstanding.

Other New Deal programs also addressed the needs of rural America. When Roosevelt became president, 90 percent of rural Americans lacked electricity. Beginning in 1935, the Rural Electrification Administration (REA) made low-cost loans available to local cooperatives for power plants and transmission lines to serve rural communities. Within ten years, the REA delivered electricity to nine out of ten farms, giving rural Americans access for the first time to modern electric conveniences.

Agricultural Initiatives

Farmers had been mired in a depression since the end of World War I. Farmers tried to compensate for low crop prices by growing more crops, hoping to boost their earnings by selling larger quantities. Instead, producing more crops pushed prices lower still. Income among farm families plunged to $167 a year, barely one-tenth of the national average.

| What were the goals and achievements of the first New Deal? | Who opposed the New Deal and why? | How did the second phase of the New Deal differ from the first? | Why did support for the New Deal decline in the late 1930s? | Conclusion: What were the achievements and limitations of the New Deal? |

This campaign poster calls Roosevelt "A Real Depression Buster" and highlights his alphabet soup of New Deal agencies.
Collection of Janice L. and David J. Frent.

New Dealers sought to cut agricultural production, thereby raising crop prices and farmers' income. Farm families—who made up one-third of all Americans—would then buy more goods and lift consumption in the entire economy. To reduce production, the Agricultural Adjustment Act (AAA) authorized the "domestic allotment plan," which paid farmers *not* to grow crops. Individual farmers who agreed not to plant crops on a portion of their fields (their "allotment") would receive a government payment compensating them for the crops they did not plant.

With the formation of the Commodity Credit Corporation, the federal government allowed farmers to hold their harvested crops off the market and wait for a higher price. In the meantime, the government stored the crop and gave farmers a "commodity loan" based on a favorable price. In effect, commodity loans addressed the problem of underconsumption by making the federal government a major consumer of agricultural goods and reducing farmers' vulnerability to low prices. New Dealers also sponsored the Farm Credit Act (FCA) to provide long-term credit on mortgaged farm property, allowing debt-ridden farmers to avoid foreclosures that were driving thousands off their land.

Crop allotments, commodity loans, and mortgage credit made farmers major beneficiaries of the New Deal. Crop prices rose impressively, farm income jumped 50 percent by 1936, and FCA loans financed 40 percent of farm mortgage debt by the end of the decade. These gains were distributed fairly equally among farmers in the corn, hog, and wheat region of the Midwest. In the South's cotton belt, however, landlords controlled the distribution of New Deal agricultural benefits and shamelessly rewarded themselves while denying benefits to many sharecroppers and tenant farmers—blacks and whites—by taking the land they had worked out of production and assigning it to the allotment program. The president of the Oklahoma Tenant Farmers' Union explained that large farmers who got "Triple-A" payments often used the money to buy tractors and then "forced their tenants and [share] croppers off the land," causing these "Americans to be starved and dispossessed of their homes in our land of plenty."

Industrial Recovery

Unlike farmers, industrialists cut production with the onset of the depression. But falling industrial production meant that millions of working people lost their jobs. Mass unemployment reduced consumer demand for industrial products, contributing to a downward spiral in both production and jobs, with no end in sight.

CHAPTER LOCATOR | How did Franklin D. Roosevelt and the Democrats win the 1932 election?

Industries responded by reducing wages for employees who still had jobs, further reducing demand—a trend made worse by competition among industrial producers. New Dealers struggled to find a way to break this cycle of unemployment and underconsumption—a way consistent with corporate profits and capitalism.

The New Deal's National Industrial Recovery Act (NIRA) opted for a government-sponsored form of industrial self-government through the National Recovery Administration (NRA), established in June 1933. The NRA encouraged industrialists in every part of the economy to agree on rules, known as codes, to define fair working conditions, to set prices, and to minimize competition. The idea behind these codes was to stabilize existing industries and maintain their workforces while avoiding what both industrialists and New Dealers termed "destructive competition," which forced employers to cut wages and jobs. Industry after industry wrote elaborate codes addressing production, pricing, and competition. In exchange for relaxing federal antitrust regulations that prohibited such business agreements, the participating businesses promised to recognize the right of working people to organize and engage in collective bargaining. To encourage consumers to patronize businesses participating in NRA codes, the New Deal mounted a public relations campaign that displayed the NRA's Blue Eagle in shop windows and on billboards throughout the nation.

New Dealers hoped that NRA codes would ensure fair treatment of workers and consumers and promotion of the general economic welfare. Instead, NRA codes tended to strengthen conventional business practices. Large corporations wrote codes that served primarily their own interests rather than the needs of workers or the welfare of the national economy. The failure of codes to cover agricultural or domestic workers led one woman to complain to Roosevelt that the NRA "never mentioned the robbery of the Housewives" by the privations caused by the depression. In the end, the NRA did little to reduce unemployment, raise consumption, or relieve the depression.

QUICK REVIEW <

How effective was the first New Deal in bringing about relief, recovery, and reform?

What were the goals and achievements of the first New Deal?

Who opposed the New Deal and why?

How did the second phase of the New Deal differ from the first?

Why did support for the New Deal decline in the late 1930s?

Conclusion: What were the achievements and limitations of the New Deal?

> Who opposed the New Deal and why?

Huey Long's ability to adapt his stump-speech style to the radio made him the one rival politician who gave Roosevelt serious concern in the mid-1930s. Corbis.

THE FIRST NEW DEAL INITIATIVES engendered fierce criticism and political opposition. From the right, Republicans and business people charged that New Deal programs were too radical, undermining private property, economic stability, and democracy. Critics on the left faulted the New Deal for its failure to allay the human suffering caused by the depression and for its timidity in attacking corporate power and greed.

Resistance to Business Reform

Business leaders lambasted Roosevelt, even though their economic prospects improved more than those of most other Americans during the depression. Although concentrated corporate power avoided reform, business leaders still conducted stridently anti–New Deal campaigns that expressed their resentment and fear of regulations, taxes, and unions. One opponent called the president "Stalin Delano Roosevelt" and insisted that the New Deal was really a "Raw Deal."

CHAPTER LOCATOR | How did Franklin D. Roosevelt and the Democrats win the 1932 election?

By 1935, two major business organizations, the National Association of Manufacturers and the Chamber of Commerce, had become openly anti–New Deal. Their critiques were amplified by the American Liberty League, founded in 1934. To League members, the AAA was a "trend toward fascist control of agriculture," relief programs marked "the end of democracy," and the NRA was a plunge into the "quicksand of visionary experimentation."

Economists who favored rational planning in the public interest and labor leaders who sought to influence wages and working conditions by organizing unions attacked the New Deal from the left. In their view, the NRA stifled enterprise by permitting monopolistic practices. Labor leaders especially resented the NRA's willingness to allow businesses to form company-controlled unions while blocking workers from organizing genuine grassroots unions to bargain for themselves.

The Supreme Court stepped into this cross fire of criticisms in May 1935 and declared that the NRA unconstitutionally conferred powers reserved to Congress on an administrative agency staffed by government appointees. The NRA codes soon lost the little authority they had. The failure of the NRA demonstrated the depth of many Americans' resistance to economic planning and the stubborn refusal of business leaders to yield to government regulations or reforms.

Casualties in the Countryside

The AAA fared better in the face of criticism than the NRA. Allotment checks for keeping land fallow and crop prices high created loyalty among farmers with enough acreage to participate. Agricultural processors and distributors, however, criticized the AAA. They objected that the program reduced the volume of crop production—the only source of their profits—while they paid a tax on processed crops that funded the very program that disadvantaged them. In 1936, the Supreme Court agreed with their contention that they were victims of an illegal tax. The AAA rebounded from the Supreme Court ruling by eliminating the offending tax and funding allotment payments from general government revenues.

Protests stirred, however, among those who did not qualify for allotments. The Southern Farm Tenants Union argued passionately that the AAA enriched large farmers and impoverished small farmers who rented rather than owned their land. One black sharecropper explained why so little New Deal money trickled down to her: "De landlord is landlord, de politicians is landlord, de judge is landlord, de shurf [sheriff] is landlord, ever'body is landlord, en we [sharecroppers] ain' got nothin'!" Such testimony showed that the AAA, like the NRA, tended to help most those who least needed help.

Displaced tenants often joined the army of migrant workers who straggled across rural America during the 1930s. Hundreds of thousands of "Okies" streamed out of the Dust Bowl of Oklahoma, Kansas, Texas, and Colorado, where chronic drought and harmful agricultural practices blasted crops and hopes. Many migrated to the lush fields and orchards of California, but few found steady or secure work. As one Okie said, "When they need us they call us migrants, and when we've picked their crop, we're bums and we got to get out."

CHRONOLOGY

1932
- Huey Long of Louisiana is elected to U.S. Senate.

1934
- Pro-business, anti–New Deal American Liberty League is founded.
- Upton Sinclair runs for governor of California.
- Dr. Francis Townsend proposes Old Age Revolving Pension plan.

1935
- Supreme Court declares the NRA unconstitutional.
- Father Charles Coughlin founds the National Union for Social Justice.
- Huey Long is assassinated.

1936
- U.S. Supreme Court strikes down parts of the AAA.

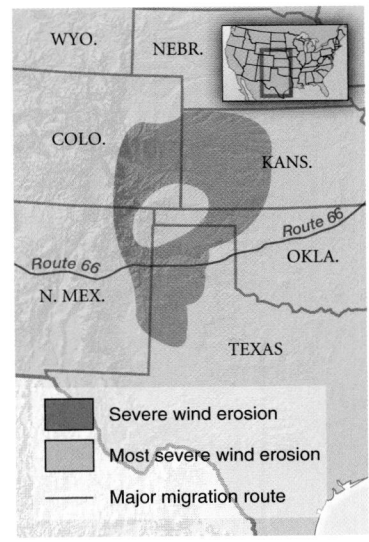

- Severe wind erosion
- Most severe wind erosion
- Major migration route

The Dust Bowl

| What were the goals and achievements of the first New Deal? | **Who opposed the New Deal and why?** | How did the second phase of the New Deal differ from the first? | Why did support for the New Deal decline in the late 1930s? | Conclusion: What were the achievements and limitations of the New Deal? |

Okie Family

This tenant farmer worked land near Eagleton, Oklahoma, but became sick with pneumonia and lost his farm. Such poor, jobless migrants were common along America's roads during the 1930s. Library of Congress.

▶ FOR MORE HELP ANALYZING THIS IMAGE, see the visual activity for this chapter in the Online Study Guide at bedfordstmartins.com/roarkunderstanding.

Politics on the Fringes

Politically, the New Deal's staunchest opponents were in the Republican Party. But the New Deal also faced challenges from the political fringes, fueled by the hardship of the depression and the hope for a cure-all.

Socialists and Communists accused the New Deal of being the handmaiden of business elites and of rescuing capitalism from its self-inflicted crisis. Socialist author Upton Sinclair ran for governor of California in 1934 on a plan he called "End Poverty in California." Sinclair demanded that the state take ownership of idle factories and unused land and give them to cooperatives of working people, a first step toward what he envisioned as a "Cooperative Commonwealth" that would put the needs of people above profits. Sinclair lost the election, ending the most serious socialist electoral challenge to the New Deal.

At its high point in the 1930s, the American Communist Party had about thirty thousand members. Individual Communists worked to organize labor unions, protect the civil rights of black people, and help the destitute, but the party preached the overthrow of "bourgeois democracy" and the destruction of capitalism in favor of Soviet-style communism. Such talk attracted few followers among the nation's millions of poor and unemployed.

More powerful radical challenges to the New Deal sprouted from homegrown roots. Many Americans felt overlooked by New Deal programs that concentrated on finance, agriculture, and industry but did little to produce jobs or aid the poor. The merciless reality of the depression also continued to erode the security of people who still had a job but worried constantly that they, too, might be pushed into the legions of the unemployed and penniless.

A Catholic priest in Detroit named Charles Coughlin spoke to and for many worried Americans in his weekly radio broadcasts, which reached a nationwide

CHAPTER LOCATOR | How did Franklin D. Roosevelt and the Democrats win the 1932 election?

672 CHAPTER 24
FORGING THE NEW DEAL, 1932–1939

audience of 40 million. Father Coughlin expressed outrage at the suffering and inequities that he blamed on Communists, bankers, and "predatory capitalists," who, he claimed, were mostly Jews. In 1932, Coughlin applauded Roosevelt's election and declared, "The New Deal is Christ's deal." But Coughlin became frustrated by Roosevelt's refusal to grant him influence, turned against the New Deal, and in 1935 founded the National Union for Social Justice, or Union Party, to challenge Roosevelt in the 1936 presidential election.

Dr. Francis Townsend was another important critic of the New Deal. Angry that many of his retired patients lived in misery, Townsend proposed in 1934 the creation of the Old Age Revolving Pension, which would pay every American over age sixty a pension of $200 a month. To receive the pension, senior citizens had to agree to spend the entire amount within thirty days, thereby stimulating the economy. Townsend organized pension clubs with more than two million paying members. When the major political parties rebuffed his impractical plan, Townsend merged his forces with Coughlin's Union Party in time for the 1936 election.

A more formidable challenge to the New Deal came from the powerful southern wing of the Democratic Party. **Huey Long**, son of a backcountry Louisiana farmer, was elected governor of the state in 1928 with his slogan "Every man a king, but no one wears a crown." Long championed the poor over the rich, country people over city folk, and the humble over elites. As governor, he delivered on his promises to provide jobs and build roads, schools, and hospitals, but he also behaved ruthlessly to achieve his goals. Journalists routinely referred to him as the "dictator of Louisiana." Swaggering and bullying to get his way, Long was elected to the U.S. Senate in 1932.

Senator Long introduced a sweeping "soak the rich" tax bill that would outlaw personal incomes of more than $1 million and inheritances of more than $5 million. When the Senate rejected his proposal, Long decided to run for president, mobilizing more than five million Americans behind his "Share Our Wealth" plan. The Share Our Wealth campaign died when Long was assassinated in 1935, but his constituency and the wide appeal of a more equitable distribution of wealth persisted.

The challenges to the New Deal from both Republicans and more radical groups stirred Democrats to solidify their winning coalition. In the midterm congressional elections of 1934—normally a time when a seated president loses support—voters gave New Dealers a landslide victory. Democrats increased their majority in the House of Representatives and gained a two-thirds majority in the Senate.

Huey Long

▶ Louisiana politician who, first as governor and then as senator, promoted a populist vision of political and social change and presented one of the most formidable challenges to the New Deal. He was assassinated in 1935.

QUICK REVIEW

What specific solutions to the crisis of the depression did critics of the New Deal propose?

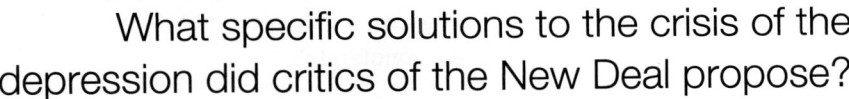

| What were the goals and achievements of the first New Deal? | Who opposed the New Deal and why? | How did the second phase of the New Deal differ from the first? | Why did support for the New Deal decline in the late 1930s? | Conclusion: What were the achievements and limitations of the New Deal? |

How did the second phase of the New Deal differ from the first?

California Farmworkers Mural

During the 1930s, artists—many of them employed by New Deal agencies—painted thousands of murals depicting the variety and vigor of American life. California-born Maxine Albro, one of the first woman muralists commissions by the WPA, painted this mural depicting farmworkers harvesting the bounty of California's fields.

THE POPULAR MANDATE for the New Deal revealed by the congressional elections persuaded Roosevelt to press ahead with bold new efforts to achieve relief, recovery, and reform. Despite the initiatives of the Hundred Days, the depression still strangled the economy. Rumbles of discontent from Father Coughlin, Huey Long, and their supporters showed that New Deal programs had fallen far short of their goals. In 1935, Roosevelt capitalized on his congressional majorities to enact major new programs that signaled the emergence of an American welfare state.

Although many citizens remained unprotected, New Deal programs provided a safety net that helped millions with jobs, relief, and government support. Underlying these programs was the idea that when people suffered because of forces beyond their control, the federal government bore responsibility to support and protect individual Americans. The safety net of welfare programs tied the political loyalty of working people to the New Deal and the Democratic Party. As a North Carolina mill worker said, "Mr. Roosevelt is the only man we ever had in the White House who would understand that my boss is a sonofabitch."

CHAPTER LOCATOR

How did Franklin D. Roosevelt and the Democrats win the 1932 election?

Relief for the Unemployed

First and foremost, millions of Americans still needed jobs. In response, Roosevelt and his advisers launched a massive work relief program. Roosevelt believed that direct government handouts crippled recipients with "spiritual and moral disintegration . . . destructive to the human spirit." Jobs, in contrast, bolstered individuals' "self-respect, . . . self-confidence, . . . courage, and determination." With a congressional appropriation of nearly $5 billion—more than all government revenues in 1934—the New Deal created the **Works Progress Administration (WPA)** to give unemployed Americans government-funded jobs on public works projects. The WPA put millions of jobless citizens to work on roads, bridges, parks, public buildings, and more. By 1936, the WPA provided jobs for 7 percent of the nation's labor force. In effect, the WPA made the federal government the employer of last resort, creating useful jobs when the private sector failed to do so. Overall, WPA jobs put 13 million Americans to work and gave them paychecks worth $10 billion.

About three out of four WPA jobs involved construction and renovation of the nation's physical infrastructure. In addition, the WPA gave jobs to thousands of artists, musicians, actors, journalists, poets, and novelists. Throughout the nation, WPA projects displayed tangible evidence of the New Deal's commitment to public welfare.

Empowering Labor

During the Great Depression, factory workers who managed to keep their jobs worried constantly about being laid off while their wages and working hours were cut. When workers tried to organize labor unions to protect themselves, municipal and state governments usually sided with employers. The New Deal dramatically reversed the federal government's stance toward unions, lending the government's support to an unprecedented wave of union organizing among the nation's working people. When the head of the United Mine Workers, John L. Lewis, told coal miners that "the President wants you to join a union," he exaggerated only a little. New Dealers believed that unions would counterbalance the power of big corporations by defending working people, maintaining wages, and replacing the violence that often accompanied strikes with economic peace and commercial stability.

Violent battles across the nation showed the determination of militant labor leaders to organize unions. In 1934, striking workers in Toledo, Minneapolis, San Francisco, and elsewhere were beaten and shot by police and the National Guard. In Congress, labor leaders lobbied for the National Labor Relations Act (NLRA), a bill sponsored by Senator Robert Wagner of New York that authorized the federal government to intervene in labor disputes and supervise the organization of labor unions. Signed into law in July 1935, the **Wagner Act**, as it came to be called, guaranteed industrial workers the right to organize unions, putting the might of federal law behind the appeals of labor leaders. The Wagner Act created the National Labor Relations Board (NLRB) to sponsor and oversee elections for union representation. If the majority of workers at a company voted for a union, then the union became the sole bargaining agent for the entire workplace, and the employer was required to negotiate with the elected union leaders.

CHRONOLOGY

1934
- In a historic shift, African American voters switch from the Republican to the Democratic Party in midterm elections.
- Indian Reorganization Act.

1935
- Works Progress Administration is created.
- National Labor Relations Act (Wagner Act).
- Committee for Industrial Organization is founded.
- Social Security Act.

1937
- Sit-down strike by United Auto Workers against General Motors.

1941
- Ford Motor Company capitulates to United Auto Workers, leaving the entire auto industry unionized.

Works Progress Administration (WPA)
▶ Federal New Deal program that provided government jobs to millions of Americans during the depression, in areas ranging from construction to the arts.

Wagner Act
▶ 1935 law that guaranteed industrial workers the right to organize into unions; also known as the National Labor Relations Act. The Wagner Act also created the National Labor Relations Board to oversee elections for union representation.

What were the goals and achievements of the first New Deal?

Who opposed the New Deal and why?

How did the second phase of the New Deal differ from the first?

Why did support for the New Deal decline in the late 1930s?

Conclusion: What were the achievements and limitations of the New Deal?

The Wagner Act and renewed labor militancy resulted in impressive increases in union membership (**Figure 24.2**) Most of the new union members were factory workers and unskilled laborers, many of them immigrants, women, and African Americans. For decades, established AFL unions had no desire to organize factory and unskilled workers, who struggled along without unions. In 1935, under the aggressive leadership of the mine workers' John L. Lewis and the head of the Amalgamated Clothing Workers, Sidney Hillman, a coalition of unskilled workers formed the Committee for Industrial Organization (CIO; later the Congress of Industrial Organizations). The CIO, helped by the Wagner Act, mobilized organizing drives in major industries, including the bitterly anti-union automobile and steel industries.

The bloody struggle by the CIO-affiliated United Auto Workers (UAW) to organize workers at General Motors climaxed in January 1937. Striking workers occupied the main assembly plant in Flint, Michigan, in a **"sit-down" strike** that slashed the plant's production of 15,000 cars a week to a mere 150. General Motors eventually surrendered and agreed to make the UAW the sole bargaining agent for all the company's workers and to refrain from interfering with union activity. Having subdued the auto industry's leading producer, the UAW expanded its campaign until, after much violence, the entire industry was unionized when the Ford Motor Company capitulated in 1941.

The CIO hoped to achieve similar success in the steel industry. But after unionizing the industry giant U.S. Steel, the CIO ran up against ruthless opposition from smaller steel firms. Following a police attack that killed ten strikers at Republic Steel outside Chicago in May 1937, the battered steelworkers halted their organizing campaign. In steel and other major industries, organizing efforts stalled until after 1941, when military mobilization created labor shortages that gave workers greater bargaining power.

"sit-down" strike

▶ A strike in which workers stop working but remain at their workplace. A sit-down strike at the General Motors Company in Flint, Michigan, in 1937 forced the company to recognize the United Auto Workers union as the bargaining agent for the workers.

FIGURE 24.2 ■ Labor Union Membership, 1930–1939

U.S. Department of Commerce, *Historical Statistics of the United States: Colonial Times to 1970* (Washington, D.C.: U.S. Government Printing Office, 1975), 178.

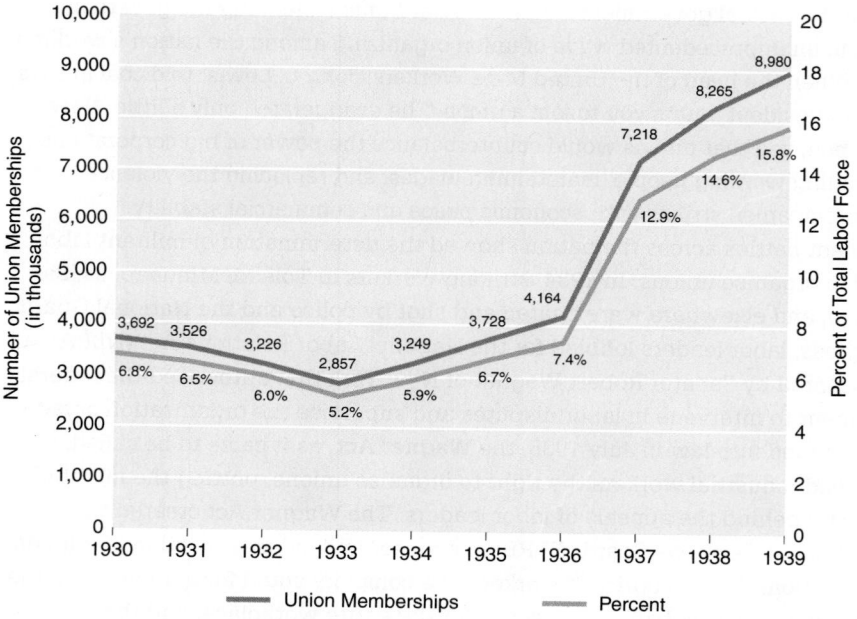

CHAPTER LOCATOR

How did Franklin D. Roosevelt and the Democrats win the 1932 election?

Social Security and Tax Reform

The single most important feature of the New Deal's emerging welfare state was **Social Security**. An ambitious, far-reaching, and permanent reform, Social Security was designed to provide a modest income to relieve the poverty of elderly people. Prompted by the popular but impractical panaceas of Dr. Townsend, Father Coughlin, and Huey Long, Roosevelt became the first president to advocate protection for the elderly. He told Congress that "it is our plain duty to provide for that security upon which welfare depends . . . and undertake the great task of furthering the security of the citizen and his family through social insurance."

The political struggle for Social Security highlighted class differences among Americans. Support for the measure came from a coalition of advocacy groups for the elderly and the poor, traditional progressives, leftists, social workers, and labor unions. Arrayed against them were economic conservatives, including the Republican Party, the American Liberty League, the National Association of Manufacturers, the Chamber of Commerce, and the American Medical Association. Despite such opposition, the large New Deal majority in Congress passed the Social Security Act in August 1935.

Social Security

▶ A federal program designed to provide a modest income for elderly people. Social Security became the longest-lasting and most far-reaching of all the New Deal programs.

Key Provisions of Social Security

Used tax contributions from workers and their employers to fund pensions for the elderly.
Stipulated that, upon reaching retirement age, workers would earn benefits based on their contributions and years of work.
Placed no means test on eligibility for benefits.
Created unemployment insurance that provided modest benefits for workers who lost their jobs.

Not all workers benefited from the Social Security Act. It excluded domestic and agricultural workers, thereby making ineligible about half of all African Americans and more than half of all employed women—about five million people in all. In addition, the law excluded workers employed by religious and nonprofit organizations, such as schools and hospitals, rendering ineligible even more working women and minorities.

In a bow to traditional beliefs about local governments' responsibility for public assistance, Social Security issued multimillion-dollar grants to the states to help support dependent children, public health services, and the blind. After the Supreme Court in 1937 upheld Social Security, the program was expanded to include benefits for dependent survivors of deceased recipients. The system gave millions of working people the assurance that, when they became too old to work, they would receive a modest income from the federal government.

Roosevelt saw in tax reform a way to redistribute wealth that would weaken conservative opposition, advance the cause of social equity, and defuse political challenges from Huey Long and Father Coughlin. In June 1935, as the Social Security Act was being debated, Roosevelt delivered a message to Congress outlining comprehensive reform. Charging that large fortunes put "great and undesirable concentration of control in [the hands of] relatively few individuals," Roosevelt urged a graduated tax on corporations, an inheritance tax, and an increase in

What were the goals and achievements of the first New Deal?	Who opposed the New Deal and why?	How did the second phase of the New Deal differ from the first?	Why did support for the New Deal decline in the late 1930s?	Conclusion: What were the achievements and limitations of the New Deal?

Mary McLeod Bethune

At the urging of Eleanor Roosevelt, Mary McLeod Bethune, a southern educational and civil rights leader, became director of the National Youth Administration's Division of Negro Affairs. The first black woman to head a federal agency, Bethune used her position to promote social change. Moorland-Spingarn Research Center, Howard University.

Mary McLeod Bethune

▶ Activist who was the highest-ranking black official in Franklin Roosevelt's administration. She was a strong advocate for the hiring of African Americans to federal New Deal jobs.

maximum personal income taxes. Congress endorsed Roosevelt's basic principle by taxing those with higher incomes at a somewhat higher rate.

Neglected Americans and the New Deal

The patchwork of New Deal reforms erected a two-tier welfare state. In the top tier, organized workers in major industries were the greatest beneficiaries of New Deal initiatives. In the bottom tier, millions of neglected Americans—women, children, and old folks, along with the unorganized, unskilled, uneducated, and unemployed—often fell through the New Deal safety net. Many working people remained more or less untouched by New Deal benefits. The average unemployment rate for the 1930s stayed high—17 percent. Workers in industries that resisted unions received little help from the Wagner Act or the WPA. Domestic workers—almost all of them women—and agricultural workers—many of them African, Hispanic, or Asian Americans—were neither unionized nor eligible for Social Security.

The New Deal neglected few citizens more than African Americans. About half of black Americans in cities were jobless. In the rural South, where the vast majority of African Americans lived, conditions were worse. New Deal agricultural policies such as the AAA favored landowners and often resulted in black sharecroppers and tenants being pushed off the land they farmed. Disfranchisement by intimidation and legal subterfuge prevented southern blacks from protesting their plight at the ballot box. Protesters risked vicious retaliation from local whites. After years of decline, lynching increased during the 1930s. In 1935, a riot in Harlem focused on white-owned businesses, dramatizing blacks' resentment and despair. Bitter critics charged that the New Deal's NRA stood for "Negro Run Around" or "Negroes Ruined Again."

Roosevelt responded to such criticisms with great caution, since New Deal reforms required the political support of powerful conservative, segregationist, southern white Democrats, who would be alienated by programs that aided blacks. Nonetheless, New Dealers still tried to attract political support from black leaders. Roosevelt's overtures to African Americans prompted northern black voters in the 1934 congressional elections to shift from the Republican to the Democratic Party, helping elect New Deal Democrats.

Eleanor Roosevelt sponsored the appointment of **Mary McLeod Bethune**—the energetic cofounder of the National Council of Negro Women—as head of the Division of Negro Affairs in the National Youth Administration. The highest-ranking black official in Roosevelt's administration, Bethune used her position to guide a small number of black professionals and civil rights activists to posts within New Deal agencies. Nicknamed the "Black Cabinet," these men and women composed the first sizable representation of African Americans in white-collar posts in the federal government, and they ultimately helped about one in four African Americans get access to New Deal relief programs.

CHAPTER LOCATOR

How did Franklin D. Roosevelt and the Democrats win the 1932 election?

Despite these gains, by 1940 African Americans still suffered severe handicaps. Most of the thirteen million black workers toiled at low-paying menial jobs, unprotected by the New Deal safety net. Making a mockery of the "separate but equal" doctrine, segregated black schools had less money and worse facilities than white schools, and only 1 percent of black students earned college degrees. In southern states, there were no black police officers or judges and hardly any black lawyers, and vigilante violence against blacks went unpunished.

Hispanic Americans fared no better. About a million Mexican Americans lived in the United States in the 1930s, most of them first- or second-generation immigrants who worked crops throughout the West. To preserve scarce jobs for U.S. citizens, the federal government choked off immigration from Mexico, while state and local officials prohibited the employment of aliens on work relief projects and deported tens of thousands of Mexican Americans, many with their American-born children. Local white administrators of many New Deal programs throughout the West discriminated against Hispanics and other people of color. A New Deal study concluded that "the Mexican is . . . segregated from the rest of the community as effectively as the Negro . . . [by] poverty and low wages."

Asian Americans had similar experiences. Asian immigrants were still excluded from U.S. citizenship and in many states were not permitted to own land. By 1930, more than half of Japanese Americans had been born in the United States, but they were still liable to discrimination. One young Asian American expressed the frustration felt by many others: "I am a fruit-stand worker. I would much rather it were doctor or lawyer . . . but my aspirations [were] frustrated long ago by circumstances [and] I am only what I am, a professional carrot washer."

Native Americans also suffered neglect from New Deal agencies. As a group, they remained the poorest of the poor. Since the Dawes Act of 1887 (see chapter 17), the federal government had encouraged Native Americans to assimilate—to abandon their Indian identities and adopt the cultural norms of the majority society. Under the leadership of the New Deal's commissioner of Indian affairs, John Collier, the New Deal's Indian Reorganization Act (IRA) of 1934 largely reversed that policy. The IRA brought little immediate benefit to Native Americans and remained a divisive issue for decades, but it provided an important foundation for Indians' economic, cultural, and political resurgence a generation later.

Singer and songwriter Woody Guthrie, the troubadour of working people, traveled the nation for eight years during the 1930s and heard other rambling men tell him "the story of their life," giving voice to experiences common among Americans neglected by the New Deal: "how the home went to pieces, how . . . the crops got to where they wouldn't bring nothing, work in factories would kill a dog . . . and—always, always [you] have to fight and argue and cuss and swear . . . to try to get a nickel more out of the rich bosses."

QUICK REVIEW

What features of a welfare state did the New Deal create and why?

| What were the goals and achievements of the first New Deal? | Who opposed the New Deal and why? | How did the second phase of the New Deal differ from the first? | Why did support for the New Deal decline in the late 1930s? | Conclusion: What were the achievements and limitations of the New Deal? |

Why did support for the New Deal decline in the late 1930s?

Distributing Surplus Food to the Needy When bountiful harvests produced surplus crops that would depress prices if they were sent to market, the New Deal arranged to distribute some of them to needy Americans. Here, farmworkers near the New Mexico border in east-central Arizona line up to receive a ration of potatoes authorized by the New Deal agent checking the box of index cards. Library of Congress.

TO ACCELERATE the sputtering economic recovery, Roosevelt shifted the emphasis of the New Deal in the mid-1930s. Instead of seeking cooperation from conservative business leaders, he decided to rely on the growing New Deal coalition to enact reforms over the strident opposition of the Supreme Court, Republicans, and corporate interests.

The Election of 1936

Roosevelt believed that the presidential election of 1936 would test his leadership and progressive ideals. The depression still had a stranglehold on the economy. Conservative leaders believed that the New Deal's failure to lift the nation out of the depression indicated that Americans were ready for a change. Left-wing critics insisted that the New Deal had missed the opportunity to displace capitalism with a socialist economy and that voters would embrace candidates who recommended more radical remedies.

Republicans chose Governor Alfred (Alf) Landon of Kansas as their presidential nominee. A moderate who had supported some New Deal measures, Landon stressed mainstream Republican proposals to achieve a balanced federal budget

CHAPTER LOCATOR

How did Franklin D. Roosevelt and the Democrats win the 1932 election?

and to ease the perils of illness and old age with old-fashioned neighborliness instead of new government bureaucracies.

Roosevelt won 60.8 percent of the popular vote, making it the widest margin of victory in a presidential election to date. Third parties—including the Socialist and Communists parties—fell pitifully short of the support they expected and never again mounted a significant challenge to the New Deal. Congressional results were equally lopsided, with Democrats outnumbering Republicans more than three to one in both houses.

In his inaugural address, Roosevelt pledged to use his mandate to help all citizens achieve a decent standard of living. He announced, "I see one third of a nation ill-housed, ill-clad, [and] ill-nourished," and he promised to devote his second term to alleviating their hardship.

Court Packing

In the afterglow of his reelection triumph, Roosevelt targeted the Supreme Court as the largest remaining obstacle to New Deal reforms. Laden with conservative justices appointed by Republican presidents, the Court had invalidated eleven New Deal measures as unconstitutional interferences with free enterprise. Now, Social Security, the Wagner Act, the Securities and Exchange Commission, and other New Deal innovations were about to be considered by justices.

To ensure that the Supreme Court's "horse and buggy" notions did not dismantle the New Deal, Roosevelt proposed a "court-packing" plan that added one new justice for each existing judge who had served for ten years and was over the age of seventy. In effect, the proposed law would give Roosevelt the power to pack the Court with up to six new justices.

But the president had not reckoned with Americans' deeply rooted deference to the independent authority of the Supreme Court. More than two-thirds of Americans believed that the Court should be free from political interference. The suggestion that individuals over age seventy had diminished mental capacity offended many elderly members of Congress, which defeated the bill in 1937.

Although Roosevelt's court-packing plan failed, Supreme Court justices got the message. After the furor abated, Chief Justice Charles Evans Hughes and fellow moderate Owen Roberts changed their views enough to keep the Court from invalidating the Wagner Act and Social Security. Then the most conservative of the elderly justices retired. Roosevelt eventually named eight justices to the Court—more than any other president, ultimately giving New Deal laws safe passage through the Court.

Reaction and Recession

Emboldened by their defeat of the court-packing plan, Republicans and southern Democrats rallied around their common conservatism to obstruct additional reforms. Democrats' arguments over whether the New Deal needed to be expanded—and if so, how—undermined the consensus among reformers and sparked antagonism between Congress and the White House. The ominous rise of belligerent regimes in Germany, Italy, Japan, and elsewhere slowed reform as some Americans began to worry more about defending the nation than changing it.

CHRONOLOGY

1936
- Roosevelt is elected to a second term in a landslide.

1937
- Congress defeats Roosevelt's "court-packing" plan.
- Farm Security Administration is created.
- National Housing Act.

1937–1938
- Roosevelt's reduction in government spending leads to a sharp economic downturn.

1938
- Fair Labor Standards Act.

What were the goals and achievements of the first New Deal?

Who opposed the New Deal and why?

How did the second phase of the New Deal differ from the first?

Why did support for the New Deal decline in the late 1930s?

Conclusion: What were the achievements and limitations of the New Deal?

Roosevelt himself favored slowing the pace of the New Deal. He believed that existing New Deal measures had steadily boosted the economy and largely eliminated the depression crisis. Roosevelt's unwarranted optimism about the economic recovery persuaded him that additional deficit spending by the federal government was no longer necessary.

Roosevelt failed to consider the stubborn realities of unemployment and poverty, and the reduction in deficit spending reversed the improving economy. Even at the high-water mark of recovery in the summer of 1937, seven million people lacked jobs. In the next few months, national income and production slipped so steeply that almost two-thirds of the economic gains since 1933 were lost by June 1938. Farm prices dropped 20 percent, and unemployment rose by more than two million. This economic reversal hurt the New Deal politically. Conservatives argued that this recession proved that New Deal measures produced only an illusion of progress. Many New Dealers insisted instead that the continuing depression demanded that Roosevelt revive federal spending and redouble efforts to stimulate the economy. In 1938, Congress heeded such pleas and enacted a massive new program of federal spending.

The recession scare of 1937–1938 taught the president the lesson that economic growth had to be carefully nurtured. The English economist John Maynard Keynes argued in his influential work *The General Theory of Employment, Interest, and Money* (1936) that only government intervention could pump enough money into the economy to restore prosperity. Roosevelt never had the inclination or time to master Keynesian theory, but he understood that escape from the depression required a plan for large-scale spending to alleviate distress and stimulate economic growth. (See "Global Comparison.")

The Last of the New Deal Reforms

From the moment he was sworn in, Roosevelt sought to expand the powers of the presidency. He believed that the president needed more authority to meet emergencies such as the depression and to administer the sprawling federal bureaucracy. In September 1938, Congress passed the Administrative Reorganization Act, which gave Roosevelt (and future presidents) new influence over the bureaucracy. Combined with a Democratic majority in Congress, a now-friendly Supreme Court, and the revival of deficit spending, the newly empowered White House seemed to be in a good position to move ahead with a revitalized New Deal.

Resistance to further reform was also on the rise, however. Conservatives argued that the New Deal had pressed government centralization too far. Even the New Deal's friends became weary of one emergency program after another while economic woes continued to shadow New Deal achievements. By the midpoint of Roosevelt's second term, restive members of Congress balked at new initiatives. Clearly, the New Deal was losing momentum, but enough support remained for one last burst of reform.

Agriculture still had strong claims on New Deal attention in the face of drought, declining crop prices, and impoverished sharecroppers and tenants. In 1937, the Agriculture Department created the Farm Security Administration (FSA) to provide housing and loans to help tenant farmers become independent. A black tenant farmer in North Carolina who received an FSA loan told a New Deal inter-

CHAPTER LOCATOR

How did Franklin D. Roosevelt and the Democrats win the 1932 election?

682 CHAPTER 24
FORGING THE NEW DEAL, 1932–1939

viewer, "I wake up in the night sometimes and think I must be half-dead and gone to heaven." But relatively few tenants received loans because the FSA was starved for funds and ran up against the major farm organizations intent on serving their own interests. For those who owned farms, the New Deal offered renewed prosperity with a second Agricultural Adjustment Act (AAA) in 1938. To moderate price swings by regulating supply, the plan combined production quotas on five staple crops—cotton, tobacco, wheat, corn, and rice—with storage loans through its Commodity Credit Corporation. The most prosperous farmers benefited most, but the act's Federal Surplus Commodities Corporation added an element of charity by issuing food stamps so that the poor could obtain surplus food. The AAA of 1938 brought stability to American agriculture and ample food to most—but not all—tables.

	Population (millions)	Gross Domestic Product (millions of dollars)
United States		
Britain		
British Colonies		
France		
French Colonies		
Italy		
Italian Colonies		
Netherlands		
Dutch Colonies		
USSR		
Japan		
Japanese Colonies		
Germany		
Austria		
Czechoslovakia		
Poland		
Hungary		
Yugoslavia		
Romania		

= 10 million people
= 10 million dollars

GLOBAL COMPARISON

National Populations and Economies, circa 1938

Throughout the Great Depression, the United States remained more productive than any other nation in the world. Despite the lingering effects of the depression, by 1938 the United States produced more than twice as much as Germany and the Soviet Union, nearly three times as much as Britain, more than four times as much as France and Japan, and more than five times as much as Italy. From the viewpoint of Germany, if the European nations listed here could be brought under German control, its economy would be greater than that of the United States and the mightiest in the world. Economically, how important were colonies to the major powers? In general, what do these data suggest about the relationship between population and gross domestic product?

| What were the goals and achievements of the first New Deal? | Who opposed the New Deal and why? | How did the second phase of the New Deal differ from the first? | Why did support for the New Deal decline in the late 1930s? | Conclusion: What were the achievements and limitations of the New Deal? |

683

Advocates for the urban poor also made modest gains after decades of neglect. New York senator Robert Wagner convinced Congress to pass the National Housing Act in 1937. By 1941, some 160,000 residences had been made available to poor people at affordable rents. The program did not come close to meeting the need for affordable housing, but for the first time, the federal government took an active role in providing decent urban housing.

The last major piece of New Deal labor legislation, the Fair Labor Standards Act of June 1938, reiterated the New Deal pledge to provide workers with a decent standard of living. After lengthy debate that revealed the waning strength of the New Deal, Congress finally agreed to intervene in the long-sacrosanct realm of worker contracts. The new law set wage and hours standards and at long last curbed the use of child labor. The minimum-wage level was modest—twenty-five cents an hour for a maximum of forty-four hours a week. And, in order to attract enough conservative votes, the act exempted merchant seamen, fishermen, domestic help, and farm laborers—relegating most women and African Americans to lower wages. Enforcement of the minimum-wage standards was weak and haphazard. Nevertheless, the Fair Labor Standards Act slowly advanced Roosevelt's inaugural promise to improve the living standards of the poorest Americans.

The final New Deal reform effort failed to make much headway against entrenched racial injustice. Although Roosevelt denounced lynching as murder, he would not jeopardize his vital base of white southern political support by demanding anti-lynching legislation, and Congress voted down attempts to make lynching a federal crime. Laws to eliminate the poll tax—used to deny blacks the opportunity to vote—encountered the same overwhelming resistance. The New Deal refused to confront racial injustice with the same vigor it brought to bear on economic hardship.

By the end of 1938, the New Deal had lost steam and encountered stiff opposition. In the congressional elections of 1938, Republicans made gains that gave them more congressional influence than they had enjoyed since 1932. New Dealers could claim unprecedented achievements since 1933, but nobody needed reminding that those achievements had not ended the depression. In his annual message to Congress in January 1939, Roosevelt signaled a halt to New Deal reforms by speaking about preserving the progress already achieved rather than extending it. Roosevelt pointed to the ominous threats posed by fascist aggressors in Germany and Japan, and he proposed defense expenditures that surpassed New Deal appropriations for relief and economic recovery.

QUICK REVIEW

How and why did political support for New Deal reforms decline?

CHAPTER LOCATOR

How did Franklin D. Roosevelt and the Democrats win the 1932 election?

Conclusion: What were the achievements and limitations of the New Deal?

THE NEW DEAL reflected Roosevelt's confidence, optimism, and energetic pragmatism. A growing majority of Americans agreed with Roosevelt that the federal government should help those in need, thereby strengthening the political coalition that propelled the New Deal. In the process of seeking relief for victims of the depression, recovery of the general economy, and basic reform of major economic institutions, the New Deal vastly expanded the size and influence of the federal government and changed the way the American people viewed Washington. New Dealers achieved significant victories, such as Social Security, labor's right to organize, and guarantees that farm prices would be maintained through controls on production and marketing. New Deal measures marked the emergence of a welfare state, but the New Deal's limited, two-tier character left many needy Americans with little aid.

Full-scale relief, recovery, and reform eluded New Deal programs, and in 1940 the depression still plagued the economy. The most durable New Deal achievements were reforms that stabilized agriculture, encouraged the organization of labor unions, and created the safety net of Social Security and fair labor standards. Perhaps the most impressive achievement of the New Deal was what did not happen. Although authoritarian governments and anticapitalist policies were common outside the United States during the 1930s, they were shunned by the New Deal coalition. Republicans and other conservatives claimed that the New Deal amounted to a form of socialism that threatened democracy and capitalism. But rather than attack capitalism and democracy, Franklin Roosevelt sought to save them, and he succeeded.

New Dealers repeatedly described their programs as a kind of warfare against the economic adversities of the 1930s. In the next decade, with the depression only partly vanquished, the Roosevelt administration had to turn from the New Deal's war against economic crisis at home to participate in a worldwide conflagration to defeat the enemies of democracy abroad.

SO NOW YOU KNOW

At the beginning of this chapter, you were asked if you knew that Social Security originated in the New Deal. Today, Social Security payments to elderly and dependent Americans account for over a third of federal government expenditures, all paid for by contributions from workers and their employers. Now that you've read the chapter, what have you learned about this program? What other New Deal programs had a long-term impact on American life?

| What were the goals and achievements of the first New Deal? | Who opposed the New Deal and why? | How did the second phase of the New Deal differ from the first? | Why did support for the New Deal decline in the late 1930s? | Conclusion: What were the achievements and limitations of the New Deal? |

685

CHAPTER 24 STUDY GUIDE

Online Study Guide
bedfordstmartins.com/roarkunderstanding

STEP 1 GETTING STARTED

Below are basic terms from this period in U.S. history. Can you identify each term below and explain why it matters? To do this exercise online or to download this chart, visit bedfordstmartins.com/roarkunderstanding.

TERM	WHO OR WHAT & WHEN	WHY IT MATTERS
Franklin D. Roosevelt, p. 660		
Great Depression, p. 661		
New Deal, p. 663		
Eleanor Roosevelt, p. 664		
Huey Long, p. 673		
Works Progress Administration, p. 675		
Wagner Act, p. 675		
"sit-down" strike, p. 676		
Social Security, p. 677		
Mary McLeod Bethune, p. 678		

STEP 2 MOVING BEYOND THE BASICS

The exercise below represents a more advanced understanding of the chapter material. Identify the following programs and legislation and decide if they were enacted to pursue the New Deal goal of relief, recovery, or reform. Describe each program and explain your reasoning for putting it into the appropriate category. Then determine the extent to which the program/legislation could be considered a success and why. To do this exercise online or to download this chart, visit bedfordstmartins.com/roarkunderstanding.

Program/legislation	Description	Relief, recovery, or reform?	How successful or unsuccessful was it?
Agricultural Adjustment Act			
Civilian Conservation Corps			
Emergency Banking Act			
Fair Labor Standards Act			
Federal Emergency Relief Administration			
Indian Reorganization Act			
National Recovery Administration			
National Youth Administration			
Public Works Administration			
Social Security Act			
Tennessee Valley Authority			
Works Progress Administration			

Now that you've reviewed various parts of the chapter, take a step back and try to see the big picture by answering these questions. Remember to use specific examples from the chapter in your answers. To do this exercise online, visit bedfordstmartins.com/roarkunderstanding.

FRANKLIN D. ROOSEVELT

▶ Why was Franklin Roosevelt so popular? Why did he win the elections of 1932 and 1936?

▶ How was Eleanor Roosevelt a part of her husband's political career?

THE NEW DEAL

▶ What were the greatest achievements of the New Deal, both generally and specifically?

▶ What were the differences between the first phase of the New Deal and the second?

LOOKING BACKWARD, LOOKING AHEAD

▶ What was distinctive about the New Deal compared with previous government reforms in the twentieth century?

▶ What was the long-term significance of the New Deal?

THE OPPOSITION

▶ Who initially opposed the New Deal and why?

▶ Why did general support for the New Deal decline?

IN YOUR OWN WORDS

Imagine that you must explain chapter 24 to someone who hasn't read it. What would be the most important points to include and why?

25
THE UNITED STATES AND THE SECOND WORLD WAR

1939–1945

> This chapter examines the involvement of the United States in World War II. It explores the events leading up to American entry into the war, the course of the war, the impact of the war on the home front, and the events that led to Allied victory.

DID YOU KNOW?

During World War II, military production in the United States was more than twice than that of Germany, Japan, and Italy combined.

> How did America respond to international developments in the 1930s?

> What led to the outbreak of war in Europe and the Pacific?

> How did the United States prepare for war?

> How did the Allies turn the tide in Europe and the Pacific?

> How did the war change life for Americans on the home front?

> How did the Allies achieve victory in World War II?

> Conclusion: Why did America emerge as a superpower at the end of the war?

Antiaircraft in Action. Noted American illustrator Dean Cornwell painted this scene for the U.S. Army.

How did America respond to international developments in the 1930s?

THE FIRST WORLD WAR left a dangerous and ultimately deadly legacy. The victors—especially Britain, France, and the United States—sought to avoid future wars at almost any cost. The defeated nations, as well as those that felt humiliated by the Versailles peace settlement—particularly Germany, Italy, and Japan— aspired to reassert their power and avenge their losses by means of renewed warfare. The aggressive, militaristic, antidemocratic regimes in Germany, Italy, and Japan seemed to most people in the United States during the 1930s a smaller threat than the economic crisis at home. Americans hoped to avoid entanglement in foreign woes and to concentrate on climbing out of the nation's economic abyss.

Roosevelt and Reluctant Isolation

Like most Americans during the 1930s, Franklin Roosevelt believed that the nation's highest priority was to attack the domestic causes and consequences of the depression. But Roosevelt had also long advocated an active role for the United States in international affairs. After World War I, Roosevelt embraced Woodrow Wilson's vision that the United States should take the lead in making the world "safe for democracy," and he continued to advocate American member- ship in the League of Nations during the isolationist 1920s.

The depression forced Roosevelt to retreat from his previous internationalism. During his 1932 presidential campaign, he pulled back from his endorsement of the League of Nations and reversed his previous support for forgiving European war debts. Once in office, Roosevelt sought to combine domestic economic recov- ery with a low-profile foreign policy that encouraged free trade and disarmament.

Roosevelt's pursuit of international amity was limited by economic circum- stances and American popular opinion. After an opinion poll demonstrated popular support for recognizing the Soviet Union, Roosevelt established formal diplomatic

CHAPTER LOCATOR | How did America respond to international developments in the 1930s? | What led to the outbreak of war in Europe and the Pacific?

CHAPTER 25
690 THE UNITED STATES AND THE SECOND WORLD WAR , 1939–1945

relations in 1933. But when the League of Nations condemned Japanese and German aggression, Roosevelt did not support the league's attempts to keep the peace because he feared jeopardizing isolationists' support for New Deal measures in Congress. America did nothing when Japan withdrew from the league and ignored the limitations on its navy imposed after World War I. The United States also looked the other way when Hitler rearmed Germany and recalled its representative to the league in 1933.

The Good Neighbor Policy

Under Franklin Roosevelt, the United States pursued "the policy of the good neighbor" in Latin America, where U.S. military forces had often intervened in local affairs. Reversing previous American policy, the Roosevelt administration asserted that no nation had the right to intervene in the internal or external affairs of another.

The good neighbor policy did not indicate a U.S. retreat from empire in Latin America. Instead, it declared that the United States would not depend on military force to exercise its influence in the region. Military nonintervention did not prevent the United States from exerting its economic influence in Latin America. In 1934, Congress passed the Reciprocal Trade Agreements Act, which gave the president the power to reduce tariffs on goods imported into the United States from nations that agreed to lower their own tariffs on U.S. exports. By 1940, twenty-two nations had agreed to reciprocal tariff reductions, helping to double U.S. exports to Latin America and contributing to the New Deal's goal of boosting the domestic economy through free trade. Although the economic power of the United States continued to overshadow that of its neighbors, the nonintervention policy planted seeds of friendship and hemispheric solidarity.

The Price of Noninvolvement

In Europe, **Adolf Hitler** rebuilt Germany's military strength, defying the terms of the Versailles peace treaty. Britain and France only made verbal protests. Emboldened, Hitler plotted to avenge defeat in World War I by recapturing territories with German inhabitants, all the while accusing Jews of polluting German purity. The venomous anti-Semitism of Hitler and his Nazi Party unified non-Jewish Germans and attracted sympathizers among many other Europeans, even in France and Britain, thereby weakening support for opposing Hitler or defending the Jews.

Across the Pacific, Japan invaded Manchuria in 1931 and planned to follow up with conquests extending throughout Southeast Asia. The Manchurian invasion bogged down in a long and vicious war when Chinese Nationalists rallied around their leader, Chiang Kai-shek, to fight against the Japanese. Preparations for new Japanese conquests continued, however. In 1936, Japan further violated naval limitation treaties by building a fleet designed to achieve naval superiority in the Pacific.

In the United States, the hostilities in Asia and Europe reinforced isolationist sentiments. Popular disillusionment with the failure of Woodrow Wilson's idealistic goals caused many Americans to question the nation's participation in World War I. In 1933, Gerald Nye, a Republican from North Dakota, chaired a Senate committee that investigated why the United States had gone to war in 1917. The Nye

CHRONOLOGY

1931
– Japan invades Manchuria.

1934
– Reciprocal Trade Agreements Act.

1935–1937
– Congress passes neutrality acts.

1936
– Nazi Germany occupies Rhineland.
– Italy conquers Ethiopia.
– Spanish civil war begins.
– Japan begins to expand naval power.

1937
– Japanese troops capture Nanking.
– Roosevelt introduces his quarantine policy.

Adolf Hitler

▶ Nazi dictator who led Germany during World War II. Hitler's territorial ambitions and racial theories led him to remilitarize Germany during the 1930s and start a general war in Europe in 1939. Hitler's forces were defeated by the Allies in 1945.

| How did the United States prepare for war? | How did the Allies turn the tide in Europe and the Pacific? | How did the war change life for Americans on the home front? | How did the Allies achieve victory in World War II? | Conclusion: Why did America emerge as a superpower at the end of the war? |

committee concluded that war profiteers had pushed America into war, and the committee's findings persuaded many Americans that it could happen again. International tensions and the Nye committee report prompted Congress to pass a series of neutrality acts between 1935 and 1937 designed to avoid entanglement in foreign wars. The neutrality acts prohibited making loans and selling arms to nations at war.

The Neutrality Act of 1937 attempted to reconcile the nation's desire for both peace and foreign trade with a "cash-and-carry" policy that required warring nations to pay cash for nonmilitary goods and to transport them in their own ships. This policy supported foreign trade and thereby benefited the nation's economy, but it also helped foreign aggressors by supplying them with goods and thereby undermining peace.

The desire for peace in France, Britain, and the United States led Germany, Italy, and Japan to launch military offensives on the assumption that the Western democracies lacked the will to oppose them. In March 1936, Nazi troops marched into the industry-rich Rhineland on Germany's western border, in blatant violation of the Treaty of Versailles. One month later, Italian armies completed their conquest of Ethiopia. In December 1937, Japanese invaders captured Nanking and celebrated their triumph in the "Rape of Nanking," a deadly rampage of murder, rape, and plunder that killed 200,000 Chinese civilians.

In Spain, a bitter civil war broke out in July 1936 when fascist rebels led by General Francisco Franco attacked the democratically elected Republican government. Both Germany and Italy reinforced Franco with soldiers, weapons, and aircraft, while the Soviet Union provided much less aid to the Republican Loyalists. Although individual Americans fought for the Loyalists in the Spanish civil war, neither the European democracies nor the U.S. government came to the Loyalists' aid, despite sympathizing with their cause. Abandoned by the Western nations, the Loyalists and their allies were defeated in 1939, and Franco built a fascist bulwark in southwestern Europe.

Hostilities in Europe, Africa, and Asia alarmed Roosevelt and other Americans. The president sought to persuade most Americans to moderate their isolationism (the desire to retreat from the world's conflicts) and find a way to support the victims of fascist aggression. Speaking in Chicago in October 1937, Roosevelt declared that the "epidemic of world lawlessness is spreading" and warned that "mere isolation or neutrality" offered no remedy for the "contagion" of war. Instead, he proposed that the United States "quarantine" aggressor nations and stop the spread of war's contagion.

Roosevelt's speech ignited a storm of protest from isolationists. The *Chicago Tribune* accused the president of seeking to replace "Americanism" with "internationalism." The strength of isolationism and the absence of congressional support for his quarantine policy disappointed Roosevelt, who remarked, "It's a terrible thing to look over your shoulder when you are trying to lead and find no one there." The popularity of isolationist sentiment convinced Roosevelt that he needed to maneuver carefully if the United States were to help prevent fascist aggressors from conquering Europe and Asia.

> **QUICK REVIEW**

How did isolationist sentiment constrain Roosevelt's foreign policy in the 1930s?

CHAPTER LOCATOR | How did America respond to international developments in the 1930s? | What led to the outbreak of war in Europe and the Pacific?

German Invasion of Poland

In 1940, German infantry reserves marched to the eastern front led by two officers on horseback. Although the German blitzkrieg massed thousands of tanks and aircraft at the front, German forces lacked sufficient trucks and other motorized vehicles to move soldiers and military supplies. The Germans' dependence on horse and foot travel limited the mobility of their troops compared with the more thoroughly motorized Allied armies. © Bettmann/Corbis.

What led to the outbreak of war in Europe and the Pacific?

BETWEEN 1939 AND 1941, fascist victories overseas eventually eroded American isolationism. Continuing German and Japanese aggression caused more and more Americans to believe that it was time for the nation to take a stand.

Nazi Aggression and War in Europe

Under the spell of isolationism, Americans passively watched Hitler's relentless campaign to dominate Europe. Hitler bullied Austria in 1938 into accepting incorporation—*Anschluss*—into the Nazi Third Reich. Next, Hitler turned his attention to Czechoslovakia's German-speaking Sudetenland. Hoping to avoid war, British prime minister Neville Chamberlain went to Munich, Germany, in September 1938 and offered Hitler terms of **appeasement** that would give the Sudetenland to Germany if Hitler agreed to leave the rest of Czechoslovakia alone. Hitler accepted Chamberlain's offer and promised that he would make no more territorial claims in Europe. But Hitler never intended to honor his promise. In March 1939, the German army conquered Czechoslovakia without firing a shot (**Map 25.1**).

In April 1939, Hitler demanded that Poland return the German territory it had been awarded after World War I. Recognizing that appeasement had failed, Britain and France assured Poland that they would go to war with Germany if Hitler launched an attack. In turn, Hitler negotiated with Soviet premier **Joseph Stalin**, offering him concessions in order to prevent the Soviet Union from joining Britain and France in opposing a German attack on Poland. Despite the enduring hatred between fascist Germany and the Communist Soviet Union, the two powers signed the Nazi-Soviet treaty of nonaggression in August 1939.

At dawn on September 1, 1939, Hitler unleashed his *blitzkrieg* (literally, "lightning war") on Poland. The attack triggered Soviet attacks on eastern Poland

appeasement
▶ British strategy aimed at avoiding a war with Germany in the late 1930s. British prime minister Neville Chamberlain believed that if concessions were offered to Hitler, peace in Europe could be maintained. The German conquest of Czechoslovakia and Poland proved Chamberlain wrong.

Joseph Stalin
▶ Soviet premier from 1922 to 1953. Despite a neutrality agreement that had allowed Germany and the Soviet Union to divide Poland in 1939, Germany invaded the Soviet Union in 1941. Under Stalin's leadership, Soviet forces stopped and then reversed Germany's advance, a defeat that played a crucial role in the ultimate Allied victory.

How did the United States prepare for war?	How did the Allies turn the tide in Europe and the Pacific?	How did the war change life for Americans on the home front?	How did the Allies achieve victory in World War II?	Conclusion: Why did America emerge as a superpower at the end of the war?

and declarations of war from France and Britain two days later. After the Nazis overran Poland, Hitler paused for a few months before launching a westward blitzkrieg. In April 1940, German forces smashed through Denmark and Norway. In May, Germany invaded the Netherlands, Belgium, Luxembourg, and France.

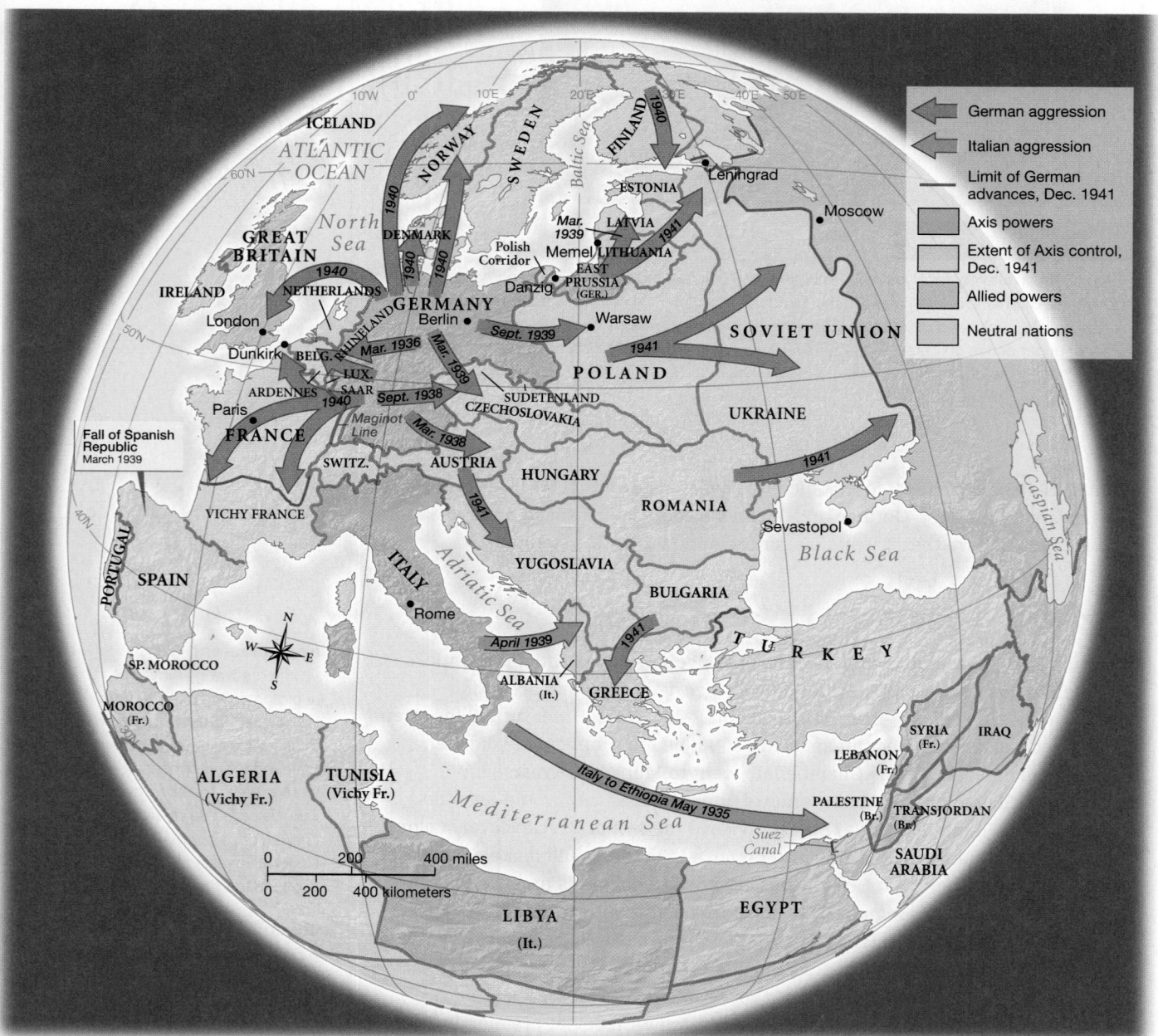

MAP 25.1 ■ Axis Aggression through 1941

For different reasons, Adolf Hitler and Benito Mussolini launched a series of surprise military strikes before 1942. Mussolini sought to re-create the Roman empire in the Mediterranean. Hitler struck to reclaim German territories occupied by France after World War I and to annex Austria. When the German dictator began his campaign to rule "inferior" peoples beyond Germany's border by attacking Poland, World War II broke out.

CHAPTER LOCATOR | How did America respond to international developments in the 1930s? | What led to the outbreak of war in Europe and the Pacific?

694 CHAPTER 25
THE UNITED STATES AND THE SECOND WORLD WAR , 1939–1945

The French believed that their Maginot Line, a concrete fortification built after World War I, would halt the German attack (see Map 25.1). But the Maginot Line did little to slow down Hitler's mechanized divisions, which wheeled around it and raced toward Paris.

The speed of the German attack trapped more than 300,000 British and French soldiers, who retreated to the French port of Dunkirk, where an improvised armada of British vessels hurriedly ferried them to safety across the English Channel. By mid-June 1940, France had signed an armistice that gave Germany control of the entire French coastline and nearly two-thirds of the countryside. A collaborationist French government was installed at Vichy in southern France. With an empire that stretched across Europe from Poland to France, Hitler seemed invincible as he poised to attack Britain.

The new British prime minister, **Winston Churchill**, vowed that Britain, unlike France, would never surrender to Hitler. "We shall fight on the seas and oceans [and] . . . in the air," he proclaimed, "whatever the cost may be, we shall fight on the beaches, . . . and in the fields and in the streets." Beginning in mid-June 1940, wave after wave of German bombers targeted British military installations and cities, killing tens of thousands of civilians. The undermanned and outgunned Royal Air Force fought as doggedly as Churchill had predicted and finally won the **Battle of Britain** by November, handing Hitler his first defeat. Victorious in the air, Britain was battered and exhausted and could not hold out for long without American help, as Churchill repeatedly wrote Roosevelt in private.

From Neutrality to the Arsenal of Democracy

When the Nazi attack on Poland ignited the war in Europe, Roosevelt issued an official proclamation of American neutrality. Most Americans condemned German aggression and favored Britain and France, but isolationism remained powerful. Roosevelt feared that if Congress did not repeal the arms embargo mandated by the Neutrality Act of 1937, France and Britain would soon succumb to the Nazis. After heated debate, Congress voted in November 1939 to revise the neutrality legislation and allow belligerent nations to buy arms, as well as nonmilitary supplies, on a cash-and-carry basis.

In practice, the revised neutrality law permitted Britain and France to purchase American war materiel and carry it across the Atlantic in their own ships, thereby shielding American vessels from attack. Roosevelt wrote a friend, "What worries me is that public opinion . . . is patting itself on the back every morning and thanking God for the Atlantic Ocean (and the Pacific Ocean)" and underestimating "the serious implications" of the European war "for our own future." Roosevelt searched for a way to aid Britain short of entering a formal alliance or declaring war against Germany. By late summer in 1940, Roosevelt concocted a scheme to deliver fifty old destroyers to Britain in exchange for American access to British bases in the Western Hemisphere. With this swap, Roosevelt took the first steps toward building a firm Anglo-American alliance against Hitler.

Roosevelt decided to run for an unprecedented third term as president in 1940. He hoped to woo voters away from their complacent isolationism to back the nation's international interests as well as New Deal reforms. But the presidential election, which Roosevelt won handily over Republican Wendell Willkie, provided no clear mandate for American involvement in the European war. Once reelected,

CHRONOLOGY

1938
- Germany annexes Austria.

1939
- German troops occupy Czechoslovakia.
- Nazi-Soviet nonaggression pact.
- **September 1.** Germany's attack on Poland begins World War II.

1940
- Germany invades Denmark, Norway, France, Belgium, Luxembourg, and the Netherlands.
- British and French evacuation from Dunkirk.
- Vichy government is installed in France.
- Battle of Britain.
- Japan, Germany, and Italy sign Tripartite Pact.

1941 Lend-Lease Act
- **June.** Germany invades Soviet Union.
- **August.** Roosevelt and Churchill issue Atlantic Charter.
- **December 7.** Japanese attack Pearl Harbor.

Winston Churchill
▶ British prime minister from 1940 to 1945, and again from 1951 to 1955. A bitter opponent of Neville Chamberlain's policy of appeasement before the war, Churchill led the British resistance to Nazi domination of Europe. As one of the "Big Three," along with Roosevelt and Stalin, Churchill participated in negotiations that shaped the postwar world.

Battle of Britain
▶ Battle for air supremacy over Britain. Starting in June 1940, in preparation for an invasion, the German air force bombed British military installations and cities, killing tens of thousands of civilians. British victory in the Battle of Britain stalled Hitler's invasion plans.

How did the United States prepare for war?	How did the Allies turn the tide in Europe and the Pacific?	How did the war change life for Americans on the home front?	How did the Allies achieve victory in World War II?	Conclusion: Why did America emerge as a superpower at the end of the war?

Roosevelt maneuvered to support Britain in every way short of war. In a fireside chat shortly after Christmas 1940, he proclaimed that it was incumbent on the United States to become "the great arsenal of democracy" and send "every ounce and every ton of munitions and supplies that we can possibly spare to help the defenders who are in the front lines."

In January 1941, Roosevelt proposed the Lend-Lease Act, which allowed the British to obtain arms from the United States without paying cash but with the promise to reimburse the United States when the war ended. The purpose of Lend-Lease, Roosevelt proclaimed, was to defend democracy and human rights throughout the world, specifically the Four Freedoms: "freedom of speech and expression . . . freedom of every person to worship God in his own way . . . freedom from want . . . [and] freedom from fear." Congress passed the Lend-Lease Act in March 1941 and started a flood of supplies to Britain that persisted throughout the war.

Stymied in his plans for an invasion of England, Hitler turned his army eastward and on June 22, 1941, launched a surprise attack on the Soviet Union. Neither Roosevelt nor Churchill had any love for Joseph Stalin or communism, but they both welcomed the Soviet Union to the anti-Nazi cause. Both Western leaders understood that Hitler's attack on Russia would provide relief for the hard-pressed British. Roosevelt quickly persuaded Congress to extend Lend-Lease to the Soviet Union, beginning the shipment of millions of tons of trucks, jeeps, and other equipment that, in all, supplied about 10 percent of Russian war materiel.

As Hitler's Wehrmacht (army) raced across the Russian plains and Nazi U-boats tried to choke off supplies to Britain and the Soviet Union, Roosevelt met with Churchill aboard a ship near Newfoundland to cement the Anglo-American alliance. In August 1941, the two leaders issued the Atlantic Charter, pledging the two nations to freedom of the seas and free trade as well as the right of national self-determination.

Japan Attacks America

Hitler exercised a measure of restraint by not provoking America directly. In contrast, Japanese ambitions in Asia clashed more openly with American interests and commitments, especially in China and the Philippines. And unlike Hitler, the Japanese high command planned to attack the United States if necessary to pursue Japan's aspirations to rule an Asian empire it termed the Greater East Asia Co-Prosperity Sphere. Appealing to widespread Asian bitterness toward such white colonial powers as the British in India and Burma, the French in Indochina (now Vietnam), and the Dutch in the East Indies (now Indonesia), the Japanese campaigned to preserve "Asia for the Asians." Japan's invasion of China—which had lasted for ten years by 1941—proved that its true goal was Asia for the Japanese (**Map 25.2**). Japan coveted the raw materials available from China and Southeast Asia and ignored American demands to stop its campaign of aggression.

In 1940, Japan signaled a new phase of its imperial designs by entering a defensive alliance with Germany and Italy—the Tripartite Pact. In 1941, U.S. naval intelligence learned that Tokyo also planned to invade the resource-rich Dutch East Indies. To thwart these plans, in July 1941 Roosevelt announced a trade embargo that denied Japan access to oil, scrap iron, and other goods essential for its war machines.

CHAPTER LOCATOR | How did America respond to international developments in the 1930s? | What led to the outbreak of war in Europe and the Pacific?

CHAPTER 25
696 THE UNITED STATES AND THE SECOND WORLD WAR , 1939–1945

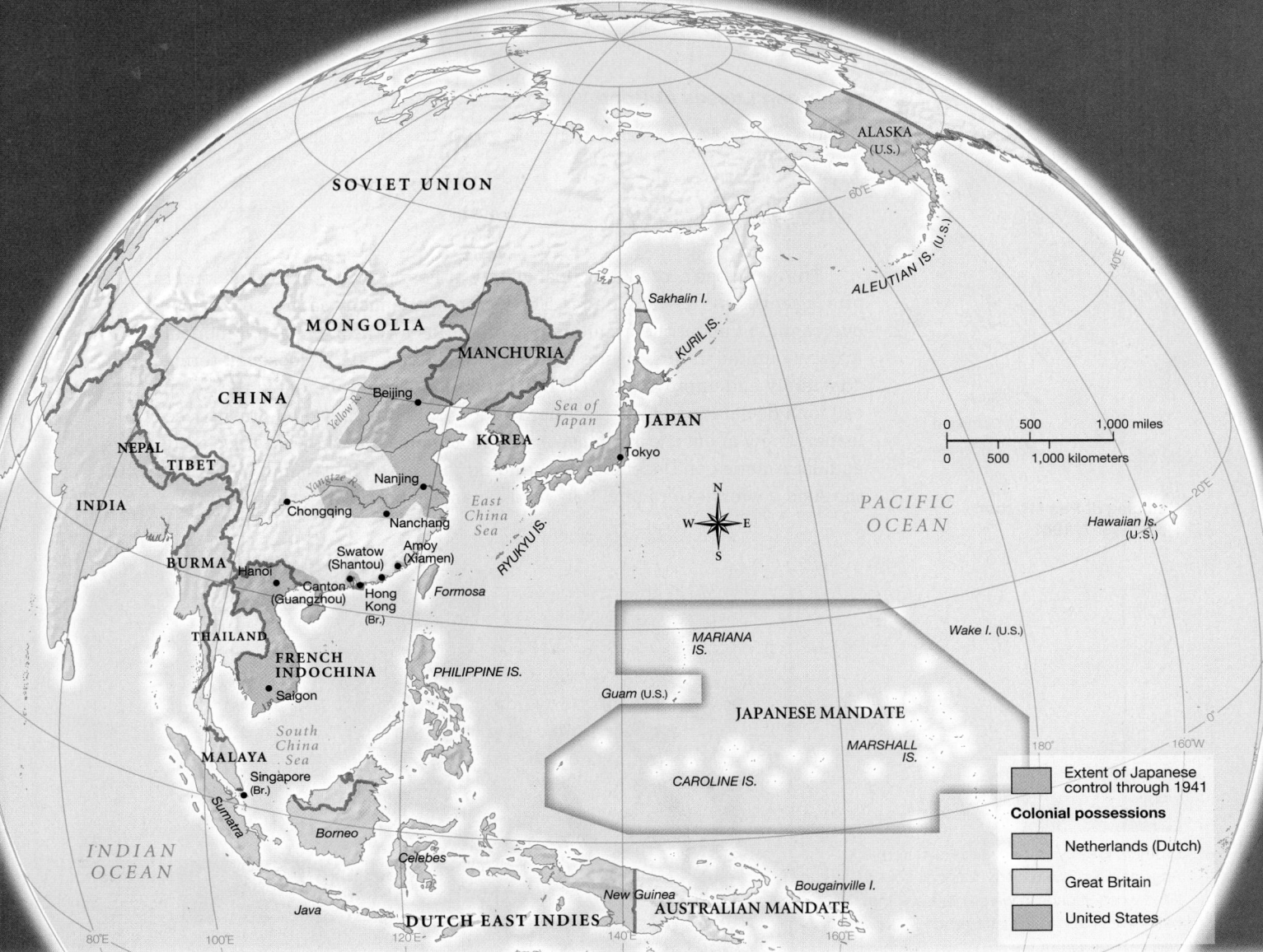

MAP 25.2 ■ Japanese Aggression through 1941
Beginning with the invasion of Manchuria in 1931, Japan sought to extend its imperialist control over most of East Asia. Japanese aggression was driven by the need for raw materials for the country's expanding industries and by the military government's devotion to martial honor.

The American embargo played into the hands of Japanese militarists headed by General Hideki Tojo, who seized control of the government in October 1941 and persuaded other leaders, including Emperor Hirohito, that swift destruction of American naval bases in the Pacific would leave Japan free to expand its empire. On December 7, 1941, Japanese aircraft attacked the U.S. Pacific Fleet at **Pearl Harbor** on the Hawaiian island of Oahu. The devastating attack almost crippled U.S. war-making capacity in the Pacific. Luckily for the United States, Japanese pilots failed to destroy the vital machine shops and oil storage facilities at Pearl Harbor, and none of the nation's aircraft carriers happened to be in port at the time of the attack.

Pearl Harbor

▶ Surprise attack by the Japanese on the U.S. fleet based in Hawaii on December 7, 1941. The attack brought America into the war against both Japan and Germany. The Japanese scored a tactical victory at Pearl Harbor, but in the long run, the attack proved a colossal blunder.

How did the United States prepare for war?	How did the Allies turn the tide in Europe and the Pacific?	How did the war change life for Americans on the home front?	How did the Allies achieve victory in World War II?	Conclusion: Why did America emerge as a superpower at the end of the war?

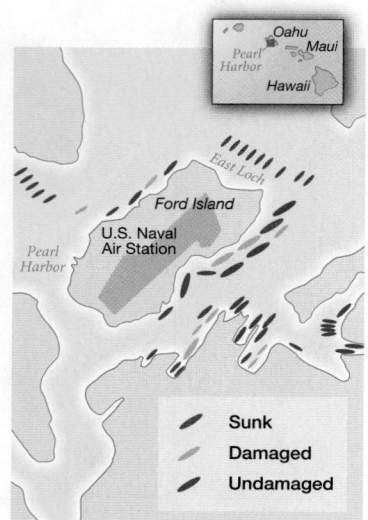

Bombing of Pearl Harbor,
December 7, 1941

Sunk
Damaged
Undamaged

American Losses at Pearl Harbor

Eighteen ships sunk or disabled, including all of the fleet's battleships.

2,400 Americans killed.

1,000 Americans wounded.

The Japanese scored a tactical victory at Pearl Harbor, but in the long run, the attack proved a colossal blunder. The victory made many Japanese commanders overconfident about their military power. Worse for the Japanese, Americans instantly united in their desire to avenge the attack, which Roosevelt termed "dastardly and unprovoked." On December 8, Congress endorsed the president's call for a declaration of war. Neither Hitler nor Benito Mussolini, Italy's fascist leader, knew about the Japanese attack in advance, but they both declared war against America on December 11, bringing the United States into all-out war with the Axis powers—Germany, Italy, and Japan—in both Europe and Asia.

Pearl Harbor Attack

Brothers Wesley and Edward Heidt from Los Angeles were one of thirty-four pairs of brothers killed when Japanese warplanes sank the battleship *Arizona* at Pearl Harbor. This pennant was salvaged from the ship's wreckage. Also included here is the official telegram informing the Heidt brothers' mother that her sons "lost their life in the service of their country." U.S.S. *Arizona* Memorial, Hawaii, National Park Service/photos by Douglas Peebles.

▶ FOR MORE HELP ANALYZING THIS IMAGE, see the visual activity for this chapter in the Online Study Guide at bedfordstmartins.com/roarkunderstanding.

> ## QUICK REVIEW

How did Roosevelt respond to the outbreak of war in Europe?

CHAPTER LOCATOR | How did America respond to international developments in the 1930s? | What led to the outbreak of war in Europe and the Pacific?

698 CHAPTER 25 THE UNITED STATES AND THE SECOND WORLD WAR , 1939–1945

African American Machine Gunners These African American soldiers prepare their machine gun for action on the side of a road near Pisa, Italy, in September 1944. They and other black soldiers who served in combat in segregated units repeatedly earned praise from their commanders for gallantry and courage under fire. As a Mississippi-born African American veteran of the Pacific theater recalled, "We had two wars to fight: prejudice . . . and those Japs." © Bettmann/Corbis.

How did the United States prepare for war?

THE TIME HAD COME, Roosevelt announced, for the prescriptions of "Dr. New Deal" to be replaced by the stronger medicines of "Dr. Win-the-War." Under Roosevelt's direction, military and civilian leaders rushed to secure the nation against possible attacks, to enlist millions of Americans in the armed forces, and to transform the American economy into the world's greatest military machine.

Home-Front Security

Shortly after declaring war against the United States, Hitler dispatched German submarines to hunt American ships along the Atlantic coast. The U-boats had devastating success for about eight months, sinking hundreds of U.S. ships and threatening to disrupt the Lend-Lease lifeline to Britain and the Soviet Union. But by mid-1942, the U.S. Navy had chased German submarines away from the East Coast and into the mid-Atlantic, reducing the direct threat to the nation.

Within the continental United States, Americans remained sheltered from the chaos and destruction the war was bringing to hundreds of millions in Europe and Asia. Nevertheless, the government worried constantly about espionage and

| How did the United States prepare for war? | How did the Allies turn the tide in Europe and the Pacific? | How did the war change life for Americans on the home front? | How did the Allies achieve victory in World War II? | Conclusion: Why did America emerge as a superpower at the end of the war? |

699

CHRONOLOGY

1940
- Congress passes the Selective Service Act to register men of military age for the draft.

1942
- U.S. economy rebounds as a result of defense spending.
- President Roosevelt orders the internment of Japanese Americans living in the West.

internal subversion. Billboards and posters warned Americans that "Enemy agents are always near; if you don't talk, they won't hear." The campaign for patriotic vigilance focused on German and Japanese foes, but Americans of Japanese descent became targets of official and popular persecution because of Pearl Harbor and long-standing racial prejudice against people of Asian descent.

About 320,000 people of Japanese descent lived in U.S. territory in 1941, two-thirds of them in Hawaii, where they largely escaped wartime persecution because they were essential and valued members of society. On the mainland, however, Japanese Americans were a tiny minority subject to frenzied wartime suspicions and persecution. Although an official military survey concluded that Japanese Americans posed no danger, popular hostility fueled a campaign to round up all mainland Japanese Americans—two-thirds of them U.S. citizens. "A Jap's a Jap. . . . It makes no difference whether he is an American citizen or not," one official declared.

On February 19, 1942, Roosevelt issued Executive Order 9066, which authorized sending all Americans of Japanese descent to ten makeshift internment camps located in remote areas of the West (**Map 25.3**). Allowed little time to secure or sell their property, Japanese Americans lost homes and businesses worth about $400 million and lived out the war penned in by barbed wire and armed guards. Although several thousand Japanese Americans served with distinction in the U.S. armed forces and no case of subversion by a Japanese American was ever uncovered, the Supreme Court, in its 1944 *Korematsu* decision, declared that Executive Order 9066's violation of constitutional rights was justified by "military necessity."

Building a Citizen Army

In 1940, Congress passed the Selective Service Act to register men of military age for a draft. In all, more than 16 million men and women served in uniform during the war, two-thirds of them draftees, mostly young men. Women were barred from combat duty, but they worked at nearly every noncombatant task, eroding traditional barriers to women's military service.

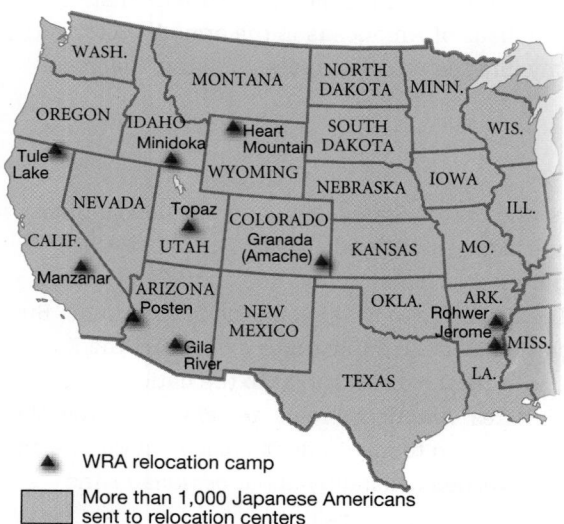

MAP 25.3 ■ Western Relocation Authority Centers

Responding to prejudice and fear of sabotage, President Roosevelt authorized the roundup and relocation of all Americans of Japanese descent in 1942. Taken from their homes in the cities and fertile farmland of the far West, Japanese Americans were confined in desolate camps scattered as far east as the Mississippi River.

▲ WRA relocation camp

More than 1,000 Japanese Americans sent to relocation centers

CHAPTER LOCATOR | How did America respond to international developments in the 1930s? | What led to the outbreak of war in Europe and the Pacific?

CHAPTER 25
700 THE UNITED STATES AND THE SECOND WORLD WAR , 1939–1945

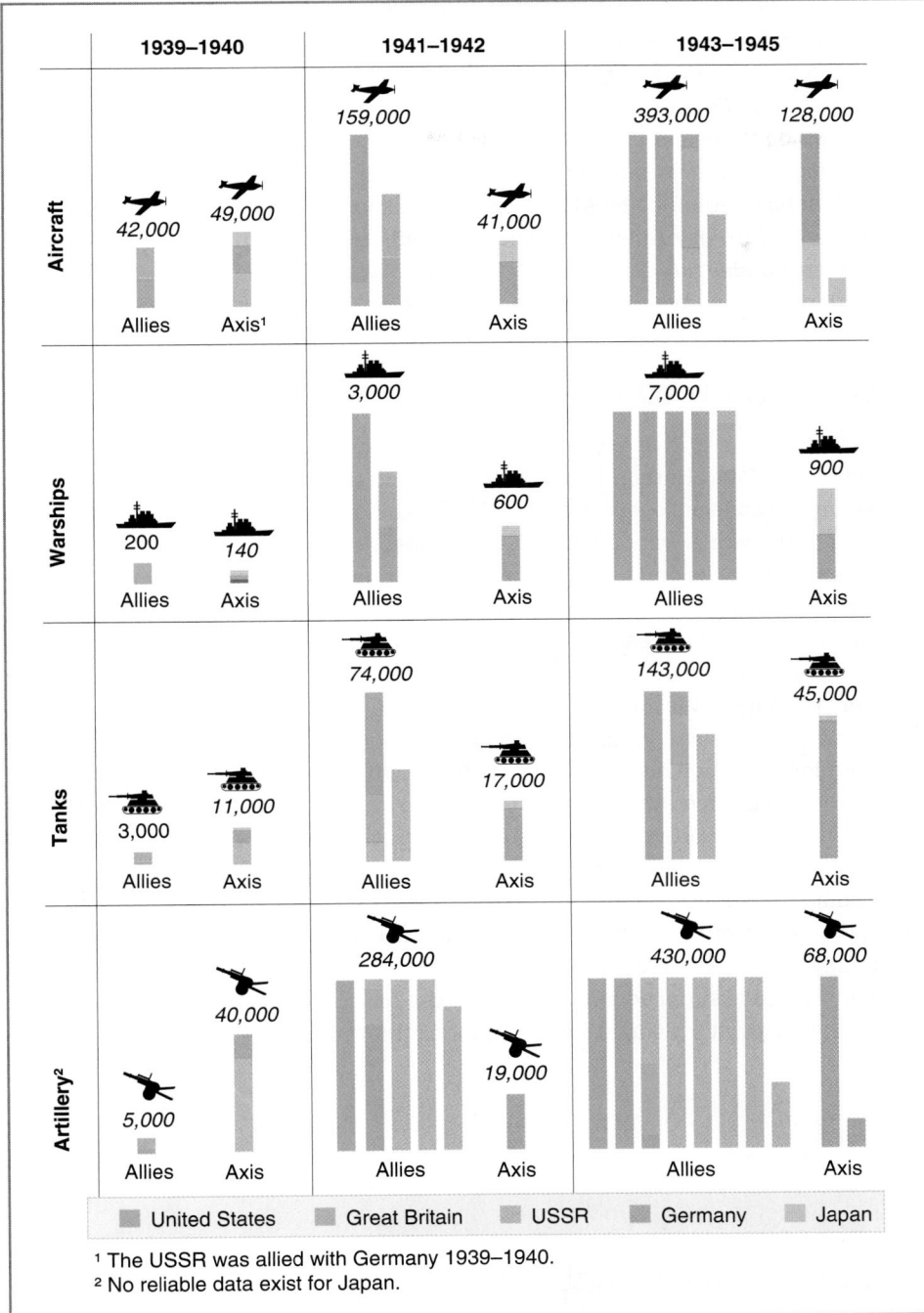

Weapons Production by the Axis and Allied Powers during World War II

This chart demonstrates the massive contribution of the United States to Allied weapons production during World War II. In the air and on the sea, U.S. weapons predominated, after 1940 accounting for more aircraft and many more warships than Britain and the Soviet Union combined. Together, the three Allied powers produced about three times as many aircraft and five to eight times as many warships as the two Axis powers. On the ground, the Soviet Union led the other Allies in the production of tanks and artillery, an outgrowth of the colossal battles on the eastern front. Overall, the Allies produced almost three times as many tanks as the Axis powers and more than seven times as many artillery pieces as Germany (no figures are available for Japan). What do these data suggest about the significance of America's entry into the war in December 1941? What do they suggest about the kind of warfare emphasized by each of the belligerents? What do they suggest about the chronology of weapons production during the war?

Legend: United States | Great Britain | USSR | Germany | Japan

[1] The USSR was allied with Germany 1939–1940.
[2] No reliable data exist for Japan.

The Selective Service Act prohibited discrimination "on account of race or color," and almost a million African Americans donned uniforms, as did half a million Mexican Americans, 25,000 Native Americans, and 13,000 Chinese Americans. The abuse and discrimination suffered by all people of color made some soldiers ask, as a Mexican American GI did on his way to the European front, "Why fight for America when you have not been treated as an American?" Only black Americans were trained in segregated camps, confined in segregated barracks,

How did the United States prepare for war?	How did the Allies turn the tide in Europe and the Pacific?	How did the war change life for Americans on the home front?	How did the Allies achieve victory in World War II?	Conclusion: Why did America emerge as a superpower at the end of the war?

and assigned to segregated units. Most black Americans were consigned to manual labor, and relatively few served in combat until late in 1944, when the need for military manpower in Europe intensified. Then, as General George Patton told black soldiers in a tank unit in Normandy, "I don't care what color you are, so long as you go up there and kill those Kraut sonsabitches."

Homosexuals also served in the armed forces, although in much smaller numbers than black Americans. Allowed to serve as long as their sexual preferences remained covert, gay Americans, like other minorities, sought to demonstrate their worth under fire. As a gay GI remarked, "Who in the hell is going to worry about [homosexuality]" in the midst of the life-or-death realities of war?

Conversion to a War Economy

In 1940, the American economy remained mired in the depression. Shortly after the attack on Pearl Harbor, Roosevelt announced the goal of converting the economy to produce "overwhelming . . . , crushing superiority of equipment in any theater of the world war." Factories were converted from making passenger cars to assembling tanks and airplanes, and production soared to record levels. By the end of the war, jobs exceeded workers, plants operated at full capacity, and the federal budget had increased tenfold to $100 billion.

To organize and oversee military production, Roosevelt called upon business leaders to come to Washington and head new government agencies such as the War Production Board, which, among other things, set production priorities and pushed for maximum output. Contracts flowed to large corporations, often on a basis that guaranteed their profits. During the first half of 1942, the government issued contracts worth more than the entire gross national product in 1941.

Overall, conversion to war production achieved Roosevelt's ambitious goal of "crushing superiority" in military goods. At a total cost of $304 billion during the war, the nation produced more than double the combined military output of Germany, Japan, and Italy. (See "Global Comparison," page 701.) This outpouring of military goods supplied not only U.S. forces but also America's allies, making good on Roosevelt's pledge to make America the "arsenal of democracy."

> **QUICK REVIEW**

How did the Roosevelt administration mobilize the human and industrial resources necessary to fight a two-front war?

CHAPTER LOCATOR | How did America respond to international developments in the 1930s? | What led to the outbreak of war in Europe and the Pacific?

CHAPTER 25
702 THE UNITED STATES AND THE SECOND WORLD WAR , 1939–1945

How did the Allies turn the tide in Europe and the Pacific?

Marine Pinned Down on Saipan Over 100,000 American GIs assaulted the Japanese garrison on Saipan in the Mariana Islands in June 1944. The battle lasted nearly a month and inflicted 14,000 casualties on American troops. The intensity of the fighting is visible on the face of the marine shown here. The suicidal defenses of the Japanese in Saipan persuaded American military planners that the final assault on the Japanese homeland would cause hundreds of thousands of American casualties. Marine Corps Photo, National Archives.

THE UNITED STATES CONFRONTED a daunting military challenge in December 1941. The attack on Pearl Harbor destroyed much of its Pacific Fleet, crippling the nation's ability to defend against Japan's offensive throughout the southern Pacific. In the Atlantic, Hitler's U-boats sank American ships, while German armies occupied most of western Europe and relentlessly advanced eastward into the Soviet Union. To fight back effectively against Germany and Japan, the United States had to coordinate military and political strategy with its allies and muster all its human and economic assets. But in 1941, nobody knew whether that would be enough.

Turning the Tide in the Pacific

In the Pacific theater, Japan's leading military strategist, Admiral Isoroku Yamamoto, believed that if his forces did not quickly conquer and secure the territories they targeted, Japan would eventually lose the war as a result of America's far greater resources. Swiftly, the Japanese assaulted American airfields in the Philippines and captured U.S. outposts on Guam and Wake Island. Singapore, the British naval base in Malaya, surrendered to the Japanese in February 1942, and most of Burma had fallen by March. All that stood in the way of Japan's domination of the southern Pacific was the American stronghold in the Philippines.

The Japanese unleashed an assault against the Philippines in January 1942 (see Map 25.5, page 715). American defenders surrendered to the Japanese in May, and the Japanese marched captured American and Filipino soldiers to a concentration camp. Thousands died during the Bataan Death March, and 16,000 more perished in the camp. By the summer of 1942, the Japanese had conquered the oil-rich Dutch East Indies and were poised to strike Australia and New Zealand.

| How did the United States prepare for war? | **How did the Allies turn the tide in Europe and the Pacific?** | How did the war change life for Americans on the home front? | How did the Allies achieve victory in World War II? | Conclusion: Why did America emerge as a superpower at the end of the war? |

CHRONOLOGY

1942
- Japan captures the Philippines.
- Battles of Coral Sea and Midway.
- **November.** U.S. forces invade North Africa.

1943
- Allied leaders meeting at Casablanca demand unconditional surrender of Axis powers.
- U.S. and British forces invade Sicily.
- U.S. and British forces take control of the Atlantic.

1944
- **June.** Allies liberate Rome.

Battle of Midway

▶ June 3–6, 1942, naval battle in the Central Pacific between American and Japanese forces. When an intelligence intercept tipped off the Americans that the Japanese were massing an invasion force aimed at Midway Island, Admiral Nimitz maneuvered U.S. ships into the Central Pacific to surprise the Japanese. American victory in the Battle of Midway reversed the balance of naval power in the Pacific and put the Japanese at a disadvantage for the rest of the war.

In the spring of 1942, U.S. forces launched a major two-pronged counteroffensive. Forces led by General Douglas MacArthur moved north from Australia and attacked the Japanese in the Philippines. Far more decisively, Admiral Chester W. Nimitz sailed his fleet west from Hawaii to retake Japanese-held islands in the mid-Pacific. On May 7–8, 1942, in the Coral Sea just north of Australia, the American fleet and carrier-based warplanes defeated a Japanese armada that was sailing around the coast of New Guinea.

Nimitz then learned from an intelligence intercept that the Japanese were massing an invasion force aimed at Midway Island, an outpost guarding the Hawaiian Islands. Nimitz maneuvered his ships into the Central Pacific to surprise the Japanese. In a furious battle that raged on June 3–6, American ships and planes delivered a devastating blow to the Japanese navy. The **Battle of Midway** reversed the balance of naval power in the Pacific and put the Japanese at a disadvantage for the rest of the war. But the Japanese still occupied and defended the many places they had conquered.

The Campaign in Europe

In early 1942, Hitler's eastern-front armies marched ever deeper into the Soviet Union while his western-front forces prepared to invade Britain. As in World War I, the Germans attempted to starve the British into submission by destroying their seaborne lifeline. In 1941 and 1942, German U-boats sank Allied ships faster than new ones could be built.

The Toll of the U-Boat Campaign

4,700 merchant vessels sunk.
200 warships sunk.
40,000 Allied seamen killed.

Until mid-1943, the outcome of the war in the Atlantic remained in doubt. Then, newly invented radar detectors and production of sufficient destroyer escorts for merchant vessels allowed the Allies to prey upon the U-boats. After suffering a 75 percent casualty rate among U-boat crews, Hitler withdrew German submarines from the North Atlantic in late May 1943. Winning the battle of the Atlantic allowed the United States to continue to supply its British and Soviet allies for the duration of the war and to reduce the imminent threat of a German invasion of Britain.

The most important strategic questions confronting the Allies were when and where to open a second front against the Nazis. Stalin demanded that America and Britain mount an immediate and massive assault across the English Channel into western France to relieve the pressure on the Soviet Union. Churchill and Roosevelt promised Stalin that they would open a second front, but they decided to strike first in southern Europe and the Mediterranean, a region of long-standing British influence.

In October and November 1942, British forces at El-Alamein in Egypt halted German general Erwin Rommel's drive to capture the Suez Canal, Britain's lifeline to the oil of the Middle East and to British colonies in India and South Asia (**Map 25.4**).

CHAPTER LOCATOR | How did America respond to international developments in the 1930s? | What led to the outbreak of war in Europe and the Pacific?

CHAPTER 25

704 THE UNITED STATES AND THE SECOND WORLD WAR , 1939–1945

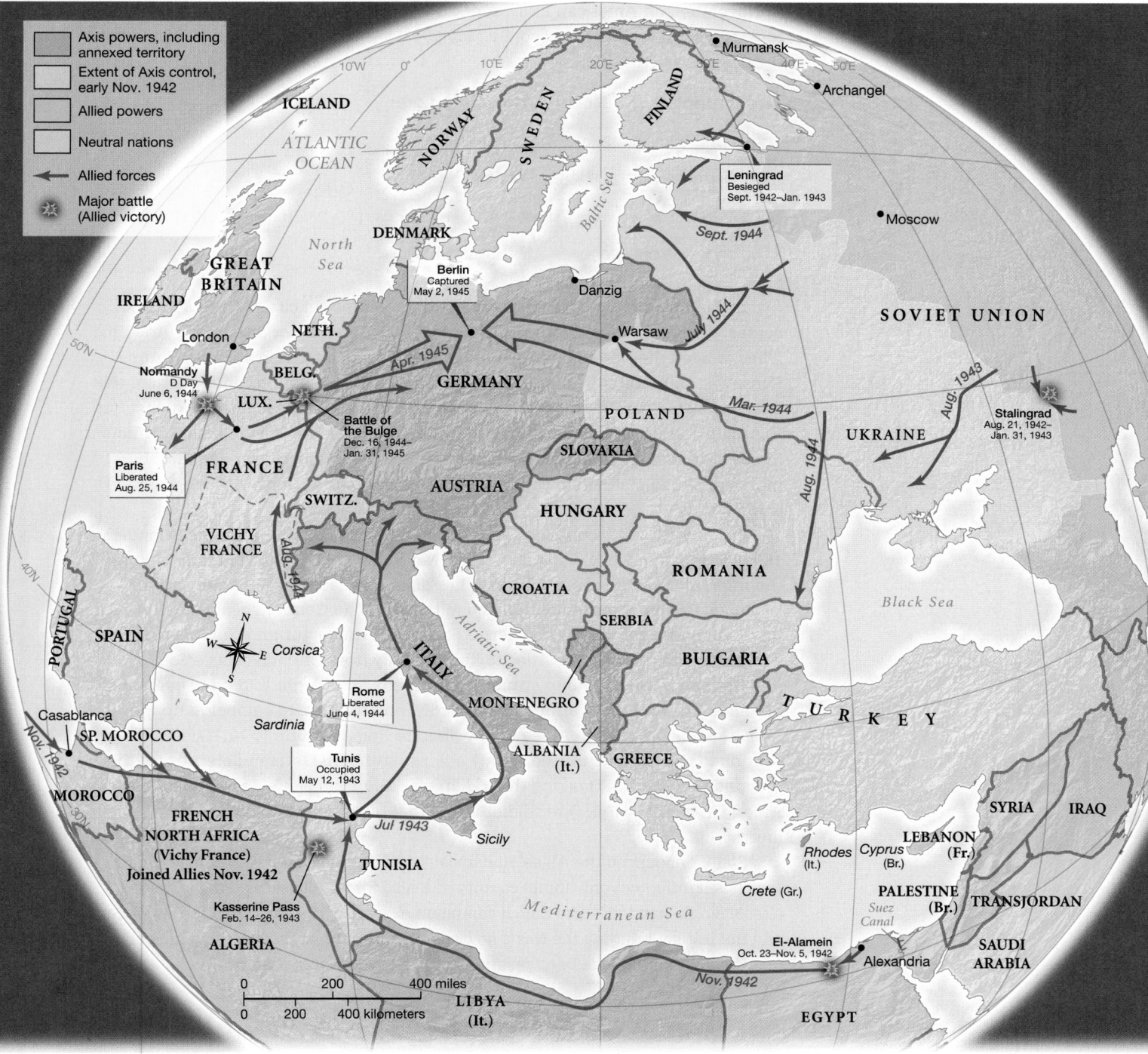

MAP 25.4 ■ The European Theater of World War II, 1942–1945
The Russian reversal of the German offensive at Stalingrad and Leningrad, combined with Allied landings in North Africa and Normandy, trapped Germany in a closing vise of Allied armies on all sides.

▶ FOR MORE HELP ANALYZING THIS MAP, see the map activity for this chapter in the Online Study Guide at bedfordstmartins.com/roarkunderstanding.

How did the United States prepare for war?	How did the Allies turn the tide in Europe and the Pacific?	How did the war change life for Americans on the home front?	How did the Allies achieve victory in World War II?	Conclusion: Why did America emerge as a superpower at the end of the war?

In November, an American army under General Dwight D. Eisenhower landed far to the west, in French Morocco. By May 1943, the Allied armies had defeated the Germans in North Africa.

The Impact of the North Africa Campaign

350,000 Axis soldiers were killed or captured.
The Germans were pushed out of Africa.
The Mediterranean was made safe for Allied shipping.
The door was opened for an Allied invasion of Italy.

In January 1943, Roosevelt traveled to the Moroccan city of Casablanca to confer with Churchill and other Allied leaders. Stalin did not attend but urged his allies to keep their promise of opening a major second front in western Europe. Roosevelt and Churchill announced that they would accept nothing less than the "unconditional surrender" of the Axis powers, ruling out peace negotiations. But Churchill and Roosevelt concluded that they needed more time to amass sufficient forces for the cross-Channel invasion of France that Stalin demanded. In the meantime, they planned to capitalize on their success in North Africa and strike against Italy.

On July 10, 1943, combined American and British amphibious forces landed 160,000 troops in Sicily. Soon afterward, Mussolini was deposed in Italy, ending the reign of Italian fascism. Quickly, the Allies invaded the mainland, and the Italian government surrendered unconditionally. The Germans responded by rushing reinforcements to Italy and seizing control of Rome, turning the Allies' Italian campaign into a series of battles to liberate Italy from German occupation.

German troops dug into strong fortifications and fought to defend every inch of Italian territory. Only after a long, deadly, and frustrating campaign up the Italian peninsula did the Allies finally liberate Rome in June 1944. Allied forces continued to push into northern Italy against stubborn German defenses for the remainder of the war, making the Italian campaign the war's deadliest for American infantrymen. One soldier wrote that his buddies "died like butchered swine."

Stalin denounced the Allies' Italian campaign because it left "the Soviet Army, which is fighting not only for its country, but also for its Allies, to do the job alone, almost single-handed." The Italian campaign exacted a high cost from the Americans and the British, bringing the Nazis no closer to surrender and consuming men and materiel that might have been reserved for a second front in France.

> **QUICK REVIEW**

How did the United States seek to counter the Japanese in the Pacific and the Germans in Europe?

CHAPTER LOCATOR | How did America respond to international developments in the 1930s? | What led to the outbreak of war in Europe and the Pacific?

706 CHAPTER 25 THE UNITED STATES AND THE SECOND WORLD WAR , 1939–1945

How did the war change life for Americans on the home front?

Pitching in at Home

This poster encourages women and children to contribute to the war effort by collecting scrap metal for recycling into weaponry. The poster highlights the middle-class prosperity of the war years, a sharp contrast to the hard times of the 1930s. Chicago Historical Society.

▶ FOR MORE HELP ANALYZING THIS IMAGE, see the visual activity for this chapter in the Online Study Guide at bedfordstmartins.com/roarkunderstanding.

THE WAR EFFORT MOBILIZED Americans as never before. Ever-increasing wartime production drew workers, both men and women, from small towns and farms to America's cities. Despite rationing and shortages, unprecedented government expenditures for war production brought prosperity to many Americans after years of depression-era poverty. The wartime ideology of human rights provided justification for the many sacrifices Americans were required to make in support of the military effort. It also established a standard of basic human equality that became a potent weapon in the campaign for equal rights at home and against the atrocities of the Holocaust perpetrated by the Nazis.

1941
- African Americans call for a Double V campaign.
- Threat of a march on Washington by African Americans leads Roosevelt to issue Executive Order 8802.

1942
- Congress of Racial Equality is founded.

1943
- 242 race riots erupt in 47 American cities.
- Zoot suit riots in Los Angeles.

1944
- GI Bill of Rights.
- Roosevelt is reelected.

1945
- Soviet troops liberate Auschwitz concentration camp.

Women and Families, Guns and Butter

Millions of American women took their places on assembly lines in defense industries. At the start of the war, about a quarter of adult women worked outside the home, most as teachers, nurses, social workers, and domestic servants. But wartime mobilization of the economy and the siphoning of millions of men into the armed forces left factories begging for women workers.

Government advertisements urged women to take industrial jobs by assuring them they were capable of work on the "Victory Line." One billboard proclaimed, "If you've sewed on buttons, or made buttonholes, on a [sewing] machine, you can learn to do spot welding on airplane parts." Millions of women responded, and by the end of the war, 18 million women worked outside the home, 50 percent more than in 1939 (**Figure 25.1**). Contributing to the war effort also paid off in wages. A Kentucky woman remembered her job at a munitions plant, where she earned "the fabulous sum of $32 a week. To us it was an absolute miracle."

The majority of married women remained at home. But they, too, supported the war effort, planting Victory Gardens to provide homegrown vegetables, saving tin cans and newspapers for recycling into war materiel, and hoarding pennies and nickels to buy war bonds. Many families scrimped to cope with the 30 percent inflation during the war, but families supported by men and women in manufacturing industries enjoyed wages that grew twice as fast as inflation.

The wartime prosperity and abundance enjoyed by most Americans contrasted with the experiences of their hard-pressed allies. Personal consumption fell by 22 percent in Britain, and food output plummeted to just one-third of prewar levels in the Soviet Union, creating widespread hunger and even starvation. Few went hungry in the United States. New Deal restraints on agricultural production were lifted, and farm output grew by 25 percent each year during the war, providing food for export to the Allies.

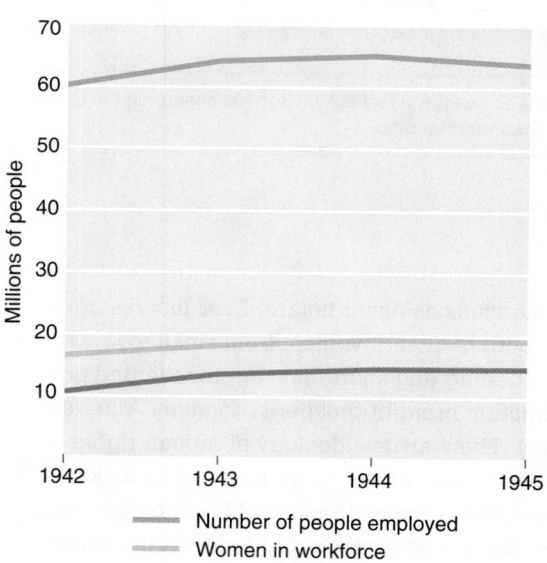

FIGURE 25.1 ■ World War II and the Economy, 1942–1945
War mobilization sent employment and union membership soaring. Women found employment in all sectors of the economy, including heavy industry. Although they lost many jobs in industry after the war, they continued to participate in the workforce in increased numbers.

Legend:
- Number of people employed
- Women in workforce
- Union membership

CHAPTER LOCATOR | How did America respond to international developments in the 1930s? | What led to the outbreak of war in Europe and the Pacific?

708
CHAPTER 25
THE UNITED STATES AND THE SECOND WORLD WAR , 1939–1945

The Double V Campaign

Fighting against the Nazis and their ideology of Aryan racial supremacy, Americans were confronted with the racial prejudice in their own country. The *Pittsburgh Courier*, a leading black newspaper, asserted that the wartime emergency called for a **Double V campaign** seeking "victory over our enemies at home and victory over our enemies on the battlefields abroad." It was time, the *Courier* proclaimed, "to persuade, embarrass, compel and shame our government and our nation . . . into a more enlightened attitude."

In 1941, African American organizations demanded that the federal government require companies receiving defense contracts to integrate their workforces. A. Philip Randolph, head of the Brotherhood of Sleeping Car Porters, promised that 100,000 African American marchers would descend on Washington if the president did not eliminate discrimination in defense industries. Roosevelt decided to risk offending his white allies in the South and in unions and issued Executive Order 8802 in mid-1941. It authorized the Committee on Fair Employment Practices to investigate and prevent racial discrimination in employment. Civil rights champions hailed the act, and Randolph called off the march.

Progress came slowly, however. In 1940, nine out of ten black Americans lived below the federal poverty line, and those who worked earned an average of just 39 percent of whites' wages. In search of better jobs and living conditions, 5.5 million black Americans migrated from the South to centers of industrial production in the North and West. Many discovered that unskilled jobs were available but that unions and employers often barred blacks from skilled trades. Severe labor shortages and government fair employment standards opened assembly-line jobs in defense plants to African Americans, causing black unemployment to drop by 80 percent during the war. But more jobs did not mean equal pay for blacks. The average income of black families rose during the war, but by the end of the conflict, it still stood at only half of what white families earned.

Blacks' migration to defense jobs intensified racial antagonisms. In 1943, 242 race riots erupted in 47 cities. In the "zoot suit riots" in Los Angeles, hundreds of white servicemen, claiming they were punishing draft dodgers, chased and beat young Mexican American men who dressed in distinctive broad-shouldered, peg-legged zoot suits. The worst mayhem occurred in Detroit, where tensions between whites and blacks over racially segregated housing ignited into a race war. Whites with clubs smashed through black neighborhoods, and blacks retaliated by destroying and looting white-owned businesses. In two days of violence, twenty-five blacks and nine whites were killed, and scores more were injured.

Racial violence created the impetus for the Double V campaign, officially supported by the National Association for the Advancement of Colored People (NAACP), which asserted black Americans' demands for the rights and privileges enjoyed by all other Americans—demands reinforced by the Allies' wartime ideology of freedom and democracy. While the NAACP focused on court challenges to segregation, a new organization founded in 1942, the Congress of Racial Equality (CORE), organized picketing and sit-ins against Jim Crow restaurants and theaters. The Double V campaign greatly expanded membership in the NAACP but achieved only limited success against racial discrimination during the war.

Double V campaign

▶ Wartime campaign in America to attack racism at home and abroad. Drawing on the wartime ideology of freedom and democracy, leading African American organizations argued that the struggle against fascism overseas had to coincide with a struggle against discrimination at home. The campaign greatly increased membership in the National Association for the Advancement of Colored People, which focused on legal challenges to segregation and discrimination.

How did the United States prepare for war? | How did the Allies turn the tide in Europe and the Pacific? | **How did the war change life for Americans on the home front?** | How did the Allies achieve victory in World War II? | Conclusion: Why did America emerge as a superpower at the end of the war?

709

Wartime Politics and the 1944 Election

Americans rallied around the war effort in unprecedented unity. Roosevelt, however, found it difficult to maintain the unity of his political coalition. Whites often resented blacks who migrated to northern cities. Many Americans complained about government price controls and the rationing of scarce goods while the war dragged on. Republicans seized the opportunity to roll back New Deal reforms. A conservative coalition of Republicans and southern Democrats succeeded in abolishing several New Deal agencies in 1942 and 1943, including the Work Projects Administration and the Civilian Conservation Corps.

In June 1944, Congress recognized the sacrifices made by millions of veterans, unanimously passing the GI Bill of Rights, which gave veterans funds for education, housing, and health care and provided loans to help them start businesses and buy homes. The GI Bill put the financial resources of the federal government behind the abstract goals of freedom and democracy for which veterans were fighting, and it empowered millions of GIs to better themselves and their families after the war.

After twelve years in the White House, Roosevelt was exhausted and gravely ill with heart disease. His poor health made the selection of a vice presidential candidate unusually important. Convinced that many Americans had soured on liberal reform, Roosevelt chose Senator Harry S. Truman of Missouri as his running mate. A reliable party man from a southern border state, Truman satisfied urban Democratic leaders while not worrying white southerners who were nervous about challenges to racial segregation.

Mass Execution of Jewish Women and Children

On October 14, 1942, Jewish women and children from the village of Mizocz in present-day Ukraine were herded into a ravine, forced to undress and lie facedown, and then shot at point-blank range by German police. This rare photograph, taken by one of the authorities at the scene, shows Germans killing the women who survived the initial gunfire. United States Holocaust Memorial Museum.

CHAPTER LOCATOR | How did America respond to international developments in the 1930s? | What led to the outbreak of war in Europe and the Pacific?

CHAPTER 25
710 THE UNITED STATES AND THE SECOND WORLD WAR , 1939–1945

The Republicans nominated as their presidential candidate the governor of New York, Thomas E. Dewey, who had made his reputation as a tough crime fighter. In the 1944 presidential campaign, Roosevelt's failing health alarmed many observers, but his frailty was outweighed by Americans' unwillingness to change presidents in the midst of the war and by Dewey's failure to persuade most voters that the New Deal was a creeping socialist menace. Voters gave Roosevelt a 53.5 percent majority, his narrowest presidential victory.

Reaction to the Holocaust

Since the 1930s, the Nazis had persecuted Jews in Germany and every German-occupied territory, causing many Jews to seek asylum beyond Hitler's reach. Roosevelt sympathized with the refugees' pleas for help, but he did not want to jeopardize his foreign policy or offend American voters. After Hitler's Anschluss in 1938, thousands of Austrian Jews sought to immigrate to the United States, but 82 percent of Americans opposed admitting them, and they were turned away. Roosevelt tried to persuade countries in Latin America and Africa to accept Jewish refugees, but none would do so.

In 1942, numerous reports that Hitler was implementing a "final solution" filtered out of German-occupied Europe. Jews and other "undesirables"—such as Gypsies, religious and political dissenters, and homosexuals—were being sent to concentration camps. Old people, children, and others deemed too weak to work were systematically slaughtered and cremated, while the able-bodied were put to work at slave labor until they died of starvation and abuse. Despite such reports, skeptical U.S. State Department officials refused to grant asylum to Jewish refugees. Most Americans, including top officials, believed that reports of the killing camps were exaggerated.

Desperate to stem the killing, the World Jewish Congress appealed to the Allies to bomb the death camps and the railroad tracks leading to them in order to hamper the killing and block further shipments of victims. Intent on achieving military victory as soon as possible, the Allies repeatedly turned down such bombing requests, arguing that the air forces could not divert resources from their military missions.

The nightmare of the **Holocaust** was all too real. When Russian troops arrived at the Auschwitz concentration camp in Poland in February 1945, they found emaciated prisoners, skeletal corpses, gas chambers, pits filled with human ashes, and loot the Nazis had stripped from the dead, including hair, gold dental fillings, and false teeth. At last, the truth about the Holocaust began to be known beyond the Germans who had perpetrated and tolerated these atrocities and the men, women, and children who had succumbed to the genocide. By then, it was too late for the 9 million victims—mostly Jews—of the Nazis' crimes against humanity.

Principal German
◆ concentration and
extermination camp

The Holocaust, 1933–1945

Holocaust
▶ German effort to murder Europe's Jews, along with other groups the Nazis deemed "undesirable." Despite reports of the ongoing genocide, the Allies did almost nothing to interfere with Hitler's "final solution." In all, some 9 million people were killed in the Holocaust, most of them Jews.

QUICK REVIEW <

How did the Second World War influence American society?

How did the United States prepare for war?

How did the Allies turn the tide in Europe and the Pacific?

How did the war change life for Americans on the home front?

How did the Allies achieve victory in World War II?

Conclusion: Why did America emerge as a superpower at the end of the war?

How did the Allies achieve victory in World War II?

D Day Invasion

"Taxi to Hell—and Back" is what Robert Sargent called his photograph of the D Day invasion of Normandy on June 6, 1944. Amid a dense fleet of landing craft, men lucky enough to have made it through rough seas and enemy fire struggle onto the beach to open a second front in Europe. Library of Congress.

BY FEBRUARY 1943, Soviet defenders defeated the German offensive against Stalingrad, turning the tide of the war in Europe. After fighting that had lasted for eighteen months, the Red Army forced Hitler's Wehrmacht to turn back toward the west. Now the Soviets and their Western allies faced the task of driving the Nazis out of eastern and western Europe. In the Pacific, the Allies had halted the expansion of the Japanese empire but now had the task of forcing the entrenched Japanese from their outposts.

From Bombing Raids to Berlin

While the Allied campaigns in North Africa and Italy were under way, British and American pilots flew bombing missions from England to German territories as a substitute for the delayed second front on the ground. During night raids, British bombers targeted general areas, hoping to hit civilians, create terror, and undermine morale. Beginning in August 1942, American pilots carried out daytime raids on industrial targets vital for the German war machine, especially oil refineries and ball bearing factories.

CHAPTER LOCATOR | How did America respond to international developments in the 1930s? | What led to the outbreak of war in Europe and the Pacific?

712 CHAPTER 25
THE UNITED STATES AND THE SECOND WORLD WAR , 1939–1945

German air defenses took a fearsome toll on Allied pilots and aircraft. In 1943, two-thirds of American airmen did not survive to complete their twenty-five-mission tours of duty. In all, 85,000 American airmen were killed. Many others were shot down and held as prisoners of war. In February 1944, the arrival of the P-51 Mustang fighter gave Allied bombers superior protection, allowing bombers to penetrate deep into Germany and pound civilian and military targets around the clock. In April 1944, the Allies began to target bridges and railroads in northwestern Europe in preparation for their cross-Channel invasion.

In November 1943, Churchill, Roosevelt, and Stalin met in Teheran to discuss wartime strategy and the second front. Roosevelt conceded to Stalin that the Soviet Union would exercise de facto control of the eastern European countries that the Red Army occupied as it pushed back the Germans. Stalin agreed to enter the war against Japan once Germany finally surrendered. Roosevelt and Churchill promised that they would at last launch a massive second-front assault in northern France in May 1944.

After frustrating delays caused by stormy weather, General Eisenhower launched the largest amphibious assault in world history on **D Day**, June 6, 1944. Rough seas and deadly fire from German machine guns slowed the assault, but Allied soldiers finally succeeded in securing the beachhead. As naval officer Tracy Sugarman recalled, "What I thought were piles of cordwood [on the beach] I later learned were the bodies of 2,500 men killed by withering fire from the Nazi gun emplacements." Sugarman reported that he and the other GIs who made the landing "were exhausted and we were exultant. We had survived D Day!"

Within a week, a flood of soldiers, tanks, and other military equipment swamped the Normandy beaches and propelled Allied forces toward Germany. On August 25, the Allies liberated Paris from four years of Nazi occupation. As Allied and Soviet armies closed on Germany in December 1944, Hitler ordered a counterattack to capture the Allies' essential supply port at Antwerp, Belgium. In the Battle of the Bulge (December 16, 1944, to January 31, 1945), German forces drove fifty-five miles into Allied lines before being stopped at Bastogne. More than 70,000 Allied soldiers were killed, including more Americans than in any other battle of the war. The Nazis lost more than 100,000 men and hundreds of tanks, fatally depleting Hitler's reserves.

In February 1945, Churchill, Stalin, and Roosevelt met secretly at the **Yalta Conference** (named for the Russian resort town where it was held) to discuss their plans for the postwar world. Seriously ill and noticeably frail, Roosevelt managed to secure Stalin's promise to permit votes of self-determination in the eastern European countries occupied by the Red Army. The Allies pledged to support Chiang Kai-shek as the leader of China. The Soviet Union obtained a role in the postwar governments of Korea and Manchuria in exchange for entering the war against Japan after the defeat of Germany.

The "Big Three" also agreed on the creation of a new international peacekeeping organization, the United Nations (UN). All nations would have a place in the UN General Assembly, but the Security Council would wield decisive power, and its permanent representatives from the Allied powers—China, France, Great Britain, the Soviet Union, and the United States—would possess a veto over UN actions. The Senate ratified the United Nations Charter in July 1945 by a vote of 89 to 2, reflecting the triumph of internationalism during the nation's mobilization for war.

CHRONOLOGY

1942
- Roosevelt authorizes Manhattan Project.

1944
- **June 6.** D Day.

1945
- **February.** Yalta Conference.
- **April 12.** Roosevelt dies; Vice President Harry Truman becomes president.
- **April 30.** Hitler commits suicide.
- **May 7.** Germany surrenders.
- **July.** United States joins United Nations.
- **August 6.** United States drops atomic bomb on Hiroshima.
- **August 9.** United States drops atomic bomb on Nagasaki.
- **August 14.** Japan surrenders, ending World War II.

D Day
▶ June 6, 1944, the date of the Allied invasion of northern France. D Day was the largest amphibious assault in world history. The invasion opened a second front against the Germans and moved the Allies closer to victory in Europe.

Yalta Conference
▶ February 1945 meeting at Yalta, a Russian resort town, during which Churchill, Stalin, and Roosevelt discussed their plans for the postwar world. Among the important decisions the Allied leaders made at the conference was the agreement to create the United Nations.

How did the United States prepare for war?	How did the Allies turn the tide in Europe and the Pacific?	How did the war change life for Americans on the home front?	**How did the Allies achieve victory in World War II?**	Conclusion: Why did America emerge as a superpower at the end of the war?

713

By April 11, Allied armies sweeping in from the west reached the banks of the Elbe River, the agreed-upon rendezvous with the Red Army, and paused while the Soviets smashed into Berlin, capturing it on May 2. Hitler had committed suicide on April 30, and the provisional German government surrendered unconditionally on May 7. The war in Europe was finally over, with the sacrifice of 135,576 American soldiers, nearly 250,000 British troops, and 9 million Russian combatants.

Roosevelt did not live to witness the end of the war. On April 12, while resting in Warm Springs, Georgia, he suffered a fatal stroke. Americans grieved for the man who had led them through years of depression and world war, and they worried aloud about his successor, Vice President Harry Truman, who would have to steer the nation to victory over Japan and protect American interests in the postwar world.

The Defeat of Japan

In 1943, British and American forces, along with Indian and Chinese allies, launched an offensive against Japanese outposts in southern Asia, pushing through Burma and into China, where the armies of Chiang Kai-shek continued to resist conquest. In the Pacific, Americans and their allies attacked Japanese strongholds by sea, air, and land, moving island by island toward the Japanese homeland (**Map 25.5**).

The island-hopping campaign began in August 1942, when American marines landed on Guadalcanal in the southern Pacific. For the next six months, a savage battle raged for control of the strategic area. Finally, during the night of February 8, 1943, Japanese forces withdrew. The terrible losses on both sides indicated to the marines how costly it would be to defeat Japan. After the battle, Joseph Steinbacher, a twenty-one-year-old from Alabama, sailed from San Francisco to New Guinea, where, he recalled, "all the cannon fodder waited to be assigned" to replace the killed and wounded.

As the Allies attacked island after island, Japanese soldiers were ordered to refuse to surrender no matter how hopeless their plight. The fierce Japanese resistance spurred remorseless Allied bombing attacks on Japanese-occupied islands, followed by amphibious landings by marines and grinding, inch-by-inch combat to root Japanese fighters out of bunkers and caves.

While the island-hopping campaign kept pressure on Japanese forces, the Allies invaded the Philippines in the fall of 1944. In the four-day Battle of Leyte Gulf, the American fleet crushed the Japanese armada, clearing the way for Allied victory in the Philippines. While the Philippine campaign was under way, American forces captured two crucial islands—Iwo Jima and Okinawa—from which they planned to launch an attack on the Japanese homeland. In desperation, Japanese leaders ordered thousands of suicide pilots, known as *kamikaze*, to crash their bomb-laden planes into Allied ships. But instead of destroying the American fleet, they demolished the last vestige of the Japanese air force. By June 1945, the Japanese were nearly defenseless on the sea and in the air. Still, their leaders prepared to fight to the death for their homeland.

Joseph Steinbacher and other GIs who had suffered "horrendous" casualties in the Philippines were now told by their commanding officer, "Men, in a few short months we are going to invade [Japan]. . . . We will be going in on the first

CHAPTER LOCATOR

How did America respond to international developments in the 1930s?

What led to the outbreak of war in Europe and the Pacific?

714 CHAPTER 25
THE UNITED STATES AND THE SECOND WORLD WAR , 1939–1945

MAP 25.5 ■ The Pacific Theater of World War II, 1941–1945

To drive the Japanese from their far-flung empire, the Allies launched two combined naval and military offensives—one to recapture the Philippines and then attack Japanese forces in China, the other to hop from island to island in the Central Pacific toward the Japanese mainland.

wave and are expecting ninety percent casualties the first day. . . . For the few of us left alive the war will be over." Steinbacher later recalled his mental attitude at that moment: "I know that I am now a walking dead man and will not have a snowball's chance in hell of making it through the last great battle to conquer the home islands of Japan."

| How did the United States prepare for war? | How did the Allies turn the tide in Europe and the Pacific? | How did the war change life for Americans on the home front? | **How did the Allies achieve victory in World War II?** | Conclusion: Why did America emerge as a superpower at the end of the war? |

Hiroshima Bombing

This rare shot taken by a news photographer in Hiroshima immediately after the atomic bomb exploded on August 6, 1945, suggests the shock and incomprehension that survivors later described as their first reactions. On August 9, another atomic bomb created similar devastation in Nagasaki. UN photo.

Hiroshima

▶ Japanese city devastated by an American-launched atomic bomb in August 1945. The bomb, developed in secret by scientists and engineers working at the government-funded Manhattan Project, killed 78,000 Japanese civilians. A second bomb was dropped on Nagasaki three days later, killing more than 100,000 people. The Japanese government surrendered on August 14, 1945, five days after the second attack.

Atomic Warfare

In mid-July 1945, as Allied forces prepared for the final assault on Japan, American scientists tested a secret weapon at a desert site near Los Alamos, New Mexico. In 1942, Roosevelt had authorized the top-secret Manhattan Project to find a way to convert nuclear energy into a super-bomb before the Germans added such a weapon to their arsenal. More than 100,000 Americans, led by scientists, engineers, and military officers at Los Alamos, worked frantically to win the race for an atomic bomb, conducting a successful test explosion on July 16, 1945.

A delegation of scientists and officials, troubled by the bomb's destructive force, secretly proposed that the United States give a public demonstration of the bomb's power, hoping to persuade Japan's leaders to surrender. But U.S. government officials quickly rejected such a demonstration. Despite Japan's numerous defeats, U.S. military advisers estimated that the invasion of Japan would cost the lives of at least 250,000 Americans.

President Truman heard about the successful bomb test when he was in Potsdam, Germany, negotiating with Stalin about postwar issues. Truman saw no reason not to use the atomic bomb against Japan if doing so would save American lives. But first he issued an ultimatum: Japan must surrender unconditionally or face utter ruin. When the Japanese failed to respond by the deadline, Truman ordered that a bomb be dropped on a Japanese city not already heavily damaged by American raids. On August 6, Colonel Paul Tibbets piloted the *Enola Gay* over **Hiroshima** and released an atomic bomb, leveling the city and incinerating 78,000 people. Three days later, after the Japanese government still refused to surrender, the United States dropped a second atomic bomb on Nagasaki, killing more than 100,000 civilians.

With American assurance that the emperor could retain his throne after the Allies took over, Japan surrendered on August 14. On a troop ship departing from Europe for what would have been the final assault on Japan, an American soldier spoke for millions of others when he heard the wonderful news that the killing was over: "We are going to grow to adulthood after all."

> ## QUICK REVIEW

Why did Truman elect to use the atomic bomb against Japan?

CHAPTER LOCATOR | How did America respond to international developments in the 1930s? | What led to the outbreak of war in Europe and the Pacific?

716 CHAPTER 25 THE UNITED STATES AND THE SECOND WORLD WAR , 1939–1945

U.S. Army Center of Military History.

Conclusion: Why did America emerge as a superpower at the end of the war?

SHORTLY AFTER PEARL HARBOR, Hitler pronounced America "a decayed country" without "much future"; a country "half Judaized, and the other half Negrified"; a country "where everything is built on the dollar" and bound to fall apart. American mobilization for World War II disproved Hitler's arrogant prophecy. At a cost of 405,399 American lives, the nation united with its allies to defeat Axis aggressors in Europe and Asia.

Wartime production lifted the nation out of the Great Depression. The gross national product soared to four times what it had been when Roosevelt became president in 1933. Jobs in defense industries eliminated chronic unemployment, provided wages for millions of women workers and African American migrants from southern farms, and boosted Americans' prosperity.

By the end of the war, the United States had emerged as a global superpower, buttressed by the military clout of the nation's nuclear monopoly. Although the war left much of the world a rubble-strewn wasteland, the American mainland had enjoyed immunity from attack. The Japanese occupation of China had left 50 million people without homes and millions more dead, maimed, and orphaned. The German offensive against the Soviet Union had killed more than 20 million Russian soldiers and civilians. Germany and Japan lay in ruins, their economies as shattered as their military forces. The Allies had killed more than 4 million Nazi soldiers and more than 1.2 million Japanese combatants, as well as hundreds of thousands of civilians.

As the dominant Western nation in the postwar world, the United States asserted its leadership in the reconstruction of Europe while occupying Japan and overseeing its economic and political recovery. America soon confronted new challenges in the tense aftermath of the war, as the Soviets seized political control of eastern Europe, a Communist revolution swept China, and national liberation movements emerged in the colonial empires of Britain and France. The surrender of the Axis powers ended the battles of World War II, but the forces unleashed by the war would shape the United States and the rest of the world for decades to come.

SO NOW YOU KNOW

During World War II, the United States' military production was more than double that of Germany, Japan, and Italy combined. This amazing level of wartime production supported the Allied victory over the Axis powers, lifted the nation out of the Great Depression, and established the United States as the dominant Western nation in the postwar world.

| How did the United States prepare for war? | How did the Allies turn the tide in Europe and the Pacific? | How did the war change life for Americans on the home front? | How did the Allies achieve victory in World War II? | **Conclusion: Why did America emerge as a superpower at the end of the war?** |

717

CHAPTER 25 STUDY GUIDE

Online Study Guide
bedfordstmartins.com/roarkunderstanding

STEP 1

GETTING STARTED

Below are basic terms from this period in American history. Can you identify each term below and explain why it matters? To do this exercise online or to download this chart, visit bedfordstmartins.com/roarkunderstanding.

TERM	WHO OR WHAT & WHEN	WHY IT MATTERS
Adolf Hitler, p. 691		
appeasement, p. 693		
Joseph Stalin, p. 693		
Winston Churchill, p. 695		
Battle of Britain, p. 695		
Pearl Harbor, p. 697		
Battle of Midway, p. 704		
Double V campaign, p. 709		
Holocaust, p. 711		
D Day, p. 713		
Yalta Conference, p. 713		
Hiroshima, p. 716		

STEP 2

MOVING BEYOND THE BASICS

The exercise below represents a more advanced understanding of the chapter material. Fill in the chart by describing important developments in the United States and their impact during World War II in the following key areas: economic activity, employment, government, politics and the New Deal, race relations, and women's roles. When you are finished, consider these questions: How did the shift to a wartime economy affect women and racial minorities? What impact did the return to full employment have on the New Deal and the political balance of power? How did the war change the size and nature of the federal government? To do this exercise online or to download this chart, visit bedfordstmartins.com/roarkunderstanding.

	Developments	Impact
Economic activity		
Employment		
Government		
Politics and the New Deal		
Race relations		
Women's roles		

Now that you've reviewed various parts of the chapter, take a step back and try to see the big picture by answering these questions. Remember to use specific examples from the chapter in your answers. To do this exercise online, visit bedfordstmartins.com/roarkunderstanding.

THE ONSET OF WORLD WAR II

▶ Why were the American people, as a whole, reluctant to become involved in World War II?

▶ How did Roosevelt use the economic power of the United States to aid Britain and the Soviet Union?

THE HOME FRONT

▶ How did the conversion to a war economy end the Great Depression? Who benefited most? What groups still struggled?

▶ What were the most important social consequences of America's involvement in World War II?

VICTORY

▶ How did the Allies achieve victory? What tensions among the Allies emerged in the final years of the war?

▶ What led to the decision to drop atomic bombs on Japan? In your opinion, was it a purely military decision, or were nonmilitary considerations important as well?

LOOKING BACKWARD, LOOKING AHEAD

▶ How did America's experience of World War I shape public opinion in 1939 and 1940 about U.S. involvement in World War II?

▶ How did World War II help set the stage for the social, economic, and political developments of the 1950s?

IN YOUR OWN WORDS

Imagine that you must explain chapter 25 to someone who hasn't read it. What would be the most important points to include and why?

ATOMIC BOMB

WORLD CONTROL

WORLD DESTRUCTION

E GOLDBERG

26

COLD WAR POLITICS IN THE TRUMAN YEARS

1945–1953

> This chapter examines American politics in the years immediately following World War II. It explores the origins and impact of the Cold War, President Truman's domestic and foreign policy agendas, and the effects of the Korean War on American domestic politics.

> What factors contributed to the Cold War?

> What obstructed Truman's domestic agenda?

> How did America's Cold War policy lead to the Korean War?

> Conclusion: What were the costs and consequences of the Cold War?

DID YOU KNOW?

The U.S. armed forces were not desegregated until after World War II.

Statement on world peace. By Pulitzer Prize–winning cartoonist Rube Goldberg, 1948.

What factors contributed to the Cold War?

Fear of communism dominated much of postwar American life and politics, even invading popular culture. Four million copies of this comic book, published by a religious organization in 1947, painted a terrifying picture of what would happen to Americans if the Soviets took over the country. Such takeover stories appeared in movies, cartoons, and magazines as well as in other comic books. Collection of Charles H. Christensen.

> ▶ FOR MORE HELP ANALYZING THIS IMAGE, see the visual activity for this chapter in the Online Study Guide at bedfordstmartins.com/roarkunderstanding.

Harry S. Truman
▶ Democratic president who assumed office in 1945 upon Franklin Roosevelt's death and won another term in 1948. Although he had an ambitious domestic agenda in the areas of civil rights and social welfare, Truman succeeded in implementing only small portions of it. Instead, he focused on foreign policy and helped make containment a major component of post–World War II American foreign policy.

WITH JAPAN'S SURRENDER in August 1945, Americans besieged the government for the return of their loved ones. Baby booties arrived at the White House with a note, "Please send my daddy home." Americans wanted to dismantle the large military establishment and expected the Allies, led by the United States and working within the United Nations, to cooperate in the management of international peace. Postwar realities quickly dashed these hopes. New threats arose as the wartime alliance forged by the United States, Great Britain, and the Soviet Union crumbled, and the United States began to develop the means to contain the spread of Soviet power around the globe.

The Cold War Begins

"The guys who came out of World War II were idealistic," reported Harold Russell, a young paratrooper who had lost both hands in a training accident.

"We felt the day had come when the wars were all over." But political leaders were less optimistic. Once the Allies had overcome a common enemy, the prewar mistrust and antagonism between the Soviet Union and the West resurfaced over their very different visions of the postwar world.

The Western Allies' delay in opening a second front in Western Europe aroused Soviet suspicions during the war. The Soviet Union had lost more than twenty million citizens and vast portions of its agricultural and industrial capacity. Soviet leader Joseph Stalin wanted to make Germany pay for Soviet economic reconstruction and to expand Soviet influence in the world. Above all, he wanted friendly governments on the Soviet Union's borders in Eastern Europe. A ruthless dictator, he also wanted to maintain his own power.

In contrast to the Soviet devastation, enemy fire had never touched the mainland of the United States, and its 405,000 dead amounted to just 2 percent of the Soviet loss. With a vastly expanded economy and a monopoly on atomic weapons, the United States was the most powerful nation on earth. That sheer power, along with U.S. economic interests, policymakers' views about how the recent war might have been avoided, and a belief in the superiority of American institutions and intentions, all affected how American leaders approached the Soviet Union.

Fearing a return of the depression, U.S. officials believed that a healthy economy depended on opportunities abroad. American companies needed access to raw materials, markets for their goods, and security for their investments overseas. These needs could be met best in countries with similar economic and political systems. As Truman put it in 1947, "The American system can survive in America only if it becomes a world system." Yet both leaders and citizens regarded their foreign policy not as a self-interested campaign to guarantee economic interests, but as the means to preserve national security and bring freedom, democracy, and capitalism to the rest of the world. Laura Briggs spoke for many Americans who believed that "it was our destiny to prove that we were the children of God and that our way was right for the world."

Recent history also shaped postwar foreign policy. Americans believed that World War II might have been avoided had Britain and France resisted rather than appeased Hitler's initial aggression. Navy Secretary James V. Forrestal argued against trying to "buy [the Soviets'] understanding and sympathy. We tried that once with Hitler." This "appeasement" analogy would be invoked repeatedly when the United States faced challenges to the international status quo.

The man with ultimate responsibility for U.S. policy came to the White House with little international experience. **Harry S. Truman** envisioned Soviet-American cooperation, as long as the Soviet Union conformed to U.S. plans for the postwar world and restrained its expansionist impulses. Proud of his ability to make quick decisions, Truman determined to be firm with the Soviets, knowing well that America's nuclear monopoly gave him the upper hand.

Soviet and American interests clashed first in Eastern Europe. Stalin insisted that the Allies' wartime agreements gave him a free hand in the countries defeated or liberated by the Red Army, just as the United States was unilaterally reconstructing governments in Italy and Japan. The Soviet dictator used harsh methods to install Communist governments in neighboring Poland and Bulgaria. Elsewhere, the Soviets initially tolerated non-Communist governments in Hungary and Czechoslovakia. In the spring of 1946, Stalin responded to pressure from the

CHRONOLOGY

1945
- Soviet and U.S. interests clash first in Eastern Europe.

1946
- George F. Kennan drafts a call for the containment of communism.
- United States grants independence to the Philippines.

1947
- National Security Act creates the National Security Council and Central Intelligence Agency.
- Truman asks for aid to Greece and Turkey and announces Truman Doctrine.

WESTMINSTER COLLEGE — Harry Truman / Winston Churchill — FULTON, MO. 1946

1948
- Congress approves the Marshall Plan for European recovery.

1948–1949
- Berlin blockade and airlift.

1949
- Communists take over mainland China; Nationalists retreat to Taiwan.
- North Atlantic Treaty Organization is formed.
- Soviet Union detonates its first atomic bomb.

1950
- Truman approves development of hydrogen bomb.

1951
- United States ends occupation of Japan and signs peace treaty and mutual security pact.

CHAPTER LOCATOR | What factors contributed to the Cold War? | What obstructed Truman's domestic agenda? | How did America's Cold War policy lead to the Korean War? | Conclusion: What were the costs and consequences of the Cold War?

723

West and removed troops from Iran on the Soviet Union's southwest border, allowing U.S. access to the rich oil fields there.

Stalin considered U.S. officials hypocritical in demanding democratic elections in Eastern Europe while supporting dictatorships friendly to U.S. interests in Latin America. The United States clung to its sphere of influence while opposing Soviet efforts to create its own. But the Western Allies were unwilling to use military force against the Soviets. They issued sharp protests but failed to prevent the Soviet Union from establishing satellite countries throughout Eastern Europe.

In 1946, the wartime Allies contended over Germany's future. Both sides wanted to demilitarize Germany, but American policymakers sought rapid industrial revival there to foster European economic recovery and thus America's own long-term prosperity. By contrast, the Soviet Union wanted Germany weak militarily and economically, and Stalin demanded heavy reparations to help rebuild the dev-

MAP 26.1 ■ The Division of Europe after World War II
The "iron curtain," a term coined by Winston Churchill to refer to the Soviet grip on Eastern and central Europe, divided the continent for nearly fifty years. Communist governments controlled the countries along the Soviet Union's western border. The only exception was Finland, which remained neutral.

astated Soviet economy. Unable to settle their differences, the Allies divided Germany. The Soviet Union installed a Communist government in the eastern section, and in December 1946, Britain, France, and the United States unified their occupation zones, beginning the process that established the Federal Republic of Germany—West Germany—in 1949 (**Map 26.1**).

The war of words escalated early in 1946. Stalin told a Moscow audience in February that capitalism inevitably produced war. One month later, Truman accompanied Winston Churchill to Fulton, Missouri, where the former prime minister denounced Soviet interference in Eastern and central Europe. "From Stettin in the Baltic to Trieste in the Adriatic, an **iron curtain** has descended across the Continent," Churchill said. Stalin saw Churchill's proposal for joint British-American action to combat Soviet aggression as "a call to war against the USSR [the Soviet Union]."

In February 1946, George F. Kennan, a career diplomat and expert on Russia, wrote a comprehensive rationale for hard-line foreign policy. Downplaying the influence of Communist ideology in Soviet policy, he instead stressed the Soviets' insecurity and Stalin's need to maintain authority at home, which he believed prompted Stalin to exaggerate threats from abroad and to expand Soviet power. Kennan believed that the Soviet Union would retreat from its expansionist efforts "in the face of superior force," recommending that the United States respond with "unalterable counterforce." He predicted that this approach, which came to be called **containment**, would eventually end in "either the breakup or the gradual mellowing of Soviet power."

Not all public figures agreed. In September 1946, Secretary of Commerce Henry A. Wallace urged greater understanding of the Soviets' concerns about their nation's security, insisting that "we have no more business in the political affairs of Eastern Europe than Russia has in the political affairs of Latin America." State Department officials were furious, and Truman fired Wallace.

The Truman Doctrine and the Marshall Plan

In 1947, the United States began to implement the doctrine of containment. It was not an easy transition; Americans approved taking a hard line against the Soviet Union, but they wanted to keep their soldiers and tax dollars at home. In addition to selling containment to the public, Truman had to gain the support of a Republican-controlled Congress, which included a forceful bloc opposed to a strong U.S. presence in Europe.

Crises in two Mediterranean countries triggered the implementation of containment. In February 1947, Britain informed the United States that its crippled economy could no longer sustain military assistance either to Greece, where the autocratic government faced a leftist uprising, or to Turkey, which was trying to resist Soviet pressures. Truman promptly sought congressional authority to send the two countries military and economic aid. Meeting with congressional leaders, Undersecretary of State Dean Acheson predicted that if Greece and Turkey fell, communism would soon consume three-fourths of the world. After a stunned silence, Michigan senator Arthur Vandenberg, the Republican foreign policy leader, warned that to get approval, Truman would have to "scare hell out of the country."

Truman did just that. Outlining what would later be called the domino theory, he warned that if Greece fell to the rebels, "confusion and disorder might well

iron curtain

▶ Metaphor first introduced in 1946 by Winston Churchill. The term refers to the line that separated Soviet-controlled Eastern Europe from the democratic nations in the rest of Europe following World War II.

containment

▶ The American commitment to resisting Soviet expansion. President Truman initiated and implemented the containment policy during the crises in Turkey and Greece in 1947. The strategy of containment shaped American foreign policy throughout the Cold War.

CHAPTER LOCATOR | What factors contributed to the Cold War? | What obstructed Truman's domestic agenda? | How did America's Cold War policy lead to the Korean War? | Conclusion: What were the costs and consequences of the Cold War?

725

Truman Doctrine

▶ First articulated by President Truman in 1947 to gain support for U.S. intervention in Greece and Turkey, the Truman Doctrine committed the nation to "support free peoples who are resisting attempted subjugation by armed minorities or by outside pressures." The doctrine was subsequently used to support American aid to any kind of government if the only alternative appeared to be communism.

Marshall Plan (European Recovery Program)

▶ Program approved by Congress in 1948 to aid European economic recovery. Between 1948 and 1953, the United States spent $13 billion to restore the economies of sixteen Western European nations. The Marshall Plan marked the first step toward the European Union and yielded economic benefits for both the United States and Europe.

spread throughout the entire Middle East" and then create instability in Europe. According to what came to be called the **Truman Doctrine**, the United States needed to "support free peoples who are resisting attempted subjugation by armed minorities or by outside pressures." Despite some congressional opposition, the administration won the day, setting a precedent for forty years of Cold War interventions that would aid any kind of government if the only alternative appeared to be communism.

A much larger assistance program for Europe followed aid to Greece and Turkey. In May 1947, Acheson described a war-ravaged Western Europe, with "factories destroyed, fields impoverished, transportation systems wrecked, populations scattered and on the borderline of starvation." American citizens were sending generous amounts of private aid, but Europe needed large-scale assistance. European economic recovery, Acheson argued, was essential to halt the growth of socialist and Communist parties in France and Italy.

In March 1948, Congress approved the European Recovery Program—known as the **Marshall Plan**, after Secretary of State George C. Marshall, who proposed the plan. Over the next five years, the United States spent $13 billion to restore the economies of sixteen Western European nations. Marshall invited all European nations and the Soviet Union to cooperate in a request for aid, but the Soviets objected to the American terms of free trade and financial disclosure and ordered their Eastern European satellites likewise to reject the offer.

Marshall Plan Bread for Greek Children Greece was one of sixteen European nations that participated in the European Recovery Program. In this photograph taken in 1949, Greek children receive loaves of bread made from the first shipment of Marshall Plan flour from the United States. © Bettmann/Corbis.

The Marshall Plan marked the first step toward the European Union. Humanitarian impulses as well as the goal of keeping Western Europe free of communism drove the adoption of this enormous aid program. But the Marshall Plan also helped boost the U.S. economy because the European nations spent most of the dollars to buy American products and Europe's economic recovery created new markets and opportunities for American investment.

In February 1948, the Soviets staged a coup and installed a Communist regime in Czechoslovakia, the last democracy left in Eastern Europe. Next, Stalin threatened Western access to Berlin. That former capital of Germany lay within Soviet-controlled East Germany, but all four Allies jointly occupied Berlin, dividing it into separate administrative units. As the Western Allies moved to organize West Germany as a separate nation, the Soviets retaliated by blocking roads and rail lines between West Germany and the Western-held sections of Berlin, cutting off food, fuel, and other essentials to two million inhabitants.

"We stay in Berlin, period," Truman vowed. To avoid a confrontation with Soviet troops, for nearly a year U.S. and British pilots airlifted 2.3 million tons of goods to sustain West Berliners. Stalin hesitated to shoot down these cargo planes, and in 1949 he lifted the blockade. The city was then divided into East Berlin, under Soviet control, and West Berlin, which became part of West Germany. For many Americans, the Berlin airlift confirmed the wisdom of containment: When challenged, the Russians backed down.

Berlin Divided, 1948

Building a National Security State

In September 1949, the United States lost its nuclear monopoly when the Soviet Union detonated its own atomic bomb. To keep the United States ahead, in January 1950 Truman approved the development of a hydrogen bomb, equivalent to five hundred atomic bombs, rejecting the arguments of several scientists who had worked on the atomic bomb and of George Kennan, who warned of an endless arms race. The "super bomb" was ready by 1954, but the U.S. advantage was brief. In November 1955, the Soviets exploded their own hydrogen bomb.

The Six-Pronged Containment Strategy

1. Atomic weapons

2. Stronger traditional military forces

3. Military alliances with other nations

4. Military and economic aid to friendly nations

5. An espionage network and secret means to subvert Communist expansion

6. A propaganda offensive to win popular admiration for the United States around the world

From the 1950s through the 1980s, deterrence formed the basis of American nuclear strategy. To deter a Soviet Union attack, the United States strove to maintain a nuclear force more powerful than the Soviets'. Because the Russians pursued a similar policy, the superpowers became locked in a nuclear weapons race. Albert Einstein, whose mathematical discoveries had laid the foundations for

CHAPTER LOCATOR | What factors contributed to the Cold War? | What obstructed Truman's domestic agenda? | How did America's Cold War policy lead to the Korean War? | Conclusion: What were the costs and consequences of the Cold War?

727

nuclear weapons, warned that the war that came after World War III would "be fought with sticks and stones."

Implementing the second component of its containment strategy, the United States beefed up its conventional military power to deter Soviet threats that might not warrant nuclear retaliation. The National Security Act of 1947 united the military branches under a single secretary of defense and created the National Security Council (NSC) to advise the president. During the Berlin crisis in 1948, Congress hiked military appropriations and enacted a peacetime draft. In addition, Congress granted permanent status to the women's military branches, though it limited their numbers and rank and banned them from combat. With 1.5 million men and women in uniform in 1950, the military strength of the United States had quadrupled since the 1930s, and defense expenditures claimed one-third of the federal budget.

Collective security, the third prong of containment strategy, marked a sharp reversal of the nation's traditional foreign policy. In 1949, the United States joined Canada and Western European nations in its first peacetime military alliance, the **North Atlantic Treaty Organization (NATO)**, designed to counter a Soviet threat to Western Europe (see Map 26.1, page 724). For the first time in its history, the United States pledged to go to war if one of its allies was attacked.

The fourth element of defense strategy involved foreign assistance programs to strengthen friendly countries, such as aid to Greece and Turkey and the Marshall Plan. In addition, in 1949 Congress approved $1 billion of military aid to its NATO allies, and the government began economic assistance to nations in other parts of the world.

The fifth ingredient of containment improved the government's espionage capacities and ability to thwart communism through covert activities. The National Security Act of 1947 created the **Central Intelligence Agency (CIA)** not only to gather information but also to perform any activities "related to intelligence affecting the national security" that the NSC might authorize. Such functions included propaganda, sabotage, economic warfare, and support for "anti-communist elements in threatened countries of the free world." In 1948, secret CIA operations helped defeat Italy's Communist Party. Subsequently, CIA agents would intervene even more actively, helping to topple legitimate foreign governments and violating the rights of U.S. citizens.

Finally, the U.S. government organized cultural exchanges and spread propaganda throughout the world. The government expanded the Voice of America, created during World War II to broadcast U.S. propaganda abroad. In addition, the State Department sent books, exhibits, jazz musicians, and other performers to foreign countries as "cultural ambassadors."

By 1950, the United States had abandoned age-old tenets of foreign policy. Isolationism and neutrality had given way to a peacetime military alliance and efforts to control events far beyond U.S. borders. The United States aggressively and successfully promoted economic recovery and a military shield for those parts of Europe not behind the iron curtain.

Superpower Rivalry around the Globe

Efforts to implement containment moved beyond Europe. In Africa, Asia, and the Middle East, World War II accelerated a tide of national liberation movements

North Atlantic Treaty Organization (NATO)

▶ Military alliance formed in 1949 among the United States, Canada, and Western European nations to counter a Soviet threat to Western Europe. For the first time in its history, the United States pledged to go to war if one of its allies was attacked.

Central Intelligence Agency (CIA)

▶ Agency created by the National Security Act of 1947 to expand the government's espionage capacities and ability to thwart communism through covert activities. CIA functions came to include propaganda, sabotage, economic warfare, and support for anti-Communist forces around the world.

against war-weakened imperial powers. By 1960, forty countries, with more than a quarter of the world's people, had won their independence. These nations, along with Latin America, came to be referred to collectively as the third world, a term denoting countries outside the Western (first world) and Soviet (second world) orbits that had not yet developed industrial economies.

Like Woodrow Wilson during World War I, Roosevelt and Truman promoted the ideal of self-determination. The United States granted independence to the Philippines in 1946 and applauded the British withdrawal from India. At the same time, both the United States and the Soviet Union cultivated governments in emerging nations that were friendly to the superpowers' own interests.

Leaders of many liberation movements, impressed with Russia's rapid economic growth, adopted socialist or Communist ideas. Although few had formal ties with the Soviet Union, American leaders saw these movements as a threatening extension of Soviet power. Seeking to hold communism at bay by fostering economic development and political stability, the Truman administration initiated the Point IV Program in 1949, providing technical aid to developing nations.

In Asia, civil war raged in China, where the Communists, led by **Mao Zedong** (Mao Tse-tung), fought the official Nationalist government under Chiang Kai-shek. While the Communists gained support among the peasants for their land reforms and valiant stand against the Japanese, Chiang's corrupt and incompetent government alienated much of the population. Siding with Chiang, the United States provided almost $3 billion in aid to the Nationalists during the civil war. Yet, recognizing the ineptness of Chiang's government, Truman and his advisers refused to divert further resources from Europe to China.

In October 1949, Mao established the People's Republic of China (PRC), and the Nationalists fled to the island of Taiwan. Fearing a U.S.-supported invasion to recapture China for the Nationalists, Mao signed a mutual defense treaty with the Soviet Union in which each nation pledged to defend the other in case of attack. The United States refused to recognize the PRC, blocked its admission to the United Nations, and supported the Nationalist government in Taiwan. Only a massive U.S. military commitment could have stopped the Chinese Communists, yet some Republicans cried that Truman and "the pro-Communists in the State Department" had "lost" China.

With China in turmoil, the administration reconsidered its plans for postwar Japan. U.S. policy shifted to helping Japan rapidly reindustrialize and secure access to natural resources and markets in Asia. In a short time, the Japanese economy was flourishing, and the official military occupation ended when the two nations signed a peace treaty and a mutual security pact in September 1951. Like West Germany, Japan now sat squarely within the American orbit.

The one place where Cold War considerations did not control American policy was Palestine. In 1943, then-Senator Harry Truman spoke passionately about Nazi Germany's annihilation of the Jews, asserting, "This is not a Jewish problem, it is an American problem—and we must . . . face it squarely and honorably." As president, he made good on his words. Jews had been migrating to Palestine, their biblical homeland, since the nineteenth century, resulting in tension and hostilities with the Palestinian Arabs. After World War II, as hundreds of thousands of European Jews sought refuge and the creation of a national homeland in Palestine, fighting escalated into terrorism on both sides.

Mao Zedong
▶ Leader of the Communists in China who toppled the Nationalist government of Chiang Kai-shek and in October 1949 established the People's Republic of China. Fearing a U.S.-supported invasion to recapture China for the Nationalists, Mao signed a mutual defense treaty with the Soviet Union.

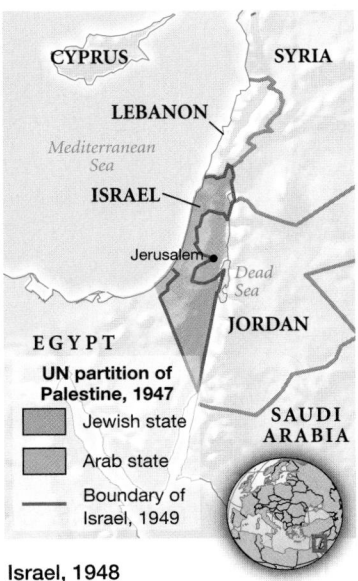
Israel, 1948

CHAPTER LOCATOR | What factors contributed to the Cold War? | What obstructed Truman's domestic agenda? | How did America's Cold War policy lead to the Korean War? | Conclusion: What were the costs and consequences of the Cold War?

729

Haganah originated in the 1910s as a paramilitary group to defend Jewish settlers in Palestine against Arabs who opposed the Zionists' expressed desire to build a Jewish state there. After Israel declared itself a nation in 1948, Haganah became the core of the Israel Defense Forces, Israel's main military organization. In this photo, Haganah troops are mobilizing in July 1948 to defend the new state from the armies of the surrounding nations of Syria, Jordan, Egypt, Lebanon, and Iraq. © Bettmann/Corbis.

Truman's foreign policy experts sought American-Arab friendship as a barrier against Soviet influence in the Middle East and as a means to secure access to Arabian oil. Uncharacteristically defying his advisers, the president responded instead to pleas from Jewish organizations, which coincided with his moral commitment to Holocaust survivors and his interest in the American Jewish vote for the 1948 election. When Jews in Palestine declared the state of Israel in May 1948, Truman quickly recognized the new country and made its defense the cornerstone of U.S. policy in the Middle East.

> QUICK REVIEW

Why did relations between the United States and the Soviet Union deteriorate after World War II?

What obstructed Truman's domestic agenda?

Truman's Whistle-Stop Campaign Harry Truman rallies a crowd from his campaign train at a stop in Bridgeport, Pennsylvania, in October 1948. Truman Library.

REFERRING TO THE CIVIL WAR GENERAL who coined the phrase "War is hell," Truman said in December 1945, "Sherman was wrong. I'm telling you I find peace is hell." Challenged by crises abroad, Truman also faced shortages, strikes, inflation, and other problems as the economy shifted to peacetime production. At the same time, he tried to expand New Deal reform with his own **Fair Deal** agenda of initiatives in civil rights, housing, education, and health care—efforts hindered by the wave of anti-Communist hysteria sweeping the country.

Reconverting to a Peacetime Economy

Despite scarcities and deprivations during World War II, most Americans enjoyed a higher standard of living than ever before. Economic experts as well as ordinary citizens worried about sustaining that standard and providing jobs for millions of returning soldiers. Truman wasted no time unveiling his plan, asking Congress to enact a twenty-one-point program of social and economic reforms. He wanted to maintain the government's power to regulate the economy while it adjusted to peacetime production, and he sought government programs to provide basic essentials such as housing and health care to those in need. "Not even President Roosevelt ever asked for as much at one sitting," exploded Republican leader Joseph W. Martin Jr.

Congress approved one of Truman's key proposals—full-employment legislation—but even that was watered down. The Employment Act of 1946 called

Fair Deal

▶ The package of initiatives proposed by President Truman in 1945. Truman hoped to follow up the accomplishments of the New Deal with initiatives in civil rights, housing, education, and health care. Republicans and southern Democrats blocked most of Truman's agenda.

CHAPTER LOCATOR | What factors contributed to the Cold War? | **What obstructed Truman's domestic agenda?** | How did America's Cold War policy lead to the Korean War? | Conclusion: What were the costs and consequences of the Cold War?

731

upon the federal government "to promote maximum employment, production, and purchasing power," thereby formalizing government's responsibility for maintaining a healthy economy. The law created the Council of Economic Advisors to assist the president, but it authorized no new powers to translate the government's obligation into effective action.

Inflation, not unemployment, turned out to be the most severe problem in the early postwar years. Consumers had $30 billion in wartime savings to spend, but shortages of meat, automobiles, housing, and other items persisted. Until industry could convert fully to civilian production and make more goods available, consumer demand would continue to drive up prices. Nonetheless, Truman's efforts to maintain price and rent controls fell to pressures from business groups and others determined to trim government powers.

Labor relations were another thorn in Truman's side. Organized labor survived the war stronger than ever, its 14.5 million members making up 35 percent of the civilian workforce. Yet union members feared the erosion of wartime gains and launched an intense struggle to preserve them. Five million workers went out on strike in 1946, affecting nearly every major industry. Workers saw corporate executives profiting at their expense. Shortly before voting to strike, a former marine and his coworkers calculated that a lavish party given by a company executive had cost more than they would earn in a whole year at the steel mill. "That sort of stuff made us realize, hell we had to bite the bullet . . . the bosses sure didn't give a damn for us." Although most Americans approved of unions in principle, they became fed up with strikes, blamed unions for shortages and rising prices, and called for government restrictions on organized labor. When the wave of strikes subsided, workers had won wage increases of about 20 percent, but the

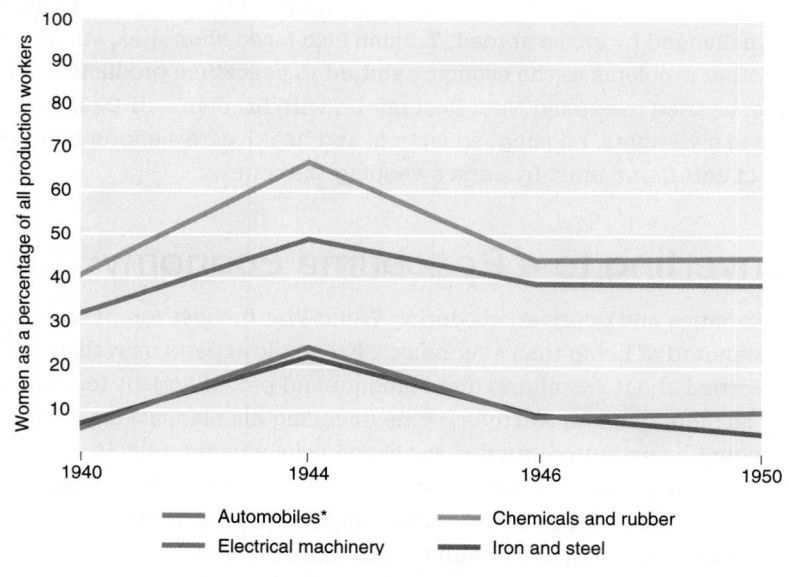

FIGURE 26.1 ■ Women Workers in Selected Industries, 1940–1950
Women demolished the idea that some jobs were "men's work" during World War II, but they failed to maintain their gains in the manufacturing sector after the war.

loss of overtime pay along with rising prices left their purchasing power only slightly higher than in 1942.

Women workers fared even less well. Polls indicated that as many as 68 to 85 percent wanted to keep their wartime jobs, but most who remained in the workforce had to settle for relatively low-paying jobs in light industry or the service sector. Displaced from her shipyard work, Marie Schreiber took a cashier's job, lamenting, "You were back to women's wages, you know . . . practically in half." Women's organizations and labor union women pushed for legislation to require equal pay for equal work, to provide child care for employed mothers, and to create a government commission to study the status of women. But at a time when women were viewed primarily as wives and mothers and a strong current of opinion resisted further expansion of federal powers, these initiatives got nowhere **(Figure 26.1)**.

By 1947, the economy had stabilized, avoiding the postwar depression that so many had feared. Wartime profits enabled businesses to expand. Consumers could now spend their wartime savings on houses, cars, and appliances that had lain beyond their reach during the depression and the war. Defense spending and foreign aid that enabled war-stricken countries to purchase American products also stimulated the economy. A soaring birthrate further sustained consumer demand. Although prosperity was far from universal, the United States entered into a remarkable economic boom that lasted through the 1960s (see chapter 27).

Another economic boost came from the only large welfare measure passed after the New Deal. **The Servicemen's Readjustment Act (GI Bill)**, enacted in 1944, offered 16 million veterans job training and education; unemployment compensation while they looked for jobs; and low-interest loans to purchase homes, farms, and small businesses. By 1948, some 1.3 million veterans had bought houses with government loans. Helping 2.2 million ex-soldiers attend college, the subsidies sparked a boom in higher education. A drugstore clerk before his military service, Don Condren was able to get an engineering degree and buy his first house. "I think the GI Bill gave the whole country an upward boost economically," he said.

Condren overlooked the disparate ways in which the GI Bill operated. Like key New Deal programs such as unemployment insurance and aid to mothers with dependent children, GI programs were administered at the state and local levels, which especially in the South routinely discriminated against African Americans. Black veterans who sought jobs for which the military had trained them were shuttled into menial labor. One decorated veteran said that the GI Bill "draws no color line," yet "my color bars me from most decent jobs, and if, instead of

The Servicemen's Readjustment Act (GI Bill)

▶ Law passed in 1944 offering America's 16 million veterans job training and education; unemployment compensation while they looked for jobs; and low-interest loans to purchase homes, farms, and small businesses. Millions of Americans benefited from the GI Bill, but its impact was uneven as minorities were denied full access to the programs it created.

Proctor Iron and Toaster

Like many manufacturers forced to convert to war production during World War II, Proctor Electric Company hoped to profit after the war from pent-up consumer demand. Even before the company had fully reconverted its plants, ads tempted consumers with products soon to come and asked them to be patient until Proctor could meet their needs, as this 1946 ad indicates.
Picture Research Consultants & Archives.

▶ FOR MORE HELP ANALYZING THIS IMAGE, see the visual activity for this chapter in the Online Study Guide at bedfordstmartins.com/roarkunderstanding.

CHAPTER LOCATOR | What factors contributed to the Cold War? | What obstructed Truman's domestic agenda? | How did America's Cold War policy lead to the Korean War? | Conclusion: What were the costs and consequences of the Cold War?

733

accepting menial work, I collect my $20 a week readjustment allowance, I am classified as a 'lazy nigger.'" Thousands of black veterans did benefit from the GI Bill, but it did not help all ex-soldiers equally.

Blacks and Mexican Americans Push for Their Civil Rights

"I spent four years in the army to free a bunch of Frenchmen and Dutchmen," an African American corporal declared, "and I'm hanged if I'm going to let the Alabama version of the Germans kick me around when I get home." Black veterans as well as civilians resolved that the return to peace would not be a return to the racial injustices of prewar America. Their political clout had grown with the migration of two million African Americans to northern and western cities, where they could vote. Pursuing civil rights through the courts and Congress, the National Association for the Advancement of Colored People (NAACP) counted half a million members.

In the postwar years, individual African Americans broke through the color barrier, achieving several "firsts." Jackie Robinson integrated major league baseball, playing for the Brooklyn Dodgers and braving abuse from fans and players to win the Rookie of the Year Award in 1947. In 1950, Ralph J. Bunche received the Nobel Peace Prize for his United Nations work, and Gwendolyn Brooks won the Pulitzer Prize for poetry.

Segregation The segregation visible on this bus was a feature of life in the South from the late nineteenth century until the 1960s. African Americans could not use white hospitals, cemeteries, schools, libraries, swimming pools, restrooms, or drinking fountains. They were relegated to balconies in movie theaters and kept apart from whites in all public meetings.
Stan Wayman/Time Life Pictures/Getty Images.

Still, for most African Americans, little had changed, especially in the South, where violence greeted their attempts to assert their rights. Armed white men turned back Medgar Evers (who would become a key civil rights leader in the 1960s) and four other veterans trying to vote in Mississippi. A mob lynched Isaac Nixon for voting in Georgia, and an all-white jury acquitted the men accused of his murder. In the South, political leaders and local vigilantes routinely intimidated potential black voters with threats of economic retaliation and violence.

The Cold War heightened American leaders' sensitivity to racial issues, as the superpowers vied for the allegiance of newly independent nations with nonwhite populations. Soviet propaganda repeatedly highlighted racial injustice in the United States. Republican senator Henry Cabot Lodge called race relations "our Achilles' heel before the world," while Secretary of State Dean Acheson noted that systematic segregation and discrimination endangered "our moral leadership of the free and democratic nations of the world."

"My very stomach turned over when I learned that Negro soldiers just back from overseas were being dumped out of army trucks in Mississippi and beaten," wrote Truman. Wrestling with the Democrats' need for northern black and liberal votes as well as southern white votes, Truman spoke more boldly on civil rights than any previous president. In 1946, he created the President's Committee on Civil Rights, and in February 1948 he asked Congress to enact the committee's recommendations. The first president to address the NAACP, Truman asserted that all Americans should have equal rights to housing, education, employment, and the ballot.

As with much of his domestic program, the president failed to act aggressively on his bold words. Congress rebuffed Truman's proposals for civil rights legislation, but some northern and western states passed laws against discrimination in employment and public accommodations. Running for reelection in 1948, Truman issued an executive order to desegregate the armed services, but it lay unimplemented until the Korean War. Despite the gap between Truman's words and what his administration actually accomplished, desegregation of the military and the administration's support of civil rights cases in the Supreme Court contributed to far-reaching changes, while his Committee on Civil Rights set an agenda for years to come.

Although discussion of race and civil rights usually focused on African Americans, Mexican Americans endured similar injustices. In 1929, they had formed the League of United Latin American Citizens (LULAC) to combat discrimination and segregation in the Southwest. Like black soldiers after World War II, Mexican American veterans believed, as one of them insisted, that "we had earned our credentials as American citizens. We had paid our dues." Problems with getting their veterans' benefits spurred a group in Corpus Christi, Texas, led by Dr. Héctor Peréz García, a combat surgeon who had earned the Bronze Star, to form the American GI Forum in 1948. It went on to become a key national organization battling discrimination against Latinos and electing sympathetic officials.

"Education is our freedom," read the GI Forum's motto, yet Mexican American children were routinely segregated in public schools. Parents filed a class action suit in Orange County, California, winning a federal court decision in 1947 that outlawed the practice of separating Mexican American and white children. In 1948, LULAC and the GI Forum achieved a similar victory over

CHAPTER LOCATOR

| What factors contributed to the Cold War? | What obstructed Truman's domestic agenda? | How did America's Cold War policy lead to the Korean War? | Conclusion: What were the costs and consequences of the Cold War? |

735

segregation in Texas schools. Such projects paralleled the efforts of the NAACP on behalf of African Americans that would culminate in the *Brown* decision in 1954 (see chapter 27). These efforts, along with challenges to discrimination in employment and efforts for political representation, demonstrated a growing mobilization of Mexican Americans in the Southwest.

The Fair Deal Flounders

Republicans capitalized on public frustrations with economic reconversion in the 1946 congressional election to capture control of Congress for the first time in fourteen years. Many had campaigned against New Deal "bureaucracy" and "radicalism" in 1946, and the new Congress was able to weaken some reform programs and enact tax cuts favoring higher-income groups.

Organized labor took the most severe blow when Congress passed the Taft-Hartley Act over Truman's veto in 1947. The law reduced the power of organized labor and made it more difficult to organize workers. For example, states could now pass "right-to-work" laws, which banned the practice of requiring all workers to join a union once a majority had voted for it. Many states, especially in the South and West, rushed to enact such laws, encouraging industries to relocate there. Taft-Hartley maintained the New Deal principle of government protection for collective bargaining, but it put the government more squarely between labor and management.

As the 1948 elections approached, Truman faced not only a resurgent Republican Party headed by its nominee, Thomas E. Dewey, but also two revolts within his own party. On the left, Henry A. Wallace, whose foreign policy views had cost him his cabinet seat, led the new Progressive Party. On the right, South Carolina governor J. Strom Thurmond headed the States' Rights Party—the Dixiecrats—formed by southern Democrats who had walked out of the 1948 Democratic Party convention when it passed a liberal civil rights plank.

Almost alone in believing he could win, Truman crisscrossed the country by train, answering supporters' cries of "Give 'em hell, Harry." So bleak were Truman's prospects that on election night, the *Chicago Daily Tribune* printed its next day's issue with the headline "DEWEY DEFEATS TRUMAN." But Truman took 303 electoral votes to Dewey's 189, and his party regained control of Congress (**Map 26.2**). His unexpected victory attested to the broad support for his foreign policy and the enduring popularity of New Deal reform.

Truman failed to turn his victory into success for his Fair Deal agenda. Congress made modest improvements in Social Security and raised the minimum wage, but it passed only one significant reform measure. The Housing Act of 1949 authorized 810,000 units of government-constructed housing over the next six years and represented a landmark commitment by the government to address the housing needs of the poor. Yet it fell far short of actual need, and slum clearance frequently displaced the poor without providing alternatives.

With southern Democrats often joining the Republicans, Congress rejected Truman's proposals for civil rights, a uni-

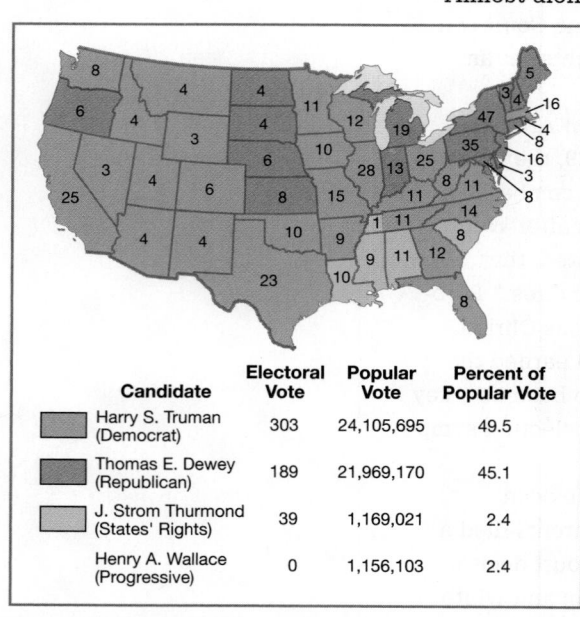

Candidate	Electoral Vote	Popular Vote	Percent of Popular Vote
Harry S. Truman (Democrat)	303	24,105,695	49.5
Thomas E. Dewey (Republican)	189	21,969,170	45.1
J. Strom Thurmond (States' Rights)	39	1,169,021	2.4
Henry A. Wallace (Progressive)	0	1,156,103	2.4

MAP 26.2 ■ The Election of 1948

versal health care program, and federal aid to education. His efforts to revise immigration policy were mixed. The McCarran-Walter Act of 1952 ended the outright ban on immigration and citizenship for Japanese and other Asians, but it also authorized the government to bar suspected Communists and homosexuals and maintained the discriminatory quota system established in the 1920s. Truman denounced that provision as "unworthy of our traditions and our ideals," but Congress overrode his veto.

By late 1950, the Korean War embroiled the president in controversy and depleted his power as a legislative leader. Truman's failure to make good on his domestic proposals set the United States apart from most European nations, which by the 1950s had in place comprehensive health, housing, and employment security programs to underwrite the material well-being of their populations.

The Domestic Chill: McCarthyism

Truman's domestic program also suffered from a wave of anticommunism that weakened liberal and leftist forces. "Red-baiting" (attempts to discredit individuals or ideas by associating them with communism) and official retaliation against leftist critics of the government had flourished during the Red scare at the end of World War I (see chapter 22). A second Red scare followed World War II, born of partisan political maneuvering, the collapse of the Soviet-American alliance, setbacks in U.S. foreign policy, and disclosures of Soviet espionage.

Republicans who had attacked the New Deal as a plot of radicals now jumped on such Cold War events as the Soviet takeover of Eastern Europe and the Communist triumph in China to accuse Democrats of fostering internal subversion. Wisconsin senator **Joseph R. McCarthy** avowed that "the Communists within our borders have been more responsible for the success of Communism abroad than Soviet Russia." McCarthy's charges—such as the allegation that retired general George C. Marshall belonged to a Communist conspiracy—were reckless and often ludicrous, but the press covered him avidly, and McCarthyism became a term synonymous with the anti-Communist crusade.

Joseph R. McCarthy

▶ Wisconsin senator who, beginning in 1950, led Senate investigations into alleged internal subversion of the United States. McCarthy's charges were reckless and often ludicrous, but the press covered him avidly, and McCarthyism became a term synonymous with the anti-Communist crusade.

Revelations of Soviet espionage gave some credibility to fears of internal communism. For example, a number of ex-Communists, including Whittaker Chambers and Elizabeth Bentley, testified that they and others had provided secret documents to the Soviets. Most alarming of all, in 1950 a British physicist working on the atomic bomb project confessed that he was a spy and implicated several Americans, including Ethel and Julius Rosenberg. The Rosenbergs pleaded innocent but were convicted of conspiracy to commit espionage and electrocuted in 1953.

Records opened in the 1990s showed that the Soviet Union did receive secret documents from Americans that probably hastened its development of nuclear weapons by a year or two. Yet the vast majority of individuals hunted down in the Red scare had done nothing more than at one time joining the Communist Party, associating with Communists, or supporting radical causes. And most of those activities had taken place long before the Cold War had made the Soviet Union an enemy.

The hunt for subversives was conducted by both Congress and the executive branch. Stung by charges of communism in the 1946 midterm elections, Truman

CHAPTER LOCATOR | What factors contributed to the Cold War? | What obstructed Truman's domestic agenda? | How did America's Cold War policy lead to the Korean War? | Conclusion: What were the costs and consequences of the Cold War?

737

issued Executive Order 9835 in March 1947, establishing loyalty review boards to investigate every federal employee. "A nightmare from which there [was] no awakening" was how State Department employee Esther Brunauer described it when she and her husband, a chemist in the navy, both lost their jobs because he had joined a Communist youth organization in the 1920s and associated with suspected radicals. Government investigators routinely violated the Bill of Rights by allowing anonymous informers to make charges and by placing the burden of proof on the accused. More than two thousand civil service employees lost their jobs, and another ten thousand resigned as Truman's loyalty program continued into the mid-1950s.

Congressional committees, such as the House Un-American Activities Committee (HUAC), also investigated individuals' past and present political associations. When those under scrutiny refused to name names, investigators charged that silence was tantamount to confession, and these "unfriendly witnesses" lost their jobs and suffered public ostracism. In 1947, HUAC investigated radical activity in Hollywood. Frank Sinatra protested, wondering if someone called for "a square deal for the underdog, will they call you a Commie? . . . Are they going to scare us into silence?" Some actors and directors cooperated, but ten refused, citing their First Amendment rights. The "Hollywood Ten" served jail sentences for contempt of Congress and then found themselves blacklisted in the movie industry.

The domestic Cold War spread beyond the nation's capital. State and local governments investigated citizens, demanded loyalty oaths, fired employees suspected of disloyalty, banned books from public libraries, and more. College professors and public school teachers lost their jobs in New York, California, and elsewhere. Because the Communist Party had helped organize unions and championed racial justice, labor and civil rights activists fell prey to McCarthyism as well. African American activist Jack O'Dell remembered that segregationists pinned the tag of Communist on "anybody who supported the right of blacks to have civil rights." McCarthyism caused untold harm to individuals innocent of breaking any law. Thousands of people were humiliated and discredited, hounded from their jobs, and in some cases even imprisoned. The anti-Communist crusade violated fundamental constitutional rights of freedom of speech and association, stifled expression of dissenting ideas, and removed unpopular causes from public contemplation.

> QUICK REVIEW

What was the impact of the Cold War on Truman's domestic agenda?

These demoralized U.S. soldiers reflect the grim situation for U.S. forces during the early months of the Korean War. Their North Korean captors forced them to march through Seoul in July 1950 carrying a banner proclaiming the righteousness of the Communist cause and attacking U.S. intervention. Wide World Photos, Inc.

How did America's Cold War policy lead to the Korean War?

THE COLD WAR ERUPTED into a shooting war in June 1950 when troops from Communist North Korea invaded South Korea. For the first time, Americans went into battle to implement containment. Confirming the global reach of the Truman Doctrine, U.S. involvement in Korea also marked the militarization of American foreign policy. The United States, in concert with the United Nations, ultimately held the line in Korea, but at a great cost in lives, dollars, and domestic unity.

Korea and the Military Implementation of Containment

The war grew out of the artificial division of Korea after World War II. Having expelled the Japanese, who had controlled Korea since 1904, the United States and the Soviet Union created two occupation zones separated by the thirty-eighth parallel (**Map 26.3,** page 740). With Moscow and Washington unable to agree on a unification plan, the United Nations sponsored elections in South Korea in July 1948. The American-favored candidate, Syngman Rhee, was elected president, and the United States withdrew most of its troops. In the fall of 1948, the Soviets established the People's Republic of North Korea under Kim Il-sung and also withdrew. Although doubting that Rhee's repressive government could sustain popular support, U.S. officials appreciated his staunch anticommunism and provided small amounts of economic and military aid to South Korea.

North and South Korean troops at the thirty-eighth parallel had engaged in skirmishes since 1948, but in June 1950, 90,000 North Koreans swept into South Korea. Assuming that the Soviet Union or China had instigated the attack (scholars learned later that they had not), Truman decided to intervene, viewing Korea as "the Greece of the Far East." With the Soviet Union boycotting the UN Security Council to protest its refusal to seat a representative from the People's Republic of

CHAPTER LOCATOR | What factors contributed to the Cold War? | What obstructed Truman's domestic agenda? | **How did America's Cold War policy lead to the Korean War?** | Conclusion: What were the costs and consequences of the Cold War?

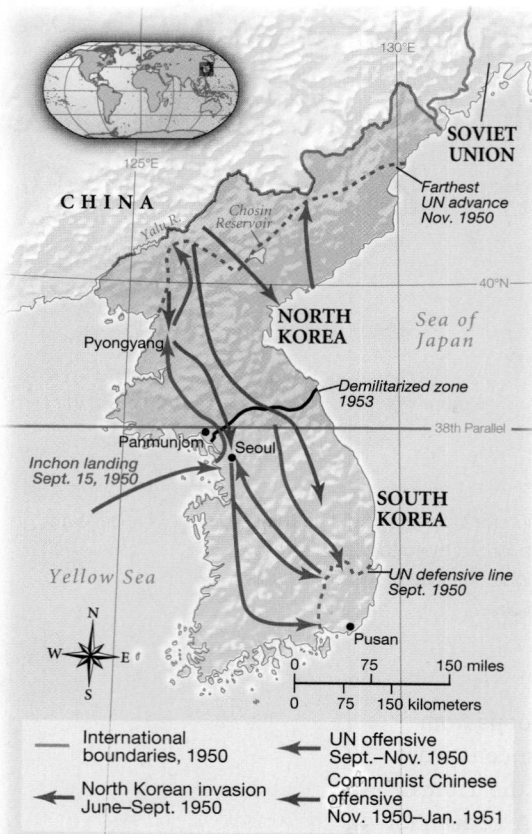

MAP 26.3 ■ The Korean War, 1950–1953
Although each side had plunged deep into enemy territory, the war ended in 1953 with the dividing line between North and South Korea nearly where it had been before the fighting began.

> ► FOR MORE HELP ANALYZING THIS MAP, see the map activity for this chapter in the Online Study Guide at bedfordstmartins.com/roarkunderstanding.

China, the United States obtained UN sponsorship of a collective effort to repel the attack. Authorized to appoint a commander for the UN force, Truman named General Douglas MacArthur, World War II hero and head of the postwar occupation of Japan.

Sixteen nations, including many NATO allies, sent troops to Korea, but the United States furnished most of the personnel and weapons, deploying almost 1.8 million troops and dictating military strategy. By failing to ask Congress for a declaration of war, Truman violated the spirit if not the letter of the Constitution. Moreover, although Congress appropriated funds to fight the war, the president's political opponents called it "Truman's war" when the military situation worsened.

The first American soldiers rushed to Korea unprepared and ill equipped, enduring severe defeats early in the war. The North Koreans took the capital of Seoul and drove deep into South Korea, forcing UN troops to retreat to Pusan. General MacArthur then launched a bold counteroffensive at Inchon, 180 miles behind North Korean lines. By mid-October, UN forces had pushed the North Koreans back to the thirty-eighth parallel. Then came the momentous decision of whether to invade North Korea and seek to unify the country.

From Containment to Rollback to Containment

"Troops could not be expected . . . to march up to a surveyor's line and stop," remarked Secretary of State Dean Acheson, reflecting popular and official support for transforming the military objective from containment to elimination of the enemy and unification of Korea. Thus, for the only time during the Cold War, the United States tried to roll back communism by force. With UN approval, Truman authorized MacArthur to cross the thirty-eighth parallel. Concerned about possible intervention by China or the Soviet Union, the president directed him to keep his troops away from the Korean-Chinese border. Disregarding the order, MacArthur sent UN forces to within forty miles of China, whereupon 300,000 Chinese soldiers crossed the Yalu River into Korea. With Chinese help, the North Koreans recaptured Seoul.

After three months of grueling battle, UN forces fought their way back to the thirty-eighth parallel. At that point, Truman decided to seek a negotiated settlement. MacArthur was furious when the goal of the war reverted to containment, which to him represented defeat. Taking his case to the public challenged both the president's authority to conduct foreign policy and the principle of civilian control of the military. Truman fired him in April 1951. Many Americans, however, sided with MacArthur. "Quite an explosion. . . . Letters of abuse by the dozens," Truman recorded in his diary. The adulation for MacArthur reflected American frustrations with containment. Why should Americans die simply to preserve the status quo? Why not destroy the enemy once and for all? In siding with MacArthur, Americans assumed that the United States was all-powerful and that stalemate in Korea resulted from the government's ineptitude or its willingness to shelter subversives.

When Congress investigated MacArthur's firing, all of the top military leaders supported the president. According to the chairman of the Joint Chiefs of Staff, MacArthur wanted to wage "the wrong war, at the wrong place, at the wrong time, with the wrong enemy." Yet Truman never recovered from the political fallout. Nor was he able to end the war. Negotiations began in July 1951, but peace talks dragged on for two more years while twelve thousand more U.S. soldiers died.

Korea, Communism, and the 1952 Election

Popular discontent with President Truman's war boosted Republican candidates in the 1952 election. Their presidential nominee, General **Dwight D. Eisenhower**, had emerged from World War II with immense popularity. As supreme commander in Europe, he won widespread acclaim for leading the Allied armies to victory over Germany. After the war, he served as army chief of staff, and in 1950 Truman appointed Eisenhower the first supreme commander of NATO forces.

Although Eisenhower believed that professional soldiers should stay out of politics, he found compelling reasons to run in 1952. The general largely agreed with Democratic foreign policy, but he deplored the Democrats' propensity to solve domestic problems with costly new federal programs. He equally disliked the foreign policy views of the leading Republican presidential contender, Senator Robert A. Taft, who attacked containment and sought to cut defense spending. Eisenhower defeated Taft for the nomination, but the old guard wrote a party platform that excoriated containment as "negative, futile, and immoral" and charged the Truman administration with shielding "traitors to the Nation in high places." By choosing thirty-nine-year-old Senator Richard M. Nixon for his running mate, Eisenhower helped to appease the right wing of the party and ensured that anticommunism would be a major theme of the campaign.

Richard Milhous Nixon grew up in southern California, worked his way through college and law school, served in the navy, and briefly practiced law. In 1946, he defeated a liberal incumbent for a seat in the House of Representatives. Nixon quickly made a name for himself as a member of HUAC and a key anti-Communist, and he won election to the Senate in 1950.

With his public approval ratings sinking, Truman decided not to run for reelection. The Democrats nominated Adlai E. Stevenson, the popular governor of Illinois, who was acceptable to both liberals and southerners. Stevenson could not escape the domestic fallout from the Korean War, however, nor could he match the widespread appeal of Eisenhower. The Republican campaign stumbled just once, over the last item of its "Korea, Communism, and Corruption" theme. When the press reported that Nixon had accepted money from a private political fund supported by wealthy Californians, Democrats jumped to the attack, even though such gifts were common and legal. While Eisenhower considered dumping Nixon from the ticket, Nixon made an emotional nationwide appeal on the new medium of television. He disclosed his finances and documented his modest standard of living. Conceding that the family pet, Checkers, might be considered an illegal gift, Nixon refused to break his daughters' hearts by returning the cocker spaniel. The overwhelmingly positive response to the "Checkers speech" kept Nixon on the ticket.

CHRONOLOGY

1948
– American and Soviet forces withdraw from divided Korea.

1950
– **June.** 90,000 North Koreans invade South Korea.

– **September.** United Nations authorizes the invasion of Korea, under U.S. general Douglas MacArthur's command.

1951
– Truman fires General Douglas MacArthur for insubordination.

1952
– Republican Dwight D. Eisenhower is elected president.

1953
– Armistice ends Korean War.

Dwight D. Eisenhower

▶ Enormously popular military figure from World War II who became the Republican presidential nominee in the 1952 election. In favor of containment and a well-funded military but wary of expensive domestic social programs, Eisenhower decided to run to curtail the influence of conservative Republicans and the Democratic Party. He won decisively and helped the Republican Party gain a narrow congressional majority.

CHAPTER LOCATOR | What factors contributed to the Cold War? | What obstructed Truman's domestic agenda? | How did America's Cold War policy lead to the Korean War? | Conclusion: What were the costs and consequences of the Cold War?

741

Shortly before the election, Eisenhower announced dramatically, "I shall go to Korea," and voters registered their confidence in his ability to end the war. Cutting sharply into traditional Democratic territory, Eisenhower won several southern states and garnered 55 percent of the popular vote overall. His coattails carried a narrow Republican majority to Congress.

An Armistice and the War's Costs

Eisenhower made good on his pledge to end the Korean War. In July 1953, the two sides reached an armistice that left Korea divided, again roughly at the thirty-eighth parallel, with North and South separated by a two-and-a-half-mile-wide demilitarized zone (see Map 26.3, page 740). The Truman administration judged the war a success for containment, since the United States had backed up its promise to help nations that were resisting communism. Both Truman and Eisenhower managed to contain what amounted to a world war—involving twenty nations altogether—within a single country and to avoid the use of nuclear weapons.

The Human Toll of the Korean War

36,000 Americans were killed, and 100,000 were wounded.

South Korea lost more than 1 million people to war-related causes.

More than 1.8 million North Koreans and Chinese were killed or wounded.

The Korean War had an enormous effect on defense policy and spending. In April 1950, two months before the war began, the National Security Council completed a top-secret report, known as NSC 68, on the United States' military strength. It warned that the survival of the nation required a massive military buildup and a tripling of the defense budget. Truman took no immediate action on these recommendations, but the Korean War brought about nearly all of the military expansion called for in NSC 68, vastly increasing U.S. capacity to act as a global power. Military spending shot up from $14 billion in 1950 to $50 billion in 1953 and remained above $40 billion thereafter. By 1953, defense spending claimed 60 percent of the federal budget, and the size of the armed forces had tripled.

To General Matthew Ridgway, MacArthur's successor as commander of the UN forces, Korea taught the lesson that U.S. forces should never again fight a land war in Asia. Nevertheless, the Korean War induced the Truman administration to expand its role in Asia by increasing aid to the French, who were fighting to hang onto their colonial empire in Indochina. As U.S. Marines retreated from a battle against Chinese soldiers in 1950, they sang, prophetically, "We're Harry's police force on call, / So put back your pack on, / The next step is Saigon, / Cheer up, me lads, bless 'em all."

> **QUICK REVIEW**

How did the Korean War shape American foreign policy in the 1950s?

The Granger Collection, New York.

Conclusion: What were the costs and consequences of the Cold War?

MORE THAN ANY DEVELOPMENT in the postwar world, the Cold War defined American politics and society for decades to come. It transformed the federal government, shifting its priorities from domestic to external affairs, greatly expanding its budget, and substantially increasing the power of the president. Military spending helped transform the nation itself, as defense contracts encouraged economic and population booms in the West and Southwest. The nuclear arms race put the people of the world at risk, consumed resources that might have been used to improve living standards, and skewed the economy toward dependence on military projects.

In sharp contrast to foreign policy, the domestic policies of the postwar years reflected continuity with the past. Most of the New Deal reforms remained in place despite Republicans' promises to turn back the clock. However, Truman's proposals for new programs in education, health, and civil rights failed to win congressional support. Consequently, the poor and minorities suffered even while a majority of Americans enjoyed a higher standard of living in an economy boosted by Cold War spending and the reconstruction of Western Europe and Japan.

Many Americans, not accustomed to paying sustained attention to foreign policy or to fighting wars without total defeat of the enemy, had difficulty accepting the terms of the Cold War. Consequently, another high cost of the Cold War was the anti-Communist hysteria that swept the nation, stifling debate and narrowing the range of ideas acceptable for political discussion. Partisan politics and Truman's warnings about the Communist menace fueled McCarthyism, but the obsession with subversion also fed on popular frustrations over the failure of containment to produce clear-cut victories. Convulsing the nation in bitter disunity, McCarthyism reflected a loss of confidence in American power. That frustration grew with the Korean War, which ended in stalemate rather than the defeat of communism. It would be a major challenge of the next administration to restore national unity and confidence.

SO NOW YOU KNOW

President Truman's order to desegregate the U.S. military in 1948 was not actually implemented until the Korean War, when commanders realized that segregation hindered military effectiveness. Many of Truman's other liberal proposals faltered because of the wave of anti-Communism that attended the Cold War.

CHAPTER LOCATOR | What factors contributed to the Cold War? | What obstructed Truman's domestic agenda? | How did America's Cold War policy lead to the Korean War? | Conclusion: What were the costs and consequences of the Cold War?

743

STEP 1
GETTING STARTED

Below are basic terms from this period in American history. Can you identify each term below and explain why it matters? To do this exercise online or to download this chart, visit bedfordstmartins.com/roarkunderstanding.

TERM	WHO OR WHAT & WHEN	WHY IT MATTERS
Harry S. Truman, p. 722		
iron curtain, p. 725		
containment, p. 725		
Truman Doctrine, p. 726		
Marshall Plan, p. 726		
North Atlantic Treaty Organization (NATO), p. 728		
Central Intelligence Agency (CIA), p. 728		
Mao Zedong, p. 729		
Fair Deal, p. 731		
The Servicemen's Readjustment Act (GI Bill), p. 733		
Joseph R. McCarthy, p. 737		
Dwight D. Eisenhower, p. 741		

STEP 2
MOVING BEYOND THE BASICS

The exercise below represents a more advanced understanding of the chapter material. Examine the key areas of conflict between the United States and the Soviet Union in the early years of the Cold War. In the chart, describe the American and Soviet actions and policies between 1945 and 1953 in Germany, Eastern Europe, Turkey and Greece, and Asia. Then, consider the following questions: What overarching strategies emerged out of the conflicts you described in the chart? What did each side come to believe about the other's strategy and ambitions? What role did mutual misunderstanding and mistrust play in the increasing tensions between the United States and the Soviet Union? To do this exercise online or to download this chart, visit bedfordstmartins.com/roarkunderstanding.

The Cold War, 1945–1953	American actions and policies	Soviet actions and policies
Germany		
Eastern Europe		
Turkey and Greece		
Asia		

Now that you've reviewed various parts of the chapter, take a step back and try to see the big picture by answering these questions. Remember to use specific examples from the chapter in your answers. To do this exercise online, visit bedfordstmartins.com/roarkunderstanding.

THE UNITED STATES AND THE POSTWAR WORLD

► What interests did American and Soviet policymakers think were at stake in Eastern Europe? How did events in the region contribute to the growing Cold War?

► What was the policy of containment? What assumptions about Soviet power and intentions were at the heart of the policy?

TRUMAN AND THE FAIR DEAL

► How did Truman propose to expand the New Deal? In what areas did he succeed, and in what areas did he fail?

► What explains the rise of McCarthyism? Why did so many Americans believe that the country faced a grave internal threat to its security?

THE KOREAN WAR

► How did the policy of containment lead to American involvement in Korea?

► What impact did the Korean War have on American domestic politics?

LOOKING BACKWARD, LOOKING AHEAD

► How did American and Soviet experiences between 1918 and 1945 lay the groundwork for the Cold War?

► How did the Cold War set the stage for American life in the 1950s?

IN YOUR OWN WORDS

Imagine that you must explain chapter 26 to someone who hasn't read it. What would be the most important points to include and why?

27
THE POLITICS AND CULTURE OF ABUNDANCE

1952–1960

> This chapter examines the politics and culture of the Eisenhower years. It explores President Eisenhower's domestic and foreign policies, the causes and consequences of the prosperity of the 1950s, and the challenges to the era's status quo, most importantly the challenge African Americans made to racial segregation and discrimination.

> What was Eisenhower's "middle way" on domestic issues?

> How did Eisenhower's foreign policy differ from Truman's?

> What fueled the prosperity of the 1950s?

> How did prosperity affect American society and culture?

> How did African Americans fight for their rights in the 1950s?

> Conclusion: What unmet challenges did peace and prosperity mask?

DID YOU KNOW?

The CIA helped to overthrow the democratically elected government of Iran in 1953.

The Margulies family of Scarsdale, New York, 1952. They are displaying all the things from their house that are made of plastic.

What was Eisenhower's "middle way" on domestic issues?

President Dwight D. Eisenhower's "middle way" earned him broad support, particularly among the white middle classes. The slogan "I Like Ike," coined for his bid for reelection, emphasized his personal appeal, which helped him easily defeat Adlai Stevenson in 1956. © Bettmann/Corbis.

MODERATION WAS THE GUIDING PRINCIPLE of Eisenhower's domestic agenda and leadership style. In 1953, he pledged a "middle way between untrammeled freedom of the individual and the demands for the welfare of the whole Nation," promising that his administration would "avoid government by bureaucracy as carefully as it avoids neglect of the helpless." Eisenhower generally resisted expanding the federal government's power, he acted reluctantly when the Supreme Court ordered schools to desegregate, and his administration terminated the federal trusteeship of dozens of Indian tribes. As a moderate Republican, however, Eisenhower supported the continuation, and in some cases the expansion, of New Deal programs. Nicknamed "Ike," the confident war hero was popular, but he was not able to lift the Republican Party to national dominance.

Modern Republicanism

In contrast to the old guard conservatives in his party who criticized containment and wanted to repeal much of the New Deal, Eisenhower preached "modern Republicanism." This meant resisting additional federal intervention in economic and social life, but not turning the clock back to the 1920s. Democratic control of Congress after the elections of 1954 further contributed to Eisenhower's moderate approach.

The new president attempted to distance himself from the anti-Communist fervor that had plagued the Truman administration. Yet Eisenhower intensified Truman's loyalty program, allowing federal executives to dismiss thousands of employees on grounds of loyalty, security, or "suitability." Moreover, Eisenhower refused to denounce Senator Joseph McCarthy publicly. In 1954, McCarthy began to destroy himself when he went after the army. As he hurled charges of communism

CHAPTER LOCATOR | What was Eisenhower's "middle way" on domestic issues?

748 CHAPTER 27 THE POLITICS AND CULTURE OF ABUNDANCE, 1952–1960

against military personnel during weeks of televised hearings, public opinion turned against him. When the army's lawyer demanded of McCarthy, "Have you left no sense of decency?" those in the hearing room applauded. A Senate vote to condemn McCarthy in December 1954 marked the end of his influence.

Eisenhower sometimes echoed the conservative Republicans' conviction that government was best left to the states and economic decisions to private business. Yet he signed laws bringing ten million more workers into Social Security, increasing the minimum wage, and continuing the federal government's modest role in financing public housing. He created a new Department of Health, Education, and Welfare, appointing as its head former Women's Army Corps commander Oveta Culp Hobby, the second woman to hold a cabinet post. And when the spread of polio neared epidemic proportions, Eisenhower obtained funds from Congress to distribute a vaccine, even though conservatives wanted to leave that responsibility to the states.

Eisenhower's greatest domestic initiative was the **Interstate Highway and Defense System Act of 1956 (Map 27.1)**. Promoted as essential to national defense and an impetus to economic growth, the act authorized the construction of a national highway system, with the federal government paying most of the costs through increased fuel and vehicle taxes. The new highways accelerated the mobility of Americans and goods and spurred suburban expansion, shopping malls, and growth in the fast-food and tourism industries; and the law substantially benefited the trucking, construction, and automobile industries that had lobbied hard for it. Unforeseen costs eventually emerged in the form of air pollution, energy consumption, declining railroads and mass transportation, and the decay of central cities.

In other areas, Eisenhower restrained federal activity in favor of state governments and private enterprise. His large tax cuts directed most benefits to business and the wealthy, and he stubbornly resisted national health insurance, federal aid to primary and secondary education, and White House leadership on behalf of civil rights. Moreover, whereas Democrats sought to keep nuclear power in government hands, Eisenhower signed legislation authorizing the private manufacture and sale of nuclear energy.

CHRONOLOGY

1953
- Republican Dwight D. Eisenhower becomes president.
- Congress begins termination of special status of American Indian tribes, and thousands continue to be relocated from reservations.

1954
- Senate condemns Senator Joseph McCarthy.

1956
- Interstate Highway and Defense System Act.
- Eisenhower is reelected to second term by a landslide.

Interstate Highway and Defense System Act of 1956

▶ Law authorizing the construction of a national highway system, with the federal government paying most of the costs through increased fuel and vehicle taxes. Promoted as essential to national defense and an impetus to economic growth, the national highway system accelerated the movement of people and goods and changed the nature of American communities.

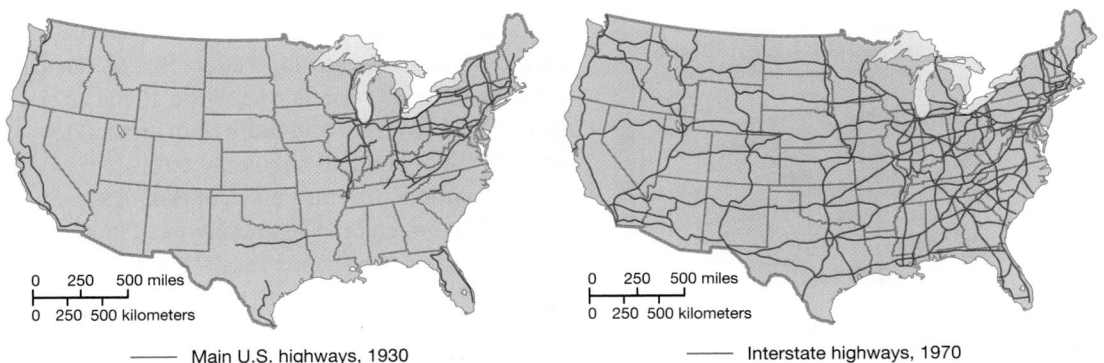

0   250   500 miles
0   250 500 kilometers

——— Main U.S. highways, 1930

0   250   500 miles
0   250 500 kilometers

——— Interstate highways, 1970

MAP 27.1 ■ The Interstate Highway System, 1930 and 1970

Built with federal funds authorized in the Interstate Highway and Defense System Act of 1956, superhighways soon crisscrossed the nation. Trucking, construction, gasoline, and travel were among the industries that prospered, but railroads suffered from the subsidized competition.

| How did Eisenhower's foreign policy differ from Truman's? | What fueled the prosperity of the 1950s? | How did prosperity affect American society and culture? | How did African Americans fight for their rights in the 1950s? | Conclusion: What unmet challenges did peace and prosperity mask? |

749

Termination and Relocation of Native Americans

Eisenhower's efforts to limit the federal government were consistent with a new direction in Indian policy, which reversed the emphasis on strengthening tribal governments and preserving Indian culture that had been established in the 1930s (see chapter 24). After World War II, when some 25,000 Indians had left their homes for military service and another 40,000 for work in defense industries, policymakers began to favor assimilating Native Americans and ending their special relationships with the government.

To some officials, the communal practices of Indians resembled socialism and stifled individual initiative. Eisenhower's commissioner of Indian affairs, Glenn Emmons, did not believe that tribal lands could produce income sufficient to lift Indians from poverty, but he also revealed the ethnocentrism of policymakers when he insisted that Indians wanted to "work and live like Americans."

By 1960, the government had implemented a three-part program of compensation, termination, and relocation. In 1946, Congress established the Indian Claims Commission to discharge outstanding claims by Native Americans for land taken by the government. When it closed in 1978, the commission had settled 285 cases, with compensation exceeding $800 million. Yet the awards were based on land values at the time the land was taken and did not include interest.

The second policy, termination, also originated in the Truman administration, when Commissioner Dillon S. Myer asserted that his Bureau of Indian Affairs should do "nothing for Indians which Indians can do for themselves." Beginning in 1953, Eisenhower signed bills transferring jurisdiction over tribal land to state and local governments and ending the trusteeship relationship between Indians and the federal government. The loss of federal hospitals, schools, and other special arrangements devastated Indian tribes. As had happened after passage of the Dawes Act in 1887 (see chapter 17), some corporate interests and individuals took advantage of the opportunity to purchase Indian land cheaply. The government abandoned termination in the 1960s after some 13,000 Indians and more than one million acres of their land had been affected.

Relocation, the third piece of Native American policy, began in 1948 and involved more than 100,000 Native Americans by 1973. The government encouraged Indians to move to cities, where relocation centers were supposed to help with housing, job training, and medical care. About one-third returned to the reservation. Most who stayed in cities faced racism, lack of adequately paying jobs for which they had skills,

Indian Relocation

As part of its new emphasis on assimilation in the late 1940s and 1950s, the Bureau of Indian Affairs distributed this leaflet to entice Native Americans to move from their reservations to cities. Either with government assistance or on their own, thousands of Indians relocated in the years after World War II. National Archives.

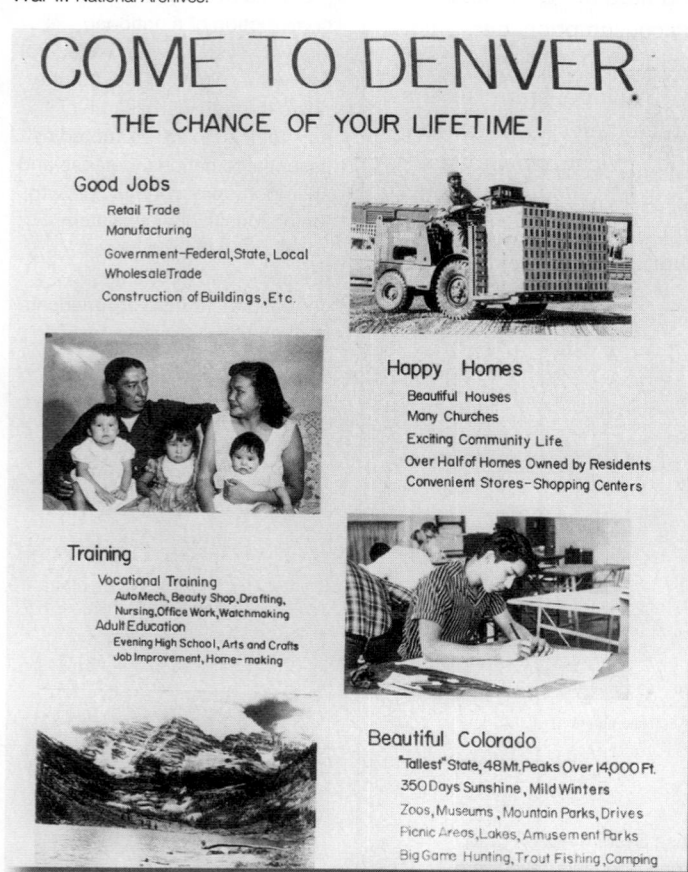

CHAPTER LOCATOR | What was Eisenhower's "middle way" on domestic issues?

poor housing, and the loss of their traditional culture. "I wish we had never left home," said one woman whose husband was out of work. "It's dirty and noisy, and people all around, crowded. . . . It seems like I never see the sky or trees."

Reflecting long-standing disagreements among Indians themselves, some who overcame these obstacles applauded the program. But most urban Indians remained in or near poverty, and even many who had welcomed relocation began to worry that "we would lose our identity as Indian people, lose our culture and our [way] of living." Within two decades, a national pan-Indian movement, a by-product of urbanization, emerged to resist assimilation and demand much more for Indians (see chapter 28).

The 1956 Election and the Second Term

Eisenhower easily defeated Adlai Stevenson in 1956, doubling his margin of 1952. Yet Democrats kept control of Congress, and in the midterm elections two years later, they all but wiped out the Republican Party, gaining a 64–34 majority in the Senate and a 282–135 advantage in the House. Although Ike captured voters' hearts, a majority of Americans remained wedded to the programs and policies of the Democrats.

Eisenhower faced more serious leadership challenges in his second term. When the economy plunged into a recession in late 1957, Eisenhower fought with Congress over the budget and vetoed bills to expand housing, urban develop-ment, and public works projects. In the end, the first Republican administration after the New Deal left the size and functions of the federal government intact, though it tipped policy somewhat more in favor of corporate interests. Unparal-leled prosperity graced the 1950s, and Eisenhower celebrated what he called the "wide diffusion of wealth and incomes" across the United States. Yet neglected amid the remarkable abundance were some forty million Americans who lived below the poverty level. Rural deprivation was particularly pronounced, as was poverty among African Americans and other minorities.

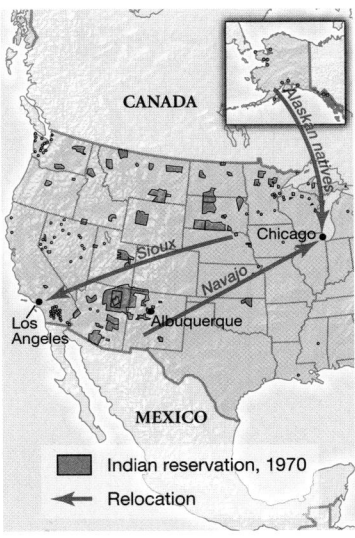

Major Indian Relocations, 1950–1970

QUICK REVIEW <

How did Eisenhower's domestic policies reflect his moderate political vision?

| How did Eisenhower's foreign policy differ from Truman's? | What fueled the prosperity of the 1950s? | How did prosperity affect American society and culture? | How did African Americans fight for their rights in the 1950s? | Conclusion: What unmet challenges did peace and prosperity mask? |

How did Eisenhower's foreign policy differ from Truman's?

The Nuclear Arms Race

Soviet Premier Nikita Khrushchev speaks at his arrival at Andrews Air Force Base in September 1959 for talks with President Eisenhower that both hoped would defuse the nuclear threat. Behind the two leaders are the Soviet ambassador, Mikhail Menshikov, and the U.S. Secretary of State, Christian Herter. At the close of their summit Eisenhower and Khrushchev issued a statement declaring that "the question of general disarmament is the most important one facing the world today." © Bettmann/Corbis.

AT HIS 1953 INAUGURATION, Eisenhower warned that "forces of good and evil are massed and armed and opposed as rarely before in history." Like Truman, he saw communism as a threat to the nation's security and economic interests. Eisenhower's foreign policy differed from Truman's, however, in three areas: its rhetoric, its means, and—after Stalin's death in 1953—its movement toward accommodation with the Soviet Union. Republican rhetoric, voiced most prominently by Secretary of State John Foster Dulles, deplored containment as "negative, futile, and immoral" because it accepted the existing Soviet sphere of control. Yet despite promises to roll back Soviet power, the Eisenhower administration continued the containment policy.

The "New Look" in Foreign Policy

To meet his goals of balancing the budget and cutting taxes, Eisenhower was determined to control military expenditures. Moreover, he feared that massive defense spending would threaten the nation's economic strength. Reflecting Americans' confidence in technology and opposition to a large peacetime army, Eisenhower's defense strategy concentrated U.S. military strength in nuclear

CHAPTER LOCATOR | What was Eisenhower's "middle way" on domestic issues?

weapons and the planes and missiles to deliver them. Instead of maintaining large ground forces of its own, the United States would give friendly nations American weapons and back them up with a nuclear arsenal. This was Eisenhower's "New Look" in foreign policy. Secretary of State Dulles believed that America's willingness to "go to the brink" of war—a strategy called brinkmanship—would block any Soviet efforts to expand.

Nuclear weapons could not stop a Soviet nuclear attack, but in response to one, they could inflict enormous destruction. This certainty of "massive retaliation" was meant to deter the Soviets from launching an attack. Because the Soviet Union could respond similarly to an American first strike, this nuclear standoff became known as **mutually assured destruction**, or **MAD**. Yet leaders of each nation sought not just balance but nuclear superiority, and they pursued an ever-escalating arms race.

Nuclear weapons, however, could not roll back the iron curtain. When a revolt against the Soviet-controlled government began in Hungary in 1956, Dulles's liberation rhetoric proved to be empty. A radio plea from Hungarian freedom fighters cried, "SOS! They just brought us a rumor that the American troops will be here within one or two hours." But help did not come. Eisenhower was unwilling to risk U.S. soldiers and possible nuclear war, and Soviet troops soon suppressed the insurrection, killing thousands of Hungarians.

Applying Containment to Vietnam

A major challenge to the containment policy came in Southeast Asia. During World War II, Ho Chi Minh, a Vietnamese nationalist, had founded a coalition called the Vietminh to fight both the occupying Japanese forces and the French colonial rulers. In 1945, the Vietminh declared Vietnam's independence from France, and when France fought to maintain its colony, the area plunged into war (see Map 29.2, page 808). Because Ho declared himself a Communist, the Truman administration quietly began to provide aid to the French.

Eisenhower viewed communism in Vietnam much as Truman had regarded it in Greece and Turkey, a view that became known as the domino theory. "You have a row of dominoes," Eisenhower explained, and "you knock over the first one, and what will happen to the last one is the certainty that it will go over very quickly." A Communist victory in Southeast Asia, he warned, could trigger the fall of Japan, Taiwan, and the Philippines. By 1954, the United States was contributing 75 percent of the cost of France's war, but Eisenhower resisted a larger role. When the French asked for troops and airplanes from the United States to avert almost certain defeat at Dien Bien Phu, Eisenhower, conscious of U.S. losses in the Korean War, said no.

Dien Bien Phu fell in May 1954 and with it the French colony of Vietnam. Two months later in Geneva, France signed a truce. The Geneva accords temporarily partitioned Vietnam at the seventeenth parallel, separating the Vietminh in the north from the puppet government established by the French in the south. Within two years, the Vietnamese people were to vote in elections for a unified government. Eisenhower began to send weapons and military advisers to South Vietnam and put the CIA to work infiltrating and destabilizing North Vietnam. Fearing a Communist victory in the elections mandated by the Geneva accords, the United States supported South Vietnamese prime minister Ngo Dinh Diem's refusal to hold the vote.

CHRONOLOGY

1953
- CIA engineers coup against government of Iran.

1954
- CIA stages coup against government of Guatemala.
- France signs Geneva accords, withdrawing from Vietnam.
- Eisenhower begins to send weapons and military advisers to South Vietnam.

1955
- Eisenhower and Khrushchev meet in Geneva.

1956
- Eisenhower pressures Britain and France to end the Suez crisis.

1957
- Soviets launch *Sputnik*.

1958
- National Aeronautics and Space Administration is established.

1960
- Soviets shoot down U.S. U-2 spy plane.

1961
- Eisenhower warns of military-industrial complex in farewell address.

mutually assured destruction (MAD)
▶ The proposition that the vast nuclear arsenals of the United States and the Soviet Union assured that both would be destroyed if either launched an attack on the other. This probability of mutually assured destruction led both superpowers to show restraint. It did not, however, prevent them from attempting to achieve nuclear superiority.

| How did Eisenhower's foreign policy differ from Truman's? | What fueled the prosperity of the 1950s? | How did prosperity affect American society and culture? | How did African Americans fight for their rights in the 1950s? | Conclusion: What unmet challenges did peace and prosperity mask? |

753

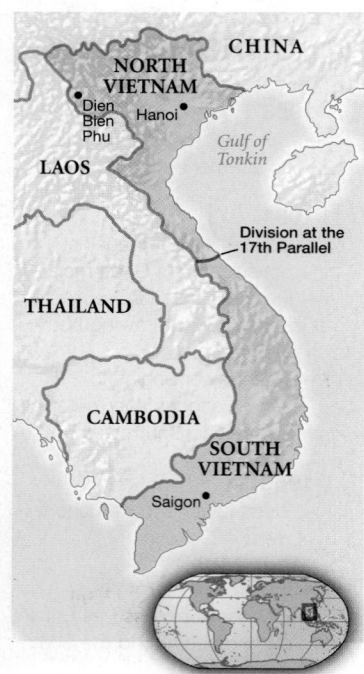

Geneva Accords, 1954

Despite massive American aid, South Vietnam's army proved unprepared for the guerrilla warfare that began in the late 1950s. With military assistance from Ho Chi Minh's government in Hanoi, Vietminh rebels in the south stepped up their guerrilla attacks on the Diem government. The insurgents gained support from the largely Buddhist peasants who were outraged by the repressive regime of the Catholic, Westernized Diem. Unwilling to abandon containment, Eisenhower left office with a deteriorating situation and a firm commitment to defend South Vietnam against communism.

Interventions in Latin America and the Middle East

While supporting friendly governments in Asia, the Eisenhower administration worked secretly to topple unfriendly ones in Latin America and the Middle East. Officials saw internal civil wars in terms of the Cold War conflict between the superpowers and tended to view nationalist uprisings as Communist threats to democracy. They also acted against governments that threatened U.S. economic interests. The Eisenhower administration took this course of action out of sight of Congress and the public, making the CIA an important arm of foreign policy.

The government of Guatemala, under the popularly elected reformist president Jacobo Arbenz, was not Soviet controlled, but it accepted support from the local Communist Party (see Map 29.1, page 805). In 1953, Arbenz moved to nationalize land owned but not cultivated by the United Fruit Company, a U.S. corporation whose annual profits were twice the size of the Guatemalan government's budget. United Fruit refused Arbenz's offer to compensate it at the value of the land the company had declared for tax purposes. Then, in response to the nationalization program, the CIA organized and supported an opposition army that overthrew the elected government and installed a military dictatorship in 1954. United Fruit kept its land, and Guatemala succumbed to a series of destructive civil wars that lasted through the 1990s.

When Cubans' desire for political and economic autonomy erupted in 1959, a CIA agent promised "to take care of Castro just like we took care of Arbenz." American companies had long controlled major Cuban resources, and decisions made in Washington directly influenced the lives of the Cuban people. An uprising in 1959 led by **Fidel Castro** drove out the U.S.-supported dictator Fulgencio Batista and led the CIA to warn Eisenhower that "Communists and other extreme radicals appear to have penetrated the Castro movement." When the United States denied Castro's requests for loans, he turned to the Soviet Union. And when U.S. companies refused Castro's offer to purchase them at their assessed value, he began to nationalize their property. Many anti-Castro Cubans fled to the United States and reported his atrocities, including the execution of hundreds of Batista's supporters. Before leaving office, Eisenhower broke off diplomatic relations with Cuba and authorized the CIA to train Cuban exiles for an invasion.

In the Middle East, the CIA intervened to oust an elected government, support an unpopular dictatorship, and maintain Western access to Iranian oil (see Map 30.3, page 841). Mohammed Mossadegh, the left-leaning democratic prime minister of Iran, accepted support from the Iranian Communist Party and

Fidel Castro
▶ Leader of the 1959 uprising against Fulgencio Batista, the Cuban dictator backed by the United States. Castro's policies, including the nationalization of American-owned industries in Cuba and the acquisition of loans from the Soviet Union, made him an enemy of the United States.

CHAPTER LOCATOR | What was Eisenhower's "middle way" on domestic issues?

CHAPTER 27
754 THE POLITICS AND CULTURE OF ABUNDANCE, 1952–1960

challenged the power of Shah Mohammad Reza Pahlavi, Iran's hereditary leader, who favored foreign oil interests and the Iranian wealthy classes. In 1951, the Iranian parliament nationalized the oil fields and refineries, then held mostly by the British.

Advisers convinced Eisenhower that Mossadegh's government left Iran vulnerable to communism, and the president wanted to keep oil-rich areas "under the control of people who are friendly." With his authorization, CIA agents instigated a coup. In August 1953, Iranian army officers captured Mossadegh and reestablished the shah's power, whereupon Iran renegotiated its oil concessions, giving U.S. companies a 40 percent share. Resentment over this use of force would poison U.S.-Iranian relations into the twenty-first century.

Elsewhere in the Middle East, the Eisenhower administration continued Truman's support of Israel but also sought to foster friendships with Arab nations to secure access to oil and to build a bulwark against communism. Yet U.S. officials demanded that smaller nations take the American side in the Cold War, even when those nations preferred neutrality. In 1955, as part of the U.S. effort to win Arab allies, Secretary of State Dulles began talks with Egypt about American support to build the Aswan Dam on the Nile River. The following year, Egypt's leader, Gamal Abdel Nasser, sought arms from Communist Czechoslovakia, formed a military alliance with other Arab nations, and recognized the People's Republic of China. In retaliation, Dulles called off the deal for the dam.

On July 26, 1956, Nasser responded by seizing the Suez Canal, then owned by Britain and France but scheduled to revert to Egypt within seven years. In response to the seizure, Israel, whose forces had been skirmishing with Egyptian troops along their common border since 1948, attacked Egypt with military help from Britain and France. Eisenhower opposed the intervention, recognizing that the Egyptians had claimed their own territory and that Nasser "embodie[d] the emotional demands of the people . . . for independence." He put economic pressure on Britain and France while calling on the United Nations to arrange a truce. The French and British soon pulled back, forcing Israel to retreat.

Despite staying out of the Suez crisis, Eisenhower made it clear that the United States would actively combat communism in the Middle East. In March 1957, Congress passed a joint resolution approving aid to any Middle Eastern nation "requesting assistance against armed aggression from any country controlled by international communism." The president invoked this Eisenhower Doctrine to send aid to Jordan in 1957 and troops to Lebanon in 1958 to counter anti-Western pressures on those governments.

The Nuclear Arms Race

While Eisenhower moved against perceived Communist inroads abroad, he also sought to reduce superpower tensions. After Stalin's death in 1953, a more moderate leadership under **Nikita Khrushchev** emerged. Like Eisenhower, who remarked

The CIA Helps Restore the Shah of Iran

In 1952, *Time* magazine called Iranian premier Mohammed Mossadegh, who was passionately committed to nationalism and democracy, "the Iranian George Washington." But Secretary of State John Foster Dulles believed that restoration of the shah's power would produce a more stable ally in an oil-rich region and he persuaded Eisenhower to approve a coup against Mossadegh. © Bettmann/Corbis.

Nikita Khrushchev

▶ More moderate Soviet leader who came to power after the death of Joseph Stalin in 1953. Khrushchev wanted to reduce defense spending and the threat of nuclear devastation. The change in leadership led to talks between Khrushchev and Eisenhower; the talks, however, failed to produce any agreements.

| How did Eisenhower's foreign policy differ from Truman's? | What fueled the prosperity of the 1950s? | How did prosperity affect American society and culture? | How did African Americans fight for their rights in the 1950s? | Conclusion: What unmet challenges did peace and prosperity mask? |

755

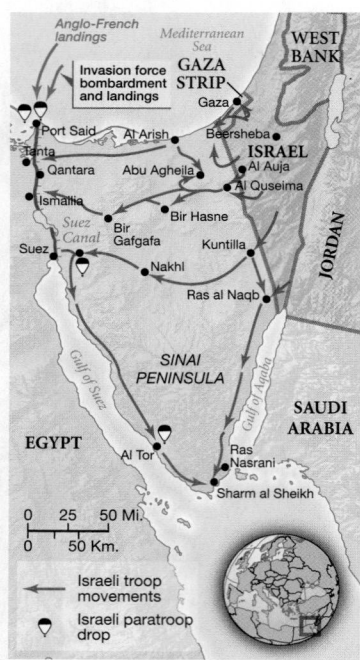

The Suez Crisis, 1956

Israeli troop movements

Israeli paratroop drop

military-industrial complex

▶ The name Eisenhower gave in his farewell address in 1961 to the combined effort of big business and the military to press for an ever-increasing share of national resources for the development of new weapons.

privately that the arms race would lead "at worst to atomic warfare, at best to robbing every people and nation on earth of the fruits of their own toil," Khrushchev wanted to reduce defense spending and the threat of nuclear devastation. Eisenhower and Khrushchev met in Geneva in 1955 at the first summit conference since the end of World War II. Although the meeting produced no new agreements, it symbolized what Eisenhower called "a new spirit of conciliation and cooperation."

In August 1957, the Soviets test-fired their first intercontinental ballistic missile and two months later beat the United States into space by launching *Sputnik*, the first artificial satellite to circle the earth. The United States launched a successful satellite of its own in January 1958, but *Sputnik* raised fears that the United States lagged behind the Soviet Union not only in missile development and space exploration but also in science and education. In response, Eisenhower established the National Aeronautics and Space Administration (NASA) and signed the National Defense Education Act, providing support for students in math, foreign languages, and science.

Eisenhower assured the public that the United States possessed nuclear superiority. In fact, during his presidency, the stockpile of nuclear weapons more than quadrupled. Yet these weapons could not guarantee security, because both superpowers possessed sufficient nuclear capacity to devastate each other. Most Americans did not follow Civil Defense Administration recommendations to construct home bomb shelters, but they did realize how precarious nuclear weapons had made their lives.

In the midst of the arms race, the superpowers continued to talk. In 1959, Khrushchev visited the United States, and Nixon went to the Soviet Union. By 1960, the two sides were close to a ban on nuclear testing. But just before a summit in Paris, a Soviet missile shot down a U-2 spy plane over Soviet territory. The State Department first denied that U.S. planes had been violating Soviet airspace, but the Soviets produced the pilot and the photos taken on his flight. Eisenhower and Khrushchev met briefly in Paris, but the U-2 incident dashed all prospects for a nuclear arms agreement.

As Eisenhower left office, he warned about the growing influence of the **military-industrial complex** in American government and life. Eisenhower had struggled against persistent pressures from defense contractors, who, in tandem with the military, sought more dollars for newer, more powerful weapons systems. In his farewell address, he warned that the "conjunction of an immense military establishment and a large arms industry . . . exercised a total influence . . . in every city, every state house, every office of the federal government." The Cold War had created a warfare state.

> QUICK REVIEW

Where and how did Eisenhower practice containment?

CHAPTER LOCATOR | What was Eisenhower's "middle way" on domestic issues?

CHAPTER 27
756 THE POLITICS AND CULTURE OF ABUNDANCE, 1952–1960

Hotpoint Air Conditioner Ad, 1955

In 1902, Willis Haviland Carrier, a twenty-six-year-old American engineer, designed the first system to control temperature and humidity and installed it in a Brooklyn printing plant. Room air conditioners began to appear in the 1930s and spread rapidly in the 1950s, making possible the industrial and population explosion in the Sun Belt. While this ad promised consumers clean as well as cool air inside the house, it failed to note that air-conditioning consumed large amounts of energy and contributed to outdoor air pollution. Hotpoint/General Electric Company.

▶ FOR MORE HELP ANALYZING THIS IMAGE, see the visual activity for this chapter in the Online Study Guide at bedfordstmartins.com/roarkunderstanding.

STIMULATED IN PART by American military spending, economic productivity *, technology* increased enormously in the 1950s. A multitude of new items came on the market, and consumption became the order of the day. Millions of Americans enjoyed new homes in the suburbs, and higher education enrollments skyrocketed. Although every section of the nation enjoyed the new abundance, the West and Southwest especially boomed in production, commerce, and population. And work itself changed. Fewer people labored on farms, service sector employment overtook manufacturing jobs, and women's employment grew. These economic shifts disadvantaged some Americans, and they did little to help the forty million who lived in poverty. Most Americans, however, enjoyed a higher standard of living, leading economist John Kenneth Galbraith to call the United States "the affluent society."

Technology Transforms Agriculture and Industry

Between 1940 and 1960, agricultural output mushroomed while the number of farmworkers declined by almost one-third. Farmers achieved unprecedented productivity through greater crop specialization, intensive use of fertilizers, and, above all, mechanization. The decline of family farms and the growth of large commercial farming, or agribusiness, were both causes and consequences of

| How did Eisenhower's foreign policy differ from Truman's? | What fueled the prosperity of the 1950s? | How did prosperity affect American society and culture? | How did African Americans fight for their rights in the 1950s? | Conclusion: What unmet challenges did peace and prosperity mask? |

mechanization. Benefiting from federal price supports begun in the New Deal, larger farmers could afford technological improvements, whereas smaller producers lacked capital to invest in the machinery necessary to compete. Consequently, average farm size more than doubled between 1940 and 1964, and the number of farms fell by more than 40 percent.

Many small farmers who hung on constituted a core of rural poverty. Southern landowners replaced sharecroppers with machines, forcing them off the land. Hundreds of thousands of African Americans joined an exodus to cities, where racial discrimination and a lack of jobs mired many in urban poverty. A Mississippi mother realized that "it was going to be machines now that harvest the crops." Considering moving to Chicago, she worried that "it might be worse up there" for her children. "I'm afraid to leave and I'm afraid to stay."

Industrial production also benefited from new technologies. Technology transformed industries such as electronics, chemicals, and air transportation and promoted the growth of television, plastics, computers, and other newer industries. American businesses enjoyed access to cheap oil, ample markets abroad, and little foreign competition. Moreover, even with Eisenhower's conservative fiscal policies, government spending reached $80 billion annually and created new jobs.

Labor unions enjoyed their greatest success during the 1950s, and real earnings for production workers rose 40 percent. The merger in 1955 of the American Federation of Labor (AFL) and the Congress of Industrial Organizations (CIO) improved labor's bargaining position. As one worker put it, "We saw continual improvement in wages, fringe benefits like holidays, vacation, medical plans . . . all sorts of things that provided more security for people." In most industrial nations, government programs underwrote their citizens' security, but in the United States company-funded programs won by unions through collective bargaining played a much larger role in providing for retirement, health care, and the like. This system resulted in wide disparities among workers, severely disadvantaging those not represented by unions and those with irregular employment.

While the absolute number of organized workers continued to grow, union membership peaked at 27.1 percent of the labor force in 1957. Technological advances eliminated jobs in heavy industry, reducing the number of workers in the steel, copper, and aluminum industries by 17 percent. "You are going to have trouble collecting union dues from all of these machines," commented a Ford manager to union leader Walter Reuther. Moreover, the economy as a whole was shifting from production to service as more workers distributed goods, performed services, provided education, and carried out government work. Unions made some headway in these fields, especially among government employees, but most service industries resisted unionization.

The growing clerical and service occupations swelled the demand for female workers. By the end of the 1950s, women held nearly one-third of all jobs. The vast majority of them worked in offices, light manufacturing, domestic service, teaching, and nursing; because these were female occupations, wages were relatively low. In 1960, the average full-time female worker earned just 60 percent of the average male worker's wages. At the bottom of the employment ladder, black women took home only 42 percent of what white men earned.

CHAPTER LOCATOR | What was Eisenhower's "middle way" on domestic issues?

CHAPTER 27
758 THE POLITICS AND CULTURE OF ABUNDANCE, 1952–1960

Burgeoning Suburbs and Declining Cities

Although suburbs had existed since the nineteenth century, nothing symbolized the affluent society more than their tremendous expansion in the 1950s. Eleven million new homes went up in the suburbs, and by 1960 one in four Americans lived there. Builder William J. Levitt adapted the factory assembly-line process when he began construction of **Levittown** in 1947, planning nearly identical units so that individual construction workers could move from house to house and perform the same single operation in each one. By 1949, families could purchase mass-produced houses in his 17,000-home development on Long Island, New York, for just under $8,000 each. Developments similar to Levittown quickly went up throughout the country. The government underwrote home ownership with low-interest mortgage guarantees through the Federal Housing Administration and the Veterans Administration and by making interest on mortgages tax deductible. Thousands of miles of interstate highway running through urban areas indirectly subsidized suburban development.

The growing suburbs helped polarize society, especially along racial lines. Each Levittown homeowner signed a contract pledging not to rent or sell to a non-Caucasian. The Supreme Court declared such covenants unenforceable in 1948, but suburban America remained dramatically segregated. Levitt commented, "We can solve a housing problem, or we can try and solve a racial problem, but we cannot combine the two."

Although some African Americans joined the suburban migration, most moved to cities in search of economic opportunity, increasing their numbers in most cities by 50 percent during the 1950s. These migrants, however, came to cities that were already in decline, losing not only population but also commerce and industry to the suburbs or to southern and western states.

Levittown

► Housing development on Long Island, New York, made up of low-cost, mass-produced houses. Begun in 1947, Levittown had 17,000 homes by 1949 and became a prime example of the suburbanization of the United States.

The Rise of the Sun Belt

No regions experienced the postwar economic and population booms more intensely than the West and Southwest. Architect Frank Lloyd Wright quipped, "Everything loose will land in Los Angeles." California overtook New York as the most populous state.

A pleasant natural environment drew new residents to the West and Southwest, but no magnet proved stronger than the promise of economic opportunity (**Map 27.2, page 760**). As railroads had fueled western growth in the nineteenth century, so the automobile and airplane spurred the post–World War II surge. The technology of air-conditioning facilitated industrial development and by 1960 cooled nearly eight million homes in the so-called Sun Belt, which stretched from Florida to California.

So important was the defense industry to the South and West that the area was later referred to as the "Gun Belt." The aerospace industry boomed in Seattle-Tacoma, Los Angeles, and Dallas–Fort Worth, and military bases helped underwrite prosperity in cities such as San Diego and San Antonio. By the 1960s, nearly one of every three California workers held a defense-related job.

The surging populations and industries soon threatened the environment. Providing sufficient water and power to cities and to agribusiness meant building dams and reservoirs on free-flowing rivers. Native Americans lost fishing sites on

| How did Eisenhower's foreign policy differ from Truman's? | **What fueled the prosperity of the 1950s?** | How did prosperity affect American society and culture? | How did African Americans fight for their rights in the 1950s? | Conclusion: What unmet challenges did peace and prosperity mask? |

759

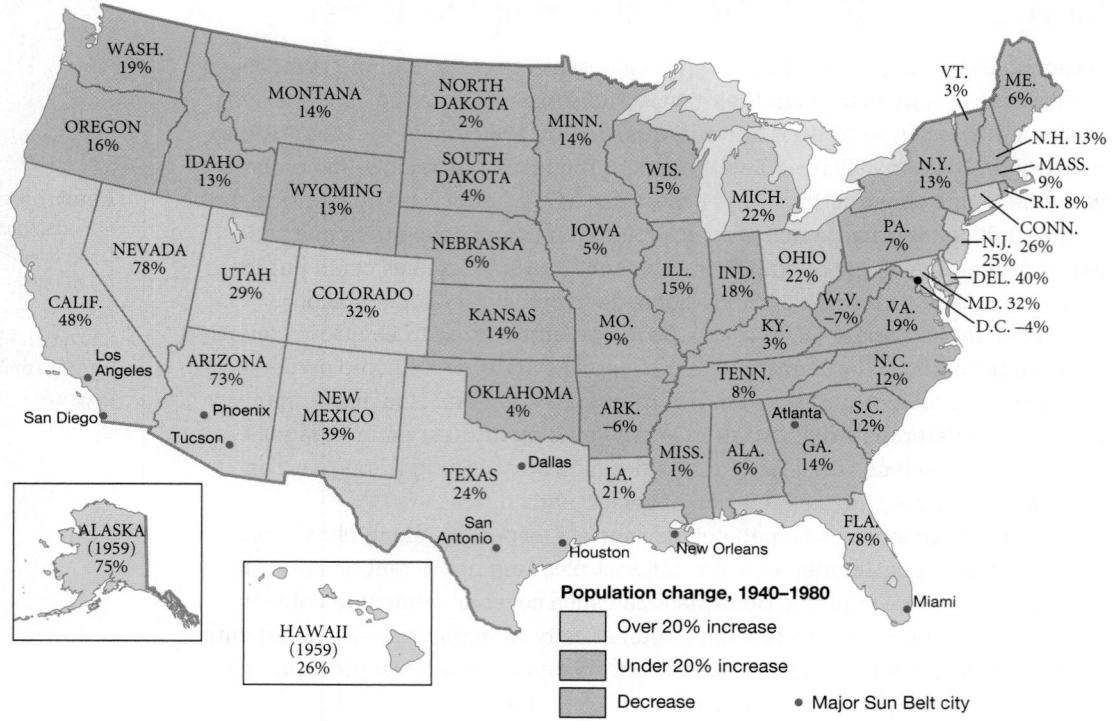

MAP 27.2 ■ The Rise of the Sun Belt, 1940–1980
The growth of defense industries, a non-unionized labor force, and the spread of air-conditioning all helped spur economic development and population growth, which made the Sun Belt the fastest-growing region of the country between 1940 and 1980.

> ► FOR MORE HELP ANALYZING THIS MAP, see the map activity for this chapter in the Online Study Guide at bedfordstmartins.com/roarkunderstanding.

the Columbia River, and dams on the Upper Missouri displaced nine hundred Indian families. Sprawling urban and suburban settlement without efficient public transportation contributed to blankets of smog over Los Angeles and other cities.

The high-technology basis of postwar economic development drew well-educated, highly skilled workers to the West, but the economic promise also attracted the poor. "We see opportunity all around us here. . . . We smell freedom here, and maybe soon we can taste it," commented a black mother in California. Between 1945 and 1960, more than one-third of the African Americans who left the South moved west.

The Mexican American population also grew, especially in California and Texas. To supply California's vast agribusiness industry, the government continued the *bracero* program begun during World War II. Until the program ended in 1964, more than 100,000 Mexicans entered the United States each year to labor in the fields—and many of them stayed, legally or illegally. But permanent Mexican immigration was not as welcome as Mexicans' low-wage labor. In 1954, the government launched a series of raids called "Operation Wetback," resulting in deportation of more than one million Mexicans. Even Mexicans with legal status felt unwelcome and vulnerable to incidents of mistaken identity.

CHAPTER LOCATOR | What was Eisenhower's "middle way" on domestic issues?

760 CHAPTER 27
THE POLITICS AND CULTURE OF ABUNDANCE, 1952–1960

At the same time, Mexican American citizens gained a small victory in their ongoing struggle for civil rights in *Hernandez v. Texas*. When a Texas jury convicted Pete Hernandez of murder, lawyers from the American GI Forum and the League of United Latin American Citizens (see chapter 26) appealed on the grounds that persons of Mexican origin had been routinely excluded from jury service. In 1954, the Supreme Court ruled unanimously that Mexican Americans constituted a distinct group and that their systematic exclusion from juries violated the constitutional guarantee of equal protection.

Free of the discrimination faced by minorities, white Americans enjoyed the fullest prosperity in the West. In April 1950, when California developers opened Lakewood, a large housing development in Los Angeles County, thirty thousand people lined up to buy houses at prices ranging from $68,000 to $85,000 in 2007 dollars. Many of the new homeowners were veterans, blue-collar and lower-level white-collar workers whose defense-based jobs at aerospace corporations enabled them to fulfill the American dream of the 1950s. A huge shopping mall, Lakewood Center, offered myriad products of the consumer culture, and the workers' children lived at commuting distance from community colleges and six state universities.

Rounding Up Undocumented Migrants

Not all Mexican Americans who wanted to work in the United States were accommodated by the *bracero* program. In 1953, Los Angeles police arrested these men, who did not have legal documents and were hiding in a freight train. © Bettmann/Corbis.

The Democratization of Higher Education

California's university system exemplified a spectacular transformation of higher education. Between 1940 and 1960, college enrollments in the United States more than doubled. Prosperity enabled more families to keep their children in school longer, and the federal government subsidized the education of more than two million veterans. The Cold War also sent millions of federal dollars to universities for defense-related research. And state governments vastly expanded the number of public colleges and universities, while municipalities began to build two-year community colleges.

Not all Americans benefited equally from the democratization of higher education. Although their college enrollments surged from 37,000 in 1941 to 90,000 in 1961, African Americans constituted only about 5 percent of all college students. For a time, the educational gap between white men and women grew. In 1940, women had earned 40 percent of undergraduate degrees, but as veterans flocked to college campuses, women's proportion fell to 25 percent in 1950 and rebounded to only 33 percent by 1960. The large veteran enrollments led colleges to relax rules that had forbidden students to marry. Unlike men, however, women tended to drop out of college after marriage and to take jobs so that their husbands could stay in school. Reflecting gender norms of the 1950s, most college women agreed that "it is natural for a woman to be satisfied with her husband's success and not crave personal achievement."

QUICK REVIEW

What factors were most important in the prosperity of the 1950s?

How did Eisenhower's foreign policy differ from Truman's?

What fueled the prosperity of the 1950s?

How did prosperity affect American society and culture?

How did African Americans fight for their rights in the 1950s?

Conclusion: What unmet challenges did peace and prosperity mask?

761

How did prosperity affect American society and culture?

TV with Scene from Ozzie and Harriet

The Adventures of Ozzie and Harriet began as a radio program in the 1940s and ran on television from 1952 to 1966. Along with other family sitcoms, it idealized white family life, in which no one got divorced or became gravely ill, no one took drugs or seriously misbehaved, fathers held white-collar jobs, mothers did not work outside the home, and husbands and wives slept in twin beds. Picture Research Consultants & Archives.

PROSPERITY IN THE 1950s intensified the transformation of the nation into a consumer society, changing the way Americans lived and converting the traditional work ethic into an ethic of consumption. People married at earlier ages, the birthrate soared, and dominant values celebrated family life and traditional gender roles. Undercurrents of rebellion, especially among young people, and women's increasing employment defied some of the dominant norms but did not greatly disrupt the complacency of the 1950s.

Consumption Rules the Day

Although the purchase and display of consumer goods was not new (see chapter 23), by the 1950s, consumption had become a reigning value, vital for economic prosperity and essential to individuals' identity and status. In place of the traditional emphasis on work and savings, the consumer culture encouraged satisfaction and happiness through the purchase and use of new products.

The consumer culture rested on a firm material base. Between 1950 and 1960, both the gross national product (the value of all goods and services produced) and median family income grew by 25 percent in constant dollars (**Figure 27.1**). Economists claimed that 60 percent of Americans enjoyed middle-class incomes in 1960. Referring to the popular ranch-style houses in the new suburbs, *House Beautiful* magazine boasted, "Our houses are all on one level, like our class structure." Though ignoring the one in five Americans who still lived in poverty, the statement reflected the increasing ability of people to consume products that made class differences less visible. By 1960, almost nine of every ten families owned a television set, nearly all had a refrigerator, and most owned at least one car. The number of shopping centers quadrupled between 1957 and 1963.

CHAPTER LOCATOR | What was Eisenhower's "middle way" on domestic issues?

762 CHAPTER 27
THE POLITICS AND CULTURE OF ABUNDANCE, 1952–1960

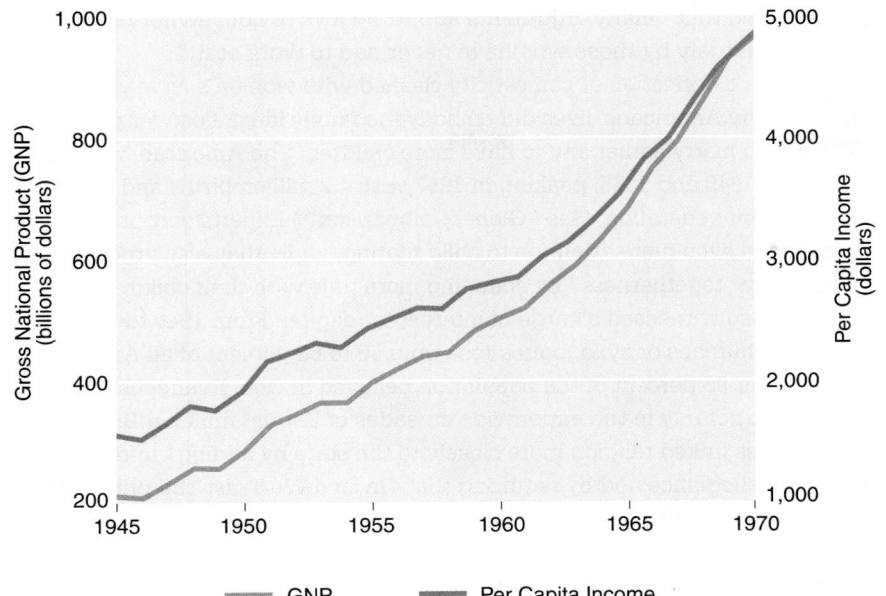

FIGURE 27.1 ■ The Postwar Economic Boom: GNP and Per Capita Income, 1945–1970
American dominance of the worldwide market, innovative technologies that led to new industries such as computers and plastics, population growth, and increases in worker productivity all contributed to the enormous economic growth of the United States after World War II.

Several forces spurred this unparalleled abundance. A population surge—from 152 million in 1950 to 180 million in 1960—expanded the demand for products and boosted industries ranging from housing to baby goods. Consumer borrowing also fueled the economic boom, as people increasingly made purchases on installment plans and began to use credit cards. In what *Life* magazine referred to as a "revolution in consumer purchasing," Americans now enjoyed their possessions while they paid for them instead of saving their money for future purchases.

Although the sheer need to support themselves and their families explained most women's employment, a desire to secure some of the new abundance sent growing numbers of women to work. In fact, married women's employment rose more than that of any other group in the 1950s. As one remarked, "My Joe can't put five kids through college . . . and the washer had to be replaced, and Ann was ashamed to bring friends home because the living room furniture was such a mess, so I went to work." The standards for family happiness imposed by the consumer culture increasingly required a second income.

The Revival of Domesticity and Religion

Despite married women's growing employment, a dominant ideology celebrated traditional family life and conventional gender roles. Both popular culture and public figures defined the ideal family as a male breadwinner, a full-time homemaker, and three or four children. Writer and feminist **Betty Friedan** gave a name to the idealization of women's domestic roles in her 1963 book *The Feminine Mystique.* Friedan criticized scholars, advertisers, and public officials for assuming that biological differences dictated different roles for men and women. According to the feminine mystique that they promulgated, women should find fulfillment in devotion to their homes, families, and serving others. Not many women directly challenged these ideas, but Edith Stern, a college-educated

Betty Friedan
► Writer and feminist who wrote *The Feminine Mystique* (1963), which criticized scholars, advertisers, and public officials for assuming that biological differences dictated different roles for men and women. According to the feminine mystique that they promulgated, women should find fulfillment in devotion to their homes, families, and serving others.

| How did Eisenhower's foreign policy differ from Truman's? | What fueled the prosperity of the 1950s? | How did prosperity affect American society and culture? | How did African Americans fight for their rights in the 1950s? | Conclusion: What unmet challenges did peace and prosperity mask? |

763

writer, maintained that "many arguments about the joys of housewifery have been advanced, largely by those who have never had to work at it."

Although the glorification of domesticity clashed with women's increasing employment, many Americans' lives did embody the family ideal. Postwar prosperity enabled people to marry earlier and to have more children. The American birthrate soared between 1945 and 1965, peaking in 1957 with 4.3 million births and producing the **baby boom** generation. (See "Global Comparison".) Experts encouraged mothers to devote even more attention to child rearing, while they also urged fathers to cultivate family "togetherness" by spending more time with their children.

The 1950s also witnessed a surge of interest in religion. From 1940 to 1960, membership in churches or synagogues rose from 50 to 63 percent of all Americans. Polls reported that 95 percent of the population believed in God. Evangelism took on new life, most notably in the nationwide crusades of Baptist minister Billy Graham. Congress linked religion more closely to the state by adding "under God" to the pledge of allegiance and by requiring that "In God We Trust" be printed on all currency. Religion helped to calm anxieties in the nuclear age, while ministers such as Graham made the Cold War a holy war, labeling communism "a great sinister anti-Christian movement masterminded by Satan." Some critics, however, questioned the depth of the religious revival, attributing the growth in church membership to a desire for conformity and a need for social outlets.

Television Transforms Culture and Politics

Just as family life and religion offered a respite from Cold War anxieties, so too did the new medium of television. By 1960, close to 90 percent of American homes

baby boom

▶ The surge in the United States' population that followed World War II. The American birthrate soared between 1945 and 1965, peaking in 1957 with 4.3 million births. The baby boom played an important role in shaping cultural, social, and economic developments in the 1950s and 1960s.

GLOBAL COMPARISON

The Baby Boom in International Perspective

The United States was not alone in welcoming bumper crops of babies in the 1950s. High fertility continued in nonindustrialized countries, while in Europe, as in the United States, birthrates rebounded from low levels during the Great Depression and World War II. Which countries had birthrates comparable to those of the United States? What might explain why countries such as Brazil, China, Iran, and Mexico had birthrates so much higher than those in the United States? What might explain why birthrates in Europe were lower than those in the United States?

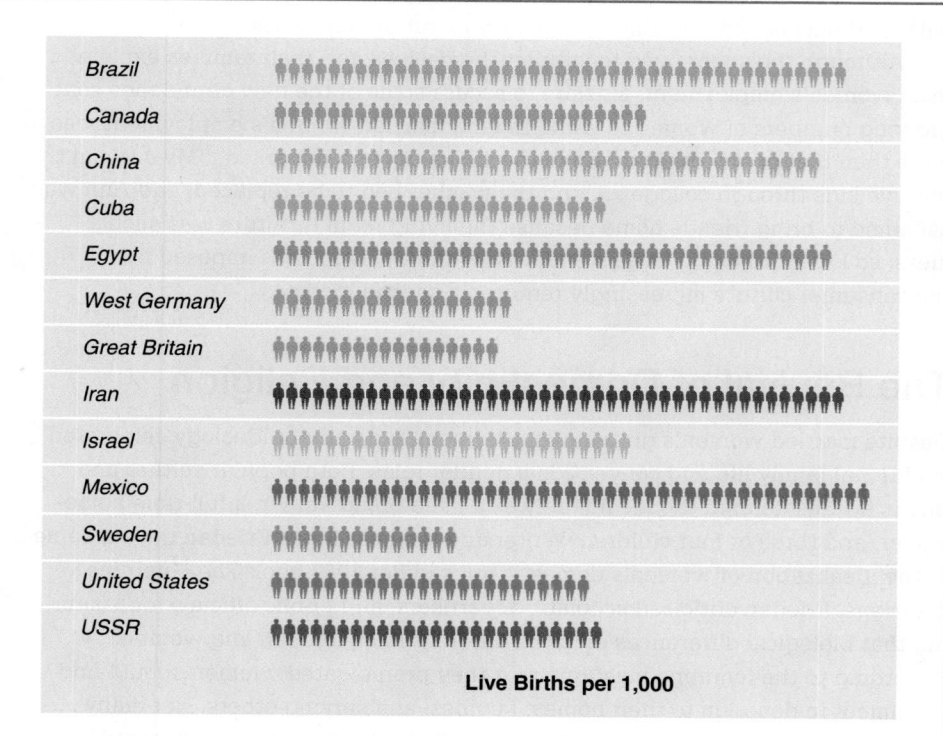

Brazil
Canada
China
Cuba
Egypt
West Germany
Great Britain
Iran
Israel
Mexico
Sweden
United States
USSR

Live Births per 1,000

boasted a television set, and the average viewer spent more than five hours each day in front of the screen. Audiences were especially attracted to situation comedies, which projected the family ideal and the feminine mystique into millions of homes. On TV, married women did not have paying jobs, and they deferred to their husbands, though they often got the upper hand through subtle manipulation.

Television also began to affect politics. Eisenhower's 1952 presidential campaign used TV ads for the first time, although he was not happy that "an old soldier should come to this." By 1960, television played a key role in election campaigns. Reflecting on his narrow victory in 1960, president-elect John F. Kennedy remarked, "We wouldn't have had a prayer without that gadget."

Television transformed politics in other ways. Money played a much larger role in elections because candidates needed to pay for expensive TV spots. The ability to appeal directly to voters in their living rooms put a premium on personal attractiveness and encouraged candidates to build their own campaign organizations, relying less on political parties. The declining strength of parties and the growing power of money in elections were not new trends, but TV helped accelerate them.

Unlike government-financed television in Europe, American TV was paid for by private enterprise. What NBC called a "selling machine in every living room" became the major vehicle for creating a consumer culture. In the mid-1950s, advertisers spent $10 billion to push their goods on TV. In 1961, Newton Minow, chairman of the Federal Communications Commission, called television a "vast wasteland." While acknowledging some of TV's great achievements, particularly documentaries and drama, Minow depicted it as "a procession of game shows, . . . formula comedies about totally unbelievable families, blood and thunder, mayhem, violence, sadism, murder . . . and cartoons." But viewers kept tuning in. In little more than a decade, television came to dominate Americans' leisure time, influence their consumption patterns, and shape their perceptions of the nation's leadership.

Countercurrents

Pockets of dissent underlay the complacency of the 1950s. Some intellectuals took exception to the materialism and conformity of the era. In *The Lonely Crowd* (1950), sociologist David Riesman lamented a shift from the "inner-directed" to the "other-directed" individual, as Americans replaced independent thinking with an eagerness to adapt to external standards of behavior and belief. Sharing that distaste for the importance of "belonging," William H. Whyte Jr., in his popular book *The Organization Man* (1956), blamed the modern corporation for making employees tailor themselves to the group. Vance Packard's 1959 best seller, *The Status Seekers*, decried "the vigorous merchandising of goods as status-symbols" and argued that "class lines . . . appear to be hardening."

Implicit in much of the critique of consumer culture was concern about the loss of traditional masculinity. Consumption itself was associated with women and their presumed greater susceptibility to manipulation. Men, required to conform in order to get ahead, moved further away from the nineteenth-century masculine ideals of individualism and aggressiveness. Moreover, the increase in married women's employment compromised the male ideal of breadwinner.

Into this gender confusion came *Playboy*, which began publication in 1953 and quickly gained a circulation of one million. The new magazine idealized masculine independence in the form of bachelorhood and assaulted the reigning middle-class

CHRONOLOGY

1953
- *Playboy* begins publication.
- Alfred Kinsey publishes *Sexual Behavior in the Human Female*.

1957
- Jack Kerouac publishes *On the Road*, a novel heralding the Beat generation.
- The baby boom, a term given to the high American birthrate, peaks with 4.3 million births.

1960
- Almost ninety percent of American families own a television set.
- The population of the United States reaches 180 million.

1963
- Betty Friedan publishes *The Feminine Mystique*, criticizing women's gender roles.

| How did Eisenhower's foreign policy differ from Truman's? | What fueled the prosperity of the 1950s? | How did prosperity affect American society and culture? | How did African Americans fight for their rights in the 1950s? | Conclusion: What unmet challenges did peace and prosperity mask? |

765

norms of domesticity and respectability. By associating the sophisticated bachelor with good wine, music, furnishings, and the like, the magazine made consumption more masculine while promoting sexual freedom, at least for men.

In fact, new research on Americans' sexual behavior disclosed that it often departed from the postwar family ideal. Two books published by Alfred Kinsey and other researchers at Indiana University—*Sexual Behavior in the Human Male* (1948) and *Sexual Behavior in the Human Female* (1953)—uncovered a surprising range of sexual conduct. In a large survey, Kinsey found that 85 percent of the men and 50 percent of the women had had sex before marriage, half of the husbands and a quarter of the wives had engaged in adultery, and significant numbers of men and women reported homosexual experiences. Although Kinsey's sampling procedures later cast doubt on his ability to generalize across the population, the books became best sellers.

Less direct challenges to mainstream standards appeared in the everyday behavior of young Americans. "Roll over Beethoven and tell Tchaikovsky the news!" belted out Chuck Berry in his 1956 hit record celebrating a new form of music that combined country sounds and black rhythm and blues—rock and roll. White teenagers lionized Elvis Presley, who shocked their parents with his tight pants, hip-rolling gestures, and sensuous rock-and-roll music. "Before there was Elvis . . . I started going crazy for 'race music,'" recalled a white man of his teenage years. "That got me into trouble with my parents and the schools." His recollection underscored African Americans' contributions to rock and roll, as well as the rebellion expressed by white youths' attraction to black music.

The most blatant revolt against conventionality came from the self-proclaimed Beat generation, a small group of primarily male literary figures based in New York City and San Francisco. Rejecting nearly everything in mainstream culture—patriotism, consumerism, technology, conventional family life, discipline—the Beats celebrated spontaneity and absolute personal freedom, including drug consumption and freewheeling sex. Jack Kerouac, who gave the Beat generation its name, published the best-selling novel *On the Road* (1957), recounting the impetuous cross-country travels of two young men. The Beats' lifestyles shocked "square" Americans, but they would provide a model for a much larger movement of youthful dissidents in the 1960s.

Bold new styles in the visual arts also showed the 1950s to be more than a decade of bland conventionality. In New York City, an artistic revolution known as "action painting" or "abstract expressionism" flowered, rejecting the idea that painting should represent recognizable forms. Jackson Pollock and other abstract expressionists, emphasizing spontaneity, poured, dripped, and threw paint on canvases or substituted sticks and other implements for brushes. The new form of painting so captivated and redirected the Western art world that New York replaced Paris as its center.

> **QUICK REVIEW**

Why did American consumption expand so dramatically in the 1950s, and what aspects of society and culture did it influence?

CHAPTER LOCATOR | What was Eisenhower's "middle way" on domestic issues?

Montgomery Civil Rights Leaders

During the Montgomery bus boycott, local white officials sought to intimidate African Americans with arrests and lawsuits. Here Rosa Parks, one of ninety-two defendants, enters the Montgomery County courthouse. Parks later said of her actions, "People always say that I didn't give up my seat because I was tired, but that isn't true," Parks recalled. "I was not tired physically. . . . I was not old. . . . I was forty-two. No, the only tired I was, was tired of giving in." Wide World Photos.

BUILDING ON THE civil rights initiatives begun during World War II, African Americans posed the most dramatic challenge to the status quo of the 1950s as they sought to overcome discrimination and segregation. Although black protest was as old as American racism, in the 1950s a grassroots movement arose that attracted national attention and the support of white liberals. Pressed by civil rights groups, the Supreme Court delivered significant institutional reforms, but the most important changes of all occurred among blacks themselves. Ordinary African Americans in substantial numbers sought their own liberation, building a movement that would transform race relations in the United States.

African Americans Challenge the Supreme Court and the President

Several factors spurred black protest in the 1950s. Between 1940 and 1960, more than three million African Americans moved from the South into areas where they had a political voice. Black leaders made sure that foreign policy officials realized how racist practices at home handicapped the United States in its competition with the Soviet Union. In the South, the very system of segregation meant that African Americans controlled certain organizational resources, such as churches and colleges, where leadership skills could be honed and networks developed.

| How did Eisenhower's foreign policy differ from Truman's? | What fueled the prosperity of the 1950s? | How did prosperity affect American society and culture? | How did African Americans fight for their rights in the 1950s? | Conclusion: What unmet challenges did peace and prosperity mask? |

Brown v. Board of Education

▶ 1954 Supreme Court ruling that overturned the "separate but equal" precedent established in *Plessy v. Ferguson* in 1896. The Court declared that separate educational facilities were inherently unequal and thus violated the Fourteenth Amendment. The ruling laid the foundation for the end of legal segregation in the United States.

The legal strategy of the major civil rights organization, the National Association for the Advancement of Colored People (NAACP), reached its crowning achievement with the Supreme Court decision in *Brown v. Board of Education* in 1954. *Brown* consolidated five separate suits that reflected the growing determination of black Americans to fight for their rights. Oliver Brown, a World War II veteran in Topeka, Kansas, filed suit because his daughter had to pass by a white school just seven blocks from their home to attend a black school more than a mile away. In Virginia, sixteen-year-old Barbara Johns initiated a student strike over conditions in her black high school, leading to another of the suits joined in *Brown*. The NAACP's lead lawyer, future Supreme Court justice Thurgood Marshall, urged the Court to overturn the "separate but equal" precedent established in *Plessy v. Ferguson* in 1896 (see chapter 21). A unanimous Court, headed by Chief Justice Earl Warren, declared, "Separate educational facilities are inherently unequal" and thus violated the Fourteenth Amendment.

School Integration in Little Rock, Arkansas

The nine African American teenagers who integrated Central High School in Little Rock, Arkansas, endured nearly three weeks of threats and hateful taunts before they even got through the doors. Here Elizabeth Eckford tries to ignore angry students and adults as she approaches the entrance to the school, only to be blocked by Arkansas National Guardsmen. Francis Miller/TimePix/Getty.

▶ FOR MORE HELP ANALYZING THIS IMAGE, see the visual activity for this chapter in the Online Study Guide at bedfordstmartins.com/roarkunderstanding.

Ultimate responsibility for enforcement of the decision lay with President Eisenhower, but he refused to endorse *Brown*. He also kept silent in 1955 when whites murdered Emmett Till, a fourteen-year-old black boy, for allegedly whistling at a white woman in Mississippi. Reflecting his own prejudice, his preference for limited federal intervention in the states, and a leadership style that favored consensus and gradual progress, Eisenhower kept his distance from civil rights issues. Such inaction fortified southern resistance to school desegregation and contributed to the gravest constitutional crisis since the Civil War.

The crisis came in Little Rock, Arkansas, in September 1957, when Governor Orval Faubus sent Arkansas National Guard troops to block the enrollment of nine black students in Little Rock's Central High School. Later, he allowed them to enter but withdrew the National Guard, leaving the students to face an angry white mob. "During those years when we desperately needed approval from our peers," Melba Patillo Beals remembered, "we were victims of the most harsh rejection imaginable." As television cameras transmitted the ugly scene, Eisenhower was forced to send regular army troops to Little Rock, the first federal military intervention in the South since Reconstruction. Paratroopers escorted the "Little Rock Nine" into the school.

Eisenhower did order the integration of public facilities in Washington, D.C., and on military bases, and he supported the first federal civil rights legislation since Reconstruction. Yet southern Democrats made sure that the Civil Rights Acts of 1957 and 1960 were little more than symbolic. Baseball star Jackie Robinson spoke for many African Americans when he wired Eisenhower in 1957, "We disagree that half a loaf is better than none. Have waited this long for a bill with meaning—can wait a little longer." Eisenhower appointed the first black professional to the White House staff, E. Frederick Morrow, but Morrow confided in his diary, "I feel ridiculous . . . trying to defend the administration's record on civil rights."

Montgomery and Mass Protest

What set the civil rights movement of the 1950s and 1960s apart from earlier acts of black protest was the large number of people involved, their willingness to confront white institutions directly, and the use of nonviolent protest and civil disobedience to bring about change. The Congress of Racial Equality (CORE) and other groups had experimented with these tactics in the 1940s, and African Americans had boycotted the segregated bus system in Baton Rouge, Louisiana, in 1953, but the first sustained protest to claim national attention began in Montgomery, Alabama, on December 1, 1955.

That day, police arrested **Rosa Parks** for violating a local segregation ordinance that required her to give up her seat so that a white man could sit down. The bus driver called the police, who promptly arrested her. Parks had long been active in the local NAACP, headed by E. D. Nixon. They had already talked about challenging bus segregation. So had the Women's Political Council (WPC), composed of black professional women and led by Jo Ann Robinson, an English professor at Alabama State College. Such local individuals and organizations, long committed to improving conditions for African Americans, laid critical foundations for the black freedom struggle throughout the South.

When word came that Parks would fight her arrest, WPC leaders mobilized teachers and students to distribute fliers calling for blacks to stay off the buses.

CHRONOLOGY

1954
– Supreme Court in *Brown v. Board of Education* rules that segregated schools are unconstitutional.

1955
– **December 1.** Rosa Parks is arrested in Montgomery, Alabama, for challenging segregation on city buses.

1955–1956
– Montgomery, Alabama, bus boycott.

1957
– Southern Christian Leadership Conference, headed by Martin Luther King Jr., is founded.
– President Eisenhower sends federal troops to enforce school integration in Little Rock, Arkansas.

Rosa Parks
▶ African American woman who was arrested on December 1, 1955, in Montgomery, Alabama, for refusing to give up her bus seat to a white man. Parks had long been active in the civil rights movement, and her decision to fight her arrest sparked the Montgomery bus boycott.

| How did Eisenhower's foreign policy differ from Truman's? | What fueled the prosperity of the 1950s? | How did prosperity affect American society and culture? | How did African Americans fight for their rights in the 1950s? | Conclusion: What unmet challenges did peace and prosperity mask? |

769

E. D. Nixon called a mass meeting at the Holt Street Baptist Church, where those assembled founded the Montgomery Improvement Association (MIA) to organize a bus boycott. The MIA arranged volunteer car pools and marshaled more than 90 percent of the black community to sustain the yearlong **Montgomery bus boycott.** Elected to head the MIA was twenty-six-year-old Martin Luther King Jr., a young Baptist pastor with a doctorate in theology from Boston University. King addressed mass meetings at churches throughout the boycott, inspiring blacks' courage and commitment by linking racial justice to Christianity. He promised, "If you will protest courageously and yet with dignity and Christian love . . . historians will have to pause and say, 'There lived a great people—a black people—who injected a new meaning and dignity into the veins of civilization.'"

Montgomery blacks summoned their courage and determination in abundance. They walked miles to get to work, contributed their meager financial resources, and stood up to intimidation and police harassment. An older woman insisted, "I'm not walking for myself, I'm walking for my children and my grandchildren." Authorities arrested several leaders, and whites firebombed King's house. Yet the movement persisted until November 1956, when the Supreme Court declared unconstitutional Alabama's laws requiring segregated buses.

King's face on the cover of *Time* magazine in February 1957 marked his rapid rise to national and international fame. In January, black clergy from across the South had chosen King to head the **Southern Christian Leadership Conference (SCLC),** newly established to coordinate local protests against segregation and disfranchisement. The prominence of King and other ministers obscured the substantial numbers and critical importance of black women in the movement. In fact, the SCLC owed much of its success to Ella Baker, a seasoned activist who came from New York to manage its office in Atlanta.

Montgomery bus boycott

▶ Yearlong boycott of Montgomery's bus system in 1955–1956 by the city's African American population aimed at ending segregation on the buses. The bus boycott brought Martin Luther King Jr. to national prominence and ended in victory when the Supreme Court declared unconstitutional Alabama's laws requiring segregated transportation.

Southern Christian Leadership Conference (SCLC)

▶ Civil rights organization made up mostly of black clergy, established in 1957 to coordinate local protests against segregation and disfranchisement. Martin Luther King Jr. became its head and Ella Baker its key organizer.

> ## QUICK REVIEW

What were the goals and strategies of civil rights activists in the 1950s?

CHAPTER LOCATOR | What was Eisenhower's "middle way" on domestic issues?

CHAPTER 27
770 THE POLITICS AND CULTURE OF ABUNDANCE, 1952–1960

Leslie Gill.

Conclusion: What unmet challenges did peace and prosperity mask?

AFFLUENCE CHANGED THE very landscape of the United States. Suburban housing developments sprang up, interstate highways began to divide cities and connect the country, farms declined in number but grew in size, and population and industry moved south and west. Daily habits and even the values of ordinary people shifted as the economy became more service oriented and the appearance of a host of new products intensified the growth of a consumer culture.

The prosperity, however, masked a number of developments and problems that Americans would face head-on in later years: rising resistance to racial injustice, a 20 percent poverty rate, married women's movement into the labor force, and the emergence of a self-conscious youth generation. In general Eisenhower tried to curb domestic programs and let private enterprise have its way. His administration maintained the welfare state inherited from the Democrats but resisted substantial further reforms.

In global affairs, Eisenhower exercised restraint on large issues, recognizing the limits of U.S. power. In the name of deterrence, he promoted the development of more destructive atomic weapons, but he withstood pressures for even larger defense budgets. Still, Eisenhower took from Truman the assumption that the United States must fight communism everywhere, and when movements in Iran, Guatemala, Cuba, and Vietnam seemed too radical, too friendly to communism, or too inimical to American economic interests, he tried to undermine them, often with secret operations and severe consequences for native populations.

Although Eisenhower presided over eight years of peace and prosperity, his foreign policy inspired anti-Americanism, established dangerous precedents for the expansion of executive power, and forged commitments and interventions that future generations would deem unwise. As Eisenhower's successors took on the struggle against communism and grappled with the domestic challenges of race, poverty, and urban decay that he had avoided, the tranquility and consensus of the 1950s would give way to the turbulence and conflict of the 1960s.

SO NOW YOU KNOW

Not only did the CIA help engineer the overthrow of a democratically elected government in Iran, but it also conducted operations in Vietnam, Latin America, and elsewhere in the Middle East and set in place Cold War policies that would have long-term repercussions for the United States.

> CHAPTER 27 STUDY GUIDE

Online Study Guide
bedfordstmartins.com/roarkunderstanding

STEP 1 GETTING STARTED

Below are basic terms from this period in American history. Can you identify each term below and explain why it matters? To do this exercise online or to download this chart, visit bedfordstmartins.com/roarkunderstanding.

TERM	WHO OR WHAT & WHEN	WHY IT MATTERS
Interstate Highway and Defense System Act of 1956, p. 749		
mutually assured destruction (MAD), p. 753		
Fidel Castro, p. 754		
Nikita Khrushchev, p. 755		
military-industrial complex, p. 756		
Levittown, p. 759		
Betty Friedan, p. 763		
baby boom, p. 764		
Brown v. Board of Education, p. 768		
Rosa Parks, p. 769		
Montgomery bus boycott, p. 770		
Southern Christian Leadership Conference (SCLC), p. 770		

STEP 2 MOVING BEYOND THE BASICS

The exercise below represents a more advanced understanding of the chapter material. Start by describing the developments that took place in each of the areas listed in the following chart. Then describe the impact of those changes on middle-class white society and culture. When you are finished, consider the society you have described as a whole. Is it fair to call it "the affluent society"? Who did not participate in the developments you described? What adjectives would you use to describe the society and culture you have depicted? To do this exercise online or to download this chart, visit bedfordstmartins.com/roarkunderstanding.

	Developments	Impact
Economic growth and consumerism		
Suburban growth/domesticity		
Culture/values		
The Cold War		

Now that you've reviewed various parts of the chapter, take a step back and try to see the big picture by answering these questions. Remember to use specific examples from the chapter in your answers. To do this exercise online, visit bedfordstmartins.com/roarkunderstanding.

THE COLD WAR IN THE 1950s

▶ What was the "New Look" in American foreign policy? In what ways, if any, did Eisenhower depart from the policies of Truman, and why did these changes occur?

▶ How did the United States use military intervention or CIA covert activities as a tool of foreign policy in the 1950s?

DOMESTIC DEVELOPMENTS

▶ What factors combined to produce enormous increases in American economic productivity in the 1950s? Who benefited the most from increased productivity? Who did not benefit? Why?

▶ How did consumption shape the culture of the 1950s?

THE CIVIL RIGHTS MOVEMENT

▶ Why was *Brown v. Board of Education* such a pivotal case in the history of the civil rights movement?

▶ What light does the Montgomery bus boycott shed on the goals and strategies of the 1950s civil rights movement?

LOOKING BACKWARD, LOOKING AHEAD

▶ Compare and contrast the culture and society of 1920s and 1950s America. What were the most important similarities? What were the most important differences?

▶ What tensions within 1950s society suggest defining aspects of 1960s America?

IN YOUR OWN WORDS

Imagine that you must explain chapter 27 to someone who hasn't read it. What would be the most important points to include and why?

28
REFORM, REBELLION, AND REACTION

1960–1974

> This chapter examines efforts to reform and transform American society and politics in the 1960s and early 1970s. It explores the domestic agenda of the Johnson administration, the role of the Supreme Court, the evolution of the black freedom movement, the movements inspired by the struggle for civil rights, the backlash against reform, and the transformation of the liberal reform agenda under President Nixon.

> What liberal reforms were advanced during the Kennedy and Johnson administrations?

> How did the civil rights movement evolve in the 1960s?

> What other rights movements emerged in the 1960s?

> What were the goals of the new wave of feminism?

> How did liberal reform fare under President Nixon?

> Conclusion: What were the achievements and limitations of liberalism?

DID YOU KNOW?

The Environmental Protection Agency (EPA) was created by Republican president Richard Nixon.

Birmingham, Alabama. Police officers attack civil rights demonstrators with fire hoses at Kelley Ingram Park in 1963.

What liberal reforms were advanced during the Kennedy and Johnson administrations?

AT THE 1960 DEMOCRATIC National Convention, John F. Kennedy announced "a New Frontier" that would confront "unsolved problems of peace and war, unconquered pockets of ignorance and prejudice, unanswered questions of poverty and surplus." Four years later, Lyndon B. Johnson invoked the ideal of a "Great Society, [which] rests on abundance and liberty for all [and] demands an end to poverty and racial injustice." Acting under the liberal faith that government should use its power to solve social and economic problems, end injustice, and promote the welfare of all citizens, the Democratic administrations of the 1960s won legislation on civil rights, poverty, education, medical care, housing, consumer protection, and environmental protection.

The Unrealized Promise of Kennedy's New Frontier

John F. Kennedy grew up in privilege, the child of an Irish Catholic businessman and diplomat. Helped by a distinguished World War II navy record, Kennedy won election to the House of Representatives in 1946 and the Senate in 1952. With a powerful political machine, his family's fortune, and a dynamic personality, Kennedy won the Democratic presidential nomination in 1960. He then stunned many Democrats by choosing as his running mate Lyndon B. Johnson of Texas, whom liberals disparaged as a typical southern conservative. In the general election, Kennedy narrowly defeated Vice President Richard M. Nixon. African American voters contributed to his victory, helping to offset the 52 percent of the white vote cast for Nixon and contributing to Kennedy's 118,550-vote margin

CHAPTER LOCATOR | What liberal reforms were advanced during the Kennedy and Johnson administrations?

776 CHAPTER 28 REFORM, REBELLION, AND REACTION, 1960–1974

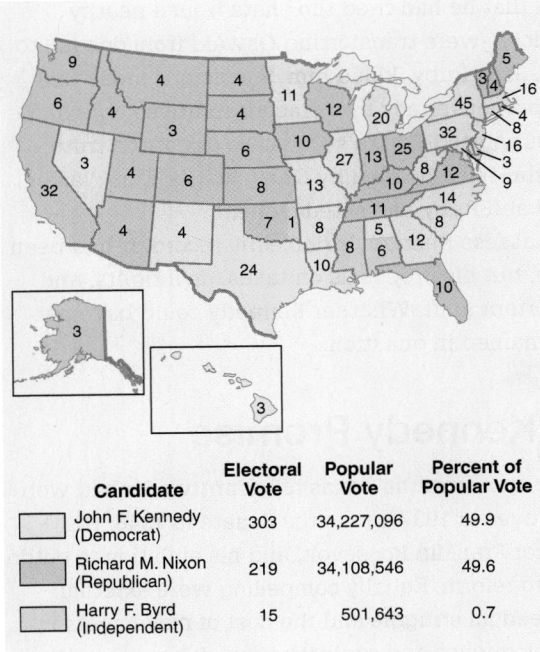

Candidate	Electoral Vote	Popular Vote	Percent of Popular Vote
John F. Kennedy (Democrat)	303	34,227,096	49.9
Richard M. Nixon (Republican)	219	34,108,546	49.6
Harry F. Byrd (Independent)	15	501,643	0.7

MAP 28.1 ■ The Election of 1960

(**Map 28.1**). Kennedy benefited from the nation's first televised presidential debates, during which he appeared cool and confident beside a nervous and pale Nixon.

The Kennedy administration projected energy, idealism, youth, and glamour, although Kennedy was in most ways a cautious, pragmatic politician. At his inauguration, he called on Americans to serve the common good. "Ask not what your country can do for you," he implored, "ask what you can do for your country." Although Kennedy's idealism inspired many, he failed to redeem campaign promises to expand the welfare state with federal education and health care programs. Moreover, he resisted leadership on behalf of racial justice until civil rights activists gave him no choice.

Moved by the desperate conditions he observed while campaigning in Appalachia, Kennedy pushed poverty onto the national agenda. In 1962, he read Michael Harrington's *The Other America*, which described the poverty that left more than one in five Americans "maimed in body and spirit, existing at levels beneath those necessary for human decency." By 1962, Kennedy had won support for a $2 billion urban renewal program, providing incentives to businesses to locate in economically depressed areas and a training program for the unemployed. In the summer of 1963, Kennedy directed aides to plan a full-scale attack on poverty and called for a comprehensive civil rights bill, marking a turning point in his domestic agenda.

Kennedy had promised to make economic growth a key objective, and he asked Congress to pass an enormous tax cut in 1963, arguing that reducing taxes would infuse money into the economy and thus increase demand and create jobs. Enacted in February 1964, the law contributed to an economic boom, as unemployment dropped to 4.1 percent, and the gross national product grew by 7 to 9 percent annually between 1964 and 1966. Some liberal critics of the tax cut, however, pointed out that it favored the well-off and that economic growth alone would not eliminate poverty. They argued instead for increased spending on social programs.

Kennedy's economic efforts were in their infancy when he fell victim to an assassin's bullet on November 22, 1963. Within minutes of the shooting—which occurred as Kennedy's motorcade passed through Dallas, Texas—radio and television broadcast the unfolding horror to the nation. Stunned Americans struggled to understand what had happened. Soon after the assassination, police arrested

CHRONOLOGY

1960
- Democrat John F. Kennedy is elected president.

1962
- Michael Harrington's *The Other America*, detailing endemic poverty in America, is published.

1963
- Supreme Court decision in *Gideon v. Wainwright* guarantees defendants the right to an attorney.
- Supreme Court decision in *Abington School District v. Schempp* bans official prayer in public schools.
- **November 22.** President Kennedy is assassinated; Lyndon B. Johnson becomes president.

1964
- Civil Rights Act, the strongest measure since Reconstruction, is passed by Congress.
- Economic Opportunity Act, part of President Johnson's War on Poverty, is passed.

1965
- Federal funding for antipoverty programs doubles.
- Immigration and Nationality Act reforms immigration policy.
- Medicare and Medicaid health care programs are passed.

1965–1966
- Congress passes most of Johnson's Great Society domestic programs.

1967
- Supreme Court decision in *Loving v. Virginia* strikes down state laws against interracial marriage.

| How did the civil rights movement evolve in the 1960s? | What other rights movements emerged in the 1960s? | What were the goals of the new wave of feminism? | How did liberal reform fare under President Nixon? | Conclusion: What were the achievements and limitations of liberalism? |

Lee Harvey Oswald and concluded that he had fired the shots from a nearby building. Two days later, while officers were transferring Oswald from one jail to another, a local nightclub operator, Jack Ruby, killed him. Suspicions arose that Ruby murdered Oswald to cover up a conspiracy by ultraconservatives who hated Kennedy, or by Communists who supported Castro's Cuba. To get at the truth, President Johnson appointed a commission headed by Chief Justice Earl Warren, which concluded that both Oswald and Ruby had acted alone.

Debate continued over how to assess Kennedy's domestic record. It had been unremarkable in his first two years, but his proposals on taxes, civil rights, and poverty in 1963 suggested an important shift. Whether Kennedy could have persuaded Congress to enact them remained in question.

Johnson Fulfills the Kennedy Promise

Lyndon B. Johnson was a self-made man from the Texas hill country who had won election to the House of Representatives in 1937 and to the Senate in 1948. His modest upbringing, his admiration for Franklin Roosevelt, and his ambition to outdo Roosevelt spurred his commitment to reform. Equally compelling were external pressures generated by the black freedom struggle and the host of movements it helped inspire. Lacking Kennedy's eloquence and sophistication, Johnson excelled behind the scenes, where he could entice, maneuver, or threaten legislators to support his objectives. The famous "Johnson treatment" became legendary. In his ability to achieve consensus around his goals, he had few peers in American history.

Johnson entreated Congress to act so that "John Fitzgerald Kennedy did not live or die in vain." He signed Kennedy's tax cut bill in February 1964. More remarkable was passage of the **Civil Rights Act of 1964**, which Kennedy had proposed in response to black protest. The strongest such measure since Reconstruction, the law required all of Johnson's political skill to pry sufficient votes from Republicans to balance the "nays" of southern Democrats. Senate Republican leader Everett Dirksen's aide reported that Johnson "never left him alone for thirty minutes."

Antipoverty legislation followed the Civil Rights Act. Johnson announced "an unconditional war on poverty" in his January 1964 State of the Union message, and Congress passed the Economic Opportunity Act of 1964 in August. The act authorized ten new programs, allocating $800 million—about 1 percent of the federal budget—for the first year. Many provisions targeted children and youths, including Head Start for preschoolers, work-study grants for college students, and the Job Corps for unemployed young people.

The "Johnson Treatment"

Abe Fortas, a distinguished lawyer who had argued a major criminal rights case, *Gideon v. Wainwright* (1963), before the Supreme Court, was a close friend of and adviser to President Johnson. This photograph of the president and Fortas taken in July 1965 illustrates how Johnson used his body as well as his voice to bend people to his will. Yoichi R. Okamoto/LBJ Library Collection.

CHAPTER LOCATOR | What liberal reforms were advanced during the Kennedy and Johnson administrations?

778 CHAPTER 28
REFORM, REBELLION, AND REACTION, 1960–1974

The Volunteers in Service to America (VISTA) program paid modest wages to volunteers working with the disadvantaged, and a legal services program provided lawyers for the poor.

The most controversial part of the law, the Community Action Program (CAP), required "maximum feasible participation" of the poor themselves in antipoverty projects. Poor people began to organize to take control of their neighborhoods and to make welfare agencies, school boards, police departments, and housing authorities more accountable to the people they served. Even though Johnson backed off from pushing thorough representation for the poor, CAP gave people usually excluded from government an opportunity to act on their own behalf and develop leadership skills.

Policymaking for a Great Society

As the 1964 election approached, Johnson projected stability and security in the midst of a booming economy. Few voters wanted to take a chance on his Republican opponent, Arizona senator Barry M. Goldwater, who attacked the welfare state and suggested using nuclear weapons if necessary to crush communism in Vietnam. Johnson achieved a record-breaking landslide of 61 percent of the popular vote, and Democrats won resounding majorities in the House (295–140) and Senate (68–32). Still, Goldwater's considerable grassroots support marked a growing movement on the right alongside the more noticeable left and liberal movements (see chapter 30).

"I want to see a whole bunch of coonskins on the wall," Johnson told his aides, using a hunting analogy to stress his ambitious legislative goals for what he called the **"Great Society."** The large Democratic majorities in Congress, his own political skills, and pressure from the black freedom struggle enabled Johnson to succeed. He persuaded Congress to act on discrimination, poverty, education, medical care, housing, consumer and environmental protection, and more.

The Economic Opportunity Act of 1964 was the opening shot in the **War on Poverty**. Congress doubled the program's funding in 1965, enacted new economic development measures for depressed regions, and authorized more than $1 billion to improve the nation's slums. Direct aid included a new food stamp program and rent supplements that provided alternatives to public housing projects for some poor families. Moreover, a movement of welfare mothers, the National Welfare Rights Organization, pushed administrators to ease restrictions on welfare recipients. The number of families receiving assistance jumped from less than one million in 1960 to three million by 1972, benefiting 90 percent of those eligible.

Central to Johnson's War on Poverty were efforts to equip the poor with the skills necessary to find jobs. His Elementary and Secondary Education Act of 1965 marked a turning point by involving the federal government in K–12 education. The measure sent federal dollars to local school districts with high poverty populations and provided equipment and supplies to private and parochial schools serving the poor. That same year, Congress passed the Higher Education Act, vastly expanding federal assistance to colleges and universities for buildings, programs, scholarships, and loans.

The federal government's responsibility for health care marked an even more significant watershed. Faced with a powerful medical lobby that opposed national

Great Society

▶ Term for President Johnson's domestic legislative agenda. Between 1964 and 1968, Johnson won passage of Great Society legislation dealing with discrimination, poverty, education, medical care, housing, consumer and environmental protection, and more. While critics pointed out shortcomings in Johnson's legislative record, the Great Society had a lasting impact on American life.

War on Poverty

▶ President Johnson's legislative effort to combat poverty in America. Key elements of the War on Poverty were included in the Economic Opportunity Act of 1964. While Johnson's efforts included substantial increases in direct aid, central to the War on Poverty were efforts to equip the poor with the skills necessary to find jobs.

How did the civil rights movement evolve in the 1960s? | What other rights movements emerged in the 1960s? | What were the goals of the new wave of feminism? | How did liberal reform fare under President Nixon? | Conclusion: What were the achievements and limitations of liberalism?

779

health insurance as "socialized medicine," Johnson focused on the elderly, who constituted a large portion of the nation's poor. Congress responded with the Medicare program, providing the elderly with universal compulsory medical insurance financed through Social Security taxes. A separate program, Medicaid, authorized federal grants to supplement state-funded medical care for poor people.

Whereas programs such as Medicare fulfilled New Deal and Fair Deal promises, the Great Society's civil rights legislation represented a break with tradition and an expansion of liberalism. The Civil Rights Act of 1964 made discrimination in employment, education, and public accommodations illegal. The **Voting Rights Act of 1965** banned literacy tests and authorized federal intervention to ensure access to the voting booth. Another form of bias fell with the Immigration and Nationality Act of 1965, which abolished quotas based on national origins that discriminated against immigrants from areas outside northern and western Europe. The law maintained caps on the total number of immigrants and for the first time limited those from the Western Hemisphere. The measure's unanticipated consequences would trigger a surge of immigration near the end of the century.

Great Society benefits reached well beyond victims of discrimination and the poor. Medicare, for example, covered the elderly, regardless of income. A groundswell of consumer activism won legislation making cars safer and raising standards for the food, drug, and cosmetics industries. Johnson insisted that the Great Society meet "not just the needs of the body but the desire for beauty and hunger for community." In 1965, he sent Congress the first presidential message on the environment, obtaining measures to control water and air pollution and to preserve the natural beauty of the American landscape. In addition, the National Arts and Humanities Act of 1965 funded artists, musicians, writers, and scholars and brought their work to public audiences.

The flood of reform legislation dwindled after 1966, when Democratic majorities in Congress diminished and a backlash against government programs arose. The Vietnam War dealt the largest blow to Johnson's ambitions, diverting his attention, spawning an antiwar movement that crippled his leadership, and devouring tax dollars that might have been used for reform (see chapter 29).

In 1968, Johnson pried out of Congress one more civil rights law, which banned discrimination in housing and jury service. He also signed the National Housing Act of 1968, which authorized an enormous increase in low-income housing—1.7 million units over three years—and left construction and ownership in private hands.

Assessing the Great Society

The reduction in poverty in the 1960s was considerable. The number of poor Americans fell from more than 20 percent of the population in 1959 to around 13 percent in 1968. Those who Johnson had said "lived on the outskirts of hope" saw new opportunities. To Rosemary Bray, what turned her family of longtime welfare recipients into taxpaying workers "was the promise of the civil rights movement and the war on poverty." A Mexican American who became a sheet metal worker through a jobs program reported that his children "will finish high school and maybe go to college. . . . I see my family and I know the chains are broken."

Certain groups, especially the aged, fared better than others. Many male-headed families rose out of poverty, but impoverishment among female-headed

Voting Rights Act of 1965
▶ Law empowering the federal government to intervene directly to enable African Americans to register to vote. As a result of the act, black voting and officeholding in the South shot up, initiating a major transformation in southern politics.

CHAPTER LOCATOR | What liberal reforms were advanced during the Kennedy and Johnson administrations?

CHAPTER 28
780 REFORM, REBELLION, AND REACTION, 1960–1974

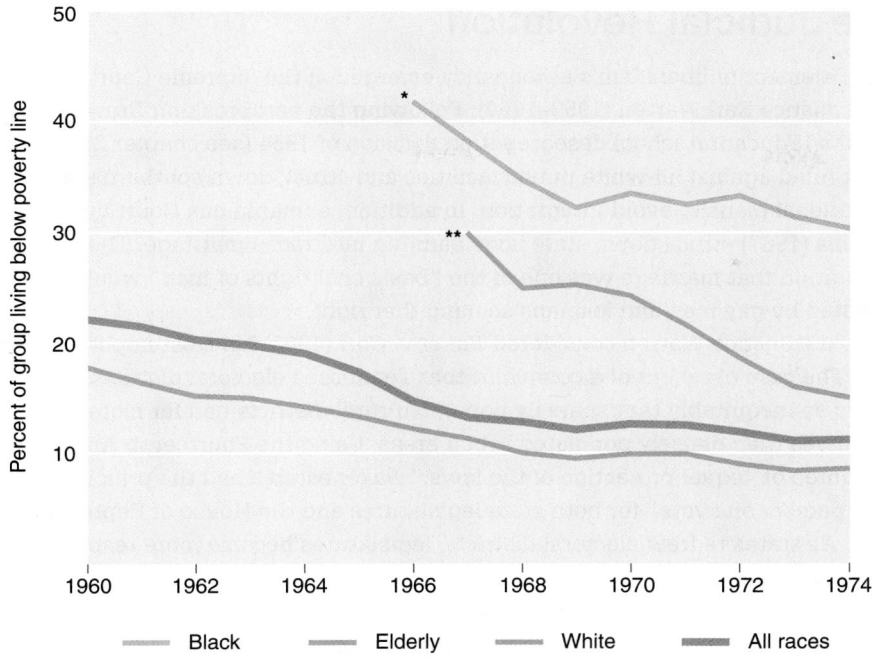

*Statistics on blacks for years 1960–1965 not available.
**Statistics on the elderly for years 1960–1966 not available.

FIGURE 28.1 ■ Poverty in the United States, 1960–1974
The short-term effects of economic growth and the Great Society's attack on poverty are seen here. Which groups experienced the sharpest decline in poverty, and what might account for the differences?

families actually increased. Whites escaped poverty faster than racial and ethnic minorities. Great Society programs contributed to a burgeoning black middle class, and the proportion of African Americans who were poor fell by 10 percentage points between 1966 and 1974. Still, one out of three remained poverty-stricken (**Figure 28.1**).

Conservative critics charged that Great Society programs discouraged initiative by giving the poor "handouts." Liberal critics claimed that focusing on training and education unjustly blamed the poor themselves for their poverty rather than an economic system that could not provide enough adequately paying jobs. Most government training programs prepared graduates for low-skilled labor and could not guarantee employment. In contrast to the New Deal, the Great Society avoided structural reform of the economy and spurned public works projects as a means of providing jobs for the disadvantaged.

Some critics argued that ending poverty required raising taxes in order to create jobs, overhaul welfare systems, and rebuild slums. Great Society programs did invest more heavily in the public sector, but they were funded from economic growth rather than from new taxes. There was no significant redistribution of income, despite large increases in subsidies for food stamps, housing, medical care, and Aid to Families with Dependent Children (AFDC). Economic prosperity allowed spending for the poor to rise and improved the lives of millions, but that spending never approached the amounts necessary to claim victory in the War on Poverty.

How did the civil rights movement evolve in the 1960s?	What other rights movements emerged in the 1960s?	What were the goals of the new wave of feminism?	How did liberal reform fare under President Nixon?	Conclusion: What were the achievements and limitations of liberalism?

The Judicial Revolution

A key element of liberalism's ascendancy emerged in the Supreme Court under Chief Justice Earl Warren (1953–1969). Following the pathbreaking *Brown v. Board of Education* school desegregation decision of 1954 (see chapter 27), the Court ruled against all-white public facilities and struck down southern states' educational plans to avoid integration. In addition, a unanimous Court in *Loving v. Virginia* (1967) struck down state laws banning interracial marriage. The justices' declaration that marriage was one of the "basic civil rights of man" would later be repeated by gay men and lesbians seeking that right.

Chief Justice Warren considered *Baker v. Carr* (1963) his most important decision. The case grew out of a complaint that Tennessee electoral districts were drawn so inequitably that sparsely populated rural districts had far more representatives than densely populated urban areas. Using the Fourteenth Amendment guarantee of "equal protection of the laws," *Baker* established the principle of "one person, one vote" for both state legislatures and the House of Representatives. As states redrew electoral districts, legislatures became more responsive to metropolitan interests.

The Warren Court also reformed the criminal justice system, using the Fourteenth Amendment to overturn a series of convictions on the grounds that the accused had been deprived of "life, liberty, or property, without due process of law." In decisions that dramatically altered law enforcement practices and the treatment of individuals accused of crimes, the Court declared that states, as well as the federal government, were subject to the Bill of Rights. *Gideon v. Wainwright* (1963) ruled that when an accused criminal could not afford to hire a lawyer, the state had to provide one. In 1966, *Miranda v. Arizona* required police officers to inform suspects of their rights upon arrest. The Court also overturned convictions based on evidence obtained by unlawful arrest, by electronic surveillance, or without a search warrant. Critics accused the justices of obstructing law enforcement and letting criminals go free; liberals argued that these rulings promoted equal treatment in the criminal justice system.

The Court's decisions on religion provoked even greater outrage. *Abington School District v. Schempp* (1963) ruled that requiring Bible reading and prayer in the schools violated the First Amendment principle of separation of church and state. Later decisions ruled against official prayer in public schools even if students were not required to participate. These decisions left students free to pray on their own but infuriated many Christians. The Court's supporters, however, declared that the religion cases protected the rights of non-Christians and atheists. Billboards demanding "Impeach Earl Warren" spoke for critics of the Court who joined a larger backlash mounting against Great Society liberalism. Nonetheless, the Court's major decisions withstood the test of time.

QUICK REVIEW

How did the Kennedy and Johnson administrations exemplify a liberal vision of the federal government?

CHAPTER LOCATOR | What liberal reforms were advanced during the Kennedy and Johnson administrations?

782 CHAPTER 28
REFORM, REBELLION, AND REACTION, 1960–1974

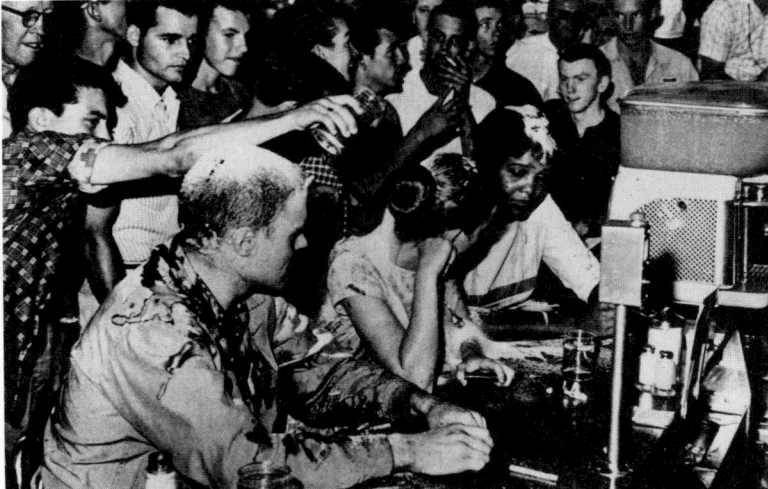

Lunch Counter Sit-in John Salter Jr., a professor at Tougaloo College, and students Joan Trumpauer and Anne Moody take part in a 1963 sit-in at the Woolworth's lunch counter in Jackson, Mississippi. Shortly before this photograph was taken, whites had thrown two students to the floor, and police had arrested one student. Salter was spattered with mustard and ketchup. State Historical Society of Wisconsin.

▶ FOR MORE HELP ANALYZING THIS IMAGE, see the visual activity for this chapter in the Online Study Guide at bedfordstmartins.com/roarkunderstanding.

BEFORE THE GREAT SOCIETY reforms—and, in fact, contributing to them— African Americans had mobilized a movement that struck down legal separation and discrimination in the South. Whereas the first Reconstruction reflected the power of northern Republicans in the aftermath of the Civil War, the second Reconstruction depended heavily on the courage and determination of black people themselves. The early black freedom struggle focused on legal rights in the South and won widespread acceptance. But when African Americans intensified their efforts for racial justice in the rest of the country and challenged the economic deprivation that equal rights left untouched, a strong backlash developed as the movement itself lost cohesion.

The Flowering of the Black Freedom Struggle

The Montgomery bus boycott of 1955–1956 gave racial issues national visibility and produced a leader in **Martin Luther King Jr.** In the 1960s, protest expanded dramatically, as blacks directly confronted the people and institutions that segregated and discriminated against them: retail establishments, public parks and libraries, buses and depots, voting registrars, and police forces.

Massive direct action began in February 1960, when four African American college students in Greensboro, North Carolina, requested service at the whites-only Woolworth's lunch counter. Within days, hundreds of young people joined them, and others launched sit-ins in thirty-one southern cities. From Southern Christian Leadership Conference (SCLC) headquarters, Ella Baker telephoned her young contacts at various colleges: "What are you going to do? It's time to move."

Martin Luther King Jr.

▶ Civil rights leader who first rose to national attention during the Montgomery bus boycott. His principles of civil disobedience and nonviolence shaped the civil rights movement from the mid-1950s through the mid-1960s. King was murdered in Memphis, Tennessee, in April 1968.

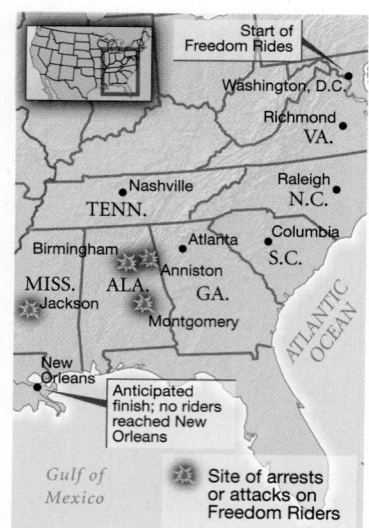

Civil Rights Freedom Rides, May 1961

March on Washington for Jobs and Freedom

▶ The largest demonstration of the civil rights movement. Inspired by the strategy of A. Philip Randolph in 1941, the 1963 March on Washington drew 250,000 people to the nation's capital. Martin Luther King Jr.'s famous "I have a dream" speech capped the day's events.

In April, Baker helped student activists form a new organization, the Student Nonviolent Coordinating Committee (SNCC). Embracing civil disobedience and the nonviolence principles of Martin Luther King Jr., activists would confront their oppressors and stand up for their rights, but they would not respond if attacked. In the words of SNCC leader James Lawson, "Nonviolence nurtures the atmosphere in which reconciliation and justice become actual possibilities." SNCC, however, rejected the top-down leadership of King and the established civil rights organizations; instead, it adopted a structure that fostered decision making and the development of leadership at the grassroots level. Although some cities quietly met student demands, more typically activists encountered violence. Hostile whites poured food over demonstrators, burned them with cigarettes, called them "niggers," and pelted them with rocks. Local police attacked protesters with dogs, clubs, fire hoses, and tear gas and arrested thousands of demonstrators.

Another wave of protest occurred in May 1961, when the Congress of Racial Equality (CORE) organized Freedom Rides to integrate interstate transportation in the South. When a group of six whites and seven blacks reached Alabama, whites bombed their bus and beat them with baseball bats so fiercely that an observer "couldn't see their faces through the blood." After a huge mob attacked the riders in Montgomery, Alabama, Attorney General Robert Kennedy dispatched federal marshals to restore order. Freedom Riders arriving in Jackson, Mississippi, were promptly arrested, and several hundred spent part of the summer in jail. All told, more than four hundred blacks and whites participated in the Freedom Rides.

In the summer of 1961, SNCC and other groups began the Voter Education Project. They, too, met violence. Whites bombed black churches, threw tenant farmers out of their homes, and beat and jailed activists. In June 1963, Mississippi NAACP leader Medgar Evers was gunned down in front of his house in Jackson. Similar violence met King's 1963 campaign in Birmingham, Alabama, to integrate public facilities and open jobs to blacks. The police attacked demonstrators with dogs, cattle prods, and fire hoses—brutalities that television broadcast around the world.

The largest demonstration drew 250,000 blacks and whites to the nation's capital in August 1963 in the **March on Washington for Jobs and Freedom**. Speaking from the Lincoln Memorial, King put his indelible stamp on the day. "I have a dream," he repeated again and again, imagining the day "when all of God's children . . . will be able to join hands and sing . . . 'Free at last, free at last; thank God Almighty, we are free at last.'"

The euphoria of the March on Washington faded as activists returned to continued violence in the South. In 1964, the Mississippi Freedom Summer Project mobilized more than a thousand northern black and white college students to conduct voter registration drives. Resistance was fierce, and by the end of the summer, southern whites had killed several activists, beaten eighty, arrested more than a thousand, and burned thirty-five black churches. Hidden resistance came from the federal government itself, as the FBI spied on King and other leaders and expanded its activities to "expose, disrupt, misdirect, discredit, or otherwise neutralize" black protest.

In March 1965, Alabama state troopers used such force to turn back a voting rights march from Selma to the state capitol in Montgomery that the incident earned the name "Bloody Sunday" and compelled President Johnson to call up the Alabama National Guard to protect the marchers. Battered and hospitalized on

CHAPTER LOCATOR | What liberal reforms were advanced during the Kennedy and Johnson administrations?

784 CHAPTER 28
REFORM, REBELLION, AND REACTION, 1960–1974

The Selma March for Voting Rights

In 1963, the Student Nonviolent Coordinating Committee (SNCC) began a campaign for voting rights in Selma, Alabama, where white officials had registered only 335 of the 15,000 African Americans of voting age. In this photo, young African Americans take part in the fifty-four-mile march from Selma to Montgomery, the state capital, with nuns, priests, and other supporters. During the march, Juanita Williams wore out her shoes (shown here), which are now displayed at the National Museum of History in Washington, D.C. Photo: Steve Shapiro/TimePix/Getty; Shoes: Smithsonian Institution, Washington, D.C.

Bloody Sunday, John Lewis, chairman of SNCC (and later a congressman), managed to make the final stretch of the Selma march to the capitol, which he counted as one of his most meaningful experiences: "[T]hat year the Voting Rights bill was passed and we all felt we'd had a part in it."

The Response in Washington

In June 1963, President Kennedy finally made good on his promise to seek strong antidiscrimination legislation. Pointing to the injustice suffered by blacks, Kennedy asked white Americans, "Who among us would then be content with the counsels of patience and delay?" Johnson took up Kennedy's commitment with passion, as scenes of violence against peaceful demonstrators appalled many television viewers across the nation. The resulting public support, the "Johnson treatment," and the president's appeal to memories of Kennedy all produced the most important civil rights law since Reconstruction.

The Civil Rights Act of 1964 guaranteed access for all Americans to public accommodations, public education, employment, and voting, and it extended constitutional protections to Indians on reservations. Title VII of the measure, banning discrimination in employment, not only attacked racial discrimination but also outlawed job discrimination against women. Because Title VII applied to every aspect of employment, including wages, hiring, and promotion, it represented a giant step for white women as well as for racial minorities.

Responding to black voter registration drives in the South, Johnson demanded legislation to remove "every remaining obstacle to the right and the opportunity to vote." In August 1965, he signed the Voting Rights Act, authorizing direct federal intervention to enable African Americans to register and vote, thereby launching a major transformation in southern politics. Black voting rates shot up dramatically (**Map 28.2**). In turn, the number of African Americans holding political office in the South increased from a handful in 1964 to more than a thousand by 1972. Such

CHRONOLOGY

1960
- Lunch counter sit-ins aimed at ending legal segregation begin in Greensboro, North Carolina, and spread to thirty-one other cities.
- Student Nonviolent Coordinating Committee (SNCC) is established.

1961
- Congress of Racial Equality organizes Freedom Rides to challenge segregation on buses.

1963
- **August.** March on Washington draws 250,000 civil rights supporters.

1964
- Congress passes Civil Rights Act.
- Mississippi Freedom Summer Project is launched to register black voters.

1965
- Selma-to-Montgomery march pushes passage of the Voting Rights Act.

1965–1968
- Urban riots erupt in Los Angeles, Newark, Detroit, Washington, D.C., and dozens of other cities across the nation.

1966
- **June.** SNCC chair Stokely Carmichael calls for "black power."

1968
- **April.** Martin Luther King Jr. is assassinated.

How did the civil rights movement evolve in the 1960s?

What other rights movements emerged in the 1960s?

What were the goals of the new wave of feminism?

How did liberal reform fare under President Nixon?

Conclusion: What were the achievements and limitations of liberalism?

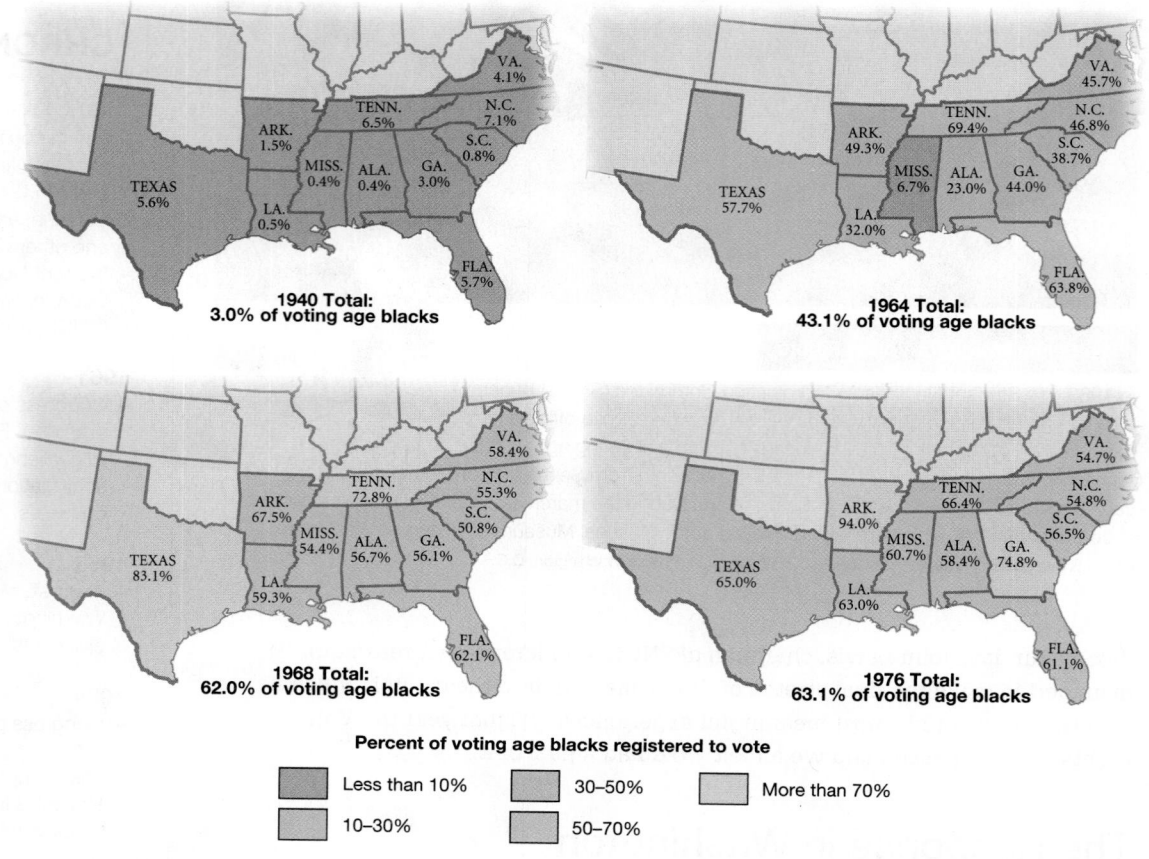

1940 Total:
3.0% of voting age blacks

VA. 4.1%
TENN. 6.5%
N.C. 7.1%
ARK. 1.5%
S.C. 0.8%
MISS. 0.4% ALA. 0.4% GA. 3.0%
TEXAS 5.6%
LA. 0.5%
FLA. 5.7%

1964 Total:
43.1% of voting age blacks

VA. 45.7%
TENN. 69.4%
N.C. 46.8%
ARK. 49.3%
S.C. 38.7%
MISS. 6.7% ALA. 23.0% GA. 44.0%
TEXAS 57.7%
LA. 32.0%
FLA. 63.8%

1968 Total:
62.0% of voting age blacks

VA. 58.4%
TENN. 72.8%
N.C. 55.3%
ARK. 67.5%
S.C. 50.8%
MISS. 54.4% ALA. 56.7% GA. 56.1%
TEXAS 83.1%
LA. 59.3%
FLA. 62.1%

1976 Total:
63.1% of voting age blacks

VA. 54.7%
TENN. 66.4%
N.C. 54.8%
ARK. 94.0%
S.C. 56.5%
MISS. 60.7% ALA. 58.4% GA. 74.8%
TEXAS 65.0%
LA. 63.0%
FLA. 61.1%

Percent of voting age blacks registered to vote

- Less than 10%
- 10–30%
- 30–50%
- 50–70%
- More than 70%

MAP 28.2 ■ The Rise of the African American Vote, 1940–1976
Voting rates of southern blacks increased gradually in the 1940s and 1950s but shot up dramatically in the deep South after the Voting Rights Act of 1965 provided for federal agents to enforce African Americans' right to vote.

> ► FOR MORE HELP ANALYZING THIS MAP, see the map activity for this chapter in the Online Study Guide at bedfordstmartins.com/roarkunderstanding.

gains translated into tangible benefits as black officials upgraded public facilities, police protection, and other basic services for their constituents.

Johnson also declared the need to realize "not just equality as a right and theory, but equality as fact and result." To this end, he issued an executive order in 1965 to require employers holding government contracts (affecting about one-third of the labor force) to take affirmative action to ensure equal opportunity. Extended to cover women in 1967, the affirmative action program required employers to counter the effects of centuries of oppression by acting forcefully to align their labor force with the available pool of qualified candidates. Most corporations came to see affirmative action as a good employment practice.

Johnson pried one final bill from a Congress increasingly resistant to reform. The Civil Rights Act of 1968 banned racial discrimination in housing and jury selection and authorized federal intervention when states failed to protect civil rights workers from violence.

Black Power and Urban Rebellions

By 1966, black protest engulfed the entire nation, demanding not just legal equality but also economic justice and abandoning nonviolence as its basic principle. These developments were not entirely new. African Americans had waged campaigns for decent jobs and housing outside the South since the 1930s. Some African Americans had always armed themselves in self-defense, and many activists doubted that their passive suffering would change the hearts of racists. Still, the black freedom struggle began to appear more threatening to the white majority. The new emphases resulted from a combination of heightened activism and unrealized promise. Legal equality could not quickly improve the material conditions of blacks, and black rage at oppressive conditions erupted in waves of urban uprisings from 1965 to 1968.

In the North, Malcolm X posed a powerful challenge to the ethos of nonviolence. Calling for black pride and autonomy, separation from the "corrupt [white] society," and self-defense against white violence, Malcolm X attracted a large following, especially in urban ghettos. At a June 1966 rally in Greenwood, Mississippi, SNCC chairman Stokely Carmichael gave the ideas espoused by Malcolm X a new name when he shouted, "We want black power." Carmichael rejected integration and assimilation because that implied white superiority. African Americans were encouraged to develop independent businesses and control their own schools, communities, and political organizations. "Black is beautiful" emphasized pride in African American culture and connections to dark-skinned people around the world. Black power quickly became the rallying cry in SNCC and CORE as well as such organizations as the Black Panther Party for Self-Defense, organized in California to combat police brutality.

The press paid inordinate attention to black radicals, and the civil rights movement encountered a severe white backlash. Although the urban riots of the mid-1960s erupted spontaneously, triggered by specific incidents of alleged police mistreatment, whites blamed black power militants. By 1966, 85 percent of the white population—up from 34 percent two years earlier—thought that African Americans were pressing for too much too quickly.

Martin Luther King Jr. agreed with black power advocates about the need for "a radical reconstruction of society," yet he clung to nonviolence and integration as the means to this end. In April 1968, the thirty-nine-year-old leader went to Memphis to support striking municipal sanitation workers. There, on April 4, he was murdered by an escaped white convict.

Although black power organizations captured the headlines, they failed to gain the massive support from African Americans that King and other leaders had attracted. Nor could they alleviate the poverty and racism entrenched in the urban North and West. Yet black power's emphasis on racial pride and its critique of American institutions resonated loudly and helped shape the protest activities of other groups.

QUICK REVIEW

How and why did the struggle for black freedom change over the course of the 1960s?

What other rights movements emerged in the 1960s?

Cesar Chavez and Dolores Huerta

Chavez and Huerta confer in Delano, California, in early 1968 during the United Farm Workers' five-year struggle with grape growers for better wages and working conditions and union recognition. The symbols surrounding them reflect the UFW's origins and connections. Arthur Schatz/TimePix/Getty Images.

> ▶ FOR MORE HELP ANALYZING THIS IMAGE, see the map activity for this chapter in the Online Study Guide at bedfordstmartins.com/roarkunderstanding.

THE CIVIL RIGHTS MOVEMENT's undeniable moral claims helped make protest more respectable, while its successes encouraged other groups with grievances. Native Americans, Latinos, college students, women, gay men and lesbians, environmentalists, and others drew on the black freedom struggle for inspiration and models of activism. Many of these groups engaged in direct-action protests, expressed their own cultural nationalism, and challenged dominant institutions and values. As a result, their grievances gained attention in the political arena, and they expanded justice and opportunity for many of their constituents.

Native American Protest

The cry "red power" reflected the influence of black radicalism on Native Americans, whose activism took on fresh militancy and goals in the 1960s. The assimilationist programs of the 1940s and 1950s, contrary to their intent, stirred a sense of Indian identity across tribal lines and a determination to preserve traditional culture. Native Americans demonstrated and occupied land and public buildings, claiming rights to natural resources and territory they had owned collectively before European settlement.

In 1969, Native American militants captured world attention when several dozen seized Alcatraz Island, an abandoned federal prison in San Francisco Bay, claiming their right of "first discovery" of this land. For nineteen months, they used the occupation to publicize injustices against Indians, promote pan-Indian cooperation, and celebrate traditional cultures. One of the organizers, Dr. LaNada Boyer, said of Alcatraz, "We were able to reestablish our identity as Indian people, as a culture, as political entities."

CHAPTER LOCATOR | What liberal reforms were advanced during the Kennedy and Johnson administrations?

In Minneapolis in 1968, two Chippewa Indians, Dennis Banks and George Mitchell, founded the **American Indian Movement (AIM)** to attack problems in cities, where about 300,000 Indians lived. AIM sought to protect Indians from police harassment, secure antipoverty funds, and establish "survival schools" to teach Indian history and values. The new movement filled many Indians with a new sense of purpose. AIM members did not have "that hangdog reservation look I was used to," Lakota activist Mary Crow Dog wrote; their visit to her South Dakota reservation "loosened a sort of earthquake inside me." AIM leaders helped organize the "Trail of Broken Treaties" caravan to the nation's capital in 1972, when activists occupied the Bureau of Indian Affairs to protest the bureau's policies and bureaucratic interference in Indians' lives.

Although these occupations failed to achieve their specific goals, Indians won the end of relocation and termination policies, greater tribal sovereignty and control over community services, protection of Indian religious practices, and a measure of respect and pride. A number of laws and court decisions restored rights to ancestral lands and compensated tribes for land seized in violation of treaties.

Latino Struggles for Justice

The fastest-growing minority group in the 1960s was Latino, or Hispanic American, an extraordinarily varied population encompassing people of Mexican, Puerto Rican, Caribbean, and other Latin American origins. (The term *Latino* stresses their common bonds as a minority group in the United States. The older, less political term *Hispanic* also includes people with origins in Spain.) People of Puerto Rican and Caribbean descent flocked to East Coast cities, but more than half of the nation's Latino population—including some six million Mexican Americans—lived in the Southwest. In addition, thousands illegally crossed the two-thousand-mile border between Mexico and the United States yearly in search of economic opportunity.

Political organization of Mexican Americans dated back to the League of United Latin American Citizens (LULAC), founded in 1929, which fought segregation and discrimination through litigation (see chapter 26). In the 1960s, however, young Mexican Americans increasingly rejected traditional politics in favor of direct action. One symbol of this generational challenge was young activists' adoption of the term *Chicano* (from *mejicano*, the Spanish word for "Mexican").

Chicano protest drew national attention to California, where **Cesar Chavez** and **Dolores Huerta** organized a movement to improve the conditions of migrant agricultural workers. As the child of migrant farmworkers, Chavez changed schools frequently and encountered indifference and discrimination. One teacher, he recalled, "hung a sign on me that said, 'I am a clown, I speak Spanish.'" After serving in World War II, Chavez began to organize voter registration drives among Mexican Americans.

In contrast to Chavez, Dolores Huerta grew up in an integrated urban neighborhood but still witnessed subtle forms of discrimination. Once, a high school teacher challenged her authorship of an essay because it was so well written. Believing that a labor union was the key to progress, she and Chavez founded the United Farm Workers (UFW) in 1962. To gain leverage for striking workers, the UFW mounted a nationwide boycott of California grapes, which drew support from millions of Americans and helped win a wage increase for the workers in

American Indian Movement (AIM)

▶ Organization established by Dennis Banks and George Mitchell in 1968 to address the problems Indians faced in American cities, including poverty and police harassment. The organization drew a large following that participated in public demonstrations and acts of civil disobedience. It contributed to Indians' successful efforts to end relocation and termination policies and to win greater control over their cultures and communities.

Cesar Chavez/ Dolores Huerta

▶ Organizers of a movement to improve the conditions of migrant agricultural workers. Huerta and Chavez founded the United Farm Workers (UFW) in 1962. The UFW's greatest success was the 1970 boycott of California grapes. Although the UFW struggled and lost membership during the 1970s, it helped politicize Mexican Americans and improve farmworkers' lives.

| How did the civil rights movement evolve in the 1960s? | What other rights movements emerged in the 1960s? | What were the goals of the new wave of feminism? | How did liberal reform fare under President Nixon? | Conclusion: What were the achievements and limitations of liberalism? |

789

1970. Although the UFW struggled and lost membership during the 1970s, it helped politicize Mexican Americans and improve farmworkers' lives.

Other Chicanos pressed the Equal Employment Opportunity Commission (EEOC), the enforcement agency of Title VII of the Civil Rights Act of 1964, to act against job discrimination against Mexican Americans. LULAC, the American GI Forum (see chapter 26), and other groups picketed government offices. President Johnson responded in 1967 by appointing Vicente T. Ximenes as the first Mexican American EEOC commissioner and by creating a special committee on Mexican American affairs.

Claiming "brown power," Chicanos organized to end discrimination in education, gain political power, and combat police brutality. In Denver, Rodolfo "Corky" Gonzales set up "freedom schools" where Chicano children learned Spanish and studied Mexican American history. The nationalist strains of Chicano protest were evident in La Raza Unida (the United Race), a political party founded in 1970 in Texas and based on cultural pride and brotherhood. Along with blacks and Native Americans, Chicanos continued to be disproportionately represented among the poor, but they gradually won more political offices, better enforcement of antidiscrimination legislation, and greater respect for their culture.

Student Rebellion, the New Left, and the Counterculture

Although materially and legally more secure than their African American, Indian, and Latino counterparts, white youths also expressed dissent, supporting the black freedom struggle and launching student protests, the antiwar movement, and the new feminist and environmental movements. They were part of a larger international phenomenon, as student movements arose around the globe.

The central organization of white student protest was Students for a Democratic Society (SDS), formed in 1960. In 1962, the organizers wrote in their statement of purpose, "We are people of this generation, bred in at least modest comfort, housed now in universities, looking uncomfortably at the world we inherit." The idealistic students criticized the complacency of their elders, the remoteness of decision makers, and the powerlessness and alienation generated by a bureaucratic society. SDS aimed to mobilize a "New Left" around the goals of civil rights, peace, and universal economic security. Other forms of student activism soon followed.

The first large-scale white student protest arose at the University of California, Berkeley, in 1964, when university officials banned students from setting up tables to recruit support for various causes. Led by whites back from civil rights work in the South, the "free speech" movement occupied the administration building, and more than seven hundred students were arrested before the California Board of Regents overturned the new restrictions.

Hundreds of student rallies and building occupations followed on campuses across the country, especially after 1965, when opposition to the Vietnam War mounted and students protested against universities' links to the military (see chapter 29). Students also changed the collegiate environment. Women at the University of Chicago, for example, charged in 1969 that all universities "discriminate against women, impede their full intellectual development, deny them places on the faculty, exploit talented women and mistreat women students." At Howard University, African American students called for a "Black Awareness Research

CHAPTER LOCATOR | What liberal reforms were advanced during the Kennedy and Johnson administrations?

790   CHAPTER 28
REFORM, REBELLION, AND REACTION, 1960–1974

Institute" and demanded that academic departments "place more emphasis on how these disciplines may be used to effect the liberation of black people."

Accomplishments of the Student Movement

Curricular reforms, such as the introduction of black studies, Latino studies, and women's studies programs
Increased financial aid for minority and poor students
Independence from paternalistic rules
A larger voice in campus decision making

Student protest bewildered and angered older Americans, even more so when it blended into a cultural revolution against nearly every conventional standard of behavior. Drawing on the ideas of the Beats of the 1950s, the "hippies," as they were called, rejected mainstream values such as materialism, order, and sexual control. Seeking personal rather than political change, they advocated "Do your own thing" and drew attention with their long hair, wildly colorful clothing, and use of illegal drugs. Across the country, thousands of radicals established communes in cities or on farms.

Rock and folk music defined both the counterculture and the political left. Music during the 1960s often carried insurgent political and social messages that reflected radical youth culture. The 1969 Woodstock Music Festival, attended by 400,000 young people, epitomized the centrality of music to the youth rebellion.

The hippies faded away in the 1970s, but many elements of the counterculture—rock music, jeans, and long hair, as well as new social attitudes—filtered into the mainstream. More tolerant approaches to sexual behaviors spawned what came to be called the "sexual revolution," with help from the birth control pill, which became available in the 1960s. Self-fulfillment became a dominant concern of many Americans, and questioning of authority became more widespread.

Gay Men and Lesbians Organize

More permissive sexual norms did not stretch easily to include tolerance of homosexuality. Gay men and lesbians avoided discrimination and ridicule only by concealing their sexual identities. Those who couldn't or wouldn't found themselves fired from jobs, arrested for their sexual activities, deprived of their children, or tagged as "perverted." Some of the first gay activism challenged the government's efforts to keep homosexuals out of the civil service. In October 1965, protesters gathered outside the White House with signs calling discrimination against homosexuals "as immoral as discrimination against Negroes and Jews." Not until ten years later, however, did the Civil Service Commission formally end its antigay policy.

A turning point in gay activism occurred in 1969 when police raided a gay bar, the Stonewall Inn, in New York City's Greenwich Village, and gay men and lesbians fought back. "Suddenly, they were not submissive anymore," a police officer remarked. Energized by the defiance shown at the Stonewall riots, gay

"Country Joe" McDonald's Guitar

The 1969 Woodstock Music Festival featured a wide variety of well-known and lesser-known artists, including the San Francisco–based Country Joe and the Fish, who inspired the crowd of 400,000 with the anti–Vietnam War song "Feel Like I'm Fixin' to Die" rag. The Oakland Museum of California.

How did the civil rights movement evolve in the 1960s?	What other rights movements emerged in the 1960s?	What were the goals of the new wave of feminism?	How did liberal reform fare under President Nixon?	Conclusion: What were the achievements and limitations of liberalism?

791

men and lesbians founded a host of new groups in the years that followed, such as the Gay Liberation Front and the National Gay and Lesbian Task Force.

In 1972, Ann Arbor, Michigan, passed the first antidiscrimination ordinance, and two years later, Elaine Noble's election to the Massachusetts legislature marked the first time an openly gay candidate won state office. In 1973, gay activists persuaded the American Psychiatric Association to remove its designation of homosexuality as a mental disease. By the mid-1970s, gay men and lesbians had established a movement through which they could claim equal rights and express pride in their identities.

A New Movement to Save the Environment

Unlike other social movements, environmentalism was organized around a cause rather than around the identity of its members. The movement that emerged in the 1950s and 1960s resembled the conservation movement born in the Progressive Era (see chapter 21). Especially in the West, post–World War II economic and population growth created increased demands for electricity and water. Environmental groups began mobilizing in the 1950s to stop the construction of dams that would disrupt national parks and wilderness areas.

The new environmentalists, however, went beyond conservationism. Polluted air and water and the use of deadly chemicals threatened the sustainability of human life itself. Biologist Rachel Carson drew national attention to the harmful effects of toxic chemicals such as the pesticide DDT in 1962 with her best seller *Silent Spring*. To the leaders of a new organization, Friends of the Earth, unlimited economic growth was "no longer healthy, but a cancer." The Sierra Club and other older conservation organizations expanded their agendas, and a host of new groups arose.

Responding to these concerns, the federal government staked out a new role in environmental regulation. Lyndon Johnson sent Congress the first presidential message on the environment and signed laws controlling air and water pollution. Richard Nixon's 1970 State of the Union message called "clean air, clean water, open spaces . . . the birthright of every American," and that year he created the **Environmental Protection Agency (EPA)** to enforce clean air and water policies and to regulate pesticides. Congress also passed the Occupational Safety and Health Act (OSHA), protecting workers against workplace accidents and disease, and the Clean Air Act of 1970, setting national standards for air quality and restricting factory and automobile emissions of carbon dioxide and other pollutants.

Nevertheless, the desire for economic growth often trumped environmental concerns. Corporations resisted restrictions. "If you're hungry and out of work, eat an environmentalist," read a union bumper sticker reflecting fears that regulations threatened jobs. Many Americans who wanted to protect the environment also valued economic expansion, personal acquisition, and convenience. Despite these conflicts, the environmental movement achieved cleaner air and water, a reduction in toxic wastes, and some preservation of endangered species and wilderness.

Environmental Protection Agency (EPA)

▶ Federal agency charged with enforcing environmental regulations. Created by President Nixon in 1970, the EPA played a key role in the push toward cleaner air, cleaner water, and a less toxic environment.

> ## QUICK REVIEW

What were the goals and achievements of the other reform movements of the 1960s and 1970s?

CHAPTER LOCATOR | What liberal reforms were advanced during the Kennedy and Johnson administrations?

CHAPTER 28
792 REFORM, REBELLION, AND REACTION, 1960–1974

Cover of the First Issue of *Ms.* Magazine

In 1972, Gloria Steinem and other journalists and writers published the premier issue of the first mass-circulation magazine for and controlled by women. *Ms.: The New Magazine for Women* ignored the recipes and fashion tips of typical women's magazines. It featured literature by women writers and articles on a broad range of feminist issues. Courtesy, Lang Communications.

BECOMING VISIBLE by the late 1960s, a multifaceted women's movement reached its high tide in the 1970s and persisted into the twenty-first century. By that time, despite a powerful countermovement, women had experienced tremendous transformations in their legal status, public opportunities, and personal and sexual relationships, and popular expectations about appropriate gender roles had shifted dramatically.

A Multifaceted Movement Emerges

Beginning in the 1940s, large demographic changes laid the preconditions for a resurgence of feminism. As more women took jobs, the importance of their paid work to the economy and their families challenged traditional views of women and awakened many women workers, especially labor union women, to the inferior conditions of their employment. The democratization of higher education brought more women to college campuses, where their aspirations exceeded the confines of domesticity and of routine, subordinate jobs.

Policy initiatives in the early 1960s reflected both these larger transformations and the efforts of women's rights activists. In 1961, Assistant Secretary of Labor Esther Peterson persuaded President Kennedy to create the President's Commission on the Status of Women (PCSW). In 1963, the commission reported widespread discrimination against women and recommended remedies. One of the PCSW's concerns was addressed even before it issued its report, when Congress passed the Equal Pay Act of 1963, making it illegal to pay women less than men for the same work.

| How did the civil rights movement evolve in the 1960s? | What other rights movements emerged in the 1960s? | **What were the goals of the new wave of feminism?** | How did liberal reform fare under President Nixon? | Conclusion: What were the achievements and limitations of liberalism? |

793

CHRONOLOGY

1963
- President's Commission on the Status of Women issues report on discrimination against women.
- Equal Pay Act makes it illegal to pay women less for the same work.

1966
- National Organization for Women is founded.

1968
- Women's liberation activists protest Miss America pageant.

1972
- Title IX of Education Amendments Act bans sex discrimination in all aspects of education.
- Congress passes Equal Rights Amendment; sends it to states for ratification.
- *Ms.* magazine begins publication.
- Phyllis Schlafly organizes a movement to oppose the Equal Rights Amendment.

1973
- Supreme Court ruling in *Roe v. Wade* protects the right to abortion.

National Organization for Women (NOW)

▶ Women's civil rights organization formed in 1966 to push the government to enforce the ban against sex discrimination contained in the 1964 Civil Rights Act. Initially, NOW focused on eliminating gender discrimination in public institutions and the workplace, but by the 1970s it also embraced many of the issues raised by more radical feminists.

Like other movements, the rise of feminism owed much to the black freedom struggle. Women gained the ban against sex discrimination in Title VII of the Civil Rights Act of 1964 and the extension of affirmative action to women by piggybacking onto civil rights measures. They soon grew impatient when the government failed to take these new policies seriously. Hoping to speed the process of change, Betty Friedan, civil rights activist Pauli Murray, several union women, and others founded the **National Organization for Women (NOW)** in 1966.

Simultaneously, a more radical feminism grew among civil rights and New Left activists. Frustrated with the unwillingness of male activists to take sexism seriously, many women walked out of New Left organizations and created their own women's liberation movement across the nation. Women's liberation began to gain public attention, especially when dozens of women picketed the Miss America beauty pageant in 1968, protesting against being forced "to compete for male approval [and] enslaved by ludicrous 'beauty' standards." Women began to speak publicly about personal experiences such as rape and abortion. Throughout the country, women joined consciousness-raising groups, where they discovered that what they had considered "personal" problems reflected an entrenched system of discrimination against and devaluation of women.

Radical feminists, who called their movement "women's liberation," differed from feminists in NOW and other more mainstream groups in several ways. NOW focused on equal treatment for women in the public sphere; women's liberation emphasized ending women's subordination in family and other personal relationships. Mainstream feminists wanted to integrate women into existing institutions; radical groups insisted that women's liberation required a total transformation of economic, political, and social institutions. Differences between these two strands of feminism blurred in the 1970s, as NOW and other mainstream groups embraced many of the issues raised by radicals.

Although NOW elected a black president, Aileen Hernandez, in 1970, the new feminism's leadership and constituency were predominantly white and middle-class. Women of color criticized white feminists for their inadequate attention to the disproportionate poverty experienced by minority women and to the additional layers of discrimination based on race or ethnicity. One black woman said, "My mother took care of rich white kids. I didn't think they were oppressed." To black women compelled to work in the lowest-paying jobs for their families' survival, employment did not necessarily look like liberation.

In addition to struggling with vast differences among women, feminism also contended with the refusal of the mass media to take women's grievances seriously. When the House of Representatives passed an equal rights amendment to the U.S. Constitution in 1970, the *New York Times* criticized it in an editorial titled "The Henpecked House." After Gloria Steinem founded *Ms.: The New Magazine for Women* in 1972, feminists had their own mass-circulation periodical controlled by women and featuring articles on a broad range of feminist issues.

Ms. reported on a multifaceted movement that included numerous organizations, reflecting the diverse experiences, backgrounds, and goals of American women. Women founded a host of organizations representing different groups of women—ethnic and racial minorities, labor union women, religious women, welfare mothers, lesbians, and more. Common threads underlay the great diversity of organizations, issues, and activities. Above all, feminism represented the

CHAPTER LOCATOR | What liberal reforms were advanced during the Kennedy and Johnson administrations?

belief that women were barred from, unequally treated in, or poorly served by the male-dominated public arena, encompassing politics, medicine, law, education, and religion. Many feminists also sought equality in the private sphere, challenging traditional norms that identified women primarily as wives and mothers or sex objects, subservient to men.

Feminist Gains Spark a Countermovement

Although it was more an effect than a cause of women's rising employment, feminism lifted female aspirations and helped lower barriers to posts monopolized by men. Between 1970 and 2000, women's share of law degrees shot up from 5 percent to nearly 50 percent, and their share of medical degrees from less than 10 percent to more than 35 percent. Women gained political offices very slowly; yet by 2008, they constituted about 16 percent of Congress and more than 20 percent of all state executives and legislators. Despite some inroads into male-dominated occupations, women still tended to concentrate in low-paying, traditionally female jobs. Employed women continued to bear primary responsibility for their homes and families, thereby working a "double day."

By the mid-1970s, feminism faced a powerful countermovement, organized around opposition to an **Equal Rights Amendment (ERA)** to the U.S. Constitution that would outlaw differential treatment of men and women under all state and federal laws. After Congress passed the ERA in 1972, Phyllis Schlafly, a conservative activist in the Republican Party, mobilized thousands of antifeminist women. These women persuaded some state legislatures to block ratification. When the time limit ran out in 1982, only thirty-five states had ratified the amendment, three short of the necessary three-fourths majority.

Powerful opposition likewise arose to feminists' quest for abortion rights. In 1973, the Supreme Court ruled in the landmark *Roe v. Wade* that the Constitution protects the right to abortion. This decision galvanized many Americans who equated abortion with murder. Abortion foes got Congress to restrict the right to abortion by denying coverage under Medicaid and other government-financed health programs, and the Supreme Court allowed states to impose additional obstacles.

Despite resistance, feminists won other lasting gains. Title IX of the Education Amendments Act of 1972 banned sex discrimination in all aspects of education, such as admissions, athletics, and hiring. Congress outlawed sex discrimination in credit in 1974, opened U.S. military academies to women in 1976, and prohibited discrimination against pregnant workers in 1978. Moreover, the Supreme Court struck down laws that treated men and women differently in Social Security, welfare and military benefits, and workers' compensation.

At the state and local levels, women won laws forcing police departments and the legal system to treat rape victims more justly and humanely. Activists also pushed the issue of domestic violence onto the public agenda, obtaining government financing for shelters for battered women and laws ensuring both greater protection for victims of domestic violence and more effective prosecution of abusers.

Equal Rights Amendment (ERA)
▶ Proposed amendment to the Constitution that would have outlawed differential treatment of men and women under all state and federal laws. Congress passed the ERA in 1972, but the amendment failed to achieve ratification within the ten-year time limit. Conservative activists were central to the effort to defeat the amendment.

Roe v. Wade
▶ 1973 Supreme Court ruling that the Constitution protects the right to abortion and that states cannot prohibit abortions in the early stages of pregnancy. The decision galvanized social conservatives and helped give the abortion issue a prominent place in the cultural conflicts of the 1980s and 1990s.

QUICK REVIEW

What were the successes and failures of the new wave of feminism?

| How did the civil rights movement evolve in the 1960s? | What other rights movements emerged in the 1960s? | **What were the goals of the new wave of feminism?** | How did liberal reform fare under President Nixon? | Conclusion: What were the achievements and limitations of liberalism? |

795

How did liberal reform fare under President Nixon?

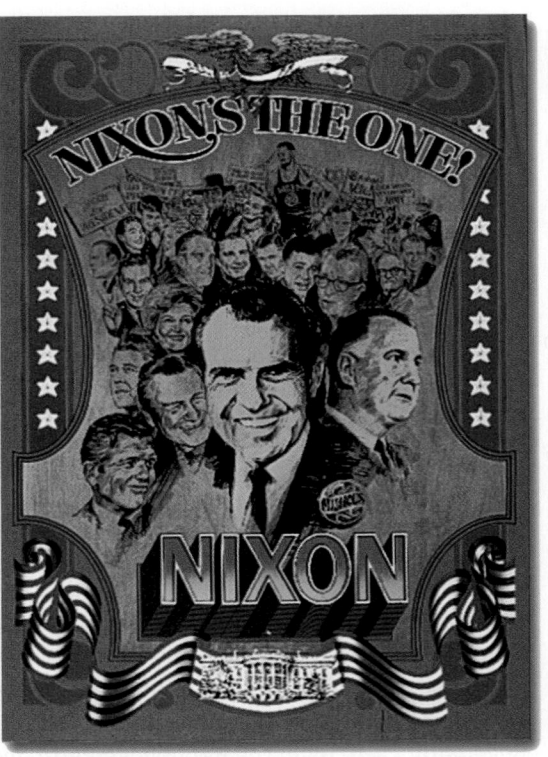

Poster for Nixon's 1968 Campaign

Seeking the presidency in 1968—a turbulent year of protests, riots, and assassinations—Richard Nixon tried to appeal to a broad spectrum of voters, reflected in this campaign poster. While his slogan "Champion of Forgotten America" spoke to white Americans alienated by the Great Society's programs for minorities and the poor, the appearance on the poster of the black Republican senator Edward Brooke and basketball player Wilt Chamberlain of the Los Angeles Lakers gave a nod to African Americans. Collection of Janice L. and David J. Frent.

OPPOSITION TO CIVIL RIGHTS MEASURES, Great Society reforms, and protest groups—along with frustrations surrounding the war in Vietnam (see chapter 29)—delivered the White House to Republican Richard M. Nixon in 1968. Nixon attacked the Great Society for "pouring billions of dollars into programs that have failed," and he promised to represent the "forgotten Americans, the non-shouters, the non-demonstrators." Nonetheless, the Nixon administration either promoted or accepted important elements of the liberal reform agenda.

Extending the Welfare State and Regulating the Economy

A number of factors shaped the liberal policies of the Nixon administration. Democrats continued to control Congress, the Republican Party contained significant numbers of liberals and moderates, and Nixon saw political advantages in accepting some liberal programs. Serious economic problems also compelled new approaches, and although Nixon's real passion lay in foreign policy, he was eager to establish his domestic legacy.

Under Nixon, existing government assistance programs in such areas as Social Security and housing grew, and new programs were created, such as a billion-dollar program that provided Pell grants for low-income students to attend college. Noting the disparity between what Nixon said and what he did, his

CHAPTER LOCATOR | What liberal reforms were advanced during the Kennedy and Johnson administrations?

speechwriter, the archconservative Pat Buchanan, grumbled, "Vigorously did we inveigh against the Great Society, enthusiastically did we fund it."

Nixon also acted contrary to his antigovernment rhetoric when economic crises and energy shortages induced him to increase the federal government's power in the marketplace. By 1970, both inflation and unemployment had surpassed 6 percent, an unprecedented combination dubbed "stagflation." Domestic troubles were compounded by the decline of American dominance in the international economy. In 1971, for the first time in decades, the United States imported more than it exported. Because the amount of dollars in foreign hands exceeded U.S. gold reserves, the nation could no longer back up its currency with gold.

In 1971, Nixon abandoned the convertibility of dollars into gold and devalued the dollar to increase exports. To protect domestic manufacturers, he imposed a 10 percent surcharge on most imports, and he froze wages and prices, thus enabling the government to stimulate the economy without fueling inflation. In the short run, these policies worked, and Nixon was resoundingly reelected in 1972. Yet by 1974, unemployment had crept back up and inflation soared, leaving to Nixon's successor the most severe economic crisis since the 1930s.

Soaring energy prices intensified stagflation. In the fall of 1973, the United States faced its first energy crisis. Arab nations, furious at the Nixon administration's support of Israel during the Yom Kippur War (see chapter 29), cut off oil shipments to the United States. Long lines formed at gas stations, where prices had nearly doubled, and many homes were cold. In response, Nixon authorized temporary emergency measures allocating petroleum and establishing a national 55-mile-per-hour speed limit to save gasoline. The energy crisis eased, but the nation had yet to come to grips with its seemingly unquenchable demand for fuel and dependence on foreign oil.

More permanently, Nixon expanded the government's regulatory role with a host of environmental protection measures. He proclaimed in 1970 that the nation must make "reparations for the damage we have done to our air, to our land and to our water." In addition to establishing the Environmental Protection Agency, he signed strong clean air legislation and measures to regulate noise pollution, oil spill cleanup, and the dumping of pesticides into the oceans. Environmentalists criticized Nixon's veto of the Clean Water Act of 1972, which Congress overrode. Yet his environmental initiatives surpassed those of previous administrations.

Responding to Demands for Social Justice

Nixon's 1968 campaign had exploited hostility to black protest and new civil rights policies to appeal to southern Democrats and white workers, but his administration had to answer to the courts and to Congress. In 1968, fourteen years after the *Brown* decision, school desegregation had barely touched the South. Nixon was reluctant to use federal power to compel integration, but the Supreme Court overruled the administration's efforts to delay court-ordered desegregation and compelled it to enforce the law. By the time Nixon left office, fewer than one in ten southern black children attended totally segregated schools.

Nixon also began to implement affirmative action among federal contractors and unions and awarded more government contracts and loans to minority

CHRONOLOGY

1968
- Republican Richard M. Nixon is elected president.

1970
- Unemployment and inflation surpass 6 percent.
- Voting Rights Act of 1965 is extended.
- Nixon establishes the Environmental Protection Agency.

1971
- Nixon takes United States off gold standard and freezes prices and wages.

1972
- Civil Rights Act of 1964 is strengthened.

1973
- Arab oil embargo.

How did the civil rights movement evolve in the 1960s? | What other rights movements emerged in the 1960s? | What were the goals of the new wave of feminism? | **How did liberal reform fare under President Nixon?** | Conclusion: What were the achievements and limitations of liberalism?

797

businesses. Congress took the initiative in other areas. In 1970, it extended the Voting Rights Act of 1965, and in 1972, it strengthened the Civil Rights Act of 1964 by enlarging the powers of the Equal Employment Opportunity Commission.

Several measures of the Nixon administration also specifically attacked sex discrimination. Although the president privately expressed patronizing attitudes about women, he confronted a growing feminist movement that included Republican women. Nixon vetoed a child care bill and publicly opposed abortion, but he signed the pathbreaking Title IX, guaranteeing equality in all aspects of education, and allowed his Labor Department to push affirmative action.

President Nixon gave more public support for justice to Native Americans than to any other group. While not bowing to radical demands, the administration dealt cautiously with extreme protests, such as the occupation of the Bureau of Indian Affairs in Washington, D.C. Nixon signed measures recognizing claims of Alaskan and New Mexican Indians and set in motion legislation restoring tribal lands and granting Indians more control over their schools and other institutions.

> QUICK REVIEW

Why and how did Republican president Richard Nixon expand the liberal reforms of previous administrations?

SO NOW YOU KNOW

Republican president Richard Nixon created the Environmental Protection Agency in 1970 in response to the demands of a new environmental movement that sought to limit the spread of toxic pollutants and to conserve nature.

CHAPTER LOCATOR | What liberal reforms were advanced during the Kennedy and Johnson administrations?

© Bob Adelman.

Conclusion: What were the achievements and limitations of liberalism?

THE GREAT SOCIETY expanded the New Deal's focus on economic security and refashioned liberalism to embrace individual rights. Yet opposition to Johnson's leadership grew so strong by 1968 that he abandoned hopes for reelection. Some Americans resented the millions of federal dollars going to the poor and minorities. Others charged that many antipoverty programs benefited industry and professionals more than they did the poor and focused more on fixing individual shortcomings than on economic reforms that would ensure adequately paying jobs for all.

When the civil rights movement attacked racial barriers and sought equality in fact as in law, it faced a powerful backlash. By the end of the 1960s, the revolution in the legal status of African Americans was complete and significant numbers began to enter the middle class, but African Americans remained, with Native Americans and Chicanos, at the bottom of the economic ladder.

The Great Society did contain successful and lasting elements. Medicare and Medicaid provided access to health care for the elderly and the poor and contributed to a sharp decline in poverty among the elderly. Federal aid for education and housing became permanent elements of national policy. Moreover, the Nixon administration implemented school desegregation in the South and affirmative action, expanded environmental regulations, and secured new rights for Native Americans and women.

Yet the perceived shortcomings of government programs contributed to social turmoil and fueled the resurgence of conservative politics. Young radicals launched direct confrontations with the government and universities that, together with racial conflict, escalated into political discord and social disorder. The war in Vietnam polarized American society as much as did racial issues or the behavior of young people, and it devoured resources that might have been used for social reform and undermined faith in presidential leadership.

How did the civil rights movement evolve in the 1960s?

What other rights movements emerged in the 1960s?

What were the goals of the new wave of feminism?

How did liberal reform fare under President Nixon?

Conclusion: What were the achievements and limitations of liberalism?

STEP 1
GETTING STARTED

Below are basic terms from this period in American history. Can you identify each term below and explain why it matters? To do this exercise online or to download this chart, visit bedfordstmartins.com/roarkunderstanding.

TERM	WHO OR WHAT & WHEN	WHY IT MATTERS
Civil Rights Act of 1964, p. 778		
Great Society, p. 779		
War on Poverty, p. 779		
Voting Rights Act of 1965, p. 780		
Martin Luther King Jr., p. 783		
March on Washington for Jobs and Freedom, p. 784		
American Indian Movement (AIM), p. 789		
Cesar Chavez/Dolores Huerta, p. 789		
Environmental Protection Agency (EPA), p. 792		
National Organization for Women (NOW), p. 794		
Equal Rights Amendment (ERA), p. 795		
Roe v. Wade, p. 795		

STEP 2
MOVING BEYOND THE BASICS

The exercise below represents a more advanced understanding of the chapter material. Fill in the chart by describing the goals, strategy and tactics, and achievements of the major rights movements of the 1960s. If significant disagreement existed within a group over goals, strategies, or tactics, make sure to include a description of those divisions. When you are finished, ask yourself the following questions: What did the various rights movements of the 1960s have in common? Which movements were most successful and why? To do this exercise online or to download this chart, visit bedfordstmartins.com/roarkunderstanding.

Rights movement	Goals	Strategy and tactics	Achievements
African Americans			
Latinos			
Native Americans			
Students			
Feminists			
Gays and lesbians			
Environmentalists			

Now that you've reviewed various parts of the chapter, take a step back and try to see the big picture by answering these questions. Remember to use specific examples from the chapter in your answers. To do this exercise online, visit bedfordstmartins.com/roarkunderstanding.

PROTEST AND REBELLION

▶ What role did students play in the civil rights struggles of the 1960s? How did the civil rights movement change toward the end of the decade?

▶ What were the key achievements of 1960s feminism? What goals did it fail to fulfill?

LYNDON JOHNSON AND THE GREAT SOCIETY

▶ What were the most important domestic achievements of the Johnson administration? What were its most important failures?

▶ What assumptions about the relationship between government and society underlay Johnson's Great Society programs?

LOOKING BACKWARD, LOOKING AHEAD

▶ How did the African American civil rights movement of the 1960s differ from the movement of the 1950s?

▶ What kinds of opposition emerged in the late 1960s to liberal reforms and radical protest? How might that trend influence politics in the decades after the 1960s?

LIBERAL REFORM IN THE NIXON ADMINISTRATION

▶ What liberal initiatives did the Nixon administration embrace, and what explains these actions?

▶ Should Richard Nixon be considered an environmentalist? Why or why not?

IN YOUR OWN WORDS

Imagine that you must explain chapter 28 to someone who hasn't read it. What would be the most important points to include and why?

29
VIETNAM AND THE LIMITS OF POWER

1961–1975

> This chapter explores U.S. foreign policy from 1961 to 1975, placing American involvement in the Vietnam War in the larger context of American politics and relations with the Soviet Union, China, and developing nations. It examines the escalation of U.S. involvement in Vietnam under Presidents Kennedy and Johnson, the polarizing effect of the war on American society and politics, and the gradual American withdrawal from Vietnam under President Nixon.

> How did American foreign policy change under Kennedy?

> Why did Johnson escalate American involvement in Vietnam?

> How did the war in Vietnam polarize the nation?

> How did American foreign policy change under Nixon?

> Conclusion: Was Vietnam an unwinnable war?

DID YOU KNOW?

The average age of a U.S. soldier in Vietnam was nineteen.

Vietnam. Marines patrol near the demilitarized zone in Vietnam during Operation Prairie, 1966.

How did American foreign policy change under Kennedy?

Preparing for the Worst during the Cuban Missile Crisis

Waiting out the tense days after President Kennedy issued the ultimatum to the Soviet Union to halt shipments of missile materials to Cuba, many Americans prepared for the worst possible outcome. Owners of Chalet Suzanne, a hotel in Lake Wales, Florida, canned several thousand cases of well water, labeled "NASK" for Nuclear Attack Survival Kit. Courtesy Chalet Suzanne Foods, Inc., Lake Wales, Florida. Photo by David Woods.

IN HIS 1961 INAUGURAL ADDRESS, John F. Kennedy declared that the United States would "pay any price, bear any burden, meet any hardship, support any friend, oppose any foe to assure the survival and the success of liberty." In this spirit, he moved quickly to pursue containment more aggressively than the Eisenhower administration had and with more flexible means.

Key Elements of Kennedy's Foreign Policy

Expansion of conventional military forces

New approaches to the third world

Escalation of the nuclear arms race

Meeting the "Hour of Maximum Danger"

John F. Kennedy

▶ Democratic president who served from 1961 until his assassination in November 1963. In foreign policy, Kennedy vigorously pursued containment, including in Vietnam. He also expanded the United States' capacity for nuclear and conventional war, asserting it as necessary in the face of Soviet aggression.

Underlying **John F. Kennedy**'s foreign policy was an assumption that the United States had "gone soft—physically, mentally, spiritually soft," as he put it in 1960. Calling the Eisenhower era "years of drift and impotency," Kennedy built up conventional ground forces to provide a more flexible response to Communist expansion, and he increased the nation's nuclear capability. In January 1961, Kennedy warned that the nation faced a grave peril: "Each day the crises multiply. . . . Each day we draw nearer the hour of maximum danger."

Although the president exaggerated the threat to national security, several developments in 1961 heightened the sense of crisis and provided a rationalization for his military buildup. Shortly before Kennedy's inauguration, Nikita Khrushchev publicly encouraged "wars of national liberation," thereby aligning the Soviet Union with independence movements in the third world that were often anti-Western. His statement reflected in part the Soviet competition with China for the allegiance of emerging nations, but U.S. officials saw in his words a threat to the status quo of containment.

Cuba, just ninety miles off the Florida coast, posed the most immediate threat to the United States. Fidel Castro's revolution had already moved Cuba into the

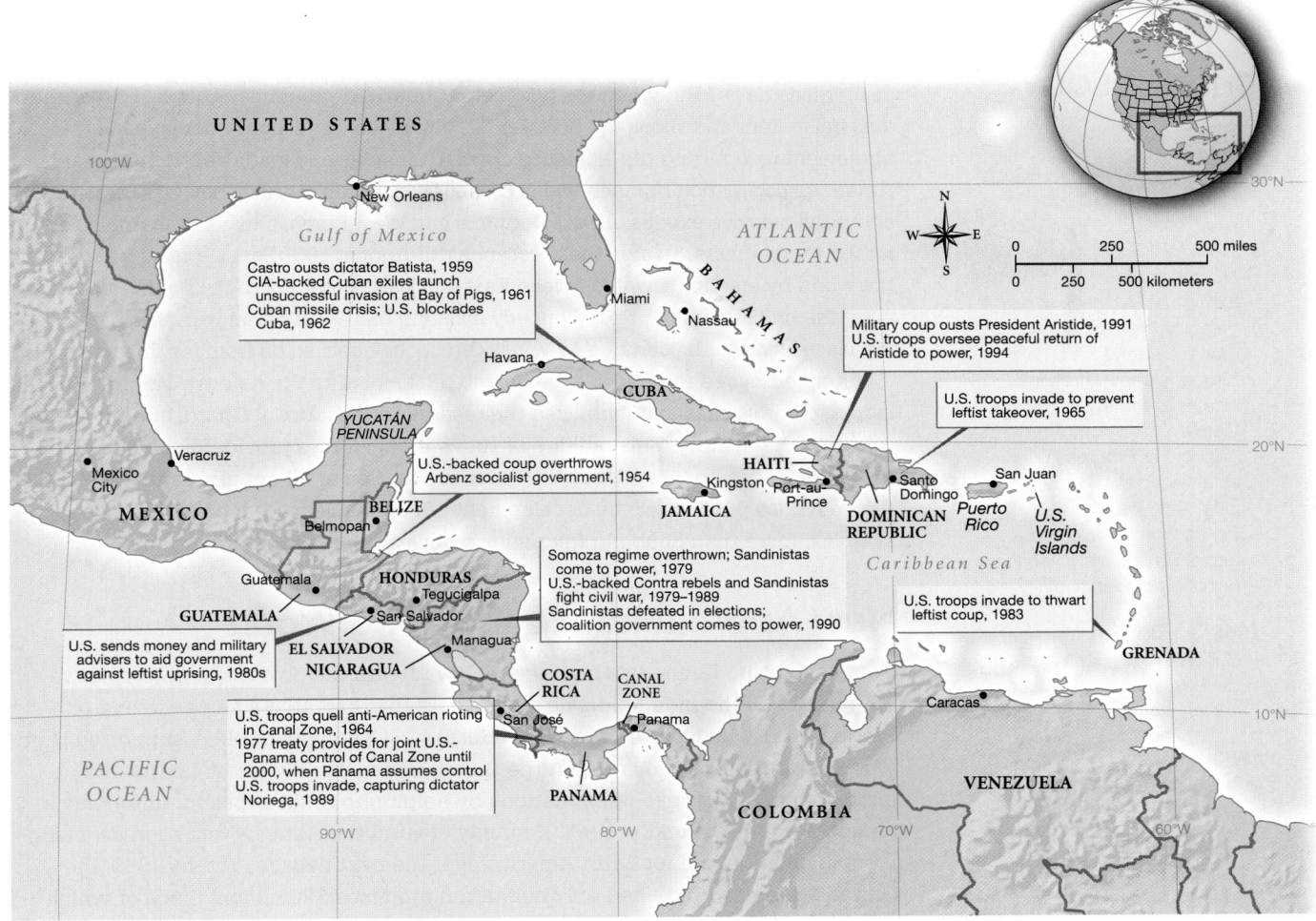

MAP 29.1 ■ U.S. Involvement in Latin America and the Caribbean, 1954–1994
During the Cold War, the United States frequently intervened in Central American and Caribbean countries to suppress Communist or leftist movements.

Soviet orbit, and President Eisenhower's CIA had been planning an invasion of the island by Cuban exiles. Kennedy ordered the invasion to proceed even though his military advisers gave it only a fair chance of success. On April 17, 1961, about 1,400 anti-Castro exiles landed at the Bay of Pigs on the south shore of Cuba (**Map 29.1**). Contrary to U.S. expectations, no popular uprising materialized to support the anti-Castro brigade. Kennedy refused to provide direct military support, and the invaders quickly fell to Castro's forces. The disaster humiliated Kennedy and the United States, posing a stark contrast to the president's inaugural promise of a new, more effective foreign policy. And it alienated Latin Americans who saw it as another example of Yankee imperialism.

Days before the Bay of Pigs invasion, the Soviet Union delivered a psychological blow when a Soviet astronaut became the first human to orbit the earth. In May 1961, Kennedy called for a huge new commitment to the space program, with the goal of sending a man to the moon by 1970. Congress authorized the Apollo program and boosted appropriations for space exploration. John H. Glenn orbited the earth in 1962, and in July 1969, two U.S. astronauts landed on the moon.

| Why did Johnson escalate American involvement in Vietnam? | How did the war in Vietnam polarize the nation? | How did American foreign policy change under Nixon? | Conclusion: Was Vietnam an unwinnable war? |

CHRONOLOGY

1961
- Bay of Pigs invasion of Cuba by U.S.-trained Cuban exiles fails.
- Berlin Wall is erected to stem the tide of Germans defecting from Communist East Germany.
- Kennedy administration increases military aid to South Vietnam.
- Alliance for Progress is established to provide aid to Latin America.
- Peace Corps is created to recruit Americans to work in developing countries.

1962
- Cuban missile crisis leads the United States to the brink of nuclear war.

1963
- The United States, the Soviet Union, and Great Britain sign limited nuclear test ban treaty.

Early in his presidency, Kennedy determined to show Khrushchev "that we can be as tough as he is." But when the two met in June 1961 in Vienna, Austria, Khrushchev was belligerent and shook the president's confidence. Khrushchev demanded an agreement recognizing the existence of two Germanys and made veiled threats about America's occupation rights in and access to West Berlin. Khrushchev was concerned about the massive exodus of East Germans into West Berlin, a major embarrassment for the Communists. To stop these escapees, in August 1961 East Germany shocked the world by erecting a wall between East and West Berlin. With the Berlin Wall stemming the tide of migration and Kennedy insisting that West Berlin was "the great testing place of Western courage and will," Khrushchev backed off from his threats.

Kennedy used the Berlin crisis to add $3.2 billion to the defense budget. He increased draft calls and mobilized the reserves and National Guard, adding 300,000 troops to the military. This buildup of conventional forces provided for a "flexible response," offering "a wider choice than humiliation or all-out nuclear action." Still, Kennedy also pushed for the development of new nuclear weapons and delivery systems, more than doubling the nation's nuclear force within three years.

New Approaches to the Third World

Complementing Kennedy's hard-line policy toward the Soviet Union were fresh approaches to the independence movements that had arisen since the end of World War II. Much more than his predecessors, Kennedy publicly supported third world aspirations, believing that the United States could win the hearts and minds of people in developing nations by helping to fulfill hopes for autonomy and democracy. To that end, in 1961 Kennedy created the Alliance for Progress, pledging $20 billion in aid for Latin America over the next decade. Yet, by 1969, the United States had provided only half of the promised $20 billion, much of which went to military projects or corrupt ruling elites.

Kennedy launched his most dramatic third world initiative in 1961 with an idea borrowed from Senator Hubert H. Humphrey: the Peace Corps. The program recruited young people to work in developing countries, attracting many who had been moved by Kennedy's appeal for idealism and sacrifice in his inaugural address. One volunteer's service eased his guilt at having been "born between clean sheets when others were issued into the dust with a birthright of hunger." By the mid-1970s, more than 60,000 volunteers had served in Latin America, Africa, and Asia. Peace Corps projects were generally welcomed, but they did not address the receiving countries' larger economic and political structures.

Kennedy also used direct military means to bring political stability to the third world. He rapidly expanded the elite special forces corps established under Eisenhower to aid groups sympathetic to the United States and fighting against Communist-leaning movements. These counterinsurgency forces, including the army's Green Berets and the navy's SEALs, were trained to wage guerrilla warfare and equipped with the latest technology. They would get their first test in Vietnam.

The Arms Race and the Nuclear Brink

The final piece of Kennedy's defense strategy was to strengthen American nuclear dominance. He upped the number of nuclear weapons based in Europe from 2,500 to 7,200 and multiplied fivefold the supply of intercontinental ballistic missiles (ICBMs).

CHAPTER LOCATOR | How did American foreign policy change under Kennedy?

806 CHAPTER 29
VIETNAM AND THE LIMITS OF POWER, 1961–1975

Concerned that this buildup would enable the United States to launch a first strike and wipe out Soviet missile sites before they could respond, the Soviet Union stepped up its own ICBM program. Thus began the most intense arms race in history.

The **Cuban missile crisis** of 1962 brought the superpowers perilously close to using their weapons when Khrushchev decided to install nuclear missiles in Cuba, while insisting to Kennedy that he had no intention of doing so. Khrushchev wanted to protect Cuba from further U.S. attempts at intervention and to balance the U.S. missiles aimed at the Soviet Union from Britain, Italy, and Turkey. On October 16, the CIA showed Kennedy aerial photographs of missile launching sites under construction in Cuba. On October 22, Kennedy announced that the military was on full alert and that the navy would turn back any Soviet vessel suspected of carrying offensive missiles to Cuba. Kennedy warned that any attack launched from Cuba would trigger a full nuclear assault against the Soviet Union.

With the superpowers on the brink of nuclear war, Kennedy and Khrushchev negotiated an agreement. The Soviets removed the missiles and pledged not to introduce new offensive weapons into Cuba. The United States promised not to invade the island. Secretly, Kennedy also agreed to remove the U.S. missiles from Turkey. The Cuban crisis led to Khrushchev's fall from power two years later, and Kennedy emerged triumphant. The image of an inexperienced president fumbling the Bay of Pigs invasion gave way to that of a strong leader bringing the United States through its "hour of maximum danger."

Having proved his toughness, Kennedy worked with Khrushchev to prevent future confrontations by installing a special "hot line" to speed top-level communication. In a major speech at American University in June 1963, Kennedy called for a reexamination of Cold War assumptions, asking Americans "not to see conflict as inevitable." Acknowledging the superpowers' differences, Kennedy stressed what they had in common: "We all breathe the same air. We all cherish our children's future and we are all mortal." In August 1963, the United States, the Soviet Union, and Great Britain signed a limited nuclear test ban treaty, reducing the threat of radioactive fallout from nuclear testing and raising hopes for further superpower accord.

A Growing War in Vietnam

In his American University speech, Kennedy criticized the idea of "a Pax Americana enforced on the world by American weapons of war," but in 1961 he began to increase the flow of those weapons into South Vietnam. Kennedy's strong anticommunism and attachment to a vigorous foreign policy prepared him to expand the commitment in Vietnam that he had inherited from Eisenhower. By the time Kennedy took office, more than $1 billion in aid and 700 U.S. military advisers had failed to stabilize South Vietnam. Two major obstacles stood in the way. First, the South Vietnamese insurgents—whom Americans called Vietcong, short for *Vietnam Cong-san* ("Vietnamese Communists")—were an indigenous force whose initiative came from within, not from the Soviet Union or China as many American officials supposed. Because the Saigon government refused to hold elections, the rebels saw no choice but to take up arms. Increasingly, Ho Chi Minh's Communist government in North Vietnam supplied them with weapons and soldiers.

Second, the South Vietnamese government and army (ARVN) refused to satisfy the demands of the insurgents but could not defeat them militarily. Ngo Dinh Diem, South Vietnamese premier from 1954 to 1963, chose self-serving military

Cuban missile crisis

▶ Urgent situation provoked by the Soviet decision in 1962 to deploy nuclear missiles in Cuba. When the Americans discovered evidence of the construction of missile launching sites in Cuba, the ensuing confrontation brought the superpowers to the brink of nuclear war. The two sides reached a negotiated settlement, with the Soviet Union agreeing to remove its missiles from Cuba and the United States agreeing to remove its missiles from Turkey.

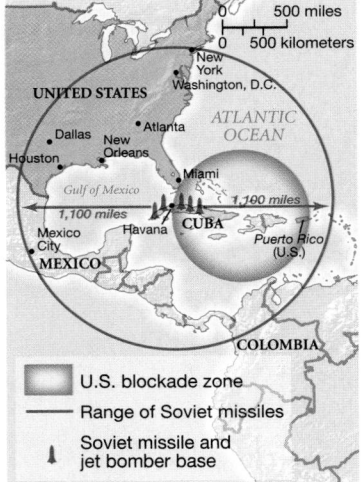

Cuban Missile Crisis, 1962

Why did Johnson escalate American involvement in Vietnam? | How did the war in Vietnam polarize the nation? | How did American foreign policy change under Nixon? | Conclusion: Was Vietnam an unwinnable war?

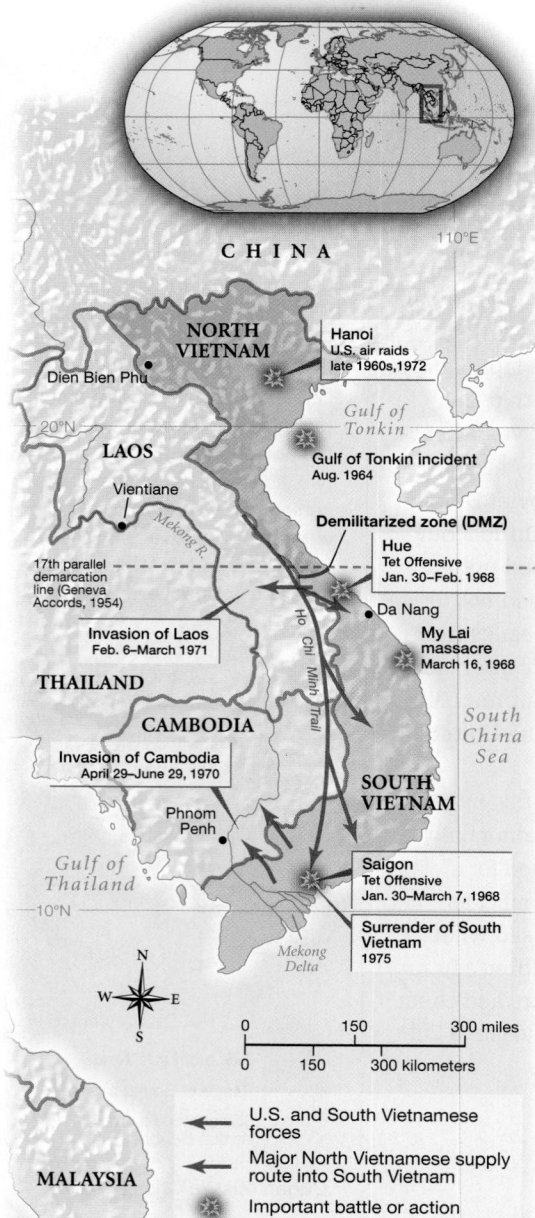

MAP 29.2 ■ The Vietnam War, 1964–1975

The United States sent 2.6 million soldiers to Vietnam and spent more than $150 billion on the longest war in American history, but it was unable to prevent the unification of Vietnam under a Communist government.

▶ FOR MORE HELP ANALYZING THIS MAP, see the map activity for this chapter in the Online Study Guide at bedfordstmartins.com/roarkunderstanding.

leaders for their personal loyalty rather than for their effectiveness. Many South Vietnamese saw Diem as a corrupt and brutal tool of the West. Even Secretary of State Dean Rusk called him "an oriental despot."

The growing intervention by North Vietnam made matters worse. In 1960, the Hanoi government established the National Liberation Front, composed of South Vietnamese rebels but directed by the northern army. In addition, Hanoi constructed a network of infiltration routes, called the Ho Chi Minh Trail, in neighboring Laos and Cambodia, through which it sent people and supplies to help liberate the South (**Map 29.2**). Violence escalated between 1960 and 1963, bringing the Saigon government close to collapse.

Kennedy responded to the deteriorating situation with measured steps, gradually escalating the U.S. commitment. By the spring of 1963, military aid had doubled, and the 9,000 Americans serving in Vietnam as military advisers occasionally participated in actual combat. The South Vietnamese government promised reform but never made good on its promises.

Reflecting racist attitudes of American superiority over nonwhite populations, officials assumed that U.S. technology and sheer power could win in Vietnam. Yet advanced weapons were ill suited to the guerrilla warfare practiced by the enemy, whose surprise attacks were designed to weaken support for the South Vietnamese government. In addition, U.S. weapons and strategy harmed the very people they were intended to save. Thousands of peasants were uprooted and resettled in "strategic hamlets," supposedly secure from the Communists. Those left in the countryside fell victim to bombs—containing the highly flammable substance napalm—dropped by the South Vietnamese air force to quell the Vietcong. In January 1962, U.S. planes began to spray herbicides such as Agent Orange to destroy the Vietcong's jungle hideouts and food supply.

With tacit permission from Washington, South Vietnamese military leaders executed a coup against Diem and his brother, who headed the secret police, on November 2, 1963. Kennedy expressed shock that the two had been murdered but indicated no change in policy. In a speech to be given on the day he was assassinated, he referred specifically to Southeast Asia and warned, "We dare not weary of the task." At his death, 16,700 Americans were stationed in Vietnam, and 100 had died there.

> QUICK REVIEW

Why did Kennedy believe that engagement in Vietnam was crucial to American foreign policy?

CHAPTER LOCATOR | How did American foreign policy change under Kennedy?

808 CHAPTER 29 VIETNAM AND THE LIMITS OF POWER, 1961–1975

Why did Johnson escalate American involvement in Vietnam?

American Soldiers Confront the South Vietnamese

The unconventional nature of the Vietnam War often resulted in U.S. soldiers harming the very people they were sent to save. In this photo, a trooper of the U.S. First Cavalry stands guard while a medic treats South Vietnamese civilians who had been wounded during a search-and-destroy mission that destroyed their hamlet near Da Nang in October 1967. © Bettmann/Corbis.

THE COLD WAR ASSUMPTIONS that had shaped Kennedy's foreign policy underlay his successor's approach to Southeast Asia and Latin America. Retaining Kennedy's key advisers—Secretary of State Dean Rusk, Secretary of Defense Robert McNamara, and National Security Adviser McGeorge Bundy—**Lyndon B. Johnson** continued the massive buildup of nuclear weapons and conventional and counterinsurgency forces. Then in 1965, Johnson made the fateful decisions to order U.S. troops into combat and to initiate sustained bombing of the North.

An All-Out Commitment in Vietnam

The president who wanted to make his mark on domestic policy was compelled to deal with the commitments his predecessors had made to stopping communism in Vietnam. Early in Johnson's administration, the public paid little attention to Vietnam and seemed willing to follow the administration's lead. Yet some advisers, politicians, and international leaders raised questions about the wisdom of a greater commitment in Vietnam. Senate majority leader Mike Mansfield wondered whether Vietnam could be won with a "limited expenditure of American lives and resources somewhere commensurate with our national interests." Senate Armed Services Committee member Richard Russell warned, "It'd take a half million men. They'd be bogged down there for ten years."

Johnson disregarded the opportunity for disengagement that these critics saw in 1964 and expanded the United States' military involvement. Along with most of his advisers, he believed that American credibility was on the line.

Lyndon B. Johnson

▶ Texas Democrat who served as U.S. president from 1963 to 1969. Johnson continued President Kennedy's buildup of nuclear weapons and conventional forces. In 1965, Johnson sent U.S. forces to prop up the South Vietnamese government, bringing the United States directly into the Vietnam War. The difficult, costly, and unpopular war in Vietnam undermined Johnson's presidency.

1963
- President Kennedy is assassinated; Lyndon B. Johnson becomes president.

1964
- Anti-American rioting in Panama Canal Zone.
- Congress grants the president broad powers to wage war in Vietnam with the Gulf of Tonkin Resolution.

1965
- Operation Rolling Thunder, the gradual intensification of the bombing of North Vietnam, begins.
- Johnson orders the first combat troops to Vietnam.
- U.S. troops invade the Dominican Republic.

Gulf of Tonkin Resolution

▶ 1964 congressional resolution granting President Johnson the authority to widen the war in Vietnam. The resolution came in the wake of a confrontation between U.S. naval forces and the North Vietnamese in the Gulf of Tonkin. Although there was much uncertainty about the precise nature of the events involved, Johnson used the confrontation as a justification for increasing American military pressure on North Vietnam.

Moreover, the president's own credibility also came into play. Like Kennedy, he feared the domestic political repercussions of disengagement without victory. His own insecurities and fear of being compared unfavorably with Kennedy precluded a course that might make him appear soft or cowardly.

Johnson understood the ineffectiveness of his South Vietnamese allies and agonized over sending young men into combat. Yet he continued to dispatch more military advisers, weapons, and economic aid and, in August 1964, seized an opportunity to increase the pressure on North Vietnam. During a routine espionage mission in the Gulf of Tonkin, off the coast of North Vietnam, two U.S. destroyers reported that North Vietnamese gunboats had fired on them (see Map 29.2, page 808). Johnson quickly ordered air strikes on North Vietnamese torpedo bases and oil storage facilities. Concealing the uncertainty about whether the second attack had even occurred and the provocative U.S. operations along the North Vietnamese coast, he won from Congress the **Gulf of Tonkin Resolution,** granting him authority to take "all necessary measures to repel any armed attacks against the forces of the United States and to prevent further aggression."

Soon after winning the election in 1964, Johnson widened the war. He rejected peace overtures from North Vietnam, which insisted on American withdrawal and a coalition government in South Vietnam as steps toward ultimate unification of the country. Instead, in February 1965, Johnson authorized Operation Rolling Thunder, a strategy of gradually intensified bombing of North Vietnam. Less than a month later, Johnson ordered the first U.S. combat troops to South Vietnam, and in July he shifted U.S. troops from defensive to offensive operations, dispatching 50,000 more soldiers (**Figure 29.1**). Although the administration downplayed the import of these decisions, they marked a critical turning point. Now it was genuinely America's war.

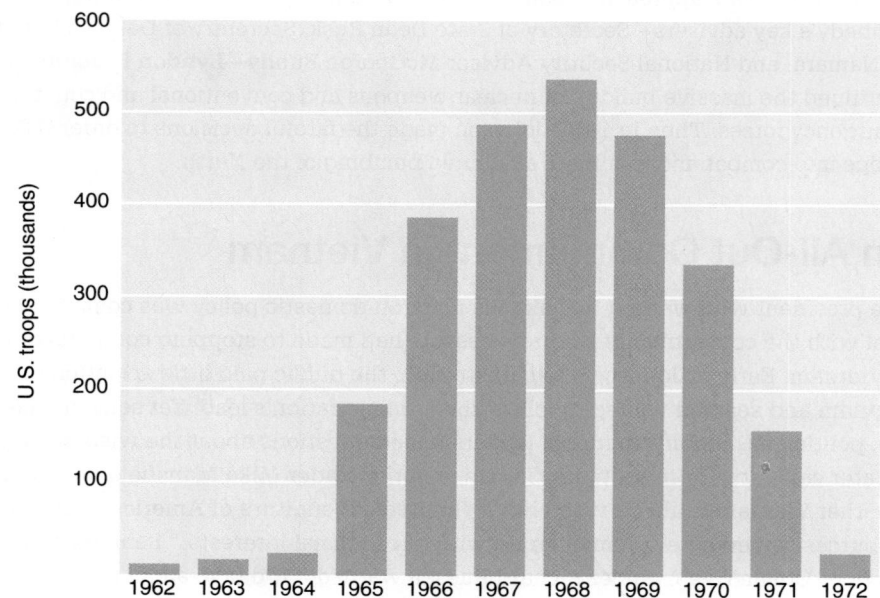

FIGURE 29.1 ■ **U.S. Troops in Vietnam, 1962–1972**
The steepest increases in the American military presence in Vietnam came in 1965 and 1966. Although troop levels declined significantly in 1971 and 1972, the United States continued massive bombing attacks.

CHAPTER LOCATOR | How did American foreign policy change under Kennedy?

Preventing Another Castro in Latin America

Closer to home, Johnson faced persistent problems in Latin America. Thirteen times during the 1960s, military coups toppled Latin American governments, and local insurgencies grew apace. The administration's response varied from case to case but centered on the determination to prevent any more Castro-type revolutions.

In 1964, riots erupted in the Panama Canal Zone, which the United States had seized and made a U.S. territory early in the twentieth century (see chapter 21). Instigated by Panamanians who viewed the United States as a colonial power, the riots left four U.S. soldiers and more than twenty Panamanians dead. Johnson sent troops to quell the disturbance, but he also initiated negotiations that eventually returned the canal to Panamanian authority in 2000.

Elsewhere, Johnson's Latin American policy generated new cries of "Yankee imperialism." In 1961, voters in the Dominican Republic ousted a longtime dictator and elected a constitutional government headed by reformist Juan Bosch, who was overthrown by a military coup two years later. In 1965, when Bosch supporters launched an uprising against the military government, Johnson sent more than 20,000 soldiers to quell what he perceived to be a leftist revolt and to take control of the island. A truce was arranged, and in 1966 Dominicans voted in a constitutional government under a moderate rightist.

This first outright show of force in Latin America in four decades damaged the administration at home and abroad. Although the administration had justified intervention on the grounds that Communists were among the rebels, it quickly became clear that they had played no significant role, and U.S. actions kept the reform-oriented Boschists from returning to power. Moreover, the president had not consulted the Dominicans or the Organization of American States (OAS), to which the United States had pledged that it would respect national sovereignty in Latin America.

The Americanized War

The military success in the Dominican Republic no doubt encouraged the president to press on in Vietnam. From 1965 to early 1968, the United States gradually escalated attacks against the North Vietnamese and their Vietcong allies. Over the course of the war, U.S. pilots dropped 3.2 million tons of explosives, more than the United States had dropped in all of World War II. Claiming monthly death tolls of more than 2,000 North Vietnamese, the intensive bombing nonetheless failed to dampen the Hanoi government's commitment.

On the ground, General William Westmoreland's strategy of attrition was designed to seek out and kill the Vietcong and soldiers in the North Vietnamese regular army. The military used helicopters extensively to conduct offensives all over South Vietnam. Because there was no battlefront as in previous wars, officials calculated progress not in territory seized but in "body counts" and

U.S. Troops in the Dominican Republic

These U.S. paratroopers were among the 20,000 troops sent to the Dominican Republic in April and May 1965. The American invasion helped restore peace but kept the popularly elected government of Juan Bosch from regaining office. Outraged Dominicans painted anti-American slogans throughout the capital, Santo Domingo, and Bosch himself said, "This was a democratic revolution smashed by the leading democracy in the world." © Bettmann/Corbis.

| Why did Johnson escalate American involvement in Vietnam? | How did the war in Vietnam polarize the nation? | How did American foreign policy change under Nixon? | Conclusion: Was Vietnam an unwinnable war? |

811

"kill ratios"—the number of enemies killed relative to the cost in American and ARVN lives.

Teenagers fought the Vietnam War. In contrast to World War II, in which the average soldier was twenty-six years old, the average soldier in Vietnam was nineteen. Men of all classes had fought in World War II, but in Vietnam, the poor and working class constituted about 80 percent of the troops. More-privileged youths avoided the draft by using college deferments or family connections to get into the National Guard. Sent from Plainville, Kansas, to Vietnam in 1965, Mike Clodfelter could not recall "a single middle-class son of the town's businessmen, lawyers, doctors, or ranchers from my high school graduating class who experienced the Armageddon of our generation."

Much more than World War II, Vietnam was a men's war. Because the United States did not undergo full mobilization for Vietnam, officials did not seek women's sacrifices for the war effort. Still, between 7,500 and 10,000 women served in Vietnam, the vast majority of them nurses.

Early in the war, African Americans constituted 31 percent of combat troops, often choosing the military over the meager opportunities in the civilian economy. Special forces ranger Arthur E. Woodley Jr. recalled, "I was just what my country needed. A black patriot. . . . The only way I could possibly make it out of the ghetto was to be the best soldier I possibly could." Death rates among black soldiers were disproportionately high until 1966, when the military adjusted personnel assignments to achieve a better racial balance.

The young troops faced extremely difficult conditions. Soldiers fought in thick jungles and swamps filled with leeches, in rain and oppressive heat. Lieutenant Philip Caputo remembered "conducting vicious manhunts through jungles and swamps where snipers harassed us constantly and booby traps cut us down one by one." The U.S. military inflicted great losses on the enemy, yet the war remained a stalemate.

The South Vietnamese government was an enormous obstacle to victory, even though in 1965 it settled into a period of stability headed by two military leaders. Graft and corruption continued to flourish in the government. In the intensified fighting and inability to distinguish friend from foe, ARVN and American troops killed and wounded thousands of South Vietnamese civilians and destroyed their villages. By 1968, nearly 30 percent of the population had become refugees. The failure to stabilize South Vietnam even as the U.S. military presence expanded enormously created grave challenges for the administration at home.

> QUICK REVIEW

How did the experiences of American troops serving in Vietnam differ from those who served in World War II?

CHAPTER LOCATOR | How did American foreign policy change under Kennedy?

812 CHAPTER 29
VIETNAM AND THE LIMITS OF POWER, 1961–1975

How did the war in Vietnam polarize the nation?

Protest in Chicago The worst violence surrounding the 1968 Democratic National Convention in Chicago came on August 28 when protesters assembled in Grant Park preparing to march to the convention site. Near the Hilton Hotel, where most of the delegates stayed, some 3,000 protesters came up against a line of police. The police attacked not only the demonstrators but also reporters, hotel guests, and bystanders with nightsticks and mace. AP Images/Michael Boyer.

SOON PRESIDENT JOHNSON was fighting a war on two fronts. Domestic opposition to the war swelled after 1965 as daily television broadcasts made it the first "living-room war." In March 1968, torn between his domestic critics and the military's clamor for more troops, Johnson announced restrictions on the bombing, a new effort at negotiations, and his decision not to pursue reelection. Throughout 1968, demonstrations, violence, and assassinations convulsed the increasingly polarized nation.

The Widening War at Home

Johnson's authorization of Operation Rolling Thunder expanded the previously quiet doubts and criticism into a mass movement against the war. In April 1965, Students for a Democratic Society (SDS) recruited 20,000 people for the first major demonstration against the war in Washington, D.C. Thousands of students protested against the presence of Reserve Officers Training Corps (ROTC) programs, CIA recruiters, and defense industry research and recruiters on their campuses. Martin Luther King Jr. deployed his moral authority, rebuking the U.S. government in 1967 as "the greatest purveyor of violence in the world today." Environmentalists attacked the use of chemical weapons, such as the deadly Agent Orange. In the spring of 1968, as many as one million students participated in a nationwide strike.

Antiwar sentiment entered society's mainstream. The *New York Times* began questioning the war in 1965, and by 1968 there were many more media critics. Clergy, business people, scientists, and physicians formed their own groups to pressure Johnson to stop the bombing and start negotiations. Prominent

CHRONOLOGY

1965
- First major demonstration against Vietnam War.

1967
- U.S. troop strength in Vietnam nears half a million, and total military deaths approach 20,000.

1968
- Demonstrations against Vietnam War increase.
- Tet Offensive, a series of attacks by North Vietnam on cities and U.S. bases in South Vietnam, begins.
- Johnson decides not to seek a second term.
- Peace negotiations between the United States and North Vietnam begin in Paris.
- Martin Luther King Jr. and Senator Robert F. Kennedy are assassinated.
- Police and protesters clash near the Democratic convention in Chicago.

Democratic senators urged Johnson to substitute negotiation for force. Although the peace movement never claimed a majority of the population, it focused media attention on the war and severely limited the administration's options. The twenty-year-old consensus around Cold War foreign policy had broken down.

Many would not fight in the war. More than 170,000 men who opposed the war on moral or religious grounds gained conscientious objector status and performed nonmilitary duties at home or in Vietnam. About 60,000 fled the country to escape the draft, and more than 200,000 were accused of failing to register or of committing other draft offenses.

Opponents of the war held diverse views. Those who saw the conflict in moral terms wanted total withdrawal, insisting that their country had no right to interfere in a civil war and stressing the suffering of the Vietnamese people. A larger segment of antiwar sentiment reflected practical considerations—the belief that the war could not be won at a bearable cost. Those activists wanted Johnson to stop bombing North Vietnam and seek negotiations. Working-class people were no more antiwar than other groups, but they recognized the class dimensions of the war and the antiwar movement. A firefighter whose son had died in Vietnam said bitterly, "It's people like us who give up our sons for the country."

The antiwar movement outraged millions of Americans who supported the war. Some members of the generation who had fought against Hitler could not understand younger men's refusal to support their government. They expressed their anger at war protesters with bumper stickers that read "America: Love It or Leave It."

By 1967, the administration realized that "discontent with the war is now wide and deep." President Johnson used various means to silence critics. His administration deceived the public by making optimistic statements and concealing officials' doubts about the possibility of victory. Johnson ordered the CIA to spy on peace advocates, and without the president's specific authorization, the FBI infiltrated the peace movement, disrupted its work, and spread false information about activists.

Pro-War Demonstrators

Advocates as well as opponents of the war in Vietnam took to the streets, as these New Yorkers did in support of the U.S. invasion of Cambodia in May 1970. Construction workers—called "hard hats"—and other union members marched with American flags and posters championing President Nixon's policies and blasting New York mayor John Lindsay for his antiwar position. Paul Fusco/Magnum Photos, Inc.

▶ FOR MORE HELP ANALYZING THIS IMAGE, see the visual activity for this chapter in the Online Study Guide at bedfordstmartins.com/roarkunderstanding.

CHAPTER LOCATOR | How did American foreign policy change under Kennedy?

CHAPTER 29
814 VIETNAM AND THE LIMITS OF POWER, 1961–1975

1968: Year of Upheaval

The year 1968 was marked by violent confrontations around the world. Protests against governments erupted from Mexico City to Paris to Tokyo, usually led by students in collaboration with workers. American society also became increasingly polarized. On one side, the so-called hawks charged that the United States was fighting with one hand tied behind its back and called for intensification of the war. The doves wanted de-escalation or withdrawal. As U.S. troop strength neared half a million and military deaths approached 20,000 by the end of 1967, most people were torn between weariness with the war and a desire to fulfill the U.S. commitment. As one woman said, "I want to get out but I don't want to give up."

Grave doubts penetrated the administration itself in 1967. Secretary of Defense Robert McNamara, a principal architect of U.S. involvement, now believed that the North Vietnamese "won't quit no matter how much bombing we do." He feared for the image of the United States, "the world's greatest superpower, killing or seriously injuring 1,000 noncombatants a week, while trying to pound a tiny, backward nation into submission on an issue whose merits are hotly disputed." McNamara did not publicly oppose the war, but in early 1968 he left the administration.

A critical turning point came with the **Tet Offensive.** On January 30, 1968, the North Vietnamese and Vietcong launched attacks on key cities and every major American base in South Vietnam. Militarily, the Communists suffered a defeat, losing ten times as many soldiers as ARVN and U.S. forces. Psychologically, however, Tet was devastating to the United States.

The Tet Offensive underscored the credibility gap between official statements and the war's actual progress. TV anchorman Walter Cronkite wondered, "What the hell is going on? I thought we were winning the war." The attacks created a million more South Vietnamese refugees as well as widespread destruction. Explaining how he had defended a village, a U.S. Army official said, "We had to destroy the town to save it." The statement epitomized for more and more Americans the brutality and senselessness of the war. Public approval of Johnson's handling of the war dropped to 26 percent.

In the aftermath of Tet, Johnson conferred with advisers in the Defense Department and an unofficial group of foreign policy experts who had been key architects of Cold War policies for two decades. Dean Acheson, Truman's secretary of state, summarized their conclusion: "We can no longer do the job we set out to do in the time we have left and we must begin to take steps to disengage."

On March 31, 1968, Lyndon Johnson announced in a televised speech that the United States would reduce its bombing of North Vietnam and pursue peace negotiations. He added the stunning declaration that he would not run for reelection. The gradual escalation of the war was over, and military strategy shifted from "Americanization" to "Vietnamization" of the war. The goal remained a non-Communist South Vietnam; the United States would simply rely more heavily on the South Vietnamese to achieve it.

Negotiations began in Paris in May 1968. The United States would not agree to recognition of the Hanoi government's National Liberation Front, to a coalition government, or to American withdrawal. The North Vietnamese would agree to nothing less. Although the talks continued, so did the fighting.

Meanwhile, violence escalated at home. Protests occurred on two hundred college campuses in the spring of 1968. In the bloodiest action, students occupied buildings at Columbia University in New York City. When negotiations failed,

Tet Offensive
▶ January 30, 1968, attack by North Vietnamese and Vietcong forces on key cities and every major American base in South Vietnam. Militarily, the Communists suffered a defeat, losing ten times as many soldiers as ARVN and U.S. forces, but the attacks cast doubts on the optimistic statements of U.S. leaders about the war.

| Why did Johnson escalate American involvement in Vietnam? | **How did the war in Vietnam polarize the nation?** | How did American foreign policy change under Nixon? | Conclusion: Was Vietnam an unwinnable war? |

university officials called in the city police, who cleared the buildings, injuring scores of demonstrators and arresting hundreds. An ensuing student strike prematurely ended the academic year.

In June, two months after the murder of Martin Luther King Jr. and the riots that followed, another assassination shook the nation. Antiwar candidate Senator Robert F. Kennedy, campaigning in California for the Democratic Party's presidential nomination, was shot by a Palestinian Arab refugee who was outraged by Kennedy's support for Israel.

In August, protesters battled the police in Chicago, where the Democratic Party had convened to nominate its presidential ticket. Several thousand demonstrators came to the city, some to support the peace candidate Senator Eugene McCarthy, others to cause disruption. On August 25, when demonstrators jeered at orders to disperse, police attacked them with tear gas and clubs. Street battles continued for three days, culminating in a police riot on the night of August 28. Taunted by the crowd, the police used mace and nightsticks, clubbing not only those who had come to provoke violence but also reporters, peaceful demonstrators, and convention delegates. Although the bloodshed in Chicago horrified those who saw it on television, it had little effect on the convention's outcome. Vice President Hubert H. Humphrey trounced the remaining antiwar candidate, McCarthy, by nearly three to one for the Democratic nomination.

In contrast to the turmoil around the **1968 Democratic convention**, the Republican convention met peacefully and nominated former vice president Richard Nixon on the first ballot. A strong third candidate entered the electoral scene when the American Independent Party nominated former Alabama governor and staunch segregationist George C. Wallace. Wallace appealed to those Americans who were dissatisfied with the reforms and rebellions of the 1960s and outraged at the assaults on traditional values. Nixon guardedly played on the resentments that fueled the Wallace campaign, calling for "law and order."

Nixon and Humphrey differed little on the central issue of Vietnam. Nixon promised "an honorable end" to the war but did not indicate how he would achieve it. Humphrey had strong reservations about U.S. policy in Vietnam, yet as vice president he was tied to Johnson's policies. With nearly 13 percent of the total popular vote, the American Independent Party produced the strongest third-party finish since 1924. Nixon edged out Humphrey by just half a million popular votes but garnered 301 electoral college votes to Humphrey's 191 and Wallace's 46. The Democrats maintained control of Congress.

The 1968 election revealed deep cracks in the coalition that had kept the Democrats in power for most of the previous thirty years. Johnson's liberal policies on race shattered a century of Democratic Party dominance in the South, which delivered all its electoral votes to Wallace and Nixon. Elsewhere, large numbers of blue-collar workers broke union ranks to vote for Wallace or Nixon, as did other groups that associated the Democrats with racial turmoil, poverty programs, changing sexual mores, and failure to turn the tide in Vietnam. These resentments would soon be mobilized into a resurging right in American politics (see chapter 30).

1968 Democratic convention

▶ Site of violent confrontations between antiwar demonstrators and Chicago police that took place in late August of that year. After taunting by some in the crowd, the police responded with mace and nightsticks, clubbing both disruptive and peaceful protesters as well as reporters and convention delegates. The bloodshed horrified those who witnessed it but had little effect on the convention's outcome.

> **QUICK REVIEW**

How did the Vietnam War affect the election of 1968?

CHAPTER LOCATOR | How did American foreign policy change under Kennedy?

816 CHAPTER 29
VIETNAM AND THE LIMITS OF POWER, 1961–1975

Nixon's trip to China was meticulously planned to dramatize the event on television and, aside from criticism from some conservatives, won overwhelming support from Americans. The Great Wall of China forms the setting for this photograph of Nixon and his wife, Pat. Nixon Presidential Materials Project, National Archives and Record Administration.

How did American foreign policy change under Nixon?

RICHARD M. NIXON took office with ambitious foreign policy goals, hoping to make his mark on history by applying his broad understanding of international relations to a changing world. Diverging from Republican orthodoxy, he made dramatic overtures to the Soviet Union and China. Yet anticommunism remained central to U.S. policy. Nixon backed repressive regimes around the world and aggressively pursued the war in Vietnam, expanding the conflict into Cambodia and Laos and ordering ferocious bombing of North Vietnam. Yet in the end, he was forced to settle for peace without victory.

Richard M. Nixon
▶ Republican president who narrowly won the 1968 election and held office until his resignation in 1974. He made dramatic overtures in pursuit of détente with both the Soviet Union and China and oversaw the eventual withdrawal of American troops from Vietnam.

Moving toward Détente with the Soviet Union and China

Well aware of the increasing conflict between the Soviet Union and China, Nixon worked with National Security Adviser **Henry A. Kissinger,** his key foreign policy adviser, to exploit the situation. Following two years of secret negotiations, in February 1972 Nixon became the nation's first president to set foot on Chinese soil. Although his visit was largely symbolic, cultural and scientific exchanges followed, and American manufacturers began to find markets in China—small steps in the process of globalization that would take giant strides in the 1990s (see chapter 31).

As Nixon and Kissinger had hoped, the warming of U.S.-Chinese relations furthered their strategy of détente, their term for easing conflict with the Soviet Union. Détente did not mean abandoning containment; instead, it involved focusing on issues of common concern, such as arms control and trade. Containment would be achieved not only by military threat but also by ensuring that the Soviets and Chinese had stakes in a stable international order. Nixon's goal was "a stronger healthy United States, Europe, Soviet Union, China, Japan, each balancing the other."

Henry A. Kissinger
▶ Key foreign policy adviser to President Nixon. Kissinger and Nixon pursued a policy of détente, their term for easing conflict with the Soviet Union. To this end, they pursued closer relationships with both China and the Soviet Union, not abandoning containment, but instead focusing on issues of common concern, such as arms control and trade.

| Why did Johnson escalate American involvement in Vietnam? | How did the war in Vietnam polarize the nation? | **How did American foreign policy change under Nixon?** | Conclusion: Was Vietnam an unwinnable war? |

817

Strategic Arms Limitation Talks (SALT)

▶ 1972 treaty between the United States and the Soviet Union in which the superpowers agreed to limit antiballistic missiles (ABMs) to two each. Limiting the capacity to mount a defense against nuclear attacks was significant because it prevented either nation from building so secure an ABM defense against a nuclear attack that it would risk a first strike.

Arms control, trade, and stability in Europe were three areas where the United States and the Soviet Union had common interests. In May 1972, Nixon visited Moscow, signing several agreements on trade and cooperation in science and space. Most significantly, Soviet and U.S. leaders concluded arms limitation treaties that had grown out of the **Strategic Arms Limitation Talks (SALT)** begun in 1969, agreeing to limit antiballistic missiles (ABMs) to two each. Giving up pursuit of a defense against nuclear weapons was a crucial move, because it prevented either nation from building so secure an ABM defense against a nuclear attack that it would risk a first strike against the other.

Although the policy of détente made little progress after 1974, U.S., Soviet, and European leaders signed a historic agreement in 1975 in Helsinki, Finland, that formally recognized the post–World War II boundaries in Europe. The Helsinki accords were controversial because they acknowledged Soviet domination over Eastern Europe—a condition that had triggered the Cold War thirty years earlier. Yet they also contained a clause committing the signing countries to recognize "the universal significance of human rights and fundamental freedoms." Dissidents in the Soviet Union and its Eastern European satellites used this official promise of rights to challenge the Soviet dictatorship.

Shoring Up Anticommunism in the Third World

Nixon promised in 1973 that "[t]he time has passed when America will make every other nation's conflict our own . . . or presume to tell the people of other nations how to manage their own affairs." Yet in Vietnam and elsewhere, Nixon and Kissinger continued to view left-wing movements as threats to U.S. interests and actively resisted social revolutions that might lead to communism.

Consequently, the Nixon administration helped to overthrow Salvador Allende, a self-proclaimed Marxist who was elected president of Chile in 1970. Since 1964, the Central Intelligence Agency (CIA) and U.S. corporations concerned about nationalization of their Chilean properties had assisted Allende's opponents. After Allende became president, Nixon ordered the CIA director to destabilize his government. In 1973, the CIA helped the Chilean military engineer a coup, killing Allende and establishing a brutal dictatorship under General Augusto Pinochet.

In other parts of the world, too, the Nixon administration stood by repressive regimes. In southern Africa, it eased pressures on white minority governments that tyrannized blacks. In the Middle East, the United States sent massive arms shipments to support the shah of Iran's harsh regime because Iran had enormous petroleum reserves and seemed a stable anti-Communist ally.

Like his predecessors, Nixon pursued a delicate balance between defending Israel's

Chile

security and seeking the goodwill of Arab nations strategically and economically important to the United States. Conflict between Israel and the Arab nations had escalated into the **Six-Day War** in 1967, when Israel attacked Egypt after that nation had massed troops on its border and cut off the sea passage to Israel's southern port. Although Syria and Jordan joined the war on Egypt's side, Israel won a stunning victory, seizing territory that amounted to twice its original size.

That decisive victory did not quell Middle Eastern turmoil. In October 1973, on the Jewish holiday Yom Kippur, Egypt and Syria surprised Israel with a full-scale attack. When the Nixon administration sided with Israel in the Yom Kippur War, Arab nations retaliated with an oil embargo that created severe shortages in the United States. After Israel repulsed the attack, Kissinger attempted to mediate between Israel and the Arab nations, but with very limited success. The Arab countries refused to recognize Israel's right to exist, Israel began to settle its citizens in territories occupied during the Six-Day War, and no solution could be found for the Palestinian refugees who had been displaced by the creation of Israel in the late 1940s. The simmering conflict contributed to anti-American sentiment among Arabs who viewed the United States as Israel's supporter.

Israeli Territorial Gains in the Six-Day War, 1967

Vietnam Becomes Nixon's War

"I'm going to stop that war. Fast," Nixon asserted. He withdrew U.S. ground troops, but he was unwilling to be the president who allowed South Vietnam to fall to the Communists. That goal was tied to the larger objective of maintaining American credibility. Regardless of the wisdom of the initial intervention, Kissinger asserted, "the commitment of 500,000 Americans has settled the importance of Vietnam. For what is involved now is confidence in American promises."

From 1969 to 1972, Nixon and Kissinger pursued a four-pronged approach. First, they tried to strengthen the South Vietnamese military and government. Second, to disarm the antiwar movement at home, Nixon gradually replaced U.S. forces with South Vietnamese soldiers and American technology and bombs. Third, the United States negotiated with both North Vietnam and the Soviet Union. Fourth, the military applied intensive bombing to persuade Hanoi to accept American terms at the bargaining table.

As part of the Vietnamization of the war, ARVN forces grew to more than a million, and the South Vietnamese air force became the fourth largest in the world. The United States also promoted land reform, village elections, and the building of schools, hospitals, and transportation facilities. Meanwhile, U.S. forces withdrew, decreasing from 543,000 in 1968 to 140,000 by the end of 1971.

In the spring of 1969, Nixon began a ferocious air war in Cambodia, carefully hiding it from Congress and the public for more than a year. Seeking to knock out North Vietnamese sanctuaries in Cambodia, Americans dropped more than 100,000 tons of bombs but succeeded only in sending the North Vietnamese to other hiding places. Echoing Johnson, Kissinger believed that a "fourth-rate power like North Vietnam" had to have a "breaking point," but the massive bombing failed to find it.

To support a new, pro-Western Cambodian government installed through a military coup in 1970 and "to show the enemy that we were still serious about our commitment in Vietnam," Nixon ordered a joint U.S.-ARVN invasion of Cambodia in April 1970. That order made Vietnam "Nixon's war" and provoked outrage at

Six-Day War

▶ 1967 conflict between Israel and the Arab nations of Egypt, Syria, and Jordan. Israel attacked Egypt after that nation had massed troops on its border and cut off the sea passage to Israel's southern port. Although Syria and Jordan joined the war on Egypt's side, Israel won a stunning victory, seizing territory that amounted to twice its original size.

| Why did Johnson escalate American involvement in Vietnam? | How did the war in Vietnam polarize the nation? | How did American foreign policy change under Nixon? | Conclusion: Was Vietnam an unwinnable war? |

819

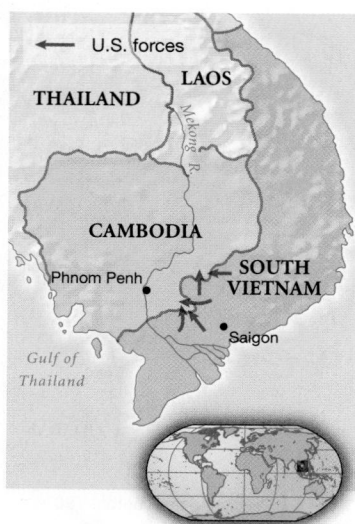

U.S. Invasion of Cambodia, 1970

Kent State University/ Jackson State College

▶ College campuses that were the sites of violent confrontations between demonstrating students and those sent to disperse them. On May 4, 1970, at Ohio's Kent State, nervous National Guard troops fired at students who were protesting the war in Vietnam, killing four and wounding ten others. On May 14, 1970, police called to Jackson State College shot into a dormitory and killed two black students.

Pentagon Papers

▶ Secret government documents published by the *New York Times* in 1971 consisting mostly of an internal study of the war begun in 1967. The documents undermined public trust in government by revealing that officials harbored considerable pessimism even as they made rosy public pronouncements about the progress of the war. Government efforts to stop publication of the documents were blocked by the Supreme Court.

home. Nixon made a belligerent speech defending his move and emphasizing the importance of U.S. credibility: "If when the chips are down, the world's most powerful nation acts like a pitiful helpless giant, the forces of totalitarianism and anarchy will threaten free nations" everywhere.

In response, more than 100,000 people protested in Washington, D.C., and students boycotted classes on hundreds of campuses. At **Kent State University** in Ohio, National Guard troops were dispatched after protesting students burned an old ROTC building. Then, at a rally there on May 4, when some students threw rocks at the troops, guardsmen fired at the students, killing four and wounding ten others. "They're starting to treat their own children like they treat us," commented a black woman in Harlem. In a confrontation at **Jackson State College** in Mississippi on May 14, police shot into a dormitory, killing two black students.

In their determination to win the war in Vietnam, Johnson and Nixon had taken extreme measures to deceive the public and silence their critics. The bombing and invasion of Cambodia infuriated enough legislators that the Senate voted to terminate the Gulf of Tonkin Resolution, which had given the president virtually a blank check in Vietnam, and to cut off funds for the Cambodian operation. The House refused to go along, but by the end of June, Nixon had pulled all U.S. troops out of Cambodia.

In 1971, Vietnam veterans became a visible part of the peace movement, the first men in U.S. history to protest a war in which they had fought. Veterans held a public investigation of "war crimes" in Vietnam, rallied in front of the Capitol, and cast away their war medals. In May 1971, veterans numbered among the 40,000 protesters who engaged in civil disobedience in an effort to shut down Washington. Officials made more than 12,000 arrests, which courts later ruled violations of protesters' rights.

After the spring of 1971, there were fewer massive antiwar demonstrations, but protest continued. Public attention focused on the court-martial of Lieutenant William Calley, which began in November 1970. During the trial, Americans learned that in March 1968, Calley's company had systematically killed every inhabitant of the hamlet of My Lai, even though they had encountered no enemy forces there. These four hundred villagers were nearly all old men, women, and children. The military covered up the atrocity for more than a year before a journalist exposed it. Eventually, twelve officers and enlisted men faced charges ranging from murder to dereliction of duty for covering up the massacre, but only Calley was convicted—of premeditated murder.

Administration policy suffered another blow in June 1971 when the *New York Times* published the ***Pentagon Papers***, an internal government study of the war begun in 1967. Even though the study did not cover the Nixon administration, government lawyers went to court to stop further publication. The Supreme Court, however, ruled that the attempt to stop publication was a violation of the First Amendment. Subsequent circulation of the *Pentagon Papers*, which revealed considerable pessimism among officials even as they made rosy promises, heightened disillusionment with the war by casting doubts on the government's credibility. More than 60 percent of Americans polled in 1971 considered it a mistake to have sent American troops to Vietnam; 58 percent believed the war to be immoral.

Military morale sank in the last years of the war. Having been exposed to the antiwar movement at home, many of the remaining soldiers had less faith in the war than their predecessors had had. Racial tensions among soldiers mounted,

CHAPTER LOCATOR | How did American foreign policy change under Kennedy?

820 CHAPTER 29
VIETNAM AND THE LIMITS OF POWER, 1961–1975

Kent State Shootings

On May 4, 1970, John Filo, a photojournalism student at Kent State University in Ohio, decided to take pictures of students demonstrating against President Nixon's recently announced decision to invade Cambodia. He observed several hundred protesters, some of whom threw rocks at National Guardsmen, who in turn sprayed tear gas toward the students. Suddenly, some guardsmen opened fire, killing four students and wounding ten. Filo took this photograph of fourteen-year-old runaway Mary Ann Vecchio sobbing over the dead body of Kent State student Jeffrey Miller. John Filo.

> ▶ FOR MORE HELP ANALYZING THIS IMAGE, see the visual activity for this chapter in the Online Study Guide at bedfordstmartins.com/roarkunderstanding.

many soldiers sought escape in illegal drugs, and enlisted men committed hundreds of "fraggings," attacks on officers. In a 1971 report, a retired Marine Corps colonel described the lack of discipline: "Our army that now remains in Vietnam [is] near mutinous."

The Peace Accords and the Legacy of Defeat

Nixon and Kissinger continued to believe that intensive firepower could bring the North Vietnamese to their knees. In March 1972, responding to a strong North Vietnamese offensive, the United States resumed sustained bombing of the North, mined Haiphong and other harbors for the first time, and announced a naval blockade. With peace talks stalled, in December Nixon ordered the most devastating bombing of North Vietnam yet.

The intense bombing was costly to both sides, but it brought renewed negotiations. On January 27, 1973, representatives of the United States, North Vietnam,

| Why did Johnson escalate American involvement in Vietnam? | How did the war in Vietnam polarize the nation? | How did American foreign policy change under Nixon? | Conclusion: Was Vietnam an unwinnable war? |

821

Evacuating South Vietnam

As Communist troops rolled south toward Saigon in the spring of 1975, desperate South Vietnamese attempted to flee along with the departing Americans. These South Vietnamese, carrying little or nothing, attempt to scale the wall of the U.S. Embassy to reach evacuation helicopters. Thousands of Vietnamese who wanted to be evacuated were left behind. AP Images.

South Vietnam, and the Vietcong signed a formal peace accord in Paris. The agreement required removal of all U.S. troops and military advisers but allowed North Vietnamese forces to remain. Both sides agreed to return prisoners of war. Nixon called the agreement "peace with honor," but in fact it allowed only a face-saving withdrawal for the United States.

Fighting resumed immediately among the Vietnamese. Nixon's efforts to support the South Vietnamese government were hampered by what came to be known as the Watergate scandal (see chapter 30). Nixon was forced to resign in 1974, and in 1975 North Vietnam launched a new offensive. On April 30, it occupied Saigon and renamed it Ho Chi Minh City to honor the Communist leader. The Americans hastily evacuated, along with 150,000 of their South Vietnamese allies.

Confusion, humiliation, and tragedy marked the rushed departure. The United States lacked sufficient transportation capabilities and time to evacuate all the South Vietnamese who had supported the South Vietnamese government and were desperate to leave. One journalist reported that his departing helicopter "took some ground fire from South Vietnamese soldiers who probably felt that the Americans had betrayed them."

During the four years it took Nixon to end the war, he had expanded the conflict into Cambodia and Laos and had launched massive bombing campaigns. Although increasing numbers of legislators criticized the war, Congress never denied the president the funds to fight it. Only after the peace accords did the legislative branch stiffen its constitutional authority in the making of war, passing the War Powers Act in November 1973. The law required the president to report to Congress within forty-eight hours of deploying military forces abroad. If Congress failed to endorse the president's action within sixty days, the troops would have to be withdrawn. The new law, however, did little to dispel the distrust of and disillusionment with the government that resulted from Americans' realization that their leaders had not told the truth about Vietnam.

The disorder that had accompanied antiwar protests and bitter divisions among Americans were other legacies of the war. Vietnam created federal budget deficits and triggered inflation that contributed to ongoing economic crises throughout the 1970s (see chapter 30).

Four presidents had declared that the survival of South Vietnam was essential for U.S. containment policy, but their dire predictions that a Communist victory in South Vietnam would set the dominoes cascading did not materialize. Although Vietnam, Laos, and Cambodia all fell within the Communist camp in the spring of 1975, Thailand, Burma, Malaysia, and the rest of Southeast Asia did not. When China and Vietnam reverted to their historically hostile relationship, the myth of a monolithic Communist power overrunning Asia evaporated.

CHAPTER LOCATOR | How did American foreign policy change under Kennedy?

The cruelest legacy of Vietnam fell on those who had served. The failure of the United States to win the war, the war's unpopularity at home, and its character as a guerrilla war denied veterans the traditional soldiers' homecoming. Many believed in the war's purposes and felt betrayed by the government for not letting them win it. Other veterans blamed the government for sacrificing the nation's youth in an immoral or unnecessary war, expressing their sense of the war's futility by referring to their dead comrades as having been "wasted." Some veterans belonging to minority groups had more reason to doubt the nobility of their purpose. A Native American soldier assigned to resettle Vietnamese civilians saw that as "just like when they moved us to the rez [reservation]. We shouldn't have done that."

Because the Vietnam War was a civil war involving guerrilla tactics, combat was especially brutal (**Table 29.1**). The terrors of conventional warfare were multiplied, and so were the motivations to commit atrocities. To demonstrate the immorality of the war, peace advocates stressed the atrocities, contributing to a distorted image of the Vietnam veteran as dehumanized and violent. Most veterans came home to public neglect; some faced harassment from antiwar activists who failed to distinguish the war from the warriors. Yet two-thirds of Vietnam veterans said that they would serve again, and most veterans readjusted well to civilian life.

Nonetheless, some suffered long after the war ended. The Veterans Administration (VA) estimated that nearly one-sixth of the veterans suffered from post-traumatic stress disorder, with its symptoms of recurring nightmares, feelings of guilt and shame, violence, drug and alcohol abuse, and suicidal tendencies. Thirty years after performing army intelligence work in Saigon, Doris Allen "still hit the floor sometimes when [she heard] loud bangs." Many of those who had served in Vietnam began to produce deformed children and fell ill themselves with cancer and other ailments. Veterans claimed a link between those illnesses and Agent Orange, a poisonous herbicide that the military had sprayed over Vietnam. Not until 1991 did Congress provide assistance to veterans with diseases linked to the poison.

By then, the climate had changed. The war began to enter the realm of popular culture, with novels, TV shows, and hit movies depicting a broad range of military experience—from soldiers reduced to brutality to men and women serving with courage and integrity. The incorporation of the Vietnam War into the collective experience was symbolized most dramatically in the Vietnam Veterans Memorial unveiled in Washington, D.C., in November 1982. Designed by Yale architecture student Maya Lin, the black, V-shaped wall inscribed with the names of 58,200 men and women lost in the war became one of the most popular sites in the nation's capital. In an article describing the memorial's dedication, a Vietnam combat veteran spoke to and for his former comrades: "Welcome home. The war is over."

TABLE 29.1 ■ Vietnam War Casualties

United States	
Battle deaths	47,434
Other deaths	10,786
Wounded	153,303
South Vietnam	
Killed in action	110,357
Military wounded	499,026
Civilians killed	415,000
Civilians wounded	913,000
Communist Regulars and Guerrillas	
Killed in action	66,000

Source: U.S. Department of Defense.

QUICK REVIEW <

What were the lasting legacies
of American involvement in Vietnam?

Why did Johnson escalate American involvement in Vietnam?	How did the war in Vietnam polarize the nation?	How did American foreign policy change under Nixon?	Conclusion: Was Vietnam an unwinnable war?

823

> Conclusion: Was Vietnam an unwinnable war?

Larry Burrows.

VIETNAM WAS AMERICA's longest war. The United States spent more than $150 billion (nearly $600 billion in 2010 dollars) and sent 2.6 million young men and women to Vietnam. Of those, 58,200 never returned, and 150,000 suffered serious injury. The war shattered consensus at home, increased presidential power at the expense of congressional authority and public accountability, weakened the economy, and contributed to the downfall of two presidents.

Even as Nixon and Kissinger took steps to ease Cold War tensions with the major Communist powers—the Soviet Union and China, which were also the main suppliers of the North Vietnamese—they also acted vigorously throughout the third world to install or prop up anti-Communist governments. They embraced their predecessors' commitment to South Vietnam as a necessary Cold War engagement: To do otherwise would threaten American credibility and make the United States appear weak. Defeat in Vietnam did not make the United States the "pitiful helpless giant" predicted by Nixon, but it did mark a relative decline of U.S. power and the impossibility of containment on a global scale.

One of the constraints on U.S. power was the tenacity of revolutionary movements determined to achieve national independence. Overestimating the effectiveness of American technological superiority, U.S. officials badly underestimated

CHAPTER LOCATOR | How did American foreign policy change under Kennedy?

the sacrifices that the enemy was willing to make and failed to realize how easily the United States could be perceived as a colonial intruder.

A second constraint on Eisenhower, Kennedy, Johnson, and Nixon was their resolve to avoid a major confrontation with the Soviet Union or China. For Johnson, who conducted the largest escalation of the war, caution was especially critical so as not to provoke direct intervention by the Communist superpowers. After China exploded its first atomic bomb in 1964, the potential heightened for the Vietnam conflict to escalate into worldwide disaster.

Third, in Vietnam the United States sought to prop up an extremely weak ally engaged in a civil war. The South Vietnamese government failed to win the support of its people, and short of taking over the South Vietnamese government and military, the United States could do little to strengthen South Vietnam's ability to resist communism.

Finally, domestic opposition to the war, which by 1968 had spread to mainstream America, constrained the options of Johnson and Nixon. As the war dragged on, with increasing American casualties and growing evidence of the damage being inflicted on innocent Vietnamese, more and more civilians wearied of the conflict. In 1973, Nixon and Kissinger bowed to the resoluteness of the enemy and the limitations of U.S. power. As the war wound down, passions surrounding it contributed to a rising conservative movement that would substantially alter the post–World War II political order.

SO NOW YOU KNOW

The Vietnam War was fought primarily by young men who faced extremely grim conditions during their one-year tours of duty and who came home to public neglect. Young men and women also organized the first major antiwar protests in 1965 and spurred an antiwar movement that broke down the consensus about Cold War foreign policy and divided the American public.

| Why did Johnson escalate American involvement in Vietnam? | How did the war in Vietnam polarize the nation? | How did American foreign policy change under Nixon? | Conclusion: Was Vietnam an unwinnable war? |

825

CHAPTER 29 STUDY GUIDE

Online Study Guide
bedfordstmartins.com/roarkunderstanding

STEP 1 GETTING STARTED

Below are basic terms from this period in American history. Can you identify each term below and explain why it matters? To do this exercise online or to download this chart, visit bedfordstmartins.com/roarkunderstanding.

TERM	WHO OR WHAT & WHEN	WHY IT MATTERS
John F. Kennedy, p. 804		
Cuban missile crisis, p. 807		
Lyndon B. Johnson, p. 809		
Gulf of Tonkin Resolution, p. 810		
Tet Offensive, p. 815		
1968 Democratic convention, p. 816		
Richard M. Nixon, p. 817		
Henry A. Kissinger, p. 817		
Strategic Arms Limitation Talks (SALT), p. 818		
Six-Day War, p. 819		
Kent State University/Jackson State College, p. 820		
Pentagon Papers, p. 820		

STEP 2 MOVING BEYOND THE BASICS

The exercise below represents a more advanced understanding of the chapter material. In the chart, list the key American policy decisions regarding Vietnam between 1961 and 1974. Then explain the rationale and impact of each decision. When you are done, consider the following questions: Why was the United States drawn ever deeper into the Vietnam conflict? At what points, if any, could policymakers have reversed course? How was U.S. involvement in Vietnam shaped by policymakers' larger vision of global politics? To do this exercise online or to download this chart, visit bedfordstmartins.com/roarkunderstanding.

	Policy Decision	Rationale	Impact
Kennedy administration			
Johnson administration			
Nixon administration			

Now that you've reviewed various parts of the chapter, take a step back and try to see the big picture by answering these questions. Remember to use specific examples from the chapter in your answers. To do this exercise online, visit bedfordstmartins.com/roarkunderstanding.

KENNEDY'S FOREIGN POLICY

► How did Kennedy's view of America's place in the world affect his foreign policy decisions in 1961 and 1962?

► How were Kennedy's decisions with respect to Vietnam shaped by the Cold War?

JOHNSON AND VIETNAM

► Why did Lyndon Johnson disregard some of his advisers who urged him to disengage from Vietnam?

► How did the divisions over Vietnam contribute to Nixon's election in 1968?

NIXON'S FOREIGN POLICY

► What impact did Nixon's strategies in Vietnam have on the United States?

► How did Nixon's approach to foreign policy differ from that of his predecessors?

LOOKING BACKWARD, LOOKING AHEAD

► How did American foreign policy in the 1950s set the stage for the escalation of U.S. involvement in Vietnam in the 1960s?

► How did American foreign policy change between 1961 and 1975? What impact did the Vietnam conflict have on these changes?

IN YOUR OWN WORDS

Imagine that you must explain chapter 29 to someone who hasn't read it. What would be the most important points to include and why?

30
THE CONSERVATIVE TURN

1969–1989

> This chapter explores the rise of conservatism as a major force in late-twentieth-century American politics. It examines the emergence of new strands of conservatism in the 1960s, the evolution of conservatism in the post-Watergate years, and its full expression in the politics and policies of Ronald Reagan.

DID YOU KNOW?

The United States' original involvement in Afghanistan occurred as part of U.S. efforts to contain the Soviet Union during the Cold War.

> How did the Nixon presidency reflect the rise of postwar conservatism?

> Why was the Watergate scandal significant?

> Why did the "outsider" presidency of Jimmy Carter fail to gain broad support?

> What conservative goals were realized in the Reagan administration?

> What strategies did liberals use to fight the conservative turn?

> How did Ronald Reagan's foreign policy affect the Cold War?

> Conclusion: What was the long-term impact of the conservative turn?

Inauguration of Ronald Reagan, 1981. Chief Justice Warren Burger administers the oath of office to President Ronald Reagan.

How did the Nixon presidency reflect the rise of postwar conservatism?

School Busing Controversy over busing as a means to integrate public schools erupted in Boston when the 1974–1975 school year started. Clashes between blacks and whites in Boston, such as this one in February 1975 outside Boston's Hyde Park High School, prompted authorities to dispatch police to protect black students. AP/Wide World.

AS WE SAW IN CHAPTER 28, Nixon acquiesced in the continuation of most Great Society programs and even approved pathbreaking environmental and minority and women's rights measures. Yet his public rhetoric and some of his actions signaled the country's rightward move in both politics and sentiment. Whereas Kennedy had appealed to Americans to contribute to the common good, Nixon invited Americans to "let each of us ask—not just what will government do for me, but what can I do for myself?" His words invoked individualism and reliance on the market and private enterprise rather than on government.

During Nixon's presidency, a new strand of conservatism, focused on "traditional values," joined the older movement that focused on anticommunism, a strong national defense, and a limited federal role in domestic affairs.

Emergence of a Grassroots Movement

Hidden beneath Lyndon Johnson's landslide victory over Arizona senator Barry Goldwater in 1964 lay a rising conservative movement. Defining his purpose as "enlarging freedom at home and safeguarding it from the forces of tyranny abroad," Goldwater argued that government intrusions into economic life hindered prosperity, stifled personal responsibility, and interfered with individuals' rights to determine their own values. Conservatives assailed big government in domestic affairs but demanded a strong military to eradicate "Godless communism."

Behind Goldwater's nomination was a growing grassroots movement. Grassroots conservatism was not limited to the West and South, but a number of Sun Belt characteristics made it especially strong in places such as Orange

CHAPTER LOCATOR | How did the Nixon presidency reflect the rise of postwar conservatism? | Why was the Watergate scandal significant?

830 CHAPTER 30 THE CONSERVATIVE TURN, 1969–1989

County, California; Dallas, Texas; and Scottsdale, Arizona. Such predominantly white areas contained relatively homogeneous, skilled, and economically comfortable populations, as well as military bases and defense production facilities. The West harbored a long-standing tradition of Protestant morality, individualism, and opposition to interference by a remote federal government. That tradition continued with the emergence of the New Right, even though it was hardly consistent with the Sun Belt's economic dependence on defense spending and on huge federal projects providing water and power for the burgeoning region. The South, which also benefited from military bases and the space program, shared the West's antipathy toward the federal government. Hostility to racial change, however, was much more central to the South's conservatism. After signing the Civil Rights Act of 1964, President Lyndon Johnson remarked privately, "I think we just delivered the South to the Republican Party." Indeed, Barry Goldwater carried five southern states in 1964.

Grassroots movements proliferated around what conservatives believed marked the "moral decline" of their nation. For example, in 1962, Mel and Norma Gabler succeeded in getting the Texas board of education to drop books that they found not in conformity with "the Christian-Judeo morals, values, and standards as given to us by God through . . . the Bible." Sex education roused the ire of Eleanor Howe in Anaheim, California, who felt that "nothing [in the sex education curriculum] depicted my values. . . . It wasn't so much the information. It was the shift in values." The Supreme Court's liberal decisions on issues such as school prayer, obscenity, and birth control also galvanized conservatives to restore "traditional values."

In the 1970s, grassroots protests against taxes grew alongside concerns about morality. As Americans struggled with inflation and unemployment, many also found themselves paying higher taxes, especially higher property taxes as the value of their homes increased. In 1978, Californians passed a popular referendum, reducing property taxes by more than one-half and limiting the state legislature's ability to raise taxes. Similar antitax crusades soon appeared in other states.

Nixon Courts the Right

In his 1968 presidential campaign, Richard Nixon exploited hostility to black protest and new civil rights policies, wooing white southerners and a considerable number of northern voters away from the Democratic Party. As president, he used this "southern strategy" to make further inroads into traditional Democratic strongholds in the 1972 election.

The Nixon administration reluctantly enforced court orders to achieve high degrees of integration in southern schools, but it resisted efforts to deal with segregation outside the South. In northern and western cities, where segregation resulted from discrimination in housing and in the drawing of school district boundaries, half of all African American children attended nearly all-black schools. After courts began to order the transfer of students between schools in white and black neighborhoods to achieve desegregation, busing became an incendiary political issue.

Violence erupted in Boston in 1974 when a district judge found that school officials had maintained what amounted to a dual system based on race and ordered busing "if necessary to achieve a unitary school system." When black

CHRONOLOGY

1964
– Barry Goldwater's nomination for president reflects growing conservative movement.

1968
– Republican Richard Nixon is elected president.

1969
– Warren E. Burger is appointed chief justice of U.S. Supreme Court.

1971
– Nixon vetoes comprehensive child care bill.

1974
– Violence erupts in Boston over school busing.

1978
– Supreme Court ruling in *Regents of University of California v. Bakke* limits affirmative action.

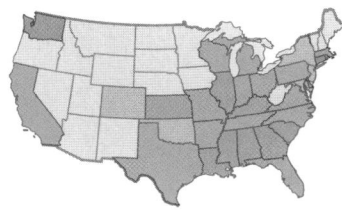

Percent of black students statewide attending schools more than 50% white

60% or more	30–40%
50–60%	20–30%
40–50%	20% or less

Integration of Public Schools, 1968

| Why did the "outsider" presidency of Jimmy Carter fail to gain broad support? | What conservative goals were realized in the Reagan administration? | What strategies did liberals use to fight the conservative turn? | How did Ronald Reagan's foreign policy affect the Cold War? | Conclusion: What was the long-term impact of the conservative turn? |

831

students began to attend the formerly all-white South Boston High School, white students boycotted classes, and angry whites threw rocks at black students disembarking from buses.

White parents and students eventually became more accepting of integration, especially after the creation of magnet schools and other new mechanisms for desegregation offered more choice. Nonetheless, integration propelled white flight to the suburbs. By 1987, the number of white students in Boston public schools was just one-third of what it had been in 1974.

Nixon's judicial appointments also reflected the southern strategy. He criticized the Supreme Court under Chief Justice Earl Warren for being "unprecedentedly politically active . . . using their interpretation of the law to remake American society according to their own social, political, and ideological precepts." When Warren resigned in 1969, Nixon replaced him with Warren E. Burger, a federal appeals court judge who was a strict constructionist—someone inclined to interpret the Constitution narrowly and to limit government intervention on behalf of individual rights. The Burger Court proved more sympathetic than the Warren Court to the president's agenda, but it continued to uphold many of the liberal programs of the 1960s. For example, the Court limited the range of affirmative action in *Regents of the University of California v. Bakke* (1978), but it allowed affirmative action programs to attack the results of past discrimination if they avoided strict quotas or racial classifications.

Nixon's southern strategy and other repercussions of the civil rights revolution of the 1960s ended the Democratic hold on the "solid South." A number of conservative southern Democrats changed their party affiliation in the 1960s and 1970s, and by 2005, Republicans held the majority of southern seats in Congress and governorships in seven southern states.

In addition to exploiting racial fears, Nixon aligned himself with those anxious about women's changing roles and new demands. In 1971, he vetoed a bill providing federal funds for day care centers with a message that combined the old and new conservatism. Parents should purchase child care services "in the private, open market," he insisted, not through government programs. He appealed to social conservatives by warning about the measure's "family-weakening implications." In response to the movement to liberalize abortion laws, Nixon sided with "defenders of the right to life of the unborn," anticipating the Republican Party's eventual embrace of the issue.

> **QUICK REVIEW**

How did Nixon's policies reflect conservatives' increasing influence on the Republican Party?

CHAPTER LOCATOR | How did the Nixon presidency reflect the rise of postwar conservatism? | Why was the Watergate scandal significant?

832 CHAPTER 30
THE CONSERVATIVE TURN, 1969–1989

Why was the Watergate scandal significant?

When Nixon was compelled to turn over tapes of White House conversations during the Watergate investigation, an eighteen-and-a-half-minute gap was discovered in a conversation between Nixon and his chief of staff, H. R. Haldeman, just three days after the Watergate break-in. Nixon's secretary, Rose Mary Woods, said that her foot must have slipped on the controls while she was transcribing the tape, using the transcription machine pictured here. Others, noting that the gap contained several separate erasings, suggested that the clumsiness of the deed linked it to Nixon.
Nixon Presidential Materials Project, National Archives and Records Administration.

NIXON WON A RESOUNDING VICTORY in the 1972 election. Two years later, however, the so-called Watergate scandal caused him to abandon his office. His successor, Gerald Ford, helped restore confidence in the presidency, but the aftermath of Watergate and severe economic problems returned the White House to the Democrats in 1976. Nonetheless, the rising conservative tide not only survived the temporary setback when Nixon resigned the presidency but also quickly challenged the Democratic administration that followed.

The Election of 1972

Nixon's ability to appeal to concerns about Vietnam, race, law and order, and traditional morality heightened his prospects for reelection in 1972. Although the war in Vietnam continued, antiwar protests diminished with the end of the draft and the decrease in American ground forces and casualties. Nixon's economic initiatives had temporarily checked inflation and unemployment (see chapter 28), and his attacks on busing and antiwar protesters had appealed to the right, positioning him favorably for the 1972 election.

A large field of contenders vied for the Democratic nomination, including New York representative Shirley Chisholm, the first African American to make a serious bid for the presidency. South Dakota senator George S. McGovern came to the Democratic convention as the clear leader and was easily nominated. Nonetheless, McGovern struggled against Nixon from the outset. Republicans portrayed him as a leftist extremist, and his support for busing, a generous welfare program, and immediate withdrawal from Vietnam alienated conservative Democrats.

Why did the "outsider" presidency of Jimmy Carter fail to gain broad support?	What conservative goals were realized in the Reagan administration?	What strategies did liberals use to fight the conservative turn?	How did Ronald Reagan's foreign policy affect the Cold War?	Conclusion: What was the long-term impact of the conservative turn?

CHRONOLOGY

1972
- Nixon campaign aides are arrested at Watergate complex.
- Nixon wins election to second term as president.

1973
- Archibald Cox is appointed independent special prosecutor to investigate Watergate.
- Vice President Spiro Agnew resigns after it is revealed he took bribes while governor of Maryland.

1974
- House Judiciary Committee votes to present impeachment charges to the House.
- Nixon resigns; Gerald R. Ford becomes president.
- Ford pardons Nixon of any crimes he may have committed while president.

1976
- Democrat Jimmy Carter is elected president.

Watergate

▶ The 1972 break-in at Democratic Party headquarters in the Watergate complex by men working for President Nixon's re-election, along with Nixon's efforts to cover it up. The Watergate scandal led to President Nixon's resignation.

Nixon achieved a landslide victory, winning 60.7 percent of the popular vote and every state except Massachusetts. Although the Democrats maintained control of Congress, Nixon won majorities among traditional Democrats—southerners, Catholics, urbanites, and blue-collar workers. Shortly after the election, however, revelations began to emerge about crimes committed to ensure the victory.

Watergate

During the early-morning hours of June 17, 1972, five men working for Nixon's reelection campaign crept into Democratic Party headquarters in the Watergate complex in Washington, D.C. Intending to repair a bugging device installed in an earlier break-in, they were discovered and arrested. Nixon and his aides then tried to cover up the intruders' connection to administration officials, setting the stage for the scandal reporters dubbed **Watergate**.

Nixon was not the first president to lie to the public or to misuse power. Every president since Franklin D. Roosevelt had enlarged the powers of his office, justifying his actions as necessary to protect national security. This expansion of executive powers weakened the traditional checks and balances on the executive branch and opened the door to abuses. No president, however, had dared go as far as Nixon, who saw opposition to his policies as a personal attack and was willing to violate the Constitution to stop it. Upon learning of the Watergate arrests, Nixon plotted to conceal links between the burglars and the White House while publicly denying any connection. In April 1973, after investigations by a grand jury and the Senate suggested that White House aides had been involved, Nixon accepted official responsibility for Watergate but denied any knowledge of the break-in or cover-up. He also announced the resignations of three White House aides and the attorney general. In May, he authorized the appointment of an independent special prosecutor, Archibald Cox, to conduct an investigation.

Meanwhile, speaking before a Senate investigating committee headed by Democrat Samuel J. Ervin of North Carolina, White House counsel John Dean described projects to harass "enemies" through tax audits and other illegal means and implicated the president in efforts to cover up the Watergate break-in. A White House aide struck the most damaging blow when he disclosed that all conversations in the Oval Office were taped. Both Cox and the Ervin committee immediately asked for the tapes related to Watergate. When Nixon refused, citing executive privilege and separation of powers, Cox and Ervin took their case to court.

Additional disclosures exposed Nixon's misuse of federal funds and tax evasion. In August 1973, Vice President Spiro Agnew resigned after an investigation revealed that he had taken bribes while governor of Maryland. Nixon's choice of House minority leader Gerald Ford of Michigan to succeed Agnew won widespread approval, but Agnew's resignation further tarnished the administration, and Nixon's popular support plummeted to 27 percent.

In February 1974, the House of Representatives voted to begin an impeachment investigation. In April, Nixon began to release edited transcripts of the tapes. The transcripts revealed Nixon's orders to aides in March 1973: "I don't give a shit what happens. I want you all to stonewall it, let them plead the Fifth Amendment, cover up or anything else, if it'll save it—save the plan."

CHAPTER LOCATOR | How did the Nixon presidency reflect the rise of postwar conservatism? | Why was the Watergate scandal significant?

In July 1974, the House Judiciary Committee voted to present articles of impeachment against the president to the House. Ordered by a unanimous Supreme Court to hand over the remaining tapes, Nixon released transcripts on August 5 that contained his conversations about how to hinder the FBI's investigation of the break-in. This was sufficient evidence to seal his fate.

In July 1974, the House Judiciary Committee considered specific charges for impeachment: (1) obstruction of justice, (2) abuse of power, (3) contempt of Congress, (4) unconstitutional waging of war by the secret bombing of Cambodia, and (5) tax evasion and the selling of political favors. The committee voted to take the first three charges to the House, where a vote of impeachment seemed certain. Ordered by a unanimous Supreme Court to hand over the remaining tapes, Nixon released transcripts on August 5 that contained his conversations about how to hinder the FBI's investigation of the break-in. This was sufficient evidence to seal his fate.

Nixon announced his resignation to a national television audience on August 8, 1974. Acknowledging some incorrect judgments, he insisted that he had always tried to do what was best for the nation. The next morning, Nixon ended an emotional farewell to his staff with some advice: "Always remember, others may hate you, but those who hate you don't win unless you hate them, and then you destroy yourself."

The Ford Presidency and the 1976 Election

Upon taking office, **Gerald R. Ford** announced, "Our long nightmare is over." But he shocked many Americans one month later when he granted Nixon a pardon "for all offenses against the United States which he . . . has committed or may have committed or taken part in" during his presidency. This sweeping pardon saved Nixon from nearly certain indictment and trial, and it provoked a tremendous outcry from Congress and the public.

Congress's efforts to guard against the types of abuses revealed in the Watergate investigations had only limited effects. The Federal Election

Gerald R. Ford

▶ House minority leader from Michigan who became Nixon's vice president in 1973 and president in 1974, when Nixon resigned. Ford was popular for his integrity and humility, but his decision to pardon Nixon provoked widespread outrage and strengthened the Democratic Party.

| Why did the "outsider" presidency of Jimmy Carter fail to gain broad support? | What conservative goals were realized in the Reagan administration? | What strategies did liberals use to fight the conservative turn? | How did Ronald Reagan's foreign policy affect the Cold War? | Conclusion: What was the long-term impact of the conservative turn? |

James Earl "Jimmy" Carter Jr.

▶ Democratic president who served from 1977 until 1981 and moved the party away from the liberalism of the 1960s. Carter's modest lifestyle, religious commitment, and status as a Washington outsider appealed to a nation reeling from the scandals of the Nixon administration. Nevertheless, his performance in office in the face of domestic and foreign crises did not inspire confidence, and he lost his bid for reelection.

Campaign Act of 1974 established public financing of presidential campaigns and imposed some restrictions on contributions to help prevent the selling of political favors. Yet politicians found other ways of raising money, such as through political action committees (PACs). Moreover, in *Buckley v. Valeo* (1976), the Supreme Court struck down limitations on campaign spending as violations of freedom of speech. Ever-larger campaign donations flowed to candidates from interest groups, corporations, labor unions, and wealthy individuals.

Special investigating committees in Congress discovered a host of illegal FBI and CIA activities stretching back to the 1950s, including harassment of political dissenters and plots to assassinate Fidel Castro and other foreign leaders. In response to these revelations, President Ford established new controls on covert operations, and Congress created permanent committees to oversee the intelligence agencies. Yet these measures did little to diminish the public's cynicism about their government.

Disillusionment grew as the Ford administration struggled with serious economic problems. Ford carried these burdens into the election campaign of 1976, while contending with a major challenge from the Republican right. Blasting Nixon's and Ford's foreign policy of détente for causing the "loss of U.S. military supremacy," California governor Ronald Reagan came close to capturing the nomination.

The Democrats nominated **James Earl "Jimmy" Carter Jr.**, former governor of Georgia. Carefully prepared on policy issues, Carter appealed to the rise of evangelical religion and alienation from government by stressing his faith as a "born-again Christian" and his distance from the government in Washington. Although he selected liberal senator Walter F. Mondale of Minnesota as his running mate, Carter's nomination nonetheless marked a rightward turn in the party.

Carter had considerable appeal as a candidate who carried his own bags, lived modestly, and taught a Bible class at his Baptist church. He also benefited from Ford's failure to solve the country's economic problems, which helped him win the traditional Democratic coalition of blacks, organized labor, and ethnic groups, and even recapture some of the white southerners who had voted for Nixon in 1972. Nonetheless, Carter received just 50 percent of the popular vote to Ford's 48 percent (**Map 30.1**).

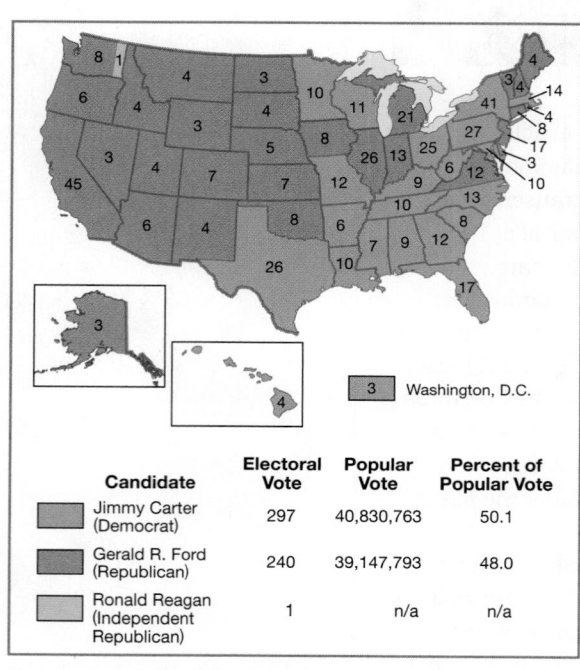

Candidate	Electoral Vote	Popular Vote	Percent of Popular Vote
Jimmy Carter (Democrat)	297	40,830,763	50.1
Gerald R. Ford (Republican)	240	39,147,793	48.0
Ronald Reagan (Independent Republican)	1	n/a	n/a

MAP 30.1 ■ The Election of 1976

> **QUICK REVIEW**

What impact, if any, did Watergate have on the political fortunes of the conservative movement?

CHAPTER LOCATOR | How did the Nixon presidency reflect the rise of postwar conservatism? | Why was the Watergate scandal significant?

CHAPTER 30
836 THE CONSERVATIVE TURN, 1969–1989

Why did the "outsider" presidency of Jimmy Carter fail to gain broad support?

Jimmy Carter's Inauguration

After his inauguration in January 1977, Jimmy Carter shunned the customary presidential limousine and instead walked with his wife, daughter, and two sons and their wives down Pennsylvania Avenue from the Capitol to the White House. Carter wanted to emphasize his opposition to some of the trappings of office that separated government from the people. Jimmy Carter Presidential Library.

JIMMY CARTER PROMISED a government that was "competent" as well as "decent, open, fair, and compassionate." He also warned Americans "that even our great Nation has its recognized limits, and that we can neither answer all questions nor solve all problems." Carter's humility and personal integrity helped revive trust in the presidency, but he lost support as he struggled with domestic and foreign crises.

Retreat from Liberalism

Jimmy Carter vowed "to help the poor and aged, to improve education, and to provide jobs," but at the same time "not to waste money." When these goals conflicted, reform took second place to budget balancing. Increasing numbers of Americans unhappy about their tax dollars being used to benefit the disadvantaged while a poor economy eroded their own material status welcomed Carter's approach. But his fiscal stringency frustrated liberal Democrats, who accused him of deserting the Democratic reform tradition stretching back to Franklin D. Roosevelt.

A number of factors hindered Carter's ability to lead. His outsider status contributed to his election but left him without strong ties to party leaders in Congress. Democrats complained of inadequate consultation and Carter's tendency to flood them with comprehensive proposals when they were more accustomed to incremental reforms. In addition, Carter refused to offer simple solutions to the American people, who were impatient for quick action to fix the economy. But the economic problems Carter inherited—unemployment, inflation, and sluggish economic growth—confounded economic doctrine. Usually, rising prices accompanied a growing economy with a strong demand for labor. Now, however, the nation faced steep inflation and high unemployment at the same time, a combination called stagflation.

| Why did the "outsider" presidency of Jimmy Carter fail to gain broad support? | What conservative goals were realized in the Reagan administration? | What strategies did liberals use to fight the conservative turn? | How did Ronald Reagan's foreign policy affect the Cold War? | Conclusion: What was the long-term impact of the conservative turn? |

1976
- Democrat Jimmy Carter is elected president.

1977
- Carter signs Panama Canal treaty.

1978
- Congress deregulates the airlines.
- Congress passes National Energy Act of 1978.

1979
- Iranian revolution overthrows the shah of Iran and institutes a fundamentalist Islamic government.
- In the Camp David accords, Egypt is the first Arab state to recognize Israel.
- Carter establishes formal diplomatic relations with China.
- Accident occurs at Three Mile Island nuclear facility.
- Hostage crisis in Iran begins.
- Soviet Union invades Afghanistan.

1980
- Congress deregulates the banking, trucking, and railroad industries.
- Inflation surpasses 13 percent.

Carter first targeted unemployment, signing bills that pumped $14 billion into the economy through public works and public service jobs programs and cut taxes by $34 billion. Unemployment receded, but then inflation surged. Working people, wrote one journalist, "winced and ached" as their paychecks bought less and less. To curb inflation, Carter curtailed federal spending, and the Federal Reserve Board tightened the money supply. Not only did these measures fail to halt inflation, which surpassed 13 percent in 1980, but they also contributed to rising unemployment, reversing the gains made in Carter's first two years.

Carter's commitment to holding down the federal budget frustrated Democrats pushing for comprehensive welfare reform, national health insurance, and a substantial jobs program that would make government the employer of last resort. Carter did sign legislation to ensure solvency in the Social Security system, but the measure increased both employer and employee contributions, thereby increasing the tax burden on lower- and middle-income Americans.

By contrast, corporations and wealthy individuals gained from new legislation, such as a sharp cut in the capital gains tax. When the Chrysler Corporation approached bankruptcy in 1979, Congress provided $1.5 billion in loan guarantees to bail out the tenth-largest corporation in the country. Congress also acted on Carter's proposals to deregulate the airlines in 1978 and the banking, trucking, and railroad industries in 1980. Carter's successor would move much further, implementing conservatives' attachment to a free market and unfettered private enterprise.

Energy and Environmental Reform

Complicating the government's efforts to deal with stagflation were the nation's enormous consumption of energy and its dependence on foreign nations to fill one-third of its energy demands. Consequently, Carter proposed a comprehensive program to conserve energy, and he elevated its importance by establishing the Department of Energy. Responding to Carter's proposal, Congress passed the National Energy Act of 1978, which penalized manufacturers of gas-guzzling automobiles and provided other incentives for conservation and development of alternative fuels, but the act fell far short of a long-term, comprehensive program.

In 1979, a new upheaval in the Middle East, the Iranian revolution, created the most severe energy crisis yet. In midsummer, shortages caused 60 percent of gasoline stations to close down, resulting in long lines and high prices. "We are struggling with a profound transition from a time of abundance to a time of

The 1980 Fuel Shortage

This billboard was sponsored by the Outdoor Advertising Association of America in 1980, while Iran held Americans hostage in Teheran and gasoline shortages and rising gas prices vexed motorists all over the country. John W. Hartman Center/Duke University Special Collections Library.

▶ FOR MORE HELP ANALYZING THIS IMAGE, see the visual activity for this chapter in the Online Study Guide at bedfordstmartins.com/roarkunderstanding.

CHAPTER LOCATOR | How did the Nixon presidency reflect the rise of postwar conservatism? | Why was the Watergate scandal significant?

growing scarcity in energy," Carter told the nation, asking Congress for additional measures to address the shortages. Congress reduced controls on the oil and gas industries to stimulate American production and imposed a windfall profits tax on producers to redistribute some of the profits they would reap from deregulation.

Carter's energy measures failed to reduce American dependence on foreign oil. European nations shared that dependence but more successfully controlled consumption. They levied high taxes on gasoline, causing people to rely more on public transportation and prompting manufacturers to produce more energy-efficient cars. In the automobile-dependent United States, however, politicians dismissed that approach. By the end of the century, the United States, with 6 percent of the world's population, would consume more than 25 percent of global oil production. (See "Global Comparison," page 840, and **Map 30.2**.)

One alternative fuel, nuclear energy, aroused opposition from a vigorous environmental movement. The perils of nuclear energy claimed international attention in March 1979, when a meltdown of the reactor core was narrowly averted at the Three Mile Island nuclear facility near Harrisburg, Pennsylvania. Popular opposition and the great expense of building nuclear power plants stalled further development of the industry. The explosion of a nuclear reactor in Chernobyl, Ukraine, in 1986 further solidified antinuclear concerns as part of the environmental movement.

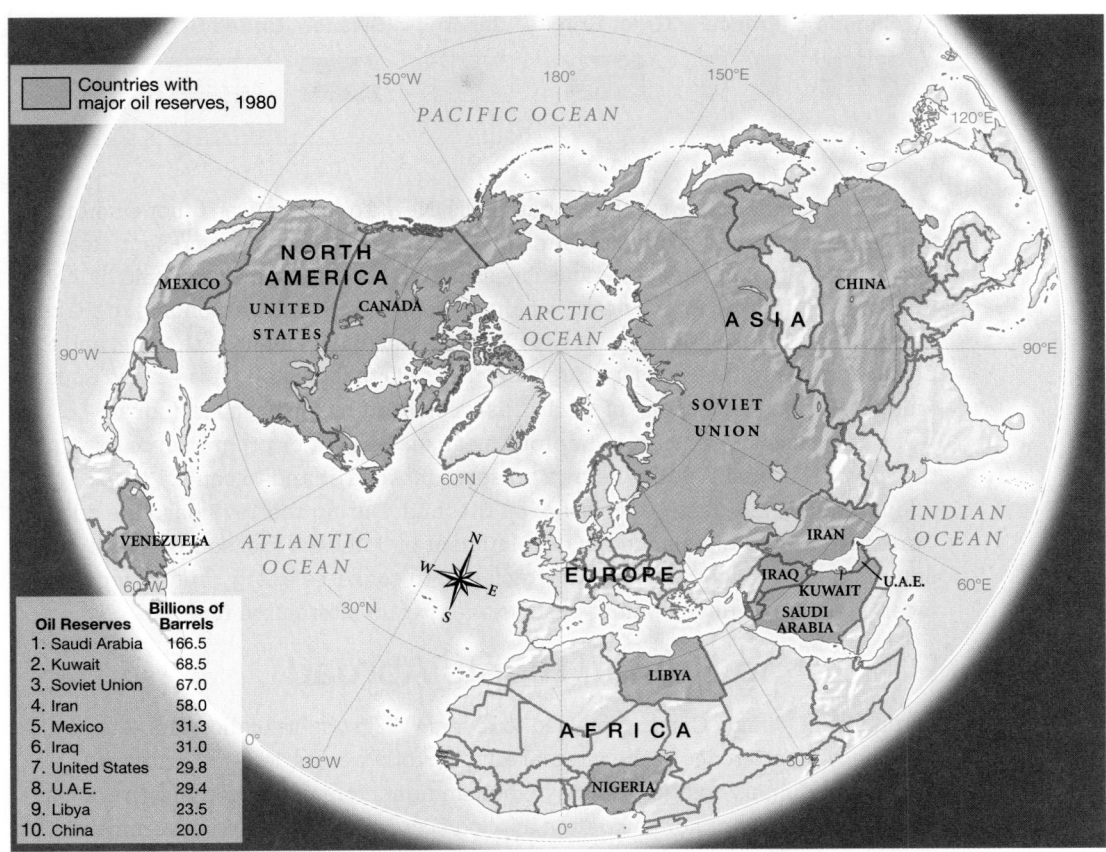

MAP 30.2 ■ Worldwide Oil Reserves, 1980

Data produced by geologists and engineers enable experts to estimate the size of "proved oil reserves," quantities that are recoverable with existing technology and costs. In 1980, the total worldwide reserves were estimated at 645 billion barrels.

| Why did the "outsider" presidency of Jimmy Carter fail to gain broad support? | What conservative goals were realized in the Reagan administration? | What strategies did liberals use to fight the conservative turn? | How did Ronald Reagan's foreign policy affect the Cold War? | Conclusion: What was the long-term impact of the conservative turn? |

Energy Consumption per Capita, 1980

Relative to most other industrialized nations, the United States consumed energy voraciously, with a per capita rate of consumption in 1980 that was more than twice as high as that of Great Britain, France, or Japan and nearly twice as high as that of the Soviet Union. A number of factors influence a nation's energy consumption (shown here in British thermal units, or Btus), including standard of living, climate, size of landmass and dispersal of population, availability and price of energy, and government policies such as support for public transportation. What country had a per capita rate of consumption even higher than that of the United States?

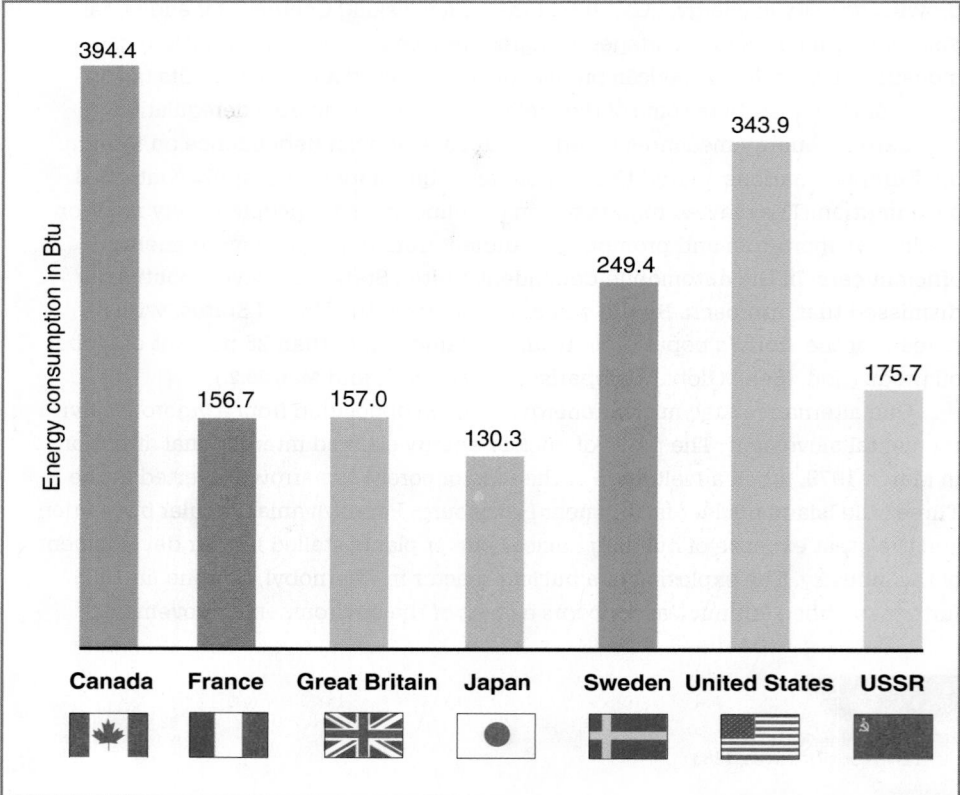

A disaster at Love Canal in Niagara Falls, New York, advanced other environmental goals by underscoring the human costs of unregulated development. Residents suffering high rates of serious illness noted that their homes sat amid highly toxic waste products from a nearby chemical company. Finally responding to the residents' claims in 1978, the State of New York agreed to help families relocate, and the Carter administration sponsored legislation in 1980 that created the so-called Superfund, $1.6 billion for cleanup of hazardous wastes left by the chemical industry.

Carter also signed bills to improve clean air and water programs; to expand the Arctic National Wildlife Refuge preserve in Alaska; and to control stripmining, which left destructive scars on the land. During the 1979 gasoline crisis, Carter attempted to balance the development of domestic fuel sources with environmental concerns, winning legislation to conserve energy and to provide incentives for the development of solar energy and alternative fuels.

Promoting Human Rights Abroad

As president, Jimmy Carter promised to reverse U.S. support of dictators, secret diplomacy, interference in the internal affairs of other countries, and excessive reliance on military solutions. Instead, human rights formed the cornerstone of his approach. The Carter administration applied economic pressure on governments that denied their citizens basic rights, denying aid or trading privileges to nations such as Chile and El Salvador, as well as to the white minority governments of Rhodesia and South Africa. Yet in other instances, Carter sacrificed human rights ideals to strategic and security considerations. He invoked no sanctions against repressive

CHAPTER LOCATOR | How did the Nixon presidency reflect the rise of postwar conservatism? | Why was the Watergate scandal significant?

840 CHAPTER 30 THE CONSERVATIVE TURN, 1969–1989

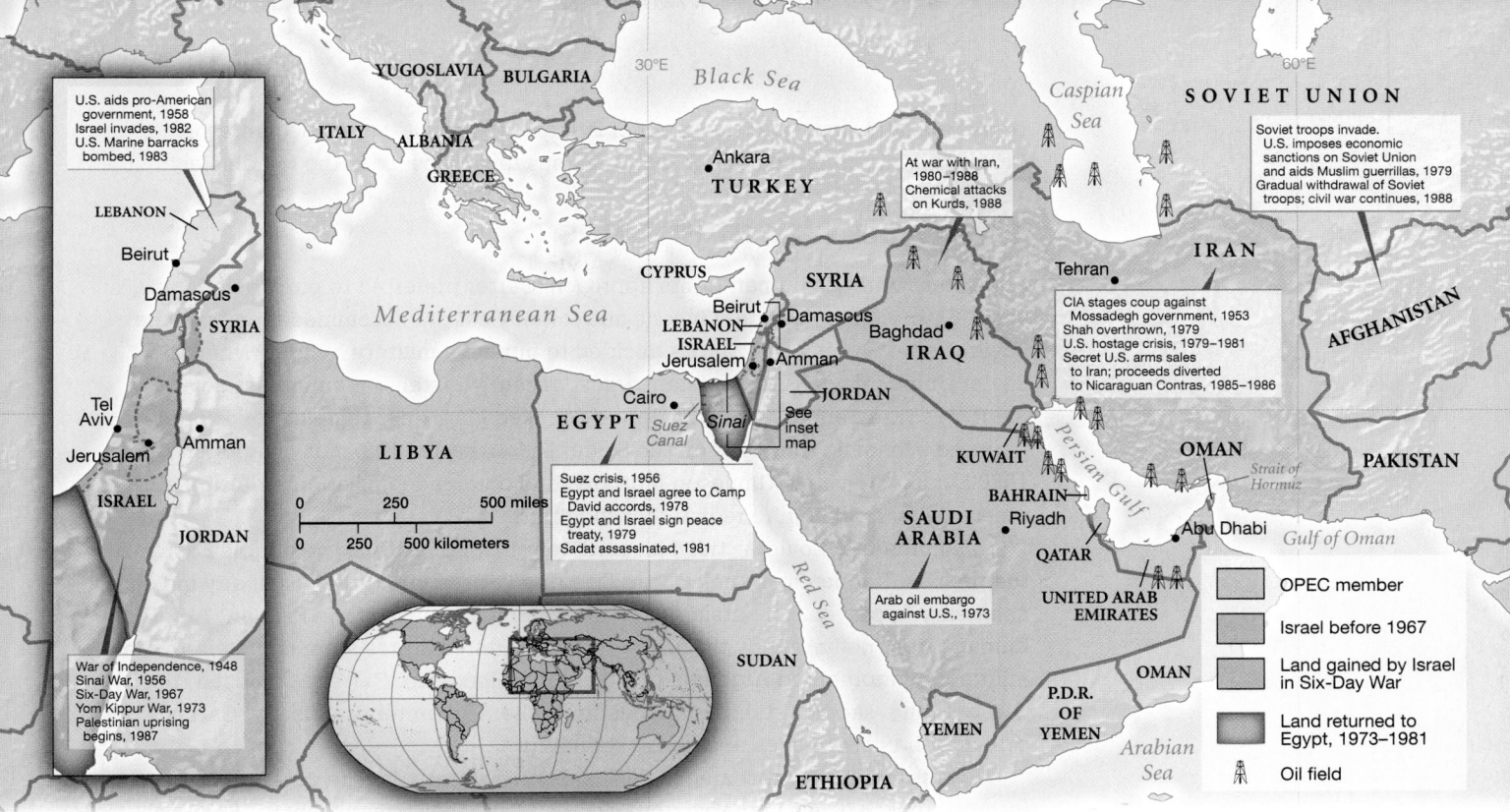

Map inset labels (Lebanon inset, left):

U.S. aids pro-American government, 1958
Israel invades, 1982
U.S. Marine barracks bombed, 1983

LEBANON
Beirut
Damascus
SYRIA
Tel Aviv
Jerusalem
Amman
ISRAEL
JORDAN

War of Independence, 1948
Sinai War, 1956
Six-Day War, 1967
Yom Kippur War, 1973
Palestinian uprising begins, 1987

Main map labels:

YUGOSLAVIA
BULGARIA
30°E
Black Sea
Caspian Sea
60°E
SOVIET UNION
ITALY
ALBANIA
GREECE
Ankara
TURKEY

At war with Iran, 1980–1988 Chemical attacks on Kurds, 1988

Soviet troops invade. U.S. imposes economic sanctions on Soviet Union and aids Muslim guerrillas, 1979 Gradual withdrawal of Soviet troops; civil war continues, 1988

CYPRUS
SYRIA
Beirut
Damascus
Baghdad
Tehran
IRAN
AFGHANISTAN
LEBANON
ISRAEL
Jerusalem
Amman
IRAQ
JORDAN
Mediterranean Sea

CIA stages coup against Mossadegh government, 1953
Shah overthrown, 1979
U.S. hostage crisis, 1979–1981
Secret U.S. arms sales to Iran; proceeds diverted to Nicaraguan Contras, 1985–1986

Cairo
EGYPT
Suez Canal
Sinai
See inset map
LIBYA

0   250   500 miles
0   250   500 kilometers

Suez crisis, 1956
Egypt and Israel agree to Camp David accords, 1978
Egypt and Israel sign peace treaty, 1979
Sadat assassinated, 1981

KUWAIT
Persian Gulf
OMAN
Strait of Hormuz
PAKISTAN
BAHRAIN
Riyadh
SAUDI ARABIA
QATAR
Abu Dhabi
Gulf of Oman

Arab oil embargo against U.S., 1973

UNITED ARAB EMIRATES
OMAN
Red Sea
SUDAN
P.D.R. OF YEMEN
YEMEN
Arabian Sea
ETHIOPIA

Legend:
OPEC member
Israel before 1967
Land gained by Israel in Six-Day War
Land returned to Egypt, 1973–1981
Oil field

► FOR MORE HELP ANALYZING THIS MAP, see the map activity for this chapter in the Online Study Guide at bedfordstmartins.com/roarkunderstanding.

MAP 30.3 ■ **The Middle East, 1948–1989**
Determination to preserve access to the rich oil reserves of the Middle East and commitment to the security of Israel were the fundamental — and often conflicting — principles of U.S. foreign policy in that region.

governments in Iran, South Korea, and the Philippines, for example, and he established formal diplomatic relations with the People's Republic of China in 1979.

Carter's human rights principles faced another test when a popular movement overthrew an oppressive dictatorship in Nicaragua. U.S. officials were uneasy about the leftist Sandinistas who led the rebellion and had ties to Cuba. Once they assumed power in 1979, however, Carter recognized the new government and sent economic aid, signaling that the way a government treated its citizens was as important as how anti-Communist and friendly to American interests it was.

Applying moral principles to relations with Panama, Carter sped up negotiations over control of the Panama Canal and in 1977 signed a treaty providing for Panama's takeover of the canal in 2000. Supporters viewed the treaty as recompense for the use of U.S. power to obtain the canal in 1903. Opponents insisted on retaining the vital waterway. "We bought it, we paid for it, it's ours," claimed Ronald Reagan during the presidential primaries of 1976. It took a massive effort by the administration to get Senate ratification of the Panama Canal treaty.

Seeking to promote peace in the Middle East, Carter seized on the courage of Egyptian president Anwar Sadat, the first Arab leader to risk his political career by talking directly with Israeli officials. In 1979, Carter invited Sadat and Israeli prime minister Menachem Begin to the presidential retreat at Camp David, Maryland. These talks led to the **Camp David accords**, whereby Egypt became the first Arab state to recognize Israel, and Israel agreed to gradual withdrawal from the Sinai Peninsula, which it had seized in the 1967 Six-Day War (**Map 30.3**). Although the issues of Palestinian self-determination in other Israeli-occupied territories (the

Camp David accords
► Agreements between Egypt and Israel reached at the 1979 talks held at Camp David. In the accords, Egypt became the first Arab state to recognize Israel, and Israel agreed to gradual withdrawal from the Sinai Peninsula, which it had seized in the 1967 Six-Day War. President Carter played a key role in bringing the two parties together and ensuring that the talks were a success.

Why did the "outsider" presidency of Jimmy Carter fail to gain broad support?	What conservative goals were realized in the Reagan administration?	What strategies did liberals use to fight the conservative turn?	How did Ronald Reagan's foreign policy affect the Cold War?	Conclusion: What was the long-term impact of the conservative turn?

841

West Bank and Gaza) and the plight of Palestinian refugees remained unresolved, Carter had nurtured the first meaningful steps toward peace in the Middle East.

The Cold War Intensifies

Consistent with his human rights approach, Carter preferred to pursue national security through nonmilitary means and initially sought accommodation with the Soviet Union. But in 1979, Carter decided to pursue a military buildup when the Soviet Union invaded Afghanistan, whose recently installed Communist government was threatened by Muslim opposition (see Map 30.3, page 841). Carter also imposed economic sanctions on the Soviet Union, barred U.S. participation in the 1980 Summer Olympic Games in Moscow, and obtained legislation requiring all nineteen-year-old men to register for the draft.

Claiming that Soviet actions jeopardized oil supplies from the Middle East, the president announced the "Carter Doctrine," threatening the use of any means necessary to prevent an outside force from gaining control of the Persian Gulf. His human rights policy fell by the wayside as the United States stepped up aid to the military dictatorship in Afghanistan's neighbor, Pakistan. Carter authorized the CIA to funnel secret aid through Pakistan to the Afghan rebels. Finally, Carter called for hefty increases in defense spending.

Events in Iran also encouraged this hard-line approach. Iranian dissidents resented the CIA's role in the overthrow of the Mossadegh government in 1953 (see chapter 27), condemned the shah's savage attempts to silence opposition, and detested his adoption of Western culture and values. These grievances erupted into a revolution in 1979 that forced the shah out of Iran and brought to power Shiite Islamic fundamentalists led by Ayatollah Ruholla Khomeini, whom the shah had exiled in 1964.

Carter's decision to allow the shah into the United States for medical treatment enraged Iranians, who believed that the United States would put the shah back in power as it had done in 1953. On November 4, 1979, a crowd broke into the U.S. Embassy in Iran's capital, Teheran, and seized sixty-six U.S. diplomats, CIA officers, citizens, and military attachés. Refusing the captors' demands that the shah be returned to Iran for trial, Carter froze Iranian assets in U.S. banks and placed an embargo on Iranian oil. In April 1980, he sent a small military operation into Iran, but the rescue mission failed.

Iran hostage crisis

▶ Crisis that began in 1979 after the Iranian revolution against the shah. Iranians broke into the U.S. Embassy in Teheran and took sixty-six Americans hostage. The hostage crisis undermined the Carter presidency and damaged his chances at reelection.

The disastrous rescue attempt and scenes of blindfolded U.S. citizens paraded before TV cameras fed Americans' feelings of impotence, simmering since the defeat in Vietnam. These frustrations in turn increased support for a more militaristic foreign policy. Opposition to Soviet-American détente, combined with the Soviet invasion of Afghanistan, nullified the thaw in superpower relations that had begun in the 1960s. The Iran hostage crisis dominated the news during the 1980 presidential campaign and contributed to Carter's defeat. Iran freed the hostages the day he left office, but relations with the United States remained tense.

> ## QUICK REVIEW

Why were so many Americans uninspired by Carter's leadership?

CHAPTER LOCATOR | How did the Nixon presidency reflect the rise of postwar conservatism? | Why was the Watergate scandal significant?

CHAPTER 30
842 THE CONSERVATIVE TURN, 1969–1989

What conservative goals were realized in the Reagan administration?

Ronald Reagan Nominated for President

Nancy and Ronald Reagan respond to cheers at the 1980 Republican National Convention, where he was nominated for president. Reagan became one of the most popular presidents of the twentieth century. Lester Sloan/Woodfin Camp & Associates.

RONALD REAGAN'S ELECTION in 1980 marked the most important turning point in politics since Franklin D. Roosevelt won the presidency in 1932. Reagan's victory established conservatism's dominance in the Republican Party, while Democrats searched for voter support by moving toward the right. The United States was not alone in this political shift. Conservatives rose to power in Britain with Prime Minister Margaret Thatcher, and they led governments in Germany, Canada, and Sweden, while socialist and social democratic governments elsewhere trimmed their welfare states.

Appealing to the New Right and Beyond

Sixty-nine-year-old **Ronald Reagan** was the oldest candidate ever nominated for the presidency. Coming first to national attention as a movie actor, he initially shared the politics of his staunchly Democratic father but moved to the right in the 1940s and 1950s and campaigned for Barry Goldwater in 1964.

Reagan's political career took off when he was elected governor of California in 1966. He ran as a conservative, but in office he displayed considerable flexibility, approving a major tax increase, a strong water pollution bill, and a liberal abortion law. Displaying similar agility in the 1980 presidential campaign, he softened earlier attacks on programs such as Social Security and chose the moderate George H. W. Bush as his running mate.

Reagan's campaign capitalized on the economic recession and the international challenges symbolized by the Americans held hostage in Iran. Repeatedly, Reagan asked voters, "Are you better off now than you were four years ago?" He promised to "take government off the backs of the people" and to restore Americans' morale and other nations' respect. Reagan won the 1980 election, and Republicans took control of the Senate for the first time since the 1950s.

Ronald Reagan

▶ Republican president who held office from 1981 until 1989. The enormously popular former actor and governor of California implemented a wide-ranging conservative agenda that rolled back taxes, industry regulations, environmental protections, and social welfare programs. Reagan also oversaw a dramatic thawing in U.S.-Soviet relations.

Why did the "outsider" presidency of Jimmy Carter fail to gain broad support?	**What conservative goals were realized in the Reagan administration?**	What strategies did liberals use to fight the conservative turn?	How did Ronald Reagan's foreign policy affect the Cold War?	Conclusion: What was the long-term impact of the conservative turn?

Christian Right

▶ Term for new conservatives who attacked what they saw as immorality in public life and who called for a return to traditional or "family" values. Jerry Falwell and Pat Robertson were key leaders of the Christian Right.

supply-side economics

▶ Economic theory that held that cutting taxes would lead to economic growth by increasing productivity and thereby increasing demand for goods and services. Despite proponents' promises to the contrary, under Ronald Reagan supply-side economics led to large increases in the federal budget deficit.

The Reagan Coalition

Free-market advocates
Militant anti-Communists
Fundamentalist Christians
White southerners
Reagan Democrats: white working-class Democrats who were disenchanted with the policies of the Democratic Party

While the economy and Iran sealed Reagan's victory, he also benefited from the burgeoning grassroots conservative movements. Reagan's support from religious conservatives, predominantly Protestants, constituted a relatively new phenomenon in politics known as the New Right or New **Christian Right**. During the 1970s, evangelical and fundamentalist Christianity claimed thousands of new adherents. Evangelical ministers such as Pat Robertson preached to huge television audiences, attacking feminism, abortion, and homosexuality and calling for the restoration of old-fashioned "family values."

Conservatives created political organizations such as the Moral Majority, founded by minister Jerry Falwell in 1979 to fight "left-wing, social-welfare bills, . . . pornography, homosexuality, [and] the advocacy of immorality in school textbooks." The Christian Coalition, founded by Pat Robertson in 1989, claimed 1.6 million members and control of the Republican Party in more than a dozen states. The organizations and publications of more traditional conservatives, who stressed limited government at home and militant anticommunism abroad, likewise flourished.

Reagan spoke for the New Right on such issues as abortion and school prayer, but he did not push hard for so-called moral or social policies. Instead, his major achievements fulfilled goals of the older right—strengthening the nation's anti-Communist posture and reducing taxes and government restraints on free enterprise. "In the present crisis," Reagan declared, "government is not the solution to our problem, government is the problem."

Reagan was extraordinarily popular, appealing even to Americans who opposed his policies but warmed to his optimism, confidence, and easygoing humor. Ignoring the darker moments of the American past, he presented a version of history that Americans could feel good about.

Unleashing Free Enterprise

Reagan's first domestic objective was a massive tax cut. In support of this objective, Reagan relied on a new theory called **supply-side economics**, which held that cutting taxes would actually increase revenue. According to this theory, tax cuts would enable businesses to expand, encourage individuals to work harder because they could keep more of their earnings, and increase the production of goods and services—the supply—which in turn would boost demand. Reagan promised that the economy would grow so much that the government would recoup the lost taxes, but instead it incurred a galloping deficit.

In the summer of 1981, Congress passed the Economic Recovery Tax Act, the largest tax reduction in U.S. history. A second measure, the Tax Reform Act of 1986, cut taxes still further. Although the 1986 law narrowed loopholes used primarily by

CHAPTER LOCATOR | How did the Nixon presidency reflect the rise of postwar conservatism? | Why was the Watergate scandal significant?

844 CHAPTER 30 THE CONSERVATIVE TURN, 1969–1989

the wealthy, affluent Americans saved far more on their tax bills than did average taxpayers, and the distribution of wealth tipped further in favor of the rich.

Carter had confined deregulation to particular industries, such as air transportation and banking, while increasing health, safety, and environmental regulations. The Reagan administration, by contrast, pursued across-the-board deregulation. It declined to enforce the Sherman Antitrust Act's limits on monopolies (see chapter 18) against an unprecedented number of business mergers and takeovers. Reagan also loosened regulations protecting employee health and safety, and he weakened labor unions. When members of the Professional Air Traffic Controllers Organization struck in 1981, Reagan fired them, destroying their union and intimidating organized labor.

Ronald Reagan blamed environmental laws for the nation's sluggish economic growth and targeted them for deregulation. His first secretary of the interior, James Watt, declared, "We will mine more, drill more, cut more timber," releasing federal lands to private exploitation. Meanwhile, the head of the Environmental Protection Agency relaxed enforcement of air and water pollution standards. Of environmentalists, Reagan wisecracked, "I don't think they'll be happy until the White House looks like a bird's nest," but their numbers grew in opposition to his policies. Popular support for environmental protection forced several officials to resign and blocked full realization of Reagan's deregulatory goals.

Deregulation of the banking industry, begun under Carter with bipartisan support, created a crisis in the savings and loan industry. Some of the newly deregulated savings and loan institutions (S&Ls) extended enormous loans to real estate developers and invested in other high-yield but risky ventures. When real estate values began to plunge, hundreds of S&Ls went bankrupt. After Congress voted to bail out the S&L industry in 1989, American taxpayers bore the burden of the largest financial scandal in U.S. history, estimated at more than $100 billion.

The S&L crisis deepened the federal deficit. The administration cut funds for food stamps, job training, student aid, and other social welfare programs, and hundreds of thousands of people lost benefits. Yet increases in defense spending far exceeded the budget cuts. Under Reagan, the nation's debt tripled to $2.3 trillion, and interest on the debt consumed one-seventh of all federal expenditures. Despite Reagan's antigovernment rhetoric, the number of federal employees increased from 2.9 million to 3.1 million during his presidency.

It took the severest recession since the 1930s to squeeze inflation out of the U.S. economy. Unemployment approached 11 percent late in 1982, and record numbers of banks and businesses closed. The threat of unemployment further undermined organized labor, forcing unions to make concessions that management insisted were necessary for industry's survival. In 1983, the economy recovered and entered a period of unprecedented growth.

That economic upswing and Reagan's own popularity posed a formidable challenge to the Democrats in the 1984 election. They nominated Carter's vice president, Walter F. Mondale, to head the ticket, but even his precedent-breaking move in choosing a woman as his running mate—New York representative Geraldine A. Ferraro—did not save the Democrats from defeat. Reagan charged his opponents with concentrating on America's failures, while he emphasized success and possibility. Democrats, he claimed, "see an America where every day is April 15th [the due date for income tax returns] . . . we see an America where every day is the Fourth of July." Reagan was reelected in a landslide victory, winning 59 percent of the popular vote and every state but Minnesota.

| Why did the "outsider" presidency of Jimmy Carter fail to gain broad support? | **What conservative goals were realized in the Reagan administration?** | What strategies did liberals use to fight the conservative turn? | How did Ronald Reagan's foreign policy affect the Cold War? | Conclusion: What was the long-term impact of the conservative turn? |

Winners and Losers in a Flourishing Economy

After the economy took off in 1983, some Americans won great fortunes. Popular culture celebrated making money and displaying wealth. Participating conspicuously in the new affluence were some members of the baby boom generation, known popularly as "yuppies," short for "young urban professionals." Though definitely a minority, these mostly white, well-educated young men and women established consumption standards that many tried to emulate. Many of the newly wealthy got rich from moving assets around rather than from producing goods, making money by manipulating debt and restructuring corporations through mergers and takeovers. Most financial wizards operated within the law, but greed sometimes led to criminal convictions.

Older industries faced increasing international pressures. German and Japanese corporations overtook U.S. manufacturing in steel, automobiles, and electronics. International competition forced the collapse of some older companies. Others moved factories and jobs abroad to be closer to foreign markets or to benefit from the low wages in countries such as Mexico and Korea. Service industries expanded and created new jobs at home, but these jobs paid substantially lower wages. The number of full-time workers earning wages below the poverty level ($12,195 for a family of four in 1990) rose from 12 percent to 18 percent of all workers in the 1980s.

The weakening of organized labor combined with the decline in manufacturing to erode the position of blue-collar workers. Chicago steelworker Ike Mazo, who contemplated the $6-an-hour jobs available to him, fumed, "It's an attack on the living standards of workers." Increasingly, a second income was needed to stave off economic decline. By 1990, nearly 60 percent of married women with young children worked outside the home. Yet even with two incomes, families struggled. Speaking of her children, Mazo's wife confessed, "I worry about their future every day. Will we be able to put them through college?" The average $10,000 gap between men's and women's annual earnings made things even harder for the nearly 20 percent of families headed by women.

In keeping with conservative philosophy, Reagan adhered to supply-side economics, insisting that a booming economy would benefit everyone. Average personal income did rise during his tenure, but the trend toward greater economic inequality that had begun in the 1970s intensified in the 1980s, encouraged in part by his tax policies. Social Security and Medicare helped to stave off destitution among the elderly. Less fortunate were other groups that the economic boom had bypassed: racial minorities, families headed by women, and children. One child in five lived in poverty.

Inequality under Reagan (1979–1987)

Personal income rose sharply for the wealthiest 20 percent of Americans.

Personal income of the poorest Americans fell by 9.8 percent.

The percentage of Americans living in poverty increased from 11.7 to 13.5, the highest poverty rate in the industrialized world.

> ## QUICK REVIEW

Why did economic inequality increase during the Reagan administration?

CHAPTER LOCATOR | How did the Nixon presidency reflect the rise of postwar conservatism? | Why was the Watergate scandal significant?

What strategies did liberals use to fight the conservative turn?

► FOR MORE HELP ANALYZING THIS IMAGE, see the visual activity for this chapter in the Online Study Guide at bedfordstmartins.com/roarkunderstanding.

"Parents & Friends of Lesbians & Gays" In June 1970, gays and lesbians marched in New York City to commemorate the first anniversary of the Stonewall riot (see chapter 28). Since then, gay pride parades have taken place throughout the United States and in other countries every year in June. Increasingly, friends, supporters, and families of homosexuals participate in the parades, as this sign from a parade in Los Angeles indicates. © Bettmann/Corbis.

THE RISE OF CONSERVATISM put liberal social movements on the defensive, as the Reagan administration moved away from the national commitment to equal opportunity undertaken in the 1960s. Feminists and minority groups fought to keep protections they had recently won, and they achieved some modest gains.

Battles in the Courts and Congress

Ronald Reagan agreed with conservatives that the nation had moved too far in guaranteeing rights to minority groups. Crying "reverse discrimination," conservatives maintained that affirmative action unfairly hurt whites. Instead they called for "color-blind" policies, ignoring statistics showing that minorities and white women still lagged far behind white men in opportunities and income. Intense mobilization by civil rights groups, educational leaders, and even corporate America prevented the administration from abandoning affirmative action, and the Supreme Court upheld important antidiscrimination policies. Moreover, against Reagan's wishes, Congress voted to extend the Voting Rights Act with veto-proof majorities. The administration did, however, limit civil rights

CHRONOLOGY

1981
- Researchers discover AIDS virus.
- Sandra Day O'Connor becomes the first woman justice on the Supreme Court.

1982
- Time limit for ratification of the Equal Rights Amendment runs out.

1984
- Supreme Court decision in *Grove City v. Bell* weakens antidiscrimination provisions of the Education Amendments Act of 1972.

enforcement by appointing conservatives to the Justice Department, the Civil Rights Commission, and other agencies and by slashing their budgets.

Congress stepped in to defend antidiscrimination programs after the Justice Department, in the case of *Grove City v. Bell* (1984), persuaded the Supreme Court to severely weaken Title IX of the Education Amendments Act of 1972, a key law promoting equal opportunity in education. In 1988, Congress passed the Civil Rights Restoration Act, which reversed the administration's victory in *Grove City* and banned any organization that practiced discrimination on the basis of race, color, national origin, sex, disability, or age from receiving government funds.

The *Grove City* decision reflected a rightward movement in the federal judiciary. With the opportunity to appoint half of the 761 federal court judges and three new Supreme Court justices, President Reagan encouraged this trend by carefully selecting conservative candidates. Thus, he turned the tide back toward strict construction—the literal interpretation of the Constitution that narrowly adheres to the words of its authors, thereby limiting judicial power to protect individual rights.

Feminism on the Defensive

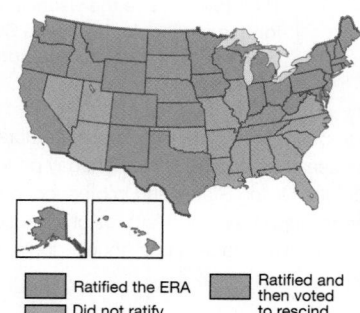

Ratified the ERA
Did not ratify the ERA
Ratified and then voted to rescind ratification

The Fight for the Equal Rights Amendment

Equal Rights Amendment (ERA)

▶ Constitutional amendment intended to guarantee women equality of rights under the law. Time ran out for ratification of the ERA in 1982.

A signal achievement of the New Right was capturing the Republican Party's position on women's rights. For the first time in its history, the Republican Party took an explicitly antifeminist tone, opposing both the **Equal Rights Amendment (ERA)** and a woman's right to abortion, key goals of women's rights activists. When the time limit for ratification of the ERA ran out in 1982, feminists suffered defeat on a key goal (see chapter 28).

Cast on the defensive, feminists focused more on women's economic and family problems, where they found some common ground with the Reagan administration. The Child Support Enforcement Amendments Act helped single and divorced mothers collect court-ordered child support payments from absent fathers. The Retirement Equity Act of 1984 benefited divorced and older women by strengthening their claims to their husbands' pensions and enabling women to qualify more easily for private retirement pensions.

Reagan eventually appointed three women to cabinet posts and, in 1981, selected the first woman, Sandra Day O'Connor, a moderate, for the Supreme Court, despite the Christian Right's objection to her support of abortion. But these actions accompanied a general decline in the number of women and minorities in high-level government positions. And with higher poverty rates than men, women suffered most from Reagan's cuts in social programs.

Although court decisions placed restrictions on women's ability to obtain abortions, feminists fought successfully to retain the basic principles of *Roe v. Wade*. Moreover, they won a key decision from the Supreme Court ruling that

CHAPTER LOCATOR | How did the Nixon presidency reflect the rise of postwar conservatism? | Why was the Watergate scandal significant?

sexual harassment in the workplace constituted sex discrimination. Feminists also made some gains at the state level in such areas as pay equity, rape, and domestic violence.

The Gay and Lesbian Rights Movement

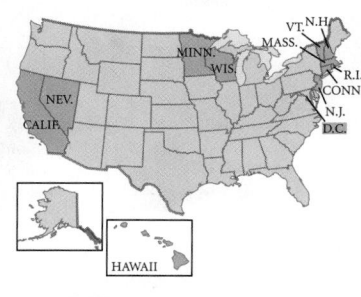

States with antidiscrimination laws

Antidiscrimination Laws for Gays and Lesbians, 1982–2000

In contrast to feminism and other social movements, gay and lesbian rights activism grew during the 1980s, galvanized in part by the discovery in 1981 of a devastating disease, **acquired immune deficiency syndrome (AIDS)**. Because initially the disease disproportionately affected male homosexuals in the United States, activists mobilized to promote public funding for AIDS education, prevention, and treatment.

The gay and lesbian rights movement helped closeted homosexuals "come out," and their visibility increased awareness, if not always acceptance, of homosexuality among the larger population. Beginning with the election of Elaine Noble to the Massachusetts legislature in 1974, several openly gay politicians won offices ranging from mayor to member of Congress, and the Democrats began to include gay rights in their party platforms. Activists organized gay rights marches throughout the country.

Popular attitudes about homosexuality moved toward greater tolerance but remained complex, leading to uneven changes in policies. Dozens of cities banned job discrimination against homosexuals, and beginning with Wisconsin in 1982, eleven states made sexual orientation a protected category under civil rights laws. Local governments and large corporations began to offer health insurance and other benefits to same-sex domestic partners.

Yet a strong countermovement challenged the drive for recognition of gay rights. The Christian Right targeted gays and lesbians as symbols of national immorality and succeeded in overturning some homosexual rights measures. Many states removed antisodomy laws from the books, but in 1986 the Supreme Court upheld the constitutionality of such laws. Until the Court reversed that opinion in 2003, more than a dozen states retained statutes that left homosexuals vulnerable to criminal charges for private consensual behavior.

acquired immune deficiency syndrome (AIDS)

▶ Deadly disease discovered in 1981. Because the disease at first disproportionately affected male homosexuals in the United States, AIDS education, prevention, and treatment became central concerns of gay rights activists.

QUICK REVIEW

What gains and setbacks did minorities, feminists, and gays and lesbians experience during the Reagan years?

Why did the "outsider" presidency of Jimmy Carter fail to gain broad support?

What conservative goals were realized in the Reagan administration?

What strategies did liberals use to fight the conservative turn?

How did Ronald Reagan's foreign policy affect the Cold War?

Conclusion: What was the long-term impact of the conservative turn?

How did Ronald Reagan's foreign policy affect the Cold War?

The Cold War Thaws U.S. president Ronald Reagan and Soviet premier Mikhail Gorbachev shake hands as they meet in June 1988 for a round of Strategic Arms Reduction Talks (START). Moving beyond the Strategic Arms Limitation Talks (SALT) of the 1970s, these negotiations aimed to reduce rather than limit nuclear warheads and the bombers that carried them. The talks culminated with a comprehensive treaty signed by Reagan's successor, George H. W. Bush, and Gorbachev in July 1991. Kenneth Jarecke/Contact Press Images.

REAGAN ACCELERATED THE ARMS BUILDUP that began under Carter and harshly censured the Soviet Union, calling it "an evil empire." Yet despite the new aggressiveness—or, as some argued, because of it—Reagan presided over the most impressive thaw in superpower conflict since the Cold War had begun. On the periphery of the Cold War, however, Reagan practiced militant anticommunism, assisting antileftist movements in Asia, Africa, and Central America and dispatching troops to the Middle East and the Caribbean.

Militarization and Interventions Abroad

Reagan expanded the military with new bombers and missiles, an enhanced nuclear force in Europe, a larger navy, and a rapid-deployment force. Throughout Reagan's presidency, defense spending averaged $216 billion a year, up from $158 billion in the Carter years and higher even than in the Vietnam era.

Reagan startled many of his own advisers in March 1983 by announcing plans for research on the Strategic Defense Initiative (SDI). Immediately dubbed "Star Wars" by critics who doubted its feasibility, the project would deploy lasers in space to destroy enemy missiles before they could reach their targets. Such a defense would upset the nuclear balance by allowing the United States to strike first and not fear retaliation. The Soviets reacted angrily because SDI violated the 1972 antiballistic missile treaty and because they would require huge investments to develop their own Star Wars technology. Subsequent administrations continued to spend billions on SDI research without producing a working system.

The U.S. military buildup could not extinguish the growing threat of terrorism by nonstate organizations that sought political objectives by attacking civilian populations. Terrorism had a long history throughout the world, but in the

CHAPTER LOCATOR | How did the Nixon presidency reflect the rise of postwar conservatism? | Why was the Watergate scandal significant?

850 CHAPTER 30 THE CONSERVATIVE TURN, 1969–1989

1970s and 1980s, Americans saw it escalate in the Middle East, where terrorist tactics were used by Palestinians after the Israeli occupation of the West Bank and by other groups hostile to Western policies. The terrorist organization Hezbollah, composed of Shiite Muslims and backed by Iran and Syria, arose in Lebanon in 1982 after Israeli forces invaded that country to stop the Palestine Liberation Organization (PLO) from using sanctuaries in Lebanon to launch attacks on Israel.

Reagan's effort to stabilize Lebanon by sending 2,000 marines to join an international peacekeeping mission failed. In April 1983, a suicide attack on the U.S. Embassy in Beirut killed 63 people, and in October a Hezbollah fighter drove a bomb-filled truck into a U.S. barracks there, killing 241 marines (see Map 30.3, page 841). The attack prompted the withdrawal of U.S. troops, and Lebanon remained in chaos, while incidents of murder, kidnapping, and hijacking by various Middle Eastern extremist groups continued.

Following a Cold War pattern begun under Eisenhower, the Reagan administration sought to contain leftist movements across the globe. In October 1983, 5,000 U.S. troops invaded Grenada, a small island nation in the Caribbean that had succumbed to a Marxist coup. In Asia, the United States moved more quietly, aiding the Afghan rebels' war against Afghanistan's Soviet-backed government. In the African nation of Angola, the United States armed rebel forces against the government supported by the Soviet Union and Cuba. Reagan also sided with the South African government, which was brutally suppressing black protest against apartheid, forcing Congress to override his veto in order to impose economic sanctions against South Africa.

Administration officials were most fearful of left-wing movements in Central America, which Reagan claimed could "destabilize the entire region from the Panama Canal to Mexico." When a leftist uprising occurred in El Salvador in 1981, the United States sent money and military advisers to prop up the authoritarian government. In neighboring Nicaragua, the administration aided the Contras (literally, "opposers"), an armed coalition seeking to unseat the left-wing Sandinistas, who had toppled a long-standing dictatorship.

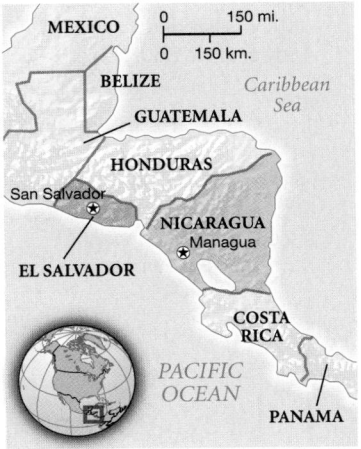

El Salvador and Nicaragua

The Iran-Contra Scandal

Fearing another Vietnam, many Americans opposed aligning the United States with reactionary forces not supported by the majority of Nicaraguans. Congress repeatedly instructed the president to stop aiding the Contras, but the administration continued to secretly provide them with weapons and training and helped wreck the Nicaraguan economy. With support for his government undermined, Nicaragua's president, Daniel Ortega, agreed to a political settlement, and when he was defeated by a coalition of all the opposition groups, he stepped aside.

Secret aid to the Contras was part of a larger project that came to be known as the **Iran-Contra scandal**. It began in 1985 when officials of the National Security Council and CIA arranged to sell arms to Iran, then in the midst of an eight-year war with neighboring Iraq, even while the United States supplied Iraq with funds and weapons. The purpose was to get Iran to pressure Hezbollah to release seven American hostages being held in Lebanon (see Map 30.3, page 841). Funds from the arms sales were then channeled to the Nicaraguan Contras. Over the objections of his secretary of state and secretary of defense, Reagan approved the

Iran-Contra scandal

▶ Reagan administration scandal that involved the sale of arms to Iran in exchange for the release of hostages held by Middle Eastern extremist groups, and the redirection of the proceeds of those sales to the Nicaraguan Contras. The Iran-Contra scandal was the most serious case of executive branch misconduct since Watergate.

| Why did the "outsider" presidency of Jimmy Carter fail to gain broad support? | What conservative goals were realized in the Reagan administration? | What strategies did liberals use to fight the conservative turn? | **How did Ronald Reagan's foreign policy affect the Cold War?** | Conclusion: What was the long-term impact of the conservative turn? |

CHRONOLOGY

1982
- Reagan sends 2,000 marines to Lebanon to join an international peacekeeping force.

1983
- Terrorist bomb kills 241 U.S. Marines in Beirut, Lebanon.
- Reagan announces plans for Strategic Defense Initiative ("Star Wars").
- United States invades Grenada.

1985
- Mikhail Gorbachev assumes power in the Soviet Union.

1986
- Iran-Contra scandal.

1987
- INF agreement eliminates all short- and medium-range missiles from Europe.

intermediate-range nuclear forces (INF) agreement

▶ Nuclear disarmament agreement reached between the United States and the Soviet Union in 1987, signifying a major thaw in the Cold War. The treaty eliminated all short- and medium-range missiles from Europe and provided for on-site inspection for the first time.

arms sales, but the three subsequently denied knowing that the proceeds were diverted to the Contras.

When news of the affair surfaced in November 1986, the Reagan administration faced serious charges. Investigations by an independent prosecutor appointed by Reagan led to a trial in which seven individuals pleaded guilty or were convicted of lying to Congress and destroying evidence. One felony conviction was later overturned on a technicality, and President George H. W. Bush pardoned the other six officials in December 1992. The independent prosecutor's final report found no evidence that Reagan had broken the law, but it concluded that he had known about the diversion of funds to the Contras and had "knowingly participated or at least acquiesced" in covering up the scandal—the most serious case of executive branch misconduct since Watergate.

A Thaw in Soviet-American Relations

A momentous reduction in Cold War tensions soon overshadowed the Iran-Contra scandal. The new Soviet-American accord depended both on Reagan's flexibility and on an innovative Soviet head of state who recognized that his country's domestic problems demanded an easing of Cold War antagonism. Mikhail Gorbachev assumed power in 1985 determined to revitalize an inefficient Soviet economy incapable of delivering basic consumer goods. Gorbachev introduced some elements of free enterprise and proclaimed a new era of *glasnost* (greater freedom of expression), eventually allowing contested elections and challenges to Communist rule.

Concerns about immense defense budgets moved both Reagan and Gorbachev to the negotiating table. With growing popular support for arms reductions, Reagan made disarmament a major goal in his last years in office and readily responded when Gorbachev took the initiative. Reagan and Gorbachev met four times between 1985 and 1988. Although Reagan's insistence on proceeding with SDI nearly killed the talks, by December 1987 the superpowers had completed an **intermediate-range nuclear forces (INF) agreement**. The INF treaty eliminated all short- and medium-range missiles from Europe and provided for on-site inspection for the first time. This was also the first time either nation had pledged to eliminate weapons already in place.

In 1988, Gorbachev further reduced tensions by announcing a gradual withdrawal from Afghanistan, which had become the Soviet equivalent of America's Vietnam. In addition, the Soviet Union, the United States, and Cuba agreed on a political settlement of the civil war in the African nation of Angola. In the Middle East, both superpowers supported a cease-fire and peace talks in the eight-year war between Iran and Iraq. Within three years, the Cold War that had defined the world for nearly half a century would be history.

> **QUICK REVIEW**

How did anticommunism shape Reagan's foreign policy?

CHAPTER LOCATOR | How did the Nixon presidency reflect the rise of postwar conservatism? | Why was the Watergate scandal significant?

Dirck Halstead/Getty Images.

Conclusion: What was the long-term impact of the conservative turn?

"OURS WAS THE FIRST REVOLUTION in the history of mankind that truly reversed the course of government," boasted Ronald Reagan in his farewell address in 1989. The word *revolution* exaggerated the change, but his administration did mark the slowdown or reversal of expanding federal budgets, programs, and regulations that had taken off in the 1930s.

Antigovernment sentiment grew along with the backlash against the reforms of the 1960s and the conduct of the Vietnam War. Watergate and other misdeeds of the Nixon administration further disillusioned Americans. Presidents Ford and Carter restored morality to the White House, but neither could solve the problems of slow economic growth, stagflation, and an increasing trade deficit. Even the Democrat Carter gave higher priority to fiscal austerity than to social reform, and he began the government's retreat from regulation of key industries.

A new conservative movement helped Reagan win the presidency and flourished during his administration. Reagan's tax cuts, combined with hefty increases in defense spending, created a federal deficit crisis that justified cuts in social welfare spending and made new federal initiatives unthinkable. Many Americans continued to support specific federal programs, but public sentiment about the government in general had taken a U-turn from the Roosevelt era. Instead of seeing the government as a helpful and problem-solving institution, many believed that not only was it ineffective at solving national problems, but it also often made things worse. As Reagan appointed new justices, the Supreme Court retreated from liberalism, curbing the government's authority to protect individual rights and regulate the economy.

With the economic recovery that set in after 1982 and his optimistic rhetoric, Reagan lifted the confidence of Americans about their nation and its promise—confidence that had eroded with the economic and foreign policy blows of the 1970s. Beginning his presidency with harsh rhetoric against the Soviet Union and a huge military buildup, Reagan helped move the two superpowers to the highest level of cooperation since the Cold War began. That cooperation signaled developments that would transform U.S.-Soviet relations—and the world—in the next decade.

SO NOW YOU KNOW

The United States began a military buildup in Afghanistan in 1979 to support Muslims who were fighting the Soviet troops sent to protect the country's newly elected Communist government. These rebels succeeded in ousting the pro-Soviet government, but the government they helped install harbored the Islamic fundamentalists who would attack the United States in 2001.

Why did the "outsider" presidency of Jimmy Carter fail to gain broad support?	What conservative goals were realized in the Reagan administration?	What strategies did liberals use to fight the conservative turn?	How did Ronald Reagan's foreign policy affect the Cold War?	Conclusion: What was the long-term impact of the conservative turn?

CHAPTER 30 STUDY GUIDE

Online Study Guide
bedfordstmartins.com/roarkunderstanding

STEP 1 GETTING STARTED

Below are terms that every college graduate should know about this period in American history. Can you identify each term below and explain why it matters? To do this exercise online or to download this chart, visit bedfordstmartins.com/roarkunderstanding.

TERM	WHO OR WHAT & WHEN	WHY IT MATTERS
Watergate, p. 834		
Gerald R. Ford, p. 835		
James Earl "Jimmy" Carter Jr., p. 836		
Camp David accords, p. 841		
Iran hostage crisis, p. 842		
Ronald Reagan, p. 843		
Christian Right, p. 844		
supply-side economics, p. 844		
Equal Rights Amendment (ERA), p. 848		
acquired immune deficiency syndrome (AIDS), p. 849		
Iran-Contra scandal, p. 851		
intermediate-range nuclear forces (INF) agreement, p. 852		

STEP 2 MOVING BEYOND THE BASICS

The exercise below represents a more advanced understanding of the chapter material. Using the chart, describe the major concerns of the groups that made up the Reagan coalition. Then describe each group's expectations of the Reagan administration. Finally, list the Reagan administration policies that addressed the major concerns of each group. When you are done, consider the following questions: What concerns and expectations, if any, did the various groups have in common? What tensions might there have been between component groups of the Reagan coalition? To do this exercise online or to download this chart, visit bedfordstmartins.com/roarkunderstanding.

Reagan coalition group	Major concerns	Expectations	Administration policies
Free-market advocates			
Militant anti-Communists			
Fundamentalist Christians			
White southerners			
Reagan Democrats			

PUTTING IT ALL TOGETHER

Now that you've reviewed various parts of the chapter, take a step back and try to see the big picture by answering these questions. Remember to use specific examples from the chapter in your answers. To do this exercise online, visit bedfordstmartins.com/roarkunderstanding.

NIXON AND WATERGATE

▶ How did the Nixon administration appeal to the conservative movement?

▶ What were Nixon's biggest mistakes in the Watergate scandal?

THE CARTER ADMINISTRATION

▶ Should Jimmy Carter be considered a liberal? Why or why not?

▶ Is it fair to describe the Carter administration as a "failed presidency"? Why or why not?

RONALD REAGAN AND THE CONSERVATIVE TURN

▶ What did voters find appealing about Ronald Reagan in 1980? What groups were most attracted to his message?

▶ What specific policies of the Reagan administration satisfied conservative goals? What did conservatives fail to win?

LOOKING BACKWARD, LOOKING AHEAD

▶ How did Reagan's experience of the Cold War during the 1950s and 1960s influence his foreign policy?

▶ In what ways does Ronald Reagan's presidency continue to shape the American political landscape?

IN YOUR OWN WORDS

Imagine that you must explain chapter 30 to someone who hasn't read it. What would be the most important points to include and why?

31
FACING THE CHALLENGES OF A CHANGING WORLD
SINCE 1989

> This chapter explores the changing nature of American politics and foreign policy from 1989 to the present. It examines the end of the Cold War during the presidency of George H. W. Bush, the domestic and foreign policies of the Clinton administration, and the George W. Bush administration's departures from previous U.S. policy in the wake of the September 11, 2001, terrorist attacks, and the election of Barack Obama.

> How did the United States respond to the end of the Cold War and tensions in the Middle East?

> What explains the Clinton administration's move to the right?

> How did President Clinton respond to the challenges of globalization?

> How did President George W. Bush change American politics and foreign policy?

> Conclusion: How have Americans debated the role of the government?

DID YOU KNOW?

By 2006, immigrants comprised 12.4 percent of the U.S. population.

New U.S. citizens. New citizens take the oath of allegiance at Monticello, Virginia, the historic home of Thomas Jefferson. July 4, 2008.

How did the United States respond to the end of the Cold War and tensions in the Middle East?

The Gulf War These soldiers arriving in Dhahran, Saudi Arabia, were part of the massive military buildup in the Persian Gulf area before the U.S.-led coalition drove Iraqi forces out of Kuwait. For the first time, women served in combat-support positions piloting planes and helicopters, directing artillery, and fighting fires. Bettman/Corbis.

VICE PRESIDENT George H. W. Bush announced his bid for the presidency in the 1988 election, declaring, "We don't need radical new directions." As president, Bush proposed few domestic initiatives. Yet as the most dramatic changes since the 1940s swept through the world, Bush confronted situations that did not fit the simpler free world versus communism framework that had guided foreign policy since World War II. Most Americans approved of Bush's handling of two challenges to U.S. foreign policy: the disintegration of the Soviet Union and its hold over Eastern Europe, and Iraq's invasion of neighboring Kuwait. But voters' concern over a sluggish economy limited Bush to one term in the White House.

Gridlock in Government

The son of a wealthy New England senator, George Herbert Walker Bush served in Congress during the 1960s and headed the CIA during the Nixon and Ford years. In 1980, Bush adjusted his more moderate policy positions to fit Reagan's conservative agenda and accepted second place on the Republican ticket. At the end of Reagan's second term, Republicans rewarded him with the presidential nomination.

Several candidates competed for the Democratic nomination in 1988. The Reverend Jesse Jackson made an impressive bid, winning several primaries and seven million votes. But a more centrist candidate, Massachusetts governor Michael Dukakis, won the nomination. On election day, Bush won 54 percent of the vote, but the Democrats gained seats in Congress.

CHAPTER LOCATOR | How did the United States respond to the end of the Cold War and tensions in the Middle East?

President Bush promised "a kinder, gentler nation" and was more inclined than Reagan to approve government activity in the private sphere. For example, he signed the Clean Air Act of 1990, the most comprehensive environmental law in history. Some forty million Americans reaped the benefits of a second regulatory measure, the Americans with Disabilities Act, in 1990. Job discrimination against people with disabilities was banned, and private businesses and public facilities had to be made handicapped accessible.

Yet Bush also needed to satisfy party conservatives. His most famous campaign pledge had been "Read my lips: no new taxes," and he opposed most proposals requiring additional federal funds. Bush vetoed thirty-six bills, including those lifting abortion restrictions, extending unemployment benefits, raising taxes, and mandating family and medical leave for workers. Press reports increasingly used the words *stalemate*, *gridlock*, and *divided government*.

Continuing a trend begun during the Reagan years, states tried to compensate for this paralysis, becoming more innovative than Washington. States passed bills to block corporate takeovers, establish parental leave policies, improve food labeling, and protect the environment. In the 1980s, a few states began to pass measures guaranteeing gay and lesbian rights. In the 1990s, dozens of cities passed ordinances requiring businesses receiving tax abatements or other city benefits to pay wages well above the federal minimum wage. And in 1999, California passed a gun control bill with much tougher restrictions on assault weapons than reformers had been able to get through Congress.

A huge federal budget deficit inherited from the Reagan administration impelled the president in 1990 to abandon his "no new taxes" pledge, outraging conservatives. The new law authorized modest tax increases for high-income Americans and higher taxes on gasoline, cigarettes, alcohol, and luxury items. Neither the new revenues nor controls on spending curbed the deficit, which was boosted by rising costs for Social Security, Medicare, and Medicaid and spending on war and natural disasters.

Bush also continued Reagan's efforts to create a more conservative Supreme Court. His first nominee, federal appeals court judge David Souter, was a moderate. But in 1991, when the only African American on the Court, Justice Thurgood Marshall, retired, Bush set off a national controversy. He nominated Clarence Thomas, a conservative black appeals court judge who had opposed affirmative action as head of the Equal Employment Opportunity Commission (EEOC) under Reagan. Charging that Thomas would not protect minority rights, civil rights groups and other liberal organizations fought the nomination. Then Anita Hill, a black law professor and former EEOC employee, shook the confirmation process by accusing Thomas of sexual harassment.

Bush and Taxes

When George H. W. Bush accepted the Republican nomination for president in 1988, he addressed an issue central to conservative politics. "Read my lips," he told convention delegates: "No new taxes." When Bush was forced to break his promise, many Republicans were outraged. Here, conservative cartoonist Scott Stantis, then at the *Arizona Republic* in Phoenix, likens Bush to Pinocchio, whose nose grew when he lied. Scott Stantis/Copley News Service.

▶ FOR MORE HELP ANALYZING THIS IMAGE, see the visual activity for this chapter in the Online Study Guide at bedfordstmartins.com/roarkunderstanding.

What explains the Clinton administration's move to the right?

How did President Clinton respond to the challenges of globalization?

How did President George W. Bush change American politics and foreign policy?

Conclusion: How have Americans debated the role of the government?

1988
- Republican George H. W. Bush is elected president.

1989
- Communism collapses in Eastern Europe.
- United States invades Panama.

1990
- Americans with Disabilities Act.
- Clean Air Act.

1991
- Persian Gulf War.
- Soviet Union dissolves.

1992
- Democrat William Jefferson "Bill" Clinton is elected president.

Colin Powell

▶ Chairman of the Joint Chiefs of Staff under President George H. W. Bush and secretary of state under President George W. Bush. In 2001, Powell became the first African American secretary of state. Disagreements between Powell and other members of the Bush administration over the Iraq War led to his resignation in 2005.

Saddam Hussein

▶ Iraqi dictator from 1979 to 2003. Hussein's decision to invade Kuwait in 1990 sparked the Persian Gulf War. In 2003, President Bush declared war on Iraq, citing Hussein's violation of UN resolutions and alleged connections to Al Qaeda. Hussein's government was quickly toppled, and he was eventually executed by Iraqi officials.

Before the Senate Judiciary Committee, Thomas angrily denied the charges, claiming that he was the victim of a "high-tech lynching for uppity blacks." Hill's testimony failed to sway the Senate, which voted narrowly to confirm Thomas, solidifying the Supreme Court's shift to the right.

Going to War in Central America and the Persian Gulf

President Bush won greater support for his actions abroad. In Central America, the United States had tolerated and, in fact, paid Panamanian dictator Manuel Noriega for helping the Contras in Nicaragua and providing the CIA with information about Communist activities in the region. But in 1989, after Noriega was indicted for drug trafficking by an American grand jury and after his troops killed an American marine, President Bush ordered 25,000 military personnel into Panama. In Operation Just Cause, U.S. forces quickly overcame Noriega's troops, sustaining 23 deaths, while hundreds of Panamanians, including many civilians, died. Chairman of the Joint Chiefs of Staff **Colin Powell** noted that "our euphoria over our victory in Just Cause was not universal." Both the United Nations and the Organization of American States censured the unilateral action by the United States.

In contrast, Bush's second military engagement rested solidly on international approval. Considering Iran to be America's major enemy in the Middle East, U.S. officials had quietly assisted the Iraqi dictator **Saddam Hussein** in the Iran-Iraq war, which began in 1980 and ended inconclusively in 1988. In August 1990, Hussein sent troops into the small, oil-rich country of Kuwait to the south (**Map 31.1**), and within days the invasion neared the Saudi Arabian border, threatening the world's largest oil reserves. President Bush quickly ordered a massive mobilization of American forces and assembled an international coalition to stand up to Iraq. He invoked principles of national self-determination and international law, but long-standing interests in Middle Eastern oil also drove the U.S. response.

The UN declared an embargo on Iraqi oil and authorized the use of force if Iraq did not withdraw from Kuwait by January 15, 1991. By then, the United States had deployed 400,000 soldiers to Saudi Arabia, joined by 265,000 troops from some two dozen other nations, including several Arab states. "The community of nations has resolutely gathered to condemn and repel lawless aggression," Bush announced. "With few exceptions, the world now stands as one."

With Iraqi forces still in Kuwait, in January 1991 Bush asked Congress to approve war. Considerable sentiment favored waiting to see if the embargo and other means would force Hussein to back down. In the end, Congress debated for three days and then authorized war by a margin of five votes in the Senate and sixty-seven in the House. On January 17, 1991, the U.S.-led coalition launched Operation Desert Storm, a forty-day bombing campaign against Iraqi military targets, power plants, oil refineries, and transportation networks. Having severely crippled Iraq by air, the coalition then stormed into Kuwait, forcing Iraqi troops to withdraw (see Map 31.1).

"By God, we've kicked the Vietnam syndrome once and for all," President George H. W. Bush exulted on March 1, 1991. Most Americans found no moral ambiguity in the **Persian Gulf War** and took pride in the display of military prowess. The

CHAPTER LOCATOR | How did the United States respond to the end of the Cold War and tensions in the Middle East?

860 CHAPTER 31
FACING THE CHALLENGES OF A CHANGING WORLD, SINCE 1989

MAP 31.1 ■ Events in the Middle East, 1989–2009

During the Persian Gulf War of 1991, Egypt, Syria, and other Middle Eastern nations joined the coalition against Iraq, and the twenty-two-member Arab League supported the war as a means to liberate Kuwait. After September 11, 2001, the Arab League approved of U.S. military operations in Afghanistan because the attacks "were an attack on the common values of the world, not just on the United States." Yet, except for the countries where the United States had military bases—Bahrain, Kuwait, Qatar, and Saudi Arabia—no Arab country supported the American invasion and occupation of Iraq in 2003. Arab hostility toward the United States also reflected the deterioration of Israeli-Palestinian relations after 1999, as Arabs charged that the United States allowed Israel to deny Palestinians land and liberty.

> ► FOR MORE HELP ANALYZING THIS MAP, see the map activity for this chapter in the Online Study Guide at bedfordstmartins.com/roarkunderstanding.

United States stood at the apex of global leadership, steering a coalition in which Arab nations fought beside their former colonial rulers.

Some Americans criticized the Bush administration for ending the war without deposing Hussein. But Bush pointed to the UN mandate limiting the mission to driving Iraqi forces out of Kuwait and to Middle Eastern leaders' concern that an invasion of Iraq would destabilize the region. His secretary of defense, Richard Cheney, doubted that coalition forces could secure a stable government to replace Hussein and considered the price of a long occupation too high.

Yet Middle Eastern stability remained elusive. Israel, which had endured Iraqi missile attacks, was more secure, but the Israeli-Palestinian conflict remained intractable. Despite military losses, Saddam Hussein remained in power and

Persian Gulf War

► 1991 war between Iraq and an international coalition headed by the United States. The war was sparked by the 1990 invasion of Kuwait by Iraqi forces. Overwhelming American military superiority led to a quick victory for coalition forces. The Iraqi dictator Saddam Hussein was, however, left in power.

| What explains the Clinton administration's move to the right? | How did President Clinton respond to the challenges of globalization? | How did President George W. Bush change American politics and foreign policy? | Conclusion: How have Americans debated the role of the government? |

turned on Iraqi Kurds and Shiite Muslims whom the United States had encouraged to rebel. And he found ways to conceal weapons development from UN inspectors before he threw them out in 1998.

The End of the Cold War

The Soviet Union supported the American position in the Persian Gulf War, marking a momentous change in relations between the United States and the Soviet Union. The progressive forces that Gorbachev had encouraged in the Communist world (see chapter 30) swept through Eastern Europe in 1989, when popular uprisings demanded an end to state repression and inefficient economic bureaucracies. Communist governments toppled like dominoes (**Map 31.2**), virtually without bloodshed, because Gorbachev refused to prop them up with Soviet armies.

Unification of East and West Germany sped to completion in 1990, and former iron curtain countries such as Hungary and Poland lined up to join NATO. Although U.S. military forces remained in Europe as part of NATO, Europe no

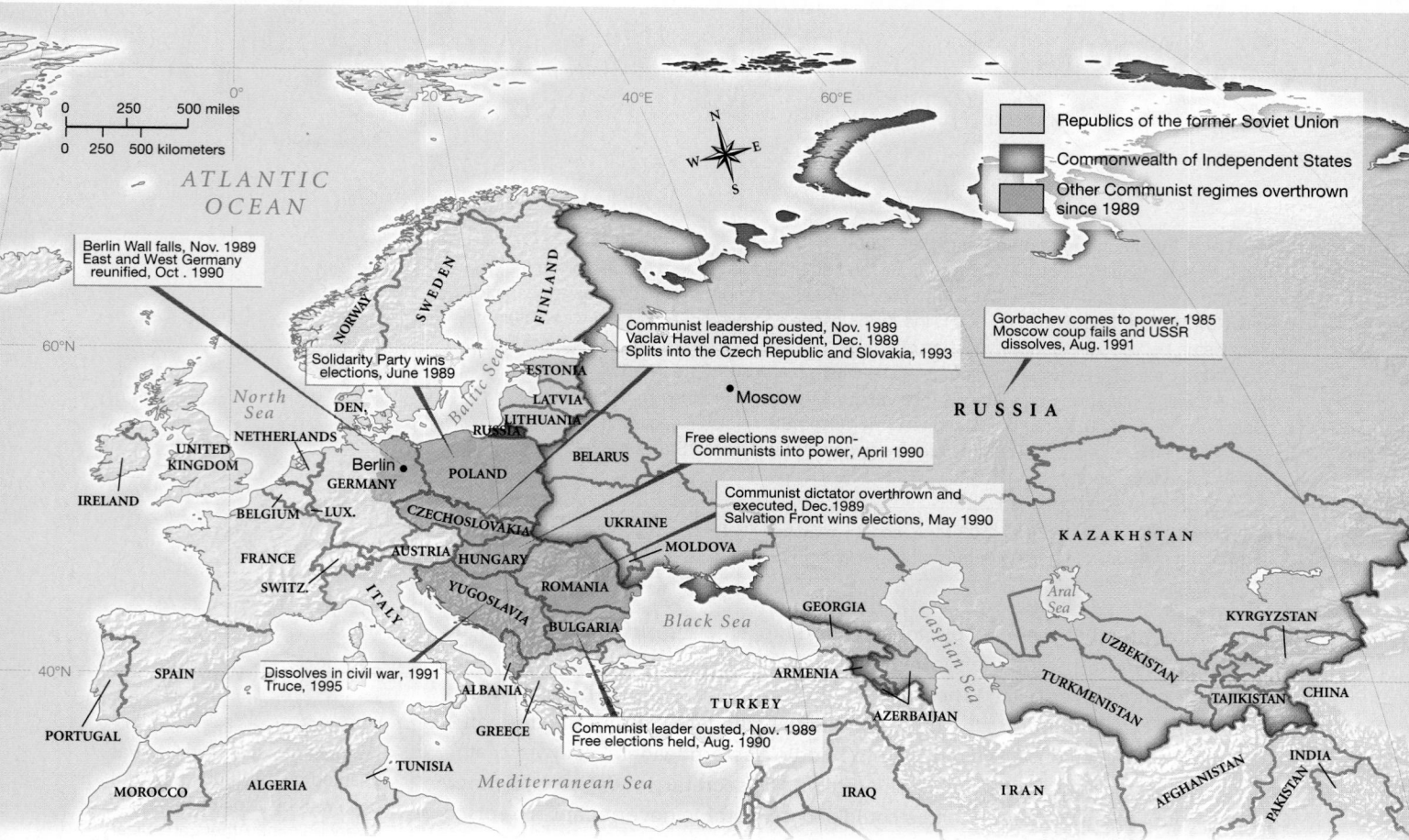

MAP 31.2 ■ Events in Eastern Europe, 1989–2002
The overthrow of Communist governments throughout Eastern Europe and the splintering of the Soviet Union into more than a dozen separate nations were among the most momentous changes in world history since World War II.

CHAPTER LOCATOR | How did the United States respond to the end of the Cold War and tensions in the Middle East?

longer depended on the United States for its security. Its economic clout also grew as Western Europe formed a common economic market in 1992.

Inspired by the liberation of Eastern Europe, republics within the Soviet Union soon sought their own independence. In December 1991, Boris Yeltsin, president of the Russian Republic, announced that Russia and eleven other republics had formed a new entity, the Commonwealth of Independent States, and other former Soviet states declared their independence. With nothing left to govern, Gorbachev resigned. The Soviet Union had dissolved.

China and North Korea resisted the liberalizing tides sweeping the world. In 1989, Chinese soldiers killed hundreds of pro-democracy demonstrators in Tiananmen Square in Beijing, and the Communist government arrested some ten thousand reformers. North Korea remained under a Communist dictatorship committed to developing nuclear weapons. "The post–Cold War world is decidedly not post-nuclear," declared one U.S. official. In 1990, the United States and the Soviet Union signed the Strategic Arms Reduction Talks treaty, which cut about 30 percent of each superpower's nuclear arsenal. And in 1996, the UN General Assembly overwhelmingly approved a total nuclear test ban treaty. Yet India and Pakistan, hostile neighbors, refused to sign the treaty, and both exploded atomic devices in 1998. Moreover, the Republican-controlled Senate defeated U.S. ratification of the test ban treaty. The potential for rogue nations and terrorist groups to develop nuclear weapons posed an ongoing threat to international peace and security.

The 1992 Election

In March 1991, Bush's chances for reelection in 1992 looked golden. With Bush's approval rating at 88 percent, most prominent Democrats opted out of the presidential race. But that did not deter William Jefferson "Bill" Clinton, who at age forty-five had served as governor of Arkansas for twelve years. Like Carter in 1976, Clinton and his running mate, Tennessee senator Albert Gore Jr., presented themselves as "New Democrats" and sought to rid the party of its liberal image.

Clinton promised to work for the "forgotten middle class," who "do the work, pay the taxes, raise the kids, and play by the rules." Disavowing the "tax and spend" label that Republicans pinned on his party, he promised a tax cut for the middle class, pledged to reinvigorate government and the economy, and vowed "to put an end to welfare as we know it." Bush was vulnerable to voters' concerns about the ailing economy, as unemployment reached 7 percent. The popularity of a third candidate, self-made Texas billionaire H. Ross Perot, revealed Americans' frustrations with government and the major parties.

Fifty-five percent of those eligible voted, just barely reversing the thirty-year decline in voter turnout. Clinton won 43 percent of the popular vote, Bush 38 percent, and Perot 19 percent—the strongest third-party finish in eighty years.

QUICK REVIEW <

What were the achievements and failures of George H. W. Bush's presidency?

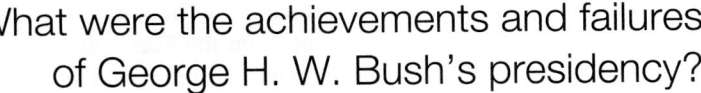

What explains the Clinton administration's move to the right?

How did President Clinton respond to the challenges of globalization?

How did President George W. Bush change American politics and foreign policy?

Conclusion: How have Americans debated the role of the government?

> # What explains the Clinton administration's move to the right?

Clinton and Gore on Tour

The gregarious Bill Clinton excelled at campaigning, and the youth of the first baby boomer candidates appealed to many. During the 1992 presidential election, Clinton and his wife, Hillary—with running mate Al Gore and his wife, Tipper—went out on bus tours as a way of demonstrating the Democrats' connection to ordinary people. Ira Wyman/Sygma/Corbis.

BILL CLINTON'S ASSERTION that "the era of big government is over" reflected the Democratic Party's move to the right that had begun with Jimmy Carter in the 1970s. Clinton did not completely abandon liberal principles. Yet his administration attended more to the concerns of middle-class Americans than to the needs of the disadvantaged.

Clinton's eight-year presidency witnessed the longest economic boom in U.S. history and ended with a budget surplus. Although various factors generated the prosperity, many Americans identified Clinton with the buoyant economy, elected him to a second term, and continued to support him even when his reckless sexual behavior resulted in impeachment. The scandal, however, crippled Clinton's leadership in his last years in office.

Clinton's Promise of Change

Clinton wanted to restore confidence in government as a force for good but also to avoid alienating antigovernment voters. The huge budget deficit that he inherited—$4.4 trillion in 1993—further precluded substantial federal initiatives. Moreover, Ross Perot's challenges denied Clinton a majority of the popular vote in both 1992 and 1996, and the Republicans controlled Congress for all but his first two years in office. Throughout most of his presidency, Clinton was burdened by investigations into past financial activities and private indiscretions.

Despite these obstacles, Clinton achieved a number of incremental reforms. He used his executive authority to ease restrictions on abortion and signed several bills that Republicans had previously blocked. Most significantly, Clinton pushed through a substantial increase in the Earned Income Tax Credit (EITC) for low-wage earners, a program begun in 1975. The EITC gave subsidies to people who worked full-time at meager wages in order to lift their family income above the poverty line. By 2003, some fifteen million low-income families were benefiting from the EITC, almost half of them minorities. One expert called it "the largest antipoverty program since the Great Society."

CHAPTER LOCATOR | How did the United States respond to the end of the Cold War and tensions in the Middle East?

Liberal Reforms under President Clinton

Family and Medical Leave Act of 1993
Violence against Women Act of 1994
Stricter air pollution controls and greater protection for national forests and parks
A minimum-wage increase
Expansion of aid for college students
Expansion of the Earned Income Tax Credit

Shortly before Clinton took office, the economy had begun to rebound, and the boom that followed helped boost his popularity through the 1990s. Economic expansion, along with budget cuts, tax increases, and declining unemployment, produced a budget surplus in 1998, the first since 1969. Despite a substantial tax cut in 1997 that reduced levies on estates and capital gains and provided tax credits for families with children and for higher education, the surplus grew.

Clinton failed, however, to provide universal health insurance or to curb skyrocketing medical costs. Under the direction of First Lady Hillary Rodham Clinton and with very little congressional consultation, the administration proposed an ambitious, complicated plan that the health care industry charged would increase taxes and government interference in medical decisions. Congress enacted piecemeal reform, such as underwriting health care for five million uninsured children, but affordable health care for all remained elusive.

Pledging to change the face of government to one that "looked like America," Clinton built on the gradual progress women and minorities had made since the 1960s, appointing the most diverse group of department heads ever assembled, including six women, three African Americans, and two Latinos. Secretary of Commerce Norman Y. Mineta became the first Asian American to hold a cabinet post. Janet Reno became the first female attorney general and Madeleine K. Albright the first female secretary of state. Clinton's judicial appointments had-

CHRONOLOGY

1992
– Democrat William Jefferson "Bill" Clinton is elected president.

1993
– Clinton announces "don't ask, don't tell" policy for gays in the military.
– Family and Medical Leave Act.

1995
– Bombing of a federal building in Oklahoma City kills 169.

1996
– Personal Responsibility and Work Opportunity Reconciliation Act.
– President Clinton is reelected.

1997
– Tax cut is enacted.

1998
– President Clinton is impeached.

1999
– Senate trial fails to approve articles of impeachment.

Clinton's Appointments

Not only did President Clinton appoint more women to high government posts than any previous president, but he also broke new ground by appointing them to offices traditionally considered to be male territory. Here Secretary of State Madeleine Albright (left) and Attorney General Janet Reno (second from right) applaud Clinton's 1999 State of the Union address with other cabinet members. AP/Wide World.

What explains the Clinton administration's move to the right?	How did President Clinton respond to the challenges of globalization?	How did President George W. Bush change American politics and foreign policy?	Conclusion: How have Americans debated the role of the government?

a similar cast, and in 1993 he named the second woman to the Supreme Court, Ruth Bader Ginsburg, whose arguments before she became an appeals court judge had won key women's rights rulings from the Supreme Court.

The Clinton Administration Moves Right

The 1994 elections swept away the Democratic majorities in Congress and helped push the Clinton administration to the right. Led by Representative Newt Gingrich of Georgia, Republicans claimed the 1994 election as a mandate for their "contract with America," a conservative platform to end "government that is too big, too intrusive, and too easy with the public's money" and to elect "a Congress that respects the values and shares the faith of the American family."

The most extreme antigovernment sentiment developed far from Washington in the form of grassroots armed militias. They celebrated white Christian supremacy and reflected conservatives' hostility to such diverse things as taxes and the United Nations. The militia movement grew after government agents stormed the headquarters of an armed religious cult in Waco, Texas, in April 1993, killing more than 80. On the second anniversary of that event, a bomb leveled a federal building in Oklahoma City, taking 169 lives in the worst terrorist attack in the nation's history up to that point.

Clinton bowed to conservative views on gay and lesbian rights, backing away from a campaign promise to lift the ban on gays in the military. When military leaders and key legislators objected, he reverted to a **"don't ask, don't tell" policy** in 1993, forbidding officials from asking military personnel about their sexual orientation but allowing the dismissal of soldiers who said they were gay or engaged in homosexual behavior. In 1996, Clinton signed the Defense of Marriage Act, prohibiting the federal government from recognizing state-licensed marriages between same-sex couples.

Nonetheless, gays and lesbians continued to make strides as attitudes about homosexuality became more tolerant. By 2006, more than half of the five hundred largest companies provided health benefits to same-sex domestic partners and included sexual orientation in their nondiscrimination policies. More than twenty-five states banned discrimination in public employment, and many of those laws extended to private employment, housing, and education. By 2009, gay marriage was legal in Massachusetts, Connecticut, Vermont, and Iowa, and several states recognized civil unions and domestic partnerships, extending to same-sex couples the rights available to married couples in legal matters such as inheritance, taxation, and medical decisions.

Clinton's efforts to cast himself as a centrist were apparent in his handling of the New Deal program Aid to Families with Dependent Children (AFDC), which most people called welfare. Public sentiment about poverty had shifted since the 1960s. Instead of blaming poverty on the lack of adequate jobs or other external circumstances, more people blamed the poor themselves and insisted that welfare programs trapped the poor in cycles of dependency.

By vetoing two welfare reform bills, Clinton forced a less punitive measure, which he signed as the 1996 election approached. The Personal Responsibility and Work Opportunity Reconciliation Act abolished AFDC. The law provided grants to the states to assist the poor, but it limited welfare payments to two years, regardless of whether the recipient could find a job, and it set a lifetime

"don't ask, don't tell" policy

▶ Military policy announced by President Clinton in 1993 that barred officials from inquiring into the sexual orientation of military personnel but permitted the dismissal of personnel who admitted to being gay or engaged in homosexual behavior. The policy represented a retreat from Clinton's campaign promise to lift the ban on gays in the military and resulted in a significant increase in discharges of homosexuals from the armed forces.

CHAPTER LOCATOR | How did the United States respond to the end of the Cold War and tensions in the Middle East?

limit of aid at five years. Reflecting growing controversy over immigration, the law also barred legal immigrants from obtaining food stamps and other benefits and allowed states to stop Medicaid for legal immigrants.

Clinton's signature on the new law denied Republicans a partisan issue in the 1996 presidential campaign. The president ran as a moderate who would save the country from extremist Republicans, while the Republican Party also moved to the center, nominating Kansan Robert Dole, a World War II hero and former Senate majority leader. Clinton won 49 percent of the votes; 41 percent went to Dole and 9 percent to third-party candidate Ross Perot. Although Clinton won reelection, voters sent a Republican majority back to Congress.

Impeaching the President

Despite his continuing popularity, Clinton's presidency was hampered by scandals and an impeachment trial. Early in his presidency, charges related to firings of White House staff, political use of FBI records, and "Whitewater"—the nickname for real estate dealings that the Clintons had conducted in Arkansas—led to an official investigation by an independent prosecutor. The president also faced a sexual harassment lawsuit filed in 1994 by a state employee. A federal court threw out that case in 1998, but another sexual scandal more seriously threatened Clinton's presidency.

In January 1998, Kenneth Starr, independent prosecutor for Whitewater, began to investigate the charge that Clinton had had sexual relations with a twenty-one-year-old White House intern and then lied about it to a federal grand jury. After vehemently denying the charge, Clinton subsequently bowed to the mounting evidence against him. Starr prepared a case for the House of Representatives, which in December 1998 voted to impeach the president for perjury and obstruction of justice. Clinton became the second president (after Andrew Johnson, in 1868) to be impeached by the House and tried by the Senate.

The Senate trial took place in early 1999. Most Americans condemned the president's behavior but approved of the job he was doing and opposed removal from office. With a two-thirds majority needed for conviction, the Senate voted 45 to 55 on the perjury count and 50 to 50 on the obstruction of justice count. A majority, including some Republicans, seemed to agree with a Clinton supporter that the president's behavior, though "indefensible, outrageous, unforgivable, shameless," did not warrant his removal from office.

The investigation that triggered events leading up to impeachment ended in 2000 when the independent prosecutor reported insufficient evidence of illegalities related to the Whitewater land deals. Although more than 60 percent of Americans gave Clinton high marks on his job performance throughout the scandal, it distracted him from domestic and international problems and precluded the possibility of significant policy advances in his last years in office.

The Booming Economy of the 1990s

Clinton's ability to weather the impeachment crisis owed much to the prosperous economy, which in 1991 began its longest period of expansion in U.S. history. The president took credit for the thriving economy, and his policies did contribute to

| What explains the Clinton administration's move to the right? | How did President Clinton respond to the challenges of globalization? | How did President George W. Bush change American politics and foreign policy? | Conclusion: How have Americans debated the role of the government? |

867

the boom. He made deficit reduction a priority, and in exchange the Federal Reserve Board and bond market traders lowered interest rates, encouraging economic expansion by making money easier to borrow. Businesses also prospered because they had squeezed down their costs through restructuring and laying off workers. Economic problems in Europe and Asia helped American firms become more competitive in the international market. And the computer revolution and the application of information technology boosted productivity.

The Booming Economy of the 1990s

Gross domestic product grew by more than one-third.
Thirteen million new jobs were created.
Inflation remained in check.
Unemployment dropped to 4 percent.
The stock market soared.

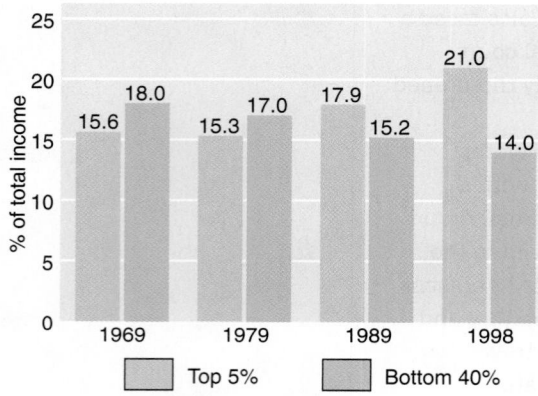

FIGURE 31.1 ■ The Growth of Inequality: Changes in Family Income, 1969–1998

For most of the post–World War II period, income increased for all groups on the economic ladder. But after 1979, the income of the poorest families actually declined, while the income of the richest 20 percent of the population grew substantially. Adapted from the *New York Times*, 1989.

People at all income levels benefited from the economic boom, but the gaps between the rich and the poor and between the wealthy and the middle class, which had been growing since the 1970s, failed to narrow (**Figure 31.1**). This persistence of inequality was linked in part to the growing use of information technology, which increased demand for highly skilled workers, while the movement of manufacturing jobs abroad diminished opportunities and wages for the less skilled. In addition, deregulation and the continuing decline of unions hurt less-skilled workers, tax cuts had favored the better-off, and the national minimum wage failed to keep up with inflation.

Although more minorities than ever attained middle-class status, in general people of color remained lowest on the economic ladder. For instance, in 2005 the median income for white households surpassed $50,000, but it stood at only $31,000 and $36,000 for African American and Latino households, respectively. In 2005, poverty afflicted about 25 percent of blacks, 22 percent of Latinos, and 11.1 percent of Asian Americans, in contrast to 8.3 percent of whites.

QUICK REVIEW

What policies of the Clinton administration reflected the president's efforts to move his party to the right?

CHAPTER LOCATOR | How did the United States respond to the end of the Cold War and tensions in the Middle East?

CHAPTER 31

868 FACING THE CHALLENGES OF A CHANGING WORLD, SINCE 1989

How did President Clinton respond to the challenges of globalization?

U.S. Troops in Kosovo In 1999, American troops joined a NATO peacekeeping unit in the former Yugoslav province of Kosovo to assist the return of the ethnic Albanians after a U.S.-led NATO bombing campaign forced the Serbian army to withdraw. Here, an Albanian boy walks beside Specialist Brent Baldwin from Jonesville, Michigan, as he patrols the town of Gnjilane in southeast Kosovo in May 2000. Wide World Photos, Inc.

AMERICA'S ECONOMIC SUCCESS in the 1990s was linked to its dominance in the world economy. From that position, President Clinton tried to shape the tremendous transformations occurring in a process called globalization—the growing integration and interdependence of national citizens and economies. Clinton agreed with George H. W. Bush that the United States must retain its economic and military dominance over all other nations. Yet no new global strategy emerged to replace the containment of communism as the decisive factor in the exercise of American power abroad.

Defining America's Place in a New World Order

In 1991, President George H. W. Bush declared a "new world order" emerging from the ashes of the Cold War. As the sole superpower, the United States was determined not to let any nation challenge its military superiority or global leadership. (See "Global Comparison," page 870.) Yet policymakers struggled to define guiding principles for deciding when and how to use the nation's military and diplomatic power in a post–Cold War world. Combating Saddam Hussein's aggression seemed the obvious course of action in 1991, but dealing with other areas of instability proved more difficult.

Africa was a case in point. In 1992, guided largely by humanitarian concern, President Bush had attached U.S. forces to a UN operation in the small northern African country of Somalia, where famine and civil war raged. In 1993, President Clinton allowed that humanitarian mission to turn into "nation building"—an effort to establish a stable government—and eighteen U.S. soldiers were killed. The outcry at home suggested that most citizens were unwilling to sacrifice lives

| What explains the Clinton administration's move to the right? | **How did President Clinton respond to the challenges of globalization?** | How did President George W. Bush change American politics and foreign policy? | Conclusion: How have Americans debated the role of the government? |

Countries with the Highest Military Expenditures, 2005

During the Cold War, the military budgets of the United States and the Soviet Union were relatively even. For example, in 1983 U.S. military expenditures stood at $217 billion, compared to $213 billion for the Soviet Union. Even before the Iraq War, which began in 2003, the U.S. military budget constituted 47 percent of total world military expenditures. That proportion rose to 48 percent in 2005, with the United States spending nearly ten times as much as its nearest competitor. The U.S. defense budget reflects the determination of Democratic and Republican administrations alike to maintain dominance in the world, even while the capacities of its traditional enemies have been greatly diminished.

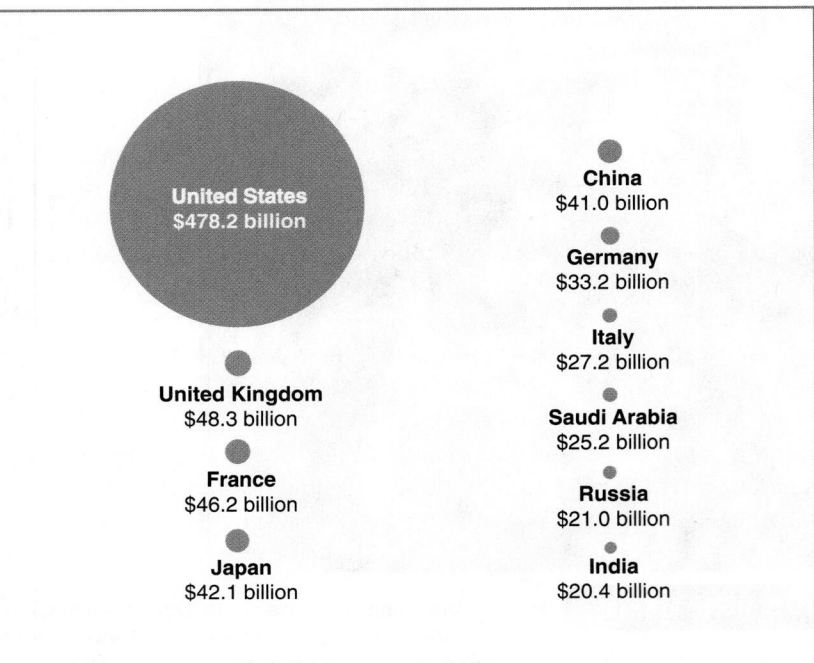

United States $478.2 billion

China $41.0 billion

Germany $33.2 billion

Italy $27.2 billion

Saudi Arabia $25.2 billion

Russia $21.0 billion

India $20.4 billion

United Kingdom $48.3 billion

France $46.2 billion

Japan $42.1 billion

when no vital interest seemed threatened. Indeed, both the United States and the United Nations stood by in 1994 when more than half a million people were massacred in a brutal civil war in the central African nation of Rwanda.

As always, the United States was more inclined to use force nearer its borders. After a military coup overthrew Jean-Bertrand Aristide, the democratically elected president of Haiti, thousands of Haitians tried to escape political violence and poverty, many on flimsy boats heading for Florida. In 1994, Clinton got the United Nations to impose economic sanctions on Haiti and to authorize intervention by U.S. troops. Hours before U.S. forces were to invade Haiti, the military leaders promised to step down. U.S. forces landed peacefully, and Aristide was restored to power. Initially a huge success, U.S. policy continued to be tested as Haiti faced grave economic challenges and political instability.

In eastern Europe, the collapse of communism ignited a severe crisis. During the Cold War, the Communist government of Yugoslavia held together a federation of six republics. After the Communists were swept out in 1989, ruthless leaders exploited ethnic differences to bolster their power, and Yugoslavia splintered into separate states and fell into civil war.

The Serbs' aggression under President Slobodan Milosevic against Bosnian Muslims in particular horrified much of the world, but European and U.S. leaders hesitated to use military force. Finally, in 1995, Clinton ordered U.S. fliers to join NATO forces in intensive bombing of Serbian military concentrations. That effort and successful offensives by the Croatian and Bosnian armies forced Milosevic to the bargaining table. After representatives from Serbia, Croatia, and Bosnia hammered out a peace treaty,

Breakup of Yugoslavia

CHAPTER LOCATOR | How did the United States respond to the end of the Cold War and tensions in the Middle East?

Clinton then agreed to send twenty thousand American troops to Bosnia as part of a NATO peacekeeping mission.

In 1998, new fighting broke out in the southern Serbian province of Kosovo, where ethnic Albanians, who constituted 90 percent of the population, demanded independence. The Serbian army retaliated, driving out one-third of Kosovo's 1.8 million Albanian Muslims. In 1999, NATO launched a U.S.-led bombing attack on Serbian targets that forced Milosevic to agree to a peace settlement. Serbians voted Milosevic out of office in October 2000, and he died in 2006 while on trial for genocide by a UN war crimes tribunal.

Elsewhere, Clinton remained willing to deploy U.S. power when he could send missiles rather than soldiers, and he was prepared to act without international support or UN sanction. In August 1998, bombs exploded at the U.S. embassies in Kenya and Tanzania, killing 12 Americans and more than 250 Africans. Clinton retaliated with missile attacks on terrorist training camps in Afghanistan and facilities in Sudan controlled by Osama bin Laden, a Saudi-born millionaire who financed the Islamic-extremist terrorist network linked to the embassy attacks. Clinton also launched air strikes against Iraq in 1993 when a plot to assassinate former president Bush was uncovered, in 1996 after Saddam Hussein attacked the Kurds in northern Iraq, and repeatedly between 1998 and 2000 after Hussein expelled UN weapons inspectors. Whereas Bush had acted in the Gulf War with the support of an international force that included Arab states, Clinton acted unilaterally and in the face of Arab opposition.

To ameliorate the Israeli-Palestinian conflict, a major source of Arab hostility toward the West, Clinton used diplomatic rather than military power. In 1993, due largely to the efforts of the Norwegian government, Yasir Arafat, head of the Palestine Liberation Organization (PLO), and Yitzhak Rabin, Israeli prime minister, recognized the existence of each other's states for the first time and agreed to Israeli withdrawal from the Gaza Strip and Jericho, allowing for Palestinian self-government there. In July 1994, Clinton presided over another turning point as Rabin and King Hussein of Jordan signed a declaration of peace. Yet difficult issues remained to be settled, and continuing violence between Israelis and Palestinians strengthened anti-American sentiment among Arabs, who saw the United States as Israel's ally.

Obstacles to Resolution of the Israeli-Palestinian Conflict

Control of Jerusalem

The fate of Palestinian refugees

200,000 Israeli settlers living in the West Bank

Debates over Globalization

Building on efforts by Presidents Reagan and Bush, Clinton sought to speed up globalization, the movement of products, capital, and labor across national borders. In November 1993, he won congressional approval of the **North American Free Trade Agreement (NAFTA),** which eliminated all tariffs and trade barriers among the United States, Canada, and Mexico. Organized labor and others fearing loss of jobs and industries to Mexico lobbied vigorously against NAFTA, and a

CHRONOLOGY

1993
- Israel and Palestine Liberation Organization sign peace accords.
- North American Free Trade Agreement.

1994
- United States sends troops to Haiti.
- General Agreement on Tariffs and Trade establishes World Trade Organization.

1998
- United States bombs Iraq and terrorist sites in Afghanistan and Sudan.

1999
- United States, with NATO, bombs Serbia.

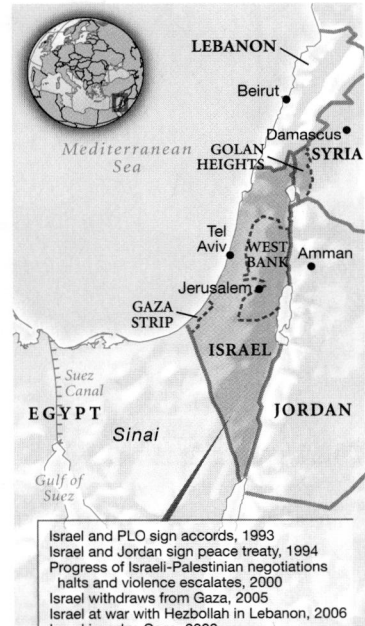

Israel and PLO sign accords, 1993
Israel and Jordan sign peace treaty, 1994
Progress of Israeli-Palestinian negotiations halts and violence escalates, 2000
Israel withdraws from Gaza, 2005
Israel at war with Hezbollah in Lebanon, 2006
Israel invades Gaza, 2008

Events in Israel since 1989

What explains the Clinton administration's move to the right?

How did President Clinton respond to the challenges of globalization?

How did President George W. Bush change American politics and foreign policy?

Conclusion: How have Americans debated the role of the government?

North American Free Trade Agreement (NAFTA)

▶ 1993 treaty that eliminated all tariffs and trade barriers among the United States, Canada, and Mexico. NAFTA was supported by President Clinton, centrist Democrats, and many Republicans. President Clinton's support of NAFTA reflected his desire to speed up globalization by seeking new measures to ease restrictions on international commerce.

Protests against the WTO

Environmentalists and animal protection advocates were among the diverse array of groups demonstrating against the World Trade Organization when it attempted to meet in Seattle, Washington, in November 1999. These activists dressed as sea turtles to protest WTO agreements permitting economic actions that they believed threatened the survival of the animals. Wide World Photos, Inc.

majority of Democrats opposed it, but Republican support ensured approval. In 1994, the Senate ratified the General Agreement on Tariffs and Trade, establishing the World Trade Organization (WTO) to enforce substantial tariff reductions and elimination of import quotas among some 135 member nations. And in 2005, Clinton's successor, George W. Bush, got Congress to lower more trade barriers with the passage of the Central American–Dominican Republic Free Trade Agreement.

The free trade issue was intensely contested. Much of corporate America welcomed the elimination of trade barriers. "Ideally, you'd have every plant you own on a barge," remarked Jack Welch, CEO of General Electric. Critics linked globalization to the loss of jobs, the weakening of unions, and the growing gap between rich and poor. Demanding "fair trade" rather than simply free trade, they wanted trade treaties to require decent wage and labor standards. Environmentalists wanted countries seeking increased commerce with the United States to eliminate or reduce pollution and to prevent the destruction of endangered species.

In November 1999, tens of thousands of activists dramatized the globalization debate when they gathered in Seattle, Washington, to protest a meeting of the WTO. Protesters charged the WTO with promoting a global economy that destroyed the environment, devastated poorer developing nations, and undercut living standards and wages for workers. Globalization controversies often centered on relationships between the United States, which dominated the world's industrial core, and the developing nations on the periphery, whose cheap labor and lax environmental standards caught the eye of investors. United Students against Sweatshops, for example, attacked the international conglomerate Nike, which paid Chinese workers $1.50 to produce a pair of shoes selling for more than $100 in the United States. Yet leaders of developing nations actively sought foreign investment, insisting that wages deemed pitiful by Americans offered people in poor nations a much better living than they could otherwise obtain. At the same time, developing countries often pointed to American hypocrisy in advocating free trade in industry while heavily subsidizing its own agricultural sector. "When countries like America, Britain and France subsidize their farmers," complained a grower in Uganda, "we get hurt."

Whereas globalization's cheerleaders argued that everyone would benefit in the long run, critics focused on the short-term victims. "International trade and global financial markets are very good at generating wealth," conceded American businessman George Soros, "but they cannot take care of other social needs, such as the preservation of peace, alleviation of poverty, protection of the environment, labor conditions, or human rights." The critics enjoyed a few successes. In 2000, President Clinton signed an executive order requiring an environmental impact review before the signing of any trade agreement. Beyond the United States, officials from the World Bank and the International Monetary Fund, along with representatives from wealthy economies, promised in 2000 to provide poor nations more debt relief and a greater voice in decisions about loans and grants. According to World Bank president James D. Wolfensohn, "Our challenge is to make globalization an instrument of opportunity and inclusion—not fear."

The Internationalization of the United States

Globalization was typically associated with the expansion of American enterprise and culture to other countries, yet the United States experienced the dynamic forces of globalization within its own borders. Already in the 1980s, Japanese, European, and Middle Eastern investors had purchased American stocks and bonds, real estate, and corporations. Local communities welcomed foreign capital, and states competed to recruit foreign automobile plants. By 2002, the paychecks of nearly 4 million American workers came from foreign-owned companies.

Globalization was transforming not just the economy but American society as well, as the United States experienced a tremendous surge of immigration. By 2006, the nation housed 35.7 million immigrants, who constituted 12.4 percent of the population. Almost half of those who arrived between 1980 and 2005 were Asians, and nearly 40 percent came from Latin America and the Caribbean. Consequently, immigration changed the racial and ethnic composition of the nation. By 2004, Asian Americans numbered 13 million, while 41 million Latinos constituted—at 14 percent—the largest minority group in the nation.

The racial composition of the new immigration heightened the century-old wariness of native-born Americans toward newcomers. Pressure for more restrictive policies stemmed from beliefs that immigrants took jobs from the native-born, suppressed wages by accepting low-paying employment, or eroded the dominant culture and language. Americans expressed particular hostility toward immigrants who were in the country illegally—an estimated 12 million in 2008—even though the economy depended on their cheap labor.

The new immigration was once again making America an international, interracial society. The largest numbers of immigrants flocked to California, New York, Texas, Florida, New Jersey, and Illinois, but new immigrants dispersed throughout the country. Taquerias, sushi bars, and Vietnamese restaurants appeared in southeastern and midwestern towns; cable TV companies added Spanish-language stations; and the international sport of soccer soared in popularity. Mixed marriages also displayed the growing fusion of cultures, recognized in 2000 on Census Bureau forms where Americans could check more than one racial category.

Like their predecessors, the majority of post-1965 immigrants were unskilled and poor, seeking economic opportunity. They took the lowest-paying jobs, including farm and yard work, child and elder care, and cleaning services—work that employers insisted native-born Americans would not do. Yet a significant number of immigrants were highly skilled workers, sought after by burgeoning high-tech industries. For example, in 1999 about one-third of the scientists and engineers employed in California's Silicon Valley had been born abroad.

QUICK REVIEW

How did President Clinton
respond to globalization?

What explains the Clinton administration's move to the right?

How did President Clinton respond to the challenges of globalization?

How did President George W. Bush change American politics and foreign policy?

Conclusion: How have Americans debated the role of the government?

How did President George W. Bush change American politics and foreign policy?

George W. Bush's Second Term

U.S. President George W. Bush (right) walks with Secretary of Defense Donald Rumsfeld, Secretary of State Condoleezza Rice, and Chairman of the Joint Chiefs of Staff Gen. Peter Pace at the White House in Washington, D.C., May 1, 2006. Jim Young/Reuters/Corbis

THE ELECTION OF GEORGE W. BUSH in 2000 marked the second time that a son of a former president gained the White House. But the younger Bush pushed a domestic agenda that was closer to Ronald Reagan's than that of George H. W. Bush. Overseas, as Islamist terrorism replaced communism as the primary threat to U.S. security, the Bush administration adopted a policy of unilateralism and preemption.

The Disputed Election of 2000

George W. Bush won the Republican nomination after a series of hard-fought primaries. The son of former president George H. W. Bush, he had served as governor of Texas since 1994. Inexperienced in national and international affairs, Bush chose for his running mate a seasoned official, Richard B. Cheney, who had served in three previous Republican administrations.

Many observers predicted that the amazingly strong economy would give the Democratic nominee, Vice President Al Gore, the edge, and he did surpass Bush by more than half a million votes. Once the polls closed, however, it became clear that Florida's 25 electoral college votes would decide the presidency. Bush's tiny margin in Florida prompted an automatic recount of the votes, which eventually gave Bush an edge of 537 votes.

Meanwhile, the Democrats asked for hand-counting of Florida ballots in several heavily Democratic counties where machine errors and confusing ballots may have left thousands of Gore votes unrecorded. The Republicans, in turn, went to court to try to stop the hand-counts. The outcome of the 2000 election hung in the balance for weeks until a bitterly divided

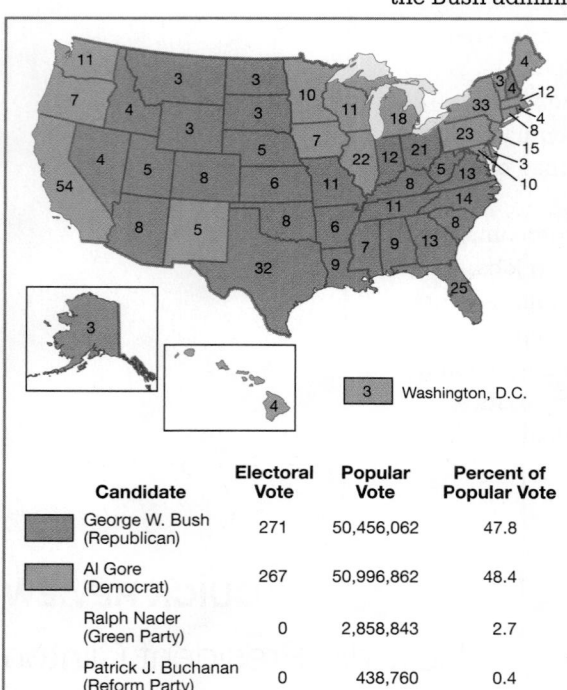

| | 3 | Washington, D.C. |

Candidate	Electoral Vote	Popular Vote	Percent of Popular Vote
George W. Bush (Republican)	271	50,456,062	47.8
Al Gore (Democrat)	267	50,996,862	48.4
Ralph Nader (Green Party)	0	2,858,843	2.7
Patrick J. Buchanan (Reform Party)	0	438,760	0.4

MAP 31.3 ■ The Election of 2000

CHAPTER LOCATOR | How did the United States respond to the end of the Cold War and tensions in the Middle East?

Supreme Court ruled five to four against further recounts, and Gore conceded the presidency to Bush on December 13, 2000 (**Map 31.3**). Despite the lack of a popular mandate, the Bush administration set out to make dramatic policy changes.

The Domestic Policies of a "Compassionate Conservative"

Bush's appointments, like Clinton's, brought significant diversity to the executive branch. He chose African Americans Colin Powell as secretary of state and Condoleezza Rice first as national security adviser and subsequently as secretary of state when Powell resigned in January 2005. Five of Bush's top-level appointees were women, including Secretary of Labor Elaine L. Chao, the first Asian American woman to serve in the cabinet.

Bush had promised to govern as a "compassionate conservative." A born-again Christian, he established the White House Office of Faith-Based and Community Initiatives to encourage religious and community groups to participate in government programs aimed at prison inmates, drug addicts, the unemployed, and others. The religious right praised the initiatives, but others charged that they violated the constitutional separation of church and state.

Bush's fiscal policies were more compassionate toward the rich than toward average Americans. In 2001, he signed a bill reducing taxes over the next ten years by $1.35 trillion. A 2003 tax law slashed another $320 billion. The laws heavily favored the rich by reducing income taxes, phasing out estate taxes, and cutting tax rates on capital gains and dividends. They also provided benefits for married couples and families with children and offered tax deductions for college expenses.

The administration insisted that the tax cuts would promote economic growth and jolt the economy out of the recession that had begun in 2000. The economy did recover, but opponents stressed inequities in the tax cuts and pointed to a mushrooming federal deficit—the highest in U.S. history—that surpassed $400 billion in 2004. The national debt rose to $9.6 trillion, making the United States increasingly dependent on China and other foreign investors, who held more than half of the debt.

Bush used regulatory powers that did not require congressional approval to weaken environmental protection as part of his larger goals of reducing government regulation, promoting economic growth, and increasing energy production. The administration opened millions of wilderness acres to mining, oil, and timber industries and relaxed environmental requirements under the Clean Air and Clean Water Acts. To worldwide dismay, the administration withdrew from the Kyoto Protocol on global warming, signed in 1997 by 178 nations to reduce greenhouse gas emissions.

Conservatives hailed Bush's appointment of two new Supreme Court justices. In 2005, John Roberts, who had served in the Reagan and George H. W. Bush administrations, was named chief justice. Bush then replaced the moderate Sandra Day O'Connor with Samuel A. Alito, a staunch conservative who won confirmation by a narrow margin.

In contrast to the partisan conflict over judicial appointments and tax and environmental policy, Bush won bipartisan support for the **No Child Left Behind (NCLB) Act** of 2002, marking the greatest change in federal education policy since the 1960s and substantially extending the role of the federal government in public

CHRONOLOGY

2000
- Republican George W. Bush is elected president.

2001
- **September 11.** Terrorists attack World Trade Center and Pentagon.
- United States attacks Afghanistan, driving out Taliban government.
- USA Patriot Act.
- $1.35 trillion tax cut.

2002
- No Child Left Behind Act.
- Department of Homeland Security is established.

2003
- United States attacks Iraq, deposing Saddam Hussein.
- Prescription drug coverage is added to Medicare.

2004
- President George W. Bush is reelected.

2005
- Hurricane Katrina.

2007
- Bush begins troop surge in Iraq.

2008
- Worst financial crisis since the Great Depression.
- Troubled Assets Relief Program is enacted.
- Democrat Barack Obama is elected president.

No Child Left Behind (NCLB) Act

▶ 2002 legislation championed by President George W. Bush that expanded the role of the federal government in public education. The law required every school to meet annual testing standards, penalized failing schools, and allowed parents to transfer their children out of such schools.

What explains the Clinton administration's move to the right?

How did President Clinton respond to the challenges of globalization?

How did President George W. Bush change American politics and foreign policy?

Conclusion: How have Americans debated the role of the government?

875

education. Promising to end, in Bush's words, "the story of children being just shuffled through the system," the law required every school to meet annual testing standards, penalized failing schools, and allowed parents to transfer their children out of such schools. NCLB authorized an increase in federal aid aimed primarily at the poorest districts, but not enough for Senator Paul Wellstone of Minnesota, one of the few critics of the education bill, who asked, "How can you reach the goal of leaving no child behind on a tin cup budget?" In addition to struggling to finance the new standards, school officials began to criticize the one-size-fits-all approach and pointed to family and community impoverishment as sources of student deficiencies.

The Bush administration's second major effort to co-opt Democratic Party issues constituted what the president hailed as "the greatest advance in health care coverage for America's seniors" since the start of Medicare in 1965. In 2003, Bush signed a bill authorizing prescription drug benefits for the elderly and at the same time expanding the role of private insurers in the Medicare system. Most Democrats opposed the legislation, charging that it left big gaps in coverage, subsidized private insurers with federal funds to compete with Medicare, banned imports of low-priced drugs, and prohibited the government from negotiating with drug companies to reduce prices. Overall, medical costs overall continued to soar, and the number of uninsured Americans surpassed 40 million in 2008.

One domestic undertaking of the Bush administration found little approval anywhere: its handling of **Hurricane Katrina,** which in August 2005 devastated the coasts of Alabama, Louisiana, and Mississippi and ultimately resulted in some 1,500 deaths. The catastrophe that ensued when New Orleans's levees broke, flooding 80 percent of the city, shook a deeply rooted assumption held by Americans, even conservatives devoted to limited government: that government owed its citizens protection from natural disasters.

New Orleans residents who were too poor or too infirm to flee the flooding spent anguished days waiting on rooftops for help; wading in filthy, toxic water; and enduring the heat, disorder, and lack of basic necessities at the convention center and Superdome, where they had been told to go for safety and protection. "How can we save the world if we can't save our own people?" wondered one Louisianan. Thousands of volunteers rescued the stranded, helped evacuees in distant cities, and traveled to the Gulf Coast to assist with reconstruction. Millions more opened their pocketbooks to aid the victims. Yet the immense private generosity and the superb response of a few groups, such as the U.S. Coast Guard, could not make up for the feeling that the nation had failed some of its citizens when they needed it most. Since so many of Katrina's hardest-hit victims were poor and black, the disaster also highlighted the severe injustices and deprivations remaining in American society.

The Globalization of Terrorism

The response to Hurricane Katrina contrasted sharply with the Bush administration's decisive reaction to the horror that had unfolded four years earlier on the morning of **September 11, 2001.** Nineteen terrorists hijacked four planes and flew three of them into the twin towers of New York City's World Trade Center and the Pentagon in Washington, D.C.; the fourth crashed in a field in Pennsylvania. The

Hurricane Katrina
▶ August 2005 hurricane that devastated the coasts of Alabama, Louisiana, and Mississippi and ultimately resulted in some 1,500 deaths, most of them among the region's poor. In the wake of the hurricane, New Orleans's levees broke, flooding 80 percent of the city. The inadequacy of the federal response to the disaster outraged the American public.

September 11, 2001
▶ Date on which nineteen terrorists hijacked four planes and flew three of them into the twin towers of New York City's World Trade Center and the Pentagon in Washington, D.C.; the fourth crashed in a field in Pennsylvania. The attacks took nearly 2,800 lives, including U.S. citizens and people from ninety countries. The attacks prompted President George W. Bush to initiate radical departures from long-standing American security and foreign policies.

CHAPTER LOCATOR | How did the United States respond to the end of the Cold War and tensions in the Middle East?

CHAPTER 31
876 FACING THE CHALLENGES OF A CHANGING WORLD, SINCE 1989

attacks took nearly 2,800 lives, including U.S. citizens and people from ninety countries.

The hijackers were members of **Al Qaeda,** an international terrorist network led by Osama bin Laden. Organized from Afghanistan, where the radical Muslim Taliban government harbored Al Qaeda, the attacks reflected several elements of globalization. Technological advances and increased mobility facilitated bin Laden's worldwide coordination of Al Qaeda. Moreover, Islamic extremists were

Al Qaeda

▶ Osama bin Laden's international terrorist organization, consisting of Islamic extremists who were enraged by the spread of Western goods, culture, and values into the Muslim world, as well as by the 1991 Persian Gulf War against Iraq and the stationing of American troops in Saudi Arabia, bin Laden's homeland. The group was responsible for the September 11, 2001, attacks on the World Trade Center and the Pentagon, which were organized from Afghanistan, as well as other attacks around the world.

▶ FOR MORE HELP ANALYZING THIS IMAGE, see the visual activity for this chapter in the Online Study Guide at bedfordstmartins.com/roarkunderstanding.

The Tribute in Light

Two pillars of light, projected by eighty-eight searchlights in the place where the World Trade Center's twin towers had stood, soared as a monument to the victims of the terrorist attacks of September 11, 2001. Turned on at the six-month anniversary of the attack, the "Tribute in Light" was dimmed one month later and has been illuminated every year since on September 11.

Daniel Derella/AP/Wide World Photos, Inc.

| What explains the Clinton administration's move to the right? | How did President Clinton respond to the challenges of globalization? | **How did President George W. Bush change American politics and foreign policy?** | Conclusion: How have Americans debated the role of the government? |

877

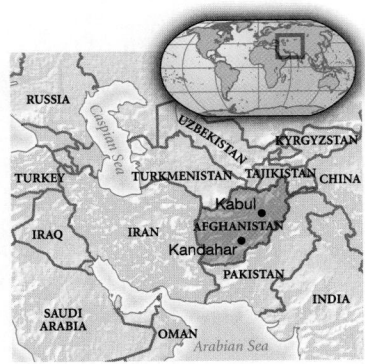

Afghanistan

USA Patriot Act

▶ 2001 law intended to increase America's ability to combat terrorism. The law gave the government new powers to monitor suspected terrorists and their associates, while allowing more exchange of information between criminal investigators and those investigating foreign threats. Critics charged that it represented an unwarranted abridgment of civil rights.

enraged by the spread of Western goods, culture, and values into the Muslim world, as well as by the 1991 Persian Gulf War against Iraq and the stationing of American troops in Saudi Arabia, bin Laden's homeland.

In the wake of the September 11 attacks, President Bush's public approval rating skyrocketed as he sought a global alliance against terrorism and won at least verbal support from most governments. On October 11, the United States and Britain began bombing Afghanistan, and American special forces aided the Northern Alliance, the Taliban government's main opposition. By December, the Taliban government was destroyed, but bin Laden had not been captured, and numerous Al Qaeda forces had escaped or remained in hiding throughout the world. Afghans elected a new national government, but although the United States still had 27,000 troops in Afghanistan seven years later, economic stability and physical security remained out of reach.

Throughout the United States, anti-immigrant sentiment revived, and anyone appearing to be Middle Eastern or practicing Islam was likely to arouse suspicion. Authorities arrested more than a thousand Arabs and Muslims, and a Justice Department study later reported that many people with no connection to terrorism spent months in jail, denied their rights. "I think America overreacted . . . by singling out Arab-named men like myself," said Shanaz Mohammed, who was jailed for eight months for an immigration violation.

In October 2001, Congress passed the **USA Patriot Act.** The law gave the government new powers to monitor suspected terrorists and their associates, while allowing more exchange of information between criminal investigators and those investigating foreign threats. It soon provoked calls for revision from both conservatives and liberals. Kathleen MacKenzie, a councilwoman in Ann Arbor, Michigan, explained why the council opposed the Patriot Act: "[A]s awful as we feel about September 11 and as concerned as we were about national safety, we felt that giving up [rights] was too high a price to pay." A security official countered, "If you don't violate someone's human rights some of the time, you probably aren't doing your job."

Insisting that presidential powers were virtually limitless in times of national crisis, Bush stretched his powers as commander in chief until he met resistance from the courts and Congress. In 2001, the administration established special military commissions to try prisoners captured in Afghanistan and taken to the U.S. military base at Guantánamo, Cuba. But in 2006, the Supreme Court ruled five to three that Congress had not authorized such tribunals and that they violated international law. That year, congressional leaders became openly critical of the administration for wiretapping phone calls made and received by U.S. residents without obtaining the warrants required by law.

The government also sought to protect Americans from future terrorist attacks through the greatest reorganization of the executive branch since 1948. In November 2002, Congress authorized the new Department of Homeland Security (DHS), combining 170,000 federal employees from twenty-two agencies that had responsibilities for various aspects of domestic security. During the new department's first six years, no terrorist attacks were launched in the United States, but doubts grew about its effectiveness when its subagency, the Federal Emergency Management Agency (FEMA), failed in the response to Hurricane Katrina.

CHAPTER LOCATOR | How did the United States respond to the end of the Cold War and tensions in the Middle East?

Chief Duties of the Department of Homeland Security

Intelligence analysis
Immigration and border security
Chemical, biological, and nuclear countermeasures
Emergency preparedness and response

Unilateralism, Preemption, and the Iraq War

The Bush administration sought collective action against the Taliban, but on most other international issues, it adopted a go-it-alone approach. In addition to withdrawing from the Kyoto Protocol on global warming and violating international rules about the treatment of military prisoners, it scrapped the 1972 Antiballistic Missile Treaty in order to develop the space-based Strategic Defense Initiative first proposed by Ronald Reagan. Bush also withdrew the nation from the UN's International Criminal Court, and he rejected an agreement to enforce bans on the development and possession of biological weapons—an agreement signed by all of America's European allies.

Nowhere was the new policy of unilateralism more striking than in a new war against Iraq, a war endorsed by Vice President Dick Cheney and Secretary of Defense Donald H. Rumsfeld, but not by Secretary of State Colin Powell. In his State of the Union message in January 2002, Bush identified Iraq, Iran, and North Korea as an "axis of evil." His words alarmed political leaders in Europe and Asia, who insisted that those three nations posed entirely different challenges and who preferred to emphasize diplomacy rather than confrontation.

Nonetheless, in June 2002 President Bush proclaimed a new policy for American security based not on containment but on preemption: "Traditional concepts of deterrence will not work against a terrorist enemy whose avowed tactics are wanton destruction and the targeting of innocents; whose so-called soldiers seek martyrdom in death and whose most potent protection is statelessness." Because nuclear, chemical, and biological weapons enabled "even weak states and small groups [to] attain a catastrophic power to strike great nations," the United States had to "be ready for preemptive action." The president's claim that the United States had the right to start a war was at odds with international law and with many Americans' understanding of their nation's ideals. It distressed most of America's great-power allies.

The Bush administration moved deliberately to apply the doctrine of preemption to Iraq, whose dictator, Saddam Hussein, appeared to be in violation of UN resolutions from the 1991 Gulf War requiring Iraq to destroy and stop further development of nuclear, chemical, and biological weapons. In November 2002, the United States persuaded the UN Security Council to pass a resolution requiring Iraq to disarm or face "serious consequences." When Iraq failed to comply fully with new UN inspections, the Bush administration decided on war. Making claims (subsequently refuted) that Hussein had links to Al Qaeda and harbored terrorists and that Iraq possessed weapons of mass destruction, the president insisted that the threat was immediate and great enough to justify preemptive action. Despite

| What explains the Clinton administration's move to the right? | How did President Clinton respond to the challenges of globalization? | **How did President George W. Bush change American politics and foreign policy?** | Conclusion: How have Americans debated the role of the government? |

879

Iraq War

Iraq War
► War launched by the United States, Britain, and a number of smaller countries in March 2003 against the government of Iraqi dictator Saddam Hussein. The U.S. invasion of Iraq proceeded in the face of considerable international opposition. Bush administration officials justified the invasion of Iraq by making claims (subsequently refuted) that Hussein had links to Al Qaeda and harbored terrorists and that Iraq possessed weapons of mass destruction. Although major combat operations in the war were declared over in May 2003, violence and instability continued to plague Iraq for years to come.

opposition from the Arab world and most major nations, the United States and Britain invaded Iraq on March 19, 2003, supported by some thirty nations (see Map 31.1, page 861). Coalition forces won an easy and decisive victory, and Bush declared the end of the **Iraq War** on May 1. Saddam Hussein was ousted and remained at large until December 2003.

Chaos followed the quick victory over Hussein. Damage from U.S. bombing and widespread looting resulting from the failure of U.S. troops to secure order and provide basic necessities left Iraqis wondering how much they had gained. "With Saddam there was tyranny, but at least you had a salary to put food on your family's table," said a young father from Hussein's hometown of Tikrit. A Baghdad hospital worker complained, "They can take our oil, but at least they should let us have electricity and water." Five years after the invasion, continuing violence had caused 2 million to flee their country and displaced 1.9 million within Iraq.

The administration had not planned adequately for the occupation and sent far fewer forces to Iraq than it had deployed in 1991 in response to Iraq's invasion of Kuwait. The 140,000 American forces in Iraq came under attack almost daily from remnants of the former Hussein regime, religious extremists, and hundreds of foreign terrorists now entering the chaotic country. Seeking to divide Iraqis and undermine the occupation, terrorists launched attacks that resulted in the deaths of tens of thousands.

The war became an issue in the presidential campaign of 2004. Massachusetts senator John Kerry, the Democratic nominee, criticized Bush's unilateralist foreign policy and the administration's conduct of the war. The president eked out a 286 to 252 victory in the electoral college, winning 50.7 percent of the popular vote to Kerry's 48.3 percent and carrying Republican majorities into Congress.

In June 2004, the United States transferred sovereignty to an interim Iraqi government, and in January 2005 about 58 percent of Iraqis eligible to vote risked their safety to elect a national assembly. The daunting challenges facing the national assembly were to write a constitution, satisfy Iraq's sharply divided political blocs, and decide to what extent Islamic religious law would shape the new government. Violence escalated against government officials, Iraqi civilians, and occupation forces. A nineteen-year-old Iraqi confined to his house by his parents, who feared he could be killed or lured into terrorist activities, said, "If I'm killed, it doesn't even matter because I'm dead right now." By 2006, when U.S. military deaths approached 3,000 and Iraqi civilian casualties reached tens of thousands, a majority of Americans told pollsters that the Iraq War was a mistake.

By 2006, Bush's conduct of the Iraq War was subject to criticism that crossed party lines and included leading military figures. Critics acknowledged that the U.S. military had felled a brutal dictator, but coalition forces were not sufficiently numerous or prepared for the turmoil that followed the invasion, nor did they find the weapons of mass destruction or links to Osama bin Laden that administration officials had insisted made the war necessary. Rather, in the chaos induced by the invasion of Iraq, more than a thousand terrorists entered Iraq—the place, according to one expert, "for fundamentalists to go . . . to stick it to the West."

The war and occupation exacted a steep price not only in dollars but also in American and Iraqi lives, U.S. relations with the other great powers, and the nation's reputation in the world, especially among Arab nations. Revelations of

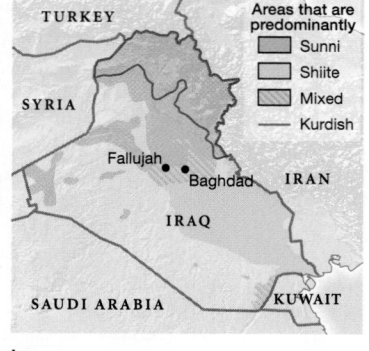

Iraq

CHAPTER LOCATOR | How did the United States respond to the end of the Cold War and tensions in the Middle East?

CHAPTER 31
880 FACING THE CHALLENGES OF A CHANGING WORLD, SINCE 1989

prisoner abuse in the Abu Ghraib prison in Iraq and in the Guantánamo detention camp housing captives from the Afghan war further tarnished the United States' image. Anti-Americanism around the world rose to its highest point in history. The budget deficit swelled, and resources were diverted to Iraq from other national security challenges, including the stabilization of Afghanistan, the elimination of bin Laden and Al Qaeda, and the threats posed by North Korea's and Iran's pursuit of nuclear weapons.

Voters registered their dissatisfaction in the 2006 congressional elections, turning control of both houses over to the Democrats for the first time since 1994. President Bush replaced Secretary of Defense Donald Rumsfeld, and the administration displayed more willingness to work with other nations in dealing with Iraq, Iran, and North Korea. Yet Bush clung to the goal of bringing democracy to the Middle East. Despite opposition from Democrats in Congress, who wanted a timetable for withdrawal from Iraq, in 2007 the administration began a troop surge that increased U.S. forces there to 160,000. The surge, along with actions by Iraqi leaders, contributed to a dramatic reduction in terrorist violence, and the administration began planning for the eventual withdrawal of U.S. forces by the end of 2011.

Barack Obama and the Promise of Change

Despite the improving situation in Iraq, President Bush's approval ratings sank below 30 percent, posing severe difficulties for the Republican Party in the 2008 elections. The Republicans nominated Senator John McCain of Arizona. McCain chose Alaska governor Sarah Palin as his running mate, the second woman to run for vice president on a major party ticket. Even more historic changes occurred in the Democratic Party when **Barack Obama** edged out Hillary Rodham Clinton, the former First Lady, in closely contested battles that continued until the last primaries in June.

Born to a white mother and a Kenyan father and raised in Hawaii and Indonesia, Obama served in the Illinois Senate and in 2004 won election to the U.S. Senate. Obama won the Democratic nomination with a combination of brilliant campaign strategy based on grassroots and Internet organizing, a charismatic personality, and the ability to speak to deep-seated longings for a new kind of politics and racial reconciliation. He won 53 percent of the popular vote and defeated McCain 365 to 173 in the electoral college, while Democrats increased their majorities in the House and Senate (**Map 31.4**).

Obama promised a series of reforms in health care, education, and the environment, but by his inauguration, he faced more immediate problems. Fueled by a breakdown in financial institutions that had accumulated trillions of dollars of bad debt, a recession hit the economy in 2008. The financial crisis was so severe that Congress passed the Bush administration's $700 billion Troubled Assets Relief Program to inject credit into the economy and shore up banks and other businesses. Home mortgage foreclosures skyrocketed, major companies went

Barack Obama

▶ The first African American to win a major political party's nomination for president and the Democratic winner of the 2008 presidential election. Obama became the forty-fourth president of the United States on January 20, 2009, and immediately set to work on the country's severe domestic and international challenges.

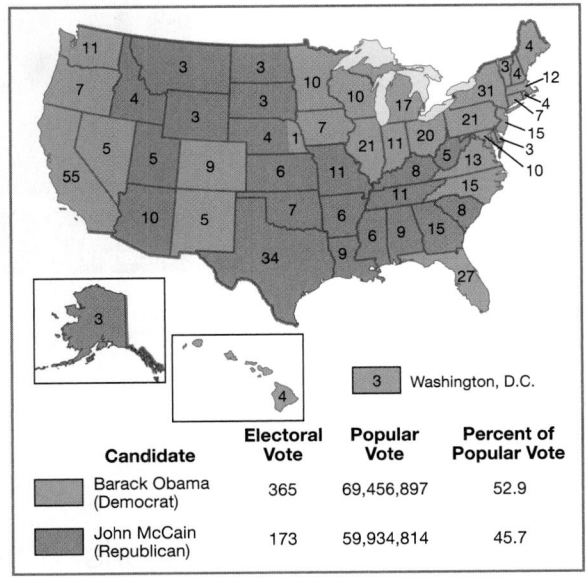

3		Washington, D.C.

Candidate	Electoral Vote	Popular Vote	Percent of Popular Vote
Barack Obama (Democrat)	365	69,456,897	52.9
John McCain (Republican)	173	59,934,814	45.7

MAP 31.4 ■ The Election of 2008

What explains the Clinton administration's move to the right?

How did President Clinton respond to the challenges of globalization?

How did President George W. Bush change American politics and foreign policy?

Conclusion: How have Americans debated the role of the government?

881

bankrupt, and unemployment surpassed ten percent. Obama attacked the recession with $787 billion worth of spending to stimulate the economy and relieve unemployment; persuaded Congress to tighten regulations on Wall Street and protect consumers; and, over unanimous Republican opposition, signed a health care law extending health insurance to 30 million. Yet, in 2010 Republicans made strong gains in the mid-term elections, which took place amidst continuing high unemployment, a huge federal deficit, and the sentiment among a minority of voters that government was taking away their liberty.

The Inauguration of Barack Obama

President Barack Obama and his wife, Michelle, walk down Pennsylvania Avenue after his inauguration at the Capitol on January 20, 2009. In his inaugural address, Obama spoke of "this winter of our hardship," referring to economic crisis, wars in Iraq and Afghanistan, and other challenges facing the nation. AP Images/Doug Mills/Pool.

> QUICK REVIEW

What impact did the terrorist attacks of September 11 have on U.S. domestic and foreign policy?

CHAPTER LOCATOR | How did the United States respond to the end of the Cold War and tensions in the Middle East?

CHAPTER 31

882 FACING THE CHALLENGES OF A CHANGING WORLD, SINCE 1989

AP Images.

Conclusion: How have Americans debated the role of the government?

THE END OF THE COLD WAR, the rise of international terrorism, and the George W. Bush administration's doctrines of preemption and unilateralism sparked new debates over the long-standing question of how the United States should act beyond its borders. Further, Americans had debated for more than two centuries what responsibilities the government could or should shoulder and what was best left to the private sector. The last three decades of the twentieth century had seen a decline in Americans' trust in government's ability to improve people's lives.

The shifting of control of the government back and forth between Republicans and Democrats from 1989 to 2008 revealed a dynamic debate over the role of government in domestic affairs. The reforms in some social areas built on a deep-rooted tradition that sought to realize the American promise of justice and human well-being. Those who mobilized against globalization worked internationally for what populists, progressives, New Deal reformers, and many activists of the 1960s had sought for the domestic population: protection of individual rights, curbs on laissez-faire capitalism, assistance for victims of rapid economic change, and fiscal policies that placed greater responsibility on those best able to pay for the collective good. Even the second Bush administration, which sought a more limited role for the federal government, expanded the government's role in public education and health care for the elderly, and a gigantic program to bail out failing businesses when a severe financial crisis hit the economy in 2008.

The United States became ever more deeply embedded in the global economy as products, information, and people crossed borders with amazing speed and frequency. Although the end of the Cold War brought about unanticipated cooperation between the United States and its former enemies, globalization also contributed to international instability and the threat of terrorism. In response to those dangers, the second Bush administration departed from the multilateral approach to foreign policy that had been built up by Republican and Democratic administrations alike since World War II. Toward the end of his second term, however, Bush worked to improve international relationships, and the unprecedented celebrations at home and abroad when Barack Obama won the presidency signaled the promise of a new era in American relations with the world.

SO NOW YOU KNOW

By 2006, the United States was home to some 35.7 million immigrants, 12.4 percent of the population. Although immigration has played a central role in the nation's history, globalization has changed the ethnic and cultural composition of the nation dramatically and has contributed to the presence of millions of illegal immigrants.

What explains the Clinton administration's move to the right?

How did President Clinton respond to the challenges of globalization?

How did President George W. Bush change American politics and foreign policy?

Conclusion: How have Americans debated the role of the government?

STEP 1 — GETTING STARTED

Below are basic terms from this period in American history. Can you identify each term below and explain why it matters? To do this exercise online or to download this chart, visit bedfordstmartins.com/roarkunderstanding.

TERM	WHO OR WHAT & WHEN	WHY IT MATTERS
Colin Powell, p. 860		
Saddam Hussein, p. 860		
Persian Gulf War, p. 861		
"don't ask, don't tell" policy, p. 866		
North American Free Trade Agreement (NAFTA), p. 872		
No Child Left Behind (NCLB) Act, p. 875		
Hurricane Katrina, p. 876		
September 11, 2001, p. 876		
Al Qaeda, p. 877		
USA Patriot Act, p. 878		
Iraq War, p. 880		
Barack Obama, p. 881		

STEP 2 — MOVING BEYOND THE BASICS

The exercise below represents a more advanced understanding of the chapter material. Reflect on the most important events and developments of the past two decades. Using the chart, describe the events that have had the most impact on recent American history. Consider events both within and outside the United States. When you are finished, consider the following questions: Were these events natural or orchestrated? What was the response of the administrations? How were these events and their effects viewed by Americans? By other nations? Which of the events and developments that you identified do you think will be most important in shaping the next twenty years of American history? Why? To do this exercise online or to download this chart, visit bedfordstmartins.com/roarkunderstanding.

Event/Development	Impact

Now that you've reviewed various parts of the chapter, take a step back and try to see the big picture by answering these questions. Remember to use specific examples from the chapter in your answers. To do this exercise online, visit bedfordstmartins.com/roarkunderstanding.

GEORGE H. W. BUSH AND THE END OF THE COLD WAR

▶ How did U.S. foreign policy change after the fall of communism in Eastern Europe and the breakup of the Soviet Union?

▶ Why did George H. W. Bush fail to win a second term as president?

THE CLINTON ADMINISTRATION

▶ Should Bill Clinton be considered a liberal? Why or why not?

▶ Why did Bill Clinton attract such intense animosity from the religious and political right?

THE GEORGE W. BUSH ADMINISTRATION

▶ What were the key components of George W. Bush's domestic agenda? How did his domestic priorities compare to those of Ronald Reagan?

▶ In what ways did Bush's foreign policy depart from that of previous administrations?

LOOKING BACKWARD, LOOKING AHEAD

▶ Compare and contrast the place of the United States in the world in 1900 and in 2005. What explains the dramatic change in America's global stature?

▶ Based on your understanding of U.S. history, consider the follow question: In fifty years' time, will the United States still be the most powerful nation in the world? Why or why not?

IN YOUR OWN WORDS

Imagine that you must explain chapter 31 to someone who hasn't read it. What would be the most important points to include and why?

SPOT ARTIFACT CREDITS

p. 3 (ceramic head): Erich Lessing/Art Resource, NY; **p. 5** (Anasazi effigy): Jerry Jacka Photography; **p. 16** (mica hand): Ohio Historical Society; **p. 21** (doll): Photo courtesy of the Oakland Museum, California; **p. 26** (knife): Photo by Michel Zabe/Banco Mexicano de Imagenes; **p. 31** (Aztec shield): Museum of Volkerkunde, Vienna; **p. 34** (saltcellar lid): Danish National Museum, Copenhagen; **p. 36** (Spanish sword): Museo del Ejercito Collección/Archivo Oronoz; **p. 42** (toucan): Werner Forman/Art Resource, NY; **p. 49** (crucifix): Courtesy of the Historical Archaeology Collections of the Florida Museum of Natural History; **p. 55** (tobacco wrapper): Colonial Williamsburg Foundation; **p. 57** (ceramic mug): Courtesy of The Association for the Preservation of Virginia Antiquities; **p. 63** (pipe): Niemeyer Nederlands Tabacologisch Musuem; **p. 75** (bell): © 1991 Mel Fisher Maritime Heritage Society, Key West, FL, Photo: Dylan Kibler; **p. 83** (psalm book): Roger Foley/Library of Congress; **p. 87** (great chair): Dedham Historical Society/ photo by Forrest Frazier; **p. 91** (dice): Courtesy of Association for the Preservation of Virginia Antiquities; **p. 104** (bayonet): Pocumtuck Valley Memorial Association, Memorial Hall Museum; **p. 111** (Poor Richard's Almanack): Courtesy, American Antiquarian Society; **p. 115** (pitcher): Pocumtuck Valley Memorial Association, Memorial Hall Museum, Deerfield, Mass.; **p. 119** (weathercock): Schoharie County Historical Society, Old Stone Fort Museum; **p. 124** (slave ship): Wilberforce House, Hull City Museums and Art Galleries, UK/Bridgeman Art Library; **p. 130** (printing press): Newport Historical Society; **p. 141** (spinning wheel): Smithsonian Institution, Washington, D.C.; **p. 144** (coin): The American Numismatic Society; **p. 150** (stamp): Courtesy of the Trustees of the British Library; **p. 155** (teapot): Northeast Auctions, Portsmouth, New Hampshire; **p. 163** (pistol): Concord Museum; **p. 163** (musket): Concord Museum; **p. 169** (seal): Collection of the Oliver Family, photo by Clive Russ; **p. 176** (red coat): Nichipor Collection/Picture Research Consultants & Archives; **p. 181** (currency): Smithsonian Institution, Washington, D.C., Photo by Douglas Mudd; **p. 189** (canteen): Fort Ticonderoga Museum; **p. 207** (penny note): Library of Congress; **p. 214** (inkwell): Independence National Historic Park; **p. 225** (George and Martha Washington's inauguration outfits): robe: gift of Mrs. Henry Wheeler de Forest in memory of her husband; suit: gift of E. Coster Wilmerding, Museum of the City of New York; **p. 227** (pitcher): Smithsonian Institution, Washington, D.C.; **p. 231** (coin): The American Numismatic Association; **p. 238** (medal): Indiana Historical Society; **p. 249** (Thomas Jefferson pitcher): Collection of Janice L. and David J. Frent; **p. 251** (compass): Smithsonian Institution, Washington, D.C.; **p. 258** (Tecumseh): Library of Congress; **p. 263** (McCoy's sampler): Chicago Historical Society; **p. 277** (Erie Canal keg): © Collection of the New-York Historical Society; **p. 288** (bank note): Miriam and Ira D. Wallach Division of Art, Prints and Photographs, The New York Public Library, Astor, Lenox and Tilden Foundations; **p. 295** (abolitionist purse): The Daughters of the American Revolution Museum, Washington, D.C. Gift of Mrs. Erwin L. Broecker; **p. 300** (miniature log cabin): National Museum of American History, Smithsonian Institution, Behring Center; **p. 307** (locomotive): National Museum of American History, Smithsonian Institutions, Behring Center; **p. 309** (plough): Courtesy Deere & Company; **p. 317** (cooking pot): Oakland Museum of California; **p. 329** Mary Cragin: Oneida Community Mansion House; **p. 337** (whip): Louisiana State Museum; **p. 350** (shoe): Valentine Museum, Cook Collection; **p. 357** (fiddle): National Museum of American History, Smithsonian Institution, Washington, D.C.; **p. 365** (Uncle Tom's Cabin poster): Granger Collection; **p. 367** (ticket): Courtesy of the American Antiquarian Society; **p. 373** (shackles): Private Collection; **p. 377** (Know-Nothing flag): Milwaukee County Historical Society; **p. 381** ("Southern Rights" flag): Kansas Historical Society; **p. 395** (soldier): Chicago History Museum; **p. 413** (flag): Smithsonian Institution, National Museum of American History, Behring Center; **p. 416** (potholder): Chicago Historical Society; **p. 427** (advertisement): Chicago Historical Society; **p. 429** (Bible): Anacostia Museum, Smithsonian Institution, Washington, D.C.; **p. 436** (ticket): Collection of Janice L. and David J. Frent; **p. 441** (plough): Courtesy Deere & Company; **p. 446** (election artifact): Collection of Janice L. and David J. Frent; **p. 455** (drum): © The Dorothea Lange Collection, Oakland Museum of California, City of Oakland. Gift of Paul S. Taylor; **p. 466** (silver bar): The Oakland Museum; **p. 481** (book): Beinecke Rare Book and Manuscript Library, Yale University; **p. 483** (telephone): Smithsonian Institution, Washington, D.C.; **p. 492** (cigarettes): Courtesy of Duke Homestead and Tobacco Museum; **p. 509** (trunk): National Park Service Collection, gift of Angelo Forgione/Picture Research Consultants & Archives; **p. 518** (sewing machine): National Museum of American History, Smithsonian Institution, Washington, D.C.;

INDEX

Aggression
Japanese, 697 (m)
before World War II, 691, 692
Agnew, Spiro T., 834
Agrarianism, transformation of, 476
Agribusiness, 475, 476, 757–758
Agricultural Adjustment Act (AAA)
first (1933), 668
second (1938), 683
Agricultural domain, in geographic regions, 510, 511 (m)
Agricultural economy, in South, 343 (m), 344
Agricultural Marketing Act (1929), 648
Agriculture. See also Farms and farming
in colonies, 129
commercial, 474–476
of Eastern Woodland peoples, 14
income (1920–1940), 651 (f)
Japanese immigrants in, 470
land policy and, 309
migrant workers and, 474
Native American societies and, 15 (i)
in New Deal, 667–668, 671, 682–683
price supports for, 629
productivity in, 308, 309
revolution in, 475
sharecropping system of, 443–444
in South, 343 (m), 493
in Southwest, 16, 23
technology and, 309, 757–758
tobacco, 62–64
in West, 474–476
workers in, 678
world market and, 230
in World War I, 609
in World War II, 708
Aguinaldo, Emilio, 562
AIDS. See Acquired immune deficiency syndrome
Aid to Families with Dependent Children (AFDC), 781, 866
AIM. See American Indian Movement
Air-conditioning, 757 (i)
in Sun Belt, 759, 760 (m)
Air force, in World War II, 697, 712–713
Airlines, deregulation of, 838
Air pollution
Carter and, 840
control of, 792
Reagan and, 845
from steamboats, 280
Akan culture, 124
Alabama, 389, 390 (m)
civil rights movement in, 784–785
Hurricane Katrina and, 876
Alamo, battle of the, 321
Alaska
Arctic National Wildlife Refuge in, 840
land bridge to, 7
Albanians, ethnic, 869 (i), 871
Albany Congress, 144–146
Albany Plan of Union, 145–146
Albright, Madeleine K., 865, 865 (i)
Albro, Maxine, 674 (i)
Albuquerque, 47
Alcatraz Island, Indian seizure of, 788
Alcohol and alcoholism. See also
Temperance; Whiskey entries
consumption in 1830, 296
Indians and, 238

prohibition and, 569–570, 635–636
WCTU statement on, 548
World War I and, 609
Alexander Hamilton (Trumbull), 230 (i)
Algeciras, Spain, conference in, 581
Algonquian Indians, 21, 22, 48 (i), 57. See also Opechancanough
Seven Years' War and, 143 (m)
Alien and Sedition Acts (1798), ***243***–244, 290
Alien Land Law (California, 1913), 591
Aliens. See Illegal immigrants
Alito, Samuel A., 875
Allende, Salvador, 818
Alliance(s). See also specific alliances
in American Revolution, 186–187, 191, 191 (i)
Tripartite Pact as, 696
World War I and, 600, 601 (m)
World War II and, 695, 722
Alliance for Progress, 806
Allies (World War I), 600, 601 (m), 605, 606–607, 606 (m). See also World War I; specific countries
loans to, 603, 647
at Paris Peace Conference, 613 (i), 614–616
Allies (World War II), 694 (m), 701 (f). See also World War II; specific countries
Casablanca meeting and, 706
D Day and, 713
NATO and, 728
postwar Germany and, 724–725
United Nations and, 713
victory by, 712–717
Allies, Indians as, 134
Allotment policy. See Dawes Allotment Act
Alphabet, Cherokee, 289
Al Qaeda, 877–878, 881
Altgeld, John Peter, 547
Amalgamated Clothing Workers, 676
Amalgamated Iron and Steel Workers, 542
Amendments to Constitution, 218, 220. See also specific amendments
Bill of Rights as, 227–228
America(s). See also Central America; Exploration; North America; South America
ancient (before 1492), 6–27
naming of, 38
origins of humans in, 6–8, 8 (f)
American Colonization Society, 297, 332
American Communist Party. See Communist Party
American Equal Rights Association, 436
American Expeditionary Force (AEF), 605, 606 (m), 607
American Federation of Labor (AFL), 522, ***524***–525, 526, 542, 546, 570, 619, 676. See also Labor unions; Strikes
in Great Depression, 653
merger with CIO, 758
in World War I, 609
American GI Forum, 735–736, 761, 790
American identity, 137
American Independent Party, 816
American Indian Movement (AIM), 789
American Indians. See Native Americans
American Liberty League, 671
Social Security and, 677

American Medical Association, 637
Social Security and, 677
American Party. See Know-Nothing Party
American Philosophical Society, 132
American Psychiatric Association, gays classified by, 792
American Railway Union (ARU), 546–547
American Red Cross, 417
American Revolution. See Revolutionary War (1775–1781)
American Sugar Refining Company, 502
Americans with Disabilities Act (1990), 859
American System, of Clay, 270
American system, of manufacturing, ***310***
American Telephone and Telegraph (AT&T), 487
American Temperance Society, 296
American Temperance Union, 297
American Tobacco Company, 576
American Woman Suffrage Association (AWSA), 549
Ames, Adelbert, 449
Amusement parks, 527 (i), 528
Amusements. See Entertainment; Leisure
Anarchism, 525, 643
unionism and, 543–544
Anasazi people, 16–17
Ancient Americans, 3–27. See also specific groups
Anderson, "Bloody Bill," 405
Anderson, Robert, 397
Andros, Edmund, 105–106
Angel of the Waters (Stebbins), 529 (i)
Anglican Church. See Church of England
Anglo-Americans
in Mexican borderlands, 319–321
in West, 468
Anglo-Saxons, and scientific racism, 490
Angola, 124, 851, 852
slaves from, 126
Animals
in ancient Americas, 9
in Columbian exchange, 39
protection of, 872 (i)
Annapolis, Maryland, 213
Annexation
of Florida, 309
of Hawaii, 555, 561
after Mexican-American War, 309, 468
of Oregon, 309
of Texas, 322, 323, 468
of Utah Territory, 319
Anschluss, 693, 711
Antebellum era
elite southern women in, 347–348
Mormons in, 319
North and South differences in, 338
Anthony, Susan B., 379, 436, 439, 494, **549**
Anthracite coal strike (1902), 576
Antiaircraft in Action (Cornwell), 688 (i)
Anti-Americanism, 881
Antiballistic missiles (ABMs), 818, 850
Antiballistic Missile Treaty (1972), 879
Antidraft riots, 417
Antietam, Battle of (1862), 403 (m), **404,** 405
Antifederalists, 217, 218, 219, 220, 221, 245, 252
Anti-imperialists, 562
Antilynching movement, 494
legislation and, 637

Antinomians, 95
Antipoverty laws, 778–779, 864
Anti-Semitism. *See also* Jews and Judaism; Nazi Germany
   in Nazi Germany, 691
Antislavery movement, 297–298, 341, 357. *See also* Abolition and abolitionism
   in election of 1848, 368
   in South, 360
Antisodomy laws, 849
Antitrust activities
   Roosevelt, Theodore, and, 576
   Taft and, 584
   U.S. Steel and, 578
   of Wilson, 587
Antiwar protests, during Vietnam War, 790, 813–816
Antwerp, Belgium, 713
Apache Indians, 23, 462–463
Apollo program, 805
Appalachian Mountains region
   movement west of, 199
   settlement and, 122, 148
Appeal . . . to the Coloured Citizens of the World, An (Walker), 297
Appeasement, before World War II, **693**
Appliances
   in 1950s, 762
   after World War II, 733 *(i)*
Appomattox Court House, Virginia, Lee's surrender at (1865), 419 *(m)*, 420, 422
Apprentices, 295
Apprenticeship laws, in black codes, 433
Arab-Israeli wars, 797, 819
Arab world, 615
   Clinton and, 871
   Eisenhower and, 755
   Israel-Palestine conflicts and, 729–730, 819, 871
   Nixon and, 797
   opinion of U.S. in, 880–881
   Persian Gulf War and, 860–862, 861 *(m)*
Arafat, Yasir, 871
Arapaho Indians, 317, 463 *(i)*, 464
Arbella (ship), 88
Arbenz, Jacobo, 754
Arbitration treaties, of Taft, 584
Archaeology, history and, 4–5
Archaic Indians, 10
   as hunters and gatherers, 9, 10–14
   warfare among, 13
Architecture
   Chicago school of, 529
   skyscrapers and, 529
Arctic National Wildlife Refuge, 840
Arctic region, Native Americans of, 21
Argonne Cemetery, 623
Arikara Indians, 462
Aristide, Jean-Bertrand, 870
Arizona, 16, 323, 373
Arizona (ship), 698 *(i)*
Arkansas, 339, 396, 397, 429
   school integration in, 768 *(i)*, 769
Armed forces. *See also* Military; Militia; specific forces, battles, and wars
   African Americans in, 176, 408 *(i)*, 410–411, 411 *(i)*, 414, 423, 605
   Bonus Marchers and, 654
   British standing army and, 148
   in Civil War, 401, 410–411, 414, 423

Continental army as, 171
desegregation of, 721, 735
Jefferson and, 252
in Revolutionary War, 175 *(i)*, 176–177
in Shays's Rebellion, 211–212
in World War I, 604–605, 605–606
in World War II, 700–702
Arminianism, 94
Armistead, William, 188 *(i)*
Armistice
   French in World War II, 695
   after Korean War, 742
   after World War I, 607, 614
Arms and armaments. *See also* Weapons
   "cash-and-carry" policy and, 692
   Iran-Contra and, 851–852
   Lend-Lease Act and, 696
   right to keep and bear, 228
Arms control, 818
Arms race. *See* Nuclear arms race
Army-McCarthy hearings, 749
Army of Northern Virginia, 404
Army of the Potomac, 403, 404, 420
Arnold, Benedict, 179, **190**
"Arsenal of democracy," U.S. as, 695–696
Art(s). *See also* specific arts and artists
   in Harlem Renaissance, 637–638
   Johnson, Lyndon B., and, 780
   Native American, 4 *(i)*
   needlework portrait of Boston Common, 114 *(i)*
Arthur, Chester A., 497
Articles of Confederation (1781–1789), 197, ***198***, 207, 213
   attempts to strengthen, 213–214
   Congress under, 199, 211
   economy and finances under, 199, 206–207
   Native Americans and, 207–208
Artifacts, 4–5
   of Woodland Indians, 18
Artisans
   slaves as, 350
   urban, 132 *(i)*
ARVN, 807–808, 819
Aryanism, in Nazi Germany, 709
Asante culture, 124
Asia, 615. *See also* specific countries
   Chinese civil war in, 729–730
   Columbus's search for, 36
   European colonies in, 696
   expansion into, 557
   human origins in, 6–8
   immigrants from, 511, 514, 643
   Roosevelt, Theodore, and, 581
   Taft and, 583
   trade with, 317
   U.S. involvement in, 742, 851
Asian Americans. *See also* specific groups
   bigotry against, 591
   in cabinet, 865, 875
   in New Deal, 679
   poverty of, 868
   in World War II, 700
Assassinations
   attempts on Castro, 836
   of Franz Ferdinand, 600, 601 *(m)*
   of Garfield, 497
   of Kennedy, John F., 777–778
   of Kennedy, Robert F., 816

   of King, Martin Luther, Jr., 787
   of Lincoln, 422
   of McKinley, 575
Assemblies. *See also* Legislatures
   colonial, 136, 151
   two-chamber, in states, 202
Assembly lines, 631, 708
Assimilation
   of Indians, 288, 289, 456, 456 *(i)*, 459, 679
   of new immigrants, 515
   of "nonwhite" groups, 470
Assumption, of state debts, 233
Astronauts, Soviet, 805
Aswan Dam, 755
Atahualpa (Incas), 42
AT&T. *See* American Telephone and Telegraph
Atchison, David Rice, 380–381
Athabascan Indians, 23
Atlanta
   fall of (1864), 419 *(m)*, 420, 421
   race riot in, 591–592
Atlanta Compromise, 591
Atlanta Constitution, 492
Atlantic Charter (1941), 696
Atlantic Ocean region. *See also* Exploration; specific countries
   Civil War in, 406
   French exploration of, 50
   slave trade in, 123–125, 124 *(m)*
   Spanish exploration of, 35
   trade in, 116 *(m)*, 130
   voyages in, 35–39
   in World War I, 606
   in World War II, 704–705, 705 *(m)*
Atomic bomb. *See also* Nuclear weapons
   in World War II, 716, 716 *(i)*
Attorney general, 227, 576
Attucks, Crispus, 156 *(i)*, 157
Audiotapes, in Watergate scandal, 833 *(i)*, 835
Auschwitz, concentration camp in, 711
Austin, Stephen F., 320
Australia, 511, 512
Austria, 615
   Hitler's *Anschluss* with, 693, 694 *(m)*, 711
Austria-Hungary, 600, 615
Automobiles and automobile industry
   Ford and, 630–631
   in 1920s, 631 *(m)*
   UAW strike in (1937), 676
"Axis of evil," Bush, George W., on, 879
Axis powers (World War II), 694 *(m)*, 698, 706. *See also* specific countries
   surrender of, 717
   weapons production by, 701 *(f)*
Ayllón, Lucas Vázquez de, 42
Aztecs. *See* Mexica

Babbitt (Lewis), 640
Baby boom, 764, 764 *(t)*
Bacon, Nathaniel, 70
Bacon's Laws (1676), 71
Bacon's Rebellion, 68, **70–71**
Baker, Ella, 770, 783
Baker, Isaac Wallace, 327 *(i)*
Baker, Newton D., 605
Baker v. Carr (1963), 782
Balance of power, 581, 630
"Balance of Power, The" (1780), 191 *(i)*

Balboa, Vasco Núñez de, 38
Balch, Emily Greene, 611
Baldwin, Brent, 869 *(i)*
Balkan region, 615
"Ballad of Pretty Boy Floyd, The," 652
Baltimore (Lord), 67
Baltimore, Maryland, 260
    Civil War in, 397
    Democratic convention in, 387
Baltimore and Ohio Railroad, 280, 522
Bambara culture, 124
"Banana republics," 557
Bank(s) and banking. *See also* Bank of the
    United States; Panics
    under Articles of Confederation, 207
    deregulation of, 845
    failures of, 648, 650, 665 *(f)*
    farmers and, 538
    growth of commercial, 231–232
    money and, 232, 282
    Morgan and, 488
    national system of, 415, 416, 586–587
    in New Deal, 665–666
    panic of 1819 and, 283
    power of bankers and, 282
    in South, 344
    state-chartered, 282
    Wilson and, 586–587
Banknotes, 207, 232, 282, 283, 292
Bank of North America, 207
Bank of the United States
    first, 233–234, 282
    Jackson and, 290–292
    second, 282, 283, 292
Bankruptcy
    of Chrysler Corporation, 838
    financial crisis of 2008– and, 882
    in 1920, 629
    of S&Ls, 845
Banks, Dennis, 789
Bank War, 291–292
Banky, Vilma, 640 *(i)*
Bannock Shoshoni Indians, 467
Baptists, 263, 295, 351, 358, 431
Barbados
    Puritans in, 89
    slavery from, 74–76
Barbary Wars (1801–1805), 255–256
Barbed wire, 473, 474
Barrios, in California, 468
Barrow plantation (1861 and 1881), 444 *(m)*
Barry, Leonora, 524
Barter, in upcountry South, 357
Barton, Clara, 417
Baruch, Bernard, 608
Baseball, 528, 638, 639 *(f)*
Bastogne, in World War II, 713
Bataan Death March, 703
Batista, Fulgencio, 754
Battle(s). *See also* Wars and warfare;
    specific battles and wars
    of Britain (1940), **695**
    of the Bulge (1944–1945), 713
    of Midway, **704**
Battle of Savage's Station, The (Sneden),
    402 *(i)*
Bay of Pigs invasion (1961), 804–805
Bayonet rule, in South, 448, 449
Beals, Melba Patillo, 769
Bear claw necklace, 255 *(i)*

Bear Flag Revolt, 321
Beat generation, 766
Beecher family. *See also* Stowe, Harriet
    Beecher
    Catharine, 264
    Lyman, 296
Begin, Menachem, 841–842
Beirut, Lebanon, 851
Beissel, Johann Conrad, 119 *(i)*
Belgium, Nazi invasion of, 694
Bell, Alexander Graham, 487
Bell, John, 376 *(m),* 387, 388–389, 388 *(m)*
Belleau Wood, battle at, 606
Benefits
    for labor, 758
    Social Security, 677–678
Bentley, Elizabeth, 737
Benton, Thomas Hart, 317, 379
Berger, Victor, 620
Beringia (land bridge), **7**–8
Berkeley, William, 69, 70
Berkman, Alexander, 543
Berlin, Germany
    division and occupation of, 724 *(m),*
        727 *(m),* 806
    in World War II, 714
Berlin airlift, 727
Berlin blockade, 727
Berlin Wall, 806
Bernard, Francis, 151, 156
Berry, Chuck, 766
Bessemer, Henry, 483–484
Bethlehem, Pennsylvania, 118 *(i)*
Bethune, Mary McLeod, 678 *(i),* **679**
Bibb, Henry, 331
Bible
    defense of slavery and, 342
    King James version of, 85
    Luther and, 49
    Puritans and, 93
    in schools, 782
Bicameral legislature, 215
Bicycles, 548 *(i)*
Biddle, Nicholas, 291 *(i)*
"Big Bonanza," 467
Big business
    railroads as, 482–483
    regulation of, 587
    tariffs and, 582–583
    in West, 475
Big house, on plantations, 345, 347 *(f)*
"Big stick" foreign policy, of Roosevelt,
    Theodore, 580–581
"Big Three," in World War II, 713
"Billion Dollar Congress," 501
Bill of Rights (U.S.), **227**–228. *See also*
    Amendments; specific Amendments
    Alien and Sedition Acts and, 243
    nullification of acts infringing on, 244
    Supreme Court on, 782
Bills of rights, in state constitutions, **202,** 203
Bimetallism system, 503
Bin Laden, Osama, 871, 877, 878, 880, 881
Biological weapons, 879
Biracialism, in South, 341
"Birds of passage" (immigrants), 513
Bird Store (New Orleans), 348 *(i)*
Birmingham, Alabama
    iron and steel industry in, 493
    racial violence in, 774 *(i),* 784

Birth control, 589 *(i),* 590, 637, 831
    pill as, 791
Birthrate, after World War II, 733, 764
Bison. *See also* Buffalo
    Archaic Indian hunters of, 9, 11–12
Black Cabinet, of Roosevelt, Franklin D., 678
Black codes, 432 *(i),* **433,** 434
Black Death, 32
Black Elk (Oglala holy man), 461
Blackfeet Indians, 23
Black Hawk (Sauk and Fox Indians), 289
Black Hawk War (1832), 289, 401
Black Hills, 460, 466 *(m)*
"Black is beautiful," 787
Black Kettle (Cheyenne leader), 458
Blacklist(s), against union members,
    544, 545
Black market, during Revolution, 183
Black Panther Party for Self-Defense, 787
Black people. *See* Africa; African
    Americans; Africans; Free blacks;
    Slaves and slavery
Black power movement, 787
Black suffrage
    Fourteenth Amendment and, 435–436
    Fifteenth Amendment and, 438–439
Black Thursday (October 24, 1929), 648
Black Tuesday (October 29, 1929), 648
Blaine, James G., 497, 498–499, 498 *(i),*
    499 *(m),* 501, 557
"Bleeding Kansas" (1850s), 380–381, 381 *(m)*
"Bleeding Sumner," 381
Blitzkrieg ("lightning war"), 693–694
Blockade runners, 417
Blockades
    of Berlin, 727
    in Civil War, 400, 406, 412
    in World War I, 602, 603
Bloody shirt, waving the, 445
"Bloody Sunday," in civil rights movement,
    784, 785
Blue-collar workers, 655
Blue Jacket (Shawnee Indians), 237, 238
"Bluestocking" (educated woman), 264
Boarding schools, for Indians, 459
Board of Trade (England), 136
Boleyn, Anne (England), 85
Bolshevism
    in Russia, 604, 606
    after World War I, 619
Bombs and bombings
    atomic bombs and, 716, 716 *(i)*
    in Cambodia, 819
    Haymarket, 524–525, 544
    in Oklahoma City, 866
    in Vietnam, 810, 811, 813, 815,
        819–820, 821
    in World War II, 712–713
Bomb shelters, 756
Bonds. *See also* Certificates of debt
    after Revolution, 232–233
Bonfield, John ("Blackjack"), 526
Bonus Marchers, 654
Book of Mormon, The, 319
Boom and bust cycles, 283
Boomtowns, 466, 477
Boonesborough, Kentucky, 186
Bootblacks, 518, 519 *(i)*
Booth, John Wilkes, 422
Borah, William, 617 *(i)*

Border(s). *See also* Boundaries
  of Mexico, 320
  of Oregon, 323
  Rio Grande as, 325–326
Borderlands
  Mexican, 319–321
  politics and, 133–136
  Spanish, 72–73
Border states (Civil War), 417
  Emancipation Proclamation and, 410
  freedom for blacks and, 408, 409
  secession and, 398
Boré, Étienne de, 343
Bosch, Juan, 811
Bosnia, 600, 870–871
Bosses (political), 498, 530–531
Boston, 88, 172, 372, 513
  police strike in (1919), 619
  school desegregation in, 830 *(i)*, 831–832
  Sons of Liberty in, 151
Boston Massacre, 156 *(i)*, **157**
Boston Port Act (1774), 160
Boston Public Library, 530
Boston Tea Party, 158 *(i)*, 159, 161
Boudry, Nancy, 350
Boundaries. *See also* Border(s)
  with Canada, 239, 323
  by 1850, 316
  after Revolutionary War, 192
  of 1763, 148
  of slave and free states, 268
  of Texas, 323, 369, 370
  western, of states, 198–199, 200 *(m)*
  after World War I (Europe), 615 *(m)*
Bow, Clara, 638
Bowdoin, James, 211, 212
Bows and arrows, 12
Boxer Protocol (1901), 556
Boxer uprising (China), 556
Boxing, 639
Boycotts
  anti-British, 155–156, 161, 162, 165
  grape, 789–790
  of Pullman cars, 546
  of UN Security Council, 739–740
Boyer, LaNada, 788
Boys. *See also* Child labor; Children; Men
  as bootblacks, 518, 519 *(i)*
Bozeman Trail, 460
Bracero program, 760, 761 *(i)*
Braddock, Edward, 146
Bradford, William, 87
Brady, Mathew, 385 *(i)*
Brains Trust, in New Deal, 664
Branch, Jacob, 350
Branches of government
  in Constitution, 216
  in Virginia Plan, 214
Brandeis, Louis, 587
Brant, Joseph (Thayendanegea), 180 *(i)*,
  181–182, 185, 192, 207–208
Bray, Rosemary, 780
Brazil
  migration to, 76 *(f)*
  sugar plantation in, 42, 74 *(i)*
Brazos River, 320
Bread riots, in Confederacy, 413
Breckinridge, John C., 376 *(m)*, 387,
  388–389, 388 *(m)*
Brest-Litovsk, treaty of (1918), 606

Briand, Aristide, 630
Bridge, Brooklyn, 508 *(i)*, 529
Brinkmanship, 753
Britain. *See* England (Britain)
***Britain, Battle of (1940),* 695**
British Empire. *See also* British North
  America; England (Britain); specific
  colonies
  borderlands and politics in, 133–136
  role of North American colonies in,
  103–106
British Guiana, Venezuela and, 557
British North America
  in 18th century, 112–137
  unifying experiences for colonists in,
  129–136
Brooklyn Bridge, 508 *(i)*, 529
Brooks, Gwendolyn, 734
Brooks, Preston, 381
Brothels, in mining camps, 327
Brotherhood of Sleeping Car Porters, 709
Brown, John, 385, 391
  Harpers Ferry raid by, 386
  Pottawatomie Creek killings by, ***381,*** 386
  trial and execution of, 386, 387 *(i)*
Brown, Joseph E., 413
Brown, William Wells, 331
"Brown power," 790
Brownsville, New York, birth control clinic
  in, 589 *(i)*, 590
***Brown v. Board of Education (1954),* 768,**
  768 *(i)*, 782
Brunauer, Esther, 738
***Bryan, William Jennings,* 552**
  election of 1896 and, 552–553, 563
  election of 1904 and, 577
  election of 1908 and, 582
  Scopes trial and, 644
  as secretary of state, 599
  on U.S expansionism, 562
  World War I and, 602
Buchanan, James, 376 *(m)*, 379, 384, 390
Buchanan, Pat, 797, 874 *(m)*
Buckley v. Valeo (1976), 836
Bucktails (pro-Jackson group), 285
Buddhists, in Vietnam, 756
Budget. *See* Federal budget
Buena Vista, Mexico, battle at, 324, 325
Buffalo. *See also* Bison
  Indians and, 23, 317, 459
  near extinction of, 459–460
  slaughter of, 317–318
Buffalo Bill (William F. Cody), 477
Buffalo soldiers, 468
Bulge, Battle of the (1944–1945), 713
Bull Moose Party. *See* Progressive Party, of
  1912
Bull Moose progressives, 587
***Bull Run, battle of (Manassas),* 402,**
  403 *(m)*
  first (1861), 402, 403 *(m)*
  second (1862), 404
"Bully pulpit," Roosevelt, Theodore, on,
  575, 575 *(i)*
Bunche, Ralph J., 734
Bundy, McGeorge, 809
Bunker Hill, battle of (1775), 172, 172 *(m)*
Bureaucracy, presidential control over, 682
Bureau of Indian Affairs, 464, 750 *(i)*
  Indian takeover of, 789, 798

Bureau of Refugees, Freedmen, and
  Abandoned Lands. *See* Freedmen's
  Bureau
Burger, Warren E., 828 *(i)*, 832, 853 *(i)*
Burgesses, 61
Burgoyne, John, 172, 178 *(m)*, 184–185
***Burial mounds,* 15**
  in Mississippi River region, 15
  of Woodland Indians, 13–14, 17–19
Burleson, Albert, 612
Burma, 696, 703, 714, 822
Burnham, Daniel, 532
Burns, Anthony, 372
Burnside, Ambrose, 404
Burr, Aaron, 242, 251
Bus boycott, in Montgomery, 767 *(i)*,
  769–770
Bush, George H. W.
  election of 1988 and, 858–859
  election of 1992 and, 863
  Iran-Contra pardons by, 852
  Iraq and, 860–861
  taxation and, 859, 859 *(i)*
  as vice president, 843
Bush, George W.
  domestic policy of, 875–876
  election of 2000 and, 874–875, 874 *(m)*
  election of 2004 and, 880
  environment and, 875
Business. *See also* Big business;
  Corporations; Finance capitalism
  civil service reform and, 497
  Clinton and, 868
  foreign-owned, 873
  in Gilded Age, 482–487, 505
  government alliance with, 578, 629–630
  mechanization in, 520
  movement to foreign markets, 846
  New Deal and, 664, 670–671
  regulation of trusts and, 502
  after World War II, 733
Busing, school, 830 *(i)*
Bute (Earl of), 148, 149
Butler, Andrew P., 381
Butler, Benjamin F., 409
Butler, Nicholas Murray, 611
Byles, Mather, 182

Cabinet. *See also* specific cabinet members
  African Americans in, 865, 875
  Asian Americans in, 865, 875
  Black Cabinet, 678
  British, 148
  women in, 749, 848, 875
Cabot, John, 38
Cabral, Pedro Álvars, 38
Cabrillo, Juan Rodríguez, 42, 47
Cahokia, 19, 19 *(m)*
Caldwell, John, 145 *(i)*
Calhoun, John C., 259, 272, ***285,*** 369
  election of 1824 and, 270–271
  election of 1836 and, 300
  nullification and, 287, 290
  on slavery, 342, 367, 382
California, 323, 326, 369, 370
  agriculture in, 474
  antitax crusade in, 831
  Chinese in, 327, 327 *(i)*, 469–470, 591
  gold rush (1849-1852) in, 326, 327, 366
  growth of, 759

California (continued)
gun control in, 859
Hispanics in, 468
Japanese in, 581, 591
manifest destiny and, 321
Mexican Americans in, 621
Mexican-American War in, 324
Mexican migration to, 321
Native Americans in, 21
Reagan as governor of, 843
reforms in, 574
Russia and, 135
Spain and, 135, 136 *(m)*
California gold rush (1849–1852), ***326***–327,
366, 465
California peoples, 12–13, 13 *(m)*
California Trail, 318 *(m)*, 322
Californios, 468
Calusa Indians, 42
Calvinism, of Puritans, 91
Cambodia, 814, 819–820, 820 *(m)*, 822
Camden, battle of (1780), 189, 189 *(m)*
Campaigns (political). *See also* Elections
in 1828 election, 284–285
in 1884 election, 498–499
Camp David accords, ***841***–842
Camp followers, 176, 184
Camp meetings, 295
Canada
boundaries with, 239, 323
British control of, 146
France and, 50, 106
free blacks and, 205, 332
immigration to, 512
Indians in, 192
loyalists in, 183
in NAFTA, 871
in Revolutionary War, 177–179, 177 *(m)*
runaway slaves in, 164, 372
Seven Years' War and, 146
War of 1812 and, 259, 260, 260 *(m)*, 261
Canals, 280
Erie Canal, 278 *(i)*, 279 *(m)*, 280
Panama Canal, 580, 580 *(m)*
Canary Islands, 36, 37
Cane Ridge, revival meeting at, 295
Cannibalism, Native American, 24
CAP. *See* Community Action Program
Cape Cod, 87
Cape of Good Hope, 34
Cape Verde Islands, 34
Capital city. *See also* Washington, DC
location along Potomac, 233
in New York, 230
in South, 233
Capital gains tax, 838
Capitalism
finance, 488–489
Roosevelt, Franklin D., and, 664
welfare, 632
Capone, Alphonse ("Al"), 636
Caputo, Philip, 812
Caravel, 34
Caribbean region, 240, 243
colonized African Americans in, 409
Columbus in, 36, 39
France and, 146
Spain and, 40
Taft and, 583
U.S. involvement in, 557, 851

Carlisle Indian School, 459
Carmichael, Stokely, 787
Carnegie, Andrew, 482, ***483***–484, 493,
511, 522
gospel of wealth and, 490
Homestead strike and, 542–545
Morgan, J. P., and, 489
Carnegie Endowment for International
Peace, 611
Carnegie Steel, 483, 489
Carney, Kate, 347
Carolina(s), 76–77, 122. *See also* North
Carolina; South Carolina
Carolina Piedmont, 182 *(m)*
Carpetbaggers, 440–441
Carranza, Venustiano, 600
Carrier, Willis Haviland, 757 *(i)*
Carson, Rachel, 792
Carter, James Earl ("Jimmy"), Jr., ***836***–837,
837 *(i)*
Cold War and, 842
election of 1976 and, 836, 836 *(m)*
election of 1980 and, 842, 843
human rights issues and, 840–842
Middle East and, 841–842
presidency of, 837–842
Carter Doctrine, 842
Cartier, Jacques, 50
Cartography, maps of New World and, 38
Cartoons. *See* specific cartoons
Casablanca meeting, 706
"Cash-and-carry" policy, 692
Cash crops, in South, 343, 357
Cash register, 520
Cass, Lewis, 367, 368, 369 *(m)*, 376 *(m)*
Caste system, 637
Castle Garden immigration station, 515
Castro, Fidel, ***754***, 804–805, 836
Casualties
in Civil War (U.S.), 404, 406, 411, 419,
420–421, 422, 423
in Iraq War, 880
in Korean War, 742
in Mexican-American War, 324, 325
at Pearl Harbor, 698
in Philippines, 714
of Philippine-U.S. conflict, 562
in Revolutionary War, 172, 179, 185
in Seven Years' War, 146
in World War I, 602, 605, 607, 607 *(f)*
in World War II North Africa
campaign, 706
Cathay Company, 50
Catholicism. *See also* Missions and
missionaries; Religion
in Democratic Party, 492, 499
in England, 84–85, 84 *(i)*, 106
Luther and, 48–49
in Maryland, 67, 130
in middle colonies, 100
missionaries and, 44, 72–73, 79
in New France, 115
vs. Protestantism, 48–49
of Smith, Alfred, 645
Catlin, George, 258 *(i)*, 317
Catt, Carrie Chapman, 610
Cattell, James McKeen, 611
Cattle. *See* Ranching
Cattle trails, 473, 474 *(m)*
Cave paintings, 6 *(i)*

Cayuga Indians, 22, 181
"Cease and desist" orders, 587
Census
of 1790 and 1800, 232
of 1810, 258
Central America. *See also* specific countries
Iran-Contra in, 851–852
leftists in, 754, 851
United Fruit in, 557
U.S. intervention in, 860
Central bank. *See also* Bank of the United
States
Hamilton on, 233–234
Central High School, Little Rock, 768 *(i)*
Central Intelligence Agency (CIA), ***728***
Chilean destabilization by, 818
Guatemala and, 754
illegal activities by, 836
Iran government and, 747, 755, 755 *(i)*
North Vietnam and, 753
operations by, 771
Central Pacific Railroad, 469
Central Park (New York City), 529 *(i)*, 530
Central Powers, 601 *(m)*, 606 *(m)*
Century of Dishonor, A (Jackson), 461
Ceremonial mounds. *See* Mound builders
Cerro Gordo, Mexico, battle at (1847), 325
Certificates of debt (public securities), 183,
232, 233
Cession. *See also* Mexican cession
of Indian land, 208, 209, 237 *(m)*, 257–258
of western lands (1782–1802), 200 *(m)*
Ceuta, 34
Chaco Canyon, 17, 17 *(i)*
Chamberlain, Neville, 693
Chamberlain, W. G., 316 *(i)*
Chamber of Commerce, 671
Social Security and, 677
Chambers, Whittaker, 737
Champlain, Lake, 146, 260
Chancellorsville, battle at (1863), 419,
419 *(m)*, 420
Chao, Elaine L., 875
Chaplin, Charlie, 638
Chapultepec, battle of (1847), 325
Charities, during Great Depression, 651
Charles I (England), 67, 85, 105
Charles I (Spain), 38, 49. *See also* Charles V
(Holy Roman Empire)
Charles II (England), 77, 100, 101, 105, 106
Charles V (Holy Roman Empire), Charles I
of Spain as, 48
Charleston, South Carolina (Charles Town),
77, 238
Democratic convention in, 386–387
Fort Sumter attack in, 397
Charles Towne. *See* Charleston
Charlottesville, capture of, 190
Charter of Privileges (Pennsylvania), 102
Charters
of Bank of the United States, 234,
282, 291
of Carolina, 77
of Massachusetts, 87–88, 92, 105, 159
of transport companies, 279
of United Nations, 713
of Virginia Company, 61
Chase, Salmon P., 369, 401, 438
Chattanooga, battle of (1863), 419 *(m)*, 420
Chavez, Cesar, 788 *(i)*, ***789***

"Checkers speech" (Nixon), 741
Chemical weapons, 808, 813
Cheney, Richard B., 874, 879
Chernobyl, nuclear accident at, 839
Cherokee Indians, 134
    removal of, 288 *(m)*, 289
Cherry Valley, battle at, 185
Chesapeake incident, 256, 256 *(m)*
Chesapeake region. *See also* Maryland;
        Tobacco; Virginia
    colonies in, 56–71, 63 *(m)*
    indentured servants in, 60, 64–67
    Puritans in, 89
    Revolutionary War in, 191
    slavery in, 77–78
    society in, 68–71
    as tobacco society, 62–67, 64 *(i)*
    War of 1812 in, 260
Chesnut, James, 359 *(i)*
Chesnut, Mary Boykin, 348, 360
Cheyenne Indians, 23, 317, 458, 460, 464
Chiang Kai-shek, 691, 713, 714, 729
Chicago
    African Americans in, 618 *(i)*, 621
    Democratic Convention (1968) in,
        813 *(i)*, 816
    Great Fire of 1871 in, 529
    Haymarket riot in, 525–526
    Hull House in, 568–569
    immigrants in, 513
    skyscrapers in, 529
    World's Columbian Exposition in,
        477, 532
"Chicago school," of architecture, 529
Chicago Tribune, 547
    on election of 1948, 736
Chicanos, 789, 790
Chickamauga, battle of (1863), 419 *(m)*, 420
Chickasaw Indians, 23, 280, 289
Chiefdoms, 15, 17–19
Chief Joseph (Nez Percé), 462
Chief justice, of Supreme Court, 227. *See
        also* specific individuals
Child, Lydia Maria, 330, 386
Childbearing, in New England, 114
Child care
    Infant Welfare Society, 566 *(i)*
    Nixon and, 798, 832
Child labor, 349–350, 495, 519 *(i)*, 577 *(i)*
    Keating-Owen Act and, 587
    in late 19th century, 518–519
    in sweatshops, 518
    in textile mills, 493, 518
Children. *See also* Child labor
    black codes, apprenticeship laws,
        and, 433
    during Civil War, 413
    education for, 295, 442
    of free blacks, 355
    of immigrants, 512 *(m)*, 513
    Indian, 459, 459 *(i)*
    in New England, 89
    in poverty, 846
    in Revolutionary War, 176
    slave, 125, 127, 127 *(i)*, 340 *(i)*, 348,
        349–350
    Social Security and, 677
    in textile mills, 493
    on western trails, 318
Children's Bureau, 583

Child Support Enforcement Amendments
        Act, 848
Chile, 818 *(m)*
    Allende in, 818
    human rights in, 840
    Spain and, 40
China
    civil war in, 729–730
    Communists vs. Nationalists in, 717
    dependence on investments from, 875
    diplomatic relations with, 841
    European trade with, 50
    Japan and, 691, 692, 696
    missionaries in, 556
    Nationalist, 691
    Nixon and, 817
    Open Door policy in, 554 *(i)*, 557, 581
    Portugal and, 34
    Soviet treaty with, 729
    Spanish-American War and, 559
    Tiananmen Square protest in, 863
    Vietnam and, 822
    in World War II, 714
    after World War II, 713
Chinese Americans. *See also* Chinese
        immigrants
    in World War II, 701
Chinese Exclusion Act (1882, 1902), **470,**
        474, 514, 591, 621
Chinese immigrants, 643
    in California, 469–470, 474
    as farm laborers, 474
    migration to cities, 514
    in mining, 327, 327 *(i)*, 467
    railroads and, 469, 514
Chippewa Indians, 22, 789
Chiricahua Apache Indians, 462–463
Chisholm, Shirley, 833
Chisholm Trail, 473, 474 *(m)*
Chivalry, in South, **347**
Chivington, John M., 458
Choctaw Indians, 23, 289
Cholera, 317, 327
Christian Coalition, 844
"Christian guardianship" (paternalism), 346
Christianity. *See also* specific religions
    in China, 556
    fundamentalist, 844
    Indians and, 58, 59, 288
    in Portugal, 33–34
    Protestant Reformation and, 48–49
    slaves and, 130, 351–352
    in Spain, 34
    white supremacists and, 866
Christian Right, 844, 848, 849
Chrysler Corporation, loans to, 838
Chumash Indians, 13, 13 *(i)*
Churches. *See also* Religion(s); specific
        religions
    black, 431
    Dutch Reformed Church, 100
    meetinghouse as, 94 *(i)*
    membership in, 295
    in New England, 97–98
    Puritan, 93–94
    social gospel and, 569
    women and, 263–264
Churchill, Winston, 695. *See also* World
        War II
    Atlantic Charter and, 696

    at Casablanca, 706
    iron curtain speech of, 724 *(m)*, 725
    at Teheran, 713
    at Yalta, 713
Church of England (Anglican), 84–85,
        88, 128
Church of Jesus Christ of Latter-Day Saints.
        See Mormons
Churubusco, battle of (1847), 325
CIA. *See* Central Intelligence Agency
Cincinnati, Ohio, 237
CIO. *See* Congress of Industrial Organiza-
        tions
Circumnavigation of globe, by Magellan,
        38–39
Cities and towns. *See also* Urban areas;
        specific locations
    African Americans in, 514, 758
    architecture of, 529–530
    bosses (political) in, 530–531
    cars in, 631
    electric lights in, 530
    free blacks in, 355
    in Gilded Age, 515–516
    growth of, 533
    immigrants in, 513, 514–515, 533
    Indians in, 750–751
    in late nineteenth century, 510–516
    mass transit in, 515
    movement to, 308
    neighborhoods in, 515
    in 1950s, 759
    population in, 313, 642 *(m)*
    poverty in, 515, 516 *(i)*
    public works in, 530
    reforms in, 531, 574
    school desegregation in, 831–832
    school enrollment in, 530
    segregation in, 515
    settlement houses in, 568–569
    slaves employed in, 349
    social geography of, 515–516
Citizens and citizenship, 856 *(i)*. *See also*
        specific groups
    Asians and, 470, 679
    for Californios, 468
    Fourteenth Amendment and, 435
    for free blacks, 382
    gender and, 493
    for Indians, 461
    Supreme Court and, 447
City government, 530–531
City upon a hill, Massachusetts Bay colony
        as, 88–89
Civil Defense Administration, 756
Civil disobedience, 784
Civilian Conservation Corps (CCC), 666
Civil liberties, World War I and, 608, 620
Civil rights
    for African Americans, 734–735
    Eisenhower and, 749, 769
    federal intervention for, 786
    of freedmen, 434
    Kennedy, John F., and, 777
    of Mexican Americans, 735–736, 761
    Nixon and, 832
    Reagan and, 848
    during reconstruction, 434
    sexual orientation as protected
        category, 849

Civil rights *(continued)*
    Truman and, 735, 736–737
    in World War II, 709
    after World War II, 733–736, 734 *(i)*
Civil Rights Act. *See also* Title VII
    of 1866, 434
    of 1875, 447
    of 1964, 778, 780, 785, 790, 798
    of 1968, 780, 786
Civil rights movement, 743, 767–770,
    783–787
    police attacks during, 774 *(i)*
Civil service, 446, 496 *(i)*
    Jackson's "spoils system" and, 286
Civil Service Commission, 498
Civil service reform, 497–***498***
Civil war(s)
    in Carolinas, 189 *(m)*
    in Guatemala, 754
    in Haiti, 240
    in Mexico, 599, 621
    in Rwanda, 870
    in Somalia, 869
    in Spain, 692
Civil War (U.S., 1861–1865), 394–423
    African Americans in, 395, 408 *(i)*,
        410–411, 411 *(i)*, 414
    battles in (1861–1862), 402–406, 403 *(m)*,
        404 *(m)*, 405 *(f)*, 405 *(m)*
    battles in (1863–1865), 418–422, 418 *(m)*,
        419 *(m)*, 420 *(f)*, 420 *(m)*
    casualties in, 404, 406, 411, 419, 420–421,
        422, 423
    diplomacy in, 399–400
    dissent during, 417
    draft in, 410, 413, 417
    in East, 402–404, 403 *(m)*
    effects of, 423
    emancipation and, 408–410
    events leading to, 366–390
    financing of, 401, 413, 501
    Fort Sumter attack and, 396 *(i)*, 397
    home fronts during, 412–414, 415–417
    Indians in, 405
    Lee's surrender and, 419 *(m)*, 420, 422
    mobilization for, 400–401
    navy in, 400, 401, 405, 406
    resources of North and South in, 399–400,
        400 *(f)*
    secession and, 389–390, 397–398
    slavery and, 399, 407, 408–409, 414
    strategy in, 400, 420
    as total war, 415
    in West, 397–398, 404–406
    women in, 412 *(i)*, 413, 416–417
Civil Works Administration (CWA), 666
Clark, George Rogers, 186, 187 *(m)*
Clark, William, 253
Classes. *See also* Elites; Middle class
    Civil War and, 413
    Social Security and, 677
Clay, Henry, 282, 283 *(i)*, 286, 291, 291 *(i)*
    American System of, 270
    "corrupt bargain" and, 271–272, 285
    election of 1824 and, 270, 271–272
    election of 1828 and, 284
    election of 1844 and, 322–323
    Missouri Compromise and, 268
    on slavery in territories, 369, 370
    as War Hawk, 259

Clayton Antitrust Act (1914), 587
Clean Air Act
    of 1970, 792
    of 1990, 859
Clean Water Act (1972), 797
"Clear and present danger" test, 620
Clemenceau, Georges, 613 *(i)*, 614
Clemens, Samuel Langhorne. *See* Twain,
    Mark
Clerical jobs, women in, 520–521, 521 *(i)*
Clermont (steamboat), 277 *(i)*, 279–280
Cleveland, Grover, 555
    election of 1884 and, 498–499, 498 *(i)*,
        499 *(m)*
    election of 1888 and, 500
    election of 1892 and, 500, 501
    gold standard and, 503–504
    on immigration restriction, 515
    Pullman strike and, 542 *(i)*, 547
    tariff issue and, 501, 502
Cleveland, Ohio, 515, 573 *(i)*, 574
Cliffs of the Upper Colorado (Moran), 454 *(i)*
Climate, in Great Plains, 472
Clinton, DeWitt, 260
Clinton, Henry, 172, 189, 190
Clinton, Hillary Rodham, 864 *(i)*, 865, 881
Clinton, William Jefferson (Bill), 864 *(i)*
    economy and, 864, 867–868
    election of 1992 and, 863
    election of 1996 and, 867
    gays in military and, 866
    globalization and, 869–872
    impeachment of, 864, 867
    Middle East and, 871
Clodfelter, Mike, 812
Closed shops, 629
Clothing. *See also* Garment industry;
    Textiles and textile industry
    in 1830s, 293 *(i)*
    empire-style, 257 *(i)*
    of Revolutionary riflemen, 175 *(i)*
    of slaves, 346
Clovis points, 9
Coal and coal industry, 308, 576, 654
Coalitions, in New Deal, 662, 662 *(m)*,
    680–681
Cobb, Howell, 389
Cobb, Thomas R. R., 342
Cockran, Bourke, 562
Codes, for New Deal workers, 669
Cody, William F. ("Buffalo Bill"), 477
Coerced labor, 44. *See also* Slaves and
    slavery
Coercive Acts (1773), 171
Coercive (Intolerable) Acts (1774),
    159–160, 161
Cold Harbor, battle of (1864), 419 *(m)*,
    420, 421
Cold War. *See also* Soviet Union
    beginning of, 725
    Carter and, 842
    end of, 852, 862–863, 862 *(m)*
    factors contributing to, 722–730
    impact of, 743
    Johnson, Lyndon B., and, 809
    Khrushchev and, 752 *(i)*
    Korean War and, 739–742
    Latin America, Middle East, and, 754–755
    new world order after, 869–871
    racial issues during, 735–736

Reagan and, 850–852
    Truman and, 721
Colfax, Schuyler, 446
Collective bargaining, in World War I, 609
Collective security, 728
    Wilson and, 616
    after World War I, 630
Colleton, John, 76–77
Collier, John, 679
Colombia, Panama Canal and, 580
Colonies and colonization. *See also* specific
    colonies and regions
    African Americans and, 297, 332, 409
    Albany Plan and, 145–146
    assemblies in, 136
    British, 79, 96 *(f)*, 112–137
    in Chesapeake region, 56–71, 63 *(m)*
    dual identity in British colonies, 137
    European in Asia, 696
    exports from, 131 *(f)*
    French, 129
    German, 615–616
    importance in 1938, 683 *(t)*
    Indian relations with, 134–135
    intercolonial political action and, 153
    land in, 112–113
    in late 17th century, 104 *(m)*
    Lower South and, 123–124
    middle colonies and, 99–102
    national liberation movements and, 717
    in New England, 86–98, 88 *(m)*
    in New Spain, 42–46, 43 *(m)*
    Portuguese, 42
    slavery in, 47
    in South, 55–79
    Spanish, 42–46, 129
    trade in, 103–104
    unifying experiences of British American,
        129–136
Colorado, 16, 323, 458, 632 *(i)*
Colored Farmers' Alliance, 539
Columbian exchange, 38–40, ***39***
"Columbia Patriot, A" (Mercy Otis
    Warren), 219
Columbia River region, 254
"Columbia's Easter Bonnet" (political
    cartoon), 558 *(i)*
Columbia University, protests at, 815–816
Columbus, Christopher, 20, ***35***–38,
    36 *(m)*, 39
Comanche Indians, 23, 317, 460
Combines (farm machine), 475
Comintern, 619
Commerce. *See also* Trade
    in British American colonies, 130
    colonial, 103–104
    in Mediterranean, 255
    in New England, 115–117
    Portuguese, 34
Commerce and Labor Department, 576
Commercial agriculture, 357, 474–476
Commercial amusements, 528
Commercial banking, growth of, 231–232
Commercial law, 282
Commission on Training Camp Activities
    (World War I), 605
Committee for Industrial Organization, 676
Committee of inspection, 180
Committee of Vigilance, in San Francisco,
    327

Committee on Civil Rights (1946). *See* President's Committee on Civil Rights
Committee on Fair Employment Practices (1941), 709
Committee on Public Information (CPI), 611
Committees (American Revolution), 180–181. *See also* specific committees
Committees of correspondence, 158, 160
Committees of public safety, 161, 180
Commodity Credit Corporation, 668, 683
Common people, 327, 356–358
Common Sense (Paine), ***172***–173, 173 *(i)*
Commonwealth, New England families as, 89
Commonwealth of Independent States (CIS), 863
Communication(s)
    mass, 635
    railroads and, 310–311
    transportation and, 303
Communism
    in China, 717
    in Czechoslovakia, 727
    in Eastern Europe, 723–724, 724 *(m)*
    Eisenhower and, 748–749, 752
    Europe after, 870
    in Great Depression, 672
    Greece, Turkey, and, 725–726, 726 *(i)*
    in Iran, 754–755
    in Italy, 728
    Korean War and, 740
    in Latin America, 754
    McCarthyism and, 737–738
    in Middle East, 754–755
    in third world, 819
    Truman and, 729
    Vietnam and, 807
    after World War I, 619–620
    after World War II, 722 *(i)*
    in Yugoslavia, 870
Communist Party, 655, 672
    in Great Depression, 654
Communities
    African American in West, 468
    utopian, 329
Community Action Program (CAP), 779
Compassionate conservatism, of Bush, George W., 875–876
Competition
    attempts to eliminate, 502
    in railroad industry, 483
    vs. regulation, 578
Complex marriage, 329
Compromise of 1850, 370, 370 *(m)*, 371, 391. *See also* Fugitive Slave Act
Compromise of 1877, 450
Computer revolution, 868
Comstock, Anthony, 590
Comstock, Henry, 465
Comstock Lode (Nevada), 366, ***465***–466, 467
Concentration camps, in Cuba, 559
Concentration policy, 318
Concord, 162–163, 163 *(m)*
Condren, Don, 733
Coney Island, New York, 527 *(i)*, ***528,*** 532
Confederacy (Civil War South)
    "belligerent" status for, 406
    birth of, 389

bread riots in, 413
centralization in, 412–413
collapse of, 421–422
Davis and, 396
diplomacy and, 406–407
draft in, 413
emancipation of slaves and, 410
industry in, 412–413
inflation in, 401, 413
Lincoln's reconstruction plan for, 428–429
mobilization of, 400–401
nationalism in, 413–414
resources of, 399–400, 400 *(f)*
secession and, 389–390, 397–398
slavery in, 399
women in, 412 *(i)*, 413
Confederacy (Tecumseh), 258
Confederate Congress, 413
Confederation government. *See* Articles of Confederation
Confederations, Iroquoisan, 22
Confiscation Act, 429
    of 1861, 409
    of 1862, 410
Conformity, Puritan, 91
Congo, slaves from, 126
Congregational Church, 130, 298
Congress (U.S.). *See also* Continental Congress
    under Articles of Confederation, 199–200
    Constitution on, 216
    election of 1876 and, 450
    election of 1932 and, 662
    ex-Confederates in, 433–434
    Reagan and, 847–848
    reconstruction plans of, 429, 434, 435–439, 446
    during Red scare, 620
    slavery and, 366–368
    Southerners in (1865-1877), 442 *(f)*
    Versailles treaty and, 616–617
    violence in, 241 *(i)*
Congressional reconstruction, 434, 435–439
Congress of Industrial Organizations (CIO), 676
    merger with AFL, 758
Congress of Racial Equality (CORE), 709, 784
Conkling, Roscoe, 497
Connecticut, 136, 198, 205
Conoco (Continental Oil Company), 632 *(i)*
Conquistadors, 41–42
"Conscientious objector" status, 228
Consciousness-raising groups, for women, 794
Conscription. *See* Draft (military)
Conservation. *See also* Environment
    environmentalists and, 792
    Roosevelt, Theodore, and, 578–579, 579 *(m)*
    Taft and, 583
Conservatives and conservatism
    grassroots, 830–831
    liberals and, 847–849
    Nixon and, 830
    Reagan and, 843–844
    Roosevelt, Theodore, on, 593
    Taft and, 582
Constitution(s)
    of Cherokees, 289

of Cuba, 561
free-state, 369
Lecompton, 384
reconstruction, in South, 433, 435 *(i)*, 437, 441–442
state, 201–202, 267
Constitution (U.S.), 197, 221. *See also* Bill of Rights; specific Amendments
    Bill of Rights and, 227–228
    democracy vs. republicanism in, 215–216
    ratification of, 216, 217–220, 218 *(m)*, 227
    slavery and, 215, 366, 371
Constitutional convention (1787), ***213***–216, 213 *(i)*
Constitutional Union Party, 387, 388 *(m)*
Consumer(s)
    Johnson, Lyndon B., and, 780
    in 1920s, 633, 634, 655
    after World War I, 618
Consumer culture, 633–634, 762–763
    advertising and, 634
    in Gilded Age, 521
    women in, 637
Consumer goods, from 1920–1930, 633 *(f)*
Consumer prices, and farm income (1865–1910), 539 *(f)*
Consumption
    in British American colonies, 130, 133
    before crash of 1929, 647–648
    mass, 634
    in 1950s, 762–763
    in World War II, 708
Containment, 725, 727
    Eisenhower and, 752
    Korean War and, 740–741
    Reagan and, 851
    strategy of, 727–728
    in Vietnam, 753–754
Continental army, 171, 172, ***176,*** 177–179, 187 *(m)*, 189, 192
    campaigns of 1777–1779 and, 185, 185 *(m)*
    at Valley Forge, 185
Continental Association, 161
Continental Congress, 186, 226. *See also* Congress (U.S.)
    Articles of Confederation and, 198–199
    debt and, 206–207
    Second, 170–172, 173, 182, 198, 198 *(i)*
    Shays's Rebellion and, 211–212
    war financing by, 183
Continental dollars, 171, 207
Continental drift, 6, 7 *(m)*
Contraband, runaway slaves as, 409
Contraception. *See* Birth control
Contract(s)
    of indenture, 66 *(i)*
    for labor, 629
    between slaveholders and ex-slaves, 429–430
Contract labor, 541
"Contract with America," 866
Contras, in Nicaragua, 851, 860
Conventions
    nominating, 300
    state (reconstruction), 435 *(i)*, 437, 441
Conversion. *See also* Puritans
    of Indians, 58
    to Protestantism, 79
    by Puritans, 97
Coode, John, 106

Davis, Paula Wright, 331
Dawes, Charles, 163 *(m)*, 630
Dawes, Henry, 461
Dawes Allotment Act (1887), *461*–462, 679, 750
Dawes Plan (1924), 630
D Day, 712 *(i),* *713*
DDT, 792
Deadwood Dick (Nat Love), 474
Dean, John, 834
Death camps, Nazi, 711
Death of Jane McCrea (Vanderlyn), 184 *(i)*
Death rate. *See* Mortality rate
Debates, Lincoln-Douglas, 383–384
Debates, presidential, 777
Debs, Eugene V., *546*–547, 588–589
    election of 1912 and, 585, 585 *(m),* 588–589
    Espionage Act and, 612
Debts. *See also* National debt
    under Articles of Confederation, 206–207
    corporate, 282
    economic panics and, 283
    of farmers, 211, 444, 476, 503, 538
    Revolutionary War, 192, 206, 239
    state, 233
Decatur, Stephen, 255
"Declaration of Dependence, A," 182
Declaration of Independence (1776), 169, 170 *(i),* 173–*174*, 202, 203, 331
"Declaration on the Causes and Necessity of Taking Up Arms, A," 171
Declaratory Act (1766), 153
Deep South, slavery in, 205
Deere, John, 309
Defender, 514
Defense. *See also* Containment
    colonial, 133–134
    in Constitution, 216
    Eisenhower and, 749, 756
    Korean War and, 742
    road and highway construction and, 749
Defense industries, 708, 709, 759
Defense of Marriage Act (1996), 866
Defense spending
    Carter and, 842
    Kennedy, John F., and, 806
    NSC 68 and, 742
    Reagan and, 850–851
    in 2005, 870 *(f)*
    after World War II, 733
Deficit, in federal budget, 845, 859, 875
Deflation, 503
Deforestation, steamboats and, 280
Deism, in colonies, *132*
Delany, Martin R., 331
Delaware (state), 172, 199, 396, 397
Delaware (Lenni Lenape) Indians, 144, 186, 187 *(m),* 208, 209, 236, 238
    Fort Wayne Treaty and, 259
Delaware River region, in Revolutionary War, 179
Demobilization
    after Civil War, 441
    after World War I, 618, 619
Democracy
    Constitution and, 215–216
    popular sovereignty and, 367
    in South, 359, 360

Democratic Party, 302. *See also* Elections; specific presidents
    collapse of reconstruction and, 448–449
    on emancipation of slaves, 408–409, 410
    in Gilded Age, 491, 492, 498–499
    National Convention of 1968, 813 *(i),* 816
    in New South, 492, 493
    "peace" Democrats in, 421
    political machines in, 530–531
    popular sovereignty and, 377, 379, 386
    Populists and, 552–553
    progressives and, 583
    South and, 442, 448–449, 832
    Watergate break-in and, 834
Democrats (Democratic Republicans), 285, *286,* 302
Demonstration(s). *See* Protest(s); Revolts and rebellions; specific demonstrations
Dempsey, Jack, 639
Denby, Charles, 556
Denmark, Nazi invasion of, 694
Departments of government. *See* specific departments
Department stores, 521
Deportation
    of Chinese immigrants, 514
    of Garvey, 637
    of loyalists, 182
    of Mexican Americans, 652
    during Red Scare (1919), 619–620
Depreciation, during Revolution, 183
Depressions (financial). *See also* Great Depression; Panics; Recessions
    in 1870s, 447, 503, 518, 522
    in 1890s, 476, 504, 518, 532, 545, 546, 550, 552, 563
Deregulation, 868
    by Carter, 838, 839
    by Reagan, 845
Desegregation
    of armed forces, 721, 735, 743
    in Korean War, 743
    Nixon and, 797
    of schools, 768–769, 797, 831–832
Desertion, in Civil War, 413, 422
De Soto, Hernando, 42, 47
Détente policy, with Soviet Union, 817, 836
Detroit
    and auto industry (1920s), 630, 632 *(m)*
    race riot in (1943), 709
Detroit, Fort, 186, 187 *(m)*
Developing nations
    Kennedy, John F., and, 806
    trade and, 872
    Truman's aid to, 729
Dew, Thomas R., 342, 347
Dewey, George, 559, 560 *(m)*
Dewey, Thomas E., 711, 736, 736 *(m)*
Dias, Bartolomeu, 34
Diaz, Porfirio, 621
Dickens, Charles, 495
Dickinson, John, 154–155, 170, 171, 172, 174
Dictatorships. *See also* Franco, Francisco; Hitler, Adolf; Mussolini, Benito; Stalin, Joseph; specific dictators
    CIA support for, 818
    in Latin America, 754
Diem, Ngo Dinh, 753, 754, 807–808

Dien Bien Phu, 753
Diet (food). *See also* Food(s)
    Columbian exchange and, 39
    of Eastern Woodland peoples, 13
    of Great Basin cultures, 12
    in New England, 115
    of slaves, 346
Dime novels, 474
Dinwiddie, Robert, 142–144
Diplomacy. *See also* Foreign policy
    in Civil War, 399–400, 406–407
    dollar, 583–584
    King Cotton, 406–407
    Monroe Doctrine and, 557
    of Roosevelt, Theodore, 580
Direct election of senators, 496–497, 541, 583
Dirksen, Everett, 778
Disarmament
    between Britain and U.S., 261
    Washington Disarmament Conference and, 630
Discovery (ship), 57
Discrimination. *See also* Integration; Race and racism; Segregation
    affirmative action and, 796, 797, 832
    against African Americans, 332, 411
    in black codes, 433
    against Californios, 468
    against Chinese immigrants, 327, 469–470
    Civil Rights Act of 1964 and, 780
    Civil Rights Act of 1968 and, 786
    in employment, 709
    against gays and lesbians, 791
    gender, 331, 518, 794, 795
    Great Society and, 780
    against immigrants, 314
    against Japanese, 581
    laws against, 735
    against Mexican Americans, 760–761
    during reconstruction, 442
    reverse, 847
Diseases. *See also* specific conditions
    AIDS as, 849
    during California gold rush, 327
    in Columbian exchange, 39
    European in Americas, 46
    Indians and, 59, 317, 458
Disfranchisement
    of African Americans, 203, 439, 591, 678
    of ex-Confederates, 441, 442
    property qualifications and, 202, 266–267
    of women, 202, 203, 379
Disqualification Act (1787), 211
Dissent. *See also* Protest(s)
    in middle colonies, 100
    World War I and, 612
Dissenters, Nazis and, 711
Distribution of wealth, New Deal and, 665
District of Columbia. *See* Washington, DC
Diversification, economic, 344
Diversity
    of Bush, George W., cabinet, 875
    of Clinton cabinet, 865, 865 *(i)*
    of colonial society, 100, 101, 107, 113
    in Pennsylvania, 101
    in West, 465, 468–470
    of workers, 517–518
Divide-and-conquer plan, 177

Divorce, 262–263, 347
Dix, Dorothea, 417
Dixiecrats, 736, 736 *(m)*
"Dole," 649
Dole, Robert, 867
"Dollar diplomacy," of Taft, 583–584, 584 *(m)*
Dolley Madison (Stuart), 257 *(i)*
Domesticity
  cult of, 527, 528
  in 1950s, 763–764
  women and, 294
Domestic markets, 310, 311
Domestic policy. *See* specific presidents
Domestic violence, 795
Dominican Republic, 583, 599
  U.S. intervention in, 811, 811 *(i)*
Dominion of New England, 105–106
Domino theory, 725–726, 753
Donelson, Fort, Battle of, 405
Donnelly, Ignatius, 551
"Don't ask, don't tell" policy, 866
Double standard, of sexual behavior, 637
Double V campaign, 709
"Doughboys," 604 *(i)*
"Doughfaces," northerners as, 373, 379
Douglas, Aaron, 638, 638 *(i)*
Douglas, Stephen A., 397
  Compromise of 1850 and, 370
  debates with Lincoln, 383–384
  election of 1860 and, 376 *(m)*, 386–387, 388, 388 *(m)*
  Freeport Doctrine of, 384
  Kansas-Nebraska Act of, 373–374
  on Lecompton constitution, 384
  popular sovereignty and, 374, 377, 384
Douglass, Frederick, 328 *(i)*, ***331,*** 369, 391
  on woman suffrage, 436
Doves (peace advocates), in Vietnam War, 815
Draft (military)
  Carter and, 842
  in Civil War, 410, 413, 417
  Continental army soldiers and, 176
  in peacetime, 728
  in Vietnam War, 814
  in World War I, 604, 604 *(i)*
  in World War II, 700–701
Dred Scott decision (Dred Scott v. Sandford), 381–383, ***382,*** 384, 385, 391
Drift and Mastery (Lippmann), 573
Drought
  in Dust Bowl, 671, 671 *(m)*
  on Great Plains (1880s–1890s), 472
Drug trafficking, by Noriega, 860
Du Bois, W. E. B., 494, ***592,*** 592 *(i)*, 605, 637
Duel, Burr-Hamilton, 251
Dukakis, Michael, 858
Dulles, John Foster, 752, 753, 755
Dunkirk, withdrawal from, 695
Dunmore (Lord), 163–164
Du Pont, 576
Duquesne, Fort, 144, 146
Dürer, Albrecht, 48–49
Dust Bowl, in Great Depression, 671, 671 *(m)*, 672 *(i)*
Dutch East India Company, 99
Dutch East Indies, 696
Dutch Reformed Church, 100
Dutch West India Company, 99

Duties
  government revenue from, 252
  Stamp Act and, 149–150
  Sugar Act and, 149–150
  Townshend, 154–155
Dynamic Sociology (Ward), 573
Dynasties, in 16th-century Europe, 48

Eagle's Nest, The (Kellogg), 364 *(i)*
Earned Income Tax Credit (EITC), 864
Earth, Columbus on, 36
East (region)
  Civil War in, 402–404, 403 *(m)*
  immigrants in, 514–515
East Berlin, 727, 806
Eastern Europe
  collapse of communism in, 862–863, 862 *(m)*
  satellite states in, 818
  World War II and, 713, 723–724
  Yalta meeting plans for, 713
Eastern front, in World War II, 693 *(i)*
Eastern Woodland Indians, 13–15, 21. *See also* Woodland Indians
East India Company (Dutch), 99
East Indies
  Dutch and, 696
  Magellan and, 39
  Portugal and, 34, 42
Eaton, William, 255–256
Eckford, Elizabeth, 768 *(i)*
Economic Opportunity Act (1964), 779
Economic Recovery Tax Act (1981), 844–845
Economic regions of world (1890s), 511 *(m)*
Economics
  laissez-faire, 490
  supply-side, 844–845
  trickle-down, 649
Economy. *See also* Depressions; Globalization; Panics; Recessions; Tariffs
  in 1920s, 647–648, 648–649
  in 1930s, 649, 655
  in 1950s, 757–758
  in 1990s, 868
  agricultural, in South, 343 *(m)*, 344
  under Articles of Confederation, 206–207
  banking and, 282
  Bank War and, 292
  boom and bust cycles in, 283
  Carter and, 837–838
  in Chesapeake colonies, 68–69
  in Civil War, 401, 412–413, 415–416, 423
  Clinton and, 864, 867–868
  colonial, 112–113
  commercial, 283
  cotton exports and, 344
  crash of 1929 and, 648
  Eisenhower and, 751
  family, 518–519
  free-labor, 312–313
  in Gilded Age, 500–504
  Great Society programs and, 779–781
  growth in, 278, 307, 308–311
  Hamilton and, 230, 232–234
  Kennedy, John F., and, 777
  manifest destiny and, 317
  market revolution and, 283
  of Mexica, 26
  mixed, 344
  national populations and, c. 1938, 683 *(t)*

  in New Deal, 664–671
  in New England, 96–97, 115–117
  in New South, 492–493
  of Philadelphia, 101
  plantation, 342–344
  postwar boom in, 762–763, 763 *(f)*
  railroads and, 310–311
  under Reagan, 844–845, 846
  in reconstruction South, 442
  after Revolution, 230–232
  during Revolution, 183
  slavery and, 205
  of West, 476
  after World War I, 618–619, 630
  in World War II, 702, 708 *(f)*, 717
  after World War II, 723, 731–734
Edison, Thomas Alva, 487
Edison General Electric, 487
Education. *See also* Higher education; School(s)
  common people and, 358
  ESEA and, 779
  freedmen and, 431
  gap between men and women, 761
  government grants for, 796
  market revolution and, 295
  NCLB and, 875–876
  NDEA and, 756
  in South, 442
  for women, 228–229, 264–265, 761
Education Amendments Act (1972), Title IX of, 795, 796, 848
Edward VI (England), 85
Edwards, Jonathan, 132, 133
EEOC. *See* Equal Employment Opportunity Commission
Egypt, 406, 704, 755, 819
  Israel and, 841–842
Eighteenth Amendment, 609, 635, 636
Eight-hour day, 495, 525, 526, 541, 583, 609, 618
Einstein, Albert, 727–728
Eisenhower, Dwight D., 741
  civil rights movement and, 749, 769
  election of 1952 and, 741–742
  election of 1956 and, 748 *(i)*, 751
  foreign policy of, 752–756
  Indian policy of, 750–751
  Latin America and, 754–755
  middle class and, 748 *(i)*
  Middle East and, 755
  modern Republicanism of, 748–749
  nuclear arms race and, 752 *(i)*, 755–756
  politics of, 741
  television and, 765
  Vietnam and, 753–754
  in World War II, 706, 713
Eisenhower Doctrine, 755
El-Alamein, battle of (1942), 704
Elbe River, 714
Elderly
  drug benefits for, 876
  income for, 846
  Medicare and, 780
  slaves as, 350
  Social Security for, 677
"Elect," Puritans as, 91
Elections. *See also* Voting and voting rights
  of 1789, 226
  of 1796, 241–242

of 1800, 244, 249, 250, 251, 251 *(m)*
of 1804, 256
of 1808, 257
of 1812, 260
of 1816, 266
of 1820, 266
of 1824, 249, 270–272, 271 *(m)*, 285, 300
of 1828, 284–285, 284 *(i)*, 285–286, 286 *(m)*, 300
of 1832, 282, 291–292, 300
of 1836, 300
of 1840, 301
of 1844, 322–323, 323 *(i)*
of 1848, 368–369, 369 *(m)*, 376 *(m)*
of 1852, 373, 375, 376 *(m)*
of 1856, 375 *(i)*, 376 *(m)*, 379
of 1860, 376 *(m)*, 386–389, 388 *(m)*
of 1862, 410
of 1864, 421
of 1865, 433
of 1866, 436–437
of 1868, 445, 445 *(m)*
of 1872, 446
of 1874, 447–448
of 1876, 449–450, 449 *(m)*, 450 *(m)*, 497
of 1878, 503
of 1880, 497
of 1884, 498–499, 498 *(i)*, 499 *(m)*, 501
of 1888, 500, 501
of 1890, 501
of 1892, 500, 501, 551, 552 *(m)*
of 1896, 550, 551–553, 553 *(m)*, 563
of 1904, 577
of 1908, 582 *(i)*
of 1910, 583
of 1912, 584–585, 585 *(m)*, 586 *(i)*, 588–589
of 1914, 587
of 1916, 587, 602, 612
of 1918, 612
of 1920, 622, 622 *(m)*
of 1924, 629–630
of 1928, 644–645, 645 *(m)*
of 1932, 661–662, 662 *(m)*
of 1934, 673
of 1936, 680–681
of 1940, 695–696
of 1944, 710
of 1946, 736
of 1948, 731, 731 *(i)*, 736, 736 *(m)*
of 1952, 741–742
of 1956, 748 *(i)*, 751
of 1960, 776–777, 804
of 1964, 779, 810, 830
of 1968, 796, 816
of 1972, 797, 833–834
of 1976, 836, 836 *(m)*
of 1980, 842, 843
of 1984, 845
of 1988, 858–859
of 1992, 863
of 1994, 866
of 1996, 867
of 2000, 874–875, 874 *(m)*
of 2004, 880
of 2008, 881, 881 *(m)*
comparison of turnout in (1868–1900 and 1968–2004), 492 *(f)*
in Mississippi (1876), 449
of president, 215–216, 242, 266–267

of senators, 496–497, 541, 583
in South, 359
television and, 765
Electoral college, 251, 585
in Constitution, 215–216
election of 1796 and, 242
election of 1824 and, 271
Electoral commission, for 1876 election, 450
Electricity, 487
Rural Electrification Administration and, 667
TVA and, 666, 667 *(m)*
Electric streetcar, 515
Elementary and Secondary Education Act (ESEA, 1965), 779
Elites. *See also* Classes
in Chesapeake colonies, 68
free black, 355
Hamilton on, 219
Mexica and, 26
southern white, 360
of southern women, 347–348
Spanish American, 45
voting rights for, 267
Elizabeth I (England), 84 *(i)*, 85
Elkins Act (1903), 576, 577
Ellis Island, 509, 510 *(i)*, **515,** 533
El Salvador
human rights in, 840
intervention in, 851
Emancipation, 298, ***354***
colonization in Africa and, 297, 409
draft and, 417
Johnson, Andrew, and, 432
Lincoln and, 408
as military necessity, 410
preliminary proclamation of, 410
proponents and opponents of, 408–409
in states, 204–205
status of slaves as contraband and, 409
Emancipation Proclamation (1863), ***410***
Embargo
on Iranian oil, 842
in World War II, 695, 696–697
Embargo Act (1807), 256
Embassies, terrorism in, 871
Emergency Banking Act (1933), 665
Emerson, Ralph Waldo, 329
Emigrant aid societies, promoting Kansas settlement, 379
Emigration
European (1870–1890), 513 *(f)*
to U.S. West, 317–318
Eminent domain, 282
Empires. *See also* Colonies and colonization
British, 103–106, 133–136
French, 135 *(m)*
Incan, 41
of Mexico, 26
Mexican, 41
Portuguese, 34
Spanish, 135, 135 *(m)*
of United States, 560–562
in West, 464, 477
after World War I, 616
Employment. *See also* Labor; Unemployment; Women; Workforce
black codes limitations on, 433
by Ford, 631
transportation improvements and, 279

of women, 763
during World War II, 709
Employment Act (1946), 731–732
Empresario, 320
Encomendero, 43, 44
Encomienda system, ***43***
Energy. *See* Electricity; Energy crisis; Oil and oil industry; specific sources
Energy crisis, 838–839
energy consumption per capita (1980) and, 840 *(f)*
Energy Department, 838
England (Britain). *See also* British Empire; Colonies and colonization; Navy, British; World War I; World War II; specific colonies
cession of land east of Mississippi, 236–237
colonial trade and, 69
colonies of, 79
cotton from South and, 400, 406
exploration by, 50
France and, 142–144, 143 *(m)*
free blacks in, 205
French Revolution and, 239
Glorious Revolution in, 106
Haiti and, 240
Hitler and, 696
immigrants from, 511, 513 *(f)*
impressment by, 256
Jay Treaty with, 239
leadership changes in, 148
loyalists in, 183, 192
militant suffragism in, 590
Ohio River region and, 143 *(m)*, 146
Oregon Country claims of, 316, 323
panic of 1837 and, 301
Puritans in, 85, 95–96
railroads in, 486 *(f)*
religion in, 84–85, 84 *(i)*
Revolutionary War and, 172, 176–177, 188–190, 191, 192, 193
school enrollment and literacy rates in, 314 *(t)*
settlement house movement from, 568
Suez Canal and, 755
Thatcher in, 843
U.S. war materiel and, 695
Venezuela/British Guiana conflict and, 557
War of 1812 with, 259–261
before World War I, 600
in World War I, 600, 603, 605
World War II and, 695, 703, 704, 708, 712
English Empire. *See* British Empire
English Reformation, 84–85
Enlightenment, 132
Enola Gay (airplane), 716
Entertainment. *See also* Leisure
commercialization of, 528
Environment
agriculture and, 476
Bush, George W., and, 875
Carter and, 839–840
Indians and, 9, 23–24
Nixon and, 792, 797
Reagan and, 845
steamboats and, 280
of Sun Belt, 759–760
Environmentalists, protests by, 790, 872 *(i)*

Environmental movement, 792, 839–840
Environmental Protection Agency (EPA), 775, **792**, 799, 845
Epidemics. *See also* specific diseases
in Columbian exchange, 39
Plains Indians and, 317
Equal Employment Opportunity Commission (EEOC), 790, 798, 859
Equality. *See also* Slaves and slavery; specific groups and rights
for African Americans, 435, 447, 709
Quaker, 101
Equal pay, demands for, 733
Equal Pay Act (1963), 793
Equal Rights Amendment (ERA)
of 1923, 636–637
of 1972, **795, 848**
Equiano, Olaudah, 125, 126 *(i)*, **133**
Erie, Lake, 146
battle at, 260
Erie Canal, 278 *(i)*, 279 *(m)*, **280**
Ervin, Samuel J., 834
Espionage Act (1917), 612
Estates, in Hudson valley, 121
Ethiopia, Italian conquest of, 692
"Ethiopian Regiment," 164
Ethnic Albanians, 869 *(i)*, 871
Ethnic groups. *See also* specific groups
in cities, 515
politics and, 491–492
Eugenics, birth control and, 637
Europe. *See also* specific countries
Civil War (U.S.) and, 400, 406–407
cotton imports (1860-1870), 407 *(f)*
exploration by, 31–51, 37 *(m)*
French and English exploration and, 49
immigrants from, 511–512, 513 *(f)*, 514–515, 643
migration from, 76 *(f)*
New World and (16th century), 48–51
Protestant Reformation in, 48–49
railroads in, 486 *(f)*
school enrollment and literacy rates in, 314 *(t)*
World War I and, 600, 601 *(m)*, 615, 615 *(m)*, 647
World War II and, 703 *(i)*, 704–705, 705 *(m)*
European Recovery Program. *See* Marshall Plan
Europeans, in 18th-century colonies, 113 *(m)*
Europeans Encountering Indians, 30 *(i)*
European Union (EU), 727
Evangelicalism, 328, 358
in 1950s, 764
Second Great Awakening and, 295–296
slaves and, 351
Evans, Hiram Wesley, 643
Evans, Matthew, 66 *(i)*
Everett, Sarah, 319
Everett, Wesley, 620
Evers, Medgar, 735
Evil empire, Reagan on, 850
Executive. *See also* President
under Articles of Confederation, 199, 200
Jefferson and, 252, 253
reorganization of, 878
Executive Orders
8802, 709

9066, 700
9835, 738
for affirmative action (1965), 786
on environment, 872
Exodusters, 474
Expansion and expansionism. *See also* Monroe Doctrine; Open door policy; Westward movement
commercial, 554–555
by 1860, 326 *(m)*
as foreign policy, 554–557
Indian land cessions to 1810 and, 237 *(m)*
missionaries and, 555–556
in North, 307
under Northwest Ordinance (1787), 210
of Pierce, 373
of railroads, 483
slavery and, 366–368
Spanish-American War and, 558–562
U.S. overseas through 1900, 561 *(m)*
of U.S. trade (1870–1900), 555 *(f)*
in West, 307, 316–321, 455–477
Expatriates, in 1920s, 639–640
Exploration. *See also* specific explorers
by Columbus, 35–38
English, 50
European, 31–51, 37 *(m)*
factors leading to, 32–33
by France, 50
by Lewis and Clark, 253–255
by Magellan, 38–39
in Mediterranean region, 32–33
by Norsemen, 32
by Portugal, 33–34
space, 756, 805
by Spain, 35–38, 40–46
Exports
colonial, 104, 131 *(f)*
of cotton, 344
embargo on, 256
expansion of, 230, 555, 555 *(f)*
to Mediterranean region, 255
from New England, 115–116
in 1930s, 691
southern crops as, 79, 342
tobacco as, 128
External taxation, 151
Extinction, of ancient large mammals, 9

Factionalism, 245, 496, 497
Factories, 310
in Confederacy, 401
labor force in, 308
slaves in, 349
textile, 280–281
welfare capitalism and, 632
women in, 519
Fair Deal, 731, 736–737
Fair Labor Standards Act (1938), 684
Fair trade, 872
Faith, salvation by, 95
Fall, Albert, 629
Fallen Timbers, battle of (1794), 238
Falwell, Jerry, 844
Families
African American, 127, 618
birth control movement and, 590
in Chesapeake region, 66–67
farm, 538 *(i)*
Farmers' Alliance and, 539

of free blacks, 355
of freedmen, 430 *(i)*, 431
in Great Depression, 651, 652
of homesteaders, 471–472
immigrant, 510 *(i)*
Mexican, 325 *(i)*
in New England, 89
in 1950s, 764
of planters, 345 *(i)*, 347
republican ideals in, 228–229
separate spheres idea and, 293–295
slave, 350, 351
of southern poor whites, 357–358
on trails, 318–319
in working class, 518–519
of yeomen, 356 *(i)*, 357
Famine, in Ireland, 314
Farewell address
of Jackson, 289
of Reagan, 853
of Washington, 241
Farm Board, 648
Farm Credit Act (FCA, 1933), 668
Farmers' Alliance, 538–540, **539,** 541
Farmers Friend Manufacturing Company, 475 *(i)*
Farms and farming. *See also* Agriculture; Rural areas; Tenant farming
agribusiness and, 757–758
commercial, 474–476
consumer prices and farm income (1865–1910), 539 *(f)*
cooperatives and, 540
electrification and, 666, 667, 667 *(m)*
expansion of markets for, 476
foreclosures in (1932–1942), 665 *(f)*
free silver issue and, 503
in Great Depression, 651, 653–654, 671, 671 *(m)*, 672 *(i)*
on Great Plains, 538 *(i)*
Homestead Act and, 416
immigrants in, 314
mechanization of, 309, 416
migratory labor and, 474
movement to cities from, 308
in New Deal, 667–668, 680 *(i)*
in New England, 115–117
in 1920s, 629, 647
poor whites as, 78
on prairie, 309
railroads and, 475, 502
sharecropping and, 443–444, 474
Shays's Rebellion and, 211–212
slaves on, 349
tariffs and, 501
technology for, 309, 475, 475 *(i)*
tenant, 357, 474
in West, 472, 474–476
whiskey tax and, 234–235
Wilson and, 587
by women, 416
World War I and, 609
yeomen and, 68, 356–357, 413
Farm Security Administration (FSA, 1937), 682–683
Fascism. *See also* Italy, in World War II; Nazi Germany
Roosevelt, Franklin D., and, 692
Faulkner, William, 640

FBI. *See* Federal Bureau of Investigation

FCA. *See* Farm Credit Act

Federal budget. *See also* Defense spending
Carter and, 838
deficit in, 845, 859, 875

Federal Bureau of Investigation (FBI), 836

Federal Communications Commission, 765

Federal Deposit Insurance Corporation (FDIC), 665

Federal Election Campaign Act (1974), 835–836

Federal Emergency Management Agency (FEMA), 878

Federal Emergency Relief Administration (FERA), 666

Federal government. *See* Government (U.S.)

Federal Hall (Philadelphia), 225 *(i)*

Federal Housing Administration, 759

Federalist Papers, The, 220
number 10, 220, 221

Federalists, 221, **241,** 244, 257, 266, 268, 302
Alien and Sedition Acts and, 243
election of 1796 and, 241–242
election of 1800 and, 251
as political party, 256
ratification of Constitution and, **217**–219, 217 *(i),* 220
after War of 1812, 261

Federal Republic of Germany. *See* West Germany

Federal Reserve Act (1913), 586–587

Federal Reserve Board, 587, 838

Federal Surplus Commodities Corporation, 683

Federal Trade Commission (FTC), **587,** 629

FEMA. *See* Federal Emergency Management Agency

Female academies, 264–265

Females. *See* Feminists and feminism; Women

Female Society of Lynn, 282

Feme covert doctrine, **262**

Feminine Mystique, The (Friedan), 763

Feminists and feminism, 636. *See also* specific individuals
countermovement against, 795–796
Fifteenth Amendment and, 439
Friedan and, 763
goals of, 793–795
Nixon and, 798
protests by, 790
Reagan and, 848–849

Fences, ranching and, 468, 473, 474

Ferdinand (Spain), 36, 37, 38, 48

Ferraro, Geraldine A., 845

Ferris, George Washington Gale, Jr., 532

Fertilizers, agricultural, 757–758

Fifteenth Amendment, 438–439

"Fifty-four Forty or Fight," 323

Filipino people, as farm laborers, 474

Fillmore, Millard, 370, 376 *(m),* 379

Films. *See* Movies

Filo, John, 821 *(i)*

"Final solution" (Hitler), 711

Finance capitalism, Morgan, J. P. and, 488–489

Finances. *See also* Business; New Deal; Stock market
under Carter, 838
for Civil War, 401, 413, 501

credit and, 283
crisis in 2008, 881–882
of presidential campaigns, 836
during Revolution, 171, 183
S&L scandal and, 845
tariffs and, 501
by U.S. government, 758

Finland, 724

Finney, Charles Grandison, 295–296

Fire, Native American uses of, 24

Fire-eaters (radical Southerners), 369, 386

Fireside chats, of Roosevelt, Franklin D., 665, 696

First Amendment, 738

First Bank of the United States, 233–234, 282

First Congress, 227, 234, 235

First Continental Congress (1774), **161**

First New Deal, 663–673

First strike capability, 807

First World War. *See* World War I

Fishing and fishing industry
common people and, 358
in New England, 96, 115
along Pacific Coast, 23
in Sun Belt, 759–760

Fitzgerald, F. Scott, 640

Fitzhugh, George, 342

Five Civilized Tribes, 405, 456

Five-Power Naval Treaty (1922), 630

Flamethrowers, 703 *(i)*

Flappers, 635 *(i),* 637

Flexible response policy, 804, 806

Florida, 72, 309, 339, 450, 642 *(m)*
de Soto in, 42
election of 2000 and, 874
invasion by Andrew Jackson, 269–270
Ponce de León in, 42
secession of, 389, 390 *(m)*

Flour milling, in middle colonies, 122

Folsom points, 11, 12

Food(s). *See also* Diet (food); Hunters and hunting; specific crops and foods
Columbian exchange and, 39
in Confederacy, 401
in Great Basin region, 12
Indian, 24, 57–58
in Massachusetts, 87
slave, 127
in Virginia colony, 59

Food Administration, in World War I, 608–609, 647

Food stamp program, 779

Football, 639

Foote, Henry S., 369

Force Bill (1833), 290

Ford, Betty, 835 *(i)*

Ford, Edsel, 628 *(i)*

Ford, Gerald R., 834, **835**–836, 835 *(i)*

Ford, Henry, 628 *(i),* **630**–631

Ford Motor Company, 631, 676

Ford's Theatre, 422

Foreclosures
farm, 665 *(f)*
in Great Depression, 652, 654

Foreign aid
Marshall Plan and, 726–727
to South Vietnam, 807, 808

Foreign investment, 872

Foreign policy. *See also* Diplomacy; specific presidents and policies
of Carter, 840–842
of Coolidge, 630
of Eisenhower, 752–756
of Harding, 630
of Johnson, Lyndon B., 809–812
of Kennedy, John F., 804–808
in late nineteenth century, 554–557
Marshall Plan and, 726
Monroe Doctrine and, 269–270, 557
new world order and, 869–871
of Nixon, 817–824
Open Door policy, 554 *(i),* 557
of Reagan, 850–852
of Roosevelt, Franklin D., 691–692
of Roosevelt, Theodore, 580–581
of Taft, 583–584
of Truman, 725–730, 743
of Wilson, 598–600

Foreign Relations Committee (Senate), 617

Forests, 577, 578, 578 *(m)*

Fort(s). *See also* specific forts
British, 239
in Ohio River region, 142–144, 144 *(m),* 237–238
along Oregon Trail, 318 *(m)*
in Seven Years' War, 146

Fortas, Abe, 778 *(i)*

Fort Wayne, Treaty of, 259

Forty-niners, 326

Founding Fathers. *See* Constitution (U.S.); specific individuals

Four Freedoms, 696

Fourier, Charles, 329

"Four-Minute Men," 611

Fourteen Points, 613, 614, 616

Fourteenth Amendment, 435–436, 437
corporations and, 490
ratification by southern states, 442
segregation and, 768 *(i)*
voting rights and, 782
women's voting rights and, 436

4th U.S. Colored Infantry, 411 *(i)*

Framers. *See* Constitution (U.S.)

France. *See also* French Revolution; World War II
Britain and, 142–144, 143 *(m)*
Caribbean islands and, 146 147 *(m)*
colonies of, 106, 129
cotton from South and, 400
exploration by, 50
fur trade and, 106
Haiti and, 240
in Indochina, 742
military forts of, 142–144, 143 *(m)*
Morocco crisis and, 581
Nazi invasion of, 694
Revolutionary War alliance with, 173, 186–187, 191, 191 *(i),* 193
Ruhr Valley occupation by, 630
Seven Years' War and, 146, 147 *(m)*
Suez Canal and, 755
trans-Mississippi region and, 253
U.S. war materiel and, 695
Vichy government in, 695
Vietnam and, 753
World War I and, 600, 603, 605–606, 606 *(m),* 609–610

France (continued)
World War II and, 695, 713
XYZ Affair and, 242–243
Franchise. *See also* Voting and voting rights
for women, 201 (i)
Franciscans, in California, 321
Franco, Francisco, 692
Frank Leslie's Illustrated Weekly, 544 (i)
Franklin, Benjamin, 138, 212
Albany Plan of Union and, 145
Enlightenment and, 132
Great Awakening and, 133
Poor Richard's Almanack of, 119 (i), 122
Second Continental Congress and, 170
Franz Ferdinand (Austria-Hungary), 600,
601 (m)
Fredericksburg, battle of (1862), 404
Free blacks, 332. *See also* African Americans
during Civil War, 417
in Continental army, 176
elite, 355
laws restricting, 354–355
as slaveholders, 355
in southern society, 354–355
in states, 204, 205
voting and, 203, 204, 267
wealth of, 313
Freedmen, 427
black codes and, 432 (i), 433, 434
education and, 431, 442, 443
as Exodusters, 474
labor by women, 440 (i), 443
labor code and, 429–430
land for, 430, 433, 437–438, 443
on plantations, 443, 444 (m)
during reconstruction, 448–449
in Republican Party, 440
search for families by, 430 (i), 431
sharecropping by, 443–444
taxes and, 433
voting rights for, 426 (i), 438–439
Freedmen's Bureau, 430, 433
Freedmen's Bureau bill
of 1865, 430
of 1866, 434
Freedom(s)
Atlantic Charter and, 696
for free blacks, 355
for freedmen, 431
religious, 93–94
for slaves, 204–205, 408–409, 414
of speech, 202, 228
in states' bills of rights, 202
for whites, 78, 333
"Freedom papers," 354 (i)
Freedom Rides, 784
Freedom schools, for Chicano children, 790
Free enterprise, 612, 629
Reagan and, 844–845
Free farmers, 68
Free labor
immigrants and, 314–315
during reconstruction, 429–430
vs. slavery, 342, 378, 429–430
woman's rights and, 331
Free-labor ideal, 312–313, 328, 333
Freeman, Elizabeth (Mum Bett), 204
Free market, 838
Freeport Doctrine, 384
Free silver, 500 (i), ***503–504,*** 541, 552

Free soil doctrine, 367
Free-Soil Party, 368, 370
Free-soil settlers, in Kansas, 380–381
Free speech, 417, 590
defense of slavery and, 360
restriction of, 620
"Free speech" movement, 790
Free states, 267, 322, 323, 361. *See also*
specific states
Free trade, 501, 872
trusts and, 486
Freewill Baptists, 263
Frémont, Jessie, 375 (i), 379
Frémont, John C., 321, 375 (i), 376 (m),
379, 409
French and Indian War. *See* Seven Years'
War
French Empire, 135 (m). *See also* New
France
French Revolution, 238–239, 240
Frick, Henry Clay, 543
Friedan, Betty, 673, 794
Friends of the Earth, 792
Frobisher, Martin, 50
Frontier
colonial, 134–135
in Revolutionary War, 192
settlers on, 471–473
Spanish, 135, 135 (m)
violence along, 70
women on, 472
Frontier thesis (Turner), 477
Fuel. *See* specific types
Fuel Administration, 609
Fugitive Slave Act (1850), 370, 371–***372,*** 391
Fugitive slave provision, of Northwest
Ordinance, 211
Fugitive slaves
in Civil War, 409, 414
Compromise of 1850 and, 370, 371–372
resistance by, 352
Revolutionary War and, 164, 192
underground railroad and, 332
Full-employment legislation, 731
Fuller, Margaret, 329
Fuller, William, 456 (i)
Fulton, Robert, 276 (i), 279
Fundamentalism
Christian, 844
Islamic, 853, 876–878
Scopes trial and, 644
Furnishing merchants, in South, 538
Furniture, 132 (i)
Fur trade, 100, 106, 134, 146, 237
Indians and, 121

Gabler, Mel and Norma, 831
Gabriel (slave), 251
Gabriel's Rebellion (1800), 251–252
Gadsden, James, 373
Gadsden Purchase (1853), 373, 373 (m)
Gage, Thomas, 160–161, 162, 172
"Gag rule," in Congress, 300
Galbraith, John Kenneth, 757
Galloway, Joseph, 161
Gama, Vasco da, 34
Gambian culture, 124
Gangs
during prohibition, 636
slave, 340, 350

Garfield, James A., 437, 497
Garment industry, mechanization of, 518
Garner family, escape from slavery, 371 (i)
Garnet, Henry Highland, 331
Garrison, William Lloyd, 297, 298 (i), 369,
386, 450
Garvey, Marcus, 637
Gary, Martin, 448
Gasoline. *See* Oil and oil industry
Gaspée (ship), 158
Gates, Horatio, 185, 189, 189 (m)
Gathering Corn in Virginia (Darley),
356 (i)
Gay Liberation Front, 792
Gay pride parades, 847 (i)
Gays and lesbians. *See also* Homosexuals
and homosexuality
Clinton's policy toward, 866
marriage by, 782, 866
in military, 866
movement for, 849
as officeholders, 792
organization by, 791–792
Gaza, 842, 871
Gender and gender issues. *See also* Men;
Women
in Chesapeake region, 65
in colonies, 155–156
equality and, 263
politics and, 229, 493–494
religion and, 263–264
separate spheres, 293–295
of slaves, 125
in Spanish colonies, 45
General Agreement on Tariffs and Trade
(GATT), 872
General Court (Massachusetts), 92
General Electric (GE), 487, 489
General Federation of Women's Clubs, 495
General Historie of Virginia, A (Smith),
54 (i)
General Managers Association (GMA),
546, 547
General Motors, 676
*General Theory of Employment, Interest,
and Money, The* (Keynes), 682
General welfare clause, in Constitution,
216, 234
Geneva Accords (1954), 753, 754 (m)
Geneva summit (1955), 756
Genoa, 32
Genocide
Milosevic trial for, 871
in Nazi Germany, 711
"Gentlemen's Agreement" (1907), with
Japan, 581
Gentry, slaveholding, ***128***
Geographic mobility, free labor and, 313
Geographic revolution, 38–40
George III (England), 148, 149, 169 (i),
172, 181
Georgia, 199
Cherokee removal and, 289
Civil War in, 421
power of planters in, 360
Revolutionary War and, 188–189,
189 (m), 190
secession and, 389, 390 (m)
Spanish exploration of, 42
German Americans, 314, 611–612, 616

Germany. *See also* Berlin entries; Nazi
Germany; West Germany
colonies of, 615–616
division of, 725
immigrants from, 118–119, 185, 314, 511,
512, 513 *(f)*
manufacturing in, 846
Morocco crisis and, 581
reparation payments of, 630
Revolutionary mercenaries (Hessians)
from, 179
U-boats of, 602
World War I and, 600, 602, 603, 605,
606, 614
after World War II, 724–725
Geronimo (Apache Indians), ***462***–463
Gettysburg, battle of (1863), ***419,*** 419 *(m),*
420, 420 *(m)*
Ghent, Treaty of (1814), 261, 270
*Ghost Dance, **463***–464, 463 *(i)*
Gibbon, John, 460
GI Bill of Rights. *See* Serviceman's
Readjustment Act (1944)
Gideon v. Wainwright (1963), 778 *(i),* 782
GI Forum. *See* American GI Forum
Gilbert, Humphrey, 50
Gilded Age, 477, 481, 505, 576–577
big business in, 482–487, 488–490
cities in, 515–516
consolidation in, 483
depression of 1890s in, 504
economy during, 500–504
free silver issue in, 503–504
gender, race, and politics in, 493–494
New South during, 492–493
politics in, 491–492
poverty in, 515, 516 *(i)*
presidential politics in, 496–499
social Darwinism and, 489–490
Supreme Court during, 488, 490
women in, 494–495
Gingrich, Newt, 866
Ginsburg, Ruth Bader, 866
Girdling, in clearing fields, 62–63
Girls. *See* Women
Glaciers, 7, 9
Glasnost, 852
Glass-Steagall Banking Act (1933), 665
Glenn, John H., 805
Globalization
Clinton and, 869–872
debates over, 871–872
United States and, 873
in World War I, 607 *(f)*
Global markets
for southern cotton, 407 *(f)*
for western agriculture, 476
Global migration, urban growth and,
510–513
Glorieta Pass, battle at (1862), 405, 405 *(m)*
Glorious Revolution (England), 106
Godspeed (ship), 57
Gold, 466 *(m)*
in Colorado, 366
Indians and discoveries of, 460
in Nevada, 465 *(i)*
from New World, 42, 45 *(f)*
Goldberg, Rube, cartoon on world peace,
720 *(i)*
Goldman, Emma, 619–620, 620 *(i)*

Goldmark, Josephine, 572
Gold rush, in California, 326–327, 366
Gold standard, 538
abandonment of, 503
vs. free silver, 500 *(i),* 503–504, 552
Goldwater, Barry M., 779, 830, 831
Goliad, massacre at (1836), 321
*Gompers, Samuel, **524***–525, 526, 619
Gonzales, Rodolfo ("Corky"), 790
Good Neighbor Policy, 691
"Goo goos," 531
Gorbachev, Mikhail, 852
Gore, Albert, Jr., 863, 864 *(i),* 874–875,
874 *(m)*
Gore, Tipper, 864 *(i)*
Gorgas, Josiah, 401
Gospel of wealth, 490
Gould, Jay, 482–483, 524
Government. *See also* Government (U.S.);
specific locations
of British colonies, 129
city, 530–531
colonial, 136
Jefferson on, 253
of Massachusetts, 87–89, 106
municipal, 530
in New England colonies, 105
of New Netherland, 100
of Pennsylvania, 102
progressivism in, 574
Puritan, 92–93
republicanism and, 201–202
state, during reconstruction, 441–442
of Virginia, 61
Woodland chiefdoms and, 17–18
Government (U.S.)
under Articles of Confederation, 198–200
branches of, 216
Bush, George H. W., and, 858–860
business and, 555, 578, 629
Civil War and, 415–416
Great Depression and, 649
Jackson and, 286
Jefferson and, 253, 273
land policy of, 309
limits and checks on, 216
stability in, 226–229
Governors, colonial, 136, 155
Gradual emancipation, 204–205, 211, 267
Grady, Henry, 492
Graham, Billy, 764
Grain, 476
in middle colonies, 122
trade in, 230
Grandfathering, black voters and, 591
Grange, 502, 538
Grange, Harold ("Red"), 639
*Grant, Ulysses S., **405***
in Civil War, 405–406, 418, 419 *(m),*
420–421, 422
corruption and, 446, 446 *(i),* 496
election of 1868 and, 445, 445 *(m)*
election of 1872 and, 446
peace policy for Indians, 458
presidency of, 445–446
reconstruction and, 445, 446–447
Grape boycott, 789–790
Graphic, The, 536 *(i)*
Grasse (Comte de), 191
Grassroots conservatism, 830–831

Graves, A. J. (Mrs.), 293
Graves, Thomas, 66 *(i)*
Great American Desert, farmers in, 472
*Great Awakening, **132***–133
Second, 295–296
Great Basin
cultures of, 12–13
Native Americans of, 21
Great Britain. *See* England (Britain)
Great Compromise, 215
Great Depression (1930s), ***661.*** *See also*
New Deal; Roosevelt, Franklin
Delano
crash of 1929 and, 648
economy during, 649, 650, 664–671
lifestyle in, 650–654
scapegoats in, 651–652
working-class militancy in, 653–654
Greater East Asia Co-Prosperity Sphere, 696
Great Fire (Chicago, 1871), 529
Great Lakes region, 280
French in, 106
Indians of, 21
Great Plains
buffalo in, 459–460
drought on, 472
Indians of, 21, 23, 317–318, 318 *(m),* 374,
457–458, 460, 463–464
in Louisiana Purchase, 253, 254 *(m)*
Spanish in, 42
Great Railroad Strike (1877), ***522***–524,
522 *(i),* 523 *(m),* 545, 546
Great Salt Lake, 319, 469
Great Sioux Reservation, 461
Great Sioux Uprising (1862), 457 *(m),* 458
*Great Society, 776, **779,** 780*–781
Great Tenochtitlan, The (Rivera), 2 *(i)*
"Great War." *See* World War I
Great White Fleet, 581
Greece, 615, 725–726, 726 *(i)*
Greeley, Horace, 401, 446, 510
Green, William, 653
Greenback Labor Party, 503, 538
Greenbacks, 503, 541
Green Berets, 806
Greene, Nathanael, 189 *(m)*
Greenhouse gases, Kyoto Protocol and, 875
Greensboro, North Carolina, Woolworth's
lunch counter sit-in and, 783
Greenville, Treaty of (1795), 236 *(i),* ***238***
Greenwich Village, 636
Grenada, invasion of, 851
Grenville, George, 149–150, 149 *(i)*
Griffith, D. W., film by, 611 *(i)*
Grimké sisters (Angelina and Sarah), 298
Grinnell, Julius S., 526
Griswold, Roger, 241 *(i)*
Grove City v. Bell (1984), 848
Guadalcanal, battle of, 714
Guadalupe Hidalgo, Treaty of (1848),
325–326, 468
Guam, 560, 561, 703
Guantánamo, Cuba
prisoners in, 878, 881
U.S. base at, 561
Guatemala, 557, 754
Guerrilla war
by Apache Indians, 462
during Civil War, 397, 405
counterinsurgency forces and, 806

Guerrilla war (continued)
   in Kansas, 381
   in Philippines, 558
   in Revolutionary War, 190
   in Vietnam War, 823
Guiteau, Charles, 497
Gulf Coast, Katrina and, 876
Gulf of Tonkin Resolution (1964), **810,** 820
Gulf Oil Company, 632 *(i)*
Gulf War. *See* Persian Gulf War
"Gun Belt," 759
Gun control, 859
Gun industry, interchangeable parts
   and, 310
Gutenberg, Johannes, 33
Guthrie, Woody, 652, 679
Gypsies, 711

Habeas corpus, Lincoln and, 397
Haganah (Israel), 730 *(i)*
Haiti, 240, 332, 599, 870
Haitian Revolution, 240, 251
Hakluyt, Richard, 57
Haldeman, H. R., 833 *(i)*
Hale, John P., 376 *(m)*
Half Breeds, 497
Halfway Covenant, 97
Hamilton, Alexander, 213, 214, 219,
   230, 500
   economy and, 230, 232–234
   election of 1796 and, 242
   election of 1800 and, 251
   Federalist Papers and, 220
   as treasury secretary, 227
   Trumbull portrait of, 230 *(i)*
   Whiskey Rebellion and, 235
Hamilton, Fort, 237
Hammond, James H., 350, 367
Hancock, John, 114 *(i)*, 151
Hancock, Winfield Scott, 497
Hanna, Mark, 553, 559
Hannastown, Pennsylvania, Indian attack
   on, 187 *(m)*
Hanoi. *See* Vietnam; Vietnam War
Harassment. *See* Sexual harassment
Harding, Florence, 622
Harding, Warren G., 622, 622 *(m)*, 628–629
Hard money, 183, 232, 234, 301
Harlan County coal strike (1931), 654, 654 *(m)*
Harlem
   migration to, 621
   riot in, 678
Harlem Renaissance, 637–**638**
Harmar, Josiah, 237
Harpers Ferry, Brown's raid on (1859), 386
Harper's Weekly, 445 *(i)*, 531
Harrington, Michael, 777
Harrison, Benjamin, 464, 500, 501
Harrison, Carter, 526
Harrison, William Henry, 258, 259, 260,
   300, 301, 322
Hartford Convention (1814), 261
Hartford Seminary, 264
Hawaii, 697, 697 *(m)*. *See also* Pearl Harbor
   annexation and, 555, 561
Hawks, in Vietnam War, 815
Hawley-Smoot tariff (1930), 648
Hay, John, 554 *(i)*, 557, 558, 581
Hayes, Rutherford B.
   election of 1876 and, 449–450

Great Railroad Strike and, 522, 523–524
   presidency of, 497
Haymarket bombing, 525–**526,** 525 *(i)*, 544
Haywood, William Dudley ("Big Bill"), 589
Hazardous waste cleanup, 840
Headright, 64
Head Start, 778
Health, Education, and Welfare,
   Department of, 749
Health issues
   Bush, George W., and, 876
   Clinton and, 865
   Johnson, Lyndon B., and, 779–780
   Truman and, 737
Hearst, William Randolph, 559
Hearts of the World (film), 611 *(i)*
Hegemony, of U.S. in Western Hemisphere,
   557
Heidt, Wesley and Edward, 698 *(i)*
Held, A. John, Jr., 626 *(i)*
Helsinki accords, 819
Hemings, Sally, 250 *(i)*
Hemingway, Ernest, 639–640
Hendrick (Mohawk Indians), 144, 145 *(i)*
Hendricks, Thomas A., 447
Henry VIII (England), 84
Henry, Fort
   battle of (Civil War), 405
   in Revolution, 187 *(m)*
Henry the Navigator, Prince (Portugal), **34**
Henry, Patrick, 151, 158, 161,
   213–214, 220
Henry Frank (steamboat), 338 *(i)*
Henry Street settlement (New York), 569
Hepburn Act (1906), 577
Heresy
   Hutchinson and, 95
   Quakers and, 97
Hernandez, Aileen, 794
Hernandez, Pete, 761
Hernandez v. Texas (1954), 761
Hessians, 179
Hezbollah, 851
Hickory Clubs, 285
Hidatsa Indians, 458
Hierarchies
   of Catholic Church, 85
   social and racial in New Spain, 45
Higginson, Thomas W., 411 *(i)*
Higher education. *See also* Universities and
   colleges; specific schools
   democratization of, 761
   in 1830s, 295
   by mid-1820s, 264–265
"Higher law" doctrine, of Seward, 388
High-tech industries
   immigrant workers in, 873
   in West, 760
Hill, Aaron (Mohawk Indians), 208
Hill, Anita, 859–860
Hillman, Sidney, 676
Hirohito (Japan), 697
Hiroshima, bombing of, **716,** 716 *(i)*
Hispanic Americans. *See also* Latinos;
   specific groups
   in New Deal, 679
   in Southwest, 468
   in Texas, 468
Hispaniola, Spanish settlement on, 40
History, archaeology and, 4–5

"History of the Standard Oil Company"
   (Tarbell), 486–487
Hitler, Adolf, **691,** 704, 717. *See also* Nazi
   Germany
   England and, 696
   League of Nations and, 691
   military strikes before 1942, 694 *(m)*
   suicide by, 714
Hobby, Oveta Culp, 749
Hobo, in Great Depression, 650
Ho Chi Minh, 753, 754, 807
Ho Chi Minh City, 822
Hohokam culture, 16
Holding companies, 502
Holidays, Puritan celebration of, 83, 91, 107
Holland, Separatists in, 87
Hollywood, HUAC investigation of, 738
"Hollywood Ten," 738
Holmes, George F., 372
Holmes, Oliver Wendell, 620
Holocaust, 707, **711,** 711 *(m)*
Holy experiment, of Penn, 101
Holy Roman Empire, 48
Home and Away:...(Krimmel), 265 *(i)*
Home front
   in Civil War, 412–414, 415–417
   in Revolutionary War, 180–183
   in World War I, 608–612
   in World War II, 702, 707–711
   World War II security and, 699–700
Homeland Security Department, 878
Homelessness
   of children, 518
   in depression of 1890s, 532
   in Great Depression, 650–651
Homespun cloth, 156
Homestead Act (1862), 416, **471,** 472 *(m)*
Homesteaders, 471–472
Homestead steelworks, 488 *(i)*, 542–545
Homo erectus, 6
Homo sapiens, 5, 6–7
Homosexuals and homosexuality. *See also*
   Gays and lesbians
   AIDS and, 849
   Kinsey on, 766
   marriage and, 782
   McCarran-Walter Act and, 737
   military and, 866
   Nazis and, 711
   in World War II armed forces, 702
Honduras, 557
Hone, Philip, 301
Honor, in South, 346–347
Hood, John B., 421
Hoover, Herbert, 628, **646**
   Bonus Marchers and, 654
   crash of 1929 and, 648–649
   election of 1928 and, 644–645, 645 *(m)*,
   646 *(i)*
   as Food Administration head,
   608–609, 647
   in Great Depression, 649
   inaugural address of, 646
   as president, 647
   as secretary of commerce, 628, 629, 647
Hoover, J. Edgar, 619–620
Hoovervilles, 652
Hopewell culture, 18–19
Hopi Indians, 17
Hopkins, Harry, 664, 666

Horsecar, 515
Horses, 12, 317
Horseshoe Bend, battle of (1814), 260
Hostages
in Iran, 838 *(i)*
in Lebanon, 851
Hot line, between U.S. and Soviet
Union, 807
Households, domestic servants in, 527–528
House of Burgesses, 61, 69, 70, 151
House of Commons, virtual representation
in, 150
House of Representatives, 215, 219, 251,
270, 834, 835
House Un-American Activities Committee
(HUAC), 738
Housing
Anasazi, 17
in Chesapeake region, 68 *(i)*
in Hudson valley, 121
for Indians, 24, 456 *(i)*
Iroquoian, 22
Johnson, Lyndon B., and, 780
in 1930s, 684
in 1950s, 759
on plantations, 347 *(f)*
residential segregation in, 515
slave, 127, 336 *(i),* 346, 347 *(f),* 349 *(i)*
sod houses, 472, 538 *(i)*
suburban, 759, 762
Housing Act (1949), 736
Houston, Sam, 321
Howe, Eleanor, 831
Howe, William, 172, 179, 183, 184–185, 189
How the Other Half Lives (Riis), 515, 516 *(i)*
HUAC. *See* House Un-American Activities
Committee
Hudson, Carrie, 349
Hudson, Henry, 99
Hudson River region, 279–280
Revolution in, 177, 178 *(m),* 179, 182 *(m),*
184
Huerta, Dolores, 788 *(i),* *789*–790
Huerta, Victoriano, 599
Hughes, Charles Evans, 602, 630, 681
Hughes, Langston, 638
Huguenots, in colonies, 130
Huitzilopochtli (god), 26
Hull House, 568–569, 570
Humanitarian missions, 869
Human rights
Carter and, 840–842
in Helsinki accords, 818
in World War II, 707
Humans
migration into Western Hemisphere, 6–8,
8 *(f)*
modern, 5
Human sacrifice, 19
by Mexica, 26
Native American, 24
Humphrey, Hubert H., 806, 816
Hunchback (ship), 408 *(i)*
Hundred Days, in New Deal, 663
Hungary, 615
Soviets and, 723
Hunkpapa Sioux Indians, 460
Hunter, David, 409
Hunter-gatherers, 10, 14, 24
ancient, 6, 8, 10–14

Archaic, 11–12
of buffalo (bison), 11–12
Eastern Woodland peoples and, 13
Paleo-Indians as, 8–9
Hunters and hunting
ancient, 6, 8, 10–14
Archaic, 11–12
of buffalo (bison), 11–12, 459–460
Paleo-Indians as, 8–9
Huron Indians, 209
Hurricane Katrina, 876, 878
Hurston, Zora Neale, 638
Hussein (Jordan), 871
Hussein, Saddam, 860–862, 869, 871,
879–880
Hutchinson, Anne, *94*–95
Hutchinson, Thomas, 156, 159
Albany Plan of Union and, 145
Boston Massacre and, 157
Stamp Act protests and, 152
Hydroelectricity, 583, 667 *(m)*
Hydrogen bomb, 727
Hymns, 358

Iberian Peninsula, 33. *See also* Portugal;
Spain
Ideas, in Columbian exchange, 39
Identity, American, 137
Igbo culture, 124
Illegal immigrants, 873
Illinois, 186, 187 *(m),* 266–267, 309, 380
Illiteracy, 358
Immigrants and immigration. *See also*
specific groups
abolition of national origins quotas
on, 780
to Chesapeake region, 65
to cities, 513
to colonies, 133–134
discrimination against, 591
as domestic servants, 527
free labor and, 314–315
in gold and silver mining, 466–467
Infnat Welfare Society and, 566 *(i)*
Jewish, 711
labor and, 676
McCarran-Walter Act and, 737
in middle colonies, 100, 118–120, 121
nativism and, 377–378
in New England, 96
new immigration, 513–514, 518, 533
to 1910, 512 *(m)*
in 1920s, 641–643
old and new immigration, 511–512
to Pennsylvania, 101
percentage in population (2006), 857, 883
racism and, 514–515
restrictions on, 514, 515, 642–643
South and, 344
in textile industry, 281
by 2006, 873
workers and, 511, 517–518
Impartial Administration of Justice Act
(1774), 160
Impeachment
of Clinton, 864, 867
of Johnson, Andrew, 438
of Nixon, 834–835
Imperialism
debate over, 560–562

Japanese, 696–698, 697 *(m)*
U.S., 562, 805
World War I and, 616
Imports
colonial, 103–104, 156
duties from, 256
of European cotton (1860–1870), 407 *(f)*
of precious metals, 45 *(f)*
tariffs and, 555 *(f)*
Impost (import tax), 207, 211
Impressment, 256, 261
in Confederacy, 413
Inauguration
of Eisenhower, 752
of Hoover, 646
of Jackson, 286
of Jefferson, 244, 245, 252
of Kennedy, 777, 804
Incan empire, 41–42
Income. *See also* Wages
EITC and, 864
farm (1865–1910), 539 *(f)*
of farm families, 667
inequality of, 868 *(f)*
per capita (1920s), 633
for women, 846
Income gap, 647
Income tax, 416, 583, 586, 678
Incorporation. *See also* Corporations
state laws of, 282
Indentured servants, 60, *64*–67, 66 *(i),*
68, 120
in New England, 89
redemptioners as, 119–120
Independence
support for, 169, 193
voting for, 174
Independence Hall, 213 *(i)*
Independent magazine, 518, 519, 523
Independent treasury system, 301
India, 406
Britain and, 696, 729
nuclear test ban treaty and, 863
Portugal and, 34
in World War II, 704
Indian(s). *See also* Native Americans;
specific groups
Archaic, 10–14
naming by Columbus, 36
Indiana, 309
Indian Claims Commission, 750
Indian country. *See* Indian Territory;
Oklahoma; West
Indian Ocean, Magellan expedition in, 39
Indian policy. *See also* Native Americans
allotment and, 461–462
concentration and, 318
of Jackson, 286, 287–289
peace policy and, 458
removal and, 286, 287–289, 288 *(m),*
456–458
reservations and, 318, 457 *(m),* 458–459,
460, 462
Indian Removal Act (1830), 288–289
Indian Reorganization Act (1934), 679
Indian Rights Association, 461
Indian Territory, 288 *(m),* 289, 405, 456,
457 *(m)*
Indian wars, in West, 209, 237–238, 318,
458, 468

Jackson State College, Mississippi, killings at, *820*
Jamaica, Spanish settlement in, 40
James (slave), 188 *(i)*
James I (England), 56–57, 61, 84 *(i)*, 85
  New Jersey, Pennsylvania, and, 101
  New York colony and, 100
James II (England), 106
James River, settlement patterns along, 67 *(m)*
Jamestown, 56 *(i)*, **57**–58
  advertisement for settlers, 60
  and Native Americans, 57–59
Japan
  aggression through 1941, 697 *(m)*
  atomic bombing of, 716, 716 *(i)*
  China and, 691, 692, 696
  immigrants from, 470, 643
  League of Nations and, 691
  Manchuria and, 691
  manufacturing in, 846
  in 1930s, 691
  Pearl Harbor and, 696–698
  postwar occupation of, 740
  Russo-Japanese War and, 581
  trade embargo against, 696–697
  U.S. treaty with, 730
  in World War I, 600
  after World War I, 616
  in World War II, 703–704, 714–715, 715 *(m)*
  after World War II, 729
Japanese Americans
  citizenship for, 679
  discrimination against, 581
  as farm laborers, 474
  World War II and, 700, 700 *(m)*
Jay, John, 212, 220, 227, 239. *See also* Jay Treaty
Jay Treaty, 239, 242
Jazz, 638
Jefferson, Fort, 237
Jefferson, Isaac, 350 *(i)*
Jefferson, Martha, 250 *(i)*
Jefferson, Mary, 350 *(i)*
Jefferson, Thomas, 171, 190, *250,* 268
  Alien and Sedition Acts and, 243–244
  Bank of the United States and, 234
  Barbary Wars and, 255–256
  Declaration of Independence and, 174
  deism of, 132
  election of 1796 and, 242
  election of 1800 and, 244, 250, 251
  election of 1804 and, 256
  Haitian Revolution and, 240
  Hemings and, 250 *(i)*
  home of, 158, 856 *(i)*
  inauguration of, 244, 245, 252
  limited government and, 253, 273
  Louisiana Purchase, Lewis and Clark expedition, and, 253–255, 254 *(m)*
  on national debt, 233
  Northwest Territory and, 208, 209 *(i)*
  portrait of, 250 *(i)*
  republicanism of, 252–253
  Revolutionary War and, 163
  as secretary of state, 227
  slavery and, 128, 269, 346, 350 *(i)*
  Virginia land claim and, 199
  on Whiskey Rebellion, 235

Jericho, 871
Jewelry, of Chumash people, 13 *(i)*
Jews and Judaism, 615. *See also* Israel
  in Democratic Party, 492
  Holocaust and, 707, 711, 711 *(m)*
  as immigrants, 512, 513
  mass execution of, 710 *(i)*
  in middle colonies, 100
  Nazi Germany and, 691
  state of Israel and, 729, 729 *(i)*
Jim Crow laws, 442, 514, 591, 709
Jobs. *See also* Employment; Labor
  discrimination against homosexuals, 849
John Adams (Trumbull), 242 *(i)*
John Brown Going to His Hanging (Pippin), 387 *(i)*
Johnson, Andrew, 432, 436 *(i)*
  assumption of presidency, 422, 432
  black codes and, 433
  Fourteenth Amendment and, 436–437
  Freedmen's Bureau and, 438
  impeachment of, 438
  reconstruction plan of, 432–433
Johnson, Hiram, 574, 585, 591, 617 *(i)*
Johnson, James Weldon, 638
Johnson, Jane, 350
Johnson, Lyndon B., 778, 778 *(i), 809*
  civil rights movement and, 784–785
  election of 1964 and, 779
  on environment, 792
  foreign policy of, 809–812
  Great Society and, 776
  Latin America and, 811
  as vice president, 776
  Vietnam War and, 780, 809–810, 811–812
Johnson, Thomas Loftin, 573 *(i)*, 574
Johnson, William, 146
Johnson-Reid Act (1924), *642*–643
Johnston, Albert Sidney, 405, 406
Johnston, Joseph, 403
Joint-stock companies, 56–57, 87
Jones, William ("Billy"), 520
Jordan, 755
Joseph, Chief (Nez Percé), 462
Journalism. *See also* Newspapers
  muckraking in, 577–578
  women in, 494–495
  yellow, 559
Judge magazine, 626 *(i)*
Judicial review, 252–253
Judiciary. *See also* Courts; Supreme Court
  under Articles of Confederation, 199
  in Constitution, 216
  revolution in, 782
Judiciary Act (1789), 252, 253
Jungle, The (Sinclair), 578, 578 *(i)*
Juries
  discrimination banned in, 761, 786
  trial by, 202
Justice Department, 619, 620
Justification by faith, 49

Kaiser, The: The Beast of Berlin (musical), 611
Kamikaze pilots, 714
Kansas
  African Americans in, 468, 474
  "Bleeding Kansas" and, 380–381, 381 *(m)*
  farm income and consumer prices in, 538
  free vs. slave state settlers in, 380–381

  slavery in, 384
  statehood for, 384
Kansas-Nebraska Act (1854), 373–***374,*** 374 *(m)*, 378, 379, 382, 383
Kaskaskia, battle at, 186
Katrina, Hurricane, 876, 878
KDKA radio, 639
Kearney, Denis, 470
Kearny, Stephen Watts, 324
Keating-Owen child labor law (1916), 587
Kelley, Florence, 572
Kellogg, E. B., 364 *(i)*
Kellogg, Frank, 630
Kellogg-Briand Pact (1928), 630
Kendall, Mary, 348
Kennan, George F., 725, 727
Kennedy, John F., 804
  assassination of, 777–778
  civil rights movement and, 785
  Cuban missile crisis and, 807
  foreign policy of, 804–808
  New Frontier of, 776–778
  television and, 765
  third world and, 806
  Vietnam and, 807–808
Kennedy, Robert F., 784, 816
Kennesaw Mountain, battle of (1864), 419 *(m)*, 420, 421
Kent State University, killings at, *820,* 821 *(i)*
Kentucky, 199, 237, 295, 405
  secession and, 396, 397–398
Kenya, U.S. embassy in, 871
Kerouac, Jack, 766
Kerry, John, 880
Kettle Hill, 560
Keynes, John Maynard, 651, 682
Khomeini, Ayatollah Ruholla, 842
Khrushchev, Nikita, 755–756
  Berlin Wall and, 806
  Cuban missile crisis and, 807
  nuclear arms race and, 752–753, 752 *(i)*
Kim Il-sung, 739
King, Martin Luther, Jr., 783
  antiwar protests and, 813
  assassination of, 787
  Montgomery bus boycott and, 770
  nonviolence principles of, 784
King, Rufus, 266
King Cotton diplomacy, 406–407
King James Bible, 85
King Philip (Metacomet, Wampanoag Indians), 103, 105, 105 *(i)*
King Philip's War (1675–1676), *103,* 104–106
Kings. *See* specific rulers
Kingsley, Bathsheba, 133
King's Mountain, battle of (1780), 189 *(m)*, 190
King William's War (1689–1697), 106
Kinsey, Alfred, 766
Kinship. *See* Families
Kiowa Indians, 317, 460
Kissinger, Henry A., 817–818, 819
Kivas (ceremonial rooms), 17, 17 *(i)*
Klan. *See* Ku Klux Klan
Klir, Joseph, 480 *(i)*
Knights of Labor, 515, 522, **524,** 525, 526, 548, 549
Know-Nothing Party, 376 *(m)*, 377–378, 377 *(i)*, 379
Knox, Henry, 227

Kofi, 204 *(i)*
Korea. *See also* Korean War; North Korea;
    South Korea
    labor in, 846
    occupation zones in, 739
    after World War II, 713, 739
Korean War (1950-1953), 737
    Cold War and, 739–742
    desegregation in, 743
    Eisenhower and, 742
    human toll of, 742
Korematsu decision, 700
Kosovo, 869 *(i)*, 871
Krimmel, John Lewis, 265 *(i)*
Ku Klux Klan, 441, 641 *(i)*, ***643***
Ku Klux Klan Act (1871), 447
Kurds, in Iraq, 862
Kuwait, Iraq and, 860
Kyoto Protocol, withdrawal from, 875

Labor. *See also* Free labor; Indentured
    servants; Labor unions; Slaves and
    slavery; Strikes; Workers
    African American, 621, 678, 709
    black codes and, 433
    Chinese, 469–470
    closed shops and, 629
    contract labor, 541
    contracts for, 629
    farm, 474
    free and unfree servants as, 68–69
    free-labor system and, 312–313
    in Great Depression, 653–654
    indentured servants as, 60, 64
    Indian, 43–44
    industrial, 542
    in manufacturing, 309–310
    Mexican, 621
    militancy in Great Depression, 653–654
    minimum wage and, 684
    NAFTA and, 871
    in New Spain, 46–47
    in 1950s, 758
    Reagan and, 845
    separate spheres concept and, 294
    slave, 349–351
    in Spanish colonies, 46–47
    Taft-Hartley Act and, 736
    in Virginia colony, 59
    Wilson and, 587
    in World War I, 608
    after World War II, 732
Labor code, during reconstruction, 429–430
Labor Department, 583
Labor force. *See* Workforce
Labor unions. *See also* Labor; Strikes;
    specific unions
    blacks in, 524
    closed shops and, 629
    decline of, 868
    membership in (1930–1939), 676 *(f)*
    middle-class progressives and, 570–572
    in mining, 467
    in New Deal, 675
    in 1930s, 675–676
    Reagan and, 845
    Sherman Antitrust Act and, 502
    in steel industry, 544
    trade unions and, 525, 526
    welfare capitalism and, 632

women and, 281, 524, 570–572
    after World War I, 618–619
    after World War II, 732–733
Ladies Association, 181
Lafayette (Marquis de), 188 *(i)*
La Follette, Robert M., 574, 585, 609, 629
Laissez-faire, 490, 496, 550
Lakes. *See also* Great Lakes region
    Champlain, 146
    Erie, 146
    Ontario, 146
    Texcoco, 25
Lakewood (housing development), 761
Lakota Sioux Indians, 458, 460
Lancaster Turnpike (1794), 231
Land. *See also* Agriculture; Conservation;
    Farms and farming; Public land
    of Californios, 468
    cession in West (1782–1802), 200 *(m)*
    in Chesapeake region, 67
    in colonies, 112–113
    conservation of, 578
    Dawes Act and, 461–462
    for freedmen, 430, 433, 437–438, 443
    as headright, 64
    Homestead Act and, 416, 471
    Indian, 70, 148, 192, 208, 236–238,
        237 *(m)*, 257–258, 456–458,
        457 *(m)*, 461–462, 750
    in New England, 93
    in Northwest Territory, 208–211, 210 *(m)*
    in Pennsylvania, 121
    public auction of, 428 *(i)*
    for railroads, 483
    return to ex-Confederates, 433
    speculation in, 142–144, 309, 538
    state claims to, 198–199
    taxes on, 448
    in West, 198–199, 292, 292 *(f)*, 472
Land bridge, between Siberia and Alaska, 7
Land-grant certificates, 183
Land grants
    to railroads, 311, 472, 473 *(m)*, 483
    to Virginia Company, 57
Landon, Alfred (Alf), 680–681
Landowners, in Chesapeake, 69
Language
    of Eastern Woodland peoples, 21
    of slaves, 126
    writing and, 5
L'Anse aux Meadows, Newfoundland, 32
Lansing, Robert, 602, 614–615
Laos, 822
Laramie, Fort
    Indian conference at, 318
    Treaty of (1851), 457, 458
    Treaty of (1868), 460, 461
La Raza Unida, 790
Las Casas, Bartolomé de, 44
Latin America. *See also* America(s); Central
    America; South America; specific
    countries
    CIA and, 771
    Good Neighbor Policy toward, 691
    interventions in, 557, 754–755
    Johnson, Lyndon B., and, 811
    Kennedy, John F., and, 806
    Nixon and, 818
    Roosevelt Corollary and, 580–581
    U.S. involvement in (1895–1941), 599 *(m)*

Latinos. *See also* Hispanic Americans;
    specific groups
    in cabinet, 865
    equal rights struggle by, 735–736,
        789–790
    poverty of, 868
Law(s). *See also* Legislation; specific laws
    in British colonies, 136
    commercial, 282
    nullification and, 243
    against southern free blacks, 354–355
    women and, 262–263
"Law and order" campaign, 816
Lawrence, Kansas, 380 *(i)*, 381
Lawson, James, 784
Lawyer-politicians, economic power of,
    282–283
League of Five Nations, 22
League of Nations, 613, 615, 616–617,
    617 *(i)*, 622, 630, 690, 691
League of United Latin-American Citizens
    (LULAC), 622, 735–736, 761, 789
League on Urban Conditions among
    Negroes, 618 *(i)*
Lebanon, 755, 851
    hostages in, 851
Lecompton constitution (Kansas), 384
Lee, Fort, capture of, 179
Lee, Richard Henry, 158
Lee, Robert E., 401, ***404***
    in Civil War, 404, 419, 419 *(m)*,
        420–421, 422
    Harpers Ferry raid and, 386
Left wing (political). *See also* Communism
    containment of, 851
    McCarthyism and, 737–738
    in 1930s, 654
Legal Tender Act (1862), 416
Legislation. *See also* Law(s); specific laws
    anti-immigrant, 642–643
    employment, 731–732
    women and, 636
Legislatures, 214. *See also* specific
    legislative bodies
    in Pennsylvania, 102
Leisure. *See also* Entertainment
    of common people, 327
    industrialization and, 527–528
    of working class, 528
Lemlich, Clara, 570
Lend-Lease Act (1941), 696, 699
Leningrad, battle at, 705 *(m)*
Lenni Lenape (Delaware) Indians. *See*
    Delaware Indians
Leopard (ship), 256
Lesbians. *See also* Gays; Homosexuals and
    homosexuality
    organization by, 791
Leslie, Frank, 544 *(i)*
Leslie's *Illustrated Weekly,* 544 *(i)*
Letters from a Farmer in Pennsylvania
    (Dickinson), 154–155, 170
Levitt, William J., 759
Levittown, New York, ***759***
Lewelling, Lorenzo, 551
Lewis, John (SNCC), 785
Lewis, John L. (United Mine Workers),
    675, 676
Lewis, Meriwether, 253–255
Lewis, Sinclair, 640

Market(s)
  for agricultural produce, 475
  colonial, 130
  domestic, 310, 311
  expansion in 1920s, 634
  foreign, 846
  overseas, 554–555
  railroad boom and, 333
  tariff and, 501
  transportation improvements and, 279
  for western agriculture, 476
  after World War II, 723
Market revolution, 277
  causes of, 278–283
  society and, 293–298
Marne River, battle at, 607
Marriage
  age of women at first, 294 (t)
  elite southern women and, 347
  by free blacks, 355
  gay and lesbian, 782, 866
  Great Depression and, 652
  interracial, 782
  in New England, 96, 114
  in Oneida community, 329
  plural (polygamy), 319, 469
  Puritan, 91
  republican, 228
  of slaves, 263, 351
  tax benefits for, 875
  woman's rights and, 262, 263
Married women. *See also* Wives
  property of, 203, 313, 347, 379
  rights of, 331, 347
  in workforce, 294, 519, 652, 708
Marshall, George C., 726, 737
Marshall, James, 326
Marshall, John, 252
Marshall, Thurgood, 768, 859
Marshall Field (store), 521
Marshall Plan, 726–727
Martin, Anna, 182
Martin, Joseph W., Jr., 731
Mary I (England), 84 (i)
Mary II (England), 106
Maryland, 199. *See also* Chesapeake
    region; Tobacco
  Catholicism in, 67, 130
  in Civil War, 404
  as English colony, 62, 136
  as proprietary colony, 104
  revolt in, 106
  secession and, 396, 397
  tobacco in, 67
Masculinity, in 1950s, 765–766
Mason, George, 203, 220
Mason, Joanna and Anthony, children of,
    90 (i)
Mason-Dixon line, 361
Massachusetts, 86 (i). *See also* New England
  Albany Plan and, 145
  charter of, 87–88, 92, 105, 159
  equality in, 204
  government of, 106
  Plymouth colony in, 87
  in Revolutionary War, 177, 178 (m)
  as royal colony, 106
  Shays's Rebellion in, 211–212
Massachusetts Bay colony, government of,
    92–93

Massachusetts Bay Company, 86 (i), *87–88*
Massachusetts Government Act (1774), 160
Massacres. *See* specific massacres
Massasoit, 105
Mass communication, 635
Mass culture, 528, 638–639
Mass media. *See also* specific media
    feminism and, 794
Mass production, 630, *631*–632
Mass transit, 515
Masters, plantation, 346–347
Materialism, of consumer culture, 762–763
Mather, Increase, 92
Mathews, John, 350
Mathews, Mary McNair, 467–468
Matrilineal descent, Iroquoian, 22
Mayan language, 40
May Day rally (Chicago, 1886), 525
Mayflower (ship), 87
Mayflower Compact, 87
Mazo, Ike, 846
McCain, John, 881
McCarran-Walter Act (1952), 737
McCarthy, Eugene, 816
McCarthy, Joseph R., and McCarthyism,
    737–738, 743, 748–749
McClellan, George B., 403, 404, 421
McClure's Magazine, 486–487
McCormick, Cyrus, 309, 416
McCormick reaper works, strike at, 525
McCrea, Jane, 184 (i)
McGovern, George S., 833
McIntosh, Fort, Treaty of (1785), 209
McKay, Claude, 638
McKinley, William, 501, 561
  assassination of, 575
  election of 1896 and, 552–553
  Spanish-American War and, 559
McKinley tariff (1890), 501, 555
McNamara, Robert, 809, 815
Meade, George G., 419
Measles, 317
Meat Inspection Act (1906), 578
Meatpacking industry, 578
Mechanization
  in business, 520
  of farming, 309, 416, 475, 757–758
  industrial, 542
  in textile industry, 280
  unskilled workers and, 514, 518
Media. *See* Mass media; specific media
Mediation, by Roosevelt, Theodore, 576
Medicaid (1965), 780
Medicare (1965), 780, 846, 865
Medicine. *See also* Diseases
  socialized, 780
Medicine Lodge Creek, Treaty of (1867), 460
Mediterranean region
  Barbary States in, 255–256
  trade and exploration in, 32–33
  in World War II, 704–706
Meetinghouse, in Hingham, Massachusetts,
    94 (i)
Mellon, Andrew, 628–629
Memphis, 406
Men. *See also* Gender
  in Great Depression, 652
  as immigrants, 513
  poverty and, 780
  separate spheres for, 293–295

Mencken, H. L., 644
Menéndez de Avilés, Pedro, 47
Mennonites, 100
Mercantilism, 70
Mercenaries (Hessians), 179
Merchant marine, in Civil War, 401
Merchants
  in Chesapeake colonies, 69
  in New England commerce, 116–117
  nonimportation and, 155
  in South, 443–444
Mergers, 488
Merrimack (frigate), 406. *See also* Virginia
    (ironclad)
Mestizos, 45
Metacomet (Wampanoag Indians). *See*
    King Philip
Metals. *See* Precious metals; specific
    metals
Methodists, 263, 295, 351, 358, 431, 491
Meuse River, battle at, 607
Mexica, 25–26, 41
Mexican Americans, 468
  civil rights of, 735–736
  as cowboys, 474
  as farm laborers, 474
  in Great Depression, 651–652
  immigration by, 621–622, 643
  land grants of, 468
  migration by, 621–622
  in New Deal, 679
  protests by, 789–790
  in Southwest, 468, 621–622
  in West, 760, 761 (i)
  in World War II, 701
Mexican-American War (1846–1848), 307 (i),
    323–326, 456, 468
  battles in, 324 (m)
  casualties in, 324, 325
  manifest destiny and, 326
  Treaty of Guadalupe Hidalgo after,
    325–326, 468
Mexican borderlands, 319–321
Mexican cession, 309, 325–326, 366 (m)
  slavery in, 367, 391
Mexican empire, 41
Mexicans, during Mexican-American War,
    325 (i)
Mexico
  agriculture from, 14
  Anglo-Americans in, 320–321
  California and, 321
  Gadsden Purchase and, 373
  independence for, 319–320
  indigenous culture of, 25–26
  labor in, 846
  in NAFTA, 871
  Pershing in, 600
  pottery from, 14
  revolution in (1911), 584
  Spanish conquest of, 40–41
  Texas and, 320–321, 320 (m), 323,
    325–326
  war news from, 306 (i)
  Wilson and, 599–600, 600 (m)
  Zimmermann telegram and, 603
Mexico City, assault on (1847), 325
Miami, Fort, 238
Miami Indians, 209, 236, 236 (i), 237,
    238, 259

Mica, 18

Michigan, 309

Middle class
  black, 621, 781
  during Civil War, 416
  domestic servants for, 527–528
  labor unions and, 570–572
  minorities in, 868
  wealthy and, 515–516
  in workforce, 519, 520–521

Middle colonies, 96 *(f)*, 99–102, 172. *See also* specific locations
  immigrants to, 118–120
  lifestyle and culture in 18th century, 118–122
  population of, 118

Middle East, 255. *See also* Iraq War (2003–); specific locations
  Arab-Israeli wars in, 797
  Carter and, 841–842
  CIA and, 771
  events in (1948-1989), 841 *(m)*
  events in (1989-2009), 861 *(m)*, 871 *(m)*
  Iranian revolution in, 838–839
  Israel and, 729–730, 729 *(m)*
  Nixon and, 818–819
  terrorism in, 851
  World War II and, 704

Middlemen, in cotton industry, 344

Middle Passage, 124 *(m)*, **125**–126

Middletown (1929), 633

Midway, Battle of, 704

Midway Plaisance, 532

Midwest, 309, 314, 472 *(m)*. *See also* specific locations

Migrant workers, 474, 476, 671, 672 *(i)*

Migration. *See also* Westward movement
  African American, 514, 618 *(i)*, 620–621, 642 *(m)*, 759, 767
  by ancient peoples, 6–8, 8 *(f)*
  by Archaic Indians, 10
  to cities, 492, 510, 758
  from Europe and Africa, 20, 76 *(f)*
  global, 510–513
  by Jews, 512, 513
  Mexican American, 621–622
  to West, 339
  west of Mississippi River, 16, 316

Miles, Nelson, 463

Militancy
  labor, 524
  working-class, 653–654

Military. *See also* Armed forces; Soldiers; specific battles and wars
  Boston Massacre and, 157
  Carter and, 842
  desegregation of, 743
  "don't ask, don't tell" policy in, 866
  equipment for (World War II), 702–703, 717
  growth of, 728
  highest world expenditures on (2005), 870 *(f)*
  of Mexica, 26
  Reagan and, 850–851
  during reconstruction, 437, 441
  in Somalia, 869
  in Sun Belt, 759
  U.S. Middle East bases, 861 *(m)*
  U.S. World War II production, 689

women in, 795
  after World War II, 722

Military districts, in South, 437 *(m)*

Military Draft Act (1917), 605

Military-industrial complex, 756

Military Reconstruction Act (1867), **437**

Militia
  in Civil War, 394 *(i)*, 397
  in Great Railroad Strike, 522, 523
  Indians and, 289
  in Massachusetts, 171, 211
  in Revolutionary War, 175, 176, 185, 189
  Whiskey Rebellion and, 235

Militia Act (1862), 410

Militia movement, 866

Miller, B. M., 653 *(i)*

Miller, Henry, 476

Miller & Lux (agribusiness), 476

"Mill girls," 280

Milliken's Bend, Battle of, 410–411

Mills, 122, 280–281, 577 *(i)*

Mill towns, 295

Milosevic, Slobodan, 870, 871

Mines and mining, 465 *(i)*, 571 *(i)*. *See also* specific metals
  "Big Bonanza" and, 467
  California gold rush and, 326–327
  camps and, 327
  Comstock Lode and, 465–466, 467
  Cripple Creek strike and, 545
  immigrants in, 466–467
  in New South, 493
  regulation of, 583
  silver and, 45 *(f)*, 503
  strikes in, 545
  towns and, 467–468
  in West, 465–468, 466 *(m)*

Mineta, Norman Y., 865

Mingo Indians, 144, 208

Miniconjou Sioux Indians, 464

Minimum wage, 609, 629, 684, 868

"Mining on the Comstock," 465 *(i)*

Minnesota, 457 *(m)*

Minorities. *See also* Ethnic groups; specific groups
  discrimination against, 760–761
  GI Bill and, 733
  in middle class, 868
  in Progressive Era, 593

Minow, Newton, 765

Minuit, Peter, 99–100

Minutemen, 162, 163

Miranda v. Arizona (1966), 782

Miscegenation, 342, 347, 348, 637

Miss America beauty pageant, 794

Missiles, 756, 852. *See also* Cuban missile crisis; Nuclear arms race

Missionary societies, 296

Missions and missionaries
  in California, 321
  in China, 556
  encomienda system and, 44
  English, 79
  Indians and, 287–288, 289
  Spanish, 72, 73, 135, 136 *(m)*

Mississippi, 389, 390 *(m)*, 449
  Hurricane Katrina and, 876

Mississippian culture, 19, 19 *(m)*

Mississippi Freedom Summer Project (1964), 784

Mississippi River region, 192, 280, 400, 406, 429
  cultures of, 15
  Spanish control of, 146, 147 *(m)*

Missouri, 380, 396, 397, 405, 409

Missouri Compromise (1820), 267–269, ***268,*** 268 *(m)*, 290, 367, 373, 374, 382

Mistresses, plantation, 347–348, 356

Mitchell, George (Chippewa Indians), 789

Mixed-race people, 240

Mobilization
  in Civil War, 400–401
  for Vietnam War, 812
  in World War I, 609

Model T Ford, 628 *(i)*

Modern Medea, The (Noble), 371 *(i)*

"Modern Republicanism" (Eisenhower), 748–749

Mogollon culture, 16

Mohammed, Shanaz, 878

Mohawk Indians, 22, 144, 180 *(i)*, 181, 185, 192

Mohawk River Valley region, Revolution in, 181, 184, 185, 187 *(m)*

Molasses
  tax on, 150
  trade in, 146

Monarchs and monarchies. *See also* specific rulers
  Spanish, 48

Mondale, Walter F., 836, 845

Money
  under Articles of Confederation, 206–207, 206 *(i)*
  banking and, 232, 282
  paper, 232, 401, 413, 503
  during Revolution, 183

Money policy, 503

Money supply, 283

"Money trust," 488, 586

Monitor (ironclad), 406

Moniz, Felipa, 35

"Monkey trial." *See* Scopes trial

Monopolies
  Reagan and, 845
  transportation company rights to, 279

Monroe, James, 251, 252, 266, 267, 268, 269
  cabinet of, 270

Monroe Doctrine (1823), 269–***270,*** 557
  Roosevelt, Theodore, and, 580–581, 581 *(m)*
  Spanish-American War and, 558
  Wilson and, 599

Monterrey, battle at (1846), 324

Montezuma (Mexico), ***41***

Montgomery, Richard, 179

Montgomery bus boycott, 767 *(i)*, 769–***770***

Montgomery Improvement Association (MIA), 770

Monticello, 350 *(i)*

Montreal, capture of, 146, 177–179, 178 *(m)*

Moody, Anne, 783 *(i)*

Moon landing, by United States, 805

Moral Majority, 844

Moral reform movement, 297

Moral suasion, 297, 495

Moran, Thomas, 454 *(i)*

Morgan, Anne, 570–571

Morgan, Daniel, 189 *(m)*

Morgan, J. P., 488, 578, 586
    depression of 1890s and, 504
    finance capitalism and, 488–489
    U.S. Steel and, 489
Morgan, J. P., and Company, 586
Mormons, 319, 468–469
Mormon Trail, 318 *(m)*
Mormon War (1857), 319
Moroccan crisis (1905), 581
Morocco, 707
Morris, Robert, 207
Morristown, New Jersey, 179
Morrow, E. Frederick, 769
Morse, Samuel F. B., 310, 310 *(i)*, 483
Mortality rate. *See also* Casualties
    during Middle Passage, 125
    in New England, 114
    in Virginia colony, 59
Mortgages, 538, 759, 881–882
Mossadegh, Mohammed (Iran),
    754–755, 842
Mothers. *See also* Wives; Women
    employment of, 733
    republican, 228–229
Mott, Lucretia, 330
Moudy, Ross, 467
Mound builders, 17–19, 19 *(m)*
Movable type, 33
Movies, 477, 611, 611 *(i)*, 638, 639 *(f)*
    during Great Depression, 652
Muckrakers, 577–578
Mugwumps, 497, 498, 499
Muir, John, 578
Mulattos, 340 *(i)*, 348
Muller v. Oregon (1908), 572
Muncie, Indiana, study of, 633
Municipal government, 529, 531. *See also*
    City government; specific forms
Munn v. Illinois (1877), 502
Murals, in 1930s, 674 *(i)*
Murray, Judith Sargent, 229, 229 *(i)*, 264
Murray, Pauli, 794
Music
    hymns as, 358
    jazz as, 638
    in 1950s, 766
    spirituals, 358
Muskogean Indians, 21, 23
Muslims
    in Afghanistan, 842
    in Iran, 842
    terrorism by, 876–878
Mussolini, Benito, 694 *(m)*, 698, 706
Mutually assured destruction (MAD), 753
Myer, Dillon S., 750

NAACP. *See* National Association for the
    Advancement of Colored People
Nader, Ralph, 874 *(m)*
NAFTA. *See* North American Free Trade
    Agreement
Nagasaki, bombing of, 716
Nahuatl language, 40–41
Names, African American, 127
Nanking, China, Japanese capture of, 692
Napalm, 808
Napoleon I Bonaparte (France), 250
Narragansett Indians, 103, 104
Narrative of the Life of Frederick Douglass,
    as Told by Himself (Douglass), 373

Narváez, Pánfilo de, 42
Nashville, battle of (1864), 419 *(m)*, 420, 421
Nasser, Gamal Abdel, 755
Nast, Thomas
    anti-Grant cartoon by, 446 *(i)*
    on Tweed ring, 531
Natchez Indians, 23
National Aeronautics and Space
    Administration (NASA), 756
National American Woman Suffrage Asso-
    ciation (NAWSA), 549, 590, 610–611
National Arts and Humanities Act
    (1965), 780
National Association for the Advancement
    of Colored People (NAACP), 567,
    592, 637, 709
    Brown decision and, 768
National Association of Manufacturers, 671
    Social Security and, 677
National Banking Act (1863), 416
National Consumers' League (NCL), 572
National debt, 292, 875. *See also* Debts
    of Britain, 147
    Jefferson and, 252
    after Revolution, 232–233
    state debts and, 233
National Defense Education Act
    (NDEA), 756
National Energy Act (1978), 838
National Farmers' Holiday Association
    (1932), 653–654
National Gay and Lesbian Task Force, 792
National Guard
    Alabama civil rights marchers and,
        784–785
    Boston police strike and, 619
    buildup of, 806
    at Homestead lockout, 543
    Jackson State shootings and, 820
    Kent State shootings and, 820, 821 *(i)*
    Little Rock desegregation and,
        768 *(i)*, 769
    in Pullman, Illinois, 542 *(i)*, 547
    in Vietnam War, 812
National Housing Act
    of 1937, 684
    of 1968, 780
National Industrial Recovery Act
    (NIRA, 1933), 669
Nationalism
    in Confederacy, 413–414
    after War of 1812, 261
Nationalist China, 691, 729
National Labor Relations (Wagner) Act
    (NLRA, 1935), 675
National Labor Relations Board (NLRB), 675
National Liberation Front (North Vietnam),
    815
National liberation movements, 717,
    728–730
National Miners Union, 654
National Negro Convention (Philadelphia),
    297
National Organization for Women
    (NOW), 794
National origins, immigration quotas
    and, 780
National parks, 579, 579 *(m)*
National Recovery Administration (NRA,
    1933), 669, 671

National Republicans (Whigs), 285, 291
National security, Carter and, 842
National Security Act (1947), 728
National Security Council (NSC), 728
    Iran-Contra and, 851–852
    NSC 68 and, 642
National security state, 727–730
National self-determination. *See* Self-
    determination
National Socialism. *See* Nazi Germany
National Union Party, 436
National War Labor Policies Board, 609
National Welfare Rights Organization, 779
National Woman's Party (NWP), 590, 636
National Woman Suffrage Association
    (NWSA), 494, 549
National Youth Administration, Division of
    Negro Affairs, 678 *(i)*
"Nation building," in Somalia, 869
Native Americans, 174. *See also* specific
    groups
    accommodation policy of, 458
    agriculture and, 15 *(i)*
    Albany Congress and, 144–146
    as allies, 134
    assimilation of, 288, 289, 456, 456 *(i)*, 459
    Black Hills gold discovery and, 460–461
    buffalo and, 317–318, 458–459
    in California, 12–13, 13 *(i)*, 321
    Catholic missionaries and, 44
    in Chesapeake region, 56 *(i)*
    Christianity and, 58, 59, 72–73
    citizenship for, 461
    in Civil War, 405
    colonies and, 134–135
    Columbian exchange and, 39
    cultures of, 11 *(m)*, 458–459
    Dawes Act and, 461–462
    discovery of precious metals and, 467
    diseases and, 317, 458
    Eastern Woodland Indians, 13–15
    encomienda system and, 43
    English colonies and, 79
    by 1500, 20–26, 22 *(m)*
    fishing sites of, 759–760
    Fort Stanwix Treaty and, 207–208,
        209, 236
    Ghost Dance of, 463–464
    Grant's peace policy for, 458
    Greenville Treaty and, 236 *(i)*, 238
    hunting weapons of, 23
    Jackson's policy toward, 286
    Jamestown and, 57–59
    King Philip's War and, 103, 105–106
    land cessions by, 208, 209, 237 *(m)*,
        257–258, 260, 457 *(m)*
    lands of, 456–458, 457 *(m)*, 461–462
    Lewis and Clark expedition and, 254,
        255 *(i)*
    in Massachusetts Bay colony, 86 *(i)*, 87
    mass execution of, 458
    Mogollon culture of, 16
    in New England, 115
    in New Spain, 45
    Nixon and, 798
    in Northwest Ordinance, 210–211
    of Pacific Coast region, 12–13
    pan-Indian movement of, 751
    Penn family and, 102
    in Pennsylvania, 121

Plains Indians, 317–318, 457, 460
Pontiac's uprising and, 148
population in 1490s, 20, 21 *(f)*
Proclamation of 1763 and, 148
protests by, 788–789
removal and, 286, 287–289, 288 *(m)*, 374, 456–458
reservations for, 457 *(m)*, 458–459, 460, 462
resistance by, 289, 458, 460–461, 462–464
Revolutionary War and, 180 *(i)*, 181–182, 184, 184 *(i)*, 185–186, 187 *(m)*, 192
Sand Creek Massacre against, 458
schools for, 459
as servants, 64
as Spanish labor, 46–47
termination and relocation of, 750–751, 751 *(m)*
trade with, 96
Trail of Tears and, 288 *(m)*, 289
treaties with, 207–208, 237, 259, 288, 289, 457
Treaty of Paris (1763) and, 146
violent conflict among, 24
in Virginia colony, 58–60, 70
warfare by, 209, 237–238, 318, 458, 468
War of 1812 and, 260, 261
in West, 236–238
westward expansion and, 317–318, 456–464
women and, 60
wooden mask by, 4 *(i)*
Wounded Knee Massacre against, 457 *(m)*, 464
Nativism, 377–378, 470, 570, 642
NATO. *See* North Atlantic Treaty Organization
Nat Turner's rebellion, 352–353, 353 *(i)*
Naturalization. *See also* Citizens and citizenship
limitations on, 470
Natural resources. *See* Resources
Nauvoo, Illinois, Mormons in, 319
Navajo Indians, 23, 462
Naval treaties, Japan and, 691
Navigation Acts, 133
    of 1650, 69, 103
    of 1651, 69, 103
    of 1660, 103
    of 1663, 103
Navy. *See also* Navy (U.S.)
British, 103, 134 *(f)*, 150, 187
French, 187, 191, 193
German, 602
Navy (U.S.)
African Americans in, 408 *(i)*
in Barbary Wars, 255
in Civil War, 400, 401, 405, 406, 408 *(i)*
Great White Fleet of, 581
Guantánamo base and, 878
in Manila, 559
at Pearl Harbor, 697–698, 698 *(m)*, 703
in Spanish-American War, 559, 560 *(m)*
in War of 1812, 260
in World War II, 703–704
Nazi Germany, 691. *See also* Germany; Hitler, Adolf; World War II
Allied attacks on, 712–714
Czechoslovakia and, 693
Holocaust in, 707, 711, 711 *(m)*

Rhineland and, 693
Soviet invasion by, 696
as Third Reich, 693
in World War II, 698, 704–706
Nazi-Soviet nonaggression treaty (1939), 693
NCL. *See* National Consumers' League
NCLB. *See* No Child Left Behind Act
NDEA. *See* National Defense Education Act
Nebraska Territory, organization of, 373–374
Necessary and proper clause, 216, 234
"Necessary evil" argument, for slavery, 342
Necessity, Fort, 144
"Negro rule," 442, 492
Neighborhoods, 515
Nelson, Knute, 562
Netherlands
American Revolution and, 191 *(i)*
Nazi invasion of, 694
Neutrality
Adams, John, on, 242
in American Revolution, 181
in Middle East, 755
U.S. policy of, 692, 695–696
in World War I, 601–602
after World War II, 724 *(m)*
Neutrality Acts (1935-1937), 692, 695
Neutrality Proclamation (1793), 239
Nevada, 323
Comstock Lode in, 366, 465–466, 467
Neville, John, 235
New Amsterdam, Puritans in, 89
New Christian Right, 844
New Deal, 660, **663**. *See also* Economy; Great Depression
achievements and limitations of, 685
agriculture in, 667–668, 671, 682–683
banking in, 665–666
coalition in, 662, 662 *(m)*, 680–681
decline of support for, 680–684
First, 663–673
goals of, 664
industrial recovery in, 668–669
neglected people during, 678–679
relief programs in, 666–667
Second, 674–679
New England. *See also* specific locations
in 17th century, 88–89, 88 *(m)*
in 18th century, 114–117
as city upon a hill, 88–89
Dominion of, 105–106
economy of, 96–97, 256
families in, 89
government of, 105
Hartford Convention and, 261
independence and, 173
Indians of, 21
land in, 93
manufacturing in, 310
mill towns in, 280–281
Native Americans in, 115
population of, 96, 96 *(f)*, 114–115
Puritans in, 86–98
religion in, 97–98, 130, 263
in Revolution, 178 *(m)*
settlement of, 86–98
slaves in, 117
society in, 90–92
textile mills in, 518
town meetings in, 92

trade in, 96
in War of 1812, 259, 260
New England Anti-Slavery Society, 297
Newfoundland, 32, 50
New France, 134
New England and, 115
New Freedom (Wilson), 585, 587
New Frontier (Kennedy), 776–778
New Guinea, 704, 714
New Hampshire, 219
New immigration, 511–512, 513–514, 518, 533
New Jersey, 101, 178 *(m)*, 179, 199, 205
loyalists in, 183
slave population in, 205 *(m)*
voting in, 201 *(i)*, 203
New Jersey Plan, 214
New Jerusalem, 263
New Left, 790–791
feminism and, 794
"New Look" (Eisenhower), 752–753
New Mexico, 320, 323, 326, 373
Civil War in, 405
Hispanics in, 468
Indians in, 16
Mexican-American War in, 324
Mogollon culture in, 16
Salado culture of, 20 *(i)*
slavery in, 369, 370
Spanish colony in, 47, 72, 73
New Nationalism (Roosevelt, T.), 585, 587
"New Negro," 635, 637–638
New Negroes (newly-arrived slaves), 126
New Netherland (New York), **99**–100
New Orleans
battle of (1815), 260–261
Civil War in, 406
Hurricane Katrina in, 876
Spanish control of, 146
New Right, Reagan and, 844
New Salem, witchcraft trials in, 98, 98 *(i)*
New South, 492–493
New Spain, 40–46, 43 *(m)*
Britain and, 134
migration to, 76 *(f)*
in 16th century, 42–46, 45 *(m)*
social and racial hierarchy in, 45
Newspapers. *See also* specific newspapers
of African Americans, 332, 514
antislavery, 298, 331
Cherokee, 289
expansion of, 285, 285 *(t)*
Stamp Act and, 152 *(i)*
New woman, 636–637
New World, 25, 31–51. *See also* America(s); specific regions
gold and silver imported into Spain, 45 *(f)*
influence of New Spain on, 48–51
New world order, 869–871
New York (city), 280
Central Park in, 529 *(i)*, 530
housing in, 112 *(i)*
immigrants in, 513, 514–515
public education in, 530
in Revolutionary War, 192
settlement houses in, 568, 569
slaves in, 121
Tammany Hall in, 530–531
travel times from (1800), 231 *(m)*
as U.S. capital, 230

New York (colony), 99–100, 172, 174
    Britain and, 100
    Puritans in, 89
    in Revolutionary War, 177, 178 *(m)*, 179
    uprising in, 106
New York (state), 199, 260, 280
    gradual emancipation law in, 205
    Love Canal and, 840
    ratification of Constitution and, 220
    slavery and, 205 *(m)*
    Treaty of Fort Stanwix and, 207, 208
New York City draft riots, 417
New York Female Moral Reform
    Society, 297
New York Journal, 559
New York Press Club, 495
New York Stock Exchange, 648
New York Times, Pentagon Papers and, 820
New York Tribune, 446
New York World, 516, 559
Nez Percé Indians, 462
Niagara, Fort, 146, 186, 208
Niagara movement (1905), 592
Nicaragua
    Contras in, 851, 860
    Iran-Contra scandal and, 851–852
    Sandinistas in, 841, 851
    Taft and, 583
    U.S. intervention in, 599
Nicholas II (Russia), 604
Nicodemas, Kansas, 468
Nigeria, 125
Night riders, 448
Nike, 872
Nimitz, Chester W., 704
Niña (ship), 36
Nineteenth Amendment, 549, ***611,*** 636
92nd Division, in World War I, 605
Nipmuck Indians, 103, 104
Nixon, E. D., 769, 770
Nixon, Isaac, lynching of, 735
Nixon, Pat, 817 *(i),* 835 *(i)*
Nixon, Richard M., 817
    anti-Communist governments and,
        818–819
    audiotapes of, 833 *(i),* 835
    China and, 817 *(i)*
    conservatism and, 830
    election of 1952 and, 741
    election of 1960 and, 776–777
    election of 1968 and, 816
    election of 1972 and, 797, 833–834
    Environmental Protection Agency and,
        775, 792, 799
    foreign policy of, 817–824
    impeachment and, 834–835
    Latin America and, 818
    liberal reforms and, 796–798
    Middle East and, 818–819
    pardon of, 835
    resignation of, 822, 833, 835
    right wing and, 831–832
    Soviet Union and, 818
    as vice president, 741–742
    Vietnam and, 814 *(i),* 819–821
    Watergate scandal and, 833–835
    welfare programs and, 796–798
Noah's Ark (Douglas), 638 *(i)*
Noble, Elaine, 792, 849
Noble, Thomas Satterwhite, 340 *(i),* 371 *(i)*

Noble and Holy Order of the Knights of
    Labor. *See* Knights of Labor
No Child Left Behind (NCLB) Act (2002),
    875–876
Nominating conventions, 300
Nonconsumption, 155
Nonimportation
    agreements among merchants, 155
    laws against British, 256
Non-Intercourse Act (1809), 259
Nonintervention policy, 691
Nonslaveholders, in South, 356–358, 359
Nonviolent protest, 784
Noriega, Manuel, 860
Normandy, D-Day invasion at, 712 *(i),* 713
Norsemen, 32
North. *See also* North (Civil War)
    African American migration to, 618 *(i),*
        620–621
    African Americans in, 514, 621
    on Brown, John, 386
    economy of, 311 *(m)*
    emancipation in, 204–205
    free labor in, 312–313
    Fugitive Slave Act (1850) and, 372
    immigrants in, 344
    mixed economy of, 344
    reconstruction and, 434, 440–441,
        446–448
    Revolutionary War in, 178 *(m)*
    South compared with, 338, 361
    Tallmadge amendments and, 268
    Wilmot Proviso and, 367
North (Civil War)
    dissent in, 417
    draft in, 410, 417
    economy of, 415–416
    emancipation and, 408–409
    home front in, 416–417
    inflation in, 401
    Lincoln's leadership of, 401
    mobilization of, 400–401
    resources of, 399, 400 *(f)*
North, Frederick (Lord), 158, 188
North Africa, World War II in, 704,
    705 *(m),* 706
North America. *See also* Latin America;
    South America; specific countries
    English exploration of, 50, 56
    European areas of influence in, 143 *(m)*
    French exploration of, 50
    Native Americans by 1500, 20–26, 22 *(m)*
    separation from Pangaea, 6–7
    after Seven Years' War, 147 *(m)*
    Spain and, 47
North American Free Trade Agreement
    (NAFTA), 871–872
North Atlantic Treaty Organization
    (NATO), 724 *(m),* ***728***
    peacekeeping by, 869 *(i),* 870–871
North Carolina, 62, 189 *(m),* 190, 396, 397.
    See also Carolina
Northern Alliance (Afghanistan), 878
Northern Securities Company, 576
North Korea, 739–740, 863, 881
North Pacific Coast Railroad, 469 *(i)*
Northup, Solomon, 373, 391
North Vietnam, 753, 754, 810, 811. *See also*
    Vietnam; Vietnam War
Northwestern Farmers' Alliance, 539

Northwest Indians, 13
Northwest Ordinance (1787), ***210–211,***
    267, 367
Northwest Passage, search for, 50, 99
Northwest Territory, 208–211, 210 *(m),* 237
Norway, Nazi invasion of, 694
NOW. *See* National Organization for
    Women
Noyes, John Humphrey, 329
NRA. *See* National Recovery Administration
NSC 68, 742
Nuclear arms race, 727, 752 *(i),* 755–756,
    806–807, 850, 852
Nuclear power
    Eisenhower and, 749
    as energy source, 839–840
    hydrogen bomb and, 727
Nuclear test ban, 756
    limited treaty for (1963), 807
    UN treaty for (1996), 863
Nuclear weapons, 717. *See also* Atomic
    bomb; Nuclear arms race
    Eisenhower and, 752–753, 756
    in Iran, 881
    Soviet, 818
    after World War II, 723
Nueces River, 323
Nullification, 290
    judicial review as, 252
    of tariff of 1828, 290
    Virginia and Kentucky Resolutions
        and, 243
Nursing, 412 *(i),* 416–417, 609
Nye, Gerald, and Nye Committee, 691–692

Oak Home Farm, San Joaquin County,
    California, 366 *(i)*
Oath of allegiance
    in Lincoln's reconstruction plan, 429
    in Wade-Davis bill, 429
Obama, Barack, 881–882, 881 *(m),* 882 *(i)*
Obama, Michelle, 882 *(i)*
Obscenity, 831
Occupation (military)
    of Germany, 724 *(m),* 725
    of Iraq, 880
    of Japan, 740
    of Korea, 739
    of South in reconstruction, 437, 437 *(m)*
Occupational Safety and Health Act
    (OSHA), 792
Occupation zones. *See* Zones of occupation
Oceans. *See also* specific ocean regions
    continental drift and, 6–7
O'Connor, Sandra Day, 848, 875
O'Dell, Jack, 738
O'Donnell, Hugh, 543
"Of Course He Wants to Vote the
    Democratic Ticket" (political
    cartoon), 445 *(i)*
Officeholders
    in antebellum South, 360
    black, 785–786
    ex-Confederates as, 433–434, 447
    gay, 792
    property qualifications for, 359
Office work, by women, 519, 520–521,
    521 *(i)*
Oglala Sioux Indians, 460, 461
Ohio company, 143

Ohio River region, 280
  cession to United States, 208
  French-British rivalry in, 142–144, 143 (m)
  Indians of, 186, 236
  in 1753, 144 (m)
  western expansion in, 237, 237 (m)
Oil and oil industry. *See also* Standard Oil
      Company
  energy shortage and, 797, 838–839
  in Iran, 842
  in Middle East, 754–755
  worldwide reserves of (1980), 839 (m)
Okies, 671, 672 (i)
Okinawa, battle at, 714
Oklahoma, 456, 472–473. *See also* Indian
      Territory
Oklahoma City, federal building bombing
      in, 866
Oklahoma Tenant Farmers' Union, 668
Old Age Revolving Pension, 673
Older Americans. *See* Elderly
Old immigration, 511–512
Old North Bridge, 163
Old Northwest, Indians in, 258–259
Oligopoly, in mining industry, 467
Olive Branch Petition (1775), 172
Oliver, Andrew, 151, 152
Olmsted, Frederick Law, 529 (i), *530,* 532
Olney, Richard B., 547
Olympic Games, Summer (1980), 842
Oñate, Juan de, 47, 468
"100% American" campaigns, 611
Oneida community, 329
Oneida Indians, 22, 181, 185
One-party political system, 266
Onondaga Indians, 22, 181
Ontario, Lake, 146
"On the Equality of the Sexes" (Murray),
      228, 229 (i)
On the Origin of Species (Darwin), 489
On the Road (Kerouac), 766
"On to Washington" movement (1894), 551
Opechancanough (Algonquian leader),
      60, 70
Open Door policy, 554 (i), *557,* 581
Open range, fencing of, 468, 473, 474
Operation Desert Storm, 860
Operation Just Cause, 860
Operation Rolling Thunder, 810, 813
"Operation Wetback," 760
Orange County, California, 830–831
Ordinance of 1784, 208–209
Ordinance of 1785, 209, 210 (m)
Ordnance Bureau (Confederacy), 401
Oregon, 309, 318–319, 322
Oregon Country, British claims to, 316, 317
Oregon Trail, 317, 318 (m), 321
Organization Man, The (Whyte), 765
Organization of American States (OAS), 811
Organized labor. *See* Labor unions
Organized Trades and Labor Unions, 524
Oriskany, battle of (1777), 181, 185
Orphans, state care of, 442
Ortega, Daniel, 851
OSHA. *See* Occupational Safety and
      Health Act
O'Sullivan, John L. (editor), 316
O'Sullivan, Mary Kenney, 570
Oswald, Lee Harvey, 778
Other America, The (Harrington), 777

Otis, Hannah, 114 (i)
Ottawa Indians, 148, 238
Ottoman Empire, after World War I, 615
Overcapitalization, 489
Overhiser, W. I., 366 (i)
Overseer, 346, 356

Pace, Peter, 874 (i)
Pacific Northwest region, peoples of,
      13, 21
Pacific Ocean region
  Balboa at, 38
  cultures of, 12–13, 23
  Hispanics in, 468
  Lewis and Clark at, 254
  Magellan in, 38–39
  trails to, 318 (m)
  World War II in, 697–698, 703–704, 703 (i),
      714–715, 715 (m)
Pacific Railroad Act (1862), 416
Packard, Vance, 765
Pahlavi, Mohammad Reza (Shah of Iran),
      755, 755 (i), 842
Paine, Thomas, 172–173
Painting
  abstract expressionism and, 766
  in 1930s, 674 (i)
Paiute Indians, 458, 462, 463, 467
Pakistan, 842, 882
  nuclear test ban treaty and, 863
Paleo-Indians, 8–9, 10
Palestine
  Cold War and, 851
  Israel and, 729–730, 819, 841–842,
      861, 871
  partition of, 729, 729 (m)
  after World War I, 615
Palestine Liberation Organization
      (PLO), 851
Palin, Sarah, 881
Palmer, A. Mitchell, 619, 620
Palo Alto, battle at (1846), 324
Panama
  Carter and, 841
  intervention in, 860
  Isthmus of, 38
Panama Canal, 580, 580 (m), 841
Panama Canal Zone, 599 (m)
  riots in, 811
Pan-American cooperation, 557
Pan-American Exposition (Buffalo, New
      York), 575
Pangaea, 6
Panics. *See also* Depressions (financial)
  of 1819, 283, 302
  of 1837, 283, 299, 301, 302
  of 1839, 301, 302
  of 1873, 447, 503, 522
  of 1893, 476, 503–504, 545
  of 1907, 578
Pan-Indian movement, 751, 788
**Pankhurst family (Emmeline, Cristabel,
      and Sylvia),** 590
Paper money. *See* Money
Pardons
  for Confederates, 433
  of Iran-Contra figures, 852
  by Johnson, Andrew, 433, 438
  of Nixon, 835
Paris, liberation in World War II, 713

Paris, Treaty of
  of 1763, 146, 148, 253
  of 1783, 169, *192,* 207, 236
  of 1898, 561–562, 561 (m)
Paris Peace Conference (1919), 613, 614–616
Parker, Alton B., 577
Parks, Rosa, 767 (i), *769–*770
Parliament (England)
  Charles I and, 85
  Navigation Acts and, 69
  taxation by, 153
Parsons, Albert, 525, 526
Partitions, of Palestine, 729, 729 (m)
Party politics. *See* Political parties
Patents, to Edison, 487
Paternalism, of planters, *346*
Patriot Act (2001). *See* USA Patriot Act
Patriotism
  in Civil War, 414, 415, 416
  in Revolutionary War, 180–181
  in World War I, 608, 611
Patriots, 155, 181, 182 (m)
Patronage, 272, 491
Patrons of Husbandry. *See* Grange
Patroonships, 100
Patton, George, 702
Paul, Alice, 590, 610
Pawnee Indians, 23, 462, 464
Payne-Aldrich bill, 582–583
Peace. *See* Armistice; Disarmament;
      specific treaties
Peace Corps, 806
"Peace" Democrats, 421
Peacekeeping forces, in Kosovo, 869 (i), 871
Peace movement. *See also* Antiwar protests
  World War I and, 611
Peace talks, with Vietnam, 821–822
Pea Ridge, battle of (1862), 405
Pearl Harbor, Japanese attack on, *697–*698,
      698 (m)
Pell grants, 796
Pendleton Civil Service Act (1883), 498
Peninsula campaign (1862), 403–404, 404 (m)
Peninsulares, 45
*Penn, William, 101–*102, 101 (i), 122
Pennsylvania, 101, 172, 179, 199, 280
  diversity in, 101–102
  emancipation in, 204–205
  Indians and land in, 121
  September 11, 2001, attacks and, 876
  settlers in, 120–122
  slave population of, 205 (m)
  Whiskey Rebellion in, 235
Pennsylvania Railroad, 483
"Penny sales," in Great Depression, 654
Penobscot Indians, 22
Pensions
  as "bonus" in Great Depression, 654
  plans for, 632
Pentagon, September 11, 2001, terrorist
      attack on, 876
Pentagon Papers, 820
People of color. *See also* specific groups
  economic status of, 868
  as immigrants, 511
People's Party (Populist Party), 540 (i),
      541, 547, 549, 563. *See also* Populist
      movement
  in election of 1892, 551, 552 (m)
  in election of 1896, 550, 552–553, 553 (m)

Pork barrel programs, 501
Port cities. *See also* specific locations
   immigrants in, 510
   Jewish immigrants in, 513
   in Revolutionary War, 176
Port Hudson, battle of (1863), 410–411
Portolá, Gaspar de, 135
Portugal
   Brazil and, 42
   exploration by, 33–34, 33 *(m)*
   migration to New World from, 76 *(f)*
   Treaty of Tordesillas and, 37
"Positive good" argument, for slavery, 342
Post office. *See* U.S. Post Office
Potato blight, in Ireland, 314
Potawatomi Indians, 238, 259
Potomac River, capital along, 233
Pottawatomie Creek massacre, 381, 386
Pottery, of Woodland peoples, 14, 18 *(i)*
Poverty
   antipoverty legislation and, 779–780
   in cities, 515, 516 *(i)*, 568
   Clinton and, 866
   in Confederacy, 413
   distribution of, 868
   free blacks in, 355
   in Great Depression, 651
   Kennedy, John F., and, 777
   in New England, 117
   in 1950s, 751
   in 1960s–1970s, 781 *(f)*
   in 1980s, 846
   prostitution and, 569
   on reservations, 458
   rural, 758
   social Darwinism and, 490
   wealth gap and, 505, 516 *(i)*
   of whites in South, 357–358
Powder Alarm, 160
Powderly, Terence V., 515, **524,** 525
Powder River valley, 460
Powell, Colin L., 860
   Iraq War and, 879
   Panama and, 860
   as secretary of state, 875
Power (energy). *See* Electricity; Energy
   crisis; Oil and oil industry
Power (political)
   after Civil War, 423
   in Constitution, 216
   of planters, 346–347, 360
   transfer of, 251
Power loom, 281 *(i)*
Powhatan (Indian leader), 56 *(i),* **57**–58, 60
Prager, Robert, lynching of, 612
Prairie, agriculture on, 309
Pratt, Richard Henry, 459
PRC. *See* People's Republic of China
Preachers, women as, 263
Precious metals, 42
   from New World, 45 *(f)*
Predestination, 91
Preemption policy, 879
Pregnancy, among female indentured
   servants, 66
Prejudice. *See also* Discrimination; specific
   groups
   abandonment of reconstruction and,
      447, 448
   against Asians, 700

in West, 468
in World War II, 709
Presbyterians, 119, 295, 491
Preservation, 578
Presidency
   election to, 215–216, 242, 266–267
   in Virginia and New Jersey Plans, 214
President. *See also* Executive; specific
      individuals
   in Constitution, 216
   title of, 227, 245
   Washington as, 227, 245
Presidential campaigns, financing of,
      835–836
Presidential debates, in 1960, 777
Presidential reconstruction, 432–433
President's Commission on the Status of
      Women (PCSW), 793
President's Committee on Civil Rights
      (1946), 735
Presidios, 135
Press, freedom of, 202, 228
Preston, John Smith, 389
Preston, Thomas, 157
Price controls
   Truman and, 732
   in World War II, 710
Price of Blood, The (Noble), 340 *(i)*
"Price Raid" (Reader), 394 *(i)*
Princeton, in Revolutionary War, 179
Printing, 33
Prisons, 441
Privateers
   Barbary, 255
   French, 243
Private property, 182, 461
Proclamation of 1763, 148
Proclamation of Amnesty and
      Reconstruction (1863), 428–429
Proctor Electric Company, 733 *(i)*
Production
   of cotton, 339
   methods of, 280–282
   in World War II, 701 *(f),* 702–703, 717
Productivity
   agricultural, 308, 309
   in factories and transportation, 308
   between 1922 and 1929, 632
Professional Air Traffic Controllers Organi-
      zation (PATCO), strike by, 845
Profiteering, in Revolution, 185
Progressive Era, 578, 591, 593
Progressive Party
   of 1912, 585, 585 *(m),* 587, 611
   election of 1924 and, 629
Progressivism, 570
   in city and state government, 574
   election of 1912 and, 584–585
   grassroots, 593
   La Follette and, 574
   limits of, 588–592
   nativism and, 570
   populism and, 585
   reform and, 568–572
   reform Darwinism and, 573
   Roosevelt, Theodore, and, 574, 575–581
   social engineering and, 573–574
   Taft and, 582–584
   Wilson and, 586–587
   woman suffrage and, 572, 590

working class and, 570–572
World War I and, 605, 608–609
Prohibition, 569–570, 609, ***635***–636, 644.
      See also Temperance
Prohibition Party, 495, 549
Propaganda, 611
   in Cold War, 728
Property. *See also* Property qualifications
   Confiscation Acts and, 429
   in Iroquoian society, 22
   liberty and, 152–153
   of loyalists, 182
   return to ex-Confederates, 433
   slaves as, 205, 263, 340 *(i),* 342
Property qualifications
   for voting, 106, 128, 201 *(i),* 202, 203,
      266–267, 284, 359, 439, 441
   women and, 263, 313
Property rights
   Homestead strike and, 543
   of married women, 203, 262, 313, 347
Prophet (Tenskwatawa), 258, 258 *(i),* 261
Prophetstown, Indiana, 259
Proprietary colonies
   Maryland as, 104
   South Carolina as, 104
Proprietors
   in Carolina, 77
   in Pennsylvania, 101, 102
Proslavery arguments, 342, 347
Prosperity. *See also* Affluence
   in 1920s, 647, 655
   in 1950s, 757–761, 762–766
   in World War II, 707
Prossor, Thomas, 251
Prostitution, 528, 569, 605
Protective tariffs, 500–502, 648. *See also*
   Tariffs
Protest(s). *See also* Civil rights movement;
      Resistance
   in China, 863
   by colonial women, 140 *(i)*
   by environmentalists, 790
   by farmers, 538–541
   by feminists, 790
   by gays and lesbians, 791–792
   by Latinos, 789–790
   in Massachusetts, 160–161
   by Native Americans, 788–789
   in 1968, 815
   against Stamp Act, 151–152
   by students, New Left, and
      Counterculture, 790–791
   against WTO, 872
Protestant Association (Maryland), 106
Protestant Reformation, 48
   England and, 84
   European order and, 48–49
Protestants and Protestantism. *See also*
      Puritans; specific groups
   in British North American colonies,
      130–133
   Calvinism and, 91
   in Chesapeake region, 67
   conversion to, 79
   in New England, 115
   in Republican Party, 491–492
   women and, 263–264
Public debt. *See* Debts
Public domain, 292

Public education. *See* Public schools
Public land, 416
Public libraries, 530
Public Opinion (journal), 515
Public parks, 529 *(i)*, 530
Public programs. *See also* Welfare
    programs; specific programs
  Carter and, 838
Public schools. *See also* School (s)
  in cities and towns, 313, 530
  in 1830s, 295
  girls in, 264
  segregation in, 581
  in South, 344, 358, 442
Public securities, 183
Public works, 551, 648–649
  in cities, 530
Pueblo Bonito, 17, 17 *(i)*
Pueblo Revolt
  of 1598, 47
  of 1680, **73**
Pueblos, 16–17, 47
Puerto Ricans, 789
Puerto Rico, 560, 561, 599 *(m)*
  Spanish settlement in, 40
Pulitzer, Joseph, 559
Pullman (town), 542 *(i)*, 545
Pullman, George M., 542 *(i)*, 545–546, 547
Pullman boycott and strike, 546–547,
  563, 570
Pullman Palace cars, 546 *(i)*
Punishment
  of loyalists, 182
  of slaves, 346, 350
Pure Food and Drug Act (1906), 578
Pure food and drug legislation, 495, 578
Puritan Revolution (England), 95–96
Puritans, 84
  Calvinism of, 91
  Congregationalism and, 130
  in England, 85, 95–96
  government by and for, 92–93
  Halfway Covenant of, 97
  holiday celebrations by, 83, 91, 107
  in Massachusetts, 88–89
  in New England, 86–98, 114
  religion of, 90–92, 93–98
Pynchon, William, 93

Qaeda, Al. *See* Al Qaeda
Quakers, 263
  in Pennsylvania, **97,** 101–102
  wealth of, 122
Quantrill, William Clarke, 405
Quartering Act (1774), 160
Quasi-War (1798–1800), 243–244
Quebec
  British capture of, 146, 147 *(m)*
  in Revolutionary War, 177–179, 178 *(m)*
Quebec Act (1774), 159
Queens. *See* specific rulers
Quincy, Josiah, 157
Quotas, on immigration, 780

Rabin, Yitzak, 871
Race and racism. *See also* Civil rights movement; Segregation; specific groups
  against Chinese immigrants, 467, 469–
    470, 514
  civil rights movement and, 767–770

Fifteenth Amendment and, 439
free blacks and, 332
Great Society programs and, 781
Hispanics and, 468
immigrants and, 514–515
Indians and, 750–751
of Johnson, Andrew, 432
Ku Klux Klan and, 441
lynchings and, 493–494, 514
mixed races and, 240
in New Deal, 678–679, 684
in New Spain, 46 *(i)*
in 1930s, 654
Nixon and, 831–832
politics of, 267
Populists and, 552
progressivism and, 591–592
reconstruction and, 441, 447–448
resistance to change, 831
scientific racism and, 490
social Darwinism and, 490
in South, 123, 342, 361
southern Democratic Party and, 448–449
U.S. imperialism and, 562
white attitudes and, 121
Wilmot Proviso and, 367, 369
during World War II, 709
Race riots
  in Atlanta, 591–592
  in Harlem, 678
  in 1943, 709
  in North, 621
  during reconstruction, 437
Racial segregation. *See* Segregation
Radar, 704
Radicalism and radicals. *See also*
    Communism
  in Great Depression, 672
  labor, 525–526
  McCarthy and, 737–738
  after World War I, 619–620
Radical reconstruction, 437–438
Radical Republicans, 434, 435, 437–438
Radio, 639
Radioactivity, from nuclear testing, 807
Railroad Administration, 609
Railroads, 280
  as big business, 482–483
  buffalo hunting and, 460
  cattle ranching and, 473
  Chinese workers on, 469, 514
  in 1860, 311 *(m)*
  expansion of, 310–311, 333, 483–484,
    484 *(m)*
  farming and, 475
  global mobility and, 511
  land grants to, 311, 472, 473 *(m)*, 483
  mileage of, 486 *(f)*
  in New South, 493
  rate system of, 538
  rebates from, 538, 576, 577
  recruitment of settlers by, 470, 472
  regulation of, 502, 583
  reorganization of, 489
  in South, 360, 401, 442
  steel and, 483–484
  strikes against, 522–524, 532, 545–547
  telegraph communication and,
    310–311, 483
  track mileage (1890), 486 *(f)*

transcontinental, 317, 416, 482
trusts in, 576
Raleigh, Walter, 48 *(i)*, 50
Rancheros, 321
Ranching, 321, 473–474
Ranchos, 321, 468
Randolph, A. Philip, 709
Randolph, Edmund, 227, 346
"Rape of Nanking," 692
Rates, railroad, 538
Ratification
  of Articles of Confederation, 198 *(i)*, 199
  of Constitution, 216, 217–220,
    218 *(m)*, 227
  of Versailles treaty, 616–617
Rationing, in World War II, 710
Raw materials, tariffs and, 501
Raza Unida, La. *See* La Raza Unida
Reader, Samuel J., 394 *(i)*
Readjusters, 493
Reagan, Nancy, 843 *(i)*
Reagan, Ronald, 828 *(i)*, **843**–848, 850–852,
  853 *(i)*
  budget deficit and, 845
  as California governor, 843
  conservative support for, 843–844
  courts, Congress, and, 847–848
  deregulation by, 845
  economy and, 844–845, 846
  election of 1976 and, 836
  election of 1980 and, 842, 843
  election of 1984 and, 845
  feminism and, 848–849
  foreign policy of, 850–852
  Iran-Contra and, 851–852
  Soviet Union and, 850–851, 852
Reapers, mechanical, 309, 416
Rebates, railroad, 538, 576, 577
Rebellions. *See* Protest(s); Revolts and
  rebellions
Recall, Populists on, 541
Recessions. *See also* Depressions;
  Economy; Panics
  in 1937–1938, 681–682
  of 2000s, 875
  in 2008, 881–882
  after World War I, 619
Reciprocal Trade Agreements Act
  (1934), 691
Reconquest, 34
Reconstruction (1863–1877), 427–451
  abandonment of, 446–448, 450
  carpetbaggers and, 440–441
  collapse of, 445–449
  congressional, 434, 435–439
  Johnson impeachment and, 438
  Johnson's plan for, 432–433
  labor code during, 429–430
  Lincoln's plan for, 428–429
  military rule during, 437–438, 437 *(m)*
  North and, 434, 440, 446–448
  politics in, 451
  presidential, 432–433
  radical, 437–438
  Redeemers and, 448, 449
  South and, 440–444, 449 *(m)*
  southern Republican Party and, 440–441,
    441–443, 448–449
  wartime, 428–429
  white supremacy and, 441, 448–449

Reconstruction Acts (1867), 438, 439
Reconstruction Amendments. *See*
　　Thirteenth Amendment; Fourteenth
　　Amendment; Fifteenth Amendment
Reconstruction Finance Corporation (RFC,
　　1932), 649, 665
Recovery, industrial, in New Deal, 664,
　　668–669
Recreation. *See* Leisure
Red Army (Soviet Union), 712, 713, 714
Red-baiting, McCarthyism and, 737–738
Redbook magazine, flappers in, 635 *(i)*
Red Cloud (Sioux chief), 460
Redcoats, in Revolutionary War, 179
Red Cross, 417, 609, 649
Redeemers, in South, 448, 449
Redemptioners, 119–120
Red Hawk (Shawnee Indians), 186
Redistricting, *Baker v. Carr* and, 782
Red scare
　　after World War I, ***619***–620
　　after World War II, 737–738
Red Stockings, 528
Reexport trade, 104
Referendum, 541
Reform and reform movements. *See also*
　　specific movements
　　abolitionism as, 297–298
　　banking and, 586–587
　　in cities, 531
　　civil service, 497–498
　　by Clinton, 864–865
　　election, 541
　　for Indians, 459, 461–462
　　moral, 297
　　in New Deal, 663–673, 682–684
　　under Nixon, 796–798
　　in politics, 496–497
　　progressive, 568–572, 574
　　Protestant Reformation and, 48–49
　　in reconstruction South, 441–442
　　Roosevelt, Theodore, and, 577–578
　　Second Great Awakening and,
　　　295–296, 302
　　settlement house movement and, 568–569
　　social Darwinism and, 489–490
　　suffrage, 267
　　temperance and, 296–297, 491 *(i)*, 495
　　by Wilson, 586–587
　　in Wisconsin government, 574
　　women and, 295, 296, 297, 298,
　　　329–331, 572
Reformation. *See* Protestant Reformation
Reform Darwinism, 573
Refugees
　　Indian, after Revolution, 192
　　Jewish, in World War II, 711
　　Palestinian, 841–842
"Refusing to Give the Lady a Seat," 617 *(i)*
Regents of the University of California v.
　　Bakke (1978), 832
Regions. *See* specific regions
Regulation
　　vs. competition, 578
　　governmental, 587, 797
　　of mines, 583
　　Reagan and, 845
　　reduction of, 629
　　of trusts, 502, 576, 578

Relief efforts
　　Cleveland on, 504
　　in 1930s, 664, 666, 675
Religion(s). *See also* Churches; specific
　　religions
　　Bill of Rights and, 228
　　in British North American colonies,
　　　130–133
　　in Chesapeake region, 67
　　common people and, 358
　　in election of 1928, 644
　　in England, 84–85, 84 *(i)*
　　of freedmen, 431
　　freedom of, 228
　　of immigrants, 514
　　Indian, 463–464
　　in middle colonies, 100, 101–102
　　in New England, 86–98
　　in 1950s, 763–764
　　in Pennsylvania, 101–102
　　politics and, 491–492
　　Protestant Reformation and, 48–49
　　of Puritans, 90–92, 93–98
　　Second Great Awakening and,
　　　295–296
　　of slaves, 351–352
　　toleration of, 93–94, 100, 101–102, 107
　　women and, 263–264
Relocation. *See also* Removal policy
　　of Indians, 289, 750–751, 751 *(m)*
　　of Japanese Americans, 700, 700 *(m)*
Remington, Frederic, 559
Removal policy, for Indians, 286, 287–289,
　　288 *(m)*, 374, 456–458
Reno, Janet, 865, 865 *(i)*
Rent controls, Truman and, 732
Reparations
　　after World War I, 630, 647
　　after World War II, 724–725
Repartimiento reform, 44
Report on Manufactures (Hamilton), 234
Report on Public Credit (Hamilton),
　　232–233, 232 *(i)*
Report on the Causes and Reasons for
　　War, 259
Representation
　　Constitution on, 215
　　New Jersey Plan on, 214
　　Virginia Plan on, 214
　　virtual, 150
Republicanism
　　Constitution and, 215–216
　　Jefferson and, 252–253
　　in late 1770s, 201–202
　　Paine on, 173
　　women's roles and, 228–229
Republican Loyalists, in Spain, 692
Republican National Convention (1980),
　　843 *(i)*
Republican Party, 302, ***378.*** *See also*
　　Elections; National Republicans
　　business and, 483
　　Christian Coalition and, 844
　　on *Dred Scott* decision, 382–383
　　economic power of, 415–416
　　Eisenhower and, 748–749
　　ex-Confederates in Congress and, 434
　　formation of, 378–379
　　in Gilded Age, 483, 491–492, 498–499
　　Liberal Party and, 446

presidential reconstruction and, 432
　　progressives in, 574, 583
　　radical reconstruction and, 437–438
　　radicals in, 434, 435, 437
　　reconstruction and, 432, 434, 437
　　slavery and, 409
　　Social Security and, 677
　　in South, 440–441, 441–443, 447,
　　　448–449, 832
　　tariff question and, 500–501
　　Versailles treaty and, 616–617
　　woman suffrage and, 611
　　World War I and, 612
Republicans (Jeffersonian), ***241,*** 270, 273
　　Alien and Sedition Acts and, 243–244
　　election of 1796 and, 242
　　after War of 1812, 261
Republican wife and mother, 228–229
Republic Steel, strike at, 676
Resaca de la Palma, battle at (1846), 324
Reservationists, in Senate, 617
Reservations (Indian), 318, 457 *(m)*,
　　458–459, 460, 462
Reserve Officers Training Corps
　　(ROTC), 813
Resistance. *See also* Revolts and
　　rebellions
　　to British taxation, 151–152
　　by Indians, 289, 458, 460–461, 462–464
　　by slaves, 352–353
Resources. *See also* specific resources
　　CCC and, 666
　　conservation of, 578–579
　　in New England, 96
　　of West, 466 *(m)*
Retirement Equity Act (1984), 848
Reuther, Walter, 758
Revel, James, 66
Revenue Act, of 1764 (Sugar Act), 150
Revere, Paul, 156 *(i)*, 163 *(m)*
Reverse discrimination, 847
Revivals and revivalism
　　common people and, 358
　　Great Awakening as, 132–133
　　in Second Great Awakening, 296
Revolts and rebellions. *See also* Resistance;
　　specific rebellions and protests
　　at Acoma pueblo, 47
　　agrarian, 538, 553
　　Bacon's Rebellion, 70
　　Bear Flag Revolt, 321
　　Boxer uprising as, 556
　　colonial, 106, 162–164
　　by farmers, 538–541
　　Gabriel's Rebellion, 251–252
　　by Germany (1918), 607
　　by Pontiac, 148
　　Shays's Rebellion, 211–212
　　by slaves, 163–164, 352–353
　　Stono rebellion, 127
　　in Texas, 321, 321 *(m)*
　　by Turner, Nat, 352–353, 353 *(i)*
　　Whiskey Rebellion, 234–235
Revolution(s)
　　in Cuba, 559
　　in France, 238–239
　　in Haiti, 240
　　in Mexico (1911), 584
　　Puritan, 95–96
　　in Russia (1917), 604

Revolutionary War (1775–1781), 169
American strategy in, 176
balance of power in, 191 *(i)*
British strategy in, 176–177, 188
British surrender at Yorktown, 191
campaigns of 1777–1779 in, 184–185,
185–186, 185 *(m)*, 188–189
casualties in, 172, 179, 185
Continental army in, 171, 172, 176
financing of, 171, 183
first year of (1775–1776), 172, 172 *(m)*,
177–179
France and, 173, 186–187
home front during, 180–183
Indians in, 180 *(i)*, 181–182, 184 *(i)*,
185–186, 187 *(m)*, 192
loyalists in, 174, 175, 177, 181–182,
182 *(m)*
in North (1775–1778), 178 *(m)*
opening of, 162–163, 163 *(m)*
peace treaty after, 192
reasons for British loss in, 193
reconciliation attempts in, 170, 172
in South, 188–192, 189 *(m)*
in West, 187 *(m)*
women in, 176, 181, 184
Rhee, Syngman, 739
Rhineland
to France, 614
Nazis in, 692
Rhode Island, 94, 199, 205, 280
laws in, 136
slaves in, 117
Rhodesia, human rights in, 840
Rice, 123, 339 *(m)*, 343
Rice, Condoleezza, 874 *(i)*, 875
Richardson, Ebenezer, 157
Richmond, Virginia, 404, 418 *(i)*, 420, 422
Ridgway, Matthew B., 742
Riesman, David, 765
Riflemen, 175 *(i)*
Rights. *See also* specific groups and rights
of African Americans, 434
in Bill of Rights, 228
colonial, 161
for Indians, 210–211, 789
Stamp Act and, 153
Right wing (political). *See also* Conservatives and conservatism
New Right and, 844
Nixon and, 831–832
Riis, Jacob, 515, 516 *(i)*, 518
Rio Grande, 323, 326, 468
Riots. *See also* Race riots
antidraft, 417
for bread, in Confederacy, 413
against Chinese immigrants, 470
against Stamp Act, 152
Rivera, Diego, 2 *(i)*
River Rouge factory (Ford), 653
Rivers and river valley regions. *See also*
specific river regions
steamboat travel and, 279 *(m)*
Road maps, 632 *(i)*
Roads and highways, 230–231,
278–279, 631
interstate highway system and,
749, 749 *(m)*
major roads (1790s), 231 *(m)*
Roanoke colony, 50, 57

Roaring Twenties, 635
Robards, Rachel Donelson. *See* Jackson,
Rachel
Roberts, John, 875
Roberts, Owen, 681
Robertson, Pat, 844
Robinson, Jackie, 734, 769
Robinson, Jo Ann, 769
Robinson, Solon, 338 *(i)*
Rochambeau (Comte de), 191
Rock and roll music, 766
Rockefeller, John D., 482, 482 *(i)*, **485**–487,
515, 555
Rockefeller, John D., Jr., 489
Rockies, 466 *(m)*
Rockingham (Marquess of), 153
Roebling, John, 508 *(i)*
Roe v. Wade (1973), **795,** 848
Rolfe, John, 58, 58 *(i)*, 62
Roman Catholicism. *See* Catholicism
Romania, after World War I, 615
Rommel, Erwin, 704
Romney, George, 180 *(i)*
Roosevelt, Eleanor, 663 *(i)*, **664,** 678, 678 *(i)*
Roosevelt, Franklin Delano, **660**–661,
660 *(i)*, 668 *(i)*. *See also* Great
Depression; New Deal; World War II
Atlantic Charter and, 696
Black Cabinet of, 678
at Casablanca, 706
death of, 714
economic programs of, 664–671
election of 1920 and, 622
election of 1932 and, 661–662, 662 *(m)*
election of 1936 and, 680–681
election of 1940 and, 695–696
election of 1944 and, 710
isolation in 1930s and, 690–691
at Teheran, 713
Roosevelt, Theodore, 559, 575 *(i)*, 593
conservation and, 578–579, 579 *(m)*
election of 1904 and, 577
election of 1912 and, 584–585, 585 *(m)*
foreign policy of, 580–581
labor-management mediation by, 576
Monroe Doctrine and, 580
New Nationalism of, 585
progressivism and, 575–581
as reformer, 577–578
Roosevelt, Franklin D., and, 661
Spanish-American War and, 560
Square Deal of, 575–577
Taft and, 583, 584
as trustbuster, 576
Washington, Booker T., and, 588 *(i)*
Wilson's reforms and, 587
Roosevelt Corollary, to Monroe Doctrine,
580–581, 581 *(m)*
Root, John Wellborn, 529
Root-Takahira agreement (1908), 581
Rosebud, battle of (1876), 460
Rosecrans, William, 420
Rosenberg, Ethel and Julius, 737
Rough Riders, 560, 575
Royal colonies
Massachusetts as, 106
Virginia as, 104
Royal government, of Virginia, 61
Royal Navy. *See* Navy, British
Ruby, Jack, 778

Ruhr Valley region, French occupation
of, 630
Rumsfeld, Donald, 874 *(i)*, 879, 881
Runaway slaves. *See* Fugitive slaves
Rural areas. *See also* Farms and farming
crash of 1929 and, 648–649
electricity and, 487, 666–667, 667 *(m)*
migration from, 510
in 1920s, 641, 643
population in, 474–475, 475 *(f)*, 642 *(m)*
poverty in, 651, 758
school enrollment in, 313
Rural Electrification Administration
(REA, 1935), 667
Rush, Benjamin, 228–229
Rush-Bagot disarmament treaty, 261
Rusk, Dean, 808, 809
Russell, Harold, 722–723
Russell, Richard, 809
Russia. *See also* Soviet Union
immigrants from, 510 *(i)*
North American exploration by, 135
Pan-Slavism and, 600
revolution of 1917 in, 604
World War I and, 600, 604, 606
Russian Republic, 863
Russo-Japanese War (1904–1905), 581
Ruth, George Herman ("Babe"), 638
Rwanda, civil war in, 870

Sacajawea (Shoshoni Indians), 254
Sacco, Nicola, 643
Sacco-Vanzetti trial, 643
"Sack of Lawrence," 381
Sacramento Valley, 321
Sacrifice. *See* Human sacrifice
Sadat, Anwar, 841–842
Saddam Hussein. *See* Hussein, Saddam
Safety, for workers, 583
Sahara Desert, Portuguese exploration
of, 34
Saigon, 807, 822 *(i)*. *See also* Vietnam;
Vietnam War
Sailors. *See also* Navy entries
African American, 408 *(i)*
impressment of, 256
St. Augustine, Florida, 47
St. Clair, Arthur, 237
Saint Domingue, 240
St. Lawrence River region, 50, 121
St. Louis, 269 *(i)*, 510
view of (1835), 269
"Saints," Puritans as, 91
St. Valentine's Day slayings, 636
Salado culture, 20 *(i)*
Salmon, 23
SALT. *See* Strategic Arms Limitation Talks
Salter, John, Jr., 783 *(i)*
Salt Lake City, invasion of, 319, 469
Salvation, 88, 94
Salvation Army, 596 *(i)*, 609
Same-sex marriage, 782
Samoset (Wampanoag Indians), 87
San Carlos Reservation, 462, 463
Sand Creek Massacre (1864), 458
San Diego, 324, 468
San Diego de Alcalá (mission), 135
Sandinistas, in Nicaragua, 841, 851
S&L crisis. *See* Savings and loan crisis
Sandoz, Jules, 464

Sandwich Islands (Hawaii). *See* Hawaii
San Francisco, 327, 465, 510, 514
Sanger, Margaret, 589 *(i)*, ***590,*** 637
Sanitation, in Revolutionary War, 172
San Jacinto, battle at, 321
San Joaquin Valley, 366 *(i)*
San Juan Hill, Roosevelt, Theodore, at, 560
San Miguel de Gualdape, 42
San Salvador, Columbus in, 36
Santa Anna, Antonio López de, 321, 324, 325
Santa Barbara region, Chumash in, 13
Santa Catalina Island, 42
Santa Fe, 47, 320, 324, 405
Santa Fe Trail, 318 *(m)*, 320
Santa Maria (ship), 36
Santee (Dakota) Indians, 458
Santee Uprising (1862), 458
Santo Domingo, 240
Sarajevo, World War I and, 600
Saratoga, battle of (1777), 178 *(m)*, 185, 185 *(m)*
Sargent, Robert, 712 *(i)*
Satak (Sitting Bear) (Kiowa chief), 460
Satellites, space, 756
Satellite states, in Eastern Europe, 818
Saturday Evening Post, 611–612, 636
Saudi Arabia
   Persian Gulf War and, 860
   U.S. soldiers in, 858 *(i)*
Sauk and Fox Indians, 289
Savannah, Georgia, fall of (1864), 419 *(m)*, 420, 421
Savings, spending after World War II, 733
Savings and loan (S&L) crisis, 845
"Scabs" (strikebreakers), 525, 543
Scalawags, 441
Scandals, during Grant administration, 446
Scandinavia, 512
Scarlet fever, 317
Schenck, Charles, 620
Schenck v. United States (1919), 620
Schneiderman, Rose, 572
School(s), 620. *See also* Education; Public schools
   desegregation of, 768–769, 797, 831–832
   enrollment in (19th century-global comparison), 314 *(t)*
   of free black elite, 355
   Indian, 459
   integration of, 830 *(i)*, 831 *(i)*
School prayer, 782, 831
Schreiber, Marie, 733
Schurz, Carl, 498
Schuylkill Canal, 280
Science. *See* Technology
Scientific management, 573–574
Scientific racism, 490
Scopes, John, 644
Scopes trial, 644
Scotland, immigrants from, 119, 513 *(f)*
Scots-Irish immigrants, 119–120
Scott, Dred, 381–382, 382 *(i)*
Scott, Tom, 484
Scott, Winfield, 325, 373, 376 *(m)*
Scottsboro Boys, 653 *(i)*, ***654***
Scottsdale, Arizona, 831
Scriven, Abream, 351
Scurvy, 327
SDS. *See* Students for a Democratic Society

Sea bridge
   European exploration and, 39
   isolation of Western Hemisphere and, 46
SEALS (U.S. Navy), 806
Searches and seizures, 228
Seasonal laborers, in industry and manufacturing, 517–518
Seattle, 619
SEC. *See* Securities and Exchange Commission
Secession, 369, 385
   of New England, 261
   of South, 389–390, 390 *(m)*, 397–398, 398 *(m)*
Second American party system, 284
"Second American Revolution," Civil War as, 423
Second Bank of the United States, 282, 283, 292
Second Continental Congress, 170–172, 173, 182, 198, 198 *(i)*
Second front, in World War II, 704, 713
Second Great Awakening, 295–296, 302
Second New Deal, 674–679
Second World War. *See* World War II
Secretaries, working women as, 520–521, 521 *(i)*
Secret ballot, Populists on, 541
Sectionalism
   antislavery petitions and, 300
   election of 1852 and, 373, 376 *(m)*
   election of 1856 and, 376 *(m)*, 379
   election of 1860 and, 376 *(m)*, 386–389, 388 *(m)*
   New South and, 492–493
   in politics, 369, 375–377, 376 *(m)*
   slavery and, 211
   Supreme Court and, 381
   War of 1812 and, 259
Securities and Exchange Commission (SEC, 1934), 666
Security. *See* Defense; National security entries
Security Council (UN), 739
Sedition Act
   of 1798, 243
   of 1918, 612
Segregation
   of armed forces, 176, 411, 605
   in California, 468, 581
   in cities, 515
   civil rights movement and, 768–770, 768 *(i)*
   Jim Crow and, 514, 591
   legality of, 591
   of Mexican American children, 735–736
   in North, 514
   of public transportation, 442
   residential and school, 831–832
   social, 515
   in South, 442, 767–770
   in World War II, 701–702
Selective Service Act
   of 1917, 604
   of 1940, 700–702
Self-determination, 598, 613, 614–615, 729
"Selling a Freeman to Pay His Fine at Monticello, Florida," 432 *(i)*
Seminole Indians, 269, 289
   free blacks and, 205

Senate (U.S.), 215
   election to, 215, 496–497, 541, 583
   slavery violence in, 381
   Versailles treaty and, 616–617
Seneca Falls, New York, woman's rights convention at, 330–331, 549
Seneca Falls Declaration of Sentiments (1848), 331
Seneca Indians, 22, 181, 185, 208
Senegambia, 126
"Sentiments of an American Woman, The," 181
"Separate but equal" doctrine, 591, 768
Separate spheres doctrine, 293–295, 637
Separation of church and state, 875
   school prayer and, 782
Separatists, 87
September 11, 2001, terrorist attacks, ***876***–878, 877 *(i)*
Serbs and Serbia, 600, 869 *(i)*, 870, 871
Servants, 527–528
   African American women as, 621
   in Chesapeake region, 68, 69, 71
   Chinese immigrants as, 514
   indentured, 60, 64–67
   Irish immigrants as, 314
   in Pennsylvania, 120
   slave labor compared with, 77
   slaves as, 347, 350
   women as, 65, 66, 295, 519
Service economy, 758
Service industries, 846
Servicemen's Readjustment Act (GI Bill, 1944), 710, 733
Service sector, women in, 295
Settlement(s). *See also* Colonies and colonization; specific locations
   African American, 468
   in Appalachian Mountains region, 122, 148
   by Archaic Indians, 4, 10, 12–13
   by Eastern Woodland peoples, 13–14
   English colonies as, 56–71
   Iroquoian, 22
   along James River, 67 *(m)*
   in middle colonies (1700–1770), 121 *(m)*
   midwestern before 1862, 472 *(m)*
   of New England, 86–98
   by Northwest people, 13
   Spanish North American, 47
Settlement houses, 568–569
Settler(s). *See also* Homesteaders
   free state vs. slave state, 380–381
   on Great Plains, 456
   Homestead Act and, 416
   Indians and, 181–182
   Indian wars and, 209, 458
   land policy and, 309
   in Mexican borderlands, 319–321
   recruitment of, 470, 472
   on transcontinental railroad, 471 *(i)*
   westward expansion by, 456–457
Seven Cities of Cíbola, 42
Seven Days Battle (1862), 402 *(i)*, 403 *(m)*, 404, 404 *(m)*
Seventeenth Amendment, 583
Seventh-Day Baptists, 119 *(i)*
Seven Years' War (1754–1763), ***142,*** 192, 193
   consequences of, 135, 142, 143 *(m)*, 144, 146–147
   North America after, 147 *(m)*

Spanish civil war, 692
Spanish Empire, 135, 135 (m). See also
    New Spain
"Speakeasy," 635
Speaker of the House, election of, 259
Special forces corps, 806
Specie payments, 283
Speculation
    in land, 142–144, 309, 472–473,
        473 (m), 538
    in mining, 465
    over national debt, 233
    in Northwest Territory, 209
    panics and, 301, 302
    in stock market, 648
Speech, freedom of, 202, 228
Speedup, 574
Spencer, Herbert, 489
Spending. See Defense spending;
    Finances
Spheres of influence
    in China, 557
    of U.S., 554, 557
    Western Hemisphere and, 557
Spies, August, 525, 526
Spies and spying, 699–700, 756
Spinning mills, 280
Spirituals, 358
Spoilsmen, 497
Spoils system, 286, **491,** 496, 497–498
Sports, 638–639
Spotsylvania Court House, battle of (1864),
    419 (m), 420, 421
Sputnik, 756
Squanto (Wampanoag Indians), 87
Square Deal, 575–577
Squatters, 309, 358, 468
Stagecoach
    companies, 231
    trips by, 279
Stagflation, 837
Stalin, Joseph, 693, 752
    Allies and, 696
    Iran and, 724
    second front and, 704, 713
    at Teheran, 713
    after World War II, 723, 725
    at Yalta, 713
Stalingrad, battle at (1942–1943), 705 (m),
    712
Stalwarts, 497
Stamp Act (1765), **150**
    protests against, 150, 151–152, 152 (i),
        159
Stamp Act Congress (1765), 152–153
Stamping mills, in mining, 467
Standardization, of parts, 310
Standard of living. See Society
Standard Oil Company, 482 (i), 485–487,
    502, 555, 576, 577
Standing Bear, Luther, 460
Standing Rock Reservation, 464
Stantis, Scott, 859 (i)
Stanton, Edwin M., 438
Stanton, Elizabeth Cady, 330–331, 330 (i),
    436, 439, 494, 549
Stanwix, Fort
    battle at (1777), 185
    Treaty of (1784), 207–***208,*** 208 (m),
        209, 236

START treaty. See Strategic Arms
    Reduction Talks treaty
Starvation, on reservations, 458
"Star Wars." See Strategic Defense
    Initiative
State(s)
    Articles of Confederation and,
        198–199, 200
    bank charters from, 282
    Constitution and, 217–219, 218 (m),
        220, 227
    constitutions of, 201–202
    elections in, 266–267
    free, 267, 322, 323, 361
    government reforms in, 574
    immigrant population in, 344 (m)
    innovation by, 859
    in labor wars, 545
    land claims of, 198–199, 200 (m)
    national assumption of debts of, 233
    in Northwest Territory, 208, 209, 210,
        210 (m)
    during reconstruction, 441–442, 447
    representation in federal government
        and, 214–215
    restoration to Union, 429, 433, 437, 442
    sexual orientation as protected civil
        right, 849
    slave, 267–268, 322, 323, 361
    slavery in, 366
    transportation subsidies from, 279
    western boundaries of, 198–200
State Department, 227, 253
State legislatures, 204–205, 215, 216, 243,
    496–497, 583, 620
States' rights, 270, 413
    federal power vs., 290
    Indian removal and, 289
    Johnson, Andrew, on, 432, 433
States' Rights Party. See Dixiecrats
Statue of Liberty, 514–515
Status Seekers, The (Packard), 765
Steamboats, 276 (i), 279–280, 279 (m), 442
Steam power, 308, 467, 475
Steamship companies, immigration and, 512
Stebbins, Emma, 529 (i)
Steel and steel industry, 485 (f)
    Morgan, J. P., in, 489, 578
    in New South, 493
    strikes in, 619, 676
    structural steel and, 529
Steeplechase Park (New York), 528
Steffens, Lincoln, 531, 574
Stein, Gertrude, 639
Steinbacher, Joseph, 714, 715
Stephens, Alexander, 389
Stephens, Harry, and family, 430 (i)
Stephenson, David, 643
Stern, Edith, 763–764
Stevens, Elizabeth Alexander, 201 (i)
Stevens, John, 201 (i)
Stevens, Thaddeus, 437
Stevenson, Adlai E., 741, 748, 751
Stewart, Maria, 297
Stock(s), 465, 468
    bank, 232, 233–234
    Standard Oil and, 486
Stock market
    crash of (1929), 648
    in San Francisco, 465

Stone Mountain, Georgia, Klan at, 643
Stonewall riots, 791–792, 847 (i)
***Stono rebellion,* 127**
Stowe, Harriet Beecher, 264
    Uncle Tom's Cabin by, 356, 372
**Strategic Arms Limitation Talks (SALT),
    818**
Strategic Arms Reduction Talks (START)
    treaty, 863
Strategic Defense Initiative (SDI), 850,
    852, 879
Streetcars, 631
Strict constructionism, by Supreme
    Court, 832
Strikebreakers, 525, 542 (i), 543, 546, 609
Strikes. See also Labor; Labor unions
    during Civil War, 416
    in coal industry, 576, 654
    by Cripple Creek miners, 545
    in Great Depression, 654, 675, 676
    Great Railroad Strike (1877), 522–524,
        522 (i), 523 (m), 545, 546
    Homestead, 542–545
    Knights of Labor and, 524
    at McCormick reaper works, 525
    by Professional Air Traffic Controllers
        Organization (PATCO), 845
    Pullman, 542 (i), 545–547
    against railroads, 522–524, 532
    in textile mills, 281
    at Triangle Shirtwaist Company,
        570–571
    after World War I, 619
    after World War II, 732–733
Stuart, Gilbert, *Dolley Madison* portrait by,
    257 (i)
Student Nonviolent Coordinating
    Committee (SNCC), 784
Students, protests by, 790–791
Students for a Democratic Society (SDS),
    790, 813
Stuyvesant, Peter, 100
Submarines
    in World War I, 602, 603
    in World War II, 699, 704
Subsidies
    for manufacturing, 234
    for transcontinental railroad, 483
    for transport companies, 279
Substitutes, in Civil War draft, 413, 417
Subtreasury plan, 541
Suburbs
    in 1950s, 759
    white flight to, 832
Subversives, McCarthyism and, 737–738
Sudetenland, 693
Suez Canal, 704, 755
    crisis over, 755, 756 (m)
Suffrage. See also Voting and voting rights;
    Woman suffrage
    black, 267, 429, 437
    expansion of southern, 359
    Fifteenth Amendment and, 438–439
    Fourteenth Amendment and, 436
    for men, 202, 203, 266–267, 359, 436, 441,
        493
    for women, 201 (i), 203, 436, 439, 469,
        494, 548, 549, 590
Suffragists, 572, 590, 608 (i), 610
Sugar Act (Revenue) Act (1764), 149–***150***

Sugar and sugar industry, 74–76, 74 (i), 77, 343, 502, 555, 560–561
Sugarman, Tracy, 713
Sullivan, John, 186
Sullivan, Louis, 529
Summit meetings, at Geneva (1955), 756
Sumner, Charles, 322, 368, 369, 381, 436, 437
Sumner, William Graham, 489, 490
Sumter, Fort, attack on, 396 (i), *397*
Sun Also Rises, The (Hemingway), 640
Sun Belt, 759–761, 760 (m)
   conservatism in, 830–831
Sunday schools, 296
Superfund, 840
Superpowers. *See also* Nuclear arms race
   global rivalry of, 728–730
   U.S. as, 717, 869
Supply ships, in Revolutionary War, 176, 193
Supply-side economics, 844–845, 846
Supreme Court (U.S.). *See also* specific cases
   antitrust law and, 502, 576
   Bush, George H. W., and, 859
   Bush, George W., and, 875
   on corporate regulation, 488, 490
   favorable business decisions by, 629
   on free speech restriction, 620
   judicial review by, 252–253
   Nixon and, 832
   progressive on, 587
   protection of corporations by, 488, 490
   on racial segregation, 591
   on railroad regulation, 502
   reconstruction and, 447
   Roosevelt, Franklin D., and, 681
   on slavery in territories, 381–383
   on Spanish and Mexican land grants, 468
   on territorial sovereignty of Cherokee, 289
   on Treaty of Fort Laramie, 461
   under Warren, 782
   women on, 848, 866
   on workday for women, 572
Surplus (financial), 292, 501
"Survival of the fittest," 490
Susan Constant (ship), 57
Sweatshops, 517 (i), 518, 872
Syria, 819, 851
Systematized shop management, 573–574

Taft, Robert A., 741
Taft, William Howard, 582–584, 582 (i), 584–585
Taft-Hartley Act (1947), 736
Taino people, 36–37, 36 (i)
Taiwan, Nationalist Chinese on, 729. *See also* China
Talcott family, 293 (i)
Taliban, 878
Talleyrand (France), 243
Tallmadge, James, Jr., 267
Tallmadge amendments, 267–268
Tammany Hall, 530–531, 531 (i), 644
Tanaghrisson (Mingo Indians), 144
Taney, Roger B., 382
Tanzania, U.S. embassy in, 871
Tarbell, Ida M., 485, 486–487

Tarhe the Crane (Wyandot Indians), 236 (i)
Tariffs, 234, 310, 629. *See also* specific tariffs
   of Abominations (1828), 290
   Clay's American System and, 270
   in 1930s, 648, 649, 691
   reform of, 501–502
   Taft and, 582–583
Taxation. *See also* Duties; specific acts
   under Articles of Confederation, 197, 199, 207, 211
   in black codes, 433
   Bush, George H. W., on, 859, 859 (i)
   Bush, George W., and, 875
   California antitax crusade and, 831
   Carter and, 838
   Civil War and, 401, 416
   Clinton and, 865
   Eisenhower and, 749
   EITC and, 864
   external and internal, 151
   of free blacks, 204
   by Grenville, 149–150
   income, 416, 583, 586
   Jefferson and, 252
   Kennedy, John F., and, 777
   national debt and, 233
   in New Deal, 673
   during reconstruction, 448
   without representation, 193
   resistance to British, 151–152
   Roosevelt, Franklin D., and, 677–678
   on slaves, 360
   in territories, 210
   Townshend duties as, 154–155
   in Virginia, 71
   on wealthy, 647
   for welfare, 781
   of whiskey, 234–235
   of windfall profits, 839
Tax Reform Act (1986), 844–845
Taylor, Frederick Winslow, 573–574
Taylor, Horace, 482 (i)
Taylor, Zachary, 368–369, 369 (m), 370, 376 (m)
   in Mexican-American War, *323,* 324, 325
Tea Act (1773), 159
Teachers and teaching, 264, 265, 295, 313
Teapot Dome scandal, 629
Tea tax, 158
Technocrats, 573
Technology. *See also* Nuclear arms race; specific types
   agricultural, 309, 757–758
   in Columbian exchange, 39
   for farming, 475, 475 (i)
   industrial, 758
   mechanization and, 757–758
   for mining, 467
   navigation and, 33
   printing and, 33
Tecumseh (Shawnee Indians), *258*–259, 260, 261, 289
Teheran
   hostage crisis in, 842
   wartime meeting in, 713
Tejanos, 320, 468, 474
Telegraph, 310, 310 (i), 416, 483
Telephone, 487
Television, 764–765, 777

Temperance movement, 296–297, 491 (i), 495, 528, 570. *See also* Prohibition
Tenant farming, 357, 474, 672 (i), 682–683
Tennent, William, 132
Tennessee, 396, 397, 405, 429, 436
Tennessee Coal and Iron Company, 578, 584
Tennessee River region, in Civil War, 405
Tennessee Valley Authority (TVA), 666, 667 (m)
Tenochtitlán, 2 (i), 25, 41
Tenskwatawa (Prophet, Shawnee Indians), 258, 258 (i), 261
Tenure of Office Act (1867), 436 (i), 438
Territories. *See also* Indian Territory; Northwest Territory
   federal land policy and, 309
   government in, 381
   popular sovereignty in, 367–368
   slavery in, 366–368, 369–370, 370 (m), 373–374, 382
   stages for statehood in, 210
Terrorism
   Afghanistan and, 853, 871
   Iraq and, 879–880
   by Klan, 441, 447
   by nonstate organizations, 850–851
   of September 11, 2001, 876–878, 877 (i)
   southern Democratic party and, 448–449
   in U.S. embassies, 871
Tet Offensive, 815
Teton Sioux Indians, 23
Texas, 314, 339, 369, 370, 456
   annexation of, 322, 323, 468
   border with Mexico, 323, 325–326
   Hispanics in, 468, 735–736
   Lone Star Republic in, 321
   Mexican Americans in, 468, 621, 622
   and Mexico (1830s), 320–321, 320 (m)
   rebellion in, 321
   secession of, 389, 390 (m)
   Spain and, 42
   Tejanos in, 468, 474
   textbooks and morality in, 831
Texas Rangers, 468
Texas War for Independence, 321, 321 (m)
Textbooks, 313, 831
Textiles and textile industry, 281 (m)
   cotton used in, 281
   in Lowell, 280–281
   mechanization in, 280, 518
   mills and, 483
   in South, 493
   women workers in, 280–281, 281 (i), 518
Thailand, 822
Thames, battle of the (1813), 260
Thatcher, Margaret, 843
Thayendanegea. See Brant, Joseph
Third parties, 302, 492. *See also* specific parties
Third Reich, Nazi Germany as, 693
Third world, 511, 511 (m), 729, 806
   anticommunism in, 818–819
Thirteen colonies, 112, 129
Thirteenth Amendment, 433
Thirty-eighth parallel, 740
This Side of Paradise (Fitzgerald), 640
Thomas, Clarence, 859
Thomas, Norman, 654
Thomas Jefferson (Trumbull), 250 (i)

Thompson, George, 298 (i)
Thoreau, Henry David, 329
Three-fifths clause, 215, 261, 268
369th Regiment, in World War I, 605
Three Mile Island, nuclear accident at, 839
Thurber, James, 640
Thurmond, J. Strom, 736, 736 (m)
Thygeson, Sylvie, 520–521
Tiananmen Square demonstrations, 863
Tibbets, Paul, 716
Ticonderoga, Fort, 146
Tientsin treaty (1858), 556
Tilden, Samuel J., 449–450, 450 (m)
Till, Emmett, 769
Tilyou, George, 528
Tippecanoe, battle of (1811), 259, 259 (m)
Title, of president, 227, 245
Title VII, of Civil Rights Act (1964), 785, 790
Title IX, of Education Amendments Act
(1972), 795, 796, 848
Tlaxcala and Tlaxcalan people, 41
Tobacco and tobacco industry
in Chesapeake region, 61, 62–67, 68
in Columbian exchange, 39
exports and, 128
free and unfree labor for, 68–69
indentured servants for, 60, 65–67
in Maryland, 67
slavery and, 127, 339 (m)
in South, 55, 343
Tocqueville, Alexis de, 338
Todd, Albert, 349
Toleration
of homosexuality, 866
religious, 93–94, 100, 101–102, 107
Tools, of Archaic Indians, 9, 11
Toombs, Robert, 368, 386
Tordesillas, Treaty of (1494), 37, 42, 56
Tories, loyalists as, 181, 190
Toronto, Canada, 260
Toussaint L'Ouverture, 240
Town meetings, in New England, 92
Townsend, Francis, 673
Townshend duties, 154–155, 158
Townships, in Northwest Territory, 209,
210 (m)
Trade. See also Slave trade
in Atlantic region, 116 (m), 124 (m)
in British colonies, 133–134, 155
in Chesapeake region, 69
during Civil War, 407
colonial, 103–104
Columbian exchange as, 39
with Cuba, 559
Dutch, 99–100
European, 33 (m)
expansion in (1870–1910), 555 (f)
free trade, 486, 501, 872
fur, 100
joint-stock companies and, 56–57
manifest destiny and, 317
in Mediterranean region, 32–33
NAFTA and, 871–872
in New England, 96, 115–117
in 1930s, 693
in Pacific Northwest, 23
in Pennsylvania, 101
in Virginia colony, 59
in West Indies, 239
in World War I, 601, 602

Trade associations, 629
Trade unions, 525, 526
Trading with the Enemy Act (1917), 612
Trail(s)
Bozeman, 460
California, 318 (m), 322
cattle, 473, 474 (m)
Chisholm, 473, 474 (m)
Oregon, 317, 318 (m), 321
Plains Indians and, 318 (m)
Santa Fe, 318 (m), 320
to West, 318 (m)
Trail of Tears, 288 (m), **289**
Transcendentalists, 328–329
Transcontinental railroads, 317, 416, 469,
470, 470 (i), 482, 483, 484 (m), 514
buffalo slaughter and, 460
slavery debate and, 373
Trans-Mississippi West, 253–254,
254 (m), 470
Transportation. See also specific types
communication and, 303
deregulation of, 838
improvements in, 278–280
productivity in, 308
routes of, in 1840, 279 (m)
segregation of, 442, 447
Travel
costs of, 279
in 1790s, 231
times from New York City (1800),
231 (m)
Treason
of Arnold, Benedict, 190
of Declaration signers, 174
by loyalists, 182
Treasury Department, 227, 253, 504, 635
Treaties. See specific treaties and wars
Treaty goods, 238
Tredegar Iron Works, 413
Trench warfare, in World War I, 604 (i), 605
Trial by jury, 202
Trials, witchcraft, 98, 98 (i)
Triangle Shirtwaist Company, 570, 571,
571 (i)
Tribute, to Mexica, 25, 26
Trickle-down economics, 649
Tripartite Pact, 696
Triple Alliance, 600
Triple Entente, 600
Tripoli, 255, 256
Troubled Assets Relief Program, 881
Troy Female Seminary, New York, 264
Trucking, highway construction and, 749
Truman, Harry S., 723
assumption of presidency, 714
atomic bomb and, 716
civil rights and, 736, 737–738
Cold War and, 721
election of 1944 and, 710
election of 1948 and, 731, 731 (i), 736,
736 (m)
Fair Deal of, 731, 736–737
foreign policy of, 725–730, 743
Israel and, 729–730
Korean War and, 737, 739–740
loyalty program of, 738
MacArthur and, 740–741
Vietnam and, 753
Truman Doctrine, 725–726

Trumbull, John, 230 (i), 242 (i), 250 (i)
Trumbull, Lyman, 434
Trumpauer, Joan, 783 (i)
Trust(s), 485–486, 502, 576, 587
"Trustbuster," Roosevelt, Theodore, as, 576
Truth, Sojourner, 331
Tubman, Harriet, 332
Tunis, 255
Turkey, 615, 725
Cuban missile crisis and, 807
Turner, Frederick Jackson, 477
Turner, Nat, 352–353, 353 (i)
Turner, West, 351
Turnpikes, 231, 279
Tuscarora Indians, 181
Tuskegee Institute, 591
TVA. See Tennessee Valley Authority
Twain, Mark (Samuel Langhorne Clemens)
on baseball, 528
on Comstock Lode, 466
on Gilded Age, 477, 481, 505
Tweed, William Marcy ("Boss"), 530–531
Twelfth Amendment, 242, 251, 271
Twelve Years a Slave (Northup), 373
"Twenty-Negro law," 413
Twenty Years at Hull-House (Addams),
568 (i)
Two Moons (Cheyenne chief), 461
Tyler, John, 322, 323
Typewriter (machine), 520, 521 (i)
"Typewriters" (secretarial workers), 520

U-boats
in World War I, **602**
in World War II, 696
Ukraine, execution of Jews in, 710 (i)
UN. See United Nations
**Uncle Tom's Cabin, or Life among the
Lowly** (Stowe), 356, **372,** 391
Underground railroad, 332, 372
Underwood tariff (1913), 586
Unemployed, The—Scene at Country
Railway Station, 536 (i)
Unemployment
Carter and, 837–838
in 1870s depression, 447, 518
in 1890s depression, 504, 518, 532,
545, 549
in Great Depression, 649, 650, 650 (i),
668–669, 678
in 1920, 629
in 1970s, 797
in panic of 1819, 283
under Reagan, 845
relief programs in 1930s and, 675
after World War I, 618
in World War II, 709
Unfree servants, 68. See also Indentured
servants; Slaves and slavery
Unilateralism, in Bush, George W., foreign
policy, 879–881
Union (U.S.). See also North (Civil War)
collapse of, 389–390
nullification and, 290
preservation of, 391, 409
Unionists, in South, 389, 396, 397, 414, 432
Union ordnance (Yorktown, Virginia), 399 (i)
Union Party, 673
Unions. See Labor unions
Union Signal, 548

United Auto Workers (UAW), 676
United Farm Workers (UFW), 788, 789–790
United Fruit Company, 557, 754
United Mine Workers (UMW), 576, 675
United Nations (UN), 713
    Charter of, 713
    China and, 729
    International Criminal Court of, 879
    nuclear test ban treaty and, 863
    Security Council and, 739
    Suez Canal and, 755
United States. *See also* Constitution (U.S.);
    Government (U.S.)
    internationalization of, 873–878
U.S. Communist Party. *See* Communist
    Party
U.S. Post Office, 230–231. *See also* Mail
    service
    birth control publication confiscated
      by, 590
    political information via, 279
U.S. Sanitary Commission, 415 *(i)*, 416
U.S. Steel, 489, 578, 584
United States v. Cruikshank (1876), 447
United States v. E. C. Knight Company
    (1895), 502
Universal education, 313
Universal male suffrage, 266, 441, 493
Universal Negro Improvement Association
    (UNIA), 637
Universal woman suffrage act (1870), 469
Universities and colleges. *See also* Higher
    education; specific schools
    in World War I, 611
University of California (Berkeley), free
    speech movement at, 790
University of Wisconsin, 574
University Settlement House, 568
Unskilled workers, 514, 518, 526, 589
Upcountry, of South, 357 *(m)*
Upcountry yeomen, 357
Upper class, in southern politics, 360
Upper South, 123, 339, 339 *(m)*. *See also*
    South
    emancipation in, 354
    secession and, 389–390, 396, 397–398,
      398 *(m)*
Uprisings. *See* Revolts and rebellions
Urban areas. *See also* Cities and towns
    electricity in, 487
    Hull House and, 568–569
    population in (1870–1900), 474–475,
      475 *(f)*
    population in (1920–1930), 642 *(m)*
Urbanization. *See also* Cities and towns
    of Indians, 750–751
    in late nineteenth century, 510–516
    produce markets and, 475
    South and, 344
Urban League, 618 *(i)*
Urban renewal programs, 777
USA Patriot Act (2001), **878**
USX. *See* U.S. Steel
Utah, 16, 319, 323, 370, 469
Utopians, 328–329
U-2 incident, 756

Vagrancy, black codes and, 433
Valentino, Rudolph, 640 *(i)*
Valley Forge, Continental army at, 185

Values, "traditional," 830
Van Bergen, Marten and Catarina, farm of,
    121 *(i)*
Van Buren, Martin, 286, 291 *(i)*, 299
    election of 1836 and, 300
    election of 1840 and, 301
    election of 1848 and, 368, 369 *(m)*, 376 *(m)*
    panic of 1837 and, 301
Vandenberg, Arthur, 725
Vanderbilt family
    Alice, 516, 516 *(i)*
    Alva, 516
    William, 516
Vanderlyn, John, 184 *(i)*
Vanzetti, Bartolomeo, 643
Vaqueros, 474
Vaux, Calvert, 529 *(i)*
Venereal disease, 569
Venezuela, 557
Venice, 32
Veracruz, in Mexican-American War, 325
Verdict, 482 *(i)*
Vermont, 199, 266
Verrazano, Giovanni da, 50
Versailles, Paris Peace Conference at, 614
Versailles treaty (1919), ***616*–**617, 691, 692
Vertical integration, trust compared with,
    485–486
Vesey, Denmark, 353, 355
Vespucci, Amerigo, 38
Veterans
    bonus for, 654
    in Great Depression, 654
    higher education for, 761
    of Mexican-American War, 367
    of Vietnam War, 820–821, 823
    after World War II, 710, 733
Veterans Administration (VA), 759
Veto, 216
    by Cleveland, 515
    by Jackson, 286, 291
    by Johnson, Andrew, 434, 438
Vice admiralty courts, 150
Vice president, 215, 242
Vichy France, 695
Vicksburg, Mississippi (1863), siege of,
    418–419, 418 *(m)*, 420
Victory Gardens, 708
Vienna summit (1961), 806
Vietcong, 807, 811
Vietminh, 753
Vietnam
    CIA and, 771
    containment policy toward, 753–754
Vietnamization policy, in Vietnam War, 815
Vietnam Veterans Memorial (1982), 823
Vietnam War (1964-1975), 802 *(i)*, 808 *(m)*.
    See also Vietnam
    age of soldiers in, 803
    antiwar movement and, 813–816
    Johnson, Lyndon B., and, 780, 809–810,
      811–812
    Kennedy, John F., and, 807–808
    legacy of, 822–823
    Nixon and, 819–821
    peace talks in, 821–822
    pro-war demonstrators in, 814 *(i)*
    veterans of, 820–821, 823
Vigilance committees, to help runaway
    slaves, 372

Villa, Francisco ("Pancho"), 600
Villages
    Archaic Indians and, 10
    of Chumash peoples, 13
    in Pacific Northwest, 13
Vincennes, Fort, battle at, 186
Violence. *See* Race riots; Wars and warfare;
    specific conflicts
Virginia, 57–61, 177, 189 *(m)*, 198, 396. *See
    also* Chesapeake region; Tobacco
    Bacon's Rebellion in, 70
    bill of rights in, 202
    as Chesapeake colony, 57–61
    Civil War in, 400, 419 *(m)*
    as "Lincoln state," 429
    map of early, 56 *(i)*
    ratification of Constitution and, 220
    Readjusters in, 493
    Revolutionary War in, 190–191
    as royal colony, 104
    secession of, 397
    settlement of western, 122
    Turner rebellion in, 352–353
Virginia (ironclad), 406
Virginia and Kentucky Resolutions (1798),
    244, 290
Virginia City, 465, 466, 467–468
Virginia colony
    indentured servants in, 60
    Indian massacre of settlers in, 60
    Native Americans in, 58–60
Virginia Company, 56–58, 61, 87
Virginia Plan, 214
Virginia Resolves (1765), 151, 214
Virtual representation, 150
Virtue, 228, 229
Voice of America, 728
Volunteers
    in Mexican-American War, 323, 325 *(i)*
    for World War I, 604 *(i)*
Volunteers in Service to America (VISTA),
    779
Voter Education Project (1961), 784
Voting and voting rights. *See also* Elec-
    tions; Woman suffrage
    for African Americans, 426 *(i)*, 438–439,
      493, 785–786, 786 *(m)*
    age for voting, 267
    black codes and, 433
    in Chesapeake colonies, 69
    in Constitution, 216, 228
    disfranchisement of blacks and, 203,
      439, 591
    in election of 1828, 284
    in election of 1860, 388–389, 388 *(m)*
    Fifteenth Amendment and, 438–439
    Fourteenth Amendment and, 436
    in Massachusetts, 92, 106
    in New South, 493
    Nineteenth Amendment and, 549, 611
    property ownership for, 201 *(i)*, 202,
      266–267, 284, 359, 439, 441
    during reconstruction, 447
    in South, 128, 359, 447, 591
    Supreme Court on, 782
    voter turnout and, 284, 301, 302, 491,
      492 *(f)*, 553
    for women, 201 *(i)*, 203, 263, 267, 436,
      439, 469, 548, 549, 590, 608, 610–611,
      610 *(m)*, 636–637

Voting Rights Act (1965), 780, 785, 798, 847
Voyages. *See also* Exploration
  to Americas, 38
  of Columbus, 35–38
  of Magellan, 38–39

Wabash v. Illinois (1886), 502
Waco, Texas, cult in, 866
Wade, Benjamin, 429
Wade-Davis bill (1864), 429
Wage labor, 429, 512. *See also* Labor
Wages. *See also* Minimum wage
  of African American women, 759
  at Ford plant, 634
  mechanization and, 310
  for men vs. women, 518
  in 1920s, 632, 647
  for organized labor, 846
  for women, 281, 282, 416, 569
  in World War I, 609
Wagner, Fort, battle of (1863), 410–411
Wagner, Robert, 675, 684
Wagner Act (NLRA, 1935), *675*–676
Wagon trains, 317, 318 *(m)*
Waite, Davis H., 545
Wake Island, 703
Wald, Lillian, 569
Waldseemüller, Martin, 38
Wales, immigrants from, 513 *(f)*
Walker, David, 297
Walker, Quok, 204
Walking city, 515
Wallace, George C., 816
Wallace, Henry A., 725, 736, 736 *(m)*
Wall Street. *See* Bank(s) and banking; Business; Great Depression; Stock market
Wampanoag Indians, 87, 204 *(i)*
  King Philip's War and, 103, 105, 105 *(i)*
Wanamaker's, 521
War bonds
  in Civil War, 401
  in World War II, 708
Ward, Lester Frank, 573
War debts. *See also* Debts
  Revolutionary, 192, 206
  Roosevelt, Franklin D., and, 690
"War" Democrats, 421
War Department, 227, 410
War guilt, German, 614
War Hawks, War of 1812 and, 259, 261
War Industries Board (WIB), 608, 612
Warm Springs, Georgia, 661
War of 1812, 258, *259*–261, 260 *(m)*, 273, 289
War of attrition (Civil War), in Virginia, 420–421
War on Poverty, 779–780
War Powers Act (1973), 822
War Production Board, 702
Warren, Earl, 768, 778, 782, 832
Warren, Mercy Otis, 219
Wars and warfare. *See also* specific battles and wars
  Indian, 317
  by Mexica, 26
  trench, 604 *(i)*, 605
Wartime reconstruction, 428–429
Washington, Booker T., 588 *(i)*, *591*
Washington, DC
  abolition of slavery and, 369, 370, 409
  burning of, 260

Coxey's army in, 550–551
  integration of public facilities in, 769
  location of, 233
  suffragist march in, 590
Washington, Fort, 237
  attack on, 177 *(i)*, 179
Washington, George, 171, 257
  cabinet of, 227
  death of, 226 *(i)*
  election of 1789 and, 226
  farewell address of, 241
  as Federalist, 241
  Hamilton and, 234
  Neutrality Proclamation and, 239
  Ohio River region and, 144, 237
  as president, 225 *(i)*, 227, 239, 245
  in Revolutionary War, 171, 172, 175 *(i)*, 179, 185, 186, 191
  Whiskey Rebellion and, 235
Washington, Martha, 252, 257
Washington Disarmament Conference (1921–1922), 630
Washington Post, on U.S. empire, 562
Wastes, cleanup of, 840
Water, travel by, 279–280, 279 *(m)*
Watergate scandal, *834*–835
Water pollution
  Carter and, 840
  control of, 792
  Reagan and, 845
Waterpower, shift to steam power from, 308
Watson, Tom, 539, 551–552
Watt, James, 845
"Waving the bloody shirt," 445
Wayne, Anthony, 236 *(i)*, 237–238
We (Lindbergh), 639
Wealth
  distribution of, 647–648, 665
  in 1860, 313
  in Gilded Age, 516, 516 *(i)*
  gospel of, 490
  of Mexica, 26
  in New England, 115–116
  Reagan and, 845
  from slave labor, 128
  social Darwinism on, 490
  in South, 360
  urban artisans and, 132 *(i)*
Wealth gap, 505, 516 *(i)*
Weapons. *See also* Atomic bomb; Nuclear arms race; Nuclear weapons
  of Archaic hunters, 11
  biological, 879
  bows and arrows as, 12
  of Indian hunters, 23
  in Vietnam War, 808
  in World War I, 602
  in World War II, 701 *(f)*, 703 *(i)*
Webster, Daniel, 282, 291, 291 *(i)*, 300, 369–370
Wedding tapestry, 110 *(i)*
Wehrmacht (German army), 696, 712
Welch, Jack, 872
Weld, Ezra Greenleaf, 328 *(i)*
Welfare capitalism, 632
Welfare programs
  AFDC and, 781
  Clinton and, 866–867
  GI Bill and, 733
  Johnson, Lyndon B., and, 778–781

Kennedy, John F., and, 777
  New Deal and, 666, 674, 678
  Nixon and, 796–798
  Reagan and, 845
Wells, Ida B., 494, 494 *(i)*, 505
Wellstone, Paul, 876
"We Owe Allegiance to No Crown" (Woodside), 248 *(i)*
Werowance (subordinate chief), 58
West, 477, 642 *(m)*. *See also* Pacific Ocean region; Sun Belt; Westward movement
  cession of lands in (1782-1802), 200 *(m)*
  Civil War in, 397–398, 404–406
  conservation in, 578–579, 579 *(m)*
  conservatism in, 831
  cowboys in, 473, 474
  diversity in, 465, 468–470
  drought in, 473
  expansion of, 455, 456
  farming in, 473, 474–476
  free labor in, 312–313
  gold discoveries in, 366, 391, 465
  homesteaders in, 471–473
  Indian land cessions and expansion to, 237 *(m)*
  Indian lands in (1850-1890), 457 *(m)*
  Indians in, 236–238, 258–259, 317–318, 456–464
  Indian wars in, 237–238, 318, 458
  land in, 198–199, 208, 292, 292 *(f)*
  manifest destiny and, 316–317, 456
  mining in, 465–468, 466 *(m)*
  Mormons in, 319
  national parks in, 579 *(m)*
  pioneers in, 317–319
  progressivism in, 574, 591
  railroads in, 471, 471 *(i)*, 472, 473 *(m)*
  ranching in, 473–474
  Revolutionary War in, 187 *(m)*
  trails to, 318 *(m)*
  trans-Mississippi, 253, 470, 484 *(m)*
  woman suffrage in, 469, 548, 610, 610 *(m)*
West Africa, 297, 332
  kinship structure in, 127
West Bank, 842, 851
West Berlin, 727, 806
West Coast. *See also* Pacific Ocean region
  Native Americans of, 21
Western Federation of Miners (WFM), 545, 589
Western Hemisphere. *See also* Latin America; specific locations
  human migrations into, 6–8, 8 *(f)*
  immigration and, 643
  indigenous people of, 25–26
  Monroe Doctrine and, 557, 599
  Roosevelt, Theodore, and, 580
  U.S. influence in, 557
Western Union, 483
West Germany, 725, 727
West India Company (Dutch), 99
West Indies
  Carolina and, 76–77
  French, 239
  sugar and slavery from, 74–76
Westinghouse, George W., 487
Westmoreland, William, 811–812
West Point, 190
West Virginia, 398

Westward movement
agriculture and, 309
in late 19th century, 455
manifest destiny and, 316–317, 456
mining and, 465–468
Native Americans and, 456–464
Northwest Ordinance and, 210
"Wetbacks," 760
Weyler, Valeriano, 559
"What a Funny Little Government"
(Taylor), 482 *(i)*
What Social Classes Owe to Each Other
(Sumner), 490
Wheat, 122, 230, 309
Wheatley, Phillis, 162 *(i)*, **164**
Wheelock, Eleazar, 180 *(i)*
Whigs (Whig Party), **286**, 299, 302
collapse of, 375–377
election of 1840 and, 301
election of 1848 and, 368–369, 369 *(m)*,
376 *(m)*
election of 1852 and, 375, 376 *(m)*
Mexican-American War and, 323
National Republicans as, 285, 291
panic of 1837 and, 301
Whiskey, taxation on, 252
Whiskey Rebellion (1794), 234–**235**
White, Hugh Lawson, 300
White, John, 48 *(i)*
White, William Allen, 559
White City (World's Columbian Exposition),
532
White-collar workers, 519–521, 610, 633,
637
White Eyes (Delaware Indians), 186
Whitefield, George, **133**
White flight, to suburbs, 832
White House, 258, 260
Office of Faith-Based and Community
Initiatives, 875
White male suffrage, 359
Whites
in Chesapeake region, 77–78
in New England, 117
new immigrants and, 514
in northern and southern colonies, 338
Plains Indians and, 318, 457–458
racism of, 121
in South, 341 *(f)*, 342, 357–358, 359–360
in southern Democratic Party, 448–449
in southern Republican Party, 441
White supremacists, 866
White supremacy
free blacks and, 332
Johnson, Andrew, and, 433
Ku Klux Klan and, 441
North and, 341
reconstruction and, 441, 448–449
in South, 341, 448–449, 493
"White terror," 441
Whitewater scandal, 867
Whitney, Eli, 230, 343
Whyte, William H., Jr., 765
Wichita Indians, 317
Wilderness, battle of the (1864), 419 *(m)*,
420, 421
Wild West show, 477
Wilhelm II (Germany), 600, 607
Wilkinson, Eliza, 181
Wilkinson, Jemima, 263

Willard, Emma Hart, 262 *(i)*, 264
Willard, Frances, 495, **548**–549, 548 *(i)*, 563
William III (of Orange, English king), 106
Williams, Roger, 93–**94**
Williamsburg, capture of, 190
Willkie, Wendell, 695
Wilmot, David, 367, 391
Wilmot Proviso (1846), **367,** 369, 379
Wilson, Woodrow, 623
election of 1912 and, 585, 586 *(i)*
election of 1916 and, 587, 602, 612
election of 1920 and, 622
foreign policy of, 598–600
Fourteen Points of, 613
at Paris Peace Conference, 613 *(i)*, 614–616
progressivism and, 586–587
segregation and, 591
Versailles treaty and, 616–617
woman suffrage and, 590, 610, 611
World War I and, 601–602, 603, 611
Windfall profits tax, 839
Winnemucca, Sarah, 458
Winthrop, John, **88**–89, 93, 95
Wiretapping, 878
Wisconsin, 309, 369, 574
sexual orientation as protected civil right
in, 849
Wisconsin glaciation, 7
Witchcraft, New Salem trials and, 98, 98 *(i)*
Wives. *See also* Married women
feme covert and, 262
of loyalists, 182
republican, 228–229
separate spheres and, 294
Wobblies. *See* Industrial Workers of the
World
Wolfensohn, James D., 872
Woman Rebel (newspaper), 590
Woman's Christian Temperance Union
(WCTU), 491 *(i)*, **495,** 548–549
Woman's Crusade, 495
"Woman's Holy War" (political cartoon),
491 *(i)*
Woman's rights movement, 379
Woman suffrage, 201 *(i)*, 331, 379, 590, 593,
610 *(m)*, 623
Fifteenth Amendment and, 438, 439
Fourteenth Amendment and, 436
movement for, 494, 528, 549
Nineteenth Amendment and, 549, 611
reform movement and, 572
in West, 469, 548, 610
Willard and, 548, 549
World War I and, 608 *(i)*, 610–611
Women. *See also* Feminists and feminism;
Gender and gender issues
in abolition movement, 298
academies for, 264–265
activism by, 329–331, 494–495
Adams, Abigail, and, 173
birth control for, 589 *(i)*, 590
in cabinet, 749, 848, 875
in Chesapeake region, 65
church governance and, 263–264
in Civil War, 412 *(i)*, 413, 416–417
in Clinton administration, 865–866, 865 *(i)*
colonial protests by, 140 *(i)*
cult of domesticity and, 527
as domestic servants, 527–528
education for, 228–229, 264–265, 761

exclusion from voting, 202–203
families headed by, 846
Farmers' Alliance and, 539
Fourteenth Amendment and, 436
French Revolution and, 238, 239 *(i)*
on frontier, 472
in garment industry, 570
in Great Awakening, 133
in Great Depression, 652
as immigrants, 513
Indian, 60, 254
Irish immigrant, 467
in Iroquoian society, 22
in Ku Klux Klan, 641 *(i)*, 643
labor unions and, 281, 524, 570–572
law and, 262–263
in mining towns, 467–468
as missionaries, 556 *(i)*
moral reform by, 297
in New England, 89
new woman and, 636–637
in nursing, 416–417, 609
as office workers, 519, 520–521, 521 *(i)*
patriotism of, 181
on plantations, 346–347
politics and, 257–258, 270, 288–289,
494–495, 548–549
polygamy and, 319, 469
poverty among, 780–781
property and, 203, 347
in public affairs, 155
Puritan, 92
as Quakers, 97
reconstruction and, 436, 439, 440 *(i)*, 441,
443
reform and, 295, 296, 297, 298
in Republican Party, 379
as republican wife and mother, 228–229
Revolution and, 176, 181, 184
rights for, 347
Second Great Awakening and, 295, 296
separate spheres doctrine and, 293–295
as servants, 65, 66
in settlement house movement, 569
sexuality and, 766
in slavery, 347, 350
Social Security and, 677
southern, 347–348, 360
in Spanish colonies, 45
strikes by, 281
on Supreme Court, 848, 866
in sweatshops, 517 *(i)*, 518
in teaching, 295, 313
in temperance movement, 491 *(i)*, 495,
548–549
in textile industry, 280–281, 493, 518
university protests by, 790
Vietnam War and, 812
voting by, 203, 263, 436, 469, 548, 549,
590, 609–611, 610 *(m)*
in westward movement, 318–319
witchcraft accusations against, 98, 98 *(i)*
in workforce, 280–282, 517 *(i)*, 519,
520 *(f)*, 610, 652, 708, 732 *(f)*, 733,
758, 763, 846
working class, 528
in World War I, 609–611
in World War II, 700, 707, 708
yeomen, 358
Women of the Ku Klux Klan (WKKK), 641 *(i)*

Women's Army Corps, 749
Women's clubs, 494–495, 528
Women's International League for Peace and Freedom (WILPF), 611
Women's liberation, 795–796
Women's Liberty Bell, 608 (i)
Women's Peace Party, 611
Women's Political Council (WPC), 769
Women's rights, 263–263. *See also* Feminists and feminism; Women
    abolition movement and, 298
    activists for, 329–331, 494–495
    conventions for, 331
Women's Trade Union League (WTUL), *570*–572
Woodland Indians, 17–19, 21, 23, 458. *See also* Eastern Woodland Indians
Woodley, Arthur E., Jr., 812
Woods, Rose Mary, 833 (i)
Woodside, John A., 248 (i)
Woodstock Music Festival, 791
Woodville, Richard Caton, cartoon by, 306 (i)
Woolworth's, lunch counter sit-ins at, 783, 783 (i)
Worcester v. Georgia (1832), 289, 290
Workday
    in coal mines, 576
    eight-hour, 495, 525, 526, 541, 583, 609, 618
    for slaves, 346, 351
    ten-hour for women, 572
Workers. *See also* Child labor; Factories; Labor; Labor unions; Strikes
    African American, 678–679, 709
    agricultural, 678, 680 (i)
    at Carnegie Steel, 485
    children as, 518–519
    Chinese, 469 (i)
    diversity of, 517–518
    in Farmers' Alliance, 539
    in Great Depression, 675–676
    industrial, 542
    migrant, 474, 476
    in mining, 467
    in New Deal, 669
    in 1920s, 647
    in 1950s, 758
    in Progressive Era, 593
    in Pullman, 545–547
    in railroad industry, 483
    Social Security and, 677–678
    in sweatshop, 517 (i)
    systematized shop management and, 573–574
    in textile industry, 280–281
    wages for, 846
    white-collar, 519–521
    Wilson and, 587
    women as, 280–282, 440 (i), 517 (i), 519, 520–521, 520 (f), 637, 708
    World War I and, 609, 618–619

Workers' compensation, 587
Workforce. *See also* Labor; Workers
    factory workers in, 308
    women in, 280–282, 416, 467, 519, 520–521, 520 (f), 610, 637, 652, 708, 732 (f), 733, 758, 763, 846
Working class
    families in, 518–519
    during Great Depression, 653–654
    labor unions and, 524
    leisure of, 528
    progressives and, 570–572
Workingmen's Party, 470
"Work Pays America!" (WPA poster), 658 (i)
Workplace
    at Carnegie Steel, 485
    sexual harassment in, 848–849
Works Progress Administration (WPA), 658 (i), *675*
World Bank, 872
World court, Taft and, 584
World Jewish Congress, 711
World power, U.S. as, 557
World's Columbian Exposition (Chicago, 1893), 477, *532*
World Trade Center, September 11, 2001, destruction of, 876, 877 (i)
World Trade Organization (WTO), 872, 872 (i)
World Turn'd Upside Down, The (pamphlet), 92 (i)
World War I (1914–1918), 596 (i), 597–612. *See also* Allies; specific countries and battles
    African Americans and, 605, 620–621
    alliances in, 600, 601 (m)
    anti-German attitudes in, 597, 611–612, 623
    casualties in, 602, 605, 607, 607 (f)
    domestic cost of, 623
    economy after, 618–619
    in France, 605–606, 606 (m)
    home front during, 608–612
    legacy of, 690
    opening of, 600
    patriotism during, 608, 611
    peace after, 613–617
    Red Scare after, 619–620
    Russian withdrawal from, 604, 606
    Salvation Army in, 596 (i), 609
    submarine warfare in, 602, 603
    U.S. and, 601–602, 603, 604–605
World War II (1939–1945). *See also* Allies; Casualties; specific countries and battles
    eastern front in, 693 (i)
    in Europe, 703 (i), 704–705, 705 (m)
    events leading to, 693–698
    home front in, 707–711
    Japanese American relocation during, 700, 700 (m)

mobilization for, 700–702
opening of, 693–695, 694 (m)
in Pacific, 703–704, 703 (i)
Pearl Harbor attack in, 697–698, 698 (m)
politics during, 710–711
second front in, 704, 713
security in, 699–700
U.S. military production during, 689
Worth, William, 325 (i)
Wounded Knee, South Dakota, massacre at (1890), 457 (m), **464**
Wovoka (Paiute shaman), 463
WPA. *See* Works Progress Administration
Wright, Frank Lloyd, 759
Writing
    archaeology, history, and, 5
    North American peoples and, 23
Wyandot Indians, 236 (i)
Wyoming, 323, 469, 548

Ximenes, Vicente T., 790
XYZ Affair, 242–*243*

Yalta Conference, 713
Yamamoto, Isoroku (Japan), 703
Yamasee Indians, 134
Yamasee War (1715), 134
Yellow journalism, 559
Yellowstone National Park, 579 (m)
Yellow Wolf (Nez Percé), 462
Yeltsin, Boris, 863
Yeomen, 68, 356
    during Civil War, 413
    plantation belt, 356–357
    politics and, 360
    southern, 356 (i)
    southern Republican Party and, 441, 448
    taxation and, 448
    upcountry, 357
YMCA, 605, 609
Yom Kippur War (1973), 797, 819
York, Duke of. *See* James I
Yorktown, battle of (1781), 188 (i), 189 (m), 190 (m), **191**
Young, Brigham, 319, 469
Young people
    education and training of, 295
    in Great Depression, 652
    student protests and, 790–791
    in working class, 528
Yugoslavia, 615
    breakup of, 870–871, 870 (m)
Yuppies, 846

Zemis (Taino spirits), 36, 36 (i)
Zimmermann, Arthur, 603
Zimmermann telegram, 603
Zones of occupation
    in Germany, 724 (m), 725
    in Korea, 739–740
Zoot suit riots, 709
Zuñi Indians, 17, 42

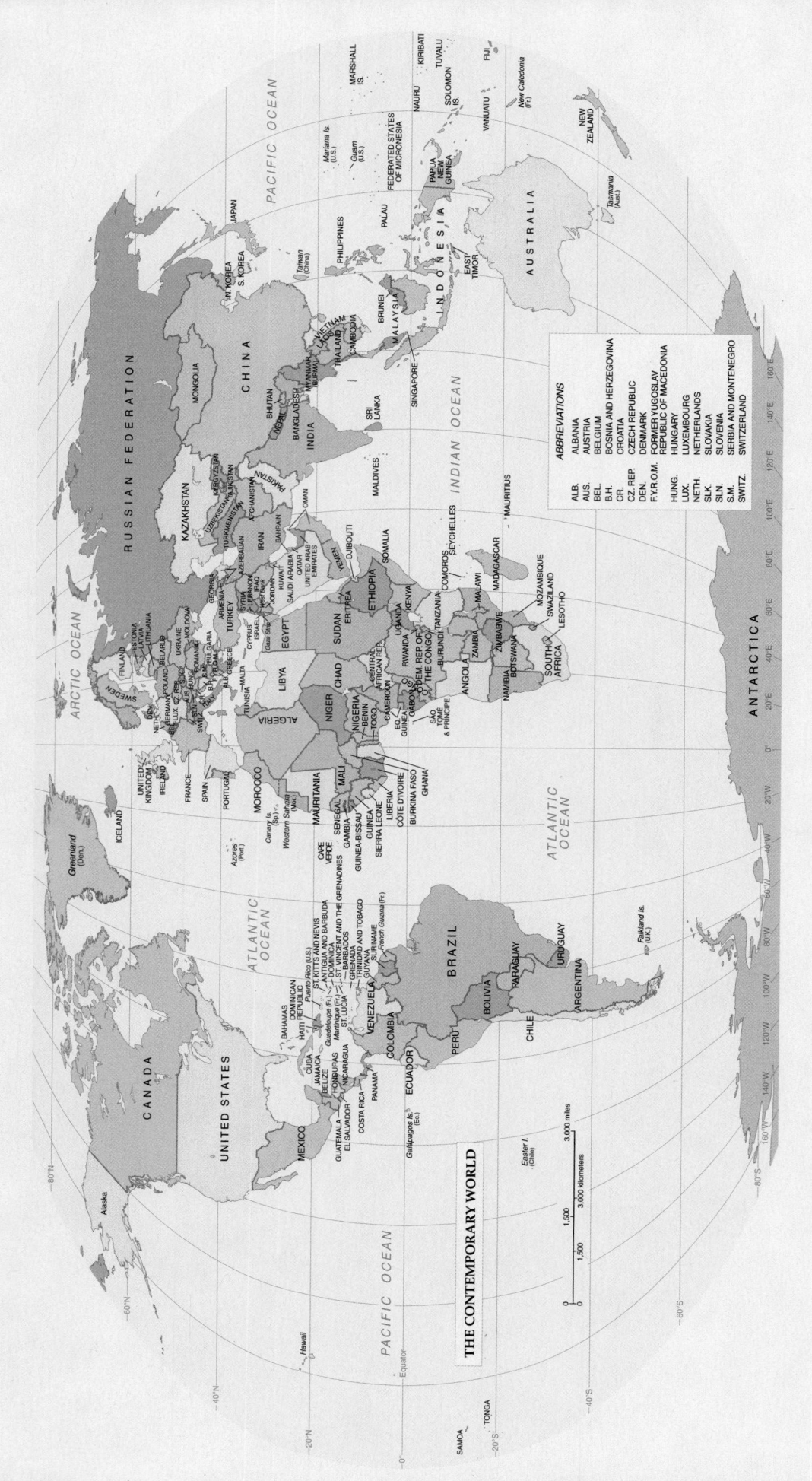

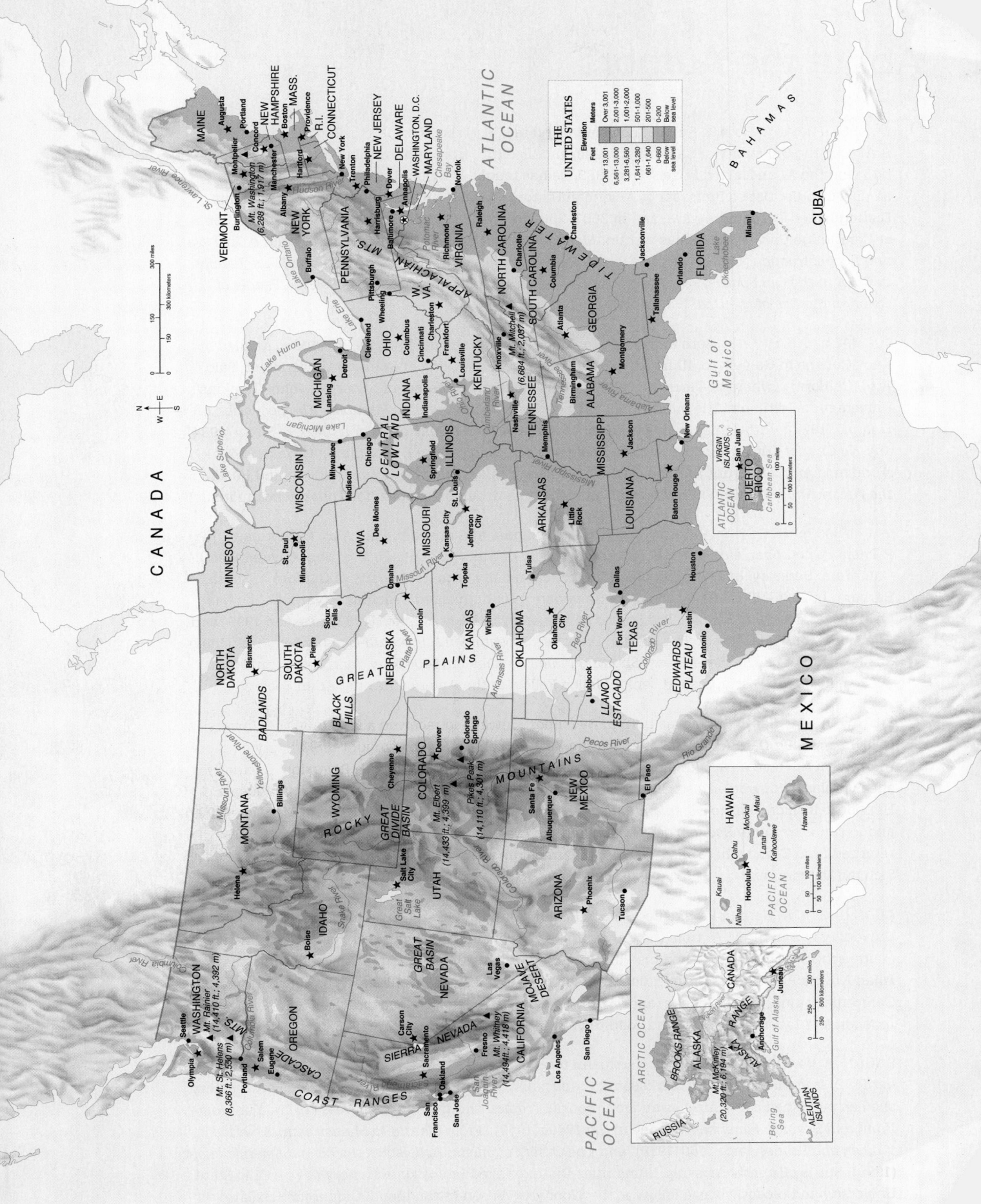

About the Authors

JAMES L. ROARK Born in Eunice, Louisiana, and raised in the West, James L. Roark received his B.A. from the University of California, Davis, and his Ph.D. from Stanford University. His dissertation won the Allan Nevins Prize. Since 1983, he has taught at Emory University, where he is Samuel Candler Dobbs Professor of American History. In 1993, he received the Emory Williams Distinguished Teaching Award, and in 2001–2002 he was Pitt Professor of American Institutions at Cambridge University. He has written *Masters without Slaves: Southern Planters in the Civil War and Reconstruction* (1977). With Michael P. Johnson, he is author of *Black Masters: A Free Family of Color in the Old South* (1984) and editor of *No Chariot Let Down: Charleston's Free People of Color on the Eve of the Civil War* (1984).

MICHAEL P. JOHNSON Born and raised in Ponca City, Oklahoma, Michael P. Johnson studied at Knox College in Galesburg, Illinois, where he received a B.A., and at Stanford University in Palo Alto, California, where he earned his Ph.D. He is currently professor of history at Johns Hopkins University in Baltimore. His publications include *Toward a Patriarchal Republic: The Secession of Georgia* (1977); with James L. Roark, *Black Masters: A Free Family of Color in the Old South* (1984) and *No Chariot Let Down: Charleston's Free People of Color on the Eve of the Civil War* (1984); *Abraham Lincoln, Slavery, and the Civil War: Selected Speeches and Writings* (2001); and *Reading the American Past: Selected Historical Documents*, the documents reader for *The American Promise*.

PATRICIA CLINE COHEN Born in Ann Arbor, Michigan, and raised in Palo Alto, California, Patricia Cline Cohen earned a B.A. at the University of Chicago and a Ph.D. at the University of California, Berkeley. In 1976, she joined the history faculty at the University of California, Santa Barbara. In 2005–2006 she received the university's Distinguished Teaching Award. Cohen has written *A Calculating People: The Spread of Numeracy in Early America* (1982; reissued 1999) and *The Murder of Helen Jewett: The Life and Death of a Prostitute in Nineteenth-Century New York* (1998). She is coauthor of *The Flash Press: Sporting Male Weeklies in 1840s New York* (2008). In 2001–2002 she was the Distinguished Senior Mellon Fellow at the American Antiquarian Society.

SARAH STAGE Sarah Stage was born in Davenport, Iowa, and received a B.A. from the University of Iowa and a Ph.D. in American studies from Yale University. She has taught U.S. history for more than twenty-five years at Williams College and the University of California, Riverside. Currently she is professor of women's studies at Arizona State University at the West campus in Phoenix. Her books include *Female Complaints: Lydia Pinkham and the Business of Women's Medicine* (1979) and *Rethinking Home Economics: Women and the History of a Profession* (1997). She recently returned from China where she had an appointment as visiting scholar at Peking University and Sichuan University.

ALAN LAWSON Born in Providence, Rhode Island, Alan Lawson received his B.A. from Brown University in and his M.A. from the University of Wisconsin. After Army service and experience as a high school teacher, he earned his Ph.D. from the University of Michigan. Since winning the Allan Nevins Prize for his dissertation, Lawson has served on the faculties of the University of California, Irvine, Smith College, and, currently, Boston College. He has written *The Failure of Independent Liberalism* (1971) and coedited *From Revolution to Republic* (1976).

SUSAN M. HARTMANN Susan M. Hartmann received her B.A. from Washington University and her Ph.D. from the University of Missouri. A specialist in modern U.S. history and women's history, she has published many articles and four books: *Truman and the 80th Congress* (1971); *The Home Front and Beyond: American Women in the 1940s* (1982); *From Margin to Mainstream: American Women and Politics since 1960* (1989); and *The Other Feminists: Activists in the Liberal Establishment* (1998). She is currently Arts and Humanities Distinguished Professor of History at The Ohio State University and recently was a fellow at the Woodrow Wilson International Center for Scholars.